C0-ACN-720

Department of State

Division of Library and Information Services

I, KURT S. BROWNING, Secretary of State of the State of Florida, do hereby certify that the copies of Title XLVII, Criminal Procedure and Corrections, Chapters 944, Section 944.291 through 948, Section 948.05, inclusive of reserved sections and chapters, as published in West's Florida Statutes Annotated, are true and correct copies of such Title and Chapters as they appear in the official Florida Statutes, as shown by the records of this office.

Given under my hand and the Great Seal of the State of Florida, at Tallahassee, the Capitol, this the 12th day of March, A.D., 2010.

Kurt S. Browning
Secretary of State

West's
FLORIDA STATUTES
ANNOTATED

Chapters 944.291 to 948.05

Under Arrangement of the
Official Florida Statutes

Volume 24

Title XLVII
Criminal Procedure and Corrections

§§ 944.291 to 948.05

WEST®
A Thomson Reuters business

Mat #41010533

PREFACE

This volume of West's Florida Statutes Annotated contains Chapters 944.291 to 948.05 of Title XLVII, Criminal Procedure and Corrections. Annotative materials have been provided to assist in the interpretation and use of the text. Italicized and other explanatory notes and credits have been specially prepared and developed to assist in the solution of questions and problems arising under the law.

The annotations in this volume from the decisions of the State and Federal Courts construing the Statutes close with cases reported in:

Southern Reporter, Third Series and Florida Cases	24 So.3d 1084
Supreme Court Reporter	130 S.Ct. 826
United States Reports	548 U.S. (part)
Lawyers' Edition, Second Series	175 L.Ed.2d (part)
Federal Reporter, Third Series	592 F.3d 131
Federal Supplement, Second Series	661 F.Supp.2d 1384
Federal Rules Decisions	262 F.R.D. 492
Federal Appendix Reporter	345 Fed.Appx. 604
Bankruptcy Reporter	421 B.R. 603
Federal Claims Reporter	90 Fed.Cl. 521
Opinions of the Attorney General	Op.Atty.Gen. 2010–03
Other Standard Reports	

Text of Laws

The text, section, chapter and title arrangement of the laws conform to FLORIDA STATUTES as prepared by the Division of Statutory Revision.

West's FLORIDA STATUTES ANNOTATED and the state edition of FLORIDA STATUTES are correlated publications and a citation to one is always a citation to the other.

The legislation incorporated in this volume is complete through the laws enacted at the 2009 Special "B" Session of the Twenty-First Legislature.

Editorial Features

The widely accepted and popular editorial features that have made West's FLORIDA STATUTES ANNOTATED an indispensable and practical working tool for Judges, Lawyers and Law Teachers, such as detailed historical and statutory notes tracing the source of the law, cross references to related and qualifying laws, complete and exhaustive annotations to the judicial constructions and interpretations by the state and federal courts and the opinions of the Attorney General, are continued in this volume.

PREFACE

Westlaw Electronic Research

A Westlaw guide covering additional resources for use in your legal research is set out following the preface of this volume. See Westlaw KeyCite to update the case history information for opinions under Notes of Decisions.

Library References

An additional feature of great practical value, included as an aid to research, consists of references classified to the various statutes citing the researcher to the West Key Number Digests, Westlaw topics, and to Corpus Juris Secundum. Through those mediums the researcher has complete access to cases of other jurisdictions relating to the same subject matter as the statute being reviewed.

Law Review Commentaries

A wealth of additional research material is also made available by means of references to pertinent articles of interest in the various Florida law reviews and journals.

THE PUBLISHER

April, 2010

RELATED PRODUCTS FROM WEST

FLORIDA PRACTICE SERIES™

Ehrhardt's Florida Evidence
Charles W. Ehrhardt

Florida Criminal Procedure
Michael E. Allen

Florida Appellate Practice
Philip J. Padovano

Florida Civil Procedure Forms
J. Allison DeFoor, II and Thomas G. Schultz

Berman's Florida Civil Procedure
Bruce J. Berman

Florida Civil Practice
Philip J. Padovano

Florida Personal Injury and Wrongful Death Actions
Thomas D. Sawaya

Florida Motor Vehicle No–Fault Law, Personal Injury Protection (PIP)
Russel Lazega

Florida Construction Law Manual
Larry R. Leiby

Florida Workers' Compensation With Forms
Patrick John McGinley

Florida DUI Handbook
David A. Demers

Florida Estate Planning
Brian McAvoy, Abraham M. Mora, and Shelly Wald

Florida Elder Law
Jerome Ira Solkoff and Scott Solkoff

Florida Insurance Law
Gregory Michael Dell, Stacey Giulianti, Russel Lazega, Theodore Leopold, Diana Martin, and Patrick John McGinley

Florida Sentencing
William H. Burgess, III

Florida Elements of an Action
Patrick John McGinley

Florida Summary Judgment and Related Termination Motions
Monique C.M. Leahy

Florida Real Estate
Manuel Farach

RELATED PRODUCTS

Florida Law of Trusts
John G. Grimsley and David Powell

OTHER WEST PRODUCTS

Florida Trial Objections
Charles W. Ehrhardt

Trawick's Florida Practice and Procedure
Henry P. Trawick, Jr.

Trawick's Florida Practice and Procedure Forms
Henry P. Trawick, Jr.

La Coe's Pleadings Under the Florida Rules of Civil Procedure with Forms
Norm La Coe

Florida Mortgages
Thomas E. Baynes, Jr.

Trawick's Redfearn Wills and Administration in Florida
Henry P. Trawick, Jr.

Florida Guardianship Law and Procedure
David C. Brennan

Florida Uniform Commercial Code Forms
Jarret C. Oeltjen

Florida Statutes Annotated

Florida Cases

Florida Business Laws Annotated
Stuart R. Cohn and Stuart D. Ames

Florida Rules of Court—State, Local & Federal

Florida KeyRules

Florida Criminal and Motor Vehicle Law

Florida Criminal Laws and Rules

Florida K–20 Education Code

Florida Family Laws and Rules

Florida Probate Code

Florida Digest

Florida Law Finder

Westlaw

WestCheck.com™

West CD–ROM Libraries™

RELATED PRODUCTS

To order any of these Florida practice tools, call your
West Representative or **1–800–328–9352**.

NEED RESEARCH HELP?

You can get quality research results with free help—call the West Reference Attorneys when you have questions concerning Westlaw or West Publications at 1–800–REF–ATTY (1–800–733–2889).

INTERNET ACCESS

Contact the West Editorial Department directly with your questions and suggestions by email at west.editor@thomson.com. Visit West's home page at west.thomson.com.

*

WESTLAW ELECTRONIC RESEARCH GUIDE

Westlaw—Expanding the Reach of Your Library

Westlaw, West's online legal research service, provides you with the same quality and integrity that you have come to expect from West books. In addition, you have quick, easy access to West's vast collection of statutes, case law materials, public records, news and business information, and other legal and nonlegal resources. West's editorial enhancements, such as case headnotes and topic and key numbers, enable you to move quickly and easily between West print resources and Westlaw for your legal research.

Accessing Databases Using the Westlaw Directory

You can use the Westlaw Directory to view all the databases on Westlaw, as well as to link to detailed information about each database. To access the Westlaw Directory, click **Directory** at the top of any Westlaw page. Browse the directory by clicking the links for the headings or subheadings in the right frame. Click a database name to access a database. You can also type all or part of a database name in the *Search for a database* text box in the left frame and click **Go**. A list of databases is displayed. To access a database, click its name.

Retrieving a Specific Document

If you know the citation of a document, use the Find service on Westlaw to quickly retrieve the document. Click **Find&Print** at the top of any Westlaw page to display the Find a Document page. Type the citation in the *Find this document by citation* text box in the left frame and click **Go**.

Find templates are available for federal and state case law, the U.S. Constitution and state constitutions, federal and state statutes and regulations, and many other materials. If you are unsure of the correct citation format, simply type the publication abbreviation in the *Find this document by citation* text box and click **Go**. A fill-in-the-blank template is displayed. For example, to display a Find template for a state's statutes, type **xx st** (where xx is a state's two-letter postal abbreviation).

To retrieve a specific case when you know one or more parties' names, click **Find&Print**. Then click **Find a Case by Party Name** in the left frame. The Find a Case by Party Name search template is displayed.

Checking Citations in KeyCite®

KeyCite is the citation research service on Westlaw. KeyCite information is available for every case in West's® National Reporter System® and more than 1 million unpublished cases; federal statutes and regulations; statutes from all 50 states; administrative decisions from selected federal agencies; regulations and administrative decisions from selected states; and other materials.

You can use KeyCite to determine whether a case, statute, regulation, or administrative decision is good law. You can also use KeyCite to retrieve citing references to a document, including cases, administrative materials, secondary sources, and briefs and other court documents. KeyCite history for a statute includes citations to recent session laws that amend or repeal the section and proposed legislation.

Click **KeyCite** at the top of any Westlaw page to get a detailed explanation of the KeyCite status flags and depth of treatment stars. Depth of treatment stars help you focus on the most important citing references.

The KeyCite Alert service allows you to monitor the status of a case, statute, regulation, or administrative decision and sends you updates when its KeyCite result (i.e., history or citing references) changes.

United States Code Annotated® (USCA®)

The USCA contains the official text of the U.S. Code along with annotations that include notes of decisions, historical notes, research references, and cross-references.

State Statutes

Annotated state statutes are available for all 50 states and the District of Columbia.

Links Tab

When you are viewing a statute, the Links tab in the left frame allows you to view information related to the statute, including cases that cite the statute, legislative history, and prior versions of the statute.

- **Legislative History**

  Legislative history for federal statutes provides you with public laws, *Congressional Record* documents, committee reports, bill drafts, congressional testimony, congressional bills, and presidential messages. Legislative history for state statutes, available for 36 states and the District of Columbia, provides you with committee reports, legislative journals, transcripts of legislative proceedings, records of legislators' votes, and governors' messages.

- **Graphical Statutes®**

  This feature allows you to track changes to a statute in an easy-to-read graphical display, which includes enacting public laws, relevant legislative history materials, and prior versions.

- **Versions**

  You can view prior versions of the USCA and selected state statutes that were effective on a specific date.

- **50 State Surveys**

  These surveys allow you to see how a particular legal topic has been addressed by comparable state statutes in any of the 50 states and the District of Columbia.

WESTLAW GUIDE

RegulationsPlus®

USCA® sections are linked to related **Code of Federal Regulations (CFR)** provisions to allow seamless viewing between the two Codes. Additional features include a full-service CFR Index of more than 1 million references created by West attorney-editors, arranged by topic and linked directly to CFR sections, plus CFR Notes of Decisions, linked to the caselaw and to West Key Numbers and Topics.

ResultsPlus®

After you run a search in a statutes database, Westlaw automatically creates a ResultsPlus list of additional documents and West topic and key numbers that have a high statistical likelihood of matching the concepts in your search. Click a document title in the list to view the full text of the document.

Additional Information

Westlaw is available on the Web at westlaw.com.

For search assistance, call the West Reference Attorneys at
1–800–REF–ATTY (1–800–733–2889).

For technical assistance, call West Customer Technical Support at
1–800–WESTLAW (1–800–937–8529).

*

FLORIDA STATUTES

The Attorney General of Florida, pursuant to the Legislative mandate expressed in the Act approved May 25, 1939, Laws 1939, c. 19140, prepared a "revision, compilation and consolidation of all the General Statutes of Florida in force, of a permanent nature" which, by Act approved June 6, 1941, Laws 1941, c. 20719, except as otherwise provided therein was "adopted and enacted as statute law" under the title of Florida Statutes 1941.

In preparing Florida Statutes 1941, the Attorney General of Florida followed a modern numbering system for the various subdivisions of the law, which would serve to perpetuate the usefulness of the Statute, and eliminate for many years the necessity of further general revisions of Florida Law. This meant that through this action of the Attorney General, pursuant to legislative mandate, a policy of revision, from time to time, of various subjects of the law could be carried out accurately and economically.

Laws 1943, c. 22012 created a Statutory Revision Department, under the direct supervision and control of the Attorney General, charged with the duty among other things of maintaining various legislative services and of publishing the Florida Statutes. Laws 1949, c. 25369 created a Legislative Reference Bureau and a Legislative Council, completely separate from the Attorney General, for the purpose of securing and promoting research and reference services. In 1967, the Statutory Revision Department was removed from the office of the Attorney General and established as a part of the Legislative Reference Bureau (Laws 1967, c. 67–472). In 1969, the Legislative Reference Bureau was renamed the Legislative Service Bureau and the Statutory Revision Department became the Statutory Revision Service within the Bureau (Laws 1969, c. 69–52). In 1971, the Legislative Service Bureau was discontinued and the Statutory Revision Service became the Division of Statutory Revision under the Joint Legislative Management Committee. The division was placed under the Office of Legislative Services in 1998.

The biennial publication of an official edition of the Florida Statutes was initiated in 1949. Since 1999, the Florida Statutes has been published in its entirety annually. This practice has implemented the state's continuous revision program by consolidating at regular intervals the general and permanent law in force in Florida.

A significant feature of the statutory revision program has been the adoption and reenactment by the legislature of the preceding edition of the Florida Statutes. See, for example, Florida Statutes, section 11.2421.

The sections of the Statutes are identified by a decimal numbering system. Chapters are arranged by subject matter and assigned numbers. After the chapters of the Florida Statutes are arranged by subject matter, each is assigned a whole number. Each section within a chapter is identified by a whole decimal number consisting of the chapter number followed by digits appearing to the right of the decimal point. For example, "s. 16.01" would identify a section in chapter 16 of the Florida Statutes. Various designations thus indicate the hierarchical arrangement of textual subdivisions. Chapters are identified by whole Arabic numbers; sections, by numbers containing a decimal point; subsections, by whole Arabic numbers enclosed by parentheses; paragraphs, by lowercase letters enclosed by parentheses; subparagraphs, by whole Arabic numbers followed by a period; sub-subparagraphs, by Roman numerals in parentheses; and sub-sub-sub-subparagraphs by uppercase letters in parentheses.

West's Florida Statutes Annotated constitutes a companion publication which by means of bound volumes, pocket parts, annotated pamphlets, and session law service pamphlets, provides the Bench and Bar with the complete and up to date text of the Statutes, and with all the supplementary annotative materials necessary in research for the understanding and resolution of problems covered by the Statutes.

TABLE OF CONTENTS

TITLE 47 (XLVII)
CRIMINAL PROCEDURE AND CORRECTIONS

Complete List of Chapters in Title XLVII, Criminal Procedure and Corrections, see page 1

Section Analysis, see beginning of each Chapter.

Index to Title XLVII, Criminal Procedure and Corrections, see volume containing end of Title XLVII

*

ABBREVIATIONS

Am.Bus.L.J.	American Business Law Journal
Am.Jur.	American Jurisprudence
Am.Jur.2d	American Jurisprudence, Second Series
Am.Jur.Pl. & Prac.Forms	American Jurisprudence Pleading and Practice Forms
Am.Jur.Proof of Facts	American Jurisprudence Proof of Facts
Am.Jur.Proof of Facts 2d	American Jurisprudence Proof of Facts, Second Series
Am.Jur.Proof of Facts 3d	American Jurisprudence Proof of Facts, Third Series
Am.Jur.Trials	American Jurisprudence Trials
App.	Appendix
Art.	Article
B.R.	Bankruptcy Reporter
Barry L.Rev.	Barry Law Review
c.	Chapter of Act
Ch.	Chapter
Comp.Gen.Laws	Compiled General Laws
Comp.Gen.Laws Supp.	Compiled General Laws Supplement
C.J.S.	Corpus Juris Secundum
Cl.	Clause
Cl.Ct.	Claims Court Reporter
Const.	Constitution
Eff.	Effective
F.2d	Federal Reporter, Second Series
F.3d	Federal Reporter, Third Series
F.R.D.	Federal Rules Decisions
F.Supp.	Federal Supplement
F.Supp.2d	Federal Supplement, Second Series
Fed.Appx.	Federal Appendix Reporter
Fletcher	Fletcher Cyclopedia Law of Private Corporations
Fla.	Florida Reporter
Fla.B.J.	Florida Bar Journal
Fla.Coastal L.J.	Florida Coastal Law Journal
Fla.J.Int'l L.	Florida Journal of International Law
Fla.Jur.	Florida Jurisprudence
Fla.Jur.2d	Florida Jurisprudence, Second Series
Fla.Jur.Forms Legal & Bus.	Florida Jurisprudence Forms Legal and Business
Fla.L.Rev.	Florida Law Review
Fla.Pl. & Prac.	Florida Pleading and Practice
Fla.Pl. & Prac.Forms	Florida Pleading and Practice Forms
Fla.Prac.Series	Florida Practice Series
Fla.St.U.L.Rev.	Florida State University Law Review
Fla.St.	Florida Statutes
Fla.St. 19__, Supp.	Florida Statutes Supplement
Fla.Tax Rev.	Florida Tax Review
Gen.St.	General Statutes
ILSA J.Int'l & Comp.L.	ILSA Journal of International & Comparative Law
J.Land Use & Envt'l L.	Journal of Land Use & Environmental Law
J.Mar.L. & Com.	Journal of Maritime Law & Commerce
J.Tech.L. & Pol'y	Journal of Technology Law & Policy
J.Transnat'l L. & Pol'y	Journal of Transnational Law & Policy

ABBREVIATIONS

(🔑) (Key Number)	State Digest and other units of the American Digest System
La Coe's Fla.Rules of Civ.Proc.	La Coe's Florida Rules of Civil Procedure
La Coe's Forms for Pl.Under Fla. Rules of Civ.Proc.	La Coe's Forms for Pleading Under Florida Rules of Civil Procedure
L.Ed.2d	Lawyers' Edition, 2nd Series
Miami L.Q.	Miami Law Quarterly
No.	Number
Nova L.J.	Nova Law Journal
Nova L.Rev.	Nova Law Review
Op.Atty.Gen.	Opinions of the Attorney General
Par.	Paragraph
PEB	Permanent Editorial Board for the Uniform Commercial Code
P.L.	Public Law
Psychol. Pub. Pol'y & L.	Psychology, Public Policy & Law
Rev.St.	Revised Statutes
Rev.Gen.St.	Revised General Statutes
St.Thomas L.Rev.	Saint Thomas Law Review
§	Section of the Act
So.	Southern Reporter
So.2d	Southern Reporter, Second Series
Stetson L.Rev.(Fla.)	Stetson Law Review
Subsec.	Subsection
Subd.	Subdivision
S.Ct.	Supreme Court Reporter
Trawick, Fla.Prac. & Proc.	Trawick's Florida Practice and Procedure
Trawick, Fla.Prac. & Proc. Forms	Trawick's Florida Practice and Procedure Forms
U.L.A.	Uniform Laws Annotated
U.S.	United States Reports
U.S.C.A.	United States Code Annotated
U.Fla.J.L. & Pub.Pol'y	University of Florida Journal of Law & Public Policy
U.Fla.L.Rev.	University of Florida Law Review
U.Miami Bus.L.Rev.	University of Miami Business Law Review
U.Miami Ent. & Sports L.Rev.	University of Miami Entertainment & Sports Law Review
U.Miami Inter-Am.L.Rev.	University of Miami Inter-American Law Review
U.Miami Int'l & Comp. L.Rev.	University of Miami International & Comparative Law Review
U.Miami L.Rev.	University of Miami Law Review

EFFECTIVE DATES

The following table shows the date of adjournment and the general effective date of laws enacted at sessions of the legislature beginning with the year 1945:

Year	Session	Adjournment Date	Effective Date
1945	Regular	6–1–45	7–31–45
1945	Extra	7–24–45	9–22–45
1947	Regular	6–6–47	8–5–47
1948	Extra	9–14, 15–48	11–14–48
1949	Regular	6–3–49	8–2–49
1949	Extra	9–24–49	11–23–49
1951	Regular	6–1–51	7–31–51
1953	Regular	6–5–53	8–4–53
1955	Regular	6–3–55	8–2–55
1956	1st Extra	8–1–56	9–30–56
1956	2nd Extra	11–6–56	1–5–57
1957	Regular	6–8–57	8–7–57
1957	Extra	10–9–57	12–8–57
1959	Regular	6–5–59	8–4–59
1961	Regular	6–2–61	8–1–61
1962	1st Extra	8–11–62	10–10–62
1962	2nd Extra	11–28–62	1–27–63
1963	Extra	2–1–63	4–2–63
1963	Regular	6–19–63	8–18–63
1965	Regular	6–4–65	8–3–65
1965	1st Extra	6–24–65	8–3–65
1965	2nd Extra	7–14–65	9–12–65
1966	1st Extra	3–9–66	5–8–66
1967	Regular	7–14–67	9–12–67
1967	1st Extra	1–28–67	3–29–67
1967	2nd Extra	7–28–67	9–26–67
1967	3rd Extra	8–18–67	10–17–67
1967	4th Extra	9–1–67	10–31–67
1968	1st Extra	2–16–68	4–16–68
1969	1st Regular	6–6–69	8–5–69
1969	Special	12–10–69	2–8–70
1970	2nd Regular	6–5–70	8–4–70
1970	Special	6–13–70	No legislation
1970	Special	10–9–70	12–8–70
1971	1st Extra	2–4–71	4–3–71
1971	1st Regular	6–4–71	8–3–71
1971	2nd Extra	6–24–71	8–23–71
1971	3rd Extra	12–9–71	2–7–72
1972	2nd Regular	4–7–72	6–6–72
1972	"E" Special	4–8–72	No legislation
1972	"F" Special	4–11–72	6–10–72
1972	Special (3rd Leg.)	12–1–72	*
1973	1st Regular	6–6–73	8–5–73
1974	Special	1–30–74	No legislation
1974	2nd Regular	5–31–74	7–30–74
1974	Special (4th Leg.)	11–19–74	*
1975	1st Regular	6–5–75	8–4–75
1976	2nd Regular	6–4–76	8–3–76

EFFECTIVE DATES

Year	Session	Adjournment Date	Effective Date
1977	1st Regular	6–3–77	8–2–77
1977	"A" Special	6–16–77	*
1977	"B" Special	6–24–77	*
1977	"C" Special	12–13–77	No legislation
1978	2nd Regular	6–2–78	8–1–78
1978	"D" Special	6–8–78	8–7–78
1978	"A" Special (6th Leg.)	12–6–78	*
1979	1st Regular	6–6–79	8–5–79
1979	"B" Special	6–6–79	8–5–79
1979	"C" Special	12–4–79	*
1980	2nd Regular	6–7–80	8–6–80
1980	"D" Special	6–11–80	8–10–80
1980	"E" Special	6–30–80	*
1980	"A" Special (7th Leg.)	11–18–80	*
1981	1st Regular	6–5–81	8–4–81
1981	"B" Special	6–17–81	8–16–81
1982	2nd Regular	3–25–82	5–24–82
1982	"C" Special		No legislation
1982	"D" Special	4–7–82	6–6–82
1982	"E" Special	4–7–82	6–6–82
1982	"F" Special	4–7–82	6–6–82
1982	"G" Special	5–21–82	7–20–82
1982	"H" Special	6–22–82	8–21–82
1983	"A" Special	3–3–83	5–2–83
1983	1st Regular	6–13–83	8–12–83
1983	"B" Special	6–24–83	8–23–83
1983	"C" Special	7–13–83	9–11–83
1984	2nd Regular	6–1–84	7–31–84
1984	"A" Special	12–7–84	2–5–85
1985	1st Regular	5–31–85	7–30–85
1986	2nd Regular	6–7–86	8–6–86
1986	"B" Special	6–19–86	8–18–86
1987	"A" Special (10th Leg.)	2–4–87	*
1987	1st Regular	6–6–87	8–5–87
1987	"B" Special	10–8–87	*
1987	"C" Special	10–14–87	*
1987	"D" Special	12–10–87	*
1988	"E" Special	2–4–88	*
1988	2nd Regular	6–7–88	8–6–88
1988	"F" Special	6–8–88	8–7–88
1989	1st Regular	6–3–89	8–2–89
1989	"A" Special	6–3–89	8–2–89
1989	"B" Special	6–20–89	8–19–89
1989	"C" Special	10–11–89	No legislation
1989	"D" Special	11–18–89	*
1990	2nd Regular	6–2–90	8–1–90
1990	"A" Special	11–20–90	*
1991	"B" Special	1–22–91	*
1991	1st Regular	5–2–91	7–1–91
1991	"C" Special	6–6–91	*
1991	"D" Special	12–13–91	*
1992	2nd Regular	3–13–92	5–12–92
1992	"E" Special	4–1–92	*
1992	"F" Special	4–1–92	*
1992	"G" Special	4–10–92	6–9–92
1992	"H" Special	7–10–92**	**

EFFECTIVE DATES

Year	Session	Adjournment Date	Effective Date
1992	"A" Special (13th Leg.)	12–11–92	*
1993	1st Regular	4–4–93	6–3–93
1993	"B" Special	5–28–93	7–27–93
1993	"C" Special	11–11–93	*
1994	2nd Regular	4–15–94	6–14–94
1994	"D" Special	6–9–94	No legislation
1995	1st Regular	5–11–95	7–10–95
1996	2nd Regular	5–4–96	7–3–96
1997	1st Regular	5–2–97	7–1–97
1997	"A" Special	11–7–97	*
1998	2nd Regular	5–1–98	6–30–98
1999	1st Regular	3–2–99	6–29–99
2000	"A" Special	1–7–00	*
2000	2nd Regular	5–5–00	7–4–00
2001	1st Regular	5–4–01	7–3–01
2001	"B" Special	10–31–01	*
2001	"C" Special	12–6–01	*
2002	2nd Regular	3–22–02	5–21–02
2002	"D" Special	4–5–02	No legislation
2002	"E" Special	5–13–02	*
2003	1st Regular	5–2–03	7–1–03
2003	"A" Special	5–27–03	*
2003	"B" Special	6–27–03	*
2003	"C" Special	7–21–03	No legislation
2003	"D" Special	8–13–03	*
2003	"E" Special	10–24–03	*
2004	2nd Regular	4–30–04	6–29–04
2004	"A" Special	12–16–04	*
2005	1st Regular	5–6–05	7–5–05
2005	"B" Special	12–8–05	*
2006	2nd Regular	5–5–06	7–4–06
2007	"A" Special	1–22–07	*
2007	1st Regular	5–4–07	7–3–07
2007	"B" Special	6–14–07	*
2007	"C" Special	10–12–07	*
2007	"D" Special	10–29–07	*
2008	2nd Regular	5–2–08	7–1–08
2009	1st Regular	5–4–09	7–3–09
2009	"A" Special	1–14–09	*
2009	"B" Special	12–8–09	*

* No legislation for which general effective date applicable.

** This session "expired" rather than "adjourned".

*

CITE THIS BOOK

Thus: West's F.S.A. § _______

*

WEST'S FLORIDA STATUTES ANNOTATED

TITLE XLVII

CRIMINAL PROCEDURE AND CORRECTIONS

Chapters 944.291 to 948.05 appear in this volume

CHAPTER 944

STATE CORRECTIONAL SYSTEM

Section

944.291. Prisoner released by reason of gain-time allowances or attainment of provisional release date

(1) Notwithstanding any provision of law to the contrary, a prisoner who has served his or her term or terms, less allowable gain-time deductions as provided by law, or who has attained his or her provisional release date shall, upon release, be placed under further supervision and control of the department. Any released prisoner who is not under further supervision and control of the department or who is not subject to any statute relating to parole shall be eligible, on a voluntary basis, for any assistance available to him or her through any parole or probation office under the department.

(2) Any prisoner who is convicted of a crime committed on or after October 1, 1988, which crime is contained in category 1, category 2, category 3, or category 4 of Rule 3.701 and Rule 3.988, Florida Rules of Criminal Procedure, and who has served at least one prior felony commitment at a state or federal correctional institution, or is sentenced as a habitual or violent habitual offender pursuant to s. 775.084, may only be released under conditional release supervision as described in chapter 947. Not fewer than 90 days prior to the tentative release date or provisional release date, whichever is earlier, the department shall provide the commission with the name and inmate identification number for each eligible inmate.

Laws 1967, c. 67–421, § 1; Laws 1974, c. 74–112, § 21; Laws 1977, c. 77–120, § 50; Laws 1978, c. 78–223, § 1; Laws 1979, c. 79–3, § 59; Laws 1981, c. 81–229, § 1; Laws 1988, c. 88–122, § 10; Laws 1989, c. 89–531, § 7. Amended by Laws 1997, c. 97–102, § 1645, eff. July 1, 1997.

Historical and Statutory Notes

Amendment Notes:

Prior to amendment in 1974, this section provided:

"(1)(a) A prisoner who has served his term or terms, less allowable statutory gain time deductions and extra good time allowances as provided by law, shall, upon release, be deemed as if released on parole until the expiration of the maximum term or terms for which he was actually sentenced or such lesser time as may be determined by the Florida parole and probation commission pursuant to § 947.13.

"(b) The provisions of this section shall not apply to prisoners who have not earned at least one hundred eighty days' gain time.

"(2) A prisoner so released shall be under the supervision and control of the parole and probation commission in accordance with the appropriate provisions of Chapter 947, pertaining to paroles and parolees and their supervision, disposition, and control."

Laws 1974, c. 74–112, substantially reworded this section to provide:

"(1) A prisoner who has served his term or terms, less allowable statutory gain-time deductions and extra good-time allowances, as provided by law, shall, upon release, be under the supervision and control of the commission as if on parole, but in no event shall such supervision extend beyond the maximum term or terms for which he was actually sentenced.

"(2) The provisions of this section shall not apply to prisoners who, at the time of sentence, could not have earned at least 180 days' gain-time."

Laws 1977, c. 77–120, a reviser's bill, amended subsec. (1) of this section to conform with Laws 1975, c. 75–49, which created the department of offender rehabilitation (see § 20.315) and transferred to the department certain functions performed by the division of corrections of the department of health and rehabilitative services and the parole and probation commission of the department of offender rehabilitation.

Laws 1978, c. 78–223, amending subsec. (1), substituted "and shall be subject to all statutes relating to parole" for "as if on parole" and "2 years as determined by the Parole and Probation Commission" for "the maximum term of years for which he was actually sentenced".

Laws 1979, c. 79–3, a reviser's bill, provided for substitution of references to the department and secretary of "corrections" for the department and secretary of "offender rehabilitation" to conform with Laws 1978, c. 78–53.

Laws 1981, c. 81–229, § 1, rewrote this section to read:

"A prisoner who has served his term or terms, less allowable statutory gain-time deductions and extra good-time allowances, as provided by law, shall not, upon release, be under further supervision and control of the department and shall not be subject to any statute relating to parole. However, any such released prisoner shall be eligible, on a voluntary basis, for any assistance available to him through any parole or probation office under the department."

Section 1 of Laws 1981, c. 81–229 contained the following provisions:

"Any person who was released pursuant to this section prior to the effective date of this act shall be discharged on such date from further supervision by the department, and any warrant which has been issued by the Parole and Probation Commission against any such person shall be rescinded.

"Any prisoner in the custody of the department who had previously been released pursuant to this section and who is in custody because of a technical violation of any condition of release pursuant to this section shall be discharged on the effective date of this act, and the warrant issued by the Parole and Probation Commission against him shall be rescinded."

Laws 1988, c. 88–122, § 10, eff. July 1, 1988, designated subsec. (1), rewrote the provisions therein, and added subsec. (2).

Laws 1989, c. 89–531, § 7, eff. Oct. 1, 1989, added "or attainment of provisional release date" to the section heading; in subsec. (1), made the subsection effective regardless of any provision of law to the contrary, made the subsection applicable to prisoners who have attained their provisional release dates, made placement under department supervision and control mandatory rather than discretionary; and deleted the provision that prisoners be subject to any statute relating to parole; and in subsec. (2), inserted the reference to provisional release dates in the last sentence.

Laws 1997, c. 97–102, eff. July 1, 1997, removed gender-specific references applicable to human beings from volume 4 of the Florida Statutes without substantive changes in legal effect.

Cross References

Basic release assistance, see § 944.706.

Law Review and Journal Commentaries

Parole revocation: Due process or star chamber? Richard A. Belz, 52 Fla.Bar J. 22 (1978).

Prisoners' gain time. 21 U.Fla.L.Rev. 103 (1968).

Rules of criminal procedure. Thomas A. Wills, 22 U.Miami L.Rev. 240, 272 (1967).

Library References

Prisons ⚷248.
Westlaw Topic No. 310.
C.J.S. Prisons and Rights of Prisoners § 152.

Research References

Encyclopedias

Generally; Release on Gain-Time Allowances, FL Jur. 2d Prisons & Prisoners § 211.

Conditional Release; Prior Felons or Habitual Offenders; Sexual Predators, FL Jur. 2d Prisons & Prisoners § 212.

Treatises and Practice Aids

16 Florida Practice Series § 10:12, Release by Reason of Gain Time Allowances or Attainment of Provisional Release Date.

Notes of Decisions

---

1. Construction and application

Statutes governing conditional release of inmates and gain-time credits create no duty on the part of the Parole Commission or the Department of Corrections (DOC) for the benefit of any private person, including inmates or parolees and thus afford no basis for an action by any aggrieved individual for alleged negligence or errors in their application or enforcement. Andrews v. Florida Parole Com'n, App. 1 Dist., 768 So.2d 1257 (2000), review granted 789 So.2d 343, review dismissed as improvidently granted 791 So.2d 1093. Action ⚷ 3; Pardon And Parole ⚷ 56; Prisons ⚷ 309

Parole Commission has broad authority to either grant or deny releasee credit for time spent on conditional release when that release is revoked due to violation of terms and conditions of release. Rivera v. Singletary, 707 So.2d 326 (1998). Prisons ⚷ 248

Statutes which allow gain time for good conduct and extra good time allowances are meant to reward those prisoners who have made an effort to conduct themselves during incarceration in a manner the prison authorities deem proper. Williams v. State, App. 4 Dist., 370 So.2d 1164 (1979). Prisons ⚷ 244

When a prisoner is released under this section after he has served his term or terms, less allowances for statutory gain time deductions and extra good time allowances, he is subject to the provisions of §§ 949.10, 949.11 and 949.12, which, among other things, provide that the arrest of a parolee on a felony charge in this state shall be prima facie evidence of the violation of the terms and conditions of his parole and require a parole revocation hearing within ten days after such arrest. Op.Atty.Gen., 073–473, Dec. 19, 1973.

2. Due process

Inmate's placement on Conditional Release did not violate due process on ground that it improperly took away liberty interest in the gain time he had been awarded, as inmate only had conditional liberty interest in gain time, and if inmate lost gain time it would only be after due process of law. Duncan v. Moore, 754 So.2d 708 (2000). Constitutional Law ⚷ 4830; Prisons ⚷ 248

3. Double jeopardy

Requiring that a Conditional Release eligible inmate finish his sentence by satisfactorily completing a period of post-prison supervision equal to the amount of gain time awarded did not violate double jeopardy. Duncan v. Moore, 754 So.2d 708 (2000). Double Jeopardy ⚷ 31

Returning a Conditional Release violator to prison to continue serving his sentence without credit for the prior awarded gain time does not constitute a violation of double jeopardy, as long as releasee's underlying criminal offense was committed on or after effective date of statute providing for forfeiture of gain time upon Conditional Release revocation. Duncan v. Moore, 754 So.2d 708 (2000). Double Jeopardy ⚷ 31

4. Retroactive application

Subjecting inmate to Conditional Release was not an ex post facto violation, where Conditional Release statute and its corresponding gain time forfeiture statute had gone into effect years before inmate committed his crime, and thus, there was no retrospective application of a later-enacted statute to inmate. Duncan v. Moore, 754 So.2d 708 (2000). Constitutional Law ⚷ 2816; Prisons ⚷ 248

5. Prior sentence gain-time credits

Prisoner who served prior sentence and was released and placed on probation was entitled to credit not only for time he was actually incarcerated on prior sentence, but also for all gain-time that he earned prior to his release, when he was sentenced for violation of probation imposed as part of that prior sentence. Bolden v. State, App. 1 Dist., 557 So.2d 630 (1990). Sentencing And Punishment ⚷ 2041

6. Mandatory minimum sentence

Person sentenced pursuant to § 775.087, is required to serve a minimum term of three years imprisonment before being eligible for parole. Such person is still entitled to both statutory and extra gain time allowances even to the extent that the individual may be released from incarceration on mandatory conditional release prior to service of three years' imprisonment. Op.Atty.Gen., 075–202, July 9, 1975.

7. Parole release date

Department of Corrections (DOC) was entitled to accept the Parole Commission's arrest warrants as lawful, as they were regular on their face and issued by a legal body having authority to issue warrants, and, therefore, was not liable for false imprisonment of parolee due to Commission's miscalculation of the date of release from supervision. Andrews v. Florida Parole Com'n, App. 1 Dist., 768 So.2d 1257 (2000), review granted 789 So.2d 343, review dismissed as improvidently granted 791 So.2d 1093. States ⚷ 112.2(4)

8. Revocation of gain-time

Retention of earned gain time was dependent not only upon satisfactory behavior while in prison but also upon satisfactory behavior while under Conditional Release supervision. Duncan v. Moore, 754 So.2d 708 (2000). Prisons ⚷ 248

Under amended statutes in effect at time of prisoner's offenses, Department of Corrections had authority, upon prisoner's return to prison after violating terms and conditions of his control release, to forfeit prisoner's previously awarded basic and incentive gain time. Dowdy v. Singletary, 704 So.2d 1052 (1998). Prisons ⚷ 248

Revoking gain time was improper for grand theft that was not subject to Conditional Release Act, even though defendant served sentence concurrently with sentences for robbery, battery on law enforcement officer, and resistance of arrest with violence subject to the Act; thus, last date of conditional release supervision should have been calculated with reference only to sentences that were subject to the Act. Cooper v. Florida Parole Com'n, App. 4 Dist., 691 So.2d 521 (1997), review granted 698 So.2d 848, approved 701 So.2d 543, rehearing denied. Prisons ⚷ 248

9. Prisoner consent to terms of release

Fact that prisoner did not sign consent certificate or verbally agree to conditions of his mandatory conditional release did not preclude his subsequent reincarceration for violation of the terms of that release. Division of Corrections, State Parole and Probation Commission v. Tamargo, App. 2 Dist., 329 So.2d 422 (1976). Prisons ⚷ 248

10. Duties of parole commission

Parole Commission acted within the scope of its quasi-judicial duties when it placed inmate on conditional release, had jurisdiction over him and the terms of conditional release, and, therefore, enjoyed judicial immunity from liability for false imprisonment, even though the Commission miscalculated the date of release from supervision resulting in incarceration for eleven months beyond the time permitted. Andrews v. Florida Parole Com'n, App. 1 Dist., 768 So.2d 1257 (2000), review granted 789 So.2d 343, review dismissed as improvidently granted 791 So.2d 1093. Pardon And Parole ⚷ 56

11. Supervision

Fact that this section required that prisoner be under the supervision of the Department of Offender Rehabilitation, as if on parole, until the expiration of the period of time he would have served in prison had he not been given credit for gain time and good time did not result in double punishment for the same crime; prisoner who objected that such provision was illegal and resulted in "double jeopardy" was in fact serving only one sentence, a portion of which was in prison and the remainder of which was out of prison but subject to supervision. Williams v. State, App. 4 Dist., 370 So.2d 1164 (1979). Double Jeopardy ⚷ 31

Lack of possibility of rehabilitation within a 180-day period, so that any revocation of mandatory conditional release of prisoner who has accumulated less than 180 days of statutory gain time will serve only to disrupt his civilian life and embitter him, provides rational basis for statutory requirement that prisoner who has accumulated more than 180 days' gain time be subject to supervision upon obtaining mandatory conditional release whereas those who have failed to accumulate 180 days' gain time are not subject to supervision. Division of Corrections, State Parole and Probation Commission v. Tamargo, App. 2 Dist., 329 So.2d 422 (1976). Prisons ⚷ 248

12. Payment for supervision

The monthly contribution or payment duty imposed by § 945.30, as amended by Laws 1977, c. 77-321 and Laws 1977, c. 77-428, applies to those persons released on so-called mandatory conditional release (those who have been released by virtue of statutory gain-time deductions or allowances). Op.Atty.Gen., 078-54, March 29, 1978.

The $10 monthly payment duly imposed by § 945.30, applies only to persons placed on parole by the parole and probation commission and persons placed on probation by the courts. It does not apply to those persons on so-called mandatory conditional release (those who have been released by virtue of statutory gain-time allowances or deductions). Op.Atty.Gen., 077-39, May 2, 1977.

13. Habitual offenders

Legislature intended that prisoners sentenced as habitual offenders, if released by reason of gain-time allowances, be released conditionally under supervision. Lincoln v. Florida Parole Com'n, App. 1 Dist., 643 So.2d 668 (1994). Prisons ⚷ 248

Sentence in habitual offender sentencing statute, stating that provisions of chapter on parole and probation commission shall not apply to habitual felony offenders, does not preclude habitual offenders' placement on conditional release when incentive gain-time makes further incarceration unlawful; statute specifically applying conditional release program to habitual and violent habitual offenders controls over such sentence, which addresses application of the parole and probation chapter only generally, particularly where such chapter did not contain act relating to conditional release program until subsequent to the amendment adding such sentence; sentence's reference to parole and probation chapter refers to other forms of early release, notably parole, and not to conditional release program. Lincoln v. Florida Parole Com'n, App. 1 Dist., 643 So.2d 668 (1994). Prisons ⚷ 248

14. Conditional release

Unlike probation, conditional release is not part of a criminal sentence, and therefore, it cannot be mandated or waived by the sentencing judge. Logan v. State, App. 5 Dist., 964 So.2d 209 (2007). Prisons ⚷ 248

15. Habeas corpus

If petitioner lacked eligibility for conditional release, he had no right to discharge by writ of habeas corpus prior to expiration of the full term of his sentence, despite contention that conditional release was revoked without authority. Lincoln v. Florida Parole Com'n, App. 1 Dist., 643 So.2d 668 (1994). Habeas Corpus ⚷ 517

Where prisoner's jail term had not yet expired, habeas corpus was not available to test intention of department of offender rehabilitation to apply, after prisoner's release, supervision restriction enacted in this section which did not become effective until after adjudication of prisoner's guilt. Thompson v. Wainwright, App. 1 Dist., 328 So.2d 487 (1976). Habeas Corpus ⚷ 223

16. Mandamus

A prisoner or releasee who is not claiming entitlement to immediate release from incarceration may challenge the Parole Commission's determination that he or she meets the statutory criteria for conditional release by petition for writ of mandamus. Logan v. State, App. 5 Dist., 964 So.2d 209 (2007). Prisons ⚷ 315

17. Review

Where defendant, resentenced pursuant to order of federal habeas corpus court, was not yet entitled to release with or without parole, any judicial intervention in the administration of the sentence would be premature. Baker v. State, App. 4 Dist., 270 So.2d 424 (1972). Criminal Law ⚷ 1134.25

Where defendant appealing from resentencing which had been directed by federal habeas corpus court did not raise before trial court question whether or not he would be released unconditionally or on parole, record provided no basis for reviewing court to pass on the question. Baker v. State, App. 4 Dist., 270 So.2d 424 (1972). Criminal Law ⚷ 1042.3(1)

944.292. Suspension of civil rights

(1) Upon conviction of a felony as defined in s. 10, Art. X of the State Constitution, the civil rights of the person convicted shall be suspended in

Florida until such rights are restored by a full pardon, conditional pardon, or restoration of civil rights granted pursuant to s. 8, Art. IV of the State Constitution.

(2) This section shall not be construed to deny a convicted felon access to the courts, as guaranteed by s. 21, Art. I of the State Constitution, until restoration of her or his civil rights.

Laws 1974, c. 74–112, § 28; Laws 1976, c. 76–139, § 1; Laws 1988, c. 88–138, § 1. Amended by Laws 1997, c. 97–102, § 1646, eff. July 1, 1997.

Historical and Statutory Notes

Amendment Notes:

Laws 1976, c. 76–139, rewrote this section which, as it appears in Fla.St.1975, provided:

"Effective July 1, 1974, upon conviction for a felony, the civil rights of the person convicted shall be suspended until he is discharged from parole or released from the custody of the department without parole, at which time such civil rights are automatically reinstated. The only civil rights which shall be suspended by conviction are the rights to vote, hold public office, and serve on a jury."

Laws 1988, c. 88–138, § 1, eff. June 28, 1988, designated subsec. (1), and added subsec. (2).

Laws 1997, c. 97–102, eff. July 1, 1997, removed gender-specific references applicable to human beings from volume 4 of the Florida Statutes without substantive changes in legal effect.

Cross References

Disqualification from jury service upon conviction of felony, see § 40.013.

Disqualification from voting and holding office upon conviction of felony, see Const. Art. 6, § 4; § 97.041.

Labor by prisoner, no restoration of civil rights, see §§ 946.002, 946.514.

Pardon or release, requisites for restoration of civil rights, see § 940.05.

Restoration of civil rights, authority of governor, see § 940.01.

Library References

Convicts ⚷21, 22.
Westlaw Topic No. 98.
C.J.S. Convicts §§ 1 to 24.

Research References

ALR Library

49 ALR 1381, Convict or Prisoner as Within Workmen's Compensation Act.

Encyclopedias

Florida Change of Name Statute, FL Jur. 2d Names § 12.

Access to Courts, Generally, FL Jur. 2d Prisons & Prisoners § 73.

Treatises and Practice Aids

16 Florida Practice Series § 6:98, Direct and Collateral Consequences and Special Sanctions--Loss of Civil Liberties Upon Conviction of a Felony.

United States Supreme Court

Prisoners, destruction of personal property by guards, remedies, see Hudson v. Palmer, 1984, 104 S.Ct. 3194, 468 U.S. 517, 82 L.Ed.2d 393, on remand 744 F.2d 22.

Notes of Decisions

1. Validity

This section, to extent that it deprives person convicted of crime of bringing or defending civil action in state courts until his civil rights are restored, is unconstitutional. Sabin v. Butter, App. 3 Dist., 493 So.2d 469 (1986). Convicts ⚷ 21; Convicts ⚷ 22

This section unconstitutionally barred individual convicted of felony, who had not had his "civil rights" restored under any of the procedures set out in section, from prosecuting civil lawsuit for personal injuries sustained in automobile accident under Const. Art. 1, § 21. Collins v. Cote, App. 4 Dist., 490 So.2d 164 (1986). Constitutional Law ⚷ 2312; Convicts ⚷ 21; Convicts ⚷ 22

"Civil death" statute [West's F.S.A. § 944.292] which suspends civil rights of convicted felon and bars prisoner's suit against sheriff who allegedly could have prevented attack by fellow prisoner is unconstitutional denial of right of access to courts guaranteed by Federal and State Constitutions. McCuiston v. Wanicka, App. 2 Dist., 483 So.2d 489 (1986). Constitutional Law ⚷ 2325; Prisons ⚷ 309

Dismissal of malpractice action by felon against his former defense counsel on authority of West's F.S.A. § 944.292, which provides that civil rights of a person convicted are suspended until restored by full pardon, conditional pardon, or restoration of civil rights, was unconstitutional application of the statute. Lloyd v. Farkash, App. 1 Dist., 476 So.2d 305 (1985). Convicts ⚷ 21; Convicts ⚷ 22

The provision authorizing suspension and automatic reinstatement of civil rights of convicted persons contained in this section constituted a clear infringement upon the exclusive constitutional power of the governor and cabinet to restore civil rights. In re Advisory Opinion of Governor Civil Rights, 306 So.2d 520 (1975). Constitutional Law ⚷ 2392; Convicts ⚷ 22

2. Construction and application

State has constitutional authority to deny basic civil rights, including right to vote and to serve on jury, to person convicted of felony; however, convicted prisoner does not forfeit all constitutional protections by reason of conviction and confinement. Singletary v. Costello, App. 4 Dist., 665 So.2d 1099 (1996). Constitutional Law ⚷ 1460; Convicts ⚷ 21; Elections ⚷ 90; Prisons ⚷ 111

Constitutional and statutory restrictions on the exercise of civil and political rights and privileges by a person convicted of a felony apply regardless of the age of the person at the time of conviction. The operation of such constitutional and statutory provisions is not affected by the fact that a person was a minor (and thus not yet able to exercise such rights and privileges) at the time of conviction. Op.Atty. Gen., 078–45, March 10, 1978.

The requirement that a convicted felon's civil rights be restored before certain civil or political rights or privileges may be exercised, and the procedures for restoration of civil rights by the governor and three members of the cabinet, apply regardless of a person's age at the time of a felony conviction. Op.Atty.Gen., 078–45, March 10, 1978.

3. Marriage

In state prison inmate's civil rights action against Florida department of corrections and its director challenging constitutionality of prison regulation restricting inmate marriages, substantial fact issues existed as to whether regulation was rationally related to state's security and rehabilitation interests, precluding summary judgment against inmate. Bradbury v. Wainwright, C.A.11 (Fla.)1983, 718 F.2d 1538. Federal Civil Procedure ⚷ 2491.5

Evidence, in proceeding in which department of corrections denied prison inmate permission to be married, was sufficient to support department's determination that the proposed marriage would adversely affect prison security and inmate's rehabilitation interests and, thus, supported denial of permission to be married. Holden v. Florida Dept. of Corrections, App. 1 Dist., 400 So.2d 142 (1981). Marriage ⚷ 9; Prisons ⚷ 291(7)

This section did not automatically suspend right of convicted felons to marry. Holden v. Florida Dept. of Corrections, App. 1 Dist., 400 So.2d 142 (1981). Marriage ⚷ 9

4. Possession of firearms

Right to possess a firearm is a "civil right" under this section providing for suspension of convicted felon's civil rights. Thompson v. State, App. 2 Dist., 438 So.2d 1005 (1983). Weapons ⚷ 4

Defendant had not had his "civil rights" restored, for purposes of F.S.A. § 790.23 governing crime of possession of firearm by convicted felon when alleged unlawful possession occurred, although under the governor's discretionary clemency power defendant was restored to his preconviction rights, in light of fact that when defendant was convicted as a felon, one of rights that he previously held as a citizen, right to possess firearm was taken away and defendant could no longer legally possess or own a firearm which was clearly a "civil right" that he no longer possessed and the governor's restoring all other preconviction rights did not include the right to process or own a firearm. Williams v. State, App. 1 Dist., 402 So.2d 78 (1981). Weapons ⚷ 4

Section 790.23 proscribing possession of weapons by convicted felon was not unconstitutional by virtue of its exemption of persons who, although they have been convicted of felony, have had their civil rights restored. Crossley v. State, 334 So.2d 17 (1976). Weapons ⚷ 3

5. Civil actions

Order abating convicted felon's petition for name change, on grounds that this section prevented convicted felon from maintaining civil action until his civil rights had been restored, was unconstitutional denial of access to courts; clarifying *Watts v. Buck*, 454 So.2d 1079 (Fla. App.). Dinkens v. Circuit Court of Tenth Judicial Circuit., App. 2 Dist., 489 So.2d 46 (1986). Constitutional Law ⚷ 2314; Convicts ⚷ 21; Convicts ⚷ 22; Names ⚷ 20

Convicted felon's right to bring legal malpractice action against his criminal defense attorney was suspended by this section until restoration of his civil rights. Watts v. Buck, App. 2 Dist., 454 So.2d 1079 (1984). Prisons ⚷ 309

Trial court properly denied convicted felon's motion for appointment of counsel in his legal malpractice action against his criminal defense attorney, where felon's right to bring the legal malpractice action was suspended until restoration of his civil rights. Watts v. Buck, App. 2 Dist., 454 So.2d 1079 (1984). Trial ⚷ 21

6. Name change petitions

Petitioner for a name change was entitled to an evidentiary hearing as to the dates of his felony convictions and as to whether his civil rights were ever suspended or, if suspended, were fully restored; name change petition was facially sufficient, and it was impossible to determine from the record whether petitioner's prior felony convictions resulted in suspension of his civil rights, and whether they occurred prior to effective date of statute requiring petitioners for a name change to show that their civil rights were never suspended or were fully restored. Finfrock v. State, App. 4 Dist., 932 So.2d 437 (2006). Names ⚷ 20

944.293. Initiation of restoration of civil rights

With respect to those persons convicted of a felony, the following procedure shall apply: Prior to the time an offender is discharged from supervision, an authorized agent of the department shall obtain from the Governor the necessary application and other forms required for the restoration of civil rights. The authorized agent shall assist the offender in completing these forms and shall ensure that the application and all necessary material are forwarded to the Governor before the offender is discharged from supervision.

Laws 1974, c. 74–112, § 29; Laws 1976, c. 76–139, § 1; Laws 1979, c. 79–3, § 60.

Historical and Statutory Notes

Amendment Notes:

Laws 1976, c. 76–139, deleted "prior to July 1, 1974," preceding "the following procedure shall apply", and substituted "governor" for "pardon board" in two instances.

Laws 1979, c. 79–3, a reviser's bill, provided for substitution of references to the department and secretary of "corrections" for the department and secretary of "offender rehabilitation" to conform with Laws 1978, c. 78–53.

Cross References

Labor by prisoner, no restoration of civil rights, see §§ 946.002, 946.514.
Pardon or release, requisites for restoration of civil rights, see § 940.05.
Restoration of civil rights, authority of governor, see § 940.01.

Library References

Convicts ⚷21.
Westlaw Topic No. 98.
C.J.S. Convicts §§ 1 to 6, 8 to 24.

Research References

ALR Library

10 ALR 6th 31, Validity, Construction, and Application of State Criminal Disenfranchisement Provisions.

Notes of Decisions

Construction and application 1

1. Construction and application

Department of Corrections failed to comply with requirement of statute to provide "other forms required for the restoration of civil rights" to offenders prior to their discharge, and thus, issuance of writ of writ of mandamus to require Department to provide forms and offer assistance was warranted; legislature chose to use word "shall" throughout statute, such that Department's statutory obligations were not discretionary, and provisions of statute required Department to provide requisite forms to offenders prior to their discharge, to offer its help to offenders in completing forms, and to respond with assistance when requested by offenders. Florida Caucus of Black State Legislators, Inc. v. Crosby, App. 1 Dist., 877 So.2d 861 (2004). Prisons ⚷ 241

Constitutional and statutory restrictions on the exercise of civil and political rights and privileges by a person convicted of a felony apply regardless of the age of the person at the time of conviction. The operation of such constitutional and statutory provisions is not affected by the fact that a person was a minor (and thus not yet able to exercise such rights and privileges) at the time of conviction. Op.Atty. Gen., 078–45, March 10, 1978.

The requirement that a convicted felon's civil rights be restored before certain civil or political rights or privileges may be exercised, and the procedures for restoration of civil rights by the governor and three members of the cabinet, apply regardless of a person's age at the time of a felony conviction. Op.Atty.Gen., 078–45, March 10, 1978.

944.30. Repealed by Laws 1988, c. 88–122, § 11, eff. July 1, 1988

Historical and Statutory Notes

Repealed § 944.30, which related to commutation of a life sentence to a sentence of a term of years, was derived from:

Laws 1986, c. 86–183, § 23.
Laws 1979, c. 79–3, § 61.
Laws 1977, c. 77–120, § 51.
Laws 1961, c. 61–530, § 18.
Laws 1957, c. 57–121, § 28.

944.31. Inspector general; inspectors; power and duties

The inspector general shall be responsible for prison inspection and investigation, internal affairs investigations, and management reviews. The office of the inspector general shall be charged with the duty of inspecting the penal and correctional systems of the state. The office of the inspector general shall inspect each correctional institution or any place in which state prisoners are housed, worked, or kept within the state, with reference to its physical conditions, cleanliness, sanitation, safety, and comfort; the quality and supply of all bedding; the quality, quantity, and diversity of food served and the manner in which it is served; the number and condition of the prisoners confined therein; and the general conditions of each institution. The office of inspector general shall see that all the rules and regulations issued by the department are strictly observed and followed by all persons connected with the correctional systems of the state. The office of the inspector general shall coordinate and supervise the work of inspectors throughout the state. The inspector general and inspectors may enter any place where prisoners in this state are kept and shall be immediately admitted to such place as they desire and may consult and confer with any prisoner privately and without molestation. The inspector general and inspectors shall be responsible for criminal and administrative investigation of matters relating to the Department of Corrections. The secretary may designate persons within the office of the inspector general as law enforcement officers to conduct any criminal investigation that occurs on property owned or leased by the department or involves matters over which the department has jurisdiction. A person designated as a law enforcement officer must be certified pursuant to s. 943.1395 and must have a minimum of 3 years' experience as an inspector in the inspector general's office or as a law enforcement officer. The department shall maintain a memorandum of understanding with the Department of Law Enforcement for the notification and investigation of mutually agreed-upon predicate events that shall include, but are not limited to, suspicious deaths and organized criminal activity. During investigations, the inspector general and inspectors may consult and confer with any prisoner or staff member privately and without molestation and persons designated as law enforcement officers under this section shall have the authority to arrest, with or without a warrant, any prisoner of or visitor to a state correctional institution for a violation of the criminal laws of the state involving an offense classified as a felony that occurs on property owned or leased by the department and may arrest offenders who have escaped or absconded from custody. Persons designated as law enforcement officers have the authority to arrest with or without a warrant a staff member of the department, including any contract employee, for a violation of the criminal laws of the state involving an offense classified as a felony under this chapter or chapter 893 on property owned or leased by the department. A person designated as a law enforcement officer under this section may make arrests of persons against whom arrest warrants have been issued, including arrests of offenders who have escaped or absconded from custody. The arrested person shall be surrendered without delay to the sheriff of the county in which the arrest is made, with a formal complaint subsequently made against her or him in accordance with law.

Laws 1957, c. 57–121, § 29; Laws 1961, c. 61–192, § 6; Laws 1961, c. 61–530, § 18; Laws 1969, c. 69–106, §§ 19, 35; Laws 1977, c. 77–120, § 52; Laws 1979, c. 79–3, § 62; Laws 1985, c. 85–330, § 2; Laws 1987, c. 87–226, § 75; Laws 1995, c. 95–325, § 18. Amended by Laws 1996, c. 96–312, § 26, eff. July 1, 1996; Laws 1997, c. 97–102, § 1856, eff. July 1, 1997; Laws 1999, c. 99–271, § 2, eff. June 29, 1999; Laws 2002, c. 2002–75, § 1, eff. April 23, 2002.

Historical and Statutory Notes

Amendment Notes:

Laws 1961, c. 61–192, § 6, rewrote the former first three sentences into the first two sentences without change in substance except that the specific provision for six inspectors was deleted and substituted the "division of corrections" for the "board" to hire the inspectors.

Laws 1961, c. 61–530, § 18, substituted "division" for "department".

Laws 1969, c. 69–106, §§ 19, 35, transferred all powers, duties and functions of the division of corrections of the board of commissioners of state institutions to the division of adult corrections of the department of health and rehabilitative services.

Laws 1977, c. 77–120, a reviser's bill, amended this section to conform with Laws 1975, c. 75–49, which created the department of offender rehabilitation (see § 20.315) and transferred to the department certain functions performed by the division of correction of the department of health and rehabilitative services and the parole and probation commission of the department of offender rehabilitation.

Laws 1979, c. 79–3, a reviser's bill, provided for substitution of references to the department and secretary of "corrections" for the department and secretary of "offender rehabilitation" to conform with Laws 1978, c. 78–53.

Laws 1985, c. 85–330, § 2, eff. July 1, 1985, rewrote the section.

Laws 1987, c. 87–226, was a reviser's correction bill amending this section to ratify prior editorial action to improve clarity.

Laws 1995, c. 95–325, § 18, eff. July 1, 1995, deleted provisions which had made the inspector general responsible for jail and stockade inspections.

Laws 1996, c. 96–312, § 26, eff. July 1, 1996, in the third sentence, following "which state", deleted "or county".

Laws 1997, c. 97–102, eff. July 1, 1997, removed gender-specific references applicable to human beings from volume 4 of the Florida Statutes without substantive changes in legal effect.

Laws 1999, c. 99–271, § 2, eff. June 29, 1999, in the first sentence, following "investigations,", deleted "inmate grievances".

Laws 2002, c. 2002–75, § 1, rewrote this section, which formerly read:

"The inspector general shall be responsible for prison inspection and investigation, internal affairs investigations, and management reviews. The office of the inspector general shall be charged with the duty of inspecting the penal and correctional systems of the state. The office of the inspector general shall inspect each correctional institution or any place in which state prisoners are housed, worked, or kept within the state, with reference to its physical conditions, cleanliness, sanitation, safety, and comfort; the quality and supply of all bedding; the quality, quantity, and diversity of food served and the manner in which it is served; the number and condition of the prisoners confined therein; and the general conditions of each institution. The office of inspector general shall see that all the rules and regulations issued by the department are strictly observed and followed by all persons connected with the correctional systems of the state. The office of the inspector general shall coordinate and supervise the work of inspectors throughout the state. The inspector general and inspectors may enter any place where prisoners in this state are kept and shall be immediately admitted to such place as they desire and may consult and confer with any prisoner privately and without molestation. The inspector general and inspectors shall be responsible for criminal and administrative investigation of matters relating to the Department of Corrections. In such investigations, the inspector general and inspectors may consult and confer with any prisoner or staff member privately and without molestation and shall have the authority to detain any person for violations of the criminal laws of the state. Such detention shall be made only on properties owned or leased by the department, and the detained person shall be surrendered without delay to the sheriff of the county in which the detention is made, with a formal complaint subsequently made against her or him in accordance with law."

Law Review and Journal Commentaries

Disciplinary and punitive transfer decisions and due process values. Bruce R. Jacob, K. M. Sharma, 12 Stetson L.Rev. (Fla.) 1 (1982).

Library References

Prisons ⚷102.
Westlaw Topic No. 310.

C.J.S. Prisons and Rights of Prisoners §§ 5 to 7, 14, 17, 22 to 23, 50 to 53, 55, 59, 78.

Research References

Encyclopedias

Generally; State Facilities, FL Jur. 2d Prisons & Prisoners § 46.

944.32. Reports of prison inspectors; recordation; inspection

Upon completing an inspection of a correctional institution the inspector shall make a full and complete report on such forms as shall be provided by the department. One copy of each report shall be filed with the department, one copy shall be sent to the officer in charge of the correctional institution, and as many other copies as the department shall require; these reports shall be matters of public record and subject to inspection by the public at any time.

Laws 1957, c. 57–121, § 30; Laws 1961, c. 61–530, § 18; Laws 1977, c. 77–120, § 53; Laws 1979, c. 79–3, § 63; Laws 1991, c. 91–225, § 19; Laws 1995, c. 95–325, § 19. Amended by Laws 1996, c. 96–312, § 27, eff. July 1, 1996.

Historical and Statutory Notes

Amendment Notes:

Laws 1961, c. 61–530, § 18, substituted "division" for "department".

Laws 1977, c. 77–120, a reviser's bill, amended this section to conform with Laws 1975, c. 75–49, which created the department of offender rehabilitation (see § 20.315) and transferred to the department certain functions performed by the division of corrections of the department of health and rehabilitative services and the parole and probation commission of the department of offender rehabilitation.

Laws 1979, c. 79–3, a reviser's bill, provided for substitution of references to the department and secretary of "corrections" for the department and secretary of "offender rehabilitation" to conform with Laws 1978, c. 78–53.

Laws 1991, c. 91–225, § 19, eff. July 1, 1991, substituted "shall be sent to the officer in charge of the jail or correctional institution, one copy shall be sent to the board of county commissioners of the county" for "with the clerk of circuit court of the county" preceding "where", and deleted "shall at all times be open to inspection in the office of the clerk of the circuit court, and" following "reports" in the last sentence.

Laws 1995, c. 95–325, § 19, eff. July 1, 1995, deleted references to jails throughout.

Laws 1996, c. 96–312, § 27, eff. July 1, 1996, in the second sentence, following "institution,", deleted "one copy shall be sent to the board of county commissioners of the county where the inspection is made".

Library References

Prisons ⚷102.
Westlaw Topic No. 310.

C.J.S. Prisons and Rights of Prisoners §§ 5 to 7, 14, 17, 22 to 23, 50 to 53, 55, 59, 78.

Research References

Encyclopedias

Inspection Reports, FL Jur. 2d Prisons & Prisoners § 48.

Other State Records, FL Jur. 2d Records & Recording Acts § 61.

944.33. Failure of inspector to make report; false report; penalty

If any prison inspector shall fail to make a report of his or her findings, he or she shall be immediately discharged and shall not be again employed in such capacity. If any prison inspector shall knowingly make a false report of his or her findings, he or she shall be guilty of a felony of the third degree, punishable as provided in s. 775.082, s. 775.083, or s. 775.084.

Laws 1957, c. 57–121, § 31; Laws 1971, c. 71–136, § 1166. Amended by Laws 1997, c. 97–102, § 1647, eff. July 1, 1997.

Historical and Statutory Notes

Amendment Notes:

Laws 1971, c. 71–136, § 1166, made the offense defined by this section a "felony of the third degree, punishable as provided in § 775.082, § 775.083, or § 775.084" in lieu of provision that offenders "be punished by imprisonment in the state correctional system for not more than 3 years or by fine of not more than $5,000, or by both."

Laws 1997, c. 97–102, eff. July 1, 1997, removed gender-specific references applicable to human beings from volume 4 of the Florida Statutes without substantive changes in legal effect.

Library References

Prisons ⚷102, 439.
Westlaw Topic No. 310.

C.J.S. Prisons and Rights of Prisoners §§ 5 to 7, 14, 17, 22 to 23, 50 to 53, 55, 59, 78, 123 to 125, 127.

Research References

Encyclopedias

Inspection Reports, FL Jur. 2d Prisons & Prisoners § 48.

944.331. Inmate grievance procedure

The department shall establish by rule an inmate grievance procedure that must conform to the Minimum Standards for Inmate Grievance Procedures as promulgated by the United States Department of Justice pursuant to 42 U.S.C. s. 1997e. The department's office of general counsel shall oversee the grievance procedures established by the department.

Laws 1985, c. 85–288, § 3. Amended by Laws 1999, c. 99–271, § 3, eff. June 29, 1999.

Historical and Statutory Notes

Amendment Notes:

Laws 1999, c. 99–271, § 3, eff. June 29, 1999, in the first sentence, substituted "that must" for "which shall"; and added the second sentence.

Library References

Prisons ⚷273, 279.
Westlaw Topic No. 310.

C.J.S. Prisons and Rights of Prisoners §§ 23, 26 to 44, 47, 76, 78 to 88, 123, 125, 127, 136 to 141, 150.

Notes of Decisions

Administrative remedies 1

1. Administrative remedies

Exhaustion of administrative remedies is a prerequisite to filing a claim under statutes making private contractors liable in tort for claims arising with respect to the care and custody of inmates. Adlington v. Mosley, App. 4 Dist., 757 So.2d 573 (2000). Prisons ⚷ 317

Remand was required for determination of whether inmate grievance procedure was available during relevant time period to inmate, who filed complaint against correctional facility employee pursuant to statutes making private contractors liable in tort for claims arising with respect to care and custody of inmates, and if so, inmate was required to exhaust that procedure before filing civil tort complaint, but if not, his failure to exhaust would be excused. Adlington v. Mosley, App. 4 Dist., 757 So.2d 573 (2000). Appeal And Error ⚷ 1178(1)

944.34. Repealed by Laws 1985, c. 85–288, § 27, eff. July 1, 1985

Historical and Statutory Notes

Repealed § 944.34, which related to order and punishment, was derived from Laws 1957, c. 57–121, § 32.

944.35. Authorized use of force; malicious battery and sexual misconduct prohibited; reporting required; penalties

(1)(a) An employee of the department is authorized to apply physical force upon an inmate only when and to the extent that it reasonably appears necessary:

1. To defend himself or herself or another against such other imminent use of unlawful force;

2. To prevent a person from escaping from a state correctional institution when the officer reasonably believes that person is lawfully detained in such institution;

3. To prevent damage to property;

4. To quell a disturbance;

5. To overcome physical resistance to a lawful command; or

6. To administer medical treatment only by or under the supervision of a physician or his or her designee and only:

a. When treatment is necessary to protect the health of other persons, as in the case of contagious or venereal diseases; or

b. When treatment is offered in satisfaction of a duty to protect the inmate against self-inflicted injury or death.

As part of the correctional officer training program, the Criminal Justice Standards and Training Commission shall develop a course specifically designed to explain the parameters of this subsection and to teach the proper methods and techniques in applying authorized physical force upon an inmate.

(b) Following any use of force, a qualified health care provider shall examine any person physically involved to determine the extent of injury, if any, and shall prepare a report which shall include, but not be limited to, a statement of whether further examination by a physician is necessary. Any noticeable physical injury shall be examined by a physician, and the physician shall prepare a report documenting the extent and probable cause of the injury and the treatment prescribed. Such report shall be completed within 5 working days of the incident and shall be submitted to the warden for appropriate investigation.

(2) Each employee of the department who either applies physical force or was responsible for making the decision to apply physical force upon an inmate or an offender supervised by the department in the community pursuant to this subsection shall prepare, date, and sign an independent report within 1 working day of the incident. The report shall be delivered to the warden or the circuit administrator, who shall forward the report with all appropriate documentation to the office of the inspector general. The inspector general shall conduct a review and make recommendations regarding the appropriateness or inappropriateness of the use of force. If the inspector general finds that the use of force was appropriate, the employee's report, together with the inspector general's written determination of the appropriateness of the force used and the reasons therefor, shall be forwarded to the circuit administrator or warden upon completion of the review. If the inspector general finds that the use of force was inappropriate, the inspector general shall conduct a complete investigation into the incident and forward the findings of fact to the appropriate regional director for further action. Copies of the employee's report and the inspector general's review shall be kept in the files of the inmate or the offender supervised by the department in the community. A notation of each incident involving use of force and the outcome based on the inspector general's evaluation shall be kept in the employee's file.

(3)(a)1. Any employee of the department who, with malicious intent, commits a battery upon an inmate or an offender supervised by the department in the community, commits a misdemeanor of the first degree, punishable as provided in s. 775.082 or s. 775.083.

2. Any employee of the department who, with malicious intent, commits a battery or inflicts cruel or inhuman treatment by neglect or otherwise, and in so doing causes great bodily harm, permanent disability, or permanent disfigurement to an inmate or an offender supervised by the department in the community, commits a felony of the third degree, punishable as provided in s. 775.082, s. 775.083, or s. 775.084.

(b) 1. As used in this paragraph, the term "sexual misconduct" means the oral, anal, or vaginal penetration by, or union with, the sexual organ of another or the anal or vaginal penetration of another by any other object, but does not include an act done for a bona fide medical purpose or an internal search conducted in the lawful performance of the employee's duty.

2. Any employee of the department who engages in sexual misconduct with an inmate or an offender supervised by the department in the community, without committing the crime of sexual battery, commits a felony of the third degree, punishable as provided in s. 775.082, s. 775.083, or s. 775.084.

3. The consent of the inmate or offender supervised by the department in the community to any act of sexual misconduct may not be raised as a defense to a prosecution under this paragraph.

4. This paragraph does not apply to any employee of the department who is legally married to an inmate or an offender supervised by the department in the community, nor does it apply to any employee who has no knowledge, and would have no reason to believe, that the person with whom the employee has engaged in sexual misconduct is an inmate or an offender under community supervision of the department.

(c) Notwithstanding prosecution, any violation of the provisions of this subsection, as determined by the Public Employees Relations Commission, shall constitute sufficient cause under s. 110.227 for dismissal from employment with the department, and such person shall not again be employed in any capacity in connection with the correctional system.

(d) Each employee who witnesses, or has reasonable cause to suspect, that an inmate or an offender under the supervision of the department in the community has been unlawfully abused or is the subject of sexual misconduct pursuant to this subsection shall immediately prepare, date, and sign an independent report specifically describing the nature of the force used or the nature of the sexual misconduct, the location and time of the incident, and the persons involved. The report shall be delivered to the inspector general of the department with a copy to be delivered to the warden of the institution or the regional administrator. The inspector general shall immediately conduct an appropriate investigation, and, if probable cause is determined that a violation of this subsection has occurred, the respective state attorney in the circuit in which the incident occurred shall be notified.

(4)(a) Any employee required to report pursuant to this section who knowingly or willfully fails to do so, or who knowingly or willfully prevents another person from doing so, commits a misdemeanor of the first degree, punishable as provided in s. 775.082 or s. 775.083.

(b) Any person who knowingly or willfully submits inaccurate, incomplete, or untruthful information with regard to reports required in this section commits a misdemeanor of the first degree, punishable as provided in s. 775.082 or s. 775.083.

(c) Any person who knowingly or willfully coerces or threatens any other person with the intent to alter either testimony or a written report regarding an incident where force was used or an incident of sexual misconduct commits a felony of the third degree, punishable as provided in s. 775.082, s. 775.083, or s. 775.084.

As part of the correctional officer training program, the Criminal Justice Standards and Training Commission shall develop course materials for inclusion in the appropriate required course specifically designed to explain the parameters of this subsection and to teach sexual assault identification and prevention methods and techniques.

Laws 1957, c. 57–121, § 33; Laws 1985, c. 85–288, § 5; Laws 1986, c. 86–163, § 85; Laws 1991, c. 91–224, § 228. Amended by Laws 1996, c. 96–312, § 6, eff. Oct. 1, 1996; Laws 1997, c. 97–78, § 15, eff. May 23, 1997; Laws 2000, c. 2000–161, § 15, eff. July 4, 2000; Laws 2001, c. 2001–92, § 2, eff. Oct. 1, 2001; Laws 2002, c. 2002–75, § 2, eff. April 23, 2002.

Historical and Statutory Notes

Amendment Notes:

Laws 1985, c. 85–288, § 5, eff. July 1, 1985, rewrote this section, which formerly read:

"It is unlawful for any corporal punishment, any cruel or inhuman punishment, or any punishment by which the flesh of the body is broken, bruised, or lacerated to be inflicted upon any prisoner at any time. Any person who violates the provisions of this section shall be discharged immediately and shall not again be employed in any capacity in connection with the correctional system and shall be punished as provided by law for whatever offense he may have committed in perpetrating the act. No prisoner shall be punished because of any report or representation which he may have made to any inspector."

Laws 1986, c. 86–163, § 85, eff. July 1, 1986, substituted in the third sentence of the subsec. (3) "public employees relations" for "career service" commission.

Laws 1991, c. 91–224, a reviser's bill, modified provisions for punishment of misdemeanors as contained in this section by deleting reference to punishment pursuant to § 775.084 to conform with Laws 1988, c. 88–131 which deleted all references to misdemeanors from § 775.084.

Laws 1996, c. 96–312, § 6, eff. Oct. 1, 1996, rewrote this section, which formerly read:

"(1) An employee of the department is authorized to apply physical force to the person of an inmate only when and to the extent that it reasonably appears necessary:

"(a) To defend himself or another against such other imminent use of unlawful force;

"(b) To prevent the escape from a state correctional institution of a person whom the officer reasonably believes to be lawfully detained in such institution;

"(c) To prevent damage to property;

"(d) To quell a disturbance;

"(e) To overcome physical resistance to a lawful command; or

"(f) To administer medical treatment only by or under the supervision of a physician or his designee and only:

"1. When treatment is necessary to protect the health of other persons, as in the case of contagious or venereal diseases; or

"2. When treatment is offered in satisfaction of a duty to protect the inmate against self-inflicted injury or death.

"(2) Following any use of force, a qualified health care provider shall examine any person physically involved to determine the extent of injury, if any, and shall prepare a report which shall include, but not be limited to, a statement of whether further examination by a physician is necessary. Any noticeable physical injury shall be examined by a physician and the physician shall prepare a report documenting the extent and probable cause of the injury and the treatment prescribed. Such report shall be completed within 5 working days of the incident and shall be submitted to the superintendent for appropriate investigation.

"(3) Any employee of the department who, with malice aforethought, commits a battery to the person of an inmate shall be guilty of a misdemeanor of the first degree, punishable as provided in s. 775.082 or s. 775.083. Any employee of the department who inflicts cruel or inhuman treatment by neglect or otherwise, and in so doing causes great bodily harm, permanent disability, or permanent disfigurement to the person of an inmate, shall be guilty of a felony of the third degree, punishable as provided in s. 775.082, s. 775.083, or s. 775.084. Notwithstanding prosecution, any violation of the provisions of this subsection, as determined by the Public Employees Relations Commission, shall constitute sufficient cause under s. 110.227 for dismissal from employment with the department, and such person shall not again be employed in any capacity in connection with the correctional system.

"(4) Each employee of the department who applies physical force to the person of an inmate or who was responsible for making the decision to apply physical force to the person of an inmate pursuant to subsection (1) shall prepare, date, and sign an independent report within 5 working days of the incident. The report shall be delivered to the superintendent, who shall have an investigation made and shall approve or disapprove the force used. The employee's report, together with the superintendent's written approval or disapproval of the force used and his reasons therefor, shall be forwarded within 5 working days of the date of the completion of the investigation to the regional director. The regional director shall, in writing, concur in the superintendent's evaluation or disapprove it. Copies of the employee's report, the superintendent's evaluation, and the regional director's review shall be kept in the files of both the inmate and the employee.

"(5) Each employee who witnesses, or has reasonable cause to suspect, that an inmate has been unlawfully abused pursuant to subsection (3) shall immediately prepare, date, and sign an independent report specifically describing the nature of the force used, the location and time of the incident, and the persons involved. The report shall be delivered to the inspector general of the department with a copy to be delivered to the superintendent of the institution. The inspector general shall immediately conduct an appropriate investigation, and, if probable cause is determined that a violation of this statute has occurred, the respective state attorney in the circuit in which the institution is located shall be notified.

"(6) Any employee required to report pursuant to this section who knowingly or willfully fails to do so, or who knowingly or willfully prevents another person from doing so, shall be guilty of a misdemeanor of the first degree, punishable as provided in s. 775.082 or s. 775.083.

"(7)(a) Any person who knowingly or willfully submits inaccurate, incomplete, or untruthful information with regard to reports required in this section shall be guilty of a misdemeanor of the first degree, punishable as provided in s. 775.082 or s. 775.083.

"(b) Any person who knowingly or willfully coerces or threatens any other person with the intent to alter either testimony or a written report regarding an incident where force was used shall be guilty of a felony of the third degree, punishable as provided in s. 775.082, s. 775.083, or s. 775.084.

"(8) The Criminal Justice Standards and Training Commission shall include as part of the correctional officer training program as provided in s. 943.14 a course specifically designed to explain the parameters of this section and to teach the proper methods and techniques in applying authorized physical force to the person of an inmate."

The introductory clause of Laws 1996, c. 96–312, § 6, provided, "Effective for offenses committed on or after October 1, 1996..."

Laws 1997, c. 97–78, § 15, eff. May 23, 1997, in subsec. (2), in the next-to-last sentence, preceding "the inmate" deleted "both"; following "community" deleted ", and the employee"; and added the last sentence.

Laws 2000, c. 2000–161, a reviser's bill, substituted references to warden for references to superintendent.

Laws 2001, c. 2001–92, § 2, in subsec. (3)(b)3., substituted "may" for "shall"; and, in subsec. (4), added the last paragraph, relating to training course materials.

Laws 2002, c. 2002–75, § 2, rewrote subsec. (2), which formerly read:

"(2) Each employee of the department who either applies physical force or was responsible for making the decision to apply physical force upon an inmate or an offender supervised by the department in the community pursuant to this subsection shall prepare, date, and sign an independent report within 5 working days of the incident. The report shall be delivered to the warden or the regional administrator, who shall have an investigation made and shall approve or disapprove the force used. The employee's report, together with the warden's or regional administrator's written approval or disapproval of the force used and the reasons therefor, shall be forwarded within 5 working days of the date of the completion of the investigation to the regional director. The regional director shall, in writing, concur in the warden's or regional administrator's evaluation or disapprove it. Copies of the employee's report, the warden's or regional administrator's evaluation, and the regional director's review shall be kept in the files of the inmate or the offender supervised by the department in the community. A notation of each incident involving use of force and the outcome based on the warden's or regional director's evaluation and the regional administrator's review shall be kept in the employee's file."

Library References

Prisons ⚷124.
Westlaw Topic No. 310.
C.J.S. Prisons and Rights of Prisoners §§ 44, 58, 60.

Research References

Encyclopedias

Generally; State Facilities, FL Jur. 2d Prisons & Prisoners § 46.

Sanctions and Liability for Duress, Battery Against, or Cruel and Unusual Treatment Of, Inmates or Supervised Offenders, FL Jur. 2d Prisons & Prisoners § 82.

Examination and Reporting Requirements, FL Jur. 2d Prisons & Prisoners § 85.

Reporting Requirements, FL Jur. 2d Prisons & Prisoners § 88.

Treatises and Practice Aids

16 Florida Practice Series § 3:15, Completing the 1994 Guidelines Scoresheet--Victim Injury (Section III).

16 Florida Practice Series § 4:19, Completing the 1995 Guidelines Scoresheet--Victim Injury (Section III).

16 Florida Practice Series § 5:19, Completing the Criminal Punishment Code Scoresheet--Victim Injury (Section III)--Sexual Penetration and Sexual Contact.

22 Florida Practice Series App. A, Florida Rules of Criminal Procedure.

Notes of Decisions

Summary judgment 1

1. Summary judgment

Whether conduct of defendant, as an individual employed by county as supervisor of "women's annex" of county jail, in giving tacit approval to plaintiff's continued imprisonment in a so called "safety cell," as it was equipped, and without medical evaluation, was contrary to requirements of several county regulations, statutory provisions, and to state and federal prohibitions against "cruel and unusual punishment" was question of fact precluding summary judgment on issue of negligence. Donner v. Hetherington, App. 3 Dist., 370 So.2d 1225 (1979). Judgment ⚷ 181(27)

944.36. Permitting inmates to escape

Any agent, employee, or officer of the department having supervision over state inmates being worked under the provisions of law who willfully permits any prisoner to escape shall be guilty of a felony of the third degree, punishable as provided in s. 775.082, s. 775.083, or s. 775.084.

Laws 1957, c. 57–121, § 34; Laws 1961, c. 61–530, § 18; Laws 1971, c. 71–136, § 1167; Laws 1977, c. 77–120, § 54; Laws 1979, c. 79–3, § 64; Laws 1985, c. 85–288, § 6.

Historical and Statutory Notes

Amendment Notes:

Laws 1961, c. 61–530, § 18, substituted "division" for "department".

Laws 1971, c. 71–136, § 1167, made the offense defined by this section a "felony of the third degree, punishable as provided in § 775.082, § 775.083, or § 775.084" in lieu of the provision that offenders "shall be punished by imprisonment in the state correctional system for not exceeding five years, or by fine not exceeding $5,000, or by both."

Laws 1977, c. 77–120, a reviser's bill, amended this section to conform with Laws 1975, c. 75–49, which created the department of offender rehabilitation (see § 20.315) and transferred to the department certain functions performed by the division of corrections of the department of health and rehabilitative services and the parole and probation commission of the department of offender rehabilitation.

Laws 1979, c. 79–3, a reviser's bill, provided for substitution of references to the department and secretary of "corrections" for the department and secretary of "offender rehabilitation" to conform with Laws 1978, c. 78–53.

Laws 1985, c. 85–288, § 6, eff. July 1, 1985, rewrote this section.

Cross References

Intentional or negligent aiding of escape by prisoners, see § 843.09 et seq.

Library References

Escape ⚷3.
Westlaw Topic No. 151.

Research References

Encyclopedias

Escape or Attempted Escape; Aiding Escaped Prisoners, FL Jur. 2d Prisons & Prisoners § 222.

944.37. Acceptance of unauthorized compensation; penalty

No officer or employee of the department shall receive, directly or indirectly, from any prisoner or from anyone on behalf of such prisoner, any gift, reward, or any compensation whatsoever for his or her services or supplies other than that prescribed or authorized by law or the department. Whoever violates this section shall be guilty of a misdemeanor of the first degree, punishable as provided in s. 775.083.

Laws 1957, c. 57–121, § 35; Laws 1961, c. 61–530, § 18; Laws 1971, c. 71–136, § 1168; Laws 1977, c. 77–120, § 55; Laws 1979, c. 79–3, § 65. Amended by Laws 1997, c. 97–102, § 1648, eff. July 1, 1997.

Historical and Statutory Notes

Amendment Notes:

Laws 1961, c. 61–530, § 18, substituted "division" for "department".

Laws 1971, c. 71–136, § 1168, made the offense defined by this section a "misdemeanor of the first degree, punishable as provided in § 775.083" in lieu of provision that offenders "shall be punished by fine of not exceeding $5,000."

Laws 1977, c. 77–120, a reviser's bill, amended this section to conform with Laws 1975, c. 75–49, which created the department of offender rehabilitation (see § 20.315) and transferred to the department certain functions performed by the division of corrections of the department of health and rehabilitative services and the parole and probation commission of the department of offender rehabilitation.

Laws 1979, c. 79–3, a reviser's bill, provided for substitution of references to the department and secretary of "corrections" for the department and secretary of "offender rehabilitation" to conform with Laws 1978, c. 78–53.

Laws 1997, c. 97–102, eff. July 1, 1997, removed gender-specific references applicable to human beings from volume 4 of the Florida

Statutes without substantive changes in legal effect.

Cross References

Leasing of county prisoners to work for private interests, prohibition, see § 951.10.
Prohibition of sale of goods made by prisoners, see § 946.518.

Law Review and Journal Commentaries

Conflicts of interest. 18 U.Fla.L.Rev. 675 (1966).

Library References

Prisons ⚷439.
Westlaw Topic No. 310.
C.J.S. Prisons and Rights of Prisoners §§ 123 to 125, 127.

Research References

Encyclopedias

Employee's Receipt of Gift from Prisoner, FL Jur. 2d Prisons & Prisoners § 216.

944.38. Acceptance of remuneration from contractor; dealing or barter with prisoners; interest in contract; penalty

(1)(a) An officer or employee of the department may not receive any compensation whatsoever, directly or indirectly, for any act or service that she or he may do or perform for or on behalf of any officer or employee or agent, or employee of a contractor. An officer or employee of the department or the state may not have an interest, directly or indirectly, in any contract or purchase made, or authorized to be made, by anyone for or on behalf of the department.

(b) This subsection does not prevent an officer or employee of the department from accepting other employment or following any pursuit that does not interfere with the full and faithful discharge by the officer or employee of his or her duties to the department. This subsection does not prevent an officer or employee of the department from accepting secondary employment with an entity contracting with the department if the officer or employee does not have responsibilities or involvement with the department's award or management of the contract or with the process of making referrals to or evaluating the contracting entity.

(2) An officer or employee of the department or of the state, or any contractor, or employee of a contractor, may not, without permission of the department, make any gift or present to a prisoner, receive a gift or present from any prisoner, or have any barter or dealings with any prisoner.

(3) For any violation of the provisions of this section the officer or employee of the state shall be discharged from her or his office or service; and every contractor, or employee, or agent of a contractor engaged therein, and a party thereto, shall be expelled from the institutional grounds, and not again permitted within the same as a contractor, agent, or employee.

Laws 1957, c. 57–121, § 36; Laws 1961, c. 61–530, § 18; Laws 1969, c. 69–106, §§ 19, 35; Laws 1977, c. 77–120, § 56; Laws 1979, c. 79–3, § 66. Amended by Laws 1997, c. 97–102, § 1649, eff. July 1, 1997; Laws 2004, c. 2004–51, § 1, eff. May 12, 2004.

Historical and Statutory Notes

Amendment Notes:

Laws 1961, c. 61–530, § 18, substituted "division" for "department".

Laws 1969, c. 69–106, §§ 19, 35, transferred all powers, duties and functions of the division of corrections of the board of commissioners of state institutions to the division of adult corrections of the department of health and rehabilitative services.

Laws 1977, c. 77–120, a reviser's bill, amended subsecs. (1) and (2) of this section to conform with Laws 1975, c. 75–49, which created the department of offender rehabilitation (see § 20.315) and transferred to the department certain functions performed by the division of corrections of the department of health and rehabilitative services and the parole and probation commission of the department of offender rehabilitation.

Laws 1979, c. 79–3, a reviser's bill, provided for substitution of references to the department and secretary of "corrections" for the department and secretary of "offender rehabilitation" to conform with Laws 1978, c. 78–53.

Laws 1997, c. 97–102, eff. July 1, 1997, removed gender-specific references applicable to human beings from volume 4 of the Florida Statutes without substantive changes in legal effect.

Laws 2004, c. 2004–51, § 1, rewrote subsec. (1); and in subsec. (2), made nonsubstantive language changes. Subsec. (1) formerly read:

"(1) No officer or employee of the department shall receive any compensation whatsoever, directly or indirectly, for any act or service which she or he may do or perform for or on behalf of any officer or employee or agent, or employee of a contractor; nor shall any officer or employee of the department or the state be interested, directly or indirectly, in any contract or purchase made, or authorized to be made, by anyone for or on behalf of the department."

Law Review and Journal Commentaries

Conflicts of interest. 18 U.Fla.L.Rev. 675 (1966).

Library References

Prisons ⚷391, 396, 402.
Westlaw Topic No. 310.
C.J.S. Prisons and Rights of Prisoners §§ 12 to 15, 17, 22.

Research References

Encyclopedias

Generally; Residence, FL Jur. 2d Cvl. Servts. & Pub. Officers & Employees § 114.

Receipt or Acceptance of Unauthorized Gifts; Employees' Interests in Contracts or Purchases of Department, FL Jur. 2d Prisons & Prisoners § 42.

944.39. Interference with prisoners; penalty

Any person who, without authority, interferes with or in any way interrupts the work of any prisoner under the custody of the department or who in any way interferes with the discipline or good conduct of any prisoner shall be guilty of a misdemeanor of the second degree, punishable as provided in s. 775.082 or s. 775.083. No person shall, by disguise, misrepresentation of identity or other illicit means, attempt to gain admission to or enter upon the grounds of any state correctional institution for the purpose of visiting any prisoner in violation of the general visiting policy adopted by the department. A person, upon conviction of an offense as outlined in this section, shall be guilty of a misdemeanor of the second degree, punishable as provided in s. 775.082 or s. 775.083. Any peace officer or any correctional officer of the department or any prison inspector or any employee of the department may arrest without warrant any person violating the provisions of this section.

Laws 1957, c. 57–121, § 37; Laws 1961, c. 61–192, § 7; Laws 1961, c. 61–530, § 18; Laws 1969, c. 69–106, §§ 19, 35; Laws 1971, c. 71–136, § 1169; Laws 1977, c. 77–120, § 57; Laws 1979, c. 79–3, § 67; Laws 1995, c. 95–283, § 16.

Historical and Statutory Notes

Amendment Notes:

Laws 1961, c. 61–192, § 7, divided the first sentence by ending the first sentence at the words "guilty of a misdemeanor"; and substituted "No person shall, by disguise, misrepresentation of identity or other illicit means, attempt to gain admission to or enter upon the grounds of any state correctional institution for the purpose of visiting any prisoner in violation of the general visiting policy adopted by the board. A person, upon conviction of an offense as outlined in this section," for "and upon conviction thereof" preceding "shall be punished by imprisonment".

Laws 1961, c. 61–530, § 18, substituted "division" for "department".

Laws 1969, c. 69–106, §§ 19, 35, transferred all powers, duties and functions of the division of corrections of the board of commissioners of state institutions to the division of adult corrections of the department of health and rehabilitative services.

Laws 1971, c. 71–136, § 1169, made the offense defined by this section a "misdemeanor of the second degree, punishable as provided in § 775.082 or § 775.083" in lieu of provision that the offender "shall be punished by imprisonment in the county jail for a term of not more than 6 months or by a fine of not more than $200.00 or by both fine and imprisonment."

Laws 1977, c. 77–120, a reviser's bill, amended this section to conform with Laws 1975, c. 75–49, which created the department of offender rehabilitation (see § 20.315) and transferred to the department certain functions performed by the division of corrections of the department of health and rehabilitative services and the parole and probation commission of the department of offender rehabilitation.

Laws 1979, c. 79–3, a reviser's bill, provided for substitution of references to the department and secretary of "corrections" for the department and secretary of "offender rehabilitation" to conform with Laws 1978, c. 78–53.

Laws 1995, c. 95–283, § 16, eff. June 15, 1995, in the last sentence, substituted "correctional officer" for "officer or guard".

Cross References

Interference with county prisoners, penalty, see § 951.19.

Library References

Obstructing Justice ⚷7.
Westlaw Topic No. 282.

C.J.S. Obstructing Justice or Governmental Administration §§ 4, 10, 12 to 29, 31 to 32, 38.

Research References

Encyclopedias

Interference With Prisoners or Correctional Officers; Inciting or Assaulting Prisoners, FL Jur. 2d Prisons & Prisoners § 215.

944.40. Escapes; penalty

Any prisoner confined in any prison, jail, private correctional facility, road camp, or other penal institution, whether operated by the state, a county, or a municipality, or operated under a contract with the state, a county, or a municipality, working upon the public roads, or being transported to or from a place of confinement who escapes or attempts to escape from such confinement commits a felony of the second degree, punishable as provided in s. 775.082, s. 775.083, or s. 775.084. The punishment of imprisonment imposed under this section shall run consecutive to any former sentence imposed upon any prisoner.

Laws 1957, c. 57–121, § 38; Laws 1965, c. 65–224, § 1; Laws 1969, c. 69–332, § 1; Laws 1971, c. 71–136, § 1170. Amended by Laws 1999, c. 99–271, § 5, eff. June 29, 1999.

Historical and Statutory Notes

Amendment Notes:

Laws 1965, c. 65–224, § 1, provided, in the last sentence, for the punishment of imprisonment to "run consecutive" to any former sentence for punishment to "be in addition" to any former sentence.

Laws 1969, c. 69–332, § 1, provided that escape constitute a felony by deleting, from the first sentence, the words "if the charge or conviction under which said prisoner is incarcerated constitutes a felony under the laws of the jurisdiction which has caused his incarceration he" following "escape from such confinement", and also deleted the words "; or if the charge or conviction under which said prisoner is incarcerated constitutes a misdemeanor, he shall be guilty of a misdemeanor and upon conviction thereof shall be punished by imprisonment of not more than 90 days." following "imprisonment of not more than 10 years".

Laws 1971, c. 71–136, § 1170, made the offense defined by this section a "felony of the second degree, punishable as provided in § 775.082, § 775.083, or § 775.084" in lieu of provision that the offender "shall be punished by imprisonment of not more than ten years".

Laws 1999, c. 99–271, § 5, eff. June 29, 1999, in the first sentence, inserted "private correctional facility," and "whether operated by the"; substituted "a municipality, or operated under a contract with the state, a county, or municipality" for "municipal", and "commits" for "shall be guilty".

Cross References

Background screening tests related to employment in the Department of Juvenile Justice, see § 435.04.
Escape, effect on gain-time, see §§ 944.275, 944.28, 951.21.
Felony murder, escape as underlying felony, see § 782.04.
Forfeiture of prisoner's earnings upon escape, see § 946.002.
Harboring or aiding escapees, see § 944.46.
Intentional or negligent aiding of escape by prisoners, offenses and penalties, see § 843.09 et seq.
Juvenile facility, escape from, see § 985.721.
Possession or use of weapon during escape, minimum sentence, see § 775.087.
Use of force to prevent escape, see § 776.07.
Work release, escape from extended limits of confinement, see §§ 945.091, 951.24.

Law Review and Journal Commentaries

Criminal law and procedure. Thomas A. Wills, 22 U.Miami L.Rev. 240, 241 (1967).

Florida's escape statute: A literal interpretation? 16 Stetson L.Rev. 479 (1987).

Survey of criminal law in Florida. Thomas A. Wills, 16 U.Miami L.Rev. 225, 236 (1961).

Library References

Escape ⚷1 to 13.
Westlaw Topic No. 151.
C.J.S. Escape and Related Offenses; Rescue §§ 1 to 30, 39, 41 to 51.

Research References

ALR Library

119 ALR, Federal 319, What Constitutes "Violent Felony" for Purpose of Sentence Enhancement Under Armed Career Criminal Act (18 U.S.C.A. § 924(e)(1)).

54 ALR 5th 141, Duress, Necessity, or Conditions of Confinement as Justification for Escape from Prison.

46 ALR 5th 523, Validity, Construction, and Application of Juvenile Escape Statutes.

50 ALR 4th 1081, Lesser-Related State Offense Instructions: Modern Status.

76 ALR 3rd 658, Failure of Prisoner to Return at Expiration of Work Furlough or Other Permissive Release Period as Crime of Escape.

169 ALR 315, Comment Note.--Duty in Instructing Jury in Criminal Prosecution to Explain and Define Offense Charged.

91 ALR 884, Motion for Summary Judgment as Searching Record.

Encyclopedias

Waiver of Right to Challenge, FL Jur. 2d Juries § 245.

Effect of Particular Crime Convicted For; Placement as Condition of Probation or Community Control, FL Jur. 2d Prisons & Prisoners § 108.

Generally; Leaving Place of Confinement for Work or Voluntary Service at Public or Nonprofit Agency or Faith-Based Service Group, FL Jur. 2d Prisons & Prisoners § 175.

Escape or Attempted Escape; Aiding Escaped Prisoners, FL Jur. 2d Prisons & Prisoners § 222.

Treatises and Practice Aids

16 Florida Practice Series § 6:91, Enhancement of Penalty and Reclassification of Offense--Habitual Felony Offender, Habitual Violent Felony Offender, Three-Time Violent Felony Offender, and Violent Career Criminal--Violent...

16 Florida Practice Series § 6:196, Capital Sentencing--Regulation of Execution.

22 Florida Practice Series § 5:6, Application for an Interception Order.

United States Supreme Court

Escape, dismissal of pending appeals, see Estelle v. Dorrough, U.S.Tex.1975, 95 S.Ct. 1173, 420 U.S. 534, 43 L.Ed.2d 377, rehearing denied 95 S.Ct. 1589, 421 U.S. 921, 43 L.Ed.2d 790, on remand 512 F.2d 1061.

Escape from prison, defense of necessity or duress, see U. S. v. Bailey, U.S.Dist.Col.1980, 100 S.Ct. 624, 444 U.S. 394, 62 L.Ed.2d 575, on remand 675 F.2d 1292, 219 U.S.App.D.C. 67.

Notes of Decisions

---

1. Validity

This section imposing penalty for escape from incarceration was not unconstitutionally overbroad. Norton v. Wainwright, N.D.Fla.1971, 324 F.Supp. 379. Escape ⚷ 1

This section imposing penalty for escape from incarceration was not void for vagueness. Norton v. Wainwright, N.D.Fla.1971, 324 F.Supp. 379. Escape ⚷ 1

This section which imposes penalty for escape from incarceration and which provides harsher punishment for an escaped felon than for an escaped misdemeanant does not deny an escapee equal protection of the law. Rebon v. State, App. 2 Dist., 203 So.2d 202 (1967). Constitutional Law ⚷ 3243; Escape ⚷ 13

2. Double jeopardy

Convictions for both resisting arrest without violence and escape, although arising out of same acts, did not violate double jeopardy, as offenses did not require identical elements of proof, offenses were not degrees of same crime, and offense of arresting offense without violence was not subsumed in escape offense. Clark v. State, App. 4 Dist., 920 So.2d 634 (2005), rehearing denied, review denied 917 So.2d 192. Double Jeopardy ⚷ 139.1

3. Common law

Escape from lawful confinement is in itself a substantive offense, identifiable at common law as "prison break", and brought forward as a part of our law by this section. Ducksworth v. Boyer, 125 So.2d 844 (1960). Escape ⚷ 4

4. Elements of offense

Defendant was subject of a valid arrest, an element of escape, where the arresting officer intended to arrest defendant and communicated this intention to defendant when she notified him that she had a warrant for his arrest and asked defendant to place his hands behind his back, and defendant understood the officer's intention and acquiesced to the officer's authority by turning around placing his hands behind his back before running away. McKinnon v. State, App. 5 Dist., 17 So.3d 860 (2009). Arrest ⚷ 68(3)

There can be no escape from a mere detention. Hebert v. State, App. 4 Dist., 962 So.2d 1068 (2007), review denied 973 So.2d 1123. Escape ⚷ 1

In prosecution for burglary with intent to escape, it was legally impossible for defendant to have intended to commit underlying offense of escape by entering or remaining in building; escape was complete as matter of law prior to defendant's alleged entry of building when he broke away from correction officers. Gaskin v. State, App. 3 Dist., 869 So.2d 646 (2004). Burglary ⚷ 3; Escape ⚷ 1

To prove the crime of escape, there must first be a valid arrest. Thomas v. State, App. 4 Dist., 805 So.2d 102 (2002).

Valid "arrest" consists of the following four factors enumerated by the supreme court: (1) a purpose or intention to effect an arrest under a real or pretended authority, (2) an actual or constructive seizure or detention of the person to be arrested by a person having present power to control the person arrested, (3) a communication by the arresting officer to the person whose arrest is sought, of an intention or purpose then and there to effect an arrest, and (4) an understanding by the person whose arrest is sought that it is the intention of the arresting officer then and there to arrest and detain him. Thomas v. State, App. 4 Dist., 805 So.2d 102 (2002). Arrest ⚷ 68(3)

Escape is technically completed on an inmate's intentional act of leaving the established area of custody. Ayendes v. State, App. 1 Dist., 385 So.2d 698 (1980), petition for review denied 392 So.2d 1371. Escape ⚷ 1

When state has established its right to legal custody and conscious and intentional act of defendant of leaving established area of such custody, offense of escape is prima facie established. Watford v. State, App. 1 Dist., 353 So.2d 1263 (1978). Escape ⚷ 10

Two elements to crime of escape are the physical act of leaving custody coupled with intent to avoid lawful confinement. Lewis v. State, App. 2 Dist., 318 So.2d 529 (1975), certiorari denied 334 So.2d 608. Escape ⚷ 1

Elements of crime of escape are physical act of leaving or not being in custody and intent to avoid lawful confinement. Helton v. State, App. 1 Dist., 311 So.2d 381 (1975). Escape ⚷ 1

5. Knowledge of arrest

For purposes of crime of armed escape, trier of fact's determination that defendant understood he was being arrested at time of his escape should rest on analysis of whether reasonable person or average citizen in similar circumstances would think they were under arrest. Sweeney v. State, App. 4 Dist., 633 So.2d 66 (1994), review denied 645 So.2d 455, denial of post-conviction relief affirmed 722 So.2d 928, rehearing denied, review denied 733 So.2d 517. Escape ⚷ 1

6. Intent

State had no prima facie case of escape against defendant who was placed in back seat of police car by an officer and left when car door was opened, due to fact that defendant had no criminal intent to escape from lawful confinement, where defendant was entitled to believe that white male who opened car door was, in fact, a police officer who was authorized to release the defendant. State v. Knox, App. 3 Dist., 557 So.2d 127 (1990). Escape ⚷ 1

This section proscribing escape or attempted escape from jail or correctional facility requires proof of intent to avoid lawful confinement and recognizes narrow defense of necessity available to prisoner whose escape has been motivated by sufficiently perilous circumstances. Muro v. State, App. 3 Dist., 445 So.2d 374 (1984). Escape ⚷ 1; Escape ⚷ 5.5; Escape ⚷ 6

Intent to escape may be proven by circumstantial evidence. Helton v. State, App. 1 Dist., 311 So.2d 381 (1975). Escape ⚷ 10

7. Lawful custody or confinement—In general

Defendant's action, in leaving area following his arrest and after having been instructed by trooper to remain and wait for another patrol car, while arresting trooper pursued defendant's companion, was sufficient to support defendant's conviction for escape. Johnson v. State, App. 1 Dist., 536 So.2d 1045 (1988), review denied 542 So.2d 1333. Escape ⚷ 2

Failure of defendant to surrender for service of jail term could not be violation of this section, which requires prior confinement of prisoner. Williamson v. State, App. 3 Dist., 388 So.2d 1345 (1980). Escape ⚷ 1

Essential element of crime of escape is that the defendant escaped from "lawful custody." Warren v. State, App. 2 Dist., 371 So.2d 219 (1979). Escape ⚷ 1

Defendant, who admitted that he was in lawful custody and that he fled from scene without permission of arresting officer, did not have to be in penal institution at time of escape to be found guilty of escape nor did distraction caused by interference of third person who prevented arresting officer from immediately taking defendant to jail alter possibility of defendant's conviction. State v. Akers, App. 2 Dist., 367 So.2d 700 (1979). Escape ⚷ 1

Where fugitive was clearly in "lawful" confinement once the Governor's warrant of arrest was served upon him, fugitive committed crime of escape when he left the jail without permission four days later even though he was confined for more than the prescribed 30 days pending the issuance of Governor's warrant. State v. Fulkerson, App. 2 Dist., 300 So.2d 276 (1974). Escape ⚷ 4

Where state never established that defendant was prisoner "convicted and sentenced" in accordance with law at time he departed from confines of county convict camp, defendant was erroneously convicted of escape under this section. Brochu v. State, App. 1 Dist., 258 So.2d 286 (1972). Escape ⚷ 10

8. —— Validity of arrest, lawful custody or confinement

Police officer did not effect an arrest of defendant by telling him that he was under arrest and instructing him to put weapon down, and thus defendant could not have committed the crime of escape when he fled; evidence demonstrated nothing more than a show of authority, because the required physical touching or submission to the officer's authority, which were required for arrest, were absent. Hebert v. State, App. 4 Dist., 962 So.2d 1068 (2007), review denied 973 So.2d 1123. Arrest ⚷ 68(3); Escape ⚷ 1

A valid arrest exists, such that an escape conviction can be sustained, when the following four factors are present: (1) a purpose or intention to effect an arrest under a real or pretended authority, (2) an actual or constructive seizure or detention of the person to be arrested by a person having present power to control the person arrested, (3) a communication by the arresting officer to the person whose arrest is sought, of an intention or purpose then and there to effect an arrest, and (4) an understanding by the person whose arrest is sought that it is the intention of the arresting officer then and there to arrest and detain him. Hebert v. State, App. 4 Dist., 962 So.2d 1068 (2007), review denied 973 So.2d 1123. Arrest ⚷ 68(3)

To be convicted of escape, there must first be valid arrest. Pollen v. State, App. 3 Dist., 834 So.2d 380 (2003), on remand 2003 WL 25731387, post-conviction relief denied 2003 WL 25731386, affirmed 861 So.2d 41. Escape ⚷ 1

Valid arrest consists of four factors: (1) purpose or intention to effect arrest under real authority; (2) actual detention of person being arrested by person having present power to control person arrested; (3) communication by arresting officer to person whose arrest is sought of intention to effect arrest; and (4) understanding by person whose arrest is sought that it is intention of arresting officer to arrest and detain him. Pollen v. State, App. 3 Dist., 834 So.2d 380 (2003), on remand 2003 WL 25731387, post-conviction relief denied 2003 WL 25731386, affirmed 861 So.2d 41. Arrest ⚷ 63.4(1)

Finding of probable cause to arrest defendant is not dispositive as to whether defendant was under valid arrest when he fled, as required for conviction for escape. Brown v. State, App. 4 Dist., 623 So.2d 800 (1993), review denied 634 So.2d 627. Escape ⚷ 1

Element of custody in crime of escape was not intended by legislature to invariably require proof of technical correctness of circumstances underlying the original arrest of prisoner, such as validity of warrant or compliance with details of statutes such as § 901.15 permitting arrests by officers without warrant. State v. Williams, 444 So.2d 13 (1984). Escape ⚷ 1

9. —— Sufficiency of custody, lawful custody or confinement

Conviction for escape does not require the state to prove that law enforcement official had completed act of acquiring total physical control of defendant in instant of escape or attempted escape so long as it is proven that official had (1) right to legal custody of defendant and (2) there was conscious and intentional act of defendant in leaving or attempting to leave established area of such custody. Applewhite v. State, App. 5 Dist., 874 So.2d 1276 (2004), review denied 895 So.2d 1066. Escape ⚷ 1

Defendant who, upon being informed that he was under arrest, ran from scene, was properly charged with escape under West's F.S.A. § 944.40, notwithstanding that he had not been restrained and arrest procedure had not progressed to point where deputy had removed handcuffs from their carrying place. State v. Ramsey, 475 So.2d 671 (1985). Escape ⚷ 1

When it was shown by state's evidence that defendant was arrested by a duly authorized officer upon authority of outstanding capiases issued by circuit court, regular on their face, and that at the time of his escape defendant was being held by duly authorized officers under authority of the capiases, defendant was in "lawful custody" so as to subject him to penalty of law for crime of escape. McGee v. State, App. 1 Dist., 435 So.2d 854 (1983), petition for review denied 444 So.2d 417. Escape ⚷ 1

Defendant, who was under custody of United States Marshall and confined in county jail pursuant to federal writ, was confined in a county detention facility within meaning of this section. Dyal v. State, App. 1 Dist., 386 So.2d 868 (1980). Escape ⚷ 1

Defendant was in lawful custody at time of his escape, so that he could be convicted under escape statutes which, inter alia, define a prisoner as any person who is under arrest and in lawful custody of any law enforcement official, since officer had probable cause to arrest defendant without a warrant for breaking and entering with intent to commit a felony. Estep v. State, App. 1 Dist., 318 So.2d 520 (1975). Escape ⚷ 1

10. —— Community release program, lawful custody or confinement

Prisoner was not a "confined inmate" within meaning of escape statute when he was released from the work release center, and because prisoner was not a "confined inmate" when he arrived at work late, the State could not show a prima facie case of escape, and thus, escape charge would be dismissed; although, by arriving at work late, prisoner might be in violation of the rules of the work release program and his privilege to participate in the program could be withdrawn, he was not subject to an escape charge. State v. Williams, App. 2 Dist., 918 So.2d 400 (2006). Escape ⚷ 1; Escape ⚷ 2

Supervised community release program was not "confinement" within meaning of this section prohibiting escape from confinement. Munn v. State, App. 2 Dist., 573 So.2d 439 (1991). Escape ⚷ 1

11. —— In-house arrest, lawful custody or confinement

Prisoner restricted to his home pursuant to in-house arrest program of county jail was not "confined" and could not be convicted of escape; prisoner was under no structured or supervised confinement. Gregory v. State, App. 2 Dist., 573 So.2d 397 (1991). Escape ⚷ 1

12. Prisoners

To be a "prisoner" under escape statute, defendant must be under arrest, i.e., held with regard to criminal charges. Villegas-Alen v. State, App. 1 Dist., 797 So.2d 1 (2000), modified on rehearing. Escape ⚷ 1

Defendant who was arrested and detained under civil authority of Immigration and Naturalization Service (INS) was not a "prisoner" as required by escape statute. Villegas-Alen v. State, App. 1 Dist., 797 So.2d 1 (2000), modified on rehearing. Escape ⚷ 1

Defendant, who had been committed to department of corrections and who was serving balance of his probation in community facility after having violated terms of his probation, was at that time a "prisoner" within meaning of criminal law and was serving a "sentence of imprisonment" when he escaped from facility. Yates v. State, App. 5 Dist., 392 So.2d 1020 (1981). Escape ⚷ 4

Within statutes in force at time, defining a prisoner as any person convicted and sentenced by the court, defendant who was incarcerated pursuant to conviction for three crimes and was awaiting sentence was not a "prisoner" and could not be guilty of escape. Burgess v. State, App. 4 Dist., 283 So.2d 399 (1973). Escape ⚷ 1

13. Law enforcement officials

Term "law enforcement official," as used in statute defining prisoner as a person who is 'in the lawful custody of any law enforcement official,' was sufficiently broad so as to include private security guard under facts in prosecution for attempted escape, where defendant, who was convicted of offense, was in custody of sheriff's office pending sentencing when he was transported to hospital for medical treatment, sheriff's office had contract with private company to escort prisoners in hospital facilities, and defendant attempted to escape from private security guard while at hospital. Williams v. State, App. 1 Dist., 770 So.2d 1263 (2000). Escape ⚷ 1; Escape ⚷ 5.5

14. Penal institution

Community correctional center, from which information charged defendant with leaving without permission after having been committed to department of corrections and sentenced to serve remainder of his probationary term because he had violated terms of his probation, was a "penal institution" within this section. Yates v. State, App. 5 Dist., 392 So.2d 1020 (1981). Escape ⚷ 4

15. Juvenile detention facilities—In general

Petition for delinquency alleging that juvenile unlawfully and feloniously escaped from lawful confinement, or while being transported to lawful confinement as a juvenile alleged to have committed a delinquent act or violation, in that child departed from police car en route to a juvenile detention facility after being taken into custody, did not allege any offense within meaning of this section, absent allegation of violation of any other statute. State v. J.A., App. 3 Dist., 384 So.2d 1347 (1980). Infants ⚷ 197

Detention facilities where juveniles are supervised pending disposition of matters for which they were taken into custody do not constitute a "penal institution" within meaning of escape statute (this section), notwithstanding that such facilities are under authority of Department of Health and Rehabilitative Services rather than auspices of a county board of commissioners. Prince v. State, App. 4 Dist., 360 So.2d 1161 (1978). Escape ⚷ 1

This section prohibiting escape does not include escape from a juvenile detention center which, pursuant to statute, is deemed to be a home rather than a penal institution; petition which attempted to allege crime for escape from a juvenile home was thus insufficient. In Interest of F. G., App. 4 Dist., 349 So.2d 727 (1977). Escape ⚷ 1; Infants ⚷ 197

16. —— Validity of statute juvenile detention facilities

Section 39.112 governing escapes from juvenile facility was not enacted in violation of Const. Art. 3, § 6, prohibiting amendment by reference to title only since that section was not an attempt to revise subject matter of this section and irreconcilable conflict between this section did not exist. State v. J.R.M., 388 So.2d 1227 (1980). Statutes ⚷ 141(2)

17. —— Intent, juvenile detention facilities

In enacting § 39.112 governing escape from any training school or secured detention facility maintained for treatment, rehabilitation, or detention of children, legislature intended to adopt by specific reference all ramifications of this section governing escape by adult prisoner from prison, jail, road camp, or other penal institution, including flight while in transit, and thus defendants could be prosecuted for being accessories after the fact to the escape of juvenile, which occurred while the juvenile was in transit between a doctor's office and a juvenile detention center. State v. Ferguson, App. 4 Dist., 395 So.2d 1182 (1981). Escape ⚷ 4

18. —— Discretion of court, juvenile detention facilities

Decision of whether to sentence a defendant as a "youthful offender" on escape charge after he had been sentenced as a "youthful offender" on a grand theft charge was in sound discretion of trial court. Miller v. State, App. 1 Dist., 411 So.2d 290 (1982). Infants ⚷ 69(3.1)

19. —— Training school, juvenile detention facilities

Jacksonville Youth Development Center was "training school" under § 39.112 providing that escape from training school constitutes escape within intent and meaning of § 944.40, even though the Center was not expressly designated as training school in rule of department of health and rehabilitative services, in that JYDC had all attributes of other institutions in state specifically designated as training schools by administrative rule. R. P. v. State, App. 1 Dist.,

389 So.2d 658 (1980), transferred to 401 So.2d 1325. Escape ⚿ 4

20. Felonious escape

Defendant's escape from lawful custody of county sheriff constituted felony whether defendant was incarcerated under felony charge or misdemeanor charge. Naylor v. State, App. 2 Dist., 250 So.2d 660 (1971). Criminal Law ⚿ 27

Where defendant was being held on pending felony charge as well as for nonfelony traffic offenses when he attempted to escape, defendant was properly charged with crime of attempting to escape. Sheptin v. State, App. 3 Dist., 210 So.2d 464 (1968), certiorari denied 212 So.2d 879, certiorari denied 89 S.Ct. 725, 393 U.S. 1071, 21 L.Ed.2d 716. Escape ⚿ 5.5

For attempted escape to constitute a felony, it must be alleged and proved that prisoner was incarcerated or confined pursuant to a felony charge or conviction. Melton v. Culver, 107 So.2d 378 (1958). Escape ⚿ 9

21. Attempted escape

This section making a person guilty of a felony of the second degree if he escapes or attempts to escape while confined in a prison, jail, road camp, or other penal institution cannot be interpreted as including an attempt in crime of escape so as to preclude a prosecution for attempted escape on ground that it is a nonexistent crime. Keel v. State, App. 1 Dist., 438 So.2d 850 (1983), cause dismissed 443 So.2d 979. Escape ⚿ 5.5

22. Escape prior to conviction

Accused could be convicted of escape based upon his escape from county jail prior to conviction and prior to amendment of this section so as to delete an escape while confined pursuant to a "charge" from operation of the statute but could not be convicted on basis of escape from county jail prior to conviction but after the amendment. Van Den Bliek v. State, App. 4 Dist., 281 So.2d 218 (1973), certiorari denied 287 So.2d 680. Escape ⚿ 1

Defendant's escape from county sheriff at time he was under charges of grand larceny and other various misdemeanors constituted criminal offense even though at time he escaped he had not been actually convicted of offenses for which he was held in custody. Naylor v. State, App. 2 Dist., 250 So.2d 660 (1971). Escape ⚿ 1

Fact that, at time of defendant's escape from jail, he had not been convicted of offense for which he was held in custody but was merely awaiting trial would not make judgment and sentence based upon defendant's plea of guilty to information charging felonious escape invalid. Harris v. State, App. 2 Dist., 217 So.2d 907 (1969). Escape ⚿ 4

23. Escape during transport of prisoners

"Transportation to a place of confinement," within meaning of escape statute, begins at the time an individual is placed under arrest. Aplewhite v. State, App. 5 Dist., 874 So.2d 1276 (2004), review denied 895 So.2d 1066. Escape ⚿ 1

"Transportation," act of which triggers felony escape charge if suspect escapes or attempts to escape, begins when suspect is placed under arrest; it has been extended to suspects who flee after being placed under arrest. Pollen v. State, App. 3 Dist., 834 So.2d 380 (2003), on remand 2003 WL 25731387, post-conviction relief denied 2003 WL 25731386, affirmed 861 So.2d 41. Escape ⚿ 4

"Transportation," act of which triggers felony escape charge if suspect escapes or attempts to escape, does not apply to suspects who have merely been detained. Pollen v. State, App. 3 Dist., 834 So.2d 380 (2003), on remand 2003 WL 25731387, post-conviction relief denied 2003 WL 25731386, affirmed 861 So.2d 41. Escape ⚿ 4

Even though defendant had not yet been handcuffed, defendant who had been placed under arrest and then fled was a prisoner and was properly convicted for escape declining to follow *Ramsey v. State,* 442 So.2d 303. Green v. State, App. 2 Dist., 470 So.2d 104 (1985), review denied 480 So.2d 1294. Escape ⚿ 1

Under this section prohibiting escape of any person being transported to or from place of confinement, motorist who was stopped for traffic violations and on whom there were two outstanding capiases, but who had not been handcuffed, had not been placed in police car, and had not been told that he was being taken to jail, although he had been informed that he was under arrest, was not being transported and thus could not be convicted of escape. Ramsey v. State, App. 5 Dist., 442 So.2d 303 (1983), quashed 475 So.2d 671 Escape ⚿ 1

Under this section prohibiting escape of prisoner being transported to or from place of confinement, question as to when transportation begins is normally factual issue to be determined by jury. Ramsey v. State, App. 5 Dist., 442 So.2d 303 (1983), quashed 475 So.2d 671. Escape ⚿ 11

Legislature intended that any person under arrest and in lawful custody of law enforcement official who escapes while being transported to or from place of confinement shall be guilty of a felony. State v. Akers, App. 2 Dist., 367 So.2d 700 (1979). Criminal Law ⚿ 27

24. Escape during confinement for civil contempt

Defendant who escaped from lawful confinement for civil contempt was punishable as for the common-law offense of prison break, even though he was not confined for a misdemeanor or a felony. Ducksworth v. Boyer, 125 So.2d 844 (1960). Escape ⚷ 4

25. Failure to return from furlough

Failure to return from period of temporary release was not "escape" within meaning of juvenile statutes, even though juvenile statute referenced adult statute defining escape, and failure to return was "escape" if committed by adult, given that failure to return was not included within general adult escape statute referenced by juvenile statute, and failure to return by adult was only considered "escape" because of separate adult statute that was not referenced by juvenile statute. J.A.G. v. State, App. 3 Dist., 825 So.2d 497 (2002). Infants ⚷ 153

Defendant did not "escape" and could not be convicted therefor when he failed to timely return from 24–hour furlough granted prior to sentencing on other offenses; there was no confinement for him to escape from. Pumphrey v. State, 527 So.2d 1382 (1988). Escape ⚷ 1

County prisoner who failed to timely return to jail from Sunday furlough and who was picked up by police was properly charged with escape, in view of statute relating to prisons and correctional institutions and statute relating to county prisoners, both of which provide that failure to return to place of confinement within time prescribed constitutes an escape. Price v. State, App. 1 Dist., 333 So.2d 84 (1976). Escape ⚷ 2

That county prisoner was simply on furlough and not working when he failed to return to place of employment within time prescribed did not preclude convicting him of escape, even though statute relating to county prisoners authorizes giving prisoners privilege of leaving jail for work or to participate in educational or vocational programs but says nothing of other purposes. Price v. State, App. 1 Dist., 333 So.2d 84 (1976). Escape ⚷ 2

An inmate who has been granted a furlough pursuant to regulations of the division of corrections, and who willfully fails to return to his place of confinement within the time prescribed, is subject to prosecution for the crime of escape under § 945.091 and this section. Op.Atty.Gen., 072–404, Nov. 16, 1972.

26. Identification of accused

Detective's testimony that he verified from inmate records that person of same name as defendant had been incarcerated in county jail, as well as other evidence, was sufficient to establish that defendant escaped from lawful custody for purpose of escape conviction. Sullivan v. State, App. 2 Dist., 430 So.2d 519 (1983). Escape ⚷ 10

In prosecution for escape, identity may be demonstrated by circumstantial evidence; receding from Fulford v. State, 113 So.2d 572. Sullivan v. State, App. 2 Dist., 430 So.2d 519 (1983). Escape ⚷ 10

Since only a prisoner can commit crime of escape, it is essential in a prosecution for escape that State establish defendant's status as a prisoner. Fouts v. State, App. 2 Dist., 374 So.2d 22 (1979). Escape ⚷ 10

Identity of name of defendant and of person shown to have been committed to state prison following felony conviction was not sufficient to establish identity of defendant with that of person previously committed to prison system, and hence state failed to prove defendant at time of his alleged escape was incarcerated under a charge or conviction of a felony. Fulford v. State, App. 2 Dist., 113 So.2d 572 (1959). Escape ⚷ 10

27. Waiver of rights of accused

Evidence affirmatively established effective waiver by accused of his right to proceed in proper person. State v. Cappetta, 216 So.2d 749 (1968), certiorari denied 89 S.Ct. 1610, 394 U.S. 1008, 22 L.Ed.2d 787. Criminal Law ⚷ 1752

Evidence established that accused voluntarily and intelligently waived his right to proceed under his own banner by fully accepting beneficial assistance of counsel which in no way prejudiced his trial. State v. Cappetta, 216 So.2d 749 (1968), certiorari denied 89 S.Ct. 1610, 394 U.S. 1008, 22 L.Ed.2d 787. Criminal Law ⚷ 1752

28. Indictment and information—In general

Information charging escape while imprisoned on felony charge, charged a felony. Gorman v. Cochran, 127 So.2d 667 (1961). Indictment And Information ⚷ 59

Escape from lawful confinement is a substantive offense, in and of itself, without regard to whether prisoner was confined pursuant to a charge or pursuant to a conviction of a crime, and person escaping from legal confinement is guilty of offense of felonious escape even though indictment under which he was confined at time of escape is subsequently dismissed, or conviction under which he was confined at time of escape is subsequently reversed or set aside on appeal. State ex rel. Wilson v. Culver, 110 So.2d 674 (1959). Escape ⚷ 1

Information alleging that party had been committed to circuit court after entering plea of not guilty in committing magistrate's court to charge of robbery and by reason of warrant and commitment was then and there confined, upon failure to give bond, in the county jail from which he feloniously escaped, was sufficient to charge a felonious escape under rule requiring that it must be alleged and proved that prisoner was incarcerated or confined pursuant to a felony charge or conviction, and information must reflect legality of custody at time escape was committed and nature of confinement under which he was being held. State ex rel. Wilson v. Culver, 110 So.2d 674 (1959). Escape ⚷ 9

29. —— Fatal variance, indictment and information

No fatal variance between information in escape prosecution and evidence adduced at trial occurred when, although information alleged that defendant escaped while confined in county adult detention center, proof showed that escape occurred after defendant became ill during booking process at detention center and was escorted by police officer to county hospital for treatment. Johnson v. State, App. 1 Dist., 357 So.2d 203 (1978), certiorari denied 362 So.2d 1054. Escape ⚷ 9

Where defendant was arrested by sheriff of county and incarcerated in county jail, and defendant was subsequently transferred for lodging to municipal jail under an intergovernmental compact between county and city, under which sheriff retained power and ability to control continued incarceration of person of defendant subject to orders of the court exercising jurisdiction over him, defendant's escape was from "lawful custody," and there was no fatal variance between information which charged that defendant escaped lawful custody of sheriff and evidence that defendant escaped while under actual confinement of municipal jail of city. Pons v. State, App. 1 Dist., 278 So.2d 336 (1973). Escape ⚷ 9

30. Notice to parent or guardian of minor

Noncompliance with requirement of § 932.38 that notice be given to parent or guardian of unmarried minor accused, invalidated conviction for escape. Williams v. Cochran, 126 So.2d 887 (1961). Infants ⚷ 68.4

31. Speedy trial

There is no special provision or exception contained in speedy trial rule (Criminal Procedure Rule 3.191) covering escapees, and therefore it was required that defendant be tried within 180 days from day on which he escaped and on which he was arrested. Strickland v. State, App. 1 Dist., 435 So.2d 934 (1983), petition for review denied 441 So.2d 633. Criminal Law ⚷ 577.11(1)

Charge of escape is a nonviolent felony, which had to be brought to trial within one year without demand under former speedy trial rule. (Criminal Procedure Rule 3.191). Arnold v. State, App. 2 Dist., 429 So.2d 819 (1983). Criminal Law ⚷ 577.6

Defendant was entitled to discharge on escape charge under former speedy trial rule (Criminal Procedure Rule 3.191) where the State failed to bring him to trial within one year after he was arrested and returned to Florida on that charge. Arnold v. State, App. 2 Dist., 429 So.2d 819 (1983). Criminal Law ⚷ 577.15(3)

Speedy trial time began running on escape charge when defendant was arrested and returned to Florida on that charge, and not at earlier time when he was charged where, at that time, he was no longer a prisoner in Florida for purposes of the rule because of the escape. Arnold v. State, App. 2 Dist., 429 So.2d 819 (1983). Criminal Law ⚷ 577.11(2)

32. Defenses—In general

Prisoner had no legal right to leave lawful custody in order to go to someplace where he could try to contact prison superintendent for an explanation of his transfer. Watford v. State, App. 1 Dist., 353 So.2d 1263 (1978). Prisons ⚷ 249; Prisons ⚷ 276

33. —— Unlawful custody, defenses

Conviction for escape was supported by evidence that defendant escaped from custody of Department of Corrections notwithstanding that convictions, on which defendant was serving sentences at time of escape, were later set aside; defendant was under lawful confinement at that time and was not entitled to self-help. Nichols v. State, App. 2 Dist., 509 So.2d 1243 (1987). Escape ⚷ 10

Unlawfulness of confinement constitutes an affirmative defense to the offense of escape, to be raised by the accused, and the state is not required to prove technical correctness of prisoner's original arrest. Marquez v. State, App. 2 Dist., 450 So.2d 345 (1984). Escape ⚷ 6; Escape ⚷ 10

Unlawfulness of confinement was affirmative defense to be raised by defendant charged with escape. State v. Williams, 444 So.2d 13 (1984). Escape ⚷ 6

Defendant was not entitled to rely on self-help to obtain release while validly incarcerated under a presumably valid conviction and sentence, even though he was incarcerated under uncounseled conviction. Lawson v. State, App. 4 Dist., 312 So.2d 522 (1975). Escape ⚷ 1

Escape conviction based on incarceration under an uncounseled conviction could stand.

Lawson v. State, App. 4 Dist., 312 So.2d 522 (1975). Escape ⚷ 1

34. —— Real, imminent, and impending danger, defenses

Defendant who was charged with escape from the close custody institution where he was serving a 20-year sentence did not meet the criteria of defense of necessity, nor did he disprove intent, where there was no evidence that the defendant had reported a threat to his life to the authorities and that the authorities had refused to take action. Bull v. State, 548 So.2d 1103 (1989). Escape ⚷ 6; Escape ⚷ 10

Testimony that officer had kicked him in the tail bone which provoked him to run so he would not have to take any further abuse or punishment from officer, and testimony of nurse employed by sheriff's department that she observed hematoma or bruise type injury in tail bone area of defendant was admissible in support of defense of necessity to charge of escape. Kent v. State, App. 5 Dist., 479 So.2d 866 (1985). Escape ⚷ 10

When state has established its right to legal custody and conscious and intentional act of defendant of leaving established area of such custody, offense of escape is prima facie established, and only viable defense to such charge is necessity involving reasonable grounds for defendant to believe that he is faced with real, imminent, and present danger of death, great bodily harm, or such type of danger to his health, if he does not temporarily leave his place of confinement. Muro v. State, App. 3 Dist., 445 So.2d 374 (1984). Escape ⚷ 6; Escape ⚷ 10

In prosecution for escape, refusal to permit defendant to testify concerning his defense that he escaped in order to avoid being homosexually raped was proper where he failed to show that he endeavored to return to custody. Holdren v. State, App. 2 Dist., 415 So.2d 39 (1982), review denied 422 So.2d 842. Escape ⚷ 6

As defense to prosecution for escape, specific and imminent threat must be personal to defendant, rather than general allegation that conditions of incarceration were intolerable. State v. Alcantaro, App. 1 Dist., 407 So.2d 922 (1981), review denied 413 So.2d 875. Escape ⚷ 6

Prisoners seeking to show necessity or duress as defense to charge of escape may not merely introduce evidence as to general conditions of confinement but must show that prisoner is faced with specific threat of death, forcible sexual attack or substantial bodily injury in immediate future, that there is no time for complaint to authority or that history shows that complaints would be futile, that there is no time or opportunity to resort to courts, that there is no evidence of violence used towards prison personnel or other "innocent" persons in escape and that prisoner immediately reported to proper authorities on attaining position of safety from immediate threat. State v. Alcantaro, App. 1 Dist., 407 So.2d 922 (1981), review denied 413 So.2d 875. Escape ⚷ 6

Trial court in escape prosecution, by dismissing escape charges because trial court had previously in unrelated case found that prison conditions amounted to cruel and unusual punishment incorrectly attempted to expand limited factual defense to crime of escape into general legal defense by allowing defense to allege unconstitutionality of prison conditions in general without showing how prison conditions specifically necessitated defendant's escape. State v. Alcantaro, App. 1 Dist., 407 So.2d 922 (1981), review denied 413 So.2d 875. Escape ⚷ 6

Only viable defense to charge of escape is necessity involving, as to defendant, reasonable grounds to believe that he is faced with real, imminent and present danger of death, great bodily harm or such type of danger to his health if he does not temporarily leave his place of confinement. Watford v. State, App. 1 Dist., 353 So.2d 1263 (1978). Escape ⚷ 6

In escape prosecution, trial court should have permitted defendant to offer testimony to effect that he was asthmatic and that he escaped in order to obtain help in getting relief from assignment to hard labor on ground that such assignment created real, imminent and impending danger to him of death or serious bodily harm; such evidence was relevant on issue of intent. Bavero v. State, App. 1 Dist., 347 So.2d 781 (1977). Escape ⚷ 10

Defendant had a right to establish as a defense to escape charge that he was forced to leave confinement to avoid a sexual assault by another inmate and that he was merely trying to reach judge to report matter. Lewis v. State, App. 2 Dist., 318 So.2d 529 (1975), certiorari denied 334 So.2d 608. Escape ⚷ 6

35. —— Surrender, defenses

Before accused, who is charged with escape, may present testimony concerning a danger prompting him to leave, he must proffer evidence of bona fide attempt to surrender or return to custody as soon as he was no longer under coercive force of the duress; receding from Lewis v. State, 318 So.2d 529. Holdren v. State, App. 2 Dist., 415 So.2d 39 (1982), review denied 422 So.2d 842. Escape ⚷ 6

36. —— Insanity, defenses

In bifurcated trial on charge of escape in which defendant filed notice of intention to rely on insanity defense, it was denial of due process to not allow defendant to show lack of intent to commit crime of escape. Washington v. State, App. 4 Dist., 371 So.2d 1108 (1979). Constitutional Law ⚷ 4651

Evidence of deliberate and stealthy nature of escape and testimony by two lay witnesses of defendant's normal and lucid conduct on night he escaped presented jury question on issue of his competence to commit the offense notwithstanding testimony of psychiatrist for defense which assertedly established insanity defense as matter of law. McClain v. State, App. 1 Dist., 327 So.2d 106 (1976). Criminal Law ⚷ 740

37. —— Intoxication, defenses

Voluntary intoxication is a defense to crime of escape in the sense that evidence of defendant's voluntary intoxication at time of alleged escape may be relied upon to establish that defendant lacked requisite intent to commit crime. Fouts v. State, App. 2 Dist., 374 So.2d 22 (1979). Criminal Law ⚷ 55

Whenever a specific or particular intent is an essential or constituent element of a criminal offense, intoxication, though voluntary, becomes a matter for consideration or as relevant evidence with reference to capacity or ability of defendant to form or entertain particular intent. Fouts v. State, App. 2 Dist., 374 So.2d 22 (1979). Criminal Law ⚷ 55

Where defendant remained outside of lawful custody for approximately one month, two weeks after specifically promising to return, defendant demonstrated requisite intent to escape, notwithstanding contention that original departure from custody was unintentional by reason of intoxication. Helton v. State, App. 1 Dist., 311 So.2d 381 (1975). Escape ⚷ 1

38. Lesser-included offenses

Resisting officer without violence is not necessarily lesser-included offense of escape; escape can be committed without resisting, obstructing, or opposing officer. Applewhite v. State, App. 5 Dist., 874 So.2d 1276 (2004), review denied 895 So.2d 1066. Indictment And Information ⚷ 191(.5)

39. Accessories

Evidence that defendant, accused of after the fact accessory liability to first-degree murder, manslaughter, and escape, was with alleged perpetrator during a prior traffic stop in another state when perpetrator ran from police was relevant to show that defendant knew perpetrator's proper name, because he had provided it to stopping officer, and that she knew he had outstanding charges. Bowen v. State, App. 2 Dist., 791 So.2d 44 (2001), rehearing denied, review denied 817 So.2d 850, on remand 2002 WL 34392015. Homicide ⚷ 956

Harmful error arising from trial for accessory after the fact to manslaughter and murder charges improperly affected jury's verdict on other accessory after the fact charges that were properly submitted to jury and entitled defendant to new trial; at trial, State relied heavily on defendant's knowledge that alleged perpetrator wore handcuff key around his neck and had vowed never to be jailed again, although that evidence was relevant primarily to support improper accessory after the fact to manslaughter charge. Bowen v. State, App. 2 Dist., 791 So.2d 44 (2001), rehearing denied, review denied 817 So.2d 850, on remand 2002 WL 34392015. Criminal Law ⚷ 1169.1(10)

Defendant had no legal duty to volunteer to police any knowledge she possessed that alleged perpetrator of manslaughter wore handcuff key on string around his neck, in prosecution for accessory after the fact manslaughter and first degree murder. Bowen v. State, App. 2 Dist., 791 So.2d 44 (2001), rehearing denied, review denied 817 So.2d 850, on remand 2002 WL 34392015. Homicide ⚷ 573(3); Homicide ⚷ 720

40. Limitations of actions

Three-year statute of limitations barred defendant's prosecution for escape, where capias was not executed for almost five years, and state's only witness, a clerical aide for sheriff's office, had no specific information regarding any search conducted to find this particular defendant but merely testified that general procedure for issuing warrants was that information was entered into computer terminal and made available to all law enforcement offices in state. Newman v. State, App. 1 Dist., 707 So.2d 811 (1998). Criminal Law ⚷ 157

41. Presumptions

Important factor in determining validity or constitutionality of presumption contained in criminal statute as in the case of the presumption contained in this section is reasonableness of relationship between presumed fact and proven fact from which it is presumed; there must be some rational relation between fact proven and ultimate fact presumed. State v. Williams, 444 So.2d 13 (1984). Criminal Law ⚷ 307

It is reasonable for jury, in prosecution for escape, to infer from proof of fact that person is actually confined as prisoner in legitimate prison or jail or is in actual custody of genuine law enforcement officer as his prisoner that such prisoner is in lawful custody. State v. Williams, 444 So.2d 13 (1984). Escape ⚷ 10

Presumption of lawful custody exists when state proves that person is confined in any institution specified in this section. State v. Williams, 444 So.2d 13 (1984). Escape ⚿ 10

State clearly established a prima facie case against defendant in prosecution for escape by showing that he was discovered to be missing about 2:30 p.m. on day in question and was apprehended outside prison walking along a road in a direction that would take him away from prison. Fouts v. State, App. 2 Dist., 374 So.2d 22 (1979). Escape ⚿ 10

42. Burden of proof

In prosecution for escape State must allege and prove that such escape was from lawful custody. Pons v. State, App., 278 So.2d 336 (1973); Fulford v. State, App., 113 So.2d 572 (1959).

In prosecution for escape, admission of testimony of law officer regarding circumstances surrounding defendant's arrest on three initial charges, disclosing the nature of such offenses and outlining factors establishing probable cause for defendant's arrest, was reversible error, since State was not required to prove technical correctness of defendant's original arrest. Marquez v. State, App. 2 Dist., 450 So.2d 345 (1984). Criminal Law ⚿ 369.1; Criminal Law ⚿ 1169.11

State was not required to prove "lawful custody" of escape charge to prove that trial judge who issued capiases upon which defendant had been arrested and was being held correctly determined existence of "probable cause" for issuance of the capiases. McGee v. State, App. 1 Dist., 435 So.2d 854 (1983), petition for review denied 444 So.2d 417. Escape ⚿ 9

To support conviction for escape under this section, state must prove beyond reasonable doubt that defendant escaped from "lawful custody." Sullivan v. State, App. 2 Dist., 430 So.2d 519 (1983). Escape ⚿ 10

Fact of defendant's prior conviction was an essential element of crime of escape inasmuch as defendant's status as a prisoner was required to be established and, hence, State was required to prove that element. Fouts v. State, App. 2 Dist., 374 So.2d 22 (1979). Escape ⚿ 1

That defendant's prior conviction was an essential element of the crime of escape and was required to be proven by State did not mean that it was proper to allow State to introduce nature of prior crime in evidence. Fouts v. State, App. 2 Dist., 374 So.2d 22 (1979). Criminal Law ⚿ 369.2(3.1)

For conviction under escape statute (this section), State need show only right to legal custody and conscious and intentional act of defendant in leaving established area of such custody. State v. Akers, App. 2 Dist., 367 So.2d 700 (1979). Escape ⚿ 1

In escape prosecution, State is not required to show that intent to escape existed prior to or even contemporaneously with the physical act of escape. Helton v. State, App. 1 Dist., 311 So.2d 381 (1975). Escape ⚿ 1

It is essential that person charged with escape be a prisoner who has been convicted and sentenced and it is not sufficient to show that, at the time of his escape, defendant was merely charged with a crime for which he was then being held. Rothrock v. Wainwright, App. 4 Dist., 286 So.2d 240 (1973). Escape ⚿ 1

To sustain a conviction for escape while serving a sentence, state is required to prove beyond a reasonable doubt that accused escaped from incarceration under a charge or conviction of a felony or misdemeanor. Fulford v. State, App. 2 Dist., 113 So.2d 572 (1959). Escape ⚿ 10

43. Admissibility of evidence

Introduction of information underlying attempted escape defendant's earlier conviction was reversible error where information recited serious crimes and thus was prejudicial; information was not necessary to prove that defendant was in lawful custody where State presented unrebutted evidence that defendant was confined in prison at time of crime. Sanders v. State, App. 4 Dist., 517 So.2d 134 (1987). Criminal Law ⚿ 369.1; Criminal Law ⚿ 1169.11

In prosecution for escape, permitting State to reveal to jury that at time of defendant's escape he was awaiting trial on another charge of escape constituted prejudicial error; defendant in no way induced, invited or waived such error, nor was he otherwise estopped to challenge it. Fouts v. State, App. 2 Dist., 375 So.2d 347 (1979). Criminal Law ⚿ 369.2(3.1); Criminal Law ⚿ 1137(1); Criminal Law ⚿ 1137(2)

In prosecution for escape where fact of defendant's prior conviction was an essential element of crime, the State should have pursued one of two options: it should have accepted offer of defendant to admit or stipulate to fact that he had been previously convicted of a crime or, if unwilling to so admit or stipulate, it should have introduced in evidence a certified copy of prior judgment of conviction with language revealing nature of prior crime excised. Fouts v. State, App. 2 Dist., 374 So.2d 22 (1979). Criminal Law ⚿ 374

It was reversible error in prosecution for escape to allow State to reveal to jury nature of crime for which defendant was serving a term of imprisonment at time of alleged escape. Fouts v. State, App. 2 Dist., 374 So.2d 22 (1979). Criminal Law ⚿ 369.2(3.1); Criminal Law ⚿ 1169.11

References to a prior irrelevant crime record are as improper in a trial for escape as in a trial for any other crime. Fouts v. State, App. 2 Dist., 374 So.2d 22 (1979). Criminal Law ⚿ 369.2(3.1)

Testimony of psychiatrist in response to hypothetical question whether conduct of a person with described behavior was consistent with reaction of someone who was undergoing LSD induced psychosis should have been admitted as relevant to issue respecting effect of LSD on defendant's mind at time of alleged escape. Fouts v. State, App. 2 Dist., 374 So.2d 22 (1979). Criminal Law ⚿ 474.2

Where there is evidence that trial from which it may be reasonably inferred that a defendant charged with escape ingested LSD prior to his unauthorized departure from premises of a correctional institution, and within a relevant time period, it is error to exclude opinion testimony of a psychiatrist as to effect of that drug on defendant's mind at time of alleged escape. Fouts v. State, App. 2 Dist., 374 So.2d 22 (1979). Criminal Law ⚿ 474.2

Trial court did not err in refusing to permit inmate charged with unlawful escape to testify that he did not intend to escape but that he left lawful custody merely to flee to someplace where he would try to contact prison superintendent for an explanation of his transfer. Watford v. State, App. 1 Dist., 353 So.2d 1263 (1978). Escape ⚿ 10

44. Sufficiency of evidence

Competent, substantial evidence supported defendant's conviction for escape; after officer told defendant that he was under arrest, defendant slapped officer's hand away and pushed officer away, and defendant began to run. Spann v. State, App. 4 Dist., 996 So.2d 873 (2008), review denied 10 So.3d 633. Escape ⚿ 1

Evidence was insufficient to prove escape in manner alleged in information, which alleged that defendant, while confined in a state or county penal institution, or working upon the public roads, or being transported to or from a place of confinement, escaped from such confinement; evidence only showed that defendant arrived at site of work-release program and left without permission or authority to do so. Crumity v. State, App. 4 Dist., 922 So.2d 276 (2006). Escape ⚿ 10

Evidence was insufficient to prove escape in manner alleged in information, which alleged that defendant, while prisoner in lawful custody of law enforcement officer and while being transported to or from place of confinement, escaped or attempted to escape from such custody; evidence only showed that defendant arrived at site of work-release program and left without permission or authority to do so, and the state never sought to amend information to conform to proof. Banasik v. State, App. 2 Dist., 889 So.2d 916 (2004). Escape ⚿ 9

Evidence did not support finding requisite for offense of escape that defendant was either under arrest or that police officer investigating theft intended to effect arrest, where officer detained defendant for misdemeanor in security office of store, officer had option of giving defendant notice to appear, and without testimony from officer as to what was communicated to defendant while they were in office, there was no evidence of valid arrest; running from officer after being detained might have amounted to resisting arrest without violence, but without more, did not establish charge of escape. Pollen v. State, App. 3 Dist., 834 So.2d 380 (2003), on remand 2003 WL 25731387, post-conviction relief denied 2003 WL 25731386, affirmed 861 So.2d 41. Escape ⚿ 10

Sufficient evidence supported finding that defendant was under "arrest," so as to support escape conviction, where officer intended to arrest defendant, he communicated that intention to defendant by stating, "you're under arrest," defendant understood that officer meant to detain him and acquiesced to that authority when he pulled over, and defendant submitted to officer's authority by requesting permission to go into house for to tell aunt he was going to jail. Thomas v. State, App. 4 Dist., 805 So.2d 102 (2002). Escape ⚿ 10

Evidence sustained conviction for armed escape since jury could have reasonably concluded that defendant understood he was being arrested at time of his escape; detective was in full police uniform at time he confronted defendant and, although detective never actually communicated words to defendant "you are under arrest," his actions communicated such intent in that detective physically touched defendant by placing his hand on defendant's shoulder in attempt to spin him around and place him against wall. Sweeney v. State, App. 4 Dist., 633 So.2d 66 (1994), review denied 645 So.2d 455, denial of post-conviction relief affirmed 722 So.2d 928, rehearing denied, review denied 733 So.2d 517. Escape ⚿ 10

Defendant's conviction for escape was not supported by evidence as evidence did not conclusively demonstrate that there had been arrest of defendant before he fled; police officer pursuing defendant ordered defendant out of garbage can in which defendant was hiding, but never communicated his intention to place defendant under arrest, defendant easily evaded officer and was able to flee unscathed, record was silent as to whether officer actually pointed his revolver at defendant, and defendant testified that he did not believe that he was in fact under arrest. Brown v. State, App. 4 Dist., 623 So.2d 800 (1993), review denied 634 So.2d 627. Escape ⚷ 10

Independent evidence of defendant's involvement in conspiracy to escape from county jail was sufficient to justify admission of out-of-court statements made by his coconspirators and was sufficient to sustain his conviction for kidnapping. Mobley v. State, 409 So.2d 1031 (1982). Criminal Law ⚷ 427(5); Kidnapping ⚷ 36

Evidence was sufficient to support escape conviction of defendant, who, after being denied furlough to see his dying, 80-year-old mother, hitchhiked to Ohio in attempt to see her. Laird v. State, App. 5 Dist., 394 So.2d 1121 (1981). Escape ⚷ 10

Evidence failed to show that at time of attempted escape the defendant was in lawful custody on a valid charge or conviction of a criminal offense. Abigando v. State, App. 1 Dist., 239 So.2d 646 (1970). Escape ⚷ 10

45. Instructions

Trial court acted within its discretion in instructing jury on definition of "transportation to place of confinement" within meaning of escape statute and that escape did not require defendant to be in total physical control of officer at time of escape; instruction was correct statement of law and was pertinent to particular facts presented in case, in that defendant ran after officer told him that he was under arrest but before officer could handcuff him. Applewhite v. State, App. 5 Dist., 874 So.2d 1276 (2004), review denied 895 So.2d 1066. Escape ⚷ 11

Defendant was not entitled in escape trial to jury instruction on permissive lesser-included offense of resisting officer without violence, where information did not specifically allege all statutory elements of resisting officer without violence. Applewhite v. State, App. 5 Dist., 874 So.2d 1276 (2004), review denied 895 So.2d 1066. Criminal Law ⚷ 795(2.26)

Judge's inadvertent omission from jury charge in escape trial of requirement that defendants had intended to avoid lawful confinement, which was part of standard instruction which court had intended to give, was reversible error. Ramadanovic v. State, App. 1 Dist., 480 So.2d 112 (1985). Criminal Law ⚷ 1172.1(3); Escape ⚷ 11

Although any sentence of incarceration or probation imposed upon conviction of escape must be consecutive, there was no requirement that jury had to be told that the sentence had to be consecutive. Lowery v. State, App. 5 Dist., 455 So.2d 1152 (1984), petition for review denied 461 So.2d 115. Criminal Law ⚷ 796

In prosecution for escape from lawful custody, trial court erred in refusing to give requested instruction on defense of necessity after having permitted introduction of testimony in support of necessity defense, which is admissible only if criteria justifying instruction thereon are satisfied. Muro v. State, App. 3 Dist., 445 So.2d 374 (1984). Escape ⚷ 11

When there is any evidence introduced at trial which supports theory of defense of necessity, defendant charged with escape is entitled to have jury instructed on law applicable to that theory when he so requests. Muro v. State, App. 3 Dist., 445 So.2d 374 (1984). Escape ⚷ 11

When evidence is offered to show that a defendant was intoxicated at time of alleged escape, though voluntarily so, jury should be instructed to consider whether defendant was so intoxicated that he could not form particular intent to escape, i.e., intent to avoid lawful confinement. Fouts v. State, App. 2 Dist., 374 So.2d 22 (1979). Criminal Law ⚷ 774

46. Sentence and punishment—In general

The defendant's prior conviction under Florida law for escape by failure to return to a work release program did not constitute a violent felony conviction, for purposes of sentencing the defendant as an armed career criminal in his sentencing for being a felon in possession of a firearm. George v. U.S., M.D.Fla.2009, 2009 WL 1370858. Sentencing and Punishment ⚷ 1285

Because defendant's primary offense was escape, and not grand theft auto, to which he also pled no contest, trial court erroneously calculated defendant's sentencing points utilizing the 1.5 multiplier. Jimerson v. State, App. 4 Dist., 724 So.2d 170 (1998). Sentencing And Punishment ⚷ 780

Judgment reciting that defendant was convicted of offense of escaping from the custody of the commissioner of agriculture was patently void and sentence entered thereon was likewise void where judgment was entered after custody of prisoners had been placed in department of corrections of board of commissioners of state institutions; however, judgment and sentence would be reversed without prejudice to right of court to enter an amended or new judgment and sentence on criminal charge of escaping from proper custody. Davis v. State, App. 2 Dist., 257 So.2d 79 (1972). Criminal Law ⚷ 1186.7; Escape ⚷ 13

Sentence of five years in state prison imposed upon defendant convicted of escape, being within ten-year maximum sentence provided by law, was proper. Naylor v. State, App. 2 Dist., 250 So.2d 660 (1971). Escape ⚷ 13

Fact that trial judge, in receiving plea of guilty and passing sentence, referred to crime charged as "escape", not "felonious escape", did not make judgment and sentence invalid, where information correctly charged offense of felonious escape, and such was the offense to which defendant pleaded guilty and upon which he was sentenced. Harris v. State, App. 2 Dist., 217 So.2d 907 (1969). Criminal Law ⚷ 990.1

Defendant who was subjected to original sentence and later sentenced for escape from confinement under original sentence could not serve escape sentence so long as any former sentence was in effect. Sterns v. Wainwright, 195 So.2d 860 (1967). Sentencing And Punishment ⚷ 1129

Service of sentence once begun will not be interrupted in absence of some specific court order. Sterns v. Wainwright, 195 So.2d 860 (1967). Sentencing And Punishment ⚷ 1155

Upon vacation of original sentence, after date of imposition of escape sentence, original sentence was voided from its inception and escape sentence was then activated as of date it was prescribed, and defendant, who was later resentenced on original charge, with credit for time served on original charge, was not entitled to credit for period of escape sentence, although escape sentence itself was purportedly vacated after it had been served. Sterns v. Wainwright, 195 So.2d 860 (1967). Sentencing And Punishment ⚷ 1129; Sentencing And Punishment ⚷ 1175

47. —— Intent, sentence and punishment

Intent of Legislature, in enacting this section providing penalty of imprisonment for crime of escape, was to prescribe penalty which would be added to all penalties previously imposed as deterrent to prisoner inclined to break jail. Tirko v. Wainwright, 178 So.2d 697 (1965). Escape ⚷ 13

48. —— Credit for time spent in jail, sentence and punishment

Crime of escape constitutes exception to § 921.161 governing credit for time spent in county jail before sentence, and trial court properly refused jail time credit for time served in jail by defendant pending completion of his trial for escape. Hagans v. State, App. 1 Dist., 395 So.2d 308 (1981). Escape ⚷ 13

Crime of escape constitutes overriding exception to statute governing credit for time spent in county jail before sentence. Danforth v. State, App. 1 Dist., 316 So.2d 304 (1975). Escape ⚷ 13

Time awaiting escape trial is mandatory continuation of defendant's original sentence. Danforth v. State, App. 1 Dist., 316 So.2d 304 (1975). Sentencing And Punishment ⚷ 1177

Trial court did not err in failing to give defendants credit for time served in jail prior to being sentenced for crime of escape. Danforth v. State, App. 1 Dist., 316 So.2d 304 (1975). Escape ⚷ 13

That defendant was serving illegal sentence at time he committed offense of escape did not entitle him to credit against sentence imposed for escape for length of time he served under unlawful conviction but any equitable considerations arising were for Parole Commission or Pardon Board. In re Allen, App. 1 Dist., 140 So.2d 640 (1962). Sentencing And Punishment ⚷ 1181

49. —— Concurrent sentences, sentence and punishment

Trial court had discretion to impose either concurrent or consecutive sentence for escape where defendant escaped while being held for sentences which had not yet been imposed. Bush v. State, App. 1 Dist., 519 So.2d 1014 (1987), review denied 528 So.2d 1181. Sentencing And Punishment ⚷ 595

This section providing that punishment imposed under escape statute shall run consecutively to any former sentence imposed upon any prisoner is mandatory, so that sentence of five years imposed for escape, " * * * [t]o run concurrent with sentence imposed * * *," would be set aside and cause would be remanded for imposition of proper sentence. Rowe v. State, App. 2 Dist., 299 So.2d 621 (1974). Escape ⚷ 13

Sentences for breaking and entering and for escape could not be served concurrently. White v. State, 240 So.2d 150 (1970). Sentencing And Punishment ⚷ 564

50. —— Consecutive sentences, sentence and punishment

Section 944.40, providing that, on conviction of escape, punishment of imprisonment imposed is to run consecutively to any former sentence imposed upon any prisoner, controls over any apparent conflict with § 921.16, providing that court may direct that sentence imposed be served concurrently with sentence imposed by court of another state or of the United States, and trial court in sentencing for escape properly imposed sentence to be served consecutively to North Carolina sentences which defendant was currently serving. Farrow v. State, App. 5 Dist., 464 So.2d 689 (1985). Sentencing And Punishment ⚷ 633

One year sentence, which was imposed after prisoner's second escape, but which was to commence after completion of initial five year sentence for felony, was not proper sentence, in view of intervening sentence for first escape, and was required to be set aside. Tirko v. Wainwright, 178 So.2d 697 (1965). Escape ⚷ 13

This section providing that punishment of imprisonment for crime of escape shall be in addition to any former sentence imposed upon prisoner means that any sentence for escape must run consecutively to any other sentence or sentences to which offender is subject at time of escape. Tirko v. Wainwright, 178 So.2d 697 (1965). Escape ⚷ 13

51. —— Failure to report for confinement, sentence and punishment

The new rule announced in the Supreme Court's decisions in *Begay v. United States* and *Chambers v. United States*, that the offense of escape by failing to report for confinement no longer constituted a violent felony conviction, for purposes of sentencing of defendants convicted of possession of a firearm by a prohibited person as armed career criminals, constituted a new substantive rule, and thus, it applied retroactively to the defendant's case on collateral review of his sentencing as an armed career criminal for being a felon in possession of a firearm based on his prior conviction under Florida law for escape by failure to return to a work release program. George v. U.S., M.D.Fla.2009, 650 F.Supp.2d 1196. Courts ⚷ 100(1)

52. —— General sentences, sentence and punishment

General sentence imposed on defendant, who was convicted of the separate offenses of escape and resisting arrest without violence, was improper, particularly where such sentence was in excess of the maximum sentence allowed under § 843.02, for resisting arrest without violence. Ramirez v. State, App. 2 Dist., 391 So.2d 356 (1980). Sentencing And Punishment ⚷ 644

53. Habeas corpus

Fact that sentence imposed on prisoner for escape was required to be set aside did not entitle prisoner, who had completed serving other terms for which he had been imprisoned, to discharge in habeas corpus proceeding, but entitled him only to be presented before trial judge for valid sentence for such escape. Tirko v. Wainwright, 178 So.2d 697 (1965). Habeas Corpus ⚷ 793

Guilty plea to information charging escape while imprisoned on felony charge precluded contention in habeas corpus proceeding that prisoner was not incarcerated under felony charge on escape. Gorman v. Cochran, 127 So.2d 667 (1961). Habeas Corpus ⚷ 276

54. Pending appeals

Defendant's appeal from order revoking probation and sentencing defendant to three years in the penitentiary was dismissed where defendant was fugitive from justice at time appeal was pending. Jones v. State, App. 3 Dist., 362 So.2d 149 (1978). Criminal Law ⚷ 1131(5)

55. Review

For purposes of the proceedings on defendant's motion to vacate, set aside, or correct his sentence for being a felon in possession of a firearm, the defendant procedurally defaulted his challenge to the classification of his prior conviction under Florida law for escape as a violent felony conviction, for purposes of his sentencing as an armed career; although defendant argued at sentencing that his prior conviction for escape was not a violent felony for purposes of classifying him as an armed career criminal, he failed to argue that issue on direct appeal of his sentence, and he failed to show cause and prejudice excusing the default. George v. U.S., M.D.Fla.2009, 650 F.Supp.2d 1196. Criminal Law ⚷ 1429(2)

Characterizing juvenile's escape from detention facility as second-degree felony and imposing 12 years' imprisonment was fundamental error which could be raised on appeal, even though juvenile did not complain of error in sentencing court. Trueblood v. State, App. 1 Dist., 610 So.2d 12 (1992). Criminal Law ⚷ 1042.3(1); Escape ⚷ 1; Escape ⚷ 13

District Court of Appeal was powerless to reverse or amend five-year sentence imposed following conviction for escape where such sentence was within legal limits; however, sentence, which was imposed upon defendant for hitchhiking to see dying, 80-year-old mother after his request for furlough to see her was denied, might have been tempered with mercy and understanding. Laird v. State, App. 5 Dist., 394 So.2d 1121 (1981). Criminal Law ⚷ 1184(4.1)

Record on appeal from conviction for escape failed to affirmatively demonstrate prejudice or harm as result of admission of testimony of witnesses whose names had not been furnished defendant pursuant to rule. Pons v. State, App. 1 Dist., 278 So.2d 336 (1973). Criminal Law ⚷ 1166(11)

944.401. Renumbered as 985.3141 and amended by Laws 1998, c. 98–207, § 4, eff. May 24, 1998

944.402. Reward for capture of escapee from correctional institution

The warden of a state correctional institution may pay a reward in an amount not greater than $100 from institutional funds to each person who is directly responsible for the capture of an inmate who has escaped from the institution. The warden of the institution from which the inmate escaped shall determine the amount of the reward. Employees of state, county, and municipal law enforcement or correctional agencies who are engaged in the apprehension, detection, or detention of prisoners are not eligible to receive such rewards.

Laws 1988, c. 88–169, § 1. Amended by Laws 2000, c. 2000–161, § 16, eff. July 4, 2000.

Historical and Statutory Notes

Amendment Notes:

Laws 2000, c. 2000–161, a reviser's bill, substituted references to warden for references to superintendent.

Library References

Rewards ⚷0.5 to 15.
Westlaw Topic No. 340.
C.J.S. Rewards and Bounties §§ 1 to 47.

Research References

Encyclopedias

Offer of Reward, FL Jur. 2d Contracts § 29.

944.405. Warrant for retaking offender who has escaped from custody or absconded from rehabilitative community reentry program, or who is ineligible for release

(1) If there is reasonable justification to believe that an offender has escaped from the custody of the department or has absconded from a rehabilitative community reentry program before the offender has satisfied his or her sentence or combined sentences, or if it is determined an offender was released in error, or if it is subsequently determined the offender was statutorily ineligible for release, the secretary of the department or the secretary's designated representative may issue a warrant for retaking the offender into custody until he or she has served the remainder of the sentence or combined sentences.

(2) An offender who is arrested as provided in subsection (1) is ineligible for bond, bail, or release on his or her own recognizance.

(3) A warrant issued under subsection (1) is in effect until the offender has been returned to the custody of the department, or until the sentence is deemed satisfied, whichever occurs first.

(4) The issuance of a warrant pursuant to this section does not negate or interfere with the right to issuance of a warrant under any other provision of law.

Laws 1987, c. 87–211, § 1; Laws 1991, c. 91–110, § 51; Laws 1993, c. 93–406, § 34. Amended by Laws 1997, c. 97–102, § 1650, eff. July 1, 1997.

Historical and Statutory Notes

Amendment Notes:

Laws 1991, c. 91–110, a reviser's bill, amended subsec. (3) of this section correctively.

Laws 1993, c. 93–406, § 34, eff. June 17, 1993, in subsec. (1), deleted "of Corrections" after "department", made gender references neutral, inserted "or if it is determined an offender was released in error, or if it is subsequently determined the offender was statutorily ineligible for release," and substituted "the secretary's" for "his".

Laws 1997, c. 97–102, eff. July 1, 1997, removed gender-specific references applicable to human beings from volume 4 of the Florida Statutes without substantive changes in legal effect.

Library References

Bail ⚷43.
Criminal Law ⚷217.
Westlaw Topic Nos. 49, 110.
C.J.S. Bail;release and Detention Pending §§ 21, 26 to 32.
C.J.S. Criminal Law §§ 448, 450.

Notes of Decisions

Credits 1

---

1. Credits

Prisoner was not entitled to sentence credit for time he spent at liberty after his mistaken release from custody; prisoner was entitled to credit only if he was released without any fault on his part, prisoner knew or should have known that his release was in error and did not attempt to call the error to the attention of authorities. Gaines v. Florida Parole Com'n, App. 1 Dist., 962 So.2d 1040 (2007). Sentencing And Punishment ⚷ 1169

944.41. Repealed by Laws 1971, c. 71–355, § 177

Historical and Statutory Notes

The repealed section, which related to the penalty for assault by a life prisoner, was derived from Laws 1957, c. 57–313, § 1.

944.42. Repealed by Laws 1996, c. 96–293, § 7, eff. Oct. 1, 1996

Historical and Statutory Notes

The repealed section, which related to assaults by prisoners serving less than life sentences, was derived from:

Laws 1971, c. 71–136, § 1171.
Laws 1957, c. 57–313, § 2.

944.43. Repealed by Laws 1981, c. 81–88, § 1

Historical and Statutory Notes

The repealed section, pertaining to possession of a weapon by a prisoner, was derived from:

Laws 1979, c. 79–3, § 68.
Laws 1977, c. 77–120, § 58.
Laws 1971, c. 71–136, § 1172.
Laws 1969, c. 69–106, §§ 19, 35.
Laws 1961, c. 61–530, § 18.
Laws 1959, c. 59–1, § 13.
Laws 1957, c. 57–313, § 3.

See, now, F.S.A. § 944.47.

944.44. Holding persons as hostages; penalty

Any prisoner who holds as hostage any person within any correctional institution or anywhere while under the jurisdiction of the department, or who by force, or threat of force holds any person or persons against their will in defiance of official orders, shall be guilty of a felony of the second degree, punishable as provided in s. 775.082, s. 775.083, or s. 775.084.

Laws 1957, c. 57–313, § 4; Laws 1961, c. 61–530, § 18; Laws 1971, c. 71–136, § 1173; Laws 1977, c. 77–120, § 59; Laws 1979, c. 79–3, § 69.

Historical and Statutory Notes

Amendment Notes:

Laws 1961, c. 61–530, § 18, substituted the "division" for "department".

Laws 1971, c. 71–136, § 1173, made the offense defined by this section a "felony of the second degree, punishable as provided in § 775.082, § 775.083, or § 775.084" in lieu of provision that offenders "shall be imprisoned in a state correctional institution for a term of not more than 10 years."

Laws 1977, c. 77–120, a reviser's bill, amended this section to conform with Laws 1975, c. 75–49, which created the department of offender rehabilitation (see § 20.315) and transferred to the department certain functions performed by the division of corrections of the department of health and rehabilitative services and the parole and probation commission of the department of offender rehabilitation.

Laws 1979, c. 79–3, a reviser's bill, provided for substitution of references to the department and secretary of "corrections" for the department and secretary of "offender rehabilitation" to conform with Laws 1978, c. 78–53.

Library References

Prisons ⚷436.
Westlaw Topic No. 310.
C.J.S. Prisons and Rights of Prisoners § 61.

Research References

Encyclopedias

Holding Persons Hostage, FL Jur. 2d Prisons & Prisoners § 220.

944.45. Mutiny, riot, strike; penalty

Whoever instigates, contrives, willfully attempts to cause, assists, or conspires to cause any mutiny, riot, or strike in defiance of official orders, in any state correctional institution, shall be guilty of a felony of the second degree, punishable as provided in s. 775.082, s. 775.083, or s. 775.084.

Laws 1957, c. 57–313, § 5; Laws 1971, c. 71–136, § 1174.

Historical and Statutory Notes

Amendment Notes:

Laws 1971, c. 71–136, § 1174, made the offense defined by this section a "felony of the second degree, punishable as provided in § 775.082, § 775.083, or § 775.084" in lieu of provision that offenders "be imprisoned for not more than 10 years".

Library References

Riot ⚷1 to 8.
Westlaw Topic No. 341.
C.J.S. Riot; Insurrection §§ 1 to 29.

Research References

Encyclopedias

Riot or Incitement to Riot, FL Jur. 2d Prisons & Prisoners § 221.

Notes of Decisions

Admissibility of evidence 1

1. Admissibility of evidence

Exclusion of evidence in inmates' trial for riot at correctional institution of abuses perpetrated by correctional officers upon inmates after riot was quelled was abuse of discretion where evidence was relevant to both credibility of correctional officers and to inmates right to present evidence in support of their defense and where exclusion of evidence deprived jury of complete picture of events related to inmates' defense. Smiley v. State, App. 1 Dist., 627 So.2d 1192 (1993). Riot ⚷ 6

944.46. Harboring, concealing, aiding escaped prisoners; penalty

Whoever harbors, conceals, maintains, or assists, or gives any other aid to any prisoner after his or her escape from any state correctional institution, knowing that he or she is an escaped prisoner, shall be guilty of a felony of the third degree, punishable as provided in s. 775.082, s. 775.083, or s. 775.084.

Laws 1957, c. 57–313, § 6; Laws 1971, c. 71–136, § 1175. Amended by Laws 1997, c. 97–102, § 1651, eff. July 1, 1997.

Historical and Statutory Notes

Amendment Notes:

Laws 1971, c. 71–136, § 1175, made the offense defined by this section a "felony of the third degree, punishable as provided in § 775.082, § 775.083, or § 775.084" in lieu of provision that offenders "shall be imprisoned in a state correctional institution for not more than 7 years".

Laws 1997, c. 97–102, eff. July 1, 1997, removed gender-specific references applicable to human beings from volume 4 of the Florida Statutes without substantive changes in legal effect.

Cross References

Escape, see § 944.40.

Library References

Compounding Offenses ⚷3.5, 4 to 6.
Westlaw Topic No. 88.
C.J.S. Compounding Offenses §§ 5, 10 to 12.
C.J.S. Escape and Related Offenses; Rescue § 31.

Research References

ALR Library

58 ALR 3rd 851, What Constitutes Termination of Felony for Purpose of Felony-Murder Rule.

21 ALR 3rd 116, Homicide by Automobile as Murder.

Encyclopedias

Homicide Outside of Common Design, 3 Am. Jur. Proof of Facts 2d 551.

Escape or Attempted Escape; Aiding Escaped Prisoners, FL Jur. 2d Prisons & Prisoners § 222.

Notes of Decisions

Sufficiency of evidence 1

1. Sufficiency of evidence

Following his escape from prison, defendant committed third-degree felony murder, with the underlying felony being harboring, concealing, or aiding an escaped prisoner, where defendant and accomplice were eluding police and the victim was stuck and killed by car in which defendant was a passenger. Sigler v. State, App. 4 Dist., 805 So.2d 32 (2001), rehearing denied, review denied 823 So.2d 126. Homicide ⚷ 601

944.47. Introduction, removal, or possession of certain articles unlawful; penalty

(1)(a) Except through regular channels as authorized by the officer in charge of the correctional institution, it is unlawful to introduce into or upon the grounds of any state correctional institution, or to take or attempt to take or send or attempt to send therefrom, any of the following articles which are hereby declared to be contraband for the purposes of this section, to wit:

1. Any written or recorded communication or any currency or coin given or transmitted, or intended to be given or transmitted, to any inmate of any state correctional institution.

2. Any article of food or clothing given or transmitted, or intended to be given or transmitted, to any inmate of any state correctional institution.

3. Any intoxicating beverage or beverage which causes or may cause an intoxicating effect.

4. Any controlled substance as defined in s. 893.02(4) or any prescription or nonprescription drug having a hypnotic, stimulating, or depressing effect.

5. Any firearm or weapon of any kind or any explosive substance.

6. Any cellular telephone or other portable communication device intentionally and unlawfully introduced inside the secure perimeter of any state correctional institution without prior authorization or consent from the officer in charge of such correctional institution. As used in this subparagraph, the term "portable communication device" means any device carried, worn, or stored which is designed or intended to receive or transmit verbal or written messages, access or store data, or connect electronically to the Internet or any other electronic device and which allows communications in any form. Such devices include, but are not limited to, portable two-way pagers, hand-held radios, cellular telephones, Blackberry-type devices, personal digital assistants or PDA's, laptop computers, or any components of these devices which are intended to be used to assemble such devices. The term also includes any new technology that is developed for similar purposes. Excluded from this definition is any device having communication capabilities which has been approved or issued by the department for investigative or institutional security purposes or for conducting other state business.

(b) It is unlawful to transmit or attempt to transmit to, or cause or attempt to cause to be transmitted to or received by, any inmate of any state correctional institution any article or thing declared by this subsection to be contraband, at any place which is outside the grounds of such institution, except through regular channels as authorized by the officer in charge of such correctional institution.

(c) It is unlawful for any inmate of any state correctional institution or any person while upon the grounds of any state correctional institution to be in actual or constructive possession of any article or thing declared by this section to be contraband, except as authorized by the officer in charge of such correctional institution.

(2) A person who violates any provision of this section as it pertains to an article of contraband described in subparagraph (1)(a)1., subparagraph (1)(a)2., or subparagraph (1)(a)6. commits a felony of the third degree, punishable as provided in s. 775.082, s. 775.083, or s. 775.084. In all other cases, a violation of a provision of this section constitutes a felony of the second degree, punishable as provided in s. 775.082, s. 775.083, or s. 775.084.

Laws 1957, c. 57–313, § 7; Laws 1961, c. 61–192, § 8; Laws 1965, c. 65–225, § 1; Laws 1967, c. 67–160, § 1; Laws 1969, c. 69–106, §§ 19, 35; Laws 1971, c. 71–136, § 1176; Laws 1977, c. 77–120, § 60; Laws 1978, c. 78–42, § 1; Laws 1979, c. 79–3, § 70; Laws 1981, c. 81–88, § 2; Laws 1982, c. 82–124, § 1; Laws 1983, c. 83–216, § 184; Laws 1984, c. 84–1, § 1; Laws 1991, c. 91–110, § 52. Amended by Laws 2008, c. 2008–250, § 4, eff. Oct. 1, 2008.

Historical and Statutory Notes

Amendment Notes:

Laws 1957, c. 57–313, § 7, enacted this section which, as it appears in Fla.St.1957 reads:

"Whoever, contrary to any rule or regulation promulgated by the department of corrections, and approved by the board of commissioners of state institutions and filed with the secretary of state in the manner provided by law, introduces or attempts to introduce into or upon the grounds of any state correctional institution or takes or attempts to take therefrom anything whatsoever, shall be guilty of a felony and imprisoned in a state correctional institution not more than 10 years."

Laws 1961, c. 61–192, § 8, rewrote the section which, as it appears in Fla.St.1961 provides:

"(1) It is unlawful to introduce into or upon the grounds of any correctional or penal institution under the supervision or control of the board of commissioners of state institutions or to take or attempt to take or send therefrom any of the following articles which are hereby declared to be contraband for the purposes of this act, to wit: any communication or any currency or coin given or transmitted or intended to be given or transmitted to any inmate of any correctional or penal institution under the supervision and direction of the board of commissioners of state institutions; any article of food or clothing; any intoxicating beverage or beverage which causes or may cause an intoxicating effect; any narcotic or hypnotic or excitative drug or any drug of whatever kind or nature including nasal inhalators of any variety, sleeping pills or barbiturates of any variety that create or may create a hypnotic effect if taken internally; and any firearm or any instrumentality customarily used as a dangerous weapon, except through regular channels as authorized by the officer in charge of each correctional or penal institution.

"(2) Whoever violates any provision of this section shall upon conviction be sentenced to the custody of the division of corrections for a term not to exceed 5 years."

Laws 1965, c. 65–225, § 1, designated subsec. (1) as par. (a) of subsec. (1) and added a par. (b) thereto.

Laws 1967, c. 67–160, § 1, deleted, from subsec. (1)(a), the words "but not limited to" preceding "nasal inhalators", and also deleted the words "that create or may create a hypnotic effect if taken internally;" preceding "and any firearm".

Laws 1969, c. 69–106, §§ 19, 35, transferred all powers, duties and functions of the board of commissioners of state institutions to the division of adult corrections of the department of health and rehabilitative services.

Laws 1971, c. 71–136, § 1176, made the offense defined by subsec. (2) of this section a "felony of the third degree, punishable as provided in § 775.082, § 775.083, or § 775.084" in lieu of provision that offenders "shall be sentenced to the custody of the division for a term not to exceed five years."

Laws 1977, c. 77–120, a reviser's bill, amended subsec. (1) (a) of this section to conform with Laws 1975, c. 75–49, which created the department of offender rehabilitation (see § 20.315) and transferred to the department certain functions performed by the division of corrections of the department of health and rehabilitative services and the parole and probation commission of the department of offender rehabilitation.

Laws 1978, c. 78–42, amending subsec. (1) (a), inserted "written as recorded" preceding "communication" and provided for any controlled substance as defined in § 893.02(3).

Laws 1979, c. 79–3, a reviser's bill, provided for substitution of references to the department and secretary of "corrections" for the department and secretary of "offender rehabilitation" to conform with Laws 1978, c. 78–53.

As so amended, Fla.St.1979, § 944.47 provided:

"(1)(a) It is unlawful to introduce into or upon the grounds of any correctional or penal institution under the supervision or control of the department, or to take or attempt to take or send therefrom, any of the following articles which are hereby declared to be contraband for the purposes of this section, to wit:

"1. Any written or recorded communication or any currency or coin given or transmitted or intended to be given or transmitted to any inmate of any correctional or penal institution under the supervision and direction of the department;

"2. Any article of food or clothing;

"3. Any intoxicating beverage or beverage which causes or may cause an intoxicating effect;

"4. Any narcotic or hypnotic or excitative drug or any drug of whatever kind or nature including, but not limited to, nasal inhalators of any variety, sleeping pills, barbiturates of any variety, and any controlled substance as defined in s. 893.02(3); and

"5. Any firearm or any instrumentality customarily used as a dangerous weapon;

"except through regular channels as authorized by the officer in charge of each correctional or penal institution.

"(b) It is unlawful to transmit or attempt to transmit or cause or attempt to cause to be transmitted to, or received by, any inmate of any state correctional institution any article or thing declared by this subsection to be contraband, at any place which is outside of the grounds of such institution, except through regular channels as authorized by the officer in charge of such institution.

"(2) Whoever violates any provision of this section shall be guilty of a felony of the third degree, punishable as provided in s. 775.082, s. 775.083, or s. 775.084."

Laws 1981, c. 81–88, § 1, rewrote pars. (a) and (b) and added par. (c) to subsec. (1).

Laws 1982, c. 82–124, § 1, rewrote subsec. (2).

Laws 1983, c. 83–216, was a reviser's correction bill, amending subsec. (2), to improve clarity and facilitate correct interpretation.

Laws 1984, c. 84–1, § 1, inserted "or attempt to send" in subsec. (1)(a), and redefined provisions pertaining to prohibited drugs in subsec. (1)(a)4.

Laws 1991, c. 91–110, a reviser's bill, amended subsec. (1)(a) of this section correctively to conform to the renumbering of § 893.02(3) as § 893.02(4).

Laws 2008, c. 2008–250, § 4, in subsec. (1)(a), added 6., relating to cellular phones and portable communications devices; and in subsec. (2), inserted a reference to subparagraph (1)(a)6., and made a nonsubstantive language change.

Cross References

Contraband, county detention facilities, see § 951.22.
Firearms, possession in motor vehicles, restriction by employers prohibited, see § 790.251.
Public school personnel, disqualification from employment, see § 1012.315.

Library References

Prisons ⚷433 to 435, 440.
Westlaw Topic No. 310.
C.J.S. Prisons and Rights of Prisoners §§ 59, 61 to 62.

Research References

ALR Library

1 ALR 6th 549, Propriety of Lesser-Included-Offense Charge in State Prosecution of Narcotics Defendant--Marijuana Cases.

45 ALR 5th 767, Validity, Construction, and Application of State Statute Criminalizing Possession of Contraband by Individual in Penal or Correctional Institution.

Encyclopedias

Introduction or Possession of Contraband, FL Jur. 2d Prisons & Prisoners § 217.

Introduction or Possession of Contraband--Drugs and Controlled Substances, FL Jur. 2d Prisons & Prisoners § 218.

Introduction or Possession of Contraband--Firearms and Weapons, FL Jur. 2d Prisons & Prisoners § 219.

United States Supreme Court

Prisoners, destruction of personal property by guards, remedies, see Hudson v. Palmer, 1984, 104 S.Ct. 3194, 468 U.S. 517, 82 L.Ed.2d 393, on remand 744 F.2d 22.

Notes of Decisions

---

1. Validity

Statute prohibiting removal of contraband from state correctional institution is not unconstitutionally vague. State v. Fleming, App. 1 Dist., 606 So.2d 1229 (1992). Prisons ⚷ 440

Defendant who was convicted of introducing contraband into prison could challenge constitutionality of only those portions of this section with which he was charged, since he was unaffected by other provisions. Greenway v. State, 413 So.2d 23 (1982). Constitutional Law ⚷ 701

This section proscribing the introduction of contraband into prison was not unconstitutionally vague as applied to defendant who attempted to smuggle two marijuana cigarettes into prison. Greenway v. State, 413 So.2d 23 (1982). Prisons ⚷ 132

This section to be sufficiently certain so as to accord with constitutional standards of due process need not furnish a detailed plan and specifications of acts or conduct prohibited, since impossible standards are not required. Wells v. State, 402 So.2d 402 (1981). Constitutional Law ⚷ 3905

Where legislature mandated that officer in charge of penal institution was person qualified to designate regular channels of entry into prison, where items of contraband were outlined by legislature, and where prison administrator was required to keep out items within that outline which, based on his experience in prison system, were potentially harmful, prison administration acted clearly within legislative guidelines when it kept marijuana from being introduced freely into prison. Clark v. State, 395 So.2d 525 (1981). Prisons ⚷ 132

2. Construction and application

Prison entrance is functional equivalent of border in that it is official boundary where traffic may conveniently by stopped and inspected. Clark v. State, 395 So.2d 525 (1981). Prisons ⚷ 103

Stringent control of contraband is crucial for safety of guards as well as prisoners; therefore, strict methods to effect control must apply, to some degree, to all who enter prison. Clark v. State, 395 So.2d 525 (1981). Prisons ⚷ 132; Prisons ⚷ 383

Possession of marijuana is not lesser included offense or lesser degree of offense of bringing cannabis upon grounds of penal institution. London v. State, App. 4 Dist., 347 So.2d 639 (1977). Indictment And Information ⚷ 189(1)

3. Double jeopardy

When there was single occurrence of inmate's possession of excess currency as proscribed by statute, regardless of amount involved, it was but one offense and charging defendant with one count of possession of United States currency in a denomination greater then $5 and second count for possession of United States currency in a total amount greater then $30 violated double jeopardy. Campbell v. State, App. 4 Dist., 586 So.2d 84 (1991). Double Jeopardy ⚷ 139.1

Conviction of controlled substance on grounds of a state correctional institution and possession of controlled substance violated double jeopardy rights where convictions were based on the same incident; conviction of possession, as the less serious offense was vacated. Henry v. State, App. 5 Dist., 492 So.2d 485 (1986). Double Jeopardy ⚷ 146

To have charged and convicted defendant of possession of cocaine and possession of cocaine upon grounds of state correctional institution amounted to violation of his right against double jeopardy, where all elements of simple possession offense were contained within elements of possession of contraband offense within prison. Ruiz v. State, App. 1 Dist., 488 So.2d 895 (1986). Double Jeopardy ⚷ 162

4. Standing

Defendant did not have standing to challenge, as vague, provisions of this section under which she was not charged, and where her conduct was clearly illegal and proscribed by that section in understandable terms, she had no standing to challenge statute as overbroad. Wells v. State, 402 So.2d 402 (1981). Constitutional Law ⚷ 699

Since defendant's bringing marijuana into prison was clearly illegal and proscribed in understandable terms, defendant had no standing to challenge this section governing introduction and removal of certain articles from correctional institution on theory that that section was overbroad in that it criminalized legal as well as illegal activity. Clark v. State, 395 So.2d 525 (1981). Constitutional Law ⚷ 801

Where defendant did not show that he alone was arrested for bringing marijuana into prison while other people who brought marijuana into prison were not arrested, defendant did not have standing to challenge this section governing introduction or removal of certain articles from correctional institutions on theory statute was overbroad in that it allowed selective enforcement. Clark v. State, 395 So.2d 525 (1981). Constitutional Law ⚷ 801

5. Multiple offenses

Defendant could not be charged with multiple offenses for possession of two prison-made knives. State v. Watts, 462 So.2d 813 (1985). Criminal Law ⚷ 29(15)

6. Amendments

Where acts constituting a conspiracy occurred both before and after effective date of amendment to this section which increased penalty for introduction of contraband into state penal institution from third-degree felony to second-degree felony, thereby causing conspiracy to commit that crime to become a felony, rather than a simple misdemeanor, mere fact that conspiracy commenced before effective date of amendment did not render application of amendment to defendant's crime an impermissible retroactive application of the law. Jenkins v. State, App. 1 Dist., 444 So.2d 1108 (1984). Prisons ⚷ 433; Prisons ⚷ 440

7. Elements of offense

In prosecution for possession of contraband in state correctional institution, defendant, whose theory of defense was unwitting possession of the contraband, was entitled to instruction that knowledge of presence of the contraband was essential element of the crime charged. Howard v. State, App. 1 Dist., 467 So.2d 445 (1985). Prisons ⚷ 433

8. Possession

Mere presence of marijuana cigarette in open cigarette pack found in defendant's cell sometime after he had been checked into jail was not sufficient to support "possession of contraband in county jail" conviction, where defendant admitted that he owned pack, but denied having any knowledge of marijuana cigarette therein, and testified that pack had been passed among other prisoners. Stemm v. State, App. 1 Dist., 523 So.2d 760 (1988). Prisons ⚷ 434

9. Place of possession

For purposes of this section, it did not matter whether inmate was on or off premises while in possession of methadone, cocaine, and drug paraphernalia, so that prisoner arrested in parking lot of lounge who was off premises pursuant to work release program could be prosecuted under this section. State v. Pollard, App. 2 Dist., 556 So.2d 1145 (1989). Prisons ⚷ 434

Defendant, an inmate at correctional institution, could be convicted for possession of contraband by a prisoner, even though he was not on the grounds of correctional institution at time he was observed in possession of marijuana. Brooks v. State, App. 1 Dist., 529 So.2d 313 (1988). Prisons ⚷ 434

10. Explosives

Definitions in § 552.081 regulating manufacture, distribution and use of explosives among general public being inapplicable to § 944.47 under which defendant was charged with inmate possession of contraband, the statutes were not to be construed in pari materia. DeFriest v. State, App. 1 Dist., 453 So.2d 133 (1984). Prisons ⚷ 435

Statutory definition of "explosive" contained in § 790.001 dealing with weapons and firearms among general public does not apply to § 944.47 regulating conduct at state correctional institutions, and, in prosecution for inmate possession of contraband, trial court's refusal to instruct jury on the first-mentioned definition was proper. DeFriest v. State, App. 1 Dist., 453 So.2d 133 (1984). Prisons ⚷ 435

Whatever the purpose of excluding shotgun shells, cartridges, ammunition for firearms and the like from statutory definition of "explosive" in § 790.001 dealing with weapons and firearms among general public, there was no reason to exclude such items from "explosive substance" as term is used in § 944.47 providing penalty for inmate possession of contraband, and trial court in prosecution under the latter statute properly declined to instruct on such exclusions. DeFriest v. State, App. 1 Dist., 453 So.2d 133 (1984). Prisons ⚷ 435

11. Clothing

"Clothing," for purposes of statute which prohibits introduction of contraband into correctional facility and defines "clothing" as type of contraband, is defined as things worn to cover body and limbs. State v. Becton, App. 5 Dist., 665 So.2d 358 (1995). Prisons ⚷ 440

Gold chain necklace which had been brought into prison was not "contraband" for purposes of statute prohibiting introduction of contraband into correctional facility; necklace did not constitute "clothing" included within contraband definition in statute, as it was not worn to cover body and limbs, and was also not "currency" qualifying as contraband under statute as it was not in circulation as medium of exchange in prison, even though cigarettes, magazines, candy and food, drugs, and favors were regularly exchanged in prison. State v. Becton, App. 5 Dist., 665 So.2d 358 (1995). Prisons ⚷ 440

12. Currency

"Currency," for purposes of statute which prohibits introduction of contraband into correctional facility and defines "currency" as type of contraband, is money or other commodity which is in circulation as medium of exchange. State v. Becton, App. 5 Dist., 665 So.2d 358 (1995). Prisons ⚷ 440

13. Weapons

For purposes of statute prohibiting the introduction of a weapon into a state correctional institution, instrument is a "weapon" if it is designed and constructed for use as a weapon, or, if the instrument is capable of being used as a weapon, defendant used, threatened to use, or intended to use it as a weapon. State v. Fleming, App. 1 Dist., 606 So.2d 1229 (1992). Prisons ⚷ 440

Jury question was presented as to whether box cutter possessed by prison employee, who allegedly brought it with him from his other job in a grocery store, was a "weapon," even though he did not brandish or use it in a threatening manner while in the institution. State v. Fleming, App. 1 Dist., 606 So.2d 1229 (1992). Prisons ⚷ 440

Pocket knife qualified as a "weapon" under this section. Staffins v. State, App. 1 Dist., 521 So.2d 382 (1988). Prisons ⚷ 435

14. Search and seizure

Anal cavity search of prison inmate, who was returning from an outside work detail, upon receipt of information by prison officials from a reliable confidential source within prison that inmate would smuggle marijuana into prison concealed in his anal cavity, was reasonable and within constitutional limits in view of facts that information received from reliable confidential source provided prison officials with compelling justification to search inmate, and that search was conducted in a reasonable fashion under proper medical conditions. Vera v. State, App. 3 Dist., 400 So.2d 1008 (1981). Prisons ⚷ 137

Essential to validity of a search made to prevent entry of forbidden articles into a designated area is that it not only be reasonable at its inception, but also that scope of the search be reasonable related to purpose which justified it in the first instance. Williams v. State, App. 1 Dist., 400 So.2d 988 (1981), review denied 411 So.2d 385. Searches And Seizures ⚷ 53.1

Warrantless search of person and possessions of prison visitor, which disclosed certain drugs in her sweater pocket, was not unreasonable and thus not constitutionally invalid because governmental interest to be protected, prevention introduction of contraband into a prison or correction facility, substantially outweighed governmental intrusion of privacy suffered by the visitor at a time and a place when she had only minimal expectation of privacy. Williams v. State, App. 1 Dist., 400 So.2d 988 (1981), review denied 411 So.2d 385. Prisons ⚷ 385

15. Border searches

Although inspection at border may reveal contraband, enabling officials to stop contraband at border instead of having to detect illegal goods once dispersed inside border, inspection must be reasonable and must not violate rights under U.S.C.A. Const. Amend. 4 of individual who crosses boundary. Clark v. State, 395 So.2d 525 (1981). Customs Duties ⚷ 126(1)

16. Defenses

This section prohibiting possession of weapon by prison inmate does not bar temporary possession of weapon taken from possession of would-be aggressor when it is used to defend attacked inmate against imminent peril of death or serious bodily injury; receding from *Carter v. State*, 312 So.2d 494, and *Dardy v. State*, 324 So.2d 178. Mungin v. State, App. 1 Dist., 458 So.2d 293 (1984), petition for review denied 464 So.2d 556. Criminal Law ⚷ 38

Authorization by the officer in charge of correctional institution is an affirmative defense to a charge of possession of a weapon by state prisoner; defendant has burden of going forward with evidence that the affirmative defense exists and once defendant has presented competent evidence of the existence of the defense, burden of proof remains with the state and state must then prove the nonexistence of the defense beyond a reasonable doubt. Wright v. State, App. 1 Dist., 442 So.2d 1058 (1983), petition for review denied 450 So.2d 489. Prisons ⚷ 435

No reason appears why duress may not be defense to charge of introducing contraband into correctional institution but defendant's proffer was not sufficiently detailed to permit judgment whether excluded testimony tended to show duress in fact and thus justified submitting issue to jury. Moyers v. State, App. 1 Dist., 400 So.2d 769 (1981), affirmed 406 So.2d 1120. Criminal Law ⚷ 670

17. Estoppel and bar

Defendant's conviction for bringing cannabis upon grounds of penal institution was not barred by his prior conviction for possession of same marijuana. London v. State, App. 4 Dist., 347 So.2d 639 (1977). Double Jeopardy ⚷ 146

18. Indictment or information

State's error in charging defendant found to be in possession of cocaine residue while confined in county jail under statute governing possession of contraband in a state correctional facility, rather than statute governing possession of contraband in a county detention facility, did not require reversal of defendant's conviction, but rather remand for correction of judgment; offense was correctly labeled a third-degree felony, defendant failed to raise issue before trial court, and defendant did not allege that he was misled or prejudiced by the error. Johnson v. State, App. 2 Dist., 873 So.2d 478 (2004). Criminal Law ⚷ 1167(1); Criminal Law ⚷ 1181.5(3.1)

Indictment alleging that inmate had in his possession or under his control a weapon, specifically a homemade knife, was not insufficient, for failure to include word "knowingly." State v. Sutton, App. 1 Dist., 416 So.2d 852 (1982). Prisons ⚷ 435

In prosecution for attempted unlawful introduction of contraband into a penal institution, there was no error in trial court's denial of defendant's motion for judgment of acquittal, which was made on grounds that offense did not track exact words of the statute. Pearson v. State, App. 4 Dist., 371 So.2d 569 (1979). Indictment And Information ⚷ 110(2)

Information which charged inmate in particular prison with unlawful introduction of contraband into a place of detention was not insufficient because it did not identify the particular prison as part of the Florida division of corrections. Machin v. State, App. 3 Dist., 270 So.2d 464 (1972). Prisons ⚷ 433

19. Judicial notice

In prosecution for possession of weapon by prison inmate, trial court did not err in taking judicial notice of regulation of department of corrections, although defendant asserted he was given inadequate notice of prosecution's intent to rely on regulation, in that defendant was not prejudiced, he had been furnished text of rule by information approximately three months prior to trial, and rule, set forth as it was in court file and published in administrative code, informed court sufficiently for it, upon written request, to take judicial notice. Rogers v. State, App. 1 Dist., 413 So.2d 1270 (1982). Criminal Law ⚷ 304(17)

20. Presumptions

If premises in which a contraband substance is found is within exclusive possession of a defendant charged with introduction of contraband to a penal institution, it may be inferred that defendant had knowledge of presence of the contraband together with ability to maintain control over it. Williams v. State, App., 413 So.2d 1263 (1982); State v. Craig, App., 413 So.2d 863 (1982).

Evidence that premises on which contraband was found were in defendant prison inmate's exclusive possession and control permitted inference of his knowledge of, and ability to maintain control over, contraband. DeFriest v. State, App. 1 Dist., 453 So.2d 133 (1984). Prisons ⚷ 433

Testimony of expert witness that he examined .22 caliber ammunition and shell casings taken from defendant's cell, that some of the ammunition contained viable propellant powder and that the powder was definitely an "explosive substance" made prima facie case that defendant inmate possessed explosive substance. DeFriest v. State, App. 1 Dist., 453 So.2d 133 (1984). Criminal Law ⚷ 494

21. Burden of proof

Defendant, who introduced evidence that he was issued screwdriver and was authorized to use it in his job of investigating manhole covers, could not be convicted of possession of a weapon by state prisoner where State failed to prove that defendant was not authorized to possess alleged weapon, a screwdriver; furthermore, defendant could not be convicted since State failed to prove that the screwdriver was a weapon. Wright v. State, App. 1 Dist., 442 So.2d 1058 (1983), petition for review denied 450 So.2d 489. Prisons ⚷ 435

In order to sustain conviction for introduction of contraband into a state correctional facility, when the premises on which contraband was found were not in the defendant's exclusive control, state must prove the defendant knew of the contraband. Doby v. State, App. 1 Dist., 352 So.2d 1236 (1977). Prisons ⚷ 433

22. Admissibility of evidence

In prosecution for possession of contraband, evidence of possible unauthorized access to prison barbershop in which inmate worked was relevant to inmate's claim that, although he was only inmate with authorized access to a locker in which contraband was found, contraband may have been placed in locker by someone else. Floyd v. State, App. 1 Dist., 514 So.2d 413 (1987). Prisons ⚷ 433

Where facts in prosecution for possession of weapon by prison inmate indicated that inmate came into temporary possession of knife after its forced removal from his aggressor, trial court erred in excluding proffered defense testimony relating to defenses of self-defense, necessity, and duress. Mungin v. State, App. 1 Dist., 458 So.2d 293 (1984), petition for review denied 464 So.2d 556. Weapons ⚷ 17(3)

In prosecution for possession of a weapon by a state prisoner, trial court did not abuse its discretion in allowing state to reopen evidence so that it could introduce applicable rule of the department of corrections, which defined a prohibited instrument, required by this section. Jones v. State, App. 1 Dist., 392 So.2d 18 (1980). Criminal Law ⚷ 686(1)

23. Sufficiency of evidence

Evidence was legally insufficient to sustain convictions on two counts, rather than one count, of possession of contraband in state correctional facility. Lleo v. State, App. 1 Dist., 601 So.2d 1292 (1992). Prisons ⚷ 433

Evidence of defendant's mere possession of marijuana in correctional institution was insufficient for conviction of introducing narcotic or hypnotic or excitative drug into or upon grounds of any correctional or penal institution. Parrish v. State, App. 2 Dist., 423 So.2d 617 (1982). Prisons ⚷ 434

Evidence was sufficient to support conviction of defendant for possession of a weapon by a state prisoner. Jones v. State, App. 1 Dist., 392 So.2d 18 (1980). Prisons ⚷ 435

Evidence that envelopes of marijuana were found secreted in defendant's wheelchair upon his return to correctional institute from furlough was insufficient to show that defendant knew the marijuana was in his chair and thus did not sustain conviction for possession of marijuana and introduction of contraband into a state correctional facility where a number of other inmates often had access to the wheelchair out of defendant's presence and there was no direct evidence to connect defendant to the marijuana. Doby v. State, App. 1 Dist., 352 So.2d 1236 (1977). Controlled Substances ⚷ 80; Prisons ⚷ 434

24. Instructions—In general

Omission from jury charge of an instruction as to knowledge of possession, held to be an essential element of the crime of introducing contraband into or upon grounds of a correctional institution, was not fundamental error denying defendant an essentially fair trial in absence of evidence that a more complete instruction would have resulted in a different verdict. Pratt v. State, App. 1 Dist., 429 So.2d 366 (1983). Criminal Law ⚷ 1038.1(4)

In prosecution for introduction of contraband to a penal institution, trial court erroneously instructed jury that defendant did not have to have knowledge that she was in possession of the contraband in order to be found guilty. Williams v. State, App. 1 Dist., 413 So.2d 1263 (1982). Prisons ⚷ 440

25. —— Included offenses, instructions

In prosecution for possession of contraband in a state facility, defendant was entitled to instruction on permissive lesser included offense of possession of less than 20 grams of marijuana, where there was sufficient evidence for jury to reasonably conclude that marijuana involved weighed less than 20 grams. Jarrell v. State, App. 2 Dist., 576 So.2d 793 (1991). Criminal Law ⚷ 795(2.26)

In prosecution for possession of contraband in a state facility, failure to instruct on possession of less than 20 grams of marijuana, as a permissive lesser included offense supported by pleadings and evidence, was reversible error, where that offense was the next-lower lesser included offense of the crime for which defendant was convicted. Jarrell v. State, App. 2 Dist., 576 So.2d 793 (1991). Criminal Law ⚷ 1173.2(4)

Defendant charged with possessing cannabis upon grounds of correctional facility was entitled to instruction on lesser included offense of simple possession, notwithstanding complete lack of evidence that defendant possessed cannabis at some place other than correctional institution. Jess v. State, App. 5 Dist., 523 So.2d 1268 (1988). Criminal Law ⚷ 795(2.70)

Defendant who was charged with introduction and possession of contraband upon grounds of state correctional facility was entitled to jury instruction on lesser included offense of misdemeanor possession of less than 20 grams of cannabis, where defendant, who was incarcerated, had approximately 2.3 grams of cannabis in his possession when he returned to correctional facility. Wilcott v. State, 509 So.2d 261 (1987). Criminal Law ⚷ 795(2.70)

26. Sentence and punishment—In general

Reference to "trial transcript" in motion to correct consecutive habitual felony offender (HFO) sentences did not meet threshold allegation requirements, where defendant failed to explain how anything in transcript would demonstrate that his convictions for aggravated assault on a law enforcement officer and possession of contraband in prison arose from the same criminal episode. Martinez v. State, App. 4 Dist., 976 So.2d 68 (2008), rehearing denied, review denied 991 So.2d 387. Sentencing And Punishment ⚷ 2277

Where defendant's possession of two knives was simultaneous in time and essentially simultaneous in space, defendant was subject to a single prosecution under F.S.A. § 944.47 providing, inter alia, that it is unlawful for any inmate of any state correctional institution to be in possession of any firearm or weapon of any kind; therefore, defendant was vulnerable to but one judgment, and could not be concurrently sentenced on two counts of possession. Watts v. State, App. 1 Dist., 440 So.2d 505 (1983), approved 462 So.2d 813. Sentencing And Punishment ⚷ 539

Where defendant was convicted for possession of hashish and attempted unlawful introduction of contraband into a penal institution, trial court erred in imposing a single term, a general term of probation; defendant was entitled to a set term of probation in each case to run consecutively or concurrently with the term set in the other case. Pearson v. State, App. 4 Dist., 371 So.2d 569 (1979). Sentencing And Punishment ⚷ 1913; Sentencing And Punishment ⚷ 1938

27. —— Scoresheet errors, sentence and punishment

Defendant's sentence was illegal because the guidelines scoresheet was incorrectly calculated; defendant's primary offense of conspiracy to introduce marijuana into a correctional facility should have been scored as a level-one offense, and not a level-four offense, and likewise, defendant's two additional offenses of solicitation to introduce marijuana should have been scored as level-one offenses, rather than level-two offenses. Urquhart v. State, App. 1 Dist., 967 So.2d 397 (2007). Sentencing And Punishment ⚷ 686

28. —— Consecutive sentences, sentence and punishment

Mandatory consecutive sentencing upon conviction for possession of contraband in a state facility is proper, despite contention that legislature cannot rob trial judge of all discretion as to whether to impose consecutive or concurrent sentence. Jarrell v. State, App. 2 Dist., 576 So.2d 793 (1991). Constitutional Law ⚷ 2371; Sentencing And Punishment ⚷ 505

29. Dismissal

Question of whether prison inmate had knowledge of knife's presence in his mattress was an ultimate fact question which could not be appropriately resolved on motion to dismiss information charging defendant with possession of a weapon by a prison inmate. State v. Craig, App. 1 Dist., 413 So.2d 863 (1982). Weapons ⚷ 17(5)

Since defendant, charged with possession of a weapon by a prison inmate, had exclusive control over cell and its contents from September 10, 1980, when he was searched, through September 14, 1980, when a homemade knife was found imbedded in his mattress, and since knowledge of the knife's presence and the ability of defendant to maintain control over it could be inferred, there were sufficient facts to raise issues which had to be resolved by the trier of fact, and it was thus error to grant defendant's motion to dismiss. State v. Craig, App. 1 Dist., 413 So.2d 863 (1982). Weapons ⚷ 17(5)

It was undisputed fact that defendant, a state prisoner, was in possession of a metal pipe, but whether that pipe was customarily used or designed to be used as a dangerous weapon was a disputed fact, one which was properly resolved by the trier of fact in prosecution for possession of a weapon by a state prisoner, and not to be resolved by a motion to dismiss. Jones v. State, App. 1 Dist., 392 So.2d 18 (1980). Prisons ⚷ 435

30. Verdict

Defendant's conviction for possession of contraband in state correctional institution was not legally inconsistent with jury verdict of not guilty, by reason of insanity, on charge of aggravated battery; while evidence of a delusional disorder could have shown that defendant lacked intent necessary for aggravated battery, defendant could have had intent necessary to possess contraband. Lleo v. State, App. 1 Dist., 601 So.2d 1292 (1992). Criminal Law ⚷ 878(4)

944.471. Short title

Sections 944.471–944.473 may be cited as the "Drug–Free Corrections Act of 1992."

Laws 1992, c. 92–310, § 18.

Research References

Encyclopedias

Drug and Alcohol Testing, FL Jur. 2d Prisons & Prisoners § 101.

944.472. Drug-free corrections; legislative findings and purposes

(1) Findings.—The Legislature finds that:

(a) Inmate substance abuse can cause a multitude of security and programmatic problems, including staff corruption, development of an unsafe and unproductive workplace, and the inability of inmate substance abusers to profit from vocational, educational, and substance abuse treatment programs.

(b) Maintaining a healthy and productive corrections workforce with safe conditions free from the effects of substance abuse is important to correctional employers, employees, inmates, and the public.

(c) Certain substance abuse testing standards are necessary to ensure uniform and economical application of policy throughout the state's institutions and to protect both inmates and employers participating in random and reasonable suspicion substance abuse testing programs.

(d) In balancing the interests of correctional employers, employees, inmates, and the public, it is in the best interest of all concerned to establish standards to ensure uniform, fair, economical, and accurate substance abuse testing in the state correctional system.

(2) Purposes.—The purposes of the Drug–Free Corrections Act of 1992 are to:

(a) Promote the goal of a drug-free correctional system through fair, economical, and reasonable methods of random and reasonable suspicion substance abuse testing of inmates for the protection of inmates, employees, employers, and the public.

(b) Establish an aggressive, routine random substance abuse testing program and a reasonable suspicion substance abuse testing program to identify substance-abusing inmates, determine appropriate treatment, and provide a strong deterrent to future substance abuse.

Laws 1992, c. 92–310, § 19. Amended by Laws 1997, c. 97–78, § 16, eff. May 23, 1997.

Historical and Statutory Notes

Amendment Notes:

Laws 1997, c. 97–78, § 16, eff. May 23, 1997, in subsecs. (1)(c) and (2)(a), inserted and reasonable suspicion"; and, in subsec. (2)(b), inserted "and a reasonable suspicion substance abuse testing program".

944.473. Inmate substance abuse testing program

(1) Rules and procedures.—The department shall establish programs for random and reasonable suspicion drug and alcohol testing by urinalysis or other noninvasive procedure for inmates to effectively identify those inmates abusing drugs, alcohol, or both. The department shall also adopt rules relating to fair, economical, and accurate operations and procedures of a random inmate substance abuse testing program and a reasonable suspicion substance abuse testing program by urinalysis or other noninvasive procedure which enumerate penalties for positive test results, including but not limited to the forfeiture of both basic and incentive gain-time, and which do not limit the number of times an inmate may be tested in any one fiscal or calendar year.

(2) Substance abuse treatment programs.—

(a) An inmate who meets the criteria established by the department shall participate in substance abuse program services when such services are available. A right to substance abuse program services is not stated, intended, or otherwise implied by this chapter.

(b) Upon arrival at a department's reception center for initial processing, each inmate shall be screened and assessed to determine if the inmate meets the department's criteria for mandated participation in a substance-abuse program. Criteria for mandated substance abuse program services shall be based on:

1. The presence of a diagnosed psychoactive substance dependence or use disorder;

2. The severity of the addiction;

3. A history of criminal behavior related to substance abuse;

4. A recommendation by a sentencing authority for substance abuse program services;

5. Unsuccessful participation in community-based substance abuse services;

6. Sentencing by a drug court or drug division; and

7. Other classification or program criteria that the department finds will ensure security and optimal program placement.

(c) When selecting contract providers to administer substance abuse treatment programs, the department shall make every effort to consider qualified faith-based service groups on an equal basis with other private organizations.

(3) Reporting requirement.—The department shall, as part of its annual report, report the number of random and reasonable suspicion substance abuse tests administered in the fiscal year, the number of positive results obtained, the number of negative results obtained, the number of inmates requesting and participating in substance abuse treatment programs as the result of a positive random or reasonable suspicion substance abuse test, and the number of repeat substance abuse offenders.

Laws 1992, c. 92–310, § 20. Amended by Laws 1997, c. 97–78, § 17, eff. May 23, 1997; Laws 2001, c. 2001–110, § 4, eff. July 1, 2001.

Historical and Statutory Notes

Amendment Notes:

Laws 1997, c. 97–78, § 17, in subsecs. (1) and (3), inserted provisions relating to reasonable suspicion drug abuse testing.

Laws 2001, c. 2001–110, § 4, rewrote subsec. (2), which formerly read:

"(2) Substance abuse treatment programs.—If substance abuse treatment is requested by an inmate, the department shall place the inmate in a substance abuse treatment program, if available and appropriate."

Library References

Prisons ⚷137, 201.
Westlaw Topic No. 310.

C.J.S. Prisons and Rights of Prisoners §§ 12, 58, 60, 72 to 73, 76, 78 to 88, 91, 123, 125, 127, 136.

Research References

Encyclopedias

Drug and Alcohol Testing, FL Jur. 2d Prisons & Prisoners § 101.

Rehabilitation; Substance Abuse Treatment, FL Jur. 2d Prisons & Prisoners § 121.

Notes of Decisions

Pleadings 2
Validity 1

1. Validity

Watchdog organization and its members had taxpayer standing to attack the constitutionality of statutes authorizing use of state funds to pay for faith-based substance abuse transitional housing programs to inmates, provided by allegedly sectarian religious institutions pursuant to contracts between institutions and Department of Corrections (DOC), as state was using legislative appropriations allegedly to aid these institutions. Council for Secular Humanism, Inc. v. McNeil, App. 1 Dist., 2009 WL 4782384 (2009). States ⚷ 168.5

Watchdog organization and its members lacked taxpayer standing to attack on constitutional grounds contracts entered into by Department of Corrections (DOC) and purported sectarian religious institutions that contracted with DOC to provide faith-based substance abuse transitional housing programs to inmates, as this attack was not a challenge to the legislature's taxing and spending powers, but was a challenge to the downstream performance of contracts by the institutions and the DOC's oversight of the contracts. Council for Secular Humanism, Inc. v. McNeil, App. 1 Dist., 2009 WL 4782384 (2009). States ⚷ 168.5

2. Pleadings

Watchdog organization and its members stated claim for violation of State Constitution's no-aid provision against secretary of Department of Corrections (DOC), in his official capacity, and purported sectarian religious institutions that contracted with DOC to provide faith-based substance abuse transitional housing programs to inmates, by alleging that programs were state-funded, pursuant to statute, and that they were fundamentally carried out in a sectarian manner, to promote the institutions' religious mission. Council for Secular Humanism, Inc. v. McNeil, App. 1 Dist., 2009 WL 4782384 (2009). Constitutional Law ⚷ 1426; Prisons ⚷ 220

944.4731. Addiction–Recovery Supervision Program

(1) This section may be cited as the "Addiction–Recovery Supervision Program Act."

(2)(a) Any offender released from a state correctional facility who is convicted of a crime committed on or after July 1, 2001, must be given addiction-recovery supervision if the offender has:

1. A history of substance abuse or addiction;

2. Participated in any drug treatment;

3. No current or previous convictions for a violent offense;

4. No current or previous convictions for drug trafficking or for the unlawful sale of a controlled substance;

5. No current or previous convictions for a property offense, except for a conviction for:

a. Passing worthless checks, forgery, uttering, or counterfeiting;

b. Third degree felony grand theft, excluding a theft relating to firearms; or

c. Third degree felony burglary of an unoccupied structure or conveyance; and

6. No current or previous conviction for a traffic offense involving injury or death.

(b) An offender released under addiction-recovery supervision shall be subject to specified terms and conditions, including payment of the costs of supervision under s. 948.09 and any other court-ordered payments, such as child support and restitution. If an offender has received a term of probation or community control to be served after release from incarceration, the period of probation or community control may not be substituted for addiction-recovery supervision and shall follow the term of addiction-recovery supervision. A panel of not fewer than two parole commissioners shall establish the terms and conditions of supervision, and the terms and conditions must be included in the supervision order. In setting the terms and conditions of supervision, the parole commission shall weigh heavily the program requirements, including, but not limited to, work at paid employment while participating in treatment and traveling restrictions. The commission shall also determine whether an offender violates the terms and conditions of supervision and whether a violation warrants revocation of addiction-recovery supervision pursuant to s. 947.141. The parole commission shall review the offender's record for the purpose of establishing the terms and conditions of supervision. The parole commission may impose any special conditions it considers warranted from its review of the record. The length of supervision may not exceed the maximum penalty imposed by the court.

(c) The Legislature finds that offenders released from state prison into the community who meet the criteria for participating in the addiction-recovery supervision program possess the greatest potential for successful substance abuse recovery through treatment and transition assistance.

(3)(a) Each fiscal year, and contingent upon funding, the department shall enter into contracts with multiple providers who are private organizations, including faith-based service groups, to operate substance abuse transition housing programs, including providers that:

1. Provide postrelease housing, programming, treatment, and other transitional services;

2. Emphasize job placement and gainful employment for program participants;

3. Provide a curriculum related to substance abuse treatment which uses a cognitive behavior model or 12–step model of addiction recovery;

4. Provide for a length of stay of not more than 12 months; and

5. Use community volunteers in operating the program to the greatest extent possible.

(b) The department shall allow providers to use innovative approaches to treatment and shall authorize a high level of flexibility in operating a program. The department shall ensure that an offender's faith orientation, or lack thereof, will not be considered in determining admission to a faith-based program and that the program does not attempt to convert an offender toward a particular faith or religious preference.

(4) When facilitating job placement for an offender under this program, the provider shall make every effort to secure suitable employment that provides adequate wages, a potential for advancement, and a likelihood of stable and long-term employment. To measure the success of postrelease job placement, the department shall, as part of its annual report, track for 1 year offenders who successfully complete the program and shall determine their employment status.

(5) Each contract entered into under this section for operating a substance abuse transition housing program must invite innovation, minimize bureaucracy, and permit the private organization or faith-based provider to petition the department to waive any rule, policy, or procedure that is inconsistent with the mission of the private organization or faith-based provider.

(6) Six months before an offender is released, the chaplain and transition assistance specialist at the institution where the offender is incarcerated shall initiate the prerelease screening process in addition to the basic release orientation required under s. 944.705.

(a) The transition assistance specialist and the chaplain shall provide a list of contracted private providers, including faith-based providers, to the offender and facilitate the application process. The transition assistance specialist shall inform the offender of program availability and assess the offender's need and suitability for substance abuse transition housing assistance. If an offender is approved for placement, the specialist shall assist the offender and coordinate the release of the offender with the selected program. If an offender requests and is approved for placement in a contracted faith-based substance abuse transition housing program, the specialist must consult with the chaplain prior to such placement. A right to substance abuse program services is not stated, intended, or otherwise implied by this section.

(b) If an offender has participated in a faith-based program while incarcerated or housed at a community correctional center and the same or a similar faith-based provider offers a contracted substance abuse transition housing program, the department shall make every attempt to maintain this continuum of care.

(7) While participating in a substance abuse transition housing program, an offender shall:

(a) Adhere to all conditions of supervision enforced by the commission and the program provider. Failure to comply with such rules or conditions may result in revocation of supervision pursuant to s. 947.141.

(b) Pay fees to defray program costs, costs of supervision required under s. 948.09, and any restitution or obligations for child support.

(c) Participate in a cognitive behavior model or 12–step model of recovery.

(8) The commission may adopt rules pursuant to ss. 120.536(1) and 120.54 as necessary for administering this section.

Added by Laws 2001, c. 2001–110, § 5, eff. July 1, 2001. Amended by Laws 2004, c. 2004–373, § 39, eff. July 1, 2004.

Historical and Statutory Notes

Amendment Notes:

Laws 2004, c. 2004–373, § 39, reenacted subsections (2)(b) and (7)(b) of this section for the purpose of incorporating the amendment to § 948.09 in references thereto.

Library References

Prisons ⚷248.
Westlaw Topic No. 310.
C.J.S. Prisons and Rights of Prisoners § 152.

Research References

Treatises and Practice Aids

16 Florida Practice Series § 10:16, Post Release--Addiction Recovery Supervision.

16 Florida Practice Series § 10:17, Violation of Conditional Release, Control Release, Conditional Medical Release, or Addiction Recovery Supervision.

Notes of Decisions

1. Validity

Watchdog organization and its members had taxpayer standing to attack the constitutionality of statutes authorizing use of state funds to pay for faith-based substance abuse transitional housing programs to inmates, provided by allegedly sectarian religious institutions pursuant to contracts between institutions and Department of Corrections (DOC), as state was using legislative appropriations allegedly to aid these institutions. Council for Secular Humanism, Inc. v. McNeil, App. 1 Dist., 2009 WL 4782384 (2009). States ⚷ 168.5

Watchdog organization and its members lacked taxpayer standing to attack on constitutional grounds contracts entered into by Department of Corrections (DOC) and purported sectarian religious institutions that contracted with DOC to provide faith-based substance abuse transitional housing programs to inmates, as this attack was not a challenge to the legislature's taxing and spending powers, but was a challenge to the downstream performance of contracts by the institutions and the DOC's oversight of the contracts. Council for Secular Humanism, Inc. v. McNeil, App. 1 Dist., 2009 WL 4782384 (2009). States ⚷ 168.5

2. Pleadings

Watchdog organization and its members stated claim for violation of State Constitution's no-aid provision against secretary of Department of Corrections (DOC), in his official capacity, and purported sectarian religious institutions that contracted with DOC to provide faith-based substance abuse transitional housing programs to inmates, by alleging that programs were state-funded, pursuant to statute, and that they were fundamentally carried out in a sectarian manner, to promote the institutions' religious mission. Council for Secular Humanism, Inc. v. McNeil, App. 1 Dist., 2009 WL 4782384 (2009). Constitutional Law ⚷ 1426; Prisons ⚷ 220

944.474. Legislative intent; employee wellness program; drug and alcohol testing

(1) It is the intent of the Legislature that the state correctional system provide a safe and secure environment for both inmates and staff. A healthy workforce is a productive workforce, and security of the state correctional system can best be provided by strong and healthy employees. The Department of Corrections may develop and implement an employee wellness program.

The program may include, but is not limited to, wellness education, smoking cessation, nutritional education, and overall health-risk reduction, including the effects of using drugs and alcohol.

(2) Under no circumstances shall employees of the department test positive for illegal use of controlled substances. An employee of the department may not be under the influence of alcohol while on duty. In order to ensure that these prohibitions are adhered to by all employees of the department and notwithstanding s. 112.0455, the department may develop a program for the random drug testing of all employees. The department may randomly evaluate employees for the contemporaneous use or influence of alcohol through the use of alcohol tests and observation methods. Notwithstanding s. 112.0455(5)(a), the department may develop a program for the reasonable suspicion drug testing of employees who are in safety- sensitive or special risk positions, as defined in s. 112.0455(5), for the controlled substances listed in s. 893.03(3)(d). The reasonable suspicion drug testing authorized by this subsection shall be conducted in accordance with s. 112.0455, but may also include testing upon reasonable suspicion based on violent acts or violent behavior of an employee who is on or off duty. The department shall adopt rules pursuant to ss. 120.536(1) and 120.54 that are necessary to administer this subsection.

Added by Laws 1996, c. 96–312, § 9, eff. July 1, 1996. Amended by Laws 2006, c. 2006–116, § 1, eff. July 1, 2006.

Historical and Statutory Notes

Amendment Notes:

Laws 2006, c. 2006–116, § 1, rewrote subsec. (2), which formerly read:

"(2) Under no circumstances shall employees of the department test positive for illegal use of controlled substances. An employee of the department may not be under the influence of alcohol while on duty. In order to ensure that these prohibitions are adhered to by all employees of the department and notwithstanding s. 112.0455, the department may develop a program for the random drug testing of all employees. The department may randomly evaluate employees for the contemporaneous use or influence of alcohol through the use of alcohol tests and observation methods."

Library References

Prisons ⚷391.
Westlaw Topic No. 310.

C.J.S. Prisons and Rights of Prisoners §§ 12 to 15, 17, 22.

Research References

Encyclopedias

Employee Wellness Program; Drug or Alcohol Use and Testing, FL Jur. 2d Prisons & Prisoners § 34.

Notes of Decisions

Random drug testing 1

---

1. Random drug testing

The Department of Corrections is specifically authorized by § 944.474(2), Florida Statutes (1996 Supp.), to develop a program for the random drug testing of all employees without the necessity of reasonable suspicion of illegal drug use. Op.Atty.Gen. 96–81, October 10, 1996.

944.48. Service of sentence

Whenever any prisoner is convicted under the provisions of ss. 944.41–944.47 [1] the punishment of imprisonment imposed shall be served consecutively to any former sentence imposed upon any prisoner convicted hereunder.

Laws 1957, c. 57–313, § 8.

[1] Section 944.41 was repealed by Laws 1971, c. 71–355, § 177, and § 944.43 was repealed by Laws 1981, c. 81–88, § 1.

Library References

Sentencing and Punishment ⚷637.
Westlaw Topic No. 350H.

Notes of Decisions

Construction and application 1

1. Construction and application

Mandatory consecutive sentencing upon conviction for possession of contraband in a state facility is proper, despite contention that legislature cannot rob trial judge of all discretion as to whether to impose consecutive or concurrent sentence. Jarrell v. State, App. 2 Dist., 576 So.2d 793 (1991). Constitutional Law ⚷ 2371; Sentencing And Punishment ⚷ 505

944.485. Subsistence fees with respect to certain prisoners; time of adoption; requirements

(1) In recognition of the fact that many prisoners in the correctional system have sources of income and assets outside of the correctional system, which may include bank accounts, inheritances, real estate, social security payments, veteran's payments, and other types of financial resources, and in recognition of the fact that the daily subsistence cost of incarcerating prisoners in the correctional system is a great burden on the taxpayers of the state, each prisoner in the state correctional system, except those who have entered into an agreement under s. 947.135 prior to October 1, 1978:

(a) Shall disclose all revenue or assets as a condition of parole or other release eligibility.

(b) Shall pay from such income and assets, except where such income is exempt by state or federal law, all or a fair portion of the prisoner's daily subsistence costs, based upon the inmate's ability to pay, the liability or potential liability of the inmate to the victim or the guardian or the estate of the victim, and the needs of his or her dependents.

(2)(a) Any prisoner who is directed to pay all or a fair portion of daily subsistence costs is entitled to reasonable advance notice of the assessment and shall be afforded an opportunity to present reasons for opposition to the assessment.

(b) An order directing payment of all or a fair portion of a prisoner's daily subsistence costs may survive against the estate of the prisoner.

Laws 1978, c. 78–441, § 1; Laws 1992, c. 92–298, § 1. Amended by Laws 1997, c. 97–102, § 1652, eff. July 1, 1997.

Historical and Statutory Notes

Amendment Notes:

Laws 1992, c. 92–298, § 1, eff. Oct. 1, 1992, at the beginning of the section heading, deleted "Department to adopt plan for"; in subsec. (1), in par. (a), inserted "or other release"; in subsec. (2), designated par. (a) and added par. (b); and deleted subsec. (3).

Laws 1997, c. 97–102, eff. July 1, 1997, removed gender-specific references applicable to human beings from volume 4 of the Florida Statutes without substantive changes in legal effect.

Law Review and Journal Commentaries

Prison reimbursement statutes: Trend toward requiring inmates to pay their own way. 44 Drake L.Rev. 325 (1996).

Library References

Prisons ⚷417.
Westlaw Topic No. 310.

C.J.S. Prisons and Rights of Prisoners §§ 5, 44, 58, 60.

Research References

Encyclopedias

Use of Earnings for Reimbursement of Prison Expenses, FL Jur. 2d Prisons & Prisoners § 166.

United States Supreme Court

Prisoners, attachment of social security benefits, see Bennett v. Arkansas, 1988, 108 S.Ct. 1204, 485 U.S. 395, 99 L.Ed.2d 455, on remand 295 Ark. 472, 748 S.W.2d 668.

Notes of Decisions

---

1. Validity

Right of disclosural privacy is not violated by requirement of this section, as condition of parole eligibility, that prisoners disclose their assets and income and be assessed cost of their subsistence in prison. Ivory v. Wainwright, 393 So.2d 542 (1980), appeal dismissed 102 S.Ct. 79, 454 U.S. 806, 70 L.Ed.2d 75. Pardon And Parole ⚷ 48.1

This section requiring, as condition of parole eligibility, that prisoners disclose their assets and income and be assessed cost of their subsistence in prison contained sufficient standards and guidelines to satisfy constitutional provision governing delegation and separation of powers. Ivory v. Wainwright, 393 So.2d 542 (1980), appeal dismissed 102 S.Ct. 79, 454 U.S. 806, 70 L.Ed.2d 75. Constitutional Law ⚷ 2415(5); Pardon And Parole ⚷ 43

This section requiring that, as condition of parole eligibility, prisoners disclose their assets and income and be assessed cost of their subsistence in prison is not ex post facto legislation on ground that it operates to increase punishment for prisoners whose crimes were committed prior to its effective date, as purpose of the statute is not punitive; nor does this section work a deprivation of property without procedural due process since parole is neither a deprivation of liberty nor of property. Ivory v. Wainwright, 393 So.2d 542 (1980), appeal dismissed 102 S.Ct. 79, 454 U.S. 806, 70 L.Ed.2d 75. Constitutional Law ⚷ 2823; Pardon And Parole ⚷ 43

Requirement that prisoner in state correctional system shall disclose all revenue or assets as a condition of parole eligibility did not result in prejudice to prisoner under First and Fifth Amendment guarantees of the United States Constitution. Panzavecchia v. Crockett, App. 1 Dist., 379 So.2d 1047 (1980). Constitutional Law ⚷ 1194; Constitutional Law ⚷ 4838; Criminal Law ⚷ 393(1)

2. Parole

Parole in Florida is granted by sovereign as a matter of grace rather than of right, and state may offer such grace under and subject to such conditions as it may consider most conducive to accomplish the desired purpose. Panzavecchia v. Crockett, App. 1 Dist., 379 So.2d 1047 (1980). Pardon And Parole ⚷ 46

3. Actions and proceedings

Order to show cause issued on petition for writ of mandamus to compel parole and probation commission to reinstate presumptive parole release date previously given petitioner would be discharged and writ would be denied where claims raised by petitioner with respect to his removal from further parole consideration for failure to file a financial disclosure affidavit were devoid of merit. Gerlock v. Florida Parole and Probation Commission, App. 1 Dist., 411 So.2d 1386 (1982). Mandamus ⚷ 73(1)

Assertion that financial disclosure requirement of this section providing that, as condition of parole eligibility, prisoners disclose their assets and income violated privilege against self-incrimination was raised prematurely in proceeding challenging that section on its face; U.S.C.A. Const. Amend. 5 claim could appropriately be raised by individual inmates on their disclosure forms. Ivory v. Wainwright, 393 So.2d 542 (1980), appeal dismissed 102 S.Ct. 79, 454 U.S. 806, 70 L.Ed.2d 75. Constitutional Law ⚷ 978

944.49. Renumbered as 946.002 in Fla.St.1983

944.50. Renumbered as 946.002 in Fla.St.1983

944.51. Repealed by Laws 1967, c. 67–100, § 2

Historical and Statutory Notes

The repealed section, which related to state road department prison camp supervision, was derived from Laws 1957, c. 57–121, § 41.

944.511. Repealed by Laws 1971, c. 71–355, § 178

Historical and Statutory Notes

The repealed section which related to employees of the road prison operation, and which provided for a five day work week, was derived from Laws 1969, c. 69–106, §§ 19, 23 and Laws 1963, c. 63–450, §§ 1, 2.

944.512. State lien on proceeds from literary or other type of account of crime for which convicted

(1) A lien prior in dignity to all others shall exist in favor of the state upon royalties, commissions, proceeds of sale, or any other thing of value payable to or accruing to a convicted felon or a person on her or his behalf, including any person to whom the proceeds may be transferred or assigned by gift or otherwise, from any literary, cinematic, or other account of the crime for which she or he was convicted. A conviction shall be defined as a guilty verdict by a jury or judge, or a guilty or nolo contendere plea by the defendant, regardless of adjudication of guilt. The lien shall attach at the time of the conviction in county or circuit court. In the event of an appeal, the funds will be held in the Revolving Escrow Trust Fund of the Department of Legal Affairs until the appeal is resolved.

(2) The proceeds of such account shall be distributed in the following order:

(a) Twenty-five percent to the dependents of the convicted felon. If there are no dependents, this portion shall be distributed to the Crimes Compensation Trust Fund to be distributed as awards for crime victims.

(b) Twenty-five percent to the victim or victims of the crime or to their dependents, to the extent of their damages as determined by the court in the lien enforcement proceedings. If there are no victims or dependents, or if their damages are less than 25 percent of the proceeds, this portion, or its remainder, shall be distributed to the Crimes Compensation Trust Fund to be distributed as awards to crime victims.

(c) After payments have been made pursuant to paragraph (a) or paragraph (b), an amount equal to pay all court costs in the prosecution of the convicted felon, which shall include, but not be limited to, jury fees and expenses, court reporter fees, and reasonable per diem for the prosecuting attorneys for the state, shall go to the General Revenue Fund. Additional costs shall be assessed for the computed per capita cost of imprisonment or supervision by the state or county correctional system. Such costs shall be determined and certified by the prosecuting attorney and the imprisoning entity and subject to review by the Auditor General.

(d) The rest, residue, and remainder to the Crimes Compensation Trust Fund to be distributed as awards to crime victims.

(3) A judge may place a lien prior in dignity to all others in favor of the state or county upon any financial settlement payable to or accruing to a convicted offender or person on her or his behalf, as a result of injury incurred during or at the time of a violation of the state law, or as a result of an attempt to flee apprehension for the offense for which the offender was convicted. A conviction is defined as in subsection (1). The lien shall be attached by order of the judge at the time of the conviction in county or circuit court. In the event of an appeal, the funds shall be held in the Revolving Escrow Trust Fund of the Department of Legal Affairs until the appeal is resolved.

(4) The proceeds of such account shall be distributed in the following order:

(a) Payment of all medical care, treatment, hospitalization, and transportation resulting from said injury.

(b) Payment to the victim or victims of the crime or to their dependents, to the extent of their damages as determined by the court in the lien enforcement proceeding.

(c) Payment of all court costs in the prosecution of the convicted felon, which shall include, but not be limited to, jury fees and expense, court reporter fees, and reasonable per diem for the prosecuting attorneys and public defenders.

(d) Payment of cost of incarceration in state or county facilities.

(e) The rest, residue, remainder to the injured party.

(5) The department is hereby authorized and directed to report to the Department of Legal Affairs the existence or reasonably expected existence of circumstances which would be covered by this section. Upon such notification, the Department of Legal Affairs is authorized and directed to take such legal action as is necessary to perfect and enforce the lien created by this section.

Laws 1977, c. 77–45, §§ 1 to 3; Laws 1979, c. 79–3, § 73; Laws 1979, c. 79–400, § 302; Laws 1988, c. 88–96, § 8; Laws 1990, c. 90–211, § 18. Amended by Laws 1997, c. 97–102, § 1653, eff. July 1, 1997; Laws 2001, c. 2001–266, § 130, eff. July 1, 2001.

Historical and Statutory Notes

Amendment Notes:

Laws 1979, c. 79–3, a reviser's bill, provided for substitution of references to the department and secretary of "corrections" for the department and secretary of "offender rehabilitation" to conform with Laws 1978, c. 78–53.

Laws 1979, c. 79–400, a reviser's bill, conformed the sections of Fla.St.1977 to additions, substitutions, and deletions editorially supplied therein in order to remove inconsistencies, redundancies, unnecessary repetition and otherwise clarify the statutes and facilitate their correct interpretation.

Laws 1988, c. 88–96, § 8, added the second through fourth sentences of subsec. (1) and changed the distribution of proceeds in subsec. (2).

Laws 1988, c. 88–96, § 15, provided that the act "shall take effect upon the effective date [January 3, 1989] of the amendment to the State Constitution contained in [1987] Senate Joint Resolution No. 135, which is to be submitted to the electors of this state for approval at the general election to be held in November 1988."

The electorate ratified the amendment to Const. Art. 1, § 16, proposed by 1987, S.J.R. No. 135, relating to rights of crime victims, at the November 8, 1988 general election. See Const.Art. 1, § 16.

Laws 1990, c. 90–211, § 18, eff. Oct. 1, 1990, inserted subsecs. (3) and (4); and redesignated former subsec. (3) as subsec. (5).

Laws 1990, c. 90–211, § 19, provides:

"Except as otherwise provided herein, this act shall take effect October 1, 1990, and shall apply to offenses committed on or after such date."

Laws 1997, c. 97–102, eff. July 1, 1997, removed gender-specific references applicable to human beings from volume 4 of the Florida Statutes without substantive changes in legal effect.

Laws 2001, c. 2001–266, § 3, in subsec. (2)(c), inserted "and certified by the prosecuting attorney and the imprisoning entity and subject to review" following "determined".

Library References

Criminal Law ⚿1221.
Westlaw Topic No. 110.
C.J.S. Criminal Law § 2411.

Research References

ALR Library

60 ALR 4th 1210, Validity, Construction, and Application of "Son of Sam" Laws Regulating or Prohibiting Distribution of Crime-Related Book, Film, of Comparable Revenues to Criminals.

Encyclopedias

Earnings from Sale of Literary, Cinematic, or Other Account of Crime, FL Jur. 2d Prisons & Prisoners § 164.

Earnings from Personal Injury Settlements, FL Jur. 2d Prisons & Prisoners § 165.

Use of Earnings for Reimbursement of Prison Expenses, FL Jur. 2d Prisons & Prisoners § 166.

Treatises and Practice Aids

16 Florida Practice Series § 8:5, Restitution from Property and Assets of the Defendant.

16 Florida Practice Series § 1:58, Sentencing Alternatives--Unusual Punishments.

United States Supreme Court

Free speech and free press, Son of Sam laws, victim compensation, financial burdens on speakers based on speech content, see Simon & Schuster, Inc. v. Members of New York State Crime Victims Bd., U.S.N.Y.1991, 112 S.Ct. 501, 502 U.S. 105, 116 L.Ed.2d 476.

Notes of Decisions

---

1. Construction and application

District Court of Appeal would quash trial court's action that purported to grant "lien" in favor of state, based on statute, in closed criminal case, on any proceeds received by defendant from any literary, cinematic or other account of his offenses; there were no royalties, commissions, proceeds of sale, or any other thing of value payable to or accruing to defendant or to anyone else as result of his criminal activity and, even assuming existence of res, any such lien under statute would attach automatically. Rolling v. State, App. 5 Dist., 655 So.2d 230 (1995). Liens ⚷ 8

2. Injunction

No temporary injunction prior to conviction is allowed under "Son of Sam" law imposing lien in favor of state upon proceeds payable to convicted felon from any literary, cinematic, or other account of the crime. Rolling v. State ex rel. Butterworth, App. 1 Dist., 630 So.2d 635 (1994). Injunction ⚷ 138.31

944.514. Repealed by Laws 1983, c. 83–209, § 6, eff. June 23, 1983

Historical and Statutory Notes

The repealed section, which related to private employment of inmates and disposition of proceeds therefrom, was derived from Laws 1983, c. 83–216, § 185; Laws 1981, c. 81–125, § 2.

944.516. Money or other property received for personal use or benefit of inmate; deposit; disposition of unclaimed trust funds

The Department of Corrections shall protect the financial interest of the state with respect to claims which the state may have against inmates in state institutions under its supervision and control and shall administer money and other property received for the personal benefit of such inmates. In carrying out the provisions of this section, the department may delegate any of its enumerated powers and duties affecting inmates of an institution to the warden or regional director who shall personally, or through designated employees of his or her personal staff under his or her direct supervision, exercise such powers or perform such duties.

(1) The Department of Corrections may:

(a) Accept and administer as a trust any money or other property received for the personal use or benefit of any inmate.

(b) Deposit money so received in banks qualified as state depositories.

(c) Withdraw any such money and use it to meet the current needs of the inmate as they may exist from time to time.

(d) As trustee, invest in the manner authorized by law for fiduciaries such moneys not required to be used for current needs of the inmate.

(e) Commingle such moneys for the purpose of deposit or investment.

(f) Use interest earned from investments to replace any funds belonging to an inmate which have been stolen, lost, or otherwise misappropriated from the inmate's trust account through no fault of the state and which cannot be replaced by appropriated funds, insurance payments, or other available resources. Such use of interest may be made only if, pursuant to a thorough investigation as part of the normal auditing process, the internal auditor of the department recommends in a written report that such use is appropriate. The report may also recommend other action, including prosecution, with respect to any missing funds. If the internal auditor of the department concludes that the department is at fault, the loss shall be replaced out of department funds; interest from the inmate trust fund may not be used to replace such loss.

(g) Establish, by rule, a limit on each inmate's trust account, including the interest earned thereon, and deduct from any moneys in the inmate's trust account exceeding that limit moneys sufficient to pay for the cost of postage of any mail sent by the inmate which postage the state is not constitutionally required to pay.

(h) Charge an administrative processing fee of up to $6 each month to inmates for banking services. Such fees shall be deposited into the department's Grants and Donations Trust Fund and shall be used to offset the cost of the department's operations. If the inmate account has a zero balance at the end of the billing cycle, a hold will be established to collect the processing fee when available.

(2) The department shall require documentation through an accounting of receipts for expenditures by inmates placed on extended limits of confinement pursuant to s. 945.091. However, the department may allow such inmates an amount up to $25 per week which may not require documentation and which may be used for discretionary needs. The $25 per week may be increased by $5 biennially, beginning in fiscal year 1985–1986, up to a total of $50.

(3) Moneys received by the department in payment of claims of the state against inmates shall be transmitted to the Chief Financial Officer for deposit into the General Revenue Fund.

(4) Upon the death of any inmate in an institution affected by the provisions of this section, any unclaimed money held for the inmate in trust by the department or by the Chief Financial Officer shall be applied first to the payment of any unpaid state claim against the inmate, and any balance remaining unclaimed for a period of 1 year shall escheat to the state as unclaimed funds held by fiduciaries.

(5) When an inmate is transferred between department facilities, is released from the custody of the department, dies, or escapes during incarceration, and the inmate has an unexpended inmate trust fund account balance of less than $1, that balance shall be transferred to the General Revenue Fund.

Laws 1981, c. 81–315, § 1; Laws 1984, c. 84–100, § 1; Laws 1985, c. 85–288, § 7; Laws 1990, c. 90–337, § 24; Laws 1995, c. 95–283, § 19. Amended by Laws 1997, c. 97–102, § 1654, eff. July 1, 1997; Laws 2000, c. 2000–161, § 17, eff. July 4, 2000; Laws 2003, c. 2003–179, § 7, eff. July 1, 2003; Laws 2003, c. 2003–261, § 1929, eff. June 26, 2003; Laws 2004, c. 2004–248, § 21, eff. July 1, 2004.

Historical and Statutory Notes

Amendment Notes:

Laws 1984, c. 84–100, § 1, added subsec. (1)(f).

Laws 1985, c. 85–288, § 7, eff. July 1, 1985, interpolated subsec. (2) and renumbered former subsecs. (2) and (3) as subsecs. (3) and (4).

Laws 1990, c. 90–337, § 24, in subsec. (1), added par. (g).

Laws 1990, c. 90–337, § 24, provided therein that the amendment take effect July 1, 1990; however, approval by the governor occurred subsequent thereto. The Florida Supreme Court in an advisory opinion to the governor of July 19, 1979 (374 So.2d 959) stated in part "* * * the effective date provided in the bill is inoperative unless the bill becomes law on or before that date" and concludes that under such circumstances the provision of Const. Art. 3, § 9, that the law take effect on the sixtieth day after adjournment sine die of the session of the legislature in which enacted, is applicable.

Laws 1995, c. 95–283, § 19, eff. June 15, 1995, added subsec. (5).

Laws 1997, c. 97–102, eff. July 1, 1997, removed gender-specific references applicable to human beings from volume 4 of the Florida Statutes without substantive changes in legal effect.

Laws 2000, c. 2000–161, a reviser's bill, substituted reference to warden for reference to superintendent.

Laws 2003, c. 2003–179, § 7, in subsec. (5), substituted a reference to the General Revenue Fund for a reference to the Inmate Welfare Trust Fund.

Laws 2003, c. 2003–261, § 1929, in subsecs. (3) and (4), substituted "Chief Financial Officer" for "Treasurer".

Laws 2004, c. 2004–248, § 21, inserted subsec. (1)(h), relating to administrative processing fees for inmate banking services.

Library References

Escheat ⚷3.
Prisons ⚷117.
Westlaw Topic Nos. 152, 310.
C.J.S. Convicts §§ 4 to 5.
C.J.S. Escheat §§ 11, 14.

Research References

Encyclopedias

Personal Funds of Inmates, FL Jur. 2d Prisons & Prisoners § 169.

United States Supreme Court

Prisoners, destruction of personal property by guards, remedies, see Hudson v. Palmer, 1984, 104 S.Ct. 3194, 468 U.S. 517, 82 L.Ed.2d 393, on remand 744 F.2d 22.

944.52. Legal adviser

The Department of Legal Affairs shall be the legal adviser of the Department of Corrections.

Laws 1957, c. 57–121, § 42; Laws 1961, c. 61–530, § 18; Laws 1969, c. 69–106, §§ 11, 35; Laws 1977, c. 77–120, § 63; Laws 1979, c. 79–3, § 74.

Historical and Statutory Notes

Amendment Notes:

Laws 1961, c. 61–530, § 18, substituted the "division" for "department".

Laws 1969, c. 69–106, §§ 11, 35, transferred all powers, duties and functions of the attorney general to the department of legal affairs.

Laws 1977, c. 77–120, a reviser's bill, amended this section to conform with Laws 1975, c. 75–49, which created the department of offender rehabilitation (see § 20.315) and transferred to the department certain functions performed by the division of corrections of the department of health and rehabilitative services and the parole and probation commission of the department of offender rehabilitation.

Laws 1979, c. 79–3, a reviser's bill, provided for substitution of references to the department and secretary of "corrections" for the department and secretary of "offender rehabilitation" to conform with Laws 1978, c. 78–53.

944.53. Repealed by Laws 1965, c. 65–195, § 2

Historical and Statutory Notes

The repealed section, which provided for the reproduction of records on film, etc., was derived from Laws 1957, c. 57–122, § 1; Laws 1961, c. 61–530, § 18.

See, now, F.S.A. § 402.19.

944.54. Repealed by Laws 1983, c. 83–131, § 42

Historical and Statutory Notes

The repealed section, pertaining to transportation furnished prisoners upon release, was derived from Laws 1959, c. 59–317, §§ 1, 2, and Laws 1978, c. 78–14, § 1.

944.55. Repealed by Laws 1973, c. 73–333, § 183

Historical and Statutory Notes

The repealed section, pertaining to a reward in connection with the return to custody of escapee, Marie Dean Arrington, was derived from:

Laws 1970, c. 70–441, §§ 1, 2.
Laws 1969, c. 69–359, §§ 1 to 4.
Laws 1969, c. 69–106, §§ 19, 35.

944.551. Repealed by Laws 1985, c. 85–288, § 27, eff. July 1, 1985

Historical and Statutory Notes

Repealed § 944.551, which related to vocational education and career development services, was derived from:

Laws 1984, c. 84–336, § 112.
Laws 1979, c. 79–7, § 47.
Laws 1979, c. 79–3, § 75.
Laws 1977, c. 77–147, § 474.
Laws 1977, c. 77–120, § 64.
Laws 1974, c. 74–112, § 15.

944.56. Repealed by Laws 1977, c. 77–120, § 65

Historical and Statutory Notes

The repealed section, which created the vocational training and employment opportunities advisory council, was derived from Laws 1974, c. 74–112, § 16.

944.57. Repealed by Laws 1985, c. 85–288, § 27, eff. July 1, 1985

Historical and Statutory Notes

Repealed § 944.57, which related to manpower development programs, was derived from:

Laws 1979, c. 79–3, § 76.
Laws 1977, c. 77–120, § 66.
Laws 1974, c. 74–112, § 17.

944.58. Repealed by Laws 1981, c. 81–24, § 23

Historical and Statutory Notes

Repealed §§ 944.58 to 944.593, which related to the correctional standards council and the powers, duties and functions thereof, were derived from:

Laws 1979, c. 79–400, § 303.
Laws 1978, c. 78–323, § 4.
Laws 1977, c. 77–210, §§ 1 to 3.
Laws 1977, c. 77–174, § 1.
Laws 1977, c. 77–120, § 67.
Laws 1977, c. 77–116, § 1.
Laws 1977, c. 77–104, § 254.
Laws 1975, c. 75–271, § 1.
Laws 1974, c. 74–107, §§ 2 to 19.

944.59. Repealed by Laws 1981, c. 81–24, § 23

Historical and Statutory Notes

See Historical and Statutory Notes following F.S.A. § 944.58.

944.591. Repealed by Laws 1981, c. 81–24, § 23

Historical and Statutory Notes

See Historical and Statutory Notes following F.S.A. § 944.58.

944.592. Repealed by Laws 1981, c. 81–24, § 23

Historical and Statutory Notes

See Historical and Statutory Notes following F.S.A. § 944.58.

944.593. Repealed by Laws 1981, c. 81–24, § 23

Historical and Statutory Notes

See Historical and Statutory Notes following F.S.A. § 944.58.

944.596. Transfer of convicted foreign citizens or nationals under treaty

When a treaty is in effect between the United States and a foreign country providing for the transfer of a convicted offender who is a citizen or national of a foreign country to the foreign country of which she or he is a citizen or national, the Governor or the Governor's designee is authorized, subject to the terms of such treaty, to consent to the transfer of such convicted offender. Laws 1979, c. 79–75, § 1. Amended by Laws 1997, c. 97–102, § 1655, eff. July 1, 1997.

Historical and Statutory Notes

Amendment Notes:

Laws 1997, c. 97–102, eff. July 1, 1997, removed gender-specific references applicable to human beings from volume 4 of the Florida Statutes without substantive changes in legal effect.

Library References

Prisons ⚷226.
Westlaw Topic No. 310.
C.J.S. Prisons and Rights of Prisoners §§ 128 to 136.

United States Code Annotated

Transfer of offenders to and from foreign countries, see 18 U.S.C.A. § 4100 et seq.

944.597. Transportation and return of prisoners by private transport company

(1) The department is authorized to contract with private transport companies for the transportation of prisoners both within and beyond the limits of this state. Each prisoner shall be taken into custody by the transport company for the purpose of transportation and then delivered by the same transport company to the proper law enforcement official upon arriving at the point of destination. Any private transport company transporting a prisoner pursuant to this section shall be considered an independent contractor and shall be solely liable for the prisoner while she or he is in the custody of such company.

(2) The department shall include, but shall not be limited to, the following requirements in any contract with any transport company:

(a) That the transport company shall maintain adequate liability coverage with respect to the transportation of prisoners;

(b) That personnel employed with the transport company who are based in the state shall meet the minimum standards in accordance with s. 943.13 and that personnel employed with the transport company based outside of Florida shall meet the minimum standards for a correctional officer or law enforcement officer in the state where the employee is based;

(c) That the transport company shall adhere to standards which provide for humane treatment of prisoners while in the custody of the transport company;

(d) That the transport company shall submit reports to the department regarding incidents of escape, use of force, and accidents involving prisoners in the custody of the transport company.

(3) Any company providing transport of inmates, pursuant to this section shall hold a Class "B" license pursuant to chapter 493, and any employee of such a company shall hold a Class "D" and Class "G" license pursuant to chapter 493.

(4) The department shall advertise for and receive competitive bids for the transportation of prisoners and award the contract to the lowest and best bidder.

Laws 1985, c. 85–340, § 7. Amended by Laws 1997, c. 97–102, § 1656, eff. July 1, 1997.

Historical and Statutory Notes

Amendment Notes:

Laws 1997, c. 97–102, eff. July 1, 1997, removed gender-specific references applicable to human beings from volume 4 of the Florida Statutes without substantive changes in legal effect.

Library References

Prisons ⚿224.
Westlaw Topic No. 310.
C.J.S. Prisons and Rights of Prisoners §§ 128 to 136.

Research References

Encyclopedias

Transportation of Prisoners by Private Transport Company, FL Jur. 2d Prisons & Prisoners § 97.

944.598. Repealed by Laws 1993, c. 93–406, § 32, eff. June 17, 1993

Historical and Statutory Notes

Repealed § 944.598, which related to the emergency release of prisoners, was derived from:

Laws 1992, c. 92–47, § 10.
Laws 1989, c. 89–526, § 48.
Laws 1989, c. 89–526, § 9.
Laws 1989, c. 89–281, § 2.
Laws 1988, c. 88–122, § 53.
Laws 1986, c. 86–46, § 1.
Laws 1983, c. 83–131, §§ 3, 5.

See, now, F.S.A. § 947.146.

944.601. Renumbered as 944.706 by Laws 1987, c. 87–298, § 9, eff. Jan. 1, 1988

944.602. Agency notification before release of mentally retarded inmates

Before the release by parole, release by reason of gain-time allowances provided for in s. 944.291, or expiration of sentence of any inmate who has been diagnosed as mentally retarded as defined in s. 393.063, the Department of Corrections shall notify the Agency for Persons with Disabilities in order that sufficient time be allowed to notify the inmate or the inmate's representative, in writing, at least 7 days prior to the inmate's release, of available community services.

Laws 1983, c. 83–274, § 8. Amended by Laws 1997, c. 97–102, § 1657, eff. July 1, 1997; Laws 1999, c. 99–8, § 311, eff. June 29, 1999; Laws 2006, c. 2006–227, § 64, eff. July 1, 2006.

Historical and Statutory Notes

Amendment Notes:

Laws 1997, c. 97–102, eff. July 1, 1997, removed gender-specific references applicable to human beings from volume 4 of the Florida Statutes without substantive changes in legal effect.

Laws 1999, c. 99–8, § 311, eff. June 29, 1999, substituted "Department of Children and Family Services" for "Department of Health and Rehabilitative Services".

Laws 2006, c. 2006–227, § 64, substituted "Agency notification" for "Notification of Department of Children and Family Services" in the section heading; and substituted "Agency for Persons with Disabilities" for "Department of Children and Family Services" following "notify the".

Library References

Pardon and Parole ⚷66.
Prisons ⚷241.
Westlaw Topic Nos. 284, 310.
C.J.S. Pardon and Parole § 60.
C.J.S. Prisons and Rights of Prisoners § 153.

Research References

Encyclopedias

Prisoners Receiving Mental Health Treatment; Mentally Retarded Prisoners, FL Jur. 2d Prisons & Prisoners § 201.

944.605. Inmate release; notification

(1) Within 6 months before the release of an inmate from the custody of the Department of Corrections or a private correctional facility by expiration of sentence under s. 944.275, any release program provided by law, or parole under chapter 947, or as soon as possible if the offender is released earlier than anticipated, notification of such anticipated release date shall be made known by the Department of Corrections to the chief judge of the circuit in which the offender was sentenced, the appropriate state attorney, the original arresting law enforcement agency, the Department of Law Enforcement, and the sheriff as chief law enforcement officer of the county in which the inmate plans to reside. In addition, unless otherwise requested by the victim, the victim's parent or guardian if the victim is a minor, the lawful representative of the victim or of the victim's parent or guardian if the victim is a minor, the victim's next of kin in the case of a homicide, the state attorney or the Department of Corrections, whichever is appropriate, shall notify such person within 6 months before the inmate's release, or as soon as possible if the offender is released

earlier than anticipated, when the name and address of such victim, or the name and address of the parent, guardian, next of kin, or lawful representative of the victim has been furnished to the agency. The state attorney shall provide the latest address documented for the victim, or for the victim's parent, guardian, next of kin, or lawful representative, as applicable, to the sheriff with the other documents required by law for the delivery of inmates to those agencies for service of sentence. Upon request, within 30 days after an inmate is approved for community work release, the state attorney, the victim, the victim's parent or guardian if the victim is a minor, the victim's next of kin in the case of a homicide, or the lawful representative of the victim or of the victim's parent or guardian if the victim is a minor shall be notified that the inmate has been approved for community work release. This section does not imply any repeal or modification of any provision of law relating to notification of victims.

(2) Within 60 days before the anticipated release of an inmate under subsection (1), a digitized photograph of the inmate to be released shall be made by the Department of Corrections or a private correctional facility, whichever has custody of the inmate. If a private correctional facility makes the digitized photograph, this photograph shall be provided to the Department of Corrections. Additionally, the digitized photograph, whether made by the Department of Corrections or a private correctional facility, shall be placed in the inmate's file. The Department of Corrections shall make the digitized photograph available electronically to the Department of Law Enforcement as soon as the digitized photograph is in the department's database and must be in a format that is compatible with the requirements of the Florida Crime Information Center. The department shall provide a copy of the digitized photograph to a local law enforcement agency upon request.

(3) If an inmate is to be released after having served one or more sentences for a conviction of robbery, sexual battery, home-invasion robbery, or carjacking, or an inmate to be released has a prior conviction for robbery, sexual battery, home-invasion robbery, or carjacking or similar offense, in this state or in another jurisdiction, and if such prior conviction information is contained in department records, the department shall release to the sheriff of the county in which the inmate plans to reside, and, if the inmate plans to reside within a municipality, to the chief of police of that municipality, the following information, which must include, but need not be limited to:

(a) Name;

(b) Social security number;

(c) Date of birth;

(d) Race;

(e) Sex;

(f) Height;

(g) Weight;

(h) Hair and eye color;

(i) Tattoos or other identifying marks;

(j) Fingerprints; and

(k) A digitized photograph as provided in subsection (2).

The department shall release the information specified in this subsection within 6 months prior to the discharge of the inmate from the custody of the department.

(4) An inmate who refuses to submit to the taking of a digitized photograph commits a felony of the third degree, punishable as provided in s. 775.082, s. 775.083, or s. 775.084.

(5) The department shall, at least 10 days before the anticipated date of release on work release of an inmate, notify in writing the county law enforcement agency in the county in this state in which the inmate is scheduled to be released.

(6) Upon request of the victim, the personal representative of the victim, or the state attorney, the department shall notify the requesting person when an inmate has been approved for community work release within 30 days after the date of approval.

Laws 1985, c. 85–107, § 3; Laws 1988, c. 88–96, § 9; Laws 1988, c. 88–122, § 54; Laws 1991, c. 91–65, § 1; Laws 1991, c. 91–225, § 22; Laws 1992, c. 92–76, § 2. Amended by Laws 1996, c. 96–312, § 35, eff. July 1, 1996; Laws 1997, c. 97–299, § 10, eff. Oct. 1, 1997; Laws 1998, c. 98–81, § 9, eff. July 1, 1998; Laws 2001, c. 2001–124, § 3, eff. July 1, 2001; Laws 2001, c. 2001–209, § 1, eff. July 1, 2001.

Historical and Statutory Notes

Amendment Notes:

Provisions comprising this section were also classified as § 947.177 in Fla. St. 1985.

Laws 1988, c. 88–96, § 9, revised notification requirements of an inmate's anticipated release from incarceration or persons anticipating release from parole.

Laws 1988, c. 88–96, § 15, provided that the act "shall take effect upon the effective date [January 3, 1989] of the amendment to the State Constitution contained in [1987] Senate Joint Resolution No. 135, which is to be submitted to the electors of this state for approval at the general election to be held in November 1988."

The electorate ratified the amendment to Const. Art. 1, § 16, proposed by 1987, S.J.R. No. 135, relating to rights of crime victims, at the November 8, 1988 general election. See Const. Art. 1, § 16.

Laws 1988, c. 88–122, § 54, eff. July 1, 1988, substituted the commission name of "parole" for "parole and probation".

Laws 1991, c. 91–65, § 1, eff. May 12, 1991, designated subsec. (1); and added subsec. (2), which relates to exit photos.

Laws 1991, c. 91–225, § 22, eff. July 1, 1991, in subsec. (1), inserted references to the Control Release Authority throughout, and substituted "the Parole Commission or the Control Release Authority is the appropriate agency for any type of release it grants, and the Department of Corrections is the appropriate agency for any type of release it authorizes" for "the appropriate agency for parole releases is the Parole Commission and the appropriate agency for releases by expiration of sentence or by any other release program provided by law is the Department of Corrections" at the end of the fifth sentence.

Laws 1992, c. 92–76, § 2, eff. Oct. 1, 1992, in subsec. (2), substituted "120 days" for "90 days"; and inserted the exception.

Laws 1996, c. 96–312, § 35, eff. July 1, 1996, rewrote this section, which formerly read:

"(1) Within 6 months prior to the release of an inmate from the custody of the Department of Corrections by expiration of sentence under s. 944.275, any release program provided by law, or parole under chapter 947, notification of such anticipated release date shall be made known by the appropriate agency to the original sentencing judge, the appropriate state attorney, the original arresting law enforcement agency, and the sheriff as chief law enforcement officer of the county in which the inmate plans to reside. If the original sentencing judge is no longer available, such notice shall be sent to the chief judge of the circuit in which the offender was sentenced. In addition, unless otherwise requested by the victim or the personal representative of the victim, the state attorney, the Department of Corrections, the Control Release Authority, or the Parole Commission, whichever is appropriate, shall notify such person within 6 months prior to the inmate's release, if the name and address of such victim or representative of the victim has been furnished to the agency. The state attorney shall provide the latest address documented for the victim to the sheriff with the other documents required by law for the delivery of inmates to those agencies for service of sentence. For the purposes of this section, the Parole Commission or the Control Release Authority is the appropriate agency for any type of release it grants, and the Department of Corrections is the appropriate agency for any type of release it authorizes. The Department of Corrections, the Control Release Authority, and the Parole Commission shall adopt rules to provide for the timely notification of releases under s. 944.598. This section shall not be construed to imply any repeal or modification of any provision of law relating to notification of victims.

"(2) Within 120 days prior to the anticipated release of an inmate under subsection (1), except for an inmate pursuant to s. 944.606, an exit photo of the inmate to be released shall be taken and placed in the inmate's file."

Laws 1997, c. 97–299, § 10, eff. Oct. 1, 1997, rewrote this section, which formerly read:

"(1) Within 6 months before the release of an inmate from the custody of the Department of Corrections by expiration of sentence under s. 944.275, any release program provided by law, or parole under chapter 947, notification of such anticipated release date shall be made known by the appropriate agency to the original sentencing judge, the appropriate state attorney, the original arresting law enforcement agency, and the sheriff as chief law enforcement officer of the county in which the inmate plans to reside. If the original sentencing judge is no longer available, such notice shall be sent to the chief judge of the circuit in which the offender was sentenced. In addition, unless otherwise requested by the victim or the personal representative of the victim, the state attorney, the Department of Corrections, the Control Release Authority, or the Parole Commission, whichever is appropriate, shall notify such person within 6 months before the inmate's release, if the name and address of such victim or representative of the victim has been furnished to the agency. The state attorney shall provide the latest address documented for the victim to the sheriff with the other documents required by law for the delivery of inmates to those agencies for service of sentence. For the purposes of this section, the Parole Commission or the Control Release Authority is the appropriate agency for any type of release it grants, and the Department of Corrections is the appropriate agency for any type of release it authorizes. This section does not imply any repeal or modification of any provision of law relating to notification of victims.

"(2) Within 120 days before the anticipated release of an inmate under subsection (1), except for an inmate for which notification is required under subsection (3) or s. 944.606, an exit photo of the inmate to be released shall be taken and placed in the inmate's file.

"(3) If an inmate is to be released after having served one or more sentences for a conviction of robbery, sexual battery, home-invasion robbery, or carjacking, or an inmate to be released has a prior conviction for robbery, sexual battery, home-invasion robbery, or carjacking or similar offense, in this state or in another jurisdiction, and if such prior conviction information is contained in department records, the appropriate releasing agency shall release to the sheriff of the county in which the inmate plans to reside, and, if the inmate plans to reside within a municipality, to the chief of police of that municipality, the following information, which must include, but need not be limited to:

"(a) Name;

"(b) Social security number;

"(c) Date of birth;

"(d) Race;

"(e) Sex;

"(f) Height;

"(g) Weight;

"(h) Hair and eye color;

"(i) Tattoos or other identifying marks;

"(j) Fingerprints; and

"(k) A photograph taken not more than 90 days before the date of the inmate's release.

"The department, the Parole Commission, or the Control Release Authority shall release the information specified in this subsection within 6 months prior to the discharge of the inmate from the custody of the department."

Laws 1998, c. 98–81, § 9, added subsec. (4).

Laws 2001, c. 2001–124, § 3, rewrote subsec. (1); in subsec. (3), in the first paragraph, substituted "department" for "appropriate releasing agency"; in the last paragraph, following "department" deleted ", the Parole Commission, or the Control Release Authority"; and added subsecs. (5) and (6). Subsec. (1) formerly read:

"(1) Within 6 months before the release of an inmate from the custody of the Department of Corrections or a private correctional facility by expiration of sentence under s. 944.275, any release program provided by law, or parole under chapter 947, or as soon as possible if the offender is released earlier than anticipated, notification of such anticipated release date shall be made known by the appropriate agency to the chief judge of the circuit in which the offender was sentenced, the appropriate state attorney, the original arresting law enforcement agency, the Department of Law Enforcement, and the sheriff as chief law enforcement officer of the county in which the inmate plans to reside. In addition, unless otherwise requested by the victim or the personal representative of the victim, the state attorney, the Department of Corrections, the Control Release Authority, or the Parole Commission, whichever is appropriate, shall notify such person within 6 months before the inmate's release, or as soon as possible if the offender is released earlier than anticipated, when the name and address of such victim or representative of the victim has been furnished to the agency. The state attorney shall provide the latest address documented for the victim to the sheriff with the other documents required by law for the delivery of inmates to those agencies for service of sentence. For the purposes of this section, the Parole Commission or the Control Release Authority is the appropriate agency for any type of release it grants, and the Department of Corrections is the appropriate agency for any type of release it authorizes. This section does not imply any repeal or modification of any provision of law relating to notification of victims."

Laws 2001, c. 2001-209, § 1, rewrote this section, which formerly read:

"(1) Within 6 months before the release of an inmate from the custody of the Department of Corrections or a private correctional facility by expiration of sentence under s. 944.275, any release program provided by law, or parole under chapter 947, or as soon as possible if the offender is released earlier than anticipated, notification of such anticipated release date shall be made known by the appropriate agency to the chief judge of the circuit in which the offender was sentenced, the appropriate state attorney, the original arresting law enforcement agency, the Department of Law Enforcement, and the sheriff as chief law enforcement officer of the county in which the inmate plans to reside. In addition, unless otherwise requested by the victim or the personal representative of the victim, the state attorney, the Department of Corrections, the Control Release Authority, or the Parole Commission, whichever is appropriate, shall notify such person within 6 months before the inmate's release, or as soon as possible if the offender is released earlier than anticipated, when the name and address of such victim or representative of the victim has been furnished to the agency. The state attorney shall provide the latest address documented for the victim to the sheriff with the other documents required by law for the delivery of inmates to those agencies for service of sentence. For the purposes of this section, the Parole Commission or the Control Release Authority is the appropriate agency for any type of release it grants, and the Department of Corrections is the appropriate agency for any type of release it authorizes. This section does not imply any repeal or modification of any provision of law relating to notification of victims.

"(2) Within 60 days before the anticipated release of an inmate under subsection (1), a digitized photograph of the inmate to be released shall be made by the Department of Corrections or a private correctional facility, whichever has custody of the inmate. If a private correctional facility makes the digitized photograph, this photograph shall be provided to the Department of Corrections. Additionally, the digitized photograph, whether made by the Department of Corrections or a private correctional facility, shall be placed in the inmate's file. The Department of Corrections shall make the digitized photograph available electronically to the Department of Law Enforcement as soon as the digitized photograph is in the department's database and must be in a format that is compatible with the requirements of the Florida Crime Information Center. The department shall provide a copy of the digitized photograph to a local law enforcement agency upon request.

"(3) If an inmate is to be released after having served one or more sentences for a conviction of robbery, sexual battery, home-invasion robbery, or carjacking, or an inmate to be released has a prior conviction for robbery, sexual battery, home-invasion robbery, or carjacking or similar offense, in this state or in another jurisdiction, and if such prior conviction information is contained in department records, the appropriate releasing agency shall release to the sheriff of the county in which the inmate plans to reside, and, if the inmate plans to reside within a municipality, to the chief of police of that municipality, the following information, which must include, but need not be limited to:

"(a) Name;

"(b) Social security number;

"(c) Date of birth;

"(d) Race;

"(e) Sex;

"(f) Height;

"(g) Weight;

"(h) Hair and eye color;

"(i) Tattoos or other identifying marks;

"(j) Fingerprints; and

"(k) A digitized photograph as provided in subsection (2) .

"The department, the Parole Commission, or the Control Release Authority shall release the information specified in this subsection within 6 months prior to the discharge of the inmate from the custody of the department.

"(4) An inmate who refuses to submit to the taking of a digitized photograph commits a felony of the third degree, punishable as provided in s. 775.082, s. 775.083, or s. 775.084."

Cross References

Victim notification of community work release of inmate, see § 960.001.

Library References

Criminal Law ⚿1222.1.
Mental Health ⚿469.
Westlaw Topic Nos. 110, 257A.
C.J.S. Criminal Law §§ 2401, 2406 to 2409.
C.J.S. Mental Health §§ 290 to 291, 299.

Research References

Encyclopedias

Generally; Leaving Place of Confinement for Work or Voluntary Service at Public or Nonprofit Agency or Faith-Based Service Group, FL Jur. 2d Prisons & Prisoners § 175.

Particular Offenders; Information Required, FL Jur. 2d Prisons & Prisoners § 205.

United States Code Annotated

Sex offender registration, supervised release, see 18 U.S.C.A. § 3583.

944.606. Sexual offenders; notification upon release

(1) As used in this section:

(a) "Convicted" means there has been a determination of guilt as a result of a trial or the entry of a plea of guilty or nolo contendere, regardless of whether adjudication is withheld. A conviction for a similar offense includes, but is not limited to, a conviction by a federal or military tribunal, including courts-martial conducted by the Armed Forces of the United States, and includes a conviction or entry of a plea of guilty or nolo contendere resulting in a sanction in any state of the United States or other jurisdiction. A sanction includes, but is not limited to, a fine; probation; community control; parole; conditional release; control release; or incarceration in a state prison, federal prison, private correctional facility, or local detention facility.

(b) "Sexual offender" means a person who has been convicted of committing, or attempting, soliciting, or conspiring to commit, any of the criminal offenses proscribed in the following statutes in this state or similar offenses in another jurisdiction: s. 787.01, s. 787.02, or s. 787.025(2)(c), where the victim is a minor and the defendant is not the victim's parent or guardian; s. 794.011, excluding s. 794.011(10); s. 794.05; s. 796.03; s. 796.035; s. 800.04; s. 825.1025; s. 827.071; s. 847.0133; s. 847.0135, excluding s. 847.0135(6); s. 847.0137; s. 847.0138; s. 847.0145; or s. 985.701(1); or any similar offense committed in this state which has been redesignated from a former statute number to one of those listed in this subsection, when the department has received verified information regarding such conviction; an offender's computerized criminal history record is not, in and of itself, verified information.

(c) "Electronic mail address" has the same meaning as provided in s. 668.602.

(d) "Instant message name" means an identifier that allows a person to communicate in real time with another person using the Internet.

(2) The Legislature finds that sexual offenders, especially those who have committed their offenses against minors, often pose a high risk of engaging in sexual offenses even after being released from incarceration or commitment and that protection of the public from sexual offenders is a paramount governmental interest. Sexual offenders have a reduced expectation of privacy because of the public's interest in public safety and in the effective operation of government. Releasing sexual offender information to law enforcement agencies and to persons who request such information, and releasing such information to the public by a law enforcement agency or public agency, will further the governmental interests of public safety.

(3)(a) The department must provide information regarding any sexual offender who is being released after serving a period of incarceration for any offense, as follows:

1. The department must provide: the sexual offender's name, any change in the offender's name by reason of marriage or other legal process, and any alias, if known; the correctional facility from which the sexual offender is released; the sexual offender's social security number, race, sex, date of birth, height, weight, and hair and eye color; date and county of sentence and each crime for which the offender was sentenced; a copy of the offender's fingerprints and a digitized photograph taken within 60 days before release; the date of release of the sexual offender; any electronic mail address and any instant message name required to be provided pursuant to s. 943.0435(4)(d); home telephone number and any cellular telephone number; and the offender's intended residence address, if known. The department shall notify the Department of Law Enforcement if the sexual offender escapes, absconds, or dies. If the sexual offender is in the custody of a private correctional facility, the facility shall take the digitized photograph of the sexual offender within 60 days before the sexual offender's release and provide this photograph to the Department of Corrections and also place it in the sexual offender's file. If the sexual offender is in the custody of a local jail, the custodian of the local jail shall register the offender within 3 business days after intake of the offender for any reason and upon release, and shall notify the Department of Law Enforcement of the sexual offender's release and provide to the Department of Law Enforcement the information specified in this paragraph and any information specified in subparagraph 2. that the Department of Law Enforcement requests.

2. The department may provide any other information deemed necessary, including criminal and corrections records, nonprivileged personnel and treatment records, when available.

(b) The department must provide the information described in subparagraph (a)1. to:

1. The sheriff of the county from where the sexual offender was sentenced;

2. The sheriff of the county and, if applicable, the police chief of the municipality, where the sexual offender plans to reside;

3. The Florida Department of Law Enforcement;

4. When requested, the victim of the offense, the victim's parent or legal guardian if the victim is a minor, the lawful representative of the victim or of the victim's parent or guardian if the victim is a minor, or the next of kin if the victim is a homicide victim; and

5. Any person who requests such information,

either within 6 months prior to the anticipated release of a sexual offender, or as soon as possible if an offender is released earlier than anticipated. All such information provided to the Department of Law Enforcement must be available electronically as soon as the information is in the agency's database and must be in a format that is compatible with the requirements of the Florida Crime Information Center.

(c) Upon request, the department must provide the information described in subparagraph (a)2. to:

1. The sheriff of the county from where the sexual offender was sentenced; and

2. The sheriff of the county and, if applicable, the police chief of the municipality, where the sexual offender plans to reside,

either within 6 months prior to the anticipated release of a sexual offender, or as soon as possible if an offender is released earlier than anticipated.

(d) Upon receiving information regarding a sexual offender from the department, the Department of Law Enforcement, the sheriff or the chief of police shall provide the information described in subparagraph (a)1. to any individual who requests such information and may release the information to the public in any manner deemed appropriate, unless the information so received is confidential or exempt from s. 119.07(1) and s. 24(a), Art. I of the State Constitution.

(4) This section authorizes the department or any law enforcement agency to notify the community and the public of a sexual offender's presence in the community. However, with respect to a sexual offender who has been found to be a "sexual predator" under chapter 775, the Florida Department of Law Enforcement or any other law enforcement agency must inform the community and the public of the sexual predator's presence in the community, as provided in chapter 775.

(5) An elected or appointed official, public employee, school administrator or employee, or agency, or any individual or entity acting at the request or upon the direction of any law enforcement agency, is immune from civil liability for damages resulting from the release of information under this section.

Laws 1992, c. 92–76, § 3; Laws 1995, c. 95–283, § 20. Amended by Laws 1996, c. 96–312, § 10, eff. July 1, 1996; Laws 1996, c. 96–388, § 65, eff. Oct. 1, 1996; Laws 1997, c. 97–299, § 11, eff. Oct. 1, 1997; Laws 1998, c. 98–81, § 10, eff. Oct. 1, 1998; Laws 1999, c. 99–3, § 119, eff. June 29, 1999; Laws 1999, c. 99–201, § 10, eff. Oct. 1, 1999; Laws 2000, c. 2000–207, § 4, eff. July 1, 2000; Laws 2000, c. 2000–246, § 3, eff. Oct. 1, 2000; Laws 2001, c. 2001–209, § 5, eff. July 1, 2001; Laws 2002, c. 2002–58,

§ 5, eff. July 1, 2002; Laws 2004, c. 2004–371, § 3, eff. July 1, 2004; Laws 2006, c. 2006–200, § 4, eff. July 1, 2006; Laws 2006, c. 2006–299, § 5, eff. July 1, 2006; Laws 2007, c. 2007–5, § 161, eff. July 3, 2007; Laws 2007, c. 2007–143, § 11, eff. Oct. 1, 2007; Laws 2007, c. 2007–209, § 6, eff. July 1, 2007; Laws 2009, c. 2009–194, § 4, eff. July 1, 2009.

Historical and Statutory Notes

Amendment Notes:

Laws 1995, c. 95–283, § 20, eff. June 15, 1995, added subsecs. (3) and (4).

Laws 1996, c. 96–312, § 10, eff. July 1, 1996, in subsec. (2)(b), in the second sentence, added ", except that such notice may be provided as soon as practical in the event of an immediate release ordered by the court".

Laws 1996, c. 96–388, § 65, eff. July 1, 1996, rewrote this section and section heading, which formerly read:

"944.606. Sex offender; notification upon release

"(1) The Legislature finds that sex offenders pose a high risk of engaging in sex offenses even after being released from incarceration or commitment and that protection of the public from sex offenders is a paramount governmental interest. Persons found to have committed a sex offense described in subsection (2) have a reduced expectation of privacy because of the public's interest in public safety and in the effective operation of government. Release of information about sexual offenders described in subsection (2) to public agencies will further the governmental interests of public safety.

"(2)(a) The department, the Parole Commission, and the Control Release Authority shall submit the information about any sex offender as provided by this section to the sheriff of the county from which the person was sentenced, to the sheriff of the county in which the person plans to reside and, if applicable, to the chief of police of the municipality in which the inmate plans to reside. The information shall be submitted for any sex offender who is being released after having served one or more sentences for a felony conviction of chapter 794, s. 800.04, s. 827.071, or s. 847.0145, or a prior conviction for a similar offense in this state or another jurisdiction if such prior conviction information is contained in department records.

"(b) The information shall include, but not be limited to: the offender's name, social security number, race, sex, date of birth, height, weight, and hair and eye color; date and county of sentence and each crime for which the offender was sentenced; a copy of the offender's fingerprints and a photograph taken within 90 days of release; and the offender's intended residence address, if known. The department, the Parole Commission, or the Control Release Authority shall release this information within 6 months prior to the discharge from the custody of the department.

"(3) The department or any law enforcement agency that receives verified information, regardless of the source, about persons found to have committed a sexual offense described in subsection (2) is authorized to publicly release such information in the interest of public safety.

"(4) Any information received by the department or a law enforcement agency under subsections (1) and (2) is verified per se, and the department, a law enforcement agency, or an officer or employee of the department or a law enforcement agency who releases such information is immune from civil liability. The department, a law enforcement agency, or an officer or employee of the department or a law enforcement agency who releases information about persons found to have committed a sexual offense described in subsection (2), when such information was received from sources other than those described in subsections (1) and (2) but was verified by a copy of a judgment of conviction or similar court order, is deemed to have acted in good faith and is immune from civil liability. A computerized criminal history, by itself, is not sufficient verification for a grant of civil immunity under this section."

Laws 1997, c. 97–299, § 11, eff. Oct. 1, 1997, rewrote this section, which formerly read:

"(1) As used in this section:

"(a) 'Conviction' means a determination of guilt that is the result of a plea or a trial, regardless of whether adjudication is withheld.

"(b) 'Sexual offender' means a person who has been convicted of a felony violation of chapter 794, s. 800.04, s. 827.071, or s. 847.0145, or a violation of a similar law of another jurisdiction, when the department has received verified information regarding such conviction; an offender's computerized criminal history record is not, in and of itself, verified information.

"(2) The Legislature finds that sexual offenders pose a high risk of engaging in sexual offenses even after being released from incarceration or commitment and that protection of the public from sexual offenders is a paramount governmental interest. Sexual offenders have a reduced expectation of privacy because of the public's interest in public safety and in the effective operation of government. Releasing sexual offender information to law enforcement agencies and to persons who request such information will further the governmental interests of public safety.

"(3)(a) The department must provide information regarding any sexual offender who is being released after serving a period of incarceration for any offense, as follows:

"1. The department must provide: the sexual offender's name, social security number, race, sex, date of birth, height, weight, and hair and eye color; date and county of sentence and each crime for which the offender was sentenced; a copy of the offender's fingerprints and a photograph taken within 90 days of release; and the offender's intended residence address, if known.

"2. The department may provide any other information deemed necessary, including criminal and corrections records, nonprivileged personnel and treatment records, when available.

"(b) The department must provide the information described in subparagraph (a)1. to:

"1. The sheriff of the county from where the sexual offender was sentenced;

"2. The sheriff of the county and, if applicable, the police chief of the municipality, where the sexual offender plans to reside; and

"3. Any person who requests such information,

"either within 6 months prior to the anticipated release of a sexual offender, or as soon as possible if an offender is released earlier than anticipated.

"(c) Upon request, the department must provide the information described in subparagraph (a)2. to:

"1. The sheriff of the county from where the sexual offender was sentenced; and

"2. The sheriff of the county and, if applicable, the police chief of the municipality, where the sexual offender plans to reside,

"either within 6 months prior to the anticipated release of a sexual offender, or as soon as possible if an offender is released earlier than anticipated.

"(d) Upon receiving information regarding a sexual offender from the department, the sheriff or the chief of police shall provide the information described in subparagraph (a)1. to any individual who requests such information.

"(4) This section does not authorize the department or any law enforcement agency to notify the community and the public of a sexual offender's presence in the community. However, with respect to a sexual offender who has been found to be a 'sexual predator' under chapter 775, the Florida Department of Law Enforcement or any other law enforcement agency must inform the community and the public of the sexual predator's presence in the community, as provided in chapter 775.

"(5) An elected or appointed official, public employee, or agency is immune from civil liability for damages resulting from the release of information under this section."

Laws 1998, c. 98–81, § 10, rewrote the section, which formerly read:

"(1) As used in this section:

"(a) 'Conviction' means a determination of guilt that is the result of a plea or a trial, regardless of whether adjudication is withheld.

"(b) 'Sexual offender' means a person who has been convicted of a felony violation of chapter 794, s. 800.04, s. 827.071, or s. 847.0145, or a violation of a similar law of another jurisdiction, when the department has received verified information regarding such conviction; an offender's computerized criminal history record is not, in and of itself, verified information.

"(2) The Legislature finds that sexual offenders, especially those who have committed their offenses against minors, often pose a high risk of engaging in sexual offenses even after being released from incarceration or commitment and that protection of the public from sexual offenders is a paramount governmental interest. Sexual offenders have a reduced expectation of privacy because of the public's interest in public safety and in the effective operation of government. Releasing sexual offender information to law enforcement agencies and to persons who request such information, and releasing such information to the public by a law enforcement agency or public agency, will further the governmental interests of public safety.

"(3)(a) The department must provide information regarding any sexual offender who is being released after serving a period of incarceration for any offense, as follows:

"1. The department must provide: the sexual offender's name and any alias, if known; the correctional facility from which the sexual offender is released; the sexual offender's social security number, race, sex, date of birth, height, weight, and hair and eye color; date and county of sentence and each crime for which the offender was sentenced; a copy of the offender's fingerprints and a digitized photograph taken within 60 days before release; the date of release of the sexual offender; and the offender's intended residence address, if known. If the sexual offender is in the custody of a private correctional facility, the facility shall take the digitized photograph of the sexual offender within 60 days before the sexual offender's release and provide this photograph to the Department of Corrections and also place it in the sexual offender's file.

"2. The department may provide any other information deemed necessary, including criminal and corrections records, nonprivileged personnel and treatment records, when available.

"(b) The department must provide the information described in subparagraph (a)1. to:

"1. The sheriff of the county from where the sexual offender was sentenced;

"2. The sheriff of the county and, if applicable, the police chief of the municipality, where the sexual offender plans to reside;

"3. The Florida Department of Law Enforcement; and

"4. Any person who requests such information,

"either within 6 months prior to the anticipated release of a sexual offender, or as soon as possible if an offender is released earlier than anticipated. All such information provided to the Department of Law Enforcement must be available electronically as soon as the information is in the agency's database and must be in a format that is compatible with the requirements of the Florida Crime Information Center.

"(c) Upon request, the department must provide the information described in subparagraph (a)2. to:

"1. The sheriff of the county from where the sexual offender was sentenced; and

"2. The sheriff of the county and, if applicable, the police chief of the municipality, where the sexual offender plans to reside,

"either within 6 months prior to the anticipated release of a sexual offender, or as soon as possible if an offender is released earlier than anticipated.

"(d) Upon receiving information regarding a sexual offender from the department, the Department of Law Enforcement, the sheriff or the chief of police shall provide the information described in subparagraph (a)1. to any individual who requests such information and may release the information to the public in any manner deemed appropriate, unless the information so received is confidential or exempt from s. 119.07(1) and s. 24(a), Art. I of the State Constitution.

"(4) This section authorizes the department or any law enforcement agency to notify the community and the public of a sexual offender's presence in the community. However, with respect to a sexual offender who has been found to be a 'sexual predator' under chapter 775, the Florida Department of Law Enforcement or any other law enforcement agency must inform the community and the public of the sexual predator's presence in the community, as provided in chapter 775. Release of information pursuant to this section does not constitute unauthorized public disclosure of information that relates to sexual predators under chapter 775.

"(5) An elected or appointed official, public employee, or agency is immune from civil liability for damages resulting from the release of information under this section."

Laws 1999, c. 99-3, § 119, eff. June 29, 1999, amended the section to improve clarity and facilitate correct interpretation.

Laws 1999, c. 99-201, § 10, reenacted subsec. (1)(b) for the purpose of incorporating amendments to § 800.04 in references thereto.

Laws 2000, c. 2000-207, § 4, rewrote subsec. (1); in subsec. (3), in par. (a)1, in the first sentence, inserted "any change in the offender's name by reason of marriage or other legal process"; and inserted the second sentence. Subsection (1) formerly read:

"(1) As used in this section:

"(a) 'Conviction' means a determination of guilt which is the result of a trial or the entry of a plea of guilty or nolo contendere, regardless of whether adjudication is withheld. A conviction for a violation of a similar law of another jurisdiction includes, but is not limited to, a conviction by a federal or military tribunal, including courts-martial conducted by the Armed Forces of the United States, and includes a conviction in any state of the United States.

"(b) 'Sexual offender' means a person who has been convicted of committing, or attempting, soliciting, or conspiring to commit, any of the criminal offenses proscribed in the following statutes in this state or similar offenses in another jurisdiction: s. 787.01 or s. 787.02, where the victim is a minor and the defendant is not the victim's parent; s. 787.025; chapter 794; s. 796.03; s. 800.04; s. 825.1025; s. 827.071; s. 847.0133; s. 847.0135; s. 847.0145; or any similar offense committed in this state which has been redesignated from a former statute number to one of those listed in this subsection, when the department has received verified information regarding such conviction; an offender's computerized criminal history record is not, in and of itself, verified information."

Laws 2000, c. 2000-246, § 3, reenacted subsec. (1)(b) for the purpose of incorporating the amendment to § 800.04 in a reference thereto.

Laws 2001, c. 2001-209, § 5, designated the existing text of subsec. (3)(b)4. as subsec. (3)(b)5.; and inserted a new subsec. (3)(b)4.

Laws 2002, c. 2002-58, § 5, in subsec. (1)(b), inserted "s. 847.0137; s. 847.0138;" following "s. 847.0135".

Laws 2004, c. 2004–371, § 3, in subsec. (1)(a), inserted "or entry of a plea of guilty or nolo contendere resulting in a sanction" following "conviction" in the second sentence, and added the last sentence, relating to what constitutes a sanction.

Laws 2006, c. 2006–200, § 4, in subsec. (1)(b), inserted "s. 796.035;" following "s. 796.03;", and inserted "or s. 985.4045(1);" following "s. 847.0145;".

Laws 2006, c. 2006–299, § 5, in subsec. (1)(b), substituted a reference to § 787.025(2)(c) for a reference to § 787.025.

Laws 2007, c. 2007–5, a reviser's bill, deleted obsolete and expired provisions, corrected grammatical and typographical errors, and made other similar changes.

Laws 2007, c. 2007–143, § 11, in subsec. (1), added pars. (c) and (d), defining "Electronic mail address" and "Instant message name" respectively; in subsec. (3)(a), inserted references to electronic mail addresses and instant message names.

Laws 2007, c. 2007–209, § 6, in subsec. (1)(b), in the first sentence, inserted "or guardian" following "victim's parent", substituted references to chapter 794 and § 794.05 for references to § 794.011 and § 794.0235, and inserted a reference to § 847.0135(4); and in subsec. (3)(a)1., in the last sentence, inserted "register the offender within 3 business days after intake of the offender for any reason and upon release, and shall" following "custodian of the local jail shall".

Laws 2009, c. 2009–194, § 4, in subsec. (1)(b) changed the reference to s. 847.0135(4) to refer to s. 847.0135(6); and in subsec. (3)(a)1. added "home telephone number and any cellular telephone number," following "s. 943.0435(4)(d);".

Cross References

Juvenile records and confidential information, see § 985.04.

Library References

Mental Health ⚷469.
Westlaw Topic No. 257A.
C.J.S. Mental Health §§ 290 to 291, 299.

Research References

Encyclopedias

Sex Offenders; Information Required, FL Jur. 2d Prisons & Prisoners § 206.

Sex Offenders; Information Required--Where Offender is in Local Jail, FL Jur. 2d Prisons & Prisoners § 207.

Treatises and Practice Aids

16 Florida Practice Series § 6:106, Direct and Collateral Consequences and Special Sanctions--Sexual Offender/Sexual Predator Sanctions--Mandatory Designation.

United States Code Annotated

Child protection, sex offender registration and notification, crime information databases, access, see 42 U.S.C.A. § 16961.

Child protection, sex offender registration and notification, generally, see 42 U.S.C.A. §§ 16911 to 16929.

Child protection, sex offender registration and notification, Project Safe Childhood program, see 42 U.S.C.A. § 16942.

Civil commitment, sexually dangerous persons, see 18 U.S.C.A. § 4248.

Sex offender registration, failure to register, see 18 U.S.C.A. § 2250.

Sex offender registration, supervised release, see 18 U.S.C.A. § 3583.

Notes of Decisions

1. Validity

Sexual offender notification and registration requirements satisfy compelling state interest of providing benefit to public safety and are least intrusive method to accomplish this goal, and thus, sexual offender designation and corresponding sanctions do not violate constitutional right to privacy. Johnson v. State, App. 5 Dist., 795 So.2d 82 (2000), clarified. Constitutional Law ⚷ 1245; Mental Health ⚷ 433(2)

Defendant abandoned claim that sexual offender notification and registration requirements violated right to privacy, where, even if his initial and reply briefs could be construed as raising this claim, argument was not developed. Johnson v. State, App. 5 Dist., 795 So.2d 82 (2000), clarified. Mental Health ⚷ 467

2. Release of information

A law enforcement agency could release or disseminate information contained in its public records relating to sexual offenders that were not otherwise exempt or confidential without a request. Op.Atty.Gen. 97–09, February 10, 1997.

3. Notification of public

The Sheriff of Columbia County is authorized to develop a program for community notification of the presence of a sexual predator or offender utilizing the placement of a decal on the vehicle of these offenders. Op.Atty.Gen., 2006–06, March 8, 2006.

4. Probation violation

The Department of Corrections does not have the statutory authority to institute violation of probation proceedings based upon its inability to acquire sex offender's address prior to his release from prison. King v. State, App. 5 Dist., 990 So.2d 1191 (2008). Sentencing and Punishment ⚷ 2009

944.607. Notification to Department of Law Enforcement of information on sexual offenders

(1) As used in this section, the term:

(a) "Sexual offender" means a person who is in the custody or control of, or under the supervision of, the department or is in the custody of a private correctional facility:

1. On or after October 1, 1997, as a result of a conviction for committing, or attempting, soliciting, or conspiring to commit, any of the criminal offenses proscribed in the following statutes in this state or similar offenses in another jurisdiction: s. 787.01, s. 787.02, or s. 787.025(2)(c), where the victim is a minor and the defendant is not the victim's parent or guardian; s. 794.011, excluding s. 794.011(10); s. 794.05; s. 796.03; s. 796.035; s. 800.04; s. 825.1025; s. 827.071; s. 847.0133; s. 847.0135, excluding s. 847.0135(6); s. 847.0137; s. 847.0138; s. 847.0145; or s. 985.701(1); or any similar offense committed in this state which has been redesignated from a former statute number to one of those listed in this paragraph; or

2. Who establishes or maintains a residence in this state and who has not been designated as a sexual predator by a court of this state but who has been designated as a sexual predator, as a sexually violent predator, or by another sexual offender designation in another state or jurisdiction and was, as a result of such designation, subjected to registration or community or public notification, or both, or would be if the person were a resident of that state or jurisdiction, without regard as to whether the person otherwise meets the criteria for registration as a sexual offender.

(b) "Conviction" means a determination of guilt which is the result of a trial or the entry of a plea of guilty or nolo contendere, regardless of whether adjudication is withheld. Conviction of a similar offense includes, but is not limited to, a conviction by a federal or military tribunal, including courts-martial conducted by the Armed Forces of the United States, and includes a conviction or entry of a plea of guilty or nolo contendere resulting in a sanction in any state of the United States or other jurisdiction. A sanction includes, but is not limited to, a fine; probation; community control; parole; conditional release; control release; or incarceration in a state prison, federal prison, private correctional facility, or local detention facility.

(c) "Institution of higher education" means a career center, community college, college, state university, or independent postsecondary institution.

(d) "Change in enrollment or employment status" means the commencement or termination of enrollment or employment or a change in location of enrollment or employment.

(e) "Electronic mail address" has the same meaning as provided in s. 668.602.

(f) "Instant message name" means an identifier that allows a person to communicate in real time with another person using the Internet.

(2) The clerk of the court of that court which convicted and sentenced the sexual offender for the offense or offenses described in subsection (1) shall forward to the department and the Department of Law Enforcement a certified copy of any order entered by the court imposing any special condition or restriction on the sexual offender which restricts or prohibits access to the victim, if the victim is a minor, or to other minors. The Department of Law Enforcement may include on its Internet site such special conditions or restrictions.

(3) If a sexual offender is not sentenced to a term of imprisonment, the clerk of the court shall ensure that the sexual offender's fingerprints are taken and forwarded to the Department of Law Enforcement within 48 hours after the court sentences the offender. The fingerprint card shall be clearly marked "Sexual Offender Registration Card."

(4) A sexual offender, as described in this section, who is under the supervision of the Department of Corrections but is not incarcerated must register with the Department of Corrections within 3 business days after sentencing for a registerable offense and otherwise provide information as required by this subsection.

(a) The sexual offender shall provide his or her name; date of birth; social security number; race; sex; height; weight; hair and eye color; tattoos or other identifying marks; any electronic mail address and any instant message name required to be provided pursuant to s. 943.0435(4)(d); and permanent or legal residence and address of temporary residence within the state or out of state while the sexual offender is under supervision in this state, including any rural route address or post office box. The Department of Corrections shall verify the address of each sexual offender in the manner described in ss. 775.21 and 943.0435. The department shall report to the Department of Law Enforcement any failure by a sexual predator or sexual offender to comply with registration requirements.

(b) If the sexual offender is enrolled, employed, or carrying on a vocation at an institution of higher education in this state, the sexual offender shall provide the name, address, and county of each institution, including each campus attended, and the sexual offender's enrollment or employment status. Each change in enrollment or employment status shall be reported to the department within 48 hours after the change in status. The Department of Corrections shall promptly notify each institution of the sexual offender's presence and any change in the sexual offender's enrollment or employment status.

(5) In addition to notification and transmittal requirements imposed by any other provision of law, the department shall compile information on any sexual offender and provide the information to the Department of Law Enforcement. The information shall be made available electronically to the Department of Law Enforcement as soon as this information is in the department's database and must be in a format that is compatible with the requirements of the Florida Crime Information Center.

(6) The information provided to the Department of Law Enforcement must include:

(a) The information obtained from the sexual offender under subsection (4);

(b) The sexual offender's most current address and place of permanent and temporary residence within the state or out of state while the sexual offender is under supervision in this state, including the name of the county or municipality in which the offender permanently or temporarily resides and, if known, the intended place of permanent or temporary residence upon satisfaction of all sanctions;

(c) The legal status of the sexual offender and the scheduled termination date of that legal status;

(d) The location of, and local telephone number for, any Department of Corrections' office that is responsible for supervising the sexual offender;

(e) An indication of whether the victim of the offense that resulted in the offender's status as a sexual offender was a minor;

(f) The offense or offenses at conviction which resulted in the determination of the offender's status as a sex offender; and

(g) A digitized photograph of the sexual offender which must have been taken within 60 days before the offender is released from the custody of the department or a private correctional facility by expiration of sentence under s. 944.275 or must have been taken by January 1, 1998, or within 60 days after the onset of the department's supervision of any sexual offender who is on probation, community control, conditional release, parole, provisional release, or control release or who is supervised by the department under the Interstate Compact Agreement for Probationers and Parolees. If the sexual offender is in the custody of a private correctional facility, the facility shall take a digitized photograph of the sexual offender within the time period provided in this paragraph and shall provide the photograph to the department.

If any information provided by the department changes during the time the sexual offender is under the department's control, custody, or supervision, including any change in the offender's name by reason of marriage or other legal process, the department shall, in a timely manner, update the information and provide it to the Department of Law Enforcement in the manner prescribed in subsection (2).

(7) If the sexual offender is in the custody of a local jail, the custodian of the local jail shall register the offender within 3 business days after intake of the offender for any reason and upon release, and shall forward the information to the Department of Law Enforcement. The custodian of the local jail shall also take a digitized photograph of the sexual offender while the offender remains in custody and shall provide the digitized photograph to the Department of Law Enforcement.

(8) If the sexual offender is under federal supervision, the federal agency responsible for supervising the sexual offender may forward to the Department of Law Enforcement any information regarding the sexual offender which is consistent with the information provided by the department under this section, and may indicate whether use of the information is restricted to law enforcement purposes only or may be used by the Department of Law Enforcement for purposes of public notification.

(9) A sexual offender, as described in this section, who is under the supervision of the Department of Corrections but who is not incarcerated shall, in addition to the registration requirements provided in subsection (4), register and obtain a distinctive driver's license or identification card in the manner provided in s. 943.0435(3), (4), and (5), unless the sexual offender is a sexual predator, in which case he or she shall register and obtain a distinctive driver's license or identification card as required under s. 775.21. A sexual offender who fails to comply with the requirements of s. 943.0435 is subject to the penalties provided in s. 943.0435(9).

(10)(a) The failure of a sexual offender to submit to the taking of a digitized photograph, or to otherwise comply with the requirements of this section, is a felony of the third degree, punishable as provided in s. 775.082, s. 775.083, or s. 775.084.

(b) A sexual offender who commits any act or omission in violation of this section may be prosecuted for the act or omission in the county in which the act or omission was committed, the county of the last registered address of the sexual offender, or the county in which the conviction occurred for the offense or offenses that meet the criteria for designating a person as a sexual offender.

(c) An arrest on charges of failure to register when the offender has been provided and advised of his or her statutory obligations to register under s. 943.0435(2), the service of an information or a complaint for a violation of this section, or an arraignment on charges for a violation of this section constitutes actual notice of the duty to register. A sexual offender's failure to immediately register as required by this section following such arrest, service, or arraignment constitutes grounds for a subsequent charge of failure to register. A sexual offender charged with the crime of failure to register who asserts, or intends to assert, a lack of notice of the duty to register as a defense to a charge of failure to register shall immediately register as required by this section. A sexual offender who is charged with a subsequent failure to register may not assert the defense of a lack of notice of the duty to register.

(d) Registration following such arrest, service, or arraignment is not a defense and does not relieve the sexual offender of criminal liability for the failure to register.

(11) The department, the Department of Highway Safety and Motor Vehicles, the Department of Law Enforcement, the Department of Corrections, the Department of Juvenile Justice, personnel of those departments, and any individual or entity acting at the request or upon the direction of those departments are immune from civil liability for damages for good faith compliance with this section, and shall be presumed to have acted in good faith in compiling, recording, reporting, or providing information. The presumption of good faith is not overcome if technical or clerical errors are made by the department, the Department of Highway Safety and Motor Vehicles, the Department of Law Enforcement, the Department of Juvenile Justice, personnel of those departments, or any individual or entity acting at the request or upon the direction of those departments in compiling, recording, reporting, or providing information, or, if the information is incomplete or incorrect because the information has not been provided by a person or agency required to provide the information, or because the information was not reported or was falsely reported.

(12) Any person who has reason to believe that a sexual offender is not complying, or has not complied, with the requirements of this section and who, with the intent to assist the sexual offender in eluding a law enforcement agency that is seeking to find the sexual offender to question the sexual offender about, or to arrest the sexual offender for, his or her noncompliance with the requirements of this section:

(a) Withholds information from, or does not notify, the law enforcement agency about the sexual offender's noncompliance with the requirements of this section, and, if known, the whereabouts of the sexual offender;

(b) Harbors, or attempts to harbor, or assists another person in harboring or attempting to harbor, the sexual offender; or

(c) Conceals or attempts to conceal, or assists another person in concealing or attempting to conceal, the sexual offender; or

(d) Provides information to the law enforcement agency regarding the sexual offender which the person knows to be false information,

commits a felony of the third degree, punishable as provided in s. 775.082, s. 775.083, or s. 775.084. This subsection does not apply if the sexual offender is incarcerated in or is in the custody of a state correctional facility, a private correctional facility, a local jail, or a federal correctional facility.

(13)(a) A sexual offender must report in person each year during the month of the sexual offender's birthday and during the sixth month following the sexual offender's birth month to the sheriff's office in the county in which he or she resides or is otherwise located to reregister.

(b) However, a sexual offender who is required to register as a result of a conviction for:

1. Section 787.01 or s. 787.02 where the victim is a minor and the offender is not the victim's parent or guardian;

2. Section 794.011, excluding s. 794.011(10);

3. Section 800.04(4)(b) where the victim is under 12 years of age or where the court finds sexual activity by the use of force or coercion;

4. Section 800.04(5)(b);

5. Section 800.04(5)(c)1. where the court finds molestation involving unclothed genitals or genital area;

6. Section 800.04(5)c.2. where the court finds molestation involving unclothed genitals or genital area;

7. Section 800.04(5)(d) where the court finds the use of force or coercion and unclothed genitals or genital area;

8. Any attempt or conspiracy to commit such offense; or

9. A violation of a similar law of another jurisdiction,

must reregister each year during the month of the sexual offender's birthday and every third month thereafter.

(c) The sheriff's office may determine the appropriate times and days for reporting by the sexual offender, which shall be consistent with the reporting requirements of this subsection. Reregistration shall include any changes to the following information:

1. Name; social security number; age; race; sex; date of birth; height; weight; hair and eye color; address of any permanent residence and address of any current temporary residence, within the state or out of state, including a rural route address and a post office box; any electronic mail address and any instant message name required to be provided pursuant to s. 943.0435(4)(d); date and place of any employment; vehicle make, model, color, and license tag number; fingerprints; and photograph. A post office box shall not be provided in lieu of a physical residential address.

2. If the sexual offender is enrolled, employed, or carrying on a vocation at an institution of higher education in this state, the sexual offender shall also provide to the department the name, address, and county of each institution, including each campus attended, and the sexual offender's enrollment or employment status.

3. If the sexual offender's place of residence is a motor vehicle, trailer, mobile home, or manufactured home, as defined in chapter 320, the sexual offender shall also provide the vehicle identification number; the license tag number; the registration number; and a description, including color scheme, of the motor vehicle, trailer, mobile home, or manufactured home. If the sexual offender's place of residence is a vessel, live-aboard vessel, or houseboat, as defined in chapter 327, the sexual offender shall also provide the hull identification number; the manufacturer's serial number; the name of the

vessel, live-aboard vessel, or houseboat; the registration number; and a description, including color scheme, of the vessel, live-aboard vessel or houseboat.

4. Any sexual offender who fails to report in person as required at the sheriff's office, or who fails to respond to any address verification correspondence from the department within 3 weeks of the date of the correspondence, or who fails to report electronic mail addresses or instant message names, commits a felony of the third degree, punishable as provided in s. 775.082, s. 775.083, or s. 775.084.

(d) The sheriff's office shall, within 2 working days, electronically submit and update all information provided by the sexual offender to the Department of Law Enforcement in a manner prescribed by that department.

Added by Laws 1997, c. 97–299, § 9, eff. Oct. 1, 1997. Amended by Laws 1998, c. 98–81, § 11, eff. Oct. 1, 1998; Laws 2000, c. 2000–207, § 5, eff. July 1, 2000; Laws 2000, c. 2000–246, § 3, eff. Oct. 1, 2000; Laws 2002, c. 2002–58, § 6, eff. July 1, 2002; Laws 2004, c. 2004–371, § 4, eff. July 1, 2004; Laws 2005, c. 2005–28, § 11, eff. Sept. 1, 2005; Laws 2006, c. 2006–200, § 5, eff. July 1, 2006; Laws 2006, c. 2006–299, § 6, eff. July 1, 2006; Laws 2007, c. 2007–5, § 162, eff. July 3, 2007; Laws 2007, c. 2007–143, § 12, eff. Oct. 1, 2007; Laws 2007, c. 2007–207, § 5, eff. July 1, 2007; Laws 2007, c. 2007–209, § 7, eff. July 1, 2007; Laws 2009, c. 2009–194, § 5, eff. July 1, 2009.

Historical and Statutory Notes

Amendment Notes:

Laws 1998, c. 98–81, § 11, rewrote the section, which formerly read:

"(1) As used in this section, the term:

"(a) 'Sex offender' means a person who is in the custody or control of, or under the supervision of, the department or is in the custody of a private correctional facility on or after October 1, 1997, as a result of a conviction for committing, or attempting, soliciting, or conspiring to commit, any of the criminal offenses proscribed in the following statutes in this state or analogous offenses in another jurisdiction: s. 787.025, chapter 794, s. 796.03, s. 800.04, s. 827.071, s. 847.0133, s. 847.0135, s. 847.0145, or any similar offense committed in this state which has been redesignated from a former statute number to one of those listed in this paragraph.

"(b) 'Conviction' means a determination of guilt as a result of a plea or trial, regardless of whether adjudication is withheld.

"(2) In addition to notification and transmittal requirements imposed by any other provision of law, the department shall compile information on any sex offender and provide the information to the Department of Law Enforcement. The information shall be made available electronically to the Department of Law Enforcement as soon as this information is in the department's database and must be in a format that is compatible with the requirements of the Florida Crime Information Center.

"(3) The information provided to the Department of Law Enforcement must include:

"(a) The name of the sex offender and any alias, if known;

"(b) The sex offender's most current address and place of permanent or temporary residence, including the name of the county or municipality in which the offender permanently or temporarily resides and, if known, the intended place of permanent or temporary residence upon satisfaction of all sanctions;

"(c) The legal status of the sex offender and the scheduled termination date of that legal status;

"(d) The location of, and local telephone number for, any office of probation, community control, parole, conditional release, or control release which is responsible for supervising the sex offender;

"(e) An indication of whether the victim of the offense that resulted in the offender's status as a sex offender was a minor;

"(f) A physical description of the sex offender;

"(g) The offense or offenses at conviction which resulted in the determination of the offender's status as a sex offender; and

"(h) A digitized photograph of the sex offender which must have been taken within 60 days before the offender is released from the custody of the department or a private correctional facility by expiration of sentence under s. 944.275 or must have been taken by January 1, 1998, or within 60 days after the onset of the department's supervision of any sex offender who is on probation, community control, conditional release, parole, provisional release, or control release or who is supervised by the department under the Interstate Compact Agreement for Probationers and Parolees. If the sex offender is in the custody of a private correctional facility, the facility shall take a digitized photograph of the sex offender within the time period provided in this paragraph and shall provide the photograph to the department.

"If any information provided by the department changes during the time the sex offender is under the department's control, custody, or supervision, the department shall update the information and provide it to the Department of Law Enforcement in the manner prescribed in subsection (2).

"(4) The department and its personnel are immune from civil liability for damages for good faith compliance with this section, and shall be presumed to have acted in good faith in compiling, recording, and providing information. The presumption of good faith is not overcome if technical or clerical errors are made by the department and its personnel in compiling, recording, or providing information, if the information compiled, recorded, or provided by the department and its personnel is incomplete because the information has not been provided to the department by a person or agency required to provide the information, or if the department and its personnel compile, record, or provide information that was falsely reported without the knowledge of the department and its personnel."

Laws 2000, c. 2000–207, § 5, in subsec. (1), corrected citations and added "or other jurisdiction"; in subsec. (3), inserted "of Law Enforcement"; in subsec. (4), inserted "within the state or out of state while the sexual offender is under supervision in this state"; in subsec. (6), in par. (b), inserted "within the state or out of state while the sexual offender is under supervision in this state"; in the last paragraph, inserted "including any change in the offender's name by reason of marriage or other legal process; and, in subsec. (9), corrected a citation.

Laws 2000, c. 2000–246, § 3, reenacted subsec. (1)(a) for the purpose of incorporating the amendment to § 800.04 in a reference thereto.

Laws 2002, c. 2002–58, § 6, rewrote subsecs. (1) and (4), which formerly read:

"(1) As used in this section, the term:

"(a) 'Sexual offender' means a person who is in the custody or control of, or under the supervision of, the department or is in the custody of a private correctional facility on or after October 1, 1997, as a result of a conviction for committing, or attempting, soliciting, or conspiring to commit, any of the criminal offenses proscribed in the following statutes in this state or similar offenses in another jurisdiction: s. 787.01, s. 787.02, or s. 787.025, where the victim is a minor and the defendant is not the victim's parent; chapter 794, excluding ss. 794.011(10) and 794.0235; s. 796.03; s. 800.04; s. 825.1025; s. 827.071; s. 847.0133; s. 847.0135; s. 847.0145; or any similar offense committed in this state which has been redesignated from a former statute number to one of those listed in this paragraph.

"(b) 'Conviction' means a determination of guilt which is the result of a trial or the entry of a plea of guilty or nolo contendere, regardless of whether adjudication is withheld. Conviction of a similar offense includes, but is not limited to, a conviction by a federal or military tribunal, including courts-martial conducted by the Armed Forces of the United States, and includes a conviction in any state of the United States or other jurisdiction."

"(4) A sexual offender, as described in this section, who is under the supervision of the Department of Corrections but is not incarcerated must register with the Department of Corrections and provide the following information: name; date of birth; social security number; race; sex; height; weight; hair and eye color; tattoos or other identifying marks; and permanent or legal residence and address of temporary residence within the state or out of state while the sexual offender is under supervision in this state, including any rural route address or post office box. The Department of Corrections shall verify the address of each sexual offender in the manner described in ss. 775.21 and 943.0435."

Laws 2004, c. 2004–371, § 4, in subsec. (1)(b), inserted "or entry of a plea of guilty or nolo contendere resulting in a sanction" following "conviction" in the second sentence, and inserted the third sentence relating to what constitutes a sanction; in subsec. (4), substituted "information as required by this subsection." for "the following information:", following "provide"; in subsec. (4)(a), added "The sexual offender shall provide his or her" at the beginning; in subsec. (4)(b), inserted "the sexual offender shall provide" preceding "the name"; and in subsec. (10), inserted par. (a) designation, and added pars. (b) to (d), relating to venue for prosecution, notice of obligation to register, and subsequent registration not being a defense, respectively.

Laws 2005, c. 2005–28, § 11, added subsecs. (12) and (13), relating to assistance in eluding law enforcement agencies, and reregistration, respectively.

Laws 2006, c. 2006–200, § 5, in subsec. (1)(a)1., inserted "s. 796.035;" following "s. 796.03;", and inserted "or s. 985.4045(1);" following "s. 847.0145;"; in subsec. (1)(a)2., added ", without regard as to whether the person otherwise meets the criteria for registration as a sexual offender" at the end; and in subsec. (1)(c), inserted "career center," following "means a".

Laws 2006, c. 2006–299, § 6, in subsec. (1)(a)1., substituted a reference to § 787.025(2)(c) for a reference to § 787.025.

Laws 2007, c. 2007–5, a reviser's bill, deleted obsolete and expired provisions, corrected grammatical and typographical errors, and made other similar changes.

Laws 2007, c. 2007–143, § 12, in subsec. (1), added pars. (e) and (f), defining "Electronic mail address" and "Instant message name" respectively; in subsecs. (4)(a) and (13), inserted references to electronic mail addresses and instant message names; rewrote subsec. (13)(b), which formerly read:

"[(13)](b) The sheriff's office shall, within 2 working days, electronically submit and update all information provided by the sexual offender to the Florida Department of Law Enforcement in a manner prescribed by the Florida Department of Law Enforcement. This procedure shall be implemented by December 1, 2005."

Laws 2007, c. 2007–207, § 5, in subsec. (9), in the first sentence, twice inserted "and obtain a distinctive driver's license or identification card" following "register".

Laws 2007, c. 2007–209, § 7, in subsec. (1)(a)1., inserted "or guardian" following "victim's parent", substituted references for § 794.011 and § 794.05 for references to chapter 794 and § 794.0235, and added a reference to § 847.0135(4); in subsec. (4), in the introductory paragraph, substituted "within 3 business days after sentencing for a registerable offense and otherwise provide" for "and provide" following "Department of Corrections", and in subsec. (4)(a), added the last sentence relating to reporting any failure of a sexual predator or sexual offender to comply with registration requirements; in subsec. (7), in the first sentence, substituted "within 3 business days after intake of the offender for any reason and upon release, and shall forward" for "and forward" following "shall register the offender"; in subsec. (11), in the first sentence, inserted references to the Department of Juvenile Justice following references to the Department of Corrections and the Department of Law Enforcement; and rewrote subsec. (13). Subsec. 13 formerly read:

"(13)(a) A sexual offender must report in person each year during the month of the sexual offender's birthday and during the sixth month following the sexual offender's birth month to the sheriff's office in the county in which he or she resides or is otherwise located to reregister. The sheriff's office may determine the appropriate times and days for reporting by the sexual offender, which shall be consistent with the reporting requirements of this paragraph. Reregistration shall include any changes to the following information:

"1. Name; social security number; age; race; sex; date of birth; height; weight; hair and eye color; address of any permanent residence and address of any current temporary residence, within the state or out of state, including a rural route address and a post office box; date and place of any employment; vehicle make, model, color, and license tag number; fingerprints; and photograph. A post office box shall not be provided in lieu of a physical residential address.

"2. If the sexual offender is enrolled, employed, or carrying on a vocation at an institution of higher education in this state, the sexual offender shall also provide to the department the name, address, and county of each institution, including each campus attended, and the sexual offender's enrollment or employment status.

"3. If the sexual offender's place of residence is a motor vehicle, trailer, mobile home, or manufactured home, as defined in chapter 320, the sexual offender shall also provide the vehicle identification number; the license tag number; the registration number; and a description, including color scheme, of the motor vehicle, trailer, mobile home, or manufactured home. If the sexual offender's place of residence is a vessel, live-aboard vessel, or houseboat, as defined in chapter 327, the sexual offender shall also provide the hull identification number; the manufacturer's serial number; the name of the vessel, live-aboard vessel, or houseboat; the registration number; and a description, including color scheme, of the vessel, live-aboard vessel, or houseboat.

"4. Any sexual offender who fails to report in person as required at the sheriff's office, or who fails to respond to any address verification correspondence from the department within 3 weeks of the date of the correspondence, commits a felony of the third degree, punishable as provided in s. 775.082, s. 775.083, and s. 775.084.

"(b) The sheriff's office shall, within 2 working days, electronically submit and update all information provided by the sexual offender to the Florida Department of Law Enforcement in a manner prescribed by the Florida Department of Law Enforcement. This procedure shall be implemented by December 1, 2005."

Laws 2009, c. 2009–194, § 5, in subpar. (1)(a)1. changed the reference to s. 847.0135(4) to refer to s. 847.0135(6).

Cross References

Juvenile records and confidential information, see § 985.04.
Probation or community control violation, revocation, modification, or continuance, see § 948.06.
Sexual offenders and sexual predators, licenses and identification cards, see § 322.141.

Library References

Mental Health ⚷469.
Westlaw Topic No. 257A.
C.J.S. Mental Health §§ 290 to 291, 299.

Research References

ALR Library

33 ALR 6th 91, Validity, Construction, and Application of State Statutes Imposing Criminal Penalties for Failure to Register as Required Under Sex Offender or Other Criminal Registration Statutes.

36 ALR 5th 161, State Statutes or Ordinances Requiring Persons Previously Convicted of Crime to Register With Authorities.

Encyclopedias

Requisites for Valid License, FL Jur. 2d Automobiles & Other Vehicles § 182.

Sex Offenders; Information Required, FL Jur. 2d Prisons & Prisoners § 206.

Treatises and Practice Aids

16 Florida Practice Series § 6:99, Direct and Collateral Consequences and Special Sanctions--Registration of Convicted Felons.

16 Florida Practice Series § 7:19, Violent Felony Offender of Special Concern.

16 Florida Practice Series § 7:67, Sentencing Alternatives for Violations of Probation/Community Control--General.

16 Florida Practice Series § 6:103, Direct and Collateral Consequences and Special Sanctions--Sexual Offender/Sexual Predator Sanctions--Sexual Offender.

16 Florida Practice Series § 6:104, Direct and Collateral Consequences and Special Sanctions--Sexual Offender/Sexual Predator Sanctions--Sexual Predator.

16 Florida Practice Series § 6:105, Direct and Collateral Consequences and Special Sanctions--Sexual Offender/Sexual Predator Sanctions--Mandatory Designation on Driver's License or Identification Card.

16 Florida Practice Series § 6:106, Direct and Collateral Consequences and Special Sanctions--Sexual Offender/Sexual Predator Sanctions--Mandatory Designation.

22 Florida Practice Series § 9:11, Release During and Following Trial--Pending Probation or Community Control Revocation Proceedings.

22 Florida Practice Series App. A, Florida Rules of Criminal Procedure.

United States Code Annotated

Child protection, sex offender registration and notification, crime information databases, access, see 42 U.S.C.A. § 16961.
Child protection, sex offender registration and notification, generally, see 42 U.S.C.A. §§ 16911 to 16929.
Child protection, sex offender registration and notification, Project Safe Childhood program, see 42 U.S.C.A. § 16942.
Sex offender registration, failure to register, see 18 U.S.C.A. § 2250.
Sex offender registration, supervised release, see 18 U.S.C.A. § 3583.

Notes of Decisions

1. Due process

Sexual offender registration and notification statute did not violate defendant's procedural due process rights on basis that defendant was not afforded a hearing to determine whether he was a danger to the public before being subject to the statutory requirements, where dangerousness was not relevant to the dispute; only relevant fact was whether defendant was convicted of a specific crime, and defendant was entitled to procedural due process before that conviction was entered. Givens v. State, App. 2 Dist., 851 So.2d 813 (2003), review denied 917 So.2d 193. Constitutional Law ⚷ 4343; Mental Health ⚷ 433(2)

2. Sexual offender

Defendant sentenced to sex offender probation was required to register as a sex offender prior to his release from probation, even though statute governing registration of probationers instructed that registration be done "in the manner provided" by statute governing registration of sex offenders sentenced to prison, and statute governing registration of sex offenders sentenced to prison did not require registration until after the prisoner's release; registration in the same manner did not mean registration at the same time. Dejesus v. State, App. 4 Dist., 862 So.2d 847 (2003). Mental Health ⚷ 469(5)

Defendant violated probation as sexual offender by failing to report change of residence, as required by sexual offender registration statute, even if he did not meet definition of sexual offender under that statute, given that defendant did qualify as "sexual offender" under statute governing notification to Department of Law Enforcement, which incorporated reporting requirements of registration statute. Grumet v. State, App. 4 Dist., 771 So.2d 39 (2000), review denied 790 So.2d 1103. Sentencing And Punishment ⚷ 1971(3)

3. Notice

Charging document's citation to wrong reporting statute did not mislead sex offender to his prejudice as to warrant dismissal of charge of failing to report every six months to county sheriff's office; cited statute and intended statute had same reporting requirements and contained identical language, and State included language of correct statute in charging documents. McMann v. State, App. 1 Dist., 954 So.2d 90 (2007). Indictment And Information ⚷ 108

Sexual offender notification and registration requirements satisfy compelling state interest of providing benefit to public safety and are least intrusive method to accomplish this goal, and thus, sexual offender designation and corresponding sanctions do not violate constitutional right to privacy. Johnson v. State, App. 5 Dist., 795 So.2d 82 (2000), clarified. Constitutional Law ⚷ 1245; Mental Health ⚷ 433(2)

Defendant abandoned claim that sexual offender notification and registration requirements violated right to privacy, where, even if his initial and reply briefs could be construed as raising this claim, argument was not developed. Johnson v. State, App. 5 Dist., 795 So.2d 82 (2000), clarified. Mental Health ⚷ 467

Failure of state's violation of probation affidavit to cite to sex offender statute, which required sexual offender to notify Department of Law Enforcement of change of residence, did not violate defendant's due process rights, undermine affidavit's validity, or excuse defendant's noncompliance with statute, since defendant had actual notice that notification statute applied to his status as a sexual offender, as well as constructive notice of statute's additional registration requirements, affidavit provided basic facts concerning alleged violation and operative statute that defendant violated, and defendant acknowledged in signing sex offender registration form that he understood he had to comply with Department of Highway Safety and Motor Vehicles' (DMV) registration requirement. Grumet v. State, App. 4 Dist., 771 So.2d 39 (2000), review denied 790 So.2d 1103. Constitutional Law ⚷ 4733(2); Sentencing And Punishment ⚷ 2011

4. Violations

Court had to presume that guilty knowledge or scienter or mens rea was an element of crime of violating sex offender registration statutes, which required offender to report change of address within 48 hours of change, even though statutory text did not contain explicit element of intent; sex offender registration statutes did not create a mere informational reporting requirement, but outlined a felony offense that was punishable with imprisonment. Giorgetti v. State, App. 4 Dist., 821 So.2d 417 (2002), review granted 837 So.2d 412, approved 868 So.2d 512. Mental Health ⚷ 469.5

5. Good faith effort to comply

Defendant made a good faith effort to comply with condition of his community control requiring him to register and obtain an identification card denoting his sex offender status from the Department of Highway Safety and Motor Vehicles (DHSMV) within 48 hours of his release from prison, where only reason he did not complete the registration was because he lacked $10 to obtain a new license, and defendant obtained the license after attempting to comply with the requirement three days later, as soon as he had obtained the necessary funds. Easterling v. State, App. 1 Dist., 989 So.2d 1285 (2008). Sentencing And Punishment ⚷ 1969(3)

6. Sentence and punishment

Remand for resentencing was required, after District Court of Appeal affirmed trial court's finding that defendant violated two conditions of community control, but reversed as to two charges concerning defendant's failure to register and obtain an identification card denoting his sex offender status from the Department of Highway Safety and Motor Vehicles (DHSMV) within 48 hours of his release from prison; it was not clear from the record whether the trial court would have imposed the same sentence of life imprisonment without possibility of parole based on the remaining violations for failing to be truthful with his probation officer and leaving his home and visiting the DHSMV without his probation officer's permission. Easterling v. State, App. 1 Dist., 989 So.2d 1285 (2008). Criminal Law ⚷ 1181.5(8)

944.608. Notification to Department of Law Enforcement of information on career offenders

(1) As used in this section, the term "career offender" means a person who is in the custody or control of, or under the supervision of, the department or is in the custody or control of, or under the supervision of, a private correctional facility, and who is designated as a habitual violent felony offender, a violent career criminal, or a three-time violent felony offender under s. 775.084 or as a prison releasee reoffender under s. 775.082(9).

(2) If a career offender is not sentenced to a term of imprisonment, the clerk of the court shall ensure that the career offender's fingerprints are taken and forwarded to the Department of Law Enforcement within 48 hours after the court sentences the career offender. The fingerprint card shall be clearly marked "Career Offender Registration Card."

(3) A career offender who is under the supervision of the department but is not incarcerated must register with the department and provide his or her name; date of birth; social security number; race; gender; height; weight; hair and eye color; tattoos or other identifying marks; and permanent or legal residence and address of temporary residence within the state or out of state while the career offender is under supervision in this state, including any rural route address or post office box. The department shall verify the address of each career offender.

(4) In addition to notification and transmittal requirements imposed by any other provision of law, the department shall compile information on any career offender and provide the information to the Department of Law Enforcement. The information shall be made available electronically to the Department of Law Enforcement as soon as this information is in the department's database and must be in a format that is compatible with the requirements of the Florida Crime Information Center.

(5) The information provided to the Department of Law Enforcement must include:

(a) The information obtained from the career offender under subsection (3);

(b) The career offender's most current address and place of permanent and temporary residence within the state or out of state while the career offender is under supervision in this state, including the name of the county or municipality in which the career offender permanently or temporarily resides and, if known, the intended place of permanent or temporary residence upon satisfaction of all sanctions;

(c) The legal status of the career offender and the scheduled termination date of that legal status;

(d) The location of, and local telephone number for, any Department of Corrections' office that is responsible for supervising the career offender; and

(e) A digitized photograph of the career offender, which must have been taken within 60 days before the career offender is released from the custody of the department or a private correctional facility or within 60 days after the onset of the department's supervision of any career offender who is on probation, community control, conditional release, parole, provisional release, or control release. If the career offender is in the custody or control of, or under the supervision of, a private correctional facility, the facility shall take a digitized photograph of the career offender within the time period provided in this paragraph and shall provide the photograph to the department.

(6)(a) The department shall notify the Department of Law Enforcement if the career offender escapes, absconds, or dies while in the custody or control of, or under the supervision of, the department.

(b) If any information provided by the department changes during the time the career offender is under the department's custody, control, or supervision, including any change in the career offender's name by reason of marriage or other legal process, the department shall, in a timely manner, update the information and provide it to the Department of Law Enforcement in the manner prescribed in subsection (4).

(7) A career offender who is under the supervision of the department but who is not incarcerated shall, in addition to the registration requirements provided in subsection (3), register in the manner provided in s. 775.261(4)(c), unless the career offender is a sexual predator, in which case he or she shall register as required under s. 775.21, or is a sexual offender, in which case he or she shall register as required in s. 944.607. A career offender who fails to comply with the requirements of s. 775.261(4) is subject to the penalties provided in s. 775.261(8).

(8) The failure of a career offender to submit to the taking of a digitized photograph, or to otherwise comply with the requirements of this section, is a felony of the third degree, punishable as provided in s. 775.082, s. 775.083, or s. 775.084.

(9) The department, the Department of Highway Safety and Motor Vehicles, the Department of Law Enforcement, personnel of those departments, and any individual or entity acting at the request or upon the direction of those departments are immune from civil liability for damages for good faith compliance with this section, and shall be presumed to have acted in good faith in compiling, recording, reporting, or providing information. The presumption of good faith is not overcome if technical or clerical errors are made by the department, the Department of Highway Safety and Motor Vehicles, the Department of Law Enforcement, personnel of those departments, or any individual or entity acting at the request or upon the direction of those departments in compiling, recording, reporting, or providing information, or, if the informa-

tion is incomplete or incorrect because the information has not been provided by a person or agency required to provide the information, or because the information was not reported or was falsely reported.

Added by Laws 2002, c. 2002–266, § 4, eff. July 1, 2002. Amended by Laws 2004, c. 2004–371, § 11, eff. July 1, 2004.

Historical and Statutory Notes

Amendment Notes:

Laws 2004, c. 2004–371, § 11, reenacted subsec. (7) of this section for the purpose of incorporating the amendments to §§ 775.21 and 943.607 in references thereto.

Cross References

Career offender registration act, see § 775.261.
Career offenders, registration and public notification, legislative intent, see § 775.26.

Library References

Criminal Law ⚷1222.1.
Westlaw Topic No. 110.
C.J.S. Criminal Law §§ 2401, 2406 to 2409.

944.609. Career offenders; notification upon release

(1) As used in this section, the term "career offender" means a person who is in the custody or control of, or under the supervision of, the department or is in the custody or control of, or under the supervision of a private correctional facility, who is designated as a habitual violent felony offender, a violent career criminal, or a three-time violent felony offender under s. 775.084 or as a prison releasee reoffender under s. 775.082(9).

(2) The Legislature finds that certain career offenders, by virtue of their histories of offenses, present a threat to the public and to communities. The Legislature finds that requiring these career offenders to register for the purpose of tracking the career offenders and providing for notifying the public and a community of the presence of a career offender are important aids to law enforcement agencies, the public, and communities if the career offender engages again in criminal conduct. Registration is intended to aid law enforcement agencies in timely apprehending a career offender. Registration is not a punishment, but merely a status. Notification to the public and communities of the presence of a career offender aids the public and communities in avoiding being victimized by the career offender. The Legislature intends to require the registration of career offenders and to authorize law enforcement agencies to notify the public and communities of the presence of a career offender.

(3)(a) The department must provide information regarding any career offender who is being released after serving a period of incarceration for any offense, as follows:

1. The department must provide the career offender's name, any change in the career offender's name by reason of marriage or other legal process, and any alias, if known; the correctional facility from which the career offender is released; the career offender's social security number, race, gender, date of birth, height, weight, and hair and eye color; date and county of sentence and

each crime for which the career offender was sentenced; a copy of the career offender's fingerprints and a digitized photograph taken within 60 days before release; the date of release of the career offender; and the career offender's intended residence address, if known. The department shall notify the Department of Law Enforcement if the career offender escapes, absconds, or dies. If the career offender is in the custody of a private correctional facility, the facility shall take the digitized photograph of the career offender within 60 days before the career offender's release and provide this photograph to the Department of Corrections and also place it in the career offender's file. If the career offender is in the custody of a local jail, the custodian of the local jail shall notify the Department of Law Enforcement of the career offender's release and provide to the Department of Law Enforcement the information specified in this paragraph and any information specified in subparagraph 2. which the Department of Law Enforcement requests.

2. The department may provide any other information deemed necessary, including criminal and corrections records and nonprivileged personnel and treatment records, when available.

(b) The department must provide the information described in subparagraph (a)1. to:

1. The sheriff of the county where the career offender was sentenced;

2. The sheriff of the county and, if applicable, the police chief of the municipality, where the career offender plans to reside;

3. The Department of Law Enforcement;

4. When requested, the victim of the offense, the victim's parent or legal guardian if the victim is a minor, the lawful representative of the victim or of the victim's parent or guardian if the victim is a minor, or the next of kin if the victim is a homicide victim; and

5. Any person who requests such information,

within 6 months prior to the anticipated release of a career offender or as soon as possible if a career offender is released earlier than anticipated. All such information provided to the Department of Law Enforcement must be available electronically as soon as the information is in the agency's database and must be in a format that is compatible with the requirements of the Florida Crime Information Center.

(c) Upon request, the department must provide the information described in subparagraph (a)2. to:

1. The sheriff of the county where the career offender was sentenced; and

2. The sheriff of the county and, if applicable, the police chief of the municipality, where the career offender plans to reside,

within 6 months prior to the anticipated release of a career offender or as soon as possible if a career offender is released earlier than anticipated.

(d) Upon receiving information regarding a career offender from the department, the Department of Law Enforcement, the sheriff, or the chief of police shall provide the information described in subparagraph (a)1. to any individual who requests such information and may release the information to the public in any manner deemed appropriate, unless the information is confidential or exempt from s. 119.07(1) and s. 24(a), Art. I of the State Constitution.

(4) The department or any law enforcement agency may notify the community and the public of a career offender's presence in the community. However, with respect to a career offender who has been found to be a sexual predator under s. 775.21, the Department of Law Enforcement or any other law enforcement agency must inform the community and the public of the career offender's presence in the community, as provided in s. 775.21.

(5) An elected or appointed official, public employee, school administrator or employee, or agency, or any individual or entity acting at the request or upon the direction of any law enforcement agency, is immune from civil liability for damages resulting from the good faith compliance with the requirements of this section or the release of information under this section.

Added by Laws 2002, c. 2002–266, § 5, eff. July 1, 2002. Amended by Laws 2004, c. 2004–371, § 15, eff. July 1, 2004.

Historical and Statutory Notes

Amendment Notes:

Laws 2004, c. 2004–371, § 15, reenacted subsec. (4) of this section for the purpose of incorporating the amendment to § 775.21 in a reference thereto.

Cross References

Career offender registration act, see § 775.261.
Career offenders, registration and public notification, legislative intent, see § 775.26.

Library References

Criminal Law ⚷1222.1.
Westlaw Topic No. 110.
C.J.S. Criminal Law §§ 2401, 2406 to 2409.

Research References

Treatises and Practice Aids

16 Florida Practice Series § 6:99, Direct and Collateral Consequences and Special Sanctions--Registration of Convicted Felons.

944.611. Legislative intent

The Legislature finds and declares that:

(1) It is desirable that each inmate be confined in and released from an institution or facility as close to the inmate's permanent residence or county of commitment as possible, in order to lessen the transportation expense to the public.

(2) It is the intent of the Legislature that:

(a) To the extent possible, an inmate be returned, upon release, to the same area from which the inmate was committed.

(b) An inmate being released from a community work-release program is not eligible for the provision of transportation.

(c) Transportation provided for an eligible inmate upon release shall be to one of the following points:

1. The county where parole placement has been approved and supervision is to commence.

2. Another state.

3. The county of employment within the state.

4. The county of legal residence within the state.

5. The county of original commitment within the state.

(d) Each releasee who is eligible for the provision of transportation shall be escorted to the site of embarkation by an officer of the correctional facility, who shall remain until the releasee has departed.

Laws 1983, c. 83–131, § 38. Amended by Laws 1997, c. 97–102, § 1658, eff. July 1, 1997.

Historical and Statutory Notes

Amendment Notes:

Laws 1997, c. 97–102, eff. July 1, 1997, removed gender-specific references applicable to human beings from volume 4 of the Florida Statutes without substantive changes in legal effect.

Library References

Prisons ⚷241.
Westlaw Topic No. 310.
C.J.S. Prisons and Rights of Prisoners § 153.

Research References

Encyclopedias

Transportation, FL Jur. 2d Prisons & Prisoners § 210.

944.612. Definitions for s. 944.613

As used in s. 944.613, the term:

(1) "Florida releasee" means:

(a) An inmate paroled before expiration of his or her sentence, who will be supervised at the location shown on his or her parole certificate.

(b) An inmate whose sentence has expired or who is released by means of gain-time.

(2) "Out-of-state releasee" means:

(a) An inmate being released on interstate compact pursuant to s. 949.07.

(b) An inmate whose sentence has expired and who intends to leave the state or is required to leave the state upon release.

Laws 1983, c. 83–131, § 39. Amended by Laws 1997, c. 97–102, § 1659, eff. July 1, 1997.

Historical and Statutory Notes

Amendment Notes:

Laws 1997, c. 97–102, eff. July 1, 1997, removed gender-specific references applicable to human beings from volume 4 of the Florida Statutes without substantive changes in legal effect.

Research References

Encyclopedias

Transportation, FL Jur. 2d Prisons & Prisoners § 210.

944.613. Methods of transportation

(1) Out-of-state releasee.—In instances when a releasee intends or is required to leave the state, transportation shall be provided by common carrier utilizing the most economical means. Transportation as authorized herein shall be furnished by nonnegotiable travel voucher payable to the common carrier being utilized, and in no event shall there be any cash disbursement to the releasee or any person, firm, or corporation. Such travel voucher shall not be valid for more than 5 days after its issuance. The source of any private transportation must be by a family member or friend whose purpose is to immediately transport the releasee out of this state.

(2) Florida releasee.—In instances when a releasee remains in this state but leaves the county where the correctional institution or facility of her or his confinement is located, transportation shall be provided by common carrier using the most economical means. Transportation as authorized herein shall be furnished by nonnegotiable travel voucher payable to the common carrier being utilized, and in no event shall there be any cash disbursement to the releasee or any person, firm, or corporation. Such travel voucher is to be utilized immediately by the releasee. The source of any private transportation must be a family member or friend whose purpose is to immediately transport the releasee to the approved location pursuant to section 1.[1]

Laws 1983, c. 83–131, § 40. Amended by Laws 1997, c. 97–102, § 1660, eff. July 1, 1997.

[1] Reviser's Note—1983: This cross-reference is erroneous; the intended reference may be s. 38, ch. 83–131, compiled as s. 944.611.

Historical and Statutory Notes

Amendment Notes:

Laws 1997, c. 97–102, eff. July 1, 1997, removed gender-specific references applicable to human beings from volume 4 of the Florida Statutes without substantive changes in legal effect.

Cross References

Release of county prisoners, duties of county commissioners, see § 951.04.

Library References

Prisons ⟹241.
Westlaw Topic No. 310.
C.J.S. Prisons and Rights of Prisoners § 153.

Research References

Encyclopedias

Transportation, FL Jur. 2d Prisons & Prisoners § 210.

Notes of Decisions

Transportation 1

---

1. Transportation

A prisoner who was in custody of a sheriff pending the disposition of a re-trial or his motion to vacate his sentence would have been, even though not actually incarcerated in a state prison, be entitled to discharge clothing, a release gratuity, and/or transportation from the Division of Corrections if he was acquitted and released, assuming, of course, he did not remain in prison to serve out any other uncompleted prison sentences. Op.Atty.Gen., 063–57, June 6, 1963.

944.70. Conditions for release from incarceration

(1)(a) A person who is convicted of a crime committed on or after October 1, 1983, but before January 1, 1994, may be released from incarceration only:

1. Upon expiration of the person's sentence;

2. Upon expiration of the person's sentence as reduced by accumulated gain-time;

3. As directed by an executive order granting clemency;

4. Upon attaining the provisional release date;

5. Upon placement in a conditional release program pursuant to s. 947.1405; or

6. Upon the granting of control release pursuant to s. 947.146.

(b) A person who is convicted of a crime committed on or after January 1, 1994, may be released from incarceration only:

1. Upon expiration of the person's sentence;

2. Upon expiration of the person's sentence as reduced by accumulated meritorious or incentive gain-time;

3. As directed by an executive order granting clemency;

4. Upon placement in a conditional release program pursuant to s. 947.1405 or a conditional medical release program pursuant to s. 947.149; or

5. Upon the granting of control release, including emergency control release, pursuant to s. 947.146.

(2) A person who is convicted of a crime committed on or after December 1, 1990, and who receives a control release date may not refuse to accept the terms or conditions of control release.

Added by Laws 1998, c. 98–204, § 16, eff. Oct. 1, 1998.

Library References

Pardon and Parole ⚷21, 41.
Prisons ⚷241, 248.
Westlaw Topic Nos. 284, 310.
C.J.S. Pardon and Parole §§ 1 to 2, 5, 42.
C.J.S. Prisons and Rights of Prisoners §§ 152 to 153.

Research References

Encyclopedias

Generally; Release on Gain-Time Allowances, FL Jur. 2d Prisons & Prisoners § 211.

944.701. Short title

Sections 944.701–944.708 may be cited as the "Transition Assistance Program Act."

Laws 1987, c. 87–298, § 4.

Historical and Statutory Notes

Amendment Notes:

Laws 1987, c. 87–298, § 12, provided for the repeal of §§ 944.701 to 944.708 on Oct. 1, 1990, and review by the legislature prior to that date. Laws 1988, c. 88–122, § 13, eff. July 1, 1988, repealed § 12 of Laws 1987, c. 87–298.

Research References

Encyclopedias

Transition Assistance Program Act; Release Orientation Program, FL Jur. 2d Prisons & Prisoners § 171.

944.702. Legislative intent

It is the intent of the Legislature to provide persons released from incarceration from the Department of Corrections with certain fundamental resources in the areas of employment, life skills training, job placement, and access to as many support services as possible in order to appreciably increase the likelihood of the inmate's successful reentry into free society. The Legislature intends that these support services include faith- based service groups on an equal basis with other private organizations.

Laws 1987, c. 87–298, § 5; Laws 1992, c. 92–310, § 6. Amended by Laws 2001, c. 2001–110, § 6, eff. July 1, 2001.

Historical and Statutory Notes

Amendment Notes:

Laws 1992, c. 92–310, § 6, eff. July 6, 1992, preceding "access" deleted "temporary housing, including".

Laws 2001, c. 2001–110, § 6, added the last sentence relating to faith-based service groups.

944.703. Eligible inmates

Sections 944.701–944.708 apply to all inmates released from the custody of the department. However, priority should be given to substance-addicted inmates to help break the cycle of drug abuse, prostitution, and other self-injurious criminal behavior that causes harm to families and communities. Those inmates with a detainer are eligible if the department determines that cancellation of the detainer is likely or that the incarceration for which the detainer was issued will be of short duration. The department shall confirm the detainer with the originating authority prior to release.

Laws 1987, c. 87–298, § 6; Laws 1992, c. 92–310, § 7; Laws 1995, c. 95–283, § 21. Amended by Laws 2001, c. 2001–110, § 7, eff. July 1, 2001.

Historical and Statutory Notes

Amendment Notes:

Laws 1992, c. 92–310, § 7, eff. July 6, 1992, in the first sentence, preceding "apply" deleted "shall"; in the second sentence, substituted "are" for "shall be"; and, in the third sentence, substituted "prior to release" for "as soon as the inmate's prerelease orientation assignment date is identified".

Laws 1995, c. 95–283, § 21, eff. June 15, 1995, in the first sentence, following "department" deleted "except those released from a work release program or to another state".

Laws 2001, c. 2001–110, § 7, inserted "However, priority should be given to substance-addicted inmates to help break the cycle of drug abuse, prostitution, and other self- injurious criminal behavior that causes harm to families and communities."

Library References

Prisons ⚷241.
Westlaw Topic No. 310.
C.J.S. Prisons and Rights of Prisoners § 153.

944.7031. Eligible inmates released from private correctional facilities

(1) It is the intent of the Legislature that state inmates nearing release from a private correctional facility managed under chapter 957 are eligible for assistance under ss. 944.701–944.708, and all laws that provide for or mandate transition assistance services to inmates nearing release also apply to inmates who reside in private correctional facilities.

(2) To assist an inmate nearing release from a private correctional facility, the department and the transition assistance specialist shall coordinate with a designated staff person at each private correctional facility to ensure that a state inmate released from the private correctional facility is informed of and provided with the same level of transition assistance services that are provided by the department for an inmate in a state correctional facility. Any inmate released from a private correctional facility shall also have equal access to placement consideration in a contracted substance abuse transition housing program, including those programs that have a faith-based component.

Added by Laws 2001, c. 2001–110, § 8, eff. July 1, 2001.

944.704. Staff who provide transition assistance; duties

The department shall provide a transition assistance specialist at each of the major institutions whose duties include, but are not limited to:

(1) Coordinating delivery of transition assistance program services at the institution and at the community correctional centers authorized pursuant to s. 945.091(1)(b).

(2) Assisting in the development of each inmate's postrelease plan.

(3) Obtaining job placement information.

(4) Providing a written medical discharge plan and referral to a county health department.

(5) For an inmate who is known to be HIV positive, providing a 30–day supply of all HIV/AIDS–related medication that the inmate is taking prior to release, if required under protocols of the Department of Corrections and

treatment guidelines of the United States Department of Health and Human Services.

(6) Facilitating placement in a private transition housing program, if requested by any eligible inmate. If an inmate who is nearing his or her date of release requests placement in a contracted substance abuse transition housing program, the transition assistance specialist shall inform the inmate of program availability and assess the inmate's need and suitability for transition housing assistance. If an inmate is approved for placement, the specialist shall assist the inmate and coordinate the release of the inmate with the selected program. If an inmate requests and is approved for placement in a contracted faith-based substance abuse transition housing program, the specialist must consult with the chaplain prior to such placement. In selecting inmates who are nearing their date of release for placement in a faith-based program, the department shall ensure that an inmate's faith orientation, or lack thereof, will not be considered in determining admission to the program and that the program does not attempt to convert an inmate toward a particular faith or religious preference.

(7) Providing a photo identification card to all inmates prior to their release.

The transition assistance specialist may not be a correctional officer or correctional probation officer as defined in s. 943.10.

Laws 1987, c. 87–298, § 7; Laws 1989, c. 89–526, § 30; Laws 1991, c. 91–281, § 4; Laws 1992, c. 92–310, § 8; Laws 1995, c. 95–283, § 22. Amended by Laws 2001, c. 2001–110, § 9, eff. July 1, 2001; Laws 2002, c. 2002–292, § 5, eff. July 1, 2002.

Historical and Statutory Notes

Amendment Notes:

Laws 1989, c. 89–526, § 30, eff. Oct. 1, 1989, rewrote subsec. (1), which formerly read:

"Coordinating inmate vocational assignment within the institution.";

inserted subsec. (5), relating to photo identification cards; and renumbered former subsec. (5) as subsec. (6).

Laws 1991, c. 91–281, § 4, eff. July 1, 1991, in subsec. (6), corrected the citation.

Laws 1992, c. 92–310, § 8, eff. July 6, 1992, rewrote the section, which formerly read:

"The department shall provide transition assistance coordinators at major institutions. Their duties shall include, but not be limited to:

"(1) Coordinating, in conjunction with the institution education program manager, inmate vocational assignment within the institution with the comprehensive plan for correctional education of the Correctional Education School Authority.

"(2) Coordinating delivery of transition assistance program services at the institution.

"(3) Assisting in the development of each inmate's postrelease employment plan.

"(4) Obtaining job placement information for transmittal to the Department of Labor and Employment Security.

"(5) Providing a photo identification card to all program participants prior to their release.

"(6) Performing any other duties consistent with s. 242.68(2)(g)20., relating to the Board of Correctional Education."

Laws 1995, c. 95–283, § 22, eff. June 15, 1995, in the introductory paragraph, substituted "provide a transition assistance officer" for "designate staff"; and in subsec. (1), substituted "transition" for "release".

Laws 2001, c. 2001–110, § 9, rewrote this section, which formerly read:

"The department shall provide a transition assistance officer at major institutions whose duties include, but are not limited to:

"(1) Coordinating delivery of transition assistance program services at the institution.

"(2) Assisting in the development of each inmate's postrelease plan.

"(3) Obtaining job placement information for transmittal to the Department of Labor and Employment Security.

"(4) Providing a photo identification card to all inmates prior to their release."

Laws 2002, c. 2002–292, § 5, added subsec. (4), relating to written medical–discharge plans and referrals; added subsec. (5), relating to a supply of medication to be given to inmates prior to release; and redesignated former subsecs. (4) and (5) as subsecs. (6) and (7).

Library References

Prisons ⚿241.
Westlaw Topic No. 310.
C.J.S. Prisons and Rights of Prisoners § 153.

944.705. Release orientation program

(1) The department shall provide participation in a standardized release orientation program to every eligible inmate.

(2) The release orientation program instruction must include, but is not limited to:

(a) Employment skills.

(b) Money management skills.

(c) Personal development and planning.

(d) Special needs.

(e) Community reentry concerns.

(f) Community reentry support.

(g) Any other appropriate instruction to ensure the inmate's successful reentry into the community.

(3) Any inmate who claims to be a victim of domestic violence as defined in s. 741.28 shall receive, as part of the release orientation program, referral to the nearest domestic violence center certified under chapter 39.

(4) The department shall conduct a needs assessment of every inmate to determine which, if any, basic support services the inmate needs after release.

(5) The department may contract with public or private entities, including faith-based service groups, for the provision of all or part of the services pursuant to this section.

(6)(a) The department shall notify every inmate, in no less than 18–point type in the inmate's release documents, that the inmate may be sentenced pursuant to s. 775.082(9) if the inmate commits any felony offense described in s. 775.082(9) within 3 years after the inmate's release. This notice must be prefaced by the word "WARNING" in boldfaced type.

(b) Nothing in this section precludes the sentencing of a person pursuant to s. 775.082(9), nor shall evidence that the department failed to provide this notice prohibit a person from being sentenced pursuant to s. 775.082(9). The state shall not be required to demonstrate that a person received any notice from the department in order for the court to impose a sentence pursuant to s. 775.082(9).

Laws 1987, c. 87–298, § 8; Laws 1988, c. 88–122, § 12; Laws 1989, c. 89–526, § 31; Laws 1991, c. 91–210, § 9; Laws 1992, c. 92–310, § 9; Laws 1994, c. 94–134, § 26;

Laws 1994, c. 94–135, § 26. Amended by Laws 1997, c. 97–239, § 3, eff. May 30, 1997; Laws 1998, c. 98–204, § 17, eff. Oct. 1, 1998; Laws 1998, c. 98–403, § 164, eff. Oct. 1, 1998; Laws 2001, c. 2001–110, § 10, eff. July 1, 2001.

Historical and Statutory Notes

Amendment Notes:

Laws 1988, c. 88–122, § 12, rewrote the section.

Laws 1989, c. 89–526, § 31, eff. Oct. 1, 1989, in subsec. (2), rewrote the introductory paragraph, which formerly read:

"The release orientation program shall consist of not fewer than 40 hours of prerelease or postrelease instruction that must include, but is not limited to:",

inserted par. (c), requiring instruction on personal development and planning, and redesignated former pars. (c) through (f) as pars. (d) through (g); and in subsec. (6), substituted "40 hours" for "120 hours", and inserted a reference to § 944.277.

Laws 1991, c. 91–210, § 9, eff. Jan. 1, 1992, in subsec. (3) substituted "domestic violence as defined in s. 741.30" for "spouse abuse".

Laws 1992, c. 92–310, § 9, eff. July 6, 1992, in subsec. (2), in the introductory paragraph, following "program" deleted "shall consist of both prerelease and postrelease"; following "instruction" deleted ", of which not fewer than 40 hours shall be completed prior to release. This instruction"; and deleted former subsec. (6).

Laws 1994, c. 94–134, § 26, eff. July 1, 1994, in subsec. (3), substituted "741.28" for "741.30".

Laws 1994, c. 94–135, § 26, eff. July 1, 1994, made the same change as Laws 1994, c. 94–134.

Laws 1994, c. 94–134, § 36, and Laws 1994, c. 94–135, § 36, provide:

"This act shall take effect July 1, 1994, and shall apply to offenses committed on or after that date."

Laws 1997, c. 97–239, § 3, eff. May 30, 1997, added subsec. (6).

Laws 1998, c. 98–204, § 17, in subsec. (6), corrected citations.

Laws 1998, c. 98–403, § 164, in subsec. (3), substituted "chapter 39" for "ss. 415.601-415.608".

Laws 2001, c. 2001–110, § 10, reenacted subsecs. (1) and (2) and, in subsec. (5), inserted ", including faith-based service groups," following "entities" and made a nonsubstantive change.

Library References

Prisons ⚿241.
Westlaw Topic No. 310.
C.J.S. Prisons and Rights of Prisoners § 153.

Research References

Encyclopedias

Transition Assistance Program Act; Release Orientation Program, FL Jur. 2d Prisons & Prisoners § 171.

Notes of Decisions

1. Validity

Prison Releasee Reoffender Punishment Act did not violate defendant's equal protection rights or due process rights on ground that he was not given notice that Act would apply to him when he was released from prison; Act had not yet been enacted when inmate was released. Nelson v. State, App. 2 Dist., 761 So.2d 452 (2000). Constitutional Law ⚿ 3808; Constitutional Law ⚿ 4729; Sentencing And Punishment ⚿ 1210

2. Construction and application

The Prison Releasee Reoffender Punishment Act is not limited to inmates released after its effective date; rather, it also applies to inmates released prior to the effective date. Grant v. State, 770 So.2d 655 (2000). Sentencing And Punishment ⚿ 1216

944.706. Basic release assistance

(1) Any inmate who is being released is eligible for transition assistance. Those inmates released to a detainer are eligible pursuant to s. 944.703.

(2) The department may contract with the Department of Children and Family Services, the Salvation Army, and other public or private organizations, including faith-based service groups, for the provision of basic support services for releasees.

(3) The department shall adopt rules for the development, implementation, and termination of transition assistance.

Laws 1983, c. 83–131, § 41; Laws 1985, c. 85–340, § 9; Fla.St.1985, § 944.601; Laws 1987, c. 87–298, § 9; Laws 1992, c. 92–310, § 10; Laws 1995, c. 95–283, § 23. Amended by Laws 1999, c. 99–8, § 312, eff. June 29, 1999; Laws 2001, c. 2001–110, § 11, eff. July 1, 2001.

Historical and Statutory Notes

Amendment Notes:

Laws 1985, c. 85–340, § 9, eff. June 24, 1985, rewrote subsec. (1), and substituted "thirty" for "ten" days in the first sentence of subsec. (3).

Laws 1987, c. 87–298, § 9, eff. Jan. 1, 1988, renumbered § 944.601 as this section and rewrote the provisions therein.

Laws 1992, c. 92–310, § 10, eff. July 6, 1992, rewrote the section, which formerly read:

"(1) Any inmate who is being released shall be eligible for a release assistance stipend and contract release, except when being released from a work-release program or to another state. Those inmates released to a detainer shall be eligible pursuant to s. 944.703. Selected inmates on work release who experience severe hardships may be considered for a release assistance stipend and contract release. Each contract release plan must meet departmental approval.

"(2) The department is authorized to contract with the Department of Health and Rehabilitative Services, the Salvation Army, and other public or private organizations for the provision of basic support services for releasees. The department shall contract with the Department of Labor and Employment Security for the provision of releasee job placement and disbursal of release assistance stipends.

"(3) The department shall advance the release date of a nonparole contract releasee by up to 30 days and shall forward to the Department of Labor and Employment Security a release assistance stipend of up to $200 for the purpose of motivating the releasee to participate in prerelease orientation, secure permanent employment, and secure permanent residence. The Department of Labor and Employment Security shall distribute the release assistance stipend to the releasee in accordance with the provisions of law and of the release contract. Violation of the terms of the contract may constitute grounds for the forfeiture of the release assistance stipend and the termination of the contract.

"(4) For those releasees who demonstrate that job placement is not needed, the department may forward the releasee's release assistance stipend directly to a basic support service provider. If it has been determined that the releasee does not need basic support services, the department may disburse the release assistance stipend directly to the releasee.

"(5) The department shall promulgate rules for the development, implementation, and termination of release contracts."

Laws 1995, c. 95–283, § 23, eff. June 15, 1995, rewrote the section, which formerly read:

"(1) Any inmate who is being released is eligible for release assistance, except when being released from a work-release program or to another state. Those inmates released to a detainer are eligible pursuant to s. 944.703. Selected inmates on work release who experience severe hardships may be considered for release assistance.

"(2) The department is authorized to contract with the Department of Health and Rehabilitative Services, the Salvation Army, and other public or private organizations for the provision of basic support services for releasees. The department shall contract with the Department of Labor and Employment Security for the provision of releasee job placement.

"(3) The department shall promulgate rules for the development, implementation, and termination of release assistance."

Laws 1999, c. 99–8, § 312, eff. June 29, 1999, substituted "Department of Children and Family Services" for "Department of Health and Rehabilitative Services".

Laws 2001, c. 2001–110, § 11, rewrote this section, which formerly read:

"(1) Any inmate who is being released is eligible for transition assistance. Those inmates released to a detainer are eligible pursuant to s. 944.703.

"(2) The department is authorized to contract with the Department of Children and Family Services, the Salvation Army, and other public or private organizations for the provision of basic support services for releasees. The department shall contract with the Department of Labor and Employment Security for the provision of releasee job placement.

"(3) The department shall promulgate rules for the development, implementation, and termination of transition assistance."

Cross References

Release of county prisoners, duties of county commissioners, see § 951.04.

Library References

Prisons ⚷241.
Westlaw Topic No. 310.
C.J.S. Prisons and Rights of Prisoners § 153.

Notes of Decisions

Clothing and gratuity 1

1. Clothing and gratuity

A prisoner who had been remanded to the custody of the sheriff so that he could be present at a hearing regarding his motion to vacate his sentence was not entitled to a discharge gratuity or clothing from the division of corrections. Op.Atty.Gen., 063–57, June 6, 1963.

When a prisoner was remanded to the custody of the sheriff by a court order which set aside his judgment and sentence and provided for a retrial, the division of corrections was under no duty to pay the prisoner a discharge gratuity and provide him with a suit of clothing. Op. Atty.Gen., 063–57, June 6, 1963.

944.7065. Transition course for inmates

In an effort to ensure that inmates released from the Department of Corrections successfully reenter the community, beginning December 1, 2002, each inmate released from incarceration by the department must complete a 100–hour comprehensive transition course that covers job readiness and life management skills. This requirement does not apply to inmates released in an emergency situation.

Added by Laws 2001, c. 2001–110, § 20, eff. July 1, 2001.

Library References

Prisons ⚷241.
Westlaw Topic No. 310.
C.J.S. Prisons and Rights of Prisoners § 153.

944.707. Postrelease special services; job placement services

(1) The department shall generate and provide to every releasee, identified by the prerelease needs assessment, support services such as, but not limited to, substance abuse counseling, family counseling, and employment support programs. The department may select and contract with public or private organizations, including faith-based service groups, for the provision of these basic support services. When selecting a provider, the department shall consider faith-based service groups on an equal basis with other private organizations. Provider selection criteria include, but are not limited to:

(a) The depth and scope of services provided.

(b) The geographic area to be served.

(c) The number of inmates to be served and the cost of services per inmate.

(d) The individual provider's record of success in the provision of inmate services.

(2) The department, with the assistance of the State Office on Homelessness, shall maintain and regularly update a comprehensive directory of support services offered by private organizations and faith-based service groups for the purpose of assisting transition assistance specialists and chaplains in making individualized placements and referrals.

Laws 1987, c. 87–298, § 10; Laws 1989, c. 89–526, § 32; Laws 1992, c. 92–310, § 11; Laws 1995, c. 95–283, § 24. Amended by Laws 2001, c. 2001–110, § 12, eff. July 1, 2001.

Historical and Statutory Notes

Amendment Notes:

Laws 1989, c. 89–526, § 32, eff. Oct. 1, 1989, in subsecs. (3)(a) and (4)(b), substituted "release orientation" for "pre-release orientation".

Laws 1992, c. 92–310, § 11, eff. July 6, 1992, rewrote the section, which formerly read:

"(1) The department shall attempt to generate and provide to every eligible releasee, identified by the prerelease needs assessment, support services such as, but not limited to, substance abuse counseling, family counseling, and employment support programs. The department is authorized to select and contract with public or private organizations for the provision of these basic support services. Provider selection criteria shall include, but not be limited to:

"(a) The depth and scope of services provided.

"(b) The geographic area to be served.

"(c) The number of inmates to be served and the cost of services per inmate.

"(d) The individual provider's record of success in the provision of inmate services.

"(2) The department shall provide up to 15 days' temporary housing to those releasees indicating need. The department is authorized to contract with the Salvation Army and any other public or private organization for the provision of temporary housing. In cases where the releasee demonstrates that undue hardship would result because of the unavailability of contract housing or because of family needs, the department may disburse temporary housing funds directly to the releasee in an amount not to exceed the equivalent of 15 days at a contract provider's facility.

"(3) The department shall forward the following items to the Department of Labor and Employment Security job service office located nearest to the inmate's intended residence.

"(a) The job placement information obtained at release orientation.

"(b) The inmate's basic release assistance stipend.

"(c) Referral information for the needed basic support service providers.

"(4)(a) The Department of Labor and Employment Security shall distribute the information required in subsection (3) to each eligible releasee. The basic release assistance stipend shall be given to the releasee in three portions. One portion shall be given upon the releasee initially reporting to the Department of Labor and Employment Security job service office. A second portion shall be given upon the releasee reporting to the Department of Labor and Employment Security job service office for subsequent interview, if required. The remaining portion shall be disbursed to the releasee after obtaining employment, or after diligent efforts to become employed, and participation in the counseling portions of basic support services, if provided.

"(b) The Department of Labor and Employment Security shall assign job service staff exclusively dedicated to releasee services at those offices identified by the Department of Corrections as having a high number of releasee contacts. Those offices having a fewer number of releasee contacts shall have designated staff assigned to assist releasees. The Department of Labor and Employment Security shall provide appropriate training for staff assigned to assist releasees. Staff assigned to assist releasees shall use job placement information obtained at each releasee's release orientation to attempt to secure suitable employment for the releasee prior to the releasee's arrival. Staff assigned to assist releasees shall act to maximize releasee placement opportunities in the job service office service area.

"(c) The Department of Labor and Employment Security shall provide to the Department of Corrections data relating to inmate placement, tracking, and market needs."

Laws 1995, c. 95–283, § 24, eff. June 15, 1995, in the first sentence of subsec. (1), preceding "releasee" deleted "eligible"; and in subsec. (2), substituted "The following items shall be provided" for "The department shall forward the following items".

Laws 2001, c. 2001–110, § 12, rewrote this section, which formerly read:

"(1) The department shall attempt to generate and provide to every releasee, identified by the prerelease needs assessment, support services such as, but not limited to, substance abuse counseling, family counseling, and employment support programs. The department is authorized to select and contract with public or private organizations for the provision of these basic support services. Provider selection criteria include, but are not limited to:

"(a) The depth and scope of services provided.

"(b) The geographic area to be served.

"(c) The number of inmates to be served and the cost of services per inmate.

"(d) The individual provider's record of success in the provision of inmate services.

"(2) The following items shall be provided to the Department of Labor and Employment Security job service office located nearest to the inmate's intended residence:

"(a) The job placement information obtained at release orientation.

"(b) Referral information for the needed basic support service providers.

"(3)(a) The Department of Labor and Employment Security shall assign job service staff exclusively dedicated to releasee services at those offices identified by the Department of Corrections as having a high number of releasee contacts. Those offices having a fewer number of releasee contacts shall have designated staff assigned to assist releasees. The Department of Labor and Employment Security shall provide appropriate training for staff assigned to assist releasees. Staff assigned to assist releasees shall use job placement information obtained at each releasee's release orientation to attempt to secure suitable employment for the releasee prior to the releasee's arrival. Staff assigned to assist releasees shall act to maximize releasee placement opportunities in the job service office service area.

"(b) The Department of Labor and Employment Security shall provide to the Department of Corrections data relating to inmate placement, tracking, and market needs."

Library References

Prisons ⚿241.
Westlaw Topic No. 310.
C.J.S. Prisons and Rights of Prisoners § 153.

Research References

Encyclopedias

Transition Assistance Program Act; Release Orientation Program, FL Jur. 2d Prisons & Prisoners § 171.

944.708. Rules

The Department of Corrections and the Department of Labor and Employment Security[1] shall promulgate rules to implement the provisions of ss. 944.701–944.707.

Laws 1987, c. 87–298, § 11.

[1] Laws 2002, c. 2002–194, § 69, repealed § 20.171, which created the Department of Labor and Employment Security.

Library References

Prisons ⚿241.
Westlaw Topic No. 310.
C.J.S. Prisons and Rights of Prisoners § 153.

Research References

Encyclopedias

Transition Assistance Program Act; Release Orientation Program, FL Jur. 2d Prisons & Prisoners § 171.

944.710. Definitions of terms relating to private operation of state correctional facilities and s. 944.105

As used with respect to private operation of state correctional facilities and s. 944.105, the term:

(1) "Bidder" means any individual, partnership, corporation, or unincorporated association that submits a proposal with the department to construct, lease, or operate a private correctional facility.

(2) "Department" means the Department of Corrections.

(3) "Private correctional facility" means any facility, which is not operated by the department, for the incarceration of adults or juveniles who have been sentenced by a court and committed to the custody of the department.

(4) "Private correctional officer" means any full-time or part-time employee of a private vendor whose primary responsibility is the supervision, protection, care, and control of prisoners within a private correctional facility.

(5) "Private vendor" means any individual, partnership, corporation, or unincorporated association bound by contract with the department to construct, lease, or operate a private correctional facility.

Laws 1989, c. 89–526, § 13.

Cross References

Inmate medical services, see § 945.6041.

Research References

Encyclopedias

Generally; Contracts With Private Vendors, FL Jur. 2d Prisons & Prisoners § 24.

Contract Requirements, FL Jur. 2d Prisons & Prisoners § 30.

Treatises and Practice Aids

16 Florida Practice Series § 6:56, Enhancement of Penalty and Reclassification of Offense--Reclassifications of Various Types of Batteries and Assaults--Battery of Facility Employee by Throwing, Tossing, or Expelling Certain...

944.711. Requests for proposals

The department shall develop a request for proposals to construct or construct and operate a single-cell prototype institution or any facility of the department specified in s. 945.025. Competitive proposals shall be solicited by the department pursuant to chapter 287.

Laws 1989, c. 89–526, § 14.

Library References

Prisons ⚷101.
States ⚷98.
Westlaw Topic Nos. 310, 360.
C.J.S. Prisons and Rights of Prisoners §§ 1 to 2.
C.J.S. States §§ 270, 280 to 288.

944.712. Bidder and private vendor qualifications

Any private vendor selected by the department must have the qualifications and operations and management experience to carry out the terms of the contract. In submitting a proposal, the bidder must demonstrate financial ability to fulfill the requirements of the contract and must submit an independently audited financial statement for the previous 5 years. If the contract includes construction and if the state is required to make payments for construction prior to the completion of construction, the contract shall contain a construction performance bond approved by the secretary of the Department of Corrections as adequate and appropriate for the construction portion of the contract.

Laws 1989, c. 89–526, § 15.

Library References

Prisons ⚷101.
States ⚷98.
Westlaw Topic Nos. 310, 360.
C.J.S. Prisons and Rights of Prisoners §§ 1 to 2.
C.J.S. States §§ 270, 280 to 288.

Research References

Encyclopedias

Generally; Contracts With Private Vendors, FL Jur. 2d Prisons & Prisoners § 24.

944.713. Insurance against liability

(1) A bidder must provide an adequate plan of insurance against liability, including liability for violations of an inmate's civil rights by an insurance agency licensed in this state, pursuant to chapter 287. The insurance plan shall, at a minimum, protect the department from actions of a third party, assure the private vendor's ability to fulfill the conditions of the contract, and provide adequate protection for the department against claims arising as a result of any occurrence during the term of the contract on an occurrence basis. The adequacy of the insurance plan shall be determined, at the bidder's expense, by an independent risk management or actuarial firm selected by the Department of Management Services. The risk management or actuarial firm selected must have demonstrated experience in assessing public liability of state government.

(2) The contract shall provide for indemnification of the state by the private vendor for any liabilities incurred up to the limits provided under s. 768.28(5). The contract shall provide that the private vendor, or the insurer of the private vendor, is liable to pay any claim or judgment for any one person which does not exceed the sum of $100,000 or any claim or judgment, or portions thereof, which, when totaled with all other claims or judgments arising out of the same incident or occurrence, does not exceed the sum of $200,000. In addition, the contractor must agree to defend, hold harmless, and indemnify the department against any and all actions, claims, damages and losses, including costs and attorney's fees.

Laws 1989, c. 89–526, § 16; Laws 1992, c. 92–279, § 316.

Historical and Statutory Notes

Amendment Notes:

Laws 1992, c. 92–279, § 316, eff. July 1, 1992, in subsec. (1), substituted "Department of Management Services" for "Department of General Services".

Laws 1992, c. 92–326, § 55, amended § 339 of Laws 1992, c. 92–279, by changing the general effective date of the act from Jan. 1, 1993, to July 1, 1992 (§§ 322 to 325 and 339 took effect upon the act becoming a law).

Library References

Prisons ⚷101.
States ⚷98.
Westlaw Topic Nos. 310, 360.

C.J.S. Prisons and Rights of Prisoners §§ 1 to 2.
C.J.S. States §§ 270, 280 to 288.

Research References

Encyclopedias

Generally; Contracts With Private Vendors, FL Jur. 2d Prisons & Prisoners § 24.

944.714. Quality assurance and standards of operation

(1) The level and quality of programs provided by a private vendor at a private correctional facility must be at least equal to programs provided at a correctional facility operated by the department that houses similar types of inmates and must be at a cost that provides the state with a substantial savings, as determined by a private accounting firm selected by the Department of Corrections.

(2) All private correctional officers employed by a private vendor must be certified, at the private vendor's expense, as having met the minimum qualifications established for correctional officers under s. 943.13.

(3) Pursuant to the terms of the contract, a private vendor shall design, construct, and operate a private correctional facility in accordance with the standards established by the American Correctional Association and approved by the department at the time of the contract. In addition, a private correctional facility shall meet any higher standard mandated in the full or partial settlement of any litigation challenging the constitutional conditions of confinement to which the department is a named defendant. The standards required under a contract for operating a private correctional facility may be higher than the standards required for accreditation by the American Correctional Association. A private vendor shall comply with all federal and state constitutional requirements, federal, state, and local laws, department rules, and all court orders.

Laws 1989, c. 89–526, § 17.

Library References

Prisons ⚷236.
Westlaw Topic No. 310.

C.J.S. Prisons and Rights of Prisoners §§ 1 to 2, 18, 128 to 134.

Research References

Encyclopedias

Quality Assurance and Standards of Operation, FL Jur. 2d Prisons & Prisoners § 25.

Employees of Private Correctional Facilities, FL Jur. 2d Prisons & Prisoners § 44.

944.715. Delegation of authority

(1) A private vendor shall incarcerate all inmates assigned to the private correctional facility by the department and as specified in the contract. The department may not exceed the maximum occupancy designated for the facility in the contract.

(2) Inmates incarcerated in a private correctional facility are in the legal custody of the department. A private vendor may not award gain-time or release credits, determine inmate eligibility for furlough or work release, calculate inmate release dates, approve inmate transfers, place inmates in less restrictive custody than that ordered by the department or approve inmate work assignments. A private vendor may not benefit financially from the labor of inmates except to the extent authorized under chapter 946.

Laws 1989, c. 89–526, § 18.

Library References

Prisons ⚷170 to 183, 236, 243.
Westlaw Topic No. 310.
C.J.S. Convicts §§ 16 to 24.
C.J.S. Prisons and Rights of Prisoners §§ 1 to 2, 18, 128 to 134, 142 to 144, 147 to 151.

Research References

Encyclopedias

Prisoners in Private Correctional Facilities, Generally, FL Jur. 2d Prisons & Prisoners § 91.

Inmates in Private Correctional Facilities, FL Jur. 2d Prisons & Prisoners § 146.

Generally; Leaving Place of Confinement for Work or Voluntary Service at Public or Nonprofit Agency or Faith-Based Service Group, FL Jur. 2d Prisons & Prisoners § 175.

Prisoners in Private Correctional Facilities, FL Jur. 2d Prisons & Prisoners § 200.

944.716. Contract termination and control of a correctional facility by the department

A detailed plan shall be provided by a private vendor under which the department shall assume control of a private correctional facility upon termination of the contract. The department may terminate the contract with cause after written notice of material deficiencies and after 60 workdays in order to correct the material deficiencies. If any event occurs that involves the noncompliance with or violation of contract terms and that presents a serious threat to the safety, health, or security of the inmates, employees, or the public, the department may temporarily assume control of the private correctional facility. A plan shall also be provided by a private vendor for the purchase and assumption of operations of a correctional facility by the department in the event of bankruptcy or the financial insolvency of the private vendor. The private vendor shall provide an emergency plan to address inmate disturbances, employee work stoppages, strikes, or other serious events in accordance with standards of the American Correctional Association.

Laws 1989, c. 89–526, § 19.

Library References

Prisons ⚷236.
Westlaw Topic No. 310.
C.J.S. Prisons and Rights of Prisoners §§ 1 to 2, 18, 128 to 134.

Research References

Encyclopedias

Quality Assurance and Standards of Operation, FL Jur. 2d Prisons & Prisoners § 25.

Termination of Contract or Assumption of Control of Facility by Department of Corrections, FL Jur. 2d Prisons & Prisoners § 27.

944.717. Conflicts of interest

(1) An employee of the department or any governmental entity that exercises any functions or responsibilities in the review or approval of a private correctional facility contract or the operation of a private correctional facility, or a member of the immediate family of any such person, may not solicit or accept, directly or indirectly, any personal benefit or promise of a benefit from a bidder or private vendor.

(2) A private vendor may not have any interest at the time of entering into a contract with the department, or acquire any interest at a later time, that would directly or indirectly conflict in any manner or degree with the performance of the contract. A private vendor may not, in the performance of the contract, employ any person who has any known interests which conflict with the performance of the contract.

Laws 1989, c. 89–526, § 20.

Library References

Prisons ⚷391.
States ⚷95.
Westlaw Topic Nos. 310, 360.
C.J.S. Prisons and Rights of Prisoners §§ 12 to 15, 17, 22.
C.J.S. States § 276.

Research References

Encyclopedias

Conflicts of Interest, FL Jur. 2d Prisons & Prisoners § 26.

944.718. Withdrawal of request for proposals

(1) When soliciting proposals for the construction, lease, or operation of a private correctional facility, the department may reserve the right to withdraw the request for proposals at any time and for any reason. Receipt of proposal materials by the department or submission of a proposal to the department does not confer any rights upon the proposer or obligations upon the department.

(2) The department may not award a contract to a private vendor unless the department receives a proposal from a vendor that meets or exceeds the requirements of ss. 944.710–944.719.

Laws 1989, c. 89–526, § 21.

Library References

Prisons ⚷101, 236.
States ⚷98.
Westlaw Topic Nos. 310, 360.
C.J.S. Prisons and Rights of Prisoners §§ 1 to 2, 18, 128 to 134.
C.J.S. States §§ 270, 280 to 288.

Research References

Encyclopedias

Generally; Contracts With Private Vendors, FL Jur. 2d Prisons & Prisoners § 24.

944.719. Adoption of rules, monitoring, and reporting

(1) The department shall adopt rules pursuant to chapter 120 specifying criteria for contractual arrangements and standards for the operation of correctional facilities by private vendors. Such rules shall define:

(a) Various categories of private correctional facilities.

(b) Physical facility requirements.

(c) Critical staffing levels.

(d) Minimum program offerings.

(e) Maximum capacity levels.

(f) The characteristics of inmates to be incarcerated in private correctional facilities.

(g) Circumstances under which inmates may be transported.

(h) Procedures for inmates to leave the grounds of a facility.

(i) A disciplinary system in accordance with the standards of the American Correctional Association.

(j) Comprehensive standards for conditions of confinement in accordance with the standards of the American Correctional Association.

(2) The department shall appoint a contract monitor who shall document the private vendor's adherence to the contract and compliance with rules, policies, procedures, and performance standards of the department.

(3) The private vendor shall provide a work area at the private correctional facility for use by the contract monitor appointed by the department and shall provide the monitor with access to all data, reports, and other materials that the monitor, the Auditor General, and the Office of Program Policy Analysis and Government Accountability determine are necessary to carry out monitoring and auditing responsibilities.

(4) The private vendor shall employ a person who shall monitor all aspects of the private vendor's performance under the contract. The monitor shall submit to the department periodic reports documenting adherence by the private vendor to performance standards established by the department. The monitor shall also submit a report to the Governor and the Legislature, by January 1 of each year, which shall include a report of the adherence to the contract by the private vendor and its compliance with rules, policies, procedures, and performance standards established by the department and an independently audited financial statement.

(5) The Office of Program Policy Analysis and Government Accountability shall conduct a performance audit, including a review of the annual financial audit of the private entity and shall deliver a report to the Legislature by

February 1 of the third year following any contract awarded by the department for the operation of a correctional facility by a private vendor.

(a) The report shall determine the reasonableness of the cost analysis procedures used by the department for comparing services provided under the contract and for comparing the quality of the services provided under the contract with the costs and quality of similar services provided by the department.

(b) In preparing the report, the office shall consider, in addition to other factors it determines are significant:

1. The extent to which the private vendor and the department have complied with the terms of the contract and ss. 944.710–944.719.

2. The wages and benefits that are provided to the staff of the private correctional facility as compared to wages and benefits provided to employees of the department performing comparable tasks.

Laws 1989, c. 89–526, § 22. Amended by Laws 1997, c. 97–102, § 1661, eff. July 1, 1997; Laws 1999, c. 99–333, § 17, eff. July 1, 1999; Laws 2001, c. 2001–266, § 131, eff. July 1, 2001.

Historical and Statutory Notes

Amendment Notes:

Laws 1997, c. 97–102, eff. July 1, 1997, removed gender-specific references applicable to human beings from volume 4 of the Florida Statutes without substantive changes in legal effect.

Laws 1999, c. 99–333, § 17, in subsec. (5), substituted "Office of Program Policy Analysis and Government Accountability" for "Auditor General" and "February 1 of the third" for "April 1 of the first"; and, in subsec. (5)(a), substituted "office" for "Auditor General".

Laws 2001, c. 2001–266, § 131, in subsec. (3), inserted ", and the Office of Program Policy Analysis and Government Accountability" following "General".

Library References

Prisons ⚿236.
Westlaw Topic No. 310.
C.J.S. Prisons and Rights of Prisoners §§ 1 to 2, 18, 128 to 134.

Research References

Encyclopedias

Generally; Contracts With Private Vendors, FL Jur. 2d Prisons & Prisoners § 24.

Quality Assurance and Standards of Operation, FL Jur. 2d Prisons & Prisoners § 25.

Contract Requirements, FL Jur. 2d Prisons & Prisoners § 30.

944.72. Privately Operated Institutions Inmate Welfare Trust Fund

(1) There is hereby created in the Department of Corrections the Privately Operated Institutions Inmate Welfare Trust Fund. The purpose of the trust fund shall be the benefit and welfare of inmates incarcerated in private correctional facilities under contract with the department pursuant to this chapter or the Department of Management Services pursuant to chapter 957. Moneys shall be deposited in the trust fund and expenditures made from the trust fund as provided in s. 945.215.

(2) Notwithstanding the provisions of s. 216.301 and pursuant to s. 216.351, any balance in the trust fund at the end of any fiscal year shall remain in the

trust fund at the end of the year and shall be available for carrying out the purposes of the trust fund.

Laws 1998, c. 98–386, § 1, eff. July 1, 1998. Amended by Laws 2002, c. 2002–109, § 2, eff. July 1, 2002; Laws 2004, c. 2004–248, § 7, eff. July 1, 2004.

Historical and Statutory Notes

Amendment Notes:

Laws 2002, c. 2002–109, § 2, deleted subsec. (3), which formerly read:

"(3) Pursuant to the provisions of s. 19(f)(2), Art. III of the State Constitution, the trust fund shall, unless terminated sooner, be terminated on July 1, 2002. However, prior to its scheduled termination, the trust fund shall be reviewed as provided in s. 215.3206(1) and (2)."

Laws 2004, c. 2004–248, § 7, in subsec. (1), substituted "Department of Management Services" for "Correctional Privatization Commission" following "chapter 944 or the" in the last sentence.

Library References

States ⚷127.
Westlaw Topic No. 360.
C.J.S. States §§ 386 to 387.

Research References

Encyclopedias

Privately Operated Institutions Inmate Welfare Trust Fund, FL Jur. 2d Prisons & Prisoners § 28.

Privately Operated Institutions Inmate Welfare Trust Fund, FL Jur. 2d Prisons & Prisoners § 168.

944.801. Education for state prisoners

(1) There is hereby established under the Department of Corrections a Correctional Education Program which shall be composed of the educational facilities and services of all institutions and facilities housing inmates operated by the Department of Corrections and shall be supervised by the Department of Corrections.

(2) The Department of Corrections is vested with the authority and responsibility to manage and operate the Correctional Education Program as provided by law.

(3) The responsibilities of the Correctional Education Program shall be to:

(a) Develop guidelines for collecting education-related information during the inmate reception process and for disseminating such information to the classification staff of the Department of Corrections. The information collected shall include the inmate's areas of educational or vocational interest, vocational skills, and level of education.

(b) Monitor and assess all inmate education program services and report the results of such evaluation in the annual report of activities.

(c) Develop complete and reliable statistics on the educational histories, the city/intracity area and school district where the inmate was domiciled prior to incarceration, the participation in state educational and training programs, and the occupations of inmates confined to state correctional facilities. The compiled statistics shall be summarized and analyzed in the annual report of correctional educational activities required by paragraph (f).

(d) Approve educational programs of the appropriate levels and types in the correctional institutions and develop procedures for the admission of inmate students thereto.

(e) Enter into agreements with public or private school districts, entities, community colleges, junior colleges, colleges, or universities as may be deemed appropriate for the purpose of carrying out its duties and responsibilities and ensure that agreements require minimum performance standards and standards for measurable objectives, in accordance with established Department of Education standards.

(f) Report annual activities to the Secretary of Corrections, the Commissioner of Education, the Governor, and the Legislature.

(g) Develop and maintain complete and reliable statistics on the number of general educational development (GED) certificates and vocational certificates issued by each institution in each skill area, the change in inmate literacy levels, and the number of inmate admissions to and withdrawals from education courses. The compiled statistics shall be summarized and analyzed in the annual report of correctional education activities required by paragraph (f).

(h) Develop a written procedure for selecting programs to add to or delete from the vocational curriculum. The procedure shall include labor market analyses which demonstrate the projected demand for certain occupations and the projected supply of potential employees. In conducting these analyses, the department shall evaluate the feasibility of adding vocational education programs which have been identified by the Department of Labor and Employment Security [1] or a regional coordinating council as being in undersupply in this state. The department shall periodically reevaluate the vocational education programs in major institutions to determine which of the programs support and provide relevant skills to inmates who could be assigned to a correctional work program that is operated as a Prison Industry Enhancement Program.

(i) Ensure that every inmate who has 2 years or more remaining to serve on his or her sentence at the time that he or she is received at an institution and who lacks basic and functional literacy skills as defined in s. 1004.02 attends not fewer than 150 hours of sequential instruction in a correctional adult basic education program. The basic and functional literacy level of an inmate shall be determined by the average composite test score obtained on a test approved for this purpose by the State Board of Education.

1. Upon completion of the 150 hours of instruction, the inmate shall be retested and, if a composite test score of functional literacy is not attained, the department is authorized to require the inmate to remain in the instructional program.

2. Highest priority of inmate participation shall be focused on youthful offenders and those inmates nearing release from the correctional system.

3. An inmate shall be required to attend the 150 hours of adult basic education instruction unless such inmate:

a. Is serving a life sentence or is under sentence of death.

b. Is specifically exempted for security or health reasons.

c. Is housed at a community correctional center, road prison, work camp, or vocational center.

d. Attains a functional literacy level after attendance in fewer than 150 hours of adult basic education instruction.

e. Is unable to enter such instruction because of insufficient facilities, staff, or classroom capacity.

4. The Department of Corrections shall provide classes to accommodate those inmates assigned to correctional or public work programs after normal working hours. The department shall develop a plan to provide academic and vocational classes on a more frequent basis and at times that accommodate the increasing number of inmates with work assignments, to the extent that resources permit.

5. If an inmate attends and actively participates in the 150 hours of instruction, the Department of Corrections may grant a one-time award of up to 6 additional days of incentive gain-time, which must be credited and applied as provided by law. Active participation means, at a minimum, that the inmate is attentive, responsive, cooperative, and completes assigned work.

(j) Recommend the award of additional incentive gain-time for inmates who receive a general educational development certificate or a vocational certificate.

(k) Ensure that all education staff are certified in accordance with the Department of Education standards.

(*l*) Develop goals and objectives relating to all phases of the correctional education program.

(4) Minors who are adjudicated as adults and who are in the custody or under the supervision of the Department of Corrections may receive and participate in educational services provided within the department without the parental consent of the minors.

(5) Notwithstanding s. 120.81(3), all inmates under 22 years of age who qualify for special educational services and programs pursuant to the Individuals with Disabilities Education Act, 20 U.S.C. ss. 1400 et seq., and who request a due process hearing as provided by that act shall be entitled to such hearing before the Division of Administrative Hearings. Administrative law judges shall not be required to travel to state or private correctional institutions and facilities in order to conduct these hearings.

Laws 1995, c. 95–325, § 16. Amended by Laws 1996, c. 96–314, § 2, eff. May 30, 1996; Laws 1997, c. 97–78, § 18, eff. May 23, 1997; Laws 1997, c. 97–93, § 36, eff. July 1, 1997; Laws 1999, c. 99–3, § 120, eff. June 29, 1999; Laws 1999, c. 99–260, § 1, eff. July 1, 1999; Laws 2002, c. 2002–387, § 1044, eff. Jan. 7, 2003.

[1] Laws 2002, c. 2002–194, § 69, repealed § 20.171, which created the Department of Labor and Employment Security.

Historical and Statutory Notes

Amendment Notes:

Laws 1996, c. 96–314, § 2, eff. May 30, 1996, in subsec. (3), inserted par. (c), relating to compilation of statistics, and redesignated former pars. (c) through (k) as pars. (d) through (*l*).

Laws 1997, c. 97–78, § 18, eff. May 23, 1997, added subsec. (4).

Laws 1997, c. 97–93, eff. July 1, 1997, was a reviser's bill which deleted obsolete and expired provisions, corrected cross references and citations, and corrected grammatical and other similar errors.

Laws 1999, c. 99–3, § 120, eff. June 29, 1999, amended the section to conform to the redesignation of s. 944.801(3).

Laws 1999, c. 99–260, § 1, eff. July 1, 1999, in subsec. (3)(h), added the last sentence; in subsec. (3)(i)4., added the last sentence; redesignated subsec. (4) as subsec. (5); and added a new subsec. (4).

Laws 2002, c. 2002–387, § 1044, in subsec. (3)(b), deleted "In cooperation with the Department of Education, pursuant to s. 229.565" preceding "monitor"; in subsec. (3)(c), deleted "In cooperation with the Department of Education, pursuant to s. 229.8075" preceding "develop"; and, in subsec. (3)(i), substituted "1004.02" for "239.105".

Cross References

Labor organizations, public employers, see § 447.203.

Library References

Prisons ⚷163.
Westlaw Topic No. 310.

C.J.S. Prisons and Rights of Prisoners §§ 50 to 57, 59, 63, 68 to 70, 73 to 75, 77, 94 to 96, 100 to 102, 113, 119, 121 to 122.

Research References

Encyclopedias

Generally; Education, FL Jur. 2d Prisons & Prisoners § 170.

Notes of Decisions

Individual education plans 2
Validity 1

---

1. Validity

Florida statute permitting inmates under 22 years of age qualifying for special educational services and programs pursuant to Individuals with Disabilities Education Act (IDEA) to request post-deprivation due process hearing as provided in IDEA was in conflict with IDEA, as state statute made no provision for hearing prior to deprivation and did not provide for prior parental notice as mandated by IDEA. Paul Y. By and Through Kathy Y. v. Singletary, S.D.Fla. 1997, 979 F.Supp. 1422. Schools ⚷ 155.5(1); States ⚷ 18.25

2. Individual education plans

Disabled student tried and incarcerated as adult failed to establish likelihood of success on merits of his action against state Department of Corrections seeking to require Department to implement individual education plan (IEP) previously developed for him under Individual with Disabilities Education Act (IDEA), given circumstances of student's incarceration, and was therefore not entitled to preliminary injunction requiring Department to implement his IEP pending conduct of due process hearing. Paul Y. By and Through Kathy Y. v. Singletary, S.D.Fla.1997, 979 F.Supp. 1422. Schools ⚷ 155.5(5)

944.802. Direct-support organization; definition; use of property; board of directors; audit

(1) Definition.—For the purpose of this section, the term "direct-support organization" means an organization:

(a) Which is a corporation not for profit that is incorporated under the provisions of chapter 617, exempted from filing fees, and approved by the Department of State;

(b) Organized and operated to conduct programs and activities; initiate developmental projects; raise funds; request and receive grants, gifts, and bequests of moneys; acquire, receive, hold, invest, and administer, in its own name, securities, funds, objects of value, or other property, real or personal; and make expenditures to or for the direct or indirect benefit of the Department of Corrections or individual units of the state correctional system;

(c) Determined by the Department of Corrections to be consistent with the priority issues and objectives of the Department of Corrections and in the best interest of the state; and

(d) Approved in writing by the Secretary of Corrections to operate for the direct or indirect benefit of the Department of Corrections or individual units of the state correctional system. Such approval shall be in a letter of agreement from the Department of Corrections.

(2) Use of property.—

(a) The Department of Corrections may permit, without charge, appropriate use of fixed property and facilities of the state correctional system by a direct-support organization subject to the provisions in this section. Such use must be directly in keeping with the approved purpose of the direct-support organization, and may not be made at times or places that would unreasonably interfere with opportunities for inmates and staff to use the areas for established purposes.

(b) The Department of Corrections may prescribe by rule any condition with which a direct-support organization shall comply in order to use fixed property or facilities of the state correctional system.

(c) The Department of Corrections shall not permit the use of any fixed property or facilities of the Department of Corrections by a direct-support organization that does not provide equal membership and employment opportunities to all persons regardless of race, color, religion, sex, age, or national origin.

(3) Annual audit.—The direct-support organization shall provide for an annual financial audit in accordance with s. 215.981.

Added by Laws 1996, c. 96–312, § 11, eff. July 1, 1996. Amended by Laws 2001, c. 2001–266, § 132, eff. July 1, 2001.

Historical and Statutory Notes

Amendment Notes:

Laws 2001, c. 2001–266, § 132, rewrote subsec. (3), which formerly read:

"(3) Annual audit.—The direct-support organization shall make provision for any annual postaudit of its financial accounts to be conducted by an independent certified public accountant in accordance with rules to be promulgated by the Department of Corrections. The annual audit report shall include a management letter and shall be submitted to the Auditor General and the Department of Corrections for review. The Department of Corrections and the Auditor General have the authority to require and receive from the organization or from its independent auditor any detail or supplemental data relative to the operation of the organization."

Cross References

Corrections Foundation license plates, see § 320.08058.

Research References

Encyclopedias

Direct-Support Organizations, FL Jur. 2d Prisons & Prisoners § 8.

Notes of Decisions

Contributions to correctional institutions 1

1. Contributions to correctional institutions

Where local employee clubs, established at correctional institutions throughout the state, have raised funds to pay for employee activities, the funds so raised should be placed in the Department of Corrections' Employee Benefit Trust Fund; the Department of Corrections has authority to control and disburse these funds, but it can neither transfer the funds nor transfer control of the funds to a direct-support organization. Op.Atty.Gen., 2006–18, May 5, 2006.

The Department of Corrections may not directly receive gifts or donations that are conditioned upon their use for a specified purpose or particular correctional unit, but it may, through a properly created direct-support organization, accept a donation that is conditioned upon its use for the transition assistance program at the Hillsborough Correctional Institution. Op.Atty. Gen., 2004-30, June 25, 2004.

944.803. Faith-based programs for inmates

(1) The Legislature finds and declares that faith-based programs offered in state and private correctional institutions and facilities have the potential to facilitate inmate institutional adjustment, help inmates assume personal responsibility, and reduce recidivism.

(2) It is the intent of the Legislature that the Department of Corrections and the private vendors operating private correctional facilities shall continuously:

(a) Measure recidivism rates for inmates who have participated in religious programs;

(b) Increase the number of volunteers who minister to inmates from various faith-based institutions in the community;

(c) Develop community linkages with churches, synagogues, mosques, and other faith-based institutions to assist inmates in their release back into the community; and

(d) Fund through the use of annual appropriations, in department facilities, and through inmate welfare trust funds pursuant to s. 945.215, in private facilities, an adequate number of chaplains and support staff to operate faith-based programs in correctional institutions.

(3) The department must have at least six new programs fully operational. These six programs shall be similar to and in addition to the current faith-based pilot program. The six new programs shall be a joint effort with the department and faith-based service groups within the community. The department shall ensure that an inmate's faith orientation, or lack thereof, will not be considered in determining admission to a faith-based program and that the program does not attempt to convert an inmate toward a particular faith or religious preference. The programs shall operate 24 hours a day within the existing correctional facilities. The programs must emphasize the importance of personal responsibility, meaningful work, education, substance abuse treatment, and peer support. Participation in the faith-based dormitory program

shall be voluntary. However, at least 80 percent of the inmates participating in this program must be within 36 months of release. Assignment to these programs shall be based on evaluation and the length of time the inmate is projected to be assigned to that particular institution. In evaluating an inmate for this program, priority shall be given to inmates who have shown an indication for substance abuse. A right to substance abuse program services is not stated, intended, or otherwise implied by this subsection. The department may not remove an inmate once assigned to the program except for the purposes of population management, for inmate conduct that may subject the inmate to disciplinary confinement or loss of gain-time, for physical or mental health concerns, or for security or safety concerns. To support the programming component, the department shall assign a chaplain and a full-time clerical support person dedicated to each dormitory to implement and monitor the program and to strengthen volunteer participation and support.

(4) The Department of Corrections shall assign chaplains to community correctional centers authorized pursuant to s. 945.091(1)(b). These chaplains shall strengthen volunteer participation by recruiting volunteers in the community to assist inmates in transition, and, if requested by the inmate, placement in a mentoring program or at a contracted substance abuse transition housing program. When placing an inmate in a contracted program, the chaplain shall work with the institutional transition assistance specialist in an effort to successfully place the released inmate.

(5) The department shall ensure that any faith component of any program authorized in this chapter is offered on a voluntary basis and, an offender's faith orientation, or lack thereof, will not be considered in determining admission to a faith-based program and that the program does not attempt to convert an offender toward a particular faith or religious preference.

(6) The department shall ensure that state funds are not expended for the purpose of furthering religious indoctrination, but rather, that state funds are expended for purposes of furthering the secular goals of criminal rehabilitation, the successful reintegration of offenders into the community, and the reduction of recidivism.

Added by Laws 1997, c. 97–78, § 19, eff. May 23, 1997. Amended by Laws 1998, c. 98–388, § 4, eff. July 1, 1998; Laws 2001, c. 2001–110, § 13, eff. July 1, 2001; Laws 2003, c. 2003–179, § 8, eff. July 1, 2003; Laws 2005, c. 2005–2, § 149, eff. July 5, 2005.

Historical and Statutory Notes

Amendment Notes:

Laws 1997, c. 97–78, § 20, provides:

"The Department of Corrections shall conduct an in-depth study to measure the effectiveness of faith-based programs in both public and private correctional institutions and facilities, and shall make recommendations to the Legislature on modifications or improvements to existing programs. The study shall include an examination of innovative faith-based programs existing in other states. The findings and recommendations from the study shall be reported to the Legislature by January 1, 1998."

Laws 1998, c. 98–388, § 4, rewrote subsec. (2)(d), which formerly read:

"(d) Fund through the use of the inmate welfare trust fund pursuant to s. 945.215 an adequate number of chaplains and support staff to operate chaplaincy programs in state correctional institutions."

Laws 2001, c. 2001–110, § 13, added subsecs. (3), (4), (5), and (6), relating to dormitory programs, chaplains, voluntary basis of program, and use of state funds.

Laws 2003, c. 2003–179, § 8, in subsec. (2)(d), substituted "annual appropriations, in department facilities, and through inmate welfare trust funds pursuant to s. 945.215, in private facilities," for "inmate trust funds pursuant to s. 945.215" following "use of".

Laws 2005, c. 2005–2, a reviser's bill, deleted obsolete and expired provisions, corrected grammatical and typographical errors, and made other similar changes.

Library References

Prisons ⚿151.
Westlaw Topic No. 310.

C.J.S. Prisons and Rights of Prisoners §§ 68, 70, 89 to 93.

944.8031. Inmate's family visitation; legislative intent; minimum services provided to visitors; budget requests

(1) The Legislature finds that maintaining an inmate's family and community relationships through enhancing visitor services and programs and increasing the frequency and quality of the visits is an underutilized correctional resource that can improve an inmate's behavior in the correctional facility and, upon an inmate's release from a correctional facility, will help to reduce recidivism.

(2) The department shall provide, at a minimum, the following services at designated visiting areas for approved visitors in state correctional facilities:

(a) Information relating to applicable visiting regulations, dress codes, and visiting procedures.

(b) A sheltered area, outside the security perimeter, for visitors waiting before and after visiting inmates.

(c) Food services with food choices which are nutritious and acceptable for children and youth visitors.

(d) Minimal equipment and supplies which assist staff and visitors in managing and occupying the time and meeting the needs of children and youth visitors.

(3) Upon determining any deficiencies and barriers to the effective and efficient operation of the department's visitation program and services, the secretary shall submit annual budget requests identifying capital improvements, staffing, and programmatic needs necessary to improve the quality and frequency of family visits and the visitation program and services.

Added by Laws 1999, c. 99–271, § 13, eff. June 29, 1999.

Library References

Prisons ⚿141, 382.
Westlaw Topic No. 310.

C.J.S. Prisons and Rights of Prisoners §§ 12, 54 to 55, 57 to 58, 60, 72 to 73, 91, 94 to 102, 113, 119 to 120.

944.804. Elderly offenders correctional facilities program of 2000

(1) The Legislature finds that the number and percentage of elderly offenders in the Florida prison system is increasing and will continue to increase for the foreseeable future. The current cost to incarcerate elderly offenders is approximately three times the cost of incarceration of younger inmates. Alternatives to the current approaches to housing, programming, and treating the medical

needs of elderly offenders, which may reduce the overall costs associated with this segment of the prison population, must be explored and implemented.

(2) The department shall establish and operate a geriatric facility at the site known as River Junction Correctional Institution, which shall be an institution specifically for generally healthy elderly offenders who can perform general work appropriate for their physical and mental condition. Prior to reopening the facility, the department shall make modifications to the facility which will ensure its compliance with the Americans with Disabilities Act and decrease the likelihood of falls, accidental injury, and other conditions known to be particularly hazardous to the elderly.

(a) In order to decrease long-term medical costs to the state, a preventive fitness/wellness program and diet specifically designed to maintain the mental and physical health of elderly offenders shall be developed and implemented. In developing the program, the department shall give consideration to preventive medical care for the elderly which shall include, but not be limited to, maintenance of bone density, all aspects of cardiovascular health, lung capacity, mental alertness, and orientation. Existing policies and procedures shall be reexamined and altered to encourage offenders to adopt a more healthy lifestyle and maximize their level of functioning. The program components shall be modified as data and experience are received which measure the relative success of the program components previously implemented.

(b) Consideration must be given to redirecting resources as a method of offsetting increased medical costs. Elderly offenders are not likely to reenter society as a part of the workforce, and programming resources would be better spent in activities to keep the elderly offenders healthy, alert, and oriented. Limited or restricted programming or activities for elderly offenders will increase the daily cost of institutional and health care, and programming opportunities adequate to reduce the cost of care will be provided. Programming shall include, but not be limited to, recreation, education, and counseling which is needs-specific to elderly offenders. Institutional staff shall be specifically trained to effectively supervise elderly offenders and to detect physical or mental changes which warrant medical attention before more serious problems develop.

(3) The department shall adopt rules that specify which elderly offenders shall be eligible to be housed at River Junction Correctional Institution.

(4) While developing the criteria for eligibility, the department shall use the information in existing offender databases to determine the number of offenders who would be eligible. The Legislature directs the department to consider a broad range of elderly offenders for River Junction Correctional Institution who have good disciplinary records and a medical grade that will permit them to perform meaningful work activities, including participation in an appropriate correctional work program (PRIDE) facility, if available.

(5) The department shall also submit a study based on existing offenders which projects the number of existing offenders who will qualify under the

rules. An appendix to the study shall identify the specific offenders who qualify.

Added by Laws 2000, c. 2000–214, § 2, eff. July 1, 2000.

Library References

Prisons ⚿157, 159, 190, 216.
Westlaw Topic No. 310.
C.J.S. Criminal Law §§ 2188 to 2190.
C.J.S. Prisons and Rights of Prisoners §§ 18, 68 to 70, 76, 78 to 88, 123, 125, 127, 136.

Research References

Encyclopedias

Care of Elderly Offenders, FL Jur. 2d Prisons & Prisoners § 124.

944.8041. Elderly offenders; annual review

For the purpose of providing information to the Legislature on elderly offenders within the correctional system, the department and the Correctional Medical Authority shall each submit annually a report on the status and treatment of elderly offenders in the state-administered and private state correctional systems, as well as such information on the River Junction Correctional Institution. In order to adequately prepare the reports, the department and the Department of Management Services shall grant access to the Correctional Medical Authority which includes access to the facilities, offenders, and any information the agencies require to complete their reports. The review shall also include an examination of promising geriatric policies, practices, and programs currently implemented in other correctional systems within the United States. The reports, with specific findings and recommendations for implementation, shall be submitted to the President of the Senate and the Speaker of the House of Representatives on or before December 31 of each year.

Added by Laws 2000, c. 2000–214, § 3, eff. July 1, 2000. Amended by Laws 2004, c. 2004–248, § 8, eff. July 1, 2004; Laws 2006, c. 2006–32, § 2, eff. July 1, 2006.

Historical and Statutory Notes

Amendment Notes:

Laws 2004, c. 2004–248, § 8, in the second sentence, substituted "Department of Management Services" for "Correctional Privatization Commission" preceding "shall grant".

Laws 2006, c. 2006–32, § 2, substituted "department" for "Florida Corrections Commission" following "system, the" in the first sentence, and deleted "of Corrections" following "department" and deleted "the Florida Corrections Commission and" following "access to" in the second sentence.

Library References

Prisons ⚿102.
Westlaw Topic No. 310.
C.J.S. Prisons and Rights of Prisoners §§ 5 to 7, 14, 17, 22 to 23, 50 to 53, 55, 59, 78.

Research References

Encyclopedias

State Correctional System, Generally, FL Jur. 2d Prisons & Prisoners § 1.

Definitions of "Prisoner," "County Prisoner," and "Municipal Prisoner", FL Jur. 2d Prisons & Prisoners § 2.

Definitions and Construction of Particular Terms Referring to State Correctional Facilities, FL Jur. 2d Prisons & Prisoners § 16.

Leased or Managed Work Programs; Management by Nonprofit Corporation, FL Jur. 2d Prisons & Prisoners § 155.

CHAPTER 945

DEPARTMENT OF CORRECTIONS

Section

DEPARTMENT OF CORRECTIONS
Ch. 945

For more information on using Westlaw to supplement your research, see the Westlaw Electronic Research Guide, which follows the Preface.

945.01. Definitions

As used herein, the following terms shall have the meanings ascribed to them unless the context shall clearly indicate otherwise:

(1) "Correctional system" means all prisons and other correctional institutions now existing or hereafter created under the jurisdiction of the department.

(2) "Department" means the Department of Corrections.

(3) "Secretary" means the Secretary of Corrections.

(4) "Reception center" means a temporary custodial institution for offenders committed to the department for classification and assignment to an appropriate institution in the correctional system.

Laws 1957, c. 57–213, § 1; Laws 1961, c. 61–530, § 18; Laws 1969, c. 69–106, §§ 19, 35; Laws 1970, c. 70–441, §§ 1, 2; Laws 1971, c. 71–377, § 283; Laws 1977, c. 77–120, § 68; Laws 1979, c. 79–3, § 77.

Historical and Statutory Notes

Amendment Notes:

Laws 1961, c. 61–530, § 18, substituted the "division" and "division of corrections" for "department" and "department of corrections".

Laws 1969, c. 69–106, the governmental reorganization act of 1969, provides in section 19(4) [see F.S.A. § 20.19(4)] as follows:

"All powers, duties and functions of the board of commissioners of state institutions relating to and including the division of corrections created under section 965.01(1), Florida Statutes, and chapters 944 and 945, Florida Statutes, are transferred by a type four (4) transfer to the department of health and rehabilitative services and its function shall be assigned to the division of adult corrections."

Laws 1970, c. 70–441, §§ 1, 2, amended Laws 1969, c. 69–106, § 19(2), (6) to read "Division of Corrections" in lieu of "Division of Adult Corrections" and transferred all powers, duties, and functions, accordingly.

Laws 1971, c. 71–377, § 283, repealed former subsec. (1) defining "board" which was rendered obsolete by the Governmental Reorganization Act, Laws 1969, c. 69–106, § 19; and former subsecs. (2) to (6) have been renumbered as subsecs. (1) to (5) in Fla.St.1971.

Laws 1977, c. 77–120, a reviser's bill, amended this section to conform with Laws 1975, c. 75–49, which created the department of offender rehabilitation (see § 20.315) and transferred to the department certain functions performed by the division of corrections of the department of health and rehabilitative services and the parole and probation commission of the department of offender rehabilitation.

Laws 1979, c. 79–3, a reviser's bill, provided for substitution of references to the department and secretary of "corrections" for the department and secretary of "offender rehabilitation" to conform with Laws 1978, c. 78–53.

Law Review and Journal Commentaries

Due process in correctional administrative hearings. Thompson H. Gooding, Jr., 33 U.Fla. L.R. 151 (1981).

New penal and correctional program in Florida. William C. Merritt, 12 U.Miami L.Rev. 200 (1958).

Prisoners' gain time. 21 U.Fla.L.Rev. 103 (1968).

Research References

Encyclopedias

State Correctional System, Generally, FL Jur. 2d Prisons & Prisoners § 1.

United States Supreme Court

Short-term custodial facilities, constitutionality of conditions of confinement, see Bell v. Wolfish, U.S.N.Y.1979, 99 S.Ct. 1861, 441 U.S. 520, 60 L.Ed.2d 447.

Notes of Decisions

Employees 1

---

1. Employees

The division of corrections has the authority to prescribe rules of conduct and assignment of authorized personnel of the correctional system but it has no authority to legally "commission" certain employees as inmate supervisors. Op. Atty.Gen., 074–155, May 21, 1974.

945.02. Repealed by Laws 1971, c. 71–377, § 283

Historical and Statutory Notes

Repealed § 945.02, which related to the division of corrections, was derived from Laws 1961, c. 61–530, § 18, and rendered obsolete by Laws 1969, c. 69–106, § 19, the Governmental Reorganization Act.

945.025. Jurisdiction of department

(1) The Department of Corrections shall have supervisory and protective care, custody, and control of the inmates, buildings, grounds, property, and all other matters pertaining to the following facilities and programs for the imprisonment, correction, and rehabilitation of adult offenders:

(a) Department of Corrections adult correctional institutions;

(b) Department of Corrections youthful offender institutions;

(c) Department of Corrections Mental Health Treatment Facility;

(d) Department of Corrections Probation and Restitution Center;

(e) Department of Corrections community correctional centers; and

(f) Department of Corrections vocational centers.

(2) In establishing, operating, and utilizing these facilities, the department shall attempt, whenever possible, to avoid the placement of nondangerous offenders who have potential for rehabilitation with repeat offenders or dangerous offenders. Medical, mental, and psychological problems shall be diagnosed and treated whenever possible. The Department of Children and Family Services and the Agency for Persons with Disabilities shall cooperate to ensure the delivery of services to persons under the custody or supervision of the department. When it is the intent of the department to transfer a mentally ill or retarded prisoner to the Department of Children and Family Services or the Agency for Persons with Disabilities, an involuntary commitment hearing shall be held according to the provisions of chapter 393 or chapter 394.

(3) There shall be other correctional facilities, including detention facilities of varying levels of security, work-release facilities, and community correctional

facilities, halfway houses, and other approved community residential and nonresidential facilities and programs; however, no adult correctional facility may be established by changing the use and purpose of any mental health facility or mental health institution under the jurisdiction of any state agency or department without authorization in the General Appropriation Act or other approval by the Legislature. Any community residential facility may be deemed a part of the state correctional system for purposes of maintaining custody of offenders, and for this purpose the department may contract for and purchase the services of such facilities.

(4) Nothing contained in chapter 287 shall be construed as requiring competitive bids for health services involving examination, diagnosis, or treatment.

Laws 1957, c. 57–317, § 1; Laws 1961, c. 61–127, § 1; Laws 1967, c. 67–99, § 1; Fla.St.1967, § 965.01(1); Laws 1969, c. 69–106, §§ 19, 35; Laws 1970, c. 70–441, §§ 1, 2; Laws 1974, c. 74–112, § 26; Laws 1975, c. 75–49, § 14; Laws 1976, c. 76–232, § 1; Laws 1977, c. 77–120, § 69; Laws 1977, c. 77–147, § 475; Laws 1977, c. 77–312, § 6; Laws 1979, c. 79–3, § 78; Laws 1980, c. 80–374, § 8; Laws 1983, c. 83–46, § 1; Laws 1983, c. 83–346, § 2; Laws 1987, c. 87–87, § 6; Laws 1987, c. 87–226, § 76. Amended by Laws 1999, c. 99–8, § 313, eff. June 29, 1999; Laws 2006, c. 2006–227, § 65, eff. July 1, 2006.

Historical and Statutory Notes

Amendment Notes:

Laws 1957, c. 57–317, § 1, enacted provision which was designated as section 965.01(1), which, as it appeared in Fla.St.1957, provided:

"(a) Division of Corrections.—The division of corrections shall have supervisory and protective care, custody and control of the inmates, buildings, grounds, property and all other matters pertaining to the following institutions for the imprisonment or correction of adult offenders:

"1. State prison farm at Raiford,

"2. State correctional institution at Lowell,

"3. Apalachee correctional institution,

"4. Glades state prison farm,

"5. Florida farm colony prison camp at Gainesville,

"6. Florida industrial school for girls prison camp at Ocala,

"7. Chattahoochee construction camp,

"8. State convict road force camps.

"(b) All of the duties, responsibilities, powers, and functions with respect to the state convict road force granted to the state road department by virtue of chapter 952 are hereby transferred to the board of commissioners of state institutions.

"(c) All of the duties, responsibilities, powers and functions with respect to the administration of the state prison farm granted to the commissioner of agriculture by virtue of chapter 954 are hereby transferred to the board of commissioners of state institutions.

"(d) The provisions of this subsection shall be cumulative of and shall not be construed to replace any separate measure enacted by this legislature wherein may be provided a department of corrections with like responsibilities and objectives. In any such separate measure the use of the term 'department of corrections' shall mean 'division of corrections.' "

Laws 1961, c. 61–127, § 1, amended subsec. (1) of former § 965.01 by deleting pars. (b), (c) and (d) and by rewriting par. (a) which, as it appeared in Fla.St.1961, provided:

"Division of Corrections.—The division of corrections shall have supervisory and protective care, custody and control of the inmates, buildings, grounds, property and all other matters pertaining to the following institutions for the imprisonment or correction of adult offenders:

"1. Apalachee correctional institution.

"2. Florida correctional institution.

"3. Glades correctional institution.

"4. Florida state prison.

"5. State road prisons."

Laws 1967, c. 67–99, § 1, amended subsec. (1) of former § 965.01 by substituting, in the introductory paragraph, the words "with the following jurisdiction, powers and duties:" for "which shall have jurisdiction of the hereinafter named state institutions:"; made the introductory paragraph of subsec. (1)(a) applicable to institutions for rehabilitation; substituted, in subsec. (1)(a)(5), "Division of corrections road prisons" for "State road prisons" and added, in subsec. (1)(a), institutions (6) to (9).

Former § 965.01 was renumbered as § 945.025 in Fla.St.1969, and read as follows:

"The division of adult corrections shall have supervisory and protective care, custody, and control of the inmates, buildings, grounds, property, and all other matters pertaining to the following institutions for the imprisonment, correction, and rehabilitation of adult offenders:

"(1) Apalachee Correctional Institution;

"(2) Florida Correctional Institution;

"(3) Glades Correctional Institution;

"(4) Florida State Prison;

"(5) Division of Corrections Road Prisons;

"(6) Sumter Correctional Institution;

"(7) Avon Park Correctional Institution;

"(8) Santa Fe Correctional Farm; and

"(9) Reception and Medical Center."

Laws 1969, c. 69–106, §§ 19, 35, transferred all powers, duties and functions of the division of corrections of the board of commissioners of state institutions to division of adult corrections of the department of health and rehabilitative services.

Laws 1970, c. 70–441, §§ 1, 2, amended Laws 1969, c. 69–106, § 19(2), (6) to read "Division of Corrections" in lieu of "Division of Adult Corrections" and transferred all powers, duties, and functions, accordingly.

Laws 1974, c. 74–112, § 26, inserted "facilities, and programs" in and designated the paragraphs of subsec. (1), deleted Santa Fe Correctional Farm from subsec. (1)(h), inserted the words "at Lake Butler" in subsec. (1)(i) and added subsecs. (1)(j) to (*o*), (2) and (3).

Laws 1975, c. 75–49, added the second through penultimate sentences to subsec. (3).

Laws 1976, c. 76–232, amended subsec. (3) to prohibit conversion of the G. Pierce Wood Memorial Hospital into a correctional facility as long as the hospital is used as a state mental hospital.

Laws 1977, c. 77–120, a reviser's bill, amended this section to conform with Laws 1975, c. 75–49, which created the department of offender rehabilitation (see § 20.315) and transferred to the department certain functions performed by the division of corrections of the department of health and rehabilitative services and the parole and probation commission of the department of offender rehabilitation.

Laws 1977, c. 77–147, a reviser's bill, amended this section to reflect reorganization of the department of health and rehabilitative services by Laws 1975, c. 75–48.

Laws 1977, c. 77–312, added the fourth sentence to subsec. (2).

Laws 1979, c. 79–3, a reviser's bill, provided for substitution of references to the department and secretary of "corrections" for the department and secretary of "offender rehabilitation" to conform with Laws 1978, c. 78–53.

Laws 1980, c. 80–374, § 8, added subsec. (4).

Laws 1983, c. 83–46, § 1, rewrote subsec. (1) which prior thereto provided:

"The Department of Corrections shall have supervisory and protective care, custody, and control of the inmates, buildings, grounds, property, and all other matters pertaining to the following institutions, facilities, and programs for the imprisonment, correction, and rehabilitation of adult offenders:

"(a) Apalachee Correctional Institution;

"(b) Florida Correctional Institution;

"(c) Glades Correctional Institution;

"(d) Florida State Prison;

"(e) Department of Corrections Road Prisons;

"(f) Sumter Correctional Institution;

"(g) Avon Park Correctional Institution;

"(h) Union Correctional Institution;

"(i) Reception and Medical Center at Lake Butler;

"(j) Cross City Correctional Institution;

"(k) Lake Correctional Institution;

"(*l*) Brevard Correctional Institution;

"(m) Department of Corrections Community Correctional Centers;

"(n) Department of Corrections Vocational Centers; and

"(*o*) DeSoto Correctional Institution."

Laws 1987, c. 87–87, § 6, and Laws 1987, c. 87–226, § 76, both reviser's bills, repealed subsec. (1)(e).

Laws 1999, c. 99–8, § 313, eff. June 29, 1999, substituted "Department of Children and Family Services" for "Department of Health and Rehabilitative Services".

Laws 2006, c. 2006–227, § 65, in subsec. (2), inserted references to the Agency for Persons with Disabilities throughout; and in subsec. (3), deleted the former second and third sentences, which had read, "Any facility the purpose and use of which was changed subsequent to January 1, 1975, shall be returned to its original use and purpose by July 1, 1977. However, the G. Pierce Wood Memorial Hospital located at Arcadia, DeSoto County, may not be converted into a correctional facility as long as such hospital is in use as a state mental health hospital.".

Cross References

Corrections department, see § 20.315.

Library References

Prisons ⚿100 to 102.
Westlaw Topic No. 310.

C.J.S. Prisons and Rights of Prisoners §§ 1 to 2, 5 to 7, 14, 17, 22 to 23, 50 to 53, 55, 59, 78.

Research References

Encyclopedias

State Inmates, FL Jur. 2d Prisons & Prisoners § 105.

Transfers to Department of Children and Family Services, FL Jur. 2d Prisons & Prisoners § 144.

Notes of Decisions

---

1. Validity

Provision contained in this section approving conversion of portion of G. Pierce Wood Memorial Hospital into correctional facility was constitutional, and thus such latter expression of legislature's will prevailed over prior Baker Act provisions setting forth rights of mental patients and designating such hospital as treatment facility. Askew v. Schuster, 331 So.2d 297 (1976). Statutes ⚿ 223.1

2. Certiorari

Where circuit judge entered order concerning handling of five defendants during murder trial to be held before the judge in Sumter County Courthouse directing sheriffs of his circuit and State Division of Corrections to deliver defendants in their custody to the Sumter Correctional Institution, and director attacked validity of such order, director's petition would be considered as a petition for certiorari rather than prohibition. State ex rel. Wainwright v. Booth, App. 2 Dist., 291 So.2d 74 (1974), writ discharged 300 So.2d 257. Prisons ⚿ 372

3. Standing

Where circuit judge entered order concerning handling of five defendants during murder trial to be held before judge in Sumter County Courthouse directing sheriffs of his circuit and Director of State Division of Corrections to deliver defendants in their custody to the Sumter Correctional Institution, director, though not a party to case below, had sufficient standing to file petition questioning judge's order, since order was specifically directed toward him. State ex rel. Wainwright v. Booth, App. 2 Dist., 291 So.2d 74 (1974), writ discharged 300 So.2d 257. Prisons ⚿ 372

4. Incarceration during trial

Circuit judge who was to conduct in Sumter County Courthouse the trial of five defendants for murder allegedly committed while they were incarcerated in Sumter Correctional Institution exceeded his jurisdiction in ordering Director of State Division of Corrections to deliver the defendants to Superintendent of Sumter Correctional Institution where they were to be held until further order of court and in requiring director to provide daily transportation of defendants to and from courthouse and to supply at least seven correctional officers to be responsible for courtroom security. State ex rel. Wainwright v. Booth, App. 2 Dist., 291 So.2d 74 (1974), writ discharged 300 So.2d 257. Prisons ⚿ 372

Circuit judge, who was to conduct in Sumter County Courthouse the trial of five defendants for murder allegedly committed while they were incarcerated in Sumter Correctional Institution, would be within his rights to direct sheriff of Sumter County to take special security precautions in connection with the trial, and if sheriff was not properly equipped to do so, the sheriff could then take such steps as were available to him to obtain the necessary assistance. State ex rel. Wainwright v. Booth, App. 2 Dist., 291 So.2d 74 (1974), writ discharged 300 So.2d 257. Criminal Law ⚿ 633.17

5. Conversion of properties

Under Correctional Organization Act, Governor had authority to convert part of hospital into correctional facility, based upon his finding that partial conversion of hospital was least costly means at hand to accommodate a critical increase in prison population and that substantial economic benefits would accrue to state by that action. Smith v. Askew, App. 1 Dist., 335 So.2d 314 (1976). Prisons ⚷ 415

6. Civil liability

In the event that employees of the division of corrections render emergency care in a reasonably prudent manner to a visitor injured on institutional grounds, they are immune from civil liability where treatment is provided outside of a hospital, doctor's office, or other place having proper medical equipment and without objection by the injured victim. As a state agency, the division of corrections is immune from civil liability for such injuries. Op.Atty.Gen., 074–38, Feb. 11, 1974.

945.03. Repealed by Laws 1971, c. 71–377, § 283

Historical and Statutory Notes

Repealed § 945.03, which related to the administration of the division, was derived from Laws 1957, c. 57–213, § 3, and Laws 1961, c. 61–530, § 18. Laws 1969, c. 69–106, § 19, the Governmental Reorganization Act, rendered the section obsolete.

945.031. Repealed by Laws 1985, c. 85–288, § 27, eff. July 1, 1985

Historical and Statutory Notes

Repealed § 945.031, which related to the adoption of an official seal, was derived from:
Laws 1979, c. 79–3, § 79.
Laws 1977, c. 77–120, § 70.
Laws 1969, c. 69–106, §§ 19, 35.
Laws 1965, c. 65–163, § 1.

945.0311. Employment of relatives

(1) For the purposes of this section, the term:

(a) "Department" means the Department of Corrections.

(b) "Relative" means an individual who is related to another as father, mother, son, daughter, brother, sister, uncle, aunt, first cousin, nephew, niece, husband, wife, father-in-law, mother-in-law, daughter-in-law, brother-in-law, sister-in-law, stepfather, stepmother, stepson, stepdaughter, stepbrother, stepsister, half brother, or half sister.

(c) "Organizational unit" includes:

1. A unit of a state correctional institution such as security, medical, dental, classification, maintenance, personnel, or business. A work camp, boot camp, or other annex of a state correctional institution is considered part of the institution and not a separate unit.

2. An area of a regional office such as personnel, medical, administrative services, probation and parole, or community facilities.

3. A correctional work center, road prison, or work release center.

4. A probation and parole circuit office or a suboffice within a circuit.

5. A bureau of the Office of the Secretary or of any of the assistant secretaries.

(d) "Line of authority" means any position having supervisory authority within the direct chain of command or supervisory path that organizationally links any position in the department to the secretary.

(e) "Direct supervision" means being an employee's immediate supervisor, or the rater or reviewer of the employee's performance.

(2) In the interest of security and effective management, the department may adopt rules prohibiting the employment of relatives in the same organizational unit or in positions in which one employee would be in the line of authority over the other or under the direct supervision of the other.

Laws 1995, c. 95–283, § 25.

Historical and Statutory Notes

Amendment Notes:

This section was designated as § 945.03 in Laws 1995, c. 95–283, § 25, but was redesignated as § 945.0311 in Fla.St.1995.

Library References

Prisons ⚿392.
Westlaw Topic No. 310.

C.J.S. Prisons and Rights of Prisoners §§ 13, 15.

Research References

Encyclopedias

Employment of Relatives, FL Jur. 2d Prisons & Prisoners § 38.

945.035. Notice of employment, appointment, or separation; response by the correctional officer; duty of department

(1) For the purposes of this section, the term "commission" refers to the Criminal Justice Standards and Training Commission.

(2) Pursuant to s. 943.139, the department shall immediately notify the commission in writing, on a form adopted by the commission, of the employment or appointment, or separation from employment or appointment, of any correctional officer. The department must maintain the form and submit, or electronically transmit, a copy of the form to the commission. "Separation from employment or appointment" includes any firing, termination, resignation, retirement, or voluntary or involuntary extended leave of absence of any correctional officer.

(3) In a case of separation from employment or appointment, the department shall execute and maintain an affidavit-of-separation form adopted by the commission, setting forth in detail the facts and reasons for such separation. A copy of the affidavit-of-separation form must be submitted, or electronically transmitted, to the commission. If the correctional officer is separated for failure to comply with s. 943.13, the notice must so specify. The affidavit must be executed under oath and constitutes an official statement within the purview of s. 837.06. The affidavit must include conspicuous language that intentional false execution of the affidavit constitutes a misdemeanor of the second degree. Any correctional officer who has separated from employment or appointment must be permitted to respond to the separation, in writing, to the commission,

setting forth the facts and reasons for the separation as the officer understands them.

(4) Before employing or appointing any correctional officer, the department must contact the commission to inquire as to the facts and reasons an officer became separated from any previous employing agency. The commission shall, upon request and without prejudice, provide to the department all information that is required under subsections (2) and (3) and that is in its possession.

(5) An administrator of the department who discloses information pursuant to this section is immune from civil liability in accordance with the provisions of s. 768.095.

Added by Laws 1996, c. 96–312, § 53, eff. July 1, 1996.

Library References

Prisons ⚷392, 396, 400.
Westlaw Topic No. 310.

C.J.S. Prisons and Rights of Prisoners §§ 13, 15, 123 to 125, 127.

945.04. Department of Corrections; general function; seal; use of inmate labor

(1) The Department of Corrections shall be responsible for the inmates and for the operation of, and shall have supervisory and protective care, custody, and control of, all buildings, grounds, property of, and matters connected with, the correctional system.

(2) The Department of Corrections may adopt an official seal to be used for the purpose of authenticating its official documents and for such other purposes as the department prescribes.

(3) The Department of Corrections shall maximize the use of inmate labor in the construction of inmate housing and the conduct of all maintenance projects so that such activities provide work opportunities for the optimum number of inmates in the most cost-effective manner.

Laws 1957, c. 57–213, § 4; Laws 1961, c. 61–530, § 18; Laws 1977, c. 77–120, § 70; Laws 1979, c. 79–3, § 80; Laws 1985, c. 85–288, § 8; Laws 1995, c. 95–283, § 26. Amended by Laws 1997, c. 97–93, § 19, eff. July 1, 1997; Laws 1997, c. 97–227, § 12, eff. May 30, 1997.

Historical and Statutory Notes

Amendment Notes:

Laws 1961, c. 61–530, § 18, substituted the "division" for "department".

Laws 1977, c. 77–120, a reviser's bill, amended this section to conform with Laws 1975, c. 75–49, which created the department of offender rehabilitation (see § 20.315) and transferred to the department certain functions performed by the division of corrections of the department of health and rehabilitative services and the parole and probation commission of the department of offender rehabilitation.

Laws 1979, c. 79–3, a reviser's bill, provided for substitution of references to the department and secretary of "corrections" for the department and secretary of "offender rehabilitation" to conform with Laws 1978, c. 78–53.

Laws 1985, c. 85–288, § 8, eff. July 1, 1985, designated existing provision as subsec. (1) and added subsecs. (2) and (3).

Laws 1995, c. 95–283, § 26, eff. June 15, 1995, added subsecs. (4) and (5).

Laws 1997, c. 97–93, eff. July 1, 1997, was a reviser's bill which deleted obsolete and expired provisions, corrected cross references and citations, and corrected grammatical and other similar errors.

Laws 1997, c. 97–227, § 12, eff. May 30, 1997, repealed subsecs. (4) and (5), which had related to assignment of inmates to and removal of inmates from programs.

Library References

Prisons ⚷100 to 102, 170.
Westlaw Topic No. 310.
C.J.S. Convicts §§ 16 to 19.
C.J.S. Prisons and Rights of Prisoners §§ 1 to 2, 5 to 7, 14, 17, 22 to 23, 50 to 53, 55, 59, 78.

Notes of Decisions

Construction and application 1

1. Construction and application

Administrative rule allowing Department of Corrections (DOC) to charge inmates for photographic copying services was invalid exercise of delegated legislative authority; enabling statutes upon which DOC relied in imposing fees for copy services, rather than authorizing DOC to make monetary assessments for various services, simply authorized the collection of monetary assessments, in addition to setting forth general functions and responsibilities of DOC, along with rights of inmates. Smith v. Florida Dept. of Corrections, App. 1 Dist., 920 So.2d 638 (2005), rehearing denied, review denied 923 So.2d 1162. Prisons ⚷ 417

945.043. Department-operated day care services

(1) The department shall have the authority to establish and operate child care services for department employees. Child care enhances the department's ability to recruit and retain employees in remote or understaffed areas. Child care centers must be located on or adjacent to the grounds of an institution or facility, and must be located outside the grounds of the compound area where inmates are housed. Individuals utilizing the child care services are not limited to employees of the department. Employees of other state agencies may also utilize department-operated day care centers. Furthermore, individual day care centers may enter into consortium agreements with their local city or county governments or the Federal Government, permitting centers to admit the children of those city, county, and Federal Government employees. Employees and other individuals who utilize the child care services shall be charged a fee for such services.

(2) The department is exempt from the requirements of s. 110.151.

Added by Laws 1996, c. 96–312, § 12, eff. July 1, 1996.

Library References

Prisons ⚷395.
Westlaw Topic No. 310.
C.J.S. Prisons and Rights of Prisoners §§ 5, 16.

945.045. Renumbered as 946.001 in Fla.St.1983

945.047. Licensing requirements for physicians, osteopathic physicians, and chiropractic physicians employed by the department

(1) The Department of Corrections shall employ only physicians, osteopathic physicians, or chiropractic physicians holding licenses in good standing to practice medicine in this state, except that, by October 1, 1980, no more than 10 percent of the total number of such physicians employed by the department may be exempted from the provisions of this subsection. Each such exempted physician shall hold a valid license to practice medicine, osteopathic medicine,

or chiropractic medicine in another state and shall have been certified by the appropriate board as eligible for admission for examination in this state under chapter 458, chapter 459, or chapter 460, as applicable. The appropriate board shall not certify as eligible for admission for examination any person who has been adjudged unqualified or guilty of any of the acts enumerated in the disciplinary provisions contained in chapter 458, chapter 459, or chapter 460, as applicable.

(2) No person subject to the provisions of this section shall, by virtue of his or her continued employment in accordance with such provisions, be in violation of the unauthorized practice provisions of chapter 458, chapter 459, or chapter 460 during such period of employment.

Laws 1979, c. 79–302, § 3. Amended by Laws 1997, c. 97–102, § 1662, eff. July 1, 1997; Laws 1997, c. 97–264, § 66, eff. July 1, 1997; Laws 1998, c. 98–166, § 299, eff. July 1, 1998.

Historical and Statutory Notes

Amendment Notes:

Laws 1997, c. 97–102, eff. July 1, 1997, removed gender-specific references applicable to human beings from volume 4 of the Florida Statutes without substantive changes in legal effect.

Laws 1997, c. 97–264, § 66, eff. July 1, 1997, in the second sentence, substituted "osteopathic medicine" for "osteopathy" throughout.

Laws 1998, c. 98–166, § 299, in the section heading, substituted "chiropractic physicians" for "chiropractors"; and, in subsec. (1), inserted "medicine" following "chiropractic".

Library References

Prisons ⚷392.
Westlaw Topic No. 310.
C.J.S. Prisons and Rights of Prisoners §§ 13, 15.

945.05. Repealed by Laws 1972, c. 72–24, § 1

Historical and Statutory Notes

Repealed § 945.05, which related to the advisory council on adult corrections and prison industries, was derived from:

Laws 1969, c. 69–106, §§ 19, 35.
Laws 1963, c. 63–400, § 19.
Laws 1961, c. 61–530, § 18.
Laws 1957, c. 57–213, § 5.

Laws 1972, c. 72–24, § 1, provided:

"Section 945.05, Florida Statutes, is repealed and the advisory council on adult corrections and prison industries created thereby is abolished."

945.06. Renumbered as 946.006 in Fla.St.1983

945.061. Renumbered as 946.007 in Fla.St.1983

945.062. Renumbered as 946.008 in Fla.St.1983

945.063. Renumbered as 946.009 in Fla.St.1983

945.065. Repealed by Laws 1978, c. 78–323, § 4, eff. Oct. 1, 1981; Laws 1983, c. 83–85, § 37, eff. Aug. 12, 1983

Historical and Statutory Notes

Repealed § 945.065, which related to the prison industry commission, was derived from Laws 1976, c. 76–273, § 4, and Laws 1979, c. 79–3, § 83.

945.066. Repealed by Laws 1983, c. 83–216, § 187

Historical and Statutory Notes

Repealed § 945.066, which related to the powers and duties of the prison industry commission, was derived from Laws 1976, c. 76–273, § 5.

945.07. Repealed by Laws 1967, c. 67–100, § 2

Historical and Statutory Notes

Repealed § 945.07, which related to the prison camps, was added by Laws 1957, c. 57–213, § 7, and amended by Laws 1961, c. 61–530, § 18.

945.08. Repealed by Laws 1965, c. 65–171, § 2

Historical and Statutory Notes

Repealed § 945.08, which related to the adoption of regulations for the classification of offenders and separation of prisoners by sex and race, was derived from Laws 1957, c. 57–213, § 8.

945.081. Repealed by Laws 1985, c. 85–288, § 27, eff. July 1, 1985

Historical and Statutory Notes

Repealed §§ 945.081 and 945.09, which related to classification regulations and classification of the commitment of prisoners, were derived from:

Laws 1981, c. 81–323, § 1.
Laws 1979, c. 79–3, § 85.
Laws 1977, c. 77–174, § 1.
Laws 1977, c. 77–120, §§ 72, 73.
Laws 1974, c. 74–112, § 27.
Laws 1969, c. 69–106, §§ 19, 35.
Laws 1967, c. 67–38, § 1.
Laws 1965, c. 65–171, § 1.
Laws 1961, c. 61–530, § 18.
Laws 1957, c. 57–213, § 9.

945.09. Repealed by Laws 1985, c. 85–288, § 27, eff. July 1, 1985

Historical and Statutory Notes

See Historical and Statutory Notes following F.S.A. § 945.09.

945.091. Extension of the limits of confinement; restitution by employed inmates

(1) The department may adopt rules permitting the extension of the limits of the place of confinement of an inmate as to whom there is reasonable cause to believe that the inmate will honor his or her trust by authorizing the inmate, under prescribed conditions and following investigation and approval by the secretary, or the secretary's designee, who shall maintain a written record of such action, to leave the confines of that place unaccompanied by a custodial agent for a prescribed period of time to:

(a) Visit, for a specified period, a specifically designated place or places:

1. For the purpose of visiting a dying relative, attending the funeral of a relative, or arranging for employment or for a suitable residence for use when released;

2. To otherwise aid in the rehabilitation of the inmate and his or her successful transition into the community; or

3. For another compelling reason consistent with the public interest,

and return to the same or another institution or facility designated by the Department of Corrections.

(b) Work at paid employment, participate in an education or a training program, or voluntarily serve a public or nonprofit agency or faith-based service group in the community, while continuing as an inmate of the institution or facility in which the inmate is confined, except during the hours of his or her employment, education, training, or service and traveling thereto and therefrom. An inmate may travel to and from his or her place of employment, education, or training only by means of walking, bicycling, or using public transportation or transportation that is provided by a family member or employer. Contingent upon specific appropriations, the department may transport an inmate in a state-owned vehicle if the inmate is unable to obtain other means of travel to his or her place of employment, education, or training.

1. An inmate may participate in paid employment only during the last 36 months of his or her confinement, unless sooner requested by the Parole Commission or the Control Release Authority.

2. While working at paid employment and residing in the facility, an inmate may apply for placement at a contracted substance abuse transition housing program. The transition assistance specialist shall inform the inmate of program availability and assess the inmate's need and suitability for transition housing assistance. If an inmate is approved for placement, the specialist shall assist the inmate. If an inmate requests and is approved for placement in a contracted faith-based substance abuse transition housing program, the specialist must consult with the chaplain prior to such placement. The department shall ensure that an inmate's faith orientation, or lack thereof, will not be considered in determining admission to a faith-based program and that the program does not attempt to convert an inmate toward a particular faith or religious preference.

(c) Participate in a residential or nonresidential rehabilitative program operated by a public or private nonprofit agency, including faith-based service groups, with which the department has contracted for the treatment of such inmate. The provisions of ss. 216.311 and 287.057 shall apply to all contracts between the department and any private entity providing such services. The department shall require such agency to provide appropriate supervision of inmates participating in such program. The department is authorized to terminate any inmate's participation in the program if such inmate fails to demonstrate satisfactory progress in the program as established by departmental rules.

(2) Each inmate who demonstrates college-level aptitudes by satisfactory evidence of successful completion of college-level academic coursework may be provided the opportunity to participate in college-level academic programs which may be offered at community colleges or universities. The inmate is personally responsible for the payment of all student fees incurred.

(3) The department may adopt regulations as to the eligibility of inmates for the extension of confinement, the disbursement of any earnings of these inmates, or the entering into of agreements between itself and any city or county or federal agency for the housing of these inmates in a local place of confinement. However, no person convicted of sexual battery pursuant to s. 794.011 is eligible for any extension of the limits of confinement under this section.

(4) The willful failure of an inmate to remain within the extended limits of his or her confinement or to return within the time prescribed to the place of confinement designated by the department shall be deemed as an escape from the custody of the department and shall be punishable as prescribed by law.

(5) The provisions of this section shall not be deemed to authorize any inmate who has been convicted of any murder, manslaughter, sexual battery, robbery, arson, aggravated assault, aggravated battery, kidnapping, escape, breaking and entering with intent to commit a felony, or aircraft piracy, or any attempt to commit the aforementioned crimes, to attend any classes at any state community college or any university which is a part of the State University System.

(6)(a) The department shall require inmates working at paid employment as provided in paragraph (1)(b) to use a portion of the employment proceeds to provide restitution to the aggrieved party for the damage or loss caused by the offense of the inmate, in an amount to be determined by the department, unless the department finds clear and compelling reasons not to order such restitution. If restitution or partial restitution is not ordered, the department shall state on the record in detail the reasons therefor.

(b) An offender who is required to provide restitution or reparation may petition the circuit court to amend the amount of restitution or reparation required or to revise the schedule of repayment established by the department or the Parole Commission.

(7) The department shall document and account for all forms for disciplinary reports for inmates placed on extended limits of confinement, which shall include, but not be limited to, all violations of rules of conduct, the rule or rules violated, the nature of punishment administered, the authority ordering such punishment, and the duration of time during which the inmate was subjected to confinement.

(8)(a) The department is authorized to levy fines only through disciplinary reports and only against inmates placed on extended limits of confinement. Major and minor infractions and their respective punishments for inmates placed on extended limits of confinement shall be defined by the rules of the department, provided that any fine shall not exceed $50 for each infraction deemed to be minor and $100 for each infraction deemed to be major. Such fines shall be deposited in the General Revenue Fund, and a receipt shall be given to the inmate.

(b) When the chief correctional officer determines that a fine would be an appropriate punishment for a violation of the rules of the department, both the determination of guilt and the amount of the fine shall be determined by the disciplinary committee pursuant to the method prescribed in s. 944.28(2)(c).

(c) The department shall develop rules defining the policies and procedures for the administering of such fines.

Laws 1967, c. 67–59, § 1; Laws 1969, c. 69–6, § 1; Laws 1969, c. 69–106, §§ 19, 35; Laws 1971, c. 71–112, § 1; Laws 1976, c. 76–273, § 9; Laws 1977, c. 77–120, § 74; Laws 1977, c. 77–150, § 4; Laws 1979, c. 79–3, § 86; Laws 1983, c. 83–274, § 2; Laws 1983, c. 83–290, § 2; Laws 1984, c. 84–363, § 7; Laws 1985, c. 85–288, § 9; Laws 1985, c. 85–340, § 8; Laws 1986, c. 86–46, § 2; Laws 1988, c. 88–96, § 12; Laws 1988, c. 88–122, §§ 55, 88; Laws 1990, c. 90–268, § 32; Laws 1992, c. 92–27, § 1; Laws 1993, c. 93–156, § 21; Laws 1995, c. 95–283, § 27. Amended by Laws 1996, c. 96–312, § 13, eff. July 1, 1996; Laws 1997, c. 97–102, § 1857, eff. July 1, 1997; Laws 2001, c. 2001–110, § 14, eff. July 1, 2001; Laws 2003, c. 2003–141, § 1, eff. Oct. 1, 2003; Laws 2003, c. 2003–179, § 9, eff. July 1, 2003.

Historical and Statutory Notes

Amendment Notes:

Laws 1967, c. 67–59 became law without Governor's approval.

Laws 1969, c. 69–6, § 1, deleted, from subsec. (1)(b), the first proviso which read: "provided there shall not be in excess of 2 per cent of the total prison population participating in this program at the same time and" following "traveling thereto and therefrom".

The second proviso in subsec. (1)(b), as enacted by Laws 1967, c. 67–59, § 1, appears as the second sentence in Fla.St.1969.

Laws 1969, c. 69–106, §§ 19, 35, transferred all powers, duties and functions of the board of commissioners of state institutions to the division of adult corrections of the department of health and rehabilitative services.

Laws 1971, c. 71–112, § 1, substituted, in subsec. (1), approval by the director in lieu of approval by the parole and probation commission; and, removed, in subsec. (1)(a), the twenty-four hour limit on visits.

Laws 1976, c. 76–273, substituted "secretary" for "director" in the introductory portion of subsec. (1), and substituted "18" for "12" months in the second sentence and added the provisions contained in subsec. (5).

Laws 1977, c. 77–120, a reviser's bill, amended this section to conform with Laws 1975, c. 75–49, which created the department of offender rehabilitation (see § 20.315) and transferred to the department certain functions performed by the division of corrections of the department of health and rehabilitative services and the parole and probation commission of the department of offender rehabilitation. Subsection (4) was deleted by amendment, and subsec. (5) was redesignated as subsec. (4) in Fla.St.1977.

The deleted subsection provided:

"The parole and probation commission is authorized to make investigations and recommendations pertaining to the validity of requests for visits by inmates, community attitudes towards inmates, and job opportunities for inmates and to otherwise assist the division when requested in the implementation of the program herein authorized."

Laws 1977, c. 77–150, deleted "and forward a copy of his approval to the Parole and Probation Commission" preceding ", to leave the confines of that place" in subsec. (1), and added provisions contained in subsec. (5).

Laws 1979, c. 79–3, a reviser's bill, provided for substitution of references to the department and secretary of "corrections" for the department and secretary of "offender rehabilitation" to conform with Laws 1978, c. 78–53.

Laws 1983, c. 83–274, § 2, added the second sentence to subsec. (3).

Laws 1983, c. 83–290, § 2, added a new subsec. (2), renumbered former subsecs. (2) to (5) as subsecs. (3) to (6), and deleted "burglary" from the enumeration of subsec. (5).

Laws 1984, c. 84–363, § 7, in subsec. (6)(a), in the first sentence, substituted "shall" for "may" and inserted "unless the department finds reasons not to order such restitution", and added the second sentence.

Laws 1985, c. 85–288, § 9, eff. July 1, 1985, added subsecs. (7) and (8).

Laws 1985, c. 85–340, § 8, eff. June 24, 1985, added subsec. (1)(c).

Laws 1986, c. 86–46, § 2, eff. June 2, 1986, amending subsec. (1) deleted the former third sentence and added a new third sentence in par. (c), and added par. (d).

Laws 1988, c. 88–96, § 12, inserted "to use a portion of the employment proceeds" preceding "to provide restitution" and inserted "clear and compelling" preceding "reasons" in the first sentence and inserted "in detail" preceding "the reasons therefor" in the second sentence of subsec. (6)(a).

Laws 1988, c. 88–96, § 15, provides that the act "shall take effect upon the effective date [January 3, 1989] of the amendment to the State Constitution contained in [1987] Senate Joint Resolution No. 135, which is to be submitted to the electors of this state for approval at the general election to be held in November 1988."

The electorate ratified the amendment to Const. Art. 1, § 16, proposed by 1987, S.J.R. No. 135, relating to rights of crime victims, at the November 8, 1988 general election. See Const. Art. 1, § 16.

Laws 1988, c. 88–122, § 55, eff. July 1, 1988, substituted the commission name of "parole" for "parole and probation".

Laws 1988, c. 88–122, § 88, eff. July 1, 1988, substituted in the second sentence of subsec. (1)(b) 24 months for 18 months.

Laws 1990, c. 90–268, § 32, eff. Oct. 1, 1990, reenacted subsec. (1) without change "For the purpose of incorporating the amendments to part I of chapter 287, Florida Statutes, in references thereto."

Laws 1992, c. 92–27, § 1, near the end of subsec. (b), substituted "36 months" for "24 months"; and at the end of subsec. (b), added "or the Control Release Authority".

Laws 1993, c. 93–156, § 21, eff. Oct. 1, 1993, in subsec. (3), in the second sentence, following "794.011" deleted "or any other sex offense specified in s. 917.012(1)"; and, at the end of the sentence, deleted "unless he has successfully completed a program of treatment pursuant to s. 917.012".

Laws 1995, c. 95–283, § 27, eff. June 15, 1995, in subsec. (1), in the introductory paragraph, inserted "or the deputy secretary or regional directors of the department as the secretary's designee".

Laws 1996, c. 96–312, § 13, eff. July 1, 1996, in subsec. (1), in the introductory paragraph, preceding "secretary's designee", deleted "deputy secretary or regional directors of the department as the"; and deleted a former par. (d), which read:

"Participate in a rehabilitative community reentry program on conditional release for a specified period not to exceed the last 90 days of confinement. While in a supervised release status, the inmate shall not be considered to be in the care and custody of the department or in confinement, extended or otherwise. The inmate shall be under the supervision of the department in the community as prescribed by the department. The department is authorized to terminate any inmate's participation in the program if such inmate fails to demonstrate satisfactory progress in the program as established by departmental rules and return such inmate to the institution or facility designated by the department. Inmates shall remain eligible to earn or lose gain-time as prescribed by law and rules of the department."

Laws 1997, c. 97–102, eff. July 1, 1997, removed gender-specific references applicable to human beings from volume 4 of the Florida Statutes without substantive changes in legal effect.

Laws 2001, c. 2001–110, § 14, in subsec. (1)(a)2., inserted "and his or her successful transition into the community" following "inmate"; in subsec. (1)(b), inserted "or faith-based service group" following "agency"; added subsec. (1)(b)2., relating to placement in a substance-abuse-transition housing program; and, in subsec. (1)(c), inserted ", including faith-based service groups," following "agency".

Laws 2003, c. 2003–141, § 1, in subsec. (1)(b), added "An inmate may travel to and from his or her place of employment, education, or training only by means of walking, bicycling, or using public transportation or transportation that is provided by a family member or employer. Contingent upon specific appropriations, the department may transport an inmate in a state-owned vehicle if the inmate is unable to obtain other means of travel to his or her place of employment, education, or training" following the first sentence.

Laws 2003, c. 2003–179, § 9, in subsec. (8)(a), substituted a reference to the General Revenue Fund for a reference to the Inmate Welfare Trust Fund in the last sentence.

Cross References

Employment of prisoners in correctional work programs, disposition of compensation earned, see §§ 946.002, 946.513.

Escape, see § 944.40.
Public works, use of prisoner labor, see § 946.40.
Work-release programs for county prisoners, extended limits of confinement, see § 951.24.
Work-release programs for youthful offenders, extended limits of confinement, see § 958.09.

Library References

Escape ⚷1.
Prisons ⚷117, 172, 174, 248 to 250, 274, 279.
Westlaw Topic Nos. 151, 310.
C.J.S. Convicts §§ 2, 4 to 5, 14 to 15, 20 to 23.
C.J.S. Escape and Related Offenses; Rescue §§ 1 to 4, 6 to 10, 12 to 17, 50.
C.J.S. Prisons and Rights of Prisoners §§ 23, 26 to 44, 47, 76, 78 to 88, 123, 125, 127, 136 to 141, 149 to 150, 152.

Research References

ALR Library

50 ALR 104, Constitutionality of Statutes in Relation to Treatment or Discipline of Convicts.

Encyclopedias

Violations and Effect Thereof; Disciplinary Reports and Punishment, FL Jur. 2d Prisons & Prisoners § 103.

Leaving Place of Confinement to Participate in Rehabilitative Program, FL Jur. 2d Prisons & Prisoners § 120.

Leased or Managed Work Programs; Management by Nonprofit Corporation, FL Jur. 2d Prisons & Prisoners § 155.

Earnings from Work-Release Programs, FL Jur. 2d Prisons & Prisoners § 163.

Use of Earnings for Restitution, FL Jur. 2d Prisons & Prisoners § 167.

Generally; Leaving Place of Confinement for Work or Voluntary Service at Public or Nonprofit Agency or Faith-Based Service Group, FL Jur. 2d Prisons & Prisoners § 175.

Treatises and Practice Aids

16 Florida Practice Series § 1:77, Credit for Time Served--Credit for Time Spent on Furlough.

Notes of Decisions

---

1. Restitution

Where defendant pleaded nolo contendere to charge against her pursuant to a plea bargain that she would be placed on probation for five years with special condition that she make restitution of property taken in burglary and two others, act of trial court in failing thereafter to afford defendant required hearing as to amount of restitution and, instead, delegating authority to defendant's probation supervisor was improper. Kroenke v. State, App. 2 Dist., 366 So.2d 46 (1978), certiorari denied 374 So.2d 99. Sentencing And Punishment ⚷ 1973(3)

2. Escape

Failure to return from period of temporary release was not "escape" within meaning of juvenile statutes, even though juvenile statute referenced adult statute defining escape, and failure to return was "escape" if committed by adult, given that failure to return was not included within general adult escape statute referenced by juvenile statute, and failure to return by adult was only considered "escape" because of separate adult statute that was not referenced by juvenile statute. J.A.G. v. State, App. 3 Dist., 825 So.2d 497 (2002). Infants ⚷ 153

Inmate who was charged with escape while on work release by failing to remain within the extended limits of his confinement could not be convicted of escape by failing to return within the prescribed time; thus, the trial court erroneously instructed the jury on the alternative theory. Atwell v. State, App. 1 Dist., 739 So.2d 1166 (1999). Criminal Law ⚷ 814(1); Escape ⚷ 9

Erroneously instructing the jury that failure to return within the prescribed time constituted escape from work release required reversal in prosecution of inmate for escape by failing to remain within the extended limits of his confinement; the court gave the instruction after the deliberating jury requested the court to read the instruction on escape. Atwell v. State, App. 1 Dist., 739 So.2d 1166 (1999). Criminal Law ⚷ 1172.6

County prisoner who failed to timely return to jail from Sunday furlough and who was picked up by police was properly charged with escape, in view of this section relating to prisons and correctional institutions and § 951.24 relating to county prisoners, both of which provide that failure to return to place of confinement within time prescribed constitutes an escape. Price v. State, App. 1 Dist., 333 So.2d 84 (1976). Escape ⚷ 2

That county prisoner was simply on furlough and not working when he failed to return to place of employment within time prescribed did not preclude convicting him of escape, even though § 951.24 relating to county prisoners authorizes giving prisoners privilege of leaving jail for work or to participate in educational or vocational programs but says nothing of other purposes. Price v. State, App. 1 Dist., 333 So.2d 84 (1976). Escape ⚷ 2

An inmate who has been granted a furlough pursuant to regulations of the division of corrections, and who willfully fails to return to his place of confinement within the time prescribed, is subject to prosecution for the crime of escape under this section and § 944.40. Op. Atty.Gen., 072–404, Nov. 16, 1972.

3. Indictment and information

No fatal variance between information in escape prosecution and evidence adduced at trial occurred when, although information alleged that defendant escaped while confined in county adult detention center, proof showed that escape occurred after defendant became ill during booking process at detention center and was escorted by police officer to county hospital for treatment. Johnson v. State, App. 1 Dist., 357 So.2d 203 (1978), certiorari denied 362 So.2d 1054. Escape ⚷ 9

4. Terms and conditions of confinement

Shift commander in jail which housed convicted felon had wide discretion in prescribing terms and conditions of confinement, particularly where conditions imposed related to security matters. Farmer v. Crews, M.D.Fla.1992, 804 F.Supp. 1516, affirmed 995 F.2d 236. Prisons ⚷ 123

5. Furlough

Inmate had no liberty interest, needed to claim relief in § 1983 civil rights claim, under furlough to attend funeral of inmate's father on inmate's own recognizance; any embarrassment or emotional distress from being forced to appear escorted by deputy and while wearing institutional clothing with handcuffs and leg restraints was outweighed by government's compelling interest in maintaining security. Farmer v. Crews, M.D.Fla.1992, 804 F.Supp. 1516, affirmed 995 F.2d 236. Civil Rights ⚷ 1098

945.0913. Inmates prohibited from driving state-owned vehicles to transport inmates in a work-release program

An inmate may not drive a state-owned vehicle for the purpose of transporting inmates who are participating in a work-release program authorized in s. 945.091(1)(b).

Added by Laws 2003, c. 2003–141, § 2, eff. Oct. 1, 2003.

Library References

Prisons ⚷174.
Westlaw Topic No. 310.
C.J.S. Convicts §§ 20 to 22.

Research References

Encyclopedias

Generally; Leaving Place of Confinement for Work or Voluntary Service at Public or Nonprofit Agency or Faith-Based Service Group, FL Jur. 2d Prisons & Prisoners § 175.

945.092. Limits on work-release and minimum security custody for persons who have committed the crime of escape

A person who has ever been convicted, regardless of adjudication, of the offense of escape, as prohibited by s. 944.40 or its successor, or as prohibited by a similar law of another state, is not eligible for any work-release program under s. 945.091 or for confinement in minimum security conditions.

Laws 1995, c. 95–283, § 29.

Library References

Prisons ⚿174, 223.
Westlaw Topic No. 310.
C.J.S. Convicts §§ 20 to 22.
C.J.S. Prisons and Rights of Prisoners §§ 18, 23 to 26.

Research References

Encyclopedias

Effect of Particular Crime Convicted For; Placement as Condition of Probation or Community Control, FL Jur. 2d Prisons & Prisoners § 108.

Generally; Leaving Place of Confinement for Work or Voluntary Service at Public or Nonprofit Agency or Faith-Based Service Group, FL Jur. 2d Prisons & Prisoners § 175.

945.10. Confidential information

(1) Except as otherwise provided by law or in this section, the following records and information held by the Department of Corrections are confidential and exempt from the provisions of s. 119.07(1) and s. 24(a), Art. I of the State Constitution:

(a) Mental health, medical, or substance abuse records of an inmate or an offender.

(b) Preplea, pretrial intervention, and presentence or postsentence investigative records, except as provided in s. 960.001(1)(g).

(c) Information regarding a person in the federal witness protection program.

(d) Parole Commission records which are confidential or exempt from public disclosure by law.

(e) Information which if released would jeopardize a person's safety.

(f) Information concerning a victim's statement and identity.

(g) Information which identifies an executioner, or any person prescribing, preparing, compounding, dispensing, or administering a lethal injection.

(h) Records that are otherwise confidential or exempt from public disclosure by law.

(2) The records and information specified in paragraphs (1)(a)–(h) may be released as follows unless expressly prohibited by federal law:

(a) Information specified in paragraphs (1)(b), (d), and (f) to the Office of the Governor, the Legislature, the Parole Commission, the Department of Children and Family Services, a private correctional facility or program that operates under a contract, the Department of Legal Affairs, a state attorney, the court, or a law enforcement agency. A request for records or information pursuant to this paragraph need not be in writing.

(b) Information specified in paragraphs (1)(c), (e), and (h) to the Office of the Governor, the Legislature, the Parole Commission, the Department of Children and Family Services, a private correctional facility or program that operates under contract, the Department of Legal Affairs, a state attorney, the court, or a law enforcement agency. A request for records or information pursuant to this paragraph must be in writing and a statement provided demonstrating a need for the records or information.

(c) Information specified in paragraph (1)(b) to an attorney representing an inmate under sentence of death, except those portions of the records containing a victim's statement or address, or the statement or address of a relative of the victim. A request for records of information pursuant to this paragraph must be in writing and a statement provided demonstrating a need for the records or information.

(d) Information specified in paragraph (1)(b) to a public defender representing a defendant, except those portions of the records containing a victim's statement or address, or the statement or address of a relative of the victim. A request for records or information pursuant to this paragraph need not be in writing.

(e) Information specified in paragraph (1)(b) to state or local governmental agencies. A request for records or information pursuant to this paragraph must be in writing and a statement provided demonstrating a need for the records or information.

(f) Information specified in paragraph (1)(b) to a person conducting legitimate research. A request for records and information pursuant to this paragraph must be in writing, the person requesting the records or information must sign a confidentiality agreement, and the department must approve the request in writing.

(g) Information specified in paragraph (1)(a) to the Department of Health and the county health department where an inmate plans to reside if he or she has tested positive for the presence of the antibody or antigen to human immunodeficiency virus infection.

Records and information released under this subsection remain confidential and exempt from the provisions of s. 119.07(1) and s. 24(a), Art. I of the State Constitution when held by the receiving person or entity.

(3) Due to substantial concerns regarding institutional security and unreasonable and excessive demands on personnel and resources if an inmate or an offender has unlimited or routine access to records of the Department of Corrections, an inmate or an offender who is under the jurisdiction of the department may not have unrestricted access to the department's records or to information contained in the department's records. However, except as to another inmate's or offender's records, the department may permit limited access to its records if an inmate or an offender makes a written request and demonstrates an exceptional need for information contained in the department's records and the information is otherwise unavailable. Exceptional circumstances include, but are not limited to:

(a) The inmate or offender requests documentation to resolve a conflict between the inmate's court documentation and the commitment papers or court orders received by the department regarding the inmate or offender.

(b) The inmate's or offender's release is forthcoming and a prospective employer requests, in writing, documentation of the inmate's or offender's work performance.

(c) The inmate or offender needs information concerning the amount of victim restitution paid during the inmate's or offender's incarceration.

(d) The requested records contain information required to process an application or claim by the inmate or offender with the Internal Revenue Service, the Social Security Administration, the Department of Labor and Employment Security,[1] or any other similar application or claim with a state agency or federal agency.

(e) The inmate or offender wishes to obtain the current address of a relative whose address is in the department's records and the relative has not indicated a desire not to be contacted by the inmate or offender.

(f) Other similar circumstances that do not present a threat to the security, order, or rehabilitative objectives of the correctional system or to any person's safety.

(4) The Department of Corrections shall adopt rules to prevent disclosure of confidential records or information to unauthorized persons.

(5) The Department of Corrections and the Parole Commission shall mutually cooperate with respect to maintaining the confidentiality of records that are exempt from the provisions of s. 119.07(1) and s. 24(a), Art. I of the State Constitution.

Laws 1957, c. 57–213, § 10; Laws 1961, c. 61–530, § 18; Laws 1965, c. 65–453, § 1; Laws 1969, c. 69–106, §§ 19, 35; Laws 1974, c. 74–112, § 24; Laws 1977, c. 77–104, § 255; Laws 1979, c. 79–3, § 87; Laws 1988, c. 88–118, § 1; Laws 1988, c. 88–122, § 56; Laws 1994, c. 94–83, § 1. Amended by Laws 1996, c. 96–406, § 448, eff. July 3, 1996; Laws 1998, c. 98–4, § 2, eff. March 26, 1998; Laws 1999, c. 99–8, § 314, eff. June 29, 1999; Laws 1999, c. 99–263, § 1, eff. July 1, 1999; Laws 2000, c. 2000–1, § 2, eff. 1, 14, 2000; Laws 2002, c. 2002–292, § 3, eff. July 1, 2002; Laws 2003, c. 2003–272, § 3, eff. June 26, 2003.

[1] Laws 2002, c. 2002–194, § 69, repealed § 20.171, which created the Department of Labor and Employment Security.

Historical and Statutory Notes

Amendment Notes:

Laws 1961, c. 61–530, § 18, substituted the "division" for "department".

The name "parole commission" was changed to "probation and parole commission" by authority of Laws 1965, c. 65–453, § 1. See, § 947.01.

Laws 1969, c. 69–106, §§ 19, 35, transferred all powers, duties and functions of the director of each division of the board of commissioners of state institutions to the division of adult corrections (now, division of corrections) of the department of health and rehabilitative services.

As so amended, the section provided:

"The parole and probation commission shall furnish the division with a copy of its report of presentence investigation, if one has been made, and subsequent information as same may become available, on every person committed to the custody of the division. The information furnished by the parole and probation commission shall be confidential and shall be available only to public officers and employees in the performance of a public duty. No inmate of any institution shall have access to any such information or excerpts therefrom. The division shall cooperate with the parole and probation commission as may be required for the proper performance of the functions of the parole and probation commission."

Laws 1974, c. 74–112, § 24, rewrote the section.

Laws 1977, c. 77–104, a reviser's bill, amended this section to reflect transfer of powers, etc., of the parole and probation commission and the division of corrections to the department of offender rehabilitation by Laws 1975, c. 75–49, §§ 2(5) and 2(6).

Laws 1979, c. 79–3, a reviser's bill, provided for substitution of references to the department and secretary of "corrections" for the department and secretary of "offender rehabilitation" to conform with Laws 1978, c. 78–53.

Laws 1988, c. 88–118, § 1, eff. June 16, 1988, substantially rewrote subsec. (2) to authorize the department to grant an inmate access to the files pertaining to him upon court order or upon exceptional circumstances, and to require the department to promulgate rules to administer the section.

Laws 1988, c. 88–122, § 56, eff. July 1, 1988, substituted the commission name of "parole" for "parole and probation".

Laws 1994, c. 94–83, § 1, eff. Oct. 1, 1994, rewrote the section, which formerly read:

"(1) Except as provided below, information in a presentence investigation report made by the Department of Corrections shall be confidential and shall be available only to officers and employees of the court, the Legislature, the Parole Commission, the Department of Health and Rehabilitative Services, the Department of Corrections, and public law enforcement agencies in the performance of a public duty or, with the written permission of the Department of Corrections, to parties establishing legitimate research purposes. The Department of Corrections shall promulgate rules and regulations stating what portions of its files, reports, or records are considered confidential and subject to restricted view. The Department of Corrections shall promulgate rules and regulations to prevent the disclosure of confidential information to unauthorized parties, except as provided above. However, nothing in this subsection shall alter other provisions of the law relating to the accessibility of inmate records.

"(2) Due to concerns for institutional security and unreasonable and excessive demands on agency personnel and resources if an inmate has unlimited or routine access to department records, an inmate of an institution, facility, or program of the Department of Corrections may not have access to any information contained in the records of the department unless a court of competent jurisdiction orders the department to give the inmate access to information in the records. However, the department may permit limited access to information in its records upon his written request, upon demonstration of exceptional circumstances including, but not limited to, safety concerns, and upon demonstration that the requested information is not available from another source. The department shall restrict release of information to any person except members of the news media and those listed in subsection (1) when there is reasonable cause to believe that such person may divulge such information to the inmate. The department shall adopt rules to administer this section.

"(3) The Department of Corrections and the commission shall mutually cooperate for the proper performance of the respective functions of each agency."

Laws 1996, c. 96–406 was a reviser's bill which deleted references to § 119.14 throughout Florida Statutes to conform to the repeal of § 119.14, the Open Government Sunset Review Act, by Laws 1995, c. 95–217, § 1.

Laws 1998, c. 98–4, § 2, in subsec. (1)(g), added "or a person administering a lethal injection pursuant to s. 922.105".

Laws 1999, c. 99–8, § 314, eff. June 29, 1999, substituted "Department of Children and Family Services" for "Department of Health and Rehabilitative Services".

Laws 1999, c. 99–263, § 1, eff. July 1, 1999, in subsec. (1)(b), added ", except as provided in ss. 960.001(1)(g)".

Laws 2000, c. 2000–1, § 2, rewrote subsec. (1)(g), which formerly read:

"(g) The identity of an executioner, or a person administering a lethal injection pursuant to s. 922.105."

Laws 2000, c. 2000–1, § 3, provides:

"The Legislature finds that the disclosure of information identifying a person prescribing, preparing, compounding, dispensing, or administering a lethal injection for purposes of death sentence execution would jeopardize the person's safety and welfare by exposing that person to potential harassment, intimidation, and harm and would constitute an unwarranted invasion into the person's privacy. Therefore, the Legislature finds that it is a public necessity that this information be kept confidential and exempt from disclosure under public records laws."

Laws 2000, c. 2000–1, § 4, provides:

"This act shall take effect on the same date that Senate Bill 6–A or similar legislation providing for execution of the death sentence by lethal injection takes effect, if such legislation is adopted in the same legislative session or an extension thereof."

Laws 2002, c. 2002–292, § 3, reenacted subsec. (1)(a) without making any changes thereto; in subsec. (2), substituted "(1)(a)–(h)" for "(1)(b)–(h)" following "The records and information specified in paragraphs" at the beginning of the subsection; and added subsec. (2)(g), relating to information regarding where an inmate who has tested positive for HIV plans to reside.

Laws 2003, c. 2003–272, § 3, in the first sentence of subsec. (1), substituted "held by" for "of" following "records and information"; and rewrote subsec. (1)(g), which formerly read:

"(g) The identity of an executioner, or a person prescribing, preparing, compounding, dispensing, or administering a lethal injection."

Cross References

Disclosure of presentence investigation reports, see Criminal Procedure Rules 3.712, 3.713.
Handling of persons receiving indeterminate sentences for noncapital felonies, see § 921.18 et seq.
Presentence investigation reports, generally, see § 921.231; Criminal Procedure Rules 3.710, 3.711.

Library References

Prisons ⚷340 to 342.
Records ⚷30 to 53.
Sentencing and Punishment ⚷292.
Westlaw Topic Nos. 310, 326, 350H.
C.J.S. Bankruptcy §§ 830 to 834.
C.J.S. Criminal Law §§ 587 to 591, 2071 to 2072.
C.J.S. Prisons and Rights of Prisoners §§ 5 to 6, 14, 17, 22 to 23, 45 to 53, 55, 59, 76, 78 to 88, 123, 125, 127, 136.
C.J.S. Records §§ 74, 76 to 80, 82 to 142.

Research References

ALR Library

77 ALR 1211, Right of Court to Hear Evidence for Purpose of Determining Sentence to be Imposed.

Encyclopedias

Prisoners, FL Jur. 2d Records & Recording Acts § 50.

Charges for Copies--Indigents, FL Jur. 2d Records & Recording Acts § 66.

Forms

Florida Pleading and Practice Forms § 96:10, Presentence Investigation Report.

Treatises and Practice Aids

1 Florida Practice Series § 608.4, Impeachment--Prior Inconsistent Statements.

Notes of Decisions

---

1. Validity

Subsection (2) of this section totally denying inmate access to information and files of Department of Corrections has no rational basis and unconstitutionally creates three classes of people in regard to access to information held by the Department. Diaz v. Florida Dept. of Corrections, App. 1 Dist., 519 So.2d 41 (1988), appeal dismissed 525 So.2d 877. Constitutional Law ⚷ 3242; Records ⚷ 31

2. Due process

Statute and rule requiring indigent inmate to pay a copy charge when he sought copies of his medical records so he could pursue a medical malpractice action did not deny inmate's right to due process; records were available for inmate's inspection. Brown v. McNeil, App. 1 Dist., 976 So.2d 616 (2008), rehearing denied. Constitutional Law ⚷ 4823; Records ⚷ 15

3. Construction and application

Under §§ 20.315, 947.174 and this section, should state parole and probation commission determine that particular piece of information is necessary for required determinations and that only department of corrections has resources to obtain such information for inmate's file, commission may have not only power but perhaps even duty to initiate legal action to direct department to acquire information for commission's use. Battis v. Florida Parole and Probation Commission, App. 1 Dist., 386 So.2d 295 (1980). Pardon And Parole ⚷ 57.1

Under § 947.01, as a member ex officio of the parole and probation commission, the secretary of the department of offender rehabilitation may not participate in the panel discussions or vote upon the granting or revocation of parole to or recommending clemency for a particular criminal offender. He may, however, participate in the discussion and vote upon all policy-making decisions to the same extent as any other commission member; and, pending a decision on appeal concerning the validity of Laws 1975, c. 75–49, he and his staff should be entitled to access to any of the commission's records that would be useful in deciding matters of policy. Op.Atty.Gen., 075–296, Dec. 3, 1975.

4. Corrections officers

Inmate was not entitled to view the personnel file of correctional facility employee who he alleged was terminated for "violating agency policy"; file was either exempt from disclosure under public records law as identifying information of active or former corrections officers, or was subject to discretionary disclosure under statute governing confidential information held by the Department of Corrections. Smith v. Hernandez, App. 2 Dist., 20 So.3d 905 (2009), rehearing denied, review denied 2010 WL 455511. Records ⚷ 31; Records ⚷ 58

5. Psychiatric evaluations

Issuance of writ of mandamus was not appropriate remedy to obtain access to psychiatric and psychological evaluations by members of Department of Corrections' staff where petitioner had not demonstrated that he had exhausted all adequate remedies, including administrative grievance proceeding outlined in Administrative Code. Park v. Dugger, App. 1 Dist., 548 So.2d 1167 (1989). Mandamus ⚷ 3(8)

6. Safety of individual

Exemption, in statute governing confidentiality of Department of Corrections (DOC) records, for information which if released would jeopardize a person's safety satisfied constitutional requirements for exemption to public records disclosure law, as it provided a meaningful exemption that was supported by a thoroughly articulated public policy. Bryan v. State, 753 So.2d 1244 (2000), certiorari denied 120 S.Ct. 1236, 528 U.S. 1185, 145 L.Ed.2d 1132. Records ⚷ 55

7. Presentence investigation reports

Order requiring Department of Corrections (DOC) to include confidential information in all presentence investigation reports (PSIs) provided to defendants improperly required DOC to act in contravention of statute restricting release of address of victim or victim's relatives in PSI. Singletary v. Smith, App. 2 Dist., 707 So.2d 340 (1997). Sentencing And Punishment ⚷ 297

When defendant seeks presentence investigation report (PSI) with confidential information, Department of Corrections (DOC) should furnish to trial court complete copy of PSI and give to state and defense identical copies in which all confidential information has been redacted; court may then reveal any confidential information it deems appropriate. Singletary v. Smith, App. 2 Dist., 707 So.2d 340 (1997). Sentencing And Punishment ⚷ 298

Department of Corrections (DOC) should not be involved in releasing confidential information in presentence investigation reports (PSIs) to defense or to state. Singletary v. Smith, App. 2 Dist., 707 So.2d 340 (1997). Sentencing And Punishment ⚷ 293

An attorney who represents inmates of state correctional institutions in administrative forums is not an officer of the court to whom presentence investigation reports must be made available pursuant to this section. Op.Atty.Gen. No. 84–96, Oct. 17, 1984.

8. Admissibility of evidence

Prior inconsistent statement made by defendant to his probation officer during presentence investigation interview was admissible during trial for impeachment purposes. Sheffield v. State, App. 1 Dist., 580 So.2d 790 (1991). Witnesses ⚷ 390.1

9. Mandamus

Legislature has mandated setting of presumptive parole release date by state parole and probation commission, and when commission without adequate reason fails so to act, it is answerable in mandamus. Battis v. Florida Parole and Probation Commission, App. 1 Dist., 386 So.2d 295 (1980). Mandamus ⚷ 73(1)

10. Appeal

Documents which were not part of the record and not presented to the parole and probation commission during its review of presumptive parole release date would not be considered on appeal and would be stricken from appendix to brief, despite contention that they were in prisoner's department of corrections file and should have been considered by the commission; if prisoner took issue with the factual predicates relied on by the commission, he should have done so at his review and the documents should have been presented to the commission at that time. Arlotta v. Florida Parole and Probation Com'n, App. 1 Dist., 419 So.2d 1159 (1982). Pardon And Parole ⚷ 62

945.11. Renumbered as 946.40 in Fla.St.1983

945.12. Transfers for rehabilitative treatment

(1) The Department of Corrections is authorized to transfer substance abuse impaired persons, as defined in chapter 397, and tuberculous or other prisoners

requiring specialized services to appropriate public or private facilities or programs for the purpose of providing specialized services or treatment for as long as the services or treatment is needed, but for no longer than the remainder of the prisoner's sentence.

(2) The Department of Corrections is authorized to enter into agreements with the controlling authorities of such state institutions which have or are provided with appropriate facilities for the secure confinement and treatment of substance abuse impaired persons, mentally ill persons, and tuberculous persons. In any such agreement, the department shall provide for custodial personnel to maintain proper security of persons transferred from the correctional system to any other state institution. Such custodial personnel shall be employed and paid by the department and subject to rules such as are agreed upon jointly by it and the controlling authority entering into such agreement.

(3) The department shall reimburse the institution furnishing treatment at a figure agreed upon by it and the controlling authority of such institution.

(4) When, in the opinion of the superintendent of an institution to which a prisoner has been transferred, such prisoner has been cured, or will no longer benefit from treatment at that institution, other than a mentally ill prisoner, the superintendent shall notify the department which shall, at the earliest practicable date thereafter, convey such prisoner to the appropriate classification center for reclassification.

(5) When the department plans to release a mentally ill or retarded offender, an involuntary commitment hearing shall be held as soon as possible prior to his or her release, according to the provisions of chapter 393 or chapter 394.

(6) A prisoner who has been determined by the Department of Children and Family Services and the Department of Corrections to be amenable to rehabilitative treatment for sexual deviation, and who has voluntarily agreed to participate in such rehabilitative treatment, may be transferred to the Department of Children and Family Services provided appropriate bed space is available.

(7) A "mentally ill person" is one who has an impairment of the emotional processes, of the ability to exercise conscious control of one's actions, or of the ability to perceive reality or to understand, which impairment substantially interferes with a person's ability to meet the ordinary demands of living, regardless of etiology.

Laws 1957, c. 57–213, § 12; Laws 1961, c. 61–530, § 18; Laws 1969, c. 69–106, §§ 19, 35; Laws 1974, c. 74–122, § 1; Laws 1977, c. 77–120, § 75; Laws 1977, c. 77–312, § 7; Laws 1979, c. 79–3, § 88; Laws 1979, c. 79–341, §§ 7, 10; Laws 1981, c. 81–259, § 497; Laws 1981, c. 81–293, § 11; Laws 1982, c. 82–224, § 2; Laws 1983, c. 83–109, § 2; Laws 1988, c. 88–33, § 7; Laws 1993, c. 93–39, § 45. Amended by Laws 1997, c. 97–102, § 1663, eff. July 1, 1997; Laws 1999, c. 99–8, § 315, eff. June 29, 1999.

Historical and Statutory Notes

Amendment Notes:

Fla.St.1957, § 945.12 provided:

"(1) The director is authorized to transfer drug addicts committed to the hospital of the state prison under § 398.18, to an appropriate institution for treatment. The director may transfer addicted, insane, tuberculous, or other prisoners requiring specialized medical treatment to an appropriate institution.

"(2) The board is authorized to enter into agreements with the controlling authorities of such state institutions as shall have or be provided with appropriate facilities for the secure confinement and treatment of drug addicts, alcoholics, insane, and tuberculous persons. In any such agreement the board shall provide for custodial personnel to maintain proper security of persons transferred from the correctional system to any other state institution. Such custodial personnel shall be employed and paid by the department and subject to such rules as shall be agreed upon jointly by the board and the controlling authority entering into such agreement.

"(3) The board is authorized to reimburse the institution furnishing treatment at a figure agreed upon by the board and the controlling authority of such institution.

"(4) When in the opinion of the superintendent of an institution to which a prisoner has been transferred such prisoner has been cured, or will no longer benefit from treatment at that institution, other than an insane prisoner, the superintendent shall notify the department, which shall, at the earliest practicable date thereafter, convey such prisoner to the appropriate classification center for reclassification."

Laws 1961, c. 61–530, § 18, substituted the "division" for "department".

Laws 1969, c. 69–106, §§ 19, 35, transferred all powers, duties and functions of the director of each division of the board of commissioners of state institutions to the division of adult corrections of the department of health and rehabilitative services.

Laws 1974, c. 74–122, § 1, rewrote subsec. (1) to provide for inmate transfers for rehabilitative treatment.

Laws 1977, c. 77–120, a reviser's bill, amended this section to conform with Laws 1975, c. 75–49, which created the department of offender rehabilitation (see § 20.315) and transferred to the department certain functions performed by the division of corrections of the department of health and rehabilitative services and the parole and probation commission of the department of offender rehabilitation.

As amended, subsec. (1) provided:

"The Department of Offender Rehabilitation is authorized to transfer drug dependents, as defined in chapter 397, and retarded, addicted, tuberculous, mentally ill, or other prisoners requiring specialized services to appropriate public or private facilities or programs for the purpose of providing such specialized service or treatment for as long as such service or treatment is needed, but for no longer than the remainder of the prisoner's sentence. When it is the intent of the department to transfer a mentally ill or retarded prisoner to the Department of Health and Rehabilitative Services, an involuntary commitment hearing shall be held according to the provisions of chapter 393 or chapter 394. If the committing court finds, after a hearing, that the patient does not meet the criteria for involuntary admission, he shall be returned to the Department of Offender Rehabilitation. If, at the hearing, the court concludes that the patient meets the criteria for involuntary hospitalization under s. 393.11 or s. 394.467(1), the judge shall order the patient to be transferred to a state mental health treatment facility or a retardation facility for treatment. The patient shall be retained by the Department [of Health and Rehabilitative Services] for a period not to exceed the remainder of his sentence. If the administrator of the facility and the patient's physician find that the patient no longer meets the criteria for involuntary admission, he shall be returned to the Department of Offender Rehabilitation immediately. If the patient remains hospitalized when his sentence expires, then an involuntary commitment hearing shall immediately be held in accordance with the provisions of s. 393.11 or s. 394.467."

Laws 1977, c. 77–312, added the second through seventh sentences to subsec. (1), substituted "shall" for "is authorized to" in subsec. (3), and added subsec. (5).

Laws 1979, c. 79–3, a reviser's bill, provided for substitution of references to the department and secretary of "corrections" for the department and secretary of "offender rehabilitation" to conform with Laws 1978, c. 78–53.

Laws 1979, c. 79–341, added subsec. (6).

Laws 1981, c. 81–259, a reviser's correction bill prepared pursuant to § 11.242, amended subsec. (1) of this section by inserting the department name in the third from last sentence.

Laws 1981, c. 81–293, § 11, substituted in subsec. (6)(b) 1983 for 1981 as the date for repeal of the provisions of this section.

Laws 1981, c. 81–293, provided therein that the law take effect July 1, 1981, "but that if it becomes law after that date, it shall operate retroactively to July 1, 1981"; however, approval by the governor occurred subsequent thereto. The Florida Supreme Court in an advisory opinion to the governor of July 19, 1979 (374 So.2d 959) stated in part "* * * the effective date provided in the bill is inoperative unless the bill becomes law on or before that date" and concludes that under such circumstances the provision of Const. Art. 3, § 9, that the law take effect on the sixtieth day after adjournment sine die of the session of the legislature in which enacted, is applicable.

Laws 1982, c. 82–224, § 2, effective July 1, 1984, amending subsec. (1), deleted the mentally ill and mentally retarded from mention in the first sentence and deleted the second and subsequent sentences.

Laws 1982, c. 82–224, § 3, provided that that act shall take effect July 1, 1984. Laws 1984, c. 84–361, § 29, however, amended that section to provide that Laws 1982, c. 82–224, shall take effect Jan. 1, 1985.

Laws 1983, c. 83–109, § 2, repealed subsec. (6)(b) of this section which provided for the scheduled repeal of subsec. (6) of this section on July 1, 1983.

Laws 1988, c. 88–33, § 7, eff. Oct. 1, 1988, substituted "mentally ill" for "insane" in subsec. (2) and (4), and added subsec. (7) defining "mentally ill person".

Laws 1993, c. 93–39, § 45, eff. Oct. 1, 1993, substituted "substance abuse impaired persons" for "drug dependents" in subsec. (1) and substituted the same phrase for "drug addicts, alcoholics" in subsec. (2).

Laws 1997, c. 97–102, eff. July 1, 1997, removed gender-specific references applicable to human beings from volume 4 of the Florida Statutes without substantive changes in legal effect.

Laws 1999, c. 99–8, § 315, eff. June 29, 1999, substituted "Department of Children and Family Services" for "Department of Health and Rehabilitative Services".

Cross References

Corrections Mental Health Act, admission of prisoners to mental health treatment facilities, see § 945.40 et seq.

Library References

Mental Health ⚷436, 452.
Prisons ⚷220.
Westlaw Topic Nos. 257A, 310.
C.J.S. Criminal Law §§ 2188 to 2190.
C.J.S. Mental Health §§ 269, 272 to 277, 283, 288 to 289, 292 to 299.
C.J.S. Prisons and Rights of Prisoners §§ 18, 23 to 26, 76, 78 to 88, 123, 125, 127, 136.

Research References

Encyclopedias

Prisoners, FL Jur. 2d Incompetent Persons § 163.

Duration of Inpatient Treatment; Request for Continued Placement; Discharge, FL Jur. 2d Prisons & Prisoners § 135.

Transfers to Department of Children and Family Services, FL Jur. 2d Prisons & Prisoners § 144.

United States Supreme Court

Involuntary transfer of prisoner to mental hospital, see Vitek v. Jones, 1980, 100 S.Ct. 1254, 445 U.S. 480, 63 L.Ed.2d 552.

Prisoner's right to medical treatment, see Estelle v. Gamble, U.S.Tex.1976, 97 S.Ct. 285, 429 U.S. 97, 50 L.Ed.2d 251, rehearing denied 97 S.Ct. 798, 429 U.S. 1066, 50 L.Ed.2d 785, on remand 554 F.2d 653.

Notes of Decisions

1. Implied consent

If an inmate patient is unable to give informed consent to a medical treatment due to unconsciousness or under similar circumstances, and if the medical treatment must be rendered immediately to preserve life or limb, then medical treatment may be rendered by the Division of Corrections. Under these circumstances is implied that consent exists. Op.Atty. Gen., 075–28, Feb. 12, 1975.

2. Refusal of medical treatment

The Division of Corrections may not forcibly treat an inmate patient who has refused medical treatment deemed necessary to save the inmate's life. Op.Atty.Gen., 075–28, Feb. 12, 1975.

3. Escapee medical treatment

Where an inmate has escaped from the custody of the Florida state prison system, there is no statutory authority authorizing the division of corrections to disburse funds for treatment of injuries sustained by such escapee during the period he is outside the custody and control of the Florida state prison system. Op.Atty.Gen., 073–322, Sept. 6, 1973.

4. Expenses

Medical and surgical expenses incurred in the care and treatment of prisoners were to be paid by the county where the prisoners were held; however, where a county participated in the statutory program which made provision for "hospital service for the indigent" through state and county cooperation to be administered by the state board of health, such expenses could be included in the program. Op.Atty.Gen., 059–18, Jan. 30, 1959.

945.13. Repealed by Laws 1983, c. 83–209, § 6

Historical and Statutory Notes

Repealed § 945.13, which related to maintenance of industrial plants, was derived from:
Laws 1979, c. 79–3, § 89.
Laws 1977, c. 77–120, § 76.
Laws 1969, c. 69–106, §§ 19, 35.
Laws 1957, c. 57–314, § 6.
Fla.St.1955, § 959.01.
Comp.Gen.Laws Supp.1927, § 8663.
Laws 1925, c. 10271, § 1.

945.135. Repealed by Laws 1983, c. 83–209, § 6

Historical and Statutory Notes

Repealed § 945.135, which related to operation of prison industry programs by nonprofit corporations, was derived from Laws 1982, c. 82–409, § 2 and Laws 1981, c. 81–125, §§ 1, 3.

Section 945.135 was amended by Laws 1983, c. 83–216, § 188, eff. Aug. 12, 1983, which was a reviser's correction bill. In addition Laws 1983, c. 83–265, § 2, amended the Sundown Act to provide for repeal of this section on October 1, 1987, and review of the nonprofit corporation leasing the prison industry program pursuant to the Sundown Act, § 11.611.

See, now, F.S.A. § 946.005 et seq.

945.14. Renumbered as 946.20 in Fla.St.1983

945.15. Renumbered as 946.21 in Fla.St.1983

945.16. Renumbered as 946.22 in Fla.St.1983

945.161. Renumbered as 946.24 in Fla.St.1983

945.17. Renumbered as 946.30 in Fla.St.1983

945.18. Renumbered as 946.31 in Fla.St.1983

945.19. Renumbered as 946.32 in Fla.St.1983

945.20. Renumbered as 946.33 in Fla.St.1983

945.21. Repealed by Laws 1985, c. 85–288, § 27, eff. July 1, 1985

Historical and Statutory Notes

Repealed § 645.21, which related to regulations of the department, was derived from:
Laws 1982, c. 82–76, § 2.
Laws 1979, c. 79–3, § 96.
Laws 1977, c. 77–120, § 80.
Laws 1976, c. 76–273, § 17.
Laws 1969, c. 69–106, §§ 10, 19, 35.
Laws 1961, c. 61–530, § 18.

Laws 1957, c. 57-213, § 14.

945.215. Inmate welfare and employee benefit trust funds

(1) Inmate purchases; department of corrections.—

(a) From the net proceeds from operating inmate canteens, vending machines used primarily by inmates and visitors, hobby shops, and other such facilities must be deposited in the General Revenue Fund; however, funds necessary to purchase items for resale at inmate canteens and vending machines must be deposited into local bank accounts designated by the department.

(b) All proceeds from contracted telephone commissions must be deposited in the General Revenue Fund. The department shall develop and update, as necessary, administrative procedures to verify that:

1. Contracted telephone companies accurately record and report all telephone calls made by inmates incarcerated in correctional facilities under the department's jurisdiction;

2. Persons who accept collect calls from inmates are charged the contracted rate; and

3. The department receives the contracted telephone commissions.

(c) Any funds that may be assigned by inmates or donated to the department by the general public or an inmate service organization must be deposited in the General Revenue Fund; however, the department shall not accept any donation from, or on behalf of, any individual inmate.

(d) All proceeds from the following sources must be deposited in the General Revenue Fund:

1. The confiscation and liquidation of any contraband found upon, or in the possession of, any inmate;

2. Disciplinary fines imposed against inmates;

3. Forfeitures of inmate earnings; and

4. Unexpended balances in individual inmate trust fund accounts of less than $1.

(e) Items for resale at inmate canteens and vending machines maintained at the correctional facilities shall be priced comparatively with like items for retail sale at fair market prices.

(f) Notwithstanding any other provision of law, inmates with sufficient balances in their individual inmate bank trust fund accounts, after all debts against the account are satisfied, shall be allowed to request a weekly draw of up to an amount set by the Secretary of Corrections, not to exceed $100, to be expended for personal use on canteen and vending machine items.

(2) Privately operated institutions inmate welfare trust fund; private correctional facilities.—

(a) For purposes of this subsection, privately operated institutions or private correctional facilities are those correctional facilities under contract with the department pursuant to chapter 944 or the Department of Management Services pursuant to chapter 957.

(b)1. The net proceeds derived from inmate canteens, vending machines used primarily by inmates, telephone commissions, and similar sources at private correctional facilities shall be deposited in the Privately Operated Institutions Inmate Welfare Trust Fund.

2. Funds in the Privately Operated Institutions Inmate Welfare Trust Fund shall be expended only pursuant to legislative appropriation.

(c) The Department of Management Services shall annually compile a report that documents Privately Operated Institutions Inmate Welfare Trust Fund receipts and expenditures at each private correctional facility. This report must specifically identify receipt sources and expenditures. The Department of Management Services shall compile this report for the prior fiscal year and shall submit the report by September 1 of each year to the chairs of the appropriate substantive and fiscal committees of the Senate and House of Representatives and to the Executive Office of the Governor.

(3) Employee benefit trust fund; department of corrections.—

(a) The department may establish an Employee Benefit Trust Fund. Trust fund sources may be derived from any of the following:

1. Proceeds of vending machines, staff canteens, or other such services not intended for use by inmates.

2. Net proceeds of the recycling program.

3. Donations, except for donations made by, or on behalf of, an individual inmate, and except for donations made by a person who provides, or seeks to provide, goods or services to the department under a contract or an agreement, individually or through a corporation or organization.

4. Additional trust funds and grants which may become available.

(b) Funds from the Employee Benefit Trust Fund may be used for employee appreciation programs and activities and to construct, operate, and maintain training and recreation facilities at correctional facilities for the exclusive use of department employees. Such facilities are the property of the department and must provide the maximum benefit to all interested employees, regardless of gender.

(c) The Employee Benefit Trust Fund shall be established as a separate and distinct set of accounts, which shall be maintained centrally by the department, overseen by the secretary, and subject to an annual audit by the department's inspector general.

(d) The department shall maintain sufficient data to provide an annual report, upon request, to the President of the Senate, the Speaker of the House of Representatives, and the Executive Office of the Governor on December 1 which lists the types of services provided using moneys in the trust fund and the allocations of funds spent.

(e) The department shall adopt rules under ss. 120.536(1) and 120.54 to administer this subsection.

Laws 1979, c. 79–78, § 1; Laws 1985, c. 85–288, § 10; Laws 1987, c. 87–233, § 1; Laws 1994, c. 94–273, § 5. Amended by Laws 1996, c. 96–312, § 14, eff. July 1, 1996; Laws 1997, c. 97–102, § 1858, eff. July 1, 1997; Laws 1998, c. 98–388, § 3, eff. July 1, 1998; Laws 1999, c. 99–271, § 14, eff. June 29, 1999; Laws 2000, c. 2000–328, § 4, eff. June 19, 2000; Laws 2001, c. 2001–379, § 1, eff. Dec. 17, 2001; Laws 2002, c. 2002–268, § 1, eff. July 1, 2002; Laws 2003, c. 2003–179, § 10, eff. July 1, 2003; Laws 2004, c. 2004–248, § 9, eff. July 1, 2004; Laws 2007, c. 2007–210, § 3, eff. June 20, 2007.

Historical and Statutory Notes

Amendment Notes:

Laws 1985, c. 85–288, § 10, eff. July 1, 1985, deleted provisions for donations in the first sentence of subsec. (1)(a) and rewrote the first and second sentences of subsec. (1)(b).

Laws 1987, c. 87–233, § 1, eff. July 1, 1987, amended subsec. (2) to provide for sources of trust fund and distribution.

Laws 1994, c. 94–273, § 5, eff. May 28, 1994, amending subsec. (1) rewrote par. (a), inserted a new par. (b), and redesignated the remaining paragraphs without change.

Laws 1996, c. 96–312, § 14, eff. July 1, 1996, in subsec. (1), in the third sentence of par. (a), inserted ", including a verification of telephone commissions,"; in par. (b), at the beginning, deleted "Effective for the expenditure of funds by the Department of Corrections for fiscal year 1994-1995 and, if required by this subsection," added subpars. 11 and 12 relating to employment of treatment and training program personnel, and expenses associated with those programs, respectively, and in the last paragraph of subsec. (1)(b), at the beginning, deleted "Effective for fiscal year 1994-1995 and thereafter,", at the beginning of the second sentence, deleted "Beginning in fiscal year 1994-1995,", and added the last sentence, and made conforming amendments; in par. (c), in the first sentence, substituted "that" for "which"; inserted par. (d) relating to the amount appropriated by § 946.008; renumbered pars. (d) and (e) as former pars. (e) and (f); and added pars. (g) and (h) relating to prices at canteens and vending machines, and authorization of weekly draws, respectively.

Laws 1997, c. 97–102, eff. July 1, 1997, removed gender-specific references applicable to human beings from volume 4 of the Florida Statutes without substantive changes in legal effect.

Laws 1998, c. 98–388, § 3, rewrote the section, which formerly read:

"(1)(a) All moneys held in any auxiliary, canteen, welfare, or similar fund in any state institution under the jurisdiction of the Department of Corrections shall be deposited in the Inmate Welfare Trust Fund of the department, which fund is created in the State Treasury, to be appropriated annually by the Legislature and deposited in the Department of Corrections Grants and Donations Trust Fund. However, moneys budgeted by the department for the purchase of items for resale at canteens or vending machines must be deposited into local bank accounts designated by the department. The department shall submit to the President of the Senate and the Speaker of the House of Representatives by January 1 of each year a report that documents the receipts and expenditures, including a verification of telephone commissions, from the Inmate Welfare Trust Fund for the previous fiscal year. The report must present this information by program, by institution, and by type of receipt.

"(b) Beginning with the legislative appropriation for fiscal year 1995–1996 and thereafter, the money in the Inmate Welfare Trust Fund must be used exclusively:

"1. To purchase items for resale at the inmate canteens or vending machines maintained at the correctional facilities;

"2. To employ personnel and inmates to manage, supervise, and operate the canteens and vending machines at the correctional facilities;

"3. For operating and fixed-capital expenses associated with the operation of inmate canteens and vending machines;

"4. To employ personnel to manage and supervise the proceeds from telephone commissions;

"5. To employ personnel for correctional education to provide literacy programs, vocational training, and academic programs that comply with standards of the Department of Education;

"6. For operating and fixed-capital expenses associated with the delivery to inmates of literacy programs, vocational training, and academic programs that comply with standards of the Department of Education;

"7. For operating and fixed-capital expenses associated with the operation of inmate chapels, libraries, and visiting pavilions;

"8. To employ personnel to operate the libraries, chapels, and visiting pavilions;

"9. For expenses associated with various inmate clubs;

"10. For expenses associated with legal services for inmates;

"11. To employ personnel to provide inmate substance abuse treatment and transition and life skills training programs; and

"12. For operating and fixed-capital expenses associated with the delivery of inmate substance abuse treatment and transition and life skills training programs. The total annual expenditures for items listed in subparagraphs 5. and 6. must exceed the total annual expenditures for items listed in subparagraphs 7. through 12. Funds in the Inmate Welfare Trust Fund or any other fund may not be used to purchase cable television service, to rent or purchase videocassettes, videocassette recorders, or other audiovisual or electronic equipment used primarily for recreation purposes. This paragraph does not preclude the purchase or rental of electronic or audiovisual equipment for inmate training or educational programs. The department shall develop administrative procedures to verify that contracted telephone commissions are being received, that persons who have accepted collect calls from inmates are being charged the contracted rate, and that contracted telephone companies are accurately and completely recording and reporting all inmate telephone calls made.

"(c) There shall be deposited in the Inmate Welfare Trust Fund all net proceeds from the operation of canteens, vending machines, hobby shops, and other such facilities and any moneys that may be assigned by the inmates or donated to the department by the general public or an inmate service organization for deposit in the fund. However, the department shall refuse to accept any donations from or on behalf of any individual inmate. The moneys of the fund shall constitute a trust held by the department for the benefit and welfare of the inmates of the institutions under the jurisdiction of the department.

"(d) There shall be deposited in the Inmate Welfare Trust Fund such moneys as constitute repayment of the one-time sum appropriated pursuant to s. 946.008.

"(e) Any contraband found upon, or in the possession of, any inmate in any institution under the jurisdiction of the department shall be confiscated and liquidated, and the proceeds thereof shall be deposited in the Inmate Welfare Trust Fund of the department.

"(f) The secretary of the department or the secretary's designee may invest in the manner authorized by law for fiduciaries any money in the Inmate Welfare Trust Fund of the department that in his or her opinion is not necessary for immediate use, and the interest earned and other increments derived from such investments made pursuant to this section shall be deposited in the Inmate Welfare Trust Fund of the department.

"(g) Items for resale at the inmate canteens or vending machines maintained at the correctional facilities shall be priced comparatively with like items for retail sale at fair market prices.

"(h) Notwithstanding any other provision of law, inmates with sufficient balances in their individual inmate bank trust fund accounts, after all debts against the account are satisfied, shall be allowed to request a weekly draw of up to $45 to be expended for personal use on canteen items.

"(2) The department may establish an Employee Benefit Trust Fund. Trust fund sources may be derived from any of the following:

"(a) Proceeds of vending machines or other such services not intended for use by inmates.

"(b) Donations, except donations by, or on behalf of, an individual inmate.

"(c) Additional trust funds and grants which may become available.

"Such fund shall be maintained and audited separately and apart from the Inmate Welfare Trust Fund. Portions of the fund may be used to construct training and recreation facilities at respective institutions. Such facilities shall be the property of the department and shall provide the maximum benefit to interested employees of both sexes, including teachers, clerical staff, medical and psychological services personnel, and officers and administrators."

Laws 1999, c. 99–271, § 14, eff. June 29, 1999, in subsec. (1), par. (a), inserted "and for visitation and family programs and services in such correctional facilities"; in subsec. (1)(a)2., "and visitors"; in subsec. (1)(b)5., inserted "visiting services and programs, family services and programs," where appearing; and in subsec. (c), inserted "visiting services and programs, family services and programs,".

Laws 2000, c. 2000–328, § 4, deleted subsec. (1)(a)5., which formerly read:

"5. Repayment of the one-time sum of $500,000 appropriated in fiscal year 1996–1997 from the Inmate Welfare Trust Fund for correctional work programs pursuant to s. 946.008.".

Laws 2001, c. 2001–379, § 1, in subsec. (1)(f), substituted "an amount set by the Secretary of Corrections, not to exceed $100," for "$45".

Laws 2002, c. 2002–268, § 1, added subsecs. (1)(b)9., relating to purchase, rental, maintenance and repair of electronic or audiovisual equipment, and (1)(b)10., relating to purchase, rental, maintenance and repair of wellness equipment; and rewrote subsec. (1)(d), which formerly read:

"(d) Funds in the Inmate Welfare Trust Fund or any other fund may not be used to purchase cable television service, to rent or purchase videocassettes, videocassette recorders, or other audiovisual or electronic equipment used primarily for recreation purposes. This paragraph does not preclude the purchase or rental of electronic or audiovisual equipment for inmate training or educational programs."

Laws 2003, c. 2003–179, § 10, rewrote subsec. (1), which formerly read:

"(1) Inmate welfare trust fund; department of corrections.—

"(a) The Inmate Welfare Trust Fund constitutes a trust held by the department for the benefit and welfare of inmates incarcerated in correctional facilities operated directly by the department and for visitation and family programs and services in such correctional facilities. Funds shall be credited to the trust fund as follows:

"1. All funds held in any auxiliary, canteen, welfare, or similar fund in any correctional facility operated directly by the department.

"2. All net proceeds from operating inmate canteens, vending machines used primarily by inmates and visitors, hobby shops, and other such facilities; however, funds necessary to purchase items for resale at inmate canteens and vending machines must be deposited into local bank accounts designated by the department.

"3. All proceeds from contracted telephone commissions. The department shall develop and update, as necessary, administrative procedures to verify that:

"a. Contracted telephone companies accurately record and report all telephone calls made by inmates incarcerated in correctional facilities under the department's jurisdiction;

"b. Persons who accept collect calls from inmates are charged the contracted rate; and

"c. The department receives the contracted telephone commissions.

"4. Any funds that may be assigned by inmates or donated to the department by the general public or an inmate service organization; however, the department shall not accept any donation from, or on behalf o[illegible] ual inmate.

"5. All proceeds from:

"a. The confiscation and liquidation [illegible] contraband found upon, or in the possessio[illegible] of, any inmate;

"b. Disciplinary fines imposed against inmates;

"c. Forfeitures of inmate earnings; and

"d. Unexpended balances in individual inmate trust fund accounts of less than $1.

"6. All interest earnings and other proceeds derived from investments of funds deposited in the trust fund. In the manner authorized by law for fiduciaries, the secretary of the department, or the secretary's designee, may invest any funds in the trust fund when it is determined that such funds are not needed for immediate use.

"(b) Funds in the Inmate Welfare Trust Fund must be used exclusively for the following purposes at correctional facilities operated directly by the department:

"1. To operate inmate canteens and vending machines, including purchasing items for resale at inmate canteens and vending machines; employing personnel and inmates to manage, supervise, and operate inmate canteens and vending machines; and covering other operating and fixed capital outlay expenses associated with operating inmate canteens and vending machines;

"2. To employ personnel to manage and supervise the proceeds from telephone commissions;

"3. To develop, implement, and maintain the medical copayment accounting system;

"4. To provide literacy programs, vocational training programs, and educational programs that comply with standards of the Department of Education, including employing personnel and covering other operating and fixed capital outlay expenses associated with providing such programs;

"5. To operate inmate chapels, faith-based programs, visiting pavilions, visiting services and programs, family services and programs, libraries, and law libraries, including employing personnel and covering other operating and fixed capital outlay expenses associated with operating inmate chapels, faith-based programs, visiting pavilions, visiting services and programs, family services and programs, libraries, and law libraries;

"6. To provide for expenses associated with various inmate clubs;

"7. To provide for expenses associated with legal services for inmates;

"8. To provide inmate substance abuse treatment programs and transition and life skills training programs, including employing personnel and covering other operating and fixed capital outlay expenses associated with providing such programs;

"9. To provide for the purchase, rental, maintenance, and repair of electronic or audiovisual equipment, unless otherwise prohibited by this chapter; and

"10. To provide for the purchase, rental, maintenance, and repair of wellness equipment, unless otherwise prohibited by this chapter.

"(c) The Legislature shall annually appropriate the funds deposited in the Inmate Welfare Trust Fund. It is the intent of the Legislature that total annual expenditures for providing literacy programs, vocational training programs, and educational programs exceed the combined total annual expenditures for operating inmate chapels, faith-based programs, visiting pavilions, visiting services and programs, family services and programs, libraries, and law libraries, covering expenses associated with inmate clubs, and providing inmate substance abuse treatment programs and transition and life skills training programs.

"(d) Funds in the Inmate Welfare Trust Fund or any other fund may not be used to purchase weight-training equipment, to purchase cable-television service for recreation purposes, or to rent or purchase videocassettes, videocassette recorders, or other audiovisual or electronic media or equipment used primarily for recreation purposes. This paragraph does not preclude the purchase or rental of electronic or audiovisual equipment or services for inmate training or educational programs.

"(e) Items for resale at inmate canteens and vending machines maintained at the correctional facilities shall be priced comparatively with like items for retail sale at fair market prices.

"(f) Notwithstanding any other provision of law, inmates with sufficient balances in their individual inmate bank trust fund accounts, after all debts against the account are satisfied, shall be allowed to request a weekly draw of up to an amount set by the Secretary of Corrections, not to exceed $100, to be expended for personal use on canteen and vending machine items.

"(g) The department shall annually compile a report that specifically documents Inmate Welfare Trust Fund receipts and expenditures. This report shall be compiled at both the statewide and institutional levels. The department must submit this report for the previous fiscal year by September 1 of each year to the chairs of the appropriate substantive and fiscal committees of the Senate and the House of Representatives and to the Executive Office of the Governor."

Laws 2004, c. 2004–248, § 9, in subsecs. (2)(a) and (2)(c), substituted references to the Department of Management Services for references to the Correctional Privatization Commission throughout.

Laws 2007, c. 2007–210, § 3, rewrote subsec. (3), which formerly read:

"(3) Employee Benefit Trust Fund; department of corrections.—

"(a) The department may establish an Employee Benefit Trust Fund. Trust fund sources may be derived from any of the following:

"1. Proceeds of vending machines or other such services not intended for use by inmates.

"2. Donations, except donations by, or on behalf of, an individual inmate.

"3. Additional trust funds and grants which may become available.

"(b) Funds from the Employee Benefit Trust Fund may be used to construct, operate, and maintain training and recreation facilities at correctional facilities for the exclusive use of department employees. Such facilities are the property of the department and must provide the maximum benefit to all interested employees, regardless of gender."

Library References

States ⚷126, 127.
Westlaw Topic No. 360.
C.J.S. States §§ 383 to 387.

Research References

Encyclopedias

Privately Operated Institutions Inmate Welfare Trust Fund, FL Jur. 2d Prisons & Prisoners § 28.

Privately Operated Institutions Inmate Welfare Trust Fund, FL Jur. 2d Prisons & Prisoners § 168.

945.21501. Employee Benefit Trust Fund

(1) There is hereby created in the Department of Corrections the Employee Benefit Trust Fund. The purpose of the trust fund shall be to:

(a) Construct, operate, and maintain training and recreation facilities at correctional facilities for the exclusive use of department employees. Any facility constructed using funds from the Employee Benefit Trust Fund is the property of the department and must provide the maximum benefit to all interested employees, regardless of gender.

(b) Provide funding for employee appreciation programs and activities designed to enhance the morale of employees.

Moneys shall be deposited in the trust fund as provided in s. 945.215.

(2) Notwithstanding the provisions of s. 216.301 and pursuant to s. 216.351, any balance in the trust fund at the end of any fiscal year shall remain in the trust fund at the end of the year and shall be available for carrying out the purposes of the trust fund.

(3) The department shall adopt rules pursuant to ss. 120.536(1) and 120.54 to administer this section.

Laws 1998, c. 98–384, § 1, eff. July 1, 1998. Amended by Laws 2002, c. 2002–110, § 2, eff. July 1, 2002; Laws 2007, c. 2007–210, § 4, eff. June 20, 2007.

Historical and Statutory Notes

Amendment Notes:

Laws 2002, c. 2002–110, § 2, deleted subsec. (3), which formerly read:

"(3) Pursuant to the provisions of s. 19(f)(2), Art. III of the State Constitution, the trust fund shall, unless terminated sooner, be terminated on July 1, 2002. However, prior to its scheduled termination, the trust fund shall be reviewed as provided in s. 215.3206(1) and (2)."

Laws 2007, c. 2007–210, § 4, rewrote subsec. (1); and added subsec. (3), relating to adoption of rules. Subsec. (1) formerly read:

"(1) There is hereby created in the Department of Corrections the Employee Benefit Trust Fund. The purpose of the trust fund shall be to construct, operate, and maintain training and recreation facilities at correctional facilities for the exclusive use of department employees. Moneys shall be deposited in the trust fund as provided in s. 945.215."

Library References

Prisons ⚿395.
States ⚿127.
Westlaw Topic Nos. 310, 360.
C.J.S. Prisons and Rights of Prisoners §§ 5, 16.
C.J.S. States §§ 386 to 387.

Notes of Decisions

Construction and application 1

1. Construction and application

Where local employee clubs, established at correctional institutions throughout the state, have raised funds to pay for employee activities, the funds so raised should be placed in the Department of Corrections' Employee Benefit Trust Fund; the Department of Corrections has authority to control and disburse these funds, but it can neither transfer the funds nor transfer control of the funds to a direct-support organization. Op.Atty.Gen., 2006–18, May 5, 2006.

945.21502. Repealed by Laws 2003, c. 2003–179, § 11, eff. July 1, 2003

Historical and Statutory Notes

Repealed § 945.21502, which related to the Inmate Welfare Trust Fund, was derived from Laws 2002, c. 2002–106, § 2 and Laws 1998, c. 98–385, § 1.

945.21503. Federal Grants Trust Fund

(1) The Federal Grants Trust Fund is created within the Department of Corrections.

(2) The fund is established for use as a depository for funds to be used for allowable grant activities funded by restricted program revenues. Moneys to be credited to the trust fund shall consist of grants and funding from the Federal Government, interest earnings, and cash advances from other trust funds.

Added by Laws 2006, c. 2006–20, § 1, eff. July 1, 2006. Amended by Laws 2009, c. 2009–29, § 2, eff. July 1, 2009.

Historical and Statutory Notes

Amendment Notes:

Laws 2009, c. 2009–29, § 2, deleted subsec. (3), which formerly read:

"(3) In accordance with s. 19(f)(2), Art. III of the State Constitution, the Federal Grants Trust Fund shall, unless terminated sooner, be terminated on July 1, 2010. Before its scheduled termination, the trust fund shall be reviewed as provided in s. 215.3206(1) and (2)."

945.2151. Verifying social security numbers

Prior to opening a canteen account pursuant to s. 945.215, an inmate who is eligible to receive a social security number must report his or her social security number. The department shall, in adherence with its agreement with the Social Security Administration and in a timely manner, submit sufficient and necessary information to verify that the reported inmate's social security number is accurate and properly belongs to the inmate. If the Social Security Administration is unable to verify a reported social security number for an inmate, the department shall prohibit canteen purchases by the inmate if the department concludes that the inmate was deceptive in reporting the social security number. The prohibition against purchasing canteen items will remain in effect until a verified social security number is obtained.

Added by Laws 1996, c. 96–312, § 49, eff. Oct. 1, 1996.

Library References

Prisons ⚿133.
Westlaw Topic No. 310.
C.J.S. Prisons and Rights of Prisoners §§ 50 to 57, 59, 63, 68 to 70, 73 to 75, 77, 94 to 96, 100 to 102, 113, 119, 121 to 122.

945.22. Repealed by Laws 1971, c. 71–377, § 284

Historical and Statutory Notes

Repealed § 945.22, which related to the employment of a director, superintendents and wardens, was derived from:

Laws 1969, c. 69–106, §§ 19, 35.
Laws 1959, c. 59–149, § 1.
Laws 1957, c. 57–213, § 15.

945.23. Repealed by Laws 1971, c. 71–355, § 178; Laws 1971, c. 71–377, § 285

Historical and Statutory Notes

Repealed § 945.23, which related to a civil service system in the adult corrections division, was derived from:

Laws 1969, c. 69–106, §§ 19, 31, 35.
Laws 1967, c. 67–437, § 1.
Laws 1961, c. 61–530, § 18.
Laws 1957, c. 57–213, § 16.

See, now, F.S.A. § 110.105 et seq.

945.24. Repealed by Laws 1961, c. 61–516, § 1

Historical and Statutory Notes

The repealed section, which related to supervision of religious activities, was derived from Laws 1957, c. 57–342, § 1.

945.25. Records

(1) It shall be the duty of the Department of Corrections to obtain and place in its records information as complete as practicable on every person who may be sentenced to supervision or incarceration under the jurisdiction of the department. Such information shall be obtained as soon as possible after imposition of sentence and shall, in the discretion of the department, include, among other things:

(a) A copy of the indictment or information and a complete statement of the facts of the crime for which such person has been sentenced.

(b) The court in which the person was sentenced.

(c) The terms of the sentence.

(d) The name of the presiding judge, the prosecuting officers, the investigating officers, and the attorneys for the person convicted.

(e) A copy of all probation reports which may have been made.

(f) Any social, physical, mental, psychiatric, or criminal record of such person.

(2) It shall be the duty of the court and its prosecuting officials to furnish to the department upon its request such information and also to furnish such copies of such minutes and other records as may be in their possession or under their control.

(3) Following the initial hearing provided for in s. 947.172(1), the commission shall prepare and the department shall include in the official record a copy of the seriousness-of-offense and favorable-parole-outcome scores and shall include a listing of the specific factors and information used in establishing a presumptive parole release date for the inmate.

Laws 1941, c. 20519, § 11; Laws 1969, c. 69–106, §§ 19, 35; Fla.St.1975, § 947.14(1), (2), (4), (6); Laws 1977, c. 77–120, §§ 81, 87; Laws 1978, c. 78–417, § 20; Laws 1979, c. 79–3, § 97; Laws 1988, c. 88–122, § 57; Laws 1995, c. 95–145, § 28. Amended by Laws 2004, c. 2004–335, § 26, eff. Oct. 1, 2004.

Historical and Statutory Notes

Amendment Notes:

Laws 1969, c. 69–106, §§ 19, 35, transferred all powers, duties and functions of department of public welfare to the division of family services of the department of health and rehabilitative services.

Laws 1977, c. 77–120, a reviser's bill, renumbered and amended provisions of subsecs. (1), (2), (4) and (6) of § 947.14 as this section to conform with Laws 1975, c. 75–49, which created the department of offender rehabilitation (see § 20.315) and transferred to the department certain functions performed by the division of corrections of the department of health and rehabilitative services and the parole and probation commission of the department of offender rehabilitation.

Laws 1978, c. 78–417, added subsec. (5).

Laws 1979, c. 79–3, a reviser's bill, provided for substitution of references to the department and secretary of "corrections" for the department and secretary of "offender rehabilitation" to conform with Laws 1978, c. 78–53.

Laws 1988, c. 88–122, § 57, eff. July 1, 1988, substituted the commission name of "parole" for "parole and probation".

Laws 1992, c. 92–310, § 5, provided for the repeal of former subsec. (4) of this section on July 1, 1993.

Laws 1995, c. 95–145, § 28, repealed former subsec. (4).

Laws 2004, c. 2004–335, § 26, in subsec. (1), deleted "permanent" preceding "records", substituted "practicable" for "may be practicably available" following "complete as", and substituted "be sentenced to supervision or incarceration under the jurisdiction of the department" for "become subject to parole" following "person who may" in the first sentence of the introductory paragraph; deleted former subsec. (2); and renumbered former subsecs. (3) and (4) as (2) and (3). Former subsec. (2) had read:

"The department, in its discretion, shall also obtain and place in its permanent records such information on every person who may be placed on probation, and on every person who may become subject to pardon and commutation of sentence."

Cross References

Classification summaries and progress reports regarding prisoners, use by parole officials, see §§ 921.20, 921.21.
Prisoner mental health history and treatment, records, see § 945.47.
Registration of convicted felons, contents, see § 775.13.

Library References

Prisons ⚷340.
Westlaw Topic No. 310.
C.J.S. Prisons and Rights of Prisoners §§ 5 to 6, 14, 17, 22 to 23, 50 to 53, 55, 59.

Notes of Decisions

---

1. Commitment papers

Since the department of corrections is not authorized by statute to secure additional copies of commitment papers in criminal cases and since the clerk of the circuit court or the clerk of the criminal court of record is not specifically authorized by statute to charge such state agency a fee for such additional copies, such clerk would not be entitled to charge a fee against department of corrections for furnishing such additional copies of the commitment papers in criminal cases. Op.Atty.Gen., 059–62, March 18, 1959.

The long standing policy of the clerks of the circuit court and clerks of the criminal court of record to furnish the parole commission upon request, and without charging a fee, copies of commitment papers in criminal cases, is proper. Op.Atty.Gen., 059–62, March 18, 1959.

2. Access to records

Under § 947.01, as a member ex officio of the parole and probation commission, the secretary of the department of offender rehabilitation may not participate in the panel discussions or vote upon the granting or revocation of parole to or recommending clemency for a particular criminal offender. He may, however, participate in the discussion and vote upon all policy-making decisions to the same extent as any other commission member; and, pending a decision on appeal concerning the validity of Laws 1975, c. 75–49, he and his staff should be entitled to access to any of the commission's records that would be useful in deciding matters of policy. Op.Atty.Gen., 075–296, Dec. 3, 1975.

3. Confrontation rights

Denial to probationer of opportunity to examine report of probation and parole commission at probation revocation hearing did not deprive him of right to cross-examine and confront witnesses. Blackburn v. State, App. 3 Dist., 261 So.2d 861 (1972). Criminal Law ⚷ 662.4

4. Privilege and privacy of records

An inmate's release date is the type of information falling within the Department of Corrections' statutory duty to obtain and place in its permanent records information as complete as may be practicably available on every person who may become subject to parole, for purpose of applying public records exception to the hearsay rule. Ward v. State, App. 3 Dist., 965 So.2d 308 (2007), review granted, quashed 7 So.3d 520, on remand 11 So.3d 459. Criminal Law ⚷ 429(1)

Parole Commission was not precluded from considering confidential portion of presentence investigation report in performing its parole review function. Adams v. State, App. 1 Dist., 560 So.2d 321 (1990). Pardon And Parole ⚷ 58

Report given by probation and parole commission is for confidential use and consideration by court and is not a public document. Blackburn v. State, App. 3 Dist., 261 So.2d 861 (1972). Privileged Communications And Confidentiality ⚷ 363

Florida parole and probation commission pursuant to subsection (6) of § 947.14 could make such rules as to the privacy and privilege and use of information obtained by the commission and placed in its permanent records concerning every person who may become subject to parole, probation, pardon and commutation of sentence; however, that provision, applied only to persons who may have become subject to parole, probation, pardon and commutation of sentence and did not apply to any other persons or the files and records of any other persons. If promulgated, such rule would operate to exempt such information placed in the commission's permanent records from the operation of public records law pursuant to section 119.07(2). Op.Atty.Gen., 074–247, Aug. 9, 1974.

A circuit judge handling juvenile matters may in his discretion refuse to permit the Florida parole and probation commission to inspect juvenile court records when making a pre-parole investigation or pre-sentence investigation. Op. Atty.Gen., 073–112, April 11, 1973.

5. Hearsay

An inmate's release date is the type of information falling within the Department of Corrections' statutory duty to obtain and place in its permanent records information as complete as may be practicably available on every person who may become subject to parole, for purpose of applying public records exception to the hearsay rule. Ward v. State, App. 3 Dist., 965 So.2d 308 (2007), review granted, quashed 7 So.3d 520, on remand 11 So.3d 459. Criminal Law ⚷ 429(1)

6. Discovery

Revocation of probation was arbitrary and unreasonable and denied procedural due process, where State introduced, as proof of probation violation, records which were claimed to be privileged by probation officer during discovery proceedings, in absence of reasons being given for failure to permit probationer to obtain discovery of materials or any showing of commission rules or policies regarding use of information by others. Sukert v. State, App. 3 Dist., 325 So.2d 439 (1976). Constitutional Law ⚷ 4733(2); Sentencing And Punishment ⚷ 2021

7. Habeas corpus

Prisoner's naked allegation that there were some conclusionary statements or recommendations noted on his record jacket which resulted in denial of parole, which allegation was not supported by any documentary evidence, was insufficient to support issuance of writ of habeas corpus. McNamara v. Cook, App. 4 Dist., 336 So.2d 677 (1976). Habeas Corpus ⚷ 725

8. Compensation

Judges, prosecution officials, and clerks of court are bound to furnish copies of records in their possession to the parole commission as a function of their office, without additional compensation. Op.Atty.Gen., 1941, p. 788.

945.26. Repealed by Laws 1985, c. 85–288, § 27, eff. July 1, 1985

Historical and Statutory Notes

Repealed § 945.26, which related to the Department of Corrections' powers and duties relating to parolees and probationers, was derived from:

Laws 1979, c. 79–3, § 98.
Laws 1977, c. 77–120, § 82.
Fla.St.1975, § 948.02.
Laws 1975, c. 75–301, § 4.
Laws 1965, c. 65–453, § 1.
Laws 1941, c. 20519, § 21.

945.27. Proceedings by department

(1) Whenever it becomes necessary to increase the number of prison beds by acquiring private property for the construction of new correctional facilities or for the expansion of existing facilities, and the property cannot be acquired by agreement satisfactory to the Department of Corrections and the parties interested in, or the owners of, the private property, the department is hereby empowered and authorized to exercise the right of eminent domain and to proceed to condemn the property in the same manner as provided by law for the condemnation of property.

(2) Any suit or action brought by the said department to condemn property as provided in this section shall be brought in the name of the Department of Corrections, and it shall be the duty of the Department of Legal Affairs to conduct the proceedings for, and to act as counsel for, the said department.

Laws 1977, c. 77–120, § 83; Laws 1979, c. 79–3, § 99; Laws 1994, c. 94–273, § 2; Laws 1995, c. 95–283, § 30.

Historical and Statutory Notes

Amendment Notes:

Laws 1979, c. 79–3, a reviser's bill, provided for substitution of references to the department and secretary of "corrections" for the department and secretary of "offender rehabilitation" to conform with Laws 1978, c. 78–53.

Laws 1994, c. 94–273, § 2, eff. May 28, 1994, rewrote subsec. (1) which formerly provided:

"Whenever it becomes necessary for the welfare and convenience of any of the institutions now under, or which may hereafter be placed under, the supervision and control of the Department of Corrections to acquire private property for the use of any of said institutions and the same cannot be acquired by agreement satisfactory to the said department and the parties interested in, or the owners of, said private property, the department is hereby empowered and authorized to exercise the right of eminent domain and to proceed to condemn the said property in the same manner as provided by law for the condemnation of property."

Laws 1995, c. 95–283, § 30, eff. June 15, 1995, in subsec. (1), deleted a former last sentence which required that the Board of Trustees of the Internal Improvement Trust Fund approve the institution of any condemnation action before it was filed.

Cross References

Eminent domain, generally, see Const. Art. 10, § 6; §§ 73.012 et seq., 74.011 et seq.
Sale and purchase of land for correctional facilities, see § 944.10.
Siting of additional correctional facilities, study and criteria, see § 944.095.

Library References

Eminent Domain ⚷18.
Westlaw Topic No. 148.
C.J.S. Eminent Domain §§ 47, 50.

Research References

Encyclopedias

Additional Facilities; Use, Acquisition, or Leasing of Land; Erection of Facilities, FL Jur. 2d Prisons & Prisoners § 21.

945.28. Selection of probation or parole offices by the department; public notice

(1) Beginning July 1, 1995, whenever the department is going to enter into a contract for the lease or purchase of a probation and parole office space to be used by the department, the department shall provide notice, by publication in the county in which the office space is to be located, in a newspaper of general circulation in said county, 30 days prior to signing any lease or purchasing any property to be used for office space, that the department intends to lease or purchase such property. The published notice shall include a telephone number whereby interested members of the public may communicate with the department with respect to any questions or input the public may have with regard to the proposed lease or purchase.

(2) When the site of the proposed probation and parole office space is to be located within one quarter mile of a school for children in grade 12 or lower, licensed day care center facility, park, playground, nursing home, convalescent center, hospital, association for disabled population, mental health center, youth center, group home for disabled population or youth, or other place where children or a population especially vulnerable to crime due to age or physical or mental disability regularly congregates, the department shall provide written notification to the county or city administrator in the county or city in which the office space is to be located simultaneously with the newspaper publication.

Laws 1995, c. 95–283, § 31. Amended by Laws 1997, c. 97–156, § 1, eff. July 1, 1997.

Historical and Statutory Notes

Amendment Notes:

Laws 1997, c. 97–156, § 1, eff. July 1, 1997, designated existing text as subsec. (1), and therein in the first sentence, substituted "probation and parole" for "probation or parole"; and added subsec. (2).

945.30. Renumbered as 948.09 and amended by Laws 1991, c. 91–280, § 7, eff. Oct. 1, 1991

945.31. Restitution and other payments

The department may establish bank accounts outside the State Treasury for the purpose of collecting and disbursing restitution and other court-ordered payments from persons in its custody or under its supervision, and may collect an administrative processing fee in an amount equal to 4 percent of the gross amounts of such payments. Such administrative processing fee shall be deposited in the department's Operating Trust Fund and shall be used to offset the cost of the department's services. The department is authorized to deposit or transfer into the General Revenue Fund:

(1) Offender overpayments that are less than $10 at the end of the offender's supervision.

(2) Offender funds that are not claimed within 1 year after supervision is terminated.

(3) Victim restitution payments that are not claimed within 1 year after the offender's supervision is terminated.

(4) Interest earned on balances in the COPS bank accounts.

(5) Payments that cannot be identified and are not claimed within 1 year after they are received.

Laws 1989, c. 89–526, § 11; Laws 1993, c. 93–120, § 14; Laws 1995, c. 95–283, § 32. Amended by Laws 1998, c. 98–388, § 5, eff. July 1, 1998; Laws 2003, c. 2003–136, § 1, eff. June 10, 2003.

Historical and Statutory Notes

Amendment Notes:

Laws 1993, c. 93–120, § 14, eff. July 1, 1994, substituted "department's Grants and Donations Trust Fund" for "Court–Ordered Payment Trust Fund created in s. 945.32" in the second sentence.

Laws 1995, c. 95–283, § 32, eff. June 15, 1995, in the first sentence, substituted "may establish bank accounts outside the State Treasury for the purpose of collecting and disbursing" for "shall collect and dispense".

Laws 1998, c. 98–388, § 5, substituted "Operating Trust Fund" for "Grants and Donations Trust Fund".

Laws 2003, c. 2003–136, § 1, rewrote this section, which formerly read:

"The department may establish bank accounts outside the State Treasury for the purpose of collecting and disbursing restitution and other court-ordered payments from persons in its custody or under its supervision, and may collect an administrative processing fee in an amount equal to 4 percent of the gross amounts of such payments. Such administrative processing fee shall be deposited in the department's Operating Trust Fund and shall be used to offset the cost of the department's services."

Library References

Prisons ⚷117.
Sentencing and Punishment ⚷2210.
Westlaw Topic Nos. 310, 350H.
C.J.S. Convicts §§ 4 to 5.

Research References

Encyclopedias

Use of Earnings for Restitution, FL Jur. 2d Prisons & Prisoners § 167.

Deposits and Depositories, FL Jur. 2d State of Florida § 218.

Forms

Florida Pleading and Practice Forms § 96:55, Order of Probation--Drug Offenders.

Florida Pleading and Practice Forms § 96:56, Order of Probation--Sex Offenders.

Florida Pleading and Practice Forms § 96:58, Order of Community Control--Drug Offender or Sexual Offender.

Notes of Decisions

1. Construction and application

Probation condition requiring processing fee for each payment of restitution, costs, and/or fees was discretionary and had to be pronounced orally; moreover, as Department of Corrections had statutory authority to impose fee, trial court had no authority to do so. Powell v. State, App. 2 Dist., 681 So.2d 722 (1996). Sentencing And Punishment ⚷ 1918; Sentencing And Punishment ⚷ 1975(2)

Defendant who was not in custody or under supervision of Department of Corrections could not be assessed a four percent processing fee for monthly restitution payments, pursuant to statute allowing such fees to be assessed against persons in custody or under supervision of Department. Harris v. State, App. 1 Dist., 593 So.2d 1169 (1992). Costs ⚷ 292

945.32. Repealed by Laws 1995, c. 95–145, § 29

Historical and Statutory Notes

Repealed § 945.32, which related to a court-ordered payment trust fund, was derived from Laws 1989, c. 89–526, § 12.

Laws 1993, c. 93–120, § 13, provided for the repeal of this section on July 1, 1994.

945.35. Requirement for education on human immunodeficiency virus, acquired immune deficiency syndrome, and other communicable diseases

(1) The Department of Corrections, in conjunction with the Department of Health, shall establish a mandatory introductory and continuing education program on human immunodeficiency virus, acquired immune deficiency syndrome, and other communicable diseases for all inmates. Programs shall be specifically designed for inmates while incarcerated and in preparation for release into the community. Consideration shall be given to cultural and other relevant differences among inmates in the development of educational materials and shall include emphasis on behavior and attitude change. The education program shall be continuously updated to reflect the latest medical information available.

(2) The Department of Corrections, in conjunction with the Department of Health, shall establish a mandatory education program on human immunodeficiency virus, acquired immune deficiency syndrome, and other communicable diseases with an emphasis on appropriate behavior and attitude change to be offered on an annual basis to all staff in correctional facilities, including new staff.

(3) When there is evidence that an inmate, while in the custody of the department, has engaged in behavior which places the inmate at a high risk of transmitting or contracting a human immunodeficiency disorder or other communicable disease, the department may begin a testing program which is consistent with guidelines of the Centers for Disease Control and Prevention and recommendations of the Correctional Medical Authority. For purposes of this subsection, "high-risk behavior" includes:

(a) Sexual contact with any person.

(b) An altercation involving exposure to body fluids.

(c) The use of intravenous drugs.

(d) Tattooing.

(e) Any other activity medically known to transmit the virus.

(4) The results of such tests shall become a part of that inmate's medical file, accessible only to persons designated by agency rule.

(5) If the department has reason to believe that an inmate may have intentionally or unintentionally transmitted a communicable disease to any correctional officer or any employee of the department, or to any person lawfully present in a correctional facility who is not incarcerated there, the department shall, upon request of the affected correctional officer, employee, or other person, cause the inmate who may have transmitted the communicable disease to be promptly tested for its presence and communicate the results as soon as

practicable to the person requesting the test be performed, and to the inmate tested if the inmate so requests.

(6) If the results of the test pursuant to subsection (5) indicate the presence of a communicable disease, the department shall provide appropriate access for counseling, health care, and support services to the affected correctional officer, employee, or other person, and to the inmate tested.

(7) The results of a test under subsections (5) and (6) are inadmissible against the person tested in any federal or state civil or criminal case or proceeding.

(8) The department shall promulgate rules to implement subsections (5), (6), and (7). Such rules shall require that the results of any tests are communicated only to a person requesting the test and the inmate tested. Such rules shall also provide for procedures designed to protect the privacy of a person requesting that the test be performed and the privacy of the inmate tested.

(9) The department shall establish policies consistent with guidelines of the Centers for Disease Control and Prevention and recommendations of the Correctional Medical Authority on the housing, physical contact, dining, recreation, and exercise hours or locations for inmates with immunodeficiency disorders as are medically indicated and consistent with the proper operation of its facilities.

(10) The department shall report to the Legislature by March 1 each year as to the implementation of this program and the participation by inmates and staff.

Laws 1988, c. 88–380, § 12. Amended by Laws 1997, c. 97–93, § 20, eff. July 1, 1997; Laws 1999, c. 99–8, § 316, eff. June 29, 1999; Laws 2001, c. 2001–244, § 4, eff. Oct. 1, 2001.

Historical and Statutory Notes

Amendment Notes:

Laws 1997, c. 97–93, eff. July 1, 1997, was a reviser's bill which deleted obsolete and expired provisions, corrected cross references and citations, and corrected grammatical and other similar errors.

Laws 1999, c. 99–8, § 316, eff. June 29, 1999, substituted "Department of Health" for "Department of Health and Rehabilitative Services".

Laws 2001, c. 2001–244, § 4, in the introductory paragraph and in subsecs. (1), (2), and (3), inserted "other communicable diseases"; inserted new subsecs. (5) through (8); renumbered existing subsecs. (5) and (6) as subsecs. (9) and (10), respectively; and made nonsubstantive grammatical changes.

Law Review and Journal Commentaries

State statutes dealing with HIV and AIDS: Comprehensive state-by-state summary. Paul Barron, Sara J. Goldstein and Karen L. Wishnev, 5 Law. & Sexuality 1 (1995).

Library References

Prisons ⟹138, 192, 342, 395.
Westlaw Topic No. 310.

C.J.S. Prisons and Rights of Prisoners §§ 5, 12, 16, 58, 60, 72 to 73, 76, 78 to 88, 91, 123, 125, 127, 136.

Research References

Encyclopedias

Education on HIV, Aids, and Other Communicable Diseases, FL Jur. 2d Prisons & Prisoners § 36.

Testing for HIV, Aids, and Other Communicable Diseases, FL Jur. 2d Prisons & Prisoners § 126.

Education Programs on HIV and Aids, FL Jur. 2d Prisons & Prisoners § 128.

945.355. HIV testing of inmates prior to release

(1) As used in this section, the term "HIV test" means a test ordered to determine the presence of the antibody or antigen to human immunodeficiency virus or the presence of human immunodeficiency virus infection.

(2) If an inmate's HIV status is unknown to the department, the department shall, pursuant to s. 381.004(3), perform an HIV test on the inmate not less than 60 days prior to the inmate's presumptive release date from prison by reason of parole, accumulation of gain-time credits, or expiration of sentence. An inmate who is known to the department to be HIV positive or who has been tested within the previous year and does not request retesting need not be tested under this section but is subject to subsections (4) and (5). However, an inmate who is released due to an emergency is exempt from the provisions of this section.

(3) The department shall record the results of the HIV test in the inmate's medical record.

(4) Pursuant to ss. 381.004(3) and 945.10, the department shall notify the Department of Health and the county health department where the inmate plans to reside regarding an inmate who is known to be HIV positive or has received an HIV positive test result under this section prior to the release of that inmate.

(5) Prior to the release of an inmate who is known to be HIV positive or who has received a positive HIV test result under this section, the department shall provide special transitional assistance to the inmate, which must include:

(a) Education on preventing the transmission of HIV to others and on the importance of receiving followup care and treatment.

(b) A written, individualized discharge plan that includes referrals to and contacts with the county health department and local HIV primary care services in the area where the inmate plans to reside.

(c) A 30–day supply of all HIV/AIDS–related medications that the inmate is taking prior to release under the protocols of the Department of Corrections and the treatment guidelines of the United States Department of Health and Human Services.

(6) Notwithstanding any provision of the Florida Statutes providing for a waiver of sovereign immunity, neither the state, its agencies, subdivisions nor employees of the state, its agencies, or subdivisions shall be liable to any person

for negligently causing death or personal injury arising out of complying with this section.

Added by Laws 2002, c. 2002–292, §§ 1, 6, eff. July 1, 2002. Amended by Laws 2003, c. 2003–1, § 112, eff. July 1, 2003.

Historical and Statutory Notes

Amendment Notes:

Laws 2003, c. 2003–1, a reviser's bill, deleted obsolete and expired provisions, corrected grammatical and typographical errors, and made other similar changes.

Cross References

HIV testing of inmates prior to release, see § 381.004.

Research References

Encyclopedias

Testing for HIV, Aids, and Other Communicable Diseases--Pending Release, FL Jur. 2d Prisons & Prisoners § 127.

Education Programs on HIV and Aids, FL Jur. 2d Prisons & Prisoners § 128.

HIV Testing of Inmates Prior to Release; Counseling, FL Jur. 2d Prisons & Prisoners § 209.

945.36. Exemption from health testing regulations for law enforcement personnel conducting drug tests on inmates and releasees

(1) Any law enforcement officer, state or county probation officer, or employee of the Department of Corrections, who is certified by the Department of Corrections pursuant to subsection (2), is exempt from part I of chapter 483, for the limited purpose of administering a urine screen drug test to:

(a) Persons during incarceration;

(b) Persons released as a condition of probation for either a felony or misdemeanor;

(c) Persons released as a condition of community control;

(d) Persons released as a condition of conditional release;

(e) Persons released as a condition of parole;

(f) Persons released as a condition of provisional release;

(g) Persons released as a condition of pretrial release; or

(h) Persons released as a condition of control release.

(2) The Department of Corrections shall develop a procedure for certification of any law enforcement officer, state or county probation officer, or employee of the Department of Corrections to perform a urine screen drug test on the persons specified in subsection (1).

Laws 1990, c. 90–205, § 1; Laws 1995, c. 95–211, § 79.

Historical and Statutory Notes

Amendment Notes:

Laws 1995, c. 95–211, § 79, a reviser's bill, in subsec. (2), substituted "on" for "to" following "test".

Library References

Pardon and Parole ⚷68.
Prisons ⚷138, 391.
Sentencing and Punishment ⚷1996.
Westlaw Topic Nos. 284, 310, 350H.
C.J.S. Pardon and Parole § 62.
C.J.S. Prisons and Rights of Prisoners §§ 12 to 15, 17, 22, 58, 60, 72 to 73, 91.

Research References

Encyclopedias

Drug and Alcohol Testing, FL Jur. 2d Prisons & Prisoners § 101.

945.40. Corrections Mental Health Act; short title for ss. 945.40–945.49

Sections 945.40–945.49 shall be known and may be cited as the "Corrections Mental Health Act."

Laws 1982, c. 82–224, § 1.

Historical and Statutory Notes

Amendment Notes:

Laws 1982, c. 82–224, § 3, provided that that act shall take effect July 1, 1984. Laws 1984, c. 84–361, § 29, however, amended that section to provide that Laws 1982, c. 82–224, shall take effect Jan. 1, 1985.

Cross References

Transfers of prisoners for specialized rehabilitative treatment, see § 945.12.

Research References

Encyclopedias

Prisoners, FL Jur. 2d Incompetent Persons § 163.

Inpatient Treatment, Generally; Rights of Patients, FL Jur. 2d Prisons & Prisoners § 131.

945.41. Legislative intent of ss. 945.40–945.49

It is the intent of the Legislature that mentally ill inmates in the custody of the Department of Corrections receive evaluation and appropriate treatment for their mental illness through a continuum of services. It is further the intent of the Legislature that:

(1) Inmates in the custody of the department who have mental illnesses that require hospitalization and intensive psychiatric inpatient treatment or care receive appropriate treatment or care in Department of Corrections mental health treatment facilities designated for that purpose. The Department of Corrections shall provide mental health services to inmates committed to it and may contract with any entities, persons, or agencies qualified to provide such services.

(2) Mental health treatment facilities be secure and adequately equipped and staffed for the provision of mental health services and that, to the extent possible, such services be provided in the least restrictive manner consistent with optimum improvement of the inmate's condition.

(3) Inmates who are transferred to any facility for the purpose of mental health treatment be given consideration for parole and be eligible for release by reason of gain-time allowances as provided in s. 944.291 and release by

expiration of sentence, consistent with guidelines established for that purpose by the department.

(4) Any inmate sentenced as a youthful offender, or designated as a youthful offender by the department pursuant to chapter 958, who is transferred pursuant to this act to a mental health treatment facility be separated from other inmates, if necessary, as determined by the warden of the treatment facility. In no case shall any youthful offender be placed at the Florida State Prison or the Union Correctional Institution for mental health treatment.

(5) The department may designate a mental health treatment facility for adult, youthful, and female offenders or may contract with other appropriate entities, persons, or agencies for such services.

Laws 1982, c. 82–224, § 1. Amended by Laws 1996, c. 96–422, § 2, eff. July 1, 1996; Laws 1999, c. 99–8, § 317, eff. June 29, 1999; Laws 2000, c. 2000–161, § 18, eff. July 4, 2000; Laws 2008, c. 2008–250, § 10, eff. Oct. 1, 2008.

Historical and Statutory Notes

Amendment Notes:

Laws 1982, c. 82–224, § 3, provided that that act shall take effect July 1, 1984. Laws 1984, c. 84–361, § 29, however, amended that section to provide that Laws 1982, c. 82–224, shall take effect Jan. 1, 1985.

Laws 1996, c. 96–422, § 2, eff. July 1, 1996, in subsec. (4), substituted "superintendent" for "administrator".

Laws 1999, c. 99–8, § 317, eff. June 29, 1999, substituted "Department of Children and Family Services" for "Department of Health and Rehabilitative Services".

Laws 2000, c. 2000–161, a reviser's bill, substituted reference to warden for reference to superintendent.

Laws 2008, c. 2008–250, § 10, in subsec. (1), deleted a former second sentence, which had read, "The department shall contract with the Department of Children and Family Services for the provision of mental health services in any departmental mental health treatment facility."; and in subsec. (5), substituted ", youthful, and female" for "and youthful female" following "adult", and inserted a reference to appropriate entities and persons.

Library References

Mental Health ⚷436.
Prisons ⚷194, 221.
Westlaw Topic Nos. 257A, 310.
C.J.S. Criminal Law §§ 2188 to 2190.
C.J.S. Mental Health §§ 272 to 277, 283.
C.J.S. Prisons and Rights of Prisoners §§ 18, 23 to 26, 76, 78 to 88, 123, 125, 127, 136.

945.42. Definitions; ss. 945.40–945.49

As used in ss. 945.40–945.49, the following terms shall have the meanings ascribed to them, unless the context shall clearly indicate otherwise:

(1) "Court" means the circuit court.

(2) "Crisis stabilization care" means a level of care that is less restrictive and intense than care provided in a mental health treatment facility, that includes a broad range of evaluation and treatment services provided within a highly structured setting or locked residential setting, and that is intended for inmates who are experiencing acute emotional distress and who cannot be adequately evaluated and treated in a transitional care unit or infirmary isolation management room. Such treatment is also more intense than treatment provided in a transitional care unit and is devoted principally toward rapid stabilization of acute symptoms and conditions.

(3) "Department" means the Department of Corrections.

(4) "Director" means the Director for Mental Health Services of the Department of Corrections or his or her designee.

(5) "In immediate need of care and treatment" means that an inmate is apparently mentally ill and is not able to be appropriately cared for in the institution where he or she is confined and that, but for being isolated in a more restrictive and secure housing environment, because of the apparent mental illness:

(a) 1. The inmate is demonstrating a refusal to care for himself or herself and without immediate treatment intervention is likely to continue to refuse to care for himself or herself, and such refusal poses an immediate, real, and present threat of substantial harm to his or her well-being; or

2. There is an immediate, real, and present threat that the inmate will inflict serious bodily harm on himself or herself or another person, as evidenced by recent behavior involving causing, attempting, or threatening such harm;

(b) 1. The inmate has refused voluntary placement for treatment at a mental health treatment facility after sufficient and conscientious explanation and disclosure of the purpose of placement; or

2. The inmate is unable to determine for himself or herself whether placement is necessary; and

(c) All available less restrictive treatment alternatives that would offer an opportunity for improvement of the inmate's condition have been clinically determined to be inappropriate.

(6) "In need of care and treatment" means that an inmate has a mental illness for which inpatient services in a mental health treatment facility are necessary and that, but for being isolated in a more restrictive and secure housing environment, because of the mental illness:

(a) 1. The inmate is demonstrating a refusal to care for himself or herself and without treatment is likely to continue to refuse to care for himself or herself, and such refusal poses a real and present threat of substantial harm to his or her well-being; or

2. There is a substantial likelihood that in the near future the inmate will inflict serious bodily harm on himself or herself or another person, as evidenced by recent behavior causing, attempting, or threatening such harm;

(b) 1. The inmate has refused voluntary placement for treatment at a mental health treatment facility after sufficient and conscientious explanation and disclosure of the purpose of placement; or

2. The inmate is unable to determine for himself or herself whether placement is necessary; and

(c) All available less restrictive treatment alternatives that would offer an opportunity for improvement of the inmate's condition have been clinically determined to be inappropriate.

(7) "Inmate" means any person committed to the custody of the Department of Corrections.

(8) "Mental health treatment facility" means any extended treatment or hospitalization-level unit within the corrections system which the Assistant Secretary for Health Services of the department specifically designates by rule to provide acute psychiatric care and which may include involuntary treatment and therapeutic intervention in contrast to less intensive levels of care such as outpatient mental health care, transitional mental health care, or crisis stabilization care.

(9) "Mentally ill" means an impairment of the mental or emotional processes, of the ability to exercise conscious control of one's actions, or of the ability to perceive or understand reality, which impairment substantially interferes with a person's ability to meet the ordinary demands of living, regardless of etiology, except that, for the purposes of transfer of an inmate to a mental health treatment facility, the term does not include retardation or developmental disability as defined in chapter 393, simple intoxication, or conditions manifested only by antisocial behavior or substance abuse addiction. However, an individual who is mentally retarded or developmentally disabled may also have a mental illness.

(10) "Psychiatrist" means a medical practitioner licensed pursuant to chapter 458 or chapter 459 who has primarily diagnosed and treated nervous and mental disorders for a period of not less than 3 years inclusive of psychiatric residency.

(11) "Psychological professional" means a behavioral practitioner who has an approved doctoral degree in psychology as defined in s. 490.003(3)(b) and is employed by the department or who is licensed as a psychologist pursuant to chapter 490.

(12) "Secretary" means the Secretary of Corrections.

(13) "Transitional mental health care" means a level of care that is more intensive than outpatient care, but less intensive than crisis stabilization care, and is characterized by the provision of traditional mental health treatments such as group and individual therapy, activity therapy, recreational therapy, and psychotropic medications in the context of a structured residential setting. Transitional mental health care is indicated for a person with chronic or residual symptomatology who does not require crisis stabilization care or acute psychiatric care, but whose impairment in functioning nevertheless renders him or her incapable of adjusting satisfactorily within the general inmate population.

(14) "Warden" means the warden of a state corrections facility or his or her designee.

Laws 1982, c. 82–224, § 1; Laws 1991, c. 91–225, § 26. Amended by Laws 1996, c. 96–422, § 3, eff. July 1, 1996; Laws 1997, c. 97–102, § 1859, eff. July 1, 1997; Laws 2000, c. 2000–161, § 19, eff. July 4, 2000; Laws 2008, c. 2008–250, § 11, eff. Oct. 1, 2008.

Historical and Statutory Notes

Amendment Notes:

Laws 1982, c. 82–224, § 3, provided that that act shall take effect July 1, 1984. Laws 1984, c. 84–361, § 29, however, amended that section to provide that Laws 1982, c. 82–224 shall take effect Jan. 1, 1985.

Laws 1991, c. 91–225, § 26, eff. July 1, 1991, rewrote subsec. (8); and added subsec. (14).

Laws 1996, c. 96–422, § 3, eff. July 1, 1996, deleted former subsec. (1) defining "administrator"; redesignated definitions accordingly; and changed subsec. (3) to define "director" rather than "deputy director".

Laws 1997, c. 97–102, eff. July 1, 1997, removed gender-specific references applicable to human beings from volume 4 of the Florida Statutes without substantive changes in legal effect.

Laws 2000, c. 2000–161, a reviser's bill, substituted references to warden for references to superintendent.

Laws 2008, c. 2008–250, § 11, rewrote this section, which formerly read:

"As used in ss. 945.40–945.49, the following terms shall have the meanings ascribed to them, unless the context shall clearly indicate otherwise:

"(1) 'Court' means the circuit court.

"(2) 'Department' means the Department of Corrections.

"(3) 'Director' means the Director for Mental Health Services of the Department of Corrections or his or her designee.

"(4) 'In immediate need of care and treatment' means that an inmate is apparently mentally ill and is not able to be appropriately cared for in the institution where the inmate is confined and that, without intervention, the alleged mental illness poses an immediate, real, and present threat of substantial harm to the inmate's well-being or to the safety of others.

"(5) 'In need of care and treatment' means that an inmate has a mental illness for which inpatient services in a mental health treatment facility are necessary, which mental illness poses a real and present threat of substantial harm to the inmate's well-being or to the safety of others.

"(6) 'Inmate' means any person committed to the custody of the Department of Corrections.

"(7) 'Mental health treatment facility' means the Corrections Mental Health Institution and any other institution that the Assistant Secretary for Health Services of the department specifically designates by rule to provide acute psychiatric care at the hospital level, in contrast to less intensive levels of care such as outpatient mental health care, transitional mental health care, or crisis stabilization care.

"(8) 'Mentally ill' means an impairment of the emotional processes, of the ability to exercise conscious control of one's actions, or of the ability to perceive reality or to understand, which impairment substantially interferes with a person's ability to meet the ordinary demands of living, regardless of etiology, except that, for the purposes of transfer of an inmate to a mental health treatment facility, the term does not include retardation or developmental disability as defined in chapter 393, simple intoxication, or conditions manifested only by antisocial behavior or drug addiction.

"(9) 'Psychiatrist' means a medical practitioner licensed pursuant to chapter 458 or chapter 459 who has primarily diagnosed and treated nervous and mental disorders for a period of not less than 3 years inclusive of psychiatric residency.

"(10) 'Psychologist' means a behavioral practitioner who has an approved degree in psychology that is primarily clinical in nature from a university or professional graduate school that is state-authorized or accredited by an accrediting agency approved by the United States Department of Education and who is professionally certified by the appropriate professional psychology association or is licensed as a psychologist pursuant to chapter 490.

"(11) 'Secretary' means the Secretary of Corrections.

"(12) 'Transitional mental health care' means a level of care that is more intensive than outpatient care, but less intensive than crisis stabilization care, and is characterized by the provision of traditional mental health treatments such as group and individual therapy, activity therapy, recreational therapy, and chemotherapy, in the context of a structured residential setting. Transitional mental health care is indicated for a person with chronic or residual symptomatology who does not require crisis stabilization care or acute psychiatric care at the hospital level, but whose impairments in functioning nevertheless render him or her incapable of adjusting satisfactorily within the general inmate population, even with the assistance of outpatient care.

"(13) 'Warden' means the warden of a state corrections facility or his or her designee."

Research References

Encyclopedias

Inpatient Treatment, Generally; Rights of Patients, FL Jur. 2d Prisons & Prisoners § 131.

Notes of Decisions

Construction and application 1

1. Construction and application

For the State to establish clear and convincing evidence to support the involuntary commitment of mentally ill inmate under the Corrections Mental Health Act, the evidence must be of such weight that it produces in the mind of the trier of fact a firm belief or conviction, without hesitancy, as to the truth of the allegations sought to be established. E.F. v. State, App. 3 Dist., 889 So.2d 135 (2004). Mental Health ⚷ 436.1

To transfer a mentally ill inmate involuntarily to a corrections mental health treatment facility under the Corrections Mental Health Act, the State needs to show that the inmate has a mental illness for which inpatient services in a mental health treatment facility are necessary, and that the mental illness pose a real and present threat of substantial harm to the inmate's well-being or to the safety of others. E.F. v. State, App. 3 Dist., 889 So.2d 135 (2004). Mental Health ⚷ 436.1

State failed to establish by clear and convincing evidence that mentally ill inmate's delusion that he was free man posed a real and present threat of substantial harm to inmate's well-being or to the safety of others, and thus evidence was not sufficient to involuntary commit inmate to corrections mental health treatment facility under Corrections Mental Health Act; while psychiatrist testified that he feared that inmate might try to escape and result in hitting electrical offense, inmate had never tried to escape. E.F. v. State, App. 3 Dist., 889 So.2d 135 (2004). Mental Health ⚷ 436.1

945.43. Admission of inmate to mental health treatment facility

(1) Criteria.—An inmate may be admitted to a mental health treatment facility if he or she is mentally ill and is in need of care and treatment, as defined in s. 945.42.

(2) Procedure for placement in a mental health treatment facility.—

(a) An inmate may be admitted to a mental health treatment facility after notice and hearing, upon the recommendation of the warden of the facility where the inmate is confined. The recommendation shall be entered on a petition and must be supported by the expert opinion of a psychiatrist and the second opinion of a psychiatrist or psychological professional. The petition shall be filed with the court in the county where the inmate is located.

(b) A copy of the petition shall be served on the inmate, accompanied by a written notice that the inmate may apply immediately to the court to have an attorney appointed if the inmate cannot afford one.

(c) The petition for placement may be filed in the county in which the inmate is located. The hearing shall be held in the same county, and one of the inmate's physicians at the facility where the inmate is located shall appear as a witness at the hearing.

(d) An attorney representing the inmate shall have access to the inmate and any records, including medical or mental health records, which are relevant to the representation of the inmate.

(e) If the court finds that the inmate is mentally ill and in need of care and treatment, as defined in s. 945.42, the court shall order that he or she be placed in a mental health treatment facility or, if the inmate is at a mental health treatment facility, that he or she be retained there. The court shall authorize the mental health treatment facility to retain the inmate for up to 6 months. If, at the end of that time, continued placement is necessary, the warden shall apply to the Division of Administrative Hearings in accordance with s. 945.45 for an order authorizing continued placement.

(3) Procedure for hearing on placement of an inmate in a mental health treatment facility.—

(a) The court shall serve notice on the warden of the facility where the inmate is confined and the allegedly mentally ill inmate. The notice must specify the date, time, and place of the hearing; the basis for the allegation of mental illness; and the names of the examining experts. The hearing shall be held within 5 days, and the court may appoint a general or special magistrate to preside. The court may waive the presence of the inmate at the hearing if such waiver is consistent with the best interests of the inmate and the inmate's counsel does not object. The hearing may be as informal as is consistent with orderly procedure. One of the experts whose opinion supported the petition for placement shall be present at the hearing for information purposes.

(b) If, at the hearing, the court finds that the inmate is mentally ill and in need of care and treatment, as defined in s. 945.42, the court shall order that he or she be placed in a mental health treatment facility. The court shall provide a copy of its order authorizing placement and all supporting documentation relating to the inmate's condition to the warden of the treatment facility. If the court finds that the inmate is not mentally ill, it shall dismiss the petition for placement.

(4) Refusal of placement.—The warden of an institution in which a mental health treatment facility is located may refuse to place any inmate in that treatment facility who is not accompanied by adequate court orders and documentation, as required in ss. 945.40–945.49.

Laws 1982, c. 82–224, § 1; Laws 1985, c. 85–62, § 75. Amended by Laws 1996, c. 96–422, § 4, eff. July 1, 1996; Laws 1997, c. 97–102, § 1860, eff. July 1, 1997; Laws 2000, c. 2000–161, § 20, eff. July 4, 2000; Laws 2004, c. 2004–11, § 103, eff. Oct. 1, 2004; Laws 2008, c. 2008–250, § 12, eff. Oct. 1, 2008.

Historical and Statutory Notes

Amendment Notes:

Laws 1982, c. 82–224, § 3, provided that that act shall take effect July 1, 1984. Laws 1984, c. 84–361, § 29, however, amended that section to provide that Laws 1982, c. 82–224, shall take effect Jan. 1, 1985.

Laws 1985, c. 85–62, § 75, a reviser's bill amending subsec. (2)(b), provided for the enactment of language which had been supplied as explained by footnote in the main volume without any further amendment in text.

Laws 1996, c. 96–422, § 4, eff. July 1, 1996, in subsecs. (2), (3), and (4), substituted references to director for references to deputy and references to superintendent for references to administrator.

Laws 1997, c. 97-102, eff. July 1, 1997, removed gender-specific references applicable to human beings from volume 4 of the Florida Statutes without substantive changes in legal effect.

Laws 2000, c. 2000–161, a reviser's bill, substituted references to warden for references to superintendent.

Laws 2004, c. 2004–11, § 103, in subsec. (3), substituted "general or special magistrate" for "master" preceding "to preside", in the third sentence.

Laws 2008, c. 2008–250, § 12, rewrote this section, which formerly read:

"(1) Criteria.—An inmate may be admitted to a mental health treatment facility if he or she is mentally ill and is in need of care and treatment.

"(2) Admission to a mental health treatment facility.—

"(a) An inmate may be admitted to a mental health treatment facility after notice and hearing, upon the recommendation of the warden of the facility where the inmate is confined and of the director. The recommendation shall be entered on a certificate and must be supported by the expert opinion of a psychiatrist and the second opinion of a psychiatrist or psychologist. The certificate shall be filed with the court in the county where the inmate is located and shall serve as a petition for a hearing regarding placement.

"(b) A copy of the certificate shall also be filed with the department, and copies shall be served on the inmate and the inmate's representatives, accompanied by:

"1. A written notice, in plain and simple language, that the inmate or the inmate's representative may apply at any time for a hearing on the issue of the inmate's need for treatment if he or she has previously waived such a hearing.

"2. A petition for such hearing, which requires only the signature of the inmate or the inmate's representative for completion.

"3. A written notice that the petition may be filed with the court in the county in which the inmate is hospitalized at the time and stating the name and address of the judge of such court.

"4. A written notice that the inmate or the inmate's representative may apply immediately to the court to have an attorney appointed if the inmate cannot afford one.

"(c) The petition may be filed in the county in which the inmate is being treated at any time within 6 months of the date of the certificate. The hearing shall be held in the same county, and one of the inmate's physicians at the facility shall appear as a witness at the hearing. If the court finds that the inmate is mentally ill and in need of care and treatment, it shall order that he or she be admitted to a mental health treatment facility or, if the inmate is at a mental health treatment facility, that he or she be retained there. However, the inmate may be immediately transferred to and admitted at a mental health treatment facility by executing a waiver of the hearing by express and informed consent, without awaiting the court order. The court shall authorize the mental health treatment facility to retain the inmate for up to 6 months. If, at the end of that time, continued treatment is necessary, the warden shall apply to the court for an order authorizing continued placement.

"(3) Procedure for hearing on transfer of an inmate for mental health treatment.—If the inmate does not waive a hearing or if the inmate or the inmate's representative files a petition for a hearing after having waived it, the court shall serve notice on the warden of the facility where the inmate is confined, the director, and the allegedly mentally ill inmate. The notice shall specify the date, time, and place of the hearing; the basis for the allegation of mental illness; and the names of the examining experts. The hearing shall be held within 5 days, and the court may appoint a general or special magistrate to preside. The hearing may be as informal as is consistent with orderly procedure. One of the experts whose opinion supported the recommendation shall be present at the hearing for information purposes. If, at the hearing, the court finds that the inmate is mentally ill and in need of care and treatment, it shall order that he or she be transferred to a mental health treatment facility and provided appropriate treatment. The court shall provide a copy of its order authorizing transfer and all supporting documentation relating to the inmate's condition to the warden of the treatment facility. If the court finds that the inmate is not mentally ill, it shall dismiss the petition for transfer.

"(4) Admission; when refusal allowed.—The warden of a treatment facility may refuse to admit any inmate who is not accompanied by adequate court orders and documentation, as required in ss. 945.40–945.49."

Cross References

Transfers of prisoners for specialized rehabilitative treatment, see § 945.12.

Library References

Mental Health ⟾436.
Westlaw Topic No. 257A.
C.J.S. Mental Health §§ 272 to 277, 283.

Research References

Encyclopedias

Inpatient Treatment, Generally; Rights of Patients, FL Jur. 2d Prisons & Prisoners § 131.

Hearing and Determination as to Transfer of Inmate for Mental Health Treatment, Generally, FL Jur. 2d Prisons & Prisoners § 132.

Emergency Admission of Inmate to Mental Health Treatment Facility, FL Jur. 2d Prisons & Prisoners § 133.

Notes of Decisions

Construction and application 1

---

1. Construction and application

For the State to establish clear and convincing evidence to support the involuntary commitment of mentally ill inmate under the Corrections Mental Health Act, the evidence must be of such weight that it produces in the mind of the trier of fact a firm belief or conviction, without hesitancy, as to the truth of the allegations sought to be established. E.F. v. State, App. 3 Dist., 889 So.2d 135 (2004). Mental Health ⚷ 436.1

To transfer a mentally ill inmate involuntarily to a corrections mental health treatment facility under the Corrections Mental Health Act, the State needs to show that the inmate has a mental illness for which inpatient services in a mental health treatment facility are necessary, and that the mental illness pose a real and present threat of substantial harm to the inmate's well-being or to the safety of others. E.F. v. State, App. 3 Dist., 889 So.2d 135 (2004). Mental Health ⚷ 436.1

State failed to establish by clear and convincing evidence that mentally ill inmate's delusion that he was free man posed a real and present threat of substantial harm to inmate's well-being or to the safety of others, and thus evidence was not sufficient to involuntary commit inmate to corrections mental health treatment facility under Corrections Mental Health Act; while psychiatrist testified that he feared that inmate might try to escape and result in hitting electrical offense, inmate had never tried to escape. E.F. v. State, App. 3 Dist., 889 So.2d 135 (2004). Mental Health ⚷ 436.1

945.44. Emergency placement of inmate in a mental health treatment facility

(1) Criteria.—An inmate may be placed in a mental health treatment facility on an emergency basis if he or she is mentally ill and in immediate need of care and treatment, as defined in s. 945.42.

(2) Procedure for emergency placement.—An inmate who is mentally ill and in immediate need of care and treatment that cannot be provided at the institution where he or she is confined may be placed in a mental health treatment facility on an emergency basis. The inmate may be placed immediately in a mental health treatment facility and shall be accompanied by the recommendation of the warden of the institution where the inmate is confined, which recommendation must state the need for the emergency placement and include a written opinion of a physician verifying the need for the emergency placement. Upon the emergency placement of the inmate in the facility, the inmate shall be evaluated; if he or she is determined to be in need of treatment or care, the warden shall initiate proceedings for placement of the inmate, as described in s. 945.43(2).

Laws 1982, c. 82–224, § 1. Amended by Laws 1996, c. 96–422, § 5, eff. July 1, 1996; Laws 1997, c. 97–102, § 1861, eff. July 1, 1997; Laws 2000, c. 2000–161, § 21, eff. July 4, 2000; Laws 2008, c. 2008–250, § 13, eff. Oct. 1, 2008.

Historical and Statutory Notes

Amendment Notes:

Laws 1982, c. 82–224, § 3, provided that that act shall take effect July 1, 1984. Laws 1984, c. 84–361, § 29, however, amended that section to provide that Laws 1982, c. 82–224, shall take effect Jan. 1, 1985.

Laws 1996, c. 96–422, § 5, eff. July 1, 1996, in subsec. (2), substituted reference to superintendent for reference to administrator.

Laws 1997, c. 97–102, eff. July 1, 1997, removed gender-specific references applicable to human beings from volume 4 of the Florida Statutes without substantive changes in legal effect.

Laws 2000, c. 2000–161, a reviser's bill, substituted references to warden for references to superintendent.

Laws 2008, c. 2008–250, § 13, substituted references to emergency placement for references to emergency admission and made nonsubstantive language changes throughout; and in subsec. (1), added a reference to § 945.42 at the end.

Library References

Mental Health ⚷436.
Westlaw Topic No. 257A.
C.J.S. Mental Health §§ 272 to 277, 283.

Research References

Encyclopedias

Emergency Admission of Inmate to Mental Health Treatment Facility, FL Jur. 2d Prisons & Prisoners § 133.

945.45. Continued placement of inmates in mental health treatment facilities

(1) Criteria.—An inmate may be retained in a mental health treatment facility if he or she is mentally ill and continues to be in need of care and treatment, as defined in s. 945.42.

(2) Procedure.—

(a) The warden shall, prior to the expiration of the period during which the treatment facility is authorized to retain the inmate, file a petition with the Division of Administrative Hearings for an order authorizing continued placement. The petition must be accompanied by a statement from the inmate's physician justifying the petition and providing a brief summary of the inmate's treatment during the time he or she has been placed. In addition, the warden shall submit an individualized plan for the inmate for whom he or she is requesting continued placement. The inmate may remain in a mental health treatment facility pending a hearing after the timely filing of the petition.

(b) Notification of this request for retention shall be mailed to the inmate, along with a waiver-of-hearing form and the completed petition, requesting the inmate's signature. The waiver-of-hearing form shall require express and informed consent and shall state that the inmate is entitled to an administrative hearing under the law; that the inmate is entitled to be represented by an attorney at the hearing and that, if the inmate cannot afford an attorney, one will be appointed; and that, if it is shown at the hearing that the inmate does not meet the criteria for continued placement, he or she will be transferred out of the mental health treatment facility. If the inmate does not sign the petition, or if the inmate does not sign a waiver within 15 days, the administrative law judge shall notice a hearing with regard to the inmate involved in accordance with ss. 120.569 and 120.57(1).

(3) Procedure for hearing.—

(a) The hearing on a petition for the continued placement of an inmate in a mental health treatment facility is an administrative hearing and shall be conducted in accordance with ss. 120.569 and 120.57(1), except that an order entered by the administrative law judge is final and subject to judicial review in accordance with s. 120.68. An administrative law judge shall be assigned by the Division of Administrative Hearings to conduct hearings for continued placement.

(b) The administrative law judge may appoint a private pro bono attorney in the circuit in which the treatment facility is located to represent the inmate.

(c) The administrative law judge may waive the presence of the inmate at the hearing if such waiver is consistent with the best interests of the inmate and the inmate's counsel does not object.

(d) If, at a hearing pursuant to ss. 945.40–945.49, the administrative law judge finds that the inmate no longer meets the criteria for placement, he or she shall order that the inmate be transferred out of the mental health treatment facility.

(e) If the inmate waives the hearing or if the administrative law judge finds that the inmate is in need of continued placement, the administrative law judge shall enter an order authorizing such continued placement for a period not to exceed 1 year. The same procedure shall be repeated prior to the expiration of each additional 1-year period that the inmate is retained in the mental health treatment facility.

Laws 1982, c. 82–224, § 1. Amended by Laws 1996, c. 96–410, § 321, eff. Oct. 1, 1996; Laws 1996, c. 96–422, § 6, eff. July 1, 1996; Laws 1997, c. 97–102, § 1862, eff. July 1, 1997; Laws 2000, c. 2000–161, § 22, eff. July 4, 2000; Laws 2008, c. 2008–250, § 14, eff. Oct. 1, 2008.

Historical and Statutory Notes

Amendment Notes:

Laws 1982, c. 82–224, § 3, provided that that act shall take effect July 1, 1984. Laws 1984, c. 84–361, § 29, however, amended that section to provide that Laws 1982, c. 82–224, shall take effect Jan. 1, 1985.

Laws 1996, c. 96–410, generally effective October 1, 1996, throughout Florida Statutes, corrected cross references and substituted references to administrative law judge for references to hearing officer or hearing examiner to conform to the revision of the Administrative Procedure Act.

Laws 1996, c. 96–422, § 6, eff. July 1, 1996, in subsec. (1), substituted references to superintendent for references to administrator.

Laws 1997, c. 97–102, eff. July 1, 1997, removed gender-specific references applicable to human beings from volume 4 of the Florida Statutes without substantive changes in legal effect.

Laws 2000, c. 2000–161, a reviser's bill, substituted references to warden for references to superintendent.

Laws 2008, c. 2008–250, § 14, rewrote this section, which formerly read:

"(1) If continued placement of an inmate is necessary, the warden shall, prior to the expiration of the period during which the treatment facility is authorized to retain the inmate, request an order authorizing continued placement. This request shall be accompanied by a statement from the inmate's physician justifying the request and a brief summary of the inmate's treatment during the time he or she has been placed. In addition, the warden shall submit an individualized plan for the inmate for whom he or she is requesting continued placement. Notification of this request for retention shall be mailed to the inmate and the inmate's representative along with a completed petition, requesting only a signature and a waiver-of-hearing form. The waiver-of-hearing form shall require express and informed consent and shall state that the inmate is entitled to a hearing under the law; that the inmate is entitled to be represented by an attorney at the hearing and that, if the inmate cannot afford an attorney, one will be appointed; and that, if it is shown at the hearing that the inmate does not meet the criteria for continued placement, he or she will be transferred to another facility of the department. If the inmate or the inmate's representative does not sign the petition, or if the inmate does not sign a waiver within 15 days, the administrative law judge shall notice a hearing with regard to the inmate involved in accordance with ss. 120.569 and 120.57(1).

"(2) If, at a hearing pursuant to ss. 945.40–945.49, the administrative law judge finds that the inmate no longer meets the criteria for treatment, he or she shall order that the inmate be transferred to another facility of the department.

"(3) If the inmate waives the hearing or if the administrative law judge finds that the inmate is in need of continued treatment, the administrative law judge shall enter an order authorizing such continued treatment for a period not to exceed 1 year. The same procedure shall be repeated prior to the expiration of each additional 1-year period that the inmate is retained in the mental health treatment facility.

"(4) Hearings on requests for orders authorizing continued placement filed in accordance with this section shall be conducted in accordance with the provisions of ss. 120.569 and 120.57(1), except that any order entered by the administrative law judge shall be final and subject to judicial review in accordance with s. 120.68."

Library References

Mental Health ⚿436.
Westlaw Topic No. 257A.
C.J.S. Mental Health §§ 272 to 277, 283.

Research References

Encyclopedias

Duration of Inpatient Treatment; Request for Continued Placement; Discharge, FL Jur. 2d Prisons & Prisoners § 135.

945.46. Initiation of involuntary placement proceedings with respect to a mentally ill inmate scheduled for release

(1) If an inmate who is receiving mental health treatment in the department is scheduled for release through expiration of sentence or any other means, but continues to be mentally ill and in need of care and treatment, as defined in s. 945.42, the warden is authorized to initiate procedures for involuntary placement pursuant to s. 394.467, 60 days prior to such release.

(2) In addition, the warden may initiate procedures for involuntary examination pursuant to s. 394.463 for any inmate who has a mental illness and meets the criteria of s. 394.463(1).

Laws 1982, c. 82–224, § 1. Amended by Laws 1996, c. 96–422, § 7, eff. July 1, 1996; Laws 2000, c. 2000–161, § 23, eff. July 4, 2000; Laws 2008, c. 2008–250, § 15, eff. Oct. 1, 2008.

Historical and Statutory Notes

Amendment Notes:

Laws 1982, c. 82–224, § 3, provided that that act shall take effect July 1, 1984. Laws 1984, c. 84–361, § 29, however, amended that section to provide that Laws 1982, c. 82–224, shall take effect Jan. 1, 1985.

Laws 1996, c. 96–422, § 7, eff. July 1, 1996, substituted reference to superintendent for reference to administrator.

Laws 2000, c. 2000–161, a reviser's bill, substituted reference to warden for reference to superintendent.

Laws 2008, c. 2008–250, § 15, designated the former section as subsec. (1), inserted "as defined in s. 945.42," following "treatment", and made a nonsubstantive language change; and added subsec. (2), relating to involuntary examinations.

Library References

Mental Health ⚷436.
Westlaw Topic No. 257A.
C.J.S. Mental Health §§ 272 to 277, 283.

Research References

Encyclopedias

Duration of Inpatient Treatment; Request for Continued Placement; Discharge--Inmate to be Released But in Continued Need of Care and Treatment, FL Jur. 2d Prisons & Prisoners § 136.

945.47. Discharge of inmate from mental health treatment

(1) An inmate who has been transferred for the purpose of mental health treatment shall be discharged from treatment by the warden under the following conditions:

(a) If the inmate is no longer in need of care and treatment, as defined in s. 945.42, he or she may be transferred out of the mental health treatment facility and provided with appropriate mental health services; or

(b) If the inmate's sentence expires during his or her treatment, but he or she is no longer in need of care and treatment as an inpatient, the inmate may be released with a recommendation for outpatient treatment, pursuant to the provisions of ss. 945.40–945.49.

(2) At any time that an inmate who has received mental health treatment while in the custody of the department becomes eligible for release under supervision or upon end of sentence, a record of the inmate's mental health treatment may be provided to the Parole Commission and to the Department of Children and Family Services upon request. The record shall include, at a minimum, a summary of the inmate's diagnosis, length of stay in treatment, clinical history, prognosis, prescribed medication, treatment plan, and recommendations for aftercare services.

Laws 1982, c. 82–224, § 1; Laws 1988, c. 88–122, § 59. Amended by Laws 1996, c. 96–422, § 8, eff. July 1, 1996; Laws 1997, c. 97–102, § 1863, eff. July 1, 1997; Laws 1999, c. 99–8, § 318, eff. June 29, 1999; Laws 2000, c. 2000–161, § 24, eff. July 4, 2000; Laws 2008, c. 2008–250, § 16, eff. Oct. 1, 2008.

Historical and Statutory Notes

Amendment Notes:

Laws 1982, c. 82–224, § 3, provided that that act shall take effect July 1, 1984. Laws 1984, c. 84–361, § 29, however, amended that section to provide that Laws 1982, c. 82–224, shall take effect Jan. 1, 1985.

Laws 1988, c. 88–122, § 59, eff. July 1, 1988, substituted the commission name of "parole" for "parole and probation".

Laws 1996, c. 96–422, § 8, eff. July 1, 1996, in subsec. (1), substituted references to superintendent for references to administrator.

Laws 1997, c. 97–102, eff. July 1, 1997, removed gender-specific references applicable to human beings from volume 4 of the Florida Statutes without substantive changes in legal effect.

Laws 1999, c. 99–8, § 318, eff. June 29, 1999, substituted "Department of Children and Family Services" for "Department of Health and Rehabilitative Services".

Laws 2000, c. 2000–161, a reviser's bill, substituted references to warden for references to superintendent.

Laws 2008, c. 2008–250, § 16, rewrote this section, which formerly read:

"(1) An inmate who has been transferred for the purpose of mental health treatment shall be discharged from treatment by the warden under the following conditions:

"(a) If the inmate is no longer in need of care and treatment, he or she may be transferred to another institution in the department;

"(b) If the inmate continues to be mentally ill, but is not in need of care and treatment as an inpatient, he or she may be transferred to another institution in the department and provided appropriate outpatient and aftercare services;

"(c) If the inmate's sentence expires during his or her treatment, but he or she is no longer in need of care and treatment as an inpatient, the inmate may be released with a recommendation for outpatient treatment, pursuant to the provisions of ss. 945.40–945.49; or

"(d) If the inmate's sentence expires and he or she continues to be mentally ill and in need of care and treatment, the warden shall initiate proceedings for involuntary placement, pursuant to s. 394.467.

"(2) An inmate who is involuntarily placed pursuant to s. 394.467 at the expiration of his or her sentence may be placed, by order of the court, in a facility designated by the Department of Children and Family Services as a secure, nonforensic, civil facility. Such a placement shall be conditioned upon a finding by the court of clear and convincing evidence that the inmate is manifestly dangerous to himself or herself or others. The need for such placement shall be reviewed by facility staff every 90 days. At any time that a patient is considered for transfer to a nonsecure, civil unit, the court which entered the order for involuntary placement shall be notified.

"(3) At any time that an inmate who has received mental health treatment while in the custody of the department becomes eligible for release on parole, a complete record of the inmate's treatment shall be provided to the Parole Commission and to the Department of Children and Family Services. The record shall include, at least, the inmate's diagnosis, length of stay in treatment, clinical history, prognosis, prescribed medication, and treatment plan and recommendations for aftercare services. In the event that the inmate is released on parole, the record shall be provided to the parole officer who shall assist the inmate in applying for services from a professional or an agency in the community. The application for treatment and continuation of treatment by the inmate may be made a condition of parole, as provided in s. 947.19(1); and a failure to participate in prescribed treatment may be a basis for initiation of parole violation hearings."

Library References

Mental Health ⟹438.
Westlaw Topic No. 257A.
C.J.S. Mental Health §§ 272 to 273, 276 to 277.

Research References

Encyclopedias

Duration of Inpatient Treatment; Request for Continued Placement; Discharge, FL Jur. 2d Prisons & Prisoners § 135.

Duration of Inpatient Treatment; Request for Continued Placement; Discharge--Inmate to be Released But in Continued Need of Care and Treatment, FL Jur. 2d Prisons & Prisoners § 136.

945.48. Rights of inmates provided mental health treatment; procedure for involuntary treatment

(1) Right to quality treatment.—An inmate in a mental health treatment facility has the right to receive treatment that is suited to his or her needs and that is provided in a humane psychological environment. Such treatment shall be administered skillfully, safely, and humanely with respect for the inmate's dignity and personal integrity.

(2) Right to express and informed consent.—Any inmate provided psychiatric treatment within the department shall be asked to give his or her express and informed written consent for such treatment. "Express and informed written consent" or "consent" means consent voluntarily given in writing after a conscientious and sufficient explanation and disclosure of the purpose of the proposed treatment; the common side effects of the treatment, if any; the expected duration of the treatment; and the alternative treatment available. The explanation shall enable the inmate to make a knowing and willful decision without any element of fraud, deceit, or duress or any other form of constraint or coercion.

(3) Procedure for involuntary treatment of inmates.—Involuntary mental health treatment of an inmate who refuses treatment that is deemed to be necessary for the appropriate care of the inmate and the safety of the inmate or others may be provided at a mental health treatment facility. The warden of the institution containing the mental health treatment facility shall petition the circuit court serving the county in which the mental health treatment facility is located for an order authorizing the treatment of the inmate. The inmate shall be provided with a copy of the petition along with the proposed treatment; the basis for the proposed treatment; the names of the examining experts; and the date, time, and location of the hearing. The inmate may have an attorney represent him or her at the hearing, and, if the inmate is indigent, the court shall appoint the office of the public defender or private counsel pursuant to s. 27.40(1) to represent the inmate at the hearing. An attorney representing the inmate shall have access to the inmate and any records, including medical or mental health records, which are relevant to the representation of the inmate.

(4) Procedure for the hearing on involuntary treatment of an inmate.—

(a) The hearing on the petition for involuntary treatment shall be held within 5 days after the petition is filed, and the court may appoint a general or special magistrate to preside. The inmate may testify or not, as he or she chooses, may cross-examine witnesses testifying on behalf of the facility, and may present his or her own witnesses. However, the court may waive the presence of the inmate at the hearing if such waiver is consistent with the best interests of the inmate and the inmate's counsel does not object. One of the inmate's physicians whose opinion supported the petition shall appear as a witness at the hearing.

(b) At the hearing on the issue of whether the court should authorize treatment for which an inmate has refused to give express and informed consent, the court shall determine by clear and convincing evidence whether the inmate is mentally ill as defined in this chapter; whether such treatment is essential to the care of the inmate; and whether the treatment is experimental or presents an unreasonable risk of serious, hazardous, or irreversible side effects. In arriving at the substitute judgment decision, the court must consider at least the following:

1. The inmate's expressed preference regarding treatment;
2. The probability of adverse side effects;
3. The prognosis for the inmate without treatment; and
4. The prognosis for the inmate with treatment.

(c) An order authorizing involuntary treatment shall allow such treatment for a period not to exceed 90 days following the date of the order. Unless the court is notified in writing that the inmate has provided express and informed consent in writing, that the inmate has been transferred to another institution of the department, or that the inmate is no longer in need of treatment, the warden shall, prior to the expiration of the initial 90–day order, petition the court for an order authorizing the continuation of treatment for another 90–day period. This procedure shall be repeated until the inmate provides express and informed consent or is no longer in need of treatment. Treatment may be continued pending a hearing after the timely filing of any petition.

(5) Procedure for emergency treatment.—In an emergency situation in which there is immediate danger to the health and safety of an inmate or other inmates, emergency treatment may be provided at a mental health treatment facility upon the written order of a physician for a period not to exceed 48 hours, excluding weekends and legal holidays. If, after the 48–hour period, the inmate has not given express and informed consent to the treatment initially refused, the warden shall, within 48 hours, excluding weekends and legal holidays, petition the circuit court, in accordance with the procedures described in this section, for an order authorizing the continued treatment of the inmate. In the interim, treatment may be continued upon the written order of a physician who has determined that the emergency situation continues to present a danger to the safety of the inmate or others. If an inmate must be isolated for mental health purposes, that decision must be reviewed within 72 hours by a different psychological professional or a physician other than the one making the original placement.

(6) Emergency treatment.—In addition to the other provisions of this section for mental health treatment, when the consent of the inmate cannot be obtained, the warden of a mental health treatment facility, or his or her designated representative, with the concurrence of the inmate's attending physician, may authorize emergency surgical or nonpsychiatric medical treatment if such treatment is deemed lifesaving or there is a situation threatening serious bodily harm to the inmate.

Laws 1982, c. 82–224, § 1; Laws 1986, c. 86–241, § 1; Laws 1988, c. 88–117, § 1; Laws 1991, c. 91–225, § 27. Amended by Laws 1996, c. 96–422, § 9, eff. July 1, 1996; Laws 1997, c. 97–102, § 1864, eff. July 1, 1997; Laws 2000, c. 2000–161, § 25, eff. July 4, 2000; Laws 2008, c. 2008–250, § 17, eff. Oct. 1, 2008.

Historical and Statutory Notes

Amendment Notes:

Laws 1982, c. 82–224, § 3, provided that that act shall take effect July 1, 1984. Laws 1984, c. 84–361, § 29, however, amended that section to provide that Laws 1982, c. 82–224, shall take effect Jan. 1, 1985.

Laws 1986, c. 86–241, § 1, eff. July 2, 1986, added subsec. (2)(c).

Laws 1988, c. 88–117, § 1, eff. June 16, 1988, substantially rewrote subsec. (2) to provide procedures for court-ordered treatment orders for inmates who refuse consent for the treatment of mental illness, to provide for notice, appointment of counsel, and the standard of proof.

Laws 1991, c. 91–225, § 2, eff. July 1, 1991, in subsec. (2), substituted "Involuntary mental health treatment of an inmate who refuses treatment that" for "If an inmate is a patient in a mental health treatment facility by the order of a court and refuses such treatment as" preceding "is deemed", and substituted "may be provided at an institution authorized to do so by the Assistant Secretary for Health Services" for ", such treatment may be provided" following "others" in the fourth sentence of the introductory paragraph, added the last sentence to par. (a), deleted ", is no longer at the mental health treatment facility," following "consent" in the fourth sentence of par. (b), and inserted references to the superintendent throughout pars. (a) and (b).

Laws 1996, c. 96–422, § 9, eff. July 1, 1996, in subsec. (2), deleted "or administrator" following "superintendent" in three places; and, in par. (d), substituted "superintendent" for "administrator".

Laws 1997, c. 97–102, eff. July 1, 1997, removed gender-specific references applicable to human beings from volume 4 of the Florida Statutes without substantive changes in legal effect.

Laws 2000, c. 2000–161, a reviser's bill, substituted references to warden for references to superintendent.

Laws 2008, c. 2008–250, § 17, rewrote this section, which formerly read:

"(1) Right to quality treatment.—An inmate in a mental health treatment facility has the right to receive treatment which is suited to his or her needs and which is provided in a humane psychological environment. Such treatment shall be administered skillfully, safely, and humanely with respect for the inmate's dignity and personal integrity.

"(2) Right to express and informed consent.—Any inmate provided psychiatric treatment within the department shall be asked to give his or her express and informed written consent for such treatment. 'Express and informed written consent' or 'consent' means consent voluntarily given in writing after a conscientious and sufficient explanation and disclosure of the purpose of the proposed treatment; the common side effects of the treatment, if any; the expected duration of the treatment; and the alternative treatment available. The explanation shall enable the inmate to make a knowing and willful decision without any element of fraud, deceit, or duress or any other form of constraint or coercion. Involuntary mental health treatment of an inmate who refuses treatment that is deemed to be necessary for the appropriate care of the inmate and the safety of the inmate or others may be provided at an institution authorized to do so by the Assistant Secretary for Health Services under the following circumstances:

"(a) In an emergency situation in which there is immediate danger to the health and safety of the inmate or other inmates, such treatment may be provided upon the written order of a physician for a period not to exceed 48 hours, excluding weekends and legal holidays. If, after the 48–hour period, the inmate has not given express and informed consent to the treatment initially refused, the warden shall, within 48 hours, excluding weekends and legal holidays, petition the circuit court serving the county in which the facility is located for an order authorizing the continued treatment of the inmate. In the interim, treatment may be continued upon the written order of a physician who has determined that the emergency situation continues to present a danger to the safety of the inmate or others. If an inmate must be isolated for mental health purposes, that decision must be reviewed within 72 hours by medical staff different from that making the original placement.

"(b) In a situation other than an emergency situation, the warden shall petition the court for an order authorizing the treatment of the inmate. The order shall allow such treatment for a period not to exceed 90 days from the date of the order. Unless the court is notified in writing that the inmate has provided express and informed consent in writing, that the inmate has been transferred to another institution of the department, or that the inmate is no longer in need of treatment, the warden shall, prior to the expiration of the initial 90–day order, petition the court for an order authorizing the continuation of treatment for another 90–day period. This procedure shall be repeated until the inmate provides consent or is no longer in need of treatment. Treatment may be continued pending a hearing after the filing of any petition.

"(c) At the hearing on the issue of whether the court should authorize treatment for which an inmate has refused to give express and informed consent, the court shall determine by clear and convincing evidence whether the inmate is mentally ill as defined in this chapter; whether such treatment is essential to the care of the inmate; and whether the treatment is experimental or presents an unreasonable risk of serious, hazardous, or irreversible side effects. In arriving at the substitute judgment decision, the court must consider at least the following:

"1. The inmate's expressed preference regarding treatment;

"2. The probability of adverse side effects;

"3. The prognosis for the inmate without treatment; and

"4. The prognosis for the inmate with treatment.

"The inmate and the inmate's representative shall be provided with a copy of the petition and the date, time, and location of the hearing. The inmate may have an attorney represent him or her at the hearing, and, if the inmate is indigent, the court shall appoint the office of the public defender to represent him or her at the hearing. The inmate may testify or not, as he or she chooses, may cross-examine witnesses testifying on behalf of the facility, and may present his or her own witnesses.

"(d) In addition to the above provisions, when the permission of the inmate cannot be obtained, the warden of a mental health treatment facility, or his or her designated representative, with the concurrence of the inmate's attending physician, may authorize emergency surgical or nonpsychiatric medical treatment if such treatment is deemed lifesaving or there is a situation threatening serious bodily harm to the inmate.

"(3) Status of inmate.—An inmate receiving mental health treatment shall be subject to the same standards applied to other inmates in the department, including, but not limited to, consideration for parole, release by reason of gain-time allowances as provided for in s. 944.291, and release by expiration of sentence."

Cross References

Licensing requirements for physicians attending prisoners, see § 945.047.

Library References

Mental Health ⚿436.
Westlaw Topic No. 257A.
C.J.S. Mental Health §§ 272 to 277, 283.

Research References

Encyclopedias

Consent for Treatment, FL Jur. 2d Prisons & Prisoners § 130.

Inpatient Treatment, Generally; Rights of Patients, FL Jur. 2d Prisons & Prisoners § 131.

Involuntary Mental Health Treatment of Inmate, FL Jur. 2d Prisons & Prisoners § 134.

Application to Inmates Receiving Mental Health Treatment, FL Jur. 2d Prisons & Prisoners § 181.

Prisoners Receiving Mental Health Treatment; Mentally Retarded Prisoners, FL Jur. 2d Prisons & Prisoners § 201.

945.49. Operation and administration

(1) Administration.—The department is authorized to contract with the appropriate entities, agencies, persons, and local governing bodies to provide mental health services pursuant to ss. 945.40–945.49.

(2) Rules.—The department, in cooperation with the Mental Health Program Office of the Department of Children and Family Services, shall adopt rules necessary for administration of ss. 945.40–945.49 in accordance with chapter 120.

(3) Orientation and training.—Correctional officers employed by a mental health treatment facility shall receive specialized training above and beyond that required for basic certification pursuant to chapter 943.

(4) Status of inmate.—An inmate receiving mental health treatment shall be subject to the same standards applied to other inmates in the department, including, but not limited to, consideration for parole, release by reason of gain-time allowances as provided for in s. 944.291, and release by expiration of sentence.

Laws 1982, c. 82–224, § 1. Amended by Laws 1996, c. 96–410, § 322, eff. Oct. 1, 1996; Laws 1996, c. 96–422, § 10, eff. July 1, 1996; Laws 1999, c. 99–8, § 319, eff. June 29, 1999; Laws 2008, c. 2008–250, § 18, eff. Oct. 1, 2008.

Historical and Statutory Notes

Amendment Notes:

Laws 1982, c. 82–224, § 3, provided that that act shall take effect July 1, 1984. Laws 1984, c. 84–361, § 29, however, amended that section to provide that Laws 1982, c. 82–224, shall take effect Jan. 1, 1985.

Laws 1996, c. 96–410, generally effective October 1, 1996, throughout Florida Statutes, corrected cross references and substituted references to administrative law judge for references to hearing officer or hearing examiner to conform to the revision of the Administrative Procedure Act.

Laws 1996, c. 96–422, § 10, eff. July 1, 1996, rewrote this section, which formerly read:

"(1) Administration.—The department is authorized to contract with the appropriate agencies, persons, and local governing bodies to provide mental health services pursuant to ss. 945.40–945.49.

"(2) Rules.—The department, in cooperation with the Mental Health Program Office of the Department of Health and Rehabilitative Services, shall adopt rules necessary for administration of ss. 945.40–945.49 in accordance with chapter 120.

"(3) Information on mental health services; data collection.—The department shall annually provide pertinent data and information relating to inmates who are provided mental health treatment. Such information shall include, but is not limited to, the number and characteristics of inmates receiving any mental health treatment and the type of treatment received; the number of emergency admissions to a mental health treatment facility; the number of inmates referred to a mental health treatment facility; the number of inmates refused admission to a mental health treatment facility and the reasons for refusal; and the number of inmates admitted to a mental health treatment facility and their lengths of stay.

"(4) Orientation and training.—Correctional officers employed by a mental health treatment facility shall receive specialized training above and beyond that required for basic certification pursuant to chapter 943. Such training shall be developed and administered by appropriate agencies such as, but not limited to, the Department of Health and Rehabilitative Services and the Florida Mental Health Institute, in accordance with requirements of the Criminal Justice Standards and Training Commission.

"(5) Hearing officers.—One or more hearing officers shall be assigned by the Division of Administrative Hearings to conduct hearings for continued placement."

Laws 1999, c. 99–8, § 319, eff. June 29, 1999, substituted "Department of Children and Family Services" for "Department of Health and Rehabilitative Services".

Laws 2008, c. 2008–250, § 18, in subsec. (1), inserted a reference to appropriate entities; in subsec. (3), deleted a former second sentence, which had read, "Such training shall be in accordance with requirements of the Criminal Justice Standards and Training Commission."; and rewrote subsec. (4), which formerly read:

"(4) Administrative law judges.—One or more administrative law judges shall be assigned by the Division of Administrative Hearings to conduct hearings for continued placement."

Library References

Mental Health ⚩436.
Prisons ⚩194, 221.
Westlaw Topic Nos. 257A, 310.
C.J.S. Criminal Law §§ 2188 to 2190.
C.J.S. Mental Health §§ 272 to 277, 283.
C.J.S. Prisons and Rights of Prisoners §§ 18, 23 to 26, 76, 78 to 88, 123, 125, 127, 136.

Research References

Encyclopedias

Prisoners, FL Jur. 2d Incompetent Persons § 163.

Inpatient Treatment, Generally; Rights of Patients, FL Jur. 2d Prisons & Prisoners § 131.

945.601. Correctional Medical Authority; ss. 945.601–945.6035, definitions

As used in this act:

(1) "Authority" means the State of Florida Correctional Medical Authority created in this act.

(2) "Health care provider" means:

(a) A regional research hospital or research center which is authorized by law to provide hospital services in accordance with chapter 395, which has a contractual or operating arrangement with a regional school of medicine, and which is located at that regional school of medicine;

(b) Any entity which has agreed to provide hospital services to inmates in the Department of Corrections; or

(c) Any entity licensed to provide hospital services in accordance with chapter 395.

(3) "Project" means any structure, facility, machinery, equipment, or other property suitable for use by a health facility in connection with its operations or proposed operations, including, without limitation, real property therefor; a clinic, computer facility, dining hall, firefighting facility, fire prevention facility, long-term care facility, hospital, interns' residence, laboratory, laundry, maintenance facility, nurses' residence, office, parking area, pharmacy, recreational facility, research facility, storage facility, utility, or X-ray facility, or any combination of the foregoing; and other structure or facility related thereto or required or useful for health care purposes, the conducting of research, or the operation of a health facility, including a facility or structure essential or convenient for the orderly conduct of the health facility and other similar items necessary or convenient for the operation of a particular facility or structure in the manner for which its use is intended. "Project" does not include such items as fuel, supplies, or other items which are customarily deemed to result in a current operating charge.

(4) "Quality management program" means to monitor and evaluate inmate health care and includes the following objectives:

(a) Assuring that all inmates receive appropriate and timely services in a safe environment.

(b) Assuring systematic monitoring of the treatment environment.

(c) Assisting in the reduction of professional and general liability risks.

(d) Enhancing efficient utilization of resources.

(e) Assisting in credential review and privilege delineation.

(f) Enhancing the identification of continuing educational needs.

(g) Facilitating the identification of strengths, weaknesses, and opportunities for improvement.

(h) Facilitating the coordination and integration of information systems.

(i) Assuring the resolution of identified problems.

(5) "Real property" includes all lands, including buildings, structures, improvements, and fixtures thereon; any property of any nature appurtenant thereto or used in connection therewith; and every estate, interest, and right, legal or equitable, therein, including any such interest for a term of years.
Laws 1986, c. 86–183, § 17. Amended by Laws 1996, c. 96–312, § 15, eff. July 1, 1996.

Historical and Statutory Notes

Prior Provisions for Legislative Review of Regulatory Statutes:

Laws 1987, c. 87–50, § 1 provided that this section and §§ 945.602, 945.603, and 945.6035, were repealed on Oct. 1, 1996, and would be reviewed by the Legislature prior thereto pursuant to § 11.611, the Sundown Act.

Laws 1991, c. 91–429, provided that, notwithstanding the Sundown Act or any other provision of law enacted before Jan. 14, 1992, which scheduled this section and §§ 945.602, 945.603, and 945.6035 for expiration or repeal, such provisions would not expire or stand repealed as scheduled by such laws, but were revived and readopted.

Sections 11.61 and 11.611, the sunset and sundown review provisions, were repealed effective on the day following the day of adjournment sine die of the 1993 regular session of the legislature by Laws 1991, c. 91–429.

Amendment Notes:

Laws 1996, c. 96–312, § 15, eff. July 1, 1996, added a new subsec. (4) defining quality management program, and renumbered former subsec. (4) as subsec. (5).

Library References

Prisons ⟹190.
Westlaw Topic No. 310.
C.J.S. Prisons and Rights of Prisoners §§ 76, 78 to 88, 123, 125, 127, 136.

Research References

Encyclopedias

Florida Correctional Medical Authority; Department of Corrections Contracts With Licensed Health Care Providers, FL Jur. 2d Prisons & Prisoners § 119.

945.602. State of Florida Correctional Medical Authority; creation; members

(1) There is created the State of Florida Correctional Medical Authority, which for administrative purposes shall be assigned to the Department of Health. The governing board of the authority shall be composed of nine persons appointed by the Governor subject to confirmation by the Senate. One member must be a member of the Florida Hospital Association; one member must be a member of the Florida League of Hospitals; one member must be a member of the Association of Community Hospitals and Health Systems of Florida; and one member must be a member of the Florida Medical Association. The authority shall contract with the Department of Health for the provision of administrative support services, including purchasing, personnel, general services, and budgetary matters. The authority shall not be subject to control, supervision, or direction by the Department of Health or the Department of Corrections. The authority shall annually elect one member to serve as chair. Members shall be appointed for terms of 4 years each. Each member is authorized to continue to serve upon the expiration of his or her term until a successor is duly appointed as provided in this section. Before entering upon his or her duties, each member of the authority shall take and subscribe to the oath or affirmation required by the State Constitution.

(2) A member of the authority may not be a current employee of the Department of Corrections. Not more than one member of the authority may be a former employee of the Department of Corrections, and such member, if appointed, may not be appointed to a term of office which begins within 5 years after the date of his or her last employment with the Department of Corrections.

(3) Effective for new appointments after July 1, 1996, at least one member of the authority must be a physician licensed under chapter 458, and one member of the authority may be a physician licensed under chapter 458 or chapter 459. At least two other members of the authority must have had at least 5 years' experience in health care administration.

(4) At least one member of the authority must have at least 5 years' experience in the identification and treatment of mental disorders.

(5) At least one member of the authority must be a dentist licensed under chapter 466 and have at least 5 years' experience in the practice of dentistry.

(6) At least one member of the authority must be a nurse licensed under part I of chapter 464 and have at least 5 years' experience in the practice of nursing.

(7)(a) Five members of the authority shall constitute a quorum, and the affirmative vote of a majority of the members present at a meeting of the authority shall be necessary for any action taken by the authority. No vacancy in the membership of the authority shall impair the right of a quorum to exercise all the rights and perform all the duties of the authority. Any action taken by the authority under this act may be authorized by resolution at any regular or special meeting, and each such resolution shall take effect immediately and need not be published or posted. All meetings of the authority shall be open to the public in accordance with s. 286.011.

(b) Neither the provisions of this section nor those of chapter 119, or of s. 154.207(7), shall apply to any health care provider under contract with the Department of Corrections except to the extent such provisions would apply to any similar provider not under contract with the Department of Corrections.

(c) Notwithstanding any general or special law, rule, regulation, or ordinance of any local agency to the contrary, service as a member of an authority by a trustee, director, officer, or employee of a health facility shall not in and of itself constitute a conflict of interest. However, any member of the authority who is employed by, or has received income from, a health facility under consideration by the authority or the Department of Corrections shall not vote on any matter related to such facility.

(8) Members of the authority shall receive no compensation for the performance of their duties under this act, but each member shall be paid expenses incurred while engaged in the performance of such duties pursuant to s. 112.061.

Laws 1986, c. 86–183, § 18; Laws 1989, c. 89–531, § 8; Laws 1990, c. 90–83, § 1; Laws 1992, c. 92–47, § 1. Amended by Laws 1996, c. 96–312, § 16, eff. July 1, 1996; Laws 1997, c. 97–102, § 1865, eff. July 1, 1997; Laws 1997, c. 97–237, § 116, eff. July 1, 1997; Laws 1997, c. 97–260, § 1, eff. July 1, 1997; Laws 2000, c. 2000–318, § 147, eff. July 1, 2000.

Historical and Statutory Notes

Amendment Notes:

Laws 1989, c. 89–531, § 8, eff. Oct. 1, 1989, rewrote subsec. (1), which formerly read:

"There is created in the Department of Corrections the State of Florida Correctional Medical Authority. The governing board of the authority shall be composed of five persons appointed by the Governor subject to confirmation by the Senate. The Department of Corrections shall provide administrative support and service to the authority. The authority shall not be subject to control, supervision, or direction by the department. One member shall be elected by the authority to serve as chairman for the first 2 years. Thereafter, the authority shall annually elect one member to serve as chairman. Of the members first appointed, one shall serve for 1 year, one for 2 years, one for 3 years, and one for 4 years. Thereafter, members shall be appointed for terms of 4 years each. Each member shall be authorized to continue to serve upon the expiration of his term until his successor is duly appointed as provided in this section. Before entering upon his duties, each member of the authority shall take and subscribe to the oath or affirmation required by the State Constitution.";

deleted former subsec. (2), which had read:

"No more than two members of the authority shall be past or present employees of the department or have otherwise been involved in the administration of prison facilities for 2 years prior to appointment, and at least two members shall have had at least 5 years' experience in hospital administration in the public or private sector."; renumbered former subsec. (3) as subsec. (2), and in par. (a), provided that five, rather than three, authority members would constitute a quorum; and renumbered former subsec. (4) as subsec. (3).

Section 9 of Laws 1989, c. 89–531, provides:

"In order to stagger the terms of the four members added to the State of Florida Correctional Medical Authority by section 8 of this act, of such members first appointed, the Governor shall appoint one for a term of 1 year, one for a term of 2 years, one for a term of 3 years, and one for a term of 4 years."

Laws 1990, c. 90–83, § 1, eff. June 14, 1990, inserted subsecs. (2) and (3); renumbered former subsec. (2) as subsec. (4); in subsec. (4), designated par. (b) and redesignated former par. (b) as par. (c); in par. (a) of subsec. (4), rewrote the last sentence, which formerly read, "All meetings of the authority, as well as all records, books, documents, and papers, shall be open and available to the public in accordance with s. 286.011."

Laws 1992, c. 92–47, § 1, eff. July 1, 1992, in subsec. (2), substituted "5 years" for "1 year"; inserted subsecs. (4) to (6); redesignated subsequent subsections; in subsec. (7)(a), deleted a former second sentence providing that any action could be taken by the authority with the unanimous consent of its members; and, in the last sentence of subsec. (7)(c), inserted "or the department".

Laws 1996, c. 96–312, § 16, eff. July 1, 1996, rewrote subsec. (3), which previously read:

"At least two members of the authority must be physicians licensed under chapter 458, and at least two other members of the authority must have had at least 5 years' experience in health care administration."

Laws 1997, c. 97–102, eff. July 1, 1997, removed gender-specific references applicable to human beings from volume 4 of the Florida Statutes without substantive changes in legal effect.

Laws 1997, c. 97–237, § 116, eff. July 1, 1997, in subsec. (1), transferred the Correctional Medical Authority from the Department of Corrections to the Department of Health in the first sentence, substituted a reference to the Association of Community Hospitals and Health Systems of Florida for a reference to the Association of Voluntary Hospitals in the third sentence, substituted the fourth sentence, relating to contracting for administrative support services for a former fourth sentence, which had read, "The Department of Corrections shall provide administrative support and service to the authority.", and inserted a reference to the Department of Health in the fifth sentence; in subsec. (2), substituted references to the Department of Corrections for references to the Department throughout, neutralized a gender reference, and made a nonsubstantive language change; and in subsec. (7), substituted references to the Department of Corrections for references to the Department throughout, and substituted a reference to providers for a reference to entities in par. (b).

Laws 1997, c. 97–260, § 1, eff. July 1, 1997, in subsec. (1), transferred the Correctional Medical Authority from the Department of Corrections to the Department of Health, required one member of the board to be a member of the Association of Community Hospitals and Health Systems of Florida, in lieu of being a member of the Association of Voluntary Hospitals, substituted the fourth sentence, relating to contracting for administrative support services, for a former fourth sentence, which had read, "The Department of Corrections shall provide administrative support and service to the authority.", and substituted a reference to the Department of Health and the Department of Corrections for a reference to the Department at end of the fifth sentence; in subsec. (2), substituted references to the Department of Corrections for references to the Department throughout, neutralized a gender reference, and made a nonsubstantive language change; in subsec. (7), substituted references to the Department of Corrections for references to the Department in pars. (b) and (c), and substituted a reference to providers for a reference to entities in par. (b).

Laws 2000, c. 2000–318, § 147, in subsec. (6), inserted "part I of" preceding "chapter".

Preamble (Laws 1992, c. 92–47):

"WHEREAS, it is in the best interests of the citizens of the State of Florida to resolve the Costello v. Dugger litigation and return control of the Florida Department of Corrections from the federal court to the State of Florida, and

"WHEREAS, an integral component of the settlement between the Plaintiff inmate class and the Department of Corrections, as set forth in the Memorandum of the parties dated May 30, 1991, was to assure full and complete support to the Correctional Medical Authority (CMA) as it carries out its duties under the law to monitor the delivery of health care services within the Department of Corrections and assure that quality care, as defined in the Health Care Settlement Agreement of July 20, 1981, which was confirmed by the Order Approving the Health Care Settlement Agreement of November 2, 1981, and the Consent Order of December 18, 1987, is delivered, and

"WHEREAS, the most appropriate means of assuring that quality care is delivered to inmates in the Florida Department of Corrections is to ensure both the funding and continued viability of the CMA as it completes its duties to survey physical health care of the institutions within the prison system and as it carries out its duties under law to monitor the delivery of health care services within the Florida corrections system, and

"WHEREAS, in order to carry out the appropriate and intended functions of the CMA, it is necessary and appropriate that the Legislature clarify and enhance the roles and responsibilities of the CMA, NOW, THEREFORE."

Library References

Prisons ⚷190.
Westlaw Topic No. 310.

C.J.S. Prisons and Rights of Prisoners §§ 76, 78 to 88, 123, 125, 127, 136.

Research References

Treatises and Practice Aids

21 Florida Practice Series § 55:3, Statutes Applicable to Medical Malpractice Claims.

945.603. Powers and duties of authority

The purpose of the authority is to assist in the delivery of health care services for inmates in the Department of Corrections by advising the Secretary of Corrections on the professional conduct of primary, convalescent, dental, and mental health care and the management of costs consistent with quality care, by advising the Governor and the Legislature on the status of the Department of Corrections' health care delivery system, and by assuring that adequate standards of physical and mental health care for inmates are maintained at all Department of Corrections institutions. For this purpose, the authority has the authority to:

(1) Review and advise the Secretary of Corrections on cost containment measures the Department of Corrections could implement.

(2) Review and make recommendations regarding health care for the delivery of health care services including, but not limited to, acute hospital-based services and facilities, primary and tertiary care services, ancillary and clinical services, dental services, mental health services, intake and screening services, medical transportation services, and the use of nurse practitioner and physician assistant personnel to act as physician extenders as these relate to inmates in the Department of Corrections.

(3) Develop and recommend to the Governor and the Legislature an annual budget for all or part of the operation of the State of Florida prison health care system.

(4) Review and advise the Secretary of Corrections on contracts between the Department of Corrections and third parties for quality management programs.

(5) Review and advise the Secretary of Corrections on minimum standards needed to ensure that an adequate physical and mental health care delivery system is maintained by the Department of Corrections.

(6) Review and advise the Secretary of Corrections on the sufficiency, adequacy, and effectiveness of the Department of Corrections' Office of Health Services' quality management program.

(7) Review and advise the Secretary of Corrections on the projected medical needs of the inmate population and the types of programs and resources required to meet such needs.

(8) Review and advise the Secretary of Corrections on the adequacy of preservice, inservice, and continuing medical education programs for all health care personnel and, if necessary, recommend changes to such programs within the Department of Corrections.

(9) Identify and recommend to the Secretary of Corrections the professional incentives required to attract and retain qualified professional health care staff within the prison health care system.

(10) Coordinate the development of prospective payment arrangements as described in s. 408.50 when appropriate for the acquisition of inmate health care services.

(11) Review the Department of Corrections' health services plan and advise the Secretary of Corrections on its implementation.

(12) Sue and be sued in its own name and plead and be impleaded.

(13) Make and execute agreements of lease, contracts, deeds, mortgages, notes, and other instruments necessary or convenient in the exercise of its powers and functions under this act.

(14) Employ or contract with health care providers, medical personnel, management consultants, consulting engineers, architects, surveyors, attorneys, accountants, financial experts, and such other employees, entities, or agents as may be necessary in its judgment to carry out the mandates of the Correctional Medical Authority and fix their compensation.

(15) Recommend to the Legislature such performance and financial audits of the Office of Health Services in the Department of Corrections as the authority considers advisable.

Laws 1986, c. 86–183, § 19; Laws 1988, c. 88–122, § 86; Laws 1989, c. 89–531, § 14; Laws 1990, c. 90–83, § 2; Laws 1992, c. 92–33, § 105; Laws 1992, c. 92–47, § 2. Amended by Laws 1996, c. 96–312, § 17, eff. July 1, 1996; Laws 1997, c. 97–237, § 117, eff. July 1, 1997.

Historical and Statutory Notes

Amendment Notes:

Laws 1988, c. 88–122, § 86, eff. July 1, 1988, inserted a new subsec. (8) and redesignated subsequent provisions, and added subsec. (16).

Laws 1989, c. 89–531, § 14, eff. Oct. 1, 1989, repealed former subsec. (15), which had read:

"Not later than 18 months after creation, render a report to the Governor indicating the opinion of the authority as to whether the department or an outside health care provider under contract to the department should provide basic medical services at each individual institution.";

and former subsec. (16) was redesignated as subsec. (15).

Laws 1990, c. 90–83, § 2, eff. June 14, 1990, in the introductory paragraph, inserted ", and to advise the Governor and the Legislature on the status of the department's health care delivery system".

Laws 1992, c. 92–33, § 105, eff. July 1, 1992, in subsec. (8), substituted "408.50" for "407.13".

Laws 1992, c. 92–47, § 2, eff. July 1, 1992, inserted "and duties" in the section heading; and rewrote the introductory paragraph and subsecs. (1) to (4), which formerly read:

"The purpose of the authority is to assist in the delivery of health care services for inmates in the Department of Corrections, to advise the department on the professional conduct of primary, convalescent, dental, and mental health care and the management of costs consistent with quality care, and to advise the Governor and the Legislature on the status of the department's health care delivery system. For this purpose, the authority may:

"(1) Review and make recommendations regarding health care for the delivery of health care services including, but not limited to, acute hospital-based services and facilities, primary and tertiary care services, quality assurance and peer review services, ancillary and clinical services, dental services, mental health services, intake and screening services, medical transportation services, and the use of nurse practitioner and physician assistant personnel to act as physician extenders.

"(2) Resolve medical treatment disputes between the Department of Corrections and any health care provider under contract to the department.

"(3) Develop and recommend to the Governor and the Legislature an annual budget for all or part of the operation of the prison health care system.

"(4) Approve contracts for quality assurance programs, peer review which continuously assesses standards for the quality of care, and the appropriate utilization of health care services and accounts for the expenditure of public funds."

Laws 1996, c. 96–312, § 17, eff. July 1, 1996, rewrote this section, which formerly read:

"The purpose of the authority is to assist in the delivery of health care services for inmates in the Department of Corrections by advising the department on the professional conduct of primary, convalescent, dental, and mental health care and the management of costs consistent with quality care, by advising the Governor and the Legislature on the status of the department's health care delivery system, and by assuring that adequate standards of physical and mental health care for inmates are maintained at all department institutions. For this purpose, the authority has the authority to:

"(1) Review and make recommendations regarding health care for the delivery of health care services including, but not limited to, acute hospital-based services and facilities, primary and tertiary care services, quality assurance and peer review services, ancillary and clinical services, dental services, mental health services, intake and screening services, medical transportation services, and the use of nurse practitioner and physician assistant personnel to act as physician extenders.

"(2) Develop and recommend to the Governor and the Legislature an annual budget for all or part of the operation of the prison health care system.

"(3) Approve contracts between the department and third parties for quality management, quality assurance, and peer review programs.

"(4) Review and ensure that adequate standards for the department's physical and mental health care delivery system are maintained.

"(5) Review the projected medical needs of the inmate population to permit adaptation to changing circumstances in the internal and external environment.

"(6) Establish and approve preservice, inservice, and continuing medical education programs for all health care personnel.

"(7) Identify the professional incentives that will be required to attract and retain qualified professional health care staff.

"(8) Coordinate the development of prospective payment arrangements as described in s. 408.50 when appropriate for the acquisition of inmate health care services.

"(9) Assist in the developing and implementing of a health services plan.

"(10) Adopt an official seal and alter the same at pleasure.

"(11) Sue and be sued in its own name and plead and be impleaded.

"(12) Make and execute agreements of lease, contracts, deeds, mortgages, notes, and other instruments necessary or convenient in the exercise of its powers and functions under this act.

"(13) Employ or contract with health care providers, medical personnel, management consultants, consulting engineers, architects, surveyors, attorneys, accountants, financial experts, and such other employees, entities, or agents as may be necessary in its judgment and fix their compensation.

"(14) Do all things necessary to carry out the purposes of this act.

"(15) Recommend to the Legislature such performance and financial audits of the office of health services in the Department of Corrections as the authority considers advisable."

Laws 1997, c. 97–237, § 117, eff. July 1, 1997, substituted references to the Department of Corrections and to the Secretary of Corrections for references to the Department and to the Secretary throughout; in subsec. (2), added "as these relate to inmates in the Department of Corrections" at the end; in subsec. (3), made a nonsubstantive language change; in subsec. (5), added "by the Department of Corrections" at the end; in subsec. (8), added "within the Department of Corrections" at the end; in subsec. (9), added "within the prison health care system" at the end; and in subsec. (14), inserted "to carry out the mandates of the Correctional Medical Authority" following "judgment".

Library References

Prisons ⚿190.
Westlaw Topic No. 310.
C.J.S. Prisons and Rights of Prisoners §§ 76, 78 to 88, 123, 125, 127, 136.

Research References

Encyclopedias

Florida Correctional Medical Authority; Department of Corrections Contracts With Licensed Health Care Providers, FL Jur. 2d Prisons & Prisoners § 119.

945.6031. Required reports and surveys

(1) Not less than annually, the authority shall report to the Governor and the Legislature the status of the Department of Corrections' health care delivery system. The report must include, but need not be limited to:

(a) Recommendations regarding cost containment measures the Department of Corrections could implement; and

(b) Recommendations regarding performance and financial audits of the Department of Corrections' Office of Health Services.

(2) The authority shall conduct surveys of the physical and mental health care system at each correctional institution at least triennially and shall report the survey findings for each institution to the Secretary of Corrections.

(3) Deficiencies found by the authority to be life-threatening or otherwise serious shall be immediately reported to the Secretary of Corrections. The Department of Corrections shall take immediate action to correct life-threatening or otherwise serious deficiencies identified by the authority and within 3 calendar days file a written corrective action plan with the authority indicating the actions that will be taken to address the deficiencies. Within 60 calendar days following a survey, the authority shall submit a report to the Secretary of Corrections indicating deficiencies found at the institution.

(4) Within 30 calendar days after the receipt of a survey report from the authority, the Department of Corrections shall file a written corrective action plan with the authority, indicating the actions which will be taken to address deficiencies determined by the authority to exist at an institution. Each plan shall set forth an estimate of the time and resources needed to correct identified deficiencies.

(5) The authority shall monitor the Department of Corrections' implementation of corrective actions which have been taken at each institution to address deficiencies related to the Department of Corrections' provision of physical and mental health care services found to exist by the authority.

(6) Failure of the Department of Corrections to file a corrective action plan or to timely implement the provisions of a corrective action plan correcting identified deficiencies may result in the initiation of the dispute resolution procedures by the authority pursuant to s. 945.6035.

Laws 1990, c. 90–83, § 3; Laws 1992, c. 92–47, § 3; Laws 1995, c. 95–325, § 22. Amended by Laws 1996, c. 96–312, § 18, eff. July 1, 1996; Laws 1997, c. 97–237, § 118, eff. July 1, 1997.

Historical and Statutory Notes

Prior Provisions for Legislative Review of Regulatory Statutes:

Laws 1991, c. 91–201, § 32, provided for the repeal of this section and § 945.6032 on Oct. 1, 1996, and review by the legislature prior to that date pursuant to § 11.611, the Sundown Act.

Laws 1991, c. 91–429, provided that, notwithstanding the Sundown Act or any other provision of law enacted before Jan. 14, 1992, which scheduled this section and § 945.6032 for expiration or repeal, such provisions would not expire or stand repealed as scheduled by such laws, but were revived and readopted.

Sections 11.61 and 11.611, the sunset and sundown review provisions, are repealed effective on the day following the day of adjournment sine die of the 1993 regular session of the legislature by Laws 1991, c. 91–429.

Amendment Notes:

Laws 1992, c. 92–47, § 3, eff. July 1, 1992, rewrote the section, which formerly read:

"Not less than annually, the authority shall report to the Governor and the Legislature the status of the department's health care delivery system. The authority shall conduct, or cause to be conducted, comprehensive surveys of the health care system at each correctional institution at least biennially."

Laws 1995, c. 95–325, § 22, eff. July 1, 1995, in the introductory paragraph, required surveys at least triennially, in lieu of at least biennially, in the second sentence.

Laws 1996, c. 96–312, § 18, eff. July 1, 1996, rewrote this section, which formerly read:

"Not less than annually, the authority shall report to the Governor and the Legislature the status of the department's health care delivery system. The authority shall conduct, or cause to be conducted, comprehensive surveys of the physical and mental health care system at each correctional institution at least triennially and shall report the survey findings for each institution to the department.

"(1) Not more than 30 days after an institutional exit conference, the department shall file a written, interim corrective action plan with the authority, indicating therein the actions which will be taken to address any deficiencies which are determined by the authority to exist at an institution.

"(2) Not more than 30 days after the receipt of an institutional report approved by the authority, the department shall file a written corrective action plan with the authority, indicating therein the actions which will be taken to address any deficiencies which are determined by the authority to exist at an institution. Each plan shall set forth the department estimate of the time and resources needed to eliminate identified deficiencies.

"(3) The authority shall monitor the department's implementation of corrective actions to be taken at each institution where deficiencies related to the department's provision of physical and mental health care services are found to exist by the authority.

"(4) Failure of the department to file a corrective action plan or to timely implement the provisions of a corrective action plan may result in the initiation of the dispute resolution procedures by the authority pursuant to s. 945.6035."

Laws 1997, c. 97–237, § 118, eff. July 1, 1997, substituted references to the Department of Corrections and to the Secretary of Corrections for references to the Department and to the Secretary throughout; and in subsec. (1), substituted a reference to the Department of Corrections' Office of Health Services for a reference to the Office of Health Services in par. (b).

Library References

Prisons ⚷190.
Westlaw Topic No. 310.

C.J.S. Prisons and Rights of Prisoners §§ 76, 78 to 88, 123, 125, 127, 136.

945.6032. Quality management program requirements

(1) The authority shall appoint a medical review committee pursuant to s. 766.101 to provide oversight for the Department of Corrections' inmate health care quality management program. The authority shall also designate one of its members to serve on the Department of Corrections' medical review committee in order to ensure coordination between the department and the authority with regard to issues of quality management and to enhance the authority's oversight of the Department of Corrections' quality management system.

(2) The authority's medical review committee shall review amendments to the Department of Corrections' inmate health care quality management program prior to implementation by the department.

(3) The findings and recommendations of a medical review committee created by the authority or the department pursuant to s. 766.101 are confidential and exempt from the provisions of s. 119.07(1) and s. 24(a), Art. I of the State Constitution, and any proceedings of the committee are exempt from the provisions of s. 286.011 and s. 24(b), Art. I of the State Constitution.

Laws 1990, c. 90–83, § 4; Laws 1992, c. 92–47, § 4; Laws 1994, c. 94–73, § 2. Amended by Laws 1996, c. 96–406, § 449, eff. July 3, 1996; Laws 1997, c. 97–237, § 119, eff. July 1, 1997.

Historical and Statutory Notes

Amendment Notes:

Laws 1992, c. 92–47, § 4, eff. July 1, 1992, designated subsecs. (1) and (3); inserted subsec. (2); and, in subsec. (3), substituted "or the department pursuant to" for "under".

Laws 1994, c. 94–73, § 2, eff. Oct. 1, 1994, reenacted and rewrote subsec. (3), which formerly read:

"The written or oral communication of the findings and recommendations of a medical review committee created by the authority or the department pursuant to s. 766.101 is not a waiver of the confidentiality accorded to records of the department or the authority under s. 119.07(3)(z)."

Laws 1996, c. 96–406 was a reviser's bill which deleted references to § 119.14 throughout Florida Statutes to conform to the repeal of § 119.14, the Open Government Sunset Review Act, by Laws 1995, c. 95–217, § 1.

Laws 1997, c. 97–237, § 119, eff. July 1, 1997, in subsecs. (1) and (2), substituted references to the Department of Corrections' inmate health care quality management program for references to the department's quality management program throughout, and made a nonsubstantive language change.

Library References

Prisons ⚷190.
Westlaw Topic No. 310.

C.J.S. Prisons and Rights of Prisoners §§ 76, 78 to 88, 123, 125, 127, 136.

Research References

Encyclopedias

Florida Correctional Medical Authority; Department of Corrections Contracts With Licensed Health Care Providers, FL Jur. 2d Prisons & Prisoners § 119.

Notes of Decisions

Reports 1

1. Reports

An outside physician review report prepared pursuant to the Department of Corrections' (DOC) Mortality Review Program, that provided supervision of DOC's health-care quality-management program and reviewed the death of inmate who received treatment for a severe asthma attack and died, was privileged against disclosure under the statute that protects records of medical review committees. Moore v. Golson, App. 1 Dist., 794 So.2d 752 (2001). Privileged Communications And Confidentiality ⚷ 422(1)

Purpose of Department of Corrections' (DOC) Mortality Review Program, as well as outside physician review reports, is to identify possible deficiencies in the provision of health services to inmate decedents that need to be addressed. Moore v. Golson, App. 1 Dist., 794 So.2d 752 (2001). Prisons ⚷ 342

Department of Corrections (DOC) did not waive its privilege for reports of medical review committees when it inadvertently produced a memorandum that was also prepared pursuant to its mortality review program following inmate's death, where the memorandum did not specifically mention the decedent, or disclose anything about the circumstances of his death. Moore v. Golson, App. 1 Dist., 794 So.2d 752 (2001). Privileged Communications And Confidentiality ⚷ 422(2)

945.6033. Continuing contracts with health care providers

The Department of Corrections may enter into continuing contracts with licensed health care providers, including hospitals and health maintenance organizations, for the provision of inmate health care services which the department is unable to provide in its facilities.

Laws 1988, c. 88–122, § 87.

Library References

Prisons ⚷190.
Westlaw Topic No. 310.
C.J.S. Prisons and Rights of Prisoners §§ 76, 78 to 88, 123, 125, 127, 136.

Research References

Encyclopedias

Florida Correctional Medical Authority; Department of Corrections Contracts With Licensed Health Care Providers, FL Jur. 2d Prisons & Prisoners § 119.

945.6034. Minimum health care standards

(1) The Assistant Secretary for Health Services is responsible for developing a comprehensive health care delivery system and promulgating all department health care standards. Such health care standards shall include, but are not limited to, rules relating to the management structure of the health care system and the provision of health care services to inmates, health care policies, health care plans, quality management systems and procedures, health service bulletins, and treatment protocols.

(2) The department shall submit all health care standards to the authority for review prior to adoption. The authority shall review all department health care standards to determine whether they conform to the standard of care generally accepted in the professional health community at large.

(3) The department shall comply with all adopted department health care standards. Failure of the department to comply with the standards may result in a dispute resolution proceeding brought by the authority pursuant to s.

945.6035, but shall not create a cause of action for any third parties, including inmates or former inmates.

Laws 1992, c. 92–47, § 5.

Library References

Prisons ⚿190.
Westlaw Topic No. 310.
C.J.S. Prisons and Rights of Prisoners §§ 76, 78 to 88, 123, 125, 127, 136.

Research References

Encyclopedias

Florida Correctional Medical Authority; Department of Corrections Contracts With Licensed Health Care Providers, FL Jur. 2d Prisons & Prisoners § 119.

United States Supreme Court

Cruel and unusual punishment, pro see prisoners, allegations of substantial harm, denial of medical treatment, deliberate indifference to serious medical needs, see Erickson v. Pardus, 2007, 127 S.Ct. 2197, 167 L.Ed. 2d 1081.

945.6035. Dispute resolution

(1) The authority and the Assistant Secretary for Health Services shall attempt to expeditiously resolve any disputes arising between the authority and the department regarding the physical and mental health care of inmates.

(2) If the authority and the Assistant Secretary for Health Services are unable to resolve a dispute regarding inmate physical or mental health care, the authority may submit a written notice to the Assistant Secretary for Health Services, setting forth each issue in controversy and the position of the authority. The Assistant Secretary for Health Services shall respond to the authority within 30 days after receipt of such written notice. The authority shall place the assistant secretary's response on the agenda of the next regularly scheduled meeting of the authority. If the dispute remains unresolved, the authority may submit a written report to the secretary detailing the authority's objections. The Assistant Secretary for Health Services shall submit a written report setting forth his or her position to the secretary on the issue or issues raised by the authority within 5 working days after receipt of the submission by the authority.

(3) The secretary shall review any disputes between the authority and the Assistant Secretary for Health Services, and shall provide written notice to the authority of his or her decision regarding such disputes within 40 days after the date when the authority provides written notice of the dispute to the secretary.

(4) If, at the end of the 40–day period, no resolution has been reached, the authority is authorized to appeal to the Administration Commission for a review and resolution of the dispute between the department and the authority.

(5) The authority, within 30 days after receiving written notice of the action of the secretary or, if no response is received, within 30 days after the secretary's response is due pursuant to subsection (3), may file an appeal by petition to the Administration Commission, filed with the Secretary of the Administration Commission. The petition shall set forth the issues in contro-

versy between the authority and the department, in the form and manner prescribed by the Administration Commission, and shall contain the reasons for the appeal. The department has 5 days after delivery of a copy of any such petition to file its reply with the Secretary of the Administration Commission, and the department shall also deliver a copy of its reply to the authority.

(6) The issues which may be raised by the authority on appeal to the Administration Commission are:

(a) Adoption or implementation by the department of a health care standard which does not conform to the standard of care generally accepted in the professional health community at large.

(b) Failure of the department to comply with an adopted health care standard.

(c) Failure to timely file a corrective action plan regarding all deficiencies which are determined by the authority to exist at an institution, as required pursuant to s. 945.6031.

(d) Failure to implement a corrective action plan filed pursuant to s. 945.6031.

(7) Within 30 days after receipt of a petition from the authority, the Secretary of the Administration Commission, or his or her designee, shall conduct an informal hearing to consider the matters presented in the petition and the reply, and after the informal hearing shall promptly submit a report of the findings and recommendations to the Administration Commission. Within 30 days after the informal hearing, the Administration Commission shall approve either the position of the authority or that of the department. If the position of the authority is approved, the Administration Commission shall set forth whatever remedial measures it deems appropriate and the department shall implement such remedial measures. The decision of the Administration Commission is final and binding on the authority and the department and shall not be subject to appeal pursuant to s. 120.68.

Laws 1986, c. 86–183, § 22; Laws 1992, c. 92–47, § 6. Amended by Laws 1997, c. 97–102, § 1664, eff. July 1, 1997.

Historical and Statutory Notes

Amendment Notes:

Laws 1992, c. 92–47, § 6, eff. July 1, 1992, rewrote the section, which formerly read:

"(1) If a dispute regarding medical treatment that is not otherwise resolvable between the parties arises between the Department of Corrections and a health care provider under contract with the department, either the health care provider or the department may submit the dispute in written form to the authority for resolution. The authority shall have 30 days to issue a written decision on the dispute.

"(2) The decision of the authority in any such dispute is final agency action under chapter 120, and either party may pursue such other recourse as provided by law.

"(3) This section does not apply if the dispute involves the provision of emergency medical care to a particular inmate."

Laws 1997, c. 97–102, eff. July 1, 1997, removed gender-specific references applicable to human beings from volume 4 of the Florida Statutes without substantive changes in legal effect.

Library References

Prisons ⚿190.

Westlaw Topic No. 310.

C.J.S. Prisons and Rights of Prisoners §§ 76, 78 to 88, 123, 125, 127, 136.

Research References

Encyclopedias

Florida Correctional Medical Authority; Department of Corrections Contracts With Licensed Health Care Providers, FL Jur. 2d Prisons & Prisoners § 119.

945.6036. Enforcement

(1) If the department fails to substantially comply with the dispute resolution decision of the Administration Commission or fails to implement required remedial action within 45 days after such decision or within the time period set by the Administration Commission, whichever period is longer, the authority is authorized to petition the Circuit Court in Leon County for an order requiring the department to comply. For the purposes of this section, "substantial compliance" means a firm effort to comply fully with the decision without omitting any essential part, and that any omission consists solely of an unimportant defect.

(2) If the authority fails to initiate a circuit court proceeding pursuant to this section, an inmate has the right to file a verified petition with the authority requesting that such a proceeding be initiated. The petition shall set forth with particularity the manner in which the department has failed to implement the decision of the Administration Commission, including any required remedial actions. The authority has 45 days after receipt of a verified petition to either initiate an action in circuit court pursuant to this section or advise the inmate in writing of the reason such an action will not be initiated.

(3) Within 30 days after service of the written decision of the authority setting forth its reason why an action will not be initiated by the authority pursuant to this section, an inmate may initiate an appropriate proceeding in the Circuit Court in Leon County to require the department to substantially comply with the decision of the Administration Commission.

Laws 1992, c. 92–47, § 7.

Library References

Prisons ⚷190.
Westlaw Topic No. 310.
C.J.S. Prisons and Rights of Prisoners §§ 76, 78 to 88, 123, 125, 127, 136.

945.6037. Nonemergency health care; inmate copayments

(1)(a) For each nonemergency visit by an inmate to a health care provider which is initiated by the inmate, the inmate must make a copayment of $5. A copayment may not be charged for the required initial medical history and physical examination of the inmate.

(b) The copayment for an inmate's health care must be deducted from any existing balance in the inmate's bank account. If the account balance is insufficient to cover the copayment, 50 percent of each deposit to the account must be withheld until the total amount owed has been paid.

(c) The proceeds of each copayment must be deposited in the General Revenue Fund.

(d) The department may waive all or part of the copayment for an inmate's visit to a health care provider if the health care:

1. Is provided in connection with an extraordinary event that could not reasonably be foreseen, such as a disturbance or a natural disaster;

2. Is an institutionwide health care measure that is necessary to address the spread of specific infectious or contagious diseases;

3. Is provided under a contractual obligation that is established under the Interstate Corrections Compact or under an agreement with another jurisdiction which precludes assessing such a copayment;

4. Was initiated by the health care provider or consists of routine followup care;

5. Is initiated by the inmate to voluntarily request an HIV test;

6. Produces an outcome that requires medical action to protect staff or inmates from a communicable disease; or

7. When the inmate is referred to mental health evaluation or treatment by a correctional officer, correctional probation officer, or other person supervising an inmate worker.

(2) The department may provide by rule for a supplemental copayment for a medical consultation relating to an inmate's health care and occurring outside the prison or for a prosthetic device for an inmate. The supplemental copayment must be used to defray all or part of the security costs associated with the surveillance and transport of the inmate to the outside consultation or with the fitting and maintenance of the prosthetic device. The proceeds of each supplemental copayment must be deposited into the General Revenue Fund.

(3)(a) An inmate may not be denied access to health care as a result of not paying any copayment or supplemental copayment that is provided for in this section.

(b) An inmate must not be given preferential access to health care as a result of paying any copayment or supplemental copayment that is provided for in this section.

(c) The expenses and operating capital outlay required to develop, implement, and maintain the medical copayment accounting system must be appropriated by the Legislature.

Laws 1994, c. 94–273, § 7; Laws 1995, c. 95–283, § 33. Amended by Laws 1997, c. 97–260, § 7, eff. July 1, 1997; Laws 2003, c. 2003–179, § 12, eff. July 1, 2003; Laws 2009, c. 2009–63, § 6, eff. July 1, 2009.

Historical and Statutory Notes

Amendment Notes:

Laws 1995, c. 95–283, § 33, eff. June 15, 1995, in subsec. (1)(d), added subpars. 5., 6., and 7.

Laws 1997, c. 97–260, § 7, eff. July 1, 1997, in subsec. (1), made the provisions effective Oct. 1, 1997, in lieu of Oct. 1, 1994, and required a copayment of $4, in lieu of a copayment of not less than $1 or more than $5 as set by rule by the Department of Corrections, in par. (a).

Laws 2003, c. 2003–179, § 12, rewrote subsec. (3)(c), which formerly read:

"(c) The expenses and operating capital outlay required to develop, implement, and maintain the medical copayment accounting system must be appropriated from the Inmate Welfare Trust Fund. The fiscal assistants and accountants at the correctional facilities funded from the Inmate Welfare Trust Fund are, in addition to their duties relating to the inmate canteen and bank, responsible for managing the medical copayment system."

Laws 2009, c. 2009–63, § 6, rewrote subsec. (1)(a), which formerly read:

"(1)(a) Effective October 1, 1997, for each nonemergency visit by an inmate to a health care provider which visit is initiated by the inmate, the inmate must make a copayment of $4. A copayment may not be charged for the required initial medical history and physical examination of the inmate."

Library References

Prisons ⚿117, 419.
Westlaw Topic No. 310.
C.J.S. Convicts §§ 4 to 5.
C.J.S. Prisons and Rights of Prisoners §§ 5, 76, 78 to 88, 123, 125, 127, 136.

Research References

Encyclopedias

State Prisoners, FL Jur. 2d Prisons & Prisoners § 137.

945.6038. Inmate litigation costs

(1) The department shall charge an inmate for the following and place a lien on the inmate's trust fund account if the inmate has insufficient funds at the time the charges are imposed:

(a) Costs of duplication of documents and accompanying evidentiary materials needed to initiate civil proceedings in judicial or administrative forums or that must be filed or served in a pending civil proceeding. The following costs are authorized:

1. Up to 15 cents per one-sided copy for duplicated copies of not more than 14 inches by 8 ½ inches; or

2. For all other copies, the actual cost of duplication.

(b) Postage and any special delivery charges, if required by law or rule, for mail to courts, attorneys, parties, and other persons required to be served.

(2) The department shall adopt rules pursuant to ss. 120.536(1) and 120.54 to implement this section.

(3) This section is not intended to create any legal rights or obligations that do not otherwise exist. This section is not intended to limit or preclude the department from charging for duplication of its records as allowed under chapter 119, nor is it intended to create a right to substitute a lien in lieu of payment for public records.

Added by Laws 2006, c. 2006–294, § 1, eff. July 1, 2006.

Library References

Prisons ⚿117, 420.
Westlaw Topic No. 310.
C.J.S. Convicts §§ 4 to 5.
C.J.S. Prisons and Rights of Prisoners §§ 5, 103 to 114, 121.

945.604. Medical claims

(1) Definition of "claim."—As used in this section, for a noninstitutional health care provider the term "claim " means a paper or electronic billing instrument submitted to the department which consists of the HCFA 1500 data set, or its successor, and has all mandatory entries for a physician licensed under chapter 458, chapter 459, chapter 460, chapter 461, or chapter 463 or a psychologist licensed under chapter 490, or any appropriate billing instrument that has all mandatory entries for any other noninstitutional health care provider. For an institutional health care provider, the term "claim" means a paper or electronic billing instrument submitted to the department which consists of the UB–92 data set, or its successor, with entries stated as mandatory by the National Uniform Billing Committee.

(2) Submission date.—Claims for payment or underpayment are considered submitted on the date the claim for payment is mailed or electronically transferred to the department by the health care provider. Claims for overpayment are considered submitted on the date the claim for overpayment is mailed or electronically transferred to the health care provider by the department.

(3) Claims for payment or underpayment.—

(a) Claims for payment or underpayment must be submitted to the department within 6 months after the following have occurred:

1. The discharge of the inmate for inpatient services rendered to the inmate or the date of service for outpatient services rendered to the inmate; and

2. The health care provider has been furnished with the correct name and address of the department.

(b) Claims for payment or underpayment must not duplicate a claim previously submitted unless it is determined the original claim was not received or is otherwise lost.

(c) The department is not obligated to pay claims for payment or underpayment which were not submitted in accordance with paragraph (a).

(4) Claims for overpayment.—

(a) If the department determines that it has made an overpayment to a health care provider for services rendered to an inmate, it must make a claim for such overpayment to the provider's designated location. The department shall provide a written or electronic statement specifying the basis for overpayment. The department must identify the claim or claims, or overpayment claim portion thereof, for which a claim for overpayment is submitted.

(b) The department must submit a claim for overpayment to a health care provider within 30 months after the department's payment of the claim, except that claims for overpayment may be submitted beyond that time from providers convicted of fraud pursuant to s. 817.234.

(c) Health care providers are not obligated to pay claims for overpayment which were not submitted in accordance with paragraph (b).

(d) A health care provider must pay, deny, or contest the department's claim for overpayment within 40 days after the receipt of the claim for overpayment.

(e) A health care provider that denies or contests the department's claim for overpayment or any portion of a claim shall notify the department, in writing, within 40 days after the provider receives the claim. The notice that the claim for overpayment is denied or contested must identify the contested portion of the claim and the specific reason for contesting or denying the claim and, if contested, must include a request for additional information.

(f) All contested claims for overpayment must be paid or denied within 120 days after receipt of the claim. Failure to pay or deny the claim for overpayment within 140 days after receipt creates an uncontestable obligation to pay the claim.

(g) The department may not reduce payment to the health care provider for other services unless the provider agrees to the reduction or fails to respond to the department's claim for overpayment as required by this subsection.

(5) Nonwaiver of provisions.—The provisions of this section may not be waived, voided, or nullified by contract.

Added by Laws 2009, c. 2009–63, § 7, eff. July 1, 2009.

Library References

Prisons ⚷419.
Westlaw Topic No. 310.

C.J.S. Prisons and Rights of Prisoners §§ 5, 76, 78 to 88, 123, 125, 127, 136.

945.6041. Inmate medical services

(1) As used in this section, the term:

(a) "Emergency medical transportation services" includes, but is not limited to, services rendered by ambulances, emergency medical services vehicles, and air ambulances as those terms are defined in s. 401.23.

(b) "Health care provider" has the same meaning as provided in s. 766. 105.

(2) Compensation to a health care provider to provide inmate medical services may not exceed 110 percent of the Medicare allowable rate if the health care provider does not have a contract to provide services with the department or the private correctional facility, as defined in s. 944.710, which houses the inmate. However, compensation to a health care provider may not exceed 125 percent of the Medicare allowable rate if:

(a) The health care provider does not have a contract to provide services with the department or the private correctional facility, as defined in s. 944.710, which houses the inmate; and

(b) The health care provider reported a negative operating margin for the previous year to the Agency for Health Care Administration through hospital-audited financial data.

(3) Compensation to an entity to provide emergency medical transportation services for inmates may not exceed 110 percent of the Medicare allowable rate if the entity does not have a contract with the department or a private correctional facility, as defined in s. 944.710, to provide the services.

(4) This section does not apply to charges for medical services provided at a hospital operated by the department.

Added by Laws 2009, c. 2009–63, § 8, eff. July 1, 2009.

Library References

Prisons ⚷419.
Westlaw Topic No. 310.

C.J.S. Prisons and Rights of Prisoners §§ 5, 76, 78 to 88, 123, 125, 127, 136.

945.71. Inmate training programs; intent and purposes

It is the intent of ss. 945.71–945.74 to authorize the establishment of structured disciplinary training programs within the Department of Corrections expressly intended to instill self-discipline, improve work habits, and improve self-confidence for inmates.

Laws 1992, c. 92–310, § 24.

Library References

Prisons ⚷163.
Westlaw Topic No. 310.

C.J.S. Prisons and Rights of Prisoners §§ 50 to 57, 59, 63, 68 to 70, 73 to 75, 77, 94 to 96, 100 to 102, 113, 119, 121 to 122.

Research References

Encyclopedias

Training Programs for State Inmates, FL Jur. 2d Prisons & Prisoners § 172.

945.72. Eligibility and screening of inmates

(1) The provisions of ss. 945.71–945.74 apply to all eligible inmates in state correctional institutions.

(2) Upon receipt of an inmate into the prison system, the department shall screen the inmate for the training program. To participate, an inmate must have no physical limitations which would preclude participation in strenuous activity and must not be impaired. In screening an inmate for the training program, the department shall consider the inmate's criminal history and the possible rehabilitative benefits of "shock" incarceration.

Laws 1992, c. 92–310, § 25.

Library References

Prisons ⚷163.
Westlaw Topic No. 310.

C.J.S. Prisons and Rights of Prisoners §§ 50 to 57, 59, 63, 68 to 70, 73 to 75, 77, 94 to 96, 100 to 102, 113, 119, 121 to 122.

Research References

Encyclopedias

Training Programs for State Inmates, FL Jur. 2d Prisons & Prisoners § 172.

945.73. Inmate training program operation

(1) The department shall, subject to specific legislative appropriation, develop and implement training programs for eligible inmates which include, but are not limited to, marching drills, calisthenics, a rigid dress code, work assignments, physical training, training in decisionmaking and personal development, drug counseling, education, and rehabilitation.

(2) The department shall adopt rules establishing criteria for placement in the training program and providing the requirements for successful completion of the program. Only inmates eligible for control release pursuant to s. 947.146 shall be permitted to participate in the training program. The rules shall further define the structured disciplinary program and allow for restrictions on general inmate population privileges.

(3) The inmate training program shall provide a short incarceration period of rigorous training to inmates who require a greater degree of supervision than is provided for those on community control or probation. The inmate training program is not intended to divert offenders away from probation or community control, but to divert them from long periods of incarceration when a short "shock" incarceration could produce the same deterrent effect.

(4) Upon an inmate's completion of the inmate training program, the department shall submit a report to the releasing authority that describes the inmate's performance. If the performance has been satisfactory, the releasing authority shall establish a release date which is within 30 days following program completion. As a condition of release, the inmate shall be placed on community supervision as provided in chapter 947, and shall be subject to the conditions established therefor.

(5) If an inmate in the training program becomes unmanageable, the department may place the inmate in the general inmate population to complete the remainder of his or her sentence. Any period of time in which the inmate is unable to participate in the inmate training program activities may be excluded from the specified time requirements in the inmate training program. The portion of the sentence served prior to placement in the inmate training program shall not be counted toward program completion.

(6) The department shall work cooperatively with the Control Release Authority, the Florida Parole Commission, or such other authority as may exist or be established in the future which is empowered by law to effect the release of an inmate who has successfully completed the requirements established by ss. 945.71–945.74.

(7) The department shall provide a special training program for staff selected to operate the inmate training program.

Laws 1992, c. 92–310, § 26. Amended by Laws 1997, c. 97–102, § 1665, eff. July 1, 1997.

Historical and Statutory Notes

Amendment Notes:

Laws 1997, c. 97–102, eff. July 1, 1997, removed gender-specific references applicable to human beings from volume 4 of the Florida Statutes without substantive changes in legal effect.

Library References

Prisons ⚿163.
Westlaw Topic No. 310.

C.J.S. Prisons and Rights of Prisoners §§ 50 to 57, 59, 63, 68 to 70, 73 to 75, 77, 94 to 96, 100 to 102, 113, 119, 121 to 122.

Research References

Encyclopedias

Training Programs for State Inmates, FL Jur. 2d Prisons & Prisoners § 172.

945.74. Implementation

The department shall implement the inmate training program to the fullest extent feasible within the parameters of ss. 945.71–945.74.

Laws 1992, c. 92–310, § 27. Amended by Laws 2000, c. 2000–158, § 89, eff. July 4, 2000.

Historical and Statutory Notes

Amendment Notes:

Laws 2000, c. 2000–158, § 89, repealed subsec. (2), which read:

"(2) On October 15, 1992, the department shall submit a report to the Speaker of the House of Representatives and the President of the Senate detailing the extent of implementation of the inmate training program and outlining future goals and any recommendations the department has for future legislative action."

Library References

Prisons ⚷163.
Westlaw Topic No. 310.
C.J.S. Prisons and Rights of Prisoners §§ 50 to 57, 59, 63, 68 to 70, 73 to 75, 77, 94 to 96, 100 to 102, 113, 119, 121 to 122.

Research References

Encyclopedias

Training Programs for State Inmates, FL Jur. 2d Prisons & Prisoners § 172.

945.75. Tours of state correctional facilities for juveniles

The Department of Corrections shall develop a program under which a judge may order that juveniles who have committed delinquent acts shall be allowed to tour state correctional facilities under the terms and conditions established by the department. Each county shall develop a comparable program to allow juveniles to tour county jails pursuant to a court order.

Laws 1994, c. 94–209, § 109.

Library References

Infants ⚷223.1.
Westlaw Topic No. 211.
C.J.S. Infants §§ 43, 71 to 95, 310.

Research References

Encyclopedias

State Correctional System, Generally, FL Jur. 2d Prisons & Prisoners § 1.

County and Municipal Detention Facilities, FL Jur. 2d Prisons & Prisoners § 18.

945.76. Renumbered as 741.327 and amended by Laws 2001, c. 2001–183, § 5, eff. July 1, 2001

CHAPTER 946

INMATE LABOR AND CORRECTIONAL WORK PROGRAMS

PART I. CORRECTIONAL WORK PROGRAMS, GENERALLY

PART II. LEASED OR MANAGED WORK PROGRAMS

Transfer

Laws 1983, c. 83–209, created Chapter 946 and provisions from Chapters 944, 945, and 959 were transferred to Fla.St.1983, Chapter 946, Inmate Labor and Correctional Work Programs.

Revision

Laws 1987, c. 87–286, §§ 3, 4, designated Part I, Correctional Work Programs Generally, and Part II, Leased or Managed Work Programs, reallocated and amended existing provisions, and added significant provisions to constitute the revised chapter.

PART I. CORRECTIONAL WORK PROGRAMS, GENERALLY

946.001. Repealed by Laws 1985, c. 85–288, § 27, eff. July 1, 1985

Historical and Statutory Notes

Repealed § 946.001, which related to the duty of the Department of Corrections to use inmate labor, was derived from:
Fla.St.1981, § 945.045.
Laws 1979, c. 79–3, § 81.
Laws 1977, c. 77–174, § 1.
Laws 1976, c. 76–273, § 18.

946.002. Requirement of labor; compensation; amount; crediting of account of prisoner; forfeiture; civil rights; prisoner not employee or entitled to compensation insurance benefits

(1)(a) The department shall require of every able-bodied prisoner imprisoned in any institution as many hours of faithful labor in each day and every day during his or her term of imprisonment as shall be prescribed by the rules of the department. Every able-bodied prisoner classified as medium custody or minimum custody who does not satisfactorily participate in any institutional work programs, correctional work programs, prison industry enhancement (PIE) programs, academic programs, or vocational programs shall be required to perform work for such political subdivisions of the state as might have entered into agreement with the department pursuant to s. 946.40.

(b) The department shall have as a continuous goal the reduction of inmate idleness in the prison system and shall incorporate this goal and that of maximizing the use of inmates while incarcerated in its strategic plan. A goal of the department shall be for all inmates, except those inmates who pose a serious security risk or who are unable to work, to work at least 40 hours a week. Until this goal can be accomplished, the department shall maximize the utilization of inmates within existing resources.

(2)(a) Each prisoner who is engaged in productive work in any state correctional institution, program, or facility under the jurisdiction of the department may receive for work performed such compensation as the department shall determine. Such compensation shall be in accordance with a schedule based on quality and quantity of work performed and skill required for performance, and said compensation shall be credited to the account of the prisoner or the prisoner's family.

(b) Any monetary payments made directly to the prisoner shall be used in whole or in part to satisfy restitution ordered by a court of competent jurisdiction to the victim of the criminal act.

(c) It shall be the policy of the department to require inmates receiving compensation for work performed in community programs to reimburse the state for lodging, food, transportation, and other expenses incurred for sustaining the inmate. Reimbursement shall be according to rules promulgated by the department, which shall provide that the inmate retain only a minimal amount of money for personal items and shall take into consideration compensation that may be allocated for the support of the inmate's family and for restitution for the victim of the crime committed.

(3) Said compensation shall be paid from the Department of Corrections Correctional Work Program Trust Fund. Whenever any price is fixed on any article, material, supply, or service, to be produced, manufactured, supplied, or performed in connection with the work program of the department, the compensation paid to the prisoners shall be included as an item of cost in the final price.

(4)(a) When any prisoner shall willfully violate the terms of his or her employment or the rules and regulations of the department, the department may in its discretion determine what portion of all moneys earned by the prisoner shall be forfeited by said prisoner and such forfeiture shall be redeposited to the Department of Corrections Correctional Work Program Trust Fund.

(b) When any prisoner escapes, the department shall determine what portion of the prisoner's earnings shall be forfeited, and such forfeiture shall be deposited in the State Treasury in the Inmate Welfare Fund of the department.

(5) Nothing in this section is intended to restore, in whole or in part, the civil rights of any prisoner. No prisoner compensated under this section shall be considered as an employee of the state or the department, nor shall such prisoner come within any other provision of the Workers' Compensation Act.

Laws 1957, c. 57–121, §§ 39, 40; Laws 1961, c. 61–530, § 18; Laws 1969, c. 69–106, §§ 19, 35; Laws 1976, c. 76–273, §§ 2, 16; Laws 1977, c. 77–104, § 253; Laws 1977, c. 77–120, §§ 61, 62; Laws 1979, c. 79–3, §§ 71, 72; Laws 1979, c. 79–40, § 121; Fla.St.1981, §§ 944.49, 944.50; Laws 1985, c. 85–288, § 11. Amended by Laws 1996, c. 96–312, § 20, eff. July 1, 1996; Laws 1997, c. 97–102, § 1866, eff. July 1, 1997; Laws 1999, c. 99–260, § 2, eff. July 1, 1999.

Historical and Statutory Notes

Amendment Notes:

Laws 1961, c. 61–530, § 18, substituted the "division" or "division of corrections" for "department" or "department of corrections".

Laws 1969, c. 69–106, §§ 19, 35, transferred all powers, duties and functions of the division of corrections of the board of commissioners of state institutions to the division of adult corrections of the department of health and rehabilitative services.

Laws 1976, c. 76–273, § 2, amending subsec. (2), inserted "program, or facility" and substituted "work performed" for "his work" in the first sentence, added "or the prisoner's family" at the end of the second sentence, and added the third through fifth sentences. This section was also amended by section 16 of the law, which amendment differed in that it did not add the third through fifth sentences.

Laws 1977, c. 77–104, a reviser's bill changed the name of the fund in subsec. (3).

Laws 1977, c. 77–120, a reviser's bill, amended this section to conform with Laws 1975, c. 75–49, which created the department of offender rehabilitation (see § 20.315) and transferred to the department certain functions performed by the division of corrections of the department of health and rehabilitative services and the parole and probation commission of the department of offender rehabilitation.

Laws 1979, c. 79–3, a reviser's bill, provided for substitution of references to the department and secretary of "corrections" for the department and secretary of "offender rehabilitation" to conform with Laws 1978, c. 78–53.

Laws 1979, c. 79–40, which redesignated the Workmen's Compensation Law as the Workers' Compensation Law, modified subsec. (5) reference to the law in conformance therewith.

Laws 1985, c. 85–288, § 11, eff. July 1, 1985, added the second sentence in subsec. (1).

Laws 1996, c. 96–312, § 20, eff. July 1, 1996, in subsec. (1), designated the former text as par. (a), and added par. (b), relating to department goals.

Laws 1997, c. 97–102, eff. July 1, 1997, removed gender-specific references applicable to human beings from volume 4 of the Florida Statutes without substantive changes in legal effect.

Laws 1999, c. 99–260, § 2, eff. July 1, 1999, in subsec. (1)(a), in the second sentence, inserted "programs, correctional work programs, prison industry enhancement (PIE) programs,", and following "academic", inserted "programs".

Cross References

Disposition of compensation earned by prisoners, private employment, see § 946.513.
Disposition of money and other property received for benefit of inmates, see § 944.516.
Labor by county prisoners, rules and regulations, see § 951.01.
Public works, use of prisoner labor, see § 946.40.
Restoration of civil rights, see §§ 940.01, 940.05, 944.293.
State lien on royalties or sale proceeds derived by prisoners from artistic depiction of crime for which incarcerated, see § 944.512.
Suspension of civil rights upon felony conviction, see § 944.292.
Work-release compensation subject to restitution to crime victim, see § 945.091.
Work-release compensation to county prisoners subject to charges for board, travel and other obligations, see § 951.24.

Law Review and Journal Commentaries

Inmate unions: An appraisal of prisoner rights and labor implication. Sidney Zonn, 32 U.Miami L.Rev. 613 (1978).

Library References

Prisons ⚷117, 170 to 173, 417.
Workers' Compensation ⚷387.
Westlaw Topic Nos. 310, 413.
C.J.S. Convicts §§ 4 to 5, 16 to 19.
C.J.S. Prisons and Rights of Prisoners §§ 5, 44, 58, 60.
C.J.S. Workmen's Compensation § 231.

Research References

Encyclopedias

Inmates in Private Correctional Facilities, FL Jur. 2d Prisons & Prisoners § 146.
Assignment of Inmates to Work Programs, FL Jur. 2d Prisons & Prisoners § 154.
State Prisoners, Generally, FL Jur. 2d Prisons & Prisoners § 161.
Use of Earnings for Reimbursement of Prison Expenses, FL Jur. 2d Prisons & Prisoners § 166.
Use of Earnings for Restitution, FL Jur. 2d Prisons & Prisoners § 167.

Treatises and Practice Aids

9 Florida Practice Series § 6:24, Not an Employee: Prisoners, Inmates, and Those Doing Community Service Labor Under Court Sentence.

Notes of Decisions

Construction and application 1
Employees 2
Payment to prisoners 3

1. Construction and application

Even though no department of corrections employee directly supervised inmate's work performed while on loan to the department of health and rehabilitative services, statute authorizing the department of corrections to enter into agreements with other state agencies in order that such agencies might, under supervision of the department, use services of inmates was applicable in inmate's workers' compensation action against the department of health and rehabilitative services. State, Dept. of Health and Rehabilitative Services v. O'Neal, App. 1 Dist., 400 So.2d 28 (1981). Workers' Compensation ⚷ 235

2. Employees

Department of corrections inmate who was injured while working for the department of health and rehabilitative services pursuant to agreement between the two departments remained under supervision of the department of corrections and thus was not an "employee" of the department of health and rehabilitative services such as would have rendered the latter liable for payment of workers' compensation benefits. State, Dept. of Health and Rehabilitative Services v. O'Neal, App. 1 Dist., 400 So.2d 28 (1981). Workers' Compensation ⚷ 235

3. Payment to prisoners

Statute governing prison labor does not mandate payment for inmate work, but rather provides that all able-bodied prisoners shall engage in daily labor and may receive compensation for productive work. Jackson v. Florida Dept. of Corrections, 790 So.2d 381 (2000). Prisons ⚷ 172

946.005. Renumbered as 946.501 by Laws 1987, c. 87–286, § 4, eff. July 4, 1987

946.006. Repealed by Laws 1999, c. 99–260, § 12, eff. July 1, 1999

Historical and Statutory Notes

The repealed section, which related to correctional work programs, was derived from:
Laws 1997, c. 97–102, § 1867.
Laws 1996, c. 96–312, § 41.
Laws 1995, c. 95–283, § 34.
Laws 1994, c. 94–155, § 1.
Fla.St.1981, § 945.06.
Laws 1976, c. 76–273, § 3.
Laws 1972, c. 72–24, § 2.
Laws 1969, c. 69–106, §§ 19, 35.
Laws 1957, c. 57–213, § 6.

946.0061. Repealed by Laws 1999, c. 99–260, § 12, eff. July 1, 1999

Historical and Statutory Notes

The repealed section, which provided that section 846.006(4) would not apply to correctional work programs operating under part II, was derived from Laws 1995, c. 95–283, § 35.

946.007. Repealed by Laws 1999, c. 99–260, § 12, eff. July 1, 1999

Historical and Statutory Notes

The repealed section, which related to correctional work program objectives, was derived from:
Laws 1989, c. 89–526, § 24.
Laws 1983, c. 83–216, § 186.
Fla.St.1981, § 945.061.
Laws 1979, c. 79–3, § 82.
Laws 1977, c. 77–174, § 1.
Laws 1976, c. 76–273, § 6.

946.008. Repealed by Laws 1999, c. 99–260, § 12, eff. July 1, 1999

Historical and Statutory Notes

The repealed section, which related to the financing of correctional work programs, was derived from:
Laws 1996, c. 96–312, § 41.
Fla.St.1981, § 945.062.
Laws 1976, c. 76–273, § 7.

946.009. Repealed by Laws 1997, c. 97–227, § 13, eff. May 30, 1997

Historical and Statutory Notes

The repealed section, which related to operational guidelines for correctional work programs, was derived from:
Laws 1996, c. 96–278, § 4.
Laws 1995, c. 95–325, § 17.
Laws 1991, c. 91–298, § 8.
Laws 1989, c. 89–526, § 25.
Fla.St.1981, § 945.063.
Laws 1976, c. 76–273, § 8.

946.01. Renumbered as 946.502 by Laws 1987, c. 87–286, § 4, eff. July 4, 1987

946.02. Renumbered as 946.503 by Laws 1987, c. 87–286, § 4, eff. July 4, 1987

946.03. Renumbered as 946.504 by Laws 1987, c. 87–286, § 4, eff. July 4, 1987

946.035. Renumbered as 946.505 by Laws 1987, c. 87–286, § 4, eff. July 4, 1987

946.041. Renumbered as 946.506 by Laws 1987, c. 87–286, § 4, eff. July 4, 1987

946.042. Renumbered as 946.507 by Laws 1987, c. 87–286, § 4, eff. July 4, 1987

946.044. Renumbered as 946.508 by Laws 1987, c. 87–286, § 4, eff. July 4, 1987

946.081. Renumbered as 946.509 by Laws 1987, c. 87–286, § 4, eff. July 4, 1987

946.082. Renumbered as 946.5095 by Laws 1987, c. 87–286, § 4, eff. July 4, 1987

946.083. Renumbered as 946.510 by Laws 1987, c. 87–286, § 4, eff. July 4, 1987

946.09. Renumbered as 946.511 by Laws 1987, c. 87–286, § 4, eff. July 4, 1987

946.10. Renumbered as 946.512 by Laws 1987, c. 87–286, § 4, eff. July 4, 1987

946.11. Renumbered as 946.513 by Laws 1987, c. 87–286, § 4, eff. July 4, 1987

946.14. Renumbered as 946.514 by Laws 1987, c. 87–286, § 4, eff. July 4, 1987

946.15. Renumbered as 946.515 by Laws 1987, c. 87–286, § 4, eff. July 4, 1987

946.18. Renumbered as 946.516 by Laws 1987, c. 87–286, § 4, eff. July 4, 1987

946.19. Renumbered as 946.517 by Laws 1987, c. 87–286, § 4, eff. July 4, 1987

946.20. Renumbered as 946.518 by Laws 1987, c. 87–286, § 4, eff. July 4, 1987

946.205. Institutional work

The department may cause to be cultivated by the inmates of the adult correctional institutions that are under the control and supervision of the department such food items as are grown on farms or in gardens generally, and as are needed and used in the state institutions. The department may sell any surplus food items to the corporation authorized under part II of this chapter. Any proceeds received from such sales by the department shall be deposited into the Correctional Work Program Trust Fund. The department may also use the services of inmates of the adult correctional institutions that are under the control and supervision of the department to perform such work as is needed and used within the state institutions.

Added by Laws 1999, c. 99–260, § 8, eff. July 1, 1999. Amended by Laws 2000, c. 2000–155, § 16, eff. July 4, 2000.

Historical and Statutory Notes

Amendment Notes:

Laws 2000, c. 2000–155, a reviser's bill, made conforming changes, deleted obsolete and expired provisions, corrected cross references, corrected grammatical and typographical errors, and made other, similar changes to improve clarity.

Library References

Prisons ⚷170, 183.
Westlaw Topic No. 310.
C.J.S. Convicts §§ 16 to 19, 23 to 24.

946.21. Repealed by Laws 1999, c. 99–260, § 12, eff. July 1, 1999

Historical and Statutory Notes

The repealed section, which related to the penalty for selling goods made by prisoners, was derived from:

Laws 1987, c. 87–286, § 16.
Fla.St.1981, § 945.16.
Laws 1971, c. 71–136, § 1177.
Fla.St.1955, § 959.03.
Comp.Gen.Laws Supp. 1940, § 8135(61).
Laws 1939, c. 19277, §§ 1, 2.

946.22. Renumbered as 946.519 by Laws 1987, c. 87–286, § 4, eff. July 4, 1987

946.24. Repealed by Laws 1996, c. 96–270, § 11, eff. May 29, 1996

Historical and Statutory Notes

The repealed section, which related to the sale of "FLORIDA" tags to Jaycees, was derived from:

Fla.St.1981, § 945.161.
Laws 1979, c. 79–164, § 193.
Laws 1979, c. 79–3, § 92.
Laws 1977, c. 77–120, § 78.
Laws 1969, c. 69–106, §§ 19, 35.
Laws 1959, c. 59–332, § 1.

946.25. Sale of hobbycrafts by prisoners

When, in the planning of the rehabilitation program of the Department of Corrections through its recreational facilities, plans are made for prisoners to engage in hobbies and hobbycrafts after their normal working hours and when they are not required by the warden of a state prison or correctional institution to be on their assigned duties, they may make items of a hobby or hobbycraft nature which may be disposed of by the prisoner through the institutional canteen or commissary to persons visiting the institution.

Added by Laws 1996, c. 96–270, § 10, eff. May 29, 1996; Laws 1996, c. 96–312, § 46, eff. July 1, 1996. Amended by Laws 2000, c. 2000–161, § 26, eff. July 4, 2000.

Historical and Statutory Notes

Amendment Notes:

Laws 2000, c. 2000–161, a reviser's bill, deleted "superintendent or" preceding "warden".

Library References

Prisons ⚷159, 183.
Westlaw Topic No. 310.
C.J.S. Convicts §§ 23 to 24.
C.J.S. Prisons and Rights of Prisoners § 69.

946.30. Repealed by Laws 1984, c. 84–280, § 9, eff. July 1, 1985; Laws 1987, c. 87–87, § 7

Historical and Statutory Notes

Repealed § 946.30, which related to the creation of the Department of Corrections Correctional Work Program Trust Fund, was derived from:

Fla.St.1981, § 945.17.
Laws 1979, c. 79–3, § 93.
Laws 1976, c. 76–273, § 12.
Laws 1970, c. 70–441, §§ 1, 2.
Laws 1969, c. 69–106, §§ 19, 35.
Laws 1961, c. 61–530, § 18.
Laws 1957, c. 57–314, § 1.

946.31. Sources of fund

If any general service operation of an institution is transferred to the work program operation by the Department of Corrections, all assets and liabilities of such operation shall become a part of the Correctional Work Program Trust Fund. All income, receipts, earnings, and profits from work programs operated by the department shall be credited to the Correctional Work Program Trust Fund, to be used for the purposes set forth; however, if the earned surplus in the fund at the end of any fiscal year exceeds $5 million, one-half of such amount in excess of this amount shall be deposited in the General Revenue Fund, and the other half shall be used by the department for the expansion and improvement of inmate work programs.

Laws 1957, c. 57–314, § 2; Laws 1961, c. 61–384, § 1; Laws 1961, c. 61–530, § 18; Laws 1963, c. 63–176, § 3; Laws 1969, c. 69–82, § 8; Laws 1976, c. 76–273, § 13; Laws 1977, c. 77–174, § 1; Laws 1977, c. 77–317, § 1; Fla.St.1981, § 945.18. Amended by Laws 1996, c. 96–312, § 43, eff. July 1, 1996; Laws 1999, c. 99–260, § 3, eff. July 1, 1999; Laws 2001, c. 2001–266, § 133, eff. July 1, 2001.

Historical and Statutory Notes

Amendment Notes:

Laws 1961, c. 61–384, § 1, substituted, in the first sentence, the words "the original general revenue appropriation which was made in the 1957 Session of the Legislature" for "five hundred thousand dollars ($500,000.00), which is hereby allotted and appropriated out of the general revenue fund" following "trust fund shall consist of"; and increased, in the proviso of the last sentence, a ceiling on the earned surplus not to exceed "seven hundred fifty thousand dollars" from "five hundred thousand dollars".

Laws 1961, c. 61–530, § 18, substituted the terms "division" and "division of corrections" for "department" and "department of corrections".

Laws 1963, c. 63–176, § 3, increased, in the proviso of the last sentence, the ceiling on the earned surplus not to exceed "one million five hundred thousand dollars" from "seven hundred fifty thousand dollars".

Laws 1969, c. 69–82, § 8, provided for substitution of the term "auditor general" for "state auditor".

As so amended, the section provided:

"The division of corrections industrial trust fund shall consist of the original general revenue appropriation which was made in the 1957 session of the legislature, together with all assets and liabilities as of June 30, 1957, as determined by the auditor general, of all industrial operations in existence at all correctional institutions as of that date; provided, however, that the assets and liabilities as of June 30, 1957, shall not include cash and accounts receivable which are in excess of the current encumbered obligations as of June 30, 1957, it being the intent of the legislature that after current obligations are liquidated the balance remaining in cash and receivables shall be deposited in the general revenue fund unallocated. Should any general service operation of an institution be transferred to the prison industries operation by the division, all assets and liabilities of such operation shall become a part of this fund. All income, receipts, earnings and profits from such industrial enterprises shall hereafter be credited to this revolving fund to be used for the purposes herein set forth; provided, however, that the earned surplus in the fund at the end of any biennium shall not exceed one million five hundred thousand dollars and such surplus as determined by the auditor general to be in excess of this amount shall be deposited in the general revenue fund unallocated."

Laws 1976, c. 76–273, rewrote the section, which formerly read:

"The [Department of Offender Rehabilitation] Industrial Trust Fund shall consist of the original general revenue appropriation which was made in the 1957 Session of the Legislature, together with all assets and liabilities as of June 30, 1957, as determined by the State Auditor, of all industrial operations in existence at all correctional institutions as of that date; provided, however, that the assets and liabilities as of June 30, 1957, shall not include cash and accounts receivable which are in excess of the current encumbered obligations as of June 30, 1957, it being the intent of the Legislature that after current obligations are liquidated the balance remaining in cash and receivables shall be deposited in the General Revenue Fund unallocated. Should any general service operation of an institution be transferred to the prison industries operation by the [department], all assets and liabilities of such operation shall become a part of this fund. All income, receipts, earnings, and profits from such industrial enterprises shall hereafter be credited to this revolving fund to be used for the purposes herein set forth; provided, however, that the earned surplus in the fund at the end of any biennium shall not exceed $1,500,000 and such surplus as determined by the Auditor General to be in excess of this amount shall be deposited in the General Revenue Fund unallocated."

Laws 1977, c. 77–174, a reviser's bill, amended this section to reflect language editorially substituted by the division of statutory revision.

Laws 1977, c. 77–317, substituted $5,000,000 for $1,500,000 in the second sentence.

Laws 1996, c. 96–312, § 43, eff. July 1, 1996, in the second sentence, substituted "the correctional work programs authorized pursuant to s. 946.006" for "industrial enterprises".

Laws 1999, c. 99–260, § 3, eff. July 1, 1999, in the first sentence, substituted "If" for "Should" and "is" for "be", and following "transferred to the", deleted "correctional"; in the second sentence, substituted "work programs operated by the department" for "the correctional work programs operated by the department authorized pursuant to s. 946.006 shall hereafter", following "the purposes", deleted "herein", substituted "used" for "utilized" and "inmate work programs" for "the correctional work program".

Laws 2001, c. 2001–266, § 133, deleted "as is determined by the Auditor General to be" following "amount".

Library References

States ⚷126, 127.
Westlaw Topic No. 360.
C.J.S. States §§ 383 to 387.

Research References

Encyclopedias

Generally; Pretrial Detainees, FL Jur. 2d Prisons & Prisoners § 145.

946.32. Use of fund

Except as otherwise provided by law, the funds shall be used for the purposes of financing the operation of inmate work programs herein set forth, and all costs of operation of such work programs shall be paid from this fund, including compensation of all personnel whose time or proportion of time is devoted to such work program operations. The Department of Corrections shall establish budgeting and cost accounting procedures to provide comparative analysis of each work program unit. The department shall prepare and issue annual consolidated and individual institution financial statements, including, but not limited to, balance sheets and operating statements for work programs. Any withdrawals from the Correctional Work Program Trust Fund which do not relate to the operation of inmate work programs shall be identified separately in the operating statements. The Department of Corrections shall have the authority to use moneys in the Correctional Work Program Trust Fund to enter into lease-purchase agreements for the lease of fixtures and equipment over periods of time exceeding the current fiscal year. The department shall have the authority to construct buildings or make capital improvements for the operation of the work programs. The ownership of any permanent enhancements made to facilities or work programs is vested in the Department of Corrections.

Laws 1957, c. 57–314, § 3; Laws 1969, c. 69–106, §§ 19, 35; Laws 1976, c. 76–273, § 14; Laws 1977, c. 77–174, § 1; Laws 1979, c. 79–3, § 94; Fla.St.1981, § 945.19. Amended by Laws 1996, c. 96–312, § 44, eff. July 1, 1996; Laws 1999, c. 99–260, § 4, eff. July 1, 1999.

Historical and Statutory Notes

Amendment Notes:

Laws 1969, c. 69–106, §§ 19, 35, transferred all powers, duties and functions of the board of commissioners of state institutions to the division of adult corrections of the department of health and rehabilitative services.

Laws 1976, c. 76–273, changed the use of funds from "prison industries" to "correctional work programs" in the first sentence, interpolated the second through fifth sentences, and provided for making capital improvements and deleted a maximum cost for any single project in the last sentence.

Laws 1977, c. 77–174, a reviser's bill, amended this section to reflect language editorially inserted or substituted in the interest of clarity by the division of statutory revision.

Laws 1979, c. 79–3, a reviser's bill, provided for substitution of references to the department and secretary of "corrections" for the department and secretary of "offender rehabilitation" to conform with Laws 1978, c. 78–53.

Laws 1996, c. 96–312, § 44, eff. July 1, 1996, in the first sentence, inserted "Except as otherwise provided by law,"; in the fifth sentence, following "fiscal year", deleted ", except that such agreements are subject to annual legislative appropriations"; and added the last sentence relating to ownership of facilities enhancements.

Laws 1999, c. 99–260, § 4, eff. July 1, 1999, substituted "inmate work programs" or "work programs" for "correctional work programs" throughout.

Library References

States ⚷127.
Westlaw Topic No. 360.
C.J.S. States §§ 386 to 387.

Research References

Encyclopedias

Generally; Pretrial Detainees, FL Jur. 2d Prisons & Prisoners § 145.

946.33. Disbursements from fund

The funds in the Correctional Work Program Trust Fund shall be deposited in the State Treasury and paid out only on warrants drawn by the Chief Financial

Officer, duly approved by the Department of Corrections. The department shall maintain all necessary records and accounts relative to such funds.

Laws 1957, c. 57–314, § 4; Laws 1961, c. 61–530, § 18; Laws 1969, c. 69–106, §§ 19, 35; Laws 1977, c. 77–120, § 79; Laws 1979, c. 79–3, § 95; Fla.St.1981, § 945.20. Amended by Laws 1999, c. 99–260, § 5, eff. July 1, 1999; Laws 2003, c. 2003–261, § 1930, eff. June 26, 2003.

Historical and Statutory Notes

Amendment Notes:

Laws 1961, c. 61–530, § 18, substituted the term "division of corrections" for "department of corrections".

Laws 1969, c. 69–106, §§ 19, 35, transferred all powers, duties and functions of the division of corrections and the board of commissioners of state institutions to the division of adult corrections of the department of health and rehabilitative services.

Laws 1977, c. 77–120, a reviser's bill, amended this section to conform with Laws 1975, c. 75–49, which created the department of offender rehabilitation and transferred to the department certain functions performed by the division of corrections of the department of health and rehabilitative services and the parole and probation commission of the department of offender rehabilitation.

Laws 1979, c. 79–3, a reviser's bill, provided for substitution of references to the department and secretary of "corrections" for the department and secretary of "offender rehabilitation" to conform with Laws 1978, c. 78–53.

Laws 1999, c. 99–260, § 5, eff. July 1, 1999, inserted "in the Correctional Work Program Trust Fund".

Laws 2003, c. 2003–261, § 1930, substituted "Chief Financial Officer" for "Comptroller".

Library References

States ⚷127.
Westlaw Topic No. 360.
C.J.S. States §§ 386 to 387.

Research References

Encyclopedias

Generally; Pretrial Detainees, FL Jur. 2d Prisons & Prisoners § 145.

946.40. Use of prisoners in public works

(1) The Department of Corrections shall, subject to the availability of funds appropriated for that purpose, and, in the absence of such funds, may, enter into agreements with such political subdivisions in the state, as defined by s. 1.01(8), including municipalities; with such agencies and institutions of the state; and with such nonprofit corporations as might use the services of inmates of correctional institutions and camps when it is determined by the department that such services will not be detrimental to the welfare of such inmates or the interests of the state in a program of rehabilitation. An agreement for use of fewer than 15 minimum custody inmates and medium custody inmates may provide that supervision will be either by the department or by the political subdivision, institution, nonprofit corporation, or agency using the inmates. The department is authorized to adopt rules governing work and supervision of inmates used in public works projects, which rules shall include, but shall not be limited to, the proper screening and supervision of such inmates. Inmates may be used for these purposes without being accompanied by a correctional officer, provided the political subdivision, mu-

nicipality, or agency of the state or the nonprofit corporation provides proper supervision pursuant to the rules of the Department of Corrections.

(2) The budget of the department may be reimbursed from the budget of any state agency or state institution for the services of inmates and personnel of the department in such amounts as may be determined by agreement between the department and the head of such agency or institution. However, no political subdivision of the state shall be required to reimburse the department for such services.

(3) The department shall not be required to provide supervision for minimum custody inmates or medium custody inmates unless there is adequate notice of the need for the services of at least 15 such inmates.

(4) No person convicted of sexual battery pursuant to s. 794.011 is eligible for any program under the provisions of this section.

Laws 1957, c. 57–213, § 11; Laws 1961, c. 61–530, § 18; Laws 1969, c. 69–106, §§ 19, 35; Laws 1970, c. 70–441, §§ 1, 2; Laws 1976, c. 76–273, § 10; Fla.St.1981, § 945.11; Laws 1983, c. 83–175, § 1; Laws 1985, c. 85–288, § 12; Laws 1985, c. 85–340, § 11; Laws 1987, c. 87–211, § 3; Laws 1987, c. 87–286, § 2; Laws 1991, c. 91–225, § 2; Laws 1991, c. 91–280, § 8; Laws 1992, c. 92–142, § 83; Laws 1993, c. 93–156, § 22; Laws 1994, c. 94–265, § 3; Laws 1995, c. 95–211, § 93. Amended by Laws 1997, c. 97–94, § 18, eff. July 1, 1997.

Historical and Statutory Notes

Amendment Notes:

Laws 1961, c. 61–530, § 18, substituted the "division" for "department".

Laws 1969, c. 69–106, §§ 19, 35, transferred all powers, duties and functions of the division of corrections of the board of commissioners of state institutions to the division of adult corrections of the department of health and rehabilitative services.

Laws 1970, c. 70–441, §§ 1, 2, amended Laws 1969, c. 69–106, § 19(2), (6), to read "Division of Corrections" in lieu of "Division of Adult Corrections" and transferred all powers, duties, and functions, accordingly.

Laws 1976, c. 76–273, authorized agreements in subsec. (1) and reimbursement in subsec. (2) with "political subdivisions of the state as defined by s. 1.01(9)", and deleted at the end of subsec. (2) the words "on the basis of the costs of such services to the agency or institution, whichever shall be lower".

Laws 1983, c. 83–175, § 1, amending subsec. (1), rewrote the first sentence and added the second through fourth sentences. Prior thereto, subsec. (1) provided:

"The department is authorized to enter into agreements with such political subdivisions of the state, as defined by s. 1.01(9), and with such agencies and institutions of the state as might, under supervision of employees of the department, use the services of inmates of correctional institutions and camps when it is determined by the department that such services will not be detrimental to the welfare of such inmates or the interests of the state in a program of rehabilitation."

Laws 1985, c. 85–288, § 12, eff. July 1, 1985, substituted in the first sentence of subsec. (1) "shall, subject to the availability of funds appropriated for that purpose, and, in the absence of such funds, may" for "is authorized to" and inserted in the second sentence "fewer than ten" preceding "minimum and maximum", deleted provisions for political subdivisions in the first sentence of subsec. (2) and added the second sentence thereto, and added provisions designated as subsecs. (3) and (4).

Laws 1985, c. 85–340, § 11, eff. June 24, 1985, in subsec. (1), substituted "may" for "is authorized to" in the first sentence, and inserted "fewer than 10" in the second sentence; in subsec. (2), in the first sentence, deleted "political subdivision of the state, as defined by s. 1.01(9)" following "budget of any" and deleted "political subdivision" following "head of such", and added the second sentence; and added provisions designated as subsecs. (3) to (5).

Laws 1987, c. 87–211, § 3, eff. Oct. 1, 1987, modified the statute reference in subsec. (4), rewrote the first sentence of subsec. (5), and substituted in the second sentence of subsec. (5)

"generated under" for "generated pursuant to" preceding "this subsection".

Laws 1987, c. 87–286, § 2, eff. July 4, 1987, substituted in the second sentence of subsec. (1) fifteen for ten "minimum custody inmates", and made the same substitution in subsec. (3).

Laws 1991, c. 91–225, § 2, eff. July 1, 1991, reenacted subsec. (5) without change "For the purpose of incorporating the amendment to section 945.30, Florida Statutes, in references thereto".

Laws 1991, c. 91–280, § 8, eff. Oct. 1, 1991, reenacted and amended subsec. (5) for the purpose of incorporating the amendment to § 945.30, which was renumbered as § 948.09, in references thereto.

Laws 1992, c. 92–142, § 83, eff. July 1, 1992, in subsec. (5), deleted a former second sentence authorizing extra positions within dollars generated under the subsection.

Laws 1993, c. 93–156, § 22, eff. Oct. 1, 1993, in subsec. (4), substituted "is" for "or any other sex offense specified in s. 917.012(1) shall be".

Laws 1994, c.94–265, § 3, eff. July 1, 1995, repealed subsec. (5) providing for deposit of a portion of the cost of supervision fee for administration of the inmate work program.

Laws 1995, c. 95–211, § 93, a reviser's bill, in subsec. (1), substituted a reference to § 1.01(8) for a reference to § 1.01(9) in the first sentence.

Laws 1997, c. 97–94, § 18, eff. July 1, 1997, repealed subsec. (5), which related to a portion of the supervision fee being deposited into the General Revenue Fund.

Cross References

County prisoners, labor on public works, see § 951.05.

Library References

Prisons ⚷170, 171, 175.
Westlaw Topic No. 310.
C.J.S. Convicts §§ 16 to 19, 23.

Research References

Encyclopedias

Assignment of Inmates to Work Programs, FL Jur. 2d Prisons & Prisoners § 154.

Leased or Managed Work Programs; Management by Nonprofit Corporation, FL Jur. 2d Prisons & Prisoners § 155.

Forestry Work Camps, FL Jur. 2d Prisons & Prisoners § 157.

Notes of Decisions

Construction and application 1
Liability for negligent supervision 2

---

1. Construction and application

Even though no department of corrections employee directly supervised inmate's work performed while on loan to the department of health and rehabilitative services, this section authorizing the department of corrections to enter into agreements with other state agencies in order that such agencies might, under supervision of the department, use services of inmates was applicable in inmate's workers' compensation action against the department of health and rehabilitative services. State, Dept. of Health and Rehabilitative Services v. O'Neal, App. 1 Dist., 400 So.2d 28 (1981). Workers' Compensation ⚷ 235

The Division of Corrections cannot make inmates of state prisons available to private citrus and vegetable growers for purpose of using the inmates in the harvesting of fruit and vegetables, though inmates would be paid equally with existing domestic and off-shore labor, and though citrus and vegetable growers were facing a grave problem with reference to harvesting of their crops. Op.Atty.Gen., 065–31, March 18, 1965.

2. Liability for negligent supervision

Sovereign immunity did not apply so as to preclude victim, who was raped by inmate after he left department of transportation work crew during lunch hour, from recovering against department of corrections for negligence in carrying out its operational duty under this section of supervising inmates, though contract provided that DOT was to provide supervision of inmates while in custody of DOT. Newsome v. Department of Corrections of State of Florida, App. 1 Dist., 435 So.2d 887 (1983), review denied 459 So.2d 314. States ⚷ 112.2(2)

946.41. Promotion of inmate work programs; safety signage

The department shall, to the extent possible and within existing resources, promote inmate work programs to the public which may include any or all of the following: signs clearly displayed which identify inmate work crews as inmates working in the community under the supervision of the department or another entity, signs clearly displayed on vehicles commonly utilized for the purpose of transporting inmate work crews working in the community, or signs clearly displayed by the supervising entity in public areas when inmate work crews are performing roadway maintenance or when safety signs are otherwise required. The department may also provide a uniform of distinctive design for inmate work crews in the community, including work crews under the supervision of another entity.

Laws 1995, c. 95–283, § 37.

Library References

Prisons ⚷170.
Westlaw Topic No. 310.
C.J.S. Convicts §§ 16 to 19.

Research References

Encyclopedias

Generally; Pretrial Detainees, FL Jur. 2d Prisons & Prisoners § 145.

Inmates in Private Correctional Facilities, FL Jur. 2d Prisons & Prisoners § 146.

PART II. LEASED OR MANAGED WORK PROGRAMS

946.501. Findings of fact

(1) It is the finding of the Legislature that correctional work programs of the Department of Corrections are uniquely different from other programs operated or conducted by other departments in that it is essential to the state that the work programs provide inmates with useful activities that can lead to meaningful employment after release in order to assist in reducing the return of inmates to the system.

(2) It is further the finding of the Legislature that the mission of a correctional work program is, in order of priority:

(a) To provide a joint effort between the department, the correctional work programs, and other vocational training programs to reinforce relevant education, training, and postrelease job placement and help reduce recommitment.

(b) To serve the security goals of the state through the reduction of idleness of inmates and the provision of an incentive for good behavior in prison.

(c) To reduce the cost of state government by operating enterprises primarily with inmate labor, which enterprises do not seek to unreasonably compete with private enterprise.

(d) To serve the rehabilitative goals of the state by duplicating, as nearly as possible, the operating activities of a free-enterprise type of profitmaking enterprise.

(3) It is further the finding of the Legislature that a program which duplicates as closely as possible free-world production and service operations in order to aid inmates in adjustment after release and to prepare inmates for gainful employment is in the best interests of the state, inmates, and the general public.

Laws 1983, c. 83–209, § 1; Fla.St.1985, § 946.005; Laws 1987, c. 87–286, § 4; Laws 1989, c. 89–526, § 26.

Historical and Statutory Notes

Amendment Notes:

Laws 1987, c. 87–286, § 4, eff. July 4, 1987, renumbered this section from § 946.005 without amendment in text.

Laws 1989, c. 89–526, § 26, eff. Oct. 1, 1989, rewrote subsec. (2), which formerly read:

"It is further the finding of the Legislature that the mission of a correctional work program is:

"(a) To reduce the cost of state government by operating enterprises primarily with inmate labor, which enterprises do not seek to unreasonably compete with private enterprise;

"(b) To serve the rehabilitative goals of the state by duplicating, as nearly as possible, the operating activities of a free-enterprise type of profitmaking enterprise;

"(c) To provide relevant education, training, and postrelease job placement; and

"(d) To serve the security goals of the state through the reduction of idleness of inmates and provision of an incentive for good behavior in prison."

Research References

Encyclopedias

Leased or Managed Work Programs; Management by Nonprofit Corporation, FL Jur. 2d Prisons & Prisoners § 155.

946.502. Legislative intent with respect to operation of correctional work programs

(1) It is the intent of the Legislature that a nonprofit corporation lease and manage the correctional work programs of the Department of Corrections.

(2) It is further the intent of the Legislature that, once one such nonprofit corporation is organized, no other nonprofit corporation be organized for the purpose of carrying out this part. In carrying out this part, the corporation is not an "agency" within the meaning of s. 20.03(11).

(3) It is further the intent of the Legislature that the corporation shall lease all correctional work programs from the department.

(4) It is further the intent of the Legislature that the state shall have a continuing interest in assuring continuity and stability in the operation of correctional work programs and that this part be construed in furtherance of such goals.

(5) It is further the intent of the Legislature that, although the state has a continuing interest in correctional work programs, such programs can best operate independently of state government.

(6) It is further the intent of the Legislature that the corporation will devise and operate correctional work programs to utilize inmates of all custody levels, with specific emphasis on reducing idleness among close custody inmates.

Laws 1983, c. 83–209, § 2; Laws 1983, c. 83–345, §§ 1, 2; Laws 1984, c. 84–280, § 1; Fla.St.1985, § 946.01; Laws 1987, c. 87–286, § 5; Laws 1989, c. 89–526, § 27. Amended by Laws 1996, c. 96–270, § 1, eff. May 29, 1996; Laws 2001, c. 2001–242, § 1, eff. June 15, 2001.

Historical and Statutory Notes

Amendment Notes:

Laws 1983, c. 83–345, §§ 1, 2, added provisions comprising the second sentence of subsec. (1) and comprising subsec. (5).

Laws 1984, c. 84–280, § 1, rewrote subsec. (1) which had provided:

"It is the intent of the Legislature that a nonprofit corporation, the members of which are appointed by the Governor and confirmed by the Senate, be organized pursuant to chapter 617, possessing all the powers granted by chapter 617, in order to lease, incrementally, and manage the correctional work programs of the Department of Corrections. The private nonprofit corporation organized pursuant to former s. 945.135 need not be reorganized if the previous organization was essentially in compliance with the provisions of ss. 946.01–946.19."

Laws 1987, c. 87–286, § 4, eff. July 4, 1987, renumbered this section from § 946.01 and section 5 of the 1987 law modified the statutory references in the section to reflect renumbering of the provisions of this chapter.

Laws 1989, c. 89–526, § 27, eff. Oct. 1, 1989, added subsec. (6), relating to utilization of inmates.

Laws 1996, c. 96–270, § 1, eff. May 29, 1996, in subsec. (1), deleted "be organized in order to" following "corporations"; in subsec. (2), deleted "as set forth in subsection (1)" following "is organized" in the first sentence, and substituted references to §§ 946.502 through 946.518 for references to §§ 946.502 through 946.517 throughout; and in subsec. (4), substituted a reference to §§ 946.502 through 946.518 for a reference to this act.

Laws 2001, c. 2001–242, § 1, in subsec. (2), in two instances, substituted "this part" for "ss. 946.502–946.518"; in subsec. (3), following "that" deleted ", by July 1, 1985,"; substituted "lease" for "have leased"; and in subsec. (4), substituted "this part" for "ss. 946.502–946.518".

Library References

Prisons ⚷170.
Westlaw Topic No. 310.
C.J.S. Convicts §§ 16 to 19.

Research References

Encyclopedias

Leased or Managed Work Programs; Management by Nonprofit Corporation, FL Jur. 2d Prisons & Prisoners § 155.

946.5025. Authorization of corporation to enter into contracts

The corporation established under this part may enter into contracts to operate correctional work programs with any county or municipal authority that operates a correctional facility or with a contractor authorized under chapter 944 or chapter 957 to operate a private correctional facility. The corporation has the same powers, privileges, and immunities in carrying out such contracts as it has under this chapter.

Laws 1991, c. 91–298, § 7. Amended by Laws 1996, c. 96–270, § 2, eff. May 29, 1996; Laws 2001, c. 2001–242, § 2, eff. June 15, 2001.

Historical and Statutory Notes

Amendment Notes:

Laws 1996, c. 96–270, § 2, eff. May 29, 1996, allowed the corporation to enter into contracts with authorized contractors to operate private correctional facilities in the first sentence, and made nonsubstantive language changes throughout.

Laws 2001, c. 2001–242, § 2, substituted "part" for "chapter".

Library References

Prisons ⚿170.
Westlaw Topic No. 310.
C.J.S. Convicts §§ 16 to 19.

Research References

Encyclopedias

Leased or Managed Work Programs; Management by Nonprofit Corporation, FL Jur. 2d Prisons & Prisoners § 155.

946.5026. Sovereign immunity in tort actions

The provisions of s. 768.28 shall be applicable to the corporation established under this part, which is deemed to be a corporation primarily acting as an instrumentality of the state.

Laws 1992, c. 92–310, § 28. Amended by Laws 2001, c. 2001–242, § 3, eff. June 15, 2001.

Historical and Statutory Notes

Amendment Notes:

Laws 2001, c. 2001–242, § 3, substituted "under this part" for "pursuant to s. 946.504(1)".

Library References

States ⚿112.1(3), 112.2(4).
Westlaw Topic No. 360.
C.J.S. States §§ 233, 313, 315 to 319, 321.

Research References

Encyclopedias

Leased or Managed Work Programs; Management by Nonprofit Corporation, FL Jur. 2d Prisons & Prisoners § 155.

Notes of Decisions

Instrumentalities of the state 1

---

1. Instrumentalities of the state

Managing entity of private, nonprofit corporation established independent of state to operate correctional work program for Florida Department of Corrections (DOC) is state instrumentality, where Florida legislature enacted statute specifically providing that entity be deemed instrumentality of state, state had statutory control over selection and appointment of Board of Directors, all of entity's assets would revert back to state if discontinued from use, and entity was exempt from sales tax and audited by state. Gambetta v. Prison Rehabilitative Industries and Diversified Enterprises, Inc., C.A.11 (Fla.)1997, 112 F.3d 1119. States ⚿ 84

946.503. Definitions to be used with respect to correctional work programs

As used in this part, the term:

(1) "Corporation" means the private nonprofit corporation established pursuant to s. 946.504(1), or a private nonprofit corporation whose sole member is the private nonprofit corporation established pursuant to s. 946.504(1), and at least 51 percent of the board of which contains members of the board of directors of the private nonprofit corporation established pursuant to s. 946.504(1), to carry out this part.

(2) "Correctional work program" means any program presently a part of the prison industries program operated by the department or any other correctional work program carried on at any state correctional facility presently or in the future, but the term does not include any program authorized by s. 945.091 or s. 946.40.

(3) "Department" means the Department of Corrections.

(4) "Facilities" means the buildings and land used in the operation of an industry program on state property.

(5) "Inmate" means any person incarcerated within any state, county, municipal, or private correctional facility.

(6) "Private correctional facility" means a facility authorized by chapter 944 or chapter 957.

Laws 1983, c. 83–209, § 2; Laws 1983, c. 83–345, §§ 1, 2; Laws 1984, c. 84–280, § 2; Fla.St.1985, § 946.02; Laws 1987, c. 87–286, § 6. Amended by Laws 1996, c. 96–270, § 3, eff. May 29, 1996; Laws 1997, c. 97–227, § 2, eff. May 30, 1997; Laws 2001, c. 2001–242, § 4, eff. June 15, 2001.

Historical and Statutory Notes

Amendment Notes:

Laws 1983, c. 83–345, § 2, added definition of "corporation".

Laws 1984, c. 84–280, § 2, changed statute reference in the definition of "corporation".

Laws 1987, c. 87–286, § 4, eff. July 4, 1987, renumbered this section from § 946.02 and section 6 of the 1987 law modified the statutory references in the section to reflect renumbering of the provisions of this chapter.

Laws 1996, c. 96–270, § 3, eff. May 29, 1996, substituted references to §§ 946.502 through 946.518 for references to §§ 946.502 through 946.517 throughout; in subsec. (5), inserted references to county, municipal, and private correctional facilities; and added subsec. (6), defining private correctional facility.

Laws 1997, c. 97–227, § 2, eff. May 30, 1997, in subsec. (4), substituted "and land" for ", land, equipment, and other chattels" following "buildings", and added "on state property" at the end.

Laws 2001, c. 2001–242, § 4, in the first sentence, substituted "this part" for "ss. 946.502–946.518"; and rewrote subsec. (1), which formerly read:

"(1) 'Corporation' means the private nonprofit corporation established pursuant to s. 946.504(1) to carry out ss. 946.502–946.518."

Research References

Encyclopedias

Leased or Managed Work Programs; Management by Nonprofit Corporation, FL Jur. 2d Prisons & Prisoners § 155.

946.504. Organization of corporation to operate correctional work programs; lease of facilities

(1) The department shall lease buildings and land to the nonprofit corporation authorized to operate the correctional work programs, the members of which are appointed by the Governor and confirmed by the Senate. The same appointment process shall be followed to fill any vacancy. The corporation shall be organized pursuant to chapter 617 and shall possess all the powers granted by that chapter. The Board of Trustees of the Internal Improvement Trust Fund shall enter into leases directly with the corporation, for a period of at least 20 years, for the lease of the lands that are currently under sublease with the department and used by the corporation for correctional work programs and that are identified as subject to lease numbers 3513, 2946, 2675, 2937, 2673, and 2671 with the Board of Trustees of the Internal Improvement Trust Fund. Any additional improvements to such property leased by the corporation from the Board of Trustees must have the prior approval of the Board of Trustees of the Internal Improvement Trust Fund.

(2) No sublease for land from any other agency of state government shall be in excess of that amount for which the department is obligated to pay under any lease agreement with any other agency of state government.

(3) The corporation shall negotiate with the Department of Management Services to reach and enter into an agreement for the lease of each correctional work program proposed by the corporation. The facilities to be leased and the amount of rental for such facilities shall be agreed upon by the Department of Management Services and the corporation, with consultation with the department. The length of such lease shall be mutually agreed upon among the department, the Department of Management Services, and the corporation; however, the initial lease may not exceed 7 years. The department shall continue to manage and operate the various correctional work programs until the lease between the department and the corporation is effective.

(4) If the department leases a single correctional work program at any correctional institution to the corporation, the corporation shall lease all such correctional work programs at that institution.

(5)(a) Prior to entering into any lease or other separate contract or agreement between the department and the corporation, the department shall determine that:

1. The members of the corporation were appointed by the Governor and confirmed by the Senate;

2. The articles of incorporation of the corporation have been approved by the Governor; and

3. The articles of incorporation contain a provision that prohibits any director from voting on any matter that comes before the board of directors that would result in a direct monetary gain to any director or any entity in which any director has an interest.

(b) The lease must be submitted to the Attorney General for his or her approval as to form and legality.

(c) All leases of land shall be subject to the approval of the Board of Trustees of the Internal Improvement Trust Fund.

(6)(a) Upon the effective date of each lease of each correctional work program, the department shall cause to be remitted to the corporation all funds appropriated for, associated with, or budgeted for the operation of that correctional work program, as agreed upon among the department, the Department of Management Services, and the corporation.

(b) No operating loss of any type may be transferred to the corporation.

(7) When it leases any correctional work program, the corporation shall exercise a reasonable effort to employ the personnel of the department who are currently involved in the correctional work programs being leased to the corporation.

(8) Notwithstanding any provision to the contrary, the corporation is authorized to use tax-exempt financing through the issuance of tax-exempt bonds, certificates of participation, lease-purchase agreements, or other tax-exempt financing methods for the purpose of constructing facilities or making capital improvements for correctional work programs and prison industry enhancement programs on state-owned land within state correctional institutions. Such tax-exempt financing may be funded by the General Appropriations Act. If the corporation obtains tax-exempt financing, the state retains a secured interest by holding a lien against any structure or improvement for which tax-exempt financing or state funds are used. The corporation shall include a provision in its financing contract requiring that a lien be filed by the Department of Corrections, on behalf of the state, in order to procure the issuance of tax-exempt bonds or certificates of participation; to enter into lease-purchase agreements; or to obtain any other tax-exempt financing methods for the construction or renovation of facilities related to correctional work programs or prison industry enhancement programs. The lien shall be against the property where any facility or structure is located which has been constructed or substantially renovated, in whole or in part, through the use of state funds. However, there is no requirement for the Department of Corrections to file a lien if the amount of state funds does not exceed $25,000 or 10 percent of the contract amount, whichever is less. The lien must be recorded, upon the execution of the contract authorizing such construction or renovation, in the county where the property is located. The lien must specify that the Department of Corrections has a financial interest in the property equal to the pro rata portion of the state's original investment of the then-fair-market value of the construction. The lien must also specify that the Department of Corrections' financial interest is proportionately reduced and subsequently vacated over a 20–year period of depreciation. The contract must include a provision that as a condition of receipt of state funding for this purpose, the corporation agrees that, if it disposes of the property before the state's interest is vacated, the

corporation will refund the proportionate share of the state's initial investment, as adjusted by depreciation.

Laws 1983, c. 83–209, § 2; Laws 1984, c. 84–280, § 3; Fla.St.1985, § 946.03; Laws 1987, c. 87–286, § 7; Laws 1992, c. 92–279, § 317. Amended by Laws 1996, c. 96–270, § 4, eff. May 29, 1996; Laws 1997, c. 97–102, § 1868, eff. July 1, 1997; Laws 1997, c. 97–227, § 3, eff. May 30, 1997; Laws 1999, c. 99–260, § 6, eff. July 1, 1999.

Historical and Statutory Notes

Amendment Notes:

Laws 1984, c. 84–280, § 3, redesignated subsection provisions and rewrote provisions contained in subsec. (1) which had provided:

"The department shall lease, incrementally, the buildings, land, furnishings, equipment, and other chattels used in the operation of each correctional work program operated by the department to the corporation. No sublease for land from any other agency of state government shall be in excess of that amount for which the department is obligated to pay under any lease agreement with any other agency of state government."

Laws 1987, c. 87–286, § 4, eff. July 4, 1987, renumbered this section from § 946.03 and section 7 of the 1987 law modified the statutory references in the section to reflect renumbering of the provisions of this chapter.

Laws 1992, c. 92–279, § 317, eff. Jan. 1, 1993, in subsecs. (3) and (6)(a), substituted "Department of Management Services" for "Department of General Services".

Laws 1992, c. 92–326, § 55, amended § 339 of Laws 1992, c. 92–279, by changing the general effective date of the act from Jan. 1, 1993, to July 1, 1992 (§§ 322 to 325 and 339 took effect upon the act becoming a law).

Laws 1995, c. 95–283, § 36, provides:

"It is the intent of the Legislature that the Department of Corrections cooperate with and assist the corporation created under section 946.504(1), Florida Statutes, in seeking qualification and in contracting with the private sector for substantial involvement in prison industry programs pursuant to section 946.006(3), Florida Statutes."

Laws 1996, c. 96–270, § 4, eff. May 29, 1996, in subsec. (1), deleted the former fourth sentence, which had read, "The private nonprofit corporation organized pursuant to former s. 945.135 need not be reorganized if the previous organization was essentially in compliance with the provisions of ss. 946.502–946.517."; and in subsec. (4), deleted the former second sentence, which had read, "Any rent paid by the corporation to the department shall be deposited in a Correctional Programs Trust Fund for enhancement of education and training, postrelease job placement, and other correctional purposes related to the purposes of ss. 946.502–946.517.".

Laws 1997, c. 97–102, eff. July 1, 1997, removed gender-specific references applicable to human beings from volume 4 of the Florida Statutes without substantive changes in legal effect.

Laws 1997, c. 97–227, § 3, eff. May 30, 1997, in subsec. (1), substituted "buildings and land to the nonprofit corporation authorized to operate the correctional work programs" for "the buildings, land, furnishings, equipment, and other chattels used in the operation of each correctional work program operated by the department to a nonprofit corporation" following "lease" in the first sentence.

Laws 1999, c. 99–260, § 6, eff. July 1, 1999, in subsec. (1), added the last two sentences; and added subsec. (8).

Cross References

Siting of facilities, see §§ 944.095, 944.10.

Library References

Prisons ⚷170.
Westlaw Topic No. 310.
C.J.S. Convicts §§ 16 to 19.

Research References

Encyclopedias

Leased or Managed Work Programs; Management by Nonprofit Corporation, FL Jur. 2d Prisons & Prisoners § 155.

946.505. Reversion upon dissolution of corporation or termination of lease

(1) In the event the corporation is dissolved or its lease of any correctional work program expires or is otherwise terminated, all property relating to such correctional work program which ceases to function because of such termination or dissolution, including all buildings, land, furnishings, equipment, and other chattels originally leased from the department, as well as any subsequently constructed or otherwise acquired facilities in connection with its continued operation of that program, automatically reverts to full ownership by the department unless the corporation intends to utilize such property in another correctional work program. Such a reversionary ownership interest of the state in any and all such after-acquired facilities by the corporation is in furtherance of the goals established in s. 946.502(4), and such a present ownership interest by the state is a continuing and insurable state interest.

(2) Notwithstanding any provision of subsection (1), the ownership of any permanent enhancements made to facilities or work programs is vested in the department.

Laws 1983, c. 83–209, § 2; Fla.St.1985, § 946.035; Laws 1987, c. 87–286, § 8; Laws 1994, c. 94–265, § 8. Amended by Laws 1997, c. 97–227, § 4, eff. May 30, 1997.

Historical and Statutory Notes

Amendment Notes:

Laws 1987, c. 87–286, § 4, eff. July 4, 1987, renumbered this section from § 946.035 and section 8 of the 1987 law modified the statutory references in the section to reflect renumbering of the provisions of this chapter.

Laws 1994, c. 94–265, § 8, eff. July 1, 1995, designated subsec. (1) and added subsec. (2).

Laws 1997, c. 97–227, § 4, eff. May 30, 1997, in subsec. (1), substituted "buildings, land, furnishings, equipment, and other chattels originally leased from the department, as well as any subsequently constructed or otherwise acquired facilities" for "funds, buildings, land, furnishings, equipment, and other chattels subsequently purchased or otherwise acquired by the corporation" following "including all" in the first sentence, and substituted a reference to after-acquired facilities for a reference to after-acquired property in the last sentence.

Library References

Prisons ⚷170.
Westlaw Topic No. 310.
C.J.S. Convicts §§ 16 to 19.

Research References

Encyclopedias

Leased or Managed Work Programs; Management by Nonprofit Corporation, FL Jur. 2d Prisons & Prisoners § 155.

946.506. Modification or termination of correctional work program by the corporation

This part does not prevent the corporation from modifying, altering, or terminating any correctional work program, once assumed, so long as the corporation is otherwise carrying out the provisions of this part.

Laws 1983, c. 83–209, § 2; Fla.St.1985, § 946.041; Laws 1987, c. 87–286, § 9. Amended by Laws 1996, c. 96–270, § 5, eff. May 29, 1996; Laws 2001, c. 2001–242, § 5, eff. June 15, 2001.

Historical and Statutory Notes

Amendment Notes:

Laws 1987, c. 87–286, § 4, eff. July 4, 1987, renumbered this section from § 946.041 and section 9 of the 1987 law modified the statutory references in the section to reflect renumbering of the provisions of this chapter.

Laws 1996, c. 96–270, § 5, eff. May 29, 1996, substituted references to §§ 946.502 through 946.518 for references to §§ 946.502 through 946.517 throughout, and made a nonsubstantive language change.

Laws 2001, c. 2001–242, § 5, substituted "This part does" for "Sections 946.502–46.518 do"; and substituted "this part" for "ss. 946.502–946.518".

Library References

Prisons ⚷170.
Westlaw Topic No. 310.
C.J.S. Convicts §§ 16 to 19.

Research References

Encyclopedias

Leased or Managed Work Programs; Management by Nonprofit Corporation, FL Jur. 2d Prisons & Prisoners § 155.

946.507. Repealed by Laws 1996, c. 96–270, § 11, eff. May 29, 1996

Historical and Statutory Notes

Repealed § 946.507, which related to appropriations, was derived from:
Laws 1987, c. 87–286, § 10.
Fla.St. 1985, § 946.042.
Laws 1984, c. 84–280, § 4.
Laws 1983, c. 83–209, § 2.

946.508. Repealed by Laws 1997, c. 97–94, § 19, eff. July 1, 1997

Historical and Statutory Notes

The repealed § 946.508, which related to the Correctional Work Program Revolving Trust Fund, was derived from:
Laws 1993, c. 93–260, § 13.
Laws 1987, c. 87–286, § 11.
Fla.St.1985, § 946.044.
Laws 1984, c. 84–280, § 5.

946.509. Insurance of property leased or acquired by the corporation

(1) The State Risk Management Trust Fund created under s. 284.30 shall insure all property eligible for coverage under part I of chapter 284 which is leased by the department to the corporation or which is subsequently acquired and owned or leased by the corporation and subject to the reversionary ownership interest of the state established in s. 946.505.

(2) Coverage under the State Risk Management Trust Fund of property leased to or otherwise acquired by the corporation shall be secured and maintained through the existing policy and account of the Department of Corrections with the Division of Risk Management of the Department of Financial Services. All matters, including premium calculations, assessments and payments, retrospective premium adjustments, reporting requirements, and other requirements, concerning coverage of such property under the State Risk Management Trust Fund shall be conducted as if all such property were owned solely by the department. Except as required by chapter 284, if the

corporation finds that it is more economical to do so, the corporation may secure private insurance coverage on all or a portion of the activities of or properties used by the corporation. If coverage through the State Risk Management Trust Fund is not secured, the corporation must present documentation of insurance coverage to the Division of Risk Management equal to the coverage that could otherwise be provided by the State Risk Management Trust Fund.

Laws 1983, c. 83–209, § 2; Fla.St.1985, § 946.081; Laws 1987, c. 87–286, § 12. Amended by Laws 1996, c. 96–270, § 6, eff. May 29, 1996; Laws 1996, c. 96–418, § 65, eff. Nov. 4, 1996; Laws 1997, c. 97–93, § 37, eff. July 1, 1997; Laws 1997, c. 97–227, § 5, eff. May 30, 1997; Laws 2000, c. 2000–122, § 24, eff. April 20, 2000; Laws 2001, c. 2001–242, § 6, eff. June 15, 2001; Laws 2003, c. 2003–261, § 1931, eff. June 26, 2003.

Historical and Statutory Notes

Amendment Notes:

Laws 1987, c. 87–286, § 4, eff. July 4, 1987, renumbered this section from § 946.081 and section 12 of the 1987 law modified the statutory references in the section to reflect renumbering of the provisions of this chapter.

Laws 1996, c. 96–270, § 6, eff. May 29, 1996, in subsec. (2), added the third and fourth sentences, relating to securing and documenting private insurance coverage.

Laws 1996, c. 96–418, § 65, eff. Nov. 4, 1996, modified provisions relating to trust funds.

Laws 1997, c. 97–93, eff. July 1, 1997, was a reviser's bill which deleted obsolete and expired provisions, corrected cross references and citations, and corrected grammatical and other similar errors.

Laws 1997, c. 97–227, § 6, eff. May 30, 1997, reenacted subsec. (1) for the purpose of incorporating an amendment to § 946.505 in a reference thereto.

Laws 2000, c. 2000–122, § 24, in subsec. (1), substituted "284.30" for "284.01"; and substituted "State Risk Management Trust Fund" for "State Property Insurance Trust Fund" throughout the section.

Laws 2001, c. 2001–242, § 6, in subsec. (1), following "owned" inserted "or leased".

Laws 2003, c. 2003–261, § 1931, in subsec. (2), substituted "Financial Services" for "Insurance" following "Risk Management of the Department of".

Library References

Prisons ⚿170.
Westlaw Topic No. 310.
C.J.S. Convicts §§ 16 to 19.

Research References

Encyclopedias

Leased or Managed Work Programs; Management by Nonprofit Corporation, FL Jur. 2d Prisons & Prisoners § 155.

946.5095. Elimination of hazardous conditions

Pursuant to the applicable provisions of part I of chapter 284, whenever state-insured property leased to or otherwise held by the corporation is inspected by the Division of Risk Management of the Department of Financial Services and any condition is found to exist which, in the opinion of the division, is hazardous from the standpoint of destruction by fire or other insurable causes, the corporation shall either promptly repair the property to eliminate any observed hazard or otherwise promptly remove the hazardous condition at its own expense.

Laws 1983, c. 83–209, § 2; Fla.St.1985, § 946.082; Laws 1987, c. 87–286, § 4. Amended by Laws 2003, c. 2003–261, § 1932, eff. June 26, 2003.

Historical and Statutory Notes

Amendment Notes:

Laws 1987, c. 87–286, § 4, eff. July 4, 1987, renumbered provisions of this chapter. This section was renumbered from § 946.082 without amendment in text in Fla.St.1987.

Laws 2003, c. 2003–261, § 1932, inserted "of the Department of Financial Services" following "Division of Risk Management".

Library References

Prisons ⚷170, 171.
Westlaw Topic No. 310.
C.J.S. Convicts §§ 16 to 19.

Research References

Encyclopedias

Leased or Managed Work Programs; Management by Nonprofit Corporation, FL Jur. 2d Prisons & Prisoners § 155.

946.510. Insurance by Division of Risk Management

Pursuant to the applicable provisions of chapter 284, the Division of Risk Management of the Department of Financial Services is authorized to insure the corporation under the same general terms and conditions as the Department of Corrections was insured by the division prior to the corporation leasing the correctional work programs as authorized by this chapter.

Laws 1985, c. 85–194, § 2; Fla.St.1985, § 946.083; Laws 1987, c. 87–286, § 4. Amended by Laws 2003, c. 2003–261, § 1933, eff. June 26, 2003.

Historical and Statutory Notes

Amendment Notes:

Laws 1987, c. 87–286, § 4, eff. July 4, 1987, renumbered this section from § 946.083 without amendment in text.

Laws 2003, c. 2003–261, § 1933, substituted "Financial Services" for "Insurance" following "Department of".

Library References

Prisons ⚷170.
Westlaw Topic No. 310.
C.J.S. Convicts §§ 16 to 19.

Research References

Encyclopedias

Leased or Managed Work Programs; Management by Nonprofit Corporation, FL Jur. 2d Prisons & Prisoners § 155.

946.511. Inmate labor to operate correctional work programs

(1) Inmates shall be evaluated and identified during the reception process to determine basic literacy, employment skills, academic skills, vocational skills, and remedial and rehabilitative needs. The evaluation shall prescribe education, work, and work-training for each inmate. Assignment to programs shall be based on the evaluation and the length of time the inmate will be in the custody of the department. Assignment to programs shall be reviewed every 6

months to ensure proper placement based on bed space availability. Assignment of inmates shall be governed by the following objectives and priorities:

(a) Inmates shall be assigned to meet the needs of the work requirements of the Department of Corrections, including essential operational functions and revenue-generating contracts.

(b) Inmates shall be assigned to correctional education.

(c) Inmates shall be assigned to meet all other work requirements of the department, including remaining operational functions and nonrevenue-generating contracts.

As used in this subsection, the term "revenue-generating contracts" includes contracts with the Department of Transportation, the corporation authorized to conduct the correctional work programs under this part, the corporation and private sector businesses operating programs authorized under s. 946.523, and federal, state, or local governmental entities or subdivisions authorized under s. 944.10(7).

(2) The corporation shall establish policies and procedures relating to the use of inmates in its correctional work program, which shall be submitted to the department for approval. Any policies and procedures in effect on the effective date of this act do not require approval.

Laws 1983, c. 83–209, § 2; Fla.St.1985, § 946.09; Laws 1987, c. 87–286, § 4; Laws 1989, c. 89–526, § 28; Laws 1991, c. 91–298, § 2. Amended by Laws 1997, c. 97–227, § 6, eff. May 30, 1997; Laws 2001, c. 2001–242, § 7, eff. June 15, 2001.

Historical and Statutory Notes

Amendment Notes:

Laws 1987, c. 87–286, § 4, eff. July 4, 1987, renumbered this section from § 946.09 without amendment in text.

Laws 1989, c. 89–526, § 28, eff. Oct. 1, 1989, inserted subsec. (3), relating to criteria for assigning and transferring inmates; and renumbered former subsec. (3) as subsec. (4).

Laws 1991, c. 91–298, § 2, eff. June 7, 1991, rewrote this section which had provided:

"(1) The department shall, subject to the necessary security requirements and the needs of the corporation, provide to the corporation sufficient inmate labor to operate the various correctional work programs.

"(2) The department may adopt such rules as may be necessary to govern the use of inmates by the corporation; however, such rules shall be related only to the need for security, inmate protection, and efficient operation of each institution.

"(3) The needs of the corporation will be considered when assigning and transferring prisoners to correctional institutions. The following criteria shall be used when assigning and transferring inmates:

"(a) Skills of the inmate relevant to the corporation's industries.

"(b) Security classification of the inmate relevant to the type of the corporation's industry.

"(c) Duration of availability of the inmate for employment by the corporation.

"(d) Establishment of a concept of a potentially rehabilitative inmate.

"(4) The corporation shall establish policies and procedures, subject to the approval of the department, relating to the use of inmates in correctional work programs."

Laws 1997, c. 97–227, § 6, eff. May 30, 1997, in subsec. (1), deleted "to correctional work programs, institutional labor, and public agency work programs" following "inmates" in the last sentence of the introductory paragraph, substituted "essential operational functions and revenue-generating contracts" for "existing Department of Transportation contracts" at the end of par. (a), deleted "and the corporation operating the correctional industry program" at the end of par. (b), substituted "remaining operational functions and nonrevenue-generating contracts" for "public works" at the end of par. (c), and added a concluding paragraph, defining revenue-generating contracts.

Laws 2001, c. 2001–242, § 7, in subsec. (1), rewrote the last paragraph, which formerly read:

"As used in this subsection, the term "revenue-generating contracts" includes contracts with the Department of Transportation, the corporation authorized to conduct the correctional work programs under part II, private sector businesses operating programs authorized under s. 946.006(3), and federal, state, or local governmental entities or subdivisions authorized under s. 944.10(7)."

Library References

Prisons ⚷173.
Westlaw Topic No. 310.

Research References

Encyclopedias

Assignment of Inmates to Work Programs, FL Jur. 2d Prisons & Prisoners § 154.

946.512. Inmate compensation plan

The corporation shall establish a compensation plan that provides for a specific amount to be paid to the department to be credited to an account for an inmate performing labor and a portion to be used to make any court-ordered payments, including restitution to the victim, and a specific amount to be paid to the Prison Industries Trust Fund to be used as provided in s. 946.522. Such funds, excluding victim restitution payments, court-ordered payments, and the amount credited to the account of the inmate, shall be deposited in the Prison Industries Trust Fund to be used as provided in s. 946.522.

Laws 1983, c. 83–209, § 2; Fla.St.1985, § 946.10; Laws 1987, c. 87–286, § 4; Laws 1991, c. 91–298, § 4. Amended by Laws 1997, c. 97–227, § 7, eff. May 30, 1997; Laws 2000, c. 2000–278, § 2, eff. June 14, 2000.

Historical and Statutory Notes

Amendment Notes:

Laws 1987, c. 87–286, § 4, eff. July 4, 1987, renumbered this section from § 946.10 without amendment in text.

Laws 1991, c. 91–298, § 4, eff. June 7, 1991, rewrote provisions for disposition of inmate income.

Laws 1997, c. 97–227, § 7, eff. May 30, 1997, substituted "Correctional Work Program Trust Fund to be used as provided in s. 946.32" for "Grants and Donations Trust Fund" at the end of the first and second sentences, and deleted a former third sentence, which had read, "The funds shall be appropriated annually.".

Laws 2000, c. 2000–278, § 2, rewrote this section, which formerly read:

"The corporation shall establish a compensation plan which provides for a specific amount to be paid to the department to be credited to an account for an inmate performing labor and a portion shall be used to make any court-ordered payments, including restitution to the victim, and a specific amount to be paid to the department's Correctional Work Program Trust Fund to be used as provided in s. 946.32. Such funds, excluding victim restitution payments, court-ordered payments, and the amount credited to the account of the inmate, shall be deposited in the department's Correctional Work Program Trust Fund to be used as provided in s. 946.32."

Library References

Prisons ⚷117, 172.
Westlaw Topic No. 310.
C.J.S. Convicts §§ 4 to 5.

Research References

Encyclopedias

State Prisoners, Generally, FL Jur. 2d Prisons & Prisoners § 161.

Use of Earnings for Restitution, FL Jur. 2d Prisons & Prisoners § 167.

946.513. Private employment of inmates; disposition of compensation received

(1) Notwithstanding the provisions of any other law, an inmate may be employed by the corporation or by any other private entity operating on the grounds of a correctional institution prior to the last 24 months of the inmate's confinement. Compensation received for such employment shall be credited by the department to an account for the inmate and shall be used to make any court-ordered payments, including restitution to the victim. The department rules shall provide that a portion of such compensation be credited by the department in the manner provided in s. 946.512.

(2) No inmate is eligible for unemployment compensation, whether employed by the corporation or by any other private enterprise operating on the grounds of a correctional institution or elsewhere, when such employment is part of a correctional work program or work-release program of either the corporation or the department.

Laws 1983, c. 83–209, § 2; Laws 1985, c. 85–62, § 76; Fla.St.1985, § 946.11; Laws 1987, c. 87–286, § 4; Laws 1988, c. 88–122, § 89; Laws 1991, c. 91–298, § 5. Amended by Laws 1997, c. 97–102, § 1666, eff. July 1, 1997; Laws 1997, c. 97–227, § 8, eff. May 30, 1997.

Historical and Statutory Notes

Amendment Notes:

Laws 1985, c. 85–62, § 76, a reviser's bill amending subsec. (1), provided for the enactment of language which had been supplied as explained by footnote in the main volume without any further amendment in text.

Laws 1987, c. 87–286, § 4, eff. July 4, 1987, renumbered this section from § 946.11 without amendment in text.

Laws 1988, c. 88–122, § 89, eff. July 1, 1988, substituted in the first sentence of subsec. (1) "twenty four" for "eighteen" months, and in the second sentence substituted statute reference to § 946.512 for § 946.10.

Laws 1991, c. 91–298, § 5, eff. June 7, 1991, amending subsec. (1), deleted provisions for reimbursing the state for food, lodging and related expenses, and inserted provision for victim restitution.

Laws 1997, c. 97–102, eff. July 1, 1997, removed gender-specific references applicable to human beings from volume 4 of the Florida Statutes without substantive changes in legal effect.

Laws 1997, c. 97–227, § 8, eff. May 30, 1997, reenacted subsec. (1) for the purpose of incorporating an amendment to § 946.512 in a reference thereto.

Cross References

Leasing of county prisoners to work for private interests, see § 951.10.
Work-release programs for prisoners, see §§ 945.091, 951.24.

Library References

Prisons ⚷117, 172, 173.
Unemployment Compensation ⚷22.
Westlaw Topic Nos. 310, 392T.
C.J.S. Convicts §§ 4 to 5.
C.J.S. Social Security and Public Welfare §§ 309 to 311, 314 to 316, 327 to 329, 338, 341 to 343, 345.

Research References

Encyclopedias

Use of Earnings for Restitution, FL Jur. 2d Prisons & Prisoners § 167.

946.514. Civil rights of inmates; inmates not state employees; liability of corporation for inmate injuries

(1) Nothing contained in this part is intended to restore in whole or in part the civil rights of inmates.

(2) No inmate compensated under this part or by the corporation or the department shall be considered as an employee of the state, the department, or the corporation.

(3) The corporation is liable for inmate injury to the extent specified in s. 768.28; however, the members of the board of directors are not individually liable to any inmate for any injury sustained in any correctional work program operated by the corporation.

Laws 1983, c. 83–209, § 2; Laws 1984, c. 84–280, § 6; Fla.St.1985, § 946.14; Laws 1987, c. 87–286, § 13. Amended by Laws 2001, c. 2001–242, § 8, eff. June 15, 2001.

Historical and Statutory Notes

Amendment Notes:

Laws 1984, c. 84–280, § 6, added the third sentence which was designated as subsec. (3) in Fla.St.1984, Supp.

Laws 1987, c. 87–286, § 4, eff. July 4, 1987, renumbered this section from § 946.14 and section 13 of the 1987 law modified the statutory references in the section to reflect renumbering of the provisions of this chapter.

Laws 2001, c. 2001–242, § 8, in subsecs. (1) and (2), substituted "this part" for "ss. 946.502–946.517".

Cross References

Restoration of civil rights, see §§ 940.01, 940.05, 944.293.
Suspension of civil rights upon felony conviction, see § 944.292.

Library References

Convicts ⚷22.
Prisons ⚷170, 171.
Westlaw Topic Nos. 98, 310.
C.J.S. Convicts §§ 7, 16 to 19.

Research References

Encyclopedias

Leased or Managed Work Programs; Management by Nonprofit Corporation, FL Jur. 2d Prisons & Prisoners § 155.

946.515. Use of goods and services produced in correctional work programs

(1) Any service or item manufactured, processed, grown, or produced by the corporation in a correctional work program may be furnished or sold to any legislative, executive, or judicial agency of the state, any political subdivision, any other state, any foreign entity or agent thereof, any agency of the Federal Government, to any contract vendor for such agencies or any subcontractor of the contract vendor, or to any person, firm, or business entity if not prohibited by federal law.

(2) No similar product or service of comparable price and quality found necessary for use by any state agency may be purchased from any source other than the corporation if the corporation certifies that the product is manufactured by, or the service is provided by, inmates and the product or service meets the comparable performance specifications and comparable price and quality requirements as specified under s. 287.042(1)(f) or as determined by an individual agency as provided in this section. The purchasing authority of any such state agency may make reasonable determinations of need, price, and quality with reference to products or services available from the corporation. In the event of a dispute between the corporation and any purchasing authority based upon price or quality under this section or s. 287.042(1)(f), either party may request a hearing with the Department of Management Services and if not resolved, either party may request a proceeding pursuant to ss. 120.569 and 120.57, which shall be referred to the Division of Administrative Hearings within 60 days after such request, to resolve any dispute under this section. No party is entitled to any appeal pursuant to s. 120.68.

(3) Agricultural commodities, including, but not limited to, sugar cane, vegetables, beef, and dairy products, may be sold to private entities or may be sold or disposed of as provided in subsections (1) and (2).

(4) The provisions of part I of chapter 287 do not apply to any purchases of commodities or contractual services made by any legislative, executive, or judicial agency of the state from the corporation.

(5) In addition, the corporation may contract to provide inmate services or inmate goods to private enterprise, where such services or goods are under the direct supervision of the corporation and, further, where it is determined by the Governor that the corporation by the provision of such services or goods does not unreasonably seek to compete with other businesses in this state.

(6) If, pursuant to a contract between any legislative, executive, or judicial agency of the state and any private contract vendor, a product or service is required by the Department of Management Services or on behalf of any state agency, is certified by or is available from the corporation identified in this chapter, and has been approved in accordance with subsection (2), the contract must contain the following language:

> IT IS EXPRESSLY UNDERSTOOD AND AGREED THAT ANY ARTICLES WHICH ARE THE SUBJECT OF, OR REQUIRED TO CARRY OUT, THIS CONTRACT SHALL BE PURCHASED FROM THE CORPORATION IDENTIFIED UNDER CHAPTER 946, F.S., IN THE SAME MANNER AND UNDER THE SAME PROCEDURES SET FORTH IN SECTION 946.515(2), AND (4), F.S.; AND FOR PURPOSES OF THIS CONTRACT THE PERSON, FIRM, OR OTHER BUSINESS ENTITY CARRYING OUT THE PROVISIONS OF THIS CONTRACT SHALL BE DEEMED TO BE SUBSTITUTED FOR THIS AGENCY INSOFAR AS DEALINGS WITH SUCH CORPORATION ARE CONCERNED.

(7) The provisions of s. 946.518 do not apply to this section.

Laws 1983, c. 83–209, § 2; Laws 1985, c. 85–194, § 1; Laws 1986, c. 86–183, § 46; Fla.St.1986, Supp. § 946.15; Laws 1987, c. 87–286, § 14; Laws 1991, c. 91–298, § 6;

Laws 1992, c. 92–279, § 318; Laws 1995, c. 95–283, § 38. Amended by Laws 1996, c. 96–270, § 7, eff. May 29, 1996; Laws 1996, c. 96–410, § 323, eff. Oct. 1, 1996; Laws 1997, c. 97–227, § 9, eff. May 30, 1997; Laws 1998, c. 98–279, § 105, eff. June 30, 1998; Laws 1999, c. 99–260, § 7, eff. July 1, 1999; Laws 2000, c. 2000–155, § 17, eff. July 4, 2000.

Historical and Statutory Notes

Amendment Notes:

Laws 1985, c. 85–194, § 1, eff. June 18, 1985, added at the end of subsec. (1) "or to any contract vendor for such agencies or to any subcontractor of the contract vendor.", and added subsecs. (5) and (6).

Laws 1986, c. 86–183, § 46, eff. Oct. 1, 1986, amending subsec. (6), inserted in the introduction ", if an article identified by Department of General Services commodity number certified by the corporation identified in this chapter," and made minor modifications to the contract language which follows.

Laws 1987, c. 87–286, § 4, eff. July 4, 1987, renumbered this section from § 946.15 and section 14 of the 1987 law modified the statutory references in the section to reflect renumbering of the provisions of this chapter.

Laws 1991, c. 91–298, § 6, eff. June 7, 1991, added subsec. (7) and rewrote subsecs. (2) and (6) which had read:

"(2) No similar article of comparable price and quality found necessary for use by any state agency may be purchased from any source other than the corporation if the corporation certifies that the article is available and can be furnished by it. The purchasing authority of any such state agency may make reasonable determinations of need, price, and quality with reference to articles available for sale by the corporation. In the event of a dispute between the corporation and any purchasing authority based upon price or quality, the matter shall be referred to the Governor, whose decision shall be final."

"(6) Any contract between any legislative, executive, or judicial agency of the state and any private contract vendor shall, if an article identified by Department of General Services commodity number is certified by the corporation identified in this chapter, contain the following language:

"IT IS EXPRESSLY UNDERSTOOD AND AGREED THAT ANY ARTICLES WHICH ARE THE SUBJECT OF, OR REQUIRED TO CARRY OUT, THIS CONTRACT SHALL BE PURCHASED FROM THE CORPORATION IDENTIFIED UNDER CHAPTER 946, F.S., IN THE SAME MANNER AND UNDER THE SAME PROCEDURES SET FORTH IN SECTION 946.515(2), (4), F.S.; AND FOR PURPOSES OF THIS CONTRACT THE PERSON, FIRM, OR OTHER BUSINESS ENTITY CARRYING OUT THE PROVISIONS OF THIS CONTRACT SHALL BE DEEMED TO BE SUBSTITUTED FOR THIS AGENCY INSOFAR AS DEALINGS WITH SUCH CORPORATION ARE CONCERNED."

Laws 1992, c. 92–279, § 318, eff. Jan. 1, 1993, in subsec. (6), a comma was inserted following "If" and "Department of Management Services" was substituted for "Department of General Services".

Laws 1992, c. 92–326, § 55, amended § 339 of Laws 1992, c. 92–279, by changing the general effective date of the act from Jan. 1, 1993, to July 1, 1992 (§§ 322 to 325 and 339 took effect upon the act becoming a law).

Laws 1995, c. 95–283, § 38, eff. June 15, 1995, in subsec. (3), added the second sentence; and, in subsec. (4), substituted "legislative, executive, or judicial agency of the state" for "state agency".

Laws 1996, c. 96–270, § 7, eff. May 29, 1996, in subsec. (1), substituted references to foreign entities and agents for references to foreign governments, and allowed services and products to be furnished or sold to any persons, firms, or business entities authorized by the federal government; in subsec. (3), substituted a reference to agricultural commodities for a reference to raw agricultural products at the beginning of the first sentence, and added the last sentence, relating to live tropical fish; and in subsec. (5), substituted "the corporation by the provision of such services or goods does not unreasonably seek to" for "such services or goods do not unreasonably" following "Governor that".

Laws 1996, c. 96–410, generally effective October 1, 1996, throughout Florida Statutes, corrected cross references and substituted references to administrative law judge for references to hearing officer or hearing examiner to conform to the revision of the Administrative Procedure Act.

Laws 1997, c. 97–227, § 9, eff. May 30, 1997, in subsec. (1), substituted "not prohibited" for "authorized" following "entity if".

Laws 1998, c. 98–279, a reviser's bill, corrected references relating to the Department of Management Services.

Laws 1999, c. 99–260, § 7, eff. July 1, 1999, in subsec. (3), deleted the last two sentences, which previously had read: "The corporation may contract with any political subdivision of this state to operate a fish and seafood processing plant and to spawn and grow fish and seafood for sale as provided in this subsection. However, the corporation may not breed or sell live tropical fish.".

Laws 2000, c. 2000–155, a reviser's bill, made conforming changes, deleted obsolete and expired provisions, corrected cross references, corrected grammatical and typographical errors, and made other, similar changes to improve clarity.

Cross References

Use and sale of goods and services produced by county prisoners, see § 951.25.

Library References

Prisons ⚷183.
Westlaw Topic No. 310.
C.J.S. Convicts §§ 23 to 24.

Research References

Encyclopedias

Sale to State, Political Subdivisions, or Federal and Foreign Governments, FL Jur. 2d Prisons & Prisoners § 159.

Sale to Private Entities, FL Jur. 2d Prisons & Prisoners § 160.

Status of Other Organizations or Bodies, FL Jur. 2d Taxation § 3132.

Notes of Decisions

Construction and application 1

1. Construction and application

Prison-made products may be furnished or sold to agencies or institutions of other states under provisions of this chapter. Op.Atty.Gen., 075–87, March 19, 1975.

946.516. Corporation status report and annual financial audit report

(1) The corporation shall submit to the Governor and the Legislature, on or before July 1 of each year, a report on the status of the correctional work programs, including, but not limited to, the proposed use of the profits from such programs, a breakdown of the amount of noninmate labor used, work subcontracted to other vendors, use of consultants, finished goods purchased for resale, and the number of inmates working in the correctional work programs at the time of such report. In addition, the corporation shall submit to the department, the Governor, the Legislature, and the Auditor General an annual financial audit report and such other information as may be requested by the Legislature, together with recommendations relating to provisions for reasonable tax incentives to private enterprises which employ inmates, parolees, or former inmates who have participated in correctional work programs.

(2) The department shall include, as a portion of its annual report, a report on postrelease job placement and the rate of subsequent contact with the correctional system for those inmates who have participated in the correctional work programs operated by the corporation and by the department.

(3) The corporation shall have an annual financial audit of its accounts and records by an independent certified public accountant retained by it and paid from its funds. The Auditor General or the director of the Office of Program

Policy Analysis and Government Accountability may, pursuant to his or her own authority or at the direction of the Joint Legislative Auditing Committee, conduct an audit of the corporation.

(4) The corporation shall be governed by the generally accepted accounting principles as established by the Financial Accounting Standards Board (FASB) in order to carry out the intent of s. 946.502(2) and (5).

Laws 1983, c. 83–209, § 2; Fla.St.1985, § 946.18; Laws 1987, c. 87–286, § 4; Laws 1989, c. 89–526, § 29. Amended by Laws 1996, c. 96–270, § 8, eff. May 29, 1996; Laws 1999, c. 99–333, § 15, eff. July 1, 1999; Laws 2001, c. 2001–242, § 9, eff. June 15, 2001.

Historical and Statutory Notes

Amendment Notes:

Laws 1987, c. 87–286, § 4, eff. July 4, 1987, renumbered this section from § 946.18 without amendment in text.

Laws 1989, c. 89–526, § 29, eff. Oct. 1, 1989, in subsec. (1), required the report to include a breakdown of the amount of noninmate labor used, work subcontracted to other venders, use of consultants and finished goods purchased for resale.

Laws 1996, c. 96–270, § 8, eff. May 29, 1996, in subsec. (1), deleted "the programs and funds which have been transferred to the corporation, the programs and funds to be taken over within the next year and" following "limited to,"; in subsec. (3), deleted "Beginning January 1, 1984," at the beginning, and substituted "biennially conduct a financial and performance audit of the corporation, which shall be conducted" for "conduct an annual financial audit of the corporation" following "shall" in the first sentence, and substituted "conduct additional audits" for "also conduct a biennial performance audit of the corporation for the period beginning January 1, 1983, through January 1, 1985, and, thereafter," following "shall" in the second sentence; and added subsec. (4), relating to accepted accounting principles.

Laws 1999, c. 99–333, § 15, in subsec. (1), substituted ", and the Auditor General an annual financial audit report" for "an annual independently audited financial statement"; and rewrote subsec. (3), which formally read:

"(3) The Auditor General shall biennially conduct a financial and performance audit of the corporation, which shall be conducted in conjunction with an independent audit conducted by the auditors of the corporation. The Auditor General shall conduct additional audits upon the request of the Joint Legislative Auditing Committee."

Laws 2001, c. 2001–242, § 9, in subsec. (1), in the first sentence, substituted "July" for "January".

Library References

Prisons ⚷170.
Westlaw Topic No. 310.
C.J.S. Convicts §§ 16 to 19.

Research References

Encyclopedias

Leased or Managed Work Programs; Management by Nonprofit Corporation, FL Jur. 2d Prisons & Prisoners § 155.

946.517. Corporation records

Corporation records are public records; however, proprietary confidential business information shall be confidential and exempt from the provisions of s. 119.07(1) and s. 24(a), Art. I of the State Constitution. However, the Legislature, the Chief Financial Officer, and the Governor, pursuant to their oversight and auditing functions, shall have access to all proprietary confidential business information upon request and without subpoena and shall retain the confidentiality of information so received. "Proprietary confidential business information" means information regardless of form or characteristics, that is owned or controlled by the corporation; is intended to be and is treated by the corporation as private and the disclosure of the information would cause harm to the corporation's business operations; has not been disclosed unless disclosed pursuant to a statutory provision, an order of a court or administrative body, a legislative proceeding pursuant to s. 5, Art. III of the State Constitution, or a private agreement that provides that the information may be released to the public; and, which is information regarding:

(1) Internal auditing controls and reports of internal auditors.

(2) Matters reasonably encompassed in privileged attorney-client communications.

(3) Security measures, systems, or procedures.

(4) Information concerning bids or other contractual data, banking records, and credit agreements, the disclosure of which would impair the efforts of the corporation to contract for goods or services on favorable terms.

(5) Information relating to private contractual data, the disclosure of which would impair the competitive interest of the provider of the information.

(6) Corporate officer, employee personnel, or inmate worker information unrelated to compensation, duties, qualifications, or responsibilities.

Laws 1983, c. 83–209, § 2; Fla.St.1985, § 946.19; Laws 1987, c. 87–286, § 4; Laws 1994, c. 94–331, § 1. Amended by Laws 1996, c. 96–406, § 450, eff. July 3, 1996; Laws 2003, c. 2003–261, § 1934, eff. June 26, 2003.

Historical and Statutory Notes

Amendment Notes:

Laws 1987, c. 87–286, § 4, eff. July 4, 1987, renumbered this section from § 946.19 without amendment in text.

Laws 1994, c. 94–331, § 1, eff. June 3, 1994, reenacted and rewrote this section notwithstanding the October 1, 1994, repeal specified in § 119.14 (3)(a). Prior to amendment this section provided:

"Each report of the corporation to the state or to the department is a public record, unless such report would not be a public record if prepared by the department."

Laws 1996, c. 96–406 was a reviser's bill which deleted references to § 119.14 throughout Florida Statutes to conform to the repeal of § 119.14, the Open Government Sunset Review Act, by Laws 1995, c. 95–217, § 1.

Laws 2003, c. 2003–261, § 1934, substituted "Chief Financial Officer" for "Comptroller" in the first sentence.

Library References

Records ⚷59.
Westlaw Topic No. 326.
C.J.S. Records §§ 125, 138.

Research References

Encyclopedias

Leased or Managed Work Programs; Management by Nonprofit Corporation, FL Jur. 2d Prisons & Prisoners § 155.

946.518. Sale of goods made by prisoners; when prohibited, when permitted

Goods, wares, or merchandise manufactured or mined in whole or in part by prisoners (except prisoners on parole or probation) may not be sold or offered for sale in this state by any person or by any federal authority or state or political subdivision thereof; however, this section does not forbid the sale, exchange, or disposition of such goods within the limitations set forth in s. 946.515, s. 946.523, or s. 946.524.

Laws 1939, c. 19277, §§ 1, 2; Comp.Gen.Laws Supp.1940, § 8135(61); Fla.St.1955, § 959.02; Laws 1957, c. 57–1, § 24; Laws 1961, c. 61–180, § 1; Laws 1963, c. 63–176, § 1; Laws 1969, c. 69–106, §§ 19, 35; Laws 1977, c. 77–120, § 77; Laws 1979, c. 79–3, § 90; Fla.St.1981, § 945.14; Laws 1983, c. 83–209, § 4; Fla.St.1985, § 946.20; Laws 1987, c. 87–286, § 15. Amended by Laws 1996, c. 96–270, § 9, eff. May 29, 1996; Laws 1996, c. 96–312, § 45, eff. July 1, 1996; Laws 1997, c. 97–227, § 10, eff. May 30, 1997; Laws 2000, c. 2000–155, § 18, eff. July 4, 2000; Laws 2001, c. 2001–242, § 10, eff. June 15, 2001.

Historical and Statutory Notes

Amendment Notes:

Laws 1957, c. 57–1, § 24, substituted the statutory references to "§§ 959.02 and 959.03" for "this chapter".

Former § 959.02 was transferred to § 945.14 in Fla.St.1957.

Laws 1961, c. 61–180, § 1, added subsec. (2).

Laws 1963, c. 63–176, § 1, deleted from the parenthetical phrase in subsec. (1), the words "convicts or" following "(except"; and substituted, at the end of the proviso of subsec. (1), the words "within the limitations set forth in § 945.16(1)" for "to any institution supported wholly or in part by funds derived from public taxation and operated under the supervision of the United States, the state, or any other state in the Union, or any political subdivision thereof".

Laws 1969, c. 69–106, §§ 19, 35, transferred all powers, duties and functions of the division of corrections of the board of commissioners of state institutions to the division of adult corrections of the department of health and rehabilitative services.

Laws 1977, c. 77–120, a reviser's bill, amended this section to conform with Laws 1975, c. 75–49, which created the department of offender rehabilitation and transferred to the department certain functions performed by the division of corrections of the department of health and rehabilitative services and the parole and probation commission of the department of offender rehabilitation.

Laws 1979, c. 79–3, a reviser's bill, provided for substitution of references to the department and secretary of "corrections" for the department and secretary of "offender rehabilitation" to conform with Laws 1978, c. 78–53.

Laws 1983, c. 83–209, § 4, modified at the end of subsec. (1), the statute references.

Laws 1987, c. 87–286, § 4, eff. July 4, 1987, renumbered this section from § 946.20 and section 15 of the 1987 law modified the statutory references in the section to reflect renumbering of the provisions of this chapter.

Laws 1996, c. 96–270, § 9, eff. May 29, 1996, deleted the subsection designations; deleted former subsec. (2); and made nonsubstantive language changes throughout. Former subsec. (2) had read:

"When, in the planning of the rehabilitation program of the Department of Corrections through its recreational facilities, plans are made for prisoners to engage in hobbies and hobbycrafts after their normal working hours and when they are not required by the superintendent or warden of a state prison or correctional institution to be on their assigned duties, they may make items of a hobby or hobbycraft nature which may be disposed of by the prisoner through the institutional canteen or commissary to persons visiting the institution."

Laws 1996, c. 96–312, § 45, eff. July 1, 1996, deleted subsection designations; at the beginning, deleted "No"; substituted "may not" for "shall not" and "this section and s. 946.21 do not" for "nothing in this section and s. 946.21 shall be construed to"; inserted "946.006(3)"; and deleted former subsec. (2).

Laws 1997, c. 97–227, § 10, eff. May 30, 1997, reenacted this section for the purpose of incorporating an amendment to § 946.515 in a reference thereto.

Laws 2000, c. 2000–155, a reviser's bill, made conforming changes, deleted obsolete and expired provisions, corrected cross references, corrected grammatical and typographical errors, and made other, similar changes to improve clarity.

Laws 2001, c. 2001–242, § 10, added ", s. 946.523, or s. 946.524".

Cross References

Acceptance of unauthorized compensation for prisoner labor, see § 944.37.
Leasing of county prisoners to work for private interests, prohibition, see § 951.10.
Use and sale of goods and services produced by county prisoners, see § 951.25.

Library References

Prisons ⚷183.
Westlaw Topic No. 310.
C.J.S. Convicts §§ 23 to 24.

Research References

Encyclopedias

Illegal Sales, FL Jur. 2d Consumer & Borrower Protection § 10.

Sale to State, Political Subdivisions, or Federal and Foreign Governments, FL Jur. 2d Prisons & Prisoners § 159.

Notes of Decisions

Credit memoranda or certificates 1

---

1. Credit memoranda or certificates

Board of commissioners of state institutions could agree with abattoir, slaughter house or meat packing plant to receive beef cattle produced at state prison farm in exchange for credit memoranda or certificates for delivery of dressed beef to board for use in state institutions with provision that if amount of credit memoranda or certificates be not redeemed within 60 days, that board be paid the stated amount in cash, in view of fact that cattle raising is not the growing of crops or sale of manufactured, mined goods, wares or merchandise within prohibition of § 952.10 (repealed) or former statute (now this section). Op.Atty.Gen., 056–302, Oct. 12, 1956.

946.519. Repealed by Laws 1999, c. 99–260, § 12, eff. July 1, 1999

Historical and Statutory Notes

The repealed section, which related to the use of goods and services produced in correctional work programs, was derived from:
Laws 1987, c. 87–286, § 4.
Fla.St.1985, § 946.22.
Laws 1983, c. 83–209, § 5.
Fla.St.1982, Supp. § 945.16.
1982, c. 82–409, § 1.
Laws 1979, c. 79–190, § 147.
Laws 1979, c. 79–3, § 91.
Laws 1977, c. 77–174, § 1.
Laws 1976, c. 76–273, § 11.
Laws 1971, c. 71–109, § 1.
Laws 1969, c. 69–106, §§ 19, 35.
Laws 1963, c. 63–176, § 2.
Laws 1961, c. 61–350, § 18.
Laws 1957, c. 57–213, § 13.

946.520. Assignment of inmates by Department of Corrections

(1) The department shall exert its best efforts to assign inmates to the corporation, or the private sector business authorized under this part, who have not less than 1 nor more than 5 years remaining before their tentative release dates. Beginning January 1, 1998, the department shall maintain the assignment of at least 60 percent of inmates to all correctional work programs collectively to the corporation, or to the private sector business authorized under this part, who have less than 10 years remaining before their tentative release dates. This 60–percent requirement does not apply to any correctional

work program, or private sector business authorized under this part, within an institution for any year in which, as of January 1 of that year, the average years remaining before the tentative release date of all inmates assigned to that institution exceeds 12 years.

(2) The department may not remove an inmate once assigned to the corporation or to the private sector business authorized under this part, except upon request of or consent of such corporation or private sector business or for the purposes of population management, for inmate conduct that may subject the inmate to disciplinary confinement or loss of gain-time, or for security and safety concerns specifically set forth in writing to the corporation or private sector business.

Added by Laws 1997, c. 97–227, § 11, eff. May 30, 1997. Amended by Laws 2001, c. 2001–242, § 11, eff. June 15, 2001.

Historical and Statutory Notes

Amendment Notes:

Laws 2001, c. 2001–242, § 11, in four instances, preceding "part" inserted "this", and following "part" deleted "I of this chapter".

Library References

Prisons ⚷172.
Westlaw Topic No. 310.

946.522. Prison Industries Trust Fund

(1) The Prison Industries Trust Fund is created, to be administered by the Department of Financial Services. The trust fund shall consist of moneys authorized to be deducted pursuant to 18 U.S.C. s. 1761(c) and the applicable federal guidelines, to be appropriated by the Legislature, and moneys deposited by the corporation authorized under this part to manage and operate correctional work programs. The appropriated funds shall be used by the corporation for purposes of construction or renovation of its facilities or for the expansion or establishment of correctional work programs as described in this part or for prison industries enhancement (PIE) programs as authorized under s. 946.523.

(2) The funds must be deposited in the State Treasury and may be paid out only on warrants drawn by the Chief Financial Officer upon receipt of a corporate resolution that has been duly authorized by the board of directors of the corporation authorized under this part to manage and operate correctional work programs. The corporation shall maintain all necessary records and accounts relative to such funds.

(3) The trust fund is exempt from s. 215.20.

(4) Notwithstanding s. 216.301 and pursuant to s. 216.351, any balance in the trust fund at the end of any fiscal year shall remain in the trust fund at the end of that year and shall be available for carrying out the purposes of the trust fund.

(5) Pursuant to s. 19(f)(3), Art. III of the State Constitution, the trust fund consists of assets held by the state, in a trustee capacity, as an agent or fiduciary for the corporation authorized under this part, and is not subject to termination under s. 19(f)(2), Art. III of the State Constitution.

Added by Laws 2000, c. 2000–278, § 1, eff. June 14, 2000. Amended by Laws 2003, c. 2003–261, § 1935, eff. June 26, 2003.

Historical and Statutory Notes

Amendment Notes:

Laws 2003, c. 2003–261, § 1935, in subsec. (1), substituted "Financial Services" for "Banking and Finance"; and in subsec. (2), substituted "Chief Financial Officer" for "Comptroller".

Library References

Prisons ⚷172.
States ⚷127.
Westlaw Topic Nos. 310, 360.
C.J.S. States §§ 386 to 387.

946.523. Prison industry enhancement (PIE) programs

(1) The corporation may operate or contract with the private sector for substantial involvement in a prison industry enhancement (PIE) program that includes, but is not limited to, contracts for the operation of a direct private sector business within a prison and the hiring of inmates. Any contract authorized by this subsection must be in compliance with federal law governing inmate work programs and must not result in the significant displacement of employed workers in the community. The purposes and objectives of this program are to:

(a) Increase the benefits to the general public by reimbursing the state for a portion of the costs of incarceration.

(b) Provide purposeful work for inmates.

(c) Increase job skills.

(d) Provide additional opportunities for rehabilitating inmates who are otherwise ineligible to work outside the prisons, such as maximum security inmates.

(e) Develop and establish new models for prison-based businesses that create jobs approximating conditions of private sector employment.

(f) Draw upon the economic base of operations for deposit into the Crimes Compensation Trust Fund.

(g) Substantially involve the private sector and its capital, management skills, and expertise in the design, development, and operation of businesses.

(h) Provide the financial basis for an inmate to contribute to the support of his or her family.

(i) Provide for the payment of state and federal taxes on an inmate's wages, which are paid at the rate of the prevailing or minimum wage rate.

(j) Provide savings for the inmate to have available for his or her use upon the inmate's eventual release from prison.

(2) Notwithstanding any other law to the contrary, including s. 440.15(8), private sector employers shall provide workers' compensation coverage to

inmates who participate in prison industry enhancement (PIE) programs under subsection (1). However, inmates are not entitled to unemployment compensation.

Added by Laws 1999, c. 99–260, § 9, eff. July 1, 1999. Amended by Laws 2003, c. 2003–412, § 38, eff. Oct. 1, 2003.

Historical and Statutory Notes

Amendment Notes:

Laws 2003, c. 2003–412, § 38, in subsec. (2), substituted "440.15(8)" for "440.15(9)".

Cross References

Contracts for the operation of private correctional facilities, inclusion of work and educational programs, see § 957.04.

Library References

Prisons ⚷175.
Westlaw Topic No. 310.
C.J.S. Convicts §§ 18 to 19, 23.

Research References

Encyclopedias

Leasing to Work for Private Interests; Work for Corporation Managing State Correctional Work Programs, FL Jur. 2d Prisons & Prisoners § 150.

Leased or Managed Work Programs; Management by Nonprofit Corporation, FL Jur. 2d Prisons & Prisoners § 155.

946.524. Corporation work camps

(1) The corporation may establish work camps that the corporation maintains and operates in accordance with chapter 951.

(2) The corporation may designate appropriate land that is owned or leased by the corporation, or may use state, county, or municipal land, as the site of the proposed facility. Any state lands used for the purposes authorized by this section must obtain prior approval of the Board of Trustees of the Internal Improvement Trust Fund. The work camps operated by the corporation may use inmates who are incarcerated in county or municipal jails for labor in correctional work programs or prison industry enhancement programs authorized by s. 946.523, and the corporation may enter into contracts to operate the work camps in accordance with s. 946.5025.

Added by Laws 1999, c. 99–260, § 10, eff. July 1, 1999.

Library References

Prisons ⚷170.
Westlaw Topic No. 310.
C.J.S. Convicts §§ 16 to 19.

Research References

Encyclopedias

Leasing to Work for Private Interests; Work for Corporation Managing State Correctional Work Programs, FL Jur. 2d Prisons & Prisoners § 150.

Leased or Managed Work Programs; Management by Nonprofit Corporation, FL Jur. 2d Prisons & Prisoners § 155.

946.525. Participation by the corporation in the state group health insurance and prescription drug programs

(1) The board of directors of the corporation established under this part may apply for participation in the state group health insurance program authorized in s. 110.123 and the prescription drug coverage program authorized by s. 110.12315 by submitting an application along with a $500 nonrefundable fee to the Department of Management Services.

(2) As a prerequisite to the adoption of a resolution for participation in the state group health insurance and prescription drug coverage program, the corporation shall seek proposals to provide health insurance and prescription drug coverages which coverages are equivalent to those offered currently by the corporation and coverages equivalent to the state group health insurance and prescription drug coverage program. The corporation shall review and consider all responsive proposals prior to the adoption of any resolution for participation in the state group health insurance and prescription drug coverage program.

(3) If the Department of Management Services determines that the corporation is eligible to enroll, the corporation must agree to the following terms and conditions:

(a) The minimum enrollment or contractual period will be 3 years.

(b) The corporation must pay to the Department of Management Services an initial administrative fee not less than $2.61 per enrollee per month, or such other amount established annually to fully reimburse the Department of Management Services for its costs.

(c) Termination of participation of the corporation requires written notice 1 year before the termination date.

(d) If participation is terminated, the corporation may not reapply for participation for a period of 2 years.

(e) The corporation shall reimburse the state for 100 percent of its costs, including administrative costs.

(f) If the corporation fails to make the payments required by this section to fully reimburse the state, the Department of Revenue or the Department of Financial Services shall, upon the request of the Department of Management Services, deduct the amount owed by the employer from any funds to be distributed by it to the corporation. The amounts so deducted shall be transferred to the Department of Management Services for further distribution to the trust funds in accordance with this chapter.

(g) The corporation shall furnish the Department of Management Services any information requested by the Department of Management Services which the Department of Management Services considers necessary to administer the state group health insurance program and the prescription drug program.

(4) The provisions of ss. 624.436–624.446 do not apply to the State Group Insurance Program or to this section.

(5) The Department of Management Services may adopt rules necessary to administer this section.

Added by Laws 2001, c. 2001–242, § 14. Amended by Laws 2003, c. 2003–261, § 1936, eff. June 26, 2003.

Effective Date

Laws 2001, c. 2001–242, § 17 provides that "[t]his act shall take effect upon becoming a law, except that section 14 [s. 946.525] shall take effect only when the Department of Management Services receives the favorable letters requested by section 15. If the favorable letters are not received, section 14 [s. 946.525] shall not take effect".

Historical and Statutory Notes

Amendment Notes:

Laws 2001, c. 2001–242, § 15 provides:

"The Department of Management Services shall request from the Internal Revenue Service, by October 1, 2001, a written determination letter and a favorable private letter ruling, stating that the State Group Self–Insurance Program, as amended by section 946.525, Florida Statutes, is a facially qualified plan. The department shall notify the President of the Senate and the Speaker of the House of Representatives within 30 days after the receipt of the favorable or unfavorable letters."

Laws 2003, c. 2003–261, § 1936, in subsec. (3)(f), substituted "Financial Services" for "Banking and Finance".

Research References

Encyclopedias

Leased or Managed Work Programs; Management by Nonprofit Corporation, FL Jur. 2d Prisons & Prisoners § 155.

CHAPTER 947

PAROLE COMMISSION

Constitutional Provisions

Art. 4, § 8(c) provides:

"(c) There may be created by law a parole and probation commission with power to supervise persons on probation and to grant paroles or conditional releases to persons under sentences for crime. The qualifications, method of selection and terms, not to exceed six years, of members of the commission shall be prescribed by law."

Cross References

Community juvenile justice system act, see § 39.025.
Compacts with other states, see §§ 949.07, 949.08.
Construction of chapter, see § 949.04.
Juvenile courts unaffected, see § 949.01.
Pardons, see § 940.01 et seq.
Probation and parole, see §§ 948.01 et seq., 949.01 et seq.
Severability clause, see § 949.05.
Short title, see § 949.06.
Uniform law for out-of-state probation and parole supervision, see § 949.07 et seq.

Law Review and Journal Commentaries

Probation in Florida. Vernon W. Clark, 14 U.Fla.L.Rev. 213 (1961).

947.001. Short title

This chapter shall be known and may be cited as the "Objective Parole Guidelines Act of 1978."

Laws 1978, c. 78–417, § 2.

Historical and Statutory Notes

Prior Provisions for Legislative Review:

Laws 1983, c. 83–131, § 34, as amended by Laws 1986, c. 86–183, § 37, and Laws 1988, c. 88–122, § 67, provided for the July 1, 1990, repeal of Florida Statutes, Chapter 947 as described in an enumeration of sections within the chapter which contained all sections except §§ 947.135 and 947.1746 as that chapter existed in Fla.St.1983. The repeal was subject to the legislative review of the parole and probation commission [now parole commission] as provided for in Laws 1983, c. 83–131, § 35. The above-mentioned laws were repealed by Laws 1989, c. 89–531, § 17.

Laws 1989, c. 89–531, § 17, as amended by Laws 1990, c. 90–337, § 20, which provided for repeal of chapter 947 on Oct. 1, 1993, was repealed by Laws 1993, c. 93–2, § 1.

Research References

Encyclopedias

Parole Commission, FL Jur. 2d State of Florida § 84.

947.002. Intent

(1) It is the purpose of this chapter to establish an objective means for determining and establishing parole dates for inmates.

(2) Objective parole criteria will be designed to give primary weight to the seriousness of the offender's present criminal offense and the offender's past criminal record. In considering the risk of recidivism, practice has shown that the best predictor is prior record.

(3) The chair shall be the agency head. While the commission is responsible for making decisions on the granting and revoking of parole, the chair shall establish, execute, and be held accountable for all administrative policy decisions. The routine administrative decisions are the full responsibility of the chair .

(4) Hearing examiners are assigned on the basis of caseload needs as determined by the chair.

(5) It is the intent of the Legislature that the decision to parole an inmate from the incarceration portion of the inmate's sentence is an act of grace of the state and shall not be considered a right.

Laws 1978, c. 78–417, § 1; Laws 1981, c. 81–322, § 1; Laws 1982, c. 82–171, § 2; Laws 1993, c. 93–61, § 3. Amended by Laws 1997, c. 97–102, § 1667, eff. July 1, 1997.

Historical and Statutory Notes

Amendment Notes:

Laws 1981, c. 81–322, § 1, substituted "examiners" for "examiner panels" in subsec. (5).

Laws 1982, c. 82–171, § 2, added subsec. (6).

Laws 1993, c. 93–61, § 3, eff. April 22, 1993, rewrote the section, which formerly read:

"(1) The present system lacks objective criteria for paroling and, thus, is subject to allegations of arbitrary and capricious release and, therefore, potential abuses. It is the intent of this act to establish an objective means for determining and establishing parole dates for inmates.

"(2) Objective parole criteria will be designed to give primary weight to the seriousness of the offender's present criminal offense and his past criminal record. In considering the risk of recidivism, practice has shown that the best predictor is prior record.

"(3) The functional reorganization of the commission shall begin on July 1, 1978. However, full implementation of objective parole guidelines shall be delayed until January 1, 1979, to provide sufficient time for integration of the full intent of this act.

"(4) The chairman shall be the agency head. While the commission is responsible for making decisions on the granting and revoking of parole, the chairman shall establish, execute, and be held accountable for all administrative policy decisions. The routine administrative decisions are the full responsibility of the chairman.

"(5) Hearing examiners are assigned on the basis of caseload needs as determined by the chairman.

"(6) It is the intent of the Legislature that the decision to parole an inmate from the incarceration portion of his sentence is an act of grace of the state and shall not be considered a right."

Laws 1997, c. 97–102, eff. July 1, 1997, removed gender-specific references applicable to human beings from volume 4 of the Florida Statutes without substantive changes in legal effect.

Law Review and Journal Commentaries

Civil commitment and the right to refuse treatment: resolving disputes from a due process perspective. 50 Miami U.L.Rev. 413 (Jan. 1996).

Library References

Pardon and Parole ⚷42.1, 46, 49, 55.1.
Westlaw Topic No. 284.
C.J.S. Pardon and Parole §§ 43 to 51.

Notes of Decisions

Error 3
Ex post facto 2
Hearing examiners 4
Legislative intent 1
Review 5

---

1. Legislative intent

Ultimate intent of Objective Parole Guidelines Act is to prevent arbitrary and capricious action by state parole and probation commission. Gobie v. Florida Parole and Probation Com'n, App. 1 Dist., 416 So.2d 838 (1982), review denied 424 So.2d 762. Pardon And Parole ⚷ 41

2. Ex post facto

Where habeas petitioner, at time he committed murder that led to his incarceration, was on fair notice that if he received life sentence he would be subject to parole at discretion of Florida Parole and Probation Commission, which was not changed by subsequently enacted Parole Act, and where guidelines promulgated thereunder merely stated and rationalized exercise of Commission's discretion, petitioner accordingly suffered no legislative increase in punishment by Commission's application of Parole Act in setting petitioner's presumptive parole release date, so that application of Parole Act did not violate Constitution's ex post facto clause. Paschal v. Wainwright, C.A.11 (Fla.)1984, 738 F.2d 1173. Constitutional Law ⚷ 2823; Pardon And Parole ⚷ 42.1

3. Error

No error was shown in parole and probation commission's consideration, in assessment of prisoner's past criminal record for purposes of fixing tentative release date, of an offense committed in another country, nor did the commission err, when considering aggravating circumstances bearing on the tentative release date, in giving due weight to the same circumstances which had influenced sentencing court to impose a consecutive sentence. Hipke v. Parole and Probation Commission, App. 1 Dist., 380 So.2d 494 (1980). Pardon And Parole ⚷ 58

4. Hearing examiners

Failure of petitioner to assert exhaustion of administrative remedy afforded by § 947.173 with respect to review, upon request, of presumptive parole release date determination operated to preclude petitioner from obtaining relief on his petition for writ of mandamus based on allegation that his release date was not determined by a hearing panel consisting of required two examiners. Houston v. Florida Parole & Probation Commission, App. 1 Dist., 377 So.2d 34 (1979). Mandamus ⚷ 3(8)

5. Review

State parole and probation commission should explicate its reasons for its actions in manner sufficient to permit judicial review for determination of whether commission has overreached legislative grant of discretion provided in Objective Parole Guidelines Act. Gobie v. Florida Parole and Probation Com'n, App. 1 Dist., 416 So.2d 838 (1982), review denied 424 So.2d 762. Pardon And Parole ⚷ 61

947.005. Definitions

As used in this chapter, unless the context clearly indicates otherwise:

(1) "Commission" means the Parole Commission.

(2) "Department" means the Department of Corrections.

(3) "Secretary" means the Secretary of Corrections.

(4) "Presumptive parole release date" means the tentative parole release date as determined by objective parole guidelines.

(5) "Effective parole release date" means the actual parole release date as determined by the presumptive parole release date, satisfactory institutional conduct, and an acceptable parole plan.

(6) "Tentative release date" means the date projected for the prisoner's release from custody by virtue of gain-time granted or forfeited pursuant to s. 944.275(3)(a).

(7) "Provisional release date" means the date projected for the prisoner's release from custody as determined pursuant to s. 944.277.[1]

(8) "Authority" means the Control Release Authority.

(9) "Qualified practitioner" means a psychiatrist licensed under chapter 458 or chapter 459, a psychologist licensed under chapter 490, or a social worker, a mental health counselor, or a marriage and family therapist licensed under chapter 491 who practices in accordance with his or her respective practice act.

(10) "Risk assessment" means an assessment completed by an independent qualified practitioner to evaluate the level of risk associated when a sex offender has contact with a child.

(11) "Safety plan" means a written document prepared by the qualified practitioner, in collaboration with the sex offender, the child's parent or legal guardian, and, when appropriate, the child, which establishes clear roles and responsibilities for each individual involved in any contact between the child and the sex offender.

Laws 1978, c. 78–417, § 3; Laws 1979, c. 79–3, § 101; Laws 1981, c. 81–322, § 2; Laws 1986, c. 86–183, § 24; Laws 1988, c. 88–122, § 14; Laws 1989, c. 89–526, § 1; Laws 1989, c. 89–531, § 11. Amended by Laws 2005, c. 2005–67, § 1, eff. Jan. 1, 2006; Laws 2007, c. 2007–200, § 7, eff. July 1, 2007; Laws 2007, c. 2007–209, § 8, eff. July 1, 2007.

[1] Repealed by Laws 1993, c. 93–406, § 32.

Historical and Statutory Notes

Amendment Notes:

Laws 1979, c. 79–3, a reviser's bill, provided for substitution of references to the department and secretary of "corrections" for the department and secretary of "offender rehabilitation" to conform with Laws 1978, c. 78–53.

Laws 1981, c. 81–322, § 2, repealed the definition of "Hearing examiner panel."

Laws 1986, c. 86–183, § 24, eff. Oct. 1, 1986, added definition of "board".

Laws 1988, c. 88–122, § 14, added the definition of "tentative release date" and deleted the definition of "board".

Laws 1989, c. 89–526, § 1, eff. Sept. 1, 1990, added provisions contained in subsec. (8), defining "Authority".

Section 52 of Laws 1989, c. 89–526, provides, in pertinent part:

"Sections 1 through 9 of this act shall take effect September 1, 1990. All inmates committed to the department as of September 1, 1990, shall have a control release date established by

December 1, 1990. Inmates received after September 1, 1990, shall have a control release date established within 90 days following notification by the department of receipt of the inmate."

Laws 1989, c. 89-531, § 11, eff. Oct. 1, 1989, added subsec. (7), defining "Provisional release date".

Laws 2005, c. 2005-67, § 1, added subsecs. (9), (10), and (11), defining "Qualified practitioner", "Risk assessment", and "Safety plan", respectively.

Laws 2007, c. 2007-200, § 7, in subsec. (9), at the end, substituted "practices in accordance with his or her respective practice act" for ", as determined by rule of the respective boards, has the coursework, training, qualifications, and experience to evaluate and treat sex offenders".

Laws 2007, c. 2007-209, § 8, in subsec. (9), substituted "practices in accordance with his or her respective practice act" for ", as determined by rule of the respective boards, has the coursework, training, qualifications, and experience to evaluate and treat sex offenders" at the end.

Research References

Treatises and Practice Aids

16 Florida Practice Series § 10:20, Parole--Presumptive Parole Release Date.

16 Florida Practice Series § 10:21, Parole--Effective Parole Release Date.

947.01. Parole Commission; creation; number of members

A Parole Commission is created to consist of six members who are residents of the state. Effective July 1, 1996, the membership of the commission shall be three members.

Laws 1941, c. 20519, § 1; Laws 1963, c. 63-83, § 1; Laws 1965, c. 65-453, § 1; Laws 1974, c. 74-112, § 30; Laws 1977, c. 77-120, § 84; Laws 1977, c. 77-174, § 1; Laws 1978, c. 78-417, § 4; Laws 1979, c. 79-3, § 102; Laws 1983, c. 83-131, § 23; Laws 1985, c. 85-288, § 13; Laws 1986, c. 86-183, § 25; Laws 1987, c. 87-300, § 4; Laws 1988, c. 88-122, § 15; Laws 1990, c. 90-337, § 9; Laws 1995, c. 95-283, § 39. Amended by Laws 1996, c. 96-422, § 12, eff. June 7, 1996.

Historical and Statutory Notes

Amendment Notes:

Laws 1941, c. 20519, § 35, repealed all conflicting laws and parts of laws.

Laws 1963, c. 63-83, § 1, changed the designation of the commission to "probation and parole commission" from "parole commission".

Laws 1965, c. 65-453, § 1, rewrote the first sentence which read, "A parole commission (hereinafter called commission) is hereby created, which shall consist of three citizens and residents of the state".

Laws 1974, c. 74-112, substantially rewrote this section which prior thereto provided:

"A parole and probation commission, hereafter called commission, is created to consist of five citizens who are residents of the state. Only persons who are citizens of Florida and who have resided within the state for a period of ten years or more and by their knowledge of penology and social welfare are qualified efficiently to discharge the duties and perform the work of the commission shall be eligible to appointment to said position."

Laws 1977, c. 77-120, a reviser's bill, amended this section to conform with Laws 1975, c. 75-49, which created the department of offender rehabilitation (see § 20.315) and transferred to the department certain functions performed by the division of corrections of the department of health and rehabilitative services and the parole and probation commission of the department of offender rehabilitation.

Laws 1977, c. 77-174, a reviser's bill, amended this section to reflect language editorially inserted by the division of statutory revision and indexing.

Laws 1978, c. 78-417, substituted in the second sentence of subsec. (2) "including the development and review of objective parole guidelines, but" for "only and".

Laws 1979, c. 79-3, a reviser's bill, provided for substitution of references to the department and secretary of "corrections" for the department and secretary of "offender rehabilitation" to conform with Laws 1978, c. 78-53.

Prior to the 1983 amendment the section provided:

"A Parole and Probation Commission is created to consist of eight citizens who are residents of the state. The members of the commission shall include:

"(1) Seven members who are qualified by their knowledge of penology and allied social sciences to discharge the duties and perform the work of the commission efficiently; and

"(2) One member who shall be the Secretary of Corrections. The secretary shall participate in the policymaking decisions of the commission, including the development and review of objective parole guidelines, but shall not participate in decisions on the granting and revocation of parole. The secretary shall be ineligible for appointment as chairman, shall receive no compensation for his services on the commission, and shall not be required to attend any minimum number of meetings."

Laws 1983, c. 83–131, rewrote this section.

Laws 1985, c. 85–288, § 13, eff. July 1, 1985, substituted "1987" for "1985" in subsec. (1)(b).

Laws 1986, c. 86–183, § 25, eff. Oct. 1, 1986, substituted "five" for "seven" members in the first sentence and added the second sentence to subsec. (1)(b).

Laws 1987, c. 87–300, § 4, eff. July 10, 1987, increased the membership in subsec. (1)(b) to six.

Laws 1988, c. 88–122, § 15, eff. July 1, 1988, deleted obsolete provisions from subsec. (1) and changed the membership of the commission from nine to seven members.

Laws 1990, c. 90–337, § 9, eff. July 1, 1990, in subsec. (1), increased number of members from seven to nine, and provided that effective July 1, 1990, appointments shall be made pursuant to s. 947.02(3).

Laws 1995, c. 95–283, § 39, eff. Oct. 6, 1995, rewrote subsec. (1), which formerly read:

"(a) A Parole Commission is created to consist of nine members who are residents of the state.

"(b) Effective July 1, 1990, the membership of the commission shall be nine members and appointment shall be made pursuant to s. 947.02(3)."

Laws 1996, c. 96–422, § 12, eff. June 7, 1996, rewrote this section, which formerly read:

"(1)(a) A Parole Commission is created to consist of six members who are residents of the state.

"(b) Effective October 6, 1995, the membership of the commission shall be seven appointed members. After October 6, 1995, upon the first vacant seat occurring, for any reason other than expiration of term, the membership shall be reduced to six.

"(2) The Secretary of Corrections shall act in a liaison capacity between the commission and the Department of Corrections."

Title of Act:

An Act providing for and adopting a state administered probation and parole system for the State of Florida; creating and establishing a parole commission and conferring and defining its duties, powers, and functions, including the power to make rules and regulations and the supervision of persons placed upon probation; providing for the method of appointment and removal of the members of the parole commission, its clerks and employees, regulating their compensation, and prohibiting their engaging in certain activities; providing for the purchase of supplies and materials and for the allowance of necessary travelling and other expenses; providing for the placing on parole of persons in certain cases, their discharge from parole, their rearrest with and without a warrant for violation of the terms and conditions of parole; providing for hearings on charges of violation of the terms and conditions of parole, and reimprisonment because of such violation; providing for the recommendation by the parole commission to the board of pardons for the extension of clemency to deserving persons; authorizing financial aid to indigent parolees at the time of their release; providing for the cooperation of certain public officers and agencies with the parole commission; authorizing and regulating the use by the courts of probation and suspension of imposition of sentence; permitting appeal from judgment adjudging guilt; excepting certain courts and correctional institutions from the operation of this act, and authorizing the preservation of probation officers now serving under any previous law; and making an appropriation for carrying into effect the provisions of this act; fixing an effective date thereof and repealing all laws and parts of laws in conflict herewith. Laws 1941, c. 20519.

Law Review and Journal Commentaries

New parole and probation act. James T. Vocelle, 16 Fla.L.J. 9 (1942).

New penal and correctional program in Florida. William C. Merritt, 12 U.Miami L.Rev. 200 (1958).

Parole and probation in Florida. James T. Vocelle, 18 Fla.L.J. 35 (1944).

Parole in Florida. Vernon G. Clark, 11 U.Fla. L.Rev. 68 (1958).

Purpose and operation of parole. Dr. Paul Raymond, 13 Fla.L.J. 133 (1939).

Rules of criminal procedure. Thomas A. Wills, 22 U.Miami L.Rev. 240, 272 (1967).

Library References

Pardon and Parole ⚿55.1.
Westlaw Topic No. 284.
C.J.S. Pardon and Parole §§ 45 to 47.

Research References

ALR Library

143 ALR 1486, Statute Conferring Power Upon Administrative Body in Respect to the Parole of Prisoners, or the Discharge of Parolees, as Unconstitutional Infringement of Power of Executive or Judiciary.

Notes of Decisions

1. Construction and application

Parole and probation commission was agency subject to Administrative Procedure Act (§ 120.50 et seq.). Florida Institutional Legal Services, Inc. v. Florida Parole and Probation Commission, App. 1 Dist., 391 So.2d 247 (1980). Pardon And Parole ⚿ 55.1

Under Laws 1975, c. 75–49, which transferred the functions of the division of corrections of the department of health and rehabilitative services to the new department of offender rehabilitation, the secretary of the new department (who is the same individual as the director of the old division) continues to be a member of the parole and probation commission pursuant to subsection of this section, and is authorized to perform the duties prescribed therein. Op. Atty.Gen., 075–212, July 16, 1975.

2. Powers and duties of commission

While the granting or withholding of parole is discretionary, parole and probation commission is required, as any other body, to comply with constitutional requirements; it cannot deny parole upon illegal grounds or upon improper considerations, and is answerable in mandamus if it does. Hardy v. Greadington, App. 5 Dist., 405 So.2d 768 (1981). Pardon And Parole ⚿ 49

3. Ex officio members

Under this section, as a member ex officio of the parole and probation commission, the secretary of the department of offender rehabilitation may not participate in the panel discussions or vote upon the granting or revocation of parole to or recommending clemency for a particular criminal offender. He may, however, participate in the discussion and vote upon all policy-making decisions to the same extent as any other commission member; and, pending a decision on appeal concerning the validity of Laws 1975, c. 75–49, he and his staff should be entitled to access to any of the commission's records that would be useful in deciding matters of policy. Op.Atty.Gen., 075–296, Dec. 3, 1975.

947.02. Parole Commission; members, appointment

(1) Except as provided in s. 947.021, the members of the Parole Commission shall be appointed by the Governor and Cabinet from a list of eligible applicants submitted by a parole qualifications committee. The appointments of members of the commission shall be certified to the Senate by the Governor and Cabinet for confirmation, and the membership of the commission shall include representation from minority persons as defined in s. 288.703.

(2) A parole qualifications committee shall consist of five persons who are appointed by the Governor and Cabinet. One member shall be designated as chair by the Governor and Cabinet. The committee shall provide for statewide advertisement and the receiving of applications for any position or positions on the commission and shall devise a plan for the determination of the qualifications of the applicants by investigations and comprehensive evaluations, including, but not limited to, investigation and evaluation of the character, habits, and philosophy of each applicant. Each parole qualifications committee shall exist for 2 years. If additional vacancies on the commission occur during this

2–year period, the committee may advertise and accept additional applications; however, all previously submitted applications shall be considered along with the new applications according to the previously established plan for the evaluation of the qualifications of applicants.

(3) Within 90 days before an anticipated vacancy by expiration of term pursuant to s. 947.03 or upon any other vacancy, the Governor and Cabinet shall appoint a parole qualifications committee if one has not been appointed during the previous 2 years. The committee shall consider applications for the commission seat, including the application of an incumbent commissioner if he or she applies, according to the provisions of subsection (2). The committee shall submit a list of three eligible applicants, which may include the incumbent if the committee so decides, without recommendation, to the Governor and Cabinet for appointment to the commission. In the case of an unexpired term, the appointment must be for the remainder of the unexpired term and until a successor is appointed and qualified. If more than one seat is vacant, the committee shall submit a list of eligible applicants, without recommendation, containing a number of names equal to three times the number of vacant seats; however, the names submitted shall not be distinguished by seat, and each submitted applicant shall be considered eligible for each vacancy.

(4) Upon receiving a list of eligible persons from the parole qualifications committee, the Governor and Cabinet may reject the list. If the list is rejected, the committee shall reinitiate the application and examination procedure according to the provisions of subsection (2).

(5) The provisions of s. 120.525 and chapters 119 and 286 apply to all activities and proceedings of a parole qualifications committee.

Laws 1941, c. 20519, § 1; Laws 1965, c. 65–453, § 2; Laws 1969, c. 69–106, § 33; Laws 1974, c. 74–112, § 31; Laws 1975, c. 75–207, § 1; Laws 1978, c. 78–417, § 5; Laws 1983, c. 83–131, § 24; Laws 1988, c. 88–122, § 16; Laws 1993, c. 93–61, § 1. Amended by Laws 1996, c. 96–410, § 324, eff. Oct. 1, 1996; Laws 1996, c. 96–422, § 13, eff. June 7, 1996; Laws 1997, c. 97–102, § 1869, eff. July 1, 1997.

Historical and Statutory Notes

Amendment Notes:

Laws 1965, c. 65–453, § 2, substituted, at the end of the penultimate sentence of subsec. (1), the words "above described list of eligible persons" for "three eligibles having the highest rank on said list."

Laws 1969, c. 69–106 (the governmental reorganization act of 1969) provides in section 33(2) as follows:

"All powers, duties and functions of the board of commissioners of state institutions relating to the appointment of the probation and parole commission as provided in section 947.02, Florida Statutes, shall be exercised and performed by the governor and the cabinet. Henceforth, however, each appointment shall be made from among the first three (3) eligible persons on the list of the persons eligible for said position."

Laws 1974, c. 74–112, § 31, substantially rewrote this section which prior thereto provided:

"(1) The members of the commission shall be appointed in the following manner: The governor and cabinet shall appoint an examining board which shall consist of five persons having special knowledge of penal treatment and the administration of criminal justice, and shall designate one member thereof as chairman. The governor and cabinet shall provide for the receiving of applications for the position of member of the commission and shall devise a plan for the determination, by examination and investigation, of the qualification of applicants. From such examinations and investigations said examining board shall compile a list of not more than ten persons eligible for said position of member of the commission, and the list shall expire at the end of two years. The examining board shall rank such eligibles on the list in the order of their relative fitness as determined by examination and investigation. The governor and cabinet shall make each appointment to the position of member of the commission from the first three eligible persons on the above described list of eligible persons. The members of the commission shall be certified to the senate by the governor and cabinet for confirmation.

"(2) Whenever the term of office of a member of the commission expires, the governor and cabinet may, in their discretion, reappoint the member without requiring him to take an examination."

Laws 1975, c. 75–207, substituted "the Parole and Probation Commission Qualifications Committee" for "The governor and cabinet" at the beginning and inserted "including, but not limited to the character, habits and philosophy of the applicant" at the end of the second sentence and designated the provision as subsec. (1), and added subsec. (2) which provided:

"Whenever a vacancy occurs in the membership of the commission by reason of the expiration of a member's term, the Governor and Cabinet may, in their discretion, reappoint the incumbent member to the commission."

Laws 1978, c. 78–417, rewrote subsec. (2) to read:

"Whenever a vacancy occurs in the membership of the commission by reason of the expiration of a member's term, the Parole and Probation Commission Qualifications Committee shall evaluate the incumbent member and shall recommend to the Governor and Cabinet one of the following:

"(a) That the incumbent member be reappointed without examination of new applicants;

"(b) That the incumbent be considered with other eligible persons in accordance with the selection process; or

"(c) That upon finding reasonable and sufficient cause the incumbent not be reappointed to the commission."

Laws 1983, c. 83–131, § 24, rewrote this section.

Laws 1988, c. 88–122, § 16, eff. July 1, 1988, substituted reference to the parole commission for the parole and probation commission.

Laws 1993, c. 93–61, § 1, eff. April 22, 1993, rewrote the section, which formerly read:

"(1) The members of the Parole Commission shall be appointed by the Governor and Cabinet from a list of eligible applicants submitted by a parole qualifications committee. The appointments of members of the commission shall be certified to the Senate by the Governor and Cabinet for confirmation.

"(2) A parole qualifications committee shall consist of five persons who are appointed by the Governor and Cabinet. One member shall be designated as chairman by the Governor and Cabinet. The committee shall provide for statewide advertisement and the receiving of applications for any position or positions on the commission and shall devise a plan for the determination of the qualifications of the applicants by investigations and comprehensive evaluations, including, but not limited to, investigation and evaluation of the character, habits, and philosophy of each applicant. Each parole qualifications committee shall exist for 2 years. If additional vacancies on the commission occur during this 2–year period, the committee may advertise and accept additional applications; however, all previously submitted applications shall be considered along with the new applications according to the previously established plan for the evaluation of the qualifications of applicants.

"(3) Whenever a vacancy occurs on the commission pursuant to s. 947.03(3) or by reason of the resignation, retirement, or death of a commissioner, the Governor and Cabinet shall appoint a parole qualifications committee if one has not been appointed during the previous 2 years. The committee shall consider applications for the commission seat according to the provisions of subsection (2) and shall submit the names of three eligible applicants, without recommendation, to the Governor and Cabinet for appointment to the commission for the remainder of the unexpired term or until a successor is appointed and qualified. If more than one seat is vacant, the committee shall submit the names of three eligible applicants for each seat; however, the names submitted shall not be distinguished by seat, and each submitted applicant shall be considered eligible for each vacancy.

"(4) Whenever a vacancy occurs on the commission by reason of expiration of a commissioner's term, the Governor and Cabinet shall appoint a parole qualifications committee if one has not been appointed during the previous 2 years. The committee shall consider applications for the commission seat according to the provisions of subsection (2). If a commissioner whose term has expired or will expire does not seek reappointment, the terms of subsection (3) apply. If a commissioner whose term has expired or will expire seeks reappointment, the parole qualifications committee shall recommend to the Governor and Cabinet one of the following:

"(a) That the incumbent member be reappointed to the commission. If the committee selects this option, only the name of the incumbent commissioner shall be submitted to the Governor and Cabinet.

"(b) That the incumbent be considered along with other eligible persons. If the committee selects this option, the name of the incumbent and two eligible applicants shall be submitted to the Governor and Cabinet without recommendation.

"(c) That the incumbent not be considered for reappointment. If the committee selects this option, the provisions of subsection (3) apply.

"Except for a recommendation under paragraph (a), if two or more terms expire at the same time, the names submitted shall not be distinguished by seat, and each submitted applicant shall be considered eligible for each vacancy.

"(5) Upon receiving a list of eligible persons from the parole qualifications committee, the Governor and Cabinet may reject the list. The committee shall reinitiate the application and examination procedure according to the provisions of subsection (2).

"(6) The provisions of s. 120.53 and chapters 119 and 286 apply to all activities and proceedings of a parole qualifications committee."

Laws 1996, c. 96–410, generally effective October 1, 1996, throughout Florida Statutes, corrected cross references and substituted references to administrative law judge for references to hearing officer or hearing examiner to conform to the revision of the Administrative Procedure Act.

Laws 1996, c. 96–422, § 13, eff. June 7, 1996, at the beginning of subsec. (1), added the exception.

Laws 1997, c. 97–102, eff. July 1, 1997, removed gender-specific references applicable to human beings from volume 4 of the Florida Statutes without substantive changes in legal effect.

Library References

Pardon and Parole ⚷55.1.
Westlaw Topic No. 284.
C.J.S. Pardon and Parole §§ 45 to 47.

Research References

ALR Library

143 ALR 1486, Statute Conferring Power Upon Administrative Body in Respect to the Parole of Prisoners, or the Discharge of Parolees, as Unconstitutional Infringement of Power of Executive or Judiciary.

Notes of Decisions

1. Qualifications committee

This section which provides for creation of parole and probation commission qualifications committee provides that committee is created whenever there is an appointment of member of parole and probation commission to be made or vacancy to be filled, and authorizes no exercise of executive power by committee; therefore, committee is not agency within meaning of Administrative Procedure Act (§ 120.50 et seq.) and is not subject to minimum information requirements of §§ 120.53 and 120.54. Florida Institutional Legal Services, Inc. v. Parole and Probation Com'n Qualifications Committee, App. 1 Dist., 419 So.2d 714 (1982). Pardon And Parole ⚷ 55.1

2. Compensation and benefits

Members of the parole and probation commission are state officers, not merely state employees. As such, they are not entitled by law to accrue annual or sick leave or to be paid for unused annual or sick leave upon termination of duty or service with the state or upon retirement, absent express authorization by statute. Op.Atty.Gen., 078–75, May 16, 1978.

947.021. Parole Commission; expedited appointments

Whenever the Legislature decreases the membership of the commission, all terms of office shall expire, notwithstanding any law to the contrary. Under such circumstances, the Governor and Cabinet shall expedite the appointment of commissioners. Notwithstanding the parole qualifications committee procedure in s. 947.02, members shall be directly appointed by the Governor and Cabinet. Members appointed to the commission may be selected from incumbents. Members shall be certified to the Senate by the Governor and Cabinet for confirmation, and the membership of the commission shall include representation from minority persons as defined in s. 288.703.

Added by Laws 1996, c. 96–422, § 14, eff. June 7, 1996.

Library References

Pardon and Parole ⚷55.1.
Westlaw Topic No. 284.
C.J.S. Pardon and Parole §§ 45 to 47.

947.022. Repealed by Laws 2007, c. 2007–5, § 163, eff. July 3, 2007

Historical and Statutory Notes

Repealed § 947.022, which related to the terms of Parole Commission members, was derived from Laws 1996, c. 96–422, § 17, eff. June 7, 1996.

947.03. Commissioners; tenure and removal

(1) Upon the expiration of the term of any member of the commission, a successor shall be appointed by the Governor and Cabinet for a term of 6 years, unless otherwise provided by law. No person is eligible to be appointed for more than two consecutive 6–year terms.

(2) Vacancies in the membership of the commission shall be filled by the Governor and Cabinet for the unexpired term in the manner provided for in s. 947.02.

(3) Each member appointed by the Governor and Cabinet is accountable to the Governor and Cabinet for the proper performance of the duties of his or her office. The Governor and Cabinet may remove from office any such member for malfeasance, misfeasance, neglect of duty, drunkenness, incompetence, or permanent inability to perform official duties or for pleading guilty or nolo contendere to, or being found guilty of, a felony. All such removals shall be submitted to the Senate for its consent as provided by the constitution.

Laws 1941, c. 20519, § 1; Laws 1965, c. 65–453, § 3; Laws 1969, c. 69–106, § 33; Laws 1969, c. 69–216, § 6; Laws 1979, c. 79–42, § 1; Laws 1983, c. 83–131, § 25; Laws 1986, c. 86–183, § 26; Laws 1990, c. 90–337, § 10. Amended by Laws 1996, c. 96–422, § 15, eff. June 7, 1996; Laws 1997, c. 97–102, § 1870, eff. July 1, 1997; Laws 2000, c. 2000–328, § 5, eff. June 19, 2000.

Historical and Statutory Notes

Amendment Notes:

Laws 1965, c. 65–453, § 3, rewrote subsec. (1) which read:

"The first three members of the commission shall be appointed for the terms of two, four, and six years respectively; and said board shall designate in its appointments the term for which each of said three first members is appointed. At the expiration of said terms the successors to said first members shall be appointed for terms of six years and until their successors are appointed and qualified."

Laws 1969, c. 69–216, § 6, substituted, in subsection (3), the constitutional reference "Section 7, Article IV of the State Constitution" for former "§ 15, Article IV of the constitution.".

Laws 1969, c. 69–106 (the governmental reorganization act of 1969) provides in section 33(2) as follows:

"All powers, duties and functions of the board of commissioners of state institutions relating to the appointment of the probation and parole commission as provided in section 947.02, Florida Statutes, shall be exercised and performed by the governor and the cabinet. Henceforth, however, each appointment shall be made from among the first three (3) eligible persons on the list of the persons eligible for said position."

As so amended in 1969, the section provided:

"(1) The terms of the existing three members of the commission shall not be disturbed by this section as amended. The two new members of the commission shall be appointed for terms of four and six years respectively, and the governor and cabinet shall designate in their appointments the term for which each of the members is appointed. At the expiration of the aforementioned terms the successors to the existing members and new members shall be appointed for terms of six years and until their successors are appointed and qualified.

"(2) Vacancies in the membership of the commission shall be filled by the governor and cabinet for the unexpired term in the manner hereinabove provided.

"(3) Each member shall devote his whole time and capacity to the duties of his office, and shall be subject to removal by the governor and cabinet for the same reasons that a state officer may be removed as provided in § 7, Art. IV of the state constitution. All such removals shall be submitted to the senate for its consent as provided by said section of the constitution."

Laws 1979, c. 79–42, § 1, deleted transitional member terms in subsec. (1), and provided for filing of vacancies as provided in § 947.02 rather than as provided "hereinabove".

Laws 1983, c. 83–131, § 25, rewrote subsecs. (1) and (3).

Laws 1986, c. 86–183, § 26, eff. Oct. 1, 1986, added ", unless otherwise provided by law." at the end of the second sentence and modified the number of members and their terms in the third sentence of subsec. (1).

Laws 1990, c. 90–337, § 10, eff. July 1, 1990, in subsec. (1), in the third sentence increased the terms of office from 4 to 6 years; deleted a former fourth sentence pertaining to the initial appointments; and, in the last sentence substituted "6–year" for "4–year".

Laws 1996, c. 96–422, § 15, eff. June 7, 1996, in subsec. (1), at the beginning of the first sentence and in the second sentence, added "unless otherwise provided by law".

Laws 1997, c. 97–102, eff. July 1, 1997, removed gender-specific references applicable to human beings from volume 4 of the Florida Statutes without substantive changes in legal effect.

Laws 2000, c. 2000–328, § 5, rewrote subsec. (1), which formerly read:

"(1) Unless otherwise provided by law, each commissioner serving on July 1, 1983, shall be permitted to remain in office until completion of his or her current term. Upon the expiration of the term, a successor shall be appointed in the manner prescribed pursuant to the provisions of this section, unless otherwise provided by law. Members appointed by the Governor and Cabinet shall be appointed for terms of 6 years, unless otherwise provided by law. No person is eligible to be appointed for more than two consecutive 6–year terms."

Library References

Pardon and Parole ⚷55.1.
Westlaw Topic No. 284.
C.J.S. Pardon and Parole §§ 45 to 47.

947.04. Organization of commission; officers; offices

(1) Before July 1 of each even-numbered year, the Governor and Cabinet shall select a chair who shall serve for a period of 2 years and until a successor is selected and qualified. The Governor and Cabinet shall, at the same time that a chair is selected, select a vice chair to serve during the same 2–year period as the chair, in the absence of the chair. The chair may succeed himself or herself. The chair, as chief administrative officer of the commission, has the authority and responsibility to plan, direct, coordinate, and execute the powers, duties, and responsibilities assigned to the commission, except those of granting and revoking parole as provided for in this chapter. Subject to approval by the Governor and the Cabinet, the chair may assign consenting retired commissioners or former commissioners to temporary duty when there is a workload need. Any such commissioner shall be paid $100 for each day or portion of a day spent on the work of the commission and shall be reimbursed for travel

expenses as provided in s. 112.061. The chair is authorized to provide or disseminate information relative to parole by means of documents, seminars, programs, or otherwise as he or she determines necessary. The chair shall establish, execute, and be held accountable for all administrative policy decisions. However, decisions to grant or revoke parole shall be made in accordance with the provisions of ss. 947.172, 947.174, and 947.23. The commissioners shall be directly accountable to the chair in the execution of their duties as commissioners, and the chair has authority to recommend to the Governor suspension of a commissioner who fails to perform the duties provided for by statute.

(2) Notwithstanding the provisions of s. 20.05(1)(g), the chair shall appoint administrators with responsibility for the management of commission activities in the following functional areas:

(a) Administration.

(b) Operations.

(c) Clemency.

(3) The commissioners shall select from their number a secretary who shall serve for a period of 1 year or until a successor is elected and qualified.

(4) The commission may establish and maintain field offices within existing administration buildings at facilities and institutions operated by the department. Headquarters shall be located in Tallahassee. The business of the commission shall be transacted anywhere in the state as provided in s. 947.06. The commission shall keep its official records and papers at the headquarters, which it shall furnish and equip.

(5) Acts and decisions of the chair may be modified as provided in s. 947.06.

Laws 1941, c. 20519, § 2; Laws 1978, c. 78–417, § 6; Laws 1979, c. 79–42, § 2; Laws 1982, c. 82–171, § 3; Laws 1983, c. 83–131, § 22; Laws 1985, c. 85–295, § 1; Laws 1986, c. 86–183, § 27; Laws 1987, c. 87–300, §§ 1, 2; Laws 1990, c. 90–211, § 15; Laws 1990, c. 90–337, § 21; Laws 1993, c. 93–61, § 2. Amended by Laws 1996, c. 96–422, § 18, eff. June 7, 1996; Laws 1997, c. 97–78, § 24, eff. May 23, 1997; Laws 1997, c. 97–102, § 1871, eff. July 1, 1997; Laws 2001, c. 2001–124, § 4, eff. July 1, 2001.

Historical and Statutory Notes

Amendment Notes:

Fla.St.1941, § 947.04 provided:

"(1) As soon as practicable after their appointment the members of the commission shall meet and select from their number a chairman who shall serve for a period of two years and until his successor is elected and qualified, and they shall likewise select from their number a secretary who shall serve for a period of two years and until his successor is elected and qualified.

"(2) The commission may establish and maintain offices in centrally and conveniently located places in Florida. Headquarters shall be located in the City of Tallahassee, for the transaction of business. The commission shall keep its official records and papers at said office, which it shall furnish and equip."

Laws 1978, c. 78–417, rewrote this section.

Laws 1979, c. 79–42, § 2, amending subsec. (1), deleted in the third sentence responsibility for dissemination of information relating to parole, interpolated the fourth sentence, and deleted in the last sentence authority to take necessary disciplinary action.

Laws 1982, c. 82–171, § 3, in subsec. (2) (a), deleted "and work release" following "Parole grant."

Laws 1983, c. 83–131, § 22, interpolated the fourth and fifth sentences of subsec. (1).

Laws 1985, c. 85–295, § 1, eff. June 20, 1985, added provision appearing as the second sentence of subsec. (1).

Laws 1986, c. 86–183, § 27, eff. Oct. 1, 1986, inserted "or former commissioners" in the fifth sentence of subsec. (1) and deleted "clemency" as one of the functional areas in subsec. (2).

Laws 1987, c. 87–300, § 1, eff. July 10, 1987, amending subsec. (4), authorized the commission to transact its business anywhere in the state and provided for clemency activities for the parole and probation commission by adding subsec. (2)(d) in § 2 of the 1987 law.

Laws 1990, c. 90–211, § 15, eff. July 1, 1990, in subsec. (4), in the second sentence, substituted "shall" for "may"; and added "as provided in s. 947.06".

Laws 1990, c. 90–337, § 21, in subsec. (4), in the second sentence, substituted "shall" for "may"; and added the reference to § 947.06.

Section 19 of Laws 1990, c. 90–211, provides:

"Except as otherwise provided herein, this act shall take effect October 1, 1990, and shall apply to offenses committed on or after such date."

Laws 1990, c. 90–337, § 21, provided therein that the amendment take effect July 1, 1990; however, approval by the governor occurred subsequent thereto. The Florida Supreme Court in an advisory opinion to the governor of July 19, 1979 (374 So.2d 959) stated in part "* * * the effective date provided in the bill is inoperative unless the bill becomes law on or before that date" and concludes that under such circumstances the provision of Const. Art. 3, § 9, that the law take effect on the sixtieth day after adjournment sine die of the session of the legislature in which enacted, is applicable.

Laws 1993, c. 93–61, § 2, eff. April 22, 1993, in subsec. (1), rewrote the first two sentences, which formerly read "On July 1 of each even-numbered year, the members of the commission shall meet and select from their number a chairman who shall serve for a period of 2 years and until a successor is elected and qualified. The commission shall, at the same meeting at which it selects its chairman, select a vice chairman to serve in the absence of the chairman.".

Laws 1996, c. 96–422, § 18, eff. June 7, 1996, rewrote subsec. (2), which formerly read:

"Notwithstanding the provisions of s. 20.05(7), the chairman shall appoint administrators with responsibility for the management of commission activities in the following functional areas:

"(a) Parole grant.

"(b) Parole revocation.

"(c) Administrative services.

"(d) Clemency."

Laws 1997, c. 97–78, § 24, eff. May 23, 1997, in subsec. (1), in the third sentence, following "may" deleted "not"; and inserted "or herself".

Laws 1997, c. 97–102, eff. July 1, 1997, removed gender-specific references applicable to human beings from volume 4 of the Florida Statutes without substantive changes in legal effect.

Laws 2001, c. 2001–124, § 4, in subsec. (4), preceding "offices" inserted "field"; and substituted "within existing administration buildings at facilities and institutions operated by the department" for "in centrally and conveniently located places in Florida".

Cross References

Clemency, authority of governor, see § 940.01.

Library References

Pardon and Parole ⚿55.1.
Westlaw Topic No. 284.
C.J.S. Pardon and Parole §§ 45 to 47.

Notes of Decisions

---

1. Meetings

The Florida parole and probation commission may not conduct its meetings at locations other than its headquarters where decisions are made as required by this section. Op.Atty.Gen., 84–41, April 19, 1984.

2. Vice-chairman

Pursuant to the authority granted it by §§ 947.06 and 947.07, and governing rules of parliamentary law, the parole and probation commission may provide, by properly adopted rule of internal organization and procedure for the conduct of its affairs of business, for the designation of a member of the commission as vice-chairman of the commission to act as chairman in the absence or incapacity of the chairman, including the calling of meetings of the commission. The commission may likewise by rule provide for the method of selection, term of office, and duties of the vice-chairman. Op.Atty.Gen., 076–148, June 29, 1976.

3. Ex officio members

Under § 947.01, as a member ex officio of the parole and probation commission, the secretary of the department of offender rehabilitation may not participate in the panel discussions or vote upon the granting or revocation of parole to or recommending clemency for a particular criminal offender. He may, however, participate in the discussion and vote upon all policy-making decisions to the same extent as any other commission member; and, pending a decision on appeal concerning the validity of Laws 1975, c. 75–49, he and his staff should be entitled to access to any of the commission's records that would be useful in deciding matters of policy. Op.Atty.Gen., 075–296, Dec. 3, 1975.

947.045. Federal Grants Trust Fund

The Federal Grants Trust Fund is hereby created, to be administered by the Florida Parole Commission.

(1) Funds to be credited to the trust fund shall consist of receipts from federal grants and shall be used for the various purposes for which the federal funds were intended.

(2) Notwithstanding the provisions of s. 216.301 and pursuant to s. 216.351, any balance in the trust fund at the end of any fiscal year shall remain in the trust fund at the end of the year and shall be available for carrying out the purposes of the trust fund.

Added by Laws 2005, c. 2005–90, § 1, eff. July 1, 2005. Amended by Laws 2009, c. 2009–27, § 2, eff. July 1, 2009.

Historical and Statutory Notes

Amendment Notes:

Laws 2009, c. 2009–27, § 2, deleted former subsec. (3), which had read:

"(3) In accordance with s. 19(f)(2), Art. III of the State Constitution, the Federal Grants Trust Fund shall be terminated on July 1, 2009, unless terminated sooner. Before its scheduled termination, the trust fund shall be reviewed as provided in s. 215.3206(1) and (2)."

Library References

Pardon and Parole ⚷55.1.
States ⚷127.
Westlaw Topic Nos. 284, 360.
C.J.S. Pardon and Parole §§ 45 to 47.
C.J.S. States §§ 386 to 387.

947.05. Seal

The commission shall adopt an official seal of which the courts shall take judicial notice.

Laws 1941, c. 20519, § 3.

Library References

Pardon and Parole ⚷55.1.
Westlaw Topic No. 284.
C.J.S. Pardon and Parole §§ 45 to 47.

Research References

Encyclopedias

Official Signatures and Seals, FL Jur. 2d Evidence & Witnesses § 52.

Treatises and Practice Aids

1 Florida Practice Series § 202.13, Official Seals.

947.06. Meeting; when commission may act

Text amended by Laws 2008, c. 2008–4, § 171, effective July 1, 2008, see also text amended by Laws 2008, c. 2008–4, § 172, effective July 1, 2008.

The commission shall meet at regularly scheduled intervals and from time to time as may otherwise be determined by the chair. The making of recommendations to the Governor and Cabinet in matters relating to modifications of acts and decisions of the chair as provided in s. 947.04(1) shall be by a majority vote of the commission. No prisoner shall be placed on parole except as provided in ss. 947.172 and 947.174 by a panel of no fewer than two commissioners appointed by the chair. All matters relating to the granting, denying, or revoking of parole shall be decided in a meeting at which the public shall have the right to be present. Victims of the crime committed by the inmate shall be permitted to make an oral statement or submit a written statement regarding their views as to the granting, denying, or revoking of parole. Persons not members or employees of the commission or victims of the crime committed by the inmate may be permitted to participate in deliberations concerning the granting and revoking of paroles only upon the prior written approval of the chair of the commission. To facilitate the ability of victims and other persons to attend commission meetings, the commission shall meet in various counties including, but not limited to, Broward, Duval, Escambia, Hillsborough, Leon, Miami–Dade, Orange, and Palm Beach, with the location chosen being as close as possible to the location where the parole-eligible inmate committed the offense for which the parole-eligible inmate was sentenced. The commission shall adopt rules governing the oral participation of victims and the submission of written statements by victims.

Laws 1941, c. 20519, § 4; Laws 1947, c. 23757, § 1; Laws 1978, c. 78–417, § 7; Laws 1979, c. 79–42, § 3; Laws 1986, c. 86–183, § 28; Laws 1988, c. 88–96, § 10; Laws 1990, c. 90–211, § 16 Amended by Laws 1997, c. 97–102, § 1668, eff. July 1, 1997; Laws 2008, c. 2008–4, § 171, eff. July 1, 2008.

Library References

Pardon and Parole ⚷55.1, 58 to 60.
Westlaw Topic No. 284.
C.J.S. Pardon and Parole §§ 45 to 47, 52 to 55.

947.06. Meeting; when commission may act

Text amended by Laws 2008, c. 2008–4, § 172, effective July 1, 2008, see also text amended by Laws 2008, c. 2008–4, § 171, effective July 1, 2008.

The commission shall meet at regularly scheduled intervals and from time to time as may otherwise be determined by the chair. The making of recommendations to the Governor and Cabinet in matters relating to modifications of acts and decisions of the chair as provided in s. 947.04(1) shall be by a majority vote of the commission. No prisoner shall be placed on parole except as provided in ss. 947.172 and 947.174 by a panel of no fewer than two commissioners appointed by the chair. All matters relating to the granting, denying, or revoking of parole shall be decided in a meeting at which the public shall have the right to be present. Victims of the crime committed by the inmate shall be permitted to make an oral statement or submit a written statement regarding their views as to the granting, denying, or revoking of parole. Persons not members or employees of the commission or victims of the crime committed by the inmate may be permitted to participate in deliberations concerning the granting and revoking of paroles only upon the prior written approval of the chair of the commission. To facilitate the ability of victims and other persons to attend commission meetings, the commission shall meet in counties including, but not limited to, Broward, Duval, Escambia, Hillsborough, Leon, Miami–Dade, Orange, and Palm Beach, with the location chosen being as close as possible to the location where the parolee or releasee committed the offense for which the parolee or releasee was sentenced. The commission shall adopt rules governing the oral participation of victims and the submission of written statements by victims.

Laws 1941, c. 20519, § 4; Laws 1947, c. 23757, § 1; Laws 1978, c. 78–417, § 7; Laws 1979, c. 79–42, § 3; Laws 1986, c. 86–183, § 28; Laws 1988, c. 88–96, § 10; Laws 1990, c. 90–337, § 22. Amended by Laws 1997, c. 97–102, § 1669, eff. July 1, 1997; Laws 2008, c. 2008–4, § 172, eff. July 1, 2008.

Historical and Statutory Notes

Amendment Notes:

Laws 1947, c. 23757, § 1, deleted, from the end of the second sentence, the words "other than parole of a prisoner" following "transaction of all business"; and substituted, in the last sentence, the words "vote of a majority" for "an unanimous vote" following "on parole except by". As amended, the second sentence provided: "A majority of the commission shall constitute a quorum for the transaction of all business."

Laws 1978, c. 78–417, interpolated the second sentence, deleted the former second sentence, inserted "as provided in ss. 947.172 and 947.174" and "in a meeting at which the public shall have a right to be present" in the third sentence, and added the fourth sentence.

Laws 1979, c. 79–42, § 3, substituted in the first sentence "regularly scheduled intervals" for "the call of the chairman" deleted in the second sentence "formulation and approval of the legislative budget request", and rewrote the third sentence which now appears as the third and fourth sentences.

Laws 1986, c. 86–183, § 28, eff. Oct. 1, 1986, substituted in the second sentence "relating to" for "of executive clemency and" preceding "modifications of acts".

Laws 1988, c. 88–96, § 10, interpolated the fifth sentence, inserted "or victims of the crime committed by the inmate may be permitted to" in the sixth sentence and added the seventh sentence.

Laws 1988, c. 88–96, § 15, provides that the act "shall take effect upon the effective date [January 3, 1989] of the amendment to the State Constitution contained in [1987] Senate Joint Resolution No. 135, which is to be submitted to the electors of this state for approval at the general election to be held in November 1988."

The electorate ratified the amendment to Const. Art. 1, § 16, proposed by 1987, S.J.R. No. 135, relating to rights of crime victims, at the November 8, 1988 general election. See Const. Art. 1, § 16.

Laws 1990, c. 90–337, § 22, eff. July 1, 1990, inserted the next to last sentence.

Laws 1997, c. 97–102, eff. July 1, 1997, removed gender-specific references applicable to human beings from volume 4 of the Florida Statutes without substantive changes in legal effect.

Laws 2008, c. 2008–4, a reviser's bill, deleted obsolete and expired provisions, corrected grammatical and typographical errors, and made other similar changes.

Library References

Pardon and Parole ⚷55.1, 58 to 60.
Westlaw Topic No. 284.
C.J.S. Pardon and Parole §§ 45 to 47, 52 to 55.

United States Supreme Court

Life inmates, rights to commutation of sentence before board of pardons, see Connecticut Bd. of Pardons v. Dumschat, U.S.Conn.1981, 101 S.Ct. 2460, 452 U.S. 458, 69 L.Ed.2d 158.

Notes of Decisions

1. Open meeting law

Open public meetings law applies to parole revocation meetings of the parole and probation commission. Wainwright v. Turner, 389 So.2d 1181 (1980). Pardon And Parole ⚷ 88

Decision of the State Parole and Probation Commission to take appeal from order of the division of administrative hearings which found that certain practices and procedures of Commission were rules and as such were invalid because of failure of Commission to properly adopt them was not "formal action" so as to require that decision be reached in open and public meeting under public meeting requirements of the sunshine law. Florida Parole and Probation Commission v. Thomas, App. 1 Dist., 364 So.2d 480 (1978). Pardon And Parole ⚷ 55.1

The sunshine law would apply to all meetings of the State Parole and Probation Commission. Florida Parole and Probation Commission v. Thomas, App. 1 Dist., 364 So.2d 480 (1978). Pardon And Parole ⚷ 55.1

Where the State Parole and Probation Commission never met to determine whether to appeal order of the Department of Administration which found that certain practices and procedures of Commission were rules and as such were invalid because of failure of Commission to properly adopt them and, rather, commencement of appeal was performed in normal course of business by legal department of agency, sunshine law would not be applicable. Florida Parole and Probation Commission v. Thomas, App. 1 Dist., 364 So.2d 480 (1978). Pardon And Parole ⚷ 55.1

2. Vice-chairman

Pursuant to the authority granted it by this section and § 947.07, and governing rules of parliamentary law, the parole and probation commission may provide, by properly adopted rule of internal organization and procedure for the conduct of its affairs of business, for the designation of a member of the commission as vice-chairman of the commission to act as chairman in the absence or incapacity of the chairman, including the calling of meetings of the commission. The commission may likewise by rule provide for the method of selection, term of office, and duties of the vice-chairman. Op.Atty.Gen., 076–148, June 29, 1976.

947.07. Rules

The commission has authority to adopt rules pursuant to ss. 120.536(1) and 120.54 for its governance, including among other things rules of practice and procedure and rules prescribing qualifications to be possessed by its employees.

Laws 1941, c. 20519, § 27; Laws 1947, c. 23757, § 1. Amended by Laws 1998, c. 98–200, § 228, eff. July 1, 1998.

Historical and Statutory Notes

Amendment Notes:

Laws 1998, c. 98–200, § 228, rewrote the section, which formerly read:

"The commission shall have power to make such rules and regulations as it deems best for its governance, including among other things rules of practice and procedure and rules prescribing qualifications to be possessed by its employees."

Law Review and Journal Commentaries

Purpose and operation of parole. Dr. Paul Raymond, 13 Fla.L.J. 133 (1939).

Library References

Pardon and Parole ⚷55.1.
Westlaw Topic No. 284.
C.J.S. Pardon and Parole §§ 45 to 47.

Notes of Decisions

1. Construction and application

Parole and probation commission was agency subject to Administrative Procedure Act (§ 120.50 et seq.). Florida Institutional Legal Services, Inc. v. Florida Parole and Probation Commission, App. 1 Dist., 391 So.2d 247 (1980). Pardon And Parole ⚷ 55.1

Parole and probation commission was obliged to adopt rules for preparation of agenda and was required to maintain current subject matter index, identifying for public any rule or order issued or adopted after January 1, 1975, including functional equivalents of declaratory statements issued by commission pursuant to § 120.565 and commission determinations of presumptive and effective parole release dates, parole rescission determinations, parole revocation orders, and other final agency decisions which were equivalent to "orders." Florida Institutional Legal Services, Inc. v. Florida Parole and Probation Commission, App. 1 Dist., 391 So.2d 247 (1980). Pardon And Parole ⚷ 55.1

2. Validity of rules

Validity of rule of parole and probation commission under which commission may treat consecutive and concurrent sentences in like manner when applying aggravating factors could not appropriately be initially attacked in court, adequate administrative remedy being available for such purpose. Canter v. Florida Parole and Probation Commission, App. 1 Dist., 409 So.2d 227 (1982). Pardon And Parole ⚷ 62

3. Vice-chairman

Pursuant to the authority granted it by § 947.06 and this section, and governing rules of parliamentary law, the parole and probation commission may provide, by properly adopted rule of internal organization and procedure for the conduct of its affairs of business, for the designation of a member of the commission as vice-chairman of the commission to act as chairman in the absence or incapacity of the chairman, including the calling of meetings of the commission. The commission may likewise by rule provide for the method of selection, term of office, and duties of the vice-chairman. Op.Atty.Gen., 076–148, June 29, 1976.

947.071. Rulemaking procedures; indexing of orders

(1) It is the intent of the Legislature that all rulemaking procedures by the commission be conducted pursuant to the Administrative Procedure Act, chapter 120.

(2) The only final orders of the commission which shall be indexed pursuant to chapter 120 are:

(a) Orders granting parole.

(b) Orders revoking parole.

(c) Orders restoring to supervision.

(d) Orders releasing from custody and further supervision.

(e) Early parole termination orders.

(f) Orders granting conditional release.

(g) Orders revoking conditional release.

Laws 1974, c. 74–112, § 34; Laws 1982, c. 82–171, § 4; Laws 1988, c. 88–122, § 17.

Historical and Statutory Notes

Amendment Notes:

Laws 1982, c. 82–171, § 4, added the language comprising subsec. (2).

Laws 1988, c. 88–122, § 17, eff. July 1, 1988, added pars. (f) and (g) to subsec. (2).

Library References

Pardon and Parole ⚷55.1.
Westlaw Topic No. 284.
C.J.S. Pardon and Parole §§ 45 to 47.

947.08. Repealed by Laws 1969, c. 69–20, § 2

Historical and Statutory Notes

The repealed section, which related to clerical and other assistance, was enacted by Laws 1941, c. 20519, § 5 and amended by Laws 1943, c. 21775, § 1.

947.081. Repealed by Laws 1975, c. 75–49, § 16

Historical and Statutory Notes

The repealed section, which provided for a department of community services, was derived from Laws 1968, Ex.Sess., c. 68–36, § 1.

947.082. Repealed by Laws 1988, c. 88–122, § 66, eff. July 1, 1988

Historical and Statutory Notes

The repealed section, providing for membership and functions of the board of clemency review, was derived from Laws 1986, c. 86–183, § 29, and Laws 1987, c. 87–300, § 3.

947.09. Repealed by Laws 1985, c. 85–295, § 7, eff. June 20, 1985

Historical and Statutory Notes

Repealed § 947.09, which related to competitive examinations for certain full-time employees, was derived from Laws 1943, c. 21775, § 2, and Laws 1941, c. 20519, § 6.

947.095. Repealed by Laws 1988, c. 88–122, § 66, eff. July 1, 1988

Historical and Statutory Notes

Repealed § 947.095, which related to the assignment of hearing examiners, was derived from:

Laws 1982, c. 82–171, § 5.
Laws 1981, c. 81–322, § 3.
Laws 1979, c. 79–42, § 4.
Laws 1978, c. 78–417, §§ 8, 25.

947.10. Business and political activity upon part of members and full-time employees of commission

No member of the commission and no full-time employee thereof shall, during her or his service upon or under the commission, engage in any other business or profession or hold any other public office, nor shall she or he serve as the representative of any political party, or any executive committee or other governing body thereof, or as an executive officer or employee of any political committee, organization, or association or be engaged on the behalf of any candidate for public office in the solicitation of votes or otherwise. However, this shall not be deemed to exclude the appointment of the Secretary of

Corrections to the commission under the terms and conditions set forth in this chapter.

Laws 1941, c. 20519, § 7; Laws 1974, c. 74–112, § 32; Laws 1977, c. 77–120, § 85; Laws 1979, c. 79–3, § 103; Laws 1986, c. 86–186, § 30; Laws 1988, c. 88–122, § 60. Amended by Laws 1997, c. 97–102, § 1670, eff. July 1, 1997.

Historical and Statutory Notes

Amendment Notes:

Laws 1974, c. 74–112, added the second sentence.

Laws 1977, c. 77–120, a reviser's bill, amended this section to conform with Laws 1975, c. 75–49, which created the department of offender rehabilitation (see § 20.315) and transferred to the department certain functions performed by the division of corrections of the department of health and rehabilitative services and the parole and probation commission of the department of offender rehabilitation.

Laws 1979, c. 79–3, a reviser's bill, provided for substitution of references to the department and secretary of "corrections" for the department and secretary of "offender rehabilitation" to conform with Laws 1978, c. 78–53.

Laws 1986, c. 86–183, § 30, eff. Oct. 1, 1986, added at the end of the second sentence ", nor shall this be deemed to exclude the appointment of commissioners to the Board of Clemency Review."

Laws 1988, c. 88–122, § 60, eff. July 1, 1988, deleted at the end of the section "nor shall this be deemed to exclude the appointment of commissioners to the board".

Laws 1997, c. 97–102, eff. July 1, 1997, removed gender-specific references applicable to human beings from volume 4 of the Florida Statutes without substantive changes in legal effect.

Library References

Pardon and Parole ⚷55.1.
Westlaw Topic No. 284.
C.J.S. Pardon and Parole §§ 45 to 47.

Notes of Decisions

Construction and application 1
Leaves of absence 3
Political activity 2

---

1. Construction and application

Section 216.262(1) (c) supersedes the requirement of this section that no full-time employee of the parole and probation commission shall engage in any other business or profession during his service under the commission. By reason of the provisions of said § 216.262(1) (c), such an employee may engage in another business or profession during hours outside of his normal working hours with the state, without obtaining anyone's approval. He would have to have the approval of the department of administration in order to be entitled to engage in another business or profession during his normal working hours with the state. Op.Atty. Gen., 074–46, Feb. 13, 1974.

2. Political activity

A full-time employee of the parole and probation commission may engage in passive political expression, such as carrying bumper stickers on his automobile, wearing lapel pins, etc. Op. Atty.Gen., 074–46, Feb. 13, 1974.

So far as state law is concerned, an employee of the parole and probation commission may solicit votes in behalf of a partisan candidate for public office except during a period of time when he is on duty or expected to perform services for which he receives compensation from the state. However, as a matter of federal law, he is prohibited from doing this if his principal employment is in connection with an activity of the commission which is wholly or partly financed by federal funds. Op.Atty.Gen., 074–46, Feb. 13, 1974.

3. Leaves of absence

A career service employee of the Florida parole and probation commission who is on leave of absence is still such an employee and, so far as state law is concerned, he cannot run for or hold any public office except that, with the consent of his agency head and the approval of the division of personnel, he may be a candidate for or hold a local public office which involves no interest that conflicts or interferes with his state employment. However, as a matter of federal law, and without regard to consent or approval, he may not run for any public office if his principal employment is in connection with an activity which is wholly or partly financed by federal funds. Op.Atty.Gen., 074–46, Feb. 13, 1974.

947.11. Legal adviser

The Department of Legal Affairs shall be the legal adviser of the commission.

Laws 1941, c. 20519, § 8; Laws 1969, c. 69–106, §§ 11, 35.

Historical and Statutory Notes

Amendment Notes:

Laws 1969, c. 69–106, §§ 11, 35, transferred all powers, duties and functions of the attorney general to the department of legal affairs.

Library References

Pardon and Parole ⟹55.1.
Westlaw Topic No. 284.
C.J.S. Pardon and Parole §§ 45 to 47.

947.12. Members, employees, expenses

(1) The members of the commission and its employees shall be reimbursed for travel expenses as provided in s. 112.061. All bills for expenses shall be properly receipted, audited, and approved and forwarded to the Chief Financial Officer and shall be paid in a manner and form as the bills for the expenses of the several departments of the state government are paid. All expenses, including salaries and other compensation, shall be paid from the General Revenue Fund and within the appropriation as fixed therefor by the Legislature. Such expenses shall be paid by the Chief Financial Officer upon proper warrants drawn upon vouchers and requisitions approved by the commission.

(2) The members of the examining board created in s. 947.02 shall each be paid per diem and travel expenses pursuant to s. 112.061 when traveling in the performance of their duties.

Laws 1941, c. 20519, § 9; Laws 1945, c. 22864, § 1; Laws 1947, c. 24033, § 1; Laws 1957, c. 57–401, § 8; Laws 1963, c. 63–400, § 19; Laws 1982, c. 82–171, § 6; Laws 1985, c. 85–61, § 17. Amended by Laws 2003, c. 2003–261, § 1937, eff. June 26, 2003.

Historical and Statutory Notes

Amendment Notes:

Laws 1945, c. 22864, § 1, increased, in the former first sentence of subsec. (1), the annual salary for each commission member to four thousand eight hundred dollars from four thousand dollars.

Laws 1947, c. 24033, § 1, increased, in the former first sentence of subsec. (1), the annual salary for each commission member to five thousand four hundred dollars from four thousand eight hundred dollars.

Laws 1957, c. 57–401, § 8, deleted, from subsec. (1), the former first and second sentences which read "Each member of the Commission shall receive an annual salary of five thousand four hundred dollars and each employee shall receive such an amount of salary as shall be fixed by the Commission. All salaries shall be paid in equal monthly installments, upon requisition, duly approved by the Commission, in manner and form as other salaries are paid in the several departments of the State Government."

Laws 1963, c. 63–400, § 19, substituted, in the first sentence of subsec. (1), the words "reimbursed for traveling expenses as provided in § 112.061" for "paid by the state their necessary traveling expenses in the performance of their duties".

Laws 1982, c. 82–171, § 6, amended subsec. (2) to provide that per diem and traveling expenses shall be determined pursuant to s. 112.061, instead of at a rate of $10 per day.

Laws 1985, c. 85–61, § 17, eff. July 30, 1985, a reviser's bill, amended subsec. (1) of this section to eliminate the requirement that state warrants be countersigned by the Governor in conformance with Laws 1983, c. 83–120, as implemented by 1983 H.J.R. 435, approved by the electors at the November, 1984, general election.

Laws 2003, c. 2003–261, § 1937, rewrote subsec. (1), which formerly read:

"(1) The members of the commission and its employees shall be reimbursed for travel expenses as provided in s. 112.061. All bills for expenses shall be properly receipted, audited, and approved and forwarded to the Comptroller and shall be paid in a manner and form as the bills for the expenses of the several departments of the state government are paid. All expenses, including salaries and other compensation, shall be paid from the General Revenue Fund and within the appropriation as fixed therefor by the Legislature. Such expenses shall be paid by the Treasurer upon proper warrants issued by the Comptroller of the state, drawn upon vouchers and requisitions approved by the commission, and signed by the Comptroller."

Library References

Pardon and Parole ⚷55.1.
Westlaw Topic No. 284.
C.J.S. Pardon and Parole §§ 45 to 47.

947.13. Powers and duties of commission

(1) The commission shall have the powers and perform the duties of:

(a) Determining what persons shall be placed on parole, subject to the provisions of ss. 947.172 and 947.174.

(b) Fixing the time and conditions of parole, as provided in this chapter.

(c) Determining whether a person has violated parole and taking action with respect to such a violation.

(d) Making such investigations as may be necessary.

(e) Reporting to the Board of Executive Clemency the circumstances, the criminal records, and the social, physical, mental, and psychiatric conditions and histories of persons under consideration by the board for pardon, commutation of sentence, or remission of fine, penalty, or forfeiture.

(f) Establishing the terms and conditions of persons released on conditional release under s. 947.1405, and determining subsequent ineligibility for conditional release due to a violation of the terms or conditions of conditional release and taking action with respect to such a violation.

(g) As the Control Release Authority, determining what persons will be released on control release under s. 947.146, establishing the time and conditions of control release, if any, and determining whether a person has violated the conditions of control release and taking action with respect to such a violation.

(h) Determining what persons will be released on conditional medical release under s. 947.149, establishing the conditions of conditional medical release, and determining whether a person has violated the conditions of conditional medical release and taking action with respect to such a violation.

(2)(a) The commission shall immediately examine records of the department under s. 945.25, and any other records which it obtains, and may make such other investigations as may be necessary.

(b) The Department of Children and Family Services and all other state, county, and city agencies, sheriffs and their deputies, and all peace officers shall cooperate with the commission and the department and shall aid and assist them in the performance of their duties.

Laws 1941, c. 20519, §§ 10, 11; Laws 1972, c. 72–256, § 1; Fla.St.1975, §§ 947.13, 947.14(3), (5); Laws 1977, c. 77–120, §§ 86, 87; Laws 1978, c. 78–417, § 9; Laws 1979, c. 79–3, § 104; Laws 1982, c. 82–171, § 7; Laws 1986, c. 86–183, § 31; Laws 1988, c. 88–122, § 18; Laws 1989, c. 89–526, § 46; Laws 1993, c. 93–61, § 4. Amended by Laws 1999, c. 99–8, § 320, eff. June 29, 1999; Laws 2004, c. 2004–335, § 52, eff. Oct. 1, 2004.

Historical and Statutory Notes

Amendment Notes:

Laws 1972, c. 72–256, § 1, added provisions contained in subsec. (2).

Laws 1977, c. 77–120, a reviser's bill, amended this section, deleting therefrom provisions formerly contained in subsec. (2), to conform with Laws 1975, c. 75–49, which created the department of offender rehabilitation and transferred to the department certain functions performed by the division of corrections of the department of health and rehabilitative services and the parole and probation commission of the department of offender rehabilitation. Provisions comprising subsecs. (2)(a) and (2)(b) are derived from Fla.St.1975, § 947.14(3) and (5), respectively, as those provisions were amended by Laws 1977, c. 77–120 and transferred by the division of statutory revision in Fla.St.1977.

Laws 1978, c. 78–417, inserted ", subject to the provisions of s. 947.172 and s. 947.174" at the end of subsec. (1)(a).

Laws 1979, c. 79–3, a reviser's bill, provided for substitution of references to the department and secretary of "corrections" for the department and secretary of "offender rehabilitation" to conform with Laws 1978, c. 78–53.

Laws 1982, c. 82–171, § 7, added a former subsec. (3).

Laws 1985, c. 85–295, § 2, eff. June 20, 1985, substituted near the end of former subsec. (3) "each report due sixty days after the conclusion of the preceding order" for "the initial report due January 30, 1983, and each subsequent report due thirty days past".

Laws 1986, c. 86–183, § 31, eff. Oct. 1, 1986, deleted subsec. (1)(e) pertaining to reporting to the board of pardons.

Laws 1988, c. 88–122, § 18, eff. July 1, 1988, repealed former subsec. (3) to eliminate the commission's responsibility to perform specific research functions.

Laws 1989, c. 89–526, § 46, eff. Oct. 1, 1989, in subsec. (1), added par. (e), relating to reporting to the Board of Clemency.

Laws 1993, c. 93–61, § 4, eff. April 22, 1993, in subsec. (1), rewrote par. (c), which formerly read "Determining violations of parole and what action shall be taken with reference thereto."; and added pars. (f), (g), and (h).

Laws 1999, c. 99–8, § 320, eff. June 29, 1999, substituted "Department of Children and Family Services" for "Department of Health and Rehabilitative Services".

Laws 2004, c. 2004–335, § 52, reenacted subsec. (2)(a) for the purpose of incorporating the amendment to § 945.25 in a reference thereto.

Cross References

Commutation of sentences, see § 940.01.
Pardons and remission of sentences, authority of governor, see § 940.01.

Library References

Pardon and Parole ⚷48 to 77.
Westlaw Topic No. 284.
C.J.S. Pardon and Parole §§ 45 to 63, 65 to 93.

United States Supreme Court

Life inmates rights to commutation of sentence before board of pardons, see Connecticut Bd. of Pardons v. Dumschat, U.S.Conn.1981, 101 S.Ct. 2460, 452 U.S. 458, 69 L.Ed.2d 158.

Parole board, immunity from consequences of official decisions, see Martinez v. State of Cal., U.S.Cal.1980, 100 S.Ct. 553, 444 U.S. 277, 62 L.Ed.2d 481, rehearing denied 100 S.Ct. 1285, 445 U.S. 920, 63 L.Ed.2d 606.

Notes of Decisions

---

1. Validity

Imposition of conditional release supervision by Parole Commission was not violation of separation of powers, nor invalid delegation of legislative power, where state constitution gave Commission authority to grant paroles or conditional releases, rather than reserve power for courts or legislature, and legislature provided that certain inmates must remain under supervision, as determined by Commission, after release from prison for period of time equal to amount of gain time awarded. Mayes v. Moore, 827 So.2d 967 (2002), certiorari denied 123 S.Ct. 2245, 539 U.S. 904, 156 L.Ed.2d 114. Constitutional Law ⚷ 2415(1); Constitutional Law ⚷ 2625(1); Prisons ⚷ 248

2. Construction and application

Parole Commission has broad authority in administering control release program, including authority to either grant or deny credit for time spent under supervision when it determines that releasee has violated terms of release. Gay v. Singletary, 700 So.2d 1220 (1997). Prisons ⚷ 248

Paroling authority is required to comply with constitutional requirements and cannot deny parole on illegal grounds or improper considerations. Moore v. Florida Parole and Probation Commission, 289 So.2d 719 (1974), certiorari denied 94 S.Ct. 2649, 417 U.S. 935, 41 L.Ed.2d 239. Pardon And Parole ⚷ 57.1

Prisoner is entitled to have question of his eligibility for parole determined on evidence which passes constitutional muster. Moore v. Florida Parole and Probation Commission, 289 So.2d 719 (1974), certiorari denied 94 S.Ct. 2649, 417 U.S. 935, 41 L.Ed.2d 239. Pardon And Parole ⚷ 58

There is no absolute right to parole but there is right to proper consideration for parole. Moore v. Florida Parole and Probation Commission, 289 So.2d 719 (1974), certiorari denied 94 S.Ct. 2649, 417 U.S. 935, 41 L.Ed.2d 239. Pardon And Parole ⚷ 46

Although presumptively valid as an administrative construction of a statute, parole and probation commissions granting of a blanket exemption from payment of contributions required under statute, appears to have been without authority; and, it would be neither administratively nor legally feasible for the commission to attempt to collect those contributions which were not paid during the blanket exemption. Op.Atty.Gen., 075–19, Feb. 4, 1975.

3. Legislative intent

It was intention of legislature to vest in Parole Commission power to grant and administer paroles, commit parolees to jail or grant them bond, as circumstances might suggest. Blackburn v. Jackson, 74 So.2d 80 (1954). Pardon And Parole ⚷ 55.1

4. Jurisdiction of commission

The parole commission is without power to grant paroles, conditional releases or absolute discharges to defendants who have been convicted of violation of child molester law but who have not been sentenced and who are eligible for release from state hospital. Marsh v. Garwood, 65 So.2d 15 (1953). Pardon And Parole ⚷ 44

Under statutes pertaining to the duties of the parole commission, where an individual was sentenced as distinguished from being committed, his case was not within the jurisdiction of the parole commission, and he could not be paroled. Op.Atty.Gen., 1951, p. 724.

When imposition of sentence in a criminal case has been suspended or deferred but defendant is not placed on probation, the parole commission has no jurisdiction over defendant. Op.Atty.Gen., 1949, p. 623.

5. Registration

Convicted felons who are probationers or parolees under the supervision of the parole commission are relieved from complying with the registration requirements of Laws 1937, c. 18107, which require that in counties having more than 150,000 population, persons convicted of felonies involving moral turpitude must register with sheriff, but are not relieved from complying with the requirements of Laws 1953, c. 28470, requiring the registration of certain convicted felons in counties having a population of 450,000 or more. Op.Atty.Gen., 057–226, Aug. 5, 1957.

6. Parole release date

Relator's prior conviction, which was obtained without assistance or offer of counsel despite his insolvency, was invalid under U.S.C.A. Const. Amends. 6 and 14, and therefore could not be used to increase his "salient factor score" so as to lengthen his prison term prior to parole release. Jenrette v. Wainwright, App. 3 Dist., 410 So.2d 575 (1982), review denied 419 So.2d 1201. Constitutional Law ⚿ 4801; Pardon And Parole ⚿ 53

Parole and probation commission failed to establish a proper presumptive parole release date as required by this chapter, when it set prisoner's release date at "life." Holston v. Florida Parole and Probation Commission, App. 1 Dist., 394 So.2d 1110 (1981). Pardon And Parole ⚿ 45.1

Parole and probation commission is charged with the responsibility of making sensitive decisions as to when release on parole is appropriate, based on objective parole criteria, and an inmate entitled to such consideration is entitled to a binding presumptive parole release date as mandated by clear legislative language. Holston v. Florida Parole and Probation Commission, App. 1 Dist., 394 So.2d 1110 (1981). Pardon And Parole ⚿ 58

Parole and probation commission may properly set a parole release date so distant as to be beyond the life expectancy for an inmate currently incarcerated if his criminal history so warrants. Holston v. Florida Parole and Probation Commission, App. 1 Dist., 394 So.2d 1110 (1981). Pardon And Parole ⚿ 48.1

The parole and probation commission, having no sentencing authority, may not be compelled, in fixing prisoner's tentative release date, to give retrospective credit for jail time served before prisoner was sentenced. Hipke v. Parole and Probation Commission, App. 1 Dist., 380 So.2d 494 (1980). Sentencing And Punishment ⚿ 1160

7. Conditions of parole

Although court is not precluded from recommending conditions of parole, Parole and Probation Commission alone is invested with authority under this section to impose such conditions. Shaffer v. State, App. 2 Dist., 446 So.2d 1156 (1984); Fray v. State, App. 2 Dist., 432 So.2d 764 (1983); Monk v. State, App., 427 So.2d 820 (1983); Alexander v. State, App., 425 So.2d 1197 (1983).

Trial court could not mandate payment of restitution as condition of parole. Shaffer v. State, App. 2 Dist., 446 So.2d 1156 (1984). Pardon And Parole ⚿ 54

Court erred in imposing, as condition of any future parole defendant might receive, fine and surcharge, court costs, payment of lien for court-appointed counsel fees. Fray v. State, App. 2 Dist., 432 So.2d 764 (1983). Pardon And Parole ⚿ 54

In prosecution for burglary and petit theft, trial court improperly imposed requirement of payment of a lien for court-appointed counsel, a fine, and a surcharge as a condition of parole, since parole and probation commission is solely vested with power to establish conditions of parole. Brown v. State, App. 2 Dist., 427 So.2d 271 (1983), approved 452 So.2d 931. Pardon And Parole ⚿ 54

Portions of order requiring that defendant pay fine, costs, restitution and medical bills either during incarceration or as conditions of parole amounted to improper establishment of conditions of parole. Alexander v. State, App. 2 Dist., 425 So.2d 1197 (1983). Pardon And Parole ⚿ 54

While recommendation pertaining to parole made in order relating to sentencing had no binding effect since the parole and probation commission determines who shall be placed on parole and time and conditions of parole, no error was committed when trial court made recommendation. Prince v. State, App. 1 Dist., 421 So.2d 791 (1982). Pardon And Parole ⚿ 54

8. Right to counsel

Consideration of eligibility for parole should be free from consequences of conviction in which defendant was denied his right to counsel. Moore v. Florida Parole and Probation Commission, 289 So.2d 719 (1974), certiorari denied 94 S.Ct. 2649, 417 U.S. 935, 41 L.Ed.2d 239. Pardon And Parole ⚿ 59

A circuit judge does not have the power to appoint a private attorney to represent an indigent parolee without compensation. Op.Atty. Gen., 074–97, March 28, 1974.

The Florida Parole and Probation Commission does not have the power to appoint counsel for indigent parolees facing a parole revocation hearing. Op.Atty.Gen., 074–97, March 28, 1974.

The Florida parole and probation commission should at least ask the public defenders of this state to represent indigent parolees until such time as a legislative remedy is forthcoming. Op.Atty.Gen., 074–97, March 28, 1974.

No state funds have been appropriated for the payment of fees to counsel appointed to represent indigent parolees. Op.Atty.Gen., 074–97, March 28, 1974.

9. Mandamus

Where prisoner asserted that parole and probation commission had improperly aggravated her presumptive parole date contrary to its established guidelines, mandamus, rather than habeas corpus, was the more appropriate remedy. Hardy v. Greadington, App. 5 Dist., 405 So.2d

768 (1981). Habeas Corpus ⚿ 279; Mandamus ⚿ 73(1)

Writ of mandamus will not lie in any review by District Court of Appeal of discretionary acts of Parole and Probation Commission. Baker v. Florida Parole and Probation Commission, App. 1 Dist., 384 So.2d 746 (1980). Mandamus ⚿ 73(1)

Granting of parole rests within paroling authority's discretion and mandamus will not lie to compel granting of parole. Moore v. Florida Parole and Probation Commission, 289 So.2d 719 (1974), certiorari denied 94 S.Ct. 2649, 417 U.S. 935, 41 L.Ed.2d 239. Mandamus ⚿ 73(1); Pardon And Parole ⚿ 47

Where prisoner claimed that denial of parole was based on paroling authority's improper consideration of prior convictions rendered when he was without counsel, mandamus would lie to compel paroling authority to exercise its discretion as to granting or denial of parole without consideration of such convictions. Moore v. Florida Parole and Probation Commission, 289 So.2d 719 (1974), certiorari denied 94 S.Ct. 2649, 417 U.S. 935, 41 L.Ed.2d 239. Mandamus ⚿ 73(1)

10. Review

Defendants' failure to object to imposition of restitution and sentencing barred them from contesting validity of restitution on appeal. Shaffer v. State, App. 2 Dist., 446 So.2d 1156 (1984). Criminal Law ⚿ 1042.3(5)

947.135. Mutual participation program

(1) Short title.—This act shall be known and may be cited as the "Mutual Participation Program Act of 1976."

(2) Legislative intent.—It is the intent of the Legislature to:

(a) Involve the department and the commission in program planning with the offender while the offender is incarcerated, leading to the establishment of certain criteria affecting the grant of parole and release from parole.

(b) Involve the offender in developing her or his individual rehabilitation program for the period of incarceration and parole with the department and the commission.

(c) Require establishment of criteria to be used in determining which offenders are eligible for this program.

(d) Encourage, through department and commission action, youthful offenders who are housed within institutions of the department to participate in the program.

However, no offender shall be eligible to participate in this program who was sentenced as an habitual felony offender pursuant to s. 775.084 or who was convicted of a capital or life felony as provided by s. 775.081, s. 775.082, or s. 775.083. Offenders meeting eligibility criteria may be offered the opportunity to participate in the program which will include a parole date.

(3) Mutual participation program; development; criteria; department and commission rules.—

(a) The department and the commission shall jointly develop a mutual participation program which sets forth for each eligible offender the terms of her or his institutional confinement, a parole date, and terms of parole supervision and release, provided such offender meets the criteria set forth in this act and any additional criteria established by the department and the commission.

1. The department and the commission, as a portion of the mutual participation program, shall require that each eligible offender satisfactorily work at a job within the institution or as a part of a correctional industries program or

satisfactorily participate in a vocational training or educational program offered by the department. Nothing in this subsection shall be construed to exclude eligible offenders from meeting both the work requirements and training and educational requirements when deemed appropriate by the department and commission.

2. Additional criteria shall be established and required by the commission and the department for participation in the program, including, but not limited to, vocational counseling and work-release programs; however, criteria for satisfactory participation in the program shall not include academic classroom instruction at the college level.

3. A panel of at least two members of the commission shall establish a parole date for each eligible offender, based on the satisfactory completion of the program. In no case shall such date fall after the date which would have been established under s. 947.172.

(b) The commission shall promulgate rules on criteria used to establish parole dates, conditions precedent to the granting of parole, terms of parole, and release from parole. The department and the commission shall establish such criteria relating to parole supervision, which criteria shall include, but not be limited to, the requirements for participation in vocational or counseling programs available in the community, stipulations related to employment, and other criteria considered necessary for the successful reintegration of the offender into society.

(c) Periodic written reports of the offender's progress in the program shall be submitted to the department and the commission.

Laws 1976, c. 76–274, §§ 1 to 6; Laws 1977, c. 77–174, § 1; Laws 1978, c. 78–417, § 10; Laws 1979, c. 79–3, § 105; Laws 1979, c. 79–42, § 13; Laws 1979, c. 79–164, § 194; Laws 1981, c. 81–259, § 498; Laws 1982, c. 82–171, § 8; Laws 1983, c. 83–131, § 10. Amended by Laws 1997, c. 97–102, § 1671, eff. July 1, 1997.

Historical and Statutory Notes

Amendment Notes:

Laws 1977, c. 77–174, a reviser's bill, amended subsec. (4) (b) [now subsec. (3)(b)] of this section to reflect language editorially inserted by the division of statutory revision and indexing.

Laws 1978, c. 78–417, deleted in the first sentence of subsec. (4) (a) [now subsec. (3)(a)] reference to a pilot program, and added the second sentence to subsec. (4) (a) 3 [now subsec. (3)(a)3].

Laws 1979, c. 79–3, a reviser's bill, provided for substitution of references to the department and secretary of "corrections" for the department and secretary of "offender rehabilitation" to conform with Laws 1978, c. 78–53.

Laws 1979, c. 79–42, § 13, repealed subsec. (2), which provided definitions. The subsequent subsections were renumbered accordingly.

Laws 1979, c. 79–164, a reviser's bill, corrected statutes by deletion of expired, obsolete, invalid, inconsistent or redundant provisions; modified cross references and grammar; and, otherwise improved the clarity to facilitate interpretation of the statutes.

Laws 1981, c. 81–259, a reviser's bill, deleted subsec. (5) which required promulgation of rules by September 1, 1976.

Laws 1982, c. 82–171, § 8, interpolated subsec. (2) (d), substituted "eligibility" for "these" in the last sentence of subsec. (2); and rewrote subsec. (3) (a)1, which formerly required participation in a correctional work program pursuant to s. 945.06.

Laws 1983, c. 83–131, § 10, substituted "or" for "and" preceding "satisfactorily" in the first sentence and added the second sentence in subsec. (3)(a)1; inserted "A panel of at least two members of" at the beginning of subsec. (3)(a)3; and deleted subsec. (4) providing for annual evaluation.

Laws 1983, c. 83–131, § 34, which repealed all of the sections of this chapter on July 1, 1987, subject to legislative review, did not include this section within the enumeration of sections to be repealed.

Laws 1997, c. 97–102, eff. July 1, 1997, removed gender-specific references applicable to human beings from volume 4 of the Florida Statutes without substantive changes in legal effect.

Cross References

Powers and duties relating to parolees, department of corrections, see § 947.16.
Prisoner classification summaries and progress reports provided to parole and probation commission, see §§ 921.20, 921.21.
Prisoner mental health history and treatment, records provided to Parole Commission and Department of Rehabilitative Services, see § 945.47.

Library References

Pardon and Parole ⚷55.1.
Westlaw Topic No. 284.
C.J.S. Pardon and Parole §§ 45 to 47.

Notes of Decisions

Construction and application 1

1. Construction and application

The statutory duty imposed upon the Florida parole and probation commission by § 947.16(3) that the commission conduct parole interviews with inmates "not less often than annually," was not abrogated or modified by the enactment of this section, and is not abrogated or modified when an inmate enters into a "contract parole" agreement pursuant to this section. Op.Atty.Gen., 077–73, July 27, 1977.

947.14. Renumbered as 945.25, 947.13 in Fla.St.1977

947.1405. Conditional release program

(1) This section and s. 947.141 may be cited as the "Conditional Release Program Act."

(2) Any inmate who:

(a) Is convicted of a crime committed on or after October 1, 1988, and before January 1, 1994, and any inmate who is convicted of a crime committed on or after January 1, 1994, which crime is or was contained in category 1, category 2, category 3, or category 4 of Rule 3.701 and Rule 3.988, Florida Rules of Criminal Procedure (1993), and who has served at least one prior felony commitment at a state or federal correctional institution;

(b) Is sentenced as a habitual or violent habitual offender or a violent career criminal pursuant to s. 775.084; or

(c) Is found to be a sexual predator under s. 775.21 or former s. 775.23,

shall, upon reaching the tentative release date or provisional release date, whichever is earlier, as established by the Department of Corrections, be released under supervision subject to specified terms and conditions, including payment of the cost of supervision pursuant to s. 948.09. Such supervision shall be applicable to all sentences within the overall term of sentences if an inmate's overall term of sentences includes one or more sentences that are eligible for conditional release supervision as provided herein. Effective July 1,

1994, and applicable for offenses committed on or after that date, the commission may require, as a condition of conditional release, that the releasee make payment of the debt due and owing to a county or municipal detention facility under s. 951.032 for medical care, treatment, hospitalization, or transportation received by the releasee while in that detention facility. The commission, in determining whether to order such repayment and the amount of such repayment, shall consider the amount of the debt, whether there was any fault of the institution for the medical expenses incurred, the financial resources of the releasee, the present and potential future financial needs and earning ability of the releasee, and dependents, and other appropriate factors. If any inmate placed on conditional release supervision is also subject to probation or community control, resulting from a probationary or community control split sentence within the overall term of sentences, the Department of Corrections shall supervise such person according to the conditions imposed by the court and the commission shall defer to such supervision. If the court revokes probation or community control and resentences the offender to a term of incarceration, such revocation also constitutes a sufficient basis for the revocation of the conditional release supervision on any nonprobationary or noncommunity control sentence without further hearing by the commission. If any such supervision on any nonprobationary or noncommunity control sentence is revoked, such revocation may result in a forfeiture of all gain-time, and the commission may revoke the resulting deferred conditional release supervision or take other action it considers appropriate. If the term of conditional release supervision exceeds that of the probation or community control, then, upon expiration of the probation or community control, authority for the supervision shall revert to the commission and the supervision shall be subject to the conditions imposed by the commission. A panel of no fewer than two commissioners shall establish the terms and conditions of any such release. If the offense was a controlled substance violation, the conditions shall include a requirement that the offender submit to random substance abuse testing intermittently throughout the term of conditional release supervision, upon the direction of the correctional probation officer as defined in s. 943.10(3). The commission shall also determine whether the terms and conditions of such release have been violated and whether such violation warrants revocation of the conditional release.

(3) As part of the conditional release process, the commission, through review and consideration of information provided by the department, shall determine:

(a) The amount of reparation or restitution.

(b) The consequences of the offense as reported by the aggrieved party.

(c) The aggrieved party's fear of the inmate or concerns about the release of the inmate.

(4) The commission shall provide to the aggrieved party information regarding the manner in which notice of any developments concerning the status of the inmate during the term of conditional release may be requested.

(5) Within 180 days prior to the tentative release date or provisional release date, whichever is earlier, a representative of the department shall review the inmate's program participation, disciplinary record, psychological and medical records, criminal records, and any other information pertinent to the impending release. The department shall gather and compile information necessary for the commission to make the determinations set forth in subsection (3). A department representative shall conduct a personal interview with the inmate for the purpose of determining the details of the inmate's release plan, including the inmate's planned residence and employment. The department representative shall forward the inmate's release plan to the commission and recommend to the commission the terms and conditions of the conditional release.

(6) The commission shall review the recommendations of the department, and such other information as it deems relevant, and may conduct a review of the inmate's record for the purpose of establishing the terms and conditions of the conditional release. The commission may impose any special conditions it considers warranted from its review of the release plan and recommendation. If the commission determines that the inmate is eligible for release under this section, the commission shall enter an order establishing the length of supervision and the conditions attendant thereto. However, an inmate who has been convicted of a violation of chapter 794 or found by the court to be a sexual predator is subject to the maximum level of supervision provided, with the mandatory conditions as required in subsection (7), and that supervision shall continue through the end of the releasee's original court-imposed sentence. The length of supervision must not exceed the maximum penalty imposed by the court.

(7)(a) Any inmate who is convicted of a crime committed on or after October 1, 1995, or who has been previously convicted of a crime committed on or after October 1, 1995, in violation of chapter 794, s. 800.04, s. 827.071, s. 847.0135(5), or s. 847.0145, and is subject to conditional release supervision, shall have, in addition to any other conditions imposed, the following special conditions imposed by the commission:

1. A mandatory curfew from 10 p.m. to 6 a.m. The commission may designate another 8–hour period if the offender's employment precludes the above specified time, and such alternative is recommended by the Department of Corrections. If the commission determines that imposing a curfew would endanger the victim, the commission may consider alternative sanctions.

2. If the victim was under the age of 18, a prohibition on living within 1,000 feet of a school, day care center, park, playground, designated public school bus stop, or other place where children regularly congregate. A releasee who is subject to this subparagraph may not relocate to a residence that is within 1,000 feet of a public school bus stop. Beginning October 1, 2004, the commission or the department may not approve a residence that is located within 1,000 feet of a school, day care center, park, playground, designated school bus stop, or other place where children regularly congregate for any releasee who is subject to this subparagraph. On October 1, 2004, the depart-

ment shall notify each affected school district of the location of the residence of a releasee 30 days prior to release and thereafter, if the releasee relocates to a new residence, shall notify any affected school district of the residence of the releasee within 30 days after relocation. If, on October 1, 2004, any public school bus stop is located within 1,000 feet of the existing residence of such releasee, the district school board shall relocate that school bus stop. Beginning October 1, 2004, a district school board may not establish or relocate a public school bus stop within 1,000 feet of the residence of a releasee who is subject to this subparagraph. The failure of the district school board to comply with this subparagraph shall not result in a violation of conditional release supervision.

3. Active participation in and successful completion of a sex offender treatment program with qualified practitioners specifically trained to treat sex offenders, at the releasee's own expense. If a qualified practitioner is not available within a 50–mile radius of the releasee's residence, the offender shall participate in other appropriate therapy.

4. A prohibition on any contact with the victim, directly or indirectly, including through a third person, unless approved by the victim, the offender's therapist, and the sentencing court.

5. If the victim was under the age of 18, a prohibition against contact with children under the age of 18 without review and approval by the commission. The commission may approve supervised contact with a child under the age of 18 if the approval is based upon a recommendation for contact issued by a qualified practitioner who is basing the recommendation on a risk assessment. Further, the sex offender must be currently enrolled in or have successfully completed a sex offender therapy program. The commission may not grant supervised contact with a child if the contact is not recommended by a qualified practitioner and may deny supervised contact with a child at any time. When considering whether to approve supervised contact with a child, the commission must review and consider the following:

a. A risk assessment completed by a qualified practitioner. The qualified practitioner must prepare a written report that must include the findings of the assessment and address each of the following components:

(I) The sex offender's current legal status;

(II) The sex offender's history of adult charges with apparent sexual motivation;

(III) The sex offender's history of adult charges without apparent sexual motivation;

(IV) The sex offender's history of juvenile charges, whenever available;

(V) The sex offender's offender treatment history, including a consultation from the sex offender's treating, or most recent treating, therapist;

(VI) The sex offender's current mental status;

(VII) The sex offender's mental health and substance abuse history as provided by the Department of Corrections;

(VIII) The sex offender's personal, social, educational, and work history;

(IX) The results of current psychological testing of the sex offender if determined necessary by the qualified practitioner;

(X) A description of the proposed contact, including the location, frequency, duration, and supervisory arrangement;

(XI) The child's preference and relative comfort level with the proposed contact, when age-appropriate;

(XII) The parent's or legal guardian's preference regarding the proposed contact; and

(XIII) The qualified practitioner's opinion, along with the basis for that opinion, as to whether the proposed contact would likely pose significant risk of emotional or physical harm to the child.

The written report of the assessment must be given to the commission.

b. A recommendation made as a part of the risk-assessment report as to whether supervised contact with the child should be approved;

c. A written consent signed by the child's parent or legal guardian, if the parent or legal guardian is not the sex offender, agreeing to the sex offender having supervised contact with the child after receiving full disclosure of the sex offender's present legal status, past criminal history, and the results of the risk assessment. The commission may not approve contact with the child if the parent or legal guardian refuses to give written consent for supervised contact;

d. A safety plan prepared by the qualified practitioner, who provides treatment to the offender, in collaboration with the sex offender, the child's parent or legal guardian, and the child, when age appropriate, which details the acceptable conditions of contact between the sex offender and the child. The safety plan must be reviewed and approved by the Department of Corrections before being submitted to the commission; and

e. Evidence that the child's parent or legal guardian, if the parent or legal guardian is not the sex offender, understands the need for and agrees to the safety plan and has agreed to provide, or to designate another adult to provide, constant supervision any time the child is in contact with the offender.

The commission may not appoint a person to conduct a risk assessment and may not accept a risk assessment from a person who has not demonstrated to the commission that he or she has met the requirements of a qualified practitioner as defined in this section.

6. If the victim was under age 18, a prohibition on working for pay or as a volunteer at any school, day care center, park, playground, or other place where children regularly congregate, as prescribed by the commission.

7. Unless otherwise indicated in the treatment plan provided by the sexual offender treatment program, a prohibition on viewing, owning, or possessing any obscene, pornographic, or sexually stimulating visual or auditory material, including telephone, electronic media, computer programs, or computer services that are relevant to the offender's deviant behavior pattern.

8. Effective for a releasee whose crime is committed on or after July 1, 2005, a prohibition on accessing the Internet or other computer services until the offender's sex offender treatment program, after a risk assessment is completed, approves and implements a safety plan for the offender's accessing or using the Internet or other computer services.

9. A requirement that the releasee must submit two specimens of blood to the Florida Department of Law Enforcement to be registered with the DNA database.

10. A requirement that the releasee make restitution to the victim, as determined by the sentencing court or the commission, for all necessary medical and related professional services relating to physical, psychiatric, and psychological care.

11. Submission to a warrantless search by the community control or probation officer of the probationer's or community controllee's person, residence, or vehicle.

(b) For a releasee whose crime was committed on or after October 1, 1997, in violation of chapter 794, s. 800.04, s. 827.071, s. 847.0135(5), or s. 847.0145, and who is subject to conditional release supervision, in addition to any other provision of this subsection, the commission shall impose the following additional conditions of conditional release supervision:

1. As part of a treatment program, participation in a minimum of one annual polygraph examination to obtain information necessary for risk management and treatment and to reduce the sex offender's denial mechanisms. The polygraph examination must be conducted by a polygrapher trained specifically in the use of the polygraph for the monitoring of sex offenders, where available, and at the expense of the sex offender. The results of the examination may not be used as evidence in a hearing to prove that a violation of supervision has occurred.

2. Maintenance of a driving log and a prohibition against driving a motor vehicle alone without the prior approval of the supervising officer.

3. A prohibition against obtaining or using a post office box without the prior approval of the supervising officer.

4. If there was sexual contact, a submission to, at the probationer's or community controllee's expense, an HIV test with the results to be released to the victim or the victim's parent or guardian.

5. Electronic monitoring of any form when ordered by the commission. Any person who has been placed under supervision and is electronically monitored by the department must pay the department for the cost of the electronic monitoring service at a rate that may not exceed the full cost of the monitoring service. Funds collected under this subparagraph shall be deposited into the General Revenue Fund. The department may exempt a person from the payment of all or any part of the electronic monitoring service cost if the department finds that any of the factors listed in s. 948.09(3) exist.

(8) It is the finding of the Legislature that the population of offenders released from state prison into the community who meet the conditional release criteria poses the greatest threat to the public safety of the groups of offenders under community supervision. Therefore, the Department of Corrections is to provide intensive supervision by experienced correctional probation officers to conditional release offenders. Subject to specific appropriation by the Legislature, caseloads may be restricted to a maximum of 40 conditional release offenders per officer to provide for enhanced public safety and to effectively monitor conditions of electronic monitoring or curfews, if so ordered by the commission.

(9) The commission shall adopt rules pursuant to ss. 120.536(1) and 120.54 necessary to implement the provisions of the Conditional Release Program Act.

(10) Effective for a releasee whose crime was committed on or after September 1, 2005, in violation of chapter 794, s. 800.04(4), (5), or (6), s. 827.071, or s. 847.0145, and the unlawful activity involved a victim who was 15 years of age or younger and the offender is 18 years of age or older or for a releasee who is designated as a sexual predator pursuant to s. 775.21, in addition to any other provision of this section, the commission must order electronic monitoring for the duration of the releasee's supervision.

(11) Effective for a releasee whose crime was committed on or after October 1, 2008, and who has been found to have committed the crime for the purpose of benefiting, promoting, or furthering the interests of a criminal gang, the commission shall, in addition to any other conditions imposed, impose a condition prohibiting the releasee from knowingly associating with other criminal gang members or associates, except as authorized by law enforcement officials, prosecutorial authorities, or the court, for the purpose of aiding in the investigation of criminal activity.

Laws 1988, c. 88–122, § 19; Laws 1989, c. 89–531, § 12; Laws 1990, c. 90–337, § 11; Laws 1991, c. 91–225, § 2; Laws 1991, c. 91–280, § 8; Laws 1992, c. 92–310, § 14; Laws 1993, c. 93–277, § 4; Laws 1993, c. 93–417, § 4; Laws 1994, c. 94–121, § 2; Laws 1994, c. 94–294, § 3; Laws 1995, c. 95–264, § 5; Laws 1995, c. 95–283, § 57. Amended by Laws 1996, c. 96–388, § 64, eff. July 1, 1996; Laws 1997, c. 97–78, § 10, eff. May 23, 1997; Laws 1997, c. 97–102, § 1872, eff. July 1, 1997; Laws 1997, c. 97–308, § 1, eff. Oct. 1, 1997; Laws 2000, c. 2000–246, § 3, eff. Oct. 1, 2000; Laws 2001, c. 2001–124, § 5, eff. July 1, 2001; Laws 2004, c. 2004–55, § 1, eff. Oct. 1, 2004; Laws 2004, c. 2004–371, § 16, eff. July 1, 2004; Laws 2005, c. 2005–28, § 12, eff. Sept. 1, 2005; Laws 2005, c. 2005–67, § 2, eff. Jan. 1, 2006; Laws 2008, c. 2008–172, § 27, eff. Oct. 1, 2008; Laws 2008, c. 2008–238, § 23, eff. Oct. 1, 2008; Laws 2009, c. 2009–63, § 9, eff. July 1, 2009.

Historical and Statutory Notes

Amendment Notes:

Laws 1989, c. 89–531, § 12, eff. Oct. 1, 1989, in subsec. (2), provided for release upon reaching the provisional release date, included payment of the cost of supervision as a term and condition of release, and provided inmates subject to conditional release supervision under this section would not be subject to provisional release supervision; and in subsec. (5), inserted the reference to the provisional release date in the first sentence.

Laws 1990, c. 90–337, § 11, eff. July 1, 1990, in subsec. (2), in the fourth sentence substituted "A panel of no fewer than two commissioners" for "The commission"; and inserted a fifth sentence.

Laws 1990, c. 90–337, § 22 provided therein that the amendment take effect July 1, 1990; however, approval by the governor occurred subsequent thereto. The Florida Supreme Court in an advisory opinion to the governor of July 19, 1979 (374 So.2d 959) stated in part "* * * the effective date provided in the bill is inoperative unless the bill becomes law on or before that date" and concludes that under such circumstances the provision of Const. Art. 3, § 9, that the law take effect on the sixtieth day after adjournment sine die of the session of the legislature in which enacted, is applicable.

Laws 1991, c. 91–225, § 2, eff. July 1, 1991, reenacted subsec. (2) without change "For the purpose of incorporating the amendment to section 945.30, Florida Statutes, in references thereto".

Laws 1991, c. 91–280, § 8, eff. Oct. 1, 1991, reenacted and amended subsec. (2) for the purpose of incorporating the amendment to § 945.30, which was renumbered as § 948.09, in references thereto.

Laws 1992, c. 92–310, § 14, eff. Oct. 1, 1992, in subsec. (6), inserted the fourth sentence.

Laws 1993, c. 93–277, § 4, eff. Oct. 1, 1993, in subsec. (6), inserted "or found by the court to be a sexual predator" in the fourth sentence.

Laws 1993, c. 93–417, § 4, eff. Nov. 24, 1993, in subsec. (2), inserted "and before January 1, 1994, and any inmate who is convicted of a crime committed on or after January 1, 1994," following "1988,", inserted "or was" following "crime is", and inserted "(1993)" "Procedure" in the first sentence, and deleted a former third sentence, which had read, "An inmate who is subject to conditional release supervision under this section shall not be subject to provisional release supervision.".

Laws 1994, c. 94–121, § 2, eff. May 4, 1994, reenacted subsec. (1) of this section for the purpose of incorporating the amendment to § 947.141 in a reference thereto.

Laws 1994, c. 94–294, § 3, eff. July 1, 1994, inserted in subsec. (2) the second and third sentences.

Laws 1995, c. 95–264, § 5, eff. Oct. 1, 1995, in subsec. (2), inserted the paragraph designations, and inserted par. (c), relating to sexual predators.

Laws 1995, c. 95–283, § 57, eff. June 15, 1995, in subsec. (6), in the fourth sentence, inserted "with the mandatory conditions as required in subsection (7)"; and added subsec. (7).

Laws 1996, c. 96–388, § 64, eff. July 1, 1996, in subsec. (2), substituted a reference to former § 775.23 or § 775.21 for a reference to § 775.23 at the end of subsec. (c); and in subsec. (7), substituted a reference to former § 775.23(2)(a) or (b) or § 775.21 for a reference to § 775.23 in the introductory paragraph, and substituted a reference to the DNA database for a reference to the DNA date bank at the end of par. (h).

Laws 1997, c. 97–78, § 10, eff. May 23, 1997, in subsec. (2), in par. (b), inserted "or violent career criminal"; in the flush left language, inserted the first complete sentence; and added subsec. (8).

Laws 1997, c. 97–102, eff. July 1, 1997, removed gender-specific references applicable to human beings from volume 4 of the Florida Statutes without substantive changes in legal effect.

Laws 1997, c. 97–308, § 1, eff. Oct. 1, 1997, in subsec. (2), in par. (b), inserted "or a violent career criminal"; in the flush left provisions at the end of subsec. (2), inserted the first complete sentence; and rewrote subsec. (7), which formerly read:

"Any inmate who is convicted of a crime committed on or after October 1, 1995, or has been previously convicted of a crime committed on or after October 1, 1995, and who meets the criteria of s. 775.21 or former s. 775.23(2)(a) or (b) shall have, in addition to any other conditions imposed, the following special conditions imposed by the commission:

"(a) A curfew, if appropriate, during hours set by the commission.

"(b) If the victim was under the age of 18, a prohibition on living within 1,000 feet of a school, day care center, park, playground, or other place where children regularly congregate.

"(c) Active participation in and successful completion of a sex offender treatment program, at the releasee's own expense, unless one is not available within a 50-mile radius of the releasee's residence.

"(d) A prohibition on any contact with the victim, directly or indirectly, including through a third person, unless approved by the commission.

"(e) If the victim was under the age of 18, a prohibition, until successful completion of a sex offender treatment program, on unsupervised contact with a child under the age of 18, unless authorized by the commission without another adult present who is responsible for the child's welfare, has been advised of the crime, and is approved by the commission.

"(f) If the victim was under age 18, a prohibition on working for pay or as a volunteer at any school, day care center, park, playground, or other place where children regularly congregate, as prescribed by the commission.

"(g) Unless otherwise indicated in the treatment plan provided by the sexual offender treatment program, a prohibition on viewing, owning, or possessing any obscene, pornographic, or sexually explicit material.

"(h) A requirement that the releasee must submit two specimens of blood to the Florida Department of Law Enforcement to be registered with the DNA database."

Laws 2000, c. 2000–246, § 3, reenacted subsec. (7) for the purpose of incorporating the amendment to § 800.04 in a reference thereto.

Laws 2001, c. 2001–124, § 5, in subsec. (2), in the last paragraph, inserted the fourth, fifth, sixth, and seventh full sentences; deleted the former fourth full sentence, which read "If an inmate has received a term of probation or community control supervision to be served after release from incarceration, the period of probation or community control must be substituted for the conditional release supervision."; in subsec. (3), following "commission" inserted ", through review and consideration of information provided by the department,"; rewrote subsec. (5); in subsec. (6), in the first sentence, deleted from the beginning of the sentence "Upon receipt of notice as required under s. 947.175,"; inserted "review the recommendations of the department, and such other information as it deems relevant, and may"; in the second sentence, substituted "release plan and recommendation" for "record"; in subsec. (7)(a)1., in three instances, substituted "commission" for "court"; rewrote subsecs. (7)(a)5. and (7)(b)5.; and added subsec. (9). Subsecs. (5), (7)(a)5., and (7)(b)5. formerly read:

"(5) Within 180 days prior to the tentative release date or provisional release date, whichever is earlier, a representative of the commission shall interview the inmate. The commission representative shall review the inmate's program participation, disciplinary record, psychological and medical records, and any other information pertinent to the impending release. A commission representative shall conduct a personal interview with the inmate for the purpose of determining the details of the inmate's release plan, including the inmate's planned residence and employment. The results of the interview must be forwarded to the commission in writing."

"5. If the victim was under the age of 18, a prohibition, until successful completion of a sex offender treatment program, on unsupervised contact with a child under the age of 18, unless authorized by the commission without another adult present who is responsible for the child's welfare, has been advised of the crime, and is approved by the commission."

"5. Electronic monitoring when deemed necessary by the community control or probation officer and his or her supervisor, and ordered by the court at the recommendation of the Department of Corrections."

Laws 2004, c. 2004–55, § 1, rewrote subsec. (7)(a)2., which formerly read:

"2. If the victim was under the age of 18, a prohibition on living within 1,000 feet of a school, day care center, park, playground, or other place where children regularly congregate."

Laws 2004, c. 2004–371, § 16, reenacted subsec. (2)(c) of this section for the purpose of incorporating the amendment to § 775.21 in a reference thereto.

Laws 2005, c. 2005–28, § 12, added subsec. (10), relating to electronic monitoring.

Laws 2005, c. 2005–67, § 2, rewrote subsec. (7)(a), which formerly read:

"(7)(a) Any inmate who is convicted of a crime committed on or after October 1, 1995, or who has been previously convicted of a crime committed on or after October 1, 1995, in violation of chapter 794, s. 800.04, s. 827.071, or s. 847.0145, and is subject to conditional release supervision, shall have, in addition to any other conditions imposed, the following special conditions imposed by the commission:

"1. A mandatory curfew from 10 p.m. to 6 a.m. The commission may designate another 8–hour period if the offender's employment precludes the above specified time, and such alternative is recommended by the Department of Corrections. If the commission determines that imposing a curfew would endanger the victim, the commission may consider alternative sanctions.

"2. If the victim was under the age of 18, a prohibition on living within 1,000 feet of a school, day care center, park, playground, designated public school bus stop, or other place where children regularly congregate. A releasee who is subject to this subparagraph may not relocate to a residence that is within 1,000 feet of a public school bus stop. Beginning October 1, 2004, the commission or the department may not approve a residence that is located within 1,000 feet of a school, day care center, park, playground, designated school bus stop, or other place where children regularly congregate for any releasee who is subject to this subparagraph. On October 1, 2004, the department shall notify each affected school district of the location of the residence of a releasee 30 days prior to release and thereafter, if the releasee relocates to a new residence, shall notify any affected school district of the residence of the releasee within 30 days after relocation. If, on October 1, 2004, any public school bus stop is located within 1,000 feet of the existing residence of such releasee, the district school board shall relocate that school bus stop. Beginning October 1, 2004, a district school board may not establish or relocate a public school bus stop within 1,000 feet of the residence of a releasee who is subject to this subparagraph. The failure of the district school board to comply with this subparagraph shall not result in a violation of conditional release supervision.

"3. Active participation in and successful completion of a sex offender treatment program with therapists specifically trained to treat sex offenders, at the releasee's own expense. If a specially trained therapist is not available within a 50-mile radius of the releasee's residence, the offender shall participate in other appropriate therapy.

"4. A prohibition on any contact with the victim, directly or indirectly, including through a third person, unless approved by the victim, the offender's therapist, and the sentencing court.

"5. If the victim was under the age of 18, a prohibition against direct contact or association with children under the age of 18 until all of the following conditions are met:

"a. Successful completion of a sex offender treatment program.

"b. The adult person who is legally responsible for the welfare of the child has been advised of the nature of the crime.

"c. Such adult person is present during all contact or association with the child.

"d. Such adult person has been approved by the commission.

"6. If the victim was under age 18, a prohibition on working for pay or as a volunteer at any school, day care center, park, playground, or other place where children regularly congregate, as prescribed by the commission.

"7. Unless otherwise indicated in the treatment plan provided by the sexual offender treatment program, a prohibition on viewing, owning, or possessing any obscene, pornographic, or sexually stimulating visual or auditory material, including telephone, electronic media, computer programs, or computer services that are relevant to the offender's deviant behavior pattern.

"8. A requirement that the releasee must submit two specimens of blood to the Florida Department of Law Enforcement to be registered with the DNA database.

"9. A requirement that the releasee make restitution to the victim, as determined by the sentencing court or the commission, for all necessary medical and related professional services relating to physical, psychiatric, and psychological care.

"10. Submission to a warrantless search by the community control or probation officer of the probationer's or community controllee's person, residence, or vehicle."

Laws 2008, c. 2008-172, § 27, in subsec. (7), inserted references to § 847.0135(5) throughout.

Laws 2008, c. 2008-238, § 23, added subsec. (11), relating to criminal gangs.

Laws 2009, c. 2009-63, § 9, in subsec. (7)(b)1., substituted "examination may" for "polygraph examination shall" following "results of the" in the last sentence; and rewrote subsec. (7)(b)5., which formerly read:

"[(7)][(b)]5. Electronic monitoring of any form when ordered by the commission."

Cross References

Habitual felony offenders and habitual violent felony offenders, provisions of this section apply, see § 775.084.

Law Review and Journal Commentaries

A Folly of Criminal Justice Policy-Making: The Rise and Demise of Early Release in Florida, and Its Ex Post Facto Implications. Chet Kaufman, 26 Fla.St.U.L.Rev. 361 (1999).

Library References

Prisons ⚷248.
Westlaw Topic No. 310.
C.J.S. Prisons and Rights of Prisoners § 152.

Research References

Encyclopedias

Persons Procuring or Authorizing Detention--Judicial and Quasi-Judicial Officers, FL Jur. 2d False Imprisonment & Malic. Prosecution § 6.

Proper Respondents, FL Jur. 2d Mandamus & Prohibition § 205.

Notification of School Districts, FL Jur. 2d Prisons & Prisoners § 14.

Particular Offenders; Information Required, FL Jur. 2d Prisons & Prisoners § 205.

Conditional Release; Prior Felons or Habitual Offenders; Sexual Predators, FL Jur. 2d Prisons & Prisoners § 212.

Entitlement to Credits or Gain-Time; Actions for Negligence in Application or Enforcement of Conditional Release or Gain-Time Statutes, FL Jur. 2d Prisons & Prisoners § 225.

Routes; Stops and Stopping, FL Jur. 2d Schools, Universities, & Colleges § 238.

Treatises and Practice Aids

16 Florida Practice Series § 1:44, Sentencing Alternatives--Straight Confinement.

16 Florida Practice Series § 2:22, Completing the 1983 Sentencing Guidelines Scoresheet--Total Sentence Imposed--Mandatory Sentences.

16 Florida Practice Series § 10:13, Post Release--Conditional Release.

16 Florida Practice Series § 10:17, Violation of Conditional Release, Control Release, Conditional Medical Release, or Addiction Recovery Supervision.

United States Code Annotated

Child protection, sex offender registration and notification, crime information databases, access, see 42 U.S.C.A. § 16961.

Sex offender registration, supervised release, see 18 U.S.C.A. § 3583.

United States Supreme Court

Searches and seizures, parolees, probable cause, see Samson v. California, 2006, 126 S.Ct. 2193.

Notes of Decisions

---

1. Validity

Imposition of conditional release supervision by Parole Commission was not violation of separation of powers, nor invalid delegation of legislative power, where state constitution gave Commission authority to grant paroles or conditional releases, rather than reserve power for courts or legislature, and legislature provided that certain inmates must remain under supervision, as determined by Commission, after release from prison for period of time equal to amount of gain time awarded. Mayes v. Moore, 827 So.2d 967 (2002), certiorari denied 123 S.Ct. 2245, 539 U.S. 904, 156 L.Ed.2d 114. Constitutional Law ⚷ 2415(1); Constitutional Law ⚷ 2625(1); Prisons ⚷ 248

Conditional release program was not bill of attainder, given that it did not punish specific individuals for acts already committed, but rather it provided for post-prison supervision for certain types of repeat offenders who commit certain new crimes. Mayes v. Moore, 827 So.2d 967 (2002), certiorari denied 123 S.Ct. 2245, 539 U.S. 904, 156 L.Ed.2d 114. Constitutional Law ⚷ 1100(4); Prisons ⚷ 248

Statute governing supervised release did not vest the Parole Commission with unlimited discretion to determine all conditions of release and thus was not unconstitutional as violating separation of powers doctrine; many conditions of supervision could be imposed by either the Parole Commission or the courts, and Parole Commission's discretion was limited in many ways. Gray v. State, App. 5 Dist., 791 So.2d 560 (2001), review denied 817 So.2d 847. Pardon And Parole ⚷ 43

2. Construction and application

Defendant's statement, in motion for postconviction relief, that he was unaware he would be released from prison subject to the provisions of conditional release until the actual day of his release could expose defendant to perjury prosecution if State fulfilled its statutory obligation to interview an inmate within 180 days before his or her tentative or provisional release date to determine the inmate's release plan, where postconviction motion was accompanied by defendant's oath "under penalties of perjury" that the facts stated in the motion were true and correct. Whitty v. State, App. 2 Dist., 5 So.3d 724 (2009). Perjury ⚷ 6

Conditional release is a legally-mandated substitute for sentenced, in-custody time, unlike probation, which is part of a sentence. Dwyer v. State, App. 4 Dist., 981 So.2d 606 (2008), review denied 7 So.3d 535. Prisons ⚷ 248; Sentencing And Punishment ⚷ 1820

The Department of Corrections (DOC) and the Parole Commission are two distinct agencies with different powers and duties under the Conditional Release Program Act. Department of Corrections v. Williams, App. 2 Dist., 901 So.2d 169 (2005). Pardon And Parole ⚷ 55.1; Prisons ⚷ 248

Parole Commission was not named as party in sex offender's petition for writ of prohibition challenging imposition of sex offender treatment program on conditional release, and thus trial court was not authorized to issue writ prohibiting Commission from enforcing terms of offender's conditional release; offender named an entity of the Department of Corrections (DOC) as party, which was distinct from Commission, having different powers and duties under Conditional Release Program Act. Department of Corrections v. Williams, App. 2 Dist., 901 So.2d 169 (2005). Pardon And Parole ⚷ 55.1; Prohibition ⚷ 19

Releasees eligible for conditional release supervision could be subject to terms of Conditional Release Program Act while they were also involuntarily civilly committed as violent sexual predators under provisions of Jimmy Ryce Act; although Conditional Release Program Act generally addressed release of individuals from prison and into community, Jimmy Ryce Act, which was more recent and more specific statute, specifically recognized that detainee under its provisions may have active term of conditional release. Parole Com'n v. Smith, App. 2 Dist., 896 So.2d 966 (2005), review denied 911 So.2d 793. Prisons ⚷ 248

If releasee fails to comply with terms and conditions of conditional release supervision under Conditional Release Program Act, releasee will be returned to prison and his or her gain time will be forfeited. Parole Com'n v. Smith, App. 2 Dist., 896 So.2d 966 (2005), review denied 911 So.2d 793. Prisons ⚷ 248

Conditional Release Program Act was enacted to address concerns with early release of certain classes of prisoners due to accrued gain time. Parole Com'n v. Smith, App. 2 Dist., 896 So.2d 966 (2005), review denied 911 So.2d 793. Prisons ⚷ 248

If a defendant may complete his conditional release supervision while in prison, he should be permitted to complete it while civilly committed. David v. Meadows, App. 1 Dist., 881 So.2d 653 (2004), rehearing denied. Mental Health ⚷ 465(5)

Sex offender, who was charged with violating his conditional release supervision by not participating in sex offender treatment program, could be on conditional release while civilly committed under the Jimmy Ryce Act; although trial court ruled that offenders could not be on conditional release while committed under the Jimmy Ryce Act since applicable statutes did not permit it, there were no restrictions found in the Conditional Release Program Act (CRPA) and the Jimmy Ryce Act that prohibited simultaneous compliance. David v. Meadows, App. 1 Dist., 881 So.2d 653 (2004), rehearing denied. Mental Health ⚷ 465(5)

Conditional release statute did not apply to defendant who had not served time for at least one prior felony, even though he had been twice "committed" to prison based on same conviction for attempted second degree murder; statute required that to qualify for conditional release, an inmate who was not an habitual or violent habitual offender or a violent career criminal or a sexual predator must have been convicted of one of the qualifying crimes and have served time for at least one prior felony. Jongewaard v. State, App. 5 Dist., 824 So.2d 1009 (2002). Pardon And Parole ⚷ 48.1

The Conditional Release Program Act was designed to prevent certain repeat offenders' early, unsupervised release from incarceration, by making them subject to supervision, in the event of early release, and to possible reincarceration. Gove v. Florida Parole Com'n, App. 1 Dist., 816 So.2d 1150 (2002), rehearing denied. Pardon And Parole ⚷ 50

Conditional release statute did not apply to defendant who had not completed service of first felony commitment until he was conditionally released, despite fact that defendant was released early because of gain time, where statute clearly required that to qualify for conditional release, an inmate who was not an habitual or violent habitual offender or a violent career criminal or a sexual predator must have been convicted of one of the qualifying crimes and have served time for at least one prior felony. Gove v. Florida Parole Com'n, App. 1 Dist., 816 So.2d 1150 (2002), rehearing denied. Pardon And Parole ⚷ 41

Current Parole Commission rule providing that "prior felony commitment" meant an offense or offenses which resulted in an adjudication of guilt of a felony and a sentence of incarceration was consistent with conditional release statute, presumptively valid, and thus District Court of Appeal accorded it due consideration. Gove v. Florida Parole Com'n, App. 1 Dist., 816 So.2d 1150 (2002), rehearing denied. Pardon And Parole ⚷ 55.1

Statutes governing conditional release of inmates and gain-time credits create no duty on the part of the Parole Commission or the Department of Corrections (DOC) for the benefit of any private person, including inmates or parolees and thus afford no basis for an action by any aggrieved individual for alleged negligence or errors in their application or enforcement. Andrews v. Florida Parole Com'n, App. 1 Dist., 768 So.2d 1257 (2000), review granted 789 So.2d 343, review dismissed as improvidently granted 791 So.2d 1093. Action ⚷ 3; Pardon And Parole ⚷ 56; Prisons ⚷ 309

Parole Commission may not transfer conditional release supervision from an expired conditional release sentence to the end of inmate's overall sentence and determine length of that supervision by gain time awarded and length of sentences in nonconditional release eligible cases; Commission may only transfer supervision to the end of the overall sentence for offenses committed after 1997 amendment to conditional release statute. Pressley v. Singletary, 724 So.2d 97 (1997), rehearing denied. Prisons ⚷ 248

Parole Commission has broad authority to either grant or deny releasee credit for time spent on conditional release when that release is revoked due to violation of terms and conditions of release. Rivera v. Singletary, 707 So.2d 326 (1998). Prisons ⚷ 248

Under prior version of conditional release statute, inmate who has been sentenced as a habitual or violent habitual offender but who is not convicted of category 1, category 2, category 3, or category 4 crime qualifies for conditional release. Deason v. Florida Dept. of Corrections, 705 So.2d 1374 (1998). Prisons ⚷ 245(3)

Revoking gain time was improper for grand theft that was not subject to Conditional Release Act, even though defendant served sentence concurrently with sentences for robbery, battery on law enforcement officer, and resistance of arrest with violence subject to the Act; thus, last date of conditional release supervision should have been calculated with reference only to sentences that were subject to the Act. Cooper v. Florida Parole Com'n, App. 4 Dist., 691 So.2d 521 (1997), review granted 698 So.2d 848, approved 701 So.2d 543, rehearing denied. Prisons ⚷ 248

Conditional release statute provided for habitualized sentencing as separate independent criterion for conditional release and did not additionally require conviction of crime enumerated in category 1, 2, 3, or 4 of sentencing guidelines. Deason v. State, App. 1 Dist., 688 So.2d 988 (1997), review granted 697 So.2d 510, approved 705 So.2d 1374. Prisons ⚷ 248

Sentence in habitual offender sentencing statute, stating that provisions of chapter on parole and probation commission shall not apply to habitual felony offenders, does not preclude habitual offenders' placement on conditional release when incentive gain-time makes further incarceration unlawful; statute specifically applying conditional release program to habitual and violent habitual offenders controls over such sentence, which addresses application of the parole and probation chapter only generally, particularly where such chapter did not contain act relating to conditional release program until subsequent to the amendment adding such sentence; sentence's reference to parole and probation chapter refers to other forms of early release, notably parole, and not to conditional release program. Lincoln v. Florida Parole Com'n, App. 1 Dist., 643 So.2d 668 (1994). Prisons ⚷ 248

3. Due process

Fact that conditional release statutes did not contain list of prohibited acts that could result in revocation of conditional release did not deprive inmate, who had not yet been placed on conditional release, of due process; order of conditional release would notify inmate of the conditions that applied. Brooks v. Florida Parole Com'n, App. 4 Dist., 974 So.2d 494 (2008), rehearing denied, review denied 988 So.2d 621. Constitutional Law ⚷ 4830; Prisons ⚷ 248

Conditional release program was not recidivist statute, and thus defendants were not entitled to actual notice of applicability of conditional release, nor opportunity to be heard prior to pleas, even though conditional release applied to recidivists or repeat offenders, given that conditional release did not increase maximum sentences, but rather required that sentences be completed outside prison, under supervision, as part of assistance program, that was not form of sentence, nor imposed by court, eligibility was established by statute, and placement on program was required by Parole Commission. Mayes v. Moore, 827 So.2d 967 (2002), certiorari denied 123 S.Ct. 2245, 539 U.S. 904, 156 L.Ed.2d 114. Prisons ⚷ 248

Inmate's placement on Conditional Release did not violate due process on ground that it improperly took away liberty interest in the gain time he had been awarded, as inmate only had conditional liberty interest in gain time, and if inmate lost gain time it would only be after due process of law. Duncan v. Moore, 754 So.2d 708 (2000). Constitutional Law ⚷ 4830; Prisons ⚷ 248

4. Double jeopardy

Requiring that a Conditional Release eligible inmate finish his sentence by satisfactorily completing a period of post-prison supervision equal to the amount of gain time awarded did not violate double jeopardy. Duncan v. Moore, 754 So.2d 708 (2000). Double Jeopardy ⚷ 31

Returning a Conditional Release violator to prison to continue serving his sentence without credit for the prior awarded gain time does not constitute a violation of double jeopardy, as long as releasee's underlying criminal offense was committed on or after effective date of statute providing for forfeiture of gain time upon Conditional Release revocation. Duncan v. Moore, 754 So.2d 708 (2000). Double Jeopardy ⚷ 31

5. Retroactive application

Subjecting inmate to Conditional Release was not an ex post facto violation, where Conditional Release statute and its corresponding gain time forfeiture statute had gone into effect years before inmate committed his crime, and thus, there was no retrospective application of a later-enacted statute to inmate. Duncan v. Moore, 754 So.2d 708 (2000). Constitutional Law ⚷ 2816; Prisons ⚷ 248

6. Waiver of objection

Defendant did not waive his right to object to conditional release terms by accepting terms set by Parole Commission at time of release, and thus defendant could challenge legality of conditional release upon subsequent determination that he had violated terms of conditional release; Commission's application of criteria for conditional release did not constitute a judgment or judicial order to which inmate was required or permitted to object. Gove v. Florida Parole Com'n, App. 1 Dist., 816 So.2d 1150 (2002), rehearing denied. Pardon And Parole ⚷ 65; Pardon And Parole ⚷ 92

Only sentences imposed for offenses committed after effective date of Conditional Release Program Act can be used by Parole Commission when calculating defendant's last date of conditional release supervision; three offenses committed nine months before effective date of Act could not be considered. Westlund v. Florida Parole Com'n, App. 1 Dist., 637 So.2d 52 (1994). Pardon And Parole ⚷ 67

Defendant did not waive objection to Parole Commission's use of sentences for offenses committed before effective date of Conditional Release Program Act to calculate last date of conditional release supervision by failing to challenge terms of conditional release prior to revocation; there was no judicial order or judgment from which defendant was required or allowed to object and defendant refused to sign certificate of conditional release that included improperly calculated date. Westlund v. Florida Parole Com'n, App. 1 Dist., 637 So.2d 52 (1994). Pardon And Parole ⚷ 67

7. Duties of parole commission

Parole Commission is the agency charged with the initial responsibility for interpreting statute governing Conditional Release program, which it must then apply based upon the circumstances presented by a particular inmate's record. Gray v. State, App. 5 Dist., 791 So.2d 560 (2001), review denied 817 So.2d 847. Pardon And Parole ⚷ 55.1

Parole Commission acted within the scope of its quasi-judicial duties when it placed inmate on conditional release, had jurisdiction over him and the terms of conditional release, and, therefore, enjoyed judicial immunity from liability for false imprisonment, even though the Commission miscalculated the date of release from supervision resulting in incarceration for eleven months beyond the time permitted. Andrews v. Florida Parole Com'n, App. 1 Dist., 768 So.2d 1257 (2000), review granted 789 So.2d 343, review dismissed as improvidently granted 791 So.2d 1093. Pardon And Parole ⚷ 56

Parole Commission has broad authority to grant or deny credit for time spent on conditional release supervision upon revocation of supervision. Bolden v. Florida Dept. of Corrections, App. 1 Dist., 865 So.2d 1 (2003), rehearing granted, review granted 848 So.2d 1153, review dismissed 867 So.2d 373. Prisons ⚷ 248

8. Concurrent sentences

When inmate who is serving concurrent sentences is released after accruing sufficient gain time and release on one or more sentences is conditional under Conditional Release Program Act, inmate's release status is not revoked as to all concurrent sentences, including sentences imposed for offenses that did not qualify for conditional release. Parole Com'n v. Cooper, 701 So.2d 543 (1997), rehearing denied. Prisons ⚷ 248

Inmate's last date of conditional release supervision should lawfully be calculated with reference only to sentences covered under Conditional Release Program Act; distinct sentences that inmate is serving concurrently to sentences for covered offenses do not subject inmate to further supervision under Act. Parole Com'n v. Cooper, 701 So.2d 543 (1997), rehearing denied. Prisons ⚷ 248

Concurrent sentences remained distinct sentences for purpose of eligibility under Conditional Release Act. Cooper v. Florida Parole Com'n, App. 4 Dist., 691 So.2d 521 (1997), review granted 698 So.2d 848, approved 701 So.2d 543, rehearing denied. Prisons ⚷ 248

9. Parole release date

Department of Corrections (DOC) was entitled to accept the Parole Commission's arrest warrants as lawful, as they were regular on their face and issued by a legal body having authority to issue warrants, and, therefore, was not liable for false imprisonment of parolee due to Commission's miscalculation of the date of release from supervision. Andrews v. Florida Parole Com'n, App. 1 Dist., 768 So.2d 1257 (2000), review granted 789 So.2d 343, review dismissed as improvidently granted 791 So.2d 1093. States ⚷ 112.2(4)

Department of Corrections, in calculating new release date following revocation of conditional release supervision, should not have considered, as tolled, the time that inmate served following expiration of incarcerative portion of sentence for shotgun offense while inmate awaited expiration of incarcerative portions of sentences for assault and battery offenses which arose from same 1992 criminal episode, and thus, Department was not permitted to add such "tolled" time onto sentence in calculating new release date. Bolden v. Florida Dept. of Corrections, App. 1 Dist., 865 So.2d 1 (2003), rehearing granted, review granted 848 So.2d 1153, review dismissed 867 So.2d 373. Prisons ⚷ 248

10. Length of community supervision period

Inmates who meet the statutory conditional release criteria are released to community supervision for a period equal to the amount of gain time earned while incarcerated. Dwyer v. State, App. 4 Dist., 981 So.2d 606 (2008), review denied 7 So.3d 535. Prisons ⚷ 248

11. Conditional release

"Conditional release" is a post-prison program under which a defendant who meets the specified statutory criteria may be released from prison prior to the expiration of his or her imposed sentence based on earned gain time, but remains under the supervision of the Department of Corrections for a period equal to the amount of the gain time earned while incarcerated. Chandler v. State, App. 2 Dist., 1 So.3d 284 (2009). Prisons ⚷ 248

If an offender placed on conditional release violates a condition of the release prior to the expiration of his or her full, pronounced prison term, gain time and release are revoked and the offender may be re-incarcerated for the balance of the original sentence imposed. Dwyer v. State, App. 4 Dist., 981 So.2d 606 (2008), review denied 7 So.3d 535. Prisons ⚷ 248

Conditional release is an additional post-prison supervision program for certain types of offenders that the legislature has determined to be in need of further supervision after release. Dwyer v. State, App. 4 Dist., 981 So.2d 606 (2008), review denied 7 So.3d 535. Prisons ⚷ 248

Sentencing court did not have authority to mandate or waive statutory requirement for conditional release supervision for prisoner who met statutory criteria for conditional release supervision, and thus, trial court's failure to impose conditional release supervision as part of sentence was not grounds for challenge to release to conditional release supervision. Logan v. State, App. 5 Dist., 964 So.2d 209 (2007). Prisons ⚷ 248

Inmates who meet the statutory conditional release criteria are released to community supervision for a period equal to the amount of gain time earned while incarcerated; however, if they violate a condition of release prior to the expiration of their full, pronounced prison term, gain time and release are revoked, and they may be re-incarcerated for the balance of their sentence. Logan v. State, App. 5 Dist., 964 So.2d 209 (2007). Prisons ⚷ 248

Hearing officer's finding that parolee's violation of conditional release by leaving county was not willful was supported by substantial evidence in record, and thus, precluded revocation of conditional release. Ellis v. Florida Parole Com'n, App. 1 Dist., 911 So.2d 831 (2005), rehearing denied. Pardon And Parole ⚷ 90

Parole Commission was without statutory authority to subject petitioner to conditional release supervision, where statute required that sentence for prior qualifying offense must have been served at state or federal correctional institution in order for petitioner to be subject to conditional release supervision, and petitioner served his sentence for prior qualifying offense in house of correction which, under law of state in which sentence was served, was county facility, rather than state facility. Hayes v. David, App. 1 Dist., 875 So.2d 678 (2004). Pardon And Parole ⚷ 64.1

Defendant could not be readjudicated guilty of attempted sexual battery upon a child when his probation was subsequently revoked, and thus offense could not be used to impose conditional release supervision based on adjudication for enumerated offense and prior felony commitment, where defendant had already been adjudicated guilty for offense, and at time of adjudication he had never served prior felony sentence. Mosley v. State, App. 5 Dist., 820 So.2d 395 (2002), rehearing denied. Double Jeopardy ⚷ 31; Prisons ⚷ 248

Defendant's conditional release, as an extra post-prison, probation-type program, was not a benefit, but an additional burden to him. Gove v. Florida Parole Com'n, App. 1 Dist., 816 So.2d 1150 (2002), rehearing denied. Pardon And Parole ⚷ 64.1

Conditional Release is not an early release program, but is an additional post-prison supervision program for certain types of offenders that the Legislature has determined to be in need of further supervision after release and who are entitled to accumulated gain time. Gray v. State, App. 5 Dist., 791 So.2d 560 (2001), review denied 817 So.2d 847. Pardon And Parole ⚷ 41

Retention of earned gain time was dependent not only upon satisfactory behavior while in prison but also upon satisfactory behavior while under Conditional Release supervision. Duncan v. Moore, 754 So.2d 708 (2000). Prisons ⚷ 248

Although the State cannot transfer the conditional release supervision of an expired sentence to the end of a longer sentence that is not eligible for conditional release and determine the length of that supervision by the ineligible sentence, it may use an unexpired eligible sentence to determine the length of the supervision and then toll the beginning of the supervision period until the inmate has been released from prison. Evans v. Singletary, 737 So.2d 505 (1999). Prisons ⚷ 248

Conditional release (as opposed to control release, provisional credits, and administrative gain time) is not an early release program, but is an extra post-prison probation-type program. Evans v. Singletary, 737 So.2d 505 (1999). Sentencing And Punishment ⚷ 1820

When an inmate is released due to gain time from a sentence that is eligible for conditional release, the inmate is placed on supervision for the amount of time equal to the gain time accrued, but forfeits gain time and is returned to prison to continue serving the sentence, if the inmate violates supervision. Evans v. Singletary, 737 So.2d 505 (1999). Prisons ⚷ 248

Length of conditional release supervision is equal to amount of gain time that inmate has accrued prior to release. Bolden v. Florida Dept. of Corrections, App. 1 Dist., 865 So.2d 1 (2003), rehearing granted, review granted 848 So.2d 1153, review dismissed 867 So.2d 373. Prisons ⚷ 248

12. Special conditions

Parole Commission had discretionary authority to impose special conditions on petitioner's conditional release supervision under statute permitting it to "impose any special conditions" it considered warranted from its review of the record, even though petitioner's conviction preceded effective date of statute requiring imposition of special conditions of conditional release supervision for certain sexual offenders. Velez v. State, App. 2 Dist., 23 So.3d 808 (2009). Sentencing and Punishment ⚷ 1962

Florida Parole Commission had discretionary authority to impose a curfew as a condition of the conditional release of defendant, who was convicted of robbery, kidnapping, and other crimes he committed after the conditional release program was in effect. Ortiz v. Florida Parole Com'n, App. 3 Dist., 15 So.3d 941 (2009). Pardon and Parole ⚷ 64.1

A habeas petition or mandamus petition can be utilized to challenge a condition of conditional release imposed by the Florida Parole Commission. Ortiz v. Florida Parole Com'n, App. 3 Dist., 15 So.3d 941 (2009). Habeas Corpus ⚷ 512.1; Mandamus ⚷ 73(1)

Florida Parole Commission (FPC) had authority to impose special sexual offender conditions on defendant's conditional release supervision, even though defendant's sexual battery convictions preceded effective date of statute requiring imposition of special sexual offender conditions on sexual offenders; such statute did not affect FPC's discretionary authority to "impose any special conditions it considers warranted" from its review of the record. Grace v. Florida Parole Com'n, App. 1 Dist., 985 So.2d 1213 (2008). Pardon And Parole ⚷ 64.1

13. Credit for time served

Defendant who received consecutive term of probation in first of two cases was entitled to 17 years' credit for time served in second case, including all gain time, upon resentencing in first case following arrest for violation of probation and the apparent revocation of probation, where both cases were originally sentenced together on the same scoresheet and State was unable to show that defendant was on conditional release in second case. Jefferson v. State, App. 4 Dist., 937 So.2d 833 (2006). Sentencing And Punishment ⚷ 2041

14. Jurisdiction

Parole Commission's jurisdiction to conduct conditional release revocation hearing was not affected by its failure to conduct hearing within 45 days after inmate's arrest for violation of terms of his conditional release, as required by statute, where inmate was still on conditional release supervision at time of hearing, and

Commission had jurisdiction over inmate until his conditional release supervision terminated. Gillard v. State, App. 1 Dist., 827 So.2d 316 (2002), rehearing denied, review denied 842 So.2d 844. Pardon And Parole ⚷ 82

15. Postconviction relief

Placement of defendant on statutorily-mandated conditional release did not constitute newly discovered evidence warranting exception to otherwise applicable two-year limitations period for filing motion for post-conviction relief; defendant did not allege that the statutory requirement of conditional release could not have been discovered within two years of his sentence, and conditional release was an application of long-standing statutory law. Dwyer v. State, App. 4 Dist., 981 So.2d 606 (2008), review denied 7 So.3d 535. Criminal Law ⚷ 1586

16. Review

Appeal, rather than certiorari, was the appropriate method of review for trial court's decision to grant sex offender's petition for writ of prohibition, thereby prohibiting Parole Commission from enforcing terms of offender's conditional release, as trial court's error, in issuing writ against Parole Commission despite fact that Commission was not named as a party, was not an act made in its review capacity. Department of Corrections v. Williams, App. 2 Dist., 901 So.2d 169 (2005). Pardon And Parole ⚷ 62

Although District Court of Appeal's scope of review is narrow, certiorari will lie to correct erroneous determination that inmate is subject to conditional release program. Hayes v. David, App. 1 Dist., 875 So.2d 678 (2004). Pardon And Parole ⚷ 62

947.141. Violations of conditional release, control release, or conditional medical release or addiction-recovery supervision

(1) If a member of the commission or a duly authorized representative of the commission has reasonable grounds to believe that an offender who is on release supervision under s. 947.1405, s. 947.146, s. 947.149, or s. 944.4731 has violated the terms and conditions of the release in a material respect, such member or representative may cause a warrant to be issued for the arrest of the releasee; if the offender was found to be a sexual predator, the warrant must be issued.

(2) Upon the arrest on a felony charge of an offender who is on release supervision under s. 947.1405, s. 947.146, s. 947.149, or s. 944.4731, the offender must be detained without bond until the initial appearance of the offender at which a judicial determination of probable cause is made. If the trial court judge determines that there was no probable cause for the arrest, the offender may be released. If the trial court judge determines that there was probable cause for the arrest, such determination also constitutes reasonable grounds to believe that the offender violated the conditions of the release. Within 24 hours after the trial court judge's finding of probable cause, the detention facility administrator or designee shall notify the commission and the department of the finding and transmit to each a facsimile copy of the probable cause affidavit or the sworn offense report upon which the trial court judge's probable cause determination is based. The offender must continue to be detained without bond for a period not exceeding 72 hours excluding weekends and holidays after the date of the probable cause determination, pending a decision by the commission whether to issue a warrant charging the offender with violation of the conditions of release. Upon the issuance of the commission's warrant, the offender must continue to be held in custody pending a revocation hearing held in accordance with this section.

(3) Within 45 days after notice to the Parole Commission of the arrest of a releasee charged with a violation of the terms and conditions of conditional

release, control release, conditional medical release, or addiction-recovery supervision, the releasee must be afforded a hearing conducted by a commissioner or a duly authorized representative thereof. If the releasee elects to proceed with a hearing, the releasee must be informed orally and in writing of the following:

(a) The alleged violation with which the releasee is charged.

(b) The releasee's right to be represented by counsel.

(c) The releasee's right to be heard in person.

(d) The releasee's right to secure, present, and compel the attendance of witnesses relevant to the proceeding.

(e) The releasee's right to produce documents on the releasee's own behalf.

(f) The releasee's right of access to all evidence used against the releasee and to confront and cross-examine adverse witnesses.

(g) The releasee's right to waive the hearing.

(4) Within a reasonable time following the hearing, the commissioner or the commissioner's duly authorized representative who conducted the hearing shall make findings of fact in regard to the alleged violation. A panel of no fewer than two commissioners shall enter an order determining whether the charge of violation of conditional release, control release, conditional medical release, or addiction-recovery supervision has been sustained based upon the findings of fact presented by the hearing commissioner or authorized representative. By such order, the panel may revoke conditional release, control release, conditional medical release, or addiction-recovery supervision and thereby return the releasee to prison to serve the sentence imposed, reinstate the original order granting the release, or enter such other order as it considers proper. Effective for inmates whose offenses were committed on or after July 1, 1995, the panel may order the placement of a releasee, upon a finding of violation pursuant to this subsection, into a local detention facility as a condition of supervision.

(5) Effective for inmates whose offenses were committed on or after July 1, 1995, notwithstanding the provisions of ss. 775.08, former 921.001, 921.002, 921.187, 921.188, 944.02, and 951.23, or any other law to the contrary, by such order as provided in subsection (4), the panel, upon a finding of guilt, may, as a condition of continued supervision, place the releasee in a local detention facility for a period of incarceration not to exceed 22 months. Prior to the expiration of the term of incarceration, or upon recommendation of the chief correctional officer of that county, the commission shall cause inquiry into the inmate's release plan and custody status in the detention facility and consider whether to restore the inmate to supervision, modify the conditions of supervision, or enter an order of revocation, thereby causing the return of the inmate to prison to serve the sentence imposed. The provisions of this section do not prohibit the panel from entering such other order or conducting any investigation that it deems proper. The commission may only place a person in a local detention facility pursuant to this section if there is a contractual agreement between the chief correctional officer of that county and the Department of Corrections. The agreement must provide for a per diem reimbursement for

each person placed under this section, which is payable by the Department of Corrections for the duration of the offender's placement in the facility. This section does not limit the commission's ability to place a person in a local detention facility for less than 1 year.

(6) Whenever a conditional release, control release, conditional medical release, or addiction-recovery supervision is revoked by a panel of no fewer than two commissioners and the releasee is ordered to be returned to prison, the releasee, by reason of the misconduct, shall be deemed to have forfeited all gain-time or commutation of time for good conduct, as provided for by law, earned up to the date of release. However, if a conditional medical release is revoked due to the improved medical or physical condition of the releasee, the releasee shall not forfeit gain-time accrued before the date of conditional medical release. This subsection does not deprive the prisoner of the right to gain-time or commutation of time for good conduct, as provided by law, from the date of return to prison.

(7) If a law enforcement officer has probable cause to believe that an offender who is on release supervision under s. 947.1405, s. 947.146, s. 947.149, or s. 944.4731 has violated the terms and conditions of his or her release by committing a felony offense, the officer shall arrest the offender without a warrant, and a warrant need not be issued in the case.

Laws 1988, c. 88–122, § 20; Laws 1993, c. 93–61, § 5; Laws 1993, c. 93–277, § 5; Laws 1994, c. 94–121, § 1; Laws 1995, c. 95–283, §§ 40, 58. Amended by Laws 1997, c. 97–194, § 30, eff. Oct. 1, 1998; Laws 1997, c. 97–239, § 4, eff. May 30, 1997; Laws 2001, c. 2001–110, § 15, eff. July 1, 2001; Laws 2002, c. 2002–255, § 2, eff. Oct. 1, 2002; Laws 2004, c. 2004–11, § 49, eff. Oct. 1, 2004.

Historical and Statutory Notes

Amendment Notes:

Laws 1993, c. 93–61, § 5, eff. April 22, 1993, rewrote the section, which formerly read:

"(1) If a member of the commission or a duly authorized representative of the commission has reasonable grounds to believe that an offender released under s. 947.1405 has violated the terms and conditions of his release in a material respect, such member or representative may cause a warrant to be issued for the arrest of the releasee.

"(2) Within 45 days after the arrest of a releasee charged with a violation of the terms and conditions of conditional release, the releasee must be afforded a hearing conducted by a commissioner or a duly authorized representative thereof. If the releasee elects to proceed with a hearing, he must be informed orally and in writing of the following:

"(a) The alleged violation with which he is charged.

"(b) His right to be represented by counsel.

"(c) His right to be heard in person.

"(d) His right to secure, present, and compel the attendance of witnesses relevant to the proceeding.

"(e) His right to produce documents on his own behalf.

"(f) His right of access to all evidence used against him and to confront and cross-examine adverse witnesses.

"(g) His right to waive the hearing.

"(3) Within a reasonable time following the hearing, the commissioner or his duly authorized representative who conducted the hearing shall make findings of fact in regard to the alleged violation. A majority of the commission shall enter an order determining whether the charge of violation of conditional release has been sustained based upon the findings of fact presented by the hearing commissioner or authorized representative. By such order, the commission shall revoke conditional release and thereby return the releasee to prison to serve the sentence imposed upon him, reinstate the original order granting conditional release, or enter such other order as it considers proper.

"(4) Whenever a conditional release is revoked by the commission and the releasee is ordered by the commission to be returned to prison, the releasee, by reason of his misconduct, may be deemed to have forfeited all gain-time or commutation of time for good conduct, as provided for by law, earned up to the date of his conditional release. This subsection does not deprive the prisoner of his right to gain-time or commutation of time for good conduct, as provided by law, from the date on which he is returned to prison."

Laws 1993, c. 93–277, § 5, eff. Oct. 1, 1993, in subsec. (1), added "however, if the offender was found to be a sexual predator, the warrant shall be issued".

Laws 1994, c. 94–121, § 1, eff. May 4, 1994, and applicable to arrests on charges of felony offenses committed on or after that date, in subsec. (1), substituted "who is on release supervision" for "released", "the release" for "his release", "must" for "shall", and following the semicolon, deleted "however,"; inserted a new subsec. (2) and redesignated subsequent subsections; in subsecs. (3) and (5), substituted "the releasee" for "he" or "him" and substituted "the releasee's" for "his" and made conforming changes; in subsec. (4), substituted "the commissioner's" for "his" and deleted another gender-specific reference; and, near the end of subsec. (5), substituted "date of return" for "date on which he is returned".

Laws 1995, c. 95–283, § 40, eff. June 15, 1995, in subsec. (4), added the last sentence; inserted subsec. (5); and redesignated former subsec. (5) as subsec. (6).

Laws 1995, c. 95–283, § 58, eff. June 15, 1995, reenacted subsecs. (1) and (2) of this section for the purpose of incorporating an amendment to § 947.1405 in references thereto.

Laws 1997, c. 97–194, § 30, eff. Oct. 1, 1998, in subsec. (5), corrected citations.

Laws 1997, c. 97–239, § 4, eff. May 30, 1997, in subsec. (6), in the first sentence, substituted "shall" for "may".

Laws 2001, c. 2001–110, § 15, in the heading, inserted "or addition-recovery supervision" following "release"; in subsecs. (1) and (2), inserted ", or s. 944.4731" following "947.149"; and, in subsecs. (3), (4), and (6), inserted ", or addiction-recovery supervision" following "release".

Laws 2002, c. 2002–255, § 2, added subsec. (7), relating to arrest of an offender without a warrant if an officer has probable cause to believe that the offender has violated the terms of supervised release.

Laws 2004, c. 2004–11, § 49, in subsec. (2), substituted references to trial court judge for references to magistrates throughout.

Cross References

Sexual Predators Act, see § 775.21.

Law Review and Journal Commentaries

A Folly of Criminal Justice Policy–Making: The Rise and Demise of Early Release in Florida, and Its Ex Post Facto Implications. Chet Kaufman, 26 Fla.St.U.L.Rev. 361 (1999).

Library References

Prisons ⚷248.
Westlaw Topic No. 310.
C.J.S. Prisons and Rights of Prisoners § 152.

Research References

ALR Library

95 ALR 2nd 1265, Withdrawal, Forfeiture, Modification, or Denial of Good-Time Allowance to Prisoner.

Encyclopedias

Notification of School Districts, FL Jur. 2d Prisons & Prisoners § 14.

Particular Offenders; Information Required, FL Jur. 2d Prisons & Prisoners § 205.

Treatises and Practice Aids

16 Florida Practice Series § 1:52, Sentencing Alternatives--Concurrent and Consecutive Sentencing.

16 Florida Practice Series § 10:14, Post Release--Conditional Medical Release.

16 Florida Practice Series § 10:15, Post Release--Control Release.

16 Florida Practice Series § 10:16, Post Release--Addiction Recovery Supervision.

16 Florida Practice Series § 10:17, Violation of Conditional Release, Control Release, Conditional Medical Release, or Addiction Recovery Supervision.

Notes of Decisions

---

1. Validity

Statute governing supervised release did not vest the Parole Commission with unlimited discretion to determine all conditions of release and thus was not unconstitutional as violating separation of powers doctrine; many conditions of supervision could be imposed by either the Parole Commission or the courts, and Parole Commission's discretion was limited in many ways. Gray v. State, App. 5 Dist., 791 So.2d 560 (2001), review denied 817 So.2d 847. Pardon And Parole ⚷ 43

2. Construction and application

Releasees eligible for conditional release supervision could be subject to terms of Conditional Release Program Act while they were also involuntarily civilly committed as violent sexual predators under provisions of Jimmy Ryce Act; although Conditional Release Program Act generally addressed release of individuals from prison and into community, Jimmy Ryce Act, which was more recent and more specific statute, specifically recognized that detainee under its provisions may have active term of conditional release. Parole Com'n v. Smith, App. 2 Dist., 896 So.2d 966 (2005), review denied 911 So.2d 793. Prisons ⚷ 248

3. Due process

State parole commission, in revoking prisoner's control release supervision, failed to comply with procedures mandated under Florida law, and thus violated prisoner's Fourteenth Amendment due process rights; commission effectively rejected parole examiner's factual findings regarding domestic battery incident and substituted its own findings, even though findings of examiner were supported by competent, substantial evidence. Collins v. Hendrickson, M.D.Fla.2005, 371 F.Supp.2d 1326. Constitutional Law ⚷ 4838; Pardon And Parole ⚷ 90

Fact that conditional release statutes did not contain list of prohibited acts that could result in revocation of conditional release did not deprive inmate, who had not yet been placed on conditional release, of due process; order of conditional release would notify inmate of the conditions that applied. Brooks v. Florida Parole Com'n, App. 4 Dist., 974 So.2d 494 (2008), rehearing denied, review denied 988 So.2d 621. Constitutional Law ⚷ 4830; Prisons ⚷ 248

In general, parole revocation hearings are governed by due process considerations and are subject to the requirement that they be conducted within a reasonable time. Gillard v. State, App. 1 Dist., 827 So.2d 316 (2002), rehearing denied, review denied 842 So.2d 844. Constitutional Law ⚷ 4838; Pardon And Parole ⚷ 82

4. Sentences

Parole Commission has broad authority to grant or deny credit for time spent on conditional release supervision upon revocation of supervision. Bolden v. Florida Dept. of Corrections, App. 1 Dist., 865 So.2d 1 (2003), rehearing granted, review granted 848 So.2d 1153, review dismissed 867 So.2d 373. Prisons ⚷ 248

A court may order a new sentence to run consecutive to punishment for a control-release violation. Scantling v. State, 711 So.2d 524 (1998). Sentencing And Punishment ⚷ 555

Parole Commission has broad authority to either grant or deny releasee credit for time spent on conditional release when that release is revoked due to violation of terms and conditions of release. Rivera v. Singletary, 707 So.2d 326 (1998). Prisons ⚷ 248

Sentence imposed for offense committed while on control release could be made consecutive to sentence to be served in connection with violation of control release; latter sentence was not new sentence, but continuation of sentence previously determined and imposed; receding from *Currelly v. State*. Scantling v. State, App. 1 Dist., 704 So.2d 565 (1997), review granted 700 So.2d 687, approved 711 So.2d 524. Sentencing And Punishment ⚷ 637

Parole Commission has broad authority in administering control release program, including authority to either grant or deny credit for time spent under supervision when it determines that releasee has violated terms of release. Gay v. Singletary, 700 So.2d 1220 (1997). Prisons ⚷ 248

Prisoner, who violated terms of his conditional release and was re-incarcerated, was not entitled to credit for time served while he was out of prison as conditional releasee; sentence defendant received was term of years, not a specific release date. Fleming v. State, App. 5 Dist., 697 So.2d 1322 (1997). Prisons ⚷ 248

5. Unrelated conduct

Criminal conduct alleged to have occurred prior to conduct forming basis for arrest, unrelated to such conduct, and charged separately from such conduct could not amount to violation of supervised release imposed following arrest. Kablitz v. Bieluch, App. 4 Dist., 872 So.2d 429 (2004). Bail ⚷ 75.1

Information concerning charges pending against arrestee seeking to post bond, which information was not known to committing magistrate who set bond, could not form basis for denial of release and discharge of warrant for violation of supervised release after pending charges were brought to magistrate's attention. Kablitz v. Bieluch, App. 4 Dist., 872 So.2d 429 (2004). Bail ⚷ 75.1

6. Gain time forfeiture

Upon revocation of conditional release, Department of Corrections (DOC) is not authorized to calculate inmate's new release date by using the gain time forfeited on the release eligible sentence with the most accrued gain time, so as to require inmate to serve more incarceration than imposed by sentencing judge; disapproving *Crosby v. McNeal*, 865 So.2d 617. McNeil v. Canty, 12 So.3d 215 (2009). Prisons ⚷ 248

If an offender placed on conditional release violates a condition of the release prior to the expiration of his or her full, pronounced prison term, gain time and release are revoked and the offender may be re-incarcerated for the balance of the original sentence imposed. Dwyer v. State, App. 4 Dist., 981 So.2d 606 (2008), review denied 7 So.3d 535. Prisons ⚷ 248

Upon a prisoner's return to prison following the revocation of his control release or conditional release, the Department of Corrections (DOC) is allowed to forfeit gain time that was earned prior to being placed on control release or conditional release. Davis v. State, App. 5 Dist., 943 So.2d 975 (2006). Prisons ⚷ 248

If releasee fails to comply with terms and conditions of conditional release supervision under Conditional Release Program Act, releasee will be returned to prison and his or her gain time will be forfeited. Parole Com'n v. Smith, App. 2 Dist., 896 So.2d 966 (2005), review denied 911 So.2d 793. Prisons ⚷ 248

Conditional Release Program Act was enacted to address concerns with early release of certain classes of prisoners due to accrued gain time. Parole Com'n v. Smith, App. 2 Dist., 896 So.2d 966 (2005), review denied 911 So.2d 793. Prisons ⚷ 248

An inmate waives any ex post facto argument as to forfeiture of gain time upon revocation of control release by electing to accept the terms and conditions of early release under the control release program. Knox v. State, App. 5 Dist., 873 So.2d 1250 (2004), cause dismissed 884 So.2d 22. Constitutional Law ⚷ 947; Prisons ⚷ 248

Gain time credits could be forfeited for conduct that occurred before credits were awarded nunc pro tunc, given that credits were earned prior to behavior underlying forfeiture, credits were recorded as if awarded at appropriate time in past, and conditional release statute specifically provided for forfeiture of all gain time earned up to date of release. Mayes v. Moore, 827 So.2d 967 (2002), certiorari denied 123 S.Ct. 2245, 539 U.S. 904, 156 L.Ed.2d 114. Prisons ⚷ 247

Inmate was not entitled to basic gain time on remainder of his sentence after he was returned to prison as a conditional release violator, where no new sentence was imposed. Hull v. Moore, App. 1 Dist., 790 So.2d 560 (2001). Prisons ⚷ 245(3)

Forfeiture of control release credits along with forfeiture of regular gain time upon supervision revocation did not violate ex post facto clause, although releasee committed underlying criminal offense prior to effective date of control release program, where releasee had voluntarily accepted placement on that program and then violated terms and conditions of control release; by accepting release under control release program, releasee waived any ex post facto claims. Lewis v. Moore, 753 So.2d 1242 (2000). Constitutional Law ⚷ 951; Constitutional Law ⚷ 2816; Prisons ⚷ 248

By accepting terms and conditions of early release under control release program, which included forfeiture of basic and incentive gain time upon revocation of control release, inmate waived any ex post facto argument as to forfeiture of such gain time after violation of control release. Bowles v. Singletary, 698 So.2d 1201 (1997), rehearing denied. Constitutional Law ⚷ 948

7. Revocation hearings

Parole Commission's jurisdiction to conduct conditional release revocation hearing was not affected by its failure to conduct hearing within 45 days after inmate's arrest for violation of terms of his conditional release, as required by statute, where inmate was still on conditional release supervision at time of hearing, and Commission had jurisdiction over inmate until his conditional release supervision terminated. Gillard v. State, App. 1 Dist., 827 So.2d 316 (2002), rehearing denied, review denied 842 So.2d 844. Pardon And Parole ⚷ 82

To be entitled to relief when the Parole Commission fails to conduct a conditional release revocation hearing within the statutorily mandated time period, the releasee must show that he was prejudiced by the alleged delay in addition to showing the statutory violation. Gillard v. State, App. 1 Dist., 827 So.2d 316 (2002), rehearing denied, review denied 842 So.2d 844. Pardon And Parole ⚷ 92

Conditional release revocation hearing conducted by Parole Commission beyond the 45-day statutory time period was presumptively unreasonable, but inmate was not entitled to relief absent a showing that he was prejudiced by the delay. Gillard v. State, App. 1 Dist., 827 So.2d 316 (2002), rehearing denied, review denied 842 So.2d 844. Pardon And Parole ⚷ 82; Pardon And Parole ⚷ 92

8. Release date

Department of Corrections, in calculating new release date following revocation of conditional release supervision, should not have considered, as tolled, the time that inmate served following expiration of incarcerative portion of sentence for shotgun offense while inmate awaited expiration of incarcerative portions of sentences for assault and battery offenses which arose from same 1992 criminal episode, and thus, Department was not permitted to add such "tolled" time onto sentence in calculating new release date. Bolden v. Florida Dept. of Corrections, App. 1 Dist., 865 So.2d 1 (2003), rehearing granted, review granted 848 So.2d 1153, review dismissed 867 So.2d 373. Prisons ⚷ 248

9. Sufficiency of petition

Habeas corpus petitioner adequately alleged a preliminary basis for concluding that he was denied procedural protections to which he was entitled in revocation of conditional release supervision proceedings, and thus, trial court was required to issue an order to show cause before adjudicating the merits of petitioner's claims, where plaintiff's sworn allegations included claims that he was improperly denied the assistance of counsel, denied access to the evidence against him, and denied the right to cross-examine adverse witnesses. Reyes v. Florida Parole Com'n, App. 1 Dist., 935 So.2d 594 (2006). Habeas Corpus ⚷ 670(8)

947.146. Control Release Authority

(1) There is created a Control Release Authority which shall be composed of the members of the Parole Commission and which shall have the same chair as the commission. The authority shall utilize such commission staff as it determines is necessary to carry out its purposes.

(2) The authority shall implement a system for determining the number and type of inmates who must be released into the community under control release in order to maintain the state prison system between 99 and 100 percent of its total capacity as defined in s. 944.023. No inmate has a right to control release. Control release is an administrative function solely used to manage the state prison population within total capacity. An inmate may not receive an advancement of his or her control release date by an award of control release allotments for any period of time before the date the inmate becomes statutorily eligible for control release or before the subsequent date of establishment of the inmate's advanceable control release date.

(3) Within 120 days prior to the date the state correctional system is projected pursuant to s. 216.136 to exceed 99 percent of total capacity, the authority shall determine eligibility for and establish a control release date for an appropriate number of parole ineligible inmates committed to the department and incarcerated within the state who have been determined by the authority to be eligible for discretionary early release pursuant to this section. In establishing control release dates, it is the intent of the Legislature that the authority prioritize consideration of eligible inmates closest to their tentative release date. The authority shall rely upon commitment data on the offender information system maintained by the department to initially identify inmates who are to be reviewed for control release consideration. The authority may use a method of

objective risk assessment in determining if an eligible inmate should be released. Such assessment shall be a part of the department's management information system. However, the authority shall have sole responsibility for determining control release eligibility, establishing a control release date, and effectuating the release of a sufficient number of inmates to maintain the inmate population between 99 percent and 100 percent of total capacity. Inmates who are ineligible for control release are inmates who are parole eligible or inmates who:

(a) Are serving a sentence that includes a mandatory minimum provision for a capital offense or drug trafficking offense and have not served the number of days equal to the mandatory minimum term less any jail-time credit awarded by the court;

(b) Are serving the mandatory minimum portion of a sentence enhanced under s. 775.087(2) or (3), or s. 784.07(3);

(c) Are convicted, or have been previously convicted, of committing or attempting to commit sexual battery, incest, or any of the following lewd or indecent assaults or acts: masturbating in public; exposing the sexual organs in a perverted manner; or nonconsensual handling or fondling of the sexual organs of another person;

(d) Are convicted, or have been previously convicted, of committing or attempting to commit assault, aggravated assault, battery, or aggravated battery, and a sex act was attempted or completed during commission of such offense;

(e) Are convicted, or have been previously convicted, of committing or attempting to commit kidnapping, burglary, or murder, and the offense was committed with the intent to commit sexual battery or a sex act was attempted or completed during commission of the offense;

(f) Are convicted, or have been previously convicted, of committing or attempting to commit false imprisonment upon a child under the age of 13 and, in the course of committing the offense, the inmate committed aggravated child abuse, sexual battery against the child, or a lewd or lascivious offense committed upon or in the presence of a person less than 16 years of age;

(g) Are sentenced, have previously been sentenced, or have been sentenced at any time under s. 775.084, or have been sentenced at any time in another jurisdiction as a habitual offender;

(h) Are convicted, or have been previously convicted, of committing or attempting to commit assault, aggravated assault, battery, aggravated battery, kidnapping, manslaughter, or murder against an officer as defined in s. 943.10(1), (2), (3), (6), (7), (8), or (9); against a state attorney or assistant state attorney; or against a justice or judge of a court described in Art. V of the State Constitution; or against an officer, judge, or state attorney employed in a comparable position by any other jurisdiction; or

(i) Are convicted, or have been previously convicted, of committing or attempting to commit murder in the first, second, or third degree under s.

782.04(1), (2), (3), or (4), or have ever been convicted of any degree of murder or attempted murder in another jurisdiction;

(j) Are convicted, or have been previously convicted, of DUI manslaughter under s. 316.193(3)(c)3., and are sentenced, or have been sentenced at any time, as a habitual offender for such offense, or have been sentenced at any time in another jurisdiction as a habitual offender for such offense;

(k) 1. Are serving a sentence for an offense committed on or after January 1, 1994, for a violation of the Law Enforcement Protection Act under s. 775.0823(2), (3), (4), (5), or (6), and the subtotal of the offender's sentence points is multiplied pursuant to former s. 921.0014 or s. 921.0024;

2. Are serving a sentence for an offense committed on or after October 1, 1995, for a violation of the Law Enforcement Protection Act under s. 775.0823(2), (3), (4), (5), (6), (7), (8), or (9), and the subtotal of the offender's sentence points is multiplied pursuant to former s. 921.0014 or s. 921.0024;

(*l*) Are serving a sentence for an offense committed on or after January 1, 1994, for possession of a firearm, semiautomatic firearm, or machine gun in which additional points are added to the subtotal of the offender's sentence points pursuant to former s. 921.0014 or s. 921.0024; or

(m) Are convicted, or have been previously convicted, of committing or attempting to commit manslaughter, kidnapping, robbery, carjacking, home-invasion robbery, or a burglary under s. 810.02(2).

In making control release eligibility determinations under this subsection, the authority may rely on any document leading to or generated during the course of the criminal proceedings, including, but not limited to, any presentence or postsentence investigation or any information contained in arrest reports relating to circumstances of the offense.

(4) Control release dates shall be based upon a system of uniform criteria which shall include, but not be limited to, present offenses for which the person is committed, past criminal conduct, length of cumulative sentences, and age of the offender at the time of commitment, together with any aggravating or mitigating circumstances.

(5) Whenever the inmate population drops below 99 percent of total capacity and remains below 99 percent for 90 consecutive days without requiring the release of inmates under this section, all control release dates shall become void and no inmate shall be eligible for release under any previously established control release date. An inmate shall not have a right to a control release date, nor shall the authority be required to establish or reestablish any additional control release dates except under the provisions of subsection (2).

(6) For purpose of determining eligibility for control release, the mandatory minimum portion of a concurrent sentence will begin on the date the sentence begins to run as provided in s. 921.161. The mandatory minimum portions of consecutive sentences shall be served at the beginning of the maximum sentence as established by the Department of Corrections. With respect to offenders who have more than one sentence with a mandatory minimum portion, each mandatory minimum portion of consecutive sentences shall be

served consecutively; provided, that in no case shall a sentence begin to run before the date of imposition of that sentence.

(7) The authority has the power and duty to:

(a) Extend or advance the control release date of any inmate for whom a date has been established pursuant to subsection (2), based upon one or more of the following:

1. Recently discovered information of:

a. Past criminal conduct;

b. Verified threats by inmates provided by victims, law enforcement, or the department;

c. Potential risk to or vulnerability of a victim;

d. Psychological or physical trauma to the victim due to the criminal offense;

e. Court-ordered restitution;

f. History of abuse or addiction to a chemical substance verified by a presentence or postsentence investigation report;

g. The inmate's ties to organized crime;

h. A change in the inmate's sentence structure;

i. Cooperation with law enforcement;

j. Strong community support; and

k. A documented mental condition as a factor for future criminal behavior.

2. The recommendation of the department regarding:

a. A medical or mental health-related condition; or

b. Institutional adjustment of the inmate, which may include refusal by the inmate to sign the agreement to the conditions of the release plan.

3. Total capacity of the state prison system.

(b) Authorize an individual commissioner to postpone a control release date for not more than 60 days without a hearing for any inmate who has become the subject of a disciplinary proceeding, a criminal arrest, an information, or an indictment; who has been terminated from work release; or about whom there is any recently discovered information as specified in paragraph (a).

(c) Determine the terms, conditions, and period of time of control release for persons released pursuant to this section.

(d) Determine violations of control release and what actions shall be taken with reference thereto.

(e) Provide for victim input into the decisionmaking process which may be used by the authority as aggravation or mitigation in determining which persons shall be released on control release.

(f) Make such investigations as may be necessary for the purposes of establishing, modifying, or revoking a control release date.

(g) Contract with a public defender or private counsel for representation of indigent persons charged with violating the terms of control release.

(h) Adopt such rules as the authority deems necessary for implementation of the provisions of this section.

(8) The Department of Corrections shall select and contract with public or private organizations for the provision of basic support services for inmates whose term of control release supervision does not exceed 180 days. Basic support services shall include, but not be limited to, substance abuse counseling, temporary housing, family counseling, and employment support programs.

(9) The authority shall examine such records as it deems necessary of the department, the Department of Children and Family Services, the Department of Law Enforcement, and any other such agency for the purpose of either establishing, modifying, or revoking a control release date. The victim impact statement shall be included in such records for examination. Such agencies shall provide the information requested by the authority for the purposes of fulfilling the requirements of this section.

(10) The authority shall adopt as a standard condition for all persons released pursuant to this section that such persons shall not commit a violation which constitutes a felony. The authority shall determine the appropriate terms, conditions, and lengths of supervision, if any, for persons placed on control release, except that such lengths of supervision shall be determined as provided in s. 947.24 and may not exceed the maximum period for which the person has been sentenced. If the person's conviction was for a controlled substance violation, the conditions must include a requirement that the person submit to random substance abuse testing intermittently throughout the term of supervision, and, when warranted, a requirement that the person participate in substance abuse assessment and substance abuse treatment services upon the direction of the correctional probation officer as defined in s. 943.10(3). Effective July 1, 1994, and applicable for offenses committed on or after that date, the authority may require, as a condition of control release, that the control releasee make payment of the debt due and owing to a county or municipal detention facility under s. 951.032 for medical care, treatment, hospitalization, or transportation received by the releasee while in that detention facility. The authority, in determining whether to order such repayment and the amount of such repayment, shall consider the amount of the debt, whether there was any fault of the institution for the medical expenses incurred, the financial resources of the releasee, the present and potential future financial needs and earning ability of the releasee, and dependents, and other appropriate factors. If any inmate placed on control release supervision is also subject to probation or community control, the department shall supervise such person according to the conditions imposed by the court, and the authority shall defer to such supervision. If the court revokes the probation or community control, the authority, as the result of the revocation, may vacate the grant of control release and resulting deferred control release supervision or take other action it considers appropriate. If the term of control release supervision exceeds that of the probation or community control, then supervision shall

revert to the authority's conditions upon expiration of the probation or community control.

(11) If an inmate is released on control release supervision subject to a detainer for a pending charge and the pending charge results in a new commitment to incarceration before expiration of the terms of control release supervision, the authority may vacate the grant of control release and the control release supervision or take other action it considers appropriate.

(12) When the authority has reasonable grounds to believe that an offender released under this section has violated the terms and conditions of control release, such offender shall be subject to the provisions of s. 947.141 and shall be subject to forfeiture of gain-time pursuant to s. 944.28(1).

(13) If it is discovered that any control releasee was placed on control release by error or while statutorily ineligible for such release, the order of control release may be vacated and the Control Release Authority may cause a warrant to be issued for the arrest and return of the control releasee to the custody of the Department of Corrections for service of the unserved portion of the sentence or combined sentences.

(14) Effective July 1, 1996, all control release dates established prior to such date become void and no inmate shall be eligible for release under any previously established control release date. Offenders who are under control release supervision as of July 1, 1996, shall be subject to the conditions established by the authority until such offenders have been discharged from supervision. Offenders who have warrants outstanding based on violation of supervision as of July 1, 1996, or who violate the terms of their supervision subsequent to July 1, 1996, shall be subject to the provisions of s. 947.141.

Laws 1989, c. 89–526, § 2; Laws 1990, c. 90–77, § 3; Laws 1990, c. 90–186, § 2; Laws 1990, c. 90–211, § 7; Laws 1990, c. 90–337, § 12; Laws 1991, c. 91–280, § 11; Laws 1992, c. 92–310, § 15; Laws 1993, c. 93–61, § 6; Laws 1993, c. 93–406, §§ 27, 30(1); Laws 1994, c. 94–111, § 1; Laws 1994, c. 94–121, § 2; Laws 1994, c. 94–294, § 2; Laws 1995, c. 95–184, § 27; Laws 1995, c. 95–251, § 4. Amended by Laws 1996, c. 96–422, § 19, eff. June 7, 1996; Laws 1997, c. 97–102, § 1873, eff. July 1, 1997; Laws 1997, c. 97–194, § 31, eff. Oct. 1, 1998; Laws 1998, c. 98–417, § 8, eff. Oct. 1, 1998; Laws 1999, c. 99–8, § 321, eff. June 29, 1999; Laws 1999, c. 99–12, § 3, eff. July 1, 1999; Laws 1999, c. 99–201, § 12, eff. Oct. 1, 1999; Laws 2001, c. 2001–236, § 7, eff. Oct. 1, 2001; Laws 2005, c. 2005–119, § 7, eff. Oct. 1, 2005; Laws 2007, c. 2007–212, § 3, eff. Oct. 1, 2007.

Historical and Statutory Notes

Amendment Notes:

Section 52 of Laws 1989, c. 89–526, provides, in pertinent part:

"All inmates committed to the department as of September 1, 1990, shall have a control release date established by December 1, 1990. Inmates received after September 1, 1990, shall have a control release date established within 90 days following notification by the department of receipt of the inmate."

Laws 1990, c. 90–77, § 3, eff. Oct. 1, 1990, in subsec. (4)(d), added provisions regarding offenses against a justice or judge.

Laws 1990, c. 90–186, § 2, eff. Oct. 1, 1990, reenacted subsec. (4)(g) without change "For the purpose of incorporating the amendment to section 944.277, Florida Statutes, in a reference thereto."

Laws 1990, c. 90–211, § 7, eff. Oct. 1, 1990, in subsec. (7), provided that the victim impact statement be included in such records for examination.

Laws 1990, c. 90–337, § 12, eff. July 1, 1990, rewrote the section, which formerly read:

"(1) There is created a Control Release Authority which shall be composed of the members of the Parole Commission and which shall have the same chairman as the commission. The authority shall utilize such commission staff as it determines is necessary to carry out its purposes.

"(2) The authority shall have as its primary purpose the development of a system of uniform criteria for the determination of the number and type of inmates who must be released into the community under control release in order to maintain the state prison system below 97.5 percent of its lawful capacity as defined in s. 944.096.

"(3) There shall be no award of provisional credits by the secretary of the department pursuant to s. 944.277 unless either:

"(a) The chairman of the Control Release Authority certifies in writing to the secretary of the department that the authority is unable to maintain the state prison system below 97.5 percent of its lawful capacity; or

"(b) Based upon the failure of the authority to act, the state prison system reaches 98 percent of its lawful capacity as provided in s. 944.277.

"(4) A panel of no fewer than two members of the authority shall establish a control release date for each parole ineligible inmate committed to the department within 90 days following notification by the department of receipt of the inmate, except an inmate who is convicted, or has been previously convicted, and sentenced for the following:

"(a) A capital felony;

"(b) Sexual battery pursuant to s. 794.011 or any other sex offense specified in s. 917.012(1);

"(c) An offense which is punishable by a mandatory minimum period of incarceration;

"(d) Committing or attempting to commit assault, aggravated assault, battery, aggravated battery, kidnapping, manslaughter, or murder against an officer as defined in s. 943.10(1), (2), (3), (6), (7), (8), or (9) or against a state attorney or assistant state attorney;

"(e) As a habitual felony offender pursuant to s. 775.084 or has been sentenced at any time in another jurisdiction as a habitual offender;

"(f) Committing or attempting to commit murder in the first or second degree under s. 782.04(1), (2), or (3); or

"(g) Any offense which would render the inmate ineligible for provisional credits under s. 944.277.

"(5) Control release dates shall be based upon a system of uniform criteria which shall include, but not be limited to, present offenses for which the person is committed, past criminal conduct, length of cumulative sentences, and age of the offender at the time of commitment.

"(6) The authority shall have the power and duty to:

"(a) Extend or advance the control release date of any inmate for whom a date has been established, based upon:

"1. Recently discovered information of past criminal conduct;

"2. The recommendation of the department regarding institutional adjustment of the inmate; or

"3. Lawful capacity of the state prison system.

"(b) Determine the terms, conditions, and period of time of control release for persons released pursuant to this section.

"(c) Determine violations of control release and what actions shall be taken with reference thereto.

"(d) Provide for victim input into the decisionmaking process for placing persons on control release.

"(e) Make such investigations as may be necessary for the purposes of establishing, modifying, or revoking a control release date.

"(f) Adopt such rules as the authority deems necessary for implementation of the provisions of this section.

"(7) The authority shall examine such records as it deems necessary of the department, the Department of Health and Rehabilitative Services, the Department of Law Enforcement, and any other such agency for the purpose of either establishing, modifying, or revoking a control release date. Such agencies shall provide the information requested by the authority for the purposes of fulfilling the requirements of this section.

"(8) The authority shall determine the appropriate terms, conditions, and lengths of supervision, if any, for persons placed on control release, except that such lengths of supervision shall be determined as provided in s. 947.24 and shall not exceed the maximum period for which the person has been sentenced. In the event any inmate placed on control release supervision is also subject to probation or community control, the department shall supervise such person according to the conditions imposed by the court, and the authority shall defer to such supervision. If the term of control release supervision exceeds that of the probation or community control, then supervision shall revert to the authority's conditions upon expiration of the probation or community control.

"(9) When the authority has reasonable grounds to believe that an offender released under this section has violated the terms and conditions of control release, such offender shall be subject to the provisions of s. 947.141 and shall be subject to forfeiture of gain-time pursuant to s. 944.28(1)."

Section 19 of Laws 1990, c. 90–211, provides:

"Except as otherwise provided herein, this act shall take effect October 1, 1990, and shall apply to offenses committed on or after such date."

Laws 1990, c. 90–337, § 22 provided therein that the amendment take effect July 1, 1990; however, approval by the governor occurred subsequent thereto. The Florida Supreme Court in an advisory opinion to the governor of July 19, 1979 (374 So.2d 959) stated in part "* * * the effective date provided in the bill is inoperative unless the bill becomes law on or before that date" and concludes that under such circumstances the provision of Const. Art. 3, § 9, that the law take effect on the sixtieth day after adjournment sine die of the session of the legislature in which enacted, is applicable.

Laws 1991, c. 91–280, § 11, eff. Oct. 1, 1991, in subsec. (4), in par. (h), added "against an officer, judge, or state attorney employed in a comparable position by any other jurisdiction; or"; in par. (i), added "or has ever been convicted of any degree of murder in another jurisdiction"; inserted subsec. (6); redesignated subsequent subsections accordingly; in subsec. (7), in par. (a), in subpar. 1., designated sub-subpar. a. and added sub-subpars. b. to h.; and added subsec. (12).

Laws 1992, c. 92–310, § 15, eff. July 6, 1992, in subsec. (4), in the introductory paragraph, inserted "and incarcerated within the state"; in par. (e), added "or a sex act was attempted or completed during commission of the offense"; in par. (g), inserted "or has been sentenced at any time"; added the last sentence of the subsection; in subsec. (7), in par. (a), in the introductory paragraph added "one or more of the following"; in subpar. 2., inserted sub-subpar. a. and designated sub-subpar. b.; inserted par. (g) and redesignated former par. (g) as par. (h); and, in subsec. (12), inserted "by error or".

Laws 1993, c. 93–61, § 6, eff. April 22, 1993, in subsec. (4), in the introductory paragraph, inserted "or within 90 days following the completion of proceedings revoking an offender's release and notification by the department of receipt of the inmate"; rewrote subsec. (7); in subsec. (10), made nonsubstantive changes and inserted the fourth sentence; inserted subsec. (11); and redesignated former subsecs. (11) and (12) as subsecs. (12) and (13). Subsection (7) formerly read:

"The authority has the power and duty to:

"(a) Extend or advance the control release date of any inmate for whom a date has been established, based upon one or more of the following:

"1. Recently discovered information of:

"a. Past criminal conduct;

"b. Verified threats by inmates provided by victims, law enforcement, or the department;

"c. History of abuse or addiction to a chemical substance verified by a presentence or postsentence investigation report;

"d. The inmate's ties to organized crime;

"e. A change in the inmate's sentence structure;

"f. Cooperation with law enforcement;

"g. Strong community support; and

"h. A documented mental condition as a factor for future criminal behavior.

"2. The recommendation of the department regarding:

"a. A medical or mental health-related condition; or

"b. Institutional adjustment of the inmate, which may include refusal by the inmate to sign the agreement to the conditions of the release plan.

"3. Lawful capacity of the state prison system.

"(b) Determine the terms, conditions, and period of time of control release for persons released pursuant to this section.

"(c) Determine violations of control release and what actions shall be taken with reference thereto.

"(d) Provide for victim input into the decisionmaking process for placing persons on control release.

"(e) Make such investigations as may be necessary for the purposes of establishing, modifying, or revoking a control release date.

"(f) Contract with a public defender or private counsel for representation of indigent persons charged with violating the terms of control release.

"(g) Create a periodic review process for inmates whose original control release dates are established at the maximum category.

"(h) Adopt such rules as the authority deems necessary for implementation of the provisions of this section."

Laws 1993, c. 93–406, § 27, eff. June 17, 1993, which incorporated the amendment by Laws 1993, c. 93–61, in subsec. (2), substituted "at or below 99" for "below 97.5" in the first sentence and added the last sentence relating to the advancement of the control release date by an award of control release award allotments; deleted former subsec. (3) which prohibited the award of provisional credits by the secretary of the department pursuant to § 944.277 unless certain conditions were met; redesignated former subsecs. (4) to (7) as subsecs. (3) to (6); in subsec. (3), substituted "as a violent habitual offender for a crime committed on or after October 1, 1988" for "under s. 775.084" and inserted "violent" before "habitual offender" in par. (g), inserted "or attempted murder" in par. (i), added pars. (j) to (m), and added the last sentence which made the 90-day requirement for the establishment of a control release date inapplicable to a person sentenced as a habitual felony offender in the last paragraph; inserted subsec. (7) about a state of emergency in the population of the state correctional system; in subsec. (10), inserted the first sentence which required as a standard condition for release pursuant to this section that the violation was not a felony, and inserted "and, when warranted, a requirement that the person participate in substance abuse assessment and substance abuse treatment services" in the third sentence; and made other nonsubstantive changes.

Sections 30, 31 of Laws 1993, c. 93–406, provide:

"Section 30. Effective on June 1, 1995:

"(1) The amendment to paragraph (g) of subsection (3) of s. 947.146, Florida Statutes, contained in this act shall be null and void and that paragraph shall revert to the language existing in that paragraph on April 22, 1993.

"(2) Section 28 of this act is repealed.

"(3) Section 29 of this act is repealed.

"Section 31. Before the release pursuant to this act under s. 947.146, Florida Statutes, of any inmate sentenced as a habitual felony offender pursuant to this act, the Control Release Authority shall develop a uniform procedure for the award of control release dates to inmates sentenced as habitual felony offenders. The procedure must give priority consideration for early release to habitualized offenders who have been in the state prison system on their current commitment for the longest period of time. It is the intent of the Legislature that the habitual felony offender serve at least a significant portion of the court-imposed sentence before release."

Laws 1994, c. 94–111, § 1, eff. April 25, 1994, in subsec. (2), in the first sentence, substituted "between 99 and 100 percent" for "at or below 99 percent"; and in subsec. (7), in the first sentence, substituted "100" for "99.5" and inserted "and remains in excess of 100 percent of lawful capacity for 14 days", in par. (b), substituted "between 99 and 100" for "below 100", and in par. (c), substituted "less than 100" for "99".

Laws 1994, c. 94–121, § 2, eff. May 4, 1994, reenacted subsec. (12) of this section for the purpose of incorporating the amendment to § 947.141 in a reference thereto.

Laws 1994, c. 94–294, § 2, eff. July 1, 1994, inserted the fourth and fifth sentences in subsec. (10).

Laws 1995, c. 95–184, § 27, eff. June 8, 1995, in subsec. (3), at the end of par. (b), added "or (3), or s. 784.07(3)", in par. (k), designated the former language as subpar. 1., and added subpar. 2., in par. (*l*), substituted ", semiautomatic firearm, or machine gun" for "or destructive device", and deleted "; or" from the end of the paragraph, and deleted former par. (m), which read:

"Is serving a sentence for an offense committed on or after January 1, 1994, for possession of a semiautomatic weapon, and additional points are added to the subtotal of the offender's sentence points pursuant to s. 921.0014".

Laws 1995, c. 95–251, § 4, eff. June 10, 1995, in subsec. (2), substituted references to total capacity for references to lawful capacity throughout, and substituted a reference to § 944.023 for a reference to § 944.096 at the end of the first sentence; in subsec. (3), inserted a par. (n) which was redesignated as part. (m) in Fla.St.1995, and made corresponding language and punctuation changes; in subsec. (6)(a), substituted a reference to total capacity for reference to lawful capacity in subpar. 3.; repealed former subsec. (7), which had read:

"If the population of the state correctional system, as defined in s. 944.02, exceeds 100 percent of lawful capacity and remains in excess of 100 percent of lawful capacity for 14 days, the Secretary of Corrections shall notify the chair of the Parole Commission and certify to the chair the lawful capacity of the state correctional system and the current population. Upon receiving such certification, the chair of the Parole Commission shall advise the Governor that a state of emergency exists. When the Governor verifies the state of emergency to the Control Release Authority by letter, the Control Release Authority shall establish emergency control release dates for inmates who are ineligible for parole, who are excluded from control release under paragraph (3)(a), paragraph (3)(b), paragraph (3)(g), or paragraph (3)(h), and who the authority determines are the most suitable for release. Under no circumstances shall an inmate convicted of a capital felony be eligible for emergency control release.

"(a) The authority shall extend or advance emergency control release dates pursuant to this section.

"(b) The authority shall maintain the inmate population between 99 and 100 percent of lawful capacity by releasing inmates on emergency control release as well as control release as otherwise provided in this section.

"(c) A state of emergency ceases to exist when the inmate population drops to less than 100 percent of lawful capacity and remains at or below that level for 30 consecutive days without requiring the release of inmates through the establishment of additional emergency control release dates.

"(d) Nothing in this subsection prohibits the establishment of a control release date under other provisions of this section or creates any right to an early release for any inmate. An inmate has no right to be reviewed for the establishment of an emergency control release date. The establishment of emergency control release dates under this subsection is solely an administrative function used to manage the prison population within lawful capacity.

"(e) When a state of emergency ceases to exist pursuant to paragraph (c), all emergency control release dates must be suspended and no inmate is eligible for release under any previously established emergency control release date."

and redesignated former subsecs. (8) through (13) as subsecs. (7) through (12).

Laws 1996, c. 96–422, § 19, eff. June 7, 1996, rewrote this section, which formerly read:

"(1) There is created a Control Release Authority which shall be composed of the members of the Parole Commission and which shall have the same chairman as the commission. The authority shall utilize such commission staff as it determines is necessary to carry out its purposes.

"(2) The authority has as its primary purpose the implementation of a system of uniform criteria for the determination of the number and type of inmates who must be released into the community under control release in order to maintain the state prison system between 99 and 100 percent of its total capacity as defined in s. 944.023. No inmate has a right to control release. Control release is an administrative function solely used to manage the state prison population within total capacity. An inmate may not receive an advancement of his control release date by an award of control release award allotments for any period of time before the date the inmate becomes statutorily eligible for control release or before the subsequent date of establishment of his advanceable control release date.

"(3) A panel of no fewer than two members of the authority shall establish a control release date for each parole ineligible inmate committed to the department and incarcerated within the state, within 90 days following notification by the department of receipt of the inmate or within 90 days following the completion of proceedings revoking an offender's release and notification by the department of receipt of the inmate, except an inmate who:

"(a) Is serving a sentence that includes a mandatory minimum provision for a capital offense or drug trafficking offense and has not served the number of days equal to the mandatory minimum term less any jail-time credit awarded by the court;

"(b) Is serving the mandatory minimum portion of a sentence enhanced under s. 775.087(2) or (3), or s. 784.07(3);

"(c) Is convicted, or has been previously convicted, of committing or attempting to commit sexual battery, incest, or any of the following lewd or indecent assaults or acts: masturbating in public; exposing the sexual organs in a perverted manner; or nonconsensual handling or fondling of the sexual organs of another person;

"(d) Is convicted, or has been previously convicted, of committing or attempting to commit assault, aggravated assault, battery, or aggravated battery, and a sex act was attempted or completed during commission of such offense;

"(e) Is convicted, or has been previously convicted, of committing or attempting to commit kidnapping, burglary, or murder, and the offense was committed with the intent to commit sexual battery or a sex act was attempted or completed during commission of the offense;

"(f) Is convicted, or has been previously convicted, of committing or attempting to commit false imprisonment upon a child under the age of 13 and, in the course of committing the offense, the inmate committed aggravated child abuse, sexual battery against the child, or a lewd, lascivious, or indecent assault or act upon or in the presence of the child;

"(g) Is sentenced, has previously been sentenced, or has been sentenced at any time under s. 775.084, or has been sentenced at any time in another jurisdiction as a habitual offender;

"(h) Is convicted, or has been previously convicted, of committing or attempting to commit assault, aggravated assault, battery, aggravated battery, kidnapping, manslaughter, or murder against an officer as defined in s. 943.10(1), (2), (3), (6), (7), (8), or (9); against a state attorney or assistant state attorney; or against a justice or judge of a court described in Art. V of the State Constitution; or against an officer, judge, or state attorney employed in a comparable position by any other jurisdiction; or

"(i) Is convicted, or has been previously convicted, of committing or attempting to commit murder in the first, second, or third degree under s. 782.04(1), (2), (3), or (4), or has ever been convicted of any degree of murder or attempted murder in another jurisdiction;

"(j) Is convicted, or has been previously convicted, of DUI manslaughter under s. 316.193(3)(c)3., and is sentenced, or has been sentenced at any time, as a habitual offender for such offense, or has been sentenced at any time in another jurisdiction as a habitual offender for such offense;

"(k)1. Is serving a sentence for an offense committed on or after January 1, 1994, for a violation of the Law Enforcement Protection Act under s. 775.0823(2), (3), (4), or (5), and the subtotal of the offender's sentence points is multiplied pursuant to s. 921.0014;

"2. Is serving a sentence for an offense committed on or after October 1, 1995, for a violation of the Law Enforcement Protection Act under s. 775.0823(2), (3), (4), (5), (6), (7), or (8), and the subtotal of the offender's sentence points is multiplied pursuant to s. 921.0014;

"(*l*) Is serving a sentence for an offense committed on or after January 1, 1994, for possession of a firearm, semiautomatic firearm, or machine gun in which additional points are added to the subtotal of the offender's sentence points pursuant to s. 921.0014; or

"(m) Is convicted, or has been previously convicted, of committing or attempting to commit manslaughter, kidnapping, robbery, carjacking, home-invasion robbery, or a burglary under s. 810.02(2).

"In making control release eligibility determinations under this subsection, the authority may rely on any document leading to or generated during the course of the criminal proceedings, including, but not limited to, any presentence or postsentence investigation or any information contained in arrest reports relating to circumstances of the offense. The 90–day requirement for the establishment of a control release date for all eligible inmates for control release consideration does not apply to a person sentenced as a habitual felony offender.

"(4) Control release dates shall be based upon a system of uniform criteria which shall include, but not be limited to, present offenses for which the person is committed, past criminal conduct, length of cumulative sentences, and age of the offender at the time of commitment, together with any aggravating or mitigating circumstances.

"(5) For purpose of determining eligibility for control release, the mandatory minimum portion of a concurrent sentence will begin on the date the sentence begins to run as provided in s. 921.161. The mandatory minimum portions of consecutive sentences shall be served at the beginning of the maximum sentence as established by the Department of Corrections. With respect to offenders who have more than one sentence with a mandatory minimum portion, each mandatory minimum portion of consecutive sentences shall be served consecutively; provided, that in no case shall a sentence begin to run before the date of imposition of that sentence.

"(6) The authority has the power and duty to:

"(a) Extend or advance the control release date of any inmate for whom a date has been established, based upon one or more of the following:

"1. Recently discovered information of:

"a. Past criminal conduct;

"b. Verified threats by inmates provided by victims, law enforcement, or the department;

"c. Potential risk to or vulnerability of a victim;

"d. Psychological or physical trauma to the victim due to the criminal offense;

"e. Court-ordered restitution;

"f. History of abuse or addiction to a chemical substance verified by a presentence or postsentence investigation report;

"g. The inmate's ties to organized crime;

"h. A change in the inmate's sentence structure;

"i. Cooperation with law enforcement;

"j. Strong community support; and

"k. A documented mental condition as a factor for future criminal behavior.

"2. The recommendation of the department regarding:

"a. A medical or mental health-related condition; or

"b. Institutional adjustment of the inmate, which may include refusal by the inmate to sign the agreement to the conditions of the release plan.

"3. Total capacity of the state prison system.

"(b) Authorize an individual commissioner to postpone a control release date for not more than 60 days without a hearing for any inmate who has become the subject of a disciplinary proceeding, a criminal arrest, an information, or an indictment; who has been terminated from work release; or about whom there is any recently discovered information as specified in paragraph (a).

"(c) Determine the terms, conditions, and period of time of control release for persons released pursuant to this section.

"(d) Determine violations of control release and what actions shall be taken with reference thereto.

"(e) Provide for victim input into the decisionmaking process which may be used by the authority as aggravation or mitigation in determining which persons shall be released on control release.

"(f) Make such investigations as may be necessary for the purposes of establishing, modifying, or revoking a control release date.

"(g) Contract with a public defender or private counsel for representation of indigent persons charged with violating the terms of control release.

"(h) Create a periodic review process for inmates whose original control release dates are established at the maximum category.

"(i) Adopt such rules as the authority deems necessary for implementation of the provisions of this section.

"(7) The Department of Corrections shall select and contract with public or private organizations for the provision of basic support services for inmates whose term of control release supervision does not exceed 180 days. Basic support services shall include, but not be limited to, substance abuse counseling, temporary housing, family counseling, and employment support programs.

"(8) The authority shall examine such records as it deems necessary of the department, the Department of Health and Rehabilitative Services, the Department of Law Enforcement, and any other such agency for the purpose of either establishing, modifying, or revoking a control release date. The victim impact statement shall be included in such records for examination. Such agencies shall provide the information requested by the authority for the purposes of fulfilling the requirements of this section.

"(9) The authority shall adopt as a standard condition for all persons released pursuant to this section that such persons shall not commit a violation which constitutes a felony. The authority shall determine the appropriate terms, conditions, and lengths of supervision, if any, for persons placed on control release, except that such lengths of supervision shall be determined as provided in s. 947.24 and may not exceed the maximum period for which the person has been sentenced. If the person's conviction was for a controlled substance violation, the conditions must include a requirement that the person submit to random substance abuse testing intermittently throughout the term of supervision, and, when warranted, a requirement that the person participate in substance abuse assessment and substance abuse treatment services upon the direction of the correctional probation officer as defined in s. 943.10(3). Effective July 1, 1994, and applicable for offenses committed on or after that date, the authority may require, as a condition of control release, that the control releasee make payment of the debt due and owing to a county or municipal detention facility under s. 951.032 for medical care, treatment, hospitalization, or transportation received by the releasee while in that detention facility. The authority, in determining whether to order such repayment and the amount of such repayment, shall consider the amount of the debt, whether there was any fault of the institution for the medical expenses incurred, the financial resources of the releasee, the present and potential future financial needs and earning ability of the releasee, and dependents, and other appropriate factors. If any inmate placed on control release supervision is also subject to probation or community control, the department shall supervise such person according to the conditions imposed by the court, and the authority shall defer to such supervision. If the court revokes the probation or community control, the authority, as the result of the revocation, may vacate the grant of control release and resulting deferred control release supervision or take other action it considers appropriate. If the term of control release supervision exceeds that of the probation or community control, then supervision shall revert to the authority's conditions upon expiration of the probation or community control.

"(10) If an inmate is released on control release supervision subject to a detainer for a pending charge and the pending charge results in a new commitment to incarceration before expiration of the terms of control release supervision, the authority may vacate the grant of control release and the control release supervision or take other action it considers appropriate.

"(11) When the authority has reasonable grounds to believe that an offender released under this section has violated the terms and conditions of control release, such offender shall be subject to the provisions of s. 947.141 and shall be subject to forfeiture of gain-time pursuant to s. 944.28(1).

"(12) If it is discovered that any control releasee was placed on control release by error or while statutorily ineligible for such release, the order of control release may be vacated and the Control Release Authority may cause a warrant to be issued for the arrest and return of the control releasee to the custody of the Department of Corrections for service of the unserved portion of the sentence or combined sentences."

Laws 1997, c. 97–102, eff. July 1, 1997, removed gender-specific references applicable to human beings from volume 4 of the Florida Statutes without substantive changes in legal effect.

Laws 1997, c. 97–194, § 31, eff. Oct. 1, 1998, in subsec. (3), corrected citations.

Laws 1998, c. 98–417, § 8, reenacted subsec. (3) of this section for the purpose of incorporating an amendment to § 782.04 in a reference thereto.

Laws 1999, c. 99–8, § 321, eff. June 29, 1999, substituted "Department of Children and Family Services" for "Department of Health and Rehabilitative Services".

Laws 1999, c. 99–12, § 3, eff. July 1, 1999, reenacted subsec. (3)(b) for the purpose of incorporating the amendment to s. 775.087 thereto.

Laws 1999, c. 99–201, § 12, in subsec. (3)(f), substituted "lewd or lascivious offense committed upon or in the presence of a person less than 16 years of age" for "lewd, lascivious, or indecent assault or act upon or in the presence of the child".

Laws 2001, c. 2001–236, § 7, eff. Oct. 1, 2001, reenacted subsec. (3) for the purpose of incorporating the amendment to § 782.04 in a reference thereto.

Laws 2005, c. 2005–119, § 7, reenacted subsec. (3)(j) for the purpose of incorporating the amendment to § 316.193 in a reference thereto.

Laws 2005, c. 2005–119, § 9, provides:

"This act shall take effect October 1, 2005, and shall apply to offenses committed on or after that date."

Laws 2007, c. 2007–212, § 3, in subsec. (3)(k)1., substituted "s. 775.0823(2), (3), (4), (5), or (6)," for "s. 775.0823(2), (3), (4), or (5)," following "Law Enforcement Protection Act under"; and in subsec. (3)(k)2., substituted "s. 775.0823(2), (3), (4), (5), (6), (7), (8), or (9)," for "s. 775.0823(2), (3), (4), (5), (6), (7), or (8)," following "Law Enforcement Protection Act under".

Law Review and Journal Commentaries

A Folly of Criminal Justice Policy–Making: The Rise and Demise of Early Release in Florida, and Its Ex Post Facto Implications. Chet Kaufman, 26 Fla.St.U.L.Rev. 361 (1999).

Library References

Prisons ⚷242.
Westlaw Topic No. 310.
C.J.S. Prisons and Rights of Prisoners § 153.

Research References

ALR Library

95 ALR 2nd 1265, Withdrawal, Forfeiture, Modification, or Denial of Good-Time Allowance to Prisoner.

110 ALR 1308, Constitutional Prohibition of Ex Post Facto Laws as Applicable to Statutes Relating to Joinder of Offenses or Defendants.

49 ALR 1306, Release of Prisoner on Illegal or Void Order as Affecting Further Imprisonment.

Encyclopedias

Generally; Release on Gain-Time Allowances, FL Jur. 2d Prisons & Prisoners § 211.

Treatises and Practice Aids

16 Florida Practice Series § 1:44, Sentencing Alternatives--Straight Confinement.

16 Florida Practice Series § 2:22, Completing the 1983 Sentencing Guidelines Scoresheet--Total Sentence Imposed--Mandatory Sentences.

16 Florida Practice Series § 10:11, Forfeiture of Gain Time and the Right to Earn Gain Time in the Future.

16 Florida Practice Series § 10:15, Post Release--Control Release.

16 Florida Practice Series § 10:17, Violation of Conditional Release, Control Release, Conditional Medical Release, or Addiction Recovery Supervision.

Notes of Decisions

Collateral estoppel 12
Control release date 5
Credit for time spent in program 8
Documentation 4
Habitual offenders 10
Mandamus 9
Noncapital felonies 6
Purpose 2
Retroactivity 3
Revocation of control release 11

Sexual activity with child 7
Validity 1

---

1. Validity

Florida's control release statute which implemented control release program for certain types of offenders was not ex post facto violation, though statute took effect after defendant was incarcerated and, under statute, defendant was ineligible for control release program due to nature of his offense, as statute was procedural in nature and did not affect punishment; provisions of statute were arbitrary because they were triggered by prison population levels, and no relationship existed between eligibility for control release and length of original sentence. Hock v. Singletary, C.A.11 (Fla.)1995, 41 F.3d 1470, rehearing and suggestion for rehearing en banc denied 58 F.3d 642, certiorari denied 116 S.Ct. 715, 516 U.S. 1050, 133 L.Ed.2d 668. Constitutional Law ⚿ 2816; Pardon And Parole ⚿ 42.1

Retroactive application of control release statute allowing for control release of certain prisoners in connection with level of prison populations did not violate due process as to prisoner who would be denied control release under statute due to nature of his offense; liberty interest did not vest under statute as prisoner had no reasonable expectation that prison population levels would be sufficient to trigger statute and had no reasonable expectation of release on any given date. Hock v. Singletary, C.A.11 (Fla.)1995, 41 F.3d 1470, rehearing and suggestion for rehearing en banc denied 58 F.3d 642, certiorari denied 116 S.Ct. 715, 516 U.S. 1050, 133 L.Ed.2d 668. Constitutional Law ⚿ 4830; Pardon And Parole ⚿ 42.1

Window period for bringing a single subject rule challenge to act containing sentencing guidelines and provisions addressing domestic violence injunctions opened on October 1, 1995. Heggs v. State, 759 So.2d 620 (2000), rehearing denied. Constitutional Law ⚿ 975

Defendant had standing to challenge act containing sentencing guidelines and provisions addressing domestic violence injunctions as violative of single subject rule set forth in State Constitution, where defendant committed his offenses on October 24 and November 2, 1995. Heggs v. State, 759 So.2d 620 (2000), rehearing denied. Protection Of Endangered Persons ⚿ 31; Sentencing And Punishment ⚿ 658; Statutes ⚿ 107(3); Statutes ⚿ 117(1); Statutes ⚿ 118(4)

Defendant's single subject rule challenge to act containing sentencing guidelines and provisions addressing domestic violence injunctions was reviewable for first time on appeal, as defendant's increased sentence under new guidelines implicated a fundamental due process liberty interest. Heggs v. State, 759 So.2d 620 (2000), rehearing denied. Criminal Law ⚿ 1042.3(1)

Act containing sentencing guidelines and provisions addressing domestic violence injunctions violated the single subject rule set forth in State Constitution, as it embraced civil and criminal provisions that were not logically connected; there was no legislative statement of intent to implement comprehensive legislation to solve a crisis. Heggs v. State, 759 So.2d 620 (2000), rehearing denied. Protection Of Endangered Persons ⚿ 31; Protection Of Endangered Persons ⚿ 45; Sentencing And Punishment ⚿ 658; Statutes ⚿ 107(2); Statutes ⚿ 107(3)

Domestic violence provisions could not be severed from act to save act's remaining sections on sentencing guidelines, as both the title and the body of act contained more than one subject; accordingly, act was void in its entirety as violative of single subject rule set forth in State Constitution. Heggs v. State, 759 So.2d 620 (2000), rehearing denied. Sentencing And Punishment ⚿ 658; Statutes ⚿ 64(10)

Florida Parole Commission (FPC) was authorized to place inmate on control release, even without his consent, based upon his 1992 offense. Verdelotti v. Moore, App. 1 Dist., 730 So.2d 373 (1999). Pardon And Parole ⚿ 45.1

No ex post facto violation occurred when inmates' control release dates were retrospectively subject to legislative amendments and then ultimately canceled; inmates were always on notice, as result of "sliding scale" built into program and explicit statutory provision that no inmate had a right to control release, that they might ultimately obtain no benefit from the program. Thomas v. Singletary, 729 So.2d 369 (1998), rehearing denied, certiorari denied 120 S.Ct. 200, 528 U.S. 884, 145 L.Ed.2d 169, rehearing denied 120 S.Ct. 571, 528 U.S. 1040, 145 L.Ed.2d 446. Constitutional Law ⚿ 2816; Prisons ⚿ 248

Statute establishing Parole Commission's authority over control release did not violate constitutional provision prohibiting amendment of criminal statute to affect punishment of previously committed crime as applied to permit controlled release of defendants who committed their offenses at time prior statute did not permit control release. State v. Florida Parole Com'n, App. 1 Dist., 624 So.2d 324 (1993), review denied 634 So.2d 627. Constitutional Law ⚿ 2823; Pardon And Parole ⚿ 43

2. Purpose

Under Florida law, purpose of control release statute is to address administrative problem of prison overcrowding, not to confer benefit on prison population. Hock v. Singletary, C.A.11 (Fla.)1995, 41 F.3d 1470, rehearing and suggestion for rehearing en banc denied 58 F.3d 642, certiorari denied 116 S.Ct. 715, 516 U.S. 1050, 133 L.Ed.2d 668. Pardon And Parole ⚿ 42.1

3. Retroactivity

Defendant's right under ex post facto clause to receive fair notice of punishment his offense carried was not compromised by retroactive application of statute which implemented control release program for certain types of offenders, thereby denying control release for defendant; defendant's punishment was not affected by statute due to its procedural and arbitrary nature, stemming from fact that provisions were linked to prison population levels, and defendant's punishment remained what it was when he committed offense. Hock v. Singletary, C.A.11 (Fla.)1995, 41 F.3d 1470, rehearing and suggestion for rehearing en banc denied 58 F.3d 642, certiorari denied 116 S.Ct. 715, 516 U.S. 1050, 133 L.Ed.2d 668. Constitutional Law ⚿ 2816; Pardon And Parole ⚿ 42.1

As a remedy for refusal of Department of Corrections to provide credits to inmates during periods of overcrowding, which violated ex post facto clause, inmates were entitled to number of credits that should have been awarded under statutes in effect at time of their offenses, not what other inmates were actually awarded under Control Release program. Gomez v. Singletary, 733 So.2d 499 (1998), rehearing denied, certiorari denied 120 S.Ct. 67, 528 U.S. 822, 145 L.Ed.2d 58. Prisons ⚿ 248

Under ex post facto clause, for purpose of determining inmates' entitlement to early release, inmates were subject to version of prison overcrowding statute in effect at time of each inmate's offense. Gomez v. Singletary, 733 So.2d 499 (1998), rehearing denied, certiorari denied 120 S.Ct. 67, 528 U.S. 822, 145 L.Ed.2d 58. Constitutional Law ⚿ 2816; Prisons ⚿ 242

4. Documentation

Control release eligibility may be based on any reasonably reliable official document contained in record and generated during course of criminal investigation or proceeding, including arrest report. Gramegna v. Parole Com'n, 666 So.2d 135 (1996). Pardon And Parole ⚿ 58

5. Control release date

Cancellation of petitioner's control release credits by Department of Corrections under statute defining inmates who were ineligible for control release was not ex post facto application of law, where at time he committed his crime and was sentenced as habitual offender, petitioner was not entitled to control release credits. Douglas v. Florida Parole Com'n, App. 5 Dist., 710 So.2d 142 (1998), review granted 722 So.2d 192, review dismissed as improvidently granted 743 So.2d 11. Constitutional Law ⚿ 2816; Prisons ⚿ 248

Florida Control Release Authority (FCRA) was not required to establish control release date for inmate the bulk of whose offenses were parole eligible and who was thus not entitled to control release. Scott v. State, 641 So.2d 407 (1994). Pardon And Parole ⚿ 48.1

6. Noncapital felonies

Though capital felons are still parole-eligible, "parole" no longer exists for anyone convicted of noncapital felony committed on or after October 1, 1983, though some prisoners sentenced under the sentencing guidelines are eligible under control release program, purpose of which is to alleviate prison overcrowding. Dolan v. State, App. 2 Dist., 618 So.2d 271 (1993), review denied 626 So.2d 204. Pardon And Parole ⚿ 41; Pardon And Parole ⚿ 48.1

7. Sexual activity with child

Defendant should not have been held ineligible for control release on ground that sex act was attempted or completed during commission of battery, although arrest report indicated that defendant was suspected of committing a lewd act upon child in addition to battery offense, where there was no indication that formal charges were ever brought on lewd act, and it was clear that the offenses were not connected. Maher v. Florida Parole Com'n, App. 1 Dist., 680 So.2d 491 (1996). Sentencing And Punishment ⚿ 1862

Defendant who is convicted of lewd, lascivious, or indecent assault on person under age of 16 has been convicted of nonconsensual handling or fondling of sexual organs of another person as matter of law and is ineligible for control release, regardless of claims that minor consented to conduct; by providing that consent is not defense to crime of lewd conduct with minor, Legislature has determined that child is incapable of understanding full consequences of acts enumerated in statute and cannot give meaningful, or legally significant, consent. Gramegna v. Parole Com'n, 666 So.2d 135 (1996). Pardon And Parole ⚿ 48.1

Police officer's arrest report was properly relied upon by Parole Commission in determining that fondling of minor by defendant, which was basis of his conviction for lewd conduct, was nonconsensual and rendered defendant ineligible for control release, even though information, indictment, bill of particulars, and judgment of conviction did not establish disqualifying conviction. Gramegna v. Parole

Com'n, 666 So.2d 135 (1996). Pardon And Parole ⚿ 58

Defendant convicted of engaging in "sexual activity" with child by person in familial or custodial authority was ineligible for control release, where incidents of proscribed sexual activity were nonconsensual and forcible. Fulkroad v. Florida Parole Com'n, App. 1 Dist., 632 So.2d 148 (1994). Pardon And Parole ⚿ 48.1

8. Credit for time spent in program

Department of Corrections cannot grant credit for time spent under control release supervision unless Parole Commission, as statutory Control Release Authority, instructs it to do so. Gay v. Singletary, 700 So.2d 1220 (1997). Prisons ⚿ 248

Control release supervision is not functional equivalent of time spent in prison; thus, releasee is not entitled to credit toward sentence for time spent under control release supervision. Gay v. Singletary, 700 So.2d 1220 (1997). Prisons ⚿ 248

Time spent under control release supervision is not "coercive deprivation of liberty" for purposes of entitlement to credit toward sentence. Gay v. Singletary, 700 So.2d 1220 (1997). Prisons ⚿ 248

Parole Commission has broad authority in administering control release program, including authority to either grant or deny credit for time spent under supervision when it determines that releasee has violated terms of release. Gay v. Singletary, 700 So.2d 1220 (1997). Prisons ⚿ 248

Control release was not a "coercive deprivation of liberty" and, thus, defendant, who served one year on control release after being released from custody of Department of Corrections and while awaiting disposition of appeal challenging sentence, was not entitled to receive credit for time spent in this program. Moening v. State, App. 5 Dist., 643 So.2d 1201 (1994). Sentencing And Punishment ⚿ 1165

9. Mandamus

Petition for habeas corpus which sought to require parole commission to establish control release date was treated as petition for writ of mandamus. Scott v. State, 641 So.2d 407 (1994). Mandamus ⚿ 154(2)

Mandamus is available to prisoner seeking control release date for which he has established his entitlement. King v. Florida Parole Com'n, App. 1 Dist., 614 So.2d 1183 (1993). Mandamus ⚿ 73(1)

Inmate's mandamus petition, seeking control release date, was deficient for failure to set forth allegations sufficient on their face to demonstrate his eligibility for control release program and entitlement to control release date; inmate could not merely take issue, in the abstract, with parole commission's legal interpretation of one of the disqualifying criteria applicable to him. King v. Florida Parole Com'n, App. 1 Dist., 614 So.2d 1183 (1993). Mandamus ⚿ 154(4); Pardon And Parole ⚿ 49

10. Habitual offenders

Defendant's sentence as habitual offender did not make him ineligible for control release program, where he was not sentenced as habitual violent felony offender. Ferguson v. State, App. 3 Dist., 677 So.2d 968 (1996). Pardon And Parole ⚿ 48.1

11. Revocation of control release

Forfeiture of control release credits along with forfeiture of regular gain time upon supervision revocation did not violate ex post facto clause, although releasee committed underlying criminal offense prior to effective date of control release program, where releasee had voluntarily accepted placement on that program and then violated terms and conditions of control release; by accepting release under control release program, releasee waived any ex post facto claims. Lewis v. Moore, 753 So.2d 1242 (2000). Constitutional Law ⚿ 951; Constitutional Law ⚿ 2816; Prisons ⚿ 248

Upon revocation of inmate's control release, Department of Corrections (DOC) was authorized to determine that inmate forfeited gain-time on sentence for 1992 offense. Verdelotti v. Moore, App. 1 Dist., 730 So.2d 373 (1999). Pardon And Parole ⚿ 75

Department of Corrections' (DOC) determination that inmate forfeited gain-time on sentences for 1987 offenses due to inmate's violation of conditions of control release violated ex post facto prohibitions, in light of inmate's timely objection to control release. Verdelotti v. Moore, App. 1 Dist., 730 So.2d 373 (1999). Constitutional Law ⚿ 2816; Pardon And Parole ⚿ 75

By accepting terms and conditions of early release under control release program, which included forfeiture of basic and incentive gain time upon revocation of control release, inmate waived any ex post facto argument as to forfeiture of such gain time after violation of control release. Bowles v. Singletary, 698 So.2d 1201 (1997), rehearing denied. Constitutional Law ⚿ 948

12. Collateral estoppel

Doctrine of collateral estoppel barred inmate from raising, in petition for writ of habeas corpus, his argument that forfeiture of gain time upon violation of the terms of his control release supervision constituted an ex post facto violation; inmate previously raised argument in a petition for writ of mandamus and in a proceeding before the Parole Commission, and issue was correctly resolved against inmate in both prior proceedings. Knox v. State, App. 5 Dist., 873 So.2d 1250 (2004), cause dismissed 884 So.2d 22. Habeas Corpus ⚷ 891

947.147. Victim restitution as condition of control release

If the defendant is released under control release, any restitution ordered under s. 775.089 shall be a condition of such release. The Control Release Authority may revoke the offender's control release if the defendant fails to comply with such order. In determining whether to revoke control release, the Control Release Authority shall consider the defendant's employment status, earning ability, and financial resources; the willfulness of the defendant's failure to pay; and any other special circumstances that may have a bearing on the defendant's ability to pay.

Laws 1991, c. 91–167, § 1; Laws 1993, c. 93–37, § 8.

Historical and Statutory Notes

Amendment Notes:

Laws 1993, c. 93–37, § 8, eff. Oct. 1, 1993, reenacted this section for the purpose of incorporating the amendment to § 775.089 in a reference thereto.

Section 16 of Laws 1993, c. 93–37, provides:

"This act shall take effect upon becoming a law, except that sections 1–12 and section 14 of this act shall take effect October 1, 1993, and shall apply to offenses committed on or after October 1, 1993."

Library References

Prisons ⚷242.
Westlaw Topic No. 310.
C.J.S. Prisons and Rights of Prisoners § 153.

Research References

Treatises and Practice Aids

16 Florida Practice Series § 10:15, Post Release--Control Release.

947.149. Conditional medical release

(1) The commission shall, in conjunction with the department, establish the conditional medical release program. An inmate is eligible for consideration for release under the conditional medical release program when the inmate, because of an existing medical or physical condition, is determined by the department to be within one of the following designations:

(a) "Permanently incapacitated inmate," which means an inmate who has a condition caused by injury, disease, or illness which, to a reasonable degree of medical certainty, renders the inmate permanently and irreversibly physically incapacitated to the extent that the inmate does not constitute a danger to herself or himself or others.

(b) "Terminally ill inmate," which means an inmate who has a condition caused by injury, disease, or illness which, to a reasonable degree of medical certainty, renders the inmate terminally ill to the extent that there can be no recovery and death is imminent, so that the inmate does not constitute a danger to herself or himself or others.

(2) Notwithstanding any provision to the contrary, any person determined eligible under this section and sentenced to the custody of the department may, upon referral by the department, be considered for conditional medical release by the commission, in addition to any parole consideration for which the inmate may be considered, except that conditional medical release is not authorized for an inmate who is under sentence of death. No inmate has a right to conditional medical release or to a medical evaluation to determine eligibility for such release.

(3) The authority and whether or not to grant conditional medical release and establish additional conditions of conditional medical release rests solely within the discretion of the commission, in accordance with the provisions of this section, together with the authority to approve the release plan to include necessary medical care and attention. The department shall identify inmates who may be eligible for conditional medical release based upon available medical information and shall refer them to the commission for consideration. In considering an inmate for conditional medical release, the commission may require that additional medical evidence be produced or that additional medical examinations be conducted, and may require such other investigations to be made as may be warranted.

(4) The conditional medical release term of an inmate released on conditional medical release is for the remainder of the inmate's sentence, without diminution of sentence for good behavior. Supervision of the medical releasee must include periodic medical evaluations at intervals determined by the commission at the time of release.

(5)(a) If it is discovered during the conditional medical release that the medical or physical condition of the medical releasee has improved to the extent that she or he would no longer be eligible for conditional medical release under this section, the commission may order that the releasee be returned to the custody of the department for a conditional medical release revocation hearing, in accordance with s. 947.141. If conditional medical release is revoked due to improvement in the medical or physical condition of the releasee, she or he shall serve the balance of her or his sentence with credit for the time served on conditional medical release and without forfeiture of any gain-time accrued prior to conditional medical release. If the person whose conditional medical release is revoked due to an improvement in medical or physical condition would otherwise be eligible for parole or any other release program, the person may be considered for such release program pursuant to law.

(b) In addition to revocation of conditional medical release pursuant to paragraph (a), conditional medical release may also be revoked for violation of any condition of the release established by the commission, in accordance with s. 947.141, and the releasee's gain-time may be forfeited pursuant to s. 944.28(1).

(6) The department and the commission shall adopt rules as necessary to implement the conditional medical release program.

Laws 1992, c. 92–310, § 16; Laws 1994, c. 94–121, § 2. Amended by Laws 1997, c. 97–102, § 1672, eff. July 1, 1997.

Historical and Statutory Notes

Amendment Notes:

Laws 1994, c. 94–121, § 2, eff. May 4, 1994, reenacted subsec. (5) of this section for the purpose of incorporating the amendment to § 947.141 in a reference thereto.

Laws 1997, c. 97–102, eff. July 1, 1997, removed gender-specific references applicable to human beings from volume 4 of the Florida Statutes without substantive changes in legal effect.

Cross References

Dangerous sexual felony offenders, mandatory sentencing, see § 794.0115.
Trafficking in cocaine, conditional medical release not prohibited, see § 893.135.
Violent career criminals, conditional medical release under this section not expressly prohibited, see § 775.084.

Law Review and Journal Commentaries

A Folly of Criminal Justice Policy–Making: The Rise and Demise of Early Release in Florida, and Its Ex Post Facto Implications. Chet Kaufman, 26 Fla.St.U.L.Rev. 361 (1999).

Library References

Prisons ⚷248.
Westlaw Topic No. 310.
C.J.S. Prisons and Rights of Prisoners § 152.

Research References

Encyclopedias

Early Release for Persons Convicted of Offenses Involving Possession of Firearm or Destructive Device, FL Jur. 2d Prisons & Prisoners § 202.

Generally; Release on Gain-Time Allowances, FL Jur. 2d Prisons & Prisoners § 211.

Forms

Florida Pleading and Practice Forms § 98:16.10, Petition for Writ of Habeas Corpus--Petitioner in Need of Medical Care.

Treatises and Practice Aids

16 Florida Practice Series § 1:44, Sentencing Alternatives--Straight Confinement.

16 Florida Practice Series § 3:26, Completing the 1994 Guidelines Scoresheet--Sentence Computation and Presumptive Sentencing Range--Calculating a State Prison Sentence.

16 Florida Practice Series § 4:34, Completing the 1995 Guidelines Scoresheet--Sentence Computation and Presumptive Sentencing Range--Calculating a Prison Sentence.

16 Florida Practice Series § 5:44, Completing the Criminal Punishment Code Scoresheet--Sentence Computation.

16 Florida Practice Series § 6:52, Enhancement of Penalty and Reclassification of Offense--Reclassifications of Various Types Batteries and Assaults--Assault or Battery on Emergency Medical Care Providers, Firefighters, Law...

16 Florida Practice Series § 6:91, Enhancement of Penalty and Reclassification of Offense--Habitual Felony Offender, Habitual Violent Felony Offender, Three-Time Violent Felony Offender, and Violent Career Criminal--Violent...

16 Florida Practice Series § 6:93, Enhancement of Penalty and Reclassification of Offense--10/20/Life.

16 Florida Practice Series § 6:94, Enhancement of Penalty and Reclassification of Offense--Dangerous Sexual Felony Offender.

16 Florida Practice Series § 10:14, Post Release--Conditional Medical Release.

16 Florida Practice Series § 10:17, Violation of Conditional Release, Control Release, Conditional Medical Release, or Addiction Recovery Supervision.

947.15. Reports

On or before January 1 of each year, the commission shall make a written report to the Governor and Cabinet of its activities together with a full and detailed financial statement, copies of which shall be sent to the Department of Legal Affairs and to such other officials and persons as the commission may deem advisable. One copy of said report shall become a part of the records of the commission.

Laws 1941, c. 20519, § 28; Laws 1969, c. 69–106, §§ 11, 33, 35.

Historical and Statutory Notes

Amendment Notes:

Laws 1969, c. 69–106, §§ 11, 35, transferred all powers, duties and functions of the attorney general to the department of legal affairs.

Laws 1969, c. 69–106, §§ 33, 35, provided, in subsec. (2) that "All powers, duties and functions of the board of commissioners of state institutions relating to the appointment of the probation and parole commission as provided in section 947.02, Florida Statutes, shall be exercised and performed by the governor and the cabinet. Henceforth, however, each appointment shall be made from among the first three (3) eligible persons on the list of the persons eligible for said position."

Library References

Pardon and Parole ⚷55.1.
Westlaw Topic No. 284.
C.J.S. Pardon and Parole §§ 45 to 47.

947.16. Eligibility for parole; initial parole interviews; powers and duties of commission

(1) Every person who has been convicted of a felony or who has been convicted of one or more misdemeanors and whose sentence or cumulative sentences total 12 months or more, who is confined in execution of the judgment of the court, and whose record during confinement or while under supervision is good, shall, unless otherwise provided by law, be eligible for interview for parole consideration of her or his cumulative sentence structure as follows:

(a) An inmate who has been sentenced for an indeterminate term or a term of 3 years or less shall have an initial interview conducted by a hearing examiner within 8 months after the initial date of confinement in execution of the judgment.

(b) An inmate who has been sentenced for a minimum term in excess of 3 years but of less than 6 years shall have an initial interview conducted by a hearing examiner within 14 months after the initial date of confinement in execution of the judgment.

(c) An inmate who has been sentenced for a minimum term of 6 or more years but other than for a life term shall have an initial interview conducted by a hearing examiner within 24 months after the initial date of confinement in execution of the judgment.

(d) An inmate who has been sentenced for a term of life shall have an initial interview conducted by a hearing examiner within 5 years after the initial date of confinement in execution of the judgment.

(e) An inmate who has been convicted and sentenced under ss. 958.011–958.15, or any other inmate who has been determined by the department to be a youthful offender, shall be interviewed by a parole examiner within 8 months after the initial date of confinement in execution of the judgment.

(2) The following special types of cases shall have their initial parole interview as follows:

(a) An initial interview may be postponed for a period not to exceed 90 days. Such postponement shall be for good cause, which shall include, but need not be limited to, the need for the department to obtain a presentence or postsentence investigation report or a probation or parole or mandatory conditional release violation report. The reason for postponement shall be noted in writing and included in the official record. No postponement for good cause shall result in an initial interview being conducted later than 90 days after the inmate's initially scheduled initial interview.

(b) An initial interview may be deferred for any inmate who is out to court. Such deferral shall not result in an initial interview being conducted later than 90 days after the department provides written notice to the commission that the inmate has been returned from court.

(c) An initial interview may be deferred for any inmate confined in any appropriate treatment facility within the state, public or private, by virtue of transfer from the department under any applicable law. Such deferral shall not result in an initial interview being conducted later than 90 days after the department provides written notice to the commission that the inmate has been returned to the department.

(d) An inmate designated a mentally disordered sex offender shall have an initial interview conducted within 90 days of receiving written notification by the department to the commission of the need for such interview and that the inmate's file contains all investigative reports deemed necessary by the commission to conduct such interview.

(e) Any inmate who has been determined to be an incapacitated person pursuant to s. 744.331 shall have an initial interview conducted within 90 days after the date the commission is provided with written notice that the inmate has been restored to capacity by the court.

(f) An initial interview may be held at the discretion of the commission after the entry of a commission order to revoke parole or mandatory conditional release.

(g) For purposes of determining eligibility for parole interview and release, the mandatory minimum portion of a concurrent sentence will begin on the date the sentence begins to run as provided in s. 921.161. The mandatory minimum portions of consecutive sentences shall be served at the beginning of the maximum sentence as established by the Department of Corrections. Each mandatory minimum portion of consecutive sentences shall be served consecutively; provided, that in no case shall a sentence begin to run before the date of imposition. The commission shall conduct an initial interview for an inmate serving a mandatory minimum sentence according to the following schedule:

1. An inmate serving a mandatory term of 7 years or less shall have an initial interview no sooner than 6 months prior to the expiration of the mandatory minimum portion of the sentence.

2. An inmate serving a mandatory term in excess of 7 years but of less than 15 years shall have an initial interview no sooner than 12 months prior to the expiration of the mandatory minimum portion of the sentence.

3. An inmate serving a mandatory term of 15 years or more shall have an initial interview no sooner than 18 months prior to the expiration of the mandatory minimum portion of the sentence.

(h) If an inmate is serving a sentence imposed by a county or circuit court of this state concurrently with a sentence imposed by a court of another state or of the United States, and if the department has designated the correctional institution of the other jurisdiction as the place for reception and confinement of such person, the inmate so released to another jurisdiction shall be eligible for consideration for parole, except that the commission shall determine the presumptive parole release date and the effective parole release date by requesting such person's record file from the receiving jurisdiction. Upon receiving such records, the commission panel assigned by the chair shall determine such release dates based on the relevant information in that file. The commission may concur with the parole release decision of the jurisdiction granting parole and accepting supervision. The provisions of s. 947.174 do not apply to an inmate serving a concurrent sentence in another jurisdiction pursuant to s. 921.16(2).

(3) Notwithstanding the provisions of ss. 775.021 and 921.16, if an inmate has received a consecutive sentence or sentences imposed by a court or courts of this state, the inmate shall be eligible for consideration for parole, unless otherwise expressly prohibited by law.

(4) A person who has become eligible for an initial parole interview and who may, according to the objective parole guidelines of the commission, be granted parole shall be placed on parole in accordance with the provisions of this law; except that, in any case of a person convicted of murder, robbery, burglary of a dwelling or burglary of a structure or conveyance in which a human being is present, aggravated assault, aggravated battery, kidnapping, sexual battery or attempted sexual battery, incest or attempted incest, an unnatural and lascivious act or an attempted unnatural and lascivious act, lewd and lascivious behavior, assault or aggravated assault when a sexual act is completed or attempted, battery or aggravated battery when a sexual act is completed or attempted, arson, or any felony involving the use of a firearm or other deadly weapon or the use of intentional violence, at the time of sentencing the judge may enter an order retaining jurisdiction over the offender for review of a commission release order. This jurisdiction of the trial court judge is limited to the first one-third of the maximum sentence imposed. When any person is convicted of two or more felonies and concurrent sentences are imposed, then the jurisdiction of the trial court judge as provided herein applies to the first one-third of the maximum sentence imposed for the highest felony of which the person was convicted. When any person is convicted of two or more felonies and consecutive sentences are imposed, then the jurisdiction of the trial court judge as provided herein applies to one-third of the total consecutive sentences imposed.

(a) In retaining jurisdiction for the purposes of this act, the trial court judge shall state the justification with individual particularity, and such justification shall be made a part of the court record. A copy of such justification shall be delivered to the department together with the commitment issued by the court pursuant to s. 944.16.[1]

(b) Gain-time as provided for by law shall accrue, except that an offender over whom the trial court has retained jurisdiction as provided herein shall not be released during the first one-third of her or his sentence by reason of gain-time.

(c) In such a case of retained jurisdiction, the commission, within 30 days after the entry of its release order, shall send notice of its release order to the original sentencing judge and to the appropriate state attorney. The release order shall be made contingent upon entry of an order by the appropriate circuit judge relinquishing jurisdiction as provided for in paragraphs (d) and (f). If the original sentencing judge is no longer in service, such notice shall be sent to the chief judge of the circuit in which the offender was sentenced. The chief judge may designate any circuit judge within the circuit to act in the place of the original sentencing judge. Such notice shall stay the time requirements of s. 947.1745.

(d) Within 10 days after receipt of the notice provided for in paragraph (c), the original sentencing judge or her or his replacement shall notify the commission as to whether or not the court further desires to retain jurisdiction. If the original sentencing judge or her or his replacement does not so notify the commission within the 10–day period or notifies the commission that the court does not desire to retain jurisdiction, then the commission may dispose of the matter as it sees fit.

(e) Upon receipt of notice of intent to retain jurisdiction from the original sentencing judge or her or his replacement, the commission shall, within 10 days, forward to the court its release order, the findings of fact, the parole hearing examiner's report and recommendation, and all supporting information upon which its release order was based.

(f) Within 30 days of receipt of the items listed in paragraph (e), the original sentencing judge or her or his replacement shall review the order, findings, and evidence; and, if the judge finds that the order of the commission is not based on competent substantial evidence or that the parole is not in the best interest of the community or the inmate, the court may vacate the release order. The judge or her or his replacement shall notify the commission of the decision of the court, and, if the release order is vacated, such notification shall contain the evidence relied on and the reasons for denial. A copy of such notice shall be sent to the inmate.

(g) The decision of the original sentencing judge or, in her or his absence, the chief judge of the circuit to vacate any parole release order as provided in this section is not appealable. Each inmate whose parole release order has been vacated by the court shall be reinterviewed within 2 years after the date of receipt of the vacated release order and every 2 years thereafter, or earlier by order of the court retaining jurisdiction. However, each inmate whose parole release order has been vacated by the court and who has been:

1. Convicted of murder or attempted murder;

2. Convicted of sexual battery or attempted sexual battery; or

3. Sentenced to a 25-year minimum mandatory sentence previously provided in s. 775.082,

shall be reinterviewed once within 5 years after the date of receipt of the vacated release order and once every 5 years thereafter, if the commission finds that it is not reasonable to expect that parole would be granted during the following years and states the bases for the finding in writing. For any inmate who is within 7 years of his or her tentative release date, the commission may establish a reinterview date prior to the 5-year schedule.

(h) An inmate whose parole release order has been vacated by the court may not be given a presumptive parole release date during the period of retention of jurisdiction by the court. During such period, a new effective parole release date may be authorized at the discretion of the commission without further interview unless an interview is requested by no fewer than two commissioners. Any such new effective parole release date must be reviewed in accordance with the provisions of paragraphs (c), (d), (e), (f), and (g).

(5) Within 90 days after any interview for parole, the inmate shall be advised of the presumptive parole release date. Subsequent to the establishment of the presumptive parole release date, the commission may, at its discretion, review the official record or conduct additional interviews with the inmate. However, the presumptive parole release date may not be changed except for reasons of institutional conduct or the acquisition of new information not available at the time of the initial interview.

(6) This section as amended by chapter 82–171, Laws of Florida, shall apply only to those persons convicted on or after the effective date of chapter 82–171; and this section as in effect before being amended by chapter 82–171 shall apply to any person convicted before the effective date of chapter 82–171.

Laws 1941, c. 20519, § 12; Laws 1943, c. 21775, § 3; Laws 1971, c. 71–110, §§ 1, 2; Laws 1974, c. 74–122, § 2; Laws 1977, c. 77–120, § 88; Laws 1978, c. 78–318, § 1; Laws 1978, c. 78–417, § 11; Laws 1979, c. 79–3, § 106; Laws 1979, c. 79–42, § 5; Laws 1979, c. 79–164, § 195; Laws 1979, c. 79–310, § 2; Laws 1979, c. 79–341, § 8; Laws 1981, c. 81–30, § 1; Laws 1981, c. 81–322, § 4; Laws 1982, c. 82–171, §§ 9, 19; Laws 1982, c. 82–401, §§ 1, 2; Laws 1983, c. 83–131, § 9; Laws 1983, c. 83–216, § 189; Laws 1985, c. 85–107, § 1; Laws 1985, c. 85–295, § 3; Laws 1989, c. 89–96, § 111. Amended by Laws 1997, c. 97–102, § 1673, eff. July 1, 1997; Laws 1997, c. 97–289, § 1, eff. Oct. 1, 1997.

[1] Repealed by Laws 1985, c. 85–288, § 27.

Historical and Statutory Notes

Amendment Notes:

Laws 1943, c. 21775, § 3, amended subsec. (1) by inserting the words "or one who has been convicted of one or more misdemeanors and whose sentence or cumulative sentences total twelve months or more" following "convicted of a felony"; deleted the words "for a definite term of over one year" following "judgment of the court thereof"; inserted the words "in cases where the term is eighteen months or less, has served not less than one-third of his term, and" following "not less than six months of such term and,"; and deleted, at the end of the subsection, the proviso which read: "provided, however, that no person who shall have been sentenced for the term of his natural life shall be eligible for consideration by the commission for parole unless he has sustained a good prison record".

Laws 1971, c. 71–110, §§ 1, 2, substituted, in the first sentence of subsec. (1), the words "and whose prison record * * * provided by law" in lieu of "thereof and who has served not less than six months of such term, and in cases where the term is eighteen months or less, has served not less than one-third of his term, and whose prison record is good, shall", added the second sentence to subsec. (1), and added subsec. (3).

Laws 1974, c. 74–122, § 2, amending subsec. (1), deleted the words "a jail or prison in this state" following "who is confined" in the first sentence and added the definition of the term "confined".

Laws 1977, c. 77–120, a reviser's bill, amended subsec. (1) of this section to conform with Laws 1975, c. 75–49, which created the department of offender rehabilitation (see § 20.315) and transferred to the department certain functions performed by the division of corrections of the department of health and rehabilitative services and the parole and probation commission of the department of offender rehabilitation.

Laws 1978, c. 78–318, added the subject matter contained in subsec. (3) following the proviso of the first sentence.

Laws 1978, c. 78–417, rewrote the section which, as it appears in Fla.St.1977, provided:

"(1) Every person who has been, or who may hereafter be, convicted of a felony or who has been convicted of one or more misdemeanors and whose sentence or cumulative sentences total 12 months or more, who is confined in execution of the judgment of the court, and whose record during confinement is good, shall, unless otherwise provided by law, be eligible for consideration by the commission for parole. An inmate who has been sentenced for a term of 5 years or less shall be interviewed by a member of the commission or its representative within 6 months after the initial date of confinement in execution of the judgment. An inmate who has been sentenced for a term in excess of 5 years shall be interviewed by a member of the commission or its representative within 1 years after the initial date of confinement in execution of the judgment. An inmate convicted of a capital crime shall be interviewed at the discretion of the commission. As used in this subsection, the term "confined" shall be deemed to include presence in any appropriate treatment facility, public or private, by virtue of transfer from the Department of Offender Rehabilitation under any applicable law.

"(2) Persons who have become eligible for parole and who may in the discretion of the commission be granted parole shall be placed on parole in accordance with the provisions of this law.

"(3) Within 30 days after any interview for parole, the inmate shall be advised of the decision of the commission. Subsequent to the initial interview, the inmate shall be interviewed for parole at periodic intervals not less often than annually."

Laws 1979, c. 79–3, a reviser's bill, provided for substitution of references to the department and secretary of "corrections" for the department and secretary of "offender rehabilitation" to conform with Laws 1978, c. 78–53.

Laws 1979, c. 79–42, § 5, interpolated the fifth sentence in subsec. (1), and substituted in the sixth sentence thereof "section" for "subsection".

Laws 1979, c. 79–164, a reviser's bill, corrected statutes by deletion of expired, obsolete, invalid, inconsistent or redundant provisions; modified cross references and grammar; and, otherwise improved the clarity to facilitate interpretation of the statutes.

Laws 1979, c. 79–310, § 2, deleted from subsec. (1) provision that a person is not eligible for parole consideration while serving sentence in another jurisdiction until returned to Florida to serve the remainder of the Florida sentence.

Laws 1979, c. 79–341, § 8, inserted in the first sentence of subsec. (3) "or attempted sexual battery, incest or attempted incest, an unnatural and lascivious act or an attempted unnatural and lascivious act, lewd and lascivious behavior assault or aggravated assault when a sexual act is completed or attempted, battery or aggravated battery when a sexual act is completed or attempted".

Laws 1981, c. 81–30, § 1, inserted in the first sentence of subsec. (3) "burglary of a dwelling or burglary of a structure or conveyance in which a human being is present" and, in subsec. (3)(g) added the language following "shall not be appealable."

Laws 1981, c. 81–322, § 4, deleted "panel" following "hearing examiner" in the third sentence of subsec. (1).

Laws 1982, c. 82–171, § 9, in subsec. (1) deleted the last two sentences of this subsection, which provided for interviews of inmates convicted of capital crimes, and defined the term "confined"; divided subsec. (1) into an introductory fragment and paragraphs; in the introductory fragment of subsec. (1), inserted "or while under supervision," inserted "to be ineligible for parole" and inserted "interview as follows"; in subsec. (1) (a), as designated, substituted "3 years" for "5 years" and "8 months" for "6 months," in subsec. (1) (b), as designated, substituted "3 years but less than 6" for "5" and substituted "14 months" for "1 year"; added subsecs. (1) (c), (1) (d), and (1) (e); in subsec. (3), substituted "an initial parole interview" for "parole" in the first sentence, substituted "half" for "third" in the second, third, and fourth sentences; in subsec. (3) (b), substituted "by law" for "in ss. 944.27, 944.271, and 944.29" and substituted "one-half" for "one-third"; in subsec. (3) (c), substituted "30 days of the final parole interview" for "the time requirements of s. 947.17(4)" and "judge" for "court" in the first sentence, interpolated the second and third sentences, and substituted "947.174" for "947.17(4)" in the fourth sentence, as amended; in subsecs. (3) (d), (3) (e), and (3) (f), among other changes substituted "judge or his replacement" for "court"; in the first sentence of subsec. (4), substituted "90" for "45"; and rewrote subsec. (2) which formerly provided:

"An initial hearing may be postponed for a period not to exceed 60 days. Such postponement shall be for good cause, and the reasons therefor shall be noted in writing and included in the official record. However, in no case shall such postponement result in a hearing being conducted any time later than 1 year after the initial date the inmate is confined in execution of the judgment of the court. Notwithstanding the provisions of this subsection, an initial interview may be deferred for an inmate who is out to court or transferred to the Department of Health and Rehabilitative Services for psychological or psychiatric treatment or observation. If an inmate is returned to the department within 1 year of the date of confinement in execution of the judgment, the provisions of subsection (1) shall apply. In all other cases, an initial interview shall be conducted within 3 months of the date the inmate returned to the department."

Section 19 of Laws 1982, c. 82–171 as amended by Laws 1982, c. 82–401, § 2, was designated as Fla.St.1982, Supp. § 947.16(5) to read:

"(5) This section as amended by ch. 82–171, Laws of Florida, shall apply only to those persons convicted on or after the effective date of ch. 82–171; and this section as in effect before being amended by ch. 82–171 shall apply to any person convicted before the effective date of ch. 82–171."

Laws 1982, c. 82–401, § 1, substituted "a parole examiner" for "The commission" at the beginning of subsec. (1) (e) and § 2 of the law rewrote provisions comprising subsec. (5). Section 3 of the law provided:

"This act shall take effect upon becoming a law [June 29, 1982] and shall operate retroactively to April 20, 1982."

Laws 1983, c. 83–131, § 9, amending subsec. (3), in the introductory provisions substituted "one-third" for "one-half" of the sentence in the second, third and fourth sentences, and substituted "charged and proven" for "of which the person was convicted" at the end of the third sentence; added the second sentence to subsec. (3)(a); substituted "one-third" for "one-half" in subsec. (3)(b); rewrote subsec. (3)(g); and added subsec. (3)(h).

Laws 1983, c. 83–216, was a reviser's correction bill amending subsecs. (1)(e), (2)(e) and (2)(h) to improve clarity and facilitate correct interpretation.

Laws 1985, c. 85–107, § 1, eff. June 11, 1985, near the beginning of subsec. (1) deleted "or who may hereafter be" preceding "convicted of a felony" and substituted "be eligible for interview for parole consideration of his cumulative sentence structure" for "to be ineligible for parole, be eligible for consideration for parole interview", inserted the first three sentences contained in subsec. (2)(g), and added subsec. (3).

Laws 1985, c. 85–295, § 3, eff. June 20, 1985, substantially rewrote provisions contained in subsec. (4)(c).

Laws 1989, c. 89–96, § 111, eff. Oct. 1, 1989, in subsec. (2)(e), substituted references to incapacitated person and capacity for references to mentally incompetent and competency.

Laws 1997, c. 97–102, eff. July 1, 1997, removed gender-specific references applicable to human beings from volume 4 of the Florida Statutes without substantive changes in legal effect.

Laws 1997, c. 97–289, § 1, eff. Oct. 1, 1997, in subsec. (4)(c), substituted "paragraphs (d) and (f)" for "paragraph 5(d) and (f)"; in subsec. (4)(h), in the third sentence, substituted "must" for "shall"; and, rewrote subsec. (4)(g), which formerly read:

"The decision of the original sentencing judge or, in his absence, the chief judge of the circuit to vacate any parole release order as provided in this act is not appealable. Each inmate whose parole release order has been vacated by the court shall be reinterviewed within 2 years after the date of receipt of the vacated release order and every 2 years thereafter, or earlier by order of the court retaining jurisdiction."

Cross References

Gain-time, see § 944.275.
Prisoner progress reports furnished to parole and probation commission, see § 921.21.

Law Review and Journal Commentaries

Administrative Procedure Act due process in parole determinations. 56 Fla.B.J. 285 (1982).

Criminal law reform—1971. 45 Fla.B.J. 405 (1971).

Due process in correctional administrative hearings. Thompson H. Gooding, Jr., 33 U.Fla. L.Rev. 151 (1981).

Instruction as to possibility of parole as reversible error. 7 Miami L.Q. 120 (1952).

Parole. James H. Burke, Jr., 57 Fla.B.J. 245 (1983).

Probation in Florida. Vernon W. Clark, 14 U.Fla.L.Rev. 213 (1961).

Library References

Pardon and Parole ⚷44 to 62.
Prisons ⚷243.
Westlaw Topic Nos. 284, 310.
C.J.S. Pardon and Parole §§ 44 to 57.
C.J.S. Prisons and Rights of Prisoners §§ 142 to 144, 147 to 151.

Research References

ALR Library

143 ALR 1486, Statute Conferring Power Upon Administrative Body in Respect to the Parole of Prisoners, or the Discharge of Parolees, as Unconstitutional Infringement of Power of Executive or Judiciary.

101 ALR 1402, Constitutionality of Statute Conferring on Court Power to Suspend Sentence.

Forms

Florida Pleading and Practice Forms § 96:29, Statutory Judgment and Sentence Form.

Treatises and Practice Aids

11 Florida Practice Series App. G, Judgment and Sentence Forms, Including Costs.

16 Florida Practice Series § 1:42, Judicial Discretion in the Imposition of Sentence--Post-Sentence Jurisdiction.

16 Florida Practice Series § 10:19, Parole--Eligibility for Parole.

16 Florida Practice Series § 10:20, Parole--Presumptive Parole Release Date.

United States Supreme Court

Life inmates, rights to commutation of sentence before board of pardons, see Connecticut Bd. of Pardons v. Dumschat, U.S.Conn.1981, 101 S.Ct. 2460, 452 U.S. 458, 69 L.Ed.2d 158.

Parole procedure, opportunity to be heard, and notification of reasons for denial of parole, see Greenholtz v. Inmates of Nebraska Penal and Correctional Complex, 1979, 99 S.Ct. 2100, 442 U.S. 1, 60 L.Ed.2d 668, on remand 602 F.2d 155.

Notes of Decisions

I. IN GENERAL

Subdivision Index

---

1. Validity

This section governing eligibility for parole is constitutional. Wilson v. State, 414 So.2d 512 (1982); Burwick v. State, App., 408 So.2d 722 (1982) approved 442 So.2d 944, certiorari denied 104 S.Ct. 1719, 80 L.Ed.2d 191.

Where habeas petitioner, at time he committed murder that led to his incarceration, was on fair notice that if he received life sentence he would be subject to parole at discretion of Florida Parole and Probation Commission, which was not changed by subsequently enacted Parole Act, and where guidelines promulgated thereunder merely stated and rationalized exercise of Commission's discretion, petitioner accordingly suffered no legislative increase in punishment by Commission's application of Parole Act in setting petitioner's presumptive parole release date, so that application of Parole Act did not violate Constitution's ex post facto clause. Paschal v. Wainwright, C.A.11 (Fla.)1984, 738 F.2d 1173. Constitutional Law ⚷ 2823; Pardon And Parole ⚷ 42.1

Although defendant's contention that this section was unconstitutional as applied to him was correct, District Court of Appeal could not address argument because record affirmatively showed that he did not raise issue before the trial judge. Springfield v. State, App. 2 Dist., 443 So.2d 484 (1984). Criminal Law ⚷ 1042.3(2)

This section providing that inmate shall be advised of decision of parole commission within 30 days after any interview for parole and that, subsequent to initial interview, inmate shall be interviewed for parole at periodic intervals not less often than annually, was constitutional. Dedmon v. State, App. 1 Dist., 400 So.2d 1042 (1981). Pardon And Parole ⚷ 43

2. Construction and application

Statute allowing trial court to retain jurisdiction over one-third of defendant's sentence applied, where statute was in effect at time of sentencing. Barnhill v. State, App. 5 Dist., 788 So.2d 313 (2001). Sentencing And Punishment ⚷ 226

It is Parole Commission which first, consistent with objective guidelines, interviews and established release dates for inmates who are eligible for parole. Blackwelder v. State, App. 2 Dist., 647 So.2d 991 (1994). Pardon And Parole ⚷ 48.1

A person cannot be on parole and probation at the same time for the same offense; but this proposition has no application when there are two separate offenses for which two sentences may be imposed in which case it is possible to have a prison sentence from which parole may be available and also have probation imposed. Stafford v. State, 455 So.2d 385 (1984). Pardon And Parole ⚷ 44

The 1982 amendment to this section establishing exceptions to eligibility for parole for persons who have committed certain designated crimes did not apply to offenses committed prior to effective date of that amendment. Wicker v. State, App. 2 Dist., 438 So.2d 398 (1983). Pardon And Parole ⚷ 42.1

A person cannot be on probation and parole at the same time, as probation and parole have separate identities and must be treated separately. Johnson v. State, App. 2 Dist., 419 So.2d 752 (1982), petition for review denied 427 So.2d 737. Pardon And Parole ⚷ 41; Sentencing And Punishment ⚷ 1819

Decision to parole, while critical to inmate, is not necessarily a right to which inmate is absolutely entitled. Daniels v. Florida Parole and Probation Commission, App. 1 Dist., 401 So.2d 1351 (1981), approved 444 So.2d 917. Pardon And Parole ⚷ 46

Whether a defendant who is convicted of a capital crime and receives a life sentence should be allowed a chance at parole after 25 years is a policy determination for legislature or the parole authorities rather than for courts. Miller v. State, 373 So.2d 882 (1979). Constitutional Law ⚷ 2507(3)

There is no restriction against consideration for parole in a sentence for a felony of the first degree. Wright v. State, App. 1 Dist., 342 So.2d 565 (1977). Pardon And Parole ⚷ 44; Pardon And Parole ⚷ 49

Trial court has no authority to grant parole; that power is vested solely in parole commission. Owens v. State, App. 1 Dist., 308 So.2d 171 (1975). Pardon And Parole ⚷ 45.1

Though trial court has no authority to grant parole, it is not precluded from recommending conditions of parole. Owens v. State, App. 1 Dist., 308 So.2d 171 (1975). Pardon And Parole ⚷ 64.1

By virtue of Laws 1983, c. 83–87, the legislature intended that parole be precluded for all persons convicted of crimes committed after the effective date of that act, as well as for persons sentenced under the guidelines, regardless of when their crimes occurred; however, parole will still be possible for persons who committed crimes prior to the effective date of the guidelines and who were not sentenced under guidelines, provided they otherwise satisfy the criteria of applicable statutes. Op.Atty.Gen., 84–5, Jan. 20, 1984.

Persons who were convicted prior to the effective date of sentencing guidelines and who were not sentenced under the guidelines would still be eligible for parole consideration on the former offense as long as the prerequisites of the applicable statutory provisions are met; of course, the law enacting guidelines prohibits parole consideration for the latter offenses upon which a guidelines sentence was imposed. Op. Atty.Gen., 84–5, Jan. 20, 1984.

3. Legislative intent

This section providing that a prisoner does not become eligible for parole consideration unless he has been sentenced to at least one year in prison expresses a legislative intent to limit period of incarceration which may be imposed as condition of probation to a period of less than one year. Villery v. Florida Parole and Probation Commission, 396 So.2d 1107 (1980). Sentencing And Punishment ⚷ 1976(2)

4. Parole

The term "parole" means procedure by which duly convicted defendant who has been sentenced and who is serving term of imprisonment under judgment of conviction is allowed to serve last portion of his sentence outside prison walls and under strict supervision, as preparation for his eventual return to society, and is applicable only to cases in which convicted and sentenced defendant has served part of sentence imposed. Marsh v. Garwood, 65 So.2d 15 (1953). Pardon And Parole ⚷ 41

"Parole" in not an act of amnesty and does not terminate a sentence legally imposed but is that procedure by which a prisoner who must in any event be returned to society at some future time is allowed to serve last portion of sentence outside prison under strict supervision as preparation for eventual return to society. Sellers v. Bridges, 153 Fla. 586, 15 So.2d 293 (1943). Pardon And Parole ⚷ 41

Parole is not granted as a reward for good conduct or efficient performance of duties assigned in prison, but investigation by parole commission must disclose a reasonable probability that applicant will live and conduct himself as a respectable and law-abiding person, and that his release will be compatible with his own welfare and the welfare of society. Sellers v. Bridges, 153 Fla. 586, 15 So.2d 293 (1943). Pardon And Parole ⚷ 43

5. Jurisdiction of commission

Where jurisdiction over sentence has been retained by trial court pursuant to statute, Parole Commission must notify both state attorney who prosecuted crime and original sentencing judge, or where unavailable, chief judge of circuit, in event it decides inmate should be released during retention period. Blackwelder v. State, App. 2 Dist., 647 So.2d 991 (1994). Pardon And Parole ⚷ 57.1

When a term of imprisonment is extinguished, either through invalidation of the judgment and sentence or as a result of time served, the Parole Commission is divested of jurisdiction, the parole previously granted is void ab initio, and the Commission should discharge any further interest in that parole or parole revocation. West's F.S.A. § 947.16(1). Op. Atty.Gen. 90–57, July 24, 1990.

6. Liability of commissioners

Determination to grant parole is a discretionary, planning level decision which does not subject the state to tort liability, despite enactment of § 768.28 waiving sovereign liability of state agencies or subdivision. Berry v. State, App. 4 Dist., 400 So.2d 80 (1981), review denied 411 So.2d 380. States ⚷ 112.2(1)

7. Powers and duties of commission

Parole and probation commission may properly set a parole release date so distant as to be beyond the life expectancy for an inmate currently incarcerated if his criminal history so warrants. Holston v. Florida Parole and Probation Commission, App. 1 Dist., 394 So.2d 1110 (1981). Pardon And Parole ⚷ 48.1

Parole and probation commission is charged with the responsibility of making sensitive decisions as to when release on parole is appropriate, based on objective parole criteria, and an inmate entitled to such consideration is entitled to a binding presumptive parole release date as mandated by clear legislative language. Holston v. Florida Parole and Probation Commission, App. 1 Dist., 394 So.2d 1110 (1981). Pardon And Parole ⚷ 58

Under §§ 20.315, 945.10 and 947.174, should state parole and probation commission determine that particular piece of information is necessary for required determinations and that only department of corrections has resources to obtain such information for inmate's file, commission may have not only power but perhaps even duty to initiate legal action to direct department to acquire information for commission's use. Battis v. Florida Parole and Probation Commission, App. 1 Dist., 386 So.2d 295 (1980). Pardon And Parole ⚷ 57.1

Pre and postsentence investigation report, while undoubtedly helpful, is not indispensable to establishment of presumptive parole release date and, absent such document, state parole and probation commission is nevertheless obligated to evaluate each inmate by considering whatever information is available such as FBI as FDCLE rap sheets, imposed judgments and sentences, reports concerning inmate's conduct while incarcerated and recommendations of trial judge. Battis v. Florida Parole and Probation Commission, App. 1 Dist., 386 So.2d 295 (1980). Pardon And Parole ⚷ 58

It is the prerogative of the Parole and Probation Commission to determine whether or not and under what conditions parole will be granted in a particular case. Wright v. State, App. 1 Dist., 342 So.2d 565 (1977). Pardon And Parole ⚷ 45.1

Parole authority is only exercisable to extent it has been conferred. Owens v. State, 316 So.2d 537 (1975). Pardon And Parole ⚷ 45.1

The parole commission is without power to grant paroles, conditional releases or absolute discharges to defendants who have been convicted of violation of child molester law but who have not been sentenced and who are eligible for release from state hospital. Marsh v. Garwood, 65 So.2d 15 (1953). Pardon And Parole ⚷ 44

If a trial judge imposed sentence that was within limits defined in statute denouncing offense, further relief by way of reducing term was matter purely within province of parole authorities. La Barbera v. State, 63 So.2d 654 (1953). Pardon And Parole ⚷ 45.1

A court having jurisdiction of defendant in criminal proceeding could order probation after defendant had been convicted, but it had no jurisdiction or power to place defendant on parole, in view of fact that parole was strictly a function of the executive branch of government to be exercised only after defendant had been convicted and sentenced. La Barbera v. State, 63 So.2d 654 (1953).

The parole commission does not have the authority to parole a prisoner who is absent from the state prison on escape. Op.Atty.Gen., 059–163, Aug. 19, 1959.

8. Eligibility for parole—In general

A prisoner serving consecutive sentences is eligible for parole and it is not a condition to parole that he be under a sentence he has not yet begun to serve; AGO 85–11, stating contrary rule, does not represent legislative intent. Lowry v. Parole and Probation Com'n, 473 So.2d 1248 (1985). Pardon And Parole ⚷ 51

Absent legislative authority, imposition of a long mandatory jail term which precludes a potential for parole is fundamental error. Warmble v. State, App. 3 Dist., 393 So.2d 1164 (1981), review denied 402 So.2d 613. Criminal Law ⚷ 1042.3(1)

There is no absolute right to parole but there is right to proper consideration for parole. Moore v. Florida Parole and Probation Commission, 289 So.2d 719 (1974), certiorari denied 94 S.Ct. 2649, 417 U.S. 935, 41 L.Ed.2d 239. Pardon And Parole ⚷ 46

Defendant, who pled guilty to a number of robberies, and against whom eight 20-year concurrent sentences were imposed, was not entitled to relief on appeal on theory that, if he had been given life sentence, he would be eligible for parole in less than half the time that he would be under sentences in question. Warncke v. State, App. 2 Dist., 247 So.2d 27 (1971). Pardon And Parole ⚷ 54

Parole and Probation Commission cannot parole inmate on consecutive sentence which has never begun to have been served. Op.Atty.Gen., 85–11, Feb. 13, 1985.

Misdemeanants convicted of crimes committed after October 1, 1983, are not eligible for parole consideration. Op.Atty.Gen., 84–5, Jan. 20, 1984.

A person is not eligible for probation if he was charged and convicted of an offense for which the maximum penalty prescribed by law is life imprisonment, even though the court fixed a lesser sentence in his case. Op.Atty.Gen., 1941, p. 790.

9. —— Due process, eligibility for parole

Florida presumptive parole release date did not create liberty interest or require due process protections, even if date was binding on Parole Commission. Damiano v. Florida Parole and Probation Com'n, C.A.11 (Fla.)1986, 785 F.2d 929. Constitutional Law ⚷ 4838

10. —— Discretion of commission, eligibility for parole

An abuse of discretion occurs in the denial of parole if the denial is based upon illegal grounds or improper considerations. Florida Parole Com'n v. Huckelbury, App. 1 Dist., 903 So.2d 977 (2005), rehearing denied, review denied 913 So.2d 596. Pardon And Parole ⚷ 47

Parole and Probation Commission acted in good faith and in accordance with its vested discretion when it determined to rescind written mutual participation agreement with prisoner in order to effect opinion of the Attorney General that a prisoner serving consecutive sentences is not eligible for parole if he is under a sentence he has not as yet begun to serve. Lowry v. Parole and Probation Com'n, 473 So.2d 1248 (1985). Pardon And Parole ⚷ 51

Parole and probation commission did not abuse its discretion in determining to extend release date of relator, who had been convicted as an accessory after the fact to the murder of her husband, using as an aggravating factor under section of its rules that the offense involved exceptionally brutal or heinous behavior indicating wanton cruelty, as such factor is not necessarily included within the definition of accessory after the fact. Hardy v. Greadington, App. 5 Dist., 405 So.2d 768 (1981). Pardon And Parole ⚷ 52

Absent showing of either statutory exceptions or exceptional circumstances for good cause, Florida parole and probation commission had no discretion to increase inmate's salient factor score or to add aggravating factor after it had previously entered order fixing presumptive parole release date. McKahn v. Florida Parole and Probation Commission, App. 1 Dist., 399 So.2d 476 (1981). Pardon And Parole ⚷ 63

11. —— Time of eligibility for parole

An inmate sentenced pursuant to section 948.01(4), can be eligible for parole consideration prior to the expiration of the specified period of sentence if otherwise qualified for consideration for parole under this section. Op. Atty.Gen., 074–283, Sept. 19, 1974.

12. —— Place of incarceration or treatment, eligibility for parole

A state prisoner who has been transferred to a privately operated facility, such as Spectrum House or Concept House, for the treatment of persons having drug problems is not eligible for consideration for parole so long as he is in such facility because this section, requires that he be confined in prison or jail in order to be eligible for parole consideration because such a privately operated facility is neither a prison nor a jail. Op.Atty.Gen., 073–310, Sept. 4, 1973.

Under this section a person who has been sentenced to the state prison could be eligible for parole consideration while he is still confined in the county jail awaiting removal to the state prison. Op.Atty.Gen., 071–182, July 1, 1971.

Where a man began serving his county jail sentence for misdemeanor which term expired on February 28, 1971 and on February 1, 1971 he received a consecutive five year state prison sentence for felony which he began serving on March 1, 1971, prisoner would be eligible pursuant to this section for parole consideration six months after he began serving his state prison sentence. Op.Atty.Gen., 071–101, May 12, 1971.

Where a man was sentenced by a federal court to serve 18 months in federal prison on August 7, 1970 and on August 21, 1970 he was sentenced to serve an 18 month sentence in the state prison and the sentencing court directed that it should be served concurrently with the federal sentence, and after being released from the federal prison the prisoner was received at the reception and medical center of the division of corrections on February 17, 1971, the parole eligibility under his Florida sentence commenced on February 17, 1971 with his arrival at the reception and medical center. Op.Atty. Gen., 071–101, May 12, 1971.

13. —— Twelve month minimum sentence, eligibility for parole

A convict who is serving a state prison sentence of twelve months or more and who has a consecutive six-month county jail sentence to serve after the completion of said state prison sentence is eligible for parole on both sentences if his prison record is good. Op.Atty.Gen., 074–10, Jan. 8, 1974.

To be eligible for parole under this section, a person convicted of a felony must be serving a term of at least 12 months in jail or prison. Op.Atty.Gen., 071–22, Feb. 12, 1971.

A prisoner is subject to the parole, granting authority of the parole commission, if he has been convicted of a felony, sentenced in consecutive sentences for a total of more than one year, and served six months. Op.Atty.Gen., 1941, p. 788.

14. —— Split sentences, eligibility for parole

Petitioner's election to be sentenced under guidelines precluded challenge to sentence of two years in prison, six months of community control, and two years of probation for violation of probation on ground that sentence was split sentence of prison term imposed as condition of probation in excess of 364 days. Burrell v. State, App. 2 Dist., 483 So.2d 479 (1986). Criminal Law ⚷ 1137(2)

Prisoners who are serving time in jail under a true split sentence are eligible for parole just as any other prisoner. Lewis v. State, App. 2 Dist., 402 So.2d 482 (1981). Pardon And Parole ⚷ 44

The separate treatment of parole and probation under this section adopting split sentence alternative as part of probation authority for trial judges reflects legislative intent to maintain their separate identity; probation condition of incarceration is not a "sentence," even for limited purpose of eligibility for parole. Villery v. Florida Parole and Probation Commission, 396 So.2d 1107 (1980). Sentencing And Punishment ⚷ 1976(1)

The parole and probation commission is not obliged under the terms of subsection of this section to consider eligible for parole, and interview, any persons sentenced to a period of incarceration of less than twelve months followed by a period of probation pursuant to a split sentence probation imposed under § 948.01(4). Op.Atty.Gen., 079–58, June 7, 1979.

15. —— Factors and evidence considered, eligibility for parole

Even as a prior uncounseled conviction cannot be used to penalize and accused in a subsequent prosecution or sentencing, a prior uncounseled conviction cannot be used in determining eligibility for parole. Jenrette v. Wainwright, App. 3 Dist., 410 So.2d 575 (1982), review denied 419 So.2d 1201. Pardon And Parole ⚷ 49

As use of firearm or dangerous weapon is not included within definition of second-degree murder or manslaughter, this aggravating factor could be legitimately used to enlarge the time before petitioner, convicted of manslaughter, would be released on parole. Smith v. Crockett, App. 3 Dist., 383 So.2d 1166 (1980). Pardon And Parole ⚷ 49

Consideration of eligibility for parole should be free from consequences of conviction in which defendant was denied his right to counsel. Moore v. Florida Parole and Probation Commission, 289 So.2d 719 (1974), certiorari denied 94 S.Ct. 2649, 417 U.S. 935, 41 L.Ed.2d 239. Pardon And Parole ⚷ 59

Prisoner is entitled to have question of his eligibility for parole determined on evidence which passes constitutional muster. Moore v. Florida Parole and Probation Commission, 289 So.2d 719 (1974), certiorari denied 94 S.Ct. 2649, 417 U.S. 935, 41 L.Ed.2d 239. Pardon And Parole ⚷ 58

Paroling authority is required to comply with constitutional requirements and cannot deny parole on illegal grounds or improper considerations. Moore v. Florida Parole and Probation Commission, 289 So.2d 719 (1974), certiorari denied 94 S.Ct. 2649, 417 U.S. 935, 41 L.Ed.2d 239. Pardon And Parole ⚷ 57.1

16. Presumptive parole date—In general

It was error for Parole and Probation Commission, in establishing presumptive parole release date (PPRD) after parole was revoked, to include 60 months for use of handgun during commission of offense as aggravating factor, where same factor had been used in setting previous PPRD. Harper v. Florida Parole Com'n, App. 1 Dist., 626 So.2d 336 (1993), cause dismissed 630 So.2d 1100. Pardon And Parole ⚷ 49

Prior convictions obtained without assistance of counsel prior to *Gideon* were not usable to calculate points under salient factor score to determine release date. Ruzicka v. Florida Parole and Probation Com'n, App. 1 Dist., 480 So.2d 190 (1985). Pardon And Parole ⚷ 50

Where parole and probation commission did not defer indefinitely establishment of inmate's presumptive parole release date and where commission had established such date for inmate prior to filing of his habeas corpus petition, he was not entitled to release on ground that commission had violated this section and had applied aggravating factors more than 45 days after his initial interview. Purnell v. Florida Parole and Probation Commission, App. 1 Dist., 409 So.2d 1122 (1982), review denied 417 So.2d 330. Habeas Corpus ⚷ 510(1)

This section under which parole and probation commission is given discretion to review official record or conduct additional interviews with inmate at its discretion subject to restriction that presumptive parole release dates will not be changed except for reasons of institutional conduct or acquisition of new information not available at time of initial interview does not purport to provide for second, alternative or cumulative form of PPRD review. Canter v. Florida Parole and Probation Commission, App. 1 Dist., 409 So.2d 227 (1982). Pardon And Parole ⚷ 62

Inmate had no right to seek second review of his presumptive parole release date, and his request for review of such date, which had already been reviewed by parole and probation commission pursuant to § 947.173, was properly denied even insofar as claiming right to "special review" on basis of "new information." Canter v. Florida Parole and Probation Commission, App. 1 Dist., 409 So.2d 227 (1982). Pardon And Parole ⚿ 62

Under this section, parole and probation commission is under a clear legal duty to establish, within six months or one year from the date of initial confinement, a presumptive parole release date for every inmate eligible for parole consideration, regardless of when he may actually be released on parole. Greer v. Florida Parole and Probation Commission, App. 1 Dist., 403 So.2d 1000 (1981). Pardon And Parole ⚿ 45.1

Parole and probation commission failed to establish a proper presumptive parole release date as required by this chapter, when it set prisoner's release date at "life." Holston v. Florida Parole and Probation Commission, App. 1 Dist., 394 So.2d 1110 (1981). Pardon And Parole ⚿ 45.1

Where state parole and probation commission has no information as to inmate's criminal history prior to offense for which he is presently incarcerated, he must be assigned salient factor score of zero except where burglary is present offense of conviction, in which case salient factor score of "one" is computed. Battis v. Florida Parole and Probation Commission, App. 1 Dist., 386 So.2d 295 (1980). Pardon And Parole ⚿ 53

Where there is complete lack of information which can appropriately be considered by state parole and probation commission as bearing on offense characteristic, commission must assign presumptive parole release date at lowest end of matrix range for the offense. Battis v. Florida Parole and Probation Commission, App. 1 Dist., 386 So.2d 295 (1980). Pardon And Parole ⚿ 53

If, after state parole and probation commission has computed proper matrix time range, using available information, aggravating circumstances are to be applied, commission is obligated both by statute and rule to explain aggravating factors in writing, for benefit of inmate and to facilitate appropriate review. Battis v. Florida Parole and Probation Commission, App. 1 Dist., 386 So.2d 295 (1980). Pardon And Parole ⚿ 61

17. —— Grounds for modification, presumptive parole date

When corrections in presumptive parole release date were ordered, consideration of aggravating factors by the Parole and Probation Commission was permitted; therefore, restructuring of convict's presumptive parole release date pursuant to court order was not subject to prohibition of this section, except for specified reasons of institutional conduct or new information not available at time of initial interview, against modifying established presumptive parole release date, and such restructuring was not error, even though restructuring may have added 120 months in aggravation while sentence was reduced by 12 years. Sheley v. Florida Parole and Probation Com'n, App. 1 Dist., 496 So.2d 854 (1986), review denied 506 So.2d 1043. Pardon And Parole ⚿ 63

Parole and Probation Commission acted outside scope of objective parole guidelines when it extended inmate's presumptive parole release date additional 60 months on assertion of "new information," in that subject information had already been considered and acted upon by Commission in establishing presumptive parole release date, and therefore former presumptive parole release date was reinstated, though that date had already passed, where allegedly new information, in form of mental health status report, reiterated information already considered by Commission. Florida Parole and Probation Com'n v. Cunard, App. 1 Dist., 490 So.2d 88 (1986), review denied 500 So.2d 543. Pardon And Parole ⚿ 58

Evidence supported 60–month extension as being based upon institutional conduct and new information not available at time of initial parole interview. Bell v. Florida Parole and Probation Com'n, App. 4 Dist., 473 So.2d 23 (1985). Pardon And Parole ⚿ 58

It was improper for Parole and Probation Commission to consider defendant's conviction for possession of firearm in extending defendant's presumptive parole release date on concurrent sentence for murder, after defendant had escaped from custody and been convicted of escape, where Commission, in setting defendant's pre-escape release date, initially chose not to extend defendant's release date because of firearm conviction and that conviction was not new information, even though defendant's original release date was vacated as result of his escape. Gaines v. Florida Parole and Probation Com'n, App. 4 Dist., 463 So.2d 1181 (1985), petition for review denied 475 So.2d 695. Pardon And Parole ⚿ 63

Once presumptive parole release date is established, it becomes binding on Parole and Probation Commission and is not to be changed except for reasons of institutional conduct, acquisition of new information not available at time of initial interview, or for good cause in exceptional circumstances. Florida Parole and

Probation Com'n v. Paige, 462 So.2d 817 (1985). Pardon And Parole ⚿ 63

Although presumptive parole release date once established is binding on Parole and Probation Commission except for good cause in exceptional circumstances, or for reason of institutional conduct or acquisition of new information not available at time of initial interview, Commission may correct clerical mistake or computational error made in setting the presumptive parole release date. Zatler v. State, App. 5 Dist., 457 So.2d 1083 (1984). Pardon And Parole ⚿ 60

Three factors justify changing a presumptive parole release date: new information, institutional conduct, and extraordinary circumstances. Jackson v. Florida Parole and Probation Com'n, App. 1 Dist., 424 So.2d 930 (1983). Pardon And Parole ⚿ 63

Order of the Florida parole and probation commission extending inmate's presumptive parole release date was error because it was not done in accordance with the Objective Parole Guidelines Act in that the commission failed to point out whether any circumstances given in explanation of its action were based on "newly acquired information" or, if not, whether there was "good cause in exceptional circumstances" for the commission's action. Moats v. Florida Parole and Probation Com'n, App. 1 Dist., 419 So.2d 775 (1982). Pardon And Parole ⚿ 61

Once petitioner's prior conviction, which parole and probation commission had used to establish his initial presumptive parole release date, was declared invalid, commission was not entitled to recalculate his parole release date and to reinstate aggravating factors found by hearing examiners, but not relied upon by the commission, because this section limits change in presumptive parole release dates through reasons of institutional conduct or the acquisition of new information not available at time of initial interview, so that the existence of a concurrent sentence, a factor found by the hearing examiner but not relied upon by the commission, was not new or previously unavailable information upon which the commission could rely. Jenrette v. Wainwright, App. 3 Dist., 410 So.2d 575 (1982), review denied 419 So.2d 1201. Pardon And Parole ⚿ 63

Trial court's order correcting error in sentencing after review by parole and probation commission qualified as "new information not available at the time of the initial interview" so as to furnish basis for commission, in its discretion, to determine whether such new information would warrant consideration of change in presumptive parole release date. Canter v. Florida Parole and Probation Commission, App. 1 Dist., 409 So.2d 227 (1982). Pardon And Parole ⚿ 60

18. Interviews—In general

An inmate sentenced under the provisions of § 775.087, to serve a minimum mandatory term of three full years should be interviewed for parole consideration as provided in this section as amended, regardless of the fact that such an inmate will not be eligible for parole prior to serving three full years. Op.Atty.Gen., 079–92, Oct. 10, 1979.

The statutory duty imposed upon the Florida parole and probation commission by subsection of this section that the commission conduct parole interviews with inmates "not less often than annually," was not abrogated or modified by the enactment of § 947.135, and is not abrogated or modified when an inmate enters into a "contract parole" agreement pursuant to § 947.135. Op.Atty.Gen., 077–73, July 27, 1977.

19. —— Necessity for interviews

Parole and Probation Commission was not required to hold parole interview for defendant who was serving sentence imposed under sentencing guidelines, even though defendant was also serving nonguidelines sentence. McCant v. State, Parole and Probation Com'n, App. 2 Dist., 497 So.2d 1315 (1986). Pardon And Parole ⚿ 58

If a person is convicted and sentenced for first degree murder committed after December 8, 1972, the effective date of Laws 1972, c. 72–724, contrary to § 782.04, or for rape committed after December 8, 1972, contrary to § 794.01 (repealed; now §§ 794.011 and 794.021), he stands convicted of a "capital crime", regardless of whether he is sentenced to death or life imprisonment, and it is discretionary with the parole and probation commission as to whether to interview him for parole consideration. Op.Atty.Gen., 073–92, March 29, 1973.

As of July 24, 1972, crimes which had previously been capital crimes became noncapital crimes. As to inmates previously sentenced for such crimes to imprisonment in the state prison instead of to death, the provisions of this section requiring interviews with inmates sentenced to serve prison terms were applicable after July 24, 1972. For the purpose of computing the time within which said provisions require interviews to be made, the inmate's sentence should be regarded as having commenced on July 24, 1972. Op.Atty.Gen., 073–92, March 29, 1973.

A person sentenced for a capital crime before July 24, 1972, no longer stood convicted of a capital crime after that date so that the discretionary interview provision of this section was no longer applicable. Op.Atty.Gen., 074–46, Feb. 13, 1974.

The provisions of this section, relating to interviews with persons sentenced to terms of imprisonment did not become applicable to a person who had a death sentence; he had no sentence to a term of imprisonment. However, when such a person has been re-sentenced since July 24, 1972, to be imprisoned for life or for a lesser time, such person for the first time came within the provisions of this section, relating to interviews with inmates sentenced to terms of imprisonment. Op.Atty.Gen., 073–92, March 29, 1973.

20. —— Time of interview

Under Florida law, pursuant to which decision whether to release inmate on parole is committed to discretion of Florida probation and parole commission without mandate of statute, no entitlement to or liberty interest in parole is created, and thus, since Florida parole statutes do not create protectible interest in timely initial interview, failure to accord plaintiff timely initial parole interview did not violate due process. Staton v. Wainwright, 1982, 665 F.2d 686, certiorari denied 102 S.Ct. 1757, 456 U.S. 909, 72 L.Ed.2d 166. Constitutional Law ⚷ 4838

Prisoner appealing determination of his presumptive parole release date was timely interviewed within six months of his confinement in execution of judgment and was interviewed under applicable guidelines in effect at time of interview, despite his ex post facto argument. Veri v. Florida Parole and Probation Com'n, App. 1 Dist., 436 So.2d 348 (1983). Pardon And Parole ⚷ 59

There was no reversible error in the parole and probation commission's failure to conduct an initial interview of defendant within six months after his initial date of confinement in execution of his judgment where defendant was sentenced to more than five years. Rolle v. Florida Parole and Probation Com'n, App. 1 Dist., 426 So.2d 1082 (1983). Pardon And Parole ⚷ 62

Defendant's confinement in county jail prior to delivery to custody of department of corrections constituted "confinement in execution of the judgment" as contemplated in this section which requires parole and probation commission to interview inmates with sentences of five years or less "within six months after the initial date of confinement in execution of the judgment," and thus defendant was entitled to a writ of mandamus to compel commission to interview him promptly. Hayes v. Florida Parole and Probation Com'n, App. 1 Dist., 414 So.2d 648 (1982). Pardon And Parole ⚷ 50

21. Gain-time

Where defendant, who pled guilty to robbery, was sentenced to ten years' probation with special condition that he serve five years in state prison, transcript of sentencing proceeding strongly suggested that trial judge intended that defendant would be eligible for parole within six months but department of corrections took position that, under sentence as imposed, defendant was entitled to gain time against the five-year period and was not eligible for parole, sentence was to be vacated. Cooney v. State, App. 3 Dist., 376 So.2d 926 (1979). Sentencing And Punishment ⚷ 1976(3)

22. Findings

Sentences, which indicated that defendant was to receive credit for "time served," did not set forth the specific period of credit time as required by this section. Wicker v. State, App. 2 Dist., 438 So.2d 399 (1983). Sentencing And Punishment ⚷ 1073

Where defendant did not object at trial to trial court's failure to make requisite statement of findings of fact under this section governing eligibility for parole, he failed to preserve error for purposes of appeal; however, affirmance was without prejudice to defendant's right to present issue to trial court via postconviction relief motion. Hernandez v. State, App. 4 Dist., 425 So.2d 213 (1983). Criminal Law ⚷ 1042.3(2); Criminal Law ⚷ 1433(2)

23. Sentence and punishment

A new commitment requiring the serving of a consecutive mandatory minimum sentence must be added to an inmate's cumulative sentences for which he is otherwise eligible for parole; the consecutive mandatory sentence could not begin to be served until the initial sentence had been terminated by pardon, parole, expiration, etc. Op.Atty.Gen., 84–27, March 26, 1984.

24. Conditions of probation

Six years' imprisonment, as a condition of 15 years' probation, was too long, and, thus, could not be imposed as a condition. Olcott v. State, App. 2 Dist., 378 So.2d 303 (1979). Sentencing And Punishment ⚷ 1976(2)

25. Waiver of consideration for parole

Defendant convicted of burglary and sexual battery waived any right he might have had for parole consideration by affirmatively selecting guideline considerations in sentencing. Williams v. State, App. 1 Dist., 454 So.2d 751 (1984). Pardon And Parole ⚷ 49

A state prisoner eligible for consideration for parole under this section and § 947.17 has a statutorily created right to be periodically interviewed and considered for parole. That right being personal to the inmate, is a right which he may waive either expressly, impliedly, or by conduct. A waiver by an inmate of his right to be considered for parole is a unilateral act, not requiring any act of the commission to perfect it, and not requiring the commission's approval. Upon due waiver by an inmate the commission is not required to conduct a parole interview. However, if due notice of a waiver has not been conveyed to the commission's interviewing official before convening a duly scheduled interview, the hearing examiner must make himself available at the scheduled time and place. The subsequent absence or failure of the inmate to appear, at the interview for which he has received due notice, may be treated as a waiver, unless circumstances exist which are inconsistent with an intent to waive, or are otherwise known to the examining official, or such as to put him on notice to make inquiry. Op.Atty. Gen., 078-29, Feb. 21, 1978.

26. Habeas corpus

Habeas corpus is a proper method of challenging legality of imprisonment claimed to have been rendered invalid by later events, and the proper method of challenging the validity of a presumptive parole release date when the prisoner claims his entitlement to immediate release. Jenrette v. Wainwright, App. 3 Dist., 410 So.2d 575 (1982), review denied 419 So.2d 1201. Habeas Corpus ⚷ 510(1)

Where disciplinary report was filed against prisoner after he had been notified that he had been granted parole but before he was scheduled to be released, petitioner was entitled to be afforded a parole rescission hearing consistent with due process requirements set out in Morrissey v. Brewer, and, unless such were held within 30 days of filing of opinion, writ of habeas corpus should issue and he should be placed upon parole. Demar v. Wainwright, 354 So.2d 366 (1977), certiorari denied 98 S.Ct. 3082, 436 U.S. 962, 57 L.Ed.2d 1129. Habeas Corpus ⚷ 792.1; Pardon And Parole ⚷ 86

Prisoner's naked allegation that there were some conclusionary statements or recommendations noted on his record jacket which resulted in denial of parole, which allegation was not supported by any documentary evidence, was insufficient to support issuance of writ of habeas corpus. McNamara v. Cook, App. 4 Dist., 336 So.2d 677 (1976). Habeas Corpus ⚷ 725

A parolee, though not physically confined in prison, could maintain habeas corpus to secure discharge from penal supervision under a judgment and sentence entered upon an information which wholly failed to charge an offense, since conditions of parole constituted such a restraint of freedom as rendered parolee for all practical purposes in "custody". Sellers v. Bridges, 153 Fla. 586, 15 So.2d 293 (1943). Habeas Corpus ⚷ 516.1

27. Mandamus

Where inmate had been confined in execution of three-year sentence more than six months, parole and probation commission should have granted parole interview within six months of confinement in execution of judgment and inmate was entitled to writ of mandamus to compel parole and probation commission to interview him and establish presumptive parole release date. Oishi v. Florida Parole and Probation Com'n, App. 1 Dist., 418 So.2d 329 (1982). Mandamus ⚷ 73(1); Pardon And Parole ⚷ 49

Legislature has mandated setting of presumptive parole release date by state parole and probation commission, and when commission without adequate reason fails so to act, it is answerable in mandamus. Battis v. Florida Parole and Probation Commission, App. 1 Dist., 386 So.2d 295 (1980). Mandamus ⚷ 73(1)

Granting of parole rests within paroling authority's discretion and mandamus will not lie to compel granting of parole. Moore v. Florida Parole and Probation Commission, 289 So.2d 719 (1974), certiorari denied 94 S.Ct. 2649, 417 U.S. 935, 41 L.Ed.2d 239. Mandamus ⚷ 73(1); Pardon And Parole ⚷ 47

Where prisoner claimed that denial of parole was based on paroling authority's improper consideration of prior convictions rendered when he was without counsel, mandamus would lie to compel paroling authority to exercise its discretion as to granting or denial of parole without consideration of such convictions. Moore v. Florida Parole and Probation Commission, 289 So.2d 719 (1974), certiorari denied 94 S.Ct. 2649, 417 U.S. 935, 41 L.Ed.2d 239. Mandamus ⚷ 73(1)

28. Review

Decision of trial court, declining to perform discretionary act of voluntarily relinquishing jurisdiction over criminal defendant, was not appealable. Olmstead v. State, App. 2 Dist., 569 So.2d 868 (1990). Criminal Law ⚷ 1023(14)

Where it was not clear from record before District Court of Appeal why petitioner's presumptive parole release date was changed, and where lower court because it believed mandamus was not proper never reached the substantive issues, though it did state that it believed that petition might have some merit, case would be reversed and remanded to circuit court for expeditious consideration of merits of the petition. Zatler v. State, App. 5 Dist., 457 So.2d 1083 (1984). Pardon And Parole ⚷ 62

Parole and probation commission order extending inmate's presumptive parole release date would be vacated and the case would be remanded for reconsideration and clarification of commission's decision not to parole inmate where the objective parole guidelines were not used in arriving at the date and where the commission did not provide adequate record support for the reasons it gave in denying parole to inmate and did not explain why some of the reasons given were relevant to parole prognosis. Jackson v. Florida Parole and Probation Com'n, App. 1 Dist., 424 So.2d 930 (1983). Pardon And Parole ⚷ 63

Circuit court had jurisdiction to review action of parole and probation commission determining prisoner's release date and provide relief if prisoner demonstrated entitlement thereto. Tucker v. Florida Parole & Probation Com'n, App. 2 Dist., 417 So.2d 1178 (1982). Pardon And Parole ⚷ 62

Prisoner was precluded from challenging on appeal order of the parole and probation commission setting a prospective parole release date where prisoner failed to seek proper review within 60 days of commission's action. Hall v. Florida Parole & Probation Commission, App. 1 Dist., 408 So.2d 1076 (1982). Pardon And Parole ⚷ 62

II. RETAINED JURISDICTION

Subdivision Index

---

51. Validity, retained jurisdiction

This section which permits a review of parole decisions in certain instances and for a certain period of time is not unconstitutional. Borden v. State, 402 So.2d 1176 (1981); Gains v. State, App., 417 So.2d 719 (1982) review denied 426 So.2d 26; Palmer v. State, App., 416 So.2d 878 (1982) remanded 438 So.2d 1.

Ex post facto application of retention statute (F.S.A. § 947.16) is not fundamental error and objection must be made in the trial court to preserve issue for review by direct appeal. Springfield v. State, App. 2 Dist., 443 So.2d 484 (1984). Criminal Law ⚷ 1042.3(2)

This section which permits trial court to retain jurisdiction over offenders committing certain enumerated crimes for up to one third of the maximum sentence imposed and which requires court to state the justification for retaining jurisdiction with individual particularity, is constitutional. Sellers v. State, App. 2 Dist.,

421 So.2d 782 (1982). Sentencing And Punishment ⚷ 1005

Where offense, i.e., second-degree murder, occurred on March 29, 1978 and amendatory provisions of this section governing retention of jurisdiction to review any parole release order issued during first third of the maximum sentence imposed for murder offenses did not become effective until June 19, 1978, the statute was an ex post facto law as applied to defendant. Williams v. State, 414 So.2d 509 (1982). Constitutional Law ⚷ 2823; Pardon And Parole ⚷ 42.1

This section authorizing sentencing judge to retain jurisdiction to review certain parole release orders did not violate separation of powers provision of Florida Constitution (Const. Art. 2, § 3). Burley v. State, App. 5 Dist., 408 So.2d 830 (1982). Constitutional Law ⚷ 2564; Pardon And Parole ⚷ 43

Where trial court had entered order retaining jurisdiction over defendant for review of parole commission release order, defendant had standing to challenge constitutionality of this section allowing retention of jurisdiction, though parole commission had not yet entered release order and trial court had not yet vacated such parole release order. Arnett v. State, App. 1 Dist., 397 So.2d 330 (1981), review denied 408 So.2d 1092. Constitutional Law ⚷ 700

This section allowing trial court, at time of sentencing for certain enumerated crimes, to enter order retaining jurisdiction over offender for review of parole commission release order, and not allowing appeal of trial court judge's decision to vacate parole release order, was within prerogative of legislature and did not violate due process since offender had no constitutional right to be conditionally released before expiration of valid sentence. Arnett v. State, App. 1 Dist., 397 So.2d 330 (1981), review denied 408 So.2d 1092. Constitutional Law ⚷ 4838; Pardon And Parole ⚷ 43

52. Construction and application, retained jurisdiction

Sentencing court's statutory violation by failing to provide written reasons for retaining jurisdiction over defendant does not make the sentence an "illegal sentence" within the meaning of rule permitting court to correct illegal sentence at any time; the absence of written reasons to retain jurisdiction does not involve a court's patent lack of authority or jurisdiction, a violation of the sentencing maximums provided by the legislature, or a violation of some other fundamental right resulting in a person's wrongful imprisonment; disapproving *Kirtsey v. State*, 855 So.2d 177; *Hernandez v. State*, 825 So.2d 513; *Bingham v. State*, 813 So.2d 1021; *Thames v. State*, 769 So.2d 448; *Hampton v. State*, 764 So.2d 829; and *Macias v. State*, 614 So.2d 1216. Wright v. State, 911 So.2d 81 (2005). Sentencing And Punishment ⚷ 2254

A motion to correct sentence is a proper means of challenging the legal sufficiency of order retaining jurisdiction over one-third of sentence to monitor any Parole Commission release order. Hampton v. State, App. 1 Dist., 764 So.2d 829 (2000). Sentencing And Punishment ⚷ 2254

To satisfy the requirements of statute allowing court's retention of jurisdiction over a portion of the sentence, a trial court must state with individual particularity the justification for retaining jurisdiction, which is not satisfied where a trial court merely refers generally to the circumstances surrounding the particular incidents, the nature of the offenses, the seriousness of the offenses, and the gravity of the offenses, without setting out any specific facts and circumstances of the crimes. Hampton v. State, App. 1 Dist., 764 So.2d 829 (2000). Sentencing And Punishment ⚷ 226

Sentencing court's retention of jurisdiction over one third of 60–year sentence did not cease when judge who imposed sentence left circuit court to become member of District Court of Appeal; under statute prohibiting parole without prior approval of trial judge, such retention of jurisdiction is exercised by sentencing court in its generic sense, and is not personal to judge who imposed sentence. Williams v. State, App. 1 Dist., 592 So.2d 1199 (1992). Sentencing And Punishment ⚷ 226

Trial court's retention of jurisdiction over one third of sentence was improper under West's F.S.A. § 947.16(3), which authorizes retention of jurisdiction for certain enumerated felonies, where underlying crime was escape, which is not enumerated in statute. Faircloth v. State, App. 2 Dist., 479 So.2d 779 (1985). Sentencing And Punishment ⚷ 226

Parole was no longer available to defendant who was sentenced pursuant to guidelines; thus, court erred in retaining jurisdiction over his sentence. Carter v. State, App. 2 Dist., 464 So.2d 172 (1985), affirmed 479 So.2d 117. Pardon And Parole ⚷ 44; Sentencing And Punishment ⚷ 226

Defendant was entitled to opportunity to hear and respond to trial court's order containing statement of particular reasons for retaining jurisdiction over defendant for first one-third of sentence imposed by trial court on original charge after finding defendant to be in violation of his probation. Stafford v. State, App. 4 Dist., 440 So.2d 55 (1983). Sentencing And Punishment ⚷ 226

In regard to defendant's armed robbery and aggravated assault convictions, trial judge did not abuse his discretion in retaining jurisdiction for purpose of reviewing parole release orders; judge, who stated when he announced the sentence that "This court will retain jurisdiction for the first third" and who made no change or modification in the sentence as announced at time of sentencing, had sufficiently notified defendant that court would retain jurisdiction over the sentence. Palmer v. State, App. 4 Dist., 416 So.2d 878 (1982), remanded 438 So.2d 1. Sentencing And Punishment ⚷ 226

Legislature had authority to say how sentencing judge may retain jurisdiction over an offender and thus had authority to require that it be done only with individually particularized justification. Moore v. State, App. 5 Dist., 392 So.2d 277 (1980). Sentencing And Punishment ⚷ 226

53. Purpose, retained jurisdiction

Purpose behind this section enumerating various offenses and providing that trial judge may retain jurisdiction for first one third of defendant's sentence when defendant is convicted of an enumerated offense is to prohibit parole of criminal defendant convicted of such offense without approval of the trial judge until after defendant has served first one third of sentence imposed. Williams v. State, App. 2 Dist., 374 So.2d 1086 (1979). Sentencing And Punishment ⚷ 205

Legislative intent was to limit application of this section authorizing trial judge to retain jurisdiction for first one third of defendant's sentence after conviction of an offense enumerated in the statute to such expressly enumerated offenses, and not to extend application of the statute to attempt to commit those offenses. Williams v. State, App. 2 Dist., 374 So.2d 1086 (1979). Sentencing And Punishment ⚷ 205

54. Amendment of statute, retained jurisdiction—In general

Trial court erred in retaining jurisdiction over one-half of defendant's sentence pursuant to amendment in effect at time of conviction, where law at time offense was committed permitted court to retain jurisdiction of only one-third of sentence. Montoya v. State, App. 5 Dist., 458 So.2d 341 (1984), petition for review denied 466 So.2d 218. Sentencing And Punishment ⚷ 226

Trial court's retention of jurisdiction over one-half of sentence for conviction of burglary with assault was improper ex post facto application of 1982 amendment to this section which had provided for trial court retention of jurisdiction for not more than one-third of total consecutive sentences imposed. Reid v. State, App. 2 Dist., 440 So.2d 651 (1983). Constitutional Law ⚷ 2815; Sentencing And Punishment ⚷ 226

Ex post facto application of this section was not fundamental error, and thus issue that trial court erred in retaining jurisdiction for first half of four sentences was not preserved for appellate review in absence of objection at trial level. Fredricks v. State, App. 1 Dist., 440 So.2d 433 (1983). Criminal Law ⚷ 1042.3(2)

Trial court's retention of jurisdiction over first one-third of defendant's sentence, pursuant to statute enacted subsequent to commission of crime, was ex post facto application of law. Brown v. State, App. 5 Dist., 428 So.2d 369 (1983). Constitutional Law ⚷ 2815; Sentencing And Punishment ⚷ 226

Amendment to this section pursuant to which trial court retained jurisdiction to review any parole release order, and which was enacted subsequent to commission of offenses in question, substantively altered defendant's situation to his disadvantage, and thus could not be retroactively applied to defendant in light of its ex post facto effect. Prince v. State, App. 1 Dist., 398 So.2d 976 (1981), review denied 411 So.2d 384. Constitutional Law ⚷ 2823; Pardon And Parole ⚷ 42.1

55. —— Text applicable, amendment of statute, retained jurisdiction

Amended text to this section governing eligibility for parole that was in effect at time defendant committed armed robbery permitted trial court to retain jurisdiction over only one third of defendant's 99-year sentence. Bowers v. State, App. 2 Dist., 452 So.2d 146 (1984). Sentencing And Punishment ⚷ 226

For purpose of retention of jurisdiction in case based on acts committed prior to effective date of 1982 amendment of this section, authority of court applied only to one-third of the total consecutive sentences imposed. Wicker v. State, App. 2 Dist., 438 So.2d 398 (1983). Sentencing And Punishment ⚷ 226

56. —— Offense committed prior to amendment of statute, retained jurisdiction

Statute increasing from one third to one half the length of sentence over which trial court could retain jurisdiction was properly applied to defendant whose offenses were committed prior to effective date of statute, and such application was not unconstitutional ex post facto law in regard to defendant. Cochran v. State, App. 2 Dist., 468 So.2d 248 (1985). Constitutional Law ⚷ 2816; Sentencing And Punishment ⚷ 17(2)

Application of amendment to statute permitting retention of jurisdiction for not more than one-half of sentence to defendant for offense which occurred prior to amendment was not an ex post facto law, since legal consequences of retained jurisdiction had already attached under existing statute and since defendant was convicted and sentenced after effective date of amendment increasing retention period. Powlowski v. State, App. 5 Dist., 467 So.2d 334 (1985). Constitutional Law ⚷ 2815; Sentencing And Punishment ⚷ 2057

Application of statute, limiting portion of sentence over which trial court could retain jurisdiction, to defendant who committed crime prior to effective date of statute would not be disadvantageous to defendant and was not an ex post facto application. Ivey v. State, App. 2 Dist., 453 So.2d 540 (1984). Constitutional Law ⚷ 2815; Sentencing And Punishment ⚷ 8

Provision of this section enacted in 1978 governing retention of jurisdiction over first third of probationary sentence for breaking and entering could not be applied where offense occurred prior to 1978. Dickerson v. State, App. 2 Dist., 427 So.2d 205 (1983). Sentencing And Punishment ⚷ 1828

Where this section pertaining to sentencing consequences was not passed until after criminal episode for which defendant was sentenced, application of this section constituted an ex post facto application, and jurisdiction over first one third of sentence should not have been retained. Dixon v. State, App. 4 Dist., 415 So.2d 78 (1982). Constitutional Law ⚷ 2815; Sentencing And Punishment ⚷ 8

Where two sexual batteries and four robberies for which defendant was convicted were committed on March 31, 1977, and this section providing for retention by trial court of jurisdiction over first one third of sentence did not become effective until June 19, 1978, application of this section to defendant's sentences was ex post facto and therefore violative of his constitutional rights. Stroemer v. State, App. 2 Dist., 410 So.2d 1350 (1981). Constitutional Law ⚷ 2815; Sentencing And Punishment ⚷ 16

Since this section requiring trial court to state, with particularity, its justification for retaining jurisdiction over defendant for review of any parole commission release order was enacted subsequent to the commission of the offenses for which defendant was sentenced, retroactive application of that section would be ex post facto in effect and would violate defendant's constitutional rights. Young v. State, App. 1 Dist., 406 So.2d 1249 (1981). Constitutional Law ⚷ 2823; Pardon And Parole ⚷ 42.1

In criminal prosecution, court's reservation of jurisdiction over first one third of sentence was vacated in light of fact that defendant committed the offense prior to effective date of provision of this section allowing court to reserve jurisdiction over certain criminal prosecutions. Rogers v. State, App. 2 Dist., 403 So.2d 548 (1981). Sentencing And Punishment ⚷ 211

Trial court's retention of jurisdiction under this section following conviction of defendant for second-degree murder and involuntary sexual battery constituted an ex post facto application of the statute, as the statute attached legal consequences to crimes which defendant committed before the law took effect, and affected him in a disadvantageous fashion by in effect extending his jail time. Myles v. State, App. 3 Dist., 399 So.2d 481 (1981). Constitutional Law ⚷ 2816; Sentencing And Punishment ⚷ 16

In criminal prosecution, trial court erred in retaining jurisdiction to review and veto one defendant's parole release order for first third of sentence pursuant to this section which was amended after commission of offense and which prevented defendant from being released by virtue of gain time during first one third of his sentence, where, by applying that section which did not exist at time of offense, trial judge in effect extended defendant's jail time and when defendant committed offense, defendant had statutory right to earn gain time, right that could be lost only by bad behavior. Williams v. State, App. 1 Dist., 383 So.2d 722 (1980), certified question answered 397 So.2d 663. Pardon And Parole ⚷ 42.1

Where defendant's offense of robbery was committed prior to effective date of amendment to this section allowing trial court to retain jurisdiction to review parole release order during first third of sentence of person convicted of robbery, application of such section to defendant was "ex post facto" in effect, and thus such section could not be applied to him. Rodriguez v. State, App. 2 Dist., 380 So.2d 1123 (1980). Pardon And Parole ⚷ 42.1

57. —— Sentencing following effective date, amendment of statute, retained jurisdiction

Retention statute in effect at time of conviction and sentencing applied to defendant, rather than statute in effect at time crime was committed, and thus trial court erred in retaining jurisdiction over first one half rather than first one third of sentence. Nazworth v. State, App. 5 Dist., 473 So.2d 214 (1985). Sentencing And Punishment ⚷ 16; Sentencing And Punishment ⚷ 226

There was no ex post facto violation in applying Laws 1982, c. 82–171, § 9 which amended this section to increase maximum retention period from one third to one half of sentence to crimes committed before effective date of the increase as defendant stood subject to the retention of jurisdiction of statute [this section] at time the crimes were committed and quantum of proof had not increased and defendant was convicted and sentenced after effective date of the increase; disapproving Reid v. State, 440 So.2d 651. Mills v. State, 462 So.2d 1075 (1985), certiorari denied 105 S.Ct. 3538, 473 U.S. 911, 87 L.Ed.2d 661, habeas corpus denied 574 So.2d 63, habeas corpus denied 622 So.2d 943, rehearing denied, denial of habeas corpus affirmed 63 F.3d 999, rehearing and suggestion for rehearing en banc denied 70 F.3d 1288, certiorari denied 116 S.Ct. 1837, 134 L.Ed.2d 940. Constitutional Law ⚷ 2816; Sentencing And Punishment ⚷ 226

Trial court erred in retaining jurisdiction for one half of defendant's sentences since, at time of sentencing, this section permitted retention of jurisdiction for maximum period of one third of any sentence. Crews v. State, App. 5 Dist., 456 So.2d 959 (1984), petition for review denied 464 So.2d 556. Sentencing And Punishment ⚷ 226

Court's retention of jurisdiction over one half of sentence of defendant was in error where defendant was sentenced after effective date of amendment to this section which limited court's retention of jurisdiction to one third of sentence. Ivey v. State, App. 2 Dist., 453 So.2d 540 (1984). Sentencing And Punishment ⚷ 226

Where defendant was sentenced on June 22, and amendment reducing maximum amount of jurisdiction that judge could retain from one half to one third of sentence was effective on June 15, trial court improperly retained jurisdiction over one half of 99-year sentence imposed on defendant convicted of second-degree murder. Hayes v. State, App. 2 Dist., 448 So.2d 84 (1984), modified 452 So.2d 656. Sentencing And Punishment ⚷ 17(1)

Where defendant was charged with an offense committed prior to effective date of an amendment to this section allowing trial court to retain jurisdiction to review a parole commission release order during first third of an offender's sentence, the amendment was an ex post facto law as applied to him and thus trial court's reservation of jurisdiction was to be deleted from defendant's sentence. Dominguez v. State, App. 2 Dist., 405 So.2d 736 (1981), petition for review denied 412 So.2d 464. Constitutional Law ⚷ 2823; Pardon And Parole ⚷ 42.1

Where offense for which defendant was convicted occurred almost seven months prior to effective date of amendment to this section allowing trial judge to retain jurisdiction over convicted offender for up to one third of sentence imposed, trial judge's retention of jurisdiction over defendant for first one third of sentence imposed constituted ex post facto application of the law. Bilyou v. State, 404 So.2d 744 (1981). Constitutional Law ⚷ 2815; Sentencing And Punishment ⚷ 16

Trial court's retention of jurisdiction over the first one third of defendant's sentence, under this section which was enacted after commission of the offense for which defendant was convicted but before his actual trial, constituted ex post facto application of that section, in that section attaches disadvantageous sentencing consequences of trial court's parole veto and no gain time release to those who committed crimes before the provision's effective date. State v. Williams, 397 So.2d 663 (1981). Constitutional Law ⚷ 2815; Sentencing And Punishment ⚷ 16

58. Retroactivity, retained jurisdiction

Sentencing court should have applied version of subsec. (3) of this section in effect at time defendant was convicted and sentenced rather than version in effect at time offense was committed. Heath v. State, App. 1 Dist., 558 So.2d 165 (1990). Sentencing And Punishment ⚷ 16

Where defendant was sentenced prior to effective date of West's F.S.A. § 947.16, authorizing trial court to retain jurisdiction over first third of a sentence, court's retention of jurisdiction constituted an unconstitutional ex post facto application of the statute. Surace v. State, App. 3 Dist., 476 So.2d 297 (1985).

59. Elements of offense, retained jurisdiction

That defendant used firearm in commission of robbery was insufficient for trial court to retain jurisdiction to review a parole commission release order over first one-third of consecutive 99-year and 30-year sentences for armed robbery and attempted second degree murder, since use of firearm was essential element of armed robbery. King v. State, App. 2 Dist., 835 So.2d 1224 (2003). Sentencing And Punishment ⚷ 226

That defendant shot at victim during armed robbery was insufficient to support trial court's retention of jurisdiction to review a parole commission release order over first one-third of 30-year sentence for attempted second degree murder, since discharge of weapon and shooting of victim were essential elements of second degree murder offense. King v. State, App. 2 Dist., 835 So.2d 1224 (2003). Sentencing And Punishment ⚷ 226

60. Justification, retained jurisdiction

Defendant stated facially sufficient claim that his sentence was illegal, and thus summary denial of defendant's motion to correct, reduce or modify sentence, was improper, where motion alleged that trial court illegally retained jurisdiction over one third of defendant's sentence, and record contained no individually particularized justification of retention of jurisdiction. Kirtsey v. State, App. 1 Dist., 855 So.2d 177 (2003). Sentencing And Punishment ⚷ 2305

Objective factors listed by trial judge met test for substance and reasonableness for retention of jurisdiction over one-third of 25-year sentence; factors included additional offenses, prior convictions, prior convictions for same offense, defendant's parole status at time of offense and victim injury. Thomas v. State, App. 3 Dist., 484 So.2d 1372 (1986). Sentencing And Punishment ⚷ 226

Trial court complied with explicit requirements of statute, which required trial judge to state with individual particularity the justification for retaining jurisdiction of person convicted of sexual battery, where court stated on record that it felt there was ample justification to retain jurisdiction for one third of sentence because defendant terrified and terrorized 16-year-old girl. Snow v. State, App. 1 Dist., 464 So.2d 1313 (1985). Sentencing And Punishment ⚷ 226

Trial court sufficiently stated with individual particularity justification for retaining jurisdiction, for purposes of parole review, over sentence for armed robbery. Overton v. State, App. 1 Dist., 429 So.2d 722 (1983), petition for review denied 440 So.2d 352. Sentencing And Punishment ⚷ 226

A reputation for and conviction of aggressive and injurious behavior is sufficient justification for retaining jurisdiction. Harden v. State, App. 4 Dist., 428 So.2d 316 (1983). Sentencing And Punishment ⚷ 226

Reputation for and conviction of aggressive and injurious behavior was sufficient justification for retention of jurisdiction in murder case to review parole commission release order during first third of sentence. Moore v. State, App. 5 Dist., 392 So.2d 277 (1980). Sentencing And Punishment ⚷ 226

61. Relinquishment of jurisdiction, retained jurisdiction

While statute governing parole clearly permits trial court to retain jurisdiction over sentence given to defendant for purposes of disapproving parole, statute does not confer discretion or authority on trial court to relinquish its jurisdiction absent Parole Commission's entry of release order. Blackwelder v. State, App. 2 Dist., 647 So.2d 991 (1994). Pardon And Parole ⚷ 54; Sentencing And Punishment ⚷ 226

While parole statute permits relinquishment of jurisdiction over sentence by sentencing court which has retained jurisdiction after expiration of 60-day limit under rules of criminal procedure for reduction or modification of sentence, court must do so in conformity with dictates of statute. Blackwelder v. State, App. 2 Dist., 647 So.2d 991 (1994). Pardon And Parole ⚷ 54; Sentencing And Punishment ⚷ 227

Trial court which had retained jurisdiction over one third of sentence of 75 years given to defendant following his conviction for murder was not required to relinquish jurisdiction over sentence where Parole Commission had not issued release order for inmate. Blackwelder v. State, App. 2 Dist., 647 So.2d 991 (1994). Pardon And Parole ⚷ 54; Sentencing And Punishment ⚷ 226

62. Sentencing guidelines, retained jurisdiction

Due to applicability of sentencing guidelines to defendant's convictions for second-degree murder, armed robbery, aggravated battery, and three counts of accessory after fact, court should not have retained jurisdiction over one third of defendant's sentence. Staten v. State, App. 2 Dist., 500 So.2d 297 (1986), decision disapproved 519 So.2d 622. Sentencing And Punishment ⚷ 226

Inasmuch as parole was not available to defendant who was sentenced pursuant to sentencing guidelines, trial court erred in retaining jurisdiction over his sentence. Williams v. State, App. 2 Dist., 470 So.2d 864 (1985). Sentencing And Punishment ⚷ 226

63. Nature and degree of crime or offense, retained jurisdiction

Trial court improperly retained jurisdiction over defendant's sentence for homicide solicitation that did not involve use of firearm, deadly weapon, or intentional violence. Duque v. State, App. 2 Dist., 526 So.2d 1079 (1988). Sentencing And Punishment ⚷ 226

Trial judge could retain jurisdiction over first one third of sentence for two counts of attempted second-degree murder and one count of shooting into occupied vehicle, despite attempted second-degree murder not being listed as offense authorizing retention of jurisdiction, where retention was authorized for criminal episode involving any felony involving use of firearm or other deadly weapon or use of intentional violence. Famiglietti v. State, App. 4 Dist., 499 So.2d 57 (1986), review denied 506 So.2d 1041. Sentencing And Punishment ⚷ 226

Trial court could not retain jurisdiction over sentence of defendant who had been convicted of burglary of a structure, a third-degree felony, since jurisdiction of sentences is permitted to be retained only for certain enumerated offenses including burglary of structure in which a human being is present. Walcott v. State, App. 5

Dist., 460 So.2d 915 (1984), approved 472 So.2d 741. Sentencing And Punishment ⚷ 226

Defendant's shoving of police officer did not constitute the type of intentional violence contemplated by this section allowing trial judge to retain jurisdiction over one half of defendant's sentence if crime involved use of intentional violence and victim was injured; thus, trial court erred in retaining jurisdiction over sentence of defendant, who was charged with battery of a law enforcement officer. Coleman v. State, App. 2 Dist., 460 So.2d 578 (1984). Sentencing And Punishment ⚷ 226

Record did not conclusively demonstrate that defendant was actually on probation for armed robbery, so that trial court had no jurisdiction to revoke defendant's probation, even if it could be said that defendant waived any requirement for an affidavit of violation of his probation and an arrest warrant. Bowers v. State, App. 2 Dist., 452 So.2d 146 (1984). Sentencing And Punishment ⚷ 2010

Trial court erred in retaining jurisdiction, for purposes of reviewing any parole release order, for the first third of sentence for carrying concealed weapon, in view of fact that such offense was not enumerated in statute providing that jurisdiction could be retained for reviewing parole release orders in cases involving specified offenses. Palmer v. State, App. 4 Dist., 416 So.2d 878 (1982), remanded 438 So.2d 1. Sentencing And Punishment ⚷ 226

Trial court in prosecution for third-degree felony-murder could retain jurisdiction over defendant regarding first third of 15-year sentence in order to review release order of parole and probation commission. Thomas v. State, App. 4 Dist., 409 So.2d 1185 (1982). Sentencing And Punishment ⚷ 226

Burglary was not one of the specified crimes for which trial court could retain jurisdiction for review of parole commission release order. Williamson v. State, App. 3 Dist., 388 So.2d 1345 (1980). Pardon And Parole ⚷ 62

Under this section, which provides that in any case of a person convicted of murder, robbery, aggravated assault, aggravated battery, kidnapping, sexual battery, arson, or any felony involving use of a firearm, at time of sentencing the judge may enter order retaining jurisdiction over offender for review of commission parole release order, carrying a concealed firearm is not a felony "involving the use of a firearm" since study of enumerated crimes bringing statute into play showed that legislature contemplated that firearm was to have been employed in some manner in connection with felony before court would be authorized to retain jurisdiction over defendant's sentence. Robinson v. State, App. 2 Dist., 368 So.2d 638 (1979). Sentencing And Punishment ⚷ 226

64. Attempts, retained jurisdiction—In general

Trial court order revoking defendant's probation on attempted arson and imposing five-year prison term with retention of jurisdiction over all five years contravened this section governing trial court's retention of jurisdiction over sentence, in that retention can be retained for only one third of sentence; furthermore, this section allows for retention of jurisdiction by the trial court only for certain enumerated offenses, and attempted arson is not one. Neal v. State, App. 5 Dist., 451 So.2d 1058 (1984). Sentencing And Punishment ⚷ 226

Trial court's retention of jurisdiction over attempted robbery conviction was improper since this section which permits retention of jurisdiction over sentences for certain enumerated offenses does not include attempted robbery on the list of applicable offenses. Crotzer v. State, App. 2 Dist., 425 So.2d 159 (1983). Sentencing And Punishment ⚷ 226

This section permitting trial court to retain jurisdiction over portion of defendant's sentence does not apply to attempts. McRae v. State, App. 2 Dist., 408 So.2d 775 (1982). Sentencing And Punishment ⚷ 226

Attempted escape is not one of specified crimes for which trial court judge may enter an order retaining jurisdiction over offender for review of parole commission release order as to first third of maximum sentence imposed. Johnson v. State, App. 4 Dist., 391 So.2d 781 (1980). Sentencing And Punishment ⚷ 226

Trial judge could not retain jurisdiction for first one third of defendant's sentence under this section authorizing such action after conviction of an offense enumerated in this section, where defendant was convicted of an attempt to commit an enumerated offense. Williams v. State, App. 2 Dist., 374 So.2d 1086 (1979). Sentencing And Punishment ⚷ 226

65. —— Double jeopardy, attempts, retained jurisdiction

Five-year sentence imposed upon defendant convicted of attempted manslaughter was not excessive, but order purporting to retain jurisdiction in trial court for one half of the sentence so as to permit trial court to review any decision to parole defendant aggravated defendant's previously imposed sentence in violation of defendant's constitutional right against double jeopardy. Ashley v. State, App. 3 Dist., 445 So.2d 360 (1984). Double Jeopardy ⚷ 31; Homicide ⚷ 1568

66. Juvenile offenders, retained jurisdiction

Trial judge's stating, upon imposing sentence including both prison term and probation, that defendant, who was then 16 years old, was to be "treated as a youthful offender for all purposes, especially, but not limited to, those of location and condition of imprisonment" did not preclude imposition of 99-year prison sentence following finding that defendant, an 18-year-old person, had violated probation, which was imposed on defendant's conviction for burglary with intent to commit assault. Schultz v. State, App. 2 Dist., 411 So.2d 892 (1982). Sentencing And Punishment ⚷ 2038

67. Guilty plea, retained jurisdiction—In general

Where trial judge gave defendant the opportunity to withdraw the plea after the state made a request for the trial court to retain jurisdiction over defendant for a period of one third of each sentence pursuant to state law, and where defendant discussed the matter with his attorney for 50 minutes after the state made that request, his guilty plea was not rendered defective on the theory that it was entered before he was aware that the state would recommend that the court retain jurisdiction. Miller v. Turner, 1981, 658 F.2d 348. Criminal Law ⚷ 273.1(1)

Where defendant did not file motion to vacate and set aside his sentence based on fact that in accepting guilty plea, trial court allegedly erred in failing to inform defendant that it could retain jurisdiction over one third of any sentence imposed and defendant did not move to withdraw his guilty plea, issue was not preserved for review on appeal. Cooper v. State, App. 2 Dist., 445 So.2d 698 (1984). Criminal Law ⚷ 1044.1(1)

Where defendant challenged trial court's retention of jurisdiction over one half of his sentence on grounds that he was not given notice of possibility of retention prior to guilty plea and court's stated justifications were insufficient to warrant retention of jurisdiction, but points were raised for first time on appeal, they were not reviewable by District Court of Appeal. Murray v. State, App. 2 Dist., 444 So.2d 1154 (1984). Criminal Law ⚷ 1042.3(2)

Trial court erred in retaining jurisdiction over first one-third of sentence imposed on defendant who pled guilty to two counts of armed robbery, where trial court failed to advise defendant at hearing on guilty plea that it wished to retain jurisdiction over portion of defendant's sentence. Shofner v. State, App. 1 Dist., 433 So.2d 657 (1983). Sentencing And Punishment ⚷ 226

Defendant who pled guilty to charges of kidnapping and aggravated battery could not raise on appeal issue of trial court's retention of jurisdiction over first one-third of sentences imposed, where he had neither objected to this aspect of sentence nor sought to withdraw plea on such ground below. McIntyre v. State, App. 3 Dist., 427 So.2d 1108 (1983). Criminal Law ⚷ 1042.3(2); Criminal Law ⚷ 1044.1(1)

Where defendant's eligibility for parole was undoubtedly major factor in his decision to enter guilty plea, the defendant was not informed that trial court could or would retain legal authority over defendant's parole for 20 years, fundamental fairness required that defendant be allowed to withdraw his plea. Gladon v. State, App. 4 Dist., 406 So.2d 1219 (1981). Criminal Law ⚷ 274(3.1)

68. —— Self-incrimination, guilty plea, retained jurisdiction

Retention of jurisdiction over one-third of defendant's sentence upon rape conviction was impermissible where it was partially based on defendant's refusal to admit his guilt since such reason violated defendant's constitutional privilege against self-incrimination. Harden v. State, App. 4 Dist., 428 So.2d 316 (1983). Sentencing And Punishment ⚷ 226

69. Nolo contendere or bargained plea, retained jurisdiction

Trial court was authorized to retain jurisdiction over one third of total consecutive sentences imposed on petitioner, who pleaded nolo contendere to three felonies consisting of armed robbery, auto theft, and leaving scene of accident. Stanley v. State, App. 1 Dist., 501 So.2d 90 (1987). Sentencing And Punishment ⚷ 226

In accepting defendant's nolo contendere plea, trial court had to inform him that it could retain jurisdiction over one half of any sentence imposed. Mrozowski v. State, App. 2 Dist., 444 So.2d 587 (1984). Criminal Law ⚷ 275.3

Trial court erred in retaining jurisdiction over part of defendant's sentence, where defendant was never informed by trial court of possibility that it would or could retain jurisdiction over part of his sentence, and retention of jurisdiction was not made part of plea bargain agreement. Crawford v. State, App. 2 Dist., 438 So.2d 974 (1983). Sentencing And Punishment ⚷ 226

70. Sentence and punishment, retained jurisdiction—In general

Retention of jurisdiction over portion of sentence to monitor any Parole Commission release order is a harsher penalty than a sentence for the same number of years without retention. Hampton v. State, App. 1 Dist., 764 So.2d 829 (2000). Sentencing And Punishment ⚷ 226

This section authorizing retention of jurisdiction in order to limit parole was inapplicable where defendant would be ineligible for parole for at least 25 years. Hallman v. State, 560 So.2d 223 (1990). Sentencing And Punishment ⚷ 226

Defendant was not required to be present when sentence was corrected to delete sentence for one offense and exclude another sentence in computing term of imprisonment over which trial court could retain jurisdiction. Jones v. State, App. 3 Dist., 453 So.2d 1192 (1984). Sentencing And Punishment ⚷ 342

Trial court did not err in sentencing defendant as an habitual felony offender while simultaneously retaining jurisdiction over the first one-third of that sentence even though the normal maximum sentence for the crime may have been enhanced. Valdes v. State, App. 1 Dist., 443 So.2d 223 (1983), petition for review denied 450 So.2d 489. Sentencing And Punishment ⚷ 226

Trial court's enhancement of sentence, by retaining jurisdiction to veto parole during the first one-third of the sentence, based on a finding of a deliberate act of murder was inconsistent with jury verdict which acquitted defendant on charge of first-degree murder and convicted him of second-degree murder. Owen v. State, App. 3 Dist., 441 So.2d 1111 (1983), motion denied 446 So.2d 100. Sentencing And Punishment ⚷ 226

Retention of jurisdiction which empowers a trial court to veto a parole recommendation and deny release pursuant to gain time is, in effect, an enhancement of sentence. Owen v. State, App. 3 Dist., 441 So.2d 1111 (1983), motion denied 446 So.2d 100. Sentencing And Punishment ⚷ 226

Where defendant injected issue of his consumption of alcohol as a defense to charge of first-degree murder and jury found that defendant was guilty only of second-degree murder, trial court could not enhance defendant's sentence by retaining jurisdiction to veto parole during the first one-third of the sentence, on the basis of its own finding that defendant had voluntarily consumed alcohol for the purpose of bolstering his courage. Owen v. State, App. 3 Dist., 441 So.2d 1111 (1983), motion denied 446 So.2d 100. Sentencing And Punishment ⚷ 226

Imposition of a ninety-nine-year sentence and retention of jurisdiction, for parole review purposes, over one-third of sentence did not compel mandatory minimum sentence of thirty-three and one-third years but permitted trial judge to control parole review during such maximum period of time. Overton v. State, App. 1 Dist., 429 So.2d 722 (1983), petition for review denied 440 So.2d 352. Sentencing And Punishment ⚷ 1126

Provision of this section pursuant to which trial judge retained jurisdiction for one-third of sentence to review any future parole commission release order did not affect validity of 120-year sentence which was imposed on defendant for offense of robbery and which was within applicable parameters. Smith v. State, App. 3 Dist., 405 So.2d 762 (1981). Sentencing And Punishment ⚷ 2234

Although trial court had authority to retain jurisdiction over defendant for the first third of the maximum sentence imposed for the highest enumerated felony charged and proven, it was improper to include in the sentence language ordering that defendant never be considered for release. McRae v. State, App. 2 Dist., 383 So.2d 289 (1980). Pardon And Parole ⚷ 54

71. —— Validity of sentence, sentence and punishment, retained jurisdiction

Motion to correct illegal sentence was the proper vehicle to challenge the court's reservation of jurisdiction to review a parole commission release order over first one-third of sentences for armed robbery and attempted second degree murder, since the reservation effectively imposed a harsher penalty upon defendant, resulting in a potentially improper sentence enhancement. King v. State, App. 2 Dist., 835 So.2d 1224 (2003). Sentencing And Punishment ⚷ 2254

Retention of jurisdiction does not affect "punishment" or sentence, within meaning of Const. Art. 10, § 9 that repeal or amendment of a criminal statute shall not affect prosecution or punishment for any crime previously committed, but rather has an effect which permits the trial judge to control parole review during the term of the sentence imposed; however, an increase in retention time is a disadvantage which cannot be applied ex post facto. Hayes v. State, App. 2 Dist., 452 So.2d 656 (1984). Constitutional Law ⚷ 2816; Constitutional Law ⚷ 2823; Sentencing And Punishment ⚷ 226

Given defendant's prior criminal record and viciousness of crimes of violence and threatened violence committed, sentencing defendant to prison for his natural life with possibility of parole at any time if approved by both parole commission and the trial court was not so disproportionate as to constitute cruel and unusual punishment proscribed by Federal and Florida Constitutions. Williams v. State, App. 3 Dist., 441 So.2d 1157 (1983). Sentencing And Punishment ⚷ 1482

72. —— Computation, sentence and punishment, retained jurisdiction

Trial court properly retained jurisdiction for one-half of defendant's 60-year burglary sentence, under subsection of § 947.16, which provided that trial judge shall retain jurisdiction for one-half of maximum sentence imposed for highest felony, because defendant's other concurrent sentences of death and life imprisonment were indeterminate. Echols v. State, 484 So.2d 568 (1985), certiorari denied 107 S.Ct. 241, 479 U.S. 871, 93 L.Ed.2d 166. Sentencing And Punishment ⚷ 226

It was error to include 15-year sentence for dealing in stolen property in computing term of imprisonment over which trial court could retain jurisdiction. Jones v. State, App. 3 Dist., 453 So.2d 1192 (1984). Sentencing And Punishment ⚷ 226

Under § 947.16 allowing trial court to retain jurisdiction over one third of maximum sentence, trial court could retain jurisdiction over 33 years of 99-year sentence for robbery with a firearm, which carried maximum sentence of life imprisonment, even though 33 years may have greatly exceeded one third of the reasonable life expectancy for the defendant. State v. Watson, 453 So.2d 810 (1984). Sentencing And Punishment ⚷ 226

73. —— Sentences exceeding portion of sentence over which jurisdiction retained

It was improper for trial court, which sentenced defendant for attempted sexual battery of child and for handling and fondling of child, to retain jurisdiction for period of ten years on handling and fondling charge, since § 947.16 limited trial court's retention of jurisdiction to the first one-third of the maximum sentence imposed, and handling and fondling offense was punishable by maximum sentence of 15 years of imprisonment. Bond v. State, App. 2 Dist., 462 So.2d 882 (1985). Sentencing And Punishment ⚷ 226

Defendant's failure to object, at the time of sentencing, to the trial court's retention of jurisdiction over one half of his two consecutive life sentences precluded him from challenging such retention by direct appeal. Cofield v. State, App. 1 Dist., 453 So.2d 409 (1984). Criminal Law ⚷ 1042.3(2)

74. —— Life sentences, sentence and punishment, retained jurisdiction

Sentencing court cannot retain jurisdiction over a life term because such a sentence is indeterminate. Moore v. State, App. 3 Dist., 902 So.2d 239 (2005). Sentencing And Punishment ⚷ 226

Court cannot retain jurisdiction over a life term, since such a sentence is indeterminate. Wainwright v. State, 704 So.2d 511 (1997), rehearing denied, certiorari denied 118 S.Ct. 1814, 523 U.S. 1127, 140 L.Ed.2d 952, denial of post-conviction relief affirmed 896 So.2d 695, certiorari denied 126 S.Ct. 188, 546 U.S. 878, 163 L.Ed.2d 178, dismissal of habeas corpus affirmed 2007 WL 3355559. Sentencing And Punishment ⚷ 226

Trial court's retention of jurisdiction over one third of life sentence was unauthorized by statute. Ford v. State, App. 2 Dist., 624 So.2d 863 (1993). Sentencing And Punishment ⚷ 226

Retention of jurisdiction on life sentence, which was characterized as enhancement of sentence, constituted illegal sentence which had to be corrected; there was no way to determine one-third of life sentence and, therefore, retention of jurisdiction over portion of life sentence was not possible under statute. Anderson v. State, App. 4 Dist., 584 So.2d 1127 (1991). Sentencing And Punishment ⚷ 226

Trial court's attempted retention of jurisdiction over portion of life sentence constituted an illegal sentence and was error of fundamental proportion. Mobley v. State, App. 4 Dist., 473 So.2d 692 (1985). Sentencing And Punishment ⚷ 226

Trial court erred in retaining jurisdiction over the first third of a life sentence; this section permitting such retention of jurisdiction was inoperable. Brown v. State, App. 4 Dist., 460 So.2d 988 (1984). Sentencing And Punishment ⚷ 226

Where trial court imposes a life sentence, it is improper for it to retain jurisdiction over the first third of a life sentence as it is impossible to calculate the length of time over which jurisdiction is retained. Brown v. State, App. 4 Dist., 460 So.2d 988 (1984). Sentencing And Punishment ⚷ 226

Trial court could not retain jurisdiction over one third of the life sentence as life sentence has no known termination point. Kosek v. State, App. 5 Dist., 448 So.2d 57 (1984). Sentencing And Punishment ⚷ 226

Trial court erred in retaining jurisdiction over 25 years of life sentence imposed on defendant convicted of robbery and first-degree murder. Willis v. State, App. 2 Dist., 447 So.2d 283 (1983). Sentencing And Punishment ⚷ 226

Provision of this section in effect when defendant committed offense for which he was convicted, allowing trial court to retain jurisdiction only over first third of maximum sentence imposed, was not applicable to life sentence assessed against defendant since a life span was immeasurable and, hence, no calculation of length of time jurisdiction could be retained could be made. Woodson v. State, App. 3 Dist., 439 So.2d 976 (1983). Sentencing And Punishment ⚷ 226

Trial court could not retain jurisdiction over defendant's life sentence for an indefinite period of time nor could trial court retain jurisdiction over first third of that life sentence, under provision of this section in effect when defendant committed offense for which he was convicted. Woodson v. State, App. 3 Dist., 439 So.2d 976 (1983). Sentencing And Punishment ⚷ 226

When a defendant is sentenced to life or a term of years in excess of any reasonable life expectancy, some evidence, such as mortality tables, must be presented to establish reasonable basis for trial court's determination as to period of time for which jurisdiction may be retained over sentence for purpose of reviewing defendant's release on parole. Watson v. State, App. 4 Dist., 437 So.2d 702 (1983), decision approved in part 453 So.2d 810. Pardon And Parole ⚷ 54

Where defendant was sentenced to 99 years for robbery with a firearm, the practical equivalent of a life sentence, and trial court retained jurisdiction over 33 years of sentence under this section authorizing such retention for purpose of reviewing defendant's release on parole during period up to one third of sentence imposed, such period was excessive because 33 years was not practical equivalent of ⅓ of a life sentence, as it was highly improbable that defendant had a total life expectancy of 127 years. Watson v. State, App. 4 Dist., 437 So.2d 702 (1983), decision approved in part 453 So.2d 810. Pardon And Parole ⚷ 54

For capital felony, imposition of life sentence was mandatory, and parole consideration is solely controlled by separate requirement under § 775.082 that defendant be required to serve no less than twenty-five years before becoming eligible for parole, and court could not retain jurisdiction over one-third of life sentence to review any parole release order. Cordero-Pena v. State, App. 3 Dist., 421 So.2d 661 (1982). Sentencing And Punishment ⚷ 226

75. —— Concurrent sentences, sentence and punishment, retained jurisdiction

Trial court's retention of jurisdiction over first half of both sentences imposed on defendant was not authorized by statute providing that trial court may retain jurisdiction only on first half of maximum sentence imposed. Emshwiller v. State, App. 2 Dist., 464 So.2d 1339 (1985). Sentencing And Punishment ⚷ 226

Trial court's retention of jurisdiction over one third of concurrent terms of 60 years' imprisonment imposed on defendant pursuant to two-count information was inappropriate, since sentences were imposed pursuant to sentencing guidelines and parole is no longer available to persons who are sentenced under guidelines. Hawkins v. State, App. 2 Dist., 463 So.2d 480 (1985). Sentencing And Punishment ⚷ 226

Where defendant was sentenced to two concurrent terms of 30 years for attempted murder and robbery and concurrent term of five years for grand theft, trial court could not retain jurisdiction over both of the 30-year sentences, pursuant to this section providing that when an individual is convicted of two or more felonies and concurrent sentences are imposed, jurisdiction of trial court shall apply only to first half of maximum sentence imposed for highest felony charged and proven. Maddox v. State, App. 2 Dist., 438 So.2d 959 (1983). Sentencing And Punishment ⚷ 226

76. —— Consecutive sentences, sentence and punishment, retained jurisdiction

Trial court could not retain jurisdiction over portion of each of consecutive sentences imposed, rather than over one third of total of consecutive sentences imposed. Mobley v. State, App. 2 Dist., 590 So.2d 1022 (1991). Sentencing And Punishment ⚷ 226

Under subsection of this section, sentencing court should have retained jurisdiction over one third of total of consecutive sentences imposed rather than over portion of each of consecutive sentences imposed. Heath v. State, App. 1 Dist., 558 So.2d 165 (1990). Sentencing And Punishment ⚷ 226

Sentencing forms, entered on two second-degree murder counts, each indicating that jurisdiction was retained for 15 years, after sentencing of defendant to three 15-year consecutive prison terms for convictions on two counts of attempted second-degree murder and one count of shooting into occupied vehicle were required to be clarified on remand as they could be construed to indicate total retention period of 30 years over total sentence of 45 years' imprisonment in contradiction of court's specifically expressed intention to retain jurisdiction for first one third of total sentence. Famiglietti v. State, App. 4 Dist., 499 So.2d 57 (1986), review denied 506 So.2d 1041. Criminal Law ⚷ 1181.5(8)

Trial judge was without authority to retain jurisdiction over first third of each of three consecutive sentences for robbery, under statute providing that, where defendant is convicted of two or more felonies and consecutive sentences are imposed, trial judge shall retain jurisdiction of one third of total consecutive sentences imposed. Johnson v. State, App. 1 Dist., 495 So.2d 830 (1986). Sentencing And Punishment ⚷ 226

Trial court could not retain jurisdiction over one third of robbery sentence and one third of burglary sentence, though it could retain jurisdiction over one third of total consecutive sentence imposed. Bearden v. State, App. 2 Dist., 481 So.2d 542 (1986). Sentencing And Punishment ⚷ 226

It was improper for trial court to retain jurisdiction to review parole orders over first half of each consecutive sentence; proper way to reserve jurisdiction over consecutive sentences was to enter order reserving jurisdiction over one half of total sentence. Brannin v. State, App. 1 Dist., 476 So.2d 245 (1985), approved 496 So.2d 124. Sentencing And Punishment ⚷ 226

Trial court erred in retaining jurisdiction over ten years of each of three 30-year consecutive sentences for attempted murders; court should have retained jurisdiction over one third of total 90 years to be served for the attempted murders, or 30 years. Connolly v. State, App. 2 Dist., 474 So.2d 912 (1985). Sentencing And Punishment ⚷ 226

Trial court erred in retaining jurisdiction over one third of each of defendant's consecutive sentences, instead of one third of total consecutive sentences. Mobley v. State, App. 4 Dist., 473 So.2d 692 (1985). Criminal Law ⚷ 1134.26; Sentencing And Punishment ⚷ 226

While trial court could assume jurisdiction over first third of defendant's total 320-year term comprised of two consecutive sentences of 160 years, it was not authorized to exercise jurisdiction over the first third of defendant's first 160 years of incarceration and then reclaim jurisdiction over the first third of the second term when it commenced. Brown v. State, App. 1 Dist., 458 So.2d 1216 (1984). Sentencing And Punishment ⚷ 226

On remand, trial court properly retained jurisdiction over one-third of defendant's total sentences of 60 years for attempted first-degree murder and 50 years for robbery, which were to run consecutively, that is, over one-third of 110 years. Kinney v. State, App. 2 Dist., 458 So.2d 1191 (1984). Sentencing And Punishment ⚷ 226

Where trial court's intention was to impose a maximum sentence for the crimes involved, the trial court, consistent with the sentencing plan, properly corrected its sentence of concurrent 120-year terms to be legal sentence of consecutive terms totaling 125 years, and trial court committed no sentencing error in retaining jurisdiction for half of the total of two consecutive sentences. Cruz v. State, App. 3 Dist., 458 So.2d 826 (1984). Sentencing And Punishment ⚷ 226; Sentencing And Punishment ⚷ 2333

Trial court could not retain jurisdiction for first one-third of each of the consecutive sentences imposed and was required to correct the written sentences to clarify that it retained jurisdiction over one-third of the total consecutive sentences. Ferrey v. State, App. 3 Dist., 457 So.2d 1122 (1984). Criminal Law ⚷ 1181.5(8); Sentencing And Punishment ⚷ 226

Those portions of sentencing orders retaining jurisdiction of first one third of each consecutive sentence were invalid. Dobbs v. State, App. 5 Dist., 454 So.2d 73 (1984). Sentencing And Punishment ⚷ 226

Trial court should have retained jurisdiction over one-third of total consecutive sentences and jurisdiction should have been retained over only one of the concurrent sentences for attempted murder. Martin v. State, App. 2 Dist., 452 So.2d 938 (1984). Sentencing And Punishment ⚷ 226

Retention of jurisdiction over one half of each of several consecutive sentences was improper. Parson v. State, App. 4 Dist., 450 So.2d 924 (1984). Sentencing And Punishment ⚷ 226

In retaining jurisdiction over defendant for one third of each sentence imposed, trial court violated this section limiting jurisdiction which trial court may retain to one third of total consecutive sentences imposed. Blackwell v. State, App. 2 Dist., 449 So.2d 1296 (1984). Sentencing And Punishment ⚷ 226

Trial court erroneously retained jurisdiction over one-third of each of consecutive sentences imposed on defendant. Wicker v. State, App. 2 Dist., 445 So.2d 583 (1983). Sentencing And Punishment ⚷ 226

At time when defendant committed the offenses for which he was convicted, trial court had authority to retain jurisdiction to review any parol commission release order for one third of the total consecutive sentences imposed but not for the first one third of each of the consecutive sentences imposed. Wicker v. State, App. 2 Dist., 438 So.2d 399 (1983). Pardon And Parole ⚷ 62

In prosecution for kidnapping and sexual battery, in which defendant was sentenced to serve 99 years on kidnapping charge and 30 years on sexual battery charge, trial court had authority under this section to retain jurisdiction to review any parole commission release order for one third of total consecutive sentences imposed, but not first one third of each of the consecutive sentences imposed. Adams v. State, App. 2 Dist., 435 So.2d 953 (1983). Sentencing And Punishment ⚷ 226

With respect to defendant who was sentenced to consecutive sentences of 15 years each on two counts of sexual battery, trial court erred in retaining jurisdiction over defendant's sentences for review of any parole commission release orders for a period of ten years on each count or a total of 20 years; under applicable law, trial court could not retain jurisdiction for a period greater than 15 years. Redding v. State, App. 2 Dist., 431 So.2d 706 (1983). Pardon And Parole ⚷ 54

It was not error for trial court to retain power to review and vacate any release order that parole commission might enter during defendant's lifetime by trial court's imposing six consecutive 100-year sentences for six felonies and by retaining jurisdiction for one third of each such sentence, aggregating 200 years, to review any parole release order. Harmon v. State, App. 1 Dist., 416 So.2d 835 (1982), approved 438 So.2d 369, habeas corpus denied 894 F.2d 1268, certiorari denied 111 S.Ct. 96, 498 U.S. 832, 112 L.Ed.2d 68. Sentencing And Punishment ⚷ 226

Trial court could not retain jurisdiction for first one third of each of consecutive sentences imposed, but only of one third of total consecutive sentences imposed. Goree v. State, App. 3 Dist., 411 So.2d 1352 (1982). Sentencing And Punishment ⚷ 226

77. Orders, retained jurisdiction—In general

Trial court may not modify sentence so as to retain jurisdiction for review of parole commission release order when such has not been done at time of sentencing. Lang v. State, App. 1 Dist., 616 So.2d 1171 (1993). Sentencing And Punishment ⚷ 2335

Trial court which retained jurisdiction over defendant's sentence for review of parole commission release order could modify retention portion of sentence within 60 days after sentence had been entered to comply with requirement that judge state justification for retention with particularity. Lang v. State, App. 1 Dist., 616 So.2d 1171 (1993). Sentencing And Punishment ⚷ 2312

To retain jurisdiction, sentencing court is only required to make findings on record and is not required to enter written order stating reasons for retention of jurisdiction. Thomas v. State, App. 3 Dist., 611 So.2d 1324 (1993). Sentencing And Punishment ⚷ 226; Sentencing And Punishment ⚷ 370; Sentencing And Punishment ⚷ 372

Trial judge could retain jurisdiction to veto parole for one third of defendant's sentence, pursuant to version of this section which was in effect at time offenses were committed, only upon providing written reasons. Diaz v. State, App. 3 Dist., 563 So.2d 199 (1990). Sentencing And Punishment ⚷ 226; Sentencing And Punishment ⚷ 370

A trial court which retains jurisdiction over the offender for review of a parole commission release order must indicate the extent of retention as to each offense. Marquez v. State, App. 2 Dist., 431 So.2d 618 (1983). Pardon And Parole ⚷ 54

Where trial court at sentencing in open court specifically retained jurisdiction over one third of the sentence on one count of the information but did not mention jurisdiction in connection with sentences entered on other counts but written judgments and sentences stated that jurisdiction was retained on all counts, order for retention of jurisdiction would be stricken from judgments and sentences entered in connection with all but the first count. Yates v. State, App. 2 Dist., 429 So.2d 815 (1983). Criminal Law ⚷ 1184(4.1)

Court must either relinquish its retention of jurisdiction over one-third of sentence or state its justification for individual particularity, as required by this section. Wright v. State, App. 2 Dist., 425 So.2d 64 (1982). Sentencing And Punishment ⚷ 227

In proceeding in which defendant was convicted of kidnapping and sexual battery, trial court erred in ordering that defendant "cannot be released without permission of this court," in light of fact that the court's jurisdiction was limited to the first third of the maximum sentence imposed for the most serious felony. Whigham v. State, App. 1 Dist., 404 So.2d 858 (1981). Sentencing And Punishment ⚷ 225

Though sexual battery and aggravated battery are among contemplated offenses with respect to which trial court may retain jurisdiction over defendant for the first third of his sentence, court was required either to relinquish jurisdiction over defendant or include in the record justification for retention of jurisdiction. Hicks v. State, App. 2 Dist., 388 So.2d 357 (1980), review denied 397 So.2d 778. Sentencing And Punishment ⚷ 226

78. —— Failure to specify reasons for orders, retained jurisdiction

Case would not be remanded to allow trial judge to provide written reasons supporting decision to retain jurisdiction to "veto" defendant's parole, but rather that portion of sentence would be stricken, in light of age of proceeding, nature of underlying sentence, and subsequent repeal of version of this section upon which trial judge had relied. Diaz v. State, App. 3 Dist., 563 So.2d 199 (1990). Criminal Law ⚷ 1181(2); Criminal Law ⚷ 1184(4.1)

Defendant was entitled to be apprised of reasons for trial court's retention of jurisdiction over first one-third of defendant's sentence.

Larkin v. State, App. 4 Dist., 474 So.2d 1282 (1985). Sentencing And Punishment ⚷ 226

By failing to object contemporaneously, defendant did not waive his right to appeal trial court's failure to enter written order setting forth justification for retaining jurisdiction over one third of defendant's sentence. Jenkins v. State, 466 So.2d 1068 (1985). Criminal Law ⚷ 1042.3(2)

In light of trial court's failure to enter an appropriate order setting out particular facts and circumstances justifying its retention of jurisdiction over defendant's sentence for second-degree murder, retention of jurisdiction would be vacated. Saname v. State, App. 1 Dist., 448 So.2d 14 (1984), petition for review denied 453 So.2d 45. Criminal Law ⚷ 1187

Trial court's incorporation by reference of defense counsel's memorandum regarding sentencing and defendant's presentence investigation did not cure trial court's error in retaining jurisdiction over sentence for second-degree murder without stating reasons for retaining jurisdiction with individual particularity. Saname v. State, App. 1 Dist., 448 So.2d 14 (1984), petition for review denied 453 So.2d 45. Sentencing And Punishment ⚷ 226

Circuit court improperly retained jurisdiction over first third of 120-year sentence imposed on defendant for conviction of four counts of robbery where, although state attorney agreed to prepare order detailing justification for retention of jurisdiction, order was not present in file and was apparently never submitted to court for signature. Hampton v. State, App. 4 Dist., 419 So.2d 354 (1982). Sentencing And Punishment ⚷ 226

In prosecution for first-degree burglary and involuntary sexual battery, trial judge was entitled under this section to retain jurisdiction over first one third of defendant's sentences, provided judge stated with individual particularity justification upon which retention was based; where justification was absent from record, judge was not legally empowered to retain jurisdiction, and cause had to be remanded with directions that if judge wished to retain jurisdiction, he state on record the justification. Mathis v. State, App. 2 Dist., 417 So.2d 1178 (1982). Criminal Law ⚷ 1181.5(8); Sentencing And Punishment ⚷ 226

Failure to make findings of fact supporting retention of jurisdiction over one third of probationer's sentence warranted remand. Brisco v. State, App. 2 Dist., 417 So.2d 833 (1982). Criminal Law ⚷ 1181.5(8)

Failure of trial court to state its reasons for retaining jurisdiction over defendant was error. Rosa v. State, App. 3 Dist., 412 So.2d 891 (1982). Pardon And Parole ⚷ 77.1

Trial court failed to state, with particularity, its justification for retaining jurisdiction over defendant for review of any parole commission release order. Young v. State, App. 1 Dist., 406 So.2d 1249 (1981). Pardon And Parole ⚷ 61

Part of judgment and sentence in which trial court retained jurisdiction over first one third of defendant's sentence was vacated due to trial court's failure to specify its reasons therefor as mandated by this section. Sellers v. State, App. 2 Dist., 406 So.2d 75 (1981). Criminal Law ⚷ 1181.5(1)

Trial judge was not legally empowered to retain jurisdiction over one third of defendant's sentence for conviction of second-degree murder pursuant to this section which allows trial judge to retain such jurisdiction where trial judge made no findings of fact and justification on the record before retaining jurisdiction, in that that section requires trial judge to state with individual particularity justification for retention on the record before such a retention can be made. LaChance v. State, App. 2 Dist., 396 So.2d 1234 (1981). Sentencing And Punishment ⚷ 226

79. —— Particularity of statement, orders, retained jurisdiction

Reasons given by trial court for order retaining jurisdiction over one third of defendant's sentence, which were inconsistent with jury verdict, vague, conclusory, insubstantial or unsupported by the record, were legally insufficient. Macias v. State, App. 3 Dist., 614 So.2d 1216 (1993). Sentencing And Punishment ⚷ 226

Trial court order retaining jurisdiction over one third of defendant's sentence which contains legally insufficient reasons for retaining such jurisdiction may be vacated on motion to correct illegal sentence. Macias v. State, App. 3 Dist., 614 So.2d 1216 (1993). Sentencing And Punishment ⚷ 2221

Trial court offered sufficient reasons for its retention of jurisdiction over one third of defendant's 45-year sentence for kidnapping with weapon, and, thus, defendant was not entitled to habeas corpus relief; written reasons prepared by court corresponded with reasons court expressed in defendant's presence at sentencing hearing. Harris v. State, App. 4 Dist., 584 So.2d 104 (1991). Habeas Corpus ⚷ 503.1; Sentencing And Punishment ⚷ 226; Sentencing And Punishment ⚷ 373

Trial court's retention of jurisdiction over armed robbery defendant's case, "for the same reasons that I have previously ascribed in retaining jurisdiction in the case of" codefendant, did not satisfy requirement that justification for retention of jurisdiction be stated with individual particularity. Ragan v. Dugger, App. 1 Dist.,

544 So.2d 1052 (1989). Sentencing And Punishment ⚷ 373

Trial court did not comply with requirement of subsection of this section that reason for retention of jurisdiction over sentence imposed in armed robbery prosecution be stated with individual particularity; reasons stated by trial court were that defendant showed absolutely no remorse for crime that he committed and that he was one-man crime wave that greatly endangered society. Marshall v. Dugger, App. 3 Dist., 526 So.2d 143 (1988). Sentencing And Punishment ⚷ 373

Trial court's retention of jurisdiction over parole was not based on vague and subjective factors despite trial court's expression at sentencing that "facts speak for themselves" as basis for retaining jurisdiction where trial court's statement of brutal facts of crime laid out quite clearly the basis for retention of jurisdiction. Murray v. State, 491 So.2d 1120 (1986). Sentencing And Punishment ⚷ 226

Statement on sentence that defendant had prior criminal activity was not sufficient reason to retain jurisdiction over first one third of jail sentence of defendant. Cahill v. State, App. 2 Dist., 489 So.2d 1219 (1986). Sentencing And Punishment ⚷ 226

Defendant was precluded from raising, via motion to correct sentence, issue as to illegality of trial court's retaining jurisdiction for one third of his sentence without stating the justification with individual particularity, since defendant could have raised the issue on direct appeal. Adams v. State, App. 2 Dist., 462 So.2d 884 (1985). Criminal Law ⚷ 1429(2)

Trial judge's statement that, based on what the judge knew about defendants, he would retain jurisdiction over defendants for one third of their sentences did not satisfy the requirements of this section providing for the retention of jurisdiction when the justification for the action is made a part of the court record, and cause would be remanded to permit correction of sentencing procedure. Robinson v. State, App. 4 Dist., 458 So.2d 1132 (1984), post-conviction relief granted 621 So.2d 556, denial of post-conviction relief affirmed 642 So.2d 644. Criminal Law ⚷ 1181.5(8); Sentencing And Punishment ⚷ 226

Trial court's justification for retention of jurisdiction over case of defendant convicted and sentenced on three counts of lewd and lascivious assault was stated with individual particularity as required by this section. Dobbs v. State, App. 5 Dist., 454 So.2d 73 (1984). Sentencing And Punishment ⚷ 226

In murder prosecution, trial judge did not fail to state his justification for imposing extended terms under the Habitual Offender Act (§ 775.084) with requisite particularity. McCoy v. State, App. 1 Dist., 429 So.2d 1256 (1983), petition for review denied 438 So.2d 833. Sentencing And Punishment ⚷ 1393

In proceeding in which court imposed sentence of 150 years, with 50 years retained jurisdiction over parole, for a second-degree murder offense, sentencing judge failed to state his justifications for retention of jurisdiction with sufficient particularity. Saname v. State, App. 1 Dist., 427 So.2d 1083 (1983). Sentencing And Punishment ⚷ 373

A court's failure to satisfy individual particularity requirement of this section governing retention of jurisdiction for parole is a procedural error. Alexander v. State, App. 2 Dist., 425 So.2d 1197 (1983). Pardon And Parole ⚷ 54

Statement of justification for trial court's retention of jurisdiction over first one-third of sentence for armed robbery failed to satisfy requirement under this section of "specificity and particularity" where the court referred to circumstances surrounding the incidents, nature of offenses and seriousness as well as gravity thereof without citing any facts or circumstances, notwithstanding that statement included somewhat more specific references to the conditions under which victim was submitted and losses to the victim. Abbott v. State, App. 1 Dist., 421 So.2d 24 (1982). Sentencing And Punishment ⚷ 373

Trial judge must state with particularity justification for retention of jurisdiction over individual before such retention can be made. Brisco v. State, App. 2 Dist., 417 So.2d 833 (1982). Sentencing And Punishment ⚷ 226

Trial judge was required to state with individual particularity justification for retention of jurisdiction on sentencing order. Sanders v. State, App. 2 Dist., 400 So.2d 1015 (1981). Sentencing And Punishment ⚷ 226

Each order retaining jurisdiction in trial court for review of parole commission release order during first third of sentence must be based upon articulated substantial reasonable grounds to be determined in each case "within individual particularity." Moore v. State, App. 5 Dist., 392 So.2d 277 (1980). Sentencing And Punishment ⚷ 226

80. —— Time of entry, orders, retained jurisdiction

Court's announcement, two weeks after imposition of sentence, that it intended at later date to retain jurisdiction over defendant's sentence did not comply with this section providing that, at time of sentencing, judge may enter order retaining jurisdiction; thus order entered almost two months after sentence, retaining jurisdiction over one-third of defendant's sentence, must be stricken. Neal v. State, App. 3 Dist., 414 So.2d 1146 (1982). Sentencing And Punishment ⚷ 226

Trial court lost chance to properly enter ex parte order entitled "Order Retaining Jurisdiction over Defendant for Review of Future Parole Commission Release Order Pursuant to Florida Statute 947.16." when it was not done at time of sentencing as this section requires. Griffin v. State, App. 5 Dist., 414 So.2d 17 (1982). Sentencing And Punishment ⚷ 2285

After defendant had been sentenced following conviction of second-degree murder and of robbery with a deadly weapon, trial court was without jurisdiction to retain jurisdiction for purpose of reviewing a parole commission release order where trial court failed, at time of sentencing, to enter an order retaining jurisdiction over defendant for such purposes. Hayes v. State, App. 3 Dist., 400 So.2d 519 (1981). Sentencing And Punishment ⚷ 226

Trial court's order seeking to retain jurisdiction over defendant for the first one third of defendant's sentence was entered without jurisdiction where order was not entered at time of sentencing but was entered two weeks after trial. Knight v. State, App. 5 Dist., 398 So.2d 833 (1981). Sentencing And Punishment ⚷ 2285

81. Review, retained jurisdiction—In general

Defendant could properly raise in motion to correct illegal sentence claim that trial court acted without authority in ordering that jurisdiction be retained for the first one-half of defendant's sixty-five-year sentence. Ayala-Laies v. State, App. 4 Dist., 16 So.3d 244 (2009). Sentencing and Punishment ⚷ 2251

Trial court's erroneous retention of jurisdiction over sentence for third degree burglary was preserved for appeal, even though objection was not couched in the most artful language, because objection was sufficient, to advise the trial court of defendant's objection. Walcott v. State, App. 5 Dist., 460 So.2d 915 (1984), approved 472 So.2d 741. Criminal Law ⚷ 1043(1)

Trial court erred in retaining jurisdiction over one-half of each sentence imposed upon defendant and was required to amend each sentence so as to limit such jurisdiction to not more than one-third of each sentence. Brumley v. State, App. 5 Dist., 455 So.2d 1096 (1984), approved 471 So.2d 1282. Sentencing And Punishment ⚷ 226

Authority given to judges to retain jurisdiction in individual cases is totally devoid of legislative guidelines and the authority is reviewable on appeal for substance and reasonableness and for the purpose of ensuring that other rights of the defendant are not violated in the process. Owen v. State, App. 3 Dist., 441 So.2d 1111 (1983), motion denied 446 So.2d 100. Sentencing And Punishment ⚷ 226

Having been furnished nothing other than the motion for postconviction relief and the order denying same, the District Court of Appeal had to reverse the order denying relief and remand the cause to the trial court with directions to attach that part of the record setting forth the "justification with individual particularity" for retention of jurisdiction over one-third of the 75-year sentence imposed on petitioner, or, if no such record now existed, to make one; on the present record, the trial court's retention of jurisdiction was unlawful and the motion unquestionably set forth a legal ground showing that the "sentence is otherwise subject to collateral attack." Williams v. State, App. 3 Dist., 435 So.2d 882 (1983). Criminal Law ⚷ 1086.1; Criminal Law ⚷ 1186.1

Where no reason was given for trial court's retaining of jurisdiction over entire sentence, court was directed to vacate portion of order retaining jurisdiction over entire sentence and resentence defendant in compliance with statutory requirements. McClellan v. State, App. 2 Dist., 434 So.2d 1 (1983). Criminal Law ⚷ 1181.5(8)

Where defendant appealed conviction but not 30-year sentence, with trial court retaining jurisdiction over first third, he could have raised the retention of jurisdiction issue on direct appeal and was precluded from subsequently collaterally attacking the retention of jurisdiction provision by a motion under Criminal Procedure Rule 3.850 alleging that trial judge did not state reasons for retaining jurisdiction with the required individual particularity. Pedroso v. State, App. 2 Dist., 420 So.2d 908 (1982). Criminal Law ⚷ 1429(2)

No error was shown in trial court's retaining jurisdiction over the first one third of 75-year sentence for second-degree murder. Eaton v. State, App. 4 Dist., 410 So.2d 933 (1981), approved 438 So.2d 822. Sentencing And Punishment ⚷ 226

Contention that trial judge did not state with individual particularity justification for retaining jurisdiction under this section authorizing sentencing judge to retain jurisdiction to review certain parole release orders was not preserved for review. Burley v. State, App. 5 Dist., 408 So.2d 830 (1982). Criminal Law ⚷ 1042.3(2)

Order retaining jurisdiction to review parole commission release order during first third of sentence is reviewable. Moore v. State, App. 5 Dist., 392 So.2d 277 (1980). Criminal Law ⚷ 1023(1)

82. —— Findings, review, retained jurisdiction

Statutory requirement that court state with specificity and particularity the justification for retaining jurisdiction over a portion of sentence is not met when the findings are vague, conclusory, and insubstantial, or are unsupported by the record. Hampton v. State, App. 1 Dist., 764 So.2d 829 (2000). Sentencing And Punishment ⚷ 226

Sentencing court's statement that "the reason for which I am retaining jurisdiction is that your past record of all manner of offenses, both as a juvenile and an adult, indicates to me a total disrespect for the law; that you apparently cannot live in a lawful society and require institutionalization" was insufficient to justify retention of jurisdiction over one-third of second-degree murder defendant's sentence to monitor any Parole Commission release order. Hampton v. State, App. 1 Dist., 764 So.2d 829 (2000). Sentencing And Punishment ⚷ 226

83. —— Failure to object, review, retained jurisdiction

Defendant's failure to object in trial court will not preclude appellate review if trial court has no statutory authority to retain jurisdiction over defendant's sentence; disapproving of *Cofield v. State,* 453 So.2d 409. State v. Mobley, 481 So.2d 481 (1986). Criminal Law ⚷ 1042.3(2)

Defendant was not precluded from challenging on direct appeal trial court's retention of jurisdiction over one half of his sentence for conviction of burglary of a structure, even though defendant made no objection to such retention at time of sentencing. State v. Walcott, 472 So.2d 741 (1985). Criminal Law ⚷ 1042.3(2)

Failure of defendant to contemporaneously object to trial judge's announcement in open court at sentencing, contrary to subsection of § 947.16, which had by then become effective, that he would retain jurisdiction of over one half of defendant's sentence did not preclude defendant from challenging, on direct appeal, the trial court's retention of jurisdiction for more than statutory period of one third of the sentence. State v. Brumley, 471 So.2d 1282 (1985). Criminal Law ⚷ 1042.3(2)

If trial court failed to follow mandatory requirements of this section requiring trial court to state with individual particularity the justification for retaining jurisdiction for one third of the sentence, defendant was not precluded from raising the point on appeal because he failed to object in the trial court. State v. Snow, 462 So.2d 455 (1985), on remand 464 So.2d 1313. Criminal Law ⚷ 1042.3(2)

Contemporaneous objection rule did not apply to sentencing error where it was contended that trial court erroneously retained jurisdiction over the sentence. Walcott v. State, App. 5 Dist., 460 So.2d 915 (1984), approved 472 So.2d 741. Criminal Law ⚷ 1042.3(2)

Issue of whether trial court erred in retaining jurisdiction over one-half of each sentence imposed upon defendant could be reviewed on appeal of the convictions and sentences, even though defendant made no objection in the trial court; disagreeing with Cofield v. State, 453 So.2d 409. Brumley v. State, App. 5 Dist., 455 So.2d 1096 (1984), approved 471 So.2d 1282. Criminal Law ⚷ 1042.3(2)

Trial court's failure to follow this section in retaining jurisdiction over convicted defendant for first one third of sentence was not preserved for appellate purposes, where defendant made no objection at time, and error was not of fundamental proportions. Jenkins v. State, App. 4 Dist., 448 So.2d 1060 (1984), decision approved in part, quashed in part 466 So.2d 1068. Criminal Law ⚷ 1042.3(2)

Issue that trial court's retention of jurisdiction over one half of each sentence imposed upon defendant convicted of robbery after he was charged with violating conditions of his probation constituted an ex post facto law was not preserved for appellate review, in that defendant imposed no objection to retention of jurisdiction at revocation of probation hearing or at conviction and sentencing. Mobley v. State, App. 2 Dist., 447 So.2d 328 (1984). Criminal Law ⚷ 1042.3(2)

Notwithstanding that record did not reflect objection below, District Court of Appeal addressed contention that trial court in prosecution for second-degree robbery erred in retention of jurisdiction over entire sentence of 15 years, where defendant on appeal challenged legality of sentence. McClellan v. State, App. 2 Dist., 434 So.2d 1 (1983). Criminal Law ⚷ 1042.3(2)

In order for District Court of Appeal to consider contention that retention of jurisdiction over defendant's sentence was error, on basis that it constituted ex post facto application of law, question must be preserved for appellate review by proper objection in trial court, and appeal may then be taken from adverse determination. Brown v. State, App. 5 Dist., 428 So.2d 369 (1983). Criminal Law ⚷ 1030(2)

Where defendant did not object to error of trial court in failing to satisfy individual particularity requirement when retaining jurisdiction, defendant could not raise issue on appeal. Alexander v. State, App. 2 Dist., 425 So.2d 1197 (1983). Criminal Law ⚷ 1042.3(2)

Objection to trial judge's retention of jurisdiction over first third of life sentence was not preserved for appeal since no objection was raised before trial court at time of sentence or by way of an appropriate posttrial motion. Gaskins v. State, App. 5 Dist., 415 So.2d 132 (1982). Criminal Law ⚷ 1042.3(2); Criminal Law ⚷ 1044.1(1)

The District Court of Appeal declined to decide issue that trial judge erred in retaining jurisdiction, after sentencing without specifying his reason for doing so, which issue defendant failed to present to trial court, in view of fact that issue constituted a procedural error and not a fundamental one. Sawyer v. State, App. 1 Dist., 401 So.2d 939 (1981). Criminal Law ⚷ 1028

84. —— Remand, review, retained jurisdiction

That defendant had extensive criminal record, without more, was insufficient to warrant retention of jurisdiction to review a parole commission release order over first one-third of sentences for armed robbery and attempted second degree murder, thus requiring remand for trial court to make defendant's criminal history a matter of record and to provide written reasons to justify retention of jurisdiction. King v. State, App. 2 Dist., 835 So.2d 1224 (2003). Criminal Law ⚷ 1181.5(8); Sentencing And Punishment ⚷ 226

Order denying defendant's postconviction motion without hearing did not attack any portion of record which refuted allegation that defendant was entitled to relief on ground that trial court, in retaining jurisdiction at time of sentencing failed to state, either in writing or in open court, justification for retention of jurisdiction, requiring remand for further proceedings on the postconviction motion. Buxton v. State, App. 1 Dist., 462 So.2d 16 (1984). Criminal Law ⚷ 1181.5(3.1)

Where transcript indicated that trial judge failed to retain jurisdiction over decision of parole department after defendant's conviction of rape, but clerk's notes and written order of judgment and sentence indicated opposite, case had to be remanded with directions to determine whether sentencing judge properly retained jurisdiction at time of sentencing in accordance with this section. Johnson v. State, App. 3 Dist., 423 So.2d 497 (1982). Criminal Law ⚷ 1181.5(8)

Remand was required to trial court with instructions to either relinquish retention of jurisdiction over one-third of defendant's sentence or to make findings of fact and justification, with individual particularity, to justify retention of jurisdiction where trial court failed to make findings of fact supporting retention of jurisdiction a part of the record. Kendrick v. State, App. 2 Dist., 418 So.2d 465 (1982). Criminal Law ⚷ 1181.5(8)

Trial court did not err in retaining jurisdiction over the first third of each of defendants' sentences imposed on convictions for attempted escape and rioting since defendants used intentional violence in committing such felony; however, trial judge did not make any findings justifying his retention of jurisdiction, and thus remand was required in order for trial judge to make such findings. Mobley v. State, 409 So.2d 1031 (1982). Criminal Law ⚷ 1181.5(2); Sentencing And Punishment ⚷ 226

Remedy for trial court's retaining jurisdiction over first one-third of defendant's sentence without making required findings was to remand case to enable trial court to make findings. Tompkins v. State, App. 5 Dist., 386 So.2d 597 (1980), review denied 392 So.2d 1380. Criminal Law ⚷ 1181.5(8)

947.165. Objective parole guidelines

(1) The commission shall develop and implement objective parole guidelines which shall be the criteria upon which parole decisions are made. The objective parole guidelines shall be developed according to an acceptable research method and shall be based on the seriousness of offense and the likelihood of favorable parole outcome. The guidelines shall require the commission to aggravate or aggregate each consecutive sentence in establishing the presumptive parole release date. Factors used in arriving at the salient factor score and the severity of offense behavior category shall not be applied as aggravating circumstances. If the sentencing judge files a written objection to the parole release of an inmate as provided for in s. 947.1745(6), such objection may be used by the commission as a basis to extend the presumptive parole release date.

(2) At least once a year, the commission shall review the objective parole guidelines and make any revisions considered necessary by virtue of statistical analysis of commission actions, which analysis uses acceptable research and methodology.

Laws 1978, c. 78–417, § 12; Laws 1979, c. 79–42, § 6; Laws 1979, c. 79–310, § 3; Laws 1981, c. 81–259, § 499; Laws 1982, c. 82–171, § 10; Laws 1985, c. 85–107, § 2; Laws 1986, c. 86–183, § 32; Laws 1993, c. 93–61, § 7.

Historical and Statutory Notes

Amendment Notes:

Laws 1979, c. 79–42, § 6, substituted in the first sentence of subsec. (2) "before January 1, 1980" for "by July 1, 1979", and inserted in the third sentence thereof reference to automated data requirements and provided that the priority basis be "in accordance with the provisions of s. 20.315(20)."

Laws 1979, c. 79–310, added the third sentence to subsec. (1).

Laws 1981, c. 81–259, a reviser's correction bill prepared pursuant to § 11.242, deleted provisions which had become obsolete.

Laws 1982, c. 82–171, § 10, in subsec. (2), substituted "statistical analysis of commission actions using acceptable research and methodology" for "experience" in the first sentence, and deleted the second sentence which provided that the commission shall be responsible for notifying the department of the statistical information and automated data requirements necessary for program review and monitoring.

Laws 1985, c. 85–107, § 2, eff. June 11, 1985, interpolated the third sentence in subsec. (1).

Laws 1986, c. 86–183, § 32, eff. Oct. 1, 1986, added the fifth sentence to subsec. (1).

Laws 1993, c. 93–61, § 7, eff. April 22, 1993, in subsec. (1), in the last sentence, substituted "If the sentencing judge" for "In the event the sentencing court"; and amended the citation.

Cross References

Sentencing guidelines, see Criminal Procedure Rules 3.701, Form 3.988.

Law Review and Journal Commentaries

Parole. James H. Burke, Jr., 57 Fla.B.J. 245 (1983).

Sentencing guidelines. Samuel S. Jacobson, 57 Fla.B.J. 234 (1983).

Library References

Pardon and Parole ⚷53.
Westlaw Topic No. 284.
C.J.S. Pardon and Parole §§ 48 to 51.

Research References

ALR Library

77 ALR 1211, Right of Court to Hear Evidence for Purpose of Determining Sentence to be Imposed.

United States Supreme Court

Life inmates, rights to commutation of sentence before board of pardons, see Connecticut Bd. of Pardons v. Dumschat, U.S.Conn.1981, 101 S.Ct. 2460, 452 U.S. 458, 69 L.Ed.2d 158.

Notes of Decisions

---

1. Construction and application

Application of Florida's Objective Parole Guidelines Act [West's F.S.A. §§ 947.001 to 947.24] did not violate petitioner's ex post facto rights by imposing new standards on Parole Commission's exercise of discretion. Johnson v. Wainwright, C.A.11 (Fla.)1985, 772 F.2d 826. Constitutional Law ⚷ 2823; Pardon And Parole ⚷ 42.1

Where risk categories established for offense characteristics used for parole consideration do not specifically list offense for which sentence was imposed, the parole and probation commission should consult and be bound by statutory classification of conviction. Faucett v. Florida Parole & Probation Commission, App. 1 Dist., 413 So.2d 1282 (1982). Pardon And Parole ⚷ 53

2. Presumptive parole release date—In general

Failure to use armed robbery conviction in setting severity level of prisoner's offense for purpose of setting prisoner's presumptive parole release date was error. Zygadlo v. Florida Parole and Probation Com'n, App. 1 Dist., 414 So.2d 600 (1982). Pardon And Parole ⚷ 53

Parole and probation commission, which computed inmate's presumptive parole release date using his kidnapping conviction rather than one of his robbery convictions as his offense characteristic, erred in refusing to recompute inmate's release date after trial court had corrected his kidnapping sentence to reflect correct conviction for false imprisonment. Faucett v. Florida Parole & Probation Commission, App. 1 Dist., 413 So.2d 1282 (1982). Pardon And Parole ⚷ 60

The parole and probation commission may exercise its discretion in establishing a presumptive parole release date for each entitled inmate only in limited circumstances with adequate explanation. James v. Florida Parole and Probation Commission, App. 1 Dist., 395 So.2d 197 (1981). Pardon And Parole ⚷ 52

3. —— Presentence investigation reports, presumptive parole release date

Parole Commission, in exercising its duty to establish inmate's presumptive parole release date in accordance with objective parole guidelines, is entitled to rely on information contained in presentence investigation reports as well as on any other information compiled by Department of Corrections in performance of its record-keeping duty. Adams v. State, App. 1 Dist., 560 So.2d 321 (1990). Pardon And Parole ⚷ 58

Absence of a presentence investigation report provides no grounds for parole and probation commission's failure to follow clear statutory requirements to set presumptive parole release dates. James v. Florida Parole and Probation Commission, App. 1 Dist., 395 So.2d 197 (1981). Pardon And Parole ⚷ 58

4. —— Aggravating circumstances, presumptive parole release date

Prior aggravated conviction could be used as an aggravating factor for calculation of PPRD, even though it had already been used to calculate one point of salient factor scale for probation revocation and revocation and conviction were closely related, in light of record which did not indicate why probation had been revoked, but that conviction had stemmed from aggravated battery itself. Ruzicka v. Florida Parole and Probation Com'n, App. 1 Dist., 480 So.2d 190 (1985). Pardon And Parole ⚷ 50

Action by parole and probation commission establishing defendant's presumptive parole release date was not improper on basis that aggravation for exceptionally brutal or heinous behavior was prohibited since depraved mind is an element of second-degree murder of which defendant was convicted, in that depraved mind is less than brutal or heinous, and exceptionally brutal behavior is not an element of second-degree murder. Bundy v. Florida Parole and Probation Com'n, App. 1 Dist., 419 So.2d 1181 (1982). Pardon And Parole ⚷ 49

Giving consideration to defendant's failure to make restitution to robbery victim as an aggravating factor, in establishing defendant's presumptive parole release date, was not error, in view of fact that returning the money had, at one point, been within defendant's knowledge and ability; failure to make restitution was not an element of robbery. Stewart v. Florida Parole and Probation Com'n, App. 1 Dist., 419 So.2d 1157 (1982). Pardon And Parole ⚷ 49

Order establishing presumptive parole release date was invalid where parole and probation commission aggravated presumptive parole release date for use of firearm, as the factors used in definition of armed robbery as offense of conviction could not be utilized to aggravate presumptive parole release date and additional aggravation was not permitted for factors included in definition of other convictions already used as aggravating elements. Mattingly v. Florida Parole and Probation Com'n, App. 1

Dist., 417 So.2d 1163 (1982). Pardon And Parole ⚷ 49

Where Florida parole and probation commission's statement of aggravation, in recommending a presumptive parole release date consisting of a 156-month matrix time range with a 24-month aggravation, related that prisoner's five-year federal sentence was consecutive to his Florida sentence, thereby indicating that it was imposed later in time than Florida sentence and, therefore, was not considered in determining salient factor score, commission's statement of aggravation stated with sufficient particularity a proper factor, the prisoner's federal sentence, to consider for aggravation. Jacobson v. Florida Parole and Probation Commission, App. 1 Dist., 407 So.2d 611 (1981). Pardon And Parole ⚷ 61

5. Aggravating circumstances

Since § 784.045 defines aggravated battery as either causing great bodily harm in committing battery or as using deadly weapon in committing it and only one of two actions is necessary to consummate crime, parole and probation commission did not err in increasing sentence for aggravated battery because a weapon was used in committing the offense. Lambeth v. Florida Parole and Probation Commission, App. 1 Dist., 411 So.2d 956 (1982). Pardon And Parole ⚷ 49

In sentencing under objective parole criteria, where parole and probation commission determined defendant's matrix range using armed robbery as the offense characteristic, use of aggravating factor of "shots fired" to aggravate beyond guidelines matrix range was sufficiently explained by phrase itself and was not cumulative to offense characteristic matrix calculation. Baker v. Florida Parole and Probation Commission, App. 1 Dist., 384 So.2d 746 (1980). Pardon And Parole ⚷ 61

Under objective parole criteria, in extending an inmate's term, by reason of aggravating circumstances, beyond guideline matrix range, parole and probation commission must distinguish aggravating circumstances from factors used in computing salient factor score. Baker v. Florida Parole and Probation Commission, App. 1 Dist., 384 So.2d 746 (1980). Pardon And Parole ⚷ 61

Under objective parole criteria, in extending an inmate's term, by reason of aggravating circumstances, beyond guideline matrix range, parole and probation commission must at least distinguish aggravating circumstances relied on from factors which determine offensive characteristic and, if offense is not specifically listed in guidelines, it must be explained by Commission sufficiently to indicate basis of comparison with an offense listed. Baker v. Florida Parole and Probation Commission, App. 1 Dist., 384 So.2d 746 (1980). Pardon And Parole ⚷ 61

Under objective parole criteria, in extending an inmate's term, by reason of aggravating circumstances, beyond guideline matrix range, parole and probation commission's explanation must be adequate to afford an inmate insight into why his term to be served was aggravated beyond guideline matrix range. Baker v. Florida Parole and Probation Commission, App. 1 Dist., 384 So.2d 746 (1980). Pardon And Parole ⚷ 61

6. Amendment to guidelines—In general

Use of 1982 presumptive parole release date guidelines for 1977 crimes was proper. Odom v. Florida Parole and Probation Com'n, App. 1 Dist., 433 So.2d 634 (1983). Pardon And Parole ⚷ 53

This section requiring parole and probation commission to review its procedures periodically and make any revisions considered necessary "by virtue of experience" in order to achieve statutory purposes does not contemplate that procedures for setting parole shall be fixed from time prisoner's crime was committed. Britt v. Florida Parole & Probation Com'n, App. 1 Dist., 417 So.2d 1079 (1982). Pardon And Parole ⚷ 48.1

Amendment to objective parole guidelines, increasing applicable matrix time from 18–33 months to 60–84 months, was not unconstitutional as violation of ex post facto clause, since defendant's punishment was not increased by the amendment and adoption and amendment of objective guidelines was a procedural change. Lopez v. Florida Parole and Probation Commission, App. 1 Dist., 410 So.2d 1354 (1982), certiorari denied 103 S.Ct. 207, 459 U.S. 905, 74 L.Ed.2d 166. Constitutional Law ⚷ 2823; Pardon And Parole ⚷ 53

Parole and probation commission did not exceed its authority in enacting amendments to objective parole guidelines after it became convinced that original matrix times were too low, and department of corrections was not required to provide necessary data before rule revisions. Lopez v. Florida Parole and Probation Commission, App. 1 Dist., 410 So.2d 1354 (1982), certiorari denied 103 S.Ct. 207, 459 U.S. 905, 74 L.Ed.2d 166. Pardon And Parole ⚷ 53

7. —— Validity of release date, amendment to guidelines

Application to the petitioner of the more stringent parole guidelines adopted by the parole and probation commission after the commission of the crime was not violative of the constitutional proscription against ex post facto laws. Lobo v. Florida Parole and Probation Com'n, App. 4 Dist., 433 So.2d 622 (1983); Williams v.

Florida Parole and Probation Com'n, App., 425 So.2d 1190 (1983); Gallon v. Florida Parole and Probation Com'n, App., 423 So.2d 465 (1982).

Parole and probation commission did not violate state and federal proscriptions against ex post facto laws when it fixed new presumptive parole release date for prisoner, who committed another crime after his initial presumptive parole release date had been set, based on the more stringent guideline adopted by the Commission after the new crime was committed. May v. Florida Parole and Probation Com'n, App. 1 Dist., 424 So.2d 122 (1982), affirmed 435 So.2d 834. Constitutional Law ⚿ 2823; Pardon And Parole ⚿ 63

Application of objective parole guidelines to appellant's 1965 convictions did not violate the ex post facto clause. Hopkins v. Florida Parole and Probation Com'n, App. 1 Dist., 422 So.2d 1014 (1982). Constitutional Law ⚿ 2823; Pardon And Parole ⚿ 53

Florida parole and probation commission's application of matrix time ranges which came into effect subsequent to defendant's sentencing in order to establish his presumptive parole release date did not violate ex post facto clauses of State and Federal Constitutions since defendant committed his crime at a time when parole was within discretion of the commission. Wright v. Florida Parole and Probation Com'n, App. 1 Dist., 420 So.2d 902 (1982). Constitutional Law ⚿ 2823; Pardon And Parole ⚿ 53

There was no ex post facto violation by applying a matrix time range for parole release set by rule in effect at time of setting presumptive parole release date rather than by rule in effect when crime occurred as the matrix time range does not automatically determine time served and parole and probation commission has discretion to aggravate or mitigate the matrix time. Overfield v. Florida Parole and Probation Com'n, App. 1 Dist., 418 So.2d 321 (1982). Constitutional Law ⚿ 2823; Pardon And Parole ⚿ 53

8. Rules and regulations

Administrative rule was not invalid delegation of legislative authority which caused the parole and probation commission to improperly rate defendant's offense for purposes of determining his presumptive parole release date. Roberts v. Florida Parole and Probation Com'n, App. 1 Dist., 424 So.2d 64 (1982). Constitutional Law ⚿ 2415(4); Pardon And Parole ⚿ 55.1

Parole and probation commission has broad authority to develop and implement objective parole guidelines, therefore, commission rule which provided for aggregation of offenses in computing presumptive parole release date where inmate was currently serving commitment imposed prior to his present commitment was not invalid on theory it violated this section which provided that factors used in arriving at salient factor score and severity of offense behavior category shall not be applied as aggravating circumstances. Nord v. Florida Parole and Probation Com'n, App. 1 Dist., 417 So.2d 1176 (1982). Pardon And Parole ⚿ 53

When challenge to parole and probation commission rule implicates commission's exercise of its discretion in matters requiring special knowledge, experience and services to determine technical and intricate matters of fact, or uniformity of ruling is essential to comply with purposes of statute being administered, rather than matter of law to be determined by ordinary rules of statutory construction, court will require prior resort to commission. Nord v. Florida Parole and Probation Com'n, App. 1 Dist., 417 So.2d 1176 (1982). Pardon And Parole ⚿ 62

947.168. Consideration for persons serving parole-eligible and parole-ineligible sentences

(1) A person serving a parole-eligible sentence who subsequently receives a parole-ineligible sentence shall be considered for parole on the parole-eligible sentence.

(2) A grant of parole on the parole-eligible sentence shall result in the initiation of service of the parole-ineligible sentence, which shall continue until expiration of sentence, expiration of sentence as reduced by accumulated gain-time, or an executive order granting clemency.

(3) Actual terms of parole service shall not be initiated until the satisfactory completion of the parole-ineligible sentence and subsequent review by the commission as provided in subsection (4).

(4) Following completion of the parole-ineligible sentence, the commission shall reinterview the offender and consider any new information provided by

the Department of Corrections. Upon an affirmative vote by the commission, the offender shall be released on parole and required to meet any conditions set by the commission pursuant to s. 947.19.

Laws 1986, c. 86–183, § 38; Laws 1991, c. 91–239, § 2. Amended by Laws 1997, c. 97–194, §32, eff. Oct. 1, 1998.

Historical and Statutory Notes

Amendment Notes:

Laws 1991, c. 91–239, § 2, eff. May 30, 1991, reenacted subsec. (1) of this section for the purpose of incorporating the amendment to § 921.001(10) in a reference thereto.

Laws 1997, c. 97–194, § 32, eff. Oct. 1, 1998, in subsec. (1), following "sentence" the second place it appears deleted "pursuant to s. 921.001(10)".

Library References

Pardon and Parole ⚷51.
Westlaw Topic No. 284.
C.J.S. Pardon and Parole §§ 48 to 51.

Research References

Treatises and Practice Aids

16 Florida Practice Series § 10:19, Parole--Eligibility for Parole.

947.17. Repealed by Laws 1978, c. 78–417, § 24

Historical and Statutory Notes

The repealed section, providing for procedure in granting parole, was derived from:
Laws 1977, c. 77–174, § 1.
Laws 1977, c. 77–120, § 89.
Laws 1974, c. 74–112, § 11.
Laws 1941, c. 20519, § 13.

947.172. Establishment of presumptive parole release date

(1) The hearing examiner shall conduct an initial interview in accordance with the provisions of s. 947.16. This interview shall include introduction and explanation of the objective parole guidelines as they relate to presumptive and effective parole release dates and an explanation of the institutional conduct record and satisfactory release plan for parole supervision as each relates to parole release.

(2) Based on the objective parole guidelines and any other competent evidence relevant to aggravating and mitigating circumstances, the hearing examiner shall, within 10 days after the interview, recommend in writing to a panel of no fewer than two commissioners appointed by the chair a presumptive parole release date for the inmate. The chair shall assign cases to such panels on a random basis, without regard to the inmate or to the commissioners sitting on the panel. If the recommended presumptive parole release date falls outside the matrix time ranges as determined by the objective parole guidelines, the hearing examiner shall include with the recommendation a statement in writing as to the reasons for the decision, specifying individual particularities. If a panel fails to reach a decision on a recommended presumptive parole release date, the chair or any other commissioner designated by the chair shall cast the deciding vote. Within 90 days after the date of the initial interview, the

inmate shall be notified in writing of the decision as to the inmate's presumptive parole release date.

(3) A presumptive parole release date shall become binding on the commission when agreement on the presumptive parole release date is reached. Should the presumptive parole release date fall outside the matrix time ranges as determined by the objective parole guidelines, the reasons for this decision shall be stated in writing with individual particularities.

Laws 1978, c. 78–417, §§ 13, 21; Laws 1979, c. 79–3, § 107; Laws 1979, c. 79–42, § 7; Laws 1981, c. 81–259, § 500; Laws 1981, c. 81–322, § 5; Laws 1982, c. 82–171, § 11; Laws 1985, c. 85–295, § 4. Amended by Laws 1997, c. 97–102, § 1674, eff. July 1, 1997.

Historical and Statutory Notes

Amendment Notes:

Laws 1979, c. 79–3, a reviser's bill, provided for substitution of references to the department and secretary of "corrections" for the department and secretary of "offender rehabilitation" to conform with Laws 1978, c. 78–53.

Laws 1979, c. 79–42, § 7, amended subsec. (2) to provide for a panel to recommend a presumptive parole date.

Laws 1981, c. 81–259, a reviser's bill, deleted subsec. (4) (c), an obsolete provision.

Laws 1981, c. 81–322, § 5, deleted "panel" following "hearing examiner" in the first sentence of subsec. (1), and, in subsec. (2), deleted "panel" following "hearing examiner" in the first and third sentences.

Laws 1982, c. 82–171, § 11, in subsec. (1), substituted "interview" for "hearing" and modified a statutory reference in the first sentence, substituted "interview" for "hearing" and substituted "an explanation of the institutional conduct second and satisfactory release plan for parole supervision as each relates to parole release" for "discussion relative to the inmate's institutional conduct record" in the second sentence; in subsec. (2), inserted "matrix time ranges as determined by the" in the third sentence, and substituted "90" for "45" in the fifth sentence, in subsec. (3), inserted "matrix time ranges as determined by the" in the second sentence; and deleted a former subsec. (4), which provided:

"On or before January 1, 1980, a presumptive parole release date developed pursuant to this section shall be established for each inmate in the custody of the department who will not be released from incarceration on or before January 1, 1980, by virtue of parole, accumulation of gain-time, or expiration of sentence. However, the presumptive parole release date need not be established on or before such date for:

"(a) Those inmates sentenced to a minimum term of 5 years or less who were confined in execution of the judgment of the court on or after August 1, 1979. Presumptive parole release dates for these inmates shall be established pursuant to this section.

"(b) Those inmates sentenced to a minimum term in excess of 5 years who were confined in execution of the judgment of the court on or after February 1, 1979. Presumptive parole release dates for these inmates shall be established pursuant to this section."

Laws 1985, c. 85–295, § 4, eff. June 20, 1985, substantially rewrote subsec. (2), which formerly read:

"Based on the objective parole guidelines and any other competent evidence relevant to aggravating and mitigating circumstances, the hearing examiner shall, within 10 days after the interview, recommend in writing to a panel of no fewer than two commissioners appointed by the chairman a presumptive parole release date for the inmate. The chairman shall assign cases to such panels on a random basis, without regard to the inmate or to the commissioners sitting on the panel. If the recommended presumptive parole release date falls outside the matrix time ranges as determined by the objective parole guidelines, the hearing examiner shall include a statement in writing as to the reasons for the decision, specifying individual particularities, with the recommendation; and the chairman shall sit on the panel in addition to the two or more commissioners. If a panel fails to reach a decision on a recommended presumptive parole release date, the chairman shall cast the deciding vote. Within 90 days from the date of the initial interview, the inmate shall be notified in writing of the decision as to the inmate's presumptive parole release date."

Laws 1997, c. 97–102, eff. July 1, 1997, removed gender-specific references applicable to human beings from volume 4 of the Florida Statutes without substantive changes in legal effect.

Cross References

Determination of exact period of imprisonment, indeterminate sentence, see § 921.22.

Library References

Pardon and Parole ⚷50, 60, 61.
Westlaw Topic No. 284.

C.J.S. Pardon and Parole §§ 48 to 52, 55 to 56.

Research References

Treatises and Practice Aids

16 Florida Practice Series § 10:20, Parole--Presumptive Parole Release Date.

Notes of Decisions

---

1. Construction and application

There is no prohibition against establishment of a presumptive parole release date beyond an inmate's sentence expiration date. Moats v. Florida Parole and Probation Com'n, App. 1 Dist., 419 So.2d 775 (1982). Pardon And Parole ⚷ 50

The parole and probation commission may exercise its discretion in establishing a presumptive parole release date for each entitled inmate only in limited circumstances with adequate explanation. James v. Florida Parole and Probation Commission, App. 1 Dist., 395 So.2d 197 (1981). Pardon And Parole ⚷ 52

2. Validity of release date

Parole and probation commission's method of fixing inmate's presumptive parole release date, in which consideration was given trial court's sentence as well as same aggravating circumstances that were reviewed and utilized in sentencing, did not violate double jeopardy proscriptions since inmate's release was within maximum time of his sentence. Davis v. Florida Parole and Probation Com'n, App. 1 Dist., 436 So.2d 144 (1983). Double Jeopardy ⚷ 31

3. Amendment of guidelines—In general

Use of parole guidelines which were not in effect at time inmate committed his offense was not improper as to determination of inmate's presumptive parole release date following inmate's escape from confinement and vacation of prior presumptive parole release date upon reconfinement. Schultz v. Florida Parole & Probation Com'n, App. 1 Dist., 432 So.2d 647 (1983). Pardon And Parole ⚷ 53

While repealed rule providing that concurrent convictions, not used in establishing salient factor score, are proper aggravating factors did not apply where defendant's initial interview was conducted after effective date of repeal, action of parole and probation commission in considering defendant's concurrent convictions as aggravating factors when it established his presumptive parole release date was proper on basis of rule providing, inter alia, that commission may render decision outside matrix time range based on any competent and persuasive evidence relating to aggravating or mitigating circumstances. Lamar v. Florida Parole & Probation Com'n, App. 1 Dist., 430 So.2d 948 (1983). Pardon And Parole ⚷ 58

In assigning presumptive parole release date, the parole and probation commission did not err in using amended parole guidelines in effect on date of inmate's interview. Grandin v. Parole and Probation Com'n, App. 1 Dist., 421 So.2d 828 (1982). Pardon And Parole ⚷ 53

4. —— Ex post facto, amendment of guidelines

Parole and probation commission did not violate ex post facto considerations by setting presumptive parole release date in accordance with parole guidelines adopted subsequent to date of offense. Woulard v. Florida Parole and Probation Com'n, App., 426 So.2d 66 (1983); Rodriguez v. Florida Parole and Probation Com'n, App., 425 So.2d 1194 (1983).

Parole and probation commission did not violate state and federal proscription against ex post facto laws when, in fixing new presumptive parole release date after prisoner committed another crime thereby requiring new presumptive parole release date be set, commission used more stringent guidelines adopted by it after later crime was committed. May v. Florida Parole and Probation Com'n, 435 So.2d 834 (1983). Constitutional Law ⚷ 2823; Pardon And Parole ⚷ 53

It was not an ex post facto application of the law for parole and probation commission to apply guidelines in effect at time of defendant's timely initial interview rather than guidelines in effect on date crime was committed or during six months after his confinement in determining his presumptive parole release date. Rolle v. Florida Parole and Probation Com'n, App. 1 Dist., 426 So.2d 1082 (1983). Constitutional Law ⚷ 2823; Pardon And Parole ⚷ 53

Parole and probation commission did not violate state and federal proscriptions against ex post facto laws when it fixed new presumptive parole release date for prisoner, who committed another crime after his initial presumptive parole release date had been set, based on the more stringent guideline adopted by the Commission after the new crime was committed. May v. Florida Parole and Probation Com'n, App. 1 Dist., 424 So.2d 122 (1982), affirmed 435 So.2d 834. Constitutional Law ⚷ 2823; Pardon And Parole ⚷ 63

Parole and probation commission did not violate ex post facto clause in applying new, harsher matrix time ranges for presumptive parole release dates, even though defendant committed offense long before new rules went into effect. Jordan v. Florida Parole and Probation Com'n, App. 1 Dist., 423 So.2d 450 (1982). Constitutional Law ⚷ 2823; Pardon And Parole ⚷ 53

There was no ex post facto violation by applying a matrix time range for parole release set by rule in effect at time of setting presumptive parole release date rather than by rule in effect when crime occurred as the matrix time range does not automatically determine time served and parole and probation commission has discretion to aggravate or mitigate the matrix time. Overfield v. Florida Parole and Probation Com'n, App. 1 Dist., 418 So.2d 321 (1982). Constitutional Law ⚷ 2823; Pardon And Parole ⚷ 53

Parole and probation commission did not violate state and federal proscriptions against ex post facto laws by applying matrix range for his parole release date under rule in effect at time his presumptive parole release date was set rather than rule in effect when he committed his crime. Britt v. Florida Parole & Probation Com'n, App. 1 Dist., 417 So.2d 1079 (1982).

Constitutional Law ⚷ 2823; Pardon And Parole ⚷ 53

5. Interviews—In general

Any error in failure to timely interview prisoner in connection with establishing his presumptive parole release date was harmless. Coleman v. Florida Parole and Probation Com'n, App. 1 Dist., 434 So.2d 42 (1983). Pardon And Parole ⚷ 62

6. —— Due process, interviews

Under Florida law, pursuant to which decision whether to release inmate on parole is committed to discretion of Florida probation and parole commission without mandate of statute, no entitlement to or liberty interest in parole is created, and thus, since Florida parole statutes do not create protectible interest in timely initial interview, failure to accord plaintiff timely initial parole interview did not violate due process. Staton v. Wainwright, 1982, 665 F.2d 686, certiorari denied 102 S.Ct. 1757, 456 U.S. 909, 72 L.Ed.2d 166. Constitutional Law ⚷ 4838

7. Notice—In general

State Attorney General had standing to represent interests of the People of Florida in challenging order of the parole and probation commission, establishing new presumptive parole release date for inmate, in view of fact that improper parole would result in direct injury suffered by the People, insofar as defendant had already demonstrated propensity to inflict such injury, together with fact that the commission failed to comply with public notice requirements in reviewing parole date, which constituted, in itself, irreparable public injury. State ex rel. Boyles v. Florida Parole and Probation Com'n, App. 1 Dist., 436 So.2d 207 (1983). Attorney General ⚷ 6

Failure of parole and probation commission to notify subject of his presumptive parole release date within 45 days of his initial interview did not mean that hearing examiner's recommendation of a 36-month release date was binding. Rodriguez v. Florida Parole and Probation Com'n, App. 1 Dist., 425 So.2d 1194 (1983). Pardon And Parole ⚷ 60

8. —— Due process, notice

Parole and probation commission did not violate defendant's due process rights by not giving him prior notice of parole guidelines governing his presumptive parole release date before they were adopted. Woulard v. Florida Parole and Probation Com'n, App. 1 Dist., 426 So.2d 66 (1983). Constitutional Law ⚷ 4838

9. Postsentence reports

When prisoner has not come forward with any evidence casting doubt upon information contained in postsentence investigative report, parole and probation commission may rely on such report. Farber v. Florida Parole and Probation Com'n, App. 1 Dist., 427 So.2d 1016 (1983). Pardon And Parole ⚷ 58

Normally, the parole and probation commission is entitled to rely on post sentence investigation reports to establish prior convictions; however, an inmate's presumptive parole release date should not be determined on an erroneous report. Rolle v. Florida Parole and Probation Com'n, App. 1 Dist., 426 So.2d 1082 (1983). Pardon And Parole ⚷ 59

State parole and probation commission did not act improperly in using postsentence report and preparole investigation in order to establish various prior convictions, and there was no error in calculating salient factor score in establishing presumptive parole release date. Bradbury v. Florida Parole and Probation Com'n, App. 1 Dist., 420 So.2d 901 (1982). Pardon And Parole ⚷ 49

10. Presentence reports

Parole and probation commission erred in aggravating defendant's presumptive parole relief date by 24 months on basis that presentence investigation indicated that he was actually in possession of more than 200 grams of methaqualone, where jury specifically acquitted defendant of the charge of possession of more than 200 grams of methaqualone, and convicted defendant as to the lesser included offense for possession of less than 200 grams of methaqualone. Shulman v. Florida Parole and Probation Com'n, App. 1 Dist., 429 So.2d 755 (1983). Pardon And Parole ⚷ 48.1

In calculating prisoner's presumptive parole release date, there was no error in parole and probation commission's relying on presentence investigation reports or department of law enforcement reports or FBI records to establish prior convictions. Jones v. Florida Parole and Probation Commission, App. 1 Dist., 413 So.2d 861 (1982). Pardon And Parole ⚷ 58

Parole and probation commission was required to establish a binding presumptive parole release date for petitioner within 15 days despite alleged lack of a presentence investigation report. James v. Florida Parole and Probation Commission, App. 1 Dist., 395 So.2d 197 (1981). Pardon And Parole ⚷ 58

Absence of a presentence investigation report provides no grounds for parole and probation commission's failure to follow clear statutory requirements to set presumptive parole release dates. James v. Florida Parole and Probation

Commission, App. 1 Dist., 395 So.2d 197 (1981). Pardon And Parole ⚷ 58

11. Calculating release date—In general

In assigning presumptive parole release date, number of months assigned inmate exclusive of aggravating factors was within matrix time range for his offense set forth in rules. Grandin v. Parole and Probation Com'n, App. 1 Dist., 421 So.2d 828 (1982). Pardon And Parole ⚷ 53

Florida parole and probation commission properly calculated state prison inmate's salient factor score of two, in establishing his presumptive parole release date, based on the age of his first conviction and his prior conviction for driving while intoxicated. Calloway v. Florida Parole and Probation Com'n, App. 1 Dist., 414 So.2d 655 (1982). Pardon And Parole ⚷ 53

Where state parole and probation commission has no information as to inmate's criminal history prior to offense for which he is presently incarcerated, he must be assigned salient factor score of zero except where burglary is present offense of conviction, in which case salient factor score of "one" is computed. Battis v. Florida Parole and Probation Commission, App. 1 Dist., 386 So.2d 295 (1980). Pardon And Parole ⚷ 53

Where there is complete lack of information which can appropriately be considered by state parole and probation commission as bearing on offense characteristic, commission must assign presumptive parole release date at lowest end of matrix range for the offense. Battis v. Florida Parole and Probation Commission, App. 1 Dist., 386 So.2d 295 (1980). Pardon And Parole ⚷ 53

12. —— Statutory criteria, calculating release date

Absent presence of statutory criteria, presumptive parole release date decisions are binding on the parole and probation commission. State ex rel. Boyles v. Florida Parole and Probation Com'n, App. 1 Dist., 436 So.2d 207 (1983). Pardon And Parole ⚷ 60

Defendant, who pled guilty to charge that he "in the course of committing said robbery, carried a weapon, to-wit: a knife * * *," had thereby pled guilty to robbery involving a weapon, rather than a firearm or other deadly weapon, for purposes of provision of § 812.13 providing in effect that maximum punishment for robbery while armed with weapon was 30 years and provisions of § 812.13 providing that maximum punishment for robbery while armed with firearm or deadly weapon was life imprisonment, and, thus, the former provision was applicable in establishing defendant's presumptive parole release date. Bennett v. Florida Parole and Probation Com'n, App. 1 Dist., 422 So.2d 1016 (1982). Pardon And Parole ⚷ 49

13. —— Codefendants, calculating release date

Refusal of the parole and probation commission to consider the disparity of sentence between the petitioner and his codefendants in computing the petitioner's presumptive parole release date was not an abuse of discretion. Lobo v. Florida Parole and Probation Com'n, App. 4 Dist., 433 So.2d 622 (1983). Pardon And Parole ⚷ 52

14. —— Degree of offense, calculating release date

Conduct of parole and probation commission in computing petitioner's presumptive parole release date on basis of a conviction of a second-degree felony was not error, notwithstanding that trafficking in cocaine was a first-degree felony, where offense of which petitioner was convicted, conspiracy to commit a first-degree felony, was a second-degree felony. Lobo v. Florida Parole and Probation Com'n, App. 4 Dist., 433 So.2d 622 (1983). Pardon And Parole ⚷ 49

Parole and probation commission did not err in aggravating defendant's presumptive parole release date for his conviction of attempted second-degree murder outside the matrix ranges by 12 months because a firearm was used in commission of the offense and by 24 months because offense resulted in great bodily injury to the victim. Daniels v. Florida Parole & Probation Com'n, App. 1 Dist., 431 So.2d 713 (1983). Pardon And Parole ⚷ 53

Where inmate's sentences reflected that he was convicted on two counts of "robbery" as opposed to two counts of "armed robbery" it was error for parole and probation commission to use "armed robbery" instead of "robbery" as his offense characteristic for purposes of his presumptive parole release date. Thomas v. Florida Parole and Probation Com'n, App. 1 Dist., 424 So.2d 121 (1982). Pardon And Parole ⚷ 48.1

Parole and probation commission properly aggregated two scores after separately scoring inmate for breaking and entering and for armed robbery, although offense characteristic was required to be reduced from "armed robbery" to "robbery." Thomas v. Florida Parole and Probation Com'n, App. 1 Dist., 424 So.2d 121 (1982). Pardon And Parole ⚷ 51

As regards setting a defendant's presumptive parole release date, the offense characteristic must reflect the offense for which defendant was convicted. Walsh v. Florida Parole and Probation Com'n, App. 1 Dist., 422 So.2d 967 (1982). Pardon And Parole ⚷ 53

Since the offense of which defendant was convicted, second-degree arson, cannot "be classified in more than one severity category," the correct category is simple arson, having a corresponding matrix time range of 14–25 months; accordingly, the parole and probation commission erred in characterizing defendant's offense severity as "High," the severity characteristic for aggravated arson, rather than "Low Moderate," the severity characteristic for simple arson. Walsh v. Florida Parole and Probation Com'n, App. 1 Dist., 422 So.2d 967 (1982). Pardon And Parole ⚷ 53

Where defendant was convicted of attempted first-degree murder, the parole and probation commission did not violate the administrative code when, in establishing presumptive parole release date, it assigned a matrix level in the "Greatest Most Serious III" category, which is one level lower than the matrix range for the consummated crime of first-degree murder. Riley v. Florida Parole and Probation Com'n, App. 1 Dist., 422 So.2d 933 (1982). Pardon And Parole ⚷ 53

In establishing presumptive parole release date, there was no error in applying offense characteristic for sexual battery with use of force, where rape occurred at knife point and victim was actually cut. Kennedy v. Florida Parole and Probation Com'n, App. 1 Dist., 421 So.2d 54 (1982). Pardon And Parole ⚷ 53

In determining defendant's presumptive parole release date, there was no error in classifying defendant's offense as "Category VI, Greatest (Most Serious I)," as, if offense could be classified under more than one category, most serious applicable category was to be used. Gaddy v. Florida Parole and Probation Com'n, App. 1 Dist., 416 So.2d 836 (1982). Pardon And Parole ⚷ 53

In establishing presumptive parole release date, no abuse of discretion was shown in Florida parole and probation commission's assigning an offense characteristic of "moderate" for possession of a knife during incarceration. Perkins v. Florida Parole and Probation Com'n,, App. 1 Dist., 414 So.2d 264 (1982). Pardon And Parole ⚷ 52

15. —— Included offenses, calculating release date

Application of aggravating factors for both burglary and grand theft was not error on part of the parole and probation commission in confirming prisoner's presumptive parole release date where the grand theft conviction was neither an element of the burglary nor was it used as part of the salient-factor score or in any other way connected with plotting the prisoner's matrix time range. Gallon v. Florida Parole and Probation Com'n, App. 1 Dist., 423 So.2d 465 (1982). Pardon And Parole ⚷ 49

Consummation of underlying offense in cases wherein prisoner has been convicted of an attempt is improper aggravating factor in determining prisoner's presumptive parole release date since it has already been considered in setting severity offense characteristic. Lowe v. Florida Parole and Probation Commission, App. 1 Dist., 411 So.2d 352 (1982). Pardon And Parole ⚷ 53

16. —— Record, calculating release date

Parole and probation commission, in establishing presumptive parole release date, may rely on charging documents for circumstances of prisoner's crime. Farber v. Florida Parole and Probation Com'n, App. 1 Dist., 427 So.2d 1016 (1983). Pardon And Parole ⚷ 58

Parole and probation commission erred in establishing appellant's original presumptive parole release date since record did not indicate that appellant ever was convicted of 1956 escape the commission stated it used in setting salient factor score; however, appellant's release date would be upheld because reduction in his salient factor score did not alter matrix time range for his offense. Brown v. Florida Parole and Probation Com'n, App. 1 Dist., 427 So.2d 349 (1983). Pardon And Parole ⚷ 53

Since it could not be determined from the record whether defendant had prior gambling conviction or whether postsentence investigation report was in error and a person with similar name was convicted of gambling and since defendant apparently had no knowledge that the parole and probation commission would consider gambling charge in determining his salient factor score and had no opportunity to object to its use, order of the commission finding no cause to change prior Commission action establishing presumptive parole release date would be reversed. Rolle v. Florida Parole and Probation Com'n, App. 1 Dist., 426 So.2d 1082 (1983). Pardon And Parole ⚷ 62

In proceeding in which defendant's presumptive parole release date was established, record before parole and probation commission failed to establish that defendant had pled guilty to burglary of a dwelling while armed with dangerous weapon, a first-degree felony, instead of burglary of a dwelling, a second-degree felony. Wilson v. Florida Parole and Probation Com'n, App. 1 Dist., 426 So.2d 60 (1983). Pardon And Parole ⚷ 48.1

Parole and probation commission, in establishing defendant's presumptive parole release date, considered two aggravating factors which were not supported by the record, namely, insurance loss and threats of violence. Walsh v.

Florida Parole and Probation Com'n, App. 1 Dist., 422 So.2d 967 (1982). Pardon And Parole ⚷ 58

Since record revealed that the parole commission, in part, aggravated appellant's Presumptive Parole Release Date because he was arrested for possession of opiate, but since there is no statutory or rule authority permitting aggravating of a PPRD for a mere arrest, the Commission's order refusing to change the PPRD, to the extent the establishment of the PPRD was based on the arrest, would be reversed. Perchetti v. Florida Parole and Probation Com'n, App. 1 Dist., 415 So.2d 53 (1982). Pardon And Parole ⚷ 49

17. —— Plea agreement, calculating release date

Information supporting count of indictment which was dismissed as result of plea agreement may be relied upon as aggravating or mitigating circumstance, provided it is competent and persuasive; therefore, 60-month aggravation based upon identification of defendant, who had pled guilty to armed robbery of one bank, as individual who had robbed second bank at gunpoint was not erroneous where defendant failed to establish identification relied upon by Parole and Probation Commission in establishing presumptive parole release date was not competent and persuasive. Bryant v. Florida Parole and Probation Com'n, App. 1 Dist., 426 So.2d 1133 (1983). Pardon And Parole ⚷ 50

18. —— Multiple offenses, calculating release date

Parole and probation commission may aggravate presumptive parole release date for multiple offenses with concurrent sentences, and did not err in aggravating presumptive parole release date for concurrent sentence of unlawful possession of firearm while engaged in criminal offense. Daizi v. Florida Parole and Probation Com'n, App. 4 Dist., 436 So.2d 171 (1983). Pardon And Parole ⚷ 51

Aggravation of presumptive parole release date for multiple offenses with concurrent sentences is proper. Menes v. Florida Parole and Probation Com'n, App. 1 Dist., 422 So.2d 1015 (1982). Pardon And Parole ⚷ 51

Parole and probation commission did not err in aggravating inmate's presumptive parole release date because of offense involving use of dangerous weapon, offense resulting in great bodily harm and there being multiple separate offenses. Diego v. Florida Parole and Probation Com'n, App. 1 Dist., 422 So.2d 1014 (1982). Pardon And Parole ⚷ 49

Parole and probation commission properly used most severe crime to determine salient factor score, then used other counts as aggravating factors to determine appellant's presumptive parole release date for 1965 convictions. Diego v. Florida Parole and Probation Com'n, App. 1 Dist., 422 So.2d 1014 (1982).

In assigning presumptive parole release date, the parole and probation commission properly aggravated inmate's score using concurrent sentences pursuant to rule. Grandin v. Parole and Probation Com'n, App. 1 Dist., 421 So.2d 828 (1982). Pardon And Parole ⚷ 53

There is no constitutional impediment to the Parole and Probation Commission's consideration of a prisoner's multiple offenses when it establishes his presumptive parole release date, even though the trial judge may have sentenced him concurrently on those offenses. Variance v. Florida Parole and Probation Com'n, App. 1 Dist., 420 So.2d 369 (1982). Pardon And Parole ⚷ 49

Parole and probation commission did not breach plea agreement whereby defendant was to receive concurrent sentences in return for his nolo contendere plea to five offenses where Commission aggravated defendant by a total of 83 months for four of the offenses in setting defendant's presumptive parole release date, since aggravation for multiple offenses with concurrent sentences is proper under the Administrative Code. Griggs v. Florida Parole and Probation Com'n, App. 1 Dist., 420 So.2d 367 (1982). Pardon And Parole ⚷ 53

Use of concurrent sentences as aggravating factors does not encroach on function of judiciary and does not violate separation of powers clause. Glisson v. Florida Parole and Probation Com'n, App. 1 Dist., 420 So.2d 336 (1982). Constitutional Law ⚷ 2507(3)

For purposes of defendant's presumptive parole release date, there was no error in aggravating defendant's release date for multiple separate offenses even if he was given concurrent sentences. Gaddy v. Florida Parole and Probation Com'n, App. 1 Dist., 416 So.2d 836 (1982). Pardon And Parole ⚷ 51

Aggravation for multiple offenses with concurrent sentences was proper in establishing presumptive parole release date since aggravation in each case was within matrix guidelines for each offense. Perkins v. Florida Parole and Probation Com'n,, App. 1 Dist., 414 So.2d 264 (1982). Pardon And Parole ⚷ 51

19. —— Expired sentences, calculating release date

Florida parole and probation commission erred in using an expired sentence in aggregation of petitioner's presumptive parole release date. Johnson v. Turner, App. 4 Dist., 436 So.2d 291 (1983). Pardon And Parole ⚷ 50

Expired sentence could not be used in aggregation of presumptive parole release date. Shannon v. Turner, App. 4 Dist., 432 So.2d 204 (1983). Pardon And Parole ⚿ 50

Defendant's prior convictions for burglary, petit theft and petit larceny could not be considered for aggregation purposes in establishing his presumptive parole release date after he was convicted of possession of marijuana and introduction of contraband into state prison, in view of fact that the sentence imposed for the prior offenses had expired. Lott v. Florida Parole and Probation Com'n, App. 1 Dist., 427 So.2d 340 (1983). Pardon And Parole ⚿ 49

Where defendant was serving only one commitment for robbery and five-year sentence imposed for earlier robbery had expired, offenses should not have been aggregated in setting presumptive parole release date. Jordan v. Florida Parole and Probation Com'n, App. 1 Dist., 423 So.2d 450 (1982). Pardon And Parole ⚿ 51

In calculating prisoner's presumptive parole release date, it was improper for parole and probation commission to aggregate commitment for possession of controlled substance paraphernalia with other commitments where that sentence had expired prior to imposition of sentence for other offenses. Jones v. Florida Parole and Probation Commission, App. 1 Dist., 413 So.2d 861 (1982). Pardon And Parole ⚿ 51

20. —— Recidivism, calculating release date

Inmate's status as adjudicated habitual offender could properly be assessed as aggravating factor in determining inmate's presumptive parole release date, though inmate's prior criminal conviction was factor in determining his salient factor score, as earlier step in determining presumptive parole release date. Florida Parole and Probation Com'n v. Griffin, App. 2 Dist., 497 So.2d 1242 (1986). Pardon And Parole ⚿ 49

Defendant who had previously been convicted of four or more felony convictions, at least two of which resulted in incarceration, was properly classified as a recidivist offender for purposes of formulating presumptive parole release date. Bivens v. Florida Parole & Probation Com'n, App. 1 Dist., 453 So.2d 1166 (1984). Pardon And Parole ⚿ 53

In establishing defendant's presumptive parole release date, parole and probation commission correctly aggregated defendant's times after including a point for a parole revocation in his second commitment. Schaeffer v. Florida Parole and Probation Com'n, App. 1 Dist., 434 So.2d 44 (1983). Pardon And Parole ⚿ 49

Where defendant's new offenses, for which his parole was revoked, did not result in his commitment to the department of corrections, as they were committed in North Carolina, but, rather, his murder conviction, from which he was on parole, necessitated his return to department's control, the parole and probation commission had no other choice than to treat defendant as a "new admission" on that basis and recalculate his presumptive parole release date utilizing murder conviction as his present offense of conviction. Collins v. Florida Parole and Probation Com'n, App. 1 Dist., 422 So.2d 952 (1982). Pardon And Parole ⚿ 72.1

Inmate, who challenged assignment of his presumptive parole release date, showed no error in his evaluation using "recidivist criminal factor" of guidelines. Grandin v. Parole and Probation Com'n, App. 1 Dist., 421 So.2d 828 (1982). Pardon And Parole ⚿ 53

21. —— Subsequent offenses, calculating release date

A 96-month aggravation for a concurrent "conviction for kidnapping by federal authority in 1973" was properly not considered in determining salient factor score, as it occurred subsequent to petitioner's present offense of conviction. Drake v. Wainwright, App. 1 Dist., 429 So.2d 374 (1983). Pardon And Parole ⚿ 53

Commission of an offense while on bond may be used to aggravate a presumptive parole release date. Menes v. Florida Parole and Probation Com'n, App. 1 Dist., 422 So.2d 1015 (1982). Pardon And Parole ⚿ 49

Aggravation was properly applied in establishing state prison inmate's presumptive parole release date where inmate committed present offense of conviction while on probation for a previous crime. Calloway v. Florida Parole and Probation Com'n, App. 1 Dist., 414 So.2d 655 (1982). Pardon And Parole ⚿ 49

Offenses for which state prison inmate was on probation at time he committed present offense of conviction could not be used in calculating his salient factor score in establishing his presumptive parole release date since adjudication of guilt was withheld. Calloway v. Florida Parole and Probation Com'n, App. 1 Dist., 414 So.2d 655 (1982). Pardon And Parole ⚿ 53

22. —— Vacated or invalidated sentences, calculating release date

Parole and probation commission's consideration of conviction which was later vacated in setting prisoner's presumptive parole release date was error. Zygadlo v. Florida Parole and Probation Com'n, App. 1 Dist., 414 So.2d 600 (1982). Pardon And Parole ⚿ 49

Parole and probation commission may not use invalid convictions when establishing a presumptive parole release date. Zygadlo v. Florida Parole and Probation Com'n, App. 1 Dist., 414 So.2d 600 (1982). Pardon And Parole ⚷ 49

23. —— Written explanation, calculating release date

Parole and probation commission is not required to explain in writing its choice of prison terms within guidelines matrix range determined by objective parole criteria only if factor influences commission to aggravate an inmate's term beyond guidelines must written explanation of that factor be given. Baker v. Florida Parole and Probation Commission, App. 1 Dist., 384 So.2d 746 (1980). Pardon And Parole ⚷ 61

24. —— Burden of proof, calculating release date

The parole and probation commission was required to show that particular circumstances indicated that inmate's 33-year-old convictions should be used to aggravate presumptive parole release date for present conviction. Fields v. Florida Parole and Probation Com'n, App. 1 Dist., 419 So.2d 772 (1982). Pardon And Parole ⚷ 61

25. Aggravation of parole—In general

In aggravating prisoner's presumptive parole release date (PPRD), Parole and Probation Commission properly aggregated prisoner's expired burglary sentence with his murder sentence. Taylor v. Florida Parole and Probation Com'n, App. 1 Dist., 543 So.2d 367 (1989). Pardon And Parole ⚷ 53

Establishment of presumptive parole release date by aggregating separate scores for preparole criminal episode and postparole episode was proper. Odom v. Florida Parole and Probation Com'n, App. 1 Dist., 433 So.2d 634 (1983). Pardon And Parole ⚷ 50

In establishing prisoner's presumptive parole release date, parole and probation commission properly aggravated prisoner's score using concurrent sentences. Deloach v. Florida Parole and Probation Com'n, App. 1 Dist., 423 So.2d 480 (1982). Pardon And Parole ⚷ 51

Aggravating for being on escape during commission of further offense is appropriate. Faucett v. Wainwright, App. 1 Dist., 419 So.2d 765 (1982). Pardon And Parole ⚷ 49

Since the actual shooting of a correctional officer is not essential to and is more serious than escape and attempted murder, there is no error in an additional aggravation when the parole and probation commission establishes a presumptive parole release date. Fuller v. Florida Parole and Probation Com'n, App. 1 Dist., 416 So.2d 488 (1982). Pardon And Parole ⚷ 49

Parole and probation commission had good cause to add aggravations in order to more accurately reflect severity of prisoner's offenses, thereby increasing length of time that prisoner would have to remain in prison before being paroled, where, after pleading guilty to third-degree murder and being placed in custody of department of youth services, prisoner ran away by shooting director of START program and taking portion of his gun collection and his automobile, he then robbed, at gunpoint, some people in their home and abducted a young man, robbed a cab driver, and again escaped from jail after being returned to state to answer charges. Zygadlo v. Florida Parole and Probation Com'n, App. 1 Dist., 414 So.2d 600 (1982). Pardon And Parole ⚷ 53

26. —— Purpose, aggravation of parole

One purpose for applying aggravating factors in determining presumptive parole release date is to permit parole and probation commission to reflect actual circumstances of the inmate's offense. Calloway v. Florida Parole and Probation Com'n, App. 1 Dist., 431 So.2d 300 (1983); Faucett v. Wainwright, App., 419 So.2d 765 (1982).

27. —— Factors considered, aggravation of parole

Inmate's physically assaulting victim in facial area with his fist could properly be used as aggravating factor in determining inmate's presumptive parole release date, where inmate had been charged and convicted of sexual battery with use of physical force and violence not likely to cause serious personal injury. Florida Parole and Probation Com'n v. Griffin, App. 2 Dist., 497 So.2d 1242 (1986). Pardon And Parole ⚷ 49

Defendant's narcotics conviction was not used in establishing his salient factors or for purposes of establishing his presumptive parole release date and was a proper aggravating factor. Rolle v. Florida Parole and Probation Com'n, App. 1 Dist., 426 So.2d 1082 (1983). Pardon And Parole ⚷ 53

The parole commission's aggravation of parolee's presumptive parole release date because of history of heroin abuse was appropriate. Sala v. Florida Parole and Probation Com'n, App. 1 Dist., 414 So.2d 263 (1982). Pardon And Parole ⚷ 49

The parole and probation commission could not properly consider prisoner's failure to provide information "upon apprehension" as a basis for extension of his presumptive parole release date. Bizzigotti v. Florida Parole &

Probation Commission, App. 1 Dist., 410 So.2d 1360 (1982). Pardon And Parole ⚷ 49

Under appropriate facts, use of fact that large jewelry loss occurred or that prisoner had knowledge or ability to aid in its recovery, but failed to do so, could be considered to extend prisoner's presumptive parole release date. Bizzigotti v. Florida Parole & Probation Commission, App. 1 Dist., 410 So.2d 1360 (1982). Pardon And Parole ⚷ 49

In setting presumptive parole release date for prisoner, who had been convicted of armed robbery, the parole and probation commission could properly add an aggravation because the prisoner struck the victim several times during the commission of the offense. Wickham v. Florida Parole and Probation Commission, App. 1 Dist., 410 So.2d 989 (1982). Pardon And Parole ⚷ 49

Under objective parole criteria, in extending an inmate's term, by reason of aggravating circumstances, beyond guideline matrix range, parole and probation commission must distinguish aggravating circumstances from factors used in computing salient factor score. Baker v. Florida Parole and Probation Commission, App. 1 Dist., 384 So.2d 746 (1980). Pardon And Parole ⚷ 61

In sentencing under objective parole criteria, where parole and probation commission determined defendant's matrix range using armed robbery as the offense characteristic, use of aggravating factor of "shots fired" to aggravate beyond guidelines matrix range was sufficiently explained by phrase itself and was not cumulative to offense characteristic matrix calculation. Baker v. Florida Parole and Probation Commission, App. 1 Dist., 384 So.2d 746 (1980). Pardon And Parole ⚷ 61

28. —— Evidence, aggravation of parole

Inmate's postconviction conduct, including, inmate's failure to provide information which would or could possibly alleviate injury flowing from his criminal action, if shown by competent evidence to be within both his knowledge and ability, may appropriately be considered by the parole and probation commission as an aggravating circumstance to extend the presumptive parole release date beyond matrix time frame. Bizzigotti v. Florida Parole & Probation Commission, App. 1 Dist., 410 So.2d 1360 (1982). Pardon And Parole ⚷ 49

Where evidence in defendant's robbery prosecution established that money was taken from armored car company employee en route from department store to armored car, employee identified defendant as armed offender who took money, totality of circumstances indicated that defendant had control of stolen money and defendant failed or refused to make restitution, such failure or refusal was factor which was completely and directly within rule of parole and probation commission governing aggravating offense factors, and, therefore, conclusion that defendant's conduct warranted 36 additional months incarceration was not improper. White v. Florida Parole and Probation Commission, App. 4 Dist., 394 So.2d 472 (1981). Pardon And Parole ⚷ 49

29. Date of release outside matrix time—Written explanation

It could not be determined whether Parole and Probation Commission impermissibly aggravated prisoner's new presumptive parole release date (PPRD) based on information previously known to Commission when it established original release date, or whether Commission permissibly based aggravation upon evaluation of prisoner's recent parole violations in light of information previously known and documented; thus, remand was required to allow Commission to clarify its reasons for aggravation. Taylor v. Florida Parole and Probation Com'n, App. 1 Dist., 543 So.2d 367 (1989). Pardon And Parole ⚷ 62

Parole and probation commission's statement of aggravation did not state with sufficient particularity a proper factor to consider for aggravation. Drake v. Wainwright, App. 1 Dist., 429 So.2d 374 (1983). Pardon And Parole ⚷ 61

An inmate's term may be extended beyond matrix guidelines by reason of aggravating factors, but parole and probation commission must give a written explanation for this extension. Diego v. Florida Parole and Probation Com'n, App. 1 Dist., 422 So.2d 1014 (1982). Pardon And Parole ⚷ 53

The parole and probation commission has duty under this section to specify with individual particularity reasons for going outside matrix time frame to aggravate or mitigate presumptive parole release date. Fields v. Florida Parole and Probation Com'n, App. 1 Dist., 419 So.2d 772 (1982). Pardon And Parole ⚷ 61

Parole and probation commission is obliged to adequately explain its decision to aggravate a prisoner's presumptive parole release date. Richardson v. Richardson v. Florida Parole and Probation Com'n, App. 1 Dist., 417 So.2d 727 (1982). Pardon And Parole ⚷ 61

If, after state parole and probation commission has computed proper matrix time range, using available information, aggravating circumstances are to be applied, commission is obligated both by statute and rule to explain aggravating factors in writing, for benefit of inmate and to facilitate appropriate review. Battis v. Florida Parole and Probation Commission, App. 1 Dist., 386 So.2d 295 (1980). Pardon And Parole ⚷ 61

Under objective parole criteria, in extending an inmate's term, by reason of aggravating circumstances, beyond guideline matrix range, parole and probation commission must at least distinguish aggravating circumstances relied on from factors which determine offensive characteristic and, if offense is not specifically listed in guidelines, it must be explained by Commission sufficiently to indicate basis of comparison with an offense listed. Baker v. Florida Parole and Probation Commission, App. 1 Dist., 384 So.2d 746 (1980). Pardon And Parole ⚷ 61

Under objective parole criteria, in extending an inmate's term, by reason of aggravating circumstances, beyond guideline matrix range, parole and probation commission's explanation must be adequate to afford an inmate insight into why his term to be served was aggravated beyond guideline matrix range. Baker v. Florida Parole and Probation Commission, App. 1 Dist., 384 So.2d 746 (1980). Pardon And Parole ⚷ 61

30. —— Armed offenses, date of release outside matrix time

Presumptive parole release date of defendant who was convicted of murder in the second degree was properly aggravated for commission of robbery and for use of a firearm. Calloway v. Florida Parole and Probation Com'n, App. 1 Dist., 431 So.2d 300 (1983). Pardon And Parole ⚷ 49

Where at time of armed robbery only two tellers were present in bank, 60-month aggravation of defendant's parole release date beyond matrix time frame for creating danger to other customers in the bank was erroneous. Bryant v. Florida Parole and Probation Com'n, App. 1 Dist., 426 So.2d 1133 (1983). Pardon And Parole ⚷ 50

Parole and probation commission properly aggravated defendant's presumptive parole release date for the use of a weapon in the commission of the crime for which he was convicted, second-degree murder; the aggravating factor is not included within the definition of second-degree murder. Young v. Florida Parole & Probation Com'n, App. 1 Dist., 416 So.2d 1179 (1982). Pardon And Parole ⚷ 49

Aggravating a prisoner's presumptive parole release date for use of a firearm during commission of a crime is legal. Zygadlo v. Florida Parole and Probation Com'n, App. 1 Dist., 414 So.2d 600 (1982). Pardon And Parole ⚷ 49

The parole and probation commission erred in taking notice of armed nature of attempted robbery in determining severity offense characteristic and in thereafter aggravating for consummation of the offense for purposes of determining prisoner's presumptive parole release date. Lowe v. Florida Parole and Probation Commission, App. 1 Dist., 411 So.2d 352 (1982). Pardon And Parole ⚷ 53

31. —— Discretion of commission, date of release outside matrix time

Parole commission's addition of 240 months in aggravation in calculating inmate's presumptive parole release date (PPRD), based on inmate's history of poor institutional conduct and continued assaultive behavior, was within commission's discretion, which discretion was subject only to limitations of statute governing establishment of PPRDs and rule pertaining to commission's decisions outside matrix time range, neither of which contained any specific prohibition for commission's reason given for adding this amount of aggravation. Spaziano v. Florida Parole Com'n, App. 1 Dist., 2006 WL 1565289 (2006), review granted 2009 WL 5449225. Pardon And Parole ⚷ 52

Decisions to aggravate an inmate beyond his matrix time range are within discretion of parole and probation commission, subject to limitations of this section and certain rules; if commission deems that appropriate aggravating circumstances exist in a particular case, amount of aggravation time is also discretionary, and is not required to bear any relationship to matrix time range for the offense of conviction or for the offense behavior which forms basis for the aggravation. Benton v. Florida Parole and Probation Com'n, App. 1 Dist., 418 So.2d 1127 (1982). Pardon And Parole ⚷ 53

Parole and probation commission did not abuse its discretion in assessing an aggravation 51 months above matrix time range in establishing inmate's presumptive parole release date based on fact that inmate was on bond for the offense of possession of marijuana at time he committed armed robbery for which he was convicted in that fact that inmate was "on bond" when he committed the offense of conviction was an appropriate aggravating circumstance. Benton v. Florida Parole and Probation Com'n, App. 1 Dist., 418 So.2d 1127 (1982). Pardon And Parole ⚷ 53

The parole and probation commission does have discretion in certain instances to set presumptive parole release date outside matrix time frame based on aggravating circumstance in which dangerous weapon has been used in commission of crime. Lowe v. Florida Parole and Probation Commission, App. 1 Dist., 411 So.2d 352 (1982). Pardon And Parole ⚷ 53

32. —— Sufficiency of evidence, date of release outside matrix time

Evidence before parole and probation commission supported calculation of presumptive parole release date based on aggravation for use of firearm during crime, notwithstanding defendant's unsubstantiated statement that weapon was only starter pistol. Farber v. Florida Parole and Probation Com'n, App. 1 Dist., 427 So.2d 1016 (1983). Pardon And Parole ⚷ 58

33. Time of determination

Where parole and probation commission did not defer indefinitely establishment of inmate's presumptive parole release date and where commission had established such date for inmate prior to filing of his habeas corpus petition, he was not entitled to release on ground that commission had violated § 947.16 and had applied aggravating factors more than 45 days after his initial interview. Purnell v. Florida Parole and Probation Commission, App. 1 Dist., 409 So.2d 1122 (1982), review denied 417 So.2d 330. Habeas Corpus ⚷ 510(1)

34. Amendments and corrections to release date—In general

The parole and probation commission departed from essential requirements of law in establishing new presumptive parole release date for inmate, based upon information that the commission had already considered and rejected at prior hearings, particularly in view of fact that the commission failed to include inmate's name on agenda or to show good cause or changing agenda, thus depriving interested parties from appearing and having input in the commission's decision. State ex rel. Boyles v. Florida Parole and Probation Com'n, App. 1 Dist., 436 So.2d 207 (1983). Pardon And Parole ⚷ 60

The parole and probation commission cannot modify a presumptive parole release date on its assertion of "new information," where that information has already been considered and acted upon by the commission in establishing the release date. State ex rel. Boyles v. Florida Parole and Probation Com'n, App. 1 Dist., 436 So.2d 207 (1983). Pardon And Parole ⚷ 60

Where court had ordered state parole and probation commission to recalculate prisoner's presumptive parole release date using most severe conviction as offense characteristic and had granted leave to use other convictions as aggravations, it was proper for Commission to change previous aggravations. Faucett v. Wainwright, App. 1 Dist., 419 So.2d 765 (1982). Pardon And Parole ⚷ 60

Parole and probation commission's establishment of presumptive parole release date who affirmed only because the commission provided a marginally acceptable explanation of its action in an amendment one day before prisoner filed notice of appeal. Richardson v. Florida Parole and Probation Com'n, App. 1 Dist., 417 So.2d 727 (1982). Pardon And Parole ⚷ 61

Action of parole and probation commission, subsequent to review, in lowering prisoner's salient factor score and changing his offense characteristic from kidnapping to false imprisonment, which resulted in reduction of matrix time range applicable to prisoner for purpose of setting his presumptive parole release date, but thereafter adding aggravations which increased length of time prisoner would have to remain in prison and which ultimately resulted in no change in presumptive parole release date originally set did not violate this section providing that a presumptive parole release date is binding on Commission upon agreement to such date. Zygadlo v. Florida Parole and Probation Com'n, App. 1 Dist., 414 So.2d 600 (1982). Pardon And Parole ⚷ 60

Where prisoner's presumptive parole release date was established by action of the parole and probation commission prior to prisoner's filing of his petition for writ of mandamus, this date became binding on commission and where aggravating factor adding 19 months to its date was then conceded to be inappropriate, there was no basis for commission to modify the date to restore the 19 months by considering prisoner's "Ancient Prior Record." Bizzigotti v. Florida Parole & Probation Commission, App. 1 Dist., 410 So.2d 1360 (1982). Pardon And Parole ⚷ 60

35. —— Clerical errors and mistakes, amendments and corrections to release date

Prisoner to whom state Parole and Probation Commission had mistakenly assigned presumptive parole date three years later than correct parole date, which already passed, was entitled to immediate establishment of effective parole release date. Brown v. Wainwright, 489 So.2d 718 (1986). Pardon And Parole ⚷ 48.1

This section providing that presumptive parole release date is binding on parole and probation commission when agreement is reached did not prevent correction of a mere clerical error. Harrisson v. Florida Parole and Probation Com'n, App. 4 Dist., 428 So.2d 388 (1983). Pardon And Parole ⚷ 60

Parole and probation commission may correct obvious clerical mistake or computation error made in presumptive parole release dates. Gaddy v. Florida Parole and Probation Com'n, App. 1 Dist., 416 So.2d 836 (1982).

Parole and probation commission did not err in correcting presumptive parole release date for prisoner when failure to deduct time prisoner was out of custody on escape was discovered.

Moore v. Florida Parole and Probation Com'n, App. 1 Dist., 415 So.2d 817 (1982). Pardon And Parole ⚷ 60

36. Suspension of release date

Commission, in determining whether to suspend inmate's presumptive parole release date (PPRD) and defer effective parole release date (EPRD), must give consideration to all information shown in official file, including aggravating and mitigating matters, both historical and current, and decide how and whether such matters rationally relate to inmate's fitness for release on parole at time Commission formulates its decision. Williams v. Florida Parole Com'n, App. 1 Dist., 625 So.2d 926 (1993), review denied 637 So.2d 236. Pardon And Parole ⚷ 63

Parole Commission did not abuse its discretion in suspending inmate's presumptive parole release date (PPRD) and denying parole merely because it relied on old information previously used to establish PPRD. Williams v. Florida Parole Com'n, App. 1 Dist., 625 So.2d 926 (1993), review denied 637 So.2d 236. Pardon And Parole ⚷ 63

Statutory expression of intent of legislature that, once set, presumptive release date be modified only for good cause and exceptional circumstances is applicable to decisional process leading to suspension of inmate's presumptive parole release date (PPRD) when Commission denies an effective parole release date (EPRD). Williams v. Florida Parole Com'n, App. 1 Dist., 625 So.2d 926 (1993), review denied 637 So.2d 236. Pardon And Parole ⚷ 63

When Parole Commission suspends presumptive parole release date (PPRD) and declines to set effective parole release date (EPRD), it is required by its rules to specifically state reasons for finding inmate to be ineligible for parole release and to identify information relied upon in reaching conclusion. Williams v. Florida Parole Com'n, App. 1 Dist., 625 So.2d 926 (1993), review denied 637 So.2d 236. Pardon And Parole ⚷ 63

37. Habeas corpus

Prisoner's petition for habeas corpus, treated by District Court of Appeal as petition for writ of mandamus, presented not a further challenge to legality of his sentences but rather a challenge to use of sentences within context of parole and probation commission's objective parole guidelines, and, accordingly, prisoner was not precluded by opinion of District Court of Appeal from seeking collateral relief from his sentences. Daizi v. Florida Parole and Probation Com'n, App. 4 Dist., 436 So.2d 171 (1983). Mandamus ⚷ 73(1)

Since mandamus petition did not contain definite allegations that if presumptive parole release date were properly computed, petitioner would be entitled to immediate release, court could not treat the petition as one for habeas corpus. Curry v. Wainwright, App. 5 Dist., 419 So.2d 744 (1982), transferred to 422 So.2d 1029. Habeas Corpus ⚷ 666

Contention that prison inmate failed to show by affidavit of evidence probable cause to believe that he was detained without lawful authority necessary for issuance of writ of habeas corpus was refuted by jurat at conclusion of inmate's petition which challenged determination of his presumptive parole release date; thus, writ would be granted and inmate ordered released from custody subject to standard provisions of parole. Taylor v. Wainwright, App. 5 Dist., 418 So.2d 1095 (1982), review dismissed 476 So.2d 669. Habeas Corpus ⚷ 725; Habeas Corpus ⚷ 791

Proper party respondent in action for habeas corpus relief in which determination of presumptive parole release date was challenged was secretary of department of corrections, not parole commission as would be the case if petition had been styled or treated as one seeking writ of mandamus. Taylor v. Wainwright, App. 5 Dist., 418 So.2d 1095 (1982), review dismissed 476 So.2d 669. Habeas Corpus ⚷ 662.1

Naming of Attorney General as respondent in prison inmate's petition for habeas corpus relief in which determination of his presumptive parole release date was challenged did not alter issues presented by petition and Attorney General would be stricken as unnecessary party. Taylor v. Wainwright, App. 5 Dist., 418 So.2d 1095 (1982), review dismissed 476 So.2d 669. Habeas Corpus ⚷ 662.1

38. Mandamus

Circuit Court, rather than District Court of Appeal, was proper forum in which to file petition for writ of mandamus to seek review of Parole and Probation Commission's suspension of prisoner's presumptive parole release date; denial of petition for writ of mandamus would then be properly reviewed by appeal to District Court. Johnson v. Florida Parole and Probation Com'n, App. 4 Dist., 543 So.2d 875 (1989). Mandamus ⚷ 141

Petition for writ of mandamus by inmate who was convicted of sexual battery but acquitted of kidnapping was legally sufficient to require hearing where petition alleged that statement of aggravating circumstances used by Parole and Probation Commission to establish presumptive parole release date beyond calculated matrix range was nothing more than restatement of essential elements of kidnapping statute (§ 787.01) of which petitioner had been acquitted, in that there was no significant distinction between statutory definition of kidnapping and allegation that petitioner held victim against her will in a bus. Wade v. Florida Parole and Probation Com'n, App. 1 Dist., 457 So.2d 575 (1984). Mandamus ⚷ 73(1)

Appropriate remedy for challenging presumptive parole release dates is by writ of mandamus directed against Florida Parole and Probation Commission; receding from Taylor v. Wainwright, 418 So.2d 1095. Pannier v. Wainwright, App. 5 Dist., 423 So.2d 533 (1982). Mandamus ⚷ 73(1)

First district, not fifth district, was proper venue for a petition for mandamus seeking to require Florida parole and probation commission to give credit for time served in computing petitioner's presumptive parole release date. Curry v. Wainwright, App. 5 Dist., 419 So.2d 744 (1982), transferred to 422 So.2d 1029. Mandamus ⚷ 142

Proper party respondent to prison inmate's petition seeking writ of mandamus challenging determination of his presumptive parole release date is parole commission. Taylor v. Wainwright, App. 5 Dist., 418 So.2d 1095 (1982), review dismissed 476 So.2d 669. Mandamus ⚷ 151(2)

Order to show cause issued on petition for writ of mandamus to compel parole and probation commission to reinstate presumptive parole release date previously given petitioner would be discharged and writ would be denied where claims raised by petitioner with respect to his removal from further parole consideration for failure to file a financial disclosure affidavit were devoid of merit. Gerlock v. Florida Parole and Probation Commission, App. 1 Dist., 411 So.2d 1386 (1982). Mandamus ⚷ 73(1)

Legislature has mandated setting of presumptive parole release date by state parole and probation commission, and when commission without adequate reason fails so to act, it is answerable in mandamus. Battis v. Florida Parole and Probation Commission, App. 1 Dist., 386 So.2d 295 (1980). Mandamus ⚷ 73(1)

39. Review

Establishment by parole and probation commission of presumptive parole release date for prisoners is final agency action, for purposes of judicial review. Daniels v. Florida Parole and Probation Commission, App. 1 Dist., 401 So.2d 1351 (1981), approved 444 So.2d 917. Pardon And Parole ⚷ 62

947.173. Review of presumptive parole release date

(1) An inmate may request one review of his or her initial presumptive parole release date established according to s. 947.16(1) if the inmate shows cause in writing, with individual particularities, within 60 days after the date the inmate is notified of the decision on the presumptive parole release date.

(2) A panel of no fewer than two commissioners appointed by the chair shall review the inmate's request for review and shall notify the inmate in writing of its decision within 60 days after the date of receipt of the request by the commission.

(3) The commission may affirm or modify the authorized presumptive parole release date. However, in the event of a decision to modify the presumptive parole release date, in no case shall this modified date be after the date established under the procedures of s. 947.172. It is the intent of this legislation that, once set, presumptive parole release dates be modified only for good cause in exceptional circumstances.

Laws 1978, c. 78–417, § 14; Laws 1979, c. 79–42, § 8; Laws 1979, c. 79–164, § 196; Laws 1982, c. 82–171, § 12; Laws 1993, c. 93–61, § 8. Amended by Laws 1996, c. 96–422, § 20, eff. June 7, 1996; Laws 1997, c. 97–102, § 1874, eff. July 1, 1997.

Historical and Statutory Notes

Amendment Notes:

Laws 1979, c. 79–42, § 8, provided for a panel to review requests in subsec. (2).

Laws 1979, c. 79–164, a reviser's bill, corrected statutes by deletion of expired, obsolete, invalid, inconsistent or redundant provisions; modified cross references and grammar; and, otherwise improved the clarity to facilitate interpretation of the statutes.

Laws 1982, c. 82–171, § 12, in subsec. (1), inserted "one" preceding "review of his presumptive", substituted "established according to the provisions of s. 947.16(1), 947.174, or 947.1745" for "by the commission" and substituted "of the date the inmate is notified" for "after the date".

Laws 1993, c. 93–61, § 8, eff. April 22, 1993, in subsec. (1), inserted "initial"; deleted references to §§ 947.174 and 947.1745; and substituted "after" for "of".

Laws 1996, c. 96–422, § 20, eff. June 7, 1996, in subsec. (2), deleted a former second sentence, which read, "Such panel shall not include the commissioners who authorized the original presumptive parole release date, except when that date has been established by the full commission."

Laws 1997, c. 97–102, eff. July 1, 1997, removed gender-specific references applicable to human beings from volume 4 of the Florida Statutes without substantive changes in legal effect.

Library References

Pardon and Parole ⚷62.
Westlaw Topic No. 284.
C.J.S. Pardon and Parole § 57.

Research References

Treatises and Practice Aids

16 Florida Practice Series § 10:20, Parole--Presumptive Parole Release Date.

16 Florida Practice Series § 10:21, Parole--Effective Parole Release Date.

Notes of Decisions

1. Construction and application

Parole in Florida is granted by sovereign as a matter of grace rather than of right, and state may offer such grace under and subject to such conditions as it may consider most conducive to accomplish the desired purpose. Panzavecchia v. Crockett, App. 1 Dist., 379 So.2d 1047 (1980). Pardon And Parole ⚷ 46

2. Discretion of commission

Parole commission's decision to suspend inmate's presumptive parole release date was not abuse of discretion, absent any showing that commission deviated from legal requirements imposed upon it or that it based suspension on illegal grounds or improper considerations. Florida Parole Com'n v. Huckelbury, App. 1 Dist., 903 So.2d 977 (2005), rehearing denied, review denied 913 So.2d 596. Pardon And Parole ⚷ 63

An inmate is not required to be released on parole where a presumptive parole release date is found invalid and court finds that another presumptive parole release date, which has already passed, is in fact the valid date since the ultimate decision to parole an inmate lies within sound discretion of parole and probation commission. Jackson v. Florida Parole and Probation Com'n, App. 1 Dist., 424 So.2d 930 (1983). Pardon And Parole ⚷ 47

Parole release date was properly conditioned by parole and probation commission on inmate's waiver of extradition to another state in which he had time to serve on sentence imposed there and inmate's refusal to accept terms offered constituted rejection of commission's proper offer of parole so that commission did not err in withholding parole. Todd v. Florida Parole & Probation Commission, App. 1 Dist., 410 So.2d 584 (1982). Pardon And Parole ⚷ 65

3. Time for requesting review

Inmate was required to seek review of his presumptive parole release date within 60-day period provided under this section. Myers v. Florida Parole and Probation Com'n, App. 1 Dist., 423 So.2d 481 (1982). Pardon And Parole ⚷ 62

Where parolee did not seek official review of commission's establishment of presumptive parole release date within 60 days, he was precluded from raising on appeal any issue which related to establishment of that date. Gonzales v. Florida Parole and Probation Com'n, App. 1 Dist., 421 So.2d 675 (1982). Pardon And Parole ⚷ 62

Time limit of 60 days prescribed by this section governing review of state parole and probation commission action in setting presumptive parole release date is not jurisdictional. Gobie v. Florida Parole and Probation Com'n, App. 1 Dist., 416 So.2d 838 (1982), review denied 424 So.2d 762. Pardon And Parole ⚷ 62

4. Calculation errors or clerical mistakes

When original proposed parole release date had been calculated on basis of erroneous written sentence, which was thereafter corrected and resulted in substantial reduction of incarceration, correction of error in original sentence constituted sufficient good cause to require Parole and Probation Commission to recalculate prisoner's proposed parole release date upon subsequent interview. Swanson v. Florida Parole and Probation Com'n, App. 1 Dist., 548 So.2d 269 (1989), review dismissed 553 So.2d 1166. Pardon And Parole ⚷ 50

Although presumptive parole release date once established is binding on Parole and Probation Commission except for good cause in exceptional circumstances, or for reason of institutional conduct or acquisition of new information not available at time of initial interview, Commission may correct clerical mistake or computational error made in setting the presumptive parole release date. Zatler v. State, App. 5 Dist., 457 So.2d 1083 (1984). Pardon And Parole ⚷ 60

Parole and probation commission erred in establishing prisoner's presumptive parole release date by calculating date based on offense severity of first-degree felony for second-degree felony offense of assault with intent to commit robbery. Everson v. Florida Parole & Probation Com'n, App. 1 Dist., 431 So.2d 238 (1983). Pardon And Parole ⚷ 53

Florida parole and probation commission, which took timely action to cure defects prior to time probationer sought court review of commission's action to correct its acknowledged error, had to be permitted to correct its errors and oversights in orderly manner pursuant to administrative procedures. Morris v. Florida Parole and Probation Com'n,, App. 1 Dist., 423 So.2d 491 (1982). Pardon And Parole ⚷ 60

Having placed prisoner in a lower category of offense severity rating than was proper in setting prisoner's presumptive parole release date, the parole and probation commission was permitted to raise the severity level after prisoner filed for review asserting the error. Wickham v. Florida Parole and Probation Commission, App. 1 Dist., 410 So.2d 989 (1982). Pardon And Parole ⚷ 60

Prisoner was precluded from challenging on appeal order of the parole and probation commission setting a prospective parole release date where prisoner failed to seek proper review within 60 days of commission's action. Hall v. Florida Parole & Probation Commission, App. 1 Dist., 408 So.2d 1076 (1982). Pardon And Parole ⚷ 62

5. Modification of release date

Under Florida parole statutes, Florida Parole Commission (FPC) acted within its discretion by extending parole release date beyond presumed date originally set, based on objection from sentencing court and based on finding of unsatisfactory release plan, and thus extension of release date could not constitute due process violation, regardless of fact that presumed date had been set for some years and periodically reviewed without modification. Tooma v. Florida Parole Com'n, S.D.Fla.2009, 612 F.Supp.2d 1255. Constitutional Law ⚷ 4838; Pardon and Parole ⚷ 50

Parole and Probation Commission cannot change or modify presumptive parole release date (PPRD) except for new information not available at time of initial interview, institutional conduct, or exceptional circumstances. Harper v. Florida Parole Com'n, App. 1 Dist., 626 So.2d 336 (1993), cause dismissed 630 So.2d 1100. Pardon And Parole ⚷ 49

The Parole and Probation Commission could not aggravate presumptive parole release date for burglary sentence on basis of information it had previously chosen not to use during initial interview to establish PPRD for murder sentence, even though PPRD for murder sentence had been vacated by prisoner's having exited from the incarcerative portion of his sentence when he was paroled and even though new interview was required to establish new PPRD after prisoner was convicted of burglary while on parole; previously known information was not "new information" and thus could not justify change or modification of PPRD. Williams v. Florida Parole and Probation Com'n, App. 1 Dist., 515 So.2d 1044 (1987). Pardon And Parole ⚷ 49

Once presumptive parole release date is established, it becomes binding on Parole and Probation Commission and is not to be changed except for reasons of institutional conduct, acquisition of new information not available at time of initial interview, or for good cause in exceptional circumstances. Florida Parole and

Probation Com'n v. Paige, 462 So.2d 817 (1985). Pardon And Parole ⚷ 63

Special action taken by Parole and Probation Commission on its own initiative in order to establish a proper presumptive parole release date to replace a previous "life" designation did not reopen questions already decided by Commission and, hence, foreclosed claim that salient factor score was improperly modified by use of a juvenile offense for which prisoner was placed on probation in Arkansas. Collins v. Florida Parole and Probation Com'n, App. 1 Dist., 441 So.2d 645 (1983). Pardon And Parole ⚷ 60

Order of the Florida parole and probation commission extending inmate's presumptive parole release date was error because it was not done in accordance with the Objective Parole Guidelines Act in that the commission failed to point out whether any circumstances given in explanation of its action were based on "newly acquired information" or, if not, whether there was "good cause in exceptional circumstances" for the Commission's action. Moats v. Florida Parole and Probation Com'n, App. 1 Dist., 419 So.2d 775 (1982). Pardon And Parole ⚷ 61

Where prisoner's presumptive parole release date was established by action of the parole and probation commission prior to prisoner's filing of his petition for writ of mandamus, this date became binding on commission and where aggravating factor adding 19 months to its date was then conceded to be inappropriate, there was no basis for commission to modify the date to restore the 19 months by considering prisoner's "Ancient Prior Record." Bizzigotti v. Florida Parole & Probation Commission, App. 1 Dist., 410 So.2d 1360 (1982). Pardon And Parole ⚷ 60

Absent showing of either statutory exceptions or exceptional circumstances for good cause, Florida parole and probation commission had no discretion to increase inmate's salient factor score or to add aggravating factor after it had previously entered order fixing presumptive parole release date. McKahn v. Florida Parole and Probation Commission, App. 1 Dist., 399 So.2d 476 (1981). Pardon And Parole ⚷ 63

6. Suspension of release date

Court reviewing Parole Commission's decision to suspend presumptive parole release date (PPRD) and to defer effective parole release date (EPRD) for abuse of discretion must determine from record whether Commission has deviated from legal requirements or otherwise acted improperly in reaching its decision. Williams v. Florida Parole Com'n, App. 1 Dist., 625 So.2d 926 (1993), review denied 637 So.2d 236. Pardon And Parole ⚷ 63

Parole Commission's cited reasons for suspending inmate's presumptive parole release date (PPRD) and refusing to set his effective parole release date (EPRD), while facially sufficient, were insufficient to determine whether Commission complied with its rules or otherwise acted improperly; to make determination trial court should have had available for review those portions of inmate's file that were relevant and material to reasons cited by Commission's order and issues presented in petition for mandamus; remand for further proceedings was therefore required, at which time Commission might supplement its response to circuit court's order to show cause and, if deemed necessary, present additional information at evidentiary hearing. Williams v. Florida Parole Com'n, App. 1 Dist., 625 So.2d 926 (1993), review denied 637 So.2d 236. Pardon And Parole ⚷ 63

Parole Commission's decision to suspend inmate's presumptive parole release date and defer setting effective parole release date (EPRD) can be set aside by court only for demonstrated abuse of discretion. Williams v. Florida Parole Com'n, App. 1 Dist., 625 So.2d 926 (1993), review denied 637 So.2d 236. Pardon And Parole ⚷ 63

Parole Commission did not abuse its discretion in suspending inmate's presumptive parole release date (PPRD) and denying parole merely because it relied on old information previously used to establish PPRD. Williams v. Florida Parole Com'n, App. 1 Dist., 625 So.2d 926 (1993), review denied 637 So.2d 236. Pardon And Parole ⚷ 63

Statutory expression of intent of legislature that, once set, presumptive release date be modified only for good cause and exceptional circumstances is applicable to decisional process leading to suspension of inmate's presumptive parole release date (PPRD) when Commission denies an effective parole release date (EPRD). Williams v. Florida Parole Com'n, App. 1 Dist., 625 So.2d 926 (1993), review denied 637 So.2d 236. Pardon And Parole ⚷ 63

When Parole Commission suspends presumptive parole release date (PPRD) and declines to set effective parole release date (EPRD), it is required by its rules to specifically state reasons for finding inmate to be ineligible for parole release and to identify information relied upon in reaching conclusion. Williams v. Florida Parole Com'n, App. 1 Dist., 625 So.2d 926 (1993), review denied 637 So.2d 236. Pardon And Parole ⚷ 63

7. Second or subsequent panel review

Administrative review under this section or denial of inmate's request for review of his presumptive parole release date constitutes final agency action and is appealable under § 120.68

and appellate rules, but parole and probation commission is at liberty to either ignore or summarily deny additional requests for review, and refusal to entertain or consider such additional request, or denial, would not constitute final agency action which could serve as basis for appeal to District Court of Appeal. Canter v. Florida Parole and Probation Commission, App. 1 Dist., 409 So.2d 227 (1982). Pardon And Parole ⚷ 62

Inmate had no right to seek second review of his presumptive parole release date, and his request for review of such date, which had already been reviewed by parole and probation commission pursuant to this section was properly denied even insofar as claiming right to "special review" on basis of "new information." Canter v. Florida Parole and Probation Commission, App. 1 Dist., 409 So.2d 227 (1982). Pardon And Parole ⚷ 62

8. Declaratory relief

Prisoners' petitions for declaratory statements by parole and probation commission concerning criteria used to establish prisoners' presumptive parole release date constituted unnecessary collateral attacks on nonfinal agency orders which were reviewable according to statutorily prescribed procedures; commission could, in its own discretion, answer prisoners' requests for information, but such communications would not be treated as "declaratory statements" for purposes of statute providing that agency disposition of petition for declaratory statements was final agency action. Law v. Florida Parole and Probation Commission, App. 1 Dist., 411 So.2d 1329 (1982). Pardon And Parole ⚷ 52

9. Res judicata

Inmate's habeas corpus petition, alleging that Florida parole and probation commission had illegally added aggravation factor in determining his presumptive parole release date, was barred by principle of res judicata where inmate previously had enjoyed full appellate review of challenged action by FPPC and prior habeas corpus petition seeking immediate relief on allegations similar to those in subject petition had previously been denied. Pannier v. Wainwright, App. 5 Dist., 423 So.2d 533 (1982). Habeas Corpus ⚷ 770; Habeas Corpus ⚷ 897

Where issues raised by prisoner seeking review of parole and probation commission's action declining to reconsider issues raised in his review request were identical to issues raised by defendant and considered by commission at prisoner's first review, over two years previously, issues raised by prisoner were res judicata. McClain v. Florida Parole and Probation Com'n, App. 1 Dist., 416 So.2d 1209 (1982). Judgment ⚷ 715(1)

10. Court orders

Where court had earlier ordered that state parole and probation commission credit prisoner with his newly established presumptive parole release date and commission order did not credit prisoner with such reduction, Commission was ordered to reduce prisoner's presumptive parole release date accordingly. Faucett v. Wainwright, App. 1 Dist., 419 So.2d 765 (1982). Pardon And Parole ⚷ 62

State parole and probation commission was directed by the District Court of Appeal to grant reviews of commission action setting presumptive parole release dates of inmates, setting forth in writing explanations for its actions. Gobie v. Florida Parole and Probation Com'n, App. 1 Dist., 416 So.2d 838 (1982), review denied 424 So.2d 762. Pardon And Parole ⚷ 62

Trial court's order correcting error in sentencing after review by parole and probation commission qualified as "new information not available at the time of the initial interview" so as to furnish basis for commission, in its discretion, to determine whether such new information would warrant consideration of change in presumptive parole release date. Canter v. Florida Parole and Probation Commission, App. 1 Dist., 409 So.2d 227 (1982). Pardon And Parole ⚷ 60

11. Habeas corpus

Proper remedy to obtain review of Parole Commission's decision after it sets effective parole release date (EPRD) is by habeas corpus. Williams v. Florida Parole Com'n, App. 1 Dist., 625 So.2d 926 (1993), review denied 637 So.2d 236. Habeas Corpus ⚷ 516.1; Pardon And Parole ⚷ 62

Habeas corpus proceeding challenging action of parole and probation commission declining to authorize effective parole release date and extending presumptive parole release date would not be treated as matter of administrative review absent showing that petitioner sought and received a review under this section of commission action and that whether petition was filed within 30 days of Commission action. Kirsch v. Greadington, App. 1 Dist., 425 So.2d 153 (1983). Pardon And Parole ⚷ 62

Habeas corpus petition which asserted arbitrary and erroneous application of parole release guidelines and alleged factual matters would be denied where no record was provided and petition did not show that statutory administrative remedies had been exhausted. Polk v. Crockett, App. 1 Dist., 379 So.2d 369 (1980). Habeas Corpus ⚷ 670(8)

12. Mandamus

Inmate who sought review of Parole and Probation Commission's establishment of a presumptive parole release date that was significantly later than date recommended by hearing examiner was required to file petition for writ of mandamus directed against Commission in county where Commission was headquartered, rather than writ of habeas corpus in county of incarceration. Roth v. Crosby, App. 2 Dist., 884 So.2d 407 (2004). Habeas Corpus ⚷ 516.1

The appropriate vehicle for challenging a presumptive parole release date is a petition for a writ of mandamus directed against the Parole and Probation Commission. Roth v. Crosby, App. 2 Dist., 884 So.2d 407 (2004). Mandamus ⚷ 73(1)

Prisoner was not entitled to mandamus relief with respect to 24–month extension of presumptive parole release date (PPRD) given for aggravating factor based upon new information, where reasons given for extension were facially valid, supported by the record, and authorized by statute and rule. Harper v. Florida Parole Com'n, App. 1 Dist., 626 So.2d 336 (1993), cause dismissed 630 So.2d 1100. Mandamus ⚷ 73(1)

Constitutional issues that were not raised in petition for mandamus filed by inmate challenging Parole Commission's suspension of his presumptive parole release date (PPRD), but were raised in inmate's reply to Parole Commission's response, were not properly before circuit court for decision and would not be reached on appeal; Commission was not afforded proper opportunity to respond to contentions before circuit court. Williams v. Florida Parole Com'n, App. 1 Dist., 625 So.2d 926 (1993), review denied 637 So.2d 236. Mandamus ⚷ 167; Mandamus ⚷ 187.4

Parole Commission order suspending inmate's presumptive parole release date (PPRD) and thereby refusing to set effective parole release date (EPRD) is appropriately reviewed by mandamus. Williams v. Florida Parole Com'n, App. 1 Dist., 625 So.2d 926 (1993), review denied 637 So.2d 236. Mandamus ⚷ 73(1); Pardon And Parole ⚷ 63

Review by mandamus of Parole Commission's decision suspending inmate's presumptive parole release date (PPRD) does not authorize court to substitute its judgment for Commission's delegated discretion and order inmate release on parole; court may only order Commission to reconsider its decision. Williams v. Florida Parole Com'n, App. 1 Dist., 625 So.2d 926 (1993), review denied 637 So.2d 236. Mandamus ⚷ 176; Pardon And Parole ⚷ 63

Petition for writ of mandamus seeking review of presumptive parole release date established by Parole and Probation Commission was properly denied, where petitioner failed to allege in petition, or show by providing appendix, that he had exhausted his administrative remedies. Gibson v. Florida Parole and Probation Com'n, App. 1 Dist., 450 So.2d 553 (1984). Mandamus ⚷ 154(2)

Order to show cause issued on petition for writ of mandamus to compel parole and probation commission to reinstate presumptive parole release date previously given petitioner would be discharged and writ would be denied where claims raised by petitioner with respect to his removal from further parole consideration for failure to file a financial disclosure affidavit were devoid of merit. Gerlock v. Florida Parole and Probation Commission, App. 1 Dist., 411 So.2d 1386 (1982). Mandamus ⚷ 73(1)

Petitioner who alleged that parole and probation commission improperly calculated his presumptive parole release date but who did not seek review by direct appeal, was not entitled to a writ of mandamus. Holman v. Florida Parole and Probation Com'n, App. 1 Dist., 407 So.2d 638 (1981). Mandamus ⚷ 4(5)

Where state prisoner did not file a timely appeal from Florida parole and probation commission action finding no cause to modify prisoner's presumptive parole release date, and chose to wait more than six months after final commission action before filing petition for writ of mandamus, prisoner's application for review of his presumptive parole release date was delayed for an unreasonable amount of time and writ would be denied. Jordan v. Florida Parole and Probation Commission, App. 1 Dist., 403 So.2d 591 (1981). Mandamus ⚷ 143(1)

Judicial review of final Florida parole and probation commission action establishing a presumptive parole release date is properly triggered by a timely appeal, not by a petition for writ of mandamus. Jordan v. Florida Parole and Probation Commission, App. 1 Dist., 403 So.2d 591 (1981). Pardon And Parole ⚷ 62

Apparent failure of petitioner to avail himself of administrative review, on request, of presumptive parole release date determinations precluded mandamus relief as regards allegation that method by which presumptive parole release date was determined treated concurrent sentences as if they were consecutive sentences. Dodd v. Florida Parole & Probation Commission, App. 1 Dist., 380 So.2d 556 (1980). Mandamus ⚷ 3(8)

Failure of petitioner to assert exhaustion of administrative remedy afforded by this section with respect to review, upon request, of presumptive parole release date determination operated to preclude petitioner from obtaining relief on his petition for writ of mandamus based on allegation that his release date was not determined by a hearing panel consisting of required two examiners. Houston v. Florida Parole & Probation Commission, App. 1 Dist., 377 So.2d 34 (1979). Mandamus ⚿ 3(8)

13. Review—In general

Defendant's most serious convicted offense was that of carrying a firearm in the commission of a robbery, not assault with intent to commit first-degree murder, and his presumptive parole release date should have been calculated on the basis of robbery as the most serious offense for purposes of the salient factor score. Green v. Florida Parole Com'n, App. 1 Dist., 555 So.2d 432 (1990). Pardon And Parole ⚿ 51

Judicial review of presumptive parole release dates (PPRDs) does not violate Const. Art. 2, § 3. Florida Parole Com'n v. Padovano, App. 1 Dist., 554 So.2d 1200 (1989), review denied 564 So.2d 488. Constitutional Law ⚿ 2545(4); Pardon And Parole ⚿ 62

Certiorari was appropriate method for review of challenged order of the parole and probation commission, establishing new presumptive parole release date for inmate. State ex rel. Boyles v. Florida Parole and Probation Com'n, App. 1 Dist., 436 So.2d 207 (1983). Pardon And Parole ⚿ 62

There can be no administrative appeal from determination of presumptive parole release date. Pannier v. Wainwright, App. 5 Dist., 423 So.2d 533 (1982). Pardon And Parole ⚿ 62

Issues that may be raised on appeal from Florida parole and probation commission's setting of presumptive parole release date are limited to those issues presented to Commission and thus probationer, not having met this requirement, could not present issues for initial review by the court. Morris v. Florida Parole and Probation Com'n,, App. 1 Dist., 423 So.2d 491 (1982). Pardon And Parole ⚿ 62

Documents which were not part of the record and not presented to the parole and probation commission during its review of presumptive parole release date would not be considered on appeal and would be stricken from appendix to brief, despite contention that they were in prisoner's department of corrections file and should have been considered by the commission; if prisoner took issue with the factual predicates relied on by the commission, he should have done so at his review and the documents should have been presented to the Commission at that time. Arlotta v. Florida Parole and Probation Com'n, App. 1 Dist., 419 So.2d 1159 (1982). Pardon And Parole ⚿ 62

14. —— Exhaustion of administrative remedies, review

Under § 120.68 entitling party adversely affected by final agency action to judicial review, parole commission's establishment of presumptive parole release date is "final agency action." Taylor v. Wainwright, App. 5 Dist., 418 So.2d 1095 (1982), review dismissed 476 So.2d 669. Pardon And Parole ⚿ 62

Inmate's appeal from final agency action taken by parole and probation commission is governed by Rules of Appellate Procedure and Administrative Procedure Act (§ 120.51 et seq.). Daniels v. Florida Parole and Probation Commission, App. 1 Dist., 401 So.2d 1351 (1981), approved 444 So.2d 917. Pardon And Parole ⚿ 62

Although direct right of administrative review is available to prison inmate who claims his presumptive release date was incorrectly set by parole and probation commission, it is not necessarily exclusive method of relief; mandamus yet abides as a remedy but mandamus continues subject to judicial restrictions upon its use which require prior resort to an exhaustion of administrative remedies when they are available and adequate. Daniels v. Florida Parole and Probation Commission, App. 1 Dist., 401 So.2d 1351 (1981), approved 444 So.2d 917. Mandamus ⚿ 3(8); Pardon And Parole ⚿ 62

Establishment by parole and probation commission of presumptive parole release date for prisoners is final agency action, for purposes of judicial review. Daniels v. Florida Parole and Probation Commission, App. 1 Dist., 401 So.2d 1351 (1981), approved 444 So.2d 917. Pardon And Parole ⚿ 62

15. —— Grounds, review

Information in psychiatric reports could not properly be relied upon as basis for altering defendant's presumptive parole release date where record was devoid of competent and substantial evidence indicating that psychiatric reports and information contained therein were "new information" not in fact available to Commission at date of initial interview. Wells v. Florida Parole and Probation Com'n, App. 1 Dist., 437 So.2d 767 (1983). Pardon And Parole ⚿ 58

A reinterview was not grounds to relitigate presumptive parole release date determination. Myers v. Florida Parole and Probation Com'n, App. 1 Dist., 423 So.2d 481 (1982). Pardon And Parole ⚿ 57.1

Where state parole and probation commission has amended presumptive parole release dates to be set as much as 11 years beyond previously established release dates and has done so no more than one month prior to date presumed to be parole release date, inmates are entitled to reviews in order to rebut information relied upon by commission in extending such dates. Gobie v. Florida Parole and Probation Com'n, App. 1 Dist., 416 So.2d 838 (1982), review denied 424 So.2d 762. Pardon And Parole ⚷ 62

16. —— Remand, review

Where it was not clear from record before District Court of Appeal why petitioner's presumptive parole release date was changed, and where lower court because it believed mandamus was not proper never reached the substantive issues, though it did state that it believed that petition might have some merit, case would be reversed and remanded to circuit court for expeditious consideration of merits of the petition. Zatler v. State, App. 5 Dist., 457 So.2d 1083 (1984). Pardon And Parole ⚷ 62

Where petitioners and two other prisoners who had also sought belated appeal from final action of the Parole and Probation Commission within 30-day grace period sought to reinstate appeals or to file petitions for writ of mandamus and petitioners' motions were denied while motions of the other two prisoners were granted, the notices of belated appeal and motions to reinstate would be remanded for reconsideration by the district court. Griffith v. Florida Parole & Probation Comm'n, 451 So.2d 457 (1984). Pardon And Parole ⚷ 62

Parole and probation commission order extending inmate's presumptive parole release date would be vacated and the case would be remanded for reconsideration and clarification of commission's decision not to parole inmate where the objective parole guidelines were not used in arriving at the date and where the commission did not provide adequate record support for the reasons it gave in denying parole to inmate and did not explain why some of the reasons given were relevant to parole prognosis. Jackson v. Florida Parole and Probation Com'n, App. 1 Dist., 424 So.2d 930 (1983). Pardon And Parole ⚷ 63

Review of final agency action of the parole and probation commission was not clearly available under Appellate Procedure Rule 9.110 until rendering of decision after petitioner sought review of his presumptive parole release date, and thus remand was required for circuit court to consider the petition on its merits. Tobin v. Greadington, App. 1 Dist., 414 So.2d 36 (1982). Pardon And Parole ⚷ 62

947.174. Subsequent interviews

(1)(a) For any inmate, except an inmate convicted of an offense enumerated in paragraph (b), whose presumptive parole release date falls more than 2 years after the date of the initial interview, a hearing examiner shall schedule an interview for review of the presumptive parole release date. Such interview shall take place within 2 years after the initial interview and every 2 years thereafter.

(b) For any inmate convicted of murder, attempted murder, sexual battery, attempted sexual battery, or who has been sentenced to a 25-year minimum mandatory sentence previously provided in s. 775.082, and whose presumptive parole release date is more than 5 years after the date of the initial interview, a hearing examiner shall schedule an interview for review of the presumptive parole release date. Such interview shall take place once within 5 years after the initial interview and once every 5 years thereafter if the commission finds that it is not reasonable to expect that parole will be granted at a hearing during the following years and states the bases for the finding in writing. For any inmate who is within 7 years of his or her tentative release date, the commission may establish an interview date prior to the 5-year schedule.

(c) Such interviews shall be limited to determining whether or not information has been gathered which might affect the presumptive parole release date. The provisions of this subsection shall not apply to an inmate serving a concurrent sentence in another jurisdiction pursuant to s. 921.16(2).

(2) The commission, for good cause, may at any time request that a hearing examiner conduct a subsequent hearing according to the procedures outlined in this section. Such request shall specify in writing the reasons for such review.

(3) The department shall, within a reasonable amount of time, make available and bring to the attention of the commission such information as is deemed important to the review of the presumptive parole release date, including, but not limited to, current progress reports, psychological reports, and disciplinary reports.

(4) The department or a hearing examiner may recommend that an inmate be placed in a work-release program prior to the last 18 months of her or his confinement before the presumptive parole release date. If the commission does not deny the recommendation within 30 days of the receipt of the recommendation, the inmate may be placed in such a program, and the department shall advise the commission of the fact prior to such placement.

(5) For purposes of this section, the commission shall develop and make available to all inmates guidelines which:

(a) Define what constitutes an unsatisfactory institutional record. In developing such guidelines, the commission shall consult with the department.

(b) Define what constitutes a satisfactory release plan and what constitutes verification of the plan prior to placement on parole.

Laws 1978, c. 78–417, § 15; Laws 1979, c. 79–42, § 9; Laws 1979, c. 79–310, § 4; Laws 1981, c. 81–322, § 6; Laws 1982, c. 82–171, § 13; Laws 1988, c. 88–122, § 21. Amended by Laws 1997, c. 97–102, § 1675, eff. July 1, 1997; Laws 1997, c. 97–289, § 2, eff. Oct. 1, 1997.

Historical and Statutory Notes

Amendment Notes:

Laws 1979, c. 79–42, § 9, provided in subsec. (4) that the department "or a hearing examiner panel" may recommend placement in a work-release program, and in subsec. (6) (a) provided for forwarding a statement to and determination whether or not to authorize the effective parole release date by a panel rather than by the commission.

Laws 1979, c. 79–310, § 4, added the fourth sentence to subsec. (1).

Laws 1981, c. 81–322, § 6, substituted "hearing examiner" for "hearing examiner panel" throughout the section.

Laws 1982, c. 82–171, § 13, modified subsec. (1) to provide for interviews instead of hearings, and deleted subsec. (6), which provided:

"Provided that the inmate's institutional conduct has been satisfactory, the presumptive parole release date shall become the effective parole release date as follows:

"(a) Sixty days prior to the presumptive parole release date, a hearing examiner shall conduct a final interview with the inmate in order to establish an effective parole release date. If it is determined that the inmate's institutional conduct has been unsatisfactory, a statement to this effect shall be made in writing with particularity and forwarded to a panel of no fewer than two commissioners appointed by the chairman. Within 14 days, the panel shall determine whether or not to authorize the effective parole release date, and the inmate shall be notified of the decision in writing within 30 days of the final interview.

"(b) When an effective date of parole has been established, release on that date shall be conditioned upon the completion of a satisfactory plan for parole supervision. An effective date of parole may be delayed for up to 30 days without a hearing for development and approval of release plans."

Laws 1988, c. 88–122, § 21, eff. July 1, 1988, provided for verification of plan prior to placement on parole in subsec. (5)(b).

Laws 1997, c. 97–102, eff. July 1, 1997, removed gender-specific references applicable to human beings from volume 4 of the Florida Statutes without substantive changes in legal effect.

Laws 1997, c. 97–289, § 2, eff. Oct. 1, 1997, rewrote subsec. (1), which formerly read:

"For any inmate whose presumptive parole release date falls more than 2 years after the date of the initial interview, a hearing examiner shall schedule an interview for review of the presumptive parole release date. Such interview shall take place within 2 years after the initial interview and every 2 years thereafter. Such interviews shall be limited to determining whether or not information has been gathered which might affect the presumptive parole release date. The provisions of this subsection shall not apply to an inmate serving a concurrent sentence in another jurisdiction pursuant to s. 921.16(2)."

Library References

Pardon and Parole ⚷59, 62.
Westlaw Topic No. 284.
C.J.S. Pardon and Parole §§ 55, 57.

Research References

Treatises and Practice Aids

16 Florida Practice Series § 10:19, Parole--Eligibility for Parole.

United States Supreme Court

Ex post facto, retroactive change in frequency of parole reconsideration hearings, significant risk of increased punishment, see Garner v. Jones, 2000, 120 S.Ct. 1362, 529 U.S. 244, 146 L.Ed.2d 236, on remand 211 F.3d 1225.

Notes of Decisions

---

1. Ex post facto violations

Ex post facto clause was not violated by retroactive application of statute changing subsequent parole hearings for certain prisoners from every two years to every five years; statute applied to a limited number of inmates, and statute was narrowly constructed. Tuff v. State, App. 3 Dist., 732 So.2d 461 (1999), rehearing denied, review denied 763 So.2d 1046. Constitutional Law ⚷ 2823; Pardon And Parole ⚷ 43

There was no ex post facto violation in confirmation of defendant's presumptive parole release date during his biennial review. Sheets v. Florida Parole and Probation Com'n, App. 1 Dist., 423 So.2d 464 (1982). Constitutional Law ⚷ 2823; Pardon And Parole ⚷ 42.1

Changes in Florida parole law, extending the time interval for parole hearings for certain classes of inmates upon written findings of the Florida Parole Commission, did not create a significant risk of increasing the length of an inmate's imprisonment, and thus, he failed to state a claim for an Ex Post Facto clause violation; it appeared that the statute at issue was crafted to reduce the futile work of frequently re-announcing the denial of parole to a class of prisoners who, in the Commission's broad discretion, were very unlikely to warrant it. Penoyer v. Briggs, C.A.11 (Fla.)2006, 206 Fed. Appx. 962, 2006 WL 3392755, Unreported. Constitutional Law ⚷ 2823; Pardon And Parole ⚷ 43

2. Powers and duties of commission

Under §§ 20.315, 945.10, and this section, should state parole and probation commission determine that particular piece of information is necessary for required determinations and that only department of corrections has resources to obtain such information for inmate's file, commission may have not only power but perhaps even duty to initiate legal action to direct department to acquire information for commission's use. Battis v. Florida Parole and Probation Commission, App. 1 Dist., 386 So.2d 295 (1980). Pardon And Parole ⚷ 57.1

3. Discretion of commission

Parole and probation commission did not err in using guidelines in effect on date of inmate's biennial interview nor by aggravating inmate's score using concurrent sentences. Cook v. Florida Parole and Probation Com'n, App. 1 Dist., 423 So.2d 492 (1982), certiorari denied 103 S.Ct. 1222, 459 U.S. 1218, 75 L.Ed.2d 458. Pardon And Parole ⚷ 53

Although hearing examiner recommended that inmate's presumptive parole release date be reduced by 24 months, Parole and Probation Commission was justified in its determination to reduce presumptive parole release date by only 12 months upon finding that inmate had received two disciplinary reports which were not mentioned by the examiner. Cook v. Florida

Parole and Probation Com'n, App. 1 Dist., 423 So.2d 492 (1982), certiorari denied 103 S.Ct. 1222, 459 U.S. 1218, 75 L.Ed.2d 458. Pardon And Parole ⚷ 60

4. Scope of biennial review hearing

Biennial review could not be used by defendant to litigate issues that could have been raised during initial establishment of his presumptive parole release date. Sheets v. Florida Parole and Probation Com'n, App., 423 So.2d 464 (1982); Van Poyck v. Florida Parole and Probation Com'n, App. 1 Dist., 431 So.2d 692 (1983); Cook v. Florida Parole and Probation Com'n, App., 423 So.2d 492 (1982) certiorari denied 103 S.Ct. 1222, 459 U.S. 1218, 75 L.Ed.2d 458.

Scope of a biennial review hearing is limited to determining whether new information has been gathered since initial interview which might affect the presumptive parole release date. Dornau v. Florida Parole and Probation Com'n, App. 1 Dist., 420 So.2d 894 (1982), petition for review denied 429 So.2d 5. Pardon And Parole ⚷ 59

There was no ex post facto violation in parole and probation commission's refusal to review inmate's original scoring following his biennial reinterview, and reinterview was not an excuse to relitigate establishment of presumptive parole release date. Gatto v. Florida Parole and Probation Com'n, App. 1 Dist., 415 So.2d 869 (1982). Constitutional Law ⚷ 2823; Pardon And Parole ⚷ 53

5. New information

Parole and Probation Commission was not required to mitigate convict's presumptive parole release date either on basis of *Paige* factors, or in absence of those factors; therefore, Commission's refusal, after having found no new information which might affect convict's presumptive parole release date, to consider convict for parole did not violate convict's equal protection or due process rights. Sheley v. Florida Parole and Probation Com'n, App. 1 Dist., 496 So.2d 854 (1986), review denied 506 So.2d 1043. Constitutional Law ⚷ 3821; Constitutional Law ⚷ 4838

Refusal of District Court of Appeal to consider documents not presented to the parole and probation commission during its review of presumptive parole release date would not preclude prisoner from submitting the documents to the commission for consideration as new information. Arlotta v. Florida Parole and Probation Com'n, App. 1 Dist., 419 So.2d 1159 (1982). Pardon And Parole ⚷ 60

Inmate had no right to seek second review of his presumptive parole release date, and his request for review of such which had already been reviewed by parole and probation commission pursuant to § 947.173, was properly denied even insofar as claiming right to "special review" on basis of "new information." Canter v. Florida Parole and Probation Commission, App. 1 Dist., 409 So.2d 227 (1982). Pardon And Parole ⚷ 62

6. Recommendation of examiner

Parole and probation commission did not violate defendant's due process rights when it reduced his presumptive parole release date by only 12 months instead of the 48 months recommended by hearing examiner, since hearing examiner's recommendation was not binding on commission. Dornau v. Florida Parole and Probation Com'n, App. 1 Dist., 420 So.2d 894 (1982), petition for review denied 429 So.2d 5. Constitutional Law ⚷ 4838

7. Habeas corpus

Habeas corpus would be proper remedy for challenging presumptive parole release date only after effective parole release date established pursuant to this section and § 947.18 has passed. Pannier v. Wainwright, App. 5 Dist., 423 So.2d 533 (1982). Habeas Corpus ⚷ 223

8. Review

Refusal of parole commission, upon biennial review of inmate's presumptive parole release date, to consider alleged errors committed during establishment of his parole date two years previous would be affirmed. Broxson v. Florida Parole and Probation Com'n, App. 1 Dist., 425 So.2d 169 (1983). Pardon And Parole ⚷ 60

Occasions when issues raised at first presumptive parole release date review and again at presumptive parole release date review of biennial action may properly be before court are when there is clear clerical or mathematical error in calculation of inmate's presumptive parole release date, when inmate raised constitutional issue which commission, as administrative agency, had no authority to consider, and when inmate had additional proof on new issue that would have effect on his presumptive parole release date and failed to meet standards of proof at first review. McClain v. Florida Parole and Probation Com'n, App. 1 Dist., 416 So.2d 1209 (1982). Pardon And Parole ⚷ 62

Both statutes and parole and probation commission rules grant inmates right to review of commission action establishing presumptive parole release date, and commission grants and court reviews on appeal, commission's biennial action, therefore, commission's denial of review of biennial action constituted final agency action which was appealable. McClain v. Florida Parole and Probation Com'n, App. 1 Dist., 416 So.2d 1209 (1982). Pardon And Parole ⚷ 62

947.1745. Establishment of effective parole release date

If the inmate's institutional conduct has been satisfactory, the presumptive parole release date shall become the effective parole release date as follows:

(1) Within 90 days before the presumptive parole release date, a hearing examiner shall conduct a final interview with the inmate in order to establish an effective parole release date and parole release plan. If it is determined that the inmate's institutional conduct has been unsatisfactory, a statement to this effect shall be made in writing with particularity and shall be forwarded to a panel of no fewer than two commissioners appointed by the chair.

(2) If the panel finds that the inmate's parole release plan is unsatisfactory, this finding may constitute new information and good cause in exceptional circumstances as described in s. 947.173, under which the panel may extend the presumptive parole release date for not more than 1 year. The panel may review any subsequently proposed parole release plan at any time.

(3) Within 30 days after receipt of the inmate's parole release plan, the panel shall determine whether to authorize the effective parole release date. The inmate must be notified of the decision in writing within 30 days after the decision by the panel.

(4) If an effective date of parole has been established, release on that date is conditioned upon the completion of a satisfactory plan for parole supervision. An effective date of parole may be delayed for up to 60 days by a commissioner without a hearing for the development and approval of release plans.

(5) An effective date of parole may be delayed by a commissioner for up to 60 days without a hearing based on:

(a) New information not available at the time of the effective parole release date interview.

(b) Unsatisfactory institutional conduct which occurred subsequent to the effective parole release date interview.

(c) The lack of a verified parole release plan.

(6) Within 90 days before the effective parole release date interview, the commission shall send written notice to the sentencing judge of any inmate who has been scheduled for an effective parole release date interview. If the sentencing judge is no longer serving, the notice must be sent to the chief judge of the circuit in which the offender was sentenced. The chief judge may designate any circuit judge within the circuit to act in the place of the sentencing judge. Within 30 days after receipt of the commission's notice, the sentencing judge, or the designee, shall send to the commission notice of objection to parole release, if the judge objects to such release. If there is objection by the judge, such objection may constitute good cause in exceptional circumstances as described in s. 947.173, and the commission may schedule a subsequent review within 2 years, extending the presumptive parole release date beyond that time. However, for an inmate who has been:

(a) Convicted of murder or attempted murder;

(b) Convicted of sexual battery or attempted sexual battery; or

(c) Sentenced to a 25-year minimum mandatory sentence previously provided in s. 775.082,

the commission may schedule a subsequent review under this subsection once every 5 years, extending the presumptive parole release date beyond that time if the commission finds that it is not reasonable to expect that parole would be granted at a review during the following years and states the bases for the finding in writing. For any inmate who is within 7 years of his or her release date, the commission may schedule a subsequent review prior to the 5 year schedule. With any subsequent review the same procedure outlined above will be followed. If the judge remains silent with respect to parole release, the commission may authorize an effective parole release date. This subsection applies if the commission desires to consider the establishment of an effective release date without delivery of the effective parole release date interview. Notice of the effective release date must be sent to the sentencing judge, and either the judge's response to the notice must be received or the time period allowed for such response must elapse before the commission may authorize an effective release date.

Laws 1982, c. 82–171, § 14; Laws 1983, c. 83–216, § 190; Laws 1986, c. 86–183, § 33; Laws 1988, c. 88–122, § 22; Laws 1991, c. 91–110, § 53; Laws 1993, c. 93–61, § 9. Amended by Laws 1997, c. 97–102, § 1676, eff. July 1, 1997; Laws 1997, c. 97–289, § 3, eff. Oct. 1, 1997.

Historical and Statutory Notes

Amendment Notes:

Laws 1983, c. 83–216, was a reviser's correction bill amending subsec. (3) to provide consistency of terminology within s. 947.1745, which refers to the "parole release date."

Laws 1986, c. 86–183, § 33, eff. Oct. 1, 1986, added subsec. (4).

Laws 1988, c. 88–122, § 22, eff. July 1, 1988, added subsec. (3)(c).

Laws 1991, c. 91–110, a reviser's bill, amended subsec. (4) of this section correctively.

Laws 1993, c. 93–61, § 9, eff. April 22, 1993, rewrote the section, which formerly read:

"If the inmate's institutional conduct has been satisfactory, the presumptive parole release date shall become the effective parole release date as follows:

"(1) Within 90 days prior to the presumptive parole release date, a hearing examiner shall conduct a final interview with the inmate in order to establish an effective parole release date. If it is determined that the inmate's institutional conduct has been unsatisfactory, a statement to this effect shall be made in writing with particularity and shall be forwarded to a panel of no fewer than two commissioners appointed by the chairman. Within 30 days after receipt of the recommendation, the panel shall determine whether or not to authorize the effective parole release date; and the inmate shall be notified of such decision in writing within 30 days of the decision by the panel.

"(2) When an effective date of parole has been established, release on that date shall be conditioned upon the completion of a satisfactory plan for parole supervision. An effective date of parole may be delayed for up to 60 days by a commissioner without a hearing for the development and approval of release plans.

"(3) An effective date of parole may be delayed by a commissioner for up to 60 days without a hearing based on:

"(a) New information not available at the time of the effective parole release date interview.

"(b) Unsatisfactory institutional conduct which occurred subsequent to the effective parole release date interview.

"(c) The lack of a verified parole release plan.

"(4) Within 90 days before the effective parole release date interview, the commission shall send written notice to the sentencing court of any inmate who has been scheduled for an effective parole release date interview. Within 30 days after receipt of the commission's notice, the sentencing court shall send to the commission notice of objection to parole release, provided the court objects to such release. If there is objection by the court, such objection may constitute good cause in exceptional circumstances as described in s. 947.173, and the commission may schedule a subsequent review within 2 years, extending the presumptive parole release date beyond that time. With any subsequent review the same procedure outlined above will be followed. If the court remains silent with respect to parole release, the commission may authorize an effective parole release date. The provisions of this subsection shall be applicable in the event the commission desires to consider the establishment of an effective release date without delivery of the effective parole release date interview. Notice to the sentencing court shall be sent, and either the court's response to the notice must be received or the time period allowed for such response must elapse before the commission can authorize an effective release date."

Laws 1997, c. 97–102, eff. July 1, 1997, removed gender-specific references applicable to human beings from volume 4 of the Florida Statutes without substantive changes in legal effect.

Laws 1997, c. 97–289, § 3, eff. Oct. 1, 1997, in subsec. (6), inserted the sixth sentence.

Cross References

Determination of exact period of imprisonment, indeterminate sentence, see § 921.22.

Library References

Pardon and Parole ⚷50, 54.
Westlaw Topic No. 284.
C.J.S. Pardon and Parole §§ 48 to 51.

Research References

ALR Library

143 ALR 1486, Statute Conferring Power Upon Administrative Body in Respect to the Parole of Prisoners, or the Discharge of Parolees, as Unconstitutional Infringement of Power of Executive or Judiciary.

Treatises and Practice Aids

16 Florida Practice Series § 10:19, Parole--Eligibility for Parole.

16 Florida Practice Series § 10:21, Parole--Effective Parole Release Date.

16 Florida Practice Series § 10:22, Parole--Terms and Conditions of Parole.

United States Supreme Court

Parole, deferral of hearings, ex post facto, see California Department of Corrections v. Morales, 1995, 115 S.Ct. 1597, 131 L.Ed.2d 588.

Notes of Decisions

1. Validity

State statute requiring Florida Parole Commission (FPC) to obtain input from sentencing judge concerning any objections to granting parole did not violate Ex Post Facto Clause as to prisoner whose crime preceded statute's enactment; statute did not restrict FPC's decision, i.e. FPC could reject any judicial objection provided, and thus statute did not alter or add to punishment imposed for underlying crime. Tooma v. Florida Parole Com'n, S.D.Fla.2009, 612 F.Supp.2d 1255. Constitutional Law ⚷ 2823; Pardon and Parole ⚷ 43

Retroactive application of statute requiring Parole Commission to notify sentencing judge of proposed release did not violate the ex post facto clause; even though the statute could work to the inmate's disadvantage by placing a potential obstacle to parole, the statute is procedural, rather than punitive, because the judge's objection does not foreclose parole, and the Commission still retains discretion to set an effective parole release date. Gaines v. Florida Parole

Com'n, App. 4 Dist., 743 So.2d 118 (1999). Constitutional Law ⚿ 2823; Pardon And Parole ⚿ 43

2. Construction and application

Parole Commission is not bound by any determinations of the parole examiner; a hearing examiner conducts an interview with the inmate merely to establish an Effective Parole Release Date (EPRD). Florida Parole Com'n v. Chapman, App. 4 Dist., 919 So.2d 689 (2006), review denied 941 So.2d 367. Pardon And Parole ⚿ 58

Inmate had no legal right to establishment of effective parole release date until 90 days before presumptive parole release date. Johnson v. Florida Parole Com'n, App. 1 Dist., 610 So.2d 624 (1992). Pardon And Parole ⚿ 57.1

3. Double jeopardy

Allowing sentencing court to raise objections to inmate's potential release on parole, which had legal effect of deferring his effective parole release date (EPRD) and preventing his release at presumptive parole release date (PPRD), did not violate double jeopardy, even though court had declined to retain jurisdiction to review Parole Commission release order under statute at time of sentencing; double jeopardy proscriptions did not apply to parole proceedings. Williams v. Florida Parole Com'n, App. 1 Dist., 625 So.2d 926 (1993), review denied 637 So.2d 236. Double Jeopardy ⚿ 31

4. Extending release date

Under Florida parole statutes, Florida Parole Commission (FPC) acted within its discretion by extending parole release date beyond presumed date originally set, based on objection from sentencing court and based on finding of unsatisfactory release plan, and thus extension of release date could not constitute due process violation, regardless of fact that presumed date had been set for some years and periodically reviewed without modification. Tooma v. Florida Parole Com'n, S.D.Fla.2009, 612 F.Supp.2d 1255. Constitutional Law ⚿ 4838; Pardon and Parole ⚿ 50

Parole Commission was authorized to suspend inmate's parole release date, or Effective Parole Release Date (EPRD), notwithstanding parole examiner's recommendations; although parole statute barred Commission from modifying PPRD absent reasons of institutional conduct or acquisition of new information, Commission was authorized to decline to authorize an effective parole release date absent positive findings that inmate was suitable for parole. Florida Parole Com'n v. Chapman, App. 4 Dist., 919 So.2d 689 (2006), review denied 941 So.2d 367. Pardon And Parole ⚿ 63

Parole Commission could use sentencing judge's objection to inmate's release to extend presumptive release date even though objection was essentially the same as objection by same judge used by Commission on earlier occasion to extend the release date. Florida Parole Com'n v. Jackson, App. 1 Dist., 618 So.2d 766 (1993), cause dismissed 624 So.2d 266. Pardon And Parole ⚿ 54

Habeas corpus relief requires showing a right or entitlement to immediate release from custody and is not an available remedy for improper action of parole and probation commission extending presumptive parole release date. Kirsch v. Greadington, App. 1 Dist., 425 So.2d 153 (1983). Habeas Corpus ⚿ 222

Even if action of parole and probation commission extending presumptive parole release date was illegal the inmate was not entitled to automatic release from incarceration as there is no right to parole and commission must make a finding of appropriateness of parole release. Kirsch v. Greadington, App. 1 Dist., 425 So.2d 153 (1983). Pardon And Parole ⚿ 46

5. New information

Attorney General's opinion, concluding that the Parole and Probation Commission cannot parole an inmate on a consecutive sentence which has not yet begun to be served, became effective only after inmate's effective parole release date was approved by, and thus binding on, the Commission, and the opinion could not be applied to justify rescission of the effective parole release date, in that it was not "new information" within meaning of statute, but merely a new interpretation of a statute or rule. Moore v. Wainwright, App. 3 Dist., 469 So.2d 882 (1985). Pardon And Parole ⚿ 49

6. Objection by sentencing court

Objection to presumptive parole release date (PPRD) by sentencing court, which merely referred to "the record" but did not provide specific reason for objection, constituted good cause in exceptional circumstances as required by statute authorizing parole commission to modify PPRD; the record contained psychological report which contained ample reason to regard inmate as unsuitable for parole. Florida Parole Com'n v. Snipes, App. 1 Dist., 616 So.2d 1177 (1993). Pardon And Parole ⚿ 54

Sentencing court's written objection to parole release could constitute "good cause in exceptional circumstances" and could be used by Parole and Probation Commission to extend the presumptive parole release date. Florida Parole and Probation Com'n v. Dornau, App. 1 Dist., 534 So.2d 789 (1988). Pardon And Parole ⚿ 54

Parole and Probation Commission was not required to provide an explanation of reason for length of presumptive parole release date extension based on sentencing court's objection to parole release. Florida Parole and Probation Com'n v. Dornau, App. 1 Dist., 534 So.2d 789 (1988). Pardon And Parole ⚷ 61

7. Pleadings

State prisoner's due process and ex post facto challenge to parole board's extension of his parole release date was cognizable under § 1983, and did not have to be converted to habeas corpus petition, since challenge was essentially procedural and outside core of habeas corpus; prisoner sought more transparency in board's decision-making process, and sought to be evaluated under parole eligibility procedures in existence at time of conviction, prior to enactment of statute requiring board to obtain input from sentencing judge. Tooma v. Florida Parole Com'n, S.D.Fla.2009, 612 F.Supp.2d 1255. Civil Rights ⚷ 1097; Habeas Corpus ⚷ 666

8. Mandamus

Petition for writ of habeas corpus seeking to have effective parole release date set should have been petition for writ of mandamus and it would be treated as such. Sanders v. State, Florida Parole Com'n, App. 3 Dist., 756 So.2d 236 (2000), mandate recalled 761 So.2d 1119. Mandamus ⚷ 154(2)

9. Notice

Inmate's petition alleging that sentencing judge continued to serve as a judge, despite her official retirement, raised a prima facie claim that inmate was entitled to a parole release date based on the Parole Commission's failure to notify the judge. Gaines v. Florida Parole Com'n, App. 4 Dist., 743 So.2d 118 (1999). Pardon And Parole ⚷ 57.1

10. Service

"Service" by sentencing judge for purposes of statute that requires the Parole Commission to notify and request comment from the sentencing judge, unless the judge is no longer serving, may include acting as a senior judge, at least where that judge is acting under a general appointment and not an appointment restricted to one particular case. Gaines v. Florida Parole Com'n, App. 4 Dist., 743 So.2d 118 (1999). Pardon And Parole ⚷ 57.1

947.1746. Establishment of effective parole release date

Within 30 days of the receipt of new information or upon receipt of a written recommendation from the department that an inmate be considered for mitigation of the authorized presumptive parole release date, the commission may, at its discretion, provide for a final interview to establish an effective parole release date or may review the official record and establish an effective parole release date without provision of a final interview, unless an interview is requested by no fewer than two commissioners.

Laws 1983, c. 83–131, § 27.

Historical and Statutory Notes

Amendment Notes:

Repeal of enumerated provisions of this chapter by Laws 1983, c. 83–131, § 34, as discussed in the note at the head of this chapter was not applicable to this section which was not included within the enumeration.

Library References

Pardon and Parole ⚷50.
Westlaw Topic No. 284.
C.J.S. Pardon and Parole §§ 48 to 51.

Research References

Treatises and Practice Aids

16 Florida Practice Series § 10:22, Parole--Terms and Conditions of Parole.

947.1747. Community control as a special condition of parole

Upon the establishment of an effective parole release date as provided for in ss. 947.1745 and 947.1746, the commission may, as a special condition of parole, require an inmate to be placed in the community control program of the Department of Corrections as described in s. 948.10 for a period not exceeding 6 months. In every case in which the commission decides to place an inmate on community control as a special condition of parole, the commission shall provide a written explanation of the reasons for its decision.

Laws 1988, c. 88–122, § 68. Amended by Laws 2004, c. 2004–373, § 42, eff. July 1, 2004.

Historical and Statutory Notes

Amendment Notes:

Laws 2004, c. 2004–373, § 42, reenacted this section for the purpose of incorporating the amendment to § 948.10 in a reference thereto.

Library References

Pardon and Parole ⚷64.1.
Westlaw Topic No. 284.
C.J.S. Pardon and Parole § 59.

Research References

Treatises and Practice Aids

16 Florida Practice Series § 10:22, Parole--Terms and Conditions of Parole.

947.175. Repealed by Laws 2001, c. 2001–124, § 7, eff. July 1, 2001

Historical and Statutory Notes

Repealed § 947.175, which related to notice to local agencies, was derived from:
Laws 1991, c. 91–225, § 23.
Laws 1988, c. 88–122, § 23.
Laws 1983, c. 83–131, § 26.
Laws 1979, c. 79–3, § 108.
Laws 1978, c. 78–417, § 16.
Laws 1977, c. 77–303, § 1.
Laws 1975, c. 75–49, § 15.

947.177. Repealed by Laws 2001, c. 2001–124, § 7, eff. July 1, 2001

Historical and Statutory Notes

Repealed § 947.177, which related to inmate release and notice by the Department of Corrections, Control Release Authority, or Parole Commission, was derived from:
Laws 1998, c. 98–81, § 12.
Laws 1997, c. 97–299, § 12.
Laws 1996, c. 96–312, § 36.
Laws 1992, c. 92–76, § 4.
Laws 1991, c. 91–225, § 24.
Laws 1991, c. 91–65, § 2.
Laws 1988, c. 88–122, § 24.
Laws 1985, c. 85–107, § 3.

947.18. Conditions of parole

No person shall be placed on parole merely as a reward for good conduct or efficient performance of duties assigned in prison. No person shall be placed on parole until and unless the commission finds that there is reasonable probability that, if the person is placed on parole, he or she will live and conduct himself or herself as a respectable and law-abiding person and that the person's release will be compatible with his or her own welfare and the welfare of society. No person shall be placed on parole unless and until the commission is satisfied that he or she will be suitably employed in self-sustaining employment or that he or she will not become a public charge. The commission shall determine the terms upon which such person shall be granted parole. If the person's conviction was for a controlled substance violation, one of the conditions must be that the person submit to random substance abuse testing intermittently throughout the term of supervision, upon the direction of the correctional probation officer as defined in s. 943.10(3). In addition to any other lawful condition of parole, the commission may make the payment of the debt due and owing to the state under s. 960.17 or the payment of the attorney's fees and costs due and owing to the state under s. 938.29 a condition of parole subject to modification based on change of circumstances. If the person's conviction was for a crime that was found to have been committed for the purpose of benefiting, promoting, or furthering the interests of a criminal gang, one of the conditions must be that the person be prohibited from knowingly associating with other criminal gang members or associates, except as authorized by law enforcement officials, prosecutorial authorities, or the court, for the purpose of aiding in the investigation of criminal activity.

Laws 1941, c. 20519, § 14; Laws 1977, c. 77–452, § 4; Laws 1983, c. 83–256, § 2; Laws 1988, c. 88–122, § 72; Laws 1990, c. 90–337, § 15. Amended by Laws 1996, c. 96–232, § 4, eff. Jan. 1, 1997; Laws 1997, c. 97–102, § 1875, eff. July 1, 1997; Laws 1997, c. 97–271, § 43, eff. July 1, 1997; Laws 2003, c. 2003–402, § 135, eff. July 1, 2004; Laws 2008, c. 2008–238, § 22, eff. Oct. 1, 2008.

Historical and Statutory Notes

Amendment Notes:

Laws 1977, c. 77–452, added the fifth sentence.

Laws 1983, c. 83–256, § 2, provided for the payment of attorneys fees and costs due and owing the county.

Laws 1988, c. 88–122, § 72, eff. July 1, 1988, added at the end of the fourth sentence language following "person shall be granted parole".

Laws 1990, c. 90–337, § 15, eff. Oct. 1, 1990, inserted provisions pertaining to persons convicted of controlled substance violations.

Laws 1990, c. 90–337, § 22 provided therein that the amendment take effect July 1, 1990; however, approval by the governor occurred subsequent thereto. The Florida Supreme Court in an advisory opinion to the governor of July 19, 1979 (374 So.2d 959) stated in part "* * * the effective date provided in the bill is inoperative unless the bill becomes law on or before that date" and concludes that under such circumstances the provision of Const. Art. 3, § 9, that the law take effect on the sixtieth day after adjournment sine die of the session of the legislature in which enacted, is applicable.

Laws 1996, c. 96–232, § 4, eff. Jan. 1, 1997, reenacted this section for the purpose of incorporating an amendment to § 27.56 in reference thereto.

Laws 1997, c. 97–102, eff. July 1, 1997, removed gender-specific references applicable to human beings from volume 4 of the Florida Statutes without substantive changes in legal effect.

Laws 1997, c. 97–271, § 43, eff. July 1, 1997, substituted a reference to § 938.29 for a reference to § 27.56 in the last sentence.

Laws 2003, c. 2003–402, § 135, in the last sentence, substituted "the state" for "a county".

Laws 2008, c. 2008–238, § 22, added the last sentence, relating to criminal gangs.

Cross References

Florida Crimes Compensation Act, see § 960.01 et seq.
Mental health treatment as condition of parole, see § 945.47.

Parolee contribution, supervision and rehabilitation costs, see § 948.09.
Restitution as condition of parole, see § 775.089.

Law Review and Journal Commentaries

Concern renewed for victim. Eric Smith, 52 Fla.B.J. 16 (1978).

Library References

Pardon and Parole ⚷64.1.
Westlaw Topic No. 284.
C.J.S. Pardon and Parole § 59.

Research References

Treatises and Practice Aids

16 Florida Practice Series § 10:22, Parole--Terms and Conditions of Parole.

Notes of Decisions

---

1. Discretion of commission

Parole Commission was not precluded from considering seriousness and facts of inmate's offenses as grounds for suspension of presumptive parole release date, under statute granting Commission discretion in determination of parole eligibility. Welsch v. State, App. 2 Dist., 823 So.2d 310 (2002). Pardon And Parole ⚷ 63

Order denying parole to defendant, who was convicted of forcible rape of ten-year-old girl, was within Parole Commission's discretion. Sanders v. State, Florida Parole Com'n, App. 3 Dist., 756 So.2d 236 (2000), mandate recalled 761 So.2d 1119. Pardon And Parole ⚷ 44

The ultimate parole decision is left to the discretion of the Parole Commission, which is guided by its rules. Sanders v. State, Florida Parole Com'n, App. 3 Dist., 756 So.2d 236 (2000), mandate recalled 761 So.2d 1119. Pardon And Parole ⚷ 47

Statutory law gives Parole Commission broad discretion over release of inmate on parole by obligating it to determine ultimate question of whether there is reasonable probability that inmate, if placed on parole, will live and conduct himself as respectable and law-abiding person and that his release will be compatible with his own welfare and welfare of society; although Commission may be aided in exercising this discretion by relying on or drawing inferences from evidence of past events and conduct, Commission is required by its rules to consider inmate's entire official record; and Commission must review and consider current as well as past information in file. Williams v. Florida Parole Com'n, App. 1 Dist., 625 So.2d 926 (1993), review denied 637 So.2d 236. Pardon And Parole ⚷ 47; Pardon And Parole ⚷ 58

Parole and Probation Commission did not abuse its discretion in declining to authorize recommended effective parole release date, thereby denying parole, solely upon basis of information which was previously considered, or available for consideration, in setting inmate's presumptive parole release date, even though inmate's presumptive parole release date could not be modified absent new information or unfavorable institutional conduct. Florida Parole and Probation Com'n v. Paige, 462 So.2d 817 (1985). Pardon And Parole ⚷ 58

Parole lies within sound discretion of state parole and probation commission. Gobie v. Florida Parole and Probation Com'n, App. 1 Dist., 416 So.2d 838 (1982), review denied 424 So.2d 762. Pardon And Parole ⚷ 47

2. Court recommendations

Trial court's recommendations as to conditions of parole may be either accepted or rejected by parole commission. Owens v. State, App. 1 Dist., 308 So.2d 171 (1975). Pardon And Parole ⚷ 64.1

Though trial court has no authority to grant parole, it is not precluded from recommending conditions of parole. Owens v. State, App. 1

Dist., 308 So.2d 171 (1975). Pardon And Parole ⚷ 64.1

3. Liability of commissioners

Members of the parole and probation commission were immune from damages liability to mother of eight-year-old child for their alleged failure to comply with this section in releasing prisoner on parole who subsequently killed the child. Berry v. State, App. 4 Dist., 400 So.2d 80 (1981), review denied 411 So.2d 380. Pardon And Parole ⚷ 56

4. Criminal record information

Fact that Parole Commission is authorized to deny parole release solely on basis of "old" information in inmate's file, does not relieve Parole Commission of obligation to consider new or current information in reaching its decision. Williams v. Florida Parole Com'n, App. 1 Dist., 625 So.2d 926 (1993), review denied 637 So.2d 236. Pardon And Parole ⚷ 58

Under §§ 20.315, 945.10 and 947.174, should state parole and probation commission determine that particular piece of information is necessary for required determinations and that only department of corrections has resources to obtain such information for inmate's file, commission may have not only power but perhaps even duty to initiate legal action to direct department to acquire information for commission's use. Battis v. Florida Parole and Probation Commission, App. 1 Dist., 386 So.2d 295 (1980). Pardon And Parole ⚷ 57.1

Where state parole and probation commission has no information as to inmate's criminal history prior to offense for which he is presently incarcerated, he must be assigned salient factor score of zero except where burglary is present offense of conviction, in which case salient factor score of "one" is computed. Battis v. Florida Parole and Probation Commission, App. 1 Dist., 386 So.2d 295 (1980). Pardon And Parole ⚷ 53

5. Aggravating factors

If, after state parole and probation commission has computed proper matrix time range, using available information, aggravating circumstances are to be applied, commission is obligated both by statute and rule to explain aggravating factors in writing, for benefit of inmate and to facilitate appropriate review. Battis v. Florida Parole and Probation Commission, App. 1 Dist., 386 So.2d 295 (1980). Pardon And Parole ⚷ 61

6. Release date

Suspension of defendant's presumptive parole release date on basis of information previously considered when presumptive release date was set is not an abuse of discretion. McCorvey v. Florida Parole Com'n, App. 1 Dist., 625 So.2d 1296 (1993). Pardon And Parole ⚷ 63

Parole Commission's cited reasons for suspending inmate's presumptive parole release date (PPRD) and refusing to set his effective parole release date (EPRD), while facially sufficient, were insufficient to determine whether Commission complied with its rules or otherwise acted improperly; to make determination trial court should have had available for review those portions of inmate's file that were relevant and material to reasons cited by Commission's order and issues presented in petition for mandamus; remand for further proceedings was therefore required, at which time Commission might supplement its response to circuit court's order to show cause and, if deemed necessary, present additional information at evidentiary hearing. Williams v. Florida Parole Com'n, App. 1 Dist., 625 So.2d 926 (1993), review denied 637 So.2d 236. Pardon And Parole ⚷ 63

Even if action of parole and probation commission extending presumptive parole release date was illegal the inmate was not entitled to automatic release from incarceration as there is no right to parole and commission must make a finding of appropriateness of parole release. Kirsch v. Greadington, App. 1 Dist., 425 So.2d 153 (1983). Pardon And Parole ⚷ 46

Pre and postsentence investigation report, while undoubtedly helpful, is not indispensable to establishment of presumptive parole release date and, absent such document, state parole and probation commission is nevertheless obligated to evaluate each inmate by considering whatever information is available such as FBI or FDCLE rap sheets, imposed judgments and sentences, reports concerning inmate's conduct while incarcerated and recommendations of trial judge. Battis v. Florida Parole and Probation Commission, App. 1 Dist., 386 So.2d 295 (1980). Pardon And Parole ⚷ 58

7. Denial of parole

Denying parolee, upon revocation of parole, credit for time served on parole and mandatory conditional release was not abuse of discretion of Parole and Probation Commission. Bronson v. Florida Parole and Probation Com'n, App. 1 Dist., 474 So.2d 409 (1985). Pardon And Parole ⚷ 76

Findings that respondent was in need of treatment as mentally disordered sex offender, that he suffered from psychosexual disorder and compulsion to commit sex acts against women and that he had been disciplined for fantasizing sexual feelings toward female correction employees provided sufficient basis to deny setting effective parole release date. Parole & Probation Com'n v. Bruce, 471 So.2d 7 (1985). Pardon And Parole ⚷ 49

If no reasons are present to justify changing a presumptive parole release date, parole may only be denied if parole and probation commission is unable to find that there is reasonable probability that, if placed on parole, he will live and conduct himself as respectable and law-abiding person and that his release will be compatible with his own welfare and welfare of society. Jackson v. Florida Parole and Probation Com'n, App. 1 Dist., 429 So.2d 1306 (1983). Pardon And Parole ⚷ 48.1

In exercising limited discretion remaining with parole and probation commission subsequent to enactment of Objective Parole Guidelines Act, commission may not act arbitrarily or capriciously; rather, commission's decision to deny parole by invoking this section governing conditions of parole will not be upheld unless commission explicates its reasons for its actions in manner sufficient to permit judicial review for determination of whether commission has overreached legislative grant of discretion provided in Act. Jackson v. Florida Parole and Probation Com'n, App. 1 Dist., 429 So.2d 1306 (1983). Pardon And Parole ⚷ 61

Parole and probation commission was apparently incapable of offering any reasonable basis for its conclusory statement that it was unable to find that there was a reasonable probability that, if prisoner was placed on parole, he would live and conduct himself as respectable and law-abiding citizen and that his release was incompatible with welfare of either prisoner or society; therefore, actions of commission in refusing, four days before his parole date, to grant prisoner parole and, instead, extending his presumptive parole release date by 39 years under this section governing conditions of parole was arbitrary and capricious and an abuse of discretion. Jackson v. Florida Parole and Probation Com'n, App. 1 Dist., 429 So.2d 1306 (1983). Pardon And Parole ⚷ 63

8. Court imposed conditions

Parole and probation commission, not the courts, have sole authority to establish conditions of parole. Ferrell v. State, App. 2 Dist., 437 So.2d 782 (1983); Taylor v. State, App., 426 So.2d 73 (1983).

Trial court erred to extent that it established conditions of defendant's parole. Ferrell v. State, App. 2 Dist., 437 So.2d 782 (1983). Pardon And Parole ⚷ 54

Although trial court could make recommendations concerning parole, it could not order defendant, who was convicted of second-degree murder and robbery, to pay lien in amount of $1,400 for court-appointed counsel as condition of any parole. Lee v. State, App. 2 Dist., 429 So.2d 813 (1983). Pardon And Parole ⚷ 64.1

While trial court may recommend conditions of parole, it may not impose conditions of parole, and thus trial court's order requiring defendant to pay $1,000 for court-appointed counsel as condition of any parole was improper. Hunt v. State, App. 2 Dist., 429 So.2d 811 (1983). Pardon And Parole ⚷ 54

Trial court erred when, in addition to imposing prison sentence, it ordered that $67 in court costs, $1,275 in court-appointed attorney fees, and restitution to victim be paid within five years as a condition of parole. Taylor v. State, App. 2 Dist., 426 So.2d 73 (1983). Pardon And Parole ⚷ 54

While trial court may make recommendations concerning parole, it may not impose conditions of parole. Taylor v. State, App. 2 Dist., 426 So.2d 73 (1983). Pardon And Parole ⚷ 54

Defendant, who allowed taking of his footprint by police only because his parole officer made it clear that to do otherwise would violate condition of his parole to carry out all instructions of his parole officer, did not voluntarily consent to taking of his footprint. Kinsler v. State, App. 2 Dist., 360 So.2d 24 (1978). Pardon And Parole ⚷ 68

Parolee's agreement to be bound by conditions of parole presupposes a valid imprisonment in the first instance to support the agreement, and parolee will ordinarily be required to comply with conditions of his parole and may be reincarcerated for their breach. Sellers v. Bridges, 153 Fla. 586, 15 So.2d 293 (1943). Pardon And Parole ⚷ 65

9. Ex post facto violations

Denying parole to defendant, who was convicted of forcible rape of ten-year-old girl, did not violate prohibition on ex post facto laws, where defendant was on fair notice when he committed offense that, if convicted, he would be held in prison solely at Parole Commission's discretion and he remained incarcerated at Commission's sole discretion. Sanders v. State, Florida Parole Com'n, App. 3 Dist., 756 So.2d 236 (2000), mandate recalled 761 So.2d 1119. Constitutional Law ⚷ 2823; Pardon And Parole ⚷ 42.1

10. Habeas corpus

Habeas corpus would be proper remedy for challenging presumptive parole release date only after effective parole release date established pursuant to § 947.174 and this section has passed. Pannier v. Wainwright, App. 5 Dist., 423 So.2d 533 (1982). Habeas Corpus ⚷ 223

11. Review

To facilitate judicial review of a challenge to the suspension of an inmate's presumptive parole release date, the Parole Commission must articulate with specificity the reasons for its decision and provide the information from the complete official record in the inmate's case that supports those reasons. Welsch v. State, App. 2 Dist., 823 So.2d 310 (2002). Pardon And Parole ⚷ 63

Reviewing court's jurisdiction in reviewing denial of parole is limited to determining whether Parole Commission has departed from requirements of law in reaching its decision, and to direct reconsideration of that decision in manner that complies with law if noncompliance is found. Williams v. Florida Parole Com'n, App. 1 Dist., 625 So.2d 926 (1993), review denied 637 So.2d 236. Pardon And Parole ⚷ 62

947.181. Victim restitution as condition of parole

(1)(a) The Parole Commission shall require as a condition of parole reparation or restitution to the aggrieved party for the damage or loss caused by the offense for which the parolee was imprisoned unless the commission finds reasons to the contrary. If the commission does not order restitution or orders only partial restitution, the commission shall state on the record the reasons therefor. The amount of such reparation or restitution shall be determined by the Parole Commission.

(b) If the parolee fails to make the reparation or restitution to the aggrieved party as authorized in paragraph (a), it shall be considered by the commission as a violation of parole as specified in s. 947.21 and may be cause for revocation of her or his parole.

(2) If a defendant is paroled, any restitution ordered under s. 775.089 shall be a condition of such parole. The Parole Commission may revoke parole if the defendant fails to comply with such order. In determining whether to revoke parole, the Parole Commission shall consider the defendant's employment status, earning ability, and financial resources; the willfulness of the defendant's failure to pay; and any other special circumstances that may have a bearing on the defendant's ability to pay.

Laws 1977, c. 77–150, § 3; Laws 1979, c. 79–400, § 304; Laws 1984, c. 84–363, §§ 5, 10; Laws 1988, c. 88–122, § 25; Laws 1993, c. 93–37, § 9. Amended by Laws 1997, c. 97–102, § 1677, eff. July 1, 1997.

Historical and Statutory Notes

Amendment Notes:

Laws 1979, c. 79–400, a reviser's bill, conformed the sections of Fla.St.1977 to additions, substitutions, and deletions editorially supplied therein in order to remove inconsistencies, redundancies, unnecessary repetition and otherwise clarify the statutes and facilitate their correct interpretation.

Laws 1984, c. 84–363, § 10, in subsec. (1)(a), in the first sentence, substituted "shall" for "may" and inserted "unless the commission finds reasons to the contrary", deleted the second sentence which pertained to the determination of the maximum amount of reparation or restitution, and interpolated a new second sentence.

Section 5 of Laws 1984, c. 84–363 added provisions appearing as subsec. (2) in Fla.St. 1984, Supp.

Laws 1988, c. 88–122, § 25, eff. July 1, 1988, changed the commission name from "parole and probation" to "parole".

Laws 1993, c. 93–37, § 9, eff. Oct. 1, 1993, reenacted subsec. (2) for the purpose of incorporating the amendment to § 775.089 in a reference thereto.

Section 16 of Laws 1993, c. 93–37, provides:

"This act shall take effect upon becoming a law, except that sections 1–12 and section 14 of this act shall take effect October 1, 1993, and shall apply to offenses committed on or after October 1, 1993."

Laws 1997, c. 97–102, eff. July 1, 1997, removed gender-specific references applicable to human beings from volume 4 of the Florida Statutes without substantive changes in legal effect.

Cross References

Restitution as condition of parole, see § 775.089.

Library References

Pardon and Parole ⚷64.1.
Westlaw Topic No. 284.
C.J.S. Pardon and Parole § 59.

Research References

Treatises and Practice Aids

16 Florida Practice Series § 10:22, Parole--Terms and Conditions of Parole.

Notes of Decisions

Construction and application 2
Delegation of authority 3
Validity 1

1. Validity

Statute granting parole commission the authority to impose restitution as condition of parole does not violate separation of powers provision of State Constitution by delegating judicial task to administrative agency; State Constitution explicitly gives parole commission the power to make parole determinations, thus creating exception to separation of powers provision. Harvin v. State, App. 1 Dist., 690 So.2d 652 (1997), rehearing denied, review denied 697 So.2d 1216. Constitutional Law ⚷ 2625(1); Pardon And Parole ⚷ 43

2. Construction and application

Restitution order attending probation for two minors was not erroneous because it required each to repay $172, one third of the aggregate thefts committed by the minors and another using the same credit card. Wallace v. Walton Context Bldg., App. 1 Dist., 379 So.2d 1311 (1980), rehearing granted 383 So.2d 729.

3. Delegation of authority

Written probation order, which could be interpreted to mean that Probation and Parole Commission or a probation officer was to determine amount of restitution to be paid by defendant, as well as schedule of repayment, was an unlawful delegation of responsibility exclusively that of court. McClure v. State, App. 2 Dist., 371 So.2d 196 (1979). Constitutional Law ⚷ 2574; Sentencing And Punishment ⚷ 1914

Where defendant pleaded nolo contendere to charge against her pursuant to a plea bargain that she would be placed on probation for five years with special condition that she make restitution of property taken in burglary and two others, act of trial court in failing thereafter to afford defendant required hearing as to amount of restitution and, instead, delegating authority to defendant's probation supervisor was improper. Kroenke v. State, App. 2 Dist., 366 So.2d 46 (1978), certiorari denied 374 So.2d 99. Sentencing And Punishment ⚷ 1973(3)

947.185. Application for mental retardation services as condition of parole

The Parole Commission may require as a condition of parole that any inmate who has been diagnosed as mentally retarded as defined in s. 393.063 shall, upon release, apply for services from the Agency for Persons with Disabilities.

Laws 1983, c. 83–274, § 9; Laws 1988, c. 88–122, § 26. Amended by Laws 1999, c. 99–8, § 322, eff. June 29, 1999; Laws 2006, c. 2006–227, § 66, eff. July 1, 2006.

Historical and Statutory Notes

Amendment Notes:

Laws 1988, c. 88–122, § 26, eff. July 1, 1988, changed the commission name from "parole and probation" to "parole".

Laws 1999, c. 99–8, § 322, eff. June 29, 1999, substituted "Department of Children and Family Services" for "Department of Health and Rehabilitative Services".

Laws 2006, c. 2006–227, § 66, substituted "services of the Agency for Persons with Disabilities" for "retardation services from the Department of Children and Family Services" at the end.

Law Review and Journal Commentaries

Executing the mentally retarded: The status of Florida Law. David A. Davis, 65 Fla.B.J. 12 (Feb. 1991).

Library References

Pardon and Parole ⚷64.1.
Westlaw Topic No. 284.
C.J.S. Pardon and Parole § 59.

Research References

Treatises and Practice Aids

16 Florida Practice Series § 10:22, Parole--Terms and Conditions of Parole.

947.19. Terms of parole

(1) The commission, upon authorizing an effective parole release date, shall specify in writing the terms and conditions of the parole, a certified copy of which shall be given to the parolee.

(2) A parolee may, within 120 days of receipt of the certified copy of the terms and conditions of parole, request that the commission modify the terms and conditions of parole; the parolee must specify in writing the reasons for requesting such modifications.

(3) A panel of no fewer than two commissioners appointed by the chair shall consider requests for review of the terms and conditions of parole, render a written decision to continue or to modify the terms and conditions of parole, specifying the reasons therefor, and inform the parolee of the decision in writing within 30 days of the date of receipt of request for review. Such panel shall not include those commissioners who authorized the original conditions of parole.

(4) During any period of requested review of terms and conditions of parole, the parolee shall be subject to the authorized terms and conditions of parole until such time according to the provisions of this section a decision is made to continue or modify the terms and conditions of parole.

Laws 1941, c. 20519, § 15; Laws 1945, c. 22858, § 7; Laws 1978, c. 78–417, § 17; Laws 1979, c. 79–42, § 10; Laws 1982, c. 82–171, § 15. Amended by Laws 1997, c. 97–102, § 1678, eff. July 1, 1997.

Historical and Statutory Notes

Amendment Notes:

Laws 1945, c. 22858, § 7, substituted, at the end of the second sentence, the word "parolee" for "parole".

Laws 1978, c. 78-417, reworded and combined the first two sentences and added a new second sentence to provisions designated as subsec. (1), and added subsecs. (2) to (4).

Laws 1979, c. 79-42, § 10, provided for review in subsecs. (3) and (4) by a panel rather than by the commission and added the second sentence of subsec. (3).

Laws 1982, c. 82-171, § 15, in subsec. (1), deleted the second sentence which provided: "The terms and conditions of parole shall be based on objective guidelines."; and in subsec. (2), substituted "120" for "30" days.

Laws 1997, c. 97-102, eff. July 1, 1997, removed gender-specific references applicable to human beings from volume 4 of the Florida Statutes without substantive changes in legal effect.

Cross References

Discharge of inmates from mental health treatment, see § 945.47.
Parolee contribution, supervision and rehabilitation costs, see § 948.09.
Restitution as condition of parole, see §§ 775.089, 947.181.

Library References

Pardon and Parole ⚿64.1.
Westlaw Topic No. 284.
C.J.S. Pardon and Parole § 59.

Research References

Treatises and Practice Aids

16 Florida Practice Series § 10:19, Parole--Eligibility for Parole.

16 Florida Practice Series § 10:22, Parole--Terms and Conditions of Parole.

16 Florida Practice Series § 10:24, Discharge from Parole Supervision or Release Supervision.

Notes of Decisions

Construction and application 1

1. Construction and application

Where parolee executed certificate of parole with full knowledge of its contents, agreeing to remain under supervision for six and one-half years, where he acquiesced in the terms and conditions of his parole without reservation, where he did not request a written statement of reasons for his extended term of parole nor seek administrative review, where his parole was revoked after two years of supervision had passed, and where he acted only upon his violation of the parole conditions, the Parole and Probation Commission's failure to provide written reasons for the extended term of parole beyond the standard two-year maximum was not jurisdictional; thus, parolee was still on parole at time of its revocation. Roach v. Mitchell, App. 2 Dist., 456 So.2d 963 (1984). Pardon And Parole ⚿ 78

Parole release date was properly conditioned by parole and probation commission on inmate's waiver of extradition to another state in which he had time to serve on sentence imposed there and inmate's refusal to accept terms offered constituted rejection of commission's proper offer of parole so that commission did not err in withholding parole. Todd v. Florida Parole & Probation Commission, App. 1 Dist., 410 So.2d 584 (1982). Pardon And Parole ⚿ 65

947.20. Rules of commission

The commission shall adopt general rules on the terms and conditions of parole and what shall constitute the violation thereof and may make special rules to govern particular cases. Such rules, both general and special, may include, among other things, a requirement that the parolee shall not leave the state or any definite area in Florida without the consent of the commission;

that the parolee shall contribute to the support of her or his dependents to the best of her or his ability; that the parolee shall make reparation or restitution for her or his crime; that the parolee shall not associate with persons engaged in criminal activity; and that the parolee shall carry out the instructions of her or his parole supervisor and, in general, comport herself or himself in accordance with the terms and conditions of her or his parole.

Laws 1941, c. 20519, § 15; Laws 1978, c. 78–417, § 18. Amended by Laws 1997, c. 97–102, § 1679, eff. July 1, 1997.

Historical and Statutory Notes

Amendment Notes:

Laws 1978, c. 78–417, substituted in the second sentence "not associate with persons engaged in criminal activity" for "abandon civil associates and ways" and "in accordance with terms and conditions of his parole" for "as supervisor shall determine".

Laws 1997, c. 97–102, eff. July 1, 1997, removed gender-specific references applicable to human beings from volume 4 of the Florida Statutes without substantive changes in legal effect.

Law Review and Journal Commentaries

But what about the victim? 22 U.Fla.L.Rev. 1 (1969).

Instruction as to possibility of parole as reversible error. 7 Miami L.Q. 120 (1952).

Library References

Pardon and Parole ⚿64.1.
Westlaw Topic No. 284.
C.J.S. Pardon and Parole § 59.

Notes of Decisions

Construction and application 1
Habeas corpus 2

1. Construction and application

Under this section, the commission, upon placing a person on parole, is given authority to specify the terms and conditions of his parole. Sellers v. Bridges, 153 Fla. 586, 15 So.2d 293 (1943).

The Florida parole commission has authority to require an individual, who is being considered for parole, to deposit funds to be used for transportation expenses in event of violation of parole. Op.Atty.Gen., 1948, p. 612.

2. Habeas corpus

A parolee, though not physically confined in prison, could maintain habeas corpus to secure discharge from penal supervision under a judgment and sentence entered upon an information which wholly failed to charge an offense, since conditions of parole constituted such a restraint of freedom as rendered parolee for all practical purposes in "custody". Sellers v. Bridges, 153 Fla. 586, 15 So.2d 293 (1943). Habeas Corpus ⚿ 516.1

947.21. Violations of parole

(1) A violation of the terms of parole may render the parolee liable to arrest and a return to prison to serve out the term for which the parolee was sentenced.

(2) An offender whose parole is revoked may, at the discretion of the commission, be credited with any portion of the time the offender has satisfactorily served on parole.

Laws 1941, c. 20519, § 15; Laws 1974, c. 74–112, § 22. Amended by Laws 1997, c. 97–102, § 1680, eff. July 1, 1997.

Historical and Statutory Notes

Amendment Notes:

Laws 1974, c. 74–112, § 22, deleted the former second sentence, and added subsec. (2). The former second sentence provided: "No part of the time he may have been on parole shall in such event, in any manner diminish the time of such sentence."

Laws 1997, c. 97–102, eff. July 1, 1997, removed gender-specific references applicable to human beings from volume 4 of the Florida Statutes without substantive changes in legal effect.

Law Review and Journal Commentaries

Parole revocation: Due process or star chamber? Richard A. Belz, 52 Fla.Bar J. 22 (1978).

Library References

Pardon and Parole ⚷69, 76.
Westlaw Topic No. 284.
C.J.S. Pardon and Parole §§ 65, 90 to 92.

Research References

ALR Library

28 ALR 947, Parole as Suspending Running of Sentence.

Treatises and Practice Aids

16 Florida Practice Series § 10:22, Parole--Terms and Conditions of Parole.

16 Florida Practice Series § 10:23, Parole--Violations of Parole.

United States Supreme Court

Habeas corpus, parole violation, in-custody requirement, collateral consequences, see Spencer v. Kemna, U.S.MO.1998, 118 S.Ct. 978.

Notes of Decisions

---

1. Validity

This section giving to State Parole and Probation Commission the discretion to credit or not to credit to inmate's sentence time spent on parole if parole is revoked is constitutional and does not constitute double jeopardy. Lashley v. State of Fla., M.D.Fla.1976, 413 F.Supp. 850. Double Jeopardy ⚷ 118; Pardon And Parole ⚷ 43

2. Construction and application

Acquittal in criminal case did not preclude judge from determining, within his discretion, that parole violation occurred based on same conduct for which defendant was found not guilty of criminal offense. Cavalcante v. Florida Parole and Probation Com'n, App. 1 Dist., 414 So.2d 658 (1982). Pardon And Parole ⚷ 71

Under this section, a convict whose parole had been revoked was not entitled to gained time. Dear v. Mayo, 153 Fla. 164, 14 So.2d 267 (1943), certiorari denied 64 S.Ct. 42, 320 U.S. 766, 88 L.Ed. 458.

3. Jurisdiction

Florida parole commission has authority to arrest a delinquent parolee, under its supervision, when such parolee is on parole in another state and is under Florida parole commission's supervision under terms of the interstate parole and probation compact. Op.Atty.Gen., 1953–54, p. 718.

4. Custody

The state correctional system may hold in custody pending a final hearing by the parole and probation commission, suspected parole and mandatory conditional release violators where there has been a finding of probable cause to believe they have violated the terms of their release, or where they have waived their right to a preliminary hearing, even though the commission may order the violator referred to conditional liberty. Op.Atty.Gen., 076–117, May 28, 1976.

5. Concurrent or consecutive sentences

Where parole had already been revoked when 20-year robbery sentence, with credit for all time served, was imposed, sentencing judge had power to order that robbery sentence be served, in effect concurrently, with firearms possession sentence, by ordering that credit be given in subsequent robbery sentence for "all time served," which necessarily included the already served 3-year firearms sentence. Brumit v. Wainwright, 290 So.2d 39 (1973). Pardon And Parole ⚷ 74

Where relator who had been convicted of felony and sentenced to serve prison term was out of prison on conditional pardon when he was sentenced to 5-year prison term after being convicted of another crime, failure of trial court to direct that 5-year prison sentence should run concurrently with original sentence did not in effect make sentences run consecutively since trial court had no jurisdiction to determine what parole board might do or to make order with reference to sentence which relator was not serving and at time was not required to serve. Mayo v. State ex rel. Cox, 56 So.2d 547 (1952). Sentencing And Punishment ⚷ 1129

6. Indeterminate sentences

A paroled state prisoner who was serving an indeterminate sentence of from six months to five years before parole and whose sentence was not reduced to a fixed term by the parole commission would, upon being returned to prison for a parole violation, be required to serve the remainder of his indeterminate sentence. Op. Atty.Gen., 059–208, Oct. 8, 1959.

7. Credit for time on parole

Whether credit is given for time on parole is within discretion of parole and probation commission. Schaeffer v. Florida Parole and Probation Com'n, App. 1 Dist., 434 So.2d 44 (1983). Pardon And Parole ⚷ 76

Prisoner was not entitled to have credited against sentence time spent on parole which was subsequently revoked. Coleman v. Wainwright, 323 So.2d 581 (1975). Pardon And Parole ⚷ 76

Parole is a privilege, not a right, and there is no constitutional requirement that credit for time spent on parole be applied to an individual's sentence. Coleman v. Wainwright, 323 So.2d 581 (1975). Pardon And Parole ⚷ 46; Pardon And Parole ⚷ 76

After July 1, 1974, by statutory amendment, question of credit for time satisfactorily served on parole became discretionary with Parole and Probation Commission and is not subject to collateral attack. Schell v. Wainwright, 322 So.2d 897 (1975). Pardon And Parole ⚷ 76

Prisoner, following revocation of parole, was not entitled to credit on his sentence for time spent on parole. Sharretts v. Wainwright, 312 So.2d 193 (1975). Pardon And Parole ⚷ 75

Parolee whose parole is revoked is not entitled to credit for time when he was on parole. Gibbs v. Wainwright, App. 2 Dist., 302 So.2d 175 (1974). Pardon And Parole ⚷ 76

Time prisoner was at liberty on parole could not be counted along with time he had spent in prison in determining whether he had completed his sentence of imprisonment. Porter v. State, App. 1 Dist., 212 So.2d 828 (1968). Sentencing And Punishment ⚷ 1168

Petitioner, whose parole was revoked, was not entitled to credit for time when he was on parole. Deese v. Cochran, 139 So.2d 429 (1962). Pardon And Parole ⚷ 76

An accused who was sentenced to serve four years for grand larceny and who was paroled after serving more than 27 months on condition of good behavior, was not, upon revocation of parole for violations of parole condition, entitled to have unserved portion of original sentence diminished by the time accused was out on parole, but rather the time of sentence would be computed from the date of the parole order, without gain time allowance during the parole period. Mayo v. Lukers, 53 So.2d 916 (1951). Pardon And Parole ⚷ 76

Where petitioner was sentenced to serve penitentiary term and was paroled, and petitioner remained at large without authority of law after expiration of time, as extended, for which petitioner was paroled, the time from conclusion of time, as extended, for which petitioner was paroled, until petitioner was reincarcerated, did not count on petitioner's sentence. Sheppard v. Mayo, 46 So.2d 729 (1950), certiorari denied 71 S.Ct. 484, 340 U.S. 927, 95 L.Ed. 669. Sentencing And Punishment ⚷ 1168

8. Credit for time in foreign jail

Petitioner who absconded while on parole and was held in county jail of sister state was not entitled to credit on his sentence for the time spent in the sister state's jail. Steele v. Wainwright, App. 1 Dist., 419 So.2d 657 (1982). Sentencing And Punishment ⚷ 1182

9. Condition of probation

Where probation order required defendant to live and remain at liberty without violation of any law, defendant's conviction in municipal court of crime of possession and sale of lottery tickets contrary to city ordinance sustained order revoking probation. Caston v. State, 58 So.2d 694 (1952). Sentencing And Punishment ⚷ 2004

A parolee will ordinarily be required to comply with conditions of his parole and may be reincarcerated for their breach. Sellers v. Bridges, 153 Fla. 586, 15 So.2d 293 (1943). Pardon And Parole ⚷ 72.1

10. Completion of parole

A paroled state prisoner who was serving an indeterminate sentence of from six months to five years before parole and whose parole period was set at two years will, upon satisfactory completion of the two year parole period, be forever discharged from any further imprisonment under said sentence. Op.Atty.Gen., 059–208, Oct. 8, 1959.

11. Presumptive parole release date

In establishing defendant's presumptive parole release date, parole and probation commission correctly aggregated defendant's times after including a point for a parole revocation in his second commitment. Schaeffer v. Florida Parole and Probation Com'n, App. 1 Dist., 434 So.2d 44 (1983). Pardon And Parole ⚷ 49

Binding effect of prior presumptive parole release date determination was waived by parolee's parole violations. Odom v. Florida Parole and Probation Com'n, App. 1 Dist., 433 So.2d 634 (1983). Pardon And Parole ⚷ 69

12. Revocation of parole—In general

Revocation of parole was not void because defendant had not at that time been convicted for violation of law. U.S. ex rel. Campbell v. Bishop, 1931, 47 F.2d 95. Sentencing And Punishment ⚷ 2004

Hearsay evidence introduced at preliminary hearing concerning parolee's possession of knife was sufficient to establish probable cause for revocation of parole on ground that parolee had violated parole condition he not carry a knife. Hansen v. Duggar, App. 1 Dist., 536 So.2d 1169 (1988). Pardon And Parole ⚷ 90

13. —— Effective date, revocation of parole

Where parolee was convicted of offense while on parole, revocation of parole took effect on date upon which revocation order was entered, and sentence for subsequent offense would be served after completion of original sentence, notwithstanding express order of probation and parole commission which made revocation effective as of completion of sentence for offense committed while on parole. Joseph v. State Division of Corrections, 301 So.2d 772 (1974). Pardon And Parole ⚷ 69

Incarceration of defendant, who is on probation from previous sentence, terminates interruption of sentence and recommences service of sentence and, thus, subsequent revocation of parole must be effective as of date of incarceration, since one cannot be both free on parole and incarcerated at the same time. Voulo v. Wainwright, 290 So.2d 58 (1974). Pardon And Parole ⚷ 91

Parole revocation may be made effective upon completion of a sentence imposed for an offense while prisoner is on parole or in future upon a similar future occurrence or condition; overruling Simmons v. State, 217 So.2d 343; Duchein v. Cochran, 127 So.2d 97; and Johnson v. State, 185 So.2d 466. Brumit v. Wainwright, 290 So.2d 39 (1973). Pardon And Parole ⚷ 69

Any suspension in serving of original sentence by virtue of parole ceased, and serving of sentence resumed, on date order revoking probation was entered, regardless of date upon which order stated it to be effective. Brumit v. Wainwright, 290 So.2d 39 (1973). Pardon And Parole ⚷ 91

Revocation of parole was effective as of date upon which revocation order was entered, and prisoner, even prior to formal revocation was, upon his earlier confinement, immediately recommencing initial sentence for armed robbery. Brumit v. Wainwright, 290 So.2d 39 (1973). Pardon And Parole ⚷ 69; Pardon And Parole ⚷ 73

14. —— Guilty plea, revocation of parole

Judge did not abuse his discretion in revoking defendant's parole, entered upon guilty plea to informations two years earlier, at trial for breaking and entering and possession of burglary tools, of which judge acquitted him, where defendant was apprehended at one p.m. in an alley behind a store which had been broken into with burglary tools on the ground between his hiding place and the back door of the burglarized premises and it was apparent that trial judge acquitted him because state failed to prove ownership of the burglarized premises. Ware v. State, App. 3 Dist., 219 So.2d 442 (1969). Pardon And Parole ⚷ 71

15. —— Hearings, revocation of parole

Delay of between 111 and 122 days from time that parolee was returned to custody of Department of Corrections and time of final revocation of parole was presumptively unreasonable, in view of 60–day period established by administrative regulations for final revocation hearing. Langle v. State, App. 5 Dist., 559 So.2d 657 (1990), review denied 569 So.2d 1279. Pardon And Parole ⚷ 84

Parolee was not entitled to release based upon delay in final revocation hearing, presumed to be unreasonable, in absence of showing of prejudice; parolee was in Department of Corrections' custody serving sentence on another charge during all but last few days of period of delay. Langle v. State, App. 5 Dist., 559 So.2d 657 (1990), review denied 569 So.2d 1279. Pardon And Parole ⚷ 84

While evidence seized in violation of Fourth Amendment is admissible at a parole revocation hearing, such evidence is not admissible during a criminal trial. Kinsler v. State, App. 2 Dist., 360 So.2d 24 (1978). Criminal Law ⚷ 394.4(1)

Where disciplinary report was filed against prisoner after he had been notified that he had been granted parole but before he was scheduled to be released, petitioner was entitled to be afforded a parole rescission hearing consistent with due process requirements set out in Morrissey v. Brewer, and, unless such were held within 30 days of filing of opinion, writ of habeas corpus should issue and he should be placed upon parole. Demar v. Wainwright, 354 So.2d 366 (1977), certiorari denied 98 S.Ct. 3082, 436 U.S. 962, 57 L.Ed.2d 1129. Habeas Corpus ⚷ 792.1; Pardon And Parole ⚷ 86

United States Supreme Court's decision in Morrissey v. Brewer does not require Florida to hold immediate parole revocation hearings for parolees who have been convicted of intervening offenses and are imprisoned elsewhere, either by sending its parole and probation commission out of state or by recalling prisoner parolee; however, parolee standing convicted of federal crime who is available in Florida for amount of time sufficient to conduct final parole revocation hearing should not arbitrarily be denied that right. Hofmann v. Wainwright, 332 So.2d 18 (1976), certiorari denied 97 S.Ct. 494, 429 U.S. 981, 50 L.Ed.2d 590. Pardon And Parole ⚷ 84

Where warrant charging parole violation was issued and served upon petitioner, he agreed to proceed to hearing after waiving counsel and parole commission entered its order of revocation upon finding that petitioner absconded from supervision in violation of terms of his parole, parole had not been revoked in procedure which failed to accord him all of procedural safeguards to which he was entitled. Smith v. Wainwright, App. 1 Dist., 285 So.2d 668 (1973). Pardon And Parole ⚷ 77.1; Pardon And Parole ⚷ 88

An alleged parole violation may be heard if the alleged violation comes to the attention of the court and defendant is given due notice of the alleged violation and an opportunity to be heard. Ware v. State, App. 3 Dist., 219 So.2d 442 (1969). Pardon And Parole ⚷ 85

A court does not, at a hearing for violation of parole which was originally entered as a result of a guilty plea, have to find that the terms of the parole were violated with the same exactness as was required for the original conviction. Ware v. State, App. 3 Dist., 219 So.2d 442 (1969). Pardon And Parole ⚷ 88

On due notice, defendant's parole violation could be heard, without a warrant having been issued by a magistrate, at same time as his trial for breaking and entering and possession of burglary tools. Ware v. State, App. 3 Dist., 219 So.2d 442 (1969). Pardon And Parole ⚷ 85

Person on probation is entitled to notice and hearing prior to revocation of his probation. Caston v. State, 58 So.2d 694 (1952). Sentencing And Punishment ⚷ 2013; Sentencing And Punishment ⚷ 2024

A finding by the hearing officer that, no probable cause exists at a parolee's preliminary revocation hearing does not preclude the commission from consideration of those charges at the final parole revocation hearing assuming the minimum due process requirements set forth in Morrissey v. Brewer, (1972) 408 U.S. 471, 92 S.Ct. 2593, 33 L.Ed.2d 484, are satisfied. Op. Atty.Gen., 076–128, June 3, 1976.

16. Right to counsel

Indigent defendants are not entitled to counsel in all parole revocation proceedings; rather, right to counsel should be determined on a case-by-case basis. Floyd v. Parole and Probation Com'n, 509 So.2d 919 (1987). Pardon And Parole ⚷ 89

Where warrant charging parole violation was issued and served upon petitioner, he agreed to proceed to hearing after waiving counsel and parole commission entered its order of revocation upon finding that petitioner absconded from supervision in violation of terms of his parole, parole had not been revoked in procedure which failed to accord him all of procedural safeguards to which he was entitled. Smith v. Wainwright, App. 1 Dist., 285 So.2d 668 (1973). Pardon And Parole ⚷ 77.1; Pardon And Parole ⚷ 88

Parolee was not entitled to court-appointed counsel at time of parole revocation hearing.

Johnson v. Wainwright, App. 1 Dist., 208 So.2d 505 (1968). Pardon And Parole ⚷ 89

17. Habeas corpus

Record in hearing on habeas corpus petition of prisoner, properly treated as one for mandamus relief, disclosed that petitioner was properly credited with all jail time including time spent on void sentence which was credited toward valid sentence. Coleman v. Wainwright, 323 So.2d 581 (1975). Habeas Corpus ⚷ 725

A parolee, though not physically confined in prison, could maintain habeas corpus to secure discharge from penal supervision under a judgment and sentence entered upon an information which wholly failed to charge an offense, since conditions of parole constituted such a restraint of freedom as rendered parolee for all practical purposes in "custody". Sellers v. Bridges, 153 Fla. 586, 15 So.2d 293 (1943). Habeas Corpus ⚷ 516.1

947.22. Authority to arrest parole violators with or without warrant

(1) If a member of the commission or a duly authorized representative of the commission has reasonable grounds to believe that a parolee has violated the terms and conditions of her or his parole in a material respect, such member or representative may issue a warrant for the arrest of such parolee. The warrant shall be returnable before a member of the commission or a duly authorized representative of the commission. The commission, a commissioner, or a parole examiner with approval of the parole examiner supervisor, may release the parolee on bail or her or his own recognizance, conditioned upon her or his appearance at any hearings noticed by the commission. If not released on bail or her or his own recognizance, the parolee shall be committed to jail pending hearings pursuant to s. 947.23. The commission, at its election, may have the hearing conducted by one or more commissioners or by a duly authorized representative of the commission. Any parole and probation officer, any officer authorized to serve criminal process, or any peace officer of this state is authorized to execute the warrant.

(2) Any parole and probation officer, when she or he has reasonable ground to believe that a parolee, control releasee, or conditional releasee has violated the terms and conditions of her or his parole, control release, or conditional release in a material respect, has the right to arrest the releasee or parolee without warrant and bring her or him forthwith before one or more commissioners or a duly authorized representative of the Parole Commission or Control Release Authority; and proceedings shall thereupon be had as provided herein when a warrant has been issued by a member of the commission or authority or a duly authorized representative of the commission or authority.

(3) If a law enforcement officer has probable cause to believe that a parolee has violated the terms and conditions of his or her parole, the officer shall arrest and take into custody the parolee without a warrant, and a warrant need not be issued in the case.

Laws 1941, c. 20519, § 16; Laws 1971, c. 71–111, § 1; Laws 1982, c. 82–171, § 16; Laws 1982, c. 82–193, § 1; Laws 1983, c. 83–216, § 191; Laws 1985, c. 85–295, § 5; Laws 1990, c. 90–337, § 13; Laws 1991, c. 91–280, § 12. Amended by Laws 1997, c. 97–102, § 1681, eff. July 1, 1997; Laws 2002, c. 2002–255, § 3, eff. Oct. 1, 2002.

Historical and Statutory Notes

Amendment Notes:

Laws 1971, c. 71–111, § 1, substituted, in the second sentence of subsec. (1), the words "shall be returnable * * * appearance before the commission" in lieu of "if issued by a member of the commission, shall be returnable before him and shall command that the parolee be brought before him, when he may examine such parolee and admit him to bail conditioned for his appearance before the parole commission".

Laws 1982, c. 82–171, § 16 and Laws 1982, c. 82–193, § 1, extended the authority provided under this section to the duly authorized representatives of the commission, clarified and extended the authority of individual commissioners, interpolated the third sentence of subsec. (1); and in the fourth sentence of subsec. (1), as amended, and in subsec. (2), substituted "parole and probation officer" for "parole or probation supervisor".

Laws 1983, c. 83–216, was a reviser's correction bill amending subsec. (1) to improve clarity and facilitate correct interpretation and to remove unnecessary repetition.

Laws 1985, c. 85–295, § 5, eff. June 20, 1985, substantially rewrote subsec. (1) and substituted in subsec. (2) "one or more commissioners" for "the commission, a commissioner".

Laws 1990, c. 90–337, § 13, eff. July 1, 1990, in subsec. (1), in the third sentence, inserted "a commissioner".

Laws 1990, c. 90–337, § 22 provided therein that the amendment take effect July 1, 1990; however, approval by the governor occurred subsequent thereto. The Florida Supreme Court in an advisory opinion to the governor of July 19, 1979 (374 So.2d 959) stated in part "* * * the effective date provided in the bill is inoperative unless the bill becomes law on or before that date" and concludes that under such circumstances the provision of Const. Art. 3, § 9, that the law take effect on the sixtieth day after adjournment sine die of the session of the legislature in which enacted, is applicable.

Laws 1991, c. 91–280, § 12, eff. Oct. 1, 1991, in subsec. (2), inserted references to control release or conditional release and control releasee or conditional releasee; and inserted references to the Control Release Authority.

Laws 1997, c. 97–102, eff. July 1, 1997, removed gender-specific references applicable to human beings from volume 4 of the Florida Statutes without substantive changes in legal effect.

Laws 2002, c. 2002–255, § 3, added subsec. (3), relating to arrest of parolees without a warrant if an officer has probable cause to believe that the parolee has violated the terms of parole.

Law Review and Journal Commentaries

Criminal law reform—1971. 45 Fla.Bar J. 405 (1971).

Parole revocation: Due process or star chamber? Richard A. Belz, 52 Fla.Bar J. 22 (1978).

Library References

Pardon and Parole ⚷80, 81.
Westlaw Topic No. 284.
C.J.S. Pardon and Parole §§ 71 to 74.

Research References

Forms

Florida Pleading and Practice Forms § 23:3, Arrest or Imprisonment by Law Enforcement Officer.

Florida Pleading and Practice Forms § 23:21, Complaint--Arrest and Imprisonment of Person Not on Probation on Warrant of Probation Officer--Against Probation Officer Acting Without Jurisdiction.

Treatises and Practice Aids

16 Florida Practice Series § 7:67, Sentencing Alternatives for Violations of Probation/Community Control--General.

16 Florida Practice Series § 10:23, Parole--Violations of Parole.

Notes of Decisions

---

1. Construction and application

Action of Parole Commission in considering a report not produced in evidence at a hearing to revoke parole was violation of § 947.23 requiring a hearing at which state and parolee may introduce such evidence as they deem necessary and pertinent to the charge of parole violations. Jackson v. Mayo, 73 So.2d 881 (1954). Pardon And Parole ⚷ 88

The state correctional system may hold in custody pending a final hearing by the parole and probation commission, suspected parole and mandatory conditional release violators where there has been a finding of probable cause to believe they have violated the terms of their release, or where they have waived their right to a preliminary hearing, even though the commission may order the violator referred to conditional liberty. Op.Atty.Gen., 076–117, May 28, 1976.

2. **Bail**

It was intention of legislature to vest in Parole Commission power to grant and administer paroles, commit parolees to jail or grant them bond, as circumstances might suggest. Blackburn v. Jackson, 74 So.2d 80 (1954). Pardon And Parole ⚷ 55.1

Absent showing that state Parole Commission had abused its discretion, trial court has no power or jurisdiction to grant bail to parolee who was held under parole violation warrant issued from Parole Commission. Blackburn v. Jackson, 74 So.2d 80 (1954). Bail ⚷ 42

3. **Release after violation of probation**

Where, upon being arrested and brought before the court on charge of having violated conditions of his probation, probationer is released with or without bail to await a further hearing, it is the duty of the probation and parole commission to continue to supervise the probationer under the conditions set forth in the original probation order while thus released and probationer is required to abide by the conditions of his probation while thus released. Op.Atty.Gen., 070–127, Sept. 18, 1970.

Where parolee has been arrested on charge of violating conditions of his parole and has been admitted to bail pending hearing before the probation and parole commission, it is the duty of said commission to continue to supervise such parolee while he is thus released on bail and parolee is required to abide by the conditions of his parole while thus released. Op.Atty. Gen., 070–127, Sept. 18, 1970.

947.23. Action of commission upon arrest of parolee

(1) Within 30 days after the arrest of a person charged with violation of the terms and conditions of her or his parole, the parolee shall be afforded a prompt preliminary hearing, conducted by a member of the commission or its duly authorized representative, at or near the place of violation or arrest to determine if there is probable cause or reasonable grounds to believe that the parolee has committed a violation of the terms or conditions of her or his parole. The parolee may knowingly execute a waiver of this hearing, up until the time of such hearing, provided the consequences of such action have been fully explained. If the parolee elects to proceed with the preliminary hearing:

(a) The parolee shall be afforded a timely notice of the preliminary hearing, which notice shall state the purpose of the hearing and state the alleged violation.

(b) The parolee shall be permitted to cross-examine adverse witnesses, unless it is determined that good cause exists not to allow such examination.

(c) The parolee shall be allowed to call witnesses as provided in subsection (3), and present evidence in her or his own behalf.

(d) The parolee may be represented by counsel.

The findings based on the evidence presented at the preliminary hearing shall be made available to the parolee either immediately following the preliminary hearing or within a reasonable time thereafter.

(2) If the preliminary hearing results in a finding of probable cause or reasonable grounds to believe that a violation of the terms or conditions of parole has occurred, any one or more commissioners or a duly authorized representative of the commission shall convene a final revocation hearing on the alleged violation. The parolee shall appear at the final hearing in person, and, if the parolee desires, she or he may be represented by counsel. At the

final hearing, the state and the parolee may introduce such evidence as is necessary and pertinent to the charge of parole violation.

(3) Any one or more commissioners or a duly authorized representative of the commission may administer oaths and compel the attendance of witnesses at such hearing by the issuance of summons, subpoenas, and subpoenas duces tecum. Subpoenas and subpoenas duces tecum shall be enforceable by appropriate proceedings in circuit court, and the failure to comply with a court order enforcing a subpoena or subpoena duces tecum shall constitute contempt of court. Any one or more commissioners or a duly authorized representative of the commission may issue subpoenas on behalf of the state or the parolee. The commission may decline a request to subpoena a witness whose testimony it finds would be cumulative, irrelevant, or nonprobative. The party requesting the subpoenas shall furnish to the commissioner, commissioners, or duly authorized representative of the commission the names and addresses of her or his proposed witnesses at least 10 days prior to the hearing date.

(4) At the hearing, the parolee shall be informed orally and in writing of:

(a) The violation of the terms and conditions of parole with which the parolee has been charged.

(b) The right to be represented by counsel.

(c) The right to be heard in person.

(d) The right to secure, present, and compel the attendance of witnesses as provided in subsection (3) and the production of documents on her or his behalf.

(e) The right of access to all evidence used against her or him.

(f) The right to confront and cross-examine adverse witnesses, unless the commissioner, commissioners, or duly authorized representative of the commission conducting the hearing finds specifically, and states in writing, good cause not to allow the confrontation.

(5)(a) At any such hearing convened by one or more commissioners or a duly authorized representative of the commission, the accused may waive her or his right to proceed further if, after being informed of her or his rights and after being advised of the consequences of a waiver in regard to the nature of the order which may be entered as a result of such waiver, the accused affirms, in writing, knowledge and understanding of such rights and consequences and elects, in writing, to execute the waiver.

(b) The accused violator may execute a waiver, in writing, of a final revocation hearing prior to the commencement of such hearing. Such waiver may be executed before a member of the commission or a duly authorized representative of the commission after the accused violator has been informed of her or his rights and after she or he has been advised of the consequences of a waiver. Within 14 days after the execution of a waiver, the accused may withdraw the waiver by executing a withdrawal of waiver before a notary public and forwarding the original of that withdrawal to the commission.

(6) Within a reasonable time after the hearing, the commissioner, commissioners, or duly authorized representative of the commission who conducted the hearing shall make findings of fact in regard to the alleged parole violation.

(a) If the hearing was conducted by three or more commissioners, a majority of them shall enter an order determining whether the charges of parole violation have been sustained, based on the findings of fact made by them. By such order they shall revoke the parole and return the parolee to prison to serve the sentence theretofore imposed upon her or him, reinstate the original order of parole, order the placement of the parolee into a community control program as set forth in s. 948.101, or enter such other order as is proper.

(b) If the hearing was conducted by one or two commissioners or a duly authorized representative of the commission, at least two commissioners shall enter an order determining whether or not the charges of parole violation have been sustained, based on the findings of fact made by the commissioner, commissioners, or duly authorized representative of the commission. The commissioners, by such order, shall revoke the parole and return the parolee to prison to serve the sentence theretofore imposed upon her or him, reinstate the original order of parole, order the placement of the parolee into a community control program as set forth in s. 948.101, or enter such other order as is proper.

(c) If the disposition after the revocation hearing is to place the parolee into a community control program, the commission shall be guided by the procedures and requirements provided in chapter 948 which apply to the courts regarding the development and implementation of community control.

However, any decision to revoke parole shall be based on a violation of a term or condition specifically enumerated in the parole release order. In a case in which parole is revoked, the majority of the commission or the two commissioners shall make a written statement of the evidence relied on and the reasons for revoking parole.

(7) Whenever a parole is revoked by the commission and the parolee is ordered by the commission to be returned to prison, the parolee, by reason of her or his misconduct, shall be deemed to forfeit all gain-time or commutation of time for good conduct, as provided for by law, earned up to the date of her or his release on parole. Nothing herein shall deprive the prisoner of her or his right to gain-time or commutation of time for good conduct, as provided by law, from the date the prisoner is returned to prison.

Laws 1941, c. 20519, § 17; Laws 1943, c. 21775, § 4; Laws 1974, c. 74–241, § 1; Laws 1977, c. 77–174, § 1; Laws 1978, c. 78–417, § 19; Laws 1979, c. 79–42, § 11; Laws 1982, c. 82–171, § 17; Laws 1982, c. 82–193, § 2; Laws 1983, c. 83–131, § 15; Laws 1985, c. 85–295, § 6; Laws 1989, c. 89–526, §§ 45, 47. Amended by Laws 1997, c. 97–102, § 1682, eff. July 1, 1997; Laws 2004, c. 2004–373, § 37, eff. July 1, 2004.

Historical and Statutory Notes

Amendment Notes:

Laws 1943, c. 21775, § 4, divided the second sentence in subsec. (1) by substituting "determining whether said charges of parole violation have been sustained. The commission shall in and by said order revoke" for "thereon rescinding" following "and shall enter an order"; and added subsec. (2).

Laws 1974, c. 74–241, § 1, inserted the second and third sentences in subsec. (1).

Laws 1977, c. 77–174, a reviser's bill, amended subsec. (1) of this section to reflect language editorially substituted by the division of statutory revision.

Laws 1978, c. 78–417, added the concluding proviso in subsec. (1) requiring that parole revocation be based upon a violation of a specifically enumerated term or condition.

Laws 1979, c. 79–42, § 11, rewrote and expanded this section which, as it appeared in Fla.St.1978, Supp., provided:

"(1) As soon as practicable after the arrest of a person charged with violation of the terms and conditions of his parole, such parolee shall appear before the commission in person, and if he desires he may be represented by counsel, and a hearing shall be had at which the state and the parolee may introduce such evidence as they may deem necessary and pertinent to the charge of parole violation. The commission, a member thereof, or a duly authorized representative of the commission or member thereof shall have the authority to administer oaths and compel the attendance of witnesses at said hearing by the issuance of summons and subpoenas and to issue subpoenas duces tecum, under penalty of contempt, under the commission's seal and signed by any member of the commission. The commission shall issue subpoenas on behalf of the parolee in connection with any matter which impinges in a material respect upon a finding of fact in a parole revocation case, provided the parolee furnishes to the commission the names and addresses of his proposed witnesses at least 7 days prior to the hearing date. Within a reasonable time thereafter, the commission shall make findings upon such charge of parole violation and shall enter an order determining whether said charges of parole violation have been sustained. The commission shall in and by said order revoke said parole and return said person to prison to serve the sentence theretofore imposed upon him or reinstate the original order of parole or shall enter such other order as it may deem proper; however, any decision to revoke parole shall be based on a violation of a term or condition specifically enumerated in the parole release order.

"(2) Whenever a parole is revoked by the commission and said parolee ordered by said commission to be returned to prison, the parolee, by reason of his misconduct, shall be deemed to forfeit all gain-time or commutation of time for good conduct, as provided for by s. 944.27, earned up to the date of his release on parole. Nothing herein shall deprive the prisoner of his right to gain-time or commutation of time for good conduct, as provided by s. 944.27, from the date he is returned to prison."

Laws 1982, c. 82–171, § 17, and Laws 1982, c. 82–193, § 2, extended and clarified the application of this section to individual commissioners, and to duly authorized representatives of the commission; in subsec. (1), substituted "Within 30 days" for "As soon as practicable" at the beginning of the first sentence; in subsec. (2), substituted "at the hearing" for "before the commission or commissioner" in the second sentence; in subsec. (3), deleted "under the seal of the commission and signature of a commissioner" following "hearing by the issuance" in the first sentence, and substituted "10" for "7" in the third sentence; in subsec. (6), designated a portion of the subsection as par. (a), divided par. (a) into two sentences, substituted "If the hearing has been conducted by the commission, a majority of" for "and" and inserted "based on the findings of fact made by the commission" in the first sentence, and substituted "The commission, by such order" for "by such order, the commission" in the second sentence, interpolated subsec. (6) (b), and substituted "majority of the commission or the two commissioners" for "commission" in the last sentence of subsec. (6); in subsec. (7), substituted "law" for "s. 944.27" in the first sentence, and rewrote subsec. (5) (b) which formerly provided:

"At any such hearing convened by a member of the commission, the parolee shall be informed orally and in writing of his right to have a hearing before a majority of the commission. The hearing may proceed before the member of the commission if the parolee waives, in writing, his right to have a hearing before a majority of the commission. At any such hearing so convened, the parolee, if he has waived his right to have a hearing before a majority of the commission, may also waive, in the manner provided in paragraph (a), his right to proceed further."

Laws 1983, c. 83–131, § 15, provided in pars. (a) and (b) for ordering placement of the parolee into community control programs as provided in § 948.03, and added par. (c) to subsec. (6).

Laws 1985, c. 85–295, § 6, eff. June 20, 1985, substituted throughout the section references to "any one or more commissioners or a duly authorized representative" for "the commission or member or duly authorized representative".

Laws 1989, c. 89–526, § 45, eff. Oct. 1, 1989, reenacted subsec. (6) without amendment.

Laws 1989, c. 89–526, § 47, eff. Oct. 1, 1989, in subsec. (1), inserted a reference to subsec. (3) in par. (c), and inserted "preliminary" preceding "hearing" in the concluding paragraph; in subsec. (2), changed references to the hearing to references to the final revocation hearing; in subsec. (3), made the issuance of subpoenas discretionary rather than mandatory, and allowed the commission to decline requests to subpoena certain witnesses; in subsec. (4)(d), inserted a reference to subsec. (3); and made nonsubstantive language and punctuation changes throughout.

Section 52 of Laws 1989, c. 89–526, provides, in pertinent part:

"Sections 1 through 9 of this act shall take effect September 1, 1990. All inmates committed to the department as of September 1, 1990, shall have a control release date established by December 1, 1990. Inmates received after September 1, 1990, shall have a control release date established within 90 days following notification by the department of receipt of the inmate."

Laws 1997, c. 97–102, eff. July 1, 1997, removed gender-specific references applicable to human beings from volume 4 of the Florida Statutes without substantive changes in legal effect.

Laws 2004, c. 2004–373, § 37, in subsec. (6), substituted references to § 948.101 for references to § 948.03 throughout.

Cross References

Forfeiture of gain-time and right to earn gain-time in the future, see § 944.28.
Gain-time, see § 944.275.

Law Review and Journal Commentaries

Parole and probation in Florida. James T. Vocelle, 18 Fla.L.J. 35 (1944).

Parole revocation: Due process or star chamber? Richard A. Belz, 52 Fla.Bar J. 22 (1978).

Library References

Pardon and Parole ⚷77.1 to 92.
Westlaw Topic No. 284.
C.J.S. Pardon and Parole §§ 66, 69 to 87.

Research References

Treatises and Practice Aids

16 Florida Practice Series § 10:23, Parole--Violations of Parole.

United States Supreme Court

Revocation of probation, necessity of statement by fact finder as to alternatives to incarceration considered, see Black v. Romano, U.S.Mo.1985, 105 S.Ct. 2254, 471 U.S. 606, 85 L.Ed.2d 636, rehearing denied 105 S.Ct. 3548, 473 U.S. 921, 87 L.Ed.2d 671.

Notes of Decisions

---

1. Validity

This section authorizing forfeiture of credit for time served on parole and forfeiture of all of accumulated gain time for good conduct if parole is revoked is constitutional and does not constitute double jeopardy. Lashley v. State of Fla., M.D.Fla.1976, 413 F.Supp. 850. Double Jeopardy ⚷ 31; Pardon And Parole ⚷ 43

This section was sufficient to meet federal and Florida constitutional standards for hearings for termination of parole provided it was applied as stated in decisional law. Albritton v. Wainwright, 313 So.2d 763 (1975). Pardon And Parole ⚷ 43

This section governing action of Parole and Probation Commission upon arrest of parolee was not unconstitutional on ground that the parole revocation proceedings provided for therein did not provide for minimum due process requirements. Dees v. State, 295 So.2d 296 (1974). Constitutional Law ⚷ 4838; Pardon And Parole ⚷ 43

2. Due process

Parole Commission violated parolee's right to due process when it failed to notify parolee of findings from his preliminary hearing to determine whether there was probable cause to believe that conditions of parole were violated, but parolee was required to demonstrate that he was prejudiced by violation before he was entitled to release. Taylor v. Dugger, App. 1 Dist., 567 So.2d 1000 (1990). Constitutional Law ⚷ 4838; Pardon And Parole ⚷ 87; Pardon And Parole ⚷ 92

Due process and state law require final parole revocation hearing within reasonable time. Proctor v. Wainwright, App. 1 Dist., 408 So.2d 793 (1982). Constitutional Law ⚷ 4838; Pardon And Parole ⚷ 84

Where parolee was given notice and preliminary hearing at which he admitted parole violations, was returned to prison and thereafter given notice and a final parole revocation hearing at which he agreed to proceed before one member of the Parole and Probation Commission without counsel, he was accorded the minimum requirements of due process. Sharretts v. Wainwright, 312 So.2d 193 (1975). Constitutional Law ⚷ 4838

Record reflected that parolee was afforded the minimum requirements of due process, as prescribed by the United States Supreme Court, in connection with his parole revocation, despite contention that he was entitled to two hearings and that the single parole commissioner who conducted the hearing pursuant to parolee's agreement acted as an arresting officer, prosecutor and judge. Addison v. Florida Parole Bd., App. 1 Dist., 281 So.2d 906 (1973). Constitutional Law ⚷ 4838

3. Jurisdiction

Jurisdiction of parole commission to revoke parole was not disturbed by fact that parole period had expired before parole was revoked, where infraction upon which parole was revoked had occurred during period of probation. Gibbs v. Cochran, 142 So.2d 276 (1962). Pardon And Parole ⚷ 78

4. Hearings—In general

Inmate held in federal custody as result of same conduct that violated his Florida parole was entitled to parole hearing after inmate was returned to Florida's jurisdiction when his federal sentence terminated. Gibson v. Florida Parole Com'n, App. 4 Dist., 801 So.2d 286 (2001). Pardon And Parole ⚷ 85

Record disclosed substantial compliance with state and federal standards for hearings prior to termination of parole of defendant who failed to deny that he had broken terms of parole on at least four occasions. Albritton v. Wainwright, 313 So.2d 763 (1975). Pardon And Parole ⚷ 88

Where it appeared that habeas corpus petitioner had not been afforded hearing in manner contemplated by this section, it was ordered that he be discharged unless Parole Commission granted him a hearing in manner prescribed by law and, consequent upon hearing, determined that his parole should be revoked. Senk v. Cochran, 116 So.2d 244 (1959). Habeas Corpus ⚷ 517

Parole Commission, in conducting hearings, must be guided by the basic principles of fairness which require at least the right seasonably to know the charges preferred, to meet them by competent evidence and to be heard by counsel upon the probative force of the evidence adduced by both sides. Jackson v. Mayo, 73 So.2d 881 (1954). Pardon And Parole ⚷ 88

5. —— Habeas corpus, hearings

Parolee, who was incarcerated for parole violation after he had been released subsequent to having been detained in jail for ten days after an arrest for a felony, was entitled to writ of habeas corpus since a hearing on parole revocation after his initial arrest on the felony charge had not been held within ten days. Carson v. Bishop, App. 1 Dist., 378 So.2d 882 (1979), certiorari denied 386 So.2d 634. Habeas Corpus ⚷ 517

6. —— Preliminary hearings

Director of department of corrections and rehabilitation of county and employee of the department of corrections had no duty to afford the required preliminary parole revocation hearing to parolee who had been placed in their custody and thus were immune from damages when he was transferred into the state prison system and, as a result, did not receive the prompt preliminary parole revocation hearing which had been scheduled for him while he was at the jail. Fowler v. Cross, 1981, 635 F.2d 476. Civil Rights ⚷ 1376(4)

7. —— Probable cause, hearings

Parolee waived his timely preliminary hearing to establish probable cause for revocation of his parole by his attorney's repeated requests for continuances. Hansen v. Duggar, App. 1 Dist., 536 So.2d 1169 (1988). Pardon And Parole ⚷ 87

Request or agreement for delay of preliminary hearing to determine probable cause for parole revocation need not be in writing. Hansen v. Duggar, App. 1 Dist., 536 So.2d 1169 (1988). Pardon And Parole ⚷ 87

Preliminary hearing to determine if there was probable cause to believe that parole had been violated, held in county adjacent to county in which parolee was arrested, was held at or near place of violation of arrest as required by subsec. (1) of this section. Hansen v. Dugger, App. 1 Dist., 515 So.2d 1345 (1987). Pardon And Parole ⚷ 85

Where parolee pleaded guilty to felony offense in Delaware during time he was present in that state pursuant to Florida parole, and was returned to Florida by Delaware authorities, failure to provide preliminary parole revocation hearing in Florida upon his return would not be grounds for discharge from custody since petition itself disclosed probable cause for parolee's return to Florida on parole violation charge, and he specifically waived extradition to be returned to Florida for that purpose after hearing before Delaware court. Proctor v. Wainwright, App. 1 Dist., 408 So.2d 793 (1982). Habeas Corpus ⚷ 517

Prompt preliminary or "probable cause" hearing is required for parole revocation. Proctor v. Wainwright, App. 1 Dist., 408 So.2d 793 (1982). Pardon And Parole ⚷ 87

Proof sufficient to support a criminal conviction is not required to support a discretionary order revoking parole. State ex rel. Florida Parole and Probation Commission v. Helton, App. 1 Dist., 313 So.2d 413 (1975). Pardon And Parole ⚷ 90

Parolee's acquittal on charges of receiving stolen property or auto larceny had no bearing on sufficiency of charge as grounds for revocation of parole. State ex rel. Florida Parole and Probation Commission v. Helton, App. 1 Dist., 313 So.2d 413 (1975). Pardon And Parole ⚷ 71

8. —— Notice, hearings

Because parolee requested date on which preliminary hearing to establish probable cause for revocation of parole was held, parolee received timely notice of hearing. Hansen v. Duggar, App. 1 Dist., 536 So.2d 1169 (1988). Pardon And Parole ⚷ 85

Failure to give parolee timely notice of preliminary parole revocation hearing violated subsection of this section, absent showing that parolee's attorney requested continuance of the preliminary hearing. Hansen v. Dugger, App. 1 Dist., 515 So.2d 1345 (1987). Pardon And Parole ⚷ 85

On due notice, defendant's parole violation could be heard, without a warrant having been issued by a magistrate, at same time as his trial for breaking and entering and possession of burglary tools. Ware v. State, App. 3 Dist., 219 So.2d 442 (1969). Pardon And Parole ⚷ 85

An alleged parole violation may be heard if the alleged violation comes to the attention of the court and defendant is given due notice of the alleged violation and an opportunity to be heard. Ware v. State, App. 3 Dist., 219 So.2d 442 (1969). Pardon And Parole ⚷ 85

9. —— Waiver, hearings

In those instances in which prisoner waives a preliminary hearing for termination of parole, none should be required. Albritton v. Wainwright, 313 So.2d 763 (1975). Pardon And Parole ⚷ 87

Writ of habeas corpus, issued on representation that petitioner had not had hearing contemplated by this section on charge of violating conditions of parole, was discharged upon showing by affidavit that petitioner had waived right to hearing before two or more members of parole commission. Sumrall v. Cochran, 127 So.2d 447 (1961). Habeas Corpus ⚷ 517

Affidavit of member of parole commission established that parolee had waived right to hearing before two or more members of commission on charge of violating conditions of parole. Sumrall v. Cochran, 127 So.2d 447 (1961). Pardon And Parole ⚷ 86

Where order of Board of Pardons, revoking conditional pardon, was entered without notice of hearing or chance to be heard regarding charges upon which order was based, delay of 10 years before proceeding by habeas corpus to assert alleged legal rights constituted waiver of such rights. Chastain v. Mayo, 56 So.2d 540 (1952). Habeas Corpus ⚷ 603

10. —— Time of hearings

Forty-seven-day delay between parolee's arrest and his preliminary hearing on revocation of parole for technical parole violation violated subsec. (1) of this section requiring such hearings to be held within 30 days, if parolee's attorney did not request the delay. Hansen v. Dugger, App. 1 Dist., 515 So.2d 1345 (1987). Pardon And Parole ⚷ 84

United States Supreme Court's decision in Morrissey v. Brewer does not require Florida to hold immediate parole revocation hearings for parolees who have been convicted of intervening offenses and are imprisoned elsewhere, either by sending its parole and probation commission out of state or by recalling prisoner parolee; however, parolee standing convicted of federal crime who is available in Florida for amount of time sufficient to conduct final parole revocation hearing should not arbitrarily be denied that right. Hofmann v. Wainwright, 332 So.2d 18 (1976), certiorari denied 97 S.Ct. 494, 429 U.S. 981, 50 L.Ed.2d 590. Pardon And Parole ⚷ 84

11. —— Fact-finding interviews, hearings

Parole and probation commission could delegate to hearing examiner panel the task of conducting fact-finding interviews to determine whether parole granted prisoner who was not yet released should be rescinded and there was no requirement that commission itself conduct such fact finding. Florida Institutional Legal Services, Inc. v. Florida Parole and Probation Commission, App. 1 Dist., 391 So.2d 247 (1980). Pardon And Parole ⚷ 55.1

12. —— Subpoenas, hearings

In the absence of express statutory direction or authorization, hearing examiners employed by the Florida parole and probation commission should refrain from serving subpoenas issued pursuant to this section, upon witnesses to compel their attendance at the revocation hearings required by that section. Op.Atty.Gen., 84–44, May 1, 1984.

13. —— Witnesses, hearings

At preliminary hearing to establish probable cause for revocation of parole, parolee was not entitled to cross-examine victims of alleged sexual batteries, which partially formed basis for the requested revocation, where those victims did not testify at hearing. Hansen v. Duggar, App. 1 Dist., 536 So.2d 1169 (1988). Pardon And Parole ⚷ 88

Petitioner, who failed to notify Parole and Probation Commission to subpoena his wife, was not deprived of due process or right under subsec. (1)(c) of this section to present witness at parole revocation hearing, where letter was sent to petitioner to advise him of date of final hearing and to state witnesses to be subpoenaed for hearing. Hansen v. Fontana, App. 1 Dist., 517 So.2d 714 (1987). Constitutional Law ⚷ 4838; Pardon And Parole ⚷ 88

Petitioner was not denied right to confront and cross-examine parole supervisor, where supervisor was not called as adverse witness at final hearing on parole revocation, and where supervisor's testimony at preliminary hearing was not used against petitioner. Hansen v. Fontana, App. 1 Dist., 517 So.2d 714 (1987). Pardon And Parole ⚷ 88

Subsection (1)(b) of this section permitting parolee to cross-examine adverse witnesses was violated if two witnesses who allegedly observed parolee violate condition of his parole were not present at preliminary parole revocation hearing. Hansen v. Dugger, App. 1 Dist., 515 So.2d 1345 (1987). Pardon And Parole ⚷ 88

14. —— Evidence, hearings

In probation or parole revocation proceeding after a subsequent arrest on a felony charge, question to be determined is not only by evidence of guilt of the offense for which the parolee is charged, but by evidence as to good behavior during the period of parole. State ex rel. Florida Parole and Probation Commission v. Helton, App. 1 Dist., 313 So.2d 413 (1975). Pardon And Parole ⚷ 90; Sentencing And Punishment ⚷ 2021

Parole Commission has duty to offer into evidence at a hearing such evidence as is necessary to sustain charge of violation of parole and has no right to treat as evidence material not introduced as such or to consider any information outside the record. Jackson v. Mayo, 73 So.2d 881 (1954). Pardon And Parole ⚷ 90

Action of Parole Commission in considering a report not produced in evidence at a hearing to revoke parole was violation of this section requiring a hearing at which state and parolee may introduce such evidence as they deem necessary and pertinent to the charge of parole violation. Jackson v. Mayo, 73 So.2d 881 (1954). Pardon And Parole ⚷ 88

Where the only evidence introduced before Parole Commission was the testimony of the parolee which denied or explained all of the accusations brought by Parole Commission, there was no evidence before the Commission authorizing it to revoke parole. Jackson v. Mayo, 73 So.2d 881 (1954). Pardon And Parole ⚷ 90

15. —— Findings, hearings

Oral notice to parolee that there was probable cause to believe he had violated two conditions of his parole, and that there was not probable cause as to his alleged violation of another condition, was sufficient notice to parolee of findings, absent any prejudice. Hansen v. Duggar, App. 1 Dist., 536 So.2d 1169 (1988). Pardon And Parole ⚷ 88

Parolee was not required to receive written notice of findings that preliminary hearing found probable cause to believe that he had violated conditions of his parole. Hansen v. Duggar, App. 1 Dist., 536 So.2d 1169 (1988). Pardon And Parole ⚷ 88

This section did not entitle parolee to receive, within reasonable time, statement of findings as to evidence presented at final hearing. Hansen v. Fontana, App. 1 Dist., 517 So.2d 714 (1987). Pardon And Parole ⚷ 91

Parolee was not required to show he was prejudiced by his failure to receive personal copy of findings of preliminary parole revocation hearing or allege that his attorney did not receive a copy in order to show subsec. (1) of this section was violated. Hansen v. Dugger, App. 1 Dist., 515 So.2d 1345 (1987). Pardon And Parole ⚷ 85

A court does not, at a hearing for violation of parole which was originally entered as a result of a guilty plea, have to find that the terms of the parole were violated with the same exactness as was required for the original conviction. Ware v. State, App. 3 Dist., 219 So.2d 442 (1969). Pardon And Parole ⚷ 88

A finding by the hearing officer that, no probable cause exists at a parolee's preliminary revocation hearing does not preclude the commission from consideration of those charges at the final parole revocation hearing assuming the minimum due process requirements set forth in Morrissey v. Brewer, (1972) 408 U.S. 471, 92 S.Ct. 2593, 33 L.Ed.2d 484, are satisfied. Op. Atty.Gen., 076–128, June 3, 1976.

16. Revocation of parole—In general

Parolee whose parole is revoked is not entitled to credit for time when he was on parole. Gibbs v. Wainwright, App. 2 Dist., 302 So.2d 175 (1974). Pardon And Parole ⚷ 76

Parolee's passing of worthless check and sentence for such crime during period of parole was sufficient to support revocation of parole. Gibbs v. Cochran, 142 So.2d 276 (1962). Pardon And Parole ⚷ 71

A paroled state prisoner who was serving an indeterminate sentence of from six months to five years before parole and whose sentence was not reduced to a fixed term by the parole commission would, upon being returned to prison for a parole violation, be required to serve the remainder of his indeterminate sentence. Op. Atty.Gen., 059–208, Oct. 8, 1959.

Parole which has been violated before expiration of time for which prisoner was sentenced may be revoked after expiration of such time, if prisoner has not been discharged from terms of parole. Op.Atty.Gen., 1946, p. 759.

17. —— Discretion, revocation of parole

Discretion vested in parole commission is not absolute and unlimited and does not include power to revoke parole, effective at some future time. Brumit v. Wainwright, 290 So.2d 39 (1973). Pardon And Parole ⚷ 69

Judge did not abuse his discretion in revoking defendant's parole, entered upon guilty plea to informations two years earlier, at trial for breaking and entering and possession of burglary tools, of which judge acquitted him, where defendant was apprehended at one p.m. in an alley behind a store which had been broken into with burglary tools on the ground between his hiding place and the back door of the burglarized premises and it was apparent that trial judge acquitted him because state failed to prove ownership of the burglarized premises. Ware v. State, App. 3 Dist., 219 So.2d 442 (1969). Pardon And Parole ⚷ 71

18. Release after violation of parole

Where parolee has been arrested on charge of violating conditions of his parole, and has been admitted to bail pending hearing before the probation and parole commission, it is the duty of said commission to continue to supervise such parolee while he is thus released on bail and parolee is required to abide by the conditions of his parole while thus released. Op.Atty. Gen., 070–127, Sept. 18, 1970.

19. Gain time

Where parolee was afforded due process in the revocation of parole, gain-time earned before release on parole was properly forfeited on revocation of parole. Sharretts v. Wainwright, 312 So.2d 193 (1975). Pardon And Parole ⚷ 75

Revocation of parole did not deprive prisoner of right to gain-time from the date of his return to prison. Sharretts v. Wainwright, 312 So.2d 193 (1975). Pardon And Parole ⚷ 75

By operation of provision of this section gain time is forfeited whenever a parole is revoked. Gibbs v. Wainwright, App. 2 Dist., 302 So.2d 175 (1974). Pardon And Parole ⚷ 75

Where proceedings resulting in revocation of parole were not defective, gain time which parolee otherwise would have been entitled to was validly forfeited. Shiplett v. Wainwright, App. 1 Dist., 198 So.2d 647 (1967). Pardon And Parole ⚷ 75

20. Right to counsel

Defendant was entitled to appointed counsel at probation revocation hearing. State v. Sanderson, 469 So.2d 1383 (1985). Sentencing And Punishment ⚷ 2014

Fact that parolee lacked counsel at revocation proceeding did not invalidate proceeding. Moore v. Wainwright, App. 1 Dist., 253 So.2d 736 (1971). Pardon And Parole ⚷ 89

This section allowing parolee to have representation of counsel at hearing on revocation of parole was permissive and due process did not require that indigent parolee be provided with counsel. Shiplett v. Wainwright, App. 1 Dist., 198 So.2d 647 (1967). Constitutional Law ⚷ 4838; Pardon And Parole ⚷ 89

21. Review

Upon review of probation or parole revocation, question is whether the revoking authority has abused its discretion. State ex rel. Florida Parole and Probation Commission v. Helton, App. 1 Dist., 313 So.2d 413 (1975). Criminal Law ⚷ 1156.7; Pardon And Parole ⚷ 92

947.24. Discharge from parole supervision or release supervision

(1) When a person is placed on parole, control release, or conditional release, the commission shall determine the period of time the person will be under parole supervision or release supervision in the following manner:

(a) If the person is being paroled or released under supervision from a single or concurrent sentence, the period of time the person will be under parole supervision or release supervision may not exceed 2 years unless the commission designates a longer period of time, in which case it must advise the parolee or releasee in writing of the reasons for the extended period. In any event, the period of parole supervision or release supervision may not exceed the maximum period for which the person has been sentenced.

(b) If the person is being paroled or released under supervision from a consecutive sentence or sentences, the period of time the person will be under parole supervision or release supervision will be for the maximum period for which the person was sentenced.

(2) The commission shall review the progress of each person who has been placed on parole, control release, or conditional release after 2 years of supervision in the community and biennially thereafter. The department shall provide to the commission the information necessary to conduct such a review. Such review must include consideration of whether to modify the reporting schedule, thereby authorizing the person under parole supervision or release supervision to submit reports quarterly, semiannually, or annually. The commission, after having retained jurisdiction of a person for a sufficient length of time to evidence satisfactory rehabilitation and cooperation, may further modify the terms and conditions of the person's parole, control release, or conditional release, may discharge the person from parole supervision or release supervision, may relieve the person from making further reports, or may permit the person to leave the state or country, upon finding that such action is in the best interests of the person and society.

(3) This section does not affect the rights of a parolee to request modification of the terms and conditions of parole under s. 947.19.

Laws 1941, c. 20519, § 18; Laws 1963, c. 63–83, § 1; Laws 1974, c. 74–112, § 9; Laws 1977, c. 77–104, § 256; Laws 1985, c. 85–107, § 4; Laws 1988, c. 88–122, § 27; Laws 1993, c. 93–61, § 10. Amended by Laws 2001, c. 2001–124, § 6, eff. July 1, 2001.

Historical and Statutory Notes

Amendment Notes:

Laws 1963, c. 63–83, § 1, rewrote the section which had read as follows:

"No person who has been placed on parole shall be discharged therefrom by the commission prior to the expiration of the term for which he was sentenced, or until he shall have been duly pardoned in accordance with law. The commission may, however, relieve a person on parole from making further reports and may permit such person to leave the state or country if satisfied that this is for his own best interest and for the best interest of society."

Laws 1974, c. 74–112, § 9, inserted the specified maximum parole period in the first sentence, added the second sentence, and inserted the words "discharge the person from parole, may" in the third sentence.

Laws 1977, c. 77–104, a reviser's bill, amended this section for clarity and to restore word that was originally enacted by Laws 1941, c. 20519, but that was inadvertently changed through typographical error in the amendment of this section by Laws 1963, c. 63–83.

Laws 1985, c. 85–107, § 4, eff. June 11, 1985, rewrote this section, which formerly read:

"When a person is placed on parole, the commission shall determine the period of time the person shall be on parole, such time not to exceed a maximum period of 2 years unless the commission designates a longer period of time, in which case it will advise the parolee in writing of the reasons for the extended period. In any event, the period of parole shall not exceed the maximum period for which the person has been sentenced. The commission, after having retained jurisdiction of a person for a sufficient length of time to evidence satisfactory rehabilitation and cooperation, may discharge the person from parole, may relieve a person on parole from making further reports, or may permit such person to leave the state or country, upon determination that such action is in the best interests of the person and of society."

Laws 1988, c. 88–122, § 27, eff. July 1, 1988, redesignated provisions of the section, adding thereto provisions constituting subsecs. (2) and (3) and deleting the provision formerly constituting the second sentence of subsec. (2) providing for circumstances under which the commission could relieve a person on parole from making reports.

Laws 1993, c. 93–61, § 10, eff. April 22, 1993, rewrote the section, which formerly read:

"(1) When a person is placed on parole, the commission shall determine the period of time the person shall be on parole in the following manner:

"(a) If the person is being paroled on a single or concurrent sentence, the period of time the person shall be on parole shall not exceed 2 years unless the commission designates a longer period of time, in which case it will advise the parolee in writing of the reasons for the extended period. In any event, the period of parole shall not exceed the maximum period for which the person has been sentenced.

"(b) If the person is being paroled on a consecutive sentence or sentences, the period of time the person shall be on parole shall be for the maximum period for which the person was sentenced.

"(2) The commission shall review the progress of each person who has been placed on parole after 2 years of supervision in the community and biennially thereafter. Such review must include consideration of whether to modify the reporting schedule, thereby authorizing the paroled person to submit reports quarterly, semiannually, or annually. The commission, after having retained jurisdiction of a person for a sufficient length of time to evidence satisfactory rehabilitation and cooperation, may further modify the terms and conditions of the person's parole, may discharge the person from parole, may relieve the person from making further reports, or may permit the person to leave the state or country, upon determining that such action is in the best interests of the person and of society.

"(3) This section does not affect the rights of a parolee to request modification of the terms and conditions of parole pursuant to s. 947.19."

Laws 2001, c. 2001–124, § 6, in subsec. (2), inserted the second sentence.

Law Review and Journal Commentaries

Probation in Florida. Vernon W. Clark, 14 U.Fla.L.Rev. 213 (1961).

Library References

Pardon and Parole ⚷93.
Westlaw Topic No. 284.
C.J.S. Pardon and Parole § 64.

Research References

Treatises and Practice Aids

16 Florida Practice Series § 10:15, Post Release--Control Release.

16 Florida Practice Series § 10:24, Discharge from Parole Supervision or Release Supervision.

Notes of Decisions

---

1. Construction and application

This section empowers the Parole and Probation Commission to determine the length of an individual's parole and to impose any term up to maximum period for which a person has been sentenced. Roach v. Mitchell, App. 2 Dist., 456 So.2d 963 (1984). Pardon And Parole ⚷ 67

This section providing that no person who has been placed on parole shall be discharged therefrom by commission prior to expiration of term for which he was sentenced is unambiguous and means that jurisdiction of parole commission to revoke is measured by time of original sentence and does not fluctuate because of time gained by good conduct. Easterlin v. Mayo, 69 So.2d 181 (1953). Pardon And Parole ⚷ 67

Time gained by prisoner by good behavior after incarceration was not deductible from period fixed in sentence in computing length of time prisoner was to remain on parole, and parole commission did not lose jurisdiction over prisoner because period fixed in sentence when shortened by time prisoner gained by good behavior expired prior to revocation of parole. Easterlin v. Mayo, 69 So.2d 181 (1953). Pardon And Parole ⚷ 67

2. Habeas corpus

A parolee, though not physically confined in prison, could maintain habeas corpus to secure discharge from penal supervision under a judgment and sentence entered upon an information which wholly failed to charge an offense, since conditions of parole constituted such a restraint of freedom as rendered parolee for all practical purposes in "custody". Sellers v. Bridges, 153 Fla. 586, 15 So.2d 293 (1943). Habeas Corpus ⚷ 516.1

3. Revocation of parole

Where defendant's sentence was three years in state prison to be followed by two years probation, and where defendant was released after serving only two years and two months of the three-year term, the two years of probation commenced upon defendant's release, and thus application to revoke his probation which was commenced more than two years later was untimely, even though it was within five years of the original sentence. State v. Tavel, App. 3 Dist., 407 So.2d 953 (1981), review denied 417 So.2d 331. Sentencing And Punishment ⚷ 1946; Sentencing And Punishment ⚷ 2010

4. Extension of parole

If parole period is to be longer than two years, parolee should be informed in writing of the reasons for extension; however, the absence of such written reasons does not result in loss of Parole and Probation Commission's statutory authority to impose an extended term or in loss of jurisdiction over parolee. Roach v. Mitchell, App. 2 Dist., 456 So.2d 963 (1984). Pardon And Parole ⚷ 67; Pardon And Parole ⚷ 78

Where parolee executed certificate of parole with full knowledge of its contents, agreeing to remain under supervision for six and one-half years, where he acquiesced in the terms and conditions of his parole without reservation, where he did not request a written statement of reasons for his extended term of parole nor seek administrative review, where his parole was revoked after two years of supervision had passed, and where he acted only upon his violation of the parole conditions, the Parole and Probation Commission's failure to provide written reasons for the extended term of parole beyond the standard two-year maximum was not jurisdictional; thus, parolee was still on parole at time of its revocation. Roach v. Mitchell, App. 2 Dist., 456 So.2d 963 (1984). Pardon And Parole ⚷ 78

947.25. Repealed by Laws 1988, c. 88-122, § 66, eff. July 1, 1988

Historical and Statutory Notes

Repealed § 947.25, which related to recommendations for clemency, was derived from:
Laws 1986, c. 86-183, § 34.
Laws 1974, c. 74-112, § 23.
Laws 1941, c. 20519, § 18.

947.26. Cooperation of custodian of prisoner; right of access

The warden or jailer of any jail or prison in which persons convicted of crime may be confined and all officers or employees thereof shall at all times cooperate with the commission and, upon its request, shall furnish it with such information as they may have respecting any person inquired about as will enable the commission properly to perform its duties. Such officials shall, at all reasonable times, when the public safety permits, give the members of the commission and its authorized agents and employees access to all prisoners in their charge.

Laws 1941, c. 20519, § 19; Laws 1986, c. 86–183, § 35; Laws 1988, c. 88–122, § 61. Amended by Laws 2000, c. 2000–161, § 27, eff. July 4, 2000.

Historical and Statutory Notes

Amendment Notes:

Laws 1986, c. 86–183, § 35, eff. Oct. 1, 1986, provided for the board of clemency review.

Laws 1988, c. 88–122, § 61, deleted reference to the board throughout the section.

Laws 2000, c. 2000–161, a reviser's bill, deleted "superintendent," preceding "warden".

Research References

Encyclopedias

Wardens, FL Jur. 2d Prisons & Prisoners § 33.

947.27. Expired

Historical and Statutory Notes

Laws 1941, c. 20519, § 29, which appeared as § 947.27, was an appropriation provision.

CHAPTER 948

PROBATION AND COMMUNITY CONTROL

Section

Cross References

Appeal by probationer, see § 924.06.
Clemency, see Const. Art. 4, § 8.

Compacts with other states, see §§ 949.07, 949.08.
Construction of law, see § 949.04.
Florida Corrections Code, see § 944.012 et seq.
Severability clause, see § 949.05.
Short title, see § 949.06.
Uniform law for out-of-state probation and parolee supervision, see § 949.07 et seq.

Law Review and Journal Commentaries

Capital offenses: Bifurcated trials. 24 U.Fla. L.Rev. 127 (1971).

Citizen volunteers: Workable solution to probation problem. 45 Fla.Bar J. 476 (1971).

Florida's rehabilitative sex offender laws. John Wallace Hamilton, 15 U.Fla.L.Rev. 245 (1962).

Survey of criminal law in Florida. Thomas A. Wills, 16 U.Miami L.Rev. 225 (1961).

United States Code Annotated

Probation, see 18 U.S.C.A. § 3601 et seq.

948.001. Definitions

As used in this chapter, the term:

(1) "Administrative probation" means a form of noncontact supervision in which an offender who presents a low risk of harm to the community may, upon satisfactory completion of half the term of probation, be transferred by the Department of Corrections to nonreporting status until expiration of the term of supervision.

(2) "Community control" means a form of intensive, supervised custody in the community, including surveillance on weekends and holidays, administered by officers with restricted caseloads. Community control is an individualized program in which the freedom of an offender is restricted within the community, home, or noninstitutional residential placement and specific sanctions are imposed and enforced.

(3) "Criminal quarantine community control" means intensive supervision, by officers with restricted caseloads, with a condition of 24-hour-per-day electronic monitoring, and a condition of confinement to a designated residence during designated hours.

(4) "Drug offender probation" means a form of intensive supervision which emphasizes treatment of drug offenders in accordance with individualized treatment plans administered by officers with restricted caseloads. Caseloads should be restricted to a maximum of 50 cases per officer in order to ensure an adequate level of staffing.

(5) "Probation" means a form of community supervision requiring specified contacts with parole and probation officers and other terms and conditions as provided in s. 948.03.

(6) "Qualified practitioner" means a psychiatrist licensed under chapter 458 or chapter 459, a psychologist licensed under chapter 490, or a social worker, a mental health counselor, or a marriage and family therapist licensed under

chapter 491 who practices in accordance with his or her respective practice act.

(7) "Risk assessment" means an assessment completed by an independent qualified practitioner to evaluate the level of risk associated when a sex offender has contact with a child.

(8) "Safety plan" means a written document prepared by the qualified practitioner, in collaboration with the sex offender, the child's parent or legal guardian, and, when appropriate, the child which establishes clear roles and responsibilities for each individual involved in any contact between the child and the sex offender.

(9) "Community residential drug punishment center" means a residential drug punishment center designated by the Department of Corrections. The Department of Corrections shall adopt rules as necessary to define and operate such a center.

(10) "Sex offender probation" or "sex offender community control" means a form of intensive supervision, with or without electronic monitoring, which emphasizes treatment and supervision of a sex offender in accordance with an individualized treatment plan administered by an officer who has a restricted caseload and specialized training. An officer who supervises an offender placed on sex offender probation or sex offender community control must meet as necessary with a treatment provider and polygraph examiner to develop and implement the supervision and treatment plan, if a treatment provider and polygraph examiner specially trained in the treatment and monitoring of sex offenders are reasonably available.

Laws 1983, c. 83–131, § 11; Laws 1991, c. 91–225, § 13; Laws 1992, c. 92–310, § 32; Laws 1993, c. 93–59, § 3; Laws 1993, c. 93–227, § 13; Laws 1995, c. 95–211, § 80. Amended by Laws 1997, c. 97–308, § 2, eff. Oct. 1, 1997; Laws 2004, c. 2004–373, § 1, eff. July 1, 2004; Laws 2005, c. 2005–67, § 3, eff. Jan. 1, 2006; Laws 2007, c. 2007–200, § 8, eff. July 1, 2007; Laws 2007, c. 2007–209, § 9, eff. July 1, 2007.

Historical and Statutory Notes

Amendment Notes:

Laws 1991, c. 91–225, § 13, eff. July 1, 1991, added subsec. (1); renumbered former subsec. (1) as subsec. (2); inserted subsec. (3); and renumbered former subsec. (2) as subsec. (4).

Laws 1992, c. 92–310, § 32, eff. July 6, 1992, in the definition of "drug offender probation" in the second sentence, substituted "should be" for "are".

Laws 1993, c. 93–59, § 3, eff. Oct. 1, 1993, added the definition of "community residential drug punishment center".

Laws 1993, c. 93–227, § 13, eff. Oct. 1, 1993, inserted the definition of "criminal quarantine community control" as subsec. (3); and redesignated former subsecs. (3) and (4) as subsecs. (4) and (5).

Laws 1993, c. 93–227, § 21, provides for applicability to offenses committed on or after October 1, 1993.

Laws 1993, c. 93–406, § 28, provides:

"(1) An offender designated for early release by the Control Release Authority who is serving:

"(a) A sentence for a controlled substance offense under s. 893.13(1)(e) or (1)(i), Florida Statutes (1991), for purchase or possession with intent to sell, manufacture, or deliver; or

"(b) A sentence, or has previously served a sentence, as a habitual offender under s. 775.084(1)(a), Florida Statutes, for a primary offense involving drug possession or purchase,

"may be released into supervision under s. 948.001(3) [redesignated as § 948.001(4) by Laws 1993, c. 93–227, § 13], Florida Statutes. Supervision may include a requirement that a substance abuse assessment be conducted and, when warranted, appropriate substance abuse treatment services shall be provided.

"(2) An offender designated for early release by the Control Release Authority who is serving:

"(a) A sentence for a controlled substance offense under s. 893.13(1)(e) or (1)(i), Florida Statutes (1991), for sale, manufacture, or delivery; or

"(b) A sentence, or has previously served a sentence, as a habitual offender under s. 775.084(1)(a), Florida Statutes, for a primary offense involving drug sale, manufacture, delivery, or trafficking,

"shall be released into supervision under s. 948.001(3) [redesignated as § 948.001(4) by Laws 1993, c. 93–227, § 13], Florida Statutes. Supervision may include a requirement that a substance abuse assessment be conducted and, when warranted, appropriate substance abuse treatment services shall be provided."

Laws 1993, c. 93–406, § 30, provides for the repeal of Laws 1993, c. 93–406, § 28, effective June 1, 1995.

Laws 1995, c. 95–211, § 80, a reviser's bill, in subsec. (1) substituted a reference to § 948.09 for a reference to § 945.30 at the end.

Laws 1997, c. 97–308, § 2, eff. Oct. 1, 1997, added the definition of "sex offender probation" or "sex offender community control".

Laws 2004, c. 2004–373, § 1, in subsec. (1), substituted "transferred" for "placed" preceding "by the", substituted "to" for "on" preceding "nonreporting", and deleted the second and third sentences, which formerly read, "The department is authorized to collect an initial processing fee of up to $50 for each probationer reduced to administrative probation. Such offender is exempt from further payment for cost of supervision as required in s. 948.09.".

Laws 2005, c. 2005–67, § 3, redesignated subsecs. (6) and (7) as subsecs. (9) and (10); and added new subsecs. (6), (7), and (8), defining "Qualified practitioner", "Risk assessment", and "Safety plan", respectively.

Laws 2007, c. 2007–200, § 8, in subsec. (6), at the end, substituted "practices in accordance with his or her respective practice act" for ", as determined by rule of the respective boards, has the coursework, training, qualifications, and experience to evaluate and treat sex offenders".

Laws 2007, c. 2007–209, § 9, in subsec. (6), substituted "practices in accordance with his or her respective practice act" with ", as determined by rule of the respective boards, has the coursework, training, qualifications, and experience to evaluate and treat sex offenders" at the end.

Research References

Treatises and Practice Aids

11 Florida Practice Series § 13:3, Probation, Treatment, and Educational Provisions.

16 Florida Practice Series § 6:9, Alternatives To, and Mitigation Of, Criminal Punishment Code Sentencing--Drug Offender Probation.

16 Florida Practice Series § 1:43, Sentencing Alternatives.

16 Florida Practice Series § 1:50, Sentencing Alternatives--Split Probation.

16 Florida Practice Series § 5:32, Completing the Criminal Punishment Code Scoresheet--Legal Status Violation (Section V).

16 Florida Practice Series § 7:12, Administrative Probation.

16 Florida Practice Series § 7:15, Criminal Quarantine Community Control.

16 Florida Practice Series § 7:18, Sex Offender Probation or Community Control.

United States Code Annotated

Sex offender registration, supervised release, see 18 U.S.C.A. § 3583.

Notes of Decisions

---

1. Community control

Sentence of community control as condition of probation did not constitute "nonstate prison sanction," under the sentencing guidelines; therefore, sentence of community control as condition of probation was departure sentence under the sentencing guidelines requiring written reasons for its imposition for defendant whose recommended sentence was any "nonstate prison sanction"; disapproving *Davis v. State,* 461 So.2d 1003 (Fla.App. 1 Dist.); *Louzon v. State,* 460 So.2d 551 (Fla.App. 5 Dist.). State v. Mestas, 507 So.2d 587 (1987). Sentencing And Punishment ⚿ 802; Sentencing And Punishment ⚿ 1976(1)

Community control is proper sanction to be imposed by trial court under sentencing guidelines category of any nonstate prison sanction.

Davis v. State, App. 1 Dist., 461 So.2d 1003 (1984). Sentencing And Punishment ⚷ 1930

"Community control" as used in sentencing guidelines does not encompass incarceration in state prison and is therefore properly classified as a "non-state prison sanction." Louzon v. State, App. 5 Dist., 460 So.2d 551 (1984). Sentencing And Punishment ⚷ 789

Community control is a more severe sanction than probation. Stranigan v. State, App. 2 Dist., 457 So.2d 546 (1984). Sentencing And Punishment ⚷ 1817

2. Discretion of trial court

Trial court did not abuse its discretion in finding willful and substantial violation of probation based on defendant's dismissal from court-ordered drug rehabilitation or treatment program due to nonattendance, even though sentencing judge did not specify number of attempts defendant would have to successfully complete program and time period for compliance; reasonable person would understand that he must undertake compliance with condition as soon as probation was ordered, and defendant entered program shortly after he was placed on probation, and was advised that he would be terminated from program for missing classes and that termination would be violation of probation. Lawson v. State, App. 5 Dist., 941 So.2d 485 (2006), review granted 954 So.2d 27, approved 969 So.2d 222. Sentencing And Punishment ⚷ 1977(3)

3. Administrative probation

Defendant had constructive notice of statutory condition of probation that he was to submit to random drug testing upon request of his probation officer, thus supporting revocation of probation based upon positive test results of drug test and defendant's admission to using cocaine and marijuana. Phillips v. State, App. 2 Dist., 971 So.2d 255 (2008). Sentencing And Punishment ⚷ 1920

4. Drug offender probation

Sentencing court could not impose drug offender probation regarding conviction for carrying a concealed weapon or firearm, which was not a drug-related offense set forth in statute governing drug offender probation. Beals v. State, App. 4 Dist., 14 So.3d 286 (2009). Sentencing and Punishment ⚷ 1864

5. Resentencing

Resentencing on defendant's conviction for possession of cocaine was warranted following sentencing court's reference during hearing to incorrect authority as basis for its departure from guidelines scoresheet recommendation, which effectively precluded State from contesting court's sentence or building record to support argument; court's subsequent written citation to proper authority on guidelines scoresheet rendered record unclear as to which authority sentence was based upon. State v. Williams, App. 4 Dist., 759 So.2d 1 (1998). Criminal Law ⚷ 1181.5(8)

948.01. When court may place defendant on probation or into community control

(1) Any state court having original jurisdiction of criminal actions may at a time to be determined by the court, with or without an adjudication of the guilt of the defendant, hear and determine the question of the probation of a defendant in a criminal case, except for an offense punishable by death, who has been found guilty by the verdict of a jury, has entered a plea of guilty or a plea of nolo contendere, or has been found guilty by the court trying the case without a jury.

(a) If the court places the defendant on probation or into community control for a felony, the department shall provide immediate supervision by an officer employed in compliance with the minimum qualifications for officers as provided in s. 943.13. A private entity may not provide probationary or supervision services to felony or misdemeanor offenders sentenced or placed on probation or other supervision by the circuit court.

(b) The department, in consultation with the Office of the State Courts Administrator, shall develop and disseminate to the courts uniform order of supervision forms by July 1 of each year or as necessary. The courts shall use the uniform order of supervision forms provided by the department for all persons placed on community supervision.

(2) If it appears to the court upon a hearing of the matter that the defendant is not likely again to engage in a criminal course of conduct and that the ends of justice and the welfare of society do not require that the defendant presently suffer the penalty imposed by law, the court, in its discretion, may either adjudge the defendant to be guilty or stay and withhold the adjudication of guilt. In either case, the court shall stay and withhold the imposition of sentence upon the defendant and shall place a felony defendant upon probation. If the defendant is found guilty of a nonfelony offense as the result of a trial or entry of a plea of guilty or nolo contendere, regardless of whether adjudication is withheld, the court may place the defendant on probation. In addition to court costs and fees and notwithstanding any law to the contrary, the court may impose a fine authorized by law if the offender is a nonfelony offender who is not placed on probation. However, a defendant who is placed on probation for a misdemeanor may not be placed under the supervision of the department unless the circuit court was the court of original jurisdiction.

(3) If, after considering the provisions of subsection (2) and the offender's prior record or the seriousness of the offense, it appears to the court in the case of a felony disposition that probation is an unsuitable dispositional alternative to imprisonment, the court may place the offender in a community control program as provided in s. 948.10. Or, in a case of prior disposition of a felony commitment, upon motion of the offender or the department or upon its own motion, the court may, within the period of its retained jurisdiction following commitment, suspend the further execution of the disposition and place the offender in a community control program upon such terms as the court may require. The court may consult with a local offender advisory council pursuant to s. 948.90 with respect to the placement of an offender into community control. Not later than 3 working days before the hearing on the motion, the department shall forward to the court all relevant material on the offender's progress while in custody. If this sentencing alternative to incarceration is utilized, the court shall:

(a) Determine what community-based sanctions will be imposed in the community control plan. Community-based sanctions may include, but are not limited to, rehabilitative restitution in money or in kind, curfew, revocation or suspension of the driver's license, community service, deprivation of nonessential activities or privileges, or other appropriate restraints on the offender's liberty.

(b) After appropriate sanctions for the offense are determined, develop, approve, and order a plan of community control which contains rules, requirements, conditions, and programs that are designed to encourage noncriminal functional behavior and promote the rehabilitation of the offender and the protection of the community. If the offense was a controlled substance violation, the conditions shall include a requirement that the offender submit to random substance abuse testing intermittently throughout the term of supervision, upon the direction of the correctional probation officer as defined in s. 943.10(3).

(4) The sanctions imposed by order of the court shall be commensurate with the seriousness of the offense. When community control or a program of public service is ordered by the court, the duration of community control supervision or public service may not be longer than the sentence that could have been imposed if the offender had been committed for the offense or a period not to exceed 2 years, whichever is less. When restitution or public service is ordered by the court, the amount of restitution or public service may not be greater than an amount which the offender could reasonably be expected to pay or perform.

(5) The imposition of sentence may not be suspended and the defendant thereupon placed on probation or into community control unless the defendant is placed under the custody of the department or another public or private entity. A private entity may not provide probationary or supervision services to felony or misdemeanor offenders sentenced or placed on probation or other supervision by the circuit court.

(6) When the court, under any of the foregoing subsections, places a defendant on probation or into community control, it may specify that the defendant serve all or part of the probationary or community control period in a community residential or nonresidential facility under the jurisdiction of the Department of Corrections or the Department of Children and Family Services or any public or private entity providing such services, and it shall require the payment prescribed in s. 948.09.

(7)(a) Notwithstanding s. 921.0024 and effective for offenses committed on or after July 1, 2009, the sentencing court may place the defendant into a postadjudicatory treatment-based drug court program if the defendant's Criminal Punishment Code scoresheet total sentence points under s. 921.0024 are 52 points or fewer and the defendant is a nonviolent felony offender, amenable to substance abuse treatment, and otherwise qualifies under s. 397.334(3). The satisfactory completion of the program shall be a condition of the defendant's probation or community control. As used in this subsection, the term "nonviolent felony" means a third degree felony violation under chapter 810 or any other felony offense that is not a forcible felony as defined in s. 776.08.

(b) The defendant must be fully advised of the purpose of the program, and the defendant must agree to enter the program. The original sentencing court shall relinquish jurisdiction of the defendant's case to the postadjudicatory drug court program until the defendant is no longer active in the program, the case is returned to the sentencing court due to the defendant's termination from the program for failure to comply with the terms thereof, or the defendant's sentence is completed.

Laws 1941, c. 20519, § 20; Laws 1945, c. 22858, § 7; Laws 1959, c. 59–130, § 1; Laws 1961, c. 61–498, § 1; Laws 1965, c. 65–453, § 1; Laws 1967, c. 67–28, § 1; Laws 1967, c. 67–204, § 1; Laws 1974, c. 74–112, §§ 12, 13; Laws 1975, c. 75–301, § 3; Laws 1976, c. 76–238, § 3; Laws 1977, c. 77–120, § 90; Laws 1977, c. 77–174, § 1; Laws 1979, c. 79–3, § 109; Laws 1983, c. 83–131, § 13; Laws 1985, c. 85–288, § 14; Laws

1986, c. 86–106, § 1; Laws 1987, c. 87–211, § 4; Laws 1988, c. 88–122, § 69; Laws 1989, c. 89–526, § 36; Laws 1990, c. 90–337, §§ 7, 16; Laws 1991, c. 91–225, §§ 2, 14; Laws 1991, c. 91–280, §§ 1, 15; Laws 1993, c. 93–227, § 14. Amended by Laws 1996, c. 96–322, § 17, eff. Oct. 1, 1996; Laws 1997, c. 97–78, § 21, eff. May 23, 1997; Laws 1997, c. 97–102, § 1876, eff. July 1, 1997; Laws 1997, c. 97–239, § 6, eff. May 30, 1997; Laws 1998, c. 98–81, § 13, eff. July 1, 1998; Laws 1999, c. 99–3, § 121, eff. June 29, 1999; Laws 1999, c. 99–8, § 323, eff. June 29, 1999; Laws 2000, c. 2000–246, § 3, eff. Oct. 1, 2000; Laws 2001, c. 2001–55, § 4, eff. July 1, 2001; Laws 2004, c. 2004–373, §§ 2 to 12, 40, eff. July 1, 2004; Laws 2008, c. 2008–250, § 5, eff. Oct. 1, 2008; Laws 2009, c. 2009–6, § 6, eff. Feb. 1, 2009; Laws 2009, c. 2009–63, § 10, eff. July 1, 2009; Laws 2009, c. 2009–64, § 3, eff. July 1, 2009.

Supersedure

Revised Florida Rules of Criminal Procedure were adopted December 6, 1972, to become effective February 1, 1973 (272 So.2d 65). The adopting order of the Supreme Court provided that conflicting rules and statutes are superseded and that statutes not superseded shall remain in effect as rules promulgated by the Supreme Court. For related rule provisions, see Criminal Procedure Rule 3.790.

Historical and Statutory Notes

Amendment Notes:

Laws 1941, c. 20519, § 35, repealed all conflicting laws and parts of laws.

Laws 1945, c. 22858, § 7, modified a statutory reference in former subsec. (4) [now subsec. (7)].

Laws 1959, c. 59–130, § 1, rewrote subsec. (1) which formerly read:

"The courts of the state having original jurisdiction of criminal actions, where the defendant in a criminal case has been found guilty upon verdict or plea, except for an offense punishable by death or life imprisonment, may, at a time to be determined by the court, hear and determine the question of the probation of such defendant."

The 1959 law also amended subsec. (3) [now (2)] by inserting, in the first sentence, "without adjudging the defendant to be guilty" following "in its discretion may" and substituted "withhold the adjudication of guilt and" for "suspend" following "thereupon stay and".

Laws 1961, c. 61–498, § 1, substituted, in subsec. (1), "either with or without an adjudication of the guilt of the defendant" for "without adjudging the defendant to be guilty" following "determined by the court"; substituted, in the first sentence of subsec. (3) [now (2)], "either adjudge the defendant to be guilty or" for "without adjudging the defendant to be guilty" following "in its discretion, may"; and inserted "in either case stay and withhold" following "withhold the adjudication of guilt and".

The name "parole commission" was changed to "probation and parole commission" by authority of Laws 1965, c. 65–453, § 1. See § 947.01.

Laws 1967, c. 67–28, § 1, and Laws 1967, c. 67–204, § 1, renumbered former subsec. (4) as subsec. (5) [now subsec. (7)] and inserted subsec. (4) [now subsec. (6)].

Laws 1974, c. 74–112, made referral to the parole and probation commission mandatory where the penalty for the offense may involve imprisonment in the state prison, required that the investigation report be prepared prior to sentencing and inserted the concluding words to a former subsec. (2) "pursuant to the provisions of section 921.231, Florida Statutes", added the third sentence to subsec. (3) [now subsec. (2)], substituted "for a misdemeanor as a felony, except for a capital felony" for "in the county jail" in former subsec. (4) [now subsec. (6)], and added the provisions contained in subsec. (6) [now subsec. (8)].

Laws 1975, c. 75–301, specified "circuit" court.

Laws 1975, c. 75–301, § 7, provided that the law take effect July 1, 1975: however, it was approved by the governor on July 3, 1975.

Laws 1976, c. 76–238, provided for custody in the Salvation Army or other public or private entity in former subsec. (5) [now subsec. (7)], provided for Salvation Army facility in former subsec. (6) [now subsec. (8)], and added to the end of former subsec. (6) [now subsec. (8)] the words "and it shall require the payment prescribed in s. 945.30".

Laws 1977, c. 77–120, a reviser's bill, amended subsecs. (2) [now deleted], (3) [now subsec. (2)] and former subsec. (6) [now subsec. (8)] of this section to conform with Laws 1975, c. 75–49, which created the department of offender rehabilitation (see § 20.315) and transferred to the department certain functions performed by the division of corrections of the department of health and rehabilitative services and the parole and probation commission of the department of offender rehabilitation.

Laws 1977, c. 77–174, a reviser's bill, amended a former subsec. (2) of this section to reflect language editorially inserted or substituted in the interest of clarity by the division of statutory revision.

Laws 1979, c. 79–3, a reviser's bill, provided for substitution of references to the department and secretary of "corrections" for the department and secretary of "offender rehabilitation" to conform with Laws 1978, c. 78–53.

Laws 1983, c. 83–131, § 13, interpolated subsecs. (4) to (7), renumbered former subsecs. (4) to (6) as subsecs. (8) to (10) [now subsecs. (6) to (8)], provided for programs of community control in subsecs. (8) to (10) [now subsecs. (6) to (8)], and added subsec. (11) [now subsec. (9)].

Laws 1985, c. 85–288, § 14, eff. July 1, 1985, in subsec. (3) [now subsec. (2)] deleted "under the supervision and control of the department for the duration of such probation" at the end of the first sentence and deleted the second sentence, and inserted in the third sentence "circuit court was court of original jurisdiction and the circuit"; substituted references to community control for supervision and provided for public service in subsec. (5) [now subsec. (4)]; and, in subsec. (8) [now subsec. (6)] substituted "imposed a split sentence whereby the defendant is" for "direct the defendant" in the first sentence and added at the end thereof "which may include a term of years or less" and provided for community control in the last sentence.

Laws 1986, c. 86–106, § 1, eff. June 13, 1986, inserted near the beginning of a former subsec. (6) ", or enters into the pretrial intervention program pursuant to s. 944.025".

Laws 1987, c. 87–211, § 4, eff. June 30, 1987, added subsec. (12) [now subsec. (10)] to provide circumstances in which an offender may not be placed in community control.

Laws 1988, c. 88–122, § 69, eff. July 1, 1988, inserted the penultimate sentence of subsec. (12) [now subsec. (10)].

Laws 1989, c. 89–526, § 36, eff. Oct. 1, 1989, in subsec. (1), added the last sentence, relating to supervision.

Laws 1990, c. 90–337, § 7, eff. July 1, 1990, in subsec. (1), in the second sentence inserted "the department shall supervise the offender", and added the third sentence; and, in subsec. (3) [now subsec. (2)], added the last sentence.

Laws 1990, c. 90–337, § 16, eff. Oct. 1, 1990, in subsec. (4)(b) [now subsec. (3)(b)], added the second sentence.

Laws 1990, c. 90–337, § 22 provided therein that the amendment take effect July 1, 1990; however, approval by the governor occurred subsequent thereto. The Florida Supreme Court in an advisory opinion to the governor of July 19, 1979 (374 So.2d 959) stated in part "* * * the effective date provided in the bill is inoperative unless the bill becomes law on or before that date" and concludes that under such circumstances the provision of Const. Art. 3, § 9, that the law take effect on the sixtieth day after adjournment sine die of the session of the legislature in which enacted, is applicable.

Laws 1991, c. 91–225, § 2, eff. July 1, 1991, reenacted subsec. (10) [now subsec. (8)] without change "For the purpose of incorporating the amendment to section 945.30, Florida Statutes, in references thereto".

Laws 1991, c. 91–225, § 14, eff. July 1, 1991, added provisions designated as subsecs. (11), (12), and (13).

Laws 1991, c. 91–280, § 1, eff. Oct. 1, 1991, in subsec. (1), in the next to last sentence, substituted "provide immediate supervision" for "supervise the offender and immediate supervision shall be provided"; in the last sentence, inserted "felony or misdemeanor"; deleted former subsec. (2); renumbered subsequent subsections accordingly; in present subsec. (2), rewrote the present last sentence and deleted a former last sentence; in subsec. (3), in the first sentence, corrected an internal reference and added "as provided in s. 948.10"; in subsec. (4), deleted a former last sentence that provided that an offender who participates in any work program under the provisions of this chapter will be considered an employee of the state for purposes of liability, unless otherwise provided by law; deleted a former subsec. (6); redesignated subsequent subsections accordingly; in subsecs. (7) and (8), deleted references to Salvation Army; corrected the citation at the end of subsec. (8); and, in subsec. (10), inserted references to adjudication withheld.

Former subsec. 6 read:

"Whenever an offender is required by the court to participate in any work program under the provisions of this chapter, enters into the pretrial intervention program pursuant to s. 944.025, or volunteers to work in a supervised work program conducted by a specified state, county, municipal, or community service organization or to work for the victim, either as an alternative to monetary restitution or as a part of the rehabilitative or community control program, the offender shall be considered an employee of the state for the purposes of chapter 440. In determining the average weekly wage, unless otherwise determined by a specific funding program, all remuneration received from the employer shall be considered a gratuity, and the offender shall not be entitled to any benefits otherwise payable under s. 440.15, regardless of whether he may be receiving wages and remuneration from other employment with another employer and regardless of his future wage-earning capacity. The provisions of this subsection do not apply to any person performing labor under a sentence of a court to perform community services as provided in s. 316.193."

Section 1 of Laws 1991, c. 91–280 provides that the amendment by that section is effective Oct. 1, 1991, and is applicable to offenses committed on or after that date.

Laws 1991, c. 91–280, § 15, eff. Oct. 1, 1991, in provisions contained in subsec. (3), added par. (c).

Laws 1993, c. 93–227, § 14, eff. Oct. 1, 1993, in subsec. (10), substituted "may" for "shall" in the introductory clause, substituted "prohibits" for "shall be construed to prohibit" before "placement of certain inmates", and "does" for "shall" before "not include manslaughter or burglary"; and added subsec. (14).

Application of Laws 1993, c. 93–227 to offenses committed on or after Oct. 1, 1993, see Historical and Statutory Notes under § 796.03.

Laws 1996, c. 96–322, § 17, eff. Oct. 1, 1996, reenacted subsec. (14) for the purpose of incorporating an amendment to § 775.0877 in a reference thereto.

Laws 1997, c. 97–78, § 21, eff. May 23, 1997, in subsec. (11), rewrote par. (b), which formerly read:

"If the offender does not meet the terms and conditions of probation or community control, the court shall impose a term of incarceration equal to the remaining portion of the order of probation or community control. Such term of incarceration shall be served under applicable law or county ordinance governing service of sentences in state or county jurisdiction. This paragraph does not prohibit any other sanction provided by law."

Laws 1997, c. 97–102, eff. July 1, 1997, removed gender-specific references applicable to human beings from volume 4 of the Florida Statutes without substantive changes in legal effect.

Laws 1997, c. 97–239, § 6, eff. May 30, 1997, reenacted subsecs. (9) and (13)(b) of this section for the purpose of incorporating an amendment to § 948.06 in a reference thereto.

Laws 1998, c. 98–81, § 13, added subsec. (15).

Laws 1999, c. 99–3, § 121, eff. June 29, 1999, amended the section to improve clarity and facilitate correct interpretation.

Laws 1999, c. 99–8, § 323, eff. June 29, 1999, substituted "Department of Children and Family Services" for "Department of Health and Rehabilitative Services".

Laws 2000, c. 2000–246, § 3, reenacted subsec. (15) for the purpose of incorporating the amendment to § 800.04 in a reference thereto.

Laws 2001, c. 55, § 4, in subsec. (13), substituted "s. 893.13(2)(a) or s. 893.13(6)(a)" for "chapter 893".

Laws 2004, c. 2004–373, §§ 2 to 12, renumbered former subsec. (5) as § 948.10(10), renumbered former subsec. (6) as § 948.012(1), renumbered former subsec. (9) as § 948.10(9), renumbered former subsec. (10) as § 948.10(2), renumbered former subsec. (11) as § 948.012(2), renumbered former subsec. (12) as § 948.012(3), renumbered former subsec. (13) as § 948.20, renumbered former subsec. (14) as § 948.101(3), renumbered former subsec. (15) as § 948.013(2), and rewrote this section, which formerly read:

"(1) Any court of the state having original jurisdiction of criminal actions may at a time to be determined by the court, either with or without an adjudication of the guilt of the defendant, hear and determine the question of the probation of a defendant in a criminal case, except for an offense punishable by death, who has been found guilty by the verdict of a jury, has entered a plea of guilty or a plea of nolo contendere, or has been found guilty by the court trying the case without a jury. If the court places the defendant on probation or into community control for a felony, the department shall provide immediate supervision by an officer employed in compliance with the minimum qualifications for officers as provided in s. 943.13. In no circumstances shall a private entity provide probationary or supervision services to felony or misdemeanor offenders sentenced or placed on probation or other supervision by the circuit court.

"(2) If it appears to the court upon a hearing of the matter that the defendant is not likely again to engage in a criminal course of conduct and that the ends of justice and the welfare of society do not require that the defendant presently suffer the penalty imposed by law, the court, in its discretion, may either adjudge the defendant to be guilty or stay and withhold the adjudication of guilt; and, in either case, it shall stay and withhold the imposition of sentence upon such defendant and shall place the defendant upon probation. However, no defendant placed on probation for a misdemeanor may be placed under the supervision of the department unless the circuit court was the court of original jurisdiction.

"(3) If, after considering the provisions of subsection (2) and the offender's prior record or the seriousness of the offense, it appears to the court in the case of a felony disposition that probation is an unsuitable dispositional alternative to imprisonment, the court may place the offender in a community control program as provided in s. 948.10. Or, in a case of prior disposition of a felony commitment, upon motion of the offender or the department or upon its own motion, the court may, within the period of its retained jurisdiction following commitment, suspend the further execution of the disposition and place the offender in a community control program upon such terms as the court may require. The court may consult with a local offender advisory council pursuant to s. 948.90 with respect to the placement of an offender into community control. Not later than 3 working days before the hearing on the motion, the department shall forward to the court all relevant material on the offender's progress while in custody. If this sentencing alternative to incarceration is utilized, the court shall:

"(a) Determine what community-based sanctions will be imposed in the community control plan. Community-based sanctions may include, but are not limited to, rehabilitative restitution in money or in kind, curfew, revocation or suspension of the driver's license, community service, deprivation of nonessential activities or privileges, or other appropriate restraints on the offender's liberty.

"(b) After appropriate sanctions for the offense are determined, develop, approve, and order a plan of community control which contains rules, requirements, conditions, and programs that are designed to encourage noncriminal functional behavior and promote the rehabilitation of the offender and the protection of the community. If the offense was a controlled substance violation, the conditions shall include a requirement that the offender submit to random substance abuse testing intermittently throughout the term of supervision, upon the direction of the correctional probation officer as defined in s. 943.10(3).

"(c) Require the department to provide notifications pursuant to s. 948.10(6).

"(4) The sanctions imposed by order of the court shall be commensurate with the seriousness of the offense. When community control or a program of public service is ordered by the court, the duration of community control supervision or public service may not be longer than the sentence that could have been imposed if the offender had been committed for the offense or a period not to exceed 2 years, whichever is less. When restitution or public service is ordered by the court, the amount of restitution or public service may not be greater than an amount which the offender could reasonably be expected to pay or perform.

"(5) Upon completion of the sanctions imposed in the community control plan before the expiration of the term ordered by the court, the department may petition the court to discharge the offender from community control supervision or to return the offender to a program of regular probation supervision. In considering the petition, the court should recognize the limited staff resources committed to the community control program, the purpose of the program, and the offender's successful compliance with the conditions set forth in the order of the court.

"(6) Whenever punishment by imprisonment for a misdemeanor or a felony, except for a capital felony, is prescribed, the court, in its discretion, may, at the time of sentencing, impose a split sentence whereby the defendant is to be placed on probation or, with respect to any such felony, into community control upon completion of any specified period of such sentence which may include a term of years or less. In such case, the court shall stay and withhold the imposition of the remainder of sentence imposed upon the defendant and direct that the defendant be placed upon probation or into community control after serving such period as may be imposed by the court. The period of probation or community control shall commence immediately upon the release of the defendant from incarceration, whether by parole or gain-time allowances.

"(7) In no case shall the imposition of sentence be suspended and the defendant thereupon placed on probation or into community control unless such defendant is placed under the custody of the department or another public or private entity.

"(8) When the court, under any of the foregoing subsections, places a defendant on probation or into community control, it may specify that the defendant serve all or part of the probationary or community control period in a community residential or nonresidential facility under the jurisdiction of the Department of Corrections or the Department of Children and Family Services or any public or private entity providing such services, and it shall require the payment prescribed in s. 948.09.

"(9) Procedures governing violations of community control shall be the same as those described in s. 948.06 with respect to probation.

"(10) An offender may not be placed in community control if:

"(a) Convicted of or adjudication withheld for a forcible felony as defined in s. 776.08, and

"(b) Previously convicted of or adjudication withheld for a forcible felony as defined in s. 776.08.

"Nothing in this subsection prohibits placement of certain inmates on community control pursuant to s. 947.1747. For the purposes of this subsection, a forcible felony does not include manslaughter or burglary.

"(11) The court may also impose a split sentence whereby the defendant is sentenced to a term of probation which may be followed by a period of incarceration or, with respect to a felony, into community control, as follows:

"(a) If the offender meets the terms and conditions of probation or community control, any term of incarceration may be modified by court order to eliminate the term of incarceration.

"(b) If the offender does not meet the terms and conditions of probation or community control, the court may revoke, modify, or continue the probation or community control as provided in s. 948.06. If the probation or community control is revoked, the court may impose any sentence that it could have imposed at the time the offender was placed on probation or community control. The court may not provide credit for time served for any portion of a probation or community control term toward a subsequent term of probation or community control. However, the court may not impose a subsequent term of probation or community control which, when combined with any amount of time served on preceding terms of probation or community control for offenses pending before the court for sentencing, would exceed the maximum penalty allowable as provided in s. 775.082. Such term of incarceration shall be served under applicable law or county ordinance governing service of sentences in state or county jurisdiction. This paragraph does not prohibit any other sanction provided by law.

"(12) The court may also impose split probation whereby, upon satisfactory completion of half the term of probation, the Department of Corrections may place the offender on administrative probation as defined in s. 948.001 for the remainder of the term of supervision.

"(13) If it appears to the court upon a hearing that the defendant is a chronic substance abuser whose criminal conduct is a violation of s. 893.13(2)(a) or (6)(a), the court may either adjudge the defendant guilty or stay and withhold the adjudication of guilt; and, in either case, it may stay and withhold the imposition of sentence and place the defendant on drug offender probation.

"(a) The Department of Corrections shall develop and administer a drug offender probation program which emphasizes a combination of treatment and intensive community supervision approaches and which includes provision for supervision of offenders in accordance with a specific treatment plan. The program may include the use of graduated sanctions consistent with the conditions imposed by the court. Drug offender probation status shall include surveillance and random drug testing, and may include those measures normally associated with community control, except that specific treatment conditions and other treatment approaches necessary to monitor this population may be ordered.

"(b) Offenders placed on drug offender probation are subject to revocation of probation as provided in s. 948.06.

"(14) The court may place a defendant who is being sentenced for criminal transmission of HIV in violation of s. 775.0877 on criminal quarantine community control. The Department of Corrections shall develop and administer a criminal quarantine community control program emphasizing intensive supervision with 24-hour-per-day electronic monitoring. Criminal quarantine community control status must include surveillance and may include other measures normally associated with community control, except that specific conditions necessary to monitor this population may be ordered.

"(15) Effective for an offense committed on or after July 1, 1998, a person is ineligible for placement on administrative probation if the person is sentenced to or is serving a term of probation or community control, regardless of the conviction or adjudication, for committing, or attempting, conspiring, or soliciting to commit, any of the felony offenses described in s. 787.01 or s. 787.02, where the victim is a minor and the defendant is not the victim's parent; s. 787.025; chapter 794; s. 796.03; s. 800.04; s. 825.1025(2)(b); s. 827.071; s. 847.0133; s. 847.0135; or s. 847.0145."

Laws 2004, c. 2004–373, § 40, reenacted subsec. (8) [now subsec. (6)] of this section for the purpose of incorporating the amendment to § 948.09 in a reference thereto.

Laws 2008, c. 2008–250, § 5, deleted former subsec. (3)(c), which had read:

"[(3)](c) Require the department to provide notifications pursuant to s. 948.10(7)."

Laws 2009, c. 2009–6, § 6, rewrote subsec. (6), which formerly read:

"(2) If it appears to the court upon a hearing of the matter that the defendant is not likely again to engage in a criminal course of conduct and that the ends of justice and the welfare of society do not require that the defendant presently suffer the penalty imposed by law, the court, in its discretion, may either adjudge the defendant to be guilty or stay and withhold the adjudication of guilt; and, in either case, it shall stay and withhold the imposition of sentence upon such defendant and shall place the defendant upon probation. However, no defendant placed on probation for a misdemeanor may be placed under the supervision of the department unless the circuit court was the court of original jurisdiction."

Laws 2009, c. 2009–63, § 10, rewrote subsec. (1), which formerly read:

"(1) Any court of the state having original jurisdiction of criminal actions may at a time to be determined by the court, either with or without an adjudication of the guilt of the defendant, hear and determine the question of the probation of a defendant in a criminal case, except for an offense punishable by death, who has been found guilty by the verdict of a jury, has entered a plea of guilty or a plea of nolo contendere, or has been found guilty by the court trying the case without a jury. If the court places the defendant on probation or into community control for a felony, the department shall provide immediate supervision by an officer employed in compliance with the minimum qualifications for officers as provided in s. 943.13. In no circumstances shall a private entity provide probationary or supervision services to felony or misdemeanor offenders sentenced or placed on probation or other supervision by the circuit court."

Laws 2009, c. 2009–64, § 3, added subsec. (7), relating to conditions under which the court may place defendants into a postadjudicatory treatment-based drug court program.

Cross References

Appeal by probationer, see § 924.06.

Continuing criminal enterprise, necessity of serving mandatory minimum term of imprisonment notwithstanding this section, see § 893.20.

Criminal offenders, disposition and sentencing, see § 921.187.

Investigations and recommendations regarding probation, see § 947.16.

Juvenile courts, see § 949.01.

Manslaughter resulting from motor vehicle operation or vehicular homicide, mandatory adjudication, plea of lesser included offense, see § 316.656.

Misdemeanor probation, sexual predator and sexual offender registration search, see § 943.04352.

Prohibition on withholding adjudication in felony cases, see § 775.08435.

Sentencing alternatives, probation, see § 921.187.

Treatment-based drug court programs, see § 397.334.

Law Review and Journal Commentaries

Adjudication of guilt, necessity in Florida. Granvel S. Kirkland, 12 U.Fla.L.Rev. 102 (1959).

Instruction as to possibility of parole as reversible error. 7 Miami L.Q. 120 (1952).

New parole and probation act. James T. Vocelle, 16 Fla.L.J. 9 (1942).

Parole and probation in Florida. James T. Vocelle, 18 Fla.L.J. 35 (1944).

Parole in Florida. Vernon G. Clark, 11 U.Fla. L.Rev. 68 (1958).

Recoupment of defense costs as a probation condition. 5 Stetson L.Rev. 117 (1975).

Rules of criminal procedure. Thomas A. Wills, 22 U.Miami L.Rev. 240, 272 (1967).

Sentence. Thomas A. Wills, 20 U.Miami L.Rev. 264 (1965).

Sentences in criminal cases. Thomas A. Wills, 14 U.Miami L.Rev. 501 (1960).

Sentencing alternatives to fine and imprisonment. Francis J. Merceret, 31 U.Miami L.Rev. 387 (1977).

Sentencing upon revocation of probation in Florida. 30 U.Miami L.Rev. 1063 (1976).

Library References

Sentencing and Punishment ⚷1800 to 1988, 2045 to 2085.

Westlaw Topic No. 350H.

C.J.S. Criminal Law §§ 556 to 575, 579 to 580, 2084, 2144 to 2155.

Research References

ALR Library

113 ALR 5th 597, Downward Departure Under State Sentencing Guidelines Permitting Downward Departure for Defendants With Significantly Reduced Mental Capacity, Including Alcohol or Drug Dependency.

76 ALR 5th 485, Effect of Delay in Taking Defendant Into Custody After Conviction and Sentence.

11 ALR 4th 999, Admissibility of Hearsay Evidence in Probation Revocation Hearings.

146 ALR 369, Relief in Habeas Corpus for Violation of Accused's Right to Assistance of Counsel.

147 ALR 656, Power to Impose Sentence With Direction that After Defendant Shall Have Served Part of Time He be Placed on Probation for the Remainder of Term.

141 ALR 1225, Imposition or Enforcement of Sentence Which Has Been Suspended Without Authority.

Forms

Florida Pleading and Practice Forms § 96:8, Sentencing Rehearings--Violation of Probation.

Florida Pleading and Practice Forms § 98:5, Motions to Correct or Mitigate Sentence.

Treatises and Practice Aids

6 Florida Practice Series § 14:5, The Requirement of a Prior Conviction.

16 Florida Practice Series § 6:9, Alternatives To, and Mitigation Of, Criminal Punishment Code Sentencing--Drug Offender Probation.

16 Florida Practice Series § 7:2, Jurisdiction to Impose Probation or Community Control.

16 Florida Practice Series § 1:34, Judicial Discretion in the Imposition of Sentence--Withholding Adjudication.

16 Florida Practice Series § 1:35, Judicial Discretion in the Imposition of Sentence--Withholding of Sentence.

16 Florida Practice Series § 1:42, Judicial Discretion in the Imposition of Sentence--Post-Sentence Jurisdiction.

16 Florida Practice Series § 1:43, Sentencing Alternatives.

16 Florida Practice Series § 1:50, Sentencing Alternatives--Split Probation.

16 Florida Practice Series § 5:49, Reasons for Departure--Mitigating Circumstances.

16 Florida Practice Series § 6:52, Enhancement of Penalty and Reclassification of Offense--Reclassifications of Various Types Batteries and Assaults--Assault or Battery on Emergency Medical Care Providers, Firefighters, Law...

16 Florida Practice Series § 6:57, Enhancement of Penalty and Reclassification of Offense--Reclassifications of Various Types of Batteries and Assaults--Assault or Battery on Persons 65 Years of Age or Older.

16 Florida Practice Series § 6:93, Enhancement of Penalty and Reclassification of Offense--10/20/Life.

16 Florida Practice Series § 7:13, Drug Offender Probation.

16 Florida Practice Series § 7:20, Probationary and Community Control Time Periods.

16 Florida Practice Series § 6:130, Boating Under the Influence--Property Damage, Personal Injury or Death.

22 Florida Practice Series App. A, Florida Rules of Criminal Procedure.

22 Florida Practice Series § 18:35, Sentence--Probation and Community Control.

Notes of Decisions

---

1. Validity

Florida sentencing procedure which allows court in its discretion to stay and withhold imposition of sentence upon defendant and place him on probation or direct defendant to be placed on probation upon completion of any part of specified period of sentence and which also allows court, upon finding of violation of probation, to impose any sentence which might have originally imposed before placing defendant on probation, does not violate constitutional prohibition against double jeopardy. Williams v. Wainwright, 1981, 650 F.2d 58. Double Jeopardy ⚷ 31

Drug offender probation statute was not unconstitutional delegation of legislative authority to administrative agency. Bunn v. State, App. 4 Dist., 687 So.2d 879 (1997). Constitutional Law ⚷ 2415(4); Sentencing And Punishment ⚷ 1825

Statute establishing drug offender probation is not unconstitutional delegation of legislative authority to administrative agency. Welborn v. State, App. 4 Dist., 687 So.2d 35 (1997). Constitutional Law ⚷ 2415(4); Sentencing And Punishment ⚷ 1825

Statute providing that Department of Corrections shall develop and administer drug offender probation program, which may include use of graduated sanctions, is not unconstitutional as an unlawful delegation of legislative authority to an administrative agency. Tory v. State, App. 4 Dist., 686 So.2d 689 (1996). Constitutional Law ⚷ 2415(4); Sentencing And Punishment ⚷ 1825

Sentence of probation imposed on defendant at resentencing was not presumptively vindictive on grounds it exceeded his original sentence. Jones v. State, App. 5 Dist., 617 So.2d 743 (1993). Sentencing And Punishment ⚷ 115(4)

2. Construction and application

Probation is creature of statutory law and courts are therefore limited to authority set out in applicable statute. Lynn v. State, App., 398 So.2d 977 (1981) review denied 411 So.2d 383; State v. Wilcox, App., 351 So.2d 89 (1977); Brown v. State, App., 302 So.2d 430 (1974).

Normally, probation presupposes the fact that a probationer is not in confinement. Freeman v. State, App., 382 So.2d 1307 (1980) review denied 401 So.2d 1334; Bernhardt v. State, 288 So.2d 490 (1974); Roy v. State, App., 207 So.2d 52 (1967) certiorari dismissed 211 So.2d 554.

Probation is a matter of grace, not right. Baker v. State, App., 319 So.2d 628 (1975); Pickman v. State, App., 155 So.2d 646 (1963) certiorari denied 164 So.2d 805.

Youthful offender statute under which trial court withheld adjudication of defendant's guilt for battery upon a person over the age of 65 and sentenced him to probation controlled sentencing in lieu of criminal statute that precluded such withheld adjudications; youthful offender statute indicated that it was to apply "[i]n lieu of other criminal penalties authorized by law," and provision in statute under which defendant was convicted concerning adjudication of guilt was one such penalty authorized by law. State v. Blackburn, App. 4 Dist., 965 So.2d 231 (2007), rehearing denied. Infants ⚷ 69(3.1); Sentencing And Punishment ⚷ 2065

Probation is creature of statute and courts are limited to authority set out in applicable statutes. Gearhart v. State, App. 5 Dist., 885 So.2d 415 (2004). Sentencing And Punishment ⚷ 1801

Statute permitting trial court to determine question of probation of convicted defendant, and place defendant on probation if warranted, did not apply to defendant subject to mandatory minimum three-year term of imprisonment for delivery of cocaine within 1000 feet of a school; as the later enacted and more specifically applicable statute, the cocaine delivery statute controlled. State v. Crews, App. 2 Dist., 884 So.2d 1139 (2004), on remand 2005 WL 6067013. Sentencing And Punishment ⚷ 1848

Drug offender probation for chronic substance abusers who commit non-violent drug crimes is an alternative sentencing scheme independent of the sentencing guidelines. Jones v. State, 813 So.2d 22 (2002), rehearing denied. Sentencing And Punishment ⚷ 1811

Statute permitting drug offender probation for chronic substance abusers who commit nonviolent drug crimes controlled over and was not impliedly repealed by the more general statute which prohibits the use of a defendant's substance abuse or addiction as a reason for downward departure from the sentencing guidelines. Jones v. State, 813 So.2d 22 (2002), rehearing denied. Sentencing And Punishment ⚷ 1826

State waived claim that trial court lacked authority to place defendant on drug offender probation and withhold adjudication of offense, where State agreed, at all stages of proceedings, that court could sentence defendant under statute governing when a court may place a defendant on probation or into community control. State v. Ackerman, App. 4 Dist., 785 So.2d 1229 (2001). Sentencing And Punishment ⚷ 1922

A trial court may withhold an adjudication of guilt after a plea has been accepted or after a verdict of guilty has been rendered and place defendant on probation, provided that the applicable statutory requirements are met. State v. McFadden, 772 So.2d 1209 (2000), rehearing denied. Sentencing And Punishment ⚷ 2054

Probationary period is generally not considered a "sentence." Landeverde v. State, App. 4 Dist., 769 So.2d 457 (2000). Sentencing And Punishment ⚷ 1811

Sentence and probation are discrete concepts which serve wholly different functions. Landeverde v. State, App. 4 Dist., 769 So.2d 457 (2000). Sentencing And Punishment ⚷ 1000; Sentencing And Punishment ⚷ 1811

"Probation" is a form of community supervision, with rehabilitation, rather than punishment, as its underlying purpose. Landeverde v. State, App. 4 Dist., 769 So.2d 457 (2000). Sentencing And Punishment ⚷ 1811

Probation is considered a "sentence" in those instances when drawing a distinction between the two concepts will result in a more severe punishment. Landeverde v. State, App. 4 Dist., 769 So.2d 457 (2000). Sentencing And Punishment ⚷ 1811

Trial court could not suspend entire term of sentence and place defendant on probation, without placing him under supervision of Department of Corrections or similar entity as required by statute. State v. Morrow, App. 1 Dist., 700 So.2d 391 (1997). Sentencing And Punishment ⚷ 1988

Probation is a matter of grace and its underlying concept is rehabilitation. Freeman v. State, App. 3 Dist., 382 So.2d 1307 (1980), review denied 401 So.2d 1334. Sentencing And Punishment ⚷ 1812

Probation is dependent on legislative and judicial grace. Watkins v. State, App. 2 Dist., 368 So.2d 363 (1979). Sentencing And Punishment ⚷ 1812

The required findings under the habitual criminal statute (§ 775.084) and the probation statute (this section) are inconsistent and mutually exclusive. Shead v. State, App. 3 Dist., 367 So.2d 264 (1979). Sentencing And Punishment ⚷ 1391

Probation matters must be handled in accordance with legislative act because there is no probation except by legislative action. Pickman v. State, App. 3 Dist., 155 So.2d 646 (1963), certiorari denied 164 So.2d 805. Sentencing And Punishment ⚷ 1801

3. Purpose and legislative intent

Statute permitting drug offender probation for chronic substance abusers is designed to vest discretion in a trial court to impose drug offender probation on chronic substance abusers who are charged with non-violent drug offenses. Jones v. State, 813 So.2d 22 (2002), rehearing denied. Sentencing And Punishment ⚷ 1811

Purpose of statute allowing sentencing courts to stay and withhold imposition of sentence and place defendant on probation is to avoid giving a criminal record to those persons whose prospects appear good for rehabilitation. State v. McKendry, App. 4 Dist., 614 So.2d 1158 (1993), review granted 624 So.2d 267, approved 641 So.2d 45. Sentencing And Punishment ⚷ 1824

This section indicates legislative intent to grant gain time to prison punishment of all offenders, whether by historic straight sentence, split sentence, or probation which contains condition of imprisonment. Van Tassel v. Coffman, 486 So.2d 528 (1985).

Purpose of this section permitting court to place a defendant on probation with or without adjudication of guilt is to avoid giving certain persons a criminal record when prospects are good for rehabilitation. Holland v. Florida Real Estate Commission, App. 2 Dist., 352 So.2d 914 (1977). Sentencing And Punishment ⚷ 1824; Sentencing And Punishment ⚷ 2055

4. Conflict of laws

Criminal Procedure Rule 3.790 governs only procedural aspects of probation and augments but does not supersede this section, which provides that sentence may include period of probation under expressed circumstances, and does not authorize sentence to state prison to be followed by period of probation. Robinson v. State, App. 3 Dist., 256 So.2d 390 (1972). Sentencing And Punishment ⚷ 1827

5. Jurisdiction—In general

County court lacked jurisdiction to sanction defendant for failing to perform community service, 19 months after defendant had been ordered to perform 150 hours of community service at the rate of 15 hours per month, upon adjudication of guilt following her plea to misdemeanor marijuana possession, where maximum amount of time to which defendant could have been sentenced was one year; court was divested of jurisdiction over defendant upon expiration of probationary period. West's F.S.A. §§ 775.082(4)(a), 775.091, 893.13(6)(b), 921.187(1)(a), Rivera v. State, App. 3 Dist., 939 So.2d 116 (2006), rehearing denied, review granted 965 So.2d 123, review dismissed as improvidently granted 985 So.2d 1092. Sentencing And Punishment ⚷ 1948; Sentencing And Punishment ⚷ 1982(3)

Order that placed defendant on probation and that was imposed during term subsequent to one in which original sentence was entered was void for lack of jurisdiction and constituted fundamental error even if not raised in trial court. Solomon v. State, App. 2 Dist., 341 So.2d 537 (1977). Criminal Law ⚷ 1042.3(4); Sentencing And Punishment ⚷ 1893

When trial judge did not suspend any part of the designated six-month sentence in county jail which he imposed, sentence of probation was void ab initio, and court lacked jurisdiction to revoke probation and impose a new jail sentence. Reynolds v. State, App. 3 Dist., 293 So.2d 743 (1974), certiorari denied 302 So.2d 764. Sentencing And Punishment ⚷ 1932; Sentencing And Punishment ⚷ 2001

Upon expiration of probationary period the court is divested of all jurisdiction over person of a probationer unless in the meantime the processes of the court have been set in motion for revocation or modification of probation pursuant to statute. Brooker v. State, App. 3 Dist., 207 So.2d 478 (1968). Sentencing And Punishment ⚷ 2010

A court having jurisdiction of defendant in criminal proceeding may order probation after defendant has been convicted, but it has no jurisdiction or power to place defendant on parole, in view of fact that parole is strictly a function of the executive branch of government to be exercised only after defendant has been convicted and sentenced. Marsh v. Garwood, 65 So.2d 15 (1953). Constitutional Law ⚷ 2545(4); Pardon And Parole ⚷ 45.1; Sentencing And Punishment ⚷ 1801

6. —— County courts, jurisdiction

County court lacked jurisdiction to sanction defendant for failing to perform community service, 19 months after defendant had been ordered to perform 150 hours of community service at the rate of 15 hours per month, upon adjudication of guilt following her plea to misdemeanor marijuana possession, where maximum amount of time to which defendant could have been sentenced was one year; court was divested of jurisdiction over defendant upon expiration of probationary period. West's F.S.A. §§§§ 775.082(4)(a), 775.091, 893.13(6)(b), 921.187(1)(a), Rivera v. State, App. 3 Dist., 939 So.2d 116 (2006), rehearing denied, review granted 965 So.2d 123, review dismissed as improvidently granted 985 So.2d 1092. Sentencing And Punishment ⚷ 1948; Sentencing And Punishment ⚷ 1982(3)

After January 1, 1973, a county court will have the authority to place on probation, under the supervision of the Florida parole and probation commission, a defendant in a case involving violation of a county ordinance and, if such should be done, it would be the duty of the commission to supervise the probationer. Op. Atty.Gen., 072–377, Oct. 30, 1972.

After January 1, 1973, a county court will have no authority to place a defendant on probation, under the supervision of the parole and probation commission, in a case involving the violation of a city ordinance and, if such should be done, the commission would be under no duty to supervise the probationer. Op.Atty. Gen., 072–377, Oct. 30, 1972.

7. —— Indictment or information, jurisdiction

Information charging defendant with shooting a glass bottle at a public vehicle was sufficient to charge him with crime of throwing a deadly missile; thus, circuit court had jurisdiction to enter an order of probation regarding that crime. Livolsi v. State, App. 2 Dist., 451 So.2d 542 (1984). Malicious Mischief ⚷ 4

Despite contention that information charging defendant with grand theft was fatally defective in that it failed to allege that taking was with intent to permanently deprive owner of property, circuit court did not lack subject-matter jurisdiction to place defendant on probation for that charge. Geri v. State, App. 1 Dist., 415 So.2d 782 (1982). Sentencing And Punishment ⚷ 1801

8. Trial court—Authority

Trial court lacked authority, under statute providing for probation and community control rather than incarceration for some defendants, to suspend mandatory minimum sentence for possession of short-barreled shotgun; mandatory minimum sentence statute was more specific and was enacted later than statute generally allowing for more lenient sentences. McKendry v. State, 641 So.2d 45 (1994). Sentencing And Punishment ⚷ 1864

Trial court had no authority to impose probation for misdemeanors, where original probationary term had expired. Bolton v. State, App. 2 Dist., 619 So.2d 412 (1993). Sentencing And Punishment ⚷ 1948

Trial court has no authority to grant parole; that power is vested solely in parole commission. Owens v. State, App. 1 Dist., 308 So.2d 171 (1975). Pardon And Parole ⚷ 45.1

9. —— Discretion, trial court

Upon defendant's pleading guilty to participating in an organized scheme to defraud the state medicaid program, trial court retained discretion to adjudicate appellant guilty or to withhold adjudication upon the entry of findings of fact in support of the exercise of its discretion, though state urged adjudication. Vicaria v. State, App. 1 Dist., 743 So.2d 644 (1999). Sentencing And Punishment ⚷ 2054; Sentencing And Punishment ⚷ 2065

Statute giving judge discretion to stay and withhold imposition of sentence and place defendant on probation may be invoked only when sentencing guidelines provide for range of sentencing that includes probation or where appropriate reasons exist to deviate from the guidelines. State v. McKendry, App. 4 Dist., 614 So.2d 1158 (1993), review granted 624 So.2d 267, approved 641 So.2d 45. Sentencing And Punishment ⚷ 1802

A trial judge does not have authority to either withhold or suspend a sentence indefinitely without placing defendant on probation. Phillips v. State, App. 5 Dist., 455 So.2d 656 (1984). Sentencing And Punishment ⚷ 1810

In a posttrial posture, trial court has great latitude and discretion in disposition of a criminal proceeding; with a deserving defendant in an appropriate case, it may, in a noncapital felony, after a finding of guilty or entry of plea of nolo contendere, with or without an adjudication of guilt, withhold imposition of sentence and place the defendant upon probation. State v. Jogan, App. 3 Dist., 388 So.2d 322 (1980). Sentencing And Punishment ⚷ 1802

Granting of probation rests within broad discretion of trial judge and is a matter of grace rather than right; statutory provisions setting out the procedures for extending probation privileges are not mandatory on trial judges. Arnold v. State, App. 1 Dist., 356 So.2d 862 (1978). Sentencing And Punishment ⚷ 1802; Sentencing And Punishment ⚷ 1812

Grant of probation rests within broad discretion of trial judge and is a matter of grace, not of right. Martin v. State, App. 4 Dist., 243 So.2d 189 (1971), certiorari denied 247 So.2d 63. Sentencing And Punishment ⚷ 1802; Sentencing And Punishment ⚷ 1812

A grant of probation rests within broad discretion of trial judge and is based on hope of rehabilitation rather than punishment. Pickman v. State, App. 3 Dist., 155 So.2d 646 (1963), certiorari denied 164 So.2d 805. Sentencing And Punishment ⚷ 1802; Sentencing And Punishment ⚷ 1833

10. —— Setting aside verdict, trial court

Trial court was authorized to set aside adjudication of guilt and place codefendant on probation under supervision of parole commission. State v. Dull, App. 1 Dist., 249 So.2d 758 (1971). Sentencing And Punishment ⚷ 1894

Where trial judge entered order which withheld adjudication of guilt and placed accused on probation, trial court could thereafter resume jurisdiction over the accused and enter other orders, including a judgment adjudicating guilt and passing sentence. Delaney v. State, 190 So.2d 578 (1966), appeal dismissed 87 S.Ct. 1710, 387 U.S. 426, 18 L.Ed.2d 866. Sentencing And Punishment ⚷ 1914

11. Guilty plea

Although defendant should have brought to attention of trial court the fact that order withholding adjudication of guilt and placing him on probation erroneously recited that he had entered a plea to a greater offense, District Court of Appeal would direct that order to recite that plea was to lesser included offense. Kinard v. State, App. 5 Dist., 394 So.2d 217 (1981). Criminal Law ⚷ 1042.3(4)

Where defendant secured favorable plea bargain which, inter alia, resulted in two charges not being pursued by the state, and where defendant entered plea of guilty to violation of probation pursuant to that plea bargain, court did not err in accepting the guilty plea without first determining that there was a full understanding of the significance of the guilty plea and its voluntariness and that there was a factual basis for the plea. Suggs v. State, App. 2 Dist., 304 So.2d 463 (1974). Sentencing And Punishment ⚷ 2009

Court may place on probation a defendant who has pleaded guilty or nolo contendere or been found guilty after trial without first entering a judgment of guilt. Delaney v. State, 190 So.2d 578 (1966), appeal dismissed 87 S.Ct. 1710, 387 U.S. 426, 18 L.Ed.2d 866. Sentencing And Punishment ⚷ 1890

Purpose of the procedure whereby defendant, who has pleaded guilty or has been found guilty after trial may be placed on probation without a judgment of conviction being entered is to provide for the rehabilitation of one who has committed the crime without formally and judicially branding the individual as a convicted criminal with consequent loss of civil rights and other damning consequences. Delaney v. State, 190 So.2d 578 (1966), appeal dismissed 87 S.Ct. 1710, 387 U.S. 426, 18 L.Ed.2d 866. Sentencing And Punishment ⚷ 2051

Where defendant was induced to plead guilty of buying, receiving, and aiding in concealment of stolen property by county solicitor's assurance that he would be placed on probation, which was granted for seven years, though solicitor knew of defendant's prior conviction in federal court for unlawfully receiving stolen property, his conviction on such plea could not support his sentence by circuit court to five years in penitentiary as dual offender after five years of probationary period. Ard v. State, 91 So.2d 166 (1956). Sentencing And Punishment ⚷ 1314

12. Acquittal

After defendant in a criminal case is adjudged not guilty, whether by reason of insanity or for other reason, the trial court has no authority to place him on probation and an order purporting to do so is void. Therefore, even if such an order of probation specifies that such defendant be under the supervision of the parole and probation commission during probation, said commission has no duty or authority to supervise him as a probationer. Op.Atty.Gen., 073-390, Oct. 16, 1973.

13. Conviction of crime

Defendant who had pled guilty in Florida state court of receiving stolen property, a crime punishable by imprisonment for a term exceeding one year, but who had been placed on probation under this section permitting the court to withhold adjudication of guilt and imposition of sentence while placing defendant on probation would, under Florida law, be considered convicted upon the entry of his plea of guilty so that he was no longer under indictment or information at time that he stated in writing, in connection with the purchase of the gun, that he was not, at the time of purchase, under indictment or information. U. S. v. Hartsfield, M.D.Fla.1975, 387 F.Supp. 16. Weapons ⚷ 4

When defendant is adjudged guilty, court should either sentence him or place him on probation, although there may be justifiable delay in either sentencing or probation for procedural reasons. Slay v. State, App. 1 Dist., 347 So.2d 730 (1977). Sentencing And Punishment ⚿ 377

Where there was no relationship between convictions except that they were combined for sentencing, probation in each case constituted independent judicial act, and illegality of one sentence of probation did not require that defendant be discharged from all probation. Fuller v. State, App. 3 Dist., 320 So.2d 442 (1975). Sentencing And Punishment ⚿ 1914

If court in felony prosecution exercises its discretion under this section and withholds imposition of sentence and places defendant on probation without adjudging him guilty, then he has not been convicted and does not lose any of his civil rights. Op.Atty.Gen., 064–163, Nov. 6, 1964.

A person found guilty of a felony in this state and placed on probation is not deprived of his civil rights in this state. Op.Atty.Gen., 1942, p. 784.

14. Sentence and punishment—In general

Defendant's probation order after court withheld adjudication on forgery charge did not constitute a "sentence" for purpose of determining when double jeopardy attached. Brown v. State, App. 1 Dist., 463 So.2d 1230 (1985). Double Jeopardy ⚿ 60.1

An underlying prison sentence not reasonably related to rehabilitative purposes of probation is fundamental error, and thus is amenable to appellate remedy sua sponte. Cunningham v. State, App. 3 Dist., 385 So.2d 721 (1980), review denied 402 So.2d 613. Criminal Law ⚿ 1042.3(4)

There is a clear distinction between a sentence and a condition of probation. Freeman v. State, App. 3 Dist., 382 So.2d 1307 (1980), review denied 401 So.2d 1334. Sentencing And Punishment ⚿ 1960

In prosecution for rape, probation was an alternative open to the sentencing judge. Berezovsky v. State, 350 So.2d 80 (1977), on remand 351 So.2d 764. Sentencing And Punishment ⚿ 1862

Even if trial judge's recommendation to parole commission that defendant, who was sentenced to life imprisonment for murder in the second degree, not be allowed to return to specified county if paroled was error, such error was harmless. Owens v. State, App. 1 Dist., 308 So.2d 171 (1975). Criminal Law ⚿ 1177.3(1)

There is clear distinction between "sentence," which must be preceded by adjudication of guilt, and "conditions of probation," which can be imposed independently of an adjudication of guilt and imposition or pronouncement of sentence. State v. Williams, App. 2 Dist., 237 So.2d 69 (1970). Sentencing And Punishment ⚿ 1960

This section does not authorize court to impose sentence in portions but only to pronounce the whole sentence or to defer the whole until a probation order entered in lieu of it is vacated. Ex parte Bosso, 41 So.2d 322 (1949).

Criminal court has no authority to suspend or grant probation as to a part of a sentence to be imposed, but to place a defendant on probation, the court could, after finding defendant guilty, suspend imposition of sentence until further order. Op.Atty.Gen., 1949, p. 624.

15. —— Presentence investigation report, sentence and punishment

Defendants who entered into plea negotiations and freely agreed to pay their pro rata share of the cost of the investigation as a condition of probation could not challenge that provision on appeal. Brenner v. State, App. 3 Dist., 337 So.2d 1007 (1976), rehearing denied 341 So.2d 287, certiorari denied 348 So.2d 944. Criminal Law ⚿ 1026.10(4)

Presentence investigation report was confidential, and not a public document, and defendant was not entitled to access thereto. Morgan v. State, App. 2 Dist., 142 So.2d 308 (1962), certiorari denied 146 So.2d 751. Sentencing And Punishment ⚿ 294

Trial court has no authority to require the parole and probation commission to make a presentence investigation on a defendant in a criminal case who has not pleaded guilty or nolo contendere and has not been found guilty by verdict of a jury or by the court trying the case without a jury. The commission would not be required to comply with an order requiring a presentence investigation before any of these steps take place. Op.Atty.Gen., 073–142, May 3, 1973.

A circuit court judge handling juvenile matters may in his discretion refuse to permit the Florida parole and probation commission to inspect juvenile court records when making a pre-parole investigation or pre-sentence investigation. Op.Atty.Gen., 073–112, April 11, 1973.

16. —— Validity of sentence, sentence and punishment

After defendant had entered plea of guilty to two burglary charges and was sentenced to concurrent terms of four and one-half years, and sentencing court provided that after one and one-half years had been served, remainder was to be stayed and withheld to be completed by probation, while defendant may have hoped that even upon revocation of probation he would serve no more than five years discussed in plea negotiations, or four and one-half years originally imposed, defendant had been placed on notice that he could receive 30 years, and, therefore, imposition of two concurrent 15-year terms upon probation revocation did not violate double jeopardy clause. Williams v. Wainwright, 1981, 650 F.2d 58. Double Jeopardy ⚷ 31

Trial court erroneously imposed sentence on defendant, suspended execution of that sentence, and released defendant on conditions, without formally placing him on probation under supervision of the Department of Corrections, Salvation Army or some other public or private entity. Phillips v. State, App. 5 Dist., 455 So.2d 656 (1984). Sentencing And Punishment ⚷ 1810

Where court granted defendant's petition for postconviction relief on charge of battery of a law enforcement officer, and denied his petition insofar as it related to crime of throwing a deadly missile, but failed to review the order of probation as originally rendered for both offenses, the order of probation was illegal. Livolsi v. State, App. 2 Dist., 451 So.2d 542 (1984). Sentencing And Punishment ⚷ 1913

Probation is authorized for defendant only where he has been found guilty of a criminal violation of state law; municipal ordinance violation is not a criminal violation. Pridgen v. City of Auburndale, App. 2 Dist., 430 So.2d 967 (1983). Municipal Corporations ⚷ 630; Sentencing And Punishment ⚷ 1835

17. —— General terms of probation, sentence and punishment

Trial court lacked authority to impose administrative probation, under which defendant would not have to be present to be supervised, as part of defendant's sentence from beginning of probationary period. Madrigal v. State, App. 4 Dist., 683 So.2d 1093 (1996). Sentencing And Punishment ⚷ 1988

Order of probation, which was predicated upon two findings of criminal activity but failed to distinguish whether one or both counts constituted the basis for placing defendant on a single term of five years probation, was a general order of probation, and thus, invalid. Livolsi v. State, App. 2 Dist., 451 So.2d 542 (1984). Sentencing And Punishment ⚷ 1913

Rule in Dorfman v. State, 351 So.2d 954 (Fla.1977) that a single general sentence may not be imposed for two or more crimes also operates to prohibit general terms of probation for two or more offenses. Ward v. State, App. 2 Dist., 429 So.2d 825 (1983). Sentencing And Punishment ⚷ 1913

Defendant was entitled to a set term of probation on each conviction, and trial court erred in imposing a general probation term for all three offenses. Ward v. State, App. 2 Dist., 429 So.2d 825 (1983). Sentencing And Punishment ⚷ 1913

18. —— Validity of separate sentences, sentence and punishment

Sentence being served by defendant at time of new violations of probation was not interrupted, and thus, sentence imposed for new probation violations was not illegal split-sentence. Collins v. State, App. 4 Dist., 697 So.2d 1305 (1997). Sentencing And Punishment ⚷ 2032

Defendant convicted of numerous counts of grand theft who was placed on probation as to some counts and who received no sentence as to other counts was not subjected to cruel and unusual punishment. Starling v. State, App. 5 Dist., 458 So.2d 799 (1984), petition for review denied 464 So.2d 556. Sentencing And Punishment ⚷ 1498

General order of probation predicated upon more than one conviction of criminal activity cannot stand; there must be a separate order of probation for each offense. Cervantes v. State, 442 So.2d 176 (1983). Sentencing And Punishment ⚷ 1913

In proceeding in which defendant was convicted of two crimes, placing defendant on a single term of probation was error; separate probation orders for each offense were required. Price v. State, App. 5 Dist., 393 So.2d 69 (1981). Sentencing And Punishment ⚷ 1913

Entry of written order sentencing defendant to six months in the county jail on one count and two years probation on the other count was erroneous in that the trial judge and respective counsel correctly agreed that only one sentence could be imposed under the circumstances and the judge thereupon pronounced a single sentence of six months in the county jail to be followed by two years probation; accordingly, the probationary portion of the sentencing order was void ab initio and the trial court lacked jurisdiction to revoke probation and impose a new sentence. Eaton v. State, App. 3 Dist., 307 So.2d 881 (1974). Sentencing And Punishment ⚷ 1921; Sentencing And Punishment ⚷ 2001

Where defendant was sentenced to three years' imprisonment upon conviction of two crimes, period of probation which was imposed as to a third offense which arose out of a different transaction was properly imposed even though the period of probation would begin to run upon completion of the prison term. Austile v. State, App. 2 Dist., 301 So.2d 30 (1974). Sentencing And Punishment ⚷ 1937

19. —— Modification, sentence and punishment

Although court has right to rescind or modify terms and conditions of probation at any time, absent proof of violation, court cannot change order of probation by enhancing its terms. Casterline v. State, App. 2 Dist., 703 So.2d 1071 (1997), rehearing denied, review granted 717 So.2d 538, review dismissed 736 So.2d 1151. Sentencing And Punishment ⚷ 1923

Order enhancing terms of probation, by including new conditions, was void and violated double jeopardy where order was not based on violation of existing terms of probation; accordingly, subsequent violations of enhanced condition were nullity. Casterline v. State, App. 2 Dist., 703 So.2d 1071 (1997), rehearing denied, review granted 717 So.2d 538, review dismissed 736 So.2d 1151. Double Jeopardy ⚷ 114.1

Defendant is not entitled to jail-time credit when placed on community control, but after defendant violates community control and receives prison sentence, jail time should be credited against new prison sentence. Smith v. State, App. 2 Dist., 664 So.2d 1076 (1995). Sentencing And Punishment ⚷ 2041

Trial court lacked jurisdiction to modify probation several months after it had announced unconditionally that probation was terminated subject only to receipt of proposed written restitution order to be prepared by state, where state failed to submit written order out of concern for victim objection to court's decision. Marcinek v. State, App. 4 Dist., 662 So.2d 771 (1995). Sentencing And Punishment ⚷ 1923

Probation order cannot be modified without hearing, even when jurisdiction is specifically reserved for purpose of adding special condition. Dennis v. State, App. 1 Dist., 630 So.2d 605 (1993). Sentencing And Punishment ⚷ 1923

Trial court's adjudicating probationer guilty some 26 months after court had initially placed him on probation and withheld adjudication, was a modification of original probation order and was improper, where probationer did not admit alleged violation of probation and no evidence was taken in support of violations. Knapp v. State, App. 4 Dist., 405 So.2d 786 (1981). Sentencing And Punishment ⚷ 1923

Probation orders are not subject to modification except for violation of conditions and then only upon notice and hearing. Knapp v. State, App. 4 Dist., 405 So.2d 786 (1981). Sentencing And Punishment ⚷ 1923

Modification of sentence one week after sentence was originally imposed was not "suspended sentence" as it was not made at time of original sentencing. Phillips v. State, App. 1 Dist., 394 So.2d 233 (1981). Sentencing And Punishment ⚷ 1804

Change in sentence placing defendant on probation one week after original sentence was imposed was void, and probation revocation and sentence after revocation were also void. Phillips v. State, App. 1 Dist., 394 So.2d 233 (1981). Sentencing And Punishment ⚷ 1893

Trial court had no jurisdiction to modify probation order entered in criminal case while judgment of conviction and probation order was on appeal before appellate court of competent jurisdiction. State ex rel. Salomon v. Sandstrom, App. 3 Dist., 349 So.2d 696 (1977). Criminal Law ⚷ 1083

Trial court may revoke, revise or modify for cause probation and incarceration provision at any time during period that order is in force and impose any sentence which might have been originally imposed. State v. Jones, 327 So.2d 18 (1976), on remand 330 So.2d 189. Sentencing And Punishment ⚷ 2010; Sentencing And Punishment ⚷ 2037

Where sentence of six months in jail to be followed by a one-year probation was illegal, sentence was amended by striking therefrom the provision for probation. Harris v. State, App. 3 Dist., 288 So.2d 552 (1974). Criminal Law ⚷ 1184(4.1)

20. —— Basis for departure, sentence and punishment

Resentencing on defendant's conviction for possession of cocaine was warranted following sentencing court's reference during hearing to incorrect authority as basis for its departure from guidelines scoresheet recommendation, which effectively precluded State from contesting court's sentence or building record to support argument; court's subsequent written citation to proper authority on guidelines scoresheet rendered record unclear as to which authority sentence was based upon. State v. Williams, App. 4 Dist., 759 So.2d 1 (1998). Criminal Law ⚷ 1181.5(8)

21. —— Consecutive sentences, sentence and punishment

Where there are two victims and two offenses, court may impose consecutive probationary periods for offenses separate from the offense for which the prison term was imposed, which do not exceed statutory maximum. Hope v. State, App. 4 Dist., 682 So.2d 1173 (1996). Sentencing And Punishment ⚷ 1938

Sentence consisting of consecutive terms of probation, which were consecutive to any other case and incarceration that was imposed as condition of probation and was to be concurrent with federal sentence, was improper, indefinite sentence, where no federal sentence had been imposed. Schlosser v. State, App. 2 Dist., 554 So.2d 1183 (1989). Sentencing And Punishment ⚿ 1913

Consecutive terms of probation, which were to be consecutive to any other case and incarceration that was imposed as condition of probation and that was to be served concurrently with federal sentence, did not necessarily immediately follow incarcerative portion of sentence, and, thus, sentence was invalid. Schlosser v. State, App. 2 Dist., 554 So.2d 1183 (1989). Sentencing And Punishment ⚿ 1938

22. —— Prior felony offenses, sentence and punishment

Where Florida court had withheld adjudication of guilt and imposition of sentence and placed defendant on probation, defendant was not a prior felony offender under New York Penal Law which requires a conviction before prior felony offender sentencing requirements become operable, even though subsequent felony during probationary period authorized Florida courts to consider the charge upon which adjudication had been withheld as a conviction. People v. Bell, 1975, 82 Misc.2d 1021, 372 N.Y.S.2d 169. Sentencing And Punishment ⚿ 1292

23. —— Deferment of imposition of sentence, sentence and punishment

Order withholding adjudication of guilt for assault and requiring defendant to serve two years probation was error where court had orally announced that probation would be comprised of two consecutive one year terms. Barlow v. State, App. 5 Dist., 390 So.2d 165 (1980). Sentencing And Punishment ⚿ 2070

Sentences of five years' imprisonment, with three years being withheld, and with defendants to be placed on probation at the completion of two years, were not invalid on theory that they took away defendants' rights or the prerogative of probation board to decrease the two-year incarceration. Brenner v. State, App. 3 Dist., 337 So.2d 1007 (1976), rehearing denied 341 So.2d 287, certiorari denied 348 So.2d 944. Sentencing And Punishment ⚿ 1936

Under this section empowering trial court in its discretion at sentencing to place defendant on probation upon completion of any specified portion of sentence and providing that court shall "withhold the imposition of the remainder of sentence" and direct that defendant be placed upon probation after serving such period as may be imposed by the court, the quoted phrase requires that time spent in jail be within any maximum jail sentence which could be imposed and an initial imposition of total sentence is not required. State v. Jones, 327 So.2d 18 (1976), on remand 330 So.2d 189. Sentencing And Punishment ⚿ 1945

Probationary portion of sentence of 90 days in county jail to be followed by three years probation, upon plea of guilty to crime of breaking and entering automobile, was invalid inasmuch as court did not withhold imposition of any portion of sentence imposed upon defendant. Woodruff v. State, App. 2 Dist., 309 So.2d 55 (1975). Sentencing And Punishment ⚿ 1936

Although valid term of probation could have been imposed by withholding imposition of portion of sentence for grand larceny, or by sentencing defendant to imprisonment as a condition of probation, portion of sentence which sentenced defendant to probation was a nullity and void and all actions taken pursuant thereto, including order of revocation of probation and sentence thereon, were of no force and effect. Lennard v. State, App. 4 Dist., 308 So.2d 579 (1975). Sentencing And Punishment ⚿ 1934

A court may impose a sentence of imprisonment or fine upon a defendant found guilty of an offense, or it may withhold sentence in whole or in part and place defendant on probation, but it cannot sentence defendant to probation, since withholding of sentence or a portion thereof is an indispensable prerequisite to entry of an order placing a defendant on probation. Brown v. State, App. 4 Dist., 302 So.2d 430 (1974). Sentencing And Punishment ⚿ 1931

Where defendant pleaded guilty to breaking and entering with intent to commit misdemeanor, so that court could have imposed maximum sentence of five years or placed him on probation for maximum of seven years, court did not have jurisdiction to withhold imposition of sentence from day to day and term to term, and then, 12 years later, to revoke order illegally suspending sentence and impose sentence. Helton v. State, 106 So.2d 79 (1958). Sentencing And Punishment ⚿ 1808

Under this section power to suspend imposition of sentence can be exercised by trial judge only as an incident to probation. Helton v. State, 106 So.2d 79 (1958). Sentencing And Punishment ⚿ 1810

Where defendant was adjudged guilty, order purporting to defer sentence without placing defendant on probation under supervision of parole commission was denial of due process of law and sentence imposed upon defendant a year later became effective nunc pro tunc on date that defendant was adjudged guilty. Bateh v. State, App. 1 Dist., 101 So.2d 869 (1958), certiorari discharged 110 So.2d 7, certiorari denied 80 S.Ct. 74, 361 U.S. 826, 4 L.Ed.2d 69. Constitutional Law ⚷ 4738; Sentencing And Punishment ⚷ 1167

Any action by trial court to suspending sentence indefinitely, with result that defendant would be placed on unsupervised probation, would constitute infringement upon powers lawfully delegated to execute branch of government. Bateh v. State, App. 1 Dist., 101 So.2d 869 (1958), certiorari discharged 110 So.2d 7, certiorari denied 80 S.Ct. 74, 361 U.S. 826, 4 L.Ed.2d 69. Constitutional Law ⚷ 2545(4)

Where defendant was adjudged guilty, trial court had alternative, absent some sufficient and lawful reason for temporary delay, of passing sentence forthwith or suspending imposition of sentence and placing defendant on probation under supervision and control of parole commission. Bateh v. State, App. 1 Dist., 101 So.2d 869 (1958), certiorari discharged 110 So.2d 7, certiorari denied 80 S.Ct. 74, 361 U.S. 826, 4 L.Ed.2d 69. Sentencing And Punishment ⚷ 1805; Sentencing And Punishment ⚷ 1810

Where an adult if charged with violating statute by selling narcotic drugs to a person who is under the age of 21, and where such adult pleads either guilty or nolo contendere, it was the mandatory duty of the court to judge him guilty and sentence him to serve a term of not less than ten years in the state prison instead of withholding the adjudication of guilt and placing such adult on probation. Op.Atty.Gen., 070-188, Dec. 30, 1970.

24. —— Duration of deferment of sentence, sentence and punishment

Eleven-month delay between defendant's plea and imposition of sentence, defendant not having been placed on probation, was error and denial of due process. Slay v. State, App. 1 Dist., 347 So.2d 730 (1977). Constitutional Law ⚷ 4718; Sentencing And Punishment ⚷ 382

Where there was prompt pronouncement of year sentence but it was not put into effect for period of several years thereafter, there was in effect probation but an illegal one where defendant was not placed in custody of parole commission, and period during which sentence was not put into effect extended beyond two-year period beyond the year sentence. Yates v. Buchanan, App. 3 Dist., 170 So.2d 72 (1964). Sentencing And Punishment ⚷ 1930; Sentencing And Punishment ⚷ 1950

Barring certain exceptions, sentence cannot be postponed indefinitely or for any considerable period. Yates v. Buchanan, App. 3 Dist., 170 So.2d 72 (1964). Sentencing And Punishment ⚷ 377

Where though one-year sentence was pronounced promptly, its enforcement was held off for a matter of years, it could not be put into effect thereafter, and sentence and commitment order were void. Yates v. Buchanan, App. 3 Dist., 170 So.2d 72 (1964). Sentencing And Punishment ⚷ 464

When trial judge delays sentence of convict, power to sentence convict must be exercised before lapse of extreme period for which sentence could have been imposed, and, when it is inflicted, the term cannot be projected beyond the extreme period. State v. Bateh, 110 So.2d 7 (1959), certiorari denied 80 S.Ct. 74, 361 U.S. 826, 4 L.Ed.2d 69. Sentencing And Punishment ⚷ 384; Sentencing And Punishment ⚷ 1158

Trial judge may withhold temporarily, or even from term to term, the imposition of sentence for purpose of determining motions and other matters arising between verdict and judgment, such as gaining information necessary to imposition of just sentence, or during pendency of other charges, or for other good and valid reasons, but cannot by the artifice of postponing pronouncement of sentence exercise the power to conditionally parole or pardon defendant. Helton v. State, 106 So.2d 79 (1958). Sentencing And Punishment ⚷ 379

An order that passing of sentence on defendant's plea of guilty be continued from day to day and term to term until finally disposed of was not order for probation, nor order suspending imposition of sentence during defendant's good behavior, in absence of order placing defendant under Parole Commission's supervision for probation period or imposition of terms or conditions on defendant, so that he was not entitled to hearing on question of his good behavior since entry of such order before imposition of sentence. Pinkney v. State, 160 Fla. 884, 37 So.2d 157 (1948). Sentencing And Punishment ⚷ 1815

A trial judge, deferring imposition of sentence on defendant, may impose sentence at any time, either during term in which his guilt of offense charged is admitted or established or at later term, without first according him a hearing on question of his good behavior. Pinkney v. State, 160 Fla. 884, 37 So.2d 157 (1948). Sentencing And Punishment ⚷ 2024

25. Community control—In general

Postconviction relief movant, having accepted terms of extremely beneficial plea agreement pursuant to which he was sentenced to community control, and having failed to live up to those generous terms, was estopped from challenging that agreement on ground that community control was statutorily precluded, and thus could not be revoked. McMillan v. State, App.

3 Dist., 701 So.2d 1214 (1997). Criminal Law ⚷ 1557(4)

When sentence of community control or incarceration is permitted, these alternatives are mutually exclusive and may not be imposed in combination. Williams v. State, App. 2 Dist., 659 So.2d 460 (1995). Sentencing And Punishment ⚷ 1934

Defendant could not be sentenced to combination of community control and incarceration, even though length of total combined sentence of community control and incarceration did not exceed the maximum guidelines incarcerative sentence. Felty v. State, 630 So.2d 1092 (1994). Sentencing And Punishment ⚷ 1934

Where sentencing guidelines specify incarceration or community control, these alternatives are mutually exclusive. Felty v. State, 630 So.2d 1092 (1994). Sentencing And Punishment ⚷ 1934

Defendant could not be convicted for violation of community control which was originally imposed relative to offense of possession of cocaine, as conditions of defendant's community control for cocaine offense were a nullity because defendant neither pled nolo contendere nor guilty to cocaine offense, nor was he found guilty of such offense following trial. Stelzl v. State, App. 5 Dist., 629 So.2d 984 (1993). Sentencing And Punishment ⚷ 2004

Community control can be imposed only for felonies, not for misdemeanors. Carlin v. State, App. 5 Dist., 626 So.2d 316 (1993). Sentencing And Punishment ⚷ 1838

Defendant convicted of misdemeanor offense could not be sentenced to one year of community control. Thompson v. State, App. 2 Dist., 617 So.2d 411 (1993). Sentencing And Punishment ⚷ 1838

Community control is not functional equivalent of jail. Smith v. State, App. 2 Dist., 615 So.2d 712 (1993). Sentencing And Punishment ⚷ 1167

Sentence of community control for misdemeanor offense is void. Mitchell v. State, App. 2 Dist., 614 So.2d 671 (1993), review denied 626 So.2d 207. Sentencing And Punishment ⚷ 1838

Trial court was precluded from placing defendant in community control where, while on probation for armed robbery, he committed strong arm robbery and false imprisonment. State v. Burgos, App. 4 Dist., 613 So.2d 588 (1993). Sentencing And Punishment ⚷ 1872(3)

Defendant was originally improperly sentenced to community control on misdemeanor charges of battery and trespass, rendering revocation and subsequent sentences void despite defendant's failure to object. York v. State, App. 2 Dist., 599 So.2d 199 (1992). Sentencing And Punishment ⚷ 1843; Sentencing And Punishment ⚷ 1844; Sentencing And Punishment ⚷ 2000; Sentencing And Punishment ⚷ 2032

Community control could be imposed in tandem with probation. Skeens v. State, App. 2 Dist., 542 So.2d 436 (1989), jurisdiction accepted 550 So.2d 467, approved 556 So.2d 1113. Sentencing And Punishment ⚷ 1934

Interrupted sentence involving community control and probation could not properly be imposed as result of consecutive sentences, such that defendant would serve period of community control and then period of probation on one sentence followed by period of community control and then probation on the second sentence. Sanchez v. State, App. 5 Dist., 538 So.2d 923 (1989). Sentencing And Punishment ⚷ 1938

Community control could be imposed only for felony offenses, so that trial court lacked jurisdiction to place defendant on community control for misdemeanor offense of resisting arrest without violence, and thus revocation of community control and subsequent sentence of one year in jail were void. Young v. State, App. 1 Dist., 509 So.2d 1339 (1987). Sentencing And Punishment ⚷ 1838; Sentencing And Punishment ⚷ 2006

An order of the parole and probation commission placing a parole violator in community control supersedes and replaces the original parole order. The commission does not have to formally revoke the original release order because it is forfeited or suspended, subject to reinstatement, on the finding a parole violation took place; however, the commission could adopt conditions from the original parole order compatible with statutes pertaining thereto, in its new order placing the parolee into a community control program. Op.Atty.Gen., 83–79, Oct. 26, 1983.

The parole and probation commission may order a parole violator into a community control program for a fixed period to be followed by a period of less restrictive supervision. Op. Atty.Gen., 83–79, Oct. 26, 1983.

26. —— Oral pronouncement, community control

Written order of community control which required defendant to submit to random urinalysis, breath testing, and blood testing was improper where court at sentencing orally imposed only condition that defendant submit to random urinalysis. Davis v. State, App. 4 Dist., 677 So.2d 1366 (1996). Sentencing And Punishment ⚷ 1920

Written order of community control must conform to oral pronouncements at sentencing hearing. Davis v. State, App. 4 Dist., 677 So.2d 1366 (1996). Sentencing And Punishment ⚷ 1921

27. —— Duration of community control

Defendant waived his right to enforce statutory two-year maximum on terms of community control by failing to appeal reimposition of two-years' community control, following violation of original community control, and instead accepting benefits of community control. Dupree v. State, App. 1 Dist., 708 So.2d 968 (1998). Sentencing And Punishment ⚷ 2039

Imposition of consecutive terms of two years' community control for separate offenses is permissible. Kocher v. State, App. 3 Dist., 651 So.2d 1288 (1995). Sentencing And Punishment ⚷ 1938

Both community control and probation terms together cannot exceed the statutory maximum term. Phillips v. State, App. 5 Dist., 651 So.2d 203 (1995). Sentencing And Punishment ⚷ 1946

Although it was true that defendant could be sentenced to two years community control on each of two cases and that consecutive sentence of community control was a legal sentence where separate offenses were committed, any sentence imposed had to be within sentencing guidelines. Mills v. State, App. 5 Dist., 623 So.2d 840 (1993). Sentencing And Punishment ⚷ 1946

Where defendant's maximum permitted guideline sentence was nonstate prison sanction or community control of one to three and one-half years incarceration and sentencing court did not enter departure sentence, defendant could not be sentenced to more than three and one-half years of community control, notwithstanding statutes permitting defendant to be sentenced to two years community control in each of two cases and permitting consecutive sentences of community control. Mills v. State, App. 5 Dist., 623 So.2d 840 (1993). Sentencing And Punishment ⚷ 1946

Maximum period of community control is two years. Gasiorowski v. State, App. 4 Dist., 610 So.2d 67 (1992), review denied 621 So.2d 1065. Sentencing And Punishment ⚷ 1943

Four-year sentence to community control for two counts of vehicular homicide exceeded statutory maximum of two years and was improper. Goss v. State, App. 3 Dist., 608 So.2d 541 (1992). Sentencing And Punishment ⚷ 1946

Sentence was illegal, because total term of community control imposed exceeded two years. Sipp v. State, App. 5 Dist., 604 So.2d 576 (1992). Sentencing And Punishment ⚷ 1943

Trial judge could sentence defendant to period of incarceration followed by period of community control as long as combined terms did not exceed maximum period of incarceration provided by statute. Rodriguez v. State, App. 3 Dist., 588 So.2d 1031 (1991). Sentencing And Punishment ⚷ 1946

Sentence of aggregate of six years community control imposed on defendant who pleaded nolo contendere to two counts of grand theft, two counts of uttering false or forged instrument, and one count of dealing in stolen property was improper where sentence was departure from maximum permissible sentence of community control for two years and there was no indication in record that trial court considered sentence to be departure from sentencing guidelines and no written reasons were provided for departure. Weaver v. State, App. 5 Dist., 587 So.2d 654 (1991). Sentencing And Punishment ⚷ 1946

Subsection of this section does not limit duration of community control to single two-year period when defendant is sentenced at same sentencing hearing for multiple offenses charged in single information. Crawford v. State, 567 So.2d 428 (1990). Sentencing And Punishment ⚷ 1946

Under this section, two years is the maximum permissible period of community control for any one offense, but this section does not limit duration of community control to a single two-year period when consecutive sentences are imposed at the same sentencing hearing. Sanchez v. State, App. 5 Dist., 538 So.2d 923 (1989). Sentencing And Punishment ⚷ 1946

Youthful offender sentence of three years' imprisonment followed by three years' community control for defendant was excessive because community control could not exceed two years. Lewis v. State, App. 4 Dist., 532 So.2d 1340 (1988). Infants ⚷ 69(3.1)

Defendant adjudicated guilty of multiple offenses charged in separate information could be sentenced to consecutive two-year terms of community control; duration of community control was not statutorily limited to total of two years under those circumstances. Mick v. State, App. 1 Dist., 506 So.2d 1121 (1987). Sentencing And Punishment ⚷ 1946

This section providing that when community control is imposed it shall not exceed term provided by general law applies to both probation and community control, since both community control and probation involve supervision, and thus placement of an offender on probation or into community control is limited to maximum of two years, unless exception to such general provision exists. Davis v. State, App. 1

Dist., 461 So.2d 1003 (1984). Sentencing And Punishment ⚷ 1946

Placement of an offender into community control is limited to two years. Davis v. State, App. 1 Dist., 461 So.2d 1003 (1984). Sentencing And Punishment ⚷ 1943

28. —— Credits, community control

Defendant was entitled to have his two-year community control sentence credited by four months for time already served on community control. Poulsen v. State, App. 4 Dist., 610 So.2d 710 (1992). Sentencing And Punishment ⚷ 1167

29. Split sentence or split probation—In general

Trial judge is authorized to sentence a defendant to a period of incarceration followed by a period of probation. State v. Holmes, 360 So.2d 380 (1978); Hicks v. State, App., 362 So.2d 173 (1978).

Although a typical true split sentence replaces the term of incarceration with a term of probation equal in length, a shorter term of probation is not prohibited. Morales v. State, App. 2 Dist., 901 So.2d 1032 (2005). Sentencing And Punishment ⚷ 1945

A "true split sentence" consists of a total period of confinement with part of that confinement suspended; generally; the defendant is placed on probation for the suspended portion of the confinement. Moore v. Stephens, App. 5 Dist., 804 So.2d 575 (2002), cause dismissed 817 So.2d 850, reinstatement denied. Sentencing And Punishment ⚷ 1934

A "probationary split sentence" involves a period of incarceration followed by a period of probation. Moore v. Stephens, App. 5 Dist., 804 So.2d 575 (2002), cause dismissed 817 So.2d 850, reinstatement denied. Sentencing And Punishment ⚷ 1934

The key distinction between a "true" split sentence and a "probationary" split sentence is the presence of a suspended portion of incarceration in the "true" split sentence. Moore v. Stephens, App. 5 Dist., 804 So.2d 575 (2002), cause dismissed 817 So.2d 850, reinstatement denied. Sentencing And Punishment ⚷ 1934

Statute authorized conditional suspended sentence that suspended all, not just portion, of period of incarceration; statute empowered trial courts to impose split sentence whereby defendant was placed on probation upon completion of any specified period of sentence, which could include term of years "or less," and statute did not determine minimum "or less" period of incarceration. State v. Powell, App. 2 Dist., 696 So.2d 789 (1997), review granted 697 So.2d 512, approved and remanded 703 So.2d 444. Sentencing And Punishment ⚷ 1936

Statute authorized conditional suspended sentence under which sentence was replaced with term of community control and probation that was shorter than suspended period of incarceration; statute empowering trial courts to impose split sentence did not expressly mandate that period of probation or community control had to be equal in length to suspended portion of prison sentence. State v. Powell, App. 2 Dist., 696 So.2d 789 (1997), review granted 697 So.2d 512, approved and remanded 703 So.2d 444. Sentencing And Punishment ⚷ 1946

Incarcerative portions of all counts of sentence must be completed before probationary portion of any count begins. Hatton v. State, App. 4 Dist., 689 So.2d 1195 (1997). Sentencing And Punishment ⚷ 1941

Sentence of incarceration and probation cannot exceed maximum period of incarceration provided by law. Myers v. State, App. 2 Dist., 676 So.2d 1063 (1996). Sentencing And Punishment ⚷ 1946

Period of two years of community control followed by ten years of supervised probation was not among sentencing alternatives authorized by *Poore v. State*. State v. Davis, App. 5 Dist., 657 So.2d 1224 (1995). Sentencing And Punishment ⚷ 1938

Split sentence pursuant to which defendant was treated as habitual offender under probation portion, but not under imprisonment portion, was illegal hybrid sentence. Mobley v. State, App. 2 Dist., 647 So.2d 264 (1994). Sentencing And Punishment ⚷ 1934

Reverse split sentence, under which term of incarceration is eliminated if defendant complies with conditions of community control, is downward departure from Sentencing Guidelines which requires written justifications. Disbrow v. State, 642 So.2d 740 (1994). Sentencing And Punishment ⚷ 802

Reverse split sentence, revoking defendant's probation, and sentencing defendant to two years of community control followed by terms of 5 and 13 years' incarceration, with terms of incarceration eliminated if defendant complied with conditions of community control, was downward departure under Sentencing Guidelines that was required to be supported by written reasons; defendant's recommended sentence was 17 to 40 years' incarceration, and reverse split sentence spared defendant from serving any term of incarceration. Disbrow v. State, 642 So.2d 740 (1994). Sentencing And Punishment ⚷ 802

Trial court erred in imposing single split sentence for defendant's conviction on two counts without specifying count to which sentence applied. Verble v. State, App. 1 Dist., 636 So.2d 890 (1994). Sentencing And Punishment ⚷ 1060

Improper probationary split sentence rather than true split sentence was imposed where incarcerative portion of split sentence was 40 years for life felony; proper sentence was life incarceration, suspended after service of 40 years incarceration with balance of sentence to be served on probation. Turner v. State, App. 5 Dist., 623 So.2d 1220 (1993). Sentencing And Punishment ⚷ 1934

Simultaneous terms of imprisonment and probation may not be imposed. Nobles v. State, App. 2 Dist., 605 So.2d 996 (1992). Sentencing And Punishment ⚷ 1935

Split sentence for two second-degree felonies, of 15-year sentence for one count and concurrent 10-year sentence followed by five-year probationary period for other count, was illegal since defendant would be required to serve probation on one count at time incarceration was completed on other count. Walker v. State, App. 1 Dist., 604 So.2d 913 (1992). Sentencing And Punishment ⚷ 1937

Probationary split sentence is valid sentencing alternative. Grant v. State, App. 2 Dist., 600 So.2d 19 (1992). Sentencing And Punishment ⚷ 1936

Split sentence could not be imposed for driving offense committed before statute authorizing reverse split sentences became effective. Bozeman v. State, App. 2 Dist., 598 So.2d 213 (1992). Sentencing And Punishment ⚷ 1828

Sentence of community control followed by probation, for offenses of possession of more than 20 grams of cannabis and possession of cannabis with intent to sell or deliver, was proper. Fryson v. State, App. 1 Dist., 559 So.2d 377 (1990). Controlled Substances ⚷ 100(2)

New sentencing alternatives, which abrogated holding in *Villery v. Florida Parole & Probation Commission* pertaining to split sentences, could not be applied retroactively to defendant since the new sentencing alternative was more onerous to defendant. Brown v. State, App. 5 Dist., 460 So.2d 427 (1984). Sentencing And Punishment ⚷ 17(2)

Imposition of probation and commitment to state hospital as a mentally disordered sex offender did not constitute an impermissible split sentence. Dorfman v. State, 351 So.2d 954 (1977), on remand 353 So.2d 967. Sentencing And Punishment ⚷ 1930

Despite fact that under amendment effective July 1, 1974, trial judge has specific statutory authority to impose split sentence probation for felonies as well as misdemeanors, where offense with which defendant was charged took place before July 1, 1974, trial judge did not have authority to utilize split sentence procedure in sentencing defendant to a term of three years provided that after he had served 12 months of the term he should be placed on probation for four years. Williams v. State, App. 4 Dist., 332 So.2d 33 (1976). Sentencing And Punishment ⚷ 1828

Prior to July 1, 1974, trial judge had specific statutory authority to prescribe period in county jail followed by probation for only misdemeanors, but under amendment effective July 1, 1974, trial judge has authority to impose split sentence probation upon conviction of felony. State v. Jones, 327 So.2d 18 (1976), on remand 330 So.2d 189. Sentencing And Punishment ⚷ 1936

This section granting authority to add a period of probation to be combined with jail sentence permits defendant to be placed on probation upon completion of any specified period of sentence; thus, where court in sentencing a defendant to imprisonment for designated period in county jail provides that, after serving stated portion thereof, defendant should be on probation for some period, the penalty for violation of probation would call for return of defendant to county jail for unserved balance of jail sentence, or such part as court should determine, but this section does not provide for adding period of probation to follow service of term for which defendant was committed to county jail. Hutchins v. State, App. 3 Dist., 286 So.2d 244 (1973), certiorari denied 293 So.2d 717. Sentencing And Punishment ⚷ 1936; Sentencing And Punishment ⚷ 2036

30. —— Continuous incarceration or community control, split sentence or split probation

Defendant could not be sentenced a to combination of community control and incarceration, even though length of total combined sentenced of community control and incarceration did not exceed maximum guidelines incarcerative sentence, where guidelines specified community control or incarceration. Allen v. State, App. 4 Dist., 662 So.2d 1254 (1995), rehearing and rehearing en banc denied. Sentencing And Punishment ⚷ 1934

Where sentencing guidelines specify incarceration or community control, these alternatives are mutually exclusive. Allen v. State, App. 4 Dist., 662 So.2d 1254 (1995), rehearing and rehearing en banc denied. Sentencing And Punishment ⚷ 1934

"Back-end split sentences," under which defendants served period of jail incarceration, followed by probation, with prison term suspended in event that probation was successfully served, were invalid; sentences did not follow any of the sentencing alternatives laid down by Florida Supreme Court, sentences were downward departure from sentencing guidelines for which written reasons had not been given, and sentences violated rule against imposing interrupted periods of incarceration. State v. Guilford, App. 5 Dist., 633 So.2d 548 (1994), review granted 639 So.2d 978, approved 644 So.2d 87. Sentencing And Punishment ⚷ 30; Sentencing And Punishment ⚷ 995; Sentencing And Punishment ⚷ 1936

Statute which precludes time gap in probationary split sentence does not prohibit separation between incarceration and probation as to each case of multiple-case sentence; rather, it merely bars period of freedom between portions of individual's overall sentence. Horner v. State, 617 So.2d 311 (1993). Sentencing And Punishment ⚷ 1937

Probationary term in split sentence that falls between or interrupts incarcerative sentence or sentences is illegal since probation must commence immediately upon release from incarceration and offender has right to serve uninterrupted split sentence. Walker v. State, App. 1 Dist., 604 So.2d 913 (1992). Sentencing And Punishment ⚷ 1941

Intermittent periods of incarceration or community control, interrupted by probationary periods, are not authorized by statute. Johnson v. State, App. 1 Dist., 598 So.2d 282 (1992). Sentencing And Punishment ⚷ 1934

Sentencing plan imposed by trial court which resulted in incarceration for nine years (less credit for time served) followed by probation for six years, followed by community control for two years, followed by second probationary term for arson of dwelling and burglary of dwelling with intent to commit arson was impermissible since it was not devised in such a manner that incarcerative and community control portions were served in continuous uninterrupted stretch. Johnson v. State, App. 1 Dist., 598 So.2d 282 (1992). Sentencing And Punishment ⚷ 1934

When sentencing plan involves both periods of incarceration or community control, together with periods of probation, plan must be devised in such a manner that incarcerative and community control portions are served in continuous uninterrupted stretch. Johnson v. State, App. 1 Dist., 598 So.2d 282 (1992). Sentencing And Punishment ⚷ 1936

In imposing sentence that involved incarceration and probation, trial court could not impose consecutive periods of probation when resulting period of court control would create time gap between release from incarceration and commencement of probation in regard to one sentence. Washington v. State, App. 1 Dist., 564 So.2d 563 (1990). Sentencing And Punishment ⚷ 1941

31. —— Validity of split sentence or split probation

Concurrent terms of four years in prison followed by 18 months' community control on each of two counts of grand theft of a motor vehicle exceeded five-year statutory maximum for offense, and remand for resentencing was required. Stephens v. State, App. 2 Dist., 677 So.2d 1325 (1996). Larceny ⚷ 88

Imposing simultaneous terms of imprisonment and probation is reversible error. Nobles v. State, App. 2 Dist., 605 So.2d 996 (1992). Criminal Law ⚷ 1177.3(4)

Sentence of one year and one day imprisonment, to be followed by 18 months community control and then by 30 months probation, was improper under decision holding that probation condition of incarceration which equals or exceeds one year is invalid, even though defendant received 60 days credit for jail time which was to be subtracted from the sentence of imprisonment. Andrews v. State, App. 2 Dist., 462 So.2d 18 (1984). Sentencing And Punishment ⚷ 1976(2)

Where at time of offense trial court did not have authority to use split sentence procedure unless punishment by imprisonment in county jail was prescribed, trial court did not have authority to sentence defendant, convicted of selling or delivering controlled substance, to split sentence although at time of sentencing the legislature had expanded authority to use split sentence procedure to include felonies. Bush v. State, App. 4 Dist., 338 So.2d 255 (1976). Sentencing And Punishment ⚷ 1828

Sentence placing defendant on probation upon his release from prison under prior judgment and sentence was proper despite defendant's contention that sentence to state prison cannot be followed by period of probation. Craft v. State, App. 2 Dist., 300 So.2d 307 (1974). Sentencing And Punishment ⚷ 1936

32. —— Plea bargain, split sentence or split probation

Defendant, who contended that true split sentence committing him to custody of department of corrections for term of three years but providing for two years of probation after one year in prison violated plea agreement by which State agreed that maximum period of incarceration would be one year, should have first raised any question in trial court; if he was aggrieved by trial court's construction of plea agreement; he could move trial court to permit him to withdraw his plea, and if he was aggrieved by ruling on motion to withdraw plea, he could appeal to District Court of Appeal. Medina v.

State, App. 5 Dist., 411 So.2d 323 (1982). Criminal Law ⚷ 1042.3(1)

33. —— Separate offenses, split sentence or split probation

Imposition of single split sentence upon conviction for three offenses did not create time gap in violation of statute, even though successive probationary terms were split from concurrent incarceration periods by initial probationary term, where there was no time gap between incarceration on the one hand and probation on the other. Horner v. State, 617 So.2d 311 (1993). Sentencing And Punishment ⚷ 1937

Jail term for second count of two-count conviction to be served between jail term and probationary period for first count was not an impermissible "gap in sentencing," but rather, merely interrupted probationary term. Jackson v. State, App. 2 Dist., 615 So.2d 850 (1993). Sentencing And Punishment ⚷ 1947

It was improper to sentence defendant to five years and five and one-half years probation, respectively, to run concurrently with terms of imprisonment imposed on other counts; the sentences of probation would be vacated and defendant resentenced to term of imprisonment within presumptive guidelines range. Brudie v. State, App. 2 Dist., 467 So.2d 1113 (1985). Sentencing And Punishment ⚷ 1935

A person cannot be on parole and probation at the same time for the same offense; but this proposition has no application when there are two separate offenses for which two sentences may be imposed in which case it is possible to have a prison sentence from which parole may be available and also have probation imposed. Stafford v. State, 455 So.2d 385 (1984). Pardon And Parole ⚷ 44

Rule that maximum period of incarceration which may be imposed as condition of probation is up to, but not including, one year applies only where incarceration and probation are imposed for the same offense and does not prohibit incarceration for a year or more followed by a period of probation imposed for separate offense. Tobin v. State, App. 1 Dist., 401 So.2d 938 (1981), review denied 411 So.2d 384. Sentencing And Punishment ⚷ 1937; Sentencing And Punishment ⚷ 1976(1)

34. —— Conditional probation, split sentence or split probation

A lengthy prison term, which has the effect of precluding parole before the term expires, cannot be imposed as a condition of probation especially where its purpose is to punish the defendant. Freeman v. State, App. 3 Dist., 382 So.2d 1307 (1980), review denied 401 So.2d 1334. Sentencing And Punishment ⚷ 1976(2)

A trial court retains authority to impose a short jail term or prison sentence as a special condition of probation where it is reasonably related to a rehabilitative purpose. Freeman v. State, App. 3 Dist., 382 So.2d 1307 (1980), review denied 401 So.2d 1334. Sentencing And Punishment ⚷ 1976(2)

Although short jail or prison sentence may be imposed as condition of probation if reasonably related to a rehabilitative purpose, it is doubtful whether a lengthy prison term can stand as a probationary condition when its primary if not exclusive purpose is to punish defendant. Shead v. State, App. 3 Dist., 367 So.2d 264 (1979). Sentencing And Punishment ⚷ 1976(2)

Trial court has general authority to require incarceration as condition of probation for felony and misdemeanor offenses. State v. Jones, 327 So.2d 18 (1976), on remand 330 So.2d 189. Sentencing And Punishment ⚷ 1976(2)

Probationer, who had accepted conditions of his probation, could not challenge constitutionality of one of the conditions after probation was revoked for violation of such condition. Brown v. State, App. 4 Dist., 305 So.2d 309 (1974). Constitutional Law ⚷ 945

Where defendant, who had originally been placed on probation upon condition that he spend six months in jail, had his probation revoked and had his original sentence modified by imposition of special condition that he be incarcerated for one year in the county jail on the work release program, District Court of Appeal, on appeal, was dealing with conditions of probation and not a sentence so that the condition of probation was not void as contrary to this section. Suggs v. State, App. 2 Dist., 304 So.2d 463 (1974). Sentencing And Punishment ⚷ 1976(2)

Trial court cannot, by the artifice of postponing the pronouncement of sentence, exercise the power to conditionally parole or pardon a defendant who stands convicted of a crime. Bateh v. State, App. 1 Dist., 101 So.2d 869 (1958), certiorari discharged 110 So.2d 7, certiorari denied 80 S.Ct. 74, 361 U.S. 826, 4 L.Ed.2d 69. Sentencing And Punishment ⚷ 1814

Upon duly finding that a parolee has violated the conditions of his parole, the parole and probation commission may enter a new parole order containing different and more restrictive conditions than those in the original parole order, including extension of the parole period within and not to exceed the statutorily prescribed limits. Op.Atty.Gen., 83-79, Oct. 26, 1983.

35. —— Probation after service of sentence, split sentence or split probation

The combined periods of incarceration and probation of a probationary split sentence cannot, at the time of the original sentence, exceed the maximum period of incarceration provided by statute for the offense charged. Darling v. State, App. 1 Dist., 886 So.2d 417 (2004). Sentencing And Punishment ⚷ 1946

Defendant's placement in probation restitution center could not exceed that portion of the maximum guidelines sentence remaining after deducting the period of incarceration with the Department of Corrections (DOC). Nelson v. State, App. 4 Dist., 669 So.2d 1145 (1996). Sentencing And Punishment ⚷ 1943

Sentence which ordered incarceration of defendant without habitual offender status followed by probation with habitual offender status was improper hybrid sentence and, thus, sentencing defendant to four years in prison as habitual offender for violating his probation was improper. Guion v. State, App. 2 Dist., 642 So.2d 1148 (1994). Sentencing And Punishment ⚷ 1400; Sentencing And Punishment ⚷ 2032

Imposing concurrent split sentences of incarceration totaling three and a half years, followed by total of 22 years probation, on offenses arising out of numerous thefts did not violate statute requiring probation to commence immediately upon defendant's release from incarceration whenever split sentence was imposed; there was no period of complete freedom between incarceration and probation. Horner v. State, App. 2 Dist., 597 So.2d 920 (1992), jurisdiction accepted 605 So.2d 1264, approved 617 So.2d 311. Sentencing And Punishment ⚷ 1941

While a trial judge is authorized to sentence a criminal defendant to a period of incarceration followed by a period of probation, the combined periods of incarceration and probation at the time of the original sentence cannot exceed the maximum period of incarceration provided by statute for the offense charged, and each sentence for a separate offense must be individually considered and fall within maximum if it is to be upheld. Williams v. State, App. 4 Dist., 556 So.2d 799 (1990). Sentencing And Punishment ⚷ 1946

From colloquy shown by trial transcript, it was apparent that trial court intended to impose a "true" split sentence of five years, i.e., two years' incarceration followed by three years' probation, for grand theft charge and that should have been done by utilizing the second of two "split sentence" boxes on sentence form; therefore, trial judge's checking of first "split sentence" box was redundant, confusing and erroneous and required that that part of sentence be stricken. McKee v. State, App. 5 Dist., 528 So.2d 417 (1988), review denied 537 So.2d 569. Criminal Law ⚷ 1184(4.1)

Defendant was properly sentenced to a probation period, following prison term, which was to end on a specified date; rejecting *Easton v. State,* 472 So.2d 1369 (Fla.App.3d). Pittman v. State, App. 1 Dist., 492 So.2d 741 (1986). Sentencing And Punishment ⚷ 1936

Order providing that, if defendant were to be released by virtue of gain time at any time before he served entire 22-year term, he was to be placed on probation for whatever the length of the remaining period, was wholly erroneous and would be stricken, being unauthorized by statute and improperly negating exclusive authority of the Department of Corrections to allot gain time as "reward" for good behavior, in which case defendant is no longer even on parole for the remainder of the original sentence. Easton v. State, App. 3 Dist., 472 So.2d 1369 (1985). Sentencing And Punishment ⚷ 30

Where defendant had completed service of maximum allowable term of probation on March 11, 1978, trial court's order of September 5, vacating three-year probationary term and placing defendant on probation for one year beginning August 25, 1978 was a nullity. Peyton v. State, App. 3 Dist., 383 So.2d 737 (1980). Sentencing And Punishment ⚷ 2010

Sentence of five years' probation on count charging conspiracy to commit unlawful sale or delivery of cocaine to begin after defendant served his term in county jail on count of unlawful sale of cocaine was valid. Willner v. State, App. 3 Dist., 350 So.2d 1108 (1977). Sentencing And Punishment ⚷ 1938

Sentence placing defendant on probation after completion of prison term was not illegal by virtue of fact that probationary period did not fall within stayed period of imprisonment. Hults v. State, 327 So.2d 210 (1976). Sentencing And Punishment ⚷ 1936

Sentence of five years probation to follow jail sentence in another case was valid. Sands v. State, App. 3 Dist., 313 So.2d 116 (1975). Sentencing And Punishment ⚷ 1938

Sentence of 60 days in jail, with 30 days thereof suspended, followed by two years probation, was improper and contrary to this section. Harrell v. State, App. 2 Dist., 308 So.2d 51 (1975). Sentencing And Punishment ⚷ 1936

So much of sentence as placed accused on probation, following term of imprisonment if he defaulted in payment of fine, was invalid. Owens v. State, App. 4 Dist., 306 So.2d 176 (1975). Sentencing And Punishment ⚷ 1936

That portion of sentence which made provision for probation after serving sentence of commitment to county jail was unauthorized and improper. Reino v. State, App. 3 Dist., 295 So.2d 123 (1974). Sentencing And Punishment ⚷ 1936

Probationary period imposed upon accused following service of designated sentences in county jail was unauthorized. Bryant v. State, App. 3 Dist., 290 So.2d 122 (1974), certiorari denied 300 So.2d 267. Sentencing And Punishment ⚷ 1936

Where defendant, following his voluntary plea of guilty to possession of cocaine and possession of cannabis, was sentenced to six months incarceration in the county jail, trial court could not properly impose a period of probation to follow the designated sentence. Kohn v. State, App. 3 Dist., 289 So.2d 48 (1974). Sentencing And Punishment ⚷ 1936

Portion of sentence which made provision for probation for one year, to follow after the serving of six months in the county jail, was unauthorized and improper. Cleveland v. State, App. 3 Dist., 287 So.2d 347 (1973). Sentencing And Punishment ⚷ 1936

Portion of sentence providing for probation for period of three years to follow serving of ten-month sentence in county jail was unauthorized. Hutchins v. State, App. 3 Dist., 286 So.2d 244 (1973), certiorari denied 293 So.2d 717. Sentencing And Punishment ⚷ 1936

Where trial court sentenced defendant to and he thereafter served maximum county jail term permissible by law, so that there was no time left for defendant to serve and no portion of sentence was withheld, order of probation to be served after completion of said maximum jail term was null and void and all acts taken pursuant thereto, including order of revocation of probation, were nullities and of no force and effect. Williams v. State, App. 3 Dist., 280 So.2d 518 (1973). Sentencing And Punishment ⚷ 1894; Sentencing And Punishment ⚷ 2009

So much of sentence as placed defendant on probation, following term in the state penitentiary, was illegal. Boyd v. State, App. 3 Dist., 272 So.2d 858 (1973). Sentencing And Punishment ⚷ 1936

A court has no legal authority to sentence a defendant to serve a term of imprisonment in the state prison and direct that he be placed on probation after serving said sentence, where the sentence and the probation are for the same offense. If a court should undertake to do this, its order that the defendant be placed on probation would be void from its inception and would have no binding force or effect. Op.Atty.Gen., 072–136, April 18, 1972.

36. —— Excessive sentence, split sentence or split probation

Defendant's sentence for conviction of negligent child abuse was illegal where sentence reflected a period of incarceration of 364 days followed by a period of probation of five years, since combined periods of incarceration and probation exceeded five-year maximum period of incarceration provided by statute. Howland v. State, App. 1 Dist., 420 So.2d 918 (1982). Sentencing And Punishment ⚷ 1946

Although trial judge is authorized to sentence a defendant to a period of incarceration followed by period of probation, combined periods at time of the original sentence cannot exceed maximum period of incarceration provided by statute for the offense charged. Howland v. State, App. 1 Dist., 420 So.2d 918 (1982). Sentencing And Punishment ⚷ 1946

Trial court's imposition of sentence of ten years' probation conditioned upon confinement in state penitentiary for three years as punishment for conviction of manslaughter was to be reduced to an appropriate lesser period of rehabilitative incarceration. Cunningham v. State, App. 3 Dist., 385 So.2d 721 (1980), review denied 402 So.2d 613. Sentencing And Punishment ⚷ 1976(3)

Combined periods of incarceration and probation at time of original sentence cannot exceed the maximum period of incarceration provided by statute for the offense charged, overruling State v. Jones, 327 So.2d 18. State v. Holmes, 360 So.2d 380 (1978). Sentencing And Punishment ⚷ 1946

Where maximum sentence that could have been imposed upon defendant following his conviction of burglary was 15 years, sentence of five years' imprisonment to be followed by 12 years' probation, being excessive by two years, would be modified by eliminating last two years of probationary period. Sanders v. State, App. 4 Dist., 351 So.2d 361 (1977). Criminal Law ⚷ 1184(4.1)

Order placing defendant on probation for period of seven years after his conviction of third-degree felony breaking and entering was erroneous, since maximum probationary period allowable by law was five years. Isaacs v. State, App. 4 Dist., 351 So.2d 359 (1977). Sentencing And Punishment ⚷ 1946

37. —— Length of sentence, split sentence or split probation

Guidelines sentence, which includes incarcerative portion of sentence and probationary or community control period, may not exceed statutory maximum for offense. Stephens v. State, App. 2 Dist., 677 So.2d 1325 (1996). Sentencing And Punishment ⚷ 1946

Combined terms of incarceration and probation may not exceed statutory maximum sentence. Baker v. State, App. 2 Dist., 652 So.2d 431 (1995). Sentencing And Punishment ⚷ 1946

Defendant's split sentence of eight years in prison, followed by two years of community control, followed by life probation exceeded maximum sentence of forty years. Neeb v. State, App. 2 Dist., 643 So.2d 40 (1994). Sentencing And Punishment ⚷ 1945

Where trial court imposes probationary split sentence, incarcerative portion of sentence plus probationary portion of sentence may not exceed maximum term of imprisonment which may be imposed as punishment for the crime. Kline v. State, App. 1 Dist., 642 So.2d 1146 (1994). Sentencing And Punishment ⚷ 1945

Total time imposed pursuant to split sentence cannot exceed maximum period of incarceration provided by law. Gretka v. State, App. 2 Dist., 629 So.2d 263 (1993). Sentencing And Punishment ⚷ 1946

Total duration of split sentence must fall within statutory maximum. Stephens v. State, App. 2 Dist., 627 So.2d 543 (1993). Sentencing And Punishment ⚷ 1946

Ordering that the "balance of the term" be served on probation after trial court sentenced defendant to five-year term of probation, with "special condition" that defendant serve five years in prison and that, upon release from prison, defendant would be placed on community control for two years, with balance of term to be served on probation, was illegal; term of probation was not definite and certain. Randolph v. State, App. 2 Dist., 626 So.2d 1006 (1993). Sentencing And Punishment ⚷ 1944

Imposition of community control and probation in addition to "special condition" that defendant, convicted of third-degree felony, serve five-year prison term constituted illegal sentence; probationary split sentence could not exceed statutory maximum sentence. Randolph v. State, App. 2 Dist., 626 So.2d 1006 (1993). Sentencing And Punishment ⚷ 1946

When sentencing plan involves "split sentence," combining incarceration and probation, total of incarcerative and probationary portions of sentence may not exceed maximum term provided by general law. Walker v. State, App. 1 Dist., 604 So.2d 913 (1992). Sentencing And Punishment ⚷ 1946

Probationary split sentence imposed upon defendant could not exceed statutory maximum sentence provided for underlying burglary and robbery offenses. Blizzard v. State, App. 1 Dist., 600 So.2d 542 (1992). Sentencing And Punishment ⚷ 1946

Imposition of probationary split sentence of seven years in prison to be followed by ten years' probation was not error where, although defendant contended that he had already served sentence in excess of penalty for probation violation, order granting defendant credit for time served did not show that defendant was entitled to credit in excess of probation violation penalty, and sentence was within sentencing guidelines. Grant v. State, App. 2 Dist., 600 So.2d 19 (1992). Sentencing And Punishment ⚷ 1946

When imposing probationary split sentence, trial court may impose sentence for any term provided by law, provided incarcerative portion does not exceed guidelines range, unless valid reason for departure exists. Thicklin v. State, App. 1 Dist., 599 So.2d 202 (1992). Sentencing And Punishment ⚷ 1946

Total of incarcerative and probationary portions of split sentence may not exceed term provided by general law. Arnett v. State, App. 1 Dist., 598 So.2d 235 (1992). Sentencing And Punishment ⚷ 1946

Trial court was not precluded from imposing combination of incarceration and probation totaling more than the 30 months recommended maximum sentence under the guidelines as probation is not part of the "sentence." Cigelski v. State, App. 1 Dist., 453 So.2d 840 (1984), petition for review denied 459 So.2d 1039. Sentencing And Punishment ⚷ 814

Split sentence of two and one-half years' imprisonment to be followed by two and one-half years of probation, imposed on defendant convicted of possession of controlled substance, was proper. Hollingsworth v. State, App. 5 Dist., 394 So.2d 580 (1981). Sentencing And Punishment ⚷ 1936

Sentence of five years' imprisonment to be followed by ten years' probation was authorized under this section following defendant's conviction of a second-degree felony. Wilcher v. State, App. 5 Dist., 388 So.2d 320 (1980). Sentencing And Punishment ⚷ 65

Although short jail or prison sentence may be imposed as condition of probation if reasonably related to a rehabilitative purpose, it is doubtful whether a lengthy prison term can stand as a probationary condition when its primary if not exclusive purpose is to punish defendant. Shead v. State, App. 3 Dist., 367 So.2d 264 (1979). Sentencing And Punishment ⚷ 1976(2)

In proceeding in which defendant entered nolo contendere plea to a charge of attempted second-degree murder, imposition of a "split sentence" of three years' imprisonment, to be followed by seven years' probation, was not error. Hicks v. State, App. 1 Dist., 362 So.2d

173 (1978). Sentencing And Punishment ⚿ 1936

Sentence which imposed three years probation for the offense of uttering and passing a forged instrument upon completion of a seven-year prison sentence for aggravated assault and breaking and entering was legal. Sturn v. State, App. 2 Dist., 295 So.2d 713 (1974). Sentencing And Punishment ⚿ 1936

38. —— Incarceration exceeding one year, split sentence or split probation

Villery, which held that incarceration pursuant to a split sentence which equals or exceeds one year is invalid, applies retroactively. Chaney v. State, App. 5 Dist., 452 So.2d 1148 (1984). Courts ⚿ 100(1)

Sentence of a period of incarceration of 15 years followed by ten years on probation would be vacated on ground that it violated *Villery,* which held that incarceration pursuant to a split sentence which equals or exceeds one year is invalid, and case would be remanded for resentencing. Chaney v. State, App. 5 Dist., 452 So.2d 1148 (1984). Sentencing And Punishment ⚿ 1943

Where defendant, who originally received split sentence of five years in prison, with condition that after having served two years, remainder of sentence would be suspended and defendant would be placed on probation for three years, applied to trial court for correction of his split sentence under decision which provided that incarceration pursuant to statutory split sentence alternatives which equals or exceeds one year is invalid, trial court was not precluded from imposing a sentence in excess of probationary term of three years; rather, maximum sentence court was authorized to impose was five years, the entire term previously imposed, including conditional period of incarceration. Flynn v. State, App. 1 Dist., 413 So.2d 36 (1981), review denied 412 So.2d 465. Sentencing And Punishment ⚿ 2332

Following defendant's conviction of two counts of burglary, split sentence of three years' imprisonment followed by two years' probation was unlawful. Cronce v. State, App. 4 Dist., 411 So.2d 345 (1982). Sentencing And Punishment ⚿ 1936

State Supreme Court's proscription of incarceration which equals or exceeds one year as part of split sentence alternative applies only to sentencing techniques of this section authorizing courts to place defendant on probation whenever punishment by imprisonment for misdemeanor or felony is prescribed and § 948.03 providing that enumerations of specific kinds of terms and conditions of probation are not exclusive of court adding others. Riley v. State, App. 2 Dist., 407 So.2d 967 (1981). Sentencing And Punishment ⚿ 1936

Trial judge who imposed sentence of incarceration followed by probation equalling or exceeding one year had option of either modifying such illegal sentence to provide that all or any portion of remainder of sentence would be probation or withdrawing original sentence and resentencing defendant to incarceration for whatever time offense provided, less credit for time served. Noles v. State, App. 2 Dist., 407 So.2d 370 (1981). Sentencing And Punishment ⚿ 2335

Sentence of three years' imprisonment, two years' probation and $250 fine violated rule that period of incarceration followed by probation imposed either as condition of probation or under true split sentence as authorized by this section cannot equal or exceed one year. Noles v. State, App. 2 Dist., 407 So.2d 370 (1981). Sentencing And Punishment ⚿ 1936

Rule that a probation condition of incarceration which equals or exceeds one year is invalid is applicable to this section providing that the court may direct a defendant to be placed on probation, upon completion of any portion of a sentence involving imprisonment, for the remainder of the sentence; therefore defendant, who was sentenced to five years of incarceration followed by ten years of probation, was entitled to resentencing to comply with rule. Roberts v. State, App. 5 Dist., 400 So.2d 475 (1981). Sentencing And Punishment ⚿ 1976(2)

Sentence which imposed seven years of incarceration to be followed by five years of probation on conviction of possession of cannabis with intent to deliver was violative of rule in Villery v. Florida Parole and Probation Commission, 396 So.2d 1107 (Fla.1981), retroactive in effect, that split sentences may not validly impose a requirement of incarceration for more than one year. Goodman v. State, App. 4 Dist., 399 So.2d 1120 (1981). Sentencing And Punishment ⚿ 1936

Imposition, on defendant convicted of burglary and theft, of five-year split sentence with two and one-half years to be served in prison and remaining time on probation was improper since split sentence alternative prohibits incarceration for term of more than one year. Cline v. State, App. 5 Dist., 399 So.2d 1115 (1981). Sentencing And Punishment ⚿ 1936

Probation condition of incarceration which equals or exceeds one year is invalid; probationer who has been placed on probation with period of incarceration of one year or more is entitled upon application to have probation order corrected, in manner specified in opinion, and such decision is to be applied retroactively;

receding from holding in State v. Jones, 327 So.2d 18. Villery v. Florida Parole and Probation Commission, 396 So.2d 1107 (1980). Courts ⚷ 100(1); Sentencing And Punishment ⚷ 1976(2)

Section 947.16 providing that a prisoner does not become eligible for parole consideration unless he has been sentenced to at least one year in prison expresses a legislative intent to limit period of incarceration which may be imposed as condition of probation to a period of less than one year. Villery v. Florida Parole and Probation Commission, 396 So.2d 1107 (1980). Sentencing And Punishment ⚷ 1976(2)

39. —— County jail sentence, split sentence or split probation

Sentence imposing six months in county jail, absent suspension of any portion thereof, to be followed by two years probation, was a clear violation of this section stating, inter alia, that whenever punishment by imprisonment in county jail is prescribed the court may direct defendant to be placed on probation upon completion of any specified period of such sentence, and that in such case the court shall stay and withhold imposition of remainder of sentence imposed upon defendant and direct that defendant be placed upon probation after serving such period as may be imposed by the court. Reynolds v. State, App. 3 Dist., 293 So.2d 743 (1974), certiorari denied 302 So.2d 764. Sentencing And Punishment ⚷ 1936

Sentence imposed on defendant of 360 days in the county jail followed by four years' probation was not authorized by statute and sentence of defendant, found guilty of resisting arrest with violence, must be modified to eliminate provision for probation. Harden v. State, App. 3 Dist., 293 So.2d 741 (1974), certiorari denied 304 So.2d 451. Criminal Law ⚷ 1184(4.1); Sentencing And Punishment ⚷ 1936

Sentence may not be imposed for maximum term of one year in county jail and be followed by period of probation for 18 months. Metchik v. State, App. 3 Dist., 286 So.2d 269 (1973). Sentencing And Punishment ⚷ 1943

40. —— Resentencing, split sentence or split probation

There are several approaches a court may take when it resentences a defendant whose negotiated sentence is vacated because of a violation of *Villery,* which held that incarceration pursuant to split sentence alternatives which equals or exceeds one year is invalid: state may exercise its option to accept the plea with the sentence reduced to a legal term and if state does not exercise that option, trial court may allow defendant to withdraw his plea thereby reinstating the charges originally filed against him or the court may resentence defendant within parameters of the plea bargain by either changing the period of incarceration which equals or exceeds one year to probation, or vacate probation portion of original sentence. Chaney v. State, App. 5 Dist., 452 So.2d 1148 (1984). Sentencing And Punishment ⚷ 2264

Upon sentencing defendant to three concurrent one-year terms, trial court was authorized to suspend sentence and place defendant on probation for period of two years after serving three months in county jail. Adkins v. State, App. 1 Dist., 330 So.2d 809 (1976). Sentencing And Punishment ⚷ 1937

Although this section authorizing trial court to impose sentence of certain period in prison and certain period on probation was in effect at time of defendant's sentencing for breaking and entering, this section was not in effect at time defendant committed crime, and thus sentence of three years' imprisonment with 12 years' probation for conviction of breaking and entering would be vacated, and defendant would be remanded to trial court for resentencing. Wildie v. State, App. 4 Dist., 326 So.2d 198 (1976). Criminal Law ⚷ 1187

Where trial court imposed illegal sentence of five years' probation on condition of one year in county jail, District Court of Appeal remanded to the trial court for resentencing rather than striking either the term of probation or the term of incarceration. Durham v. State, App. 3 Dist., 304 So.2d 146 (1974). Criminal Law ⚷ 1181.5(8)

Imposition of sentence of five years' imprisonment upon defendant's motion to correct illegal sentence of five years' probation with condition of one year in county jail had unconstitutional chilling effect on right of all defendants who would otherwise attack illegal sentences. Durham v. State, App. 3 Dist., 304 So.2d 146 (1974). Double Jeopardy ⚷ 115

41. —— Credit for time served, split sentence or split probation

Defendant who was sentenced to three-year prison term for admitted probation violation, after serving more than five years on original sentence for underlying sex offense conviction, was not eligible for five years' time-served credit, which would have meant his immediate release. Fulcher v. State, App. 3 Dist., 875 So.2d 647 (2004), rehearing and rehearing en banc denied, dismissed 890 So.2d 1114. Sentencing And Punishment ⚷ 2041

When a defendant is given a split sentence, serves time in prison, is released on probation, and subsequently violates that probation, she or he is entitled to credit for time served in prison on the original sentence, especially in the absence of any documentation establishing a waiver of credit during a negotiated plea for the probation violation. Fulcher v. State, App. 3 Dist., 875 So.2d 647 (2004), rehearing and rehearing en banc denied, dismissed 890 So.2d 1114. Sentencing And Punishment ⚷ 2041

Defendants were entitled to have first probationary term reduced by amount of time they spent in jail or prison, including gain time; at original sentencing hearing, trial court expressly granted credit for time served, which was more than 30 months' credit for each defendant, and defendants each spent short amount of time incarcerated after sentencing before being released on appeal bonds. Netherly v. State, App. 2 Dist., 873 So.2d 407 (2004), rehearing denied, review denied 889 So.2d 72. Sentencing And Punishment ⚷ 2041

Sentences of terms of imprisonment and probation for violation of community control to be followed by term of probation for new substantive offenses which comprised violation of community control was permissible, provided that if defendant subsequently has his second probation revoked and is ordered to serve time in prison, he will receive credit for time he served in prison on first sentence. Williams v. State, App. 2 Dist., 629 So.2d 174 (1993), cause dismissed 639 So.2d 984, review denied 642 So.2d 748. Sentencing And Punishment ⚷ 2041

Defendant who was resentenced to term of probation after he appealed his original sentence was entitled to credit for time he had already spent on probation. Jones v. State, App. 5 Dist., 617 So.2d 743 (1993). Sentencing And Punishment ⚷ 1167

Since defendant may not have been given full credit for jail time he served on original split sentences as special condition of probation revocation, proceeding would be remanded and upon remand trial court was required to conduct hearing to determine time actually served in jail by defendant on original split sentences and to give defendant appropriate credit for jail time on sentences under review. Delgado v. State, App. 3 Dist., 423 So.2d 603 (1982). Criminal Law ⚷ 1181.5(8)

Where trial court imposed split sentence of one year and one day imprisonment to be followed by three years probation upon revocation of probation it was aware that defendant had served three years in prison and fully intended that defendant serve additional year for having violated his probation, defendant was not entitled to have three years he served as special condition of prior probation order credited against subsequent sentence, with result that he would be set free, since trial court was empowered to impose sentence of sufficient length after crediting time served to carry out that intent. Toombs v. State, App. 3 Dist., 404 So.2d 766 (1981), review denied 412 So.2d 471. Sentencing And Punishment ⚷ 2041

In case of defendants who have served 364 days or more, requirement that credit for time served be given effectively precludes court from further utilization of split sentence alternative when imposing sentence for revocation of probation and leaves trial court with power to impose either any straight sentence of imprisonment it might originally have imposed or to place defendant on probation. Toombs v. State, App. 3 Dist., 404 So.2d 766 (1981), review denied 412 So.2d 471. Sentencing And Punishment ⚷ 2032

Where order withholding adjudication of guilt placed defendant on two years' probation with special condition that he remain incarcerated for first six months of probation and further specified that defendant was to be given credit for any time spent in confinement in county jail or in custody of Division of Corrections, time defendant spent in confinement was to be credited against six months' jail term and not against entire two-year probationary period, for purpose of determining date of expiration of probation. Depson v. State, App. 1 Dist., 363 So.2d 43 (1978). Sentencing And Punishment ⚷ 1948

Order of probation requiring that defendants spend nine months and 11 months and 29 days, respectively, in county jail as condition of probation was not "imposition of sentence" within § 921.161 providing that court imposing sentence shall allow defendant credit for all time he spent in county jail before sentence, and thus refusal to allow credit for time served against jail term imposed as condition of probation was not error. Bracey v. State, App. 1 Dist., 356 So.2d 72 (1978). Sentencing And Punishment ⚷ 1976(2)

There was insufficient time left on defendant's split sentence after period of imprisonment of 25 years to allow for maximum gain time and extra good time he could acquire during his five years of parole. Wright v. State, App. 1 Dist., 342 So.2d 565 (1977). Sentencing And Punishment ⚷ 1936

It is permissible under this section authorizing a split sentence for trial court to require that initial imprisonment prior to release on probation be served without credit for gain time or good time provided there is sufficient time left in sentence after period of imprisonment to allow for maximum gain time and good time that defendant could acquire during term of imprisonment. Wright v. State, App. 1 Dist., 342 So.2d 565 (1977). Sentencing And Punishment ⚷ 1936

Defendant must be given credit for time spent in jail pursuant to split sentence probation order whether it is imposed pursuant to this section granting authority to trial judge to prescribe period in county jail followed by probation or as a condition of probation. State v. Jones, 327 So.2d 18 (1976), on remand 330 So.2d 189. Sentencing And Punishment ⚷ 1167

A prisoner sentenced pursuant to provision of this section, is entitled to earn gain time under statute, for the specified period of the sentence imposed in accordance with subsection (4) of this section. Op.Atty.Gen., 074–283, Sept. 19, 1974.

An inmate sentenced pursuant to provision of this section, can be eligible for parole consideration prior to the expiration of the specified period of sentence if otherwise qualified for consideration for parole under § 947.16. Op. Atty.Gen., 074–283, Sept. 19, 1974.

42. Early release

Sentence of two concurrent 12–year sentences with proviso that if defendant was released under provisions for early release, balance of 12–year sentence was to be served on probation, was improper because such probation, when term is both indefinite and uncertain, was not authorized by this section. Fisher v. State, App. 5 Dist., 559 So.2d 362 (1990). Sentencing And Punishment ⚷ 1944

43. Release after violation of probation

Where, upon being arrested and brought before the court on charge of having violated conditions of his probation, probationer is released with or without bail to await a further hearing, it is the duty of the probation and parole commission to continue to supervise the probationer under the conditions set forth in the original probation order while thus released and probationer is required to abide by the conditions of his probation while thus released. Op.Atty.Gen., 070–127, Sept. 18, 1970.

Where parolee has been arrested on charge of violating conditions of his parole, and has been admitted to bail pending hearing before the probation and parole commission, it is the duty of said commission to continue to supervise such parolee while he is thus released on bail and parolee is required to abide by the conditions of his parole while thus released. Op.Atty. Gen., 070–127, Sept. 18, 1970.

44. Release on own recognizance

This section, as amended by s. 7, Ch. 90–337, Laws of Florida, does not appear to control the postarrest, pretrial procedures provided for in Ch. 907, which authorize the Florida Supreme Court to adopt rules governing the procedures for pretrial release; pursuant to Rule 3.131(b), Fla.R.Crim.P., the judicial officer may release the defendant on his or her own recognizance and place the defendant in the custody of a designated person or organization agreeing to supervise him or her. Op.Atty.Gen. 90–82, Oct. 4, 1990.

45. Conditional suspended sentence

Sentence of five years' incarceration suspended on condition of successful completion of two years of community control followed by three years' probation and twelve years' incarceration suspended on condition defendant successfully complete two years of community control followed by 13 years' probation, imposed as part of plea bargain upon violation of original terms of community control, was an illegal, conditional suspended, and alternative sentence; however, reimposition of sentence upon a second violation of community control was proper where the sentence did not violate statutory maximums for crimes committed and defendant benefitted from sentence without challenging its legality. Warrington v. State, App. 5 Dist., 660 So.2d 385 (1995). Sentencing And Punishment ⚷ 1934; Sentencing And Punishment ⚷ 2038

46. Withheld adjudication

In cases of withheld adjudication, Florida law holds that until defendant has successfully completed probationary term, court is not divested of its jurisdiction to later adjudicate defendant guilty. U.S. v. Gispert, S.D.Fla.1994, 864 F.Supp. 1193. Sentencing And Punishment ⚷ 2079

Defendant who purchased firearm which formed basis for felon in possession of firearm conviction after he had pled guilty to felony charge, Florida state court had withheld adjudication and placed him on probation and he had successfully completed probation was not "convicted" felon under Florida law for purposes of felon in possession of firearm statute; pursuant to Florida law, once defendant completed his probation, state court no longer retained jurisdiction to adjudicate him guilty. U.S. v. Gispert, S.D.Fla.1994, 864 F.Supp. 1193. Weapons ⚷ 4

Withholding of adjudication without ordering probation in prosecution for possession of marijuana with intent to sell exceeded scope of court's authority under statutes and rule permitting judge to withhold adjudication of guilt in felony prosecution if defendant was placed on probation. State v. Messina, App. 4 Dist., 13 So.3d 153 (2009). Sentencing and Punishment ⚷ 2079

State failed to produce evidence that defendant who was charged with three third-degree felonies had previously had adjudication withheld for a felony offense, and thus trial court could withhold adjudication on the instant felonies, despite State's contention that defendant was charged with possession of methamphetamines in another state, and that he received the equivalent of a withhold of adjudication. State v. Barfield, App. 5 Dist., 995 So.2d 1138 (2008). Sentencing and Punishment ⚷ 2066; Sentencing and Punishment ⚷ 2075

Withholding of adjudication without ordering probation in prosecution for possession of cocaine exceeded scope of court's authority under statutes and rule permitting judge to withhold adjudication of guilt in felony prosecution if defendant was placed on probation. State v. Tribble, App. 4 Dist., 984 So.2d 639 (2008). Sentencing And Punishment ⚷ 2079

Once any required pre-sentencing procedures are concluded, the options available to the trial court are either to adjudge the defendant guilty and order confinement or to withhold adjudication and place the defendant on probation; only if the trial court places the defendant on probation may the court withhold adjudication of guilt. State v. Tribble, App. 4 Dist., 984 So.2d 639 (2008). Sentencing And Punishment ⚷ 2079

47. Conditions of probation—In general

Withholding or suspending adjudication or sentence in a felony case can only be done when the defendant is put on probation. State v. Tribble, App. 4 Dist., 984 So.2d 639 (2008). Sentencing And Punishment ⚷ 2079

A court cannot impose probation as a condition of probation. Blaxton v. State, App. 2 Dist., 868 So.2d 620 (2004). Sentencing And Punishment ⚷ 1983(2)

Defendant would not be relieved of obligation of probation to reimburse county sheriff for medical expenses, as defendant waived any objection to legality of sentence containing this condition, where obligation was included as specific component of plea agreement, bargained for and voluntarily entered into by defendant. Allen v. State, App. 1 Dist., 642 So.2d 815 (1994). Criminal Law ⚷ 273.1(2)

Imposing cost which defendant did not agree to as condition of probation was error given that trial judge did not orally announce cost as special condition of probation and in absence of statutory authority in written order for imposition of payment. Stone v. State, App. 5 Dist., 642 So.2d 34 (1994), rehearing denied. Sentencing And Punishment ⚷ 1920

Cost imposed as condition of probation must be stricken on appeal unless trial judge can cite supporting statutory authority for its imposition. Stone v. State, App. 5 Dist., 642 So.2d 34 (1994), rehearing denied. Sentencing And Punishment ⚷ 1975(2)

Special condition of probation is invalid if it has no relationship to count of which offender was convicted, relates to conduct which is not in itself criminal, and requires or forbids conduct which is not reasonably related to future criminality. Forshee v. State, App. 2 Dist., 579 So.2d 388 (1991). Sentencing And Punishment ⚷ 1963

Conditions of probation imposed upon defendant convicted of obtaining property with a worthless check, requiring defendant to refrain from consuming alcoholic beverages, not to visit any bars, and submit to substance abuse counseling and treatment at his own expense, were invalid, absent supporting findings; conditions were unrelated to crime for which defendant was convicted, and did not relate to criminal activity. Mitsakos v. State, App. 2 Dist., 579 So.2d 336 (1991). Sentencing And Punishment ⚷ 1977(2); Sentencing And Punishment ⚷ 1980(2)

House arrest confining defendant to his home except for very limited circumstances could only be imposed as condition of community control and as such could not exceed two years; accordingly, oral condition of probation imposing 24 years of house arrest was illegal. Yourn v. State, App. 2 Dist., 579 So.2d 309 (1991). Sentencing And Punishment ⚷ 1976(2)

Probation order which included incarceration as condition thereof was a "sentence" so that defendant was entitled to earn gain time for time incarcerated under West's F.S.A. § 951.21. Van Tassel v. Coffman, 486 So.2d 528 (1985). Prisons ⚷ 245(3)

48. —— Drug offenders, conditions of probation

Condition of drug offender probation concerning defendant's consumption and possession of alcohol was special condition that was required to be orally announced at sentencing. Boyd v. State, App. 2 Dist., 688 So.2d 959 (1997). Sentencing And Punishment ⚷ 1918

Condition of drug offender probation requiring defendant to work at suitable employment was required to state "to the best of his ability." Boyd v. State, App. 2 Dist., 688 So.2d 959 (1997). Sentencing And Punishment ⚷ 1972(3)

Conditions of drug offender probation requiring defendant to pay for drug and alcohol testing, evaluation, treatment were special conditions required to be orally announced at sentencing. Boyd v. State, App. 2 Dist., 688 So.2d 959 (1997). Sentencing And Punishment ⚷ 1918

Condition of drug offender probation relating to alcohol evaluation and treatment was special condition required to be orally announced at sentencing. Boyd v. State, App. 2 Dist., 688 So.2d 959 (1997). Sentencing And Punishment ⚿ 1918

Conditions which pertained to regular probation and community control applied to defendant's drug offender probation, and therefore trial court was not required to orally pronounce those conditions of defendant's drug offender probation that were statutorily imposed and contained in pertinent rule of criminal procedure; however, trial court was required to orally pronounce special conditions of defendant's drug offender probation, i.e., those conditions that were neither statutorily imposed nor listed in rule. Welborn v. State, App. 4 Dist., 687 So.2d 35 (1997). Sentencing And Punishment ⚿ 1918

Defendant placed on drug offender probation is on constructive notice that some or all of the standard conditions of probation listed in statute may be imposed, and oral pronouncement of those conditions is not required, nor is oral pronouncement required for conditions identical to those contained in the Supreme Court's "Form Order of Probation," but other conditions must be stricken if not orally pronounced. Tory v. State, App. 4 Dist., 686 So.2d 689 (1996). Sentencing And Punishment ⚿ 1918

Defendant who was convicted of manufacturing cannabis and possessing paraphernalia and who was previously convicted of cultivating and possessing marijuana was chronic substance abuser and, thus, defendant was properly placed on drug offender probation. Ringling v. State, App. 2 Dist., 678 So.2d 1339 (1996). Sentencing And Punishment ⚿ 1980(2)

Indigent alcoholics who were repeat violators of § 856.01 (repealed) could have been required to take antabuse as a condition of probation, if such medication was prescribed by a physician to arrest their ingestion of alcohol, if the necessary examination, treatment and medication could have been provided by the department of health and rehabilitative services through an appropriate treatment resource under chapter 396, and if such condition of probation was designed to protect society and to rehabilitate the probationer. Op.Atty.Gen., 072–124, April 5, 1972.

49. Term of probation—In general

Order of probation or community control placement is not a fixed sentence such that defendant loses right to invoke Fifth Amendment privilege against self-incrimination, as order withholds imposition of sentence and is subject to modification. Landeverde v. State, App. 4 Dist., 769 So.2d 457 (2000). Sentencing And Punishment ⚿ 1809

When two separate and consecutive terms of probation are imposed, separate 12–month periods of incarceration may be imposed as a condition of each probation. Cigelski v. State, App. 1 Dist., 453 So.2d 840 (1984), petition for review denied 459 So.2d 1039. Sentencing And Punishment ⚿ 1976(2)

Where because it had been ordered that term of probation was to be treated separately, so that defendant could not be on parole and probation at the same time, and where at time affidavits were filed charging probation violation defendant's term of probation had not yet commenced, trial court could not revoke or modify his probation. Simmons v. State, App. 2 Dist., 445 So.2d 700 (1984). Sentencing And Punishment ⚿ 2010

Where trial judge clearly indicated that defendant's term of probation was to be treated separately, he could not be on parole and probation at the same time, and his probation could not begin until his parole expired. Simmons v. State, App. 2 Dist., 445 So.2d 700 (1984). Sentencing And Punishment ⚿ 1940

Where defendant was placed on five years concurrent probation in two cases, and those sentences of probation were consecutive to terms of imprisonment imposed in two other cases, defendant's probation did not start until he completed the sentences of imprisonment, because a defendant cannot be on probation and parole at the same time. Mackin v. State, App. 2 Dist., 427 So.2d 767 (1983). Sentencing And Punishment ⚿ 1941

50. —— Maximum term of probation

Both community control and probation terms together cannot exceed the statutory maximum term. Phillips v. State, App. 5 Dist., 651 So.2d 203 (1995). Sentencing And Punishment ⚿ 1946

Court is not authorized to extend term of probation beyond period of maximum sentence. Conrey v. State, App. 5 Dist., 624 So.2d 793 (1993). Sentencing And Punishment ⚿ 1952

Extension of probation beyond maximum five-year period allowed for third-degree felony was illegal. Conrey v. State, App. 5 Dist., 624 So.2d 793 (1993). Sentencing And Punishment ⚿ 1952

Maximum probation that can be imposed for third-degree felony is five years, and thus trial court could not legally extend original probationary term of defendant, who pled nolo contendere to second-degree grand theft, for additional three years. Servis v. State, App. 2 Dist., 588 So.2d 290 (1991). Sentencing And Punishment ⚿ 1952

Since the maximum statutory penalty for offense of possession of a short-barreled shotgun is five years, maximum period of probation which could be imposed is five years. Twining v. State, App. 2 Dist., 380 So.2d 496 (1980). Sentencing And Punishment ⚷ 1946

A term of probation cannot exceed maximum sentence which a court may impose. Swift v. State, App. 2 Dist., 362 So.2d 723 (1978). Sentencing And Punishment ⚷ 1945

A probationary term may not exceed the maximum possible sentence unless expressly provided by law. Mays v. State, App. 2 Dist., 349 So.2d 792 (1977). Sentencing And Punishment ⚷ 1945

51. —— Excessive term of probation

Court may not evade the two-year limit on community control by sentencing a defendant to a term of probation in excess of two years, with a special condition of house arrest. Bebout v. State, App. 4 Dist., 904 So.2d 613 (2005). Sentencing And Punishment ⚷ 1943

Trial court lacks authority to extend period of probation beyond maximum permissible sentence for underlying offense. Moore v. State, App. 1 Dist., 623 So.2d 795 (1993). Sentencing And Punishment ⚷ 1952

Order, entered pursuant to conviction of aggravated assault, requiring defendant to serve seven years of probation exceeded maximum allowed by two years. Almond v. State, App. 4 Dist., 350 So.2d 810 (1977), certiorari denied 358 So.2d 128. Sentencing And Punishment ⚷ 1943

Where information in case charging defendant with burglary of a structure did not allege that there was a human being in the structure at the time defendant committed the crime, placing defendant on probation for 15 years was excessive and defendant would be resentenced to probationary term not exceeding five years. Mays v. State, App. 2 Dist., 349 So.2d 792 (1977). Sentencing And Punishment ⚷ 1943

Sentence placing defendant on probation for seven years, which was in excess of five-year maximum sentence permissible for uttering a forgery, was excessive, and would be modified to five years' probation. La Quire v. State, App. 4 Dist., 345 So.2d 788 (1977). Criminal Law ⚷ 1184(4.1); Sentencing And Punishment ⚷ 1945

52. Supervision of probationers

"Court-supervised" probation subject to termination on payment of court costs was illegal sanction upon withholding of adjudication of guilt, pursuant to statute requiring persons placed on probation to be placed under supervision of Department of Corrections. State v. Luxenburg, App. 2 Dist., 13 So.3d 137 (2009). Sentencing and Punishment ⚷ 2079

Requirement of this section, that individual placed on probation be supervised by department of corrections is mandatory, and thus that portion of sentence placing defendant on unsupervised probation had to be reversed and case remanded for correction of judgment and sentence. Lynn v. State, App. 1 Dist., 398 So.2d 977 (1981), review denied 411 So.2d 383. Criminal Law ⚷ 1181.5(8)

This section providing that a defendant placed on probation for commission of a felony offense be supervised by Department of Offender Rehabilitation is mandatory and operated to require that defendant be so supervised when placed on probation upon plea of nolo contendere to felony offense of attempted burglary. State v. Wilcox, App. 2 Dist., 351 So.2d 89 (1977). Sentencing And Punishment ⚷ 1988

Provision of § 948.04 that defendants found guilty of misdemeanors who are placed on probation shall be under supervision not to exceed six months unless otherwise specified by the court does not authorize trial court to place a defendant who has been adjudicated guilty of a misdemeanor upon probation for unlimited period of time. McNulty v. State, App. 1 Dist., 339 So.2d 1155 (1976). Sentencing And Punishment ⚷ 1946

Filing of notice of appeal from order withholding adjudication of guilt and placing defendant under supervision of probation and parole commission for five years did not divest trial court and commission of all jurisdiction over defendant pending appeal and did not entitle him to order directing the court and commission to cease supervising him pending the appeal. Varnom v. State, App. 1 Dist., 198 So.2d 64 (1967). Criminal Law ⚷ 1083

A county court is authorized to place a defendant on probation, under the supervision of the parole and probation commission, in any case pending in that court, whether it involves traffic offenses such as driving while intoxicated or reckless driving, or any other misdemeanor, and if such should be done, it would be the duty of the commission to supervise such probationer. Op.Atty.Gen., 073–23, Feb. 15, 1973.

A court placing on probation a defendant who is to reside in Florida has no authority to order the probationer not to report to or be under the supervision of Florida parole and probation commission. The statutes mandatorily require that when a defendant is placed on probation, he is to be under the supervision and control of said commission unless he is permitted to reside in another state under the compact set forth in § 949.07. The court may thereafter terminate that supervision pursuant to the terms of

§ 948.05. Op.Atty.Gen., 072–223, July 13, 1972.

53. Residence of probationer

The only authority which a court has to allow a probationer to reside in another state is that granted by the compact set out in § 949.07. That compact provides that before granting such permission, opportunity shall be granted to the receiving state to investigate the home and prospective employment of the probationer. The compact further unequivocally provides that the receiving state will assume the duties of visitation and supervision over probationers of a sending state. Result is that when a court places a defendant on probation with permission to reside in another state, this must be done under the terms of said compact and the court has no authority whatever to order that the receiving state not investigate or supervise the probationer. Nevertheless, if the court later becomes satisfied that discharging the probationer from supervision in the other state will be for the best interests of justice and the welfare of society, then the court may discharge him from such supervision under the authority of § 948.05. Op.Atty.Gen., 072–223, July 13, 1972.

Where a defendant is placed on probation and is not permitted to reside in another state pursuant to the compact set forth in § 949.07, the court placing him on probation has the authority to so frame the order of probation as to permit the probationer to travel to, but not to reside in, another state on a temporary basis. If the original order of probation does not so permit, court has the authority to later amend the terms and conditions thereof in such manner as to allow the probationer to do this. Op. Atty.Gen., 072–2223.

54. Ordinance violators

A violation of a municipal ordinance of the City of Jacksonville is not a violation of state law requiring board of parole and probation commission to supervise defendants who are placed on probation unless the consolidated city council determines that the consolidated government shall be considered to be a county for purposes of violations of municipal ordinances. Op.Atty.Gen., 075–164, June 9, 1975.

55. Search and seizure

One does not absolutely forfeit protection of Fourth Amendment's prohibition of unreasonable searches and seizures merely by assuming status of probationer; however, probationary status may be taken into account in determining whether particular search was in fact reasonable. Croteau v. State, 334 So.2d 577 (1976). Sentencing And Punishment ⚷ 1992

56. Habitual offenders

Resentencing within guidelines was required for defendant who had already served incarceration portion of improper hybrid habitual offender sentences, which imposed habitual offender status on probation only, including one cell bump authorized for violations of probation. Shaw v. State, App. 2 Dist., 637 So.2d 254 (1994), review denied 648 So.2d 724. Criminal Law ⚷ 1181.5(9)

Imposing hybrid habitual offender sentences, by sentencing defendant to incarceration without habitual offender status followed by probation with habitual offender status, was error. Shaw v. State, App. 2 Dist., 637 So.2d 254 (1994), review denied 648 So.2d 724. Sentencing And Punishment ⚷ 1400

Trial judge has discretion to place habitual felony offender on probation. McKnight v. State, 616 So.2d 31 (1993). Sentencing And Punishment ⚷ 1873

Trial court may impose probation even when court has made finding that defendant is habitual offender. Bamberg v. State, App. 2 Dist., 599 So.2d 769 (1992), jurisdiction accepted 605 So.2d 1262, approved 618 So.2d 204. Sentencing And Punishment ⚷ 1873

Placing of defendant adjudicated to be habitual felony offender on straight probation in lieu of sentence constituted unauthorized and illegal sentence which state was entitled to appeal. State v. Kendrick, App. 5 Dist., 596 So.2d 1153 (1992), jurisdiction accepted 606 So.2d 1164, review dismissed 613 So.2d 5. Criminal Law ⚷ 1024(9); Sentencing And Punishment ⚷ 1873

57. Revocation of probation—In general

Due process does not require that court spell out in probation order or at sentencing hearing that if state seeks to revoke defendant's probation and increases penalty based on disobedience of criminal statutes that burden of proof is less stringent than that employed in typical criminal case. State v. Green, App. 2 Dist., 667 So.2d 959 (1996). Constitutional Law ⚷ 4731; Constitutional Law ⚷ 4733(2)

Although trial court erroneously suspended execution of defendant's sentence and released defendant on conditions without formally placing him on probation, trial court's revocation of the suspension of sentence was proper in that it had the effect of correcting the illegal sentence, even though the suspension was revoked because defendant had violated conditions of release. Phillips v. State, App. 5 Dist., 455 So.2d 656 (1984). Sentencing And Punishment ⚷ 2005

Probationer was not sentenced for purposes of application of sentencing guidelines until her probation was revoked. Duggar v. State, App. 1 Dist., 446 So.2d 222 (1984). Sentencing And Punishment ⚷ 2032

58. —— Due process, revocation of probation

In probation revocation proceeding, denial of preliminary hearing to probationer to determine if there was probable cause to believe he had violated his probation did not constitute a denial of procedural due process, in that procedural due process was satisfied by state procedure under which a probationer is arrested on warrant issued by judicial officer on probable cause supported by affidavit. Singletary v. State, App. 4 Dist., 290 So.2d 116 (1974), certiorari dismissed 293 So.2d 361. Constitutional Law ⚷ 4733(2)

Probation revocation procedure wherein probationer's arrest, confinement, hearing and sentencing occurred under canopy of the usual state criminal system court rules and statutes exceeded minimum procedural due process requirements of State and Federal Constitutions. Singletary v. State, App. 4 Dist., 290 So.2d 116 (1974), certiorari dismissed 293 So.2d 361. Constitutional Law ⚷ 4733(2)

59. —— Term of probation, revocation of probation

When affidavit and warrant charging probation violations issue within probationary term, there is no jurisdictional impediment to holding hearing thereon after expiration of such term. Peyton v. State, App. 3 Dist., 383 So.2d 737 (1980). Sentencing And Punishment ⚷ 2010

Court may only revoke probation for violations which occur during term of that probation. Swift v. State, App. 2 Dist., 362 So.2d 723 (1978). Sentencing And Punishment ⚷ 2003

Where maximum punishment which could have been imposed under applicable statute for leaving scene of accident was one year, term of probation for that offense could not exceed one year, and thus defendant's probation therefor ended on December 2, 1977 which meant that trial court, which erroneously placed defendant on probation for five years for leaving scene of an accident, erred in revoking defendant's probation for that offense since violations which served as basis for revocation occurred after December 2, 1977. Swift v. State, App. 2 Dist., 362 So.2d 723 (1978). Sentencing And Punishment ⚷ 2006

Filing, during probation period, of a separate information against defendant for some separate offense allegedly committed by him during term of probation cannot substitute for affirmative action required to be taken or initiated during term as prerequisite to revocation of probation. Brooker v. State, App. 3 Dist., 207 So.2d 478 (1968). Sentencing And Punishment ⚷ 2010

60. —— Grounds, revocation of probation

When probationer violates probation condition by committing a crime, he demonstrates his unsuitability for probation, notwithstanding his belief that he is no longer on probation. Hiers v. State, App. 5 Dist., 440 So.2d 71 (1983). Sentencing And Punishment ⚷ 2004

Imposition of probation on nol-prossed charges was a nullity, and, therefore, trial court was without jurisdiction to revoke probation and impose sentence on such charges following finding of probation violation. Walker v. State, App. 2 Dist., 382 So.2d 1231 (1980). Sentencing And Punishment ⚷ 1800

Although defendant's having driven without a license was a violation of law and therefore violation of probation requirement that he live honorably and not violate the law, where defendant was not charged with such conduct, his probation could not be revoked on the basis thereof. King v. State, App. 2 Dist., 349 So.2d 738 (1977). Sentencing And Punishment ⚷ 2011

Under its inherent power to revoke probation, circuit court properly revoked order of probation, the term of which had not yet commenced, where the Court determined that the probationer had been guilty of misconduct (while he was in county jail) occurring subsequent to the entry of the order of probation. Martin v. State, App. 4 Dist., 243 So.2d 189 (1971), certiorari denied 247 So.2d 63. Sentencing And Punishment ⚷ 2005

Probation may be revoked solely upon conviction by jury of a subsequent crime, provided the subsequent conviction is valid. Egantoff v. State, App. 2 Dist., 208 So.2d 843 (1968), certiorari denied 218 So.2d 164. Sentencing And Punishment ⚷ 2004

61. —— Affidavit, revocation of probation

Order, which revoked probation but which was found, by federal district court, to have violated due process, did not extend the date of expiration of the three-year term of probation; thus, subsequent affidavit for violation of probation, which was filed more than three years after defendant was placed on probation, was fatally untimely. Wrich v. State, App. 2 Dist., 350 So.2d 1114 (1977). Sentencing And Punishment ⚷ 1948; Sentencing And Punishment ⚷ 2010

Probation cannot be revoked for one reason when affidavit of violation states another. Mack v. State, App. 2 Dist., 342 So.2d 562 (1977). Sentencing And Punishment ⚷ 2011

62. —— Resentencing, revocation of probation

Effective sentence of ten years with credit for time served, imposed by trial court upon probation violation, did not exceed legal sentencing limits, even though original sentence imposed upon defendant for grand larceny, forgery and uttering a forged instrument was a split five-year sentence, with 11 months to be served in state penitentiary, and defendant then placed on probation for the remaining four years and one month. Williams v. State, App. 3 Dist., 392 So.2d 600 (1981). Sentencing And Punishment ⚿ 2038

Sentence of three years for aggravated assault, imposed by trial court upon revocation of three years' probation, was not improper even though the trial court had suspended the original sentence of six to 18 months when the probation was imposed, since a court may suspend some or all of a defendant's sentence in order to place him on probation. McGuirk v. State, App. 2 Dist., 382 So.2d 1235 (1980). Sentencing And Punishment ⚿ 2032

If probation is revoked after defendant has been sentenced to period of incarceration followed by a period of probation, trial judge may impose any sentence which he might have originally imposed minus jail time previously served as part of the sentence. State v. Holmes, 360 So.2d 380 (1978). Sentencing And Punishment ⚿ 2037

Where, on conviction of felonies, defendant was sentenced to confinement in county jail for one year to be followed by probation for five years, trial court on reconsideration reduced jail to 85 days then served, retaining the five-year probation period, and during the five-year period defendant committed other felonies, trial judge, upon revoking probation, had authority to impose three concurrent sentences of two years each in state penitentiary with credit for the days served in county jail. Jones v. State, App. 3 Dist., 330 So.2d 189 (1976).

Where sentencing court directs that defendant be placed on probation upon completion of specified period of sentence with remainder of jail sentence stayed and withheld and he subsequently violates probation, he may be sentenced to imprisonment by trial judge for same period of years as court could have originally imposed without necessity of establishing term of sentence and withholding a part of it at initial sentencing proceedings. Jones v. State, App. 3 Dist., 330 So.2d 189 (1976).

63. Orders

Remand for written sentencing order and correction of probation order was required, where trial judge orally sentenced defendant to one year in county jail followed by two years' probation, and probation order imposed three years' probation with special condition that defendant spend first 364 days in county jail. Eidson v. State, App. 1 Dist., 667 So.2d 247 (1995). Criminal Law ⚿ 1181.5(8)

Where oral sentencing order included provision for community control as well as provision for incarceration, written sentencing order had to be conformed to oral order to include community control. Ayers v. State, App. 2 Dist., 651 So.2d 1226 (1995). Sentencing And Punishment ⚿ 1921

Remand was required to determine which term of probation was intended by trial court where, during sentencing hearing, trial court stated that defendant would serve 24 months probation, at a separate time trial court stated that defendant would serve three years probation, and later written order provision recited term of probation would be for five years. Kinlaw v. State, App. 5 Dist., 564 So.2d 1242 (1990). Criminal Law ⚿ 1181.5(8)

Defendant was not precluded from seeking correction of probation order in trial court on remand, even though a discrepancy was not raised as an issue on appeal where there was a discrepancy between amount of restitution orally imposed and amount in probation order. Bishop v. State, App. 5 Dist., 564 So.2d 629 (1990). Criminal Law ⚿ 1192

Written order placing defendant on probation had to recite that probation would be terminated upon payment of restitution. Johnson v. State, App. 2 Dist., 561 So.2d 1254 (1990). Sentencing And Punishment ⚿ 1918

Judgment and sentencing order which imposed lien for court-appointed services as a condition of probation was improper where trial court had orally stated that it would not impose public defender lien as condition of probation and that defendant would have three years to satisfy the lien, even though the order of probation did not list lien as a condition of probation. Moore v. State, App. 2 Dist., 525 So.2d 1031 (1988). Sentencing And Punishment ⚿ 1920

General order of probation predicated on more than one conviction of criminal conduct was improper and there should be a separate order of probation for each offense. Moore v. State, App. 2 Dist., 525 So.2d 1031 (1988). Sentencing And Punishment ⚿ 1913

Order specifying that defendant was placed on probation for each offense to which he pled guilty, and that each probationary period was to run concurrently with other periods, was not improper, general order of probation. Sullivan v. State, App. 5 Dist., 525 So.2d 499 (1988). Sentencing And Punishment ⚿ 1913

Probation order, which did not describe whether one or both convictions constituted predicate for the order, was invalid. Cervantes v. State, 442 So.2d 176 (1983). Sentencing And Punishment ⚷ 1913

Order granting probation is not sentence; it is the grace of state, in lieu of sentence, granted in hopeful anticipation of defendant's rehabilitation. Loeb v. State, App. 3 Dist., 387 So.2d 433 (1980). Sentencing And Punishment ⚷ 1811; Sentencing And Punishment ⚷ 1812

Where an order of probation says nothing about whether the probationer may consult or seek the assistance of such agencies as alcoholic rehabilitation, guidance clinics, etc., the court that made such order does not have the authority to prohibit the Florida parole and probation commission from referring the probationer to such agencies without first obtaining a determination from the court that such reference is necessary. Op.Atty.Gen., 071–144, June 11, 1971.

64. Records and recordation

This section with respect to placing defendants on probation does not require elimination of all records of case when court withholds adjudication of guilt and places defendant on probation after he is found guilty or pleads guilty to offense. Mulkey v. Purdy, 234 So.2d 108 (1970). Sentencing And Punishment ⚷ 1913

Petitioner, who at age 17 pled guilty to misdemeanor of petit larceny, and was put on probation for 6 months, was not entitled to have his fingerprints, which sheriff had taken after petitioner's arrest, expunged, or to have court's docket entries of his case erased and court file thereon removed or sealed, though petitioner alleged that prospective employer informed him that it would not hire him unless such record was expunged. Purdy v. Mulkey, App. 3 Dist., 228 So.2d 132 (1969), writ discharged 234 So.2d 108. Infants ⚷ 133

65. Review

Postconviction relief petitioner did not waive challenge to improper enhancement of terms of his probation by failing to raise issue on direct appeal from original imposition of improper enhancement or by failure to appeal subsequent revocation of his probation. Casterline v. State, App. 2 Dist., 703 So.2d 1071 (1997), rehearing denied, review granted 717 So.2d 538, review dismissed 736 So.2d 1151. Double Jeopardy ⚷ 201

Defendant who pled guilty to first-degree murder and received sentence of probation could not challenge legality of probationary sentence after he violated his probation; although sentence violated statute prohibiting imposition of probation for first-degree murder offense, violation benefited defendant. Bashlor v. State, App. 1 Dist., 586 So.2d 488 (1991), review denied 598 So.2d 75. Sentencing And Punishment ⚷ 1922

Where defendant's two-year sentence for probation violation was to become effective upon completion of defendant's five-year sentence for robbery, and possible impropriety of such sentencing was not raised on petition for writ of certiorari, discharge of writ was without prejudice to defendant to pursue any postconviction relief to which he might be entitled in proper proceeding. Simmons v. State, 305 So.2d 178 (1974). Criminal Law ⚷ 1181(1)

Defendant, who was convicted of robbery and whose probation for assault with intent to commit robbery was simultaneously revoked, could not raise for first time in Supreme Court issue that probation was allegedly revoked in violation of statute. Simmons v. State, 305 So.2d 178 (1974). Criminal Law ⚷ 1042.3(4)

Order of probation was appealable. Lubash v. State, App. 3 Dist., 296 So.2d 565 (1974), certiorari denied 304 So.2d 131. Criminal Law ⚷ 1023(16)

Where sole order dispositive or defendant's rights is a probation order such order must be considered, at least for purposes of appeal, to be a final order. Delaney v. State, 190 So.2d 578 (1966), appeal dismissed 87 S.Ct. 1710, 387 U.S. 426, 18 L.Ed.2d 866. Criminal Law ⚷ 1023(12); Criminal Law ⚷ 1023(16)

Where trial judge entered order which withheld adjudication of guilt and placed accused on probation, two prior orders denying motions to quash indictment, each of which in effect upheld validity of criminal statute, traveled forward with order of probation to satisfy jurisdictional requirement of Supreme Court. Delaney v. State, 190 So.2d 578 (1966), appeal dismissed 87 S.Ct. 1710, 387 U.S. 426, 18 L.Ed.2d 866. Criminal Law ⚷ 1134.90

District Court of Appeal had jurisdiction to review order placing defendant on probation following conviction by jury even though final adjudication of guilt had been withheld. Warren v. State, App. 1 Dist., 174 So.2d 429 (1965). Criminal Law ⚷ 1023(16)

Statutes which authorize appeals from orders placing convicted defendant on probation, with or without an adjudication of guilt, are not in conflict with any of appellate rules adopted by Supreme Court and were to have same effect as if they had been separately promulgated by Supreme Court. Warren v. State, App. 1 Dist., 174 So.2d 429 (1965). Criminal Law ⚷ 1005

948.011. When court may impose fine and place on probation or into community control as an alternative to imprisonment

When the law authorizes the placing of a defendant on probation, and when the defendant's offense is punishable by both fine and imprisonment, the trial court may, in its discretion, impose a fine upon him or her and place him or her on probation or into community control as an alternative to imprisonment.

Laws 1959, c. 59–175, § 1; Laws 1983, c. 83–131, § 14. Amended by Laws 1997, c. 97–102, § 1683, eff. July 1, 1997; Laws 2004, c. 2004–373, § 13, eff. July 1, 2004.

Historical and Statutory Notes

Amendment Notes:

Laws 1983, c. 83–131, § 14, provided for placement into community control.

Laws 1997, c. 97–102, eff. July 1, 1997, removed gender-specific references applicable to human beings from volume 4 of the Florida Statutes without substantive changes in legal effect.

Laws 2004, c. 2004–373, § 13, inserted "an alternative" preceding "to imprisonment" throughout.

Cross References

Sentencing alternatives, probation, see § 921.187.

Law Review and Journal Commentaries

Probation in Florida. Vernon W. Clark, 14 U.Fla.L.Rev. 213 (1961).

Sentence. Thomas A. Wills, 20 U.Miami L.Rev. 264 (1965).

Library References

Sentencing and Punishment ⚷1930.
Westlaw Topic No. 350H.
C.J.S. Criminal Law § 2144.

Research References

Treatises and Practice Aids

16 Florida Practice Series § 1:43, Sentencing Alternatives.

16 Florida Practice Series § 1:61, Costs, Assessments, Surcharges, and Fines--Fines.

22 Florida Practice Series App. A, Florida Rules of Criminal Procedure.

Notes of Decisions

Construction and application 1

1. Construction and application

Trial court could properly impose imprisonment, fine, and probation all within one sentence on defendant who was convicted for lewd and lascivious act upon child under the age of 16. Singleton v. State, App. 1 Dist., 582 So.2d 657 (1991). Infants ⚷ 20

Defendant, who was 19 years of age, reacted improvidently and with lack of advice as to possible alternatives when he expressed his belief that he would not be able to make monetary payments required by probation conditions, and justice would be served by vacatur of prison sentences, which had been imposed on basis that defendant did not want to be on probation and did not want to pay fine or restitution, and full advisement of defendant of his legal position and of possible alternatives to probation. Holley v. State, App. 5 Dist., 483 So.2d 854 (1986). Criminal Law ⚷ 1181.5(1)

948.012. Split sentence of probation or community control and imprisonment

(1) Whenever punishment by imprisonment for a misdemeanor or a felony, except for a capital felony, is prescribed, the court, in its discretion, may, at the time of sentencing, impose a split sentence whereby the defendant is to be placed on probation or, with respect to any such felony, into community control upon completion of any specified period of such sentence which may include a term of years or less. In such case, the court shall stay and withhold the imposition of the remainder of sentence imposed upon the defendant and direct that the defendant be placed upon probation or into community control after serving such period as may be imposed by the court. The period of probation or community control shall commence immediately upon the release of the defendant from incarceration, whether by parole or gain-time allowances.

(2) The court may also impose a split sentence whereby the defendant is sentenced to a term of probation which may be followed by a period of incarceration or, with respect to a felony, into community control, as follows:

(a) If the offender meets the terms and conditions of probation or community control, any term of incarceration may be modified by court order to eliminate the term of incarceration.

(b) If the offender does not meet the terms and conditions of probation or community control, the court may revoke, modify, or continue the probation or community control as provided in s. 948.06. If the probation or community control is revoked, the court may impose any sentence that it could have imposed at the time the offender was placed on probation or community control. The court may not provide credit for time served for any portion of a probation or community control term toward a subsequent term of probation or community control. However, the court may not impose a subsequent term of probation or community control which, when combined with any amount of time served on preceding terms of probation or community control for offenses pending before the court for sentencing, would exceed the maximum penalty allowable as provided in s. 775.082. Such term of incarceration shall be served under applicable law or county ordinance governing service of sentences in state or county jurisdiction. This paragraph does not prohibit any other sanction provided by law.

(3) The court may also impose split probation whereby, upon satisfactory completion of half the term of probation, the Department of Corrections may place the offender on administrative probation for the remainder of the term of supervision.

(4) Effective for offenses committed on or after September 1, 2005, the court must impose a split sentence pursuant to subsection (1) for any person who is convicted of a life felony for lewd and lascivious molestation pursuant to s. 800.04(5)(b) if the court imposes a term of years in accordance with s. 775.082(3)(a)4.a.(II) rather than life imprisonment. The probation or community control portion of the split sentence imposed by the court for a defendant

must extend for the duration of the defendant's natural life and include a condition that he or she be electronically monitored.

Laws 1967, c. 67–204, § 1; Laws 1974, c. 74–112, § 12; Laws 1983, c. 83–131, § 13; Laws 1985, c. 85–288, § 14; Laws 1991, c. 91–225, § 14; Laws 1991, c. 91–280, § 1; Laws 1997, c. 97–78, § 21; Laws 1999, c. 99–3, § 121. Renumbered from 948.01(6), (11), (12) and amended by Laws 2004, c. 2004–373, §§ 4, 8, 9, eff. July 1, 2004. Amended by Laws 2005, c. 2005–28, § 14, eff. Sept. 1, 2005; Laws 2006, c. 2006–1, § 115, eff. July 4, 2006; Laws 2007, c. 2007–2, § 6, eff. March 12, 2007; Laws 2008, c. 2008–182, § 2, eff. July 1, 2008.

Historical and Statutory Notes

Amendment Notes:

Laws 2004, c. 2004–373, §§ 4, 8, 9, renumbered former subsecs. (6), (11), and (12) of § 948.01 as this section; and in subsec. (3), deleted a reference to § 948.001.

Laws 2005, c. 2005–28, § 14, added subsec. (4), relating to offenses committed on or after Sept. 1, 2005.

Laws 2006, c. 2006–1, a reviser's bill, deleted obsolete and expired provisions, corrected grammatical and typographical errors, and made other similar changes.

Laws 2007, c. 2007–2, § 6, reenacted subsec. (2)(b) for the purpose of incorporating the amendment to § 948.06 in a reference thereto.

Laws 2008, c. 2008–182, § 2, in subsec. (4), substituted a reference to § 775.082(3)(a)4.b(II) for a reference to § 775.082(3)(a)4.b.

Library References

Sentencing and Punishment ⚷1933.
Westlaw Topic No. 350H.

Research References

Treatises and Practice Aids

16 Florida Practice Series § 1:4, Classes of Offenses--Felonies.

16 Florida Practice Series § 1:46, Sentencing Alternatives--True Split Sentence.

16 Florida Practice Series § 1:49, Sentencing Alternatives--Reverse Split Sentence.

16 Florida Practice Series § 1:50, Sentencing Alternatives--Split Probation.

16 Florida Practice Series § 1:52, Sentencing Alternatives--Concurrent and Consecutive Sentencing.

16 Florida Practice Series § 1:69, Credit for Time Served--Jail Credit.

16 Florida Practice Series § 3:32, Completing the 1994 Guidelines Scoresheet--Total Sentence Imposed--Sentences Imposed After Revocation of Probation or Community Control.

16 Florida Practice Series § 4:40, Completing the 1995 Guidelines Scoresheet--Total Sentence Imposed--Sentences Imposed After Revocation of Probation or Community Control.

16 Florida Practice Series § 6:67, Enhancement of Penalty and Reclassification of Offense--Minimum Mandatory Sentencing--Life Felonies.

16 Florida Practice Series § 7:20, Probationary and Community Control Time Periods.

948.013. Administrative probation

(1) The Department of Corrections may establish procedures for transferring an offender to administrative probation. The department may collect an initial processing fee of up to $50 for each probationer transferred to administrative probation. The offender is exempt from further payment for the cost of supervision as required in s. 948.09.

(2) Effective for an offense committed on or after July 1, 1998, a person is ineligible for placement on administrative probation if the person is sentenced to or is serving a term of probation or community control, regardless of the conviction or adjudication, for committing, or attempting, conspiring, or solicit-

ing to commit, any of the felony offenses described in s. 787.01 or s. 787.02, where the victim is a minor and the defendant is not the victim's parent; s. 787.025; chapter 794; s. 796.03; s. 800.04; s. 825.1025(2)(b); s. 827.071; s. 847.0133; s. 847.0135; or s. 847.0145.

Laws 1998, c. 98–81, § 13; Laws 2000, c. 2000–246, § 3. Renumbered from 948.01(15) and amended by Laws 2004, c. 2004–373, § 12, effective July 1, 2004.

Historical and Statutory Notes

Amendment Notes:

Laws 2004, c. 2004–373, § 12, renumbered and rewrote former subsec. (15) of § 948.01 as this section. Subsec. (15) of § 948.01 formerly read:

"(15) Effective for an offense committed on or after July 1, 1998, a person is ineligible for placement on administrative probation if the person is sentenced to or is serving a term of probation or community control, regardless of the conviction or adjudication, for committing, or attempting, conspiring, or soliciting to commit, any of the felony offenses described in s. 787.01 or s. 787.02, where the victim is a minor and the defendant is not the victim's parent; s. 787.025; chapter 794; s. 796.03; s. 800.04; s. 825.1025(2)(b); s. 827.071; s. 847.0133; s. 847.0135; or s. 847.0145."

Library References

Sentencing and Punishment ⚷1801.
Westlaw Topic No. 350H.
C.J.S. Criminal Law § 2147.

Research References

Treatises and Practice Aids

16 Florida Practice Series § 1:43, Sentencing Alternatives.

16 Florida Practice Series § 7:12, Administrative Probation.

948.014. Requirement to submit to drawing of blood or other biological specimens

(1) As a condition of probation, community control, or any other court-ordered community supervision, the court shall order offenders to submit to the drawing of the blood or other biological specimens when required under s. 943.325 as a condition of the probation, community control, or other court-ordered community supervision.

(2) For the purposes of this section, conviction shall include a finding of guilty, or entry of a plea of nolo contendere or guilty, regardless of adjudication, or, in the case of a juvenile, the finding of delinquency.

(3) Any order issued pursuant to this section shall also require the convicted person to reimburse the appropriate agency for the costs of drawing and transmitting the blood or other biological specimens to the Department of Law Enforcement.

Laws 1995, c. 95–283, § 53; Laws 1998, c. 98–251, § 15; Laws 1999, c. 99–3, § 122. Renumbered from 948.03(10), (11) and amended by Laws 2004, c. 2004–373, §§ 23, 24 eff. July 1, 2004. Amended by Laws 2009, c. 2009–190, § 4, eff. July 1, 2009.

Historical and Statutory Notes

Amendment Notes:

Laws 2004, c. 2004–373, §§ 23 and 24, renumbered former subsec. (10) of § 948.03 as subsecs. (1) and (2), and renumbered former subsec. (11) of § 948.03 as subsec. (3); and substituted references to other biological specimens for references to specimens, and substituted references to this section for references to this subsection throughout.

Laws 2009, c. 2009–190, § 4, rewrote subsec. (1), which formerly read:

"(1) As a condition of probation, community control, or any other court-ordered community supervision, the court shall order persons convicted of offenses specified in s. 943.325 to submit to the drawing of the blood or other biological specimens as prescribed in that section as a condition of the probation, community control, or other court-ordered community supervision."

Library References

Sentencing and Punishment ⚷1983.
Westlaw Topic No. 350H.

Research References

Treatises and Practice Aids

16 Florida Practice Series § 7:10, Terms and Conditions of Probation--Standard, or General, Terms and Conditions of Probation.

948.015. Presentence investigation reports

The circuit court, when the defendant in a criminal case has been found guilty or has entered a plea of nolo contendere or guilty and has a lowest permissible sentence under the Criminal Punishment Code of any nonstate prison sanction, may refer the case to the department for investigation or recommendation. Upon such referral, the department shall make the following report in writing at a time specified by the court prior to sentencing. The full report shall include:

(1) A complete description of the situation surrounding the criminal activity with which the offender has been charged, including a synopsis of the trial transcript, if one has been made; nature of the plea agreement, including the number of counts waived, the pleas agreed upon, the sentence agreed upon, and any additional terms of agreement; and, at the offender's discretion, his or her version and explanation of the criminal activity.

(2) The offender's sentencing status, including whether the offender is a first offender, a habitual or violent offender, a youthful offender, or is currently on probation.

(3) The offender's prior record of arrests and convictions.

(4) The offender's educational background.

(5) The offender's employment background, including any military record, present employment status, and occupational capabilities.

(6) The offender's financial status, including total monthly income and estimated total debts.

(7) The social history of the offender, including his or her family relationships, marital status, interests, and activities.

(8) The residence history of the offender.

(9) The offender's medical history and, as appropriate, a psychological or psychiatric evaluation.

(10) Information about the environments to which the offender might return or to which the offender could be sent should a sentence of nonincarceration or community supervision be imposed by the court, and consideration of the offender's plan concerning employment supervision and treatment.

(11) Information about any resources available to assist the offender, such as:

(a) Treatment centers.

(b) Residential facilities.

(c) Career training programs.

(d) Special education programs.

(e) Services that may preclude or supplement commitment to the department.

(12) The views of the person preparing the report as to the offender's motivations and ambitions and an assessment of the offender's explanations for his or her criminal activity.

(13) An explanation of the offender's criminal record, if any, including his or her version and explanation of any previous offenses.

(14) A statement regarding the extent of any victim's loss or injury.

(15) A recommendation as to disposition by the court. The department shall make a written determination as to the reasons for its recommendation, and shall include an evaluation of the following factors:

(a) The appropriateness or inappropriateness of community facilities, programs, or services for treatment or supervision for the offender.

(b) The ability or inability of the department to provide an adequate level of supervision for the offender in the community and a statement of what constitutes an adequate level of supervision.

(c) The existence of other treatment modalities which the offender could use but which do not exist at present in the community.

Laws 1991, c. 91–280, § 3. Amended by Laws 1997, c. 97–102, § 1684, eff. July 1, 1997; Laws 1997, c. 97–194, § 33, eff. Oct. 1, 1998; Laws 1998, c. 98–204, § 18, eff. Oct. 1, 1998; Laws 2004, c. 2004–357, § 64, eff. July 1, 2004.

Historical and Statutory Notes

Amendment Notes:

Laws 1997, c. 97–102, eff. July 1, 1997, removed gender-specific references applicable to human beings from volume 4 of the Florida Statutes without substantive changes in legal effect.

Laws 1997, c. 97–194, § 33, eff. Oct. 1, 1998, in the introductory paragraph, substituted "Criminal Punishment Code" for "sentencing guidelines".

Laws 1998, c. 98–204, § 18, in the introductory paragraph, substituted "lowest permissible sentence" for "recommended sentence".

Laws 2004, c. 2004–357, § 64, in subsec. (11)(c), substituted "Career" for "Vocational" preceding "training".

Library References

Sentencing and Punishment ⚷275 to 301.
Westlaw Topic No. 350H.
C.J.S. Criminal Law §§ 2068 to 2074.

Research References

Forms

Florida Pleading and Practice Forms § 96:10, Presentence Investigation Report.

Treatises and Practice Aids

22 Florida Practice Series App. A, Florida Rules of Criminal Procedure.

22 Florida Practice Series § 18:32, Sentence--Presentence Investigation Report.

948.02. Renumbered as 945.26 by Laws 1977, c. 77–120, § 82

948.03. Terms and conditions of probation

(1) The court shall determine the terms and conditions of probation. Conditions specified in this section do not require oral pronouncement at the time of sentencing and may be considered standard conditions of probation. These conditions may include among them the following, that the probationer or offender in community control shall:

(a) Report to the probation and parole supervisors as directed.

(b) Permit such supervisors to visit him or her at his or her home or elsewhere.

(c) Work faithfully at suitable employment insofar as may be possible.

(d) Remain within a specified place.

(e) Make reparation or restitution to the aggrieved party for the damage or loss caused by his or her offense in an amount to be determined by the court. The court shall make such reparation or restitution a condition of probation, unless it determines that clear and compelling reasons exist to the contrary. If the court does not order restitution, or orders restitution of only a portion of the damages, as provided in s. 775.089, it shall state on the record in detail the reasons therefor.

(f) Effective July 1, 1994, and applicable for offenses committed on or after that date, make payment of the debt due and owing to a county or municipal detention facility under s. 951.032 for medical care, treatment, hospitalization, or transportation received by the felony probationer while in that detention facility. The court, in determining whether to order such repayment and the amount of such repayment, shall consider the amount of the debt, whether there was any fault of the institution for the medical expenses incurred, the financial resources of the felony probationer, the present and potential future financial needs and earning ability of the probationer, and dependents, and other appropriate factors.

(g) Support his or her legal dependents to the best of his or her ability.

(h) Make payment of the debt due and owing to the state under s. 960.17, subject to modification based on change of circumstances.

(i) Pay any application fee assessed under s. 27.52(1)(b) and attorney's fees and costs assessed under s. 938.29, subject to modification based on change of circumstances.

(j) Not associate with persons engaged in criminal activities.

(k) 1. Submit to random testing as directed by the correctional probation officer or the professional staff of the treatment center where he or she is receiving treatment to determine the presence or use of alcohol or controlled substances.

2. If the offense was a controlled substance violation and the period of probation immediately follows a period of incarceration in the state correction system, the conditions shall include a requirement that the offender submit to random substance abuse testing intermittently throughout the term of supervision, upon the direction of the correctional probation officer as defined in s. 943.10(3).

(*l*) Be prohibited from possessing, carrying, or owning any firearm unless authorized by the court and consented to by the probation officer.

(m) Be prohibited from using intoxicants to excess or possessing any drugs or narcotics unless prescribed by a physician. The probationer or community controllee shall not knowingly visit places where intoxicants, drugs, or other dangerous substances are unlawfully sold, dispensed, or used.

(n) Submit to the drawing of blood or other biological specimens as prescribed in ss. 943.325 and 948.014, and reimburse the appropriate agency for the costs of drawing and transmitting the blood or other biological specimens to the Department of Law Enforcement.

(2) The enumeration of specific kinds of terms and conditions shall not prevent the court from adding thereto such other or others as it considers proper. However, the sentencing court may only impose a condition of supervision allowing an offender convicted of s. 794.011, s. 800.04, s. 827.071, s. 847.0135(5), or s. 847.0145, to reside in another state, if the order stipulates that it is contingent upon the approval of the receiving state interstate compact authority. The court may rescind or modify at any time the terms and conditions theretofore imposed by it upon the probationer. However, if the court withholds adjudication of guilt or imposes a period of incarceration as a condition of probation, the period shall not exceed 364 days, and incarceration shall be restricted to either a county facility, a probation and restitution center under the jurisdiction of the Department of Corrections, a probation program drug punishment phase I secure residential treatment institution, or a community residential facility owned or operated by any entity providing such services.

Laws 1941, c. 20519, § 23; Laws 1977, c. 77–452, § 5; Laws 1981, c. 81–198, § 1; Laws 1983, c. 83–75, § 3; Laws 1983, c. 83–131, § 16; Laws 1983, c. 83–216, § 192; Laws 1983, c. 83–256, § 3; Laws 1984, c. 84–363, § 8; Laws 1985, c. 85–288, § 15; Laws 1987, c. 87–211, § 5; Laws 1988, c. 88–96, § 11; Laws 1988, c. 88–122, §§ 70, 71; Laws 1989, c. 89–526, § 37; Laws 1990, c. 90–287, § 10; Laws 1990, c. 90–337, §§ 8, 17; Laws 1991, c. 91–225, § 11; Laws 1991, c. 91–280, § 4; Laws 1992, c. 92–310, § 23; Laws 1993, c. 93–37, § 10; Laws 1993, c. 93–227, § 15; Laws 1994, c. 94–294, § 1; Laws 1995, c. 95–189, § 1; Laws 1995, c. 95–283, §§ 53, 59. Amended by Laws 1996, c. 96–170, § 1, eff. Oct. 1, 1996; Laws 1996, c. 96–232, § 4, eff. Jan. 1, 1997; Laws 1996, c. 96–312, § 54, eff. July 1, 1996; Laws 1996, c. 96–409, § 6, eff. Oct. 1, 1996; Laws 1997, c. 97–78, § 22, eff. May 23, 1997; Laws 1997, c. 97–102, § 1877, eff. July 1, 1997; Laws 1997, c. 97–107, § 11, eff. May 24, 1997; Laws 1997, c. 97–234, § 27, eff. July 1, 1997; Laws 1997, c. 97–271, § 44, eff. July 1, 1997; Laws 1997, c. 97–308, § 3, eff. Oct. 1, 1997; Laws 1998, c. 98–81, § 14, eff. July 1, 1998; Laws 1998,

c. 98–251, § 15, eff. July 1, 1998; Laws 1999, c. 99–3, § 122, eff. June 29, 1999; Laws 1999, c. 99–201, § 13, eff. Oct. 1, 1999; Laws 2000, c. 2000–246, § 3, eff. Oct. 1, 2000; Laws 2001, c. 2001–50, § 6, eff. July 1, 2001; Laws 2002, c. 2002–387, § 1045, eff. Jan. 7, 2003; Laws 2003, c. 2003–18, § 1, eff. July 1, 2003; Laws 2003, c. 2003–63, § 1, eff. June 2, 2003; Laws 2003, c. 2003–402, § 136, eff. July 1, 2004; Laws 2004, 2004–373, §§ 14 to 25, eff. July 1, 2004; Laws 2006, c. 2006–1, § 116, eff. July 4, 2006; Laws 2008, c. 2008–172, § 28, eff. Oct. 1, 2008.

Historical and Statutory Notes

Amendment Notes:

Laws 1977, c. 77–452, added subsec. (1) (i).

Laws 1981, c. 81–198, § 1, added new subsec. (2) and redesignated former subsec. (2) as subsec. (3).

Laws 1983, c. 83–75, § 3, deleted in subsec. (2)(c) [now subsec. (3)(c)] reference to pornographic purposes provided for in § 847.014.

Laws 1983, c. 83–131, § 16, amended the section to provide for terms and conditions in community control; deleted terms in subsec. (1)(a) pertaining to avoiding "injurious or vicious habits" and avoiding "persons or places of disreputable or harmful character" added subsec. (1)(i); interpolated subsec. (2); and redesignated former subsecs. (2) and (3) as subsecs. (3) and (4).

Laws 1983, c. 83–216, was a reviser's correction bill amending subsecs. (2) and (3) to improve clarity and to remove a surplus word.

Laws 1983, c. 83–256, § 3, added the second sentence to par. (e) and added provision designated par. (h) in subsec. (1).

Laws 1984, c. 84–363, § 8, in subsec. (1)(e), deleted "compelling and extraordinary" following "court determines that" in the second sentence, and added the third sentence.

Laws 1985, c. 85–288, § 15, eff. July 1, 1985, added the third sentence in subsec. (4) and added subsec. (5).

Laws 1987, c. 87–211, § 5, eff. Oct. 1, 1987, added subsec. (2)(d), renumbered present subsecs. (3) to (5) as subsecs. (6) to (8) [now subsecs. (3)(d), (4), (5)], and added new subsecs. (3) to (5).

Laws 1988, c. 88–96, § 11, inserted "clear and compelling" preceding "reasons" in the second sentence and substituted "restitution of only a portion of the damages, as provided in s. 775.089" for "only partial restitution" and inserted "in detail" preceding "the reasons" in the third sentence of subsec. (1)(e).

Laws 1988, c. 88–96, § 15, provides that the act "shall take effect upon the effective date [January 3, 1989] of the amendment to the State Constitution contained in [1987] Senate Joint Resolution No. 135, which is to be submitted to the electors of this state for approval at the general election to be held in November 1988."

The electorate ratified the amendment to Const. Art. 1, § 16, proposed by 1987, S.J.R. No. 135, relating to rights of crime victims, at the November 8, 1988 general election. See Const. Art. 1, § 16.

Laws 1988, c. 88–122, § 70, eff. July 1, 1988, added subsec. (9) [now subsec. (6)].

Laws 1988, c. 88–122, § 71, eff. July 1, 1988, added subsec. (1)(j).

Laws 1989, c. 89–526, § 37, eff. Oct. 1, 1989, in subsec. (5), required development of procedures to investigate noncompliance, and substituted "24 hours per day" for "during all hours of the day" in the first sentence; inserted subsec. (6), relating to contracts with local law enforcement agencies; renumbered former subsecs. (6) through (9) as subsecs. (7) through (10) [now subsecs. (4) to (7)]; and made nonsubstantive language and punctuation changes.

Laws 1990, c. 90–287, § 10, eff. Sept. 1, 1990, in subsec. (8) [now subsec. (5)] in the third sentence inserted "a probation program drug punishment phase I secure residential treatment institution"; and in subsec. (9) [now subsec. (6)], inserted a new subpar. (a)2., relettered subsequent subparagraphs, and rewrote subpar. (9)(c) [now (6)(c)], which formerly read:

"Prior to admission to such a facility, the court shall obtain an individual assessment and recommendation on the appropriate treatment needs pursuant to the Community Control Implementation Manual which shall be considered by the court in ordering such placements. Placement in such a facility or center shall not exceed 364 days. Early termination of placement shall be recommended to the court, when appropriate, by the facility or center supervisor. The Department of Corrections is authorized to contract with appropriate agencies for provision of services."

Laws 1990, c. 90–337, § 8, eff. July 1, 1990, in subsec. (10) [now subsec. (7)], deleted paragraph designations; in the first sentence, following "devices" deleted "by August 1, 1988"; in the second sentence substituted "be licensed by the FCC," for "meet the following minimum standards", and inserted "tamper-alert"; and deleted former pars. (b) and (c), pertaining to requirements for tamper resistant straps and transmitter standards.

Laws 1990, c. 90–337, § 17, eff. Oct. 1, 1990, in subsec. (1)(j), designated subpar. 1., and substituted "correctional probation" for "supervising"; and added subpar. 2.

Laws 1990, c. 90–337, § 21 provided therein that the amendment take effect July 1, 1990; however, approval by the governor occurred subsequent thereto. The Florida Supreme Court in an advisory opinion to the governor of July 19, 1979 (374 So.2d 959) stated in part "* * * the effective date provided in the bill is inoperative unless the bill becomes law on or before that date" and concludes that under such circumstances the provision of Const. Art. 3, § 9, that the law take effect on the sixtieth day after adjournment sine die of the session of the legislature in which enacted, is applicable.

Laws 1991, c. 91–225, § 11, eff. July 1, 1991, reenacted subsec. (9)(a) [now subsec. (6)(a)] without change "For the purpose of incorporating the amendment to section 944.026, Florida Statutes, in references thereto".

Laws 1991, c. 91–280, § 4, eff. Oct. 1, 1991, in subsec. (3), designated par. (a); redesignated former subsecs. (4) to (6) as pars. (b) to (d) of subsec. (3); redesignated former subsecs. (7) to (10) as subsecs. (4) to (7); and rewrote present subsec. (7), which formerly read:

"Pursuant to chapter 287, the department shall issue a request for proposal for electronic monitoring devices to be utilized by the department for purposes of electronic monitoring under this section or any other section of law which authorizes electronic monitoring. Electronic monitoring devices certified for use by the department must be licensed by the FCC, be capable of maintaining full operation on a backup power source for 8 hours, and meet such other necessary and vital specifications as may be set by the department for tamper-alert, efficient, and economical usage. The provisions of this subsection do not apply to passive devices."

Laws 1992, c. 92–310, § 23, eff. July 6, 1992, added subsec. (8).

Laws 1993, c. 93–37, § 10, eff. Oct. 1, 1993, reenacted subsec. (1)(e) for the purpose of incorporating the amendment to § 775.089 in a reference thereto.

Section 16 of Laws 1993, c. 93–37, provides:

"This act shall take effect upon becoming a law, except that sections 1–12 and section 14 of this act shall take effect October 1, 1993, and shall apply to offenses committed on or after October 1, 1993."

Laws 1993, c. 93–227, § 15, eff. Oct. 1, 1993, in subsec. (2), inserted the par. (a) designation, redesignated former pars. (2)(a) to (2)(d) as subpars. 1 to 4 of par. (a) and added par. (b), and, in subsec. (3), inserted the subpar. 1 designation and added subpar. 2 in par. (a); and made other nonsubstantive changes.

Application of Laws 1993, c. 93–227 to offenses committed on or after Oct. 1, 1993, see Historical and Statutory Notes under § 796.03.

Laws 1994, c. 94–294, § 1, eff. July 1, 1994, amending subsec. (1), inserted a new par. (f) and redesignated former pars. (f) to (j) as (g) to (k).

Laws 1995, c. 95–189, § 1, eff. July 1, 1995, in subsec. (1), added a par. (*l*) [redesignated as (n)], relating to payments to nonprofit organizations.

Laws 1995, c. 95–283, § 53, eff. June 15, 1995, added subsecs. (9) and (10) [redesignated as (10) and (11)], relating to blood specimens.

Laws 1995, c. 95–283, § 59, eff. June 15, 1995, in subsec. (1), in the introductory paragraph, inserted the second and third sentences, added pars. (*l*) and (m); inserted subsec. (5); and redesignated former subsecs. (5) to (8) as subsecs. (6) to (9).

Laws 1996, c. 96–170, § 1, eff. Oct. 1, 1996, in subsec. (1), in the introductory paragraph, corrected internal citations; inserted par. (n); and redesignated former par. (n) as par. (*o*).

Laws 1996, c. 96–232, § 4, eff. Jan. 1, 1997, reenacted subsec. (1)(i) for the purpose of incorporating an amendment to § 27.56 in reference thereto.

Laws 1996, c. 96–312, § 54, eff. July 1, 1996, in subsec. (6), added the second sentence relating to residence in another state.

Laws 1996, c. 96–409, § 6, eff. Oct. 1, 1996, in subsec. (5), added par. (i).

Laws 1997, c. 97–78, § 22, eff. May 23, 1997, in subsec. (1), in the introductory language, twice substituted "(m)" for "(n)"; and, in par. (n), added ", if such a program is available in the county of the offender's residence".

Laws 1997, c. 97–102, eff. July 1, 1997, removed gender-specific references applicable to human beings from volume 4 of the Florida Statutes without substantive changes in legal effect.

Laws 1997, c. 97–107, § 11, eff. May 24, 1997, in subsec. (1)(i), inserted "application fee assessed under § 27.52(1)(c) and".

Laws 1997, c. 97–234, § 27, eff. July 1, 1997, in subsec. (9), designated the former subsection as par. (a) and deleted a reference to § 228.0713, and added pars (b) and (c).

Laws 1997, c. 97–271, § 44, eff. July 1, 1997, in subsec. (1), par. (i), substituted "s. 938.29" for "s. 27.56".

Laws 1997, c. 97–308, § 3, eff. Oct. 1, 1997, rewrote subsec. (5), which formerly read:

"Effective for probationers or community controlees whose crime was committed on or after October 1, 1995, and who are placed under supervision for violation of chapter 794 or s. 800.04, s. 827.071, or s. 847.0145, the court must impose the following conditions in addition to all other standard and special conditions imposed:

"(a) A curfew, if appropriate, during hours set by the sentencing court.

"(b) If the victim was under the age of 18, a prohibition on living within 1,000 feet of a school, day care center, park, playground, or other place where children regularly congregate, as prescribed by the court.

"(c) Active participation in and successful completion of a sex offender treatment program, at the probationer's or community controlee's own expense, unless one is not available within a 50-mile radius of the probationer's or community controlee's residence.

"(d) A prohibition on any contact with the victim, directly or indirectly, including through a third person, unless approved by the sentencing court.

"(e) If the victim was under the age of 18, a prohibition, until successful completion of a sex offender treatment program, on unsupervised contact with a child under the age of 18, unless authorized by the sentencing court without another adult present who is responsible for the child's welfare, has been advised of the crime, and is approved by the commission.

"(f) If the victim was under age 18, a prohibition on working for pay or as a volunteer at any school, day care center, park, playground, or other place where children regularly congregate.

"(g) Unless otherwise indicated in the treatment plan provided by the sexual offender treatment program, a prohibition on viewing, owning, or possessing any obscene, pornographic, or sexually explicit material.

"(h) A requirement that the probationer or community controlee must submit two specimens of blood to the Florida Department of Law Enforcement to be registered with the DNA data bank.

"(i) A requirement that the probationer or community controlee make restitution to the victim, as ordered by the court under s. 775.089, for all necessary medical and related professional services relating to physical, psychiatric, and psychological care."

Laws 1998, c. 98–81, § 14, in subsec. (5), added the introductory paragraph.

Laws 1998, c. 98–251, § 15, reenacted subsec. (10) for the purpose of incorporating an amendment to § 943.325 in a reference thereto.

Laws 1999, c. 99–3, § 122, eff. June 29, 1999, amended the section to conform to the redesignation of subsec. (9) as subsec. (10).

Laws 1999, c. 99–201, § 13, in subsec. (4)(a), substituted "Lewd or lascivious battery, lewd or lascivious molestation, lewd or lascivious conduct, or lewd or lascivious exhibition, as defined in s. 800.04" for "A lewd, lascivious, or indecent assault or act upon, or int he presence of, a child"; in subsec. (5)(a), in the introductory language substituted "chapter 794," for "chapter 794 or"; and, reenacted subsec. (6) without change.

Laws 2000, c. 2000–246, § 3, reenacted subsections (4), (5), and (6) for the purpose of incorporating the amendment to § 800.04 in a reference thereto.

Laws 2001, c. 2001–50, § 6, added subsec. (12).

Laws 2002, c. 2002–387, § 1045, in subsec. (9)(a), substituted "1003.435" for "229.814" and, in subsec. (9)(b), substituted "1003.53" for "230.2316.

Laws 2003, c. 2003–18, § 1, in subsec. (5)(a)8., inserted "or other approved biological specimens" following "two specimens of blood".

Laws 2003, c. 2003–63, § 1, in subsec. (5)(a)2., inserted "The 1,000–foot distance shall be measured in a straight line from the offender's place of residence to the nearest boundary line of the school, day care center, park, playground, or other place where children congregate. The distance may not be measured by a pedestrian route or automobile route" following the first sentence.

Laws 2003, c. 2003–402, § 136, in subsec. (1)(i), substituted "27.52(2)(a)" for "27.52(1)(c)".

Laws 2004, c. 2004–373, §§ 14 to 25, renumbered former subsec. (2) as § 948.101(1), renumbered former subsec. (3) as § 948.11, renumbered former subsec. (4) as § 948.31, renumbered former subsec. (5) as § 948.30, renumbered former subsec. (7) as § 948.035, renumbered former subsec. (8) as § 948.036, renumbered former subsec. (9) as § 948.037, renumbered former subsec. (10) as § 948.014(1), (2), renumbered former subsec. (11) as § 948.014(3), renumbered former subsec. (12) as § 948.038, and rewrote this section, which formerly read:

"(1) The court shall determine the terms and conditions of probation or community control. Conditions specified in paragraphs (a)–(m) do not require oral pronouncement at the time of sentencing and may be considered standard conditions of probation. Conditions specified in paragraphs (a)–(m) and (2)(a) do not require oral pronouncement at sentencing and may be considered standard conditions of community control. These conditions may include among them the following, that the probationer or offender in community control shall:

"(a) Report to the probation and parole supervisors as directed.

"(b) Permit such supervisors to visit him or her at his or her home or elsewhere.

"(c) Work faithfully at suitable employment insofar as may be possible.

"(d) Remain within a specified place.

"(e) Make reparation or restitution to the aggrieved party for the damage or loss caused by his or her offense in an amount to be determined by the court. The court shall make such reparation or restitution a condition of probation, unless it determines that clear and compelling reasons exist to the contrary. If the court does not order restitution, or orders restitution of only a portion of the damages, as provided in s. 775.089, it shall state on the record in detail the reasons therefor.

"(f) Effective July 1, 1994, and applicable for offenses committed on or after that date, make payment of the debt due and owing to a county or municipal detention facility under s. 951.032 for medical care, treatment, hospitalization, or transportation received by the felony probationer while in that detention facility. The court, in determining whether to order such repayment and the amount of such repayment, shall consider the amount of the debt, whether there was any fault of the institution for the medical expenses incurred, the financial resources of the felony probationer, the present and potential future financial needs and earning ability of the probationer, and dependents, and other appropriate factors.

"(g) Support his or her legal dependents to the best of his or her ability.

"(h) Make payment of the debt due and owing to the state under s. 960.17, subject to modification based on change of circumstances.

"(i) Pay any application fee assessed under s. 27.52(2)(a) and attorney's fees and costs assessed under s. 938.29, subject to modification based on change of circumstances.

"(j) Not associate with persons engaged in criminal activities.

"(k)1. Submit to random testing as directed by the correctional probation officer or the professional staff of the treatment center where he or she is receiving treatment to determine the presence or use of alcohol or controlled substances.

"2. If the offense was a controlled substance violation and the period of probation immediately follows a period of incarceration in the state correction system, the conditions shall include a requirement that the offender submit to random substance abuse testing intermittently throughout the term of supervision, upon the direction of the correctional probation officer as defined in s. 943.10(3).

"(*l*) Be prohibited from possessing, carrying, or owning any firearm unless authorized by the court and consented to by the probation officer.

"(m) Be prohibited from using intoxicants to excess or possessing any drugs or narcotics unless prescribed by a physician. The probationer or community controllee shall not knowingly visit places where intoxicants, drugs, or other dangerous substances are unlawfully sold, dispensed, or used.

"(n) Attend an HIV/AIDS awareness program consisting of a class of not less than 2 hours or more than 4 hours in length, the cost for which shall be paid by the offender, if such a program is available in the county of the offender's residence.

"(*o*) Pay not more than $1 per month during the term of probation or community control to a nonprofit organization established for the sole purpose of supplementing the rehabilitative efforts of the Department of Corrections.

"(2)(a) The court shall require intensive supervision and surveillance for an offender placed into community control, which may include but is not limited to:

"1. Specified contact with the parole and probation officer.

"2. Confinement to an agreed-upon residence during hours away from employment and public service activities.

"3. Mandatory public service.

"4. Supervision by the Department of Corrections by means of an electronic monitoring device or system.

"(b) For an offender placed on criminal quarantine community control, the court shall require:

"1. Electronic monitoring 24 hours per day.

"2. Confinement to a designated residence during designated hours.

"(3)(a) 1. The Department of Corrections may, at its discretion, electronically monitor an offender sentenced to community control.

"2. The Department of Corrections shall electronically monitor an offender sentenced to criminal quarantine community control 24 hours per day.

"(b) Any offender placed on community control who violates the terms and conditions of community control and is restored to community control may be supervised by means of an electronic monitoring device or system.

"(c) For those offenders being electronically monitored, the Department of Corrections shall develop procedures to determine, investigate, and report the offender's noncompliance with the terms and conditions of sentence 24 hours per day. All reports of noncompliance shall be immediately investigated by a community control officer.

"(d) The Department of Corrections may contract with local law enforcement agencies to assist in the location and apprehension of offenders who are in noncompliance as reported by the electronic monitoring system. This contract is intended to provide the department a means for providing immediate investigation of noncompliance reports, especially after normal office hours.

"(4) The court shall require a diagnosis and evaluation to determine the need of a probationer or offender in community control for treatment. If the court determines that a need therefor is established by such diagnosis and evaluation process, the court shall require outpatient counseling as a term or condition of probation or community control for any person who was found guilty of any of the following, or whose plea of guilty or nolo contendere to any of the following was accepted by the court:

"(a) Lewd or lascivious battery, lewd or lascivious molestation, lewd or lascivious conduct, or lewd or lascivious exhibition, as defined in s. 800.04.

"(b) Sexual battery, as defined in chapter 794, against a child.

"(c) Exploitation of a child as provided in s. 450.151, or for prostitution.

"Such counseling shall be required to be obtained from a community mental health center, a recognized social service agency providing mental health services, or a private mental health professional or through other professional counseling. The plan for counseling for the individual shall be provided to the court for review.

"(5) Conditions imposed pursuant to this subsection, as specified in paragraphs (a) and (b), do not require oral pronouncement at the time of sentencing and shall be considered standard conditions of probation or community control for offenders specified in this subsection.

"(a) Effective for probationers or community controllees whose crime was committed on or after October 1, 1995, and who are placed under supervision for violation of chapter 794, s. 800.04, s. 827.071, or s. 847.0145, the court must impose the following conditions in addition to all other standard and special conditions imposed:

"1. A mandatory curfew from 10 p.m. to 6 a.m. The court may designate another 8–hour period if the offender's employment precludes the above specified time, and such alternative is recommended by the Department of Corrections. If the court determines that imposing a curfew would endanger the victim, the court may consider alternative sanctions.

"2. If the victim was under the age of 18, a prohibition on living within 1,000 feet of a school, day care center, park, playground, or other place where children regularly congregate, as prescribed by the court. The 1,000–foot distance shall be measured in a straight line from the offender's place of residence to the nearest boundary line of the school, day care center, park, playground, or other place where children congregate. The distance may not be measured by a pedestrian route or automobile route.

"3. Active participation in and successful completion of a sex offender treatment program with therapists specifically trained to treat sex offenders, at the probationer's or community controllee's own expense. If a specially trained therapist is not available within a 50–mile radius of the probationer's or community controllee's residence, the offender shall participate in other appropriate therapy.

"4. A prohibition on any contact with the victim, directly or indirectly, including through a third person, unless approved by the victim, the offender's therapist, and the sentencing court.

"5. If the victim was under the age of 18, a prohibition, until successful completion of a sex offender treatment program, on unsupervised contact with a child under the age of 18, unless authorized by the sentencing court without another adult present who is responsible for the child's welfare, has been advised of the crime, and is approved by the sentencing court.

"6. If the victim was under age 18, a prohibition on working for pay or as a volunteer at any school, day care center, park, playground, or other place where children regularly congregate.

"7. Unless otherwise indicated in the treatment plan provided by the sexual offender treatment program, a prohibition on viewing, owning, or possessing any obscene, pornographic, or sexually stimulating visual or auditory material, including telephone, electronic media, computer programs, or computer services that are relevant to the offender's deviant behavior pattern.

"8. A requirement that the probationer or community controllee must submit two specimens of blood or other approved biological specimens to the Florida Department of Law Enforcement to be registered with the DNA data bank.

"9. A requirement that the probationer or community controllee make restitution to the victim, as ordered by the court under s. 775.089, for all necessary medical and related professional services relating to physical, psychiatric, and psychological care.

"10. Submission to a warrantless search by the community control or probation officer of the probationer's or community controllee's person, residence, or vehicle.

"(b) Effective for a probationer or community controllee whose crime was committed on or after October 1, 1997, and who is placed on sex offender probation for a violation of chapter 794, s. 800.04, s. 827.071, or s. 847.0145, in addition to any other provision of this subsection, the court must impose the following conditions of probation or community control:

"1. As part of a treatment program, participation at least annually in polygraph examinations to obtain information necessary for risk management and treatment and to reduce the sex offender's denial mechanisms. A polygraph examination must be conducted by a polygrapher trained specifically in the use of the polygraph for the monitoring of sex offenders, where available, and shall be paid by the sex offender. The results of the polygraph examination shall not be used as evidence in court to prove that a violation of community supervision has occurred.

"2. Maintenance of a driving log and a prohibition against driving a motor vehicle alone without the prior approval of the supervising officer.

"3. A prohibition against obtaining or using a post office box without the prior approval of the supervising officer.

"4. If there was sexual contact, a submission to, at the probationer's or community controllee's expense, an HIV test with the results to be released to the victim and/or the victim's parent or guardian.

"5. Electronic monitoring when deemed necessary by the community control or probation officer and his or her supervisor, and ordered by the court at the recommendation of the Department of Corrections.

"(6) The enumeration of specific kinds of terms and conditions shall not prevent the court from adding thereto such other or others as it considers proper. However, the sentencing court may only impose a condition of supervision allowing an offender convicted of s. 794.011, s. 800.04, s. 827.071, or s. 847.0145, to reside in another state, if the order stipulates that it is contingent upon the approval of the receiving state interstate compact authority. The court may rescind or modify at any time the terms and conditions theretofore imposed by it upon the probationer or offender in community control. However, if the court withholds adjudication of guilt or imposes a period of incarceration as a condition of probation or community control, the period shall not exceed 364 days, and incarceration shall be restricted to either a county facility, a probation and restitution center under the jurisdiction of the Department of Corrections, a probation program drug punishment phase I secure residential treatment institution, or a community residential facility owned or operated by any entity providing such services.

"(7)(a) If the court imposes a period of residential treatment or incarceration as a condition of probation or community control, the residential treatment or incarceration shall be restricted to the following facilities:

"1. A Department of Corrections probation and restitution center;

"2. A probation program drug punishment treatment community;

"3. A community residential facility which is owned and operated by any public or private entity, excluding a community correctional center as defined in s. 944.026; or

"4. A county-owned facility.

"(b) It is the intent of the Legislature that a county jail be used as the last available alternative for placement of an offender as a condition of probation. However, this shall not create a right of placement for the probationer, nor shall it restrict judicial discretion in ordering such treatment or incarceration.

"(c) Prior to admission to such a facility or treatment community, the court shall obtain an individual assessment and recommendation on the appropriate treatment needs pursuant to chapter 953 or the Community Control Implementation Manual which shall be considered by the court in ordering such placements. Placement in such a facility or center, or in the phase I secure residential phase of a probation program drug punishment treatment community, shall not exceed 364 days. Early completion of an offender's placement shall be recommended to the court, when appropriate, by the facility or center supervisor, by the supervising probation officer, or by the program manager. However, with respect to the placement of a probationer pursuant to chapter 953, such placement shall not be completed until satisfactory completion of the drug punishment program. Termination for cause from such a program shall be pursuant to s. 953.25(4). The Department of Corrections is authorized to contract with appropriate agencies for provision of services.

"(8)(a) Whenever an offender is required by the court to participate in any work program under the provisions of this chapter, enters into the pretrial intervention program pursuant to s. 948.08, or volunteers to work in a supervised work program conducted by a specified state, county, municipal, or community service organization or to work for the victim, either as an alternative to monetary restitution or as a part of the rehabilitative or community control program, the offender shall be considered an employee of the state for the purposes of chapter 440.

"(b) In determining the average weekly wage, unless otherwise determined by a specific funding program, all remuneration received from the employer shall be considered a gratuity, and the offender shall not be entitled to any benefits otherwise payable under s. 440.15, regardless of whether the offender may be receiving wages and remuneration from other employment with another employer and regardless of his or her future wage-earning capacity. The provisions of this subsection do not apply to any person performing labor under a sentence of a court to perform community services as provided in s. 316.193.

"(9)(a) As a condition of community control, probation, or probation following incarceration, require an offender who has not obtained a high school diploma or high school equivalency diploma or who lacks basic or functional literacy skills, upon acceptance by an adult education program, to make a good faith effort toward completion of such basic or functional literacy skills or high school equivalency diploma, as defined in s. 1003.435, in accordance with the assessed adult general education needs of the individual offender. The court shall not revoke community control, probation, or probation following incarceration because of the offender's inability to achieve such skills or diploma but may revoke community control, probation, or probation following incarceration if the offender fails to make a good faith effort to achieve such skills or diploma. The court may grant early termination of community control, probation, or probation following incarceration upon the offender's successful completion of the approved program. As used in this subsection, "good faith effort" means the offender is enrolled in a program of instruction and is attending and making satisfactory progress toward completion of the requirements.

"(b) A juvenile on community control who is a public school student must attend a public adult education program or a dropout prevention program, pursuant to s. 1003.53, which includes a second chance school or an alternative to expulsion, if the school district where the juvenile is enrolled offers such programs, unless the principal of the school determines that special circumstances warrant continuation in the regular educational school program.

"(c) If a juvenile on community control attends a regular educational school program because a public adult education program or dropout prevention program, which includes a second chance school or an alternative to expulsion, is not available in the school district, the identity of the juvenile on community control, the nature of the felony offense committed by the juvenile, and the conditions of community control must be made known to each of the student's teachers.

"(10) As a condition of probation, community control, or any other court-ordered community supervision, the court shall order persons convicted of offenses specified in s. 943.325 to submit to the drawing of the blood specimens as prescribed in that section as a condition of the probation, community control, or other court-ordered community supervision. For the purposes of this subsection, conviction shall include a finding of guilty, or entry of a plea of nolo contendere or guilty, regardless of adjudication, or, in the case of a juvenile, the finding of delinquency.

"(11) Any order issued pursuant to subsection (10) shall also require the convicted person to reimburse the appropriate agency for the costs of drawing and transmitting the blood specimens to the Florida Department of Law Enforcement.

"(12) As a condition of probation, community control, or any other court-ordered community supervision, the court shall order a person convicted of an offense of domestic violence, as defined in s. 741.28, to attend and successfully complete a batterers' intervention program unless the court determines that the person does not qualify for the batterers' intervention program pursuant to s. 741.325. Effective July 1, 2002, the batterers' intervention program must be a program certified under s. 741.32 and the offender must pay the cost of attending the program."

Laws 2006, c. 2006–1, a reviser's bill, deleted obsolete and expired provisions, corrected grammatical and typographical errors, and made other similar changes.

Laws 2008, c. 2008–172, § 28, in subsec. (2), inserted a reference to § 847.0135(5) in the second sentence.

Cross References

Automobile accidents involving death or personal injury, see § 316.027.
Communication of terms to probationer, continuing supervision, see § 947.16.
Compacts with other states, see §§ 949.07, 949.08.
Compensation of crime victim, see § 960.001 et seq.
Imposition of conditions of probation or community control, sentencing, see § 921.187.
Probationer contribution, supervision and rehabilitation costs, see § 948.09.
Restitution as condition of probation, see §§ 775.089, 921.187.
Treatment-based drug court programs, see § 397.334.

Law Review and Journal Commentaries

Concern renewed for victim. Eric Smith, 52 Fla.B.J. 16 (1978).

Parole revocation: Due process or star chamber? Richard A. Belz, 52 Fla.B.J. 22 (1978).

Probation in Florida. Vernon W. Clark, 14 U.Fla.L.Rev. 213 (1961).

Recoupment of defense costs as a probation condition. 5 Stetson L.Rev. 117 (1975).

Sentence. Thomas A. Wills, 20 U.Miami L.Rev. 264 (1965).

Sex, lies, and polygraph machines: The portrait of Mr. Cassamassima. James M. Shaw, 57 U.Miami L.Rev. 429 (2003).

Library References

Sentencing and Punishment ⚷1960 to 1996, 2082 to 2085.
Westlaw Topic No. 350H.
C.J.S. Criminal Law §§ 567, 2151 to 2152, 2155 to 2156.

Research References

ALR Library

40 ALR 6th 419, Validity, Construction, and Application of Statutory and Municipal Enactments and Conditions of Release Prohibiting Sex Offenders from Parks.

15 ALR 6th 173, Presentence Withdrawal of Plea of Nolo Contendere or Non Vult Contendere Under State Law--Sentencing and Punishment Issues; Ineffective Assistance of Counsel.

10 ALR 6th 265, Presentence Withdrawal of Plea of Nolo Contendere or Non Vult Contendere Under State Law--Awareness of Collateral Consequences of Plea, and Competency to Enter Plea.

99 ALR 5th 557, Validity of Requirement That, as Condition of Probation, Defendant Submit to Warrantless Searches.

92 ALR 5th 35, Persons or Entities Entitled to Restitution as "Victim" Under State Criminal Restitution Statute.

65 ALR 5th 187, Propriety of Probation Condition Exposing Defendant to Public Shame or Ridicule.

15 ALR 5th 391, Measure and Elements of Restitution to Which Victim is Entitled Under State Criminal Statute.

87 ALR 4th 929, Propriety of Conditioning Probation on Defendant's Submission to Drug Testing.

26 ALR 4th 905, Power of State Court, During Same Term, to Increase Severity of Lawful Sentence--Modern Status.

89 ALR 2nd 540, Plea of Nolo Contendere or Non Vult Contendere.

147 ALR 656, Power to Impose Sentence With Direction that After Defendant Shall Have Served Part of Time He be Placed on Probation for the Remainder of Term.

59 ALR 521, Effect of Mere Oral Announcement of Sentence Without Entry Thereof in Records.

Encyclopedias

What is "Employment", FL Jur. 2d Workers' Compensation § 50.

Forms

Florida Pleading and Practice Forms § 96:55, Order of Probation--Drug Offenders.

Florida Pleading and Practice Forms § 96:58, Order of Community Control--Drug Offender or Sexual Offender.

Treatises and Practice Aids

6 Florida Practice Series § 14:4, The Victim.

9 Florida Practice Series § 6:20, Not an Employee: Other Individuals Specifically Excluded by Statute.

16 Florida Practice Series § 6:9, Alternatives To, and Mitigation Of, Criminal Punishment Code Sentencing--Drug Offender Probation.

16 Florida Practice Series § 7:6, Constitutional Rights of the Probationer or Community Controllee--Search and Seizure.

16 Florida Practice Series § 7:8, Terms and Conditions of Probation--Necessary Incidents to Probation or Community Control.

16 Florida Practice Series § 8:2, Jurisdiction.

16 Florida Practice Series § 8:6, Victims and Intervenors.

16 Florida Practice Series § 8:8, Restitution as a Condition of Probation or Community Control.

16 Florida Practice Series § 7:10, Terms and Conditions of Probation--Standard, or General, Terms and Conditions of Probation.

16 Florida Practice Series § 7:11, Special Conditions of Probation.

16 Florida Practice Series § 7:12, Administrative Probation.

16 Florida Practice Series § 7:16, Standard Terms and Conditions of Community Control and Criminal Quarantine Community Control.

16 Florida Practice Series § 7:23, Modification or Recision of Probation or Community Control--Post-Sentencing.

16 Florida Practice Series § 7:35, Revocation of Probation or Community Control--Grounds for Revocation--Revocation After Commencement of Probation or Community Control--Failure to Pay Court-Ordered Costs or Restitution.

16 Florida Practice Series § 7:48, Revocation of Probation or Community Control--Revocation Hearing.

16 Florida Practice Series § 7:77, Sentencing Alternatives for Violations of Probation/Community Control--Enhancement of Sentence.

16 Florida Practice Series § 8:38, Subjects of Restitution--Collateral Damage.

16 Florida Practice Series § 8:46, Subjects of Restitution--Interest.

United States Code Annotated

Child protection, sex offender registration and notification, crime information databases, access, see 42 U.S.C.A. § 16961.

Sex offender registration, supervised release, see 18 U.S.C.A. § 3583.

United States Supreme Court

Denial of probation after notice of grant of release, see Jago v. Van Curen, 1981, 102 S.Ct. 31, 454 U.S. 14, 70 L.Ed.2d 13.

Probation revocation, failure to pay fine or make restitution, see Bearden v. Georgia, 1983, 103 S.Ct. 2064, 461 U.S. 660, 76 L.Ed.2d 221, on remand 167 Ga.App. 334, 308 S.E.2d 63.

Probationer, self incrimination involved in disclosure to probation officer, see Minnesota v. Murphy, U.S.Minn.1984, 104 S.Ct. 1136, 465 U.S. 420, 79 L.Ed.2d 409, rehearing denied 104 S.Ct. 1932, 466 U.S. 945, 80 L.Ed.2d 477, on remand 348 N.W.2d 764.

Notes of Decisions

---

1. Construction and application

Statute permitting transfer of sex offender to another state as condition of probation only if approved by receiving state applied to defendant who was sentenced for sex offense before approval language was added but re-sentenced after it became effective. Moore v. Nelson, App. 4 Dist., 830 So.2d 918 (2002). Sentencing And Punishment ⚿ 1828; Sentencing And Punishment ⚿ 1967(3)

Attempted capital sexual battery was offense under sexual battery statute, as modified by "attempt" statute, rather than merely offense under "attempt" statute, and thus, trial court could properly impose conditions of probation upon defendant convicted of attempted capital sexual battery; receding from *Lee v. State*, 766 So.2d 374. Wilcox v. State, App. 1 Dist., 783 So.2d 1150 (2001). Sentencing And Punishment ⚿ 1960

Statute providing a list of mandatory conditions for offenders who have been placed on probation or community control for certain sex crimes did not apply to juvenile delinquency proceeding in which mandatory conditions were imposed on juvenile's probation due to his status as a sex offender, where juvenile was not adjudicated as an adult; statute did not specifically express that the conditions were to apply to juvenile delinquents, many of the mandatory conditions of probation did not have any effect upon juvenile offenders, and another statute specifically addressed remedies for the correction and treatment of juvenile sex offenders. C.C.M. v. State, App. 1 Dist., 782 So.2d 537 (2001). Infants ⚿ 132

There are two types of conditions of probation: general conditions, which are imposed upon most if not all probationers and are broadly directed toward supervision and rehabilitation, and special conditions, which may be imposed only if reasonably related to rehabilitation. Fernandez v. State, App. 4 Dist., 677 So.2d 332 (1996), review dismissed 683 So.2d 485. Sentencing And Punishment ⚿ 1960

Trial court is not mandated to impose conditions listed in statute authorizing various terms and conditions of probation. Fernandez v. State, App. 4 Dist., 677 So.2d 332 (1996), review dismissed 683 So.2d 485. Sentencing And Punishment ⚿ 1962

Trial court could properly impose imprisonment, fine, and probation all within one sentence on defendant who was convicted for lewd and lascivious act upon child under the age of 16. Singleton v. State, App. 1 Dist., 582 So.2d 657 (1991). Infants ⚿ 20

Defendant, who agreed to seven-week period of probation as alternative to bail or incarceration while awaiting presentence investigation, did not, by appearing in court for disposition hearing at expiration of seven-week period, satisfy special condition of probation and become thereupon entitled to be forever discharged. Rodriguez v. State, App. 3 Dist., 441 So.2d 1129 (1983), petition for review denied 451 So.2d 850. Sentencing And Punishment ⚿ 1953

Parole in Florida is granted by sovereign as a matter of grace rather than of right, and state may offer such grace under and subject to such conditions as it may consider most conducive to accomplish the desired purpose. Panzavecchia v. Crockett, App. 1 Dist., 379 So.2d 1047 (1980). Pardon And Parole ⚿ 46

While requirements that probationer spend some time in jail or pay a fine are not usually thought of as conditions of probation, this section is sufficiently broad to allow imposition of such conditions. Brown v. State, App. 4 Dist., 302 So.2d 430 (1974). Sentencing And Punishment ⚿ 1974(2); Sentencing And Punishment ⚿ 1976(2)

2. Purpose of probation

Purpose of probation is primarily to rehabilitate and not to punish. Kominsky v. State, App. 1 Dist., 330 So.2d 800 (1976). Sentencing And Punishment ⚿ 1811

3. Jurisdiction—In general

Trial court has authority to impose special probation conditions as part of new sentence once defendant is formally charged with probation violation and brought before court for hearing. McCord v. State, App. 3 Dist., 679 So.2d 32 (1996). Sentencing And Punishment ⚿ 2040

Even if reviewing court could relinquish jurisdiction nunc pro tunc so as to authorize trial court's consideration of motion for reduction of sentence, that would not retroactively vivify the community control imposed by the court in response to the motion at a time when it lacked jurisdiction, and there thus could be no community control which could be violated for misconduct occurring during the period of jurisdictional limbo. Figone v. Downey, App. 2 Dist., 547 So.2d 697 (1989). Criminal Law ⚿ 1083

The trial court's jurisdiction to entertain motion for return of fine, restitution payment and probation cost payment ordered as part of probationary condition, was not divested by trial court's dismissal of criminal charges against defendant on remand prior to filing of motion as court's inherent authority to correct its own prior wrongdoing still obtained. Cooper v. Gordon, App. 3 Dist., 389 So.2d 318 (1980). Criminal Law ⚿ 1192

Following reversal on appeal of defendant's conviction and remand for new trial, trial court, as part of its inherent power to correct effects of its own wrongdoing and to restore defendant to status quo ante, had jurisdiction to entertain defendant's motion for return of fine and restitution payment and costs imposed as probationary condition. Cooper v. Gordon, App. 3 Dist., 389 So.2d 318 (1980). Criminal Law ⚷ 1192

A trial court has authority to impose any valid condition of probation which would serve a useful rehabilitative purpose. Hines v. State, 358 So.2d 183 (1978). Sentencing And Punishment ⚷ 1963

Criminal court of record has full and exclusive jurisdiction to procure the presence of a defendant placed on probation by the circuit court of county before establishment of criminal court and to revoke, modify or continue probation. Op.Atty.Gen., 1949, p. 625.

4. —— Revocation of probation, jurisdiction

Trial court had jurisdiction to revoke probation, even though written probation order was entered after defendant violated the terms of her probation; probation was part of negotiated written plea agreement signed by defendant and recited in detail at the sentencing hearing, and probationer did not contest probation. Matthews v. State, App. 4 Dist., 736 So.2d 72 (1999). Sentencing And Punishment ⚷ 2010

It is exclusively within the jurisdiction of the court to set the terms and conditions upon which a probationer's probation may be revoked, and probation may be revoked only for the violation of a condition set by the court. Barber v. State, App. 3 Dist., 344 So.2d 913 (1977). Sentencing And Punishment ⚷ 2003

5. —— Valuation of property, jurisdiction

Where, although evidence would support verdict that property stolen and received was worth more than $100, information failed to allege necessary valuation required to vest jurisdiction in circuit court, and defendant was tried by jury and did not plead to factual recitation so as to tacitly amend information, Circuit Court had no jurisdiction over charged misdemeanor, and thus all orders entered in case, including order of probation and subsequent order revoking defendant's probation and sentence of prison term, were nullity and had to be reversed. Page v. State, App. 2 Dist., 376 So.2d 901 (1979). Criminal Law ⚷ 93

6. —— Subject matter, jurisdiction

Irregularities in imposition of defendant's community control would not ipso facto deprive trial court of subject matter jurisdiction with respect to new felony charges stemming from good-faith enforcement of that community control. Figone v. Downey, App. 2 Dist., 547 So.2d 697 (1989). Criminal Law ⚷ 92

Because lack of subject matter jurisdiction is fundamental error and can be raised at any time, defendant could raise it for first time on appeal of his judgment and sentence following revocation of his probation. Page v. State, App. 2 Dist., 376 So.2d 901 (1979). Criminal Law ⚷ 1033.1

7. —— Deportation, jurisdiction

Inasmuch as deportation is federal matter, trial court had no authority to order defendants deported to Cuba if they were found to be illegal aliens, which order was made as special condition of probation; however, the trial court could recommend to appropriate federal authorities that defendants be deported if court deemed it advisable. Torros v. State, App. 2 Dist., 415 So.2d 908 (1982). States ⚷ 18.43

8. Discretion of trial court

A trial court generally has authority to modify or rescind the terms or conditions of probation imposed by it; however, that discretion is not unlimited. State v. Springer, App. 5 Dist., 965 So.2d 270 (2007). Sentencing And Punishment ⚷ 1985

In a case involving sex offender probation, the trial court must impose certain legislatively mandated conditions; the statute does not allow for judicial discretion. State v. Miller, App. 5 Dist., 888 So.2d 76 (2004), rehearing denied, on subsequent appeal 17 So.3d 778. Sentencing And Punishment ⚷ 1962

Except in cases involving certain crimes, a trial court has discretion to determine which general conditions to include in a probation order. Jones v. State, App. 1 Dist., 876 So.2d 642 (2004). Sentencing And Punishment ⚷ 1962

Willful failure to actively participate in or complete sex offender treatment, or provide test results to the victim, does not necessarily preclude revocation of sex offender probation simply because the number of attempts at compliance were not specified or because the defendant is willing to undertake another attempt at compliance within the probationary period; if immediate initial attempts are unsuccessful and the defendant expresses a willingness to try again, other chances at compliance are a matter that should be left to the sound discretion of the trial court. Woodson v. State, App. 5 Dist., 864 So.2d 512 (2004), review granted 879 So.2d 626, review dismissed 889 So.2d 823. Sentencing And Punishment ⚷ 2003

In a case involving sex offender probation, the trial court must impose certain legislatively mandated conditions; the statute does not allow for judicial discretion. Woodson v. State, App. 5 Dist., 864 So.2d 512 (2004), review granted 879 So.2d 626, review dismissed 889 So.2d 823. Sentencing And Punishment ⚷ 1962

Though defendant may have some voice in determining terms of probation by appealing to court's discretion, the court's determination is subject only to test of reasonableness, and defendant's consent to such terms, if they are otherwise reasonable, is not material to their legality. Dearth v. State, App. 4 Dist., 390 So.2d 108 (1980). Sentencing And Punishment ⚿ 1963

Trial court is vested with broad discretion in determining conditions of probation, and if probationer is determined to have violated any of terms or conditions of his probation and the court desires to restore him to probation after finding such violation, the court may, at such time, impose additional conditions. Carmo v. State, App. 4 Dist., 378 So.2d 850 (1979). Sentencing And Punishment ⚿ 2040

Trial courts have broad discretion to impose various conditions of probation, but a special condition of probation cannot be imposed if it is so punitive as to be unrelated to rehabilitation. Rodriguez v. State, App. 2 Dist., 378 So.2d 7 (1979). Sentencing And Punishment ⚿ 1962; Sentencing And Punishment ⚿ 1963

Granting of probation rests within broad discretion of trial judge and is a matter of grace rather than right; statutory provisions setting out the procedures for extending probation privileges are not mandatory on trial judges. Arnold v. State, App. 1 Dist., 356 So.2d 862 (1978). Sentencing And Punishment ⚿ 1802; Sentencing And Punishment ⚿ 1812

Trial court is vested with broad discretion in determining conditions of probation, but such discretion is not unbridled. Kominsky v. State, App. 1 Dist., 330 So.2d 800 (1976). Sentencing And Punishment ⚿ 1962

Grant of probation rests within broad discretion of trial judge and is a matter of grace, not of right. Martin v. State, App. 4 Dist., 243 So.2d 189 (1971), certiorari denied 247 So.2d 63. Sentencing And Punishment ⚿ 1802; Sentencing And Punishment ⚿ 1812

The trial court in granting probation may, in its discretion, impose such terms and conditions of probation as the court deems proper and will serve to rehabilitate the defendant and protect and serve the public. Such determination and the imposition of a condition of probation is a purely judicial function which the trial court must exercise as a matter of sound judicial discretion and is presumptively valid until and unless an appellate court determines otherwise. Op.Atty.Gen., 83–38, June 22, 1983.

Where an order of probation says nothing about whether the probationer may consult or seek the assistance of such agencies as alcoholic rehabilitation, guidance, clinics, etc., the court that made such order does not have the authority to prohibit the Florida parole and probation commission from referring the probationer to such agencies without first obtaining a determination from the court that such reference is necessary. Op.Atty.Gen., 971–144, June 11, 1971.

9. Delegation of authority

Condition of community control requiring juvenile to obey all lawful and reasonable demands of his mother, including participation in church youth programs, did not constitute unlawful delegation of judicial authority to juvenile's mother; as natural guardian, mother had legal authority to direct that child participate or not participate in various youth programs or activities in accordance with her legal obligation to do those things that were in child's best interests. L.M. v. State, App. 1 Dist., 610 So.2d 1314 (1992). Constitutional Law ⚿ 2570; Infants ⚿ 225

Condition of probation which prohibited defendant convicted of RICO conspiracy from seeking employment in automobile sales or service industry without prior approval of probation officer who determined that such employment would not create potential for type of harm that led to defendant's conviction improperly delegated judicial responsibility to probation officer. Fisher v. State, App. 2 Dist., 609 So.2d 168 (1992). Constitutional Law ⚿ 2574; Sentencing And Punishment ⚿ 1988

Special condition of community control requiring defendant to follow conditions imposed by community control counselor was unlawful delegation of judicial authority. In Interest of T.L.D., App. 4 Dist., 586 So.2d 1294 (1991). Constitutional Law ⚿ 2574; Sentencing And Punishment ⚿ 1988

Only court can set conditions of probation. In Interest of T.L.D., App. 4 Dist., 586 So.2d 1294 (1991). Constitutional Law ⚿ 2574

Trial court reversibly errs when it delegates judicial responsibility to probation officer. In Interest of T.L.D., App. 4 Dist., 586 So.2d 1294 (1991). Constitutional Law ⚿ 2574; Criminal Law ⚿ 1177.3(4)

10. Constitutional rights of probationers—In general

Constitutional rights of probationers are limited by conditions of probation which are desirable for purposes of rehabilitation. Rodriguez v. State, App. 2 Dist., 378 So.2d 7 (1979). Sentencing And Punishment ⚿ 1963

U.S.C.A. Const. Amend. 1 rights of free speech and association may be limited by valid probationary conditions. Rodriguez v. State, App. 2 Dist., 378 So.2d 7 (1979). Constitutional Law ⚿ 1440; Constitutional Law ⚿ 2104

U.S.C.A. Const. Amend. 4 prohibition of unreasonable searches and seizures and the privilege against self-incrimination under U.S.C.A. Const. Amend. 5 are qualified by probationary status. Rodriguez v. State, App. 2 Dist., 378 So.2d 7 (1979). Sentencing And Punishment ⚿ 1970(2); Sentencing And Punishment ⚿ 1992

Where questions probationer refused to answer, on ground of Fifth Amendment privilege, during investigation by special prosecutor, involved separate criminal offense with which probationer, not having been convicted thereof and not having been granted immunity, could have been charged, probationer retained his right to refuse to answer such questions, and his probation, which included special condition that he was to cooperate with authorities in bringing to justice other persons involved in scheme which had led to charges brought against him, could not be revoked for exercising such right. Douglas v. State, App. 2 Dist., 376 So.2d 11 (1979). Sentencing And Punishment ⚿ 2003

11. —— Waiver, constitutional rights of probationers

Condition of probation requiring defendant to waive his rights under U.S.C.A. Const. Amend. 4 was improper and would be stricken. Kirkpatrick v. State, App. 4 Dist., 412 So.2d 903 (1982). Sentencing And Punishment ⚿ 1970(2); Sentencing And Punishment ⚿ 1992

Requirement in order placing defendant on probation that defendant had to "waive any notice of a hearing" to set a fee and impose a lien against him in order for him to obtain services of a public defender was an infringement upon defendant's constitutional right to counsel and such requirement would be stricken. McGeorge v. State, App. 5 Dist., 386 So.2d 29 (1980). Sentencing And Punishment ⚿ 1970(2)

Probationer, upon specific request and at periodic intervals may be required to identify himself and provide all necessary information for his supervision including the place of his residence and his employment, and may also be required to affirm or deny his location at a particular place and a particular time, to explain his noncriminal conduct, and to permit the search of his person and quarters by the supervisor, and failure to do so may itself be grounds for revocation of probation; agreement to accept the terms of probation effectively waives Fifth Amendment privilege against self-incrimination with respect to this information. State v. Heath, 343 So.2d 13 (1977), certiorari denied 98 S.Ct. 269, 434 U.S. 893, 54 L.Ed.2d 179. Sentencing And Punishment ⚿ 1969(2); Sentencing And Punishment ⚿ 1990; Witnesses ⚿ 305(2)

12. —— Abridgement, constitutional rights of probationers

Even constitutional rights can be abridged by conditions of probation if the conditions are reasonably related to the probationer's past or future criminality or to the rehabilitative purposes of probation. Saidi v. State, App. 5 Dist., 845 So.2d 1022 (2003). Sentencing And Punishment ⚿ 1963

Under Florida law, constitutionally protected rights can be abridged by conditions of probation if they are reasonably related to probationer's past or future criminality or to the rehabilitative purposes of probation. Wiggins v. State, App. 4 Dist., 386 So.2d 46 (1980). Sentencing And Punishment ⚿ 1963

13. Search and seizure—In general

Probationer may be required to provide all necessary information for his supervision, to confirm or deny his location at particular place at particular time, to explain his noncriminal conduct, and to submit to search of his quarters and of his person; probationer's Fifth Amendment rights relate only to separate criminal offense, and if he chooses not to answer questions about noncriminal conduct or to submit to such searches, his probation can be revoked. Cassamassima v. State, App. 5 Dist., 657 So.2d 906 (1995), certification denied. Criminal Law ⚿ 393(1); Sentencing And Punishment ⚿ 1969(2); Sentencing And Punishment ⚿ 1992

One does not absolutely forfeit protection of Fourth Amendment's prohibition of unreasonable searches and seizures merely by assuming status of probationer; however, probationary status may be taken into account in determining whether particular search was in fact reasonable. Croteau v. State, 334 So.2d 577 (1976). Sentencing And Punishment ⚿ 1992

14. —— Standing, search and seizure

Probation conditions were proper which required defendant to have no contact with named individuals, permitted law enforcement officers to search probationer and all vehicles and premises concerning which he had legal standing to give consent to search, and requiring probationer to submit to physical or chemical examinations upon request of any probation supervisor or law enforcement officer to determine systemic presence of controlled substances or unlawfully acquired drugs. Isaacs v. State, App. 4 Dist., 351 So.2d 359 (1977). Sentencing And Punishment ⚿ 1971(2); Sentencing And Punishment ⚿ 1994; Sentencing And Punishment ⚿ 1996

15. —— Consent, search and seizure

Probationer, by expressly agreeing to a condition of probation that he voluntarily submit to reasonable searches of his person, home or vehicle by probation officer or authorized police officers, had not voluntarily waived right to be protected from warrantless searches, in that such a consent could not be regarded as voluntary where the only other alternative was incarceration. Dearth v. State, App. 4 Dist., 390 So.2d 108 (1980). Sentencing And Punishment ⚷ 1994

Requirement in order placing defendant on probation that he "shall consent to a search of himself or any vehicle or premises under his control at any time by any law enforcement officer" was erroneous and would be stricken. McGeorge v. State, App. 5 Dist., 386 So.2d 29 (1980). Sentencing And Punishment ⚷ 1994

Probation condition requiring defendant to consent to search of himself or any vehicle or premises under his control at any time by any law enforcement officer was valid insofar as it permitted defendant's probation supervisors to make those searches, but was not valid insofar as it granted blanket permission for warrantless searches to other law enforcement officers. Smith v. State, App. 5 Dist., 383 So.2d 991 (1980). Sentencing And Punishment ⚷ 1995

Condition set forth unilaterally by judge in probation order which requires probationer to consent at any time to warrantless search by law enforcement officer violates Florida and United States Constitutions. Grubbs v. State, 373 So.2d 905 (1979). Sentencing And Punishment ⚷ 1994

16. —— Law enforcement officers, search and seizure

A police officer acting in good faith and in response to a probation officer's request to effect an arrest in the probation officer's presence had the authority to conduct a search of a probationer's person. Johnston v. State, App. 4 Dist., 768 So.2d 504 (2000), rehearing denied, review denied 817 So.2d 847. Sentencing And Punishment ⚷ 1990

Condition of probation that required defendant to submit to search at any time by law enforcement officer was invalid. Llanos v. State, App. 5 Dist., 401 So.2d 848 (1981). Sentencing And Punishment ⚷ 1992

Condition of probation authorizing warrantless searches by any law enforcement officer violates U.S.C.A. Const. Amend. 4, and Const. Art. 1, § 12. Balser v. State, App. 5 Dist., 399 So.2d 67 (1981). Sentencing And Punishment ⚷ 1993

In light of fact that condition of probation whereby defendant was required to submit to searches by any authorized police officer was improper, the words "and authorized police officers" was stricken from order. Gosman v. State, App. 4 Dist., 391 So.2d 339 (1980). Sentencing And Punishment ⚷ 1995

Requirement that defendant, while on probation, submit to search by any law enforcement officer and submit to physical or chemical examinations upon request of any law enforcement officer would be stricken from sentence of defendant, who was convicted for possession and sale of heroin. Thomas v. State, App. 5 Dist., 387 So.2d 540 (1980). Sentencing And Punishment ⚷ 1996

Condition of probation authorizing any law enforcement officer to search, at any time, defendant and all vehicles and premises concerning which he had legal standing to give consent to search violated search and seizure provision of the U.S.C.A. Const. Amend. 4 and F.S.A. Const. Art. 1, § 12 and thus was to be stricken. Johnson v. State, App. 5 Dist., 386 So.2d 291 (1980). Sentencing And Punishment ⚷ 1992

Special condition of probationary provision of defendant's sentence, authorizing any law enforcement officer at any time to search his person, vehicle or premises, was invalid. Jones v. State, App. 5 Dist., 384 So.2d 956 (1980), review denied 392 So.2d 1375. Sentencing And Punishment ⚷ 1992

Probation condition authorizing any probation, supervisor and any law enforcement officer to search, at any time, defendant and all vehicles and premises concerning which he had legal standing to give consent to search was valid and would be approved. Sanders v. State, App. 4 Dist., 351 So.2d 361 (1977). Sentencing And Punishment ⚷ 1994

Condition of probation requiring probationer to submit to a search by law enforcement officers as well as probation supervisor was valid and enforcible; receding from position expressed in Pace v. State, App. 4 Dist., 350 So.2d 1075 (1977). Sentencing And Punishment ⚷ 1995

Probation condition requiring defendant to "submit your person, residence or automobile to search by Probation Supervisor or law enforcement officer upon demand without search warrant," was null and void on its face. Pace v. State, App. 4 Dist., 335 So.2d 11 (1976). Sentencing And Punishment ⚷ 1993

17. —— Probation supervisors, search and seizure

Condition of probation requiring probationer to submit to warrantless search of his person, residence or automobile by any law enforcement officer or his probation supervisor was too broad insofar as it permitted warrantless searches by any law enforcement officer, but was correct insofar as it permitted such searches by probation supervisor. Elkins v.

State, App., 388 So.2d 1314 (1980); Maples v. State, App., 397 So.2d 1146 (1981).

Probation officers and detectives legally entered residence shared by probationer and defendant; probation officers had authority to enter probationer's residence to conduct warrantless probationary search to determine whether she was in violation of probation, officer's had reasonable suspicion of criminal activities by probationer based on relative of probationer who advised officer that probationer was dealing drugs out of her home, and detectives accompanied probation officers during probationary search as safety precaution. State v. Yule, App. 2 Dist., 905 So.2d 251 (2005), review denied 917 So.2d 197. Sentencing And Punishment ⚷ 1995

A probation officer has the authority to search a probationer when he has reasonable grounds to believe that the probationer has violated the terms and conditions of his probation. Johnston v. State, App. 4 Dist., 768 So.2d 504 (2000), rehearing denied, review denied 817 So.2d 847. Sentencing And Punishment ⚷ 1990

Condition in written order of probation requiring probationer to submit to a warrantless search of his person, premises or vehicle by his supervising officer at any time was valid though not pronounced at sentencing, codified in Rule of Criminal Procedure as a general condition of probation, nor found in statute relating to terms and conditions of probation, as the statute does authorize probation officer to visit probationer's home at any time, thus providing the necessary notice. Brown v. State, App. 2 Dist., 697 So.2d 928 (1997). Sentencing And Punishment ⚷ 1918; Sentencing And Punishment ⚷ 1993

Condition of probation requiring probationer to submit to warrantless search of his person, residence or car by anyone other than his probation officer was invalid. Hunte v. State, App. 5 Dist., 388 So.2d 37 (1980). Sentencing And Punishment ⚷ 1970(2)

Condition of probation order was valid insofar as it permitted defendant's probation supervisor to make warrantless searches for evidence of drugs, but it was not valid insofar as it granted blanket permission for warrantless searches to any law enforcement officer. Barber v. State, App. 5 Dist., 387 So.2d 540 (1980). Sentencing And Punishment ⚷ 1995

Probation condition that defendant submit to search at any time, by any probation supervisor and any law enforcement officer of his person and all vehicles and premises concerning which he had legal standing to consent to search was valid insofar as it related to searches by probation supervisor, but to extent such condition intended to grant greater authority to law enforcement officers to conduct a warrantless search, it was a unilateral search condition requiring defendant to consent at any time to a warrantless search, and as such was a violation of Fourth Amendment to United States Constitution and Const. Art. 1, § 12. Wood v. State, App. 5 Dist., 378 So.2d 110 (1980). Sentencing And Punishment ⚷ 1993; Sentencing And Punishment ⚷ 1995

Condition of order placing defendant on probation, which required him to permit, during period of probation, without a warrant, the search of his person, premises or vehicle by any law officer or probation officer at any time, was invalid to extent that it allowed unrestricted warrantless searches by law enforcement officers, but authorization of searches by defendant's probation officer was valid. Jessee v. State, App. 2 Dist., 375 So.2d 881 (1979). Sentencing And Punishment ⚷ 1995

18. Validity of conditions—In general

Trial court that sentenced defendant to probation under Youthful Offender Act, after defendant pled nolo contendere to lewd and lascivious battery, was required to impose mandatory sex offender probation conditions pursuant to statute governing terms and conditions of probation, even though Youthful Offender Act provided that probation could be imposed "in lieu of other criminal penalties"; provision of Youthful Offender Act defining probation specifically referred to statute governing terms and conditions of probation, and recognized that youthful offenders sentenced to probation were subject to its requirements. State v. Miller, App. 5 Dist., 888 So.2d 76 (2004), rehearing denied, on subsequent appeal 17 So.3d 778. Infants ⚷ 69(7)

Trial court, in its sentencing of defendant who was convicted of burglary, sexual battery, and kidnapping, was not required to impose sex offender conditions on order of probation involving kidnapping count, since statute mandating imposition of such conditions for certain enumerated offenses did not list kidnapping as one of those offenses. Edmondson v. State, App. 1 Dist., 816 So.2d 768 (2002). Sentencing And Punishment ⚷ 1977(1)

Although, as special probation condition, defendant convicted of leaving accident scene resulting in person's death could be required to clean victim's grave site monthly, appellate court would delete requirement that victim's family direct defendant's work on the site. Rodriguez v. State, App. 2 Dist., 684 So.2d 864 (1996). Criminal Law ⚷ 1184(4.1); Sentencing And Punishment ⚷ 1983(2)

Probation condition imposing $100 assessment for county court improvement fund was without legal basis and stricken on appeal.

Heathcoe v. State, App. 2 Dist., 654 So.2d 1258 (1995). Sentencing And Punishment ⚷ 1975(2)

There was no statutory authority for imposition of $60 fee to county "First Step" as special condition of probation and, thus, fee would be stricken. Johnson v. State, App. 5 Dist., 648 So.2d 263 (1994). Sentencing And Punishment ⚷ 1975(2)

Remand was required to trial court in order for trial court to reference statutory authority for imposing special condition of probation of payment of one dollar a month to organization or to delete it from written special conditions of probation. Gedeon v. State, App. 5 Dist., 636 So.2d 178 (1994). Criminal Law ⚷ 1181.5(8)

Condition of probation that defendant have no contact with children under age ten was too broad; condition had to be more specific so that defendant could not be charged with unintentional violation of it. Lambert v. State, App. 4 Dist., 635 So.2d 1056 (1994). Sentencing And Punishment ⚷ 1971(3)

Condition of probation that defendant have no contact with children under age ten was too broad; condition needed to be more specific so that defendant could not be charged with unintentional violation of it. Lambert v. State, App. 4 Dist., 635 So.2d 93 (1994). Sentencing And Punishment ⚷ 1971(3)

Trial court erred in imposing additional conditions of probation absent judicial determination that defendant violated terms of prior probation orders. Malone v. State, App. 4 Dist., 632 So.2d 1140 (1994). Sentencing And Punishment ⚷ 1923

Condition of probation is invalid if it has no relationship to crime of which offender was convicted, it relates to conduct which is not in itself criminal, and it requires or forbids conduct which is not reasonably related to future criminality. Richardson v. State, App. 2 Dist., 620 So.2d 257 (1993). Sentencing And Punishment ⚷ 1963

Condition of probation requiring probationer to show respect to criminal justice workers is unconstitutionally vague. Olvey v. State, App. 2 Dist., 609 So.2d 640 (1992), decision clarified on rehearing. Sentencing And Punishment ⚷ 1969(3)

Condition of probation that defendant, who pled guilty to lewd and lascivious acts and attempted sexual battery, should have no contact with children, should have specified children under age of 18 rather than 21. Baxter v. State, App. 2 Dist., 596 So.2d 460 (1991), review denied 599 So.2d 654. Sentencing And Punishment ⚷ 1971(2)

Probation condition requiring probationer to show respect to officers connected with criminal justice system was too vague to inform probationer of what conduct was acceptable or unacceptable. Knight v. State, App. 2 Dist., 593 So.2d 1202 (1992). Sentencing And Punishment ⚷ 1969(3)

All but one probation condition in written order was either stated at oral pronouncement and related to offense committed or was statutorily authorized where court announced at sentencing that it was placing defendant on "ordinary probation," and, thus, only single condition not stated at oral pronouncement as special condition and not statutorily authorized would be stricken. Vinyard v. State, App. 2 Dist., 586 So.2d 1301 (1991). Sentencing And Punishment ⚷ 1918

Condition of probation imposed on defendant convicted of handling and fondling child under age of 14, that defendant refrain from having any unsupervised contact with minors, was not unconstitutionally vague under circumstances of case. Maguire v. State, App. 2 Dist., 586 So.2d 1268 (1991), quashed 594 So.2d 306. Infants ⚷ 20

Conditions of probation are valid only if probation is valid in the first instance. Ex parte Bosso, 41 So.2d 322 (1949). Sentencing And Punishment ⚷ 1963

19. —— Attempted offenses, validity of conditions

Trial court could subject defendant who pled no contest to attempted lewd act upon a child to sex offender probation conditions, in case in which defendant agreed to imposition of conditions as part of plea bargain. State v. Thurman, App. 5 Dist., 791 So.2d 1228 (2001). Sentencing And Punishment ⚷ 1862

Community control conditions required to be imposed for offense of sexual battery could not be imposed on defendant convicted of attempted sexual battery. Lee v. State, App. 1 Dist., 766 So.2d 374 (2000). Sentencing And Punishment ⚷ 1965

20. —— Sufficiency of evidence, validity of conditions

Defendant could not be convicted for violation of community control which was originally imposed relative to offense of possession of cocaine, as conditions of defendant's community control for cocaine offense were a nullity because defendant neither pled nolo contendere nor guilty to cocaine offense, nor was he found guilty of such offense following trial. Stelzl v. State, App. 5 Dist., 629 So.2d 984 (1993). Sentencing And Punishment ⚷ 2004

Where special condition of probation is challenged on relevancy grounds, it will only be upheld if record supports at least one of the circumstances outlined in District Court of Appeals' *Rodriguez* decision. Martinez v. State, App. 2 Dist., 627 So.2d 542 (1993). Sentencing And Punishment ⚷ 1963

21. —— Relevancy, validity of conditions

Special condition of probation will be upheld, when challenged on grounds of relevancy, only if it either has relationship to crime of which offender convicted, it relates to conduct that is in itself criminal, or it requires or forbids conduct that is reasonably related to future criminality. Biller v. State, 618 So.2d 734 (1993). Sentencing And Punishment ⚷ 1963

22. —— Possession of firearms, validity of conditions

Portion of probation condition implying that felon can possess weapons otherwise prohibited with consent of probation officer was improper. Weber v. State, App. 2 Dist., 691 So.2d 1 (1995). Sentencing And Punishment ⚷ 1981(3)

Probation condition for drug violations which prohibited defendant from carrying weapons, without first procuring consent of probation officer, was invalid, as such condition implied that a felon could possess weapons otherwise prohibited with consent of his or her probation officer. Levely v. State, App. 2 Dist., 685 So.2d 847 (1995). Sentencing And Punishment ⚷ 1981(3)

Condition of probation that defendant not possess, carry, or own any weapons without first procuring consent of probation officer was improper because it implied that felon can possess otherwise prohibited weapons with the consent of his probation officer. Williams v. State, App. 2 Dist., 681 So.2d 817 (1996). Sentencing And Punishment ⚷ 1981(2)

Condition of probation prohibiting defendant from possessing firearms or possessing weapons without first procuring consent of probation officer was valid condition. Ringling v. State, App. 2 Dist., 678 So.2d 1339 (1996). Sentencing And Punishment ⚷ 1981(2)

Conditions of community control placed on defendant forbidding excessive use of intoxicants and regarding possessing or carrying firearms or weapons had to be stricken where, although defendant was found guilty of felony, trial court withheld adjudication of guilt and court failed to orally pronounce two conditions of community control at sentencing. Martin v. State, App. 2 Dist., 667 So.2d 931 (1996). Sentencing And Punishment ⚷ 1920

Condition of probation prohibiting probationer from possessing, carrying, or owning firearm was valid general condition and did not have to be pronounced orally at sentencing. Kirkland v. State, App. 1 Dist., 666 So.2d 974 (1996). Sentencing And Punishment ⚷ 1918

Probation condition stating that defendant will neither possess, carry, nor own any weapon without first securing consent of probation officer would be stricken to the extent that condition implied that felon could possess prohibited weapon or firearm with permission of his probation officer. Murphy v. State, App. 2 Dist., 666 So.2d 182 (1995). Sentencing And Punishment ⚷ 1981(3)

Probation condition prohibiting the carrying of weapons other than those enumerated in statute would be stricken as it was not orally pronounced. Murphy v. State, App. 2 Dist., 666 So.2d 182 (1995). Sentencing And Punishment ⚷ 1920

Contested condition of probation, that defendant would not possess, carry, or own firearm, was stricken where it was not orally pronounced and defendant was not convicted of a felony. Raimondo v. State, App. 2 Dist., 666 So.2d 180 (1995). Sentencing And Punishment ⚷ 1920

Condition of probation which prohibited defendant from possessing, carrying or owning weapons or firearms without first securing consent of his probation officer would be stricken, since that condition implied that defendant could possess firearm with probation officer's permission, and defendant was convicted felon and thus could not lawfully possess firearm. Luby v. State, App. 2 Dist., 648 So.2d 308 (1995). Sentencing And Punishment ⚷ 1981(3)

Portion of condition of probation improperly implying that felon could possess firearm with consent of probation officer had to be stricken. Jennings v. State, App. 2 Dist., 645 So.2d 592 (1994). Sentencing And Punishment ⚷ 1981(2)

Defendant's special probation condition implying that he would be allowed to possess firearm with his probation officer's permission must be stricken, where defendant was convicted felon who could not lawfully possess firearm. Pagan v. State, App. 2 Dist., 637 So.2d 959 (1994). Sentencing And Punishment ⚷ 1981(2)

Probation condition prohibiting possession or ownership of firearm is valid with respect to defendant who is convicted of felony possession of cocaine. Grate v. State, App. 5 Dist., 623 So.2d 591 (1993). Sentencing And Punishment ⚷ 1981(2)

Condition that defendant obtain consent of probation officer to possess firearm was improper condition of probation inasmuch as convicted felon may not lawfully possess firearm. Crawford v. State, App. 2 Dist., 616 So.2d 1158 (1993). Sentencing And Punishment ⚷ 1981(2)

Condition of defendant's probation, viz., prohibiting the possession, carrying, or use of weapons or firearms without prior consent of his probation officer, was improper and had to be stricken, since defendant was a convicted felon. Hinton v. State, App. 2 Dist., 439 So.2d 1008 (1983). Sentencing And Punishment ⚷ 1981(2)

Condition of defendant's probation requiring that she not possess, carry, or own any weapons or firearms without first securing consent of probation officer was stricken as violating F.S.A. § 790.23 prohibiting convicted felon from owning, possessing, or controlling any electric weapons or firearms. Smith v. State, App. 2 Dist., 396 So.2d 206 (1981). Sentencing And Punishment ⚷ 1981(2)

23. —— Possession of obscene materials, validity of conditions

Statute governing conditions of probation, which prohibited sexual battery defendant from viewing or possessing any obscene material did not violate due process in failing to provide sufficient notice of what was "obscene" and notice of what constituted defendant's "deviant behavior pattern;" U.S. Supreme Court had defined obscene material, and Florida statute, defining attempted sexual battery while in a position of familial or custodial authority, provided adequate notice of defendant's "deviant sexual behavior." Ertley v. State, App. 1 Dist., 785 So.2d 592 (2001). Constitutional Law ⚷ 4732; Sentencing And Punishment ⚷ 1983(2)

24. —— Waiver of confidentiality, validity of conditions

Waiver of confidentiality could not be imposed upon defendant as condition of probation where imposition of waiver was not justified by record pursuant to *Williams*. Walker v. State, App. 2 Dist., 662 So.2d 1352 (1995). Sentencing And Punishment ⚷ 1983(2)

25. —— Living conditions, validity of conditions

Requirement that defendant move from his grandmother's house and obtain his own residence within two weeks was not proper condition for probation. Tucker v. State, App. 1 Dist., 529 So.2d 818 (1988). Sentencing And Punishment ⚷ 1971(2)

It was improper to impose as a condition of probation the requirement that defendant not live with his mother; condition did not fall within statutory enumerated conditions which could be broadly imposed as conditions of probation, and the record, trial judge, and State all failed to set forth any rational relationship between crime of uttering a forgery, of which defendant was convicted, and challenged condition nor had any relationship been established between possibility of future criminal conduct and challenged condition. Cole v. State, App. 1 Dist., 521 So.2d 297 (1988). Sentencing And Punishment ⚷ 1971(2)

26. —— Deportation or leaving country, validity of conditions

Condition of probation requiring defendant to leave country was not related to offense of which defendant was convicted or to future criminality and was invalid; although entering United States other than as designated by immigration officers could constitute crime, record did not establish that defendant's presence in United States was in itself criminal. Martinez v. State, App. 2 Dist., 627 So.2d 542 (1993). Sentencing And Punishment ⚷ 1968(2)

27. —— Educational requirements, validity of conditions

Probation condition requiring defendant to obtain or make good faith effort to obtain either literacy skills or high school diploma would be stricken where defendant concededly had already obtained high school diploma and was literate. Weber v. State, App. 2 Dist., 691 So.2d 1 (1995). Sentencing And Punishment ⚷ 1983(3)

Special probation condition, which required defendant to obtain graduate equivalency degree (GED) and permitted him to "study off" his community service hours by enrolling within 30 days in GED program and remaining successfully enrolled, was orally pronounced and referred to in the order of probation and, thus, would be affirmed. Garrison v. State, App. 2 Dist., 685 So.2d 53 (1996). Sentencing And Punishment ⚷ 1918

Probation condition requiring good faith effort to obtain either literacy skills or high school diploma was special condition of probation and had to be pronounced orally. Powell v. State, App. 2 Dist., 681 So.2d 722 (1996). Sentencing And Punishment ⚷ 1918

Due process considerations required that language "insofar as possible" be deemed part of conditions of community control imposed on defendant requiring that he receive grades of A or B if he attends school because defendant's community control may not be revoked for failure to comply with condition unless trial court determines that he had ability to comply. Martin v. State, App. 2 Dist., 667 So.2d 931 (1996). Constitutional Law ⚷ 4733(1); Sentencing And Punishment ⚷ 1983(3)

Defendant could not be required, as condition of his probation after he had been convicted of dealing in stolen property, to obtain his Graduate Equivalency Diploma (GED). Priest v. State, App. 2 Dist., 626 So.2d 1005 (1993). Sentencing And Punishment ⚷ 1983(2)

28. —— Assignment of property, validity of conditions

Trial court had authority to order defendant convicted of grand theft to assign patent acquired through use of stolen research materials to victims as condition of defendant's probation, as defendant had been found financially unable to make monetary restitution and requiring defendant to assign patent was therefore only way to effectuate restitution. Taborsky v. State, App. 2 Dist., 659 So.2d 1112 (1995), rehearing denied, review denied 666 So.2d 145. Sentencing And Punishment ⚷ 1973(3)

29. —— Religious instruction, validity of conditions

Requiring a probationer or community controlee to submit to a course of religious instruction contravenes the First Amendment. L.M. v. State, App. 1 Dist., 587 So.2d 648 (1991). Constitutional Law ⚷ 1417; Sentencing And Punishment ⚷ 1983(2)

Condition of community control imposed on juvenile adjudicated delinquent, which required him to "get with the pastor" of his mother's church and enroll in any and all of the church's youth programs was error; although record below did not indicate whether any or all of the youth programs had religious content, order required juvenile to participate in such programs, regardless of content, raising possibility of First Amendment violation. L.M. v. State, App. 1 Dist., 587 So.2d 648 (1991). Constitutional Law ⚷ 1428; Infants ⚷ 225

30. —— Work and support requirements, validity of conditions

It was an improper condition of probation to require probationer to maintain full-time employment inasmuch as a downturn in the economy could prevent completion of the condition; accordingly, portion of condition requiring probationer to "work diligently" at a lawful occupation would be modified to read "seek gainful employment." Kirkland v. State, App. 1 Dist., 666 So.2d 974 (1996). Sentencing And Punishment ⚷ 1972(3)

Trial court order requiring defendant to maintain full-time employment as condition of probation was proper, where, during its oral pronouncement of sentence, the court clarified that defendant would be insulated from losing his job because he would always have one available through county work release center; the court's clarification removed the possibility that defendant could violate his probation because of economic conditions beyond his control. Brown v. State, App. 5 Dist., 666 So.2d 240 (1996). Sentencing And Punishment ⚷ 1972(3)

Probation condition requiring defendant to work diligently at lawful occupation and support any dependents to the best of his ability, as directed by his probation officer, merely combined two standards set forth in statute and did not violate due process. Gregory v. State, App. 2 Dist., 616 So.2d 174 (1993). Constitutional Law ⚷ 4732; Sentencing And Punishment ⚷ 1972(2); Sentencing And Punishment ⚷ 1983(2)

Condition of probation requiring defendant to work and support his dependents was statutorily allowed. Brown v. State, App. 2 Dist., 613 So.2d 558 (1993). Sentencing And Punishment ⚷ 1972(2); Sentencing And Punishment ⚷ 1983(2)

Provision in probation condition requiring defendant to work and support his dependents "to the best of [his] ability" met requirement of statute that a defendant only be required to work "as may be possible." Brown v. State, App. 2 Dist., 613 So.2d 558 (1993). Sentencing And Punishment ⚷ 1972(2); Sentencing And Punishment ⚷ 1983(2)

Condition of probation and community control, imposed after revocation of probation defendant was serving for attempted sexual battery, that defendant maintain employment and earn at least $800 per month, was fundamental error; condition was unreasonable in context of current job market and had no relationship to conviction. Evans v. State, App. 1 Dist., 608 So.2d 90 (1992). Criminal Law ⚷ 1042.3(4); Sentencing And Punishment ⚷ 1972(2)

31. —— Restitution, validity of conditions

Condition of probation delegating to probation officer the right to determine the rate of repayment of restitution was facially invalid. White v. State, App. 1 Dist., 606 So.2d 1265 (1992). Constitutional Law ⚷ 2574; Sentencing And Punishment ⚷ 1973(2)

32. —— Marriage requirements, validity of conditions

Lack of specificity in condition of probation which defendant was charged with violating, requiring continuation of counseling without specifying how long, was not solved by separate condition requiring evaluation for counseling and a rehabilitation program, both to be selected by the probation officer, where defendant was not charged with violation of latter condition, and no evaluation was ever performed. Larangera v. State, App. 4 Dist., 686 So.2d 697

(1996). Sentencing And Punishment ⚷ 1977(3)

Imposing a condition of probation that defendant "rectify" his marital situation and make his child "legitimate" within one year, which was tantamount to ordering him to marry the mother of the child, was beyond trial court's authority. Michalow v. State, App. 4 Dist., 362 So.2d 456 (1978). Sentencing And Punishment ⚷ 1983(2)

33. —— Fines, validity of conditions

Trial court erroneously imposed $15,000 fine as condition of probation for sale of cocaine count given statute providing that fine imposed on second-degree felony may not exceed $10,000. Jones v. State, App. 1 Dist., 617 So.2d 806 (1993). Sentencing And Punishment ⚷ 1974(2)

34. —— Consumption of alcohol, validity of conditions

In imposing probation upon revocation of defendant's community control, court improperly imposed conditions that defendant visit no bars, restaurants, or any place where alcoholic beverages were served without written permission from probation officer, and that defendant not be within three blocks of known high drug areas as determined by probation officer. Grady v. State, App. 2 Dist., 604 So.2d 1255 (1992). Sentencing And Punishment ⚷ 1967(2); Sentencing And Punishment ⚷ 1980(2)

Probation condition requiring that defendant not visit bars, restaurants, or any place where alcoholic beverages are served without permission from probation officer, after consent from judge, was improper. Strong v. State, App. 2 Dist., 599 So.2d 264 (1992). Sentencing And Punishment ⚷ 1980(2)

Special condition of probation on standard probation order from stating "you shall visit no bars" was overbroad and would be stricken. Cummings v. State, App. 2 Dist., 597 So.2d 416 (1992). Sentencing And Punishment ⚷ 1980(2)

Conditions of probation relating to alcohol use or visiting premises upon which alcohol or intoxicants were sold were unrelated to crime of grand theft for which defendant was convicted, and thus, those conditions could not stand. Stonebraker v. State, App. 2 Dist., 594 So.2d 351 (1992). Sentencing And Punishment ⚷ 1980(2)

Conditions of community control and probation that drug defendant not possess or consume alcohol, associate with persons who use alcohol, or frequent places where alcohol is main source of business were invalid. Alvarez v. State, App. 2 Dist., 593 So.2d 289 (1992). Sentencing And Punishment ⚷ 1971(2); Sentencing And Punishment ⚷ 1980(2)

Appellate court would strike condition of probation order requiring defendant to not consume any alcohol, be in possession of alcohol, associate with persons who use alcohol, or frequent places where alcohol is main source of business. Richards v. State, App. 2 Dist., 584 So.2d 157 (1991). Criminal Law ⚷ 1184(4.1); Sentencing And Punishment ⚷ 1980(2)

35. —— Use of drugs and narcotics, validity of conditions

Condition of probation requiring abstention from alcohol was reasonable, even though probationer was an alcoholic, thus, probationer's use of alcohol was a willful and substantial probation violation. Spry v. State, App. 2 Dist., 750 So.2d 123 (2000). Sentencing And Punishment ⚷ 1980(2); Sentencing And Punishment ⚷ 1980(3)

Possibility of overly broad interpretation of general condition of probation prohibiting possession of "any drugs or narcotics unless prescribed by a physician" to prohibit probationer from possessing over-the-counter medications did not render condition unconstitutionally vague. Johnson v. State, App. 2 Dist., 701 So.2d 367 (1997). Sentencing And Punishment ⚷ 1980(3)

Portion of probation condition prohibiting defendant from possessing "any drugs or narcotics unless prescribed by a physician" was too vague. Weber v. State, App. 2 Dist., 691 So.2d 1 (1995). Sentencing And Punishment ⚷ 1980(3)

Probation condition that defendant not visit places were intoxicants, drugs or other dangerous substances are unlawfully sold, dispensed or used was a general rather than a special condition of probation and was valid, but should be amended to reflect that defendant may not "knowing visit" such prohibited places. Nelson v. State, App. 4 Dist., 669 So.2d 1145 (1996). Sentencing And Punishment ⚷ 1980(3)

Probation condition, prohibiting possession and consumption of alcohol, frequenting of places where alcohol was main source of business, and association with persons who consumed alcohol, was special condition of probation, and thus was required to be orally pronounced at sentencing. Gerstenberger v. State, App. 2 Dist., 667 So.2d 1009 (1996). Sentencing And Punishment ⚷ 1918

Condition of probation prohibiting defendant from visiting places where certain substances were unlawfully sold, dispensed, or used was valid, and as a valid general condition of probation, need not have been pronounced in open court. Burdo v. State, App. 3 Dist., 667 So.2d

874 (1996), review granted 676 So.2d 412, quashed 682 So.2d 557. Sentencing And Punishment ⚷ 1918; Sentencing And Punishment ⚷ 1980(2)

Condition of probation prohibiting defendant from using intoxicants to excess was special condition that was invalid where not announced in open court. Burdo v. State, App. 3 Dist., 667 So.2d 874 (1996), review granted 676 So.2d 412, quashed 682 So.2d 557. Sentencing And Punishment ⚷ 1920; Sentencing And Punishment ⚷ 1980(2)

Condition of probation prohibiting probationer from possessing any drugs or narcotics unless prescribed by a physician was too vague and would be stricken as vague, inasmuch as it could be interpreted to prohibit probationer from possessing over-the-counter cold medication or aspirin. Kirkland v. State, App. 1 Dist., 666 So.2d 974 (1996). Sentencing And Punishment ⚷ 1980(3)

Condition of probation providing that probationer could not use intoxicants to excess was special condition of probation which trial court was required to pronounce orally at the sentencing hearing. Kirkland v. State, App. 1 Dist., 666 So.2d 974 (1996). Sentencing And Punishment ⚷ 1918

Special condition of probation which prohibited use of intoxicants was stricken from sentence where trial court failed to announce condition at sentencing. Jones v. State, App. 2 Dist., 666 So.2d 191 (1995). Sentencing And Punishment ⚷ 1920

Imposition of special condition of probation, that defendant would not use intoxicants to excess, should have been orally pronounced at sentencing. Parrish v. State, App. 2 Dist., 666 So.2d 184 (1995). Sentencing And Punishment ⚷ 1918

Condition of probation prohibiting defendant, who was convicted for sale and possession of cannabis, from using intoxicants to excess or visiting places where intoxicants, drugs or other dangerous substances were unlawfully sold, dispensed, or used was sufficiently definite and specific to inform persons of reasonable intelligence what conduct was prohibited. Gregory v. State, App. 2 Dist., 616 So.2d 174 (1993). Sentencing And Punishment ⚷ 1980(2)

Trial court could properly impose as condition of probation that defendant not use intoxicants to excess or visit places where intoxicants or drugs or other dangerous substances were unlawfully sold. Brown v. State, App. 2 Dist., 613 So.2d 558 (1993). Sentencing And Punishment ⚷ 1980(2)

Conditions of probation that defendant not use intoxicants to excess and that he not visit places where intoxicants and drugs were unlawfully used were proper for defendant convicted of substance offenses. Pratt v. State, App. 2 Dist., 601 So.2d 619 (1992). Sentencing And Punishment ⚷ 1980(2)

Condition of probation that defendant not consume any alcohol or illegal drugs was invalid as to alcohol but valid as to illegal drugs. Pratt v. State, App. 2 Dist., 601 So.2d 619 (1992). Sentencing And Punishment ⚷ 1980(2)

Special condition of defendant's probation, which prohibited defendant from using intoxicants and from visiting places where intoxicants, drugs, or other dangerous substances were unlawfully sold, dispensed, or used, was improper where special condition was entered without oral pronouncement, was not statutorily mandated, and was not related to defendant's grand theft convictions. Thomas v. State, App. 2 Dist., 599 So.2d 262 (1992). Sentencing And Punishment ⚷ 1918; Sentencing And Punishment ⚷ 1980(2)

Conditions on community control and probation that drug defendant not possess or consume illegal drugs, associate with persons who use illegal drugs, or frequent places where illegal drugs are used were valid. Alvarez v. State, App. 2 Dist., 593 So.2d 289 (1992). Sentencing And Punishment ⚷ 1971(2); Sentencing And Punishment ⚷ 1980(2)

36. —— Drug and alcohol testing, generally, validity of conditions

Portion of probation condition stating that probationer would submit to alcohol and drug testing was statutory "general condition" of probation that did not need to be orally pronounced at sentencing. Torres v. State, App. 2 Dist., 712 So.2d 1169 (1998). Sentencing And Punishment ⚷ 1918

Probation condition and community control condition requiring defendant to submit to testing for controlled substances at any time requested by his probation or community control officer, or the professional staff of any treatment center, was statutorily authorized condition and thus, did not have to be orally announced at sentencing. Joly v. State, App. 2 Dist., 702 So.2d 569 (1997). Sentencing And Punishment ⚷ 1918

Probation condition requiring defendant to submit to alcohol and controlled substance testing would be modified to strike that portion which required him to pay for such testing. Washington v. State, App. 2 Dist., 685 So.2d 858 (1996). Sentencing And Punishment ⚷ 1996

Random substance abuse testing is statutorily authorized probation condition when the offense is for controlled substances and probation immediately follows incarceration. Scott v. State, App. 2 Dist., 681 So.2d 738 (1996). Sentencing And Punishment ⚷ 1996

Trial court could not require defendant to pay for random testing, drug/alcohol evaluation, and treatment as conditions of probation. McCoy v. State, App. 2 Dist., 675 So.2d 993 (1996). Sentencing And Punishment ⚷ 1975(2)

Sentencing court's statement placing defendant on drug offender probation did not also put defendant on constructive notice of special conditions imposed, i.e., that he attend and successfully complete rehabilitation program, that he submit to drug evaluation and treatment, that he pay for random drug testing to which he was to submit at probation officer's request, and that he not use or possess alcoholic beverages for any purpose; such conditions were not statutorily prescribed. Dean v. State, App. 4 Dist., 669 So.2d 1140 (1996). Sentencing And Punishment ⚷ 1918

Trial court was not required to pronounce orally at sentencing a condition of community control requiring probationer to submit to tests to determine use of alcohol, regardless of whether alcohol use had any relation to probationer's past criminal conduct or future criminality. Brock v. State, App. 1 Dist., 667 So.2d 1014 (1996), rehearing denied, review granted 676 So.2d 1368, approved 688 So.2d 909. Sentencing And Punishment ⚷ 1918

It was error for sentencing court to impose probation condition and community control condition requiring probationer to pay for random drug testing, where such conditions were not orally pronounced at sentencing hearing. Golden v. State, App. 2 Dist., 667 So.2d 933 (1996). Sentencing And Punishment ⚷ 1920

Condition of probation requiring probationer to submit to urinalysis, breathalyzer, or blood tests when requested was unobjectionable; however, portion of condition requiring probationer to pay for the test was a special condition that had to be pronounced orally at sentencing. Kirkland v. State, App. 1 Dist., 666 So.2d 974 (1996). Sentencing And Punishment ⚷ 1918

Conditions of probation requiring defendant to pay for cost of drug and alcohol evaluation as well as cost of any needed treatment and prohibiting defendant from using intoxicants to excess were special conditions of probation which trial court was required to pronounce orally at sentencing. Augustin v. State, App. 2 Dist., 666 So.2d 218 (1995), certiorari denied 116 S.Ct. 1692, 517 U.S. 1196, 134 L.Ed.2d 792. Sentencing And Punishment ⚷ 1918

Submission to drug/alcohol evaluation and counseling as directed by probation officer was appropriate condition of probation for defendant who pled nolo contendere to sale of controlled substance. Wheatley v. State, App. 1 Dist., 629 So.2d 896 (1993). Sentencing And Punishment ⚷ 1977(2)

Trial court in grand theft prosecution would be required to delete all references in probation order pertaining to consumption of alcohol or to testing or treatment for use of alcohol. Bryant v. State, App. 5 Dist., 622 So.2d 620 (1993). Sentencing And Punishment ⚷ 1977(2); Sentencing And Punishment ⚷ 1980(2)

While probation condition prohibiting use of illegal drugs by defendant convicted of grand theft and providing for random testing for such drugs was proper, there was no basis on record to require defendant to undergo drug offender probation or drug treatment. Bryant v. State, App. 5 Dist., 622 So.2d 620 (1993). Sentencing And Punishment ⚷ 1977(2); Sentencing And Punishment ⚷ 1980(2); Sentencing And Punishment ⚷ 1996

Probation condition that defendant not use intoxicants to excess did not give probation officer discretion to impose urinalysis testing requirements and it was improper to find defendant in violation of probation for failure to submit to urinalysis. Paterson v. State, App. 1 Dist., 612 So.2d 692 (1993). Sentencing And Punishment ⚷ 1996

Defendant could be ordered to receive drug evaluation, screening, and any necessary treatment as condition of probation, irrespective of whether condition reasonably related to defendant's battery and second-degree murder convictions. Navarre v. State, App. 1 Dist., 608 So.2d 525 (1992). Sentencing And Punishment ⚷ 1977(2)

Requiring defendant to submit to random drug screening was appropriate statutory condition of probation. Astolfo v. State, App. 2 Dist., 598 So.2d 314 (1992). Sentencing And Punishment ⚷ 1996

37. —— Defendant's expense, drug and alcohol testing, validity of conditions

Trial court could not impose special probationary condition of random drug testing at defendant's expense, where random drug testing was already valid general probationary condition. Walker v. State, App. 2 Dist., 662 So.2d 1352 (1995). Sentencing And Punishment ⚷ 1996

Portion of condition of probation that random drug testing of defendant be conducted at "defendant's own expense" had to be stricken since it was not authorized by statute that authorizes imposition of condition to submit for random drug testing. Williams v. State, App. 2 Dist., 661 So.2d 59 (1995). Sentencing And Punishment ⚷ 1996

38. —— Schedule of activities, validity of conditions

Trial court properly imposed, as condition of community control sentence, requirement that defendant submit schedule of his activities to his probation officer. Johnson v. State, App. 5 Dist., 636 So.2d 792 (1994). Sentencing And Punishment ⚷ 1969(2)

39. —— Lie detector tests, validity of conditions

Probation of defendant, who had pled nolo contendere in lewd act case, should not have been conditioned on his submission to periodic lie detector tests; lie detector tests were not reliable for forensic use, and it was improper delegation of court's fact-finding authority to rely on lie detector to establish whether crime had been committed. Hart v. State, App. 5 Dist., 633 So.2d 1189 (1994). Constitutional Law ⚷ 2570; Sentencing And Punishment ⚷ 1996

40. —— Contact with others, validity of conditions

Portion of defendant's probation order forbidding her to associate with "persons who use illegal drugs" was unenforceable because it was too vague and capable of unintentional violation. Wilson v. State, App. 2 Dist., 857 So.2d 223 (2003), rehearing denied. Sentencing And Punishment ⚷ 1971(2)

Sentencing court's oral pronouncement of probation condition was vague about type of visitation that defendant was allowed to have with minors; court needed to clarify visitation that defendant was allowed to have with his own son, with minor relatives, and with other children who were not related to defendant, and needed to indicate whether visitation was to be supervised and, if so, who needed supervised visitation and who did not. McCord v. State, App. 3 Dist., 679 So.2d 32 (1996). Sentencing And Punishment ⚷ 1971(3)

Restricting contact of lewd assault defendant with persons under age 21 while defendant was on probation unduly restricted defendant's contacts with adults and, thus, condition of probation was amended to prohibit contact with persons under 18 years of age without written permission from probation officer. Sturgeon v. State, App. 2 Dist., 582 So.2d 746 (1991). Sentencing And Punishment ⚷ 1971(2)

41. —— Restricting ability to work, validity of conditions

Although special condition of probation prohibiting defendant, a licensed physician, from writing medical prescriptions while on probation impacted upon a fundamental, constitutional right, i.e., the right to earn one's livelihood by any lawful calling, condition did not abrogate such right and thus an attack on grounds of overbreadth was not appropriate. McPike v. State, App. 2 Dist., 473 So.2d 291 (1985). Sentencing And Punishment ⚷ 1972(2)

42. —— Newspaper advertisements, validity of conditions

Requirement that defendant place DUI news ad in newspaper consisting of his mug shot, name and caption "DUI-convicted" as condition of probation did not violate rehabilitational purpose; rehabilitation and punishment are not mutually exclusive ideas and can co-exist in any single, particular consequence of conviction without robbing one another of effect. Lindsay v. State, App. 4 Dist., 606 So.2d 652 (1992), review denied 618 So.2d 209. Sentencing And Punishment ⚷ 1983(2)

As condition of probation, a requirement that defendant place ad in newspaper showing his mug shot, name and caption "DUI-convicted" had reasonable relationship between defendant's conduct of driving while under influence of alcoholic beverages; humiliation arising from publicizing of fact of conviction had apparent logical connection with deterring criminal conduct. Lindsay v. State, App. 4 Dist., 606 So.2d 652 (1992), review denied 618 So.2d 209. Sentencing And Punishment ⚷ 1983(2)

Mere fact that defendant, as condition of probation, must place ad in newspaper containing his mug shot, his name and caption "DUI-convicted" while next offender does not have condition imposed upon him is no basis to strike down all impositions of this condition; there was some basis to deem this "first" DUI offense more than mere indiscretion as defendant was so impaired by alcohol that he ran his vehicle into the rear of a police car, his blood alcohol level was very high, and he continued his alcohol consumption after he took control of vehicle and operated it with open can of beer in hand. Lindsay v. State, App. 4 Dist., 606 So.2d 652 (1992), review denied 618 So.2d 209. Sentencing And Punishment ⚷ 1983(2)

43. —— Drug offenders, validity of conditions

Like defendant placed on regular probation or community control, defendant placed on drug offender probation is on constructive notice that some or all of standard conditions of probation listed in statute may be imposed by judge and, thus, oral pronouncement of standard conditions, in either case, is not required. Mosley v. State, App. 4 Dist., 677 So.2d 27 (1996), rehearing denied. Sentencing And Punishment ⚷ 1918

Two-year drug offender probation was legal condition of probation and not so egregious as to constitute fundamental error, so that defendant's failure to object on the grounds that there was no nexus between that condition and defendant's offense precluded consideration of the claim on appeal. McCarthren v. State, App. 5 Dist., 635 So.2d 1005 (1994). Criminal Law ⚷ 1042.3(4); Sentencing And Punishment ⚷ 1980(2)

44. —— Parental rights, validity of conditions

Condition of community control requiring juvenile offender to obey all lawful and reasonable demands of his mother, including participation in church youth programs, did not violate juvenile's rights under First Amendment to United States Constitution and free exercise of religion provision of State Constitution; inherent in parents' authority and control over their unemancipated child living in parents' household is parents' right to require that child attend church with them as part of child's religious and moral training. L.M. v. State, App. 1 Dist., 610 So.2d 1314 (1992). Constitutional Law ⚷ 1428; Infants ⚷ 225

45. —— Accounting of activities, validity of conditions

Defendant could not be required to maintain hourly accounting of activities in daily log as provision of community control order where condition was not pronounced orally at sentencing and was not authorized by statute. Palag v. State, App. 1 Dist., 622 So.2d 1151 (1993). Sentencing And Punishment ⚷ 1918; Sentencing And Punishment ⚷ 1983(2)

46. —— Support of stepchildren, validity of conditions

Condition of probation order requiring probationer to support his two stepdaughters had to be stricken, even though probationers may be required to support their legal dependents, since there is no legal duty to prove support for minor who is not natural or adopted and for whom care has not be contracted. Vernon v. State, App. 1 Dist., 618 So.2d 369 (1993). Sentencing And Punishment ⚷ 1983(2)

47. —— Attorneys' fees, validity of conditions

Court of Appeals would strike imposition of attorney fees for defendant's court-appointed attorney as special condition of probation; trial court never addressed issue of attorney fees in connection with case for which probation was imposed, no amount was determined, and court made no announcement about fees in that case. Galicia v. State, App. 2 Dist., 685 So.2d 850 (1995). Sentencing And Punishment ⚷ 1921

Probation condition imposing $100 state's attorney's fee against defendant was not statutorily authorized as "investigative costs incurred by law enforcement agencies" as cost of prosecution, but was an award of attorney fees for which there was no statutory rule or authorization. Turkaly v. State, App. 5 Dist., 615 So.2d 222 (1993). Costs ⚷ 308; Sentencing And Punishment ⚷ 1975(2)

48. —— Residency requirements, validity of conditions

Committing defendant to probation restitution center for indefinite period of time was error, as such placement may not exceed 364 days. Nelson v. State, App. 4 Dist., 669 So.2d 1145 (1996). Sentencing And Punishment ⚷ 1976(2)

Special condition of probation which prohibited probationer from living in particular area of city was sufficiently clear and informed person of reasonable intelligence what conduct was prohibited; condition was detailed and specific and set forth particular area where probationer was prohibited from living. Baker v. State, App. 2 Dist., 609 So.2d 167 (1992). Sentencing And Punishment ⚷ 1967(2)

49. —— Oral conditions, validity of conditions

Condition of probation prohibiting defendant from visiting "places where intoxicants, drugs, or other dangerous substances are unlawfully sold, dispensed, or used" was a general condition that was not required to be pronounced orally at sentencing in order to be included in written order; condition was more precise definition of statutory condition prohibiting association with persons engaged in criminal activities. Nank v. State, App. 2 Dist., 646 So.2d 762 (1994), rehearing denied. Sentencing And Punishment ⚷ 1918

50. Clarity of conditions

Sentence of probation, for defendant convicted of grand theft, which carried condition that defendant submit to deposition by representative of victim's insurer, was required to be remanded for further clarification; trial court had not provided guidance as to whether appearance at deposition, which insurer had indicated would be designed to discover what "really happened" to money taken from victim, would have impact on defendant's right to be free from self-incrimination. Sarrain v. State, App. 3 Dist., 632 So.2d 1063 (1994). Criminal Law ⚷ 1181.5(8); Sentencing And Punishment ⚷ 1970(2)

Condition of probation order requiring defendant to "forfeit all weapons or tools" was vague and should be stricken. Zachary v. State, App. 2 Dist., 559 So.2d 105 (1990). Sentencing And Punishment ⚷ 1983(2)

At sentencing, trial judge should clearly delineate all terms upon which he deems it necessary to condition probation and defendant should clearly state of record his objections and refusal to accept conditions of probation, failing which he should be deemed to have accepted such conditions. Bentley v. State, App. 5 Dist., 411 So.2d 1361 (1982), review denied 419 So.2d 1195. Sentencing And Punishment ⚿ 1918; Sentencing And Punishment ⚿ 1922

A probation order must sufficiently instruct probationer as to what he must do or refrain from doing while on probation. Mastick v. State, App. 3 Dist., 409 So.2d 203 (1982). Sentencing And Punishment ⚿ 1918

Probation condition that defendant "live honorably," imposed after she pleaded nolo contendere to larceny charge that she failed to report her receipt of unemployment compensation on reapplications for welfare as required, had to be stricken. Smith v. State, App. 4 Dist., 383 So.2d 959 (1980). Sentencing And Punishment ⚿ 1966(2)

Condition of probation requiring a probationer to live honorably is too vague and uncertain to apprise him of the type of conduct which would give rise to a violation of his probation, and, thus, if properly challenged, such a condition should be stricken. Norris v. State, App. 4 Dist., 383 So.2d 691 (1980), petition for review denied 388 So.2d 1116. Sentencing And Punishment ⚿ 1966(3)

Terms and conditions of probation were sufficiently set forth where defendant signed an instrument setting forth conditions of probation in three other cases and the body of this instrument referred to instant case and required restitution of money obtained in instant case. Pickman v. State, App. 3 Dist., 155 So.2d 646 (1963), certiorari denied 164 So.2d 805. Sentencing And Punishment ⚿ 1918

51. Interpretation of conditions

Probationary conditions were to be interpreted under common sense standard and would justify revocation of probation only if violation was willful. Villabol v. State, App. 2 Dist., 595 So.2d 1057 (1992), review denied 604 So.2d 489. Sentencing And Punishment ⚿ 2003

52. Reasonable conditions

Probation conditions relating to curfew, warrantless searches, driving, and use of post office box were statutorily-authorized general conditions, not special conditions, and conditions were valid as rationally related to state's broad interest in supervision and rehabilitation of offenders. Greenwood v. State, App. 1 Dist., 754 So.2d 158 (2000). Sentencing And Punishment ⚿ 1979(2); Sentencing And Punishment ⚿ 1983(2); Sentencing And Punishment ⚿ 1993

Sentencing court must not impose conditions of probation which are overbroad and can be violated unintentionally. Hughes v. State, App. 4 Dist., 667 So.2d 910 (1996), rehearing denied, review denied 676 So.2d 413. Sentencing And Punishment ⚿ 1965

Trial court may impose reasonable conditions of probation which relate to offense involved, tend to insure rehabilitation of prisoner, or protection of public; trial court, however, is not authorized to restrict unnecessarily valid exercise of valuable right or to impose conditions of probation which are overbroad. Williams v. State, App. 2 Dist., 661 So.2d 59 (1995). Sentencing And Punishment ⚿ 1963

Condition of probation or community control is valid so long as it is reasonably related to offense, to rehabilitation of defendant, or to protection of public. Cassamassima v. State, App. 5 Dist., 657 So.2d 906 (1995), certification denied. Sentencing And Punishment ⚿ 1963

Condition of probation should reasonably relate to offense involved, rehabilitation of defendant, or protection of public. Brown v. State, App. 4 Dist., 406 So.2d 1262 (1981). Sentencing And Punishment ⚿ 1963

To be valid, conditions of probation should be reasonably related to the offense involved, rehabilitation of the defendant or the protection of the public. Dearth v. State, App. 4 Dist., 390 So.2d 108 (1980). Sentencing And Punishment ⚿ 1963

Condition of probation that is reasonably related to crime for which offender has been convicted and that is directed to reasonable restraint of activity in order to diminish inclination to commit similar crimes is proper and therefore not an abuse of discretion. Russell v. State, App. 3 Dist., 342 So.2d 96 (1977). Sentencing And Punishment ⚿ 1963

53. Relationship of crime to condition—In general

Traditionally, whether a probation condition is a general condition or a special condition is determined by reference to the applicable statute and rule of criminal procedure; conditions which appear in neither the statute nor the rule are considered special and must be orally pronounced. Cole v. State, App. 4 Dist., 932 So.2d 1123 (2006). Sentencing And Punishment ⚿ 1918

When a question is raised concerning the relevancy of a special condition or probation, the record must support the imposition of the condition. Saidi v. State, App. 5 Dist., 845 So.2d 1022 (2003). Sentencing And Punishment ⚿ 1963

As a general rule, there must be a reasonable nexus between any special condition of probation and the crime committed by the offender. Saidi v. State, App. 5 Dist., 845 So.2d 1022 (2003). Sentencing And Punishment ⚷ 1963

Special conditions of probation or community control must reasonably relate to defendant's present criminal conduct or future criminality, or pertain to conduct which is itself criminal. Brock v. State, 688 So.2d 909 (1997). Sentencing And Punishment ⚷ 1963

Trial court may validly impose upon defendant general conditions of community control that are rationally related to state's need to supervise defendant regardless of whether condition is reasonably related to defendant's offense or restricts conduct which is not itself criminal. Brock v. State, 688 So.2d 909 (1997). Sentencing And Punishment ⚷ 1963

Special condition of probation is invalid if it has no relationship to crime of which offender was convicted, relates to conduct which is not in itself criminal, and requires or forbids conduct which is not reasonably related to future criminality, and special condition that is challenged on relevancy grounds will be upheld only if one of these circumstances is supported by the record. Madrigal v. State, App. 4 Dist., 683 So.2d 1093 (1996). Sentencing And Punishment ⚷ 1963

Imposition of special condition of probation which required defendant, who had been convicted of assault and weapons charges, to remain outside the United States was improper; condition did not relate to offenses of which defendant was convicted or future criminality, as no showing was made that defendant's presence in country was itself criminal. Madrigal v. State, App. 4 Dist., 683 So.2d 1093 (1996). Sentencing And Punishment ⚷ 1968(2)

Special condition of probation is constitutional if it bears relationship to crime for which offender is convicted, relates to conduct which is in itself criminal, or requires or forbids conduct which is reasonably related to future criminality. M.C.L. v. State, App. 1 Dist., 682 So.2d 1209 (1996). Sentencing And Punishment ⚷ 1963

Special condition of probation will be upheld, when challenged on grounds of relevancy, unless it has no relationship to crime of which offender was convicted, relates to conduct that is not in itself criminal, or requires or forbids conduct that is not reasonably related to future criminality. Fernandez v. State, App. 4 Dist., 677 So.2d 332 (1996), review dismissed 683 So.2d 485. Sentencing And Punishment ⚷ 1963

Condition of probation is invalid as not reasonably related to rehabilitation if it has no relationship to crime of which defendant was convicted, relates to conduct which is not in itself criminal, and requires or forbids conduct which is not reasonably related to future criminality. Zeigler v. State, App. 4 Dist., 647 So.2d 272 (1994). Sentencing And Punishment ⚷ 1963

If objection is lodged, special condition of probation will later be held invalid as not reasonably related to rehabilitation if it has no relationship to crime of which offender was convicted, relates to conduct which is not in itself criminal, and requires or forbids conduct which is not reasonably related to future criminality. Nank v. State, App. 2 Dist., 646 So.2d 762 (1994), rehearing denied. Sentencing And Punishment ⚷ 1963

When question is raised concerning relevancy of condition of probation, record must support imposition of condition by showing nexus between the condition and the crime. McCarthren v. State, App. 5 Dist., 635 So.2d 1005 (1994). Sentencing And Punishment ⚷ 1963

Fact that defendant had three-year-old conviction for possession of cocaine was too remote to show nexus between offenses of grand theft and resisting merchandise recovery and drug offender probation condition. McCarthren v. State, App. 5 Dist., 635 So.2d 1005 (1994). Sentencing And Punishment ⚷ 1980(2)

Condition of probation is invalid if it has no relation to crime, relates to conduct which is not in itself criminal, and requires or forbids conduct not reasonably related to future criminal activity. Priest v. State, App. 2 Dist., 626 So.2d 1005 (1993). Sentencing And Punishment ⚷ 1963

Rule that conditions of probation are not limited to those having some relationship to exact crime which resulted in probation but are proper to achieve any of the lawful purposes of the probation also applies to conditions of community control in juvenile cases. M.A.R. v. State, App. 5 Dist., 433 So.2d 29 (1983), petition for review denied 441 So.2d 632. Infants ⚷ 223.1

Condition of probation is invalid if it has no relationship to crime of which offender was convicted, relates to conduct which is not in itself criminal and requires or forbids conduct which is not reasonably related to future criminality. Bodden v. State, App. 1 Dist., 411 So.2d 1391 (1982). Sentencing And Punishment ⚷ 1963

This section authorizing sentencing court to impose nine enumerated conditions of probation in every case implies that there need be no relationship between conditions of probation as such and particular crime of which probationer stands convicted. Bentley v. State, App. 5 Dist., 411 So.2d 1361 (1982), review denied 419 So.2d 1195. Sentencing And Punishment ⚷ 1963

Condition of probation is invalid if it has no relationship to crime of which offender was convicted, relates to conduct which is not in itself criminal, or requires or forbids conduct which is not reasonably related to future criminality. Rodriguez v. State, App. 2 Dist., 378 So.2d 7 (1979). Sentencing And Punishment ⚷ 1963

Probation conditions must be reasonably related to offense and should provide standard of conduct essential to probationer's rehabilitation in addition to protection of public. Grubbs v. State, 373 So.2d 905 (1979). Sentencing And Punishment ⚷ 1963

54. —— Alcohol consumption, relationship of crime to condition

Probation condition that probationer not use intoxicants to excess was invalid, where condition was not reasonably related to rehabilitation and did not relate to underlying offense or to commission of future crimes. Hayes v. State, App. 4 Dist., 665 So.2d 339 (1995). Sentencing And Punishment ⚷ 1980(2)

Requirement that defendant refrain from excessive use of alcohol was inappropriate condition of probation, in light of facts that alcohol use was not related to crime of aggravated battery for which defendant had been convicted, was not in itself criminal, and was not reasonably related to future criminality. Godley v. State, App. 2 Dist., 659 So.2d 447 (1995). Sentencing And Punishment ⚷ 1980(2)

Condition of probation that defendant use no alcohol was not reasonably related to offenses or defendant's rehabilitation. Lambert v. State, App. 4 Dist., 635 So.2d 93 (1994). Sentencing And Punishment ⚷ 1980(2)

Condition of probation restricting use of alcohol may not be imposed when such use is not related to any of probationer's offense and nothing in record indicates that use of alcohol would relate to future criminality. Nunez v. State, App. 2 Dist., 633 So.2d 1146 (1994). Sentencing And Punishment ⚷ 1980(2)

Probation condition, that defendant consume no alcoholic beverages, was invalid where there was no evidence that offense was alcohol related; defendant was convicted of purchasing cocaine. Gomez-Rodriqueq v. State, App. 5 Dist., 632 So.2d 709 (1994). Sentencing And Punishment ⚷ 1980(2)

Special probation condition and alcohol restriction had to be stricken as being unrelated to conviction for attempted sexual battery on a child under twelve. Hernandez v. State, App. 2 Dist., 626 So.2d 1011 (1993). Sentencing And Punishment ⚷ 1980(2)

Trial court could not impose upon defendant convicted of aggravated assault probation which included requirement that he refrain from consuming any alcohol and from entering any bar or liquor lounge without permission from his probation officer; requirement was not related to crime involved. MacIntyre v. State, App. 5 Dist., 625 So.2d 118 (1993). Sentencing And Punishment ⚷ 1980(2)

Probation conditions that prohibited defendant from entering bar or liquor lounge without permission from probation officer and from consuming alcohol were invalid; conditions had no relation to crimes of cocaine possession, and prohibited behavior was not reasonably related to future criminality. Grate v. State, App. 5 Dist., 623 So.2d 591 (1993). Sentencing And Punishment ⚷ 1980(2)

Condition of probation which forbade use of alcohol or frequenting places where alcohol is the main source of business was invalid, considering that condition was not related to crime of possession of cannabis with intent to sell of which defendant was convicted, consumption of alcohol is not illegal, and use of alcohol was not reasonably related to future criminality. Richardson v. State, App. 2 Dist., 620 So.2d 257 (1993). Sentencing And Punishment ⚷ 1980(2)

Requirement that defendant not use or possess alcoholic beverages should not have been included as special condition of probation in sentencing defendant for carrying concealed firearm and carrying concealed weapon, where there was nothing connecting any use of alcohol with crimes of conviction, and there was nothing in record which would suggest that defendant had propensity toward alcohol or that his judgment became impaired as consequence of using it. Biller v. State, 618 So.2d 734 (1993). Sentencing And Punishment ⚷ 1980(2)

Conditions of probation which related to probationer's consumption of or presence around alcohol were invalid as they were not reasonably related to offense of burglary of dwelling with assault or battery. Baker v. State, App. 2 Dist., 609 So.2d 167 (1992). Sentencing And Punishment ⚷ 1980(2)

Trial court could not impose, as conditions of probation for robbery and kidnapping violations, requirement that defendant's consumption of alcohol be restricted and that he be prohibited from visiting premises upon which alcohol was served; conditions bore no reasonable relation to offenses for which he was committed. Beckner v. State, App. 2 Dist., 604 So.2d 842 (1992). Sentencing And Punishment ⚷ 1980(2)

Condition of probation relating to alcohol consumption was improperly imposed where it was not reasonably related to crimes of sexual battery of child and lewd and lascivious or indecent act upon child under age of 16 of which defendant was convicted. Sanchez v. State, App. 2 Dist., 600 So.2d 1256 (1992). Sentencing And Punishment ⚷ 1980(2)

The conditions of defendant's probation must be stricken to the extent they relate to the consumption of alcohol and bar defendant from places where alcohol is sold or served, where these conditions did not reasonably relate to the crimes for which defendant was convicted. Wright v. State, App. 2 Dist., 599 So.2d 767 (1992). Sentencing And Punishment ⚷ 1980(2)

Conditions of probation pertaining to consumption of alcohol and barring defendant from premises on which alcohol would be served did not reasonably relate to convictions for burglary of dwelling and grand theft and, thus, could not stand. Pope v. State, App. 2 Dist., 598 So.2d 309 (1992). Sentencing And Punishment ⚷ 1980(2)

Conditions of probation relating to alcohol and drug use, evaluation, and treatment, except those portions of conditions relating to prohibition from using or possessing illegal narcotics, marijuana, or drugs, would be stricken on ground that they were unrelated to defendant's offense of theft of motorcycle. Smith v. State, App. 2 Dist., 589 So.2d 423 (1991). Sentencing And Punishment ⚷ 1977(2); Sentencing And Punishment ⚷ 1980(2)

Probation condition prohibiting probationer from using intoxicants to excess or visiting places serving intoxicants, drugs or other substances, and condition prohibiting probationer from visiting restaurants or bars where alcohol was served would be stricken, as conditions were not reasonably related to grand theft, and record did not indicate that probationer had a problem with substance abuse. Daniels v. State, App. 2 Dist., 583 So.2d 423 (1991). Sentencing And Punishment ⚷ 1980(2)

Condition of defendant's probation—that he visit no bars, restaurants, or any other place where alcoholic beverages are served without written permission from probation officer after consent from judge—was unrelated to crime of trafficking in cocaine for which defendant was convicted, related to conduct that was not itself criminal, and delegated impermissible authority to probation officer and would thus be stricken. Edmunds v. State, App. 2 Dist., 559 So.2d 415 (1990). Constitutional Law ⚷ 2574; Sentencing And Punishment ⚷ 1980(2)

55. —— Drug and alcohol testing and treatment, relationship of crime to condition

Defendant could properly be required to undergo random drug and alcohol testing and substance abuse evaluation as condition of probation imposed following his convictions for accessory after the fact to robbery and possession of a motor vehicle, as his convictions related to drug or alcohol abuse. Fennell v. State, App. 2 Dist., 694 So.2d 873 (1997). Sentencing And Punishment ⚷ 1996

Trial court had authority, as general condition of placing probationer on community control, to order probationer to submit to random drug and alcohol testing even if substance use was not related to present offense or future criminality. Brock v. State, 688 So.2d 909 (1997). Sentencing And Punishment ⚷ 1996

Condition of probation requiring defendant to submit to drug evaluation and screening was not improper on ground it was not reasonably related to second-degree murder and battery offenses, as it is standard condition of probation that can be imposed on any probationer, irrespective of whether it reasonably relates to type of offense. West's F.S.A. § 948.03(1)(j). Curry v. State, 682 So.2d 1091 (1996). Sentencing And Punishment ⚷ 1977(2)

Defendant could not be required to undergo random alcohol testing as a condition of probation, where requirement failed to be reasonably related to rehabilitation of defendant, bore no relationship to crime for which defendant was convicted, and related to conduct that was otherwise legal. Brown v. State, App. 4 Dist., 679 So.2d 367 (1996). Sentencing And Punishment ⚷ 1996

Trial court erred in imposing condition of probation requiring defendant to get a drug evaluation and attend weekly alcohol or drug abuse treatment group meetings where nothing in the record indicated that defendant's crime was reasonably related to the use of intoxicants or illegal substances. Carter v. State, App. 4 Dist., 677 So.2d 1349 (1996). Sentencing And Punishment ⚷ 1977(2)

Condition of probation that defendant submit to random testing for alcohol, although statutorily authorized, served no discernible purpose and thus was improper, where defendant was not prohibited from using alcohol and there was nothing to suggest that defendant had alcohol problem or that use of alcohol bore reasonable relationship to nature of crime. Fernandez v. State, App. 4 Dist., 677 So.2d 332 (1996), review dismissed 683 So.2d 485. Sentencing And Punishment ⚷ 1996

Condition of probation that defendant submit to random testing for illegal substances was valid condition that did not need to be scrutinized on case-by-case basis for relevancy, as testing could be said to be related to conduct which is itself criminal, related to future criminality, or otherwise directed toward rehabilitation. Fernandez v. State, App. 4 Dist., 677

So.2d 332 (1996), review dismissed 683 So.2d 485. Sentencing And Punishment ⚷ 1996

Trial court had authority, as condition of placing probation on community control, to order probationer to submit to random alcohol and drug testing even though drug and alcohol use were not demonstrably related to past criminal conduct or future criminality. Brock v. State, App. 1 Dist., 667 So.2d 1014 (1996), rehearing denied, review granted 676 So.2d 1368, approved 688 So.2d 909. Sentencing And Punishment ⚷ 1996

Trial court was not authorized, in sentencing defendant for offense which was not alcohol or drug related, to impose special conditions of probation requiring defendant to submit to drug evaluation and treatment and abide by treatment center rules, regulations, and programs. Turner v. State, App. 2 Dist., 666 So.2d 212 (1995). Sentencing And Punishment ⚷ 1977(2)

Special condition of probation, that defendant would receive a substance abuse evaluation and treatment and bear the cost of the same, was invalid in prosecution for burglary of a structure and petit theft; condition did not have relationship to crime of which defendant was convicted, did not relate to conduct that was in itself criminal, or did not require or forbid conduct that was reasonably related to future criminality. Bell v. State, App. 4 Dist., 652 So.2d 1192 (1995). Sentencing And Punishment ⚷ 1977(2)

Requirement that defendant submit to random drug testing as condition of probation may be imposed regardless of whether it directly related to circumstances of defendant's offense. Hayes v. State, App. 1 Dist., 585 So.2d 397 (1991), review denied 593 So.2d 1052. Sentencing And Punishment ⚷ 1996

Conditions of probation imposed on defendant convicted of possession of controlled substance that he submit to urinalysis testing and that he not use intoxicants in excess were reasonably related to the offense. Rowland v. State, App. 1 Dist., 548 So.2d 812 (1989). Sentencing And Punishment ⚷ 1980(2); Sentencing And Punishment ⚷ 1996

56. —— Paternity testing, relationship of crime to condition

Defendant could not be required, as a condition of probation, to submit to testing and other procedures concerning his alleged paternity of a child; alleged paternity was completely unrelated to offense for which defendant was convicted, and paternity proceedings could not be ordered as an incident of statutory directive that defendant be directed to support legal dependents. Washington v. State, App. 4 Dist., 529 So.2d 356 (1988). Sentencing And Punishment ⚷ 1996

57. —— Possession of firearms, relationship of crime to condition

Special conditions of probation imposed on defendant for insurance fraud and making false report to law enforcement prohibiting defendant from possessing firearms and using intoxicants excessively were invalid; conditions were unrelated to insurance fraud, were not criminal activities, and did not relate to future criminality. Bourget v. State, App. 2 Dist., 634 So.2d 1109 (1994). Sentencing And Punishment ⚷ 1980(2); Sentencing And Punishment ⚷ 1981(2)

58. —— Clothing or attire, relationship of crime to condition

Condition should not have been placed on juvenile's community control forbidding him to wear jewelry, where that condition was unrelated to both charges and rehabilitation. In Interest of J.C.S., App. 4 Dist., 560 So.2d 426 (1990). Infants ⚷ 223.1

59. —— Contact with victim, relationship of crime to condition

Special condition of probation which precludes contact between perpetrator of sexual crime and his or her victim bears reasonable relation to future criminality, rendering condition valid, especially where familial relationship provided opportunity for past criminal incident. Jano v. State, App. 4 Dist., 559 So.2d 1270 (1990). Sentencing And Punishment ⚷ 1971(2)

Trial court could impose special condition of probation prohibiting defendant from having any contact with victim, who was nine-year-old daughter of defendant's girl friend, or any member of victim's family, even though defendant's own six-year-old daughter lived in same household as victim and was apparently related to victim. Russ v. State, App. 1 Dist., 519 So.2d 715 (1988). Sentencing And Punishment ⚷ 1971(2)

Conditions of probation prohibiting defendant from having contact with his child and from residing with a minor child under age of 16 were valid where defendant was convicted of negligent abuse of his child, since the conditions were reasonably related to the crime and to defendant's future criminality. Howland v. State, App. 1 Dist., 420 So.2d 918 (1982). Sentencing And Punishment ⚷ 1971(2)

60. —— Limitations on sexual relations, relationship of crime to condition

Requirement that defendant not father any children during probation period was struck from conditions of his probation. Burchell v. State, App. 2 Dist., 419 So.2d 358 (1982). Sentencing And Punishment ⚷ 1983(2)

Condition of probation of defendants, who were respectively convicted of forgery, uttering a forged instrument, and burglary of a structure, that prohibited sexual intercourse with individuals other than his or her lawfully married spouse, was invalid for failure to meet the test requiring that a condition of probation be "reasonably related" to rehabilitation, in that condition bore only a tangential relationship to underlying crimes, related to conduct not itself criminal, and required marriage and forbade extramarital sex, both of which were not reasonably related to curtailing defendants' necessity to steal to support their illegitimate children. Wiggins v. State, App. 4 Dist., 386 So.2d 46 (1980). Sentencing And Punishment ⚷ 1983(2)

61. —— Cohabitation, relationship of crime to condition

Where defendant violated prior probation by following former girlfriend and her daughter, special condition of probation that defendant not live with female unless married or related to her was invalid, as it was not related to defendant's criminal conduct and did not prohibit conduct which was criminal in itself or related to future criminal conduct. Stephens v. State, App. 1 Dist., 659 So.2d 1303 (1995). Sentencing And Punishment ⚷ 2040

Condition of probation that defendant not live with a member of the opposite sex was invalid as not relating to defendant's crime of burglary or reasonably tailored to prevent future criminal conduct. Huff v. State, App. 2 Dist., 554 So.2d 616 (1989). Sentencing And Punishment ⚷ 1971(2)

62. —— Waiver of confidentiality, relationship of crime to condition

Probation condition that defendant "will waive confidentiality" had to be stricken, since nothing in record indicated that condition was related to offenses charged of robbery and attempted robbery, and even if some how related, condition was overbroad and may have applied to certain privileges of confidentiality which were unconnected to those offenses. Williams v. State, App. 2 Dist., 661 So.2d 59 (1995). Sentencing And Punishment ⚷ 1983(2)

63. —— Ban on conceiving children, relationship of crime to condition

Imposition of special condition of probation, that defendant, convicted of stealing, not become pregnant during her term of probation unless she was married, was grossly erroneous on its face as bearing no relationship to offense for which defendant was convicted, relating to conduct which was not itself criminal, and requiring or forbidding conduct which was not reasonably related to future criminality, and in interest of justice special condition would be stricken from probation order. Thomas v. State, App. 1 Dist., 519 So.2d 1113 (1988). Sentencing And Punishment ⚷ 1983(2)

Condition of probation prohibiting defendant from fathering a child was invalid where defendant was convicted of child abuse, since condition did not reasonably relate to the crime and related to noncriminal conduct, and since condition could not reasonably relate to future criminality given other conditions prohibiting defendant from having contact with his child or from residing with minor children under the age of 16. Howland v. State, App. 1 Dist., 420 So.2d 918 (1982). Sentencing And Punishment ⚷ 1983(2)

Probation condition prohibiting custody of any children had clear relationship to the crime of child abuse of which probationer had been convicted and was therefore valid and applied to expected child conceived prior to probation order, but conditions prohibiting marriage and pregnancy added nothing to decrease the possibility of further child abuse or other criminality and were invalid. Rodriguez v. State, App. 2 Dist., 378 So.2d 7 (1979). Sentencing And Punishment ⚷ 1983(2)

64. —— Financial restrictions, relationship of crime to condition

Where, in prosecution for obtaining property of value by means of worthless checks, evidence showed that defendant had drinking problem and was generally inattentive in his check writing when he was drinking, probation conditions that defendant not have checking account, that he not be in possession of blank checks, and that he submit to physical examination for presence of drugs upon request of any probation supervisor or law enforcement officer were not unduly harsh and restrictive, but were reasonably related to offense and provided standard of conduct essentially promoting defendant's rehabilitation in addition to protection of public. Wood v. State, App. 5 Dist., 378 So.2d 110 (1980). Sentencing And Punishment ⚷ 1983(2); Sentencing And Punishment ⚷ 1996

65. —— Contact with others, relationship of crime to condition

Probation condition, which prohibited probationer from having contact with purported father of her child, was directed against probationer individually with intention of preventing further assistance to aid escape of incarcerated father, was not restriction against contact between child and father, and was reasonably related to goal of rehabilitation after conviction for aiding escape of father. Mitchell v. State, App. 1 Dist., 516 So.2d 1120 (1987). Sentencing And Punishment ⚷ 1971(2)

66. —— Ban on legal work, relationship of crime to condition

Condition of probation prohibiting defendant who was member of out-of-state bar from "being affiliated with the legal profession" was not reasonably related to offense of grand theft or defendant's rehabilitation. Pratt v. State, App. 2 Dist., 516 So.2d 328 (1987). Sentencing And Punishment ⚷ 1972(2)

67. —— Use of intoxicants, relationship of crime to condition

A probation condition limiting defendant from using intoxicants to excess is not subject to an analysis of whether it is related to the crime charged or to defendant's rehabilitation. Carter v. State, App. 4 Dist., 677 So.2d 1349 (1996). Sentencing And Punishment ⚷ 1980(2)

Condition of probation prohibiting possession and consumption of alcohol, frequenting places where alcohol was main source of business, and association with persons who consumed alcohol was not related to defendant's offenses of possession of cannabis and possession of methamphetamine, and thus was invalid. Gerstenberger v. State, App. 2 Dist., 667 So.2d 1009 (1996). Sentencing And Punishment ⚷ 1971(2); Sentencing And Punishment ⚷ 1980(2)

Special condition prohibiting defendant from using any intoxicants or using intoxicants to excess was not reasonably related to underlying offense of unemployment compensation fraud and, therefore, should not have been imposed. Jackson v. State, App. 4 Dist., 654 So.2d 234 (1995), rehearing denied. Sentencing And Punishment ⚷ 1980(2)

Condition of probation prohibiting attempted murder and armed robbery defendant from using intoxicants was invalid as not reasonably related to rehabilitation in absence of evidence relating condition to crimes for which defendant was convicted. Zeigler v. State, App. 4 Dist., 647 So.2d 272 (1994). Sentencing And Punishment ⚷ 1980(2)

68. —— Educational requirements, relationship of crime to condition

Condition of probation requiring defendant, who had pled guilty to burglary of conveyance and petit theft, to enroll in and successfully complete courses to obtain his Graduate Equivalency Diploma was invalid; condition was not reasonably related to defendant's crime, and compliance might have been impossible. Colburn v. State, App. 2 Dist., 510 So.2d 652 (1987). Sentencing And Punishment ⚷ 1983(2)

69. —— Pornography, relationship of crime to condition

Possessing pornography involving adults did not support revocation of probation imposed for possessing child pornography in the absence of evidence establishing a rational relationship between the pornographic, obscene, or sexually stimulating materials and the probationer's deviant behavior pattern; the trial court did not make any findings describing the nature of the material, its content, and how it related or was relevant to, the deviant behavior pattern. Sellers v. State, App. 5 Dist., 16 So.3d 225 (2009). Sentencing and Punishment ⚷ 1983(3)

70. Excessive conditions

Fine of $547 and sentence of 15 days' imprisonment as a condition of six months' probation were impermissibly excessive for violating city ordinance which provided for a maximum sentence of 60 days in jail and a $500 fine. Pridgen v. City of Auburndale, App. 2 Dist., 430 So.2d 967 (1983). Municipal Corporations ⚷ 643

Prison term of two years imposed on defendant as condition of 15-year probation was excessive. Smith v. State, App. 2 Dist., 396 So.2d 206 (1981). Sentencing And Punishment ⚷ 1976(2)

Defendant, who was placed on probation on condition that she be imprisoned for 18 months and who was sentenced prior to state Supreme Court decision indicating that conditioning probation on incarceration in excess of one year was unlawful, was entitled to have the excessive incarceration condition invalidated, though she failed to object in trial court to its imposition. Gonzalez v. State, App. 3 Dist., 392 So.2d 334 (1981). Criminal Law ⚷ 1042.3(4)

Sentence of seven years' probation imposed upon defendant convicted of obtaining property by worthless check was excessive, and term of probation would be reduced to five years. Heatherly v. State, App. 4 Dist., 343 So.2d 54 (1977). Sentencing And Punishment ⚷ 1856

71. Punitive conditions

Trial court abused its discretion in prosecution for grand retail theft in imposing, as a special condition of probation, requirement that defendant purchase $160 worth of earrings from department store from which she had stolen approximately $160 worth of earrings and keep them in her possession during period of probation, since, in view of her financial circumstances, effect of condition was so punitive that it was unrelated to rehabilitation. Walker

v. State, App. 1 Dist., 461 So.2d 229 (1984). Sentencing And Punishment ⚷ 1983(2)

Special condition of probation which is so punitive that it is unrelated to rehabilitation cannot be imposed in lieu of sentence. Kominsky v. State, App. 1 Dist., 330 So.2d 800 (1976). Sentencing And Punishment ⚷ 1963

72. Addition or modification of conditions—In general

To determine whether a modification is an enhancement of probation, such that modification cannot be imposed absent proof of a violation, one must look to see whether the condition as changed is more restrictive than the original condition. Berchin v. State, App. 4 Dist., 938 So.2d 659 (2006). Sentencing And Punishment ⚷ 1952

Circuit court had authority to rule on probationer's emergency motion to modify probation by transferring him from one assisted living facility to another, without the state filing a warrant of violation of probation; modification was not an enhancement, as there was no indication that new facility was more restrictive than the current facility. Berchin v. State, App. 4 Dist., 938 So.2d 659 (2006). Sentencing And Punishment ⚷ 1950

Trial court may, at any time during probationary period, modify any probation conditions with caveat that court cannot enhance penalty, or add new conditions without proof of violation. Gearhart v. State, App. 5 Dist., 885 So.2d 415 (2004). Sentencing And Punishment ⚷ 1985

Special conditions of probation imposed for two counts of attempted capital sexual battery, which were conditions set forth in statute relating to sex offenses, were related to defendant's rehabilitation or protection of public. Williams v. State, App. 1 Dist., 879 So.2d 49 (2004), rehearing denied, review denied 894 So.2d 973. Sentencing And Punishment ⚷ 1971(2)

A trial court may at any time modify community control conditions it has previously imposed, but it cannot enhance the penalty or add new conditions. Garvison v. State, App. 2 Dist., 775 So.2d 340 (2000). Sentencing And Punishment ⚷ 1985

Generally, absent proof of violation, court may not subsequently enhance terms and conditions of probation. Green v. State, App. 4 Dist., 638 So.2d 1006 (1994). Sentencing And Punishment ⚷ 1923

Trial court's purported revocation of defendant's probation in seven cases and again placing him on probation subject to same conditions except that he was, in addition, to serve 11 months and 15 days in the county jail was illegal modification of defendant's probation resulting in imposition of special conditions which, when combined with one year originally imposed, exceeded 364 days, the maximum incarceration; trial court could either modify probation orders further by deleting special condition regarding jail time or withdraw probation orders and impose sentences of imprisonment consistent with Sentencing Guidelines, giving defendant credit for all time spent in jail. McDougal v. State, App. 1 Dist., 604 So.2d 896 (1992). Sentencing And Punishment ⚷ 2009; Sentencing And Punishment ⚷ 2038

Trial court may add, at time of original sentencing, conditions of probation or community control other than those enumerated by statute. Russo v. State, App. 1 Dist., 603 So.2d 1353 (1992). Sentencing And Punishment ⚷ 1963

Any modification of conditions of probation or community control subsequent to original sentencing must be limited to term or condition previously imposed. Russo v. State, App. 1 Dist., 603 So.2d 1353 (1992). Sentencing And Punishment ⚷ 1985

Trial court had jurisdiction to hear state's motion to modify previously entered probation order to increase restitution defendant was ordered to pay. Woods v. Angel, App. 5 Dist., 556 So.2d 820 (1990). Sentencing And Punishment ⚷ 1923

This section expressly providing that enumeration of specific conditions of probation shall not prevent sentencing court from adding other conditions as it considers proper authorizes conditions of probation of same general kind, class and nature as does provision of this section expressly enumerating conditions of probation and which to sentencing judge appear reasonable and proper to accomplish purposes sought to be achieved. Bentley v. State, App. 5 Dist., 411 So.2d 1361 (1982), review denied 419 So.2d 1195. Sentencing And Punishment ⚷ 1963

Where court which found defendant guilty of sexual battery and attempted sexual battery placed defendant on probation with condition of probation being that he satisfactorily complete mentally disordered sex offender program, and thereafter the program agency reported to court that it had exhausted treatment under the program and that defendant had violated the terms of his probation, court which conducted proper hearing did not err in revoking probation and sentencing defendant to 30 years in the state penitentiary under each of the two counts. Brown v. State, App. 3 Dist., 400 So.2d 812 (1981). Sentencing And Punishment ⚷ 2003; Sentencing And Punishment ⚷ 2032

Where trial judge had placed defendant on three years' probation, trial judge was without jurisdiction, after disposition of federal charges against defendant, to amend order of probation to include a nine-month jail sentence, notwithstanding judge's attempt in original order of probation, to reserve the right to sentence the defendant to jail if, in fact, he was found guilty of the federal offense. Buckbee v. State, App. 3 Dist., 378 So.2d 39 (1979), certiorari denied 388 So.2d 1118. Sentencing And Punishment ⚷ 1923

Trial judge did not have a right to amend order of probation to impose jail time, even if defendant agreed to existence of that right, since trial judge did not have jurisdiction to amend order of probation and jurisdiction could not be conferred upon a judge by agreement of the parties. Buckbee v. State, App. 3 Dist., 378 So.2d 39 (1979), certiorari denied 388 So.2d 1118. Sentencing And Punishment ⚷ 1923

Trial judge's order formally placing defendant on probation was final and there was no right, nor could one be reserved, to add a new condition to probation, unless defendant violated a term of his probation and was granted a hearing on violation of probation. Buckbee v. State, App. 3 Dist., 378 So.2d 39 (1979), certiorari denied 388 So.2d 1118. Sentencing And Punishment ⚷ 1923

Trial court was bound by its previous order pursuant to negotiated admission of first violation of probation and, hence, erred in sentencing defendant to five years where to previously modified conditions of probation to provide for a two-year term of imprisonment if probation was subsequently revoked. Kord v. State, App. 3 Dist., 361 So.2d 800 (1978), certiorari denied 368 So.2d 1373. Sentencing And Punishment ⚷ 2036

Trial court could not unconstitutionally penalize defendant for exercising his right to appeal by modifying probation order to raise amount to be paid into county fine and forfeiture fund from $10 to $30 per month upon being advised that defendant desired to appeal. Kominsky v. State, App. 1 Dist., 330 So.2d 800 (1976). Sentencing And Punishment ⚷ 1987

Trial court may revoke, revise or modify for cause probation and incarceration provision at any time during period that order is in force and impose any sentence which might have been originally imposed. State v. Jones, 327 So.2d 18 (1976), on remand 330 So.2d 189. Sentencing And Punishment ⚷ 2010; Sentencing And Punishment ⚷ 2037

73. —— Notice and hearing, addition or modification of conditions

Extension of defendant's probation was improper, where defendant never received formal notice of purported probation violation, nor of hearing on request of Department of Corrections (DOC) to extend probation, and defendant's alleged agreement to extend term of his probation was nullity because it was accomplished through informal discussions, without hearing or advice of counsel. Gearhart v. State, App. 5 Dist., 885 So.2d 415 (2004). Sentencing And Punishment ⚷ 1923

Court could not modify its order of community control to include new condition requiring defendant to reside at probation and restitution center without providing defendant with notice and hearing, when there had been no violation of community control, even though original orders of community control and probation contained condition which stated that court retained jurisdiction to place defendant in center on recommendation of probation/community control officer without finding violation. Russo v. State, App. 1 Dist., 603 So.2d 1353 (1992). Sentencing And Punishment ⚷ 1923

Probation orders are not subject to modification except for violation of conditions and then only upon notice and hearing. Knapp v. State, App. 4 Dist., 405 So.2d 786 (1981). Sentencing And Punishment ⚷ 1923

74. —— Appeal, addition or modification of conditions

In the absence of a contemporaneous objection, a defendant may appeal a condition of probation only if it is so egregious as to be the equivalent of fundamental error. Saidi v. State, App. 5 Dist., 845 So.2d 1022 (2003). Criminal Law ⚷ 1042.3(4)

Trial court had no jurisdiction to modify probation order entered in criminal case while judgment of conviction and probation order was on appeal before appellate court of competent jurisdiction. State ex rel. Salomon v. Sandstrom, App. 3 Dist., 349 So.2d 696 (1977). Criminal Law ⚷ 1083

75. —— Double jeopardy, addition or modification of conditions

Condition of pretrial supervised release requiring defendant to obtain certain sex-offender counseling did not constitute punishment for purposes of Double Jeopardy Clause, even though trial court lacked statutory authority to impose condition, given that defendant was neither on probation nor under community control; improper imposition of condition was of short duration and limited impact, trial court was not engaged in determination of guilt or punishment when it considered pretrial release, and conditional pretrial release was remedial and not punitive. State v. Torres, App. 2 Dist., 890 So.2d 292 (2004). Double Jeopardy ⚷ 22

Trial court's entry of order of modification, extending term of defendant's probation from three years to "upon successful completion of sex offender treatment," violated double jeopardy prohibition against multiple punishments for same act, where there was no formal proof of finding by trial court of violation of probation. Gearhart v. State, App. 5 Dist., 885 So.2d 415 (2004). Double Jeopardy ⚷ 114.1

Enhancement of probation, where there is no proof of violation of probation, contravenes double jeopardy prohibition against multiple punishments for same offense. Gearhart v. State, App. 5 Dist., 885 So.2d 415 (2004). Double Jeopardy ⚷ 114.1

Sentence imposed upon defendant at post-conviction hearing conducted for purpose of clarifying defendant's original sentence deviated from and increased defendant's sentence as originally imposed, in violation of double jeopardy, where sentence as originally pronounced neither expressly nor impliedly included sex offender probation imposed at hearing; original sentence included drug offender probation with requirements of successful completion of sex offender treatment and no contact with victim. Rivera v. State, App. 2 Dist., 862 So.2d 55 (2003), rehearing denied. Double Jeopardy ⚷ 114.1

Defendant's resentencing that included five years sexual offender probation did not violate double jeopardy as enhanced sentence, where registration requirements of sexual offender probation under Florida Sexual Predators Act imposed no affirmative disability or restraint on defendant, and because its purpose was remedial and regulatory rather than punitive. Andrews v. State, App. 4 Dist., 792 So.2d 1274 (2001). Double Jeopardy ⚷ 112.1

Enhancing conditions of defendant's probation when there was no record basis for such modification placed defendant in double jeopardy. Anderson v. State, App. 3 Dist., 444 So.2d 1109 (1984). Double Jeopardy ⚷ 112.1

76. —— Due process, addition or modification of conditions

Generally, a trial court has authority to modify or rescind the terms or conditions of probation it imposes; however, the constitutional guarantees of due process and protection from double jeopardy prohibit a trial court from revoking or enhancing probation without first determining the probationer violated probation. J.D.D. v. State, App. 1 Dist., 12 So.3d 820 (2009). Constitutional Law ⚷ 4733(1); Sentencing and Punishment ⚷ 1985; Sentencing and Punishment ⚷ 1986

Defendant's due process rights were violated by amendment of terms of probation to impose more stringent visitations restrictions and to reassign original counselor, without providing defendant with hearing before amendment. Albright v. State, App. 5 Dist., 622 So.2d 1171 (1993). Constitutional Law ⚷ 4731; Constitutional Law ⚷ 4732; Sentencing And Punishment ⚷ 1923

77. —— Counseling, addition or modification of conditions

Trial court was authorized to change defendant's probationary condition of family counseling to condition of individual anger management, under statute allowing trial court, during term of probation, to modify any condition previously imposed by court. Zepeda v. State, App. 5 Dist., 658 So.2d 1201 (1995). Sentencing And Punishment ⚷ 1985

78. —— Contact with victims, addition or modification of conditions

Addition of condition to defendant's probation that defendant have no contact with victim was impermissible absent finding of violation of probation. Zepeda v. State, App. 5 Dist., 658 So.2d 1201 (1995). Sentencing And Punishment ⚷ 1986

Instruction by probation officer that probationer not go to his wife's house was not a routine supervisory direction but amounted to a new condition of probation which probation officer was without authority to prescribe; thus, it was error for trial court in probation revocation proceeding to impliedly find that probationer violated probation by visiting his wife's house. Haynes v. State, App. 1 Dist., 440 So.2d 661 (1983). Sentencing And Punishment ⚷ 1988; Sentencing And Punishment ⚷ 2003

79. —— Contact with others, addition or modification of conditions

Trial court had the discretion to modify defendant's probation to allow him to have unsupervised contact with his young son and grandchildren before defendant had completed his four year sex offender treatment program; statutes provided that the trial court had the authority to modify the terms of probation, and that unsupervised contact could be ordered prior to completion of a sex offender treatment program if authorized by the court. Wesner v. State, App. 2 Dist., 843 So.2d 1039 (2003). Sentencing And Punishment ⚷ 1987

Absent any violation of conditions of defendant's probation, trial court had no authority to amend conditions in order to add new condition limiting defendant's contact with former wife. Brenatelli v. State, App. 5 Dist., 555 So.2d 1315 (1990). Sentencing And Punishment ⚷ 1923

80. —— Use of intoxicants, addition or modification of conditions

Special condition of probation, which prohibited excessive use of intoxicants and visiting places where intoxicants or drugs are unlawfully sold, dispensed, or used and which was not orally pronounced at sentencing, would be modified to strike portion relating to excessive use of intoxicants; remainder was more precise definition of general prohibition that need not be orally pronounced. Laster v. State, App. 2 Dist., 658 So.2d 1129 (1995). Sentencing And Punishment ⚿ 1921; Sentencing And Punishment ⚿ 1980(2)

81. —— Weapons, addition or modification of conditions

Special condition of probation, which prohibited ownership or possession of "any weapons, firearms, or destructive devices" and which was not orally pronounced at sentencing, would be modified to strike reference to other weapons and destructive devices. Laster v. State, App. 2 Dist., 658 So.2d 1129 (1995). Sentencing And Punishment ⚿ 1920

Probation condition that convicted felon would not possess, carry, or own any weapons or firearms without first securing consent of probation officer, would be modified so as to prohibit the possession of firearms regardless of consent of probation officer, without regard to oral pronouncement at sentencing, as statute made it unlawful for person convicted of felony to own, possess, or have in care, custody, or control any firearm, electric weapon or device, or to carry concealed weapon, including all tear gas guns and chemical weapons or devices. Fitts v. State, App. 2 Dist., 649 So.2d 300 (1995). Sentencing And Punishment ⚿ 1981(2); Sentencing And Punishment ⚿ 1986

82. —— Correction of error, addition or modification of conditions

Order of probation, which erroneously imposed single two-year probationary period on defendant for two separate counts of battery rather than imposing two consecutive one-year probationary periods in conformity with oral announcement of trial court at time of sentencing, would be modified to conform to oral ruling of trial court. Barlow v. State, App. 5 Dist., 388 So.2d 349 (1980). Criminal Law ⚿ 1184(4.1)

83. —— Community control, addition or modification of conditions

Change in conditions of community control to allow defendant to relocate to another state was error, where order modifying sentence to allow defendant to take up residence with his mother in Virginia did not state that relocation was contingent on approval of proper Virginia authorities. State, Dept. of Corrections v. Coleman, App. 4 Dist., 766 So.2d 285 (2000). Sentencing And Punishment ⚿ 1987

Record did not support defendant's contention that sentence of community control for violation of community control illegally modified jail sentence that he had already begun serving, notwithstanding that judgment of sentence indicated that defendant received probation on "each" count; although scrivener's error may have indicated to defendant that his sentence on count for which he had received jail time was modified, record otherwise indicated that defendant received community control only on count pertaining to violation of community control and that jail sentence was not altered. Henshaw v. State, App. 2 Dist., 564 So.2d 540 (1990). Criminal Law ⚿ 1126

84. —— Probation, addition or modification of conditions

Statutory requirement that trial court prohibit probationers who committed certain specified sex-based crimes from living within 1,000 feet of any school, day care center, park, or playground, or any other place where children regularly congregate, was mandatory, and thus trial court had no authority to modify sex offender's probation to allow him to live 865 feet from playground in neighboring gated community, provided that he did not enter any portion of subdivision and its recreation area. State v. Springer, App. 5 Dist., 965 So.2d 270 (2007). Sentencing And Punishment ⚿ 1971(1); Sentencing And Punishment ⚿ 1987

85. —— Restitution, addition or modification of conditions

Trial court erred by ordering payment of additional restitution where no affidavit charging violation of probation was ever filed, nor was it contended that probationer had violated probation. Green v. State, App. 4 Dist., 638 So.2d 1006 (1994). Sentencing And Punishment ⚿ 1923

Record did not support finding that defendant violated her probation by failing to make payment of court costs and restitution, as there was no evidence of defendant's ability to work, and resultant ability to make any court-ordered payments, prior to filing of affidavit charging violation and amended affidavit; following filing of amended affidavit, examining doctor opined that defendant was then able to work. Bianco v. State, App. 4 Dist., 638 So.2d 1005 (1994). Criminal Law ⚿ 1126

Where probationary period had commenced, trial court lacked authority under this section for imposing additional condition to probation that defendant make restitution to burglary victim. Carmo v. State, App. 4 Dist., 378 So.2d 850 (1979). Sentencing And Punishment ⚿ 1923

86. —— Expiration of probation, addition or modification of conditions

Where alleged violations had occurred after expiration of probation, such violations were not a basis on which probation could be modified. Curry v. State, App. 3 Dist., 362 So.2d 36 (1978), certiorari denied 372 So.2d 471. Sentencing And Punishment ⚷ 1948

87. Rehabilitation of probationer

Trial courts may and should use conditions of probation to protect victims of domestic abuse from future violent acts, to prevent future abusive conduct, and to assist in rehabilitation. Stephens v. State, App. 1 Dist., 659 So.2d 1303 (1995). Sentencing And Punishment ⚷ 1963

Trial courts have broad discretion to impose various conditions of probation, but condition cannot be imposed if it is not reasonably related to rehabilitation. Stephens v. State, App. 1 Dist., 659 So.2d 1303 (1995). Sentencing And Punishment ⚷ 1962; Sentencing And Punishment ⚷ 1963

Trial courts have broad discretion to impose conditions of probation, but condition of probation cannot be imposed if it is not reasonably related to rehabilitation. Zeigler v. State, App. 4 Dist., 647 So.2d 272 (1994). Sentencing And Punishment ⚷ 1962; Sentencing And Punishment ⚷ 1963

Condition of probation is invalid as not reasonably related to rehabilitation if it has no relationship to crime of which defendant is convicted, relates to conduct which is not in itself criminal, and requires or forbids conduct which is not reasonably related to future criminality. Martinez v. State, App. 2 Dist., 627 So.2d 542 (1993). Sentencing And Punishment ⚷ 1963

Conditioning probation for two counts of grand theft and one count of petty theft on defendant's purchase of $145 worth of property she attempted to steal from merchants was not an abuse of discretion where the rehabilitative costs imposed were clearly not punitive under specific financial circumstances of defendant. Williams v. State, App. 1 Dist., 474 So.2d 1260 (1985). Sentencing And Punishment ⚷ 1983(2)

Propriety of special condition of probation must be evaluated in terms of whether it is reasonably related to rehabilitation. Bodden v. State, App. 1 Dist., 411 So.2d 1391 (1982). Sentencing And Punishment ⚷ 1963

Special condition of probation was not valid where the concerns which prompted imposition of such condition were not focused on the issue of probationer's rehabilitation. Bodden v. State, App. 1 Dist., 411 So.2d 1391 (1982). Sentencing And Punishment ⚷ 1963

In determining whether condition of probation is reasonably related to rehabilitation, a condition is invalid if it has no relationship to the crime of which offender was convicted, relates to conduct which is in itself not criminal, and requires or forbids conduct which is not reasonably related to future criminality. Wiggins v. State, App. 4 Dist., 386 So.2d 46 (1980). Sentencing And Punishment ⚷ 1963

88. Association with individuals—In general

Upon conviction for lewd assault on minor, it is permissible to order no contact with children as condition of probation and to require defendant to answer whether he had such contact. Cassamassima v. State, App. 5 Dist., 657 So.2d 906 (1995), certification denied. Sentencing And Punishment ⚷ 1971(2)

Condition of probation prohibiting defendant from associating with any person engaged in any criminal activity was statutorily authorized. Emond v. State, App. 2 Dist., 652 So.2d 419 (1995), review granted 660 So.2d 715, quashed 668 So.2d 599. Sentencing And Punishment ⚷ 1971(2)

Condition of probation imposed upon defendant, convicted of obtaining property by worthless check, that defendant not associate with a particular individual was not shown to have been abuse of trial court's discretion, in absence of indication in record as to trial court's reason for such condition. Heatherly v. State, App. 4 Dist., 343 So.2d 54 (1977). Sentencing And Punishment ⚷ 1971(2)

89. —— Construction, association with individuals

Special written condition of probation which prohibited defendant from associating with or contacting "known convicted felons or anyone on probation or community control" was construed to mean that defendant may not associate with known convicted felons or known persons on probation or community control. McClendon v. State, App. 5 Dist., 659 So.2d 718 (1995). Sentencing And Punishment ⚷ 1971(3)

90. —— Clarity and specificity, association with individuals

Imposition of vague condition of probation upon defendant convicted of sexual assault that he have no contact with anyone under age 18 was error. Bower v. State, App. 5 Dist., 675 So.2d 957 (1996), rehearing denied. Sentencing And Punishment ⚷ 1971(3)

Condition of probation prohibiting defendant from associating with persons who used illegal drugs was required to be stricken as too vague and capable of unintentional violation. Callaway v. State, App. 2 Dist., 658 So.2d 593 (1995). Sentencing And Punishment ⚷ 1971(3)

91. —— Overbreadth, association with individuals

Special condition of probation imposed on defendant convicted of lewd and lascivious assault on a child, that defendant not associate with or have contact in any way with any child under age of 17 or his two stepdaughters, was impermissibly broad, since possibility of unintentional violation was too great and it could prevent normal family relationship. Graham v. State, App. 5 Dist., 658 So.2d 642 (1995). Sentencing And Punishment ⚷ 1971(3)

Impermissibly broad special condition of probation imposed on defendant convicted of lewd and lascivious assault on a child, i.e., that defendant not associate with or have contact in any way with any child under age of 17, could be cured upon remand by requiring that defendant have no unsupervised contact with minors. Graham v. State, App. 5 Dist., 658 So.2d 642 (1995). Criminal Law ⚷ 1181.5(8)

Condition of defendant's probation, prohibiting him from living with a member of the opposite sex unless married, was overbroad in that its language would prohibit defendant from living with his mother or any other female relative and, thus, would be modified to permit defendant to live with his female relatives. Mays v. State, App. 2 Dist., 349 So.2d 792 (1977). Sentencing And Punishment ⚷ 1971(2)

92. —— Codefendants, association with individuals

Special condition of defendant's probation prohibiting her from associating with codefendant was valid; condition bore direct relationship to the crimes for which defendant was convicted and forbid conduct which was reasonably related to prohibiting future criminality. Allen v. State, App. 2 Dist., 645 So.2d 579 (1994). Sentencing And Punishment ⚷ 1971(2)

Prohibiting defendant from associating with former codefendant as condition of probation was not unreasonable or inconsistent with defendant's convictions for vehicular homicide, leaving scene of accident with injuries and grand theft; defendant had been seen drinking with former codefendant at bar, then getting into codefendant's car and driving while both were intoxicated. Waters v. State, App. 1 Dist., 520 So.2d 678 (1988). Sentencing And Punishment ⚷ 1971(2)

93. —— Elderly people, association with individuals

Condition of probation that defendant not associate with the elderly would be clarified to not prohibit such association at family or social gatherings. Henning v. State, App. 4 Dist., 648 So.2d 1262 (1995). Sentencing And Punishment ⚷ 1972(3)

94. —— Children, association with individuals

Condition of probation imposed on defendant convicted of committing lewd, lascivious or indecent act on a child, prohibiting him from having contact with female child under age of 16 years, unless child's parent or legal guardian was present improperly subjected defendant to unintentional violation if he was inadvertently placed in a work or social situation where young girls were present, without their parents or guardians. Rowles v. State, App. 5 Dist., 682 So.2d 1184 (1996). Sentencing And Punishment ⚷ 1971(3)

95. —— Living conditions, association with individuals

Condition of probation prohibiting defendant, convicted for possession of marijuana, from living with a member of the opposite sex who was not a relative unless written permission from probation officer was given was invalid, since condition had no relationship to crime for which defendant was convicted, related to conduct which was not in itself criminal, and required or forbade conduct that was not reasonably related to future criminality. Brodus v. State, App. 2 Dist., 449 So.2d 941 (1984). Sentencing And Punishment ⚷ 1971(2)

Trial court erred in prohibiting defendant, who pled nolo contendere to charge of carrying concealed firearm, from living with female to whom he was not married or related as condition of probation, which condition bore no reasonable relation to crime of which defendant was convicted. Wilkinson v. State, App. 5 Dist., 388 So.2d 1322 (1980). Sentencing And Punishment ⚷ 1971(2)

96. —— Gangs, association with individuals

Trial court's imposition of condition of community control that juvenile defendant not associate with gang members was proper; however, no violation of condition could occur unless juvenile knew that individuals he was associating with were gang members. In Interest of D.S., App. 4 Dist., 652 So.2d 892 (1995), rehearing denied. Infants ⚷ 225

97. Location restrictions—In general

Probation condition, that defendant not come within 250 miles of victim, was too vague to advise defendant of limits of his restrictions, as that radius was capable of being constantly redefined with no notice to defendant whenever victim left her home and, thus, that condition was illegal. Hughes v. State, App. 4 Dist., 667 So.2d 910 (1996), rehearing denied, review denied 676 So.2d 413. Sentencing And Punishment ⚿ 1967(3)

Condition of probation, precluding defendant who pled guilty to two counts of DUI manslaughter and two counts of DUI accident with damage to property from leaving county without permission of probation department for good cause shown, was justified. Eloshway v. State, App. 4 Dist., 553 So.2d 1258 (1989), review denied 564 So.2d 486. Sentencing And Punishment ⚿ 1967(2)

Order which prohibited probationer from living in or near former neighborhood did not prohibit probationer from going to former residence to do maintenance, and interpretation that it did improperly added a condition of probation to the order. Nickens v. State, App. 4 Dist., 547 So.2d 1289 (1989). Sentencing And Punishment ⚿ 1971(3)

Requirement that probationer leave county by certain time of day was not valid condition of probation; however, probationer's failure to raise contemporaneous objection to imposition of that condition at hearing prohibited him from raising challenge on appeal. Jacobsen v. State, App. 2 Dist., 536 So.2d 373 (1988). Criminal Law ⚿ 1042.3(4); Sentencing And Punishment ⚿ 1968(2)

Condition of probation was proper which provided that defendant would not be permitted to be physically on premises where assault for which he had been convicted occurred. Russell v. State, App. 3 Dist., 342 So.2d 96 (1977). Sentencing And Punishment ⚿ 1971(2)

98. —— Known criminal or drug areas, location restrictions

Condition of probation prohibiting defendant from frequenting places where illegal drugs were used was required to be stricken, since places defendant was to avoid were not specifically defined. Callaway v. State, App. 2 Dist., 658 So.2d 593 (1995). Sentencing And Punishment ⚿ 1980(3)

Probation condition prohibiting defendant from visiting places where intoxicants, drugs or other dangerous substances were unlawfully sold, dispensed, or used was valid as more precise definition of general probation conditions. Heathcoe v. State, App. 2 Dist., 654 So.2d 1258 (1995). Sentencing And Punishment ⚿ 1980(2)

Condition of probation that required defendant to stay minimum distance from known high-drug areas as determined by probation officer was improper. Henshaw v. State, App. 2 Dist., 564 So.2d 541 (1990). Sentencing And Punishment ⚿ 1967(2)

Condition of probation could not require defendant to remain at least three blocks away from known, high-drug areas. Johnson v. State, App. 2 Dist., 561 So.2d 1254 (1990). Sentencing And Punishment ⚿ 1967(2)

Court properly imposed upon narcotics defendant term of probation which forbade defendant from visiting places where narcotics and drugs were unlawfully sold, dispensed, or used. Williams v. State, App. 2 Dist., 556 So.2d 480 (1990). Sentencing And Punishment ⚿ 1980(2)

Condition of probation that defendant not be within three blocks of a "high drug area" as defined by probation officer was invalid as being too vague, absent indication in the record that the areas in question were defined specifically or in writing, and as not having relationship to defendant's crime of burglary or reasonably tailored to prevent future criminal conduct. Huff v. State, App. 2 Dist., 554 So.2d 616 (1989). Sentencing And Punishment ⚿ 1967(2)

Condition of probation banning probationer from coming within one block of high crime area known for drug trafficking was proper as an attempt to deter future criminal conduct. Johnson v. State, App. 5 Dist., 547 So.2d 1048 (1989). Sentencing And Punishment ⚿ 1967(2)

99. —— In-house control, location restrictions

Condition of 13–year probation generally requiring defendant to remain at his residence when he was not at work or at school created unlawful de facto sentence of community control. Coleman v. State, App. 5 Dist., 564 So.2d 1238 (1990). Sentencing And Punishment ⚿ 1976(2)

100. —— Oral pronouncement, known criminal or drug areas, location restrictions

Probation condition prohibiting visits to places where intoxicants are illegally sold, dispensed or used need not be orally pronounced, as it is more precise definition of general prohibition. Johnson v. State, App. 2 Dist., 664 So.2d 1053 (1995). Sentencing And Punishment ⚿ 1918

Condition placed on defendant's probation, that he not visit places where controlled substances were unlawfully sold, dispensed, or used, was clarification of statutory prohibition against associating with persons engaged in criminal activity, and thus was valid condition that need not have been orally pronounced at sentencing. Johnson v. State, App. 4 Dist., 662 So.2d 755 (1995). Sentencing And Punishment ⚿ 1918; Sentencing And Punishment ⚿ 1980(2)

Probation condition prohibiting defendant from visiting places where intoxicants are unlawfully sold, dispensed, or used would not be stricken since it was valid as a more precise definition of a general prohibition and, as such, did not need to be orally pronounced at sentencing. Williams v. State, App. 2 Dist., 658 So.2d 1172 (1995). Sentencing And Punishment ⚷ 1918; Sentencing And Punishment ⚷ 1980(2)

Portion of probation condition precluding defendant from visiting places where intoxicants, drugs or other dangerous substances were unlawfully sold was proper as precise definition of general prohibition that need not be announced in court. Brown v. State, App. 2 Dist., 658 So.2d 1058 (1995). Sentencing And Punishment ⚷ 1918

Condition of probation preventing defendant from visiting places where intoxicants, drugs, or other dangerous substances are unlawfully sold, dispensed, or used was valid condition that did not need to be pronounced in open court as it was a more precise definition of a general prohibition. Fielder v. State, App. 2 Dist., 658 So.2d 596 (1995). Sentencing And Punishment ⚷ 1918; Sentencing And Punishment ⚷ 1980(2)

Condition of probation prohibiting defendant from visiting places where intoxicants were unlawfully sold, dispensed or used was more precise definition of general condition of probation and was not required to be orally pronounced at sentencing. Callaway v. State, App. 2 Dist., 658 So.2d 593 (1995). Sentencing And Punishment ⚷ 1918

Condition of probation prohibiting defendant from visiting places where intoxicants, drugs or other dangerous substances were unlawfully sold, dispensed or used was more precise definition of general condition of probation authorized by statute and was not required to be pronounced in open court. Dexter v. State, App. 2 Dist., 654 So.2d 1248 (1995). Sentencing And Punishment ⚷ 1918

Condition of probation, that defendant not visit places where intoxicants, drugs or other dangerous substances were unlawfully sold, dispensed or used, was more precise definition of general prohibition associated with probation, and as such could be imposed without being orally pronounced. Daughtery v. State, App. 2 Dist., 654 So.2d 1209 (1995). Sentencing And Punishment ⚷ 1918

Probation condition barring defendant from visiting places where intoxicants were unlawfully sold, dispensed, or used did not have to be orally pronounced inasmuch as it was valid as more precise definition of general probation. Evans v. State, App. 2 Dist., 653 So.2d 1103 (1995). Sentencing And Punishment ⚷ 1918

Condition of probation prohibiting defendant from visiting places where certain substances were unlawfully sold, dispensed or used was not a special condition of probation, and did not need to be orally pronounced; condition was more precise definition of general condition prohibiting association with persons engaged in criminal activities. Hann v. State, App. 2 Dist., 653 So.2d 404 (1995), rehearing denied. Sentencing And Punishment ⚷ 1918

Probation condition for defendant convicted of being felon in possession of firearm, which prohibited him from visiting places where drugs or intoxicants are illegally sold, was valid general condition which did not need to be orally pronounced at sentencing. Reed v. State, App. 2 Dist., 652 So.2d 912 (1995). Sentencing And Punishment ⚷ 1918

Written condition of probation, restricting probationer from visiting places where substances were unlawfully sold, dispensed, or used, was valid condition which was not required to be orally pronounced in open court. Swinford v. State, App. 4 Dist., 651 So.2d 225 (1995). Sentencing And Punishment ⚷ 1918; Sentencing And Punishment ⚷ 1980(2)

Special condition in written order of probation which proscribed visiting places where intoxicants, drugs, or dangerous substances were dispensed or used unlawfully did not have to be orally pronounced at defendant's sentencing hearing, as it was more precise statement of statute regarding terms and conditions of probation or community control. Sheffield v. State, App. 2 Dist., 651 So.2d 160 (1995), review granted 663 So.2d 632, quashed 668 So.2d 600. Sentencing And Punishment ⚷ 1918

Portion of probation condition prohibiting probationer from visiting places where intoxicants are illegally sold, dispensed or used was valid without oral pronouncement, since it was more precise definition of general prohibition. Stark v. State, App. 2 Dist., 650 So.2d 697 (1995). Sentencing And Punishment ⚷ 1918

101. —— Sufficiency of evidence, location restrictions

In view of undisputed fact that probationer fled from hospital while under an adjudication of incompetency, evidence was insufficient to sustain revocation of probation on ground that defendant left county of residence without consent of probation supervisor in violation of condition of probation. Johnson v. State, App. 5 Dist., 378 So.2d 108 (1980). Sentencing And Punishment ⚷ 2021

102. Residence of probationer—In general

Trial court could allow probationer's residence in another state only if order so allowing stipulated that it was contingent upon approval of receiving state's Interstate Parole and Probation Compact authority, where probationer had originally been convicted of two counts of sexual battery. Moore v. Proctor, App. 4 Dist., 795 So.2d 235 (2001). Sentencing And Punishment ⚷ 1988; States ⚷ 6

Trial court improperly issued order permitting probationer to reside in another state and report to his probation officer by telephone, where order did not stipulate that it was contingent upon approval of receiving state's Interstate Parole and Probation Compact authority, and was in fact entered after receiving state's interstate compact authority had rejected department's request and requested probationer's removal from the state. Moore v. Proctor, App. 4 Dist., 795 So.2d 235 (2001). Sentencing And Punishment ⚷ 1988; States ⚷ 6

Receiving state's agreement to accept probation supervision of probationer did not moot certiorari petition filed by secretary of department of corrections, seeking quashal of trial court order allowing probationer to reside out of state and report by phone to his probation officer for failing to specify that it was contingent upon approval of receiving state's Interstate Parole and Probation Compact authority. Moore v. Proctor, App. 4 Dist., 795 So.2d 235 (2001). Criminal Law ⚷ 1131(4); States ⚷ 6

Trial court, in the exercise of its discretion, may, as a condition of probation, say where a probationer may reside, but condition must be sufficiently definite to advise probationer of limits of probation and condition must also bear some reasonable relationship to purposes of probation. Almond v. State, App. 4 Dist., 350 So.2d 810 (1977), certiorari denied 358 So.2d 128. Sentencing And Punishment ⚷ 1971(2); Sentencing And Punishment ⚷ 1971(3)

Condition of probation ordering defendant to "reside elsewhere other than Central Florida" was not sufficiently definite to advise defendant of limits of restriction, did not bear a reasonable relationship to the purposes of probation, and thus would be stricken from order of probation. Almond v. State, App. 4 Dist., 350 So.2d 810 (1977), certiorari denied 358 So.2d 128. Sentencing And Punishment ⚷ 1968(3)

While the record reflected that defendant, one of whose conditions of probation was that he not change his residence without the consent of his probation supervisor, was not cooperative in notifying his supervisor before or after he moved, his failure to obtain prior consent to a change of residence, after he and his family were removed from their residence by a writ of possession issued pursuant to a final judgment for removal obtained by his landlord, was explained away in that to seek prior consent would have been a useless act under the circumstances. Kotowski v. State, App. 3 Dist., 344 So.2d 602 (1977). Sentencing And Punishment ⚷ 1971(3)

Probationer's refusal to discuss his compliance or noncompliance with terms of his probation concerning his residence is factor judge may consider in revocation hearing. State v. Mangam, 343 So.2d 599 (1977). Sentencing And Punishment ⚷ 2019

Probationer is allowed to live outside of confinement as matter of judicial grace and it is clearly proper to require probationer to maintain specific residence, to report his movements and to report regularly to supervisor or court to assure rehabilitation of probationer and protect public. State v. Mangam, 343 So.2d 599 (1977). Sentencing And Punishment ⚷ 1969(2); Sentencing And Punishment ⚷ 1971(2)

103. —— Cohabitation restrictions, residence of probationer

Community control condition imposed on defendant convicted of drug crimes, that he not live with a member of the opposite sex who is not a relative, without written permission, was invalid. Ford v. State, App. 2 Dist., 556 So.2d 483 (1990). Sentencing And Punishment ⚷ 1971(2)

Court could not impose condition of probation which forbade defendant from living with member of opposite sex who was not relative. Williams v. State, App. 2 Dist., 556 So.2d 480 (1990). Sentencing And Punishment ⚷ 1971(2)

Condition of probation for drug crimes could not prohibit defendant from living with unrelated member of opposite sex. Kelly v. State, App. 2 Dist., 552 So.2d 312 (1989). Sentencing And Punishment ⚷ 1971(2)

Condition of probation which directed defendant, who was unmarried and residing with mother of two of his children, to legalize living arrangements within ten days or move merely required defendant to abide by law and not violate § 798.01 prohibiting living in a state of adultery and § 798.02 prohibiting man or woman not married to each other from lewdly and lasciviously associating and cohabiting together, and as such condition was not an improper condition of probation. Miller v. State, App. 1 Dist., 520 So.2d 80 (1988), review denied 531 So.2d 1354. Sentencing And Punishment ⚷ 1971(2)

104. Reports from probationers

Written condition of probation that required defendant to report daily to probation officer which was not orally pronounced at sentencing hearing was invalid, as requirement was special condition of probation not otherwise statutorily authorized. Vasquez v. State, App. 4 Dist., 663 So.2d 1343 (1995), review dismissed 666 So.2d 145. Sentencing And Punishment ⚷ 1920

Where neither probation order nor transcript of plea proceeding evidenced that as a condition of probation defendant was to report to probation intake office after completion of his six-month jail term, it was error to find him in violation of probation three years later for failure to report and to impose an additional six-month period of incarceration. Mastick v. State, App. 3 Dist., 409 So.2d 203 (1982). Sentencing And Punishment ⚷ 2003

Failure to file reports for four consecutive months as required by condition of probationary sentence and repeated failure to follow probation officer's instructions to visit job bank were substantial violations and warranted revocation. Roth v. State, App. 2 Dist., 406 So.2d 121 (1981). Sentencing And Punishment ⚷ 2003

Although Department of Offender Rehabilitation, acting through a probation officer, may require a probationer to file periodic reports even though such a requirement is not made a condition of his probation, such probation may not be revoked solely upon the ground that the probationer has failed to file the reports, unless the requirement is made a condition of his probation by the court. Barber v. State, App. 3 Dist., 344 So.2d 913 (1977). Sentencing And Punishment ⚷ 2003

Affidavit in which Texas probation supervisor stated that probationer had failed to file reports for the months of March, May, June, July, August, and September of 1975 and January and February of 1976 and probationer's own testimony that the report was correct was sufficient to sustain determination that probationer had substantially violated his probation, one condition of which was that probationer make a full and truthful report to his probation supervisor not later than the fifth day of each month. Wheeler v. State, App. 2 Dist., 344 So.2d 630 (1977). Sentencing And Punishment ⚷ 2021

Where minutes recited that court placed defendant on probation for two years to run after release on other charges and probation order put defendant on probation for two years to begin on expiration of any prison sentence then being served and where concurrent sentences then being served were revoked but defendant was shortly thereafter resentenced, probation period began to run upon his release from resentence and could be revoked less than two months thereafter for failure to report to probation supervisor in accordance with parole condition. Roy v. State, App. 2 Dist., 207 So.2d 52 (1967), certiorari dismissed 211 So.2d 554. Sentencing And Punishment ⚷ 2006

105. Probation supervisors

Probation could not be revoked for probationer's failure to contact community treatment services for counseling and therapy where that requirement was imposed by probation officer and was not encompassed by court's probation condition which directed probationer to comply with all instructions of his probation officer. Hutchinson v. State, App. 2 Dist., 428 So.2d 739 (1983). Sentencing And Punishment ⚷ 2003

Court-imposed condition of probation providing that "You will promptly and truthfully answer all inquiries directed to you by the Court or the Probation Officer, and allow the Officer to visit in your home, at your employment site or elsewhere, and you will comply with all instructions he may give you," was clear and unambiguous, and probationer's compliance with its provisions was required, and, accordingly, his failure to comply with probation officer's directive, pursuant to that court-imposed condition, to report to him in June supported revocation of his probation. Watkins v. State, App. 2 Dist., 368 So.2d 363 (1979). Sentencing And Punishment ⚷ 2003

Act of defendant in leaving county after his probation supervisor had denied him permission to do so constituted a substantial violation of his probation and was sufficient to support revocation order. Abelson v. State, App. 2 Dist., 367 So.2d 633 (1979). Sentencing And Punishment ⚷ 2003

A trial court may lawfully revoke probation based on evidence that defendant violated one of the conditions of probation but was never given prior formal notice of such condition because of his refusal to make himself reasonably available to his probation supervisor for the purpose of being informed of his probationary conditions. Mobley v. State, App. 3 Dist., 348 So.2d 373 (1977). Sentencing And Punishment ⚷ 2003

Where probation supervisor required probationer to enter halfway house whose rules stated that if any task seemed demeaning, he should feel free to leave, probationer who left facility when ordered to wear diapers and who called probation officer next morning was not guilty of violating condition of his probation on theory that he had left facility without his supervisor's permission. Bienz v. State, App. 4 Dist., 343 So.2d 913 (1977). Sentencing And Punishment ⚷ 1971(3)

Condition of probation imposed upon defendant, convicted of obtaining property by worthless check, that defendant promptly and truthfully answer all inquiries by court or probation supervisors was reasonable and lawful and was not a violation of defendant's right to remain silent. Heatherly v. State, App. 4 Dist., 343 So.2d 54 (1977). Sentencing And Punishment ⚷ 1969(2)

106. Corporate officers

Trial court exceeded authority by imposing, as condition of exterminating corporation's probation following conviction for grand theft, restriction on corporate officer's participating in exterminating business during term of corporation's probation, where no evidence was presented that corporate officer personally did any act constituting grand theft. Donald and Bales Exterminating, Inc. v. State, App. 1 Dist., 487 So.2d 78 (1986). Sentencing And Punishment ⚷ 1972(2)

107. Employment or seeking employment—In general

Condition of community control that defendant maintain full-time employment was unnecessarily imposed upon defendant who had a baby and wanted to stay home to care for the child; rather than requiring defendant to work full time, standard employment condition of statute governing available terms and conditions of probation or community control merely allowed trial court to require defendant to "work faithfully at suitable employment insofar as may be possible," which could have been construed to include being a full-time "stay-at-home mom." Gaines v. State, App. 2 Dist., 899 So.2d 513 (2005). Sentencing And Punishment ⚷ 1972(3)

Any violation by probationer of condition of probation requiring him to work diligently at lawful occupation was not willful, and thus could not provide grounds for revocation of probation, where probationer had been actively seeking employment and had held two separate positions, and, while probationer was unemployed at time affidavit of violation of probation was filed, he was attending vocational school. Reed v. State, App. 2 Dist., 865 So.2d 644 (2004). Sentencing And Punishment ⚷ 1972(3)

Probation condition requiring defendant to maintain full-time employment is fundamental error because factors out of defendant's control could prevent completion of this requirement. Reed v. State, App. 2 Dist., 865 So.2d 644 (2004). Sentencing And Punishment ⚷ 1972(2)

Trial court abused its discretion in finding probationer had violated condition of probation by failing to maintain full-time employment, where condition of probation was invalid because factors outside of probationer's control could prevent him from completing requirement. Reed v. State, App. 2 Dist., 865 So.2d 644 (2004). Sentencing And Punishment ⚷ 1972(2)

It is error to require probationer to maintain full-time employment, although trial court may require probationer to maintain or actively seek gainful employment. Miller v. State, App. 1 Dist., 691 So.2d 26 (1997). Sentencing And Punishment ⚷ 1972(3)

Special probation conditions requiring that defendant "have full employment" three months after release from prison and that he set up four bank accounts, one for each of his children, and deposit minimum of five percent of his net pay into each account would be deleted because such conditions did not allow for circumstances beyond defendant's control which could prevent his compliance; probation conditions could be violated by defendant by his inability to comply, notwithstanding that he may have made good faith efforts to do so. Taylor v. State, App. 3 Dist., 687 So.2d 33 (1997). Sentencing And Punishment ⚷ 1972(3); Sentencing And Punishment ⚷ 1983(3)

Condition of probation requiring defendant to work "faithfully at suitable employment" should have included phrase "insofar as may be possible." Washington v. State, App. 2 Dist., 686 So.2d 733 (1997). Sentencing And Punishment ⚷ 1972(3)

Probation condition requiring defendant to "work faithfully at suitable employment" would be modified to include the phrase "insofar as may be possible." Washington v. State, App. 2 Dist., 685 So.2d 858 (1996). Sentencing And Punishment ⚷ 1987

That probationer "work diligently at a lawful occupation" was invalid condition of probation, since it did not take into consideration possibility that economic conditions would prevent probationer from obtaining employment. Mathis v. State, App. 4 Dist., 683 So.2d 634 (1996). Sentencing And Punishment ⚷ 1972(2)

Oral pronouncement of sentence was vague regarding condition of probation that defendant could not take any job which would require him to wear uniform; sentencing court needed to clarify probation condition by specifically indicating types of jobs that required wearing of an uniform that would violate prohibition. McCord v. State, App. 3 Dist., 679 So.2d 32 (1996). Sentencing And Punishment ⚷ 1972(3)

Trial court improperly imposed as condition of defendant's probation that defendant obtain and maintain employment; appropriate condition was to include alternative of actively seeking gainful employment. Allen v. State, App. 5 Dist., 676 So.2d 491 (1996). Sentencing And Punishment ⚷ 1972(2)

Probation conditions dealing with intoxicants and employment were general conditions of probation that did not have to be orally pronounced. Holmes v. State, App. 2 Dist., 675 So.2d 995 (1996). Sentencing And Punishment ⚷ 1918

Probation condition regarding employment would be modified to add the language "to the best of your ability." Williams v. State, App. 2 Dist., 674 So.2d 885 (1996). Sentencing And Punishment ⚷ 1972(3)

Probation condition requiring probationer to work diligently at lawful occupation, advise his employer of his probation status, and support any dependents to best of his ability, as directed by his probation officer was proper and did not have to be modified to include the words "insofar as may be possible" to prevent probationer from being in violation because of economic circumstances beyond his control. Reiter v. State, App. 2 Dist., 674 So.2d 189 (1996). Sentencing And Punishment ⚷ 1965; Sentencing And Punishment ⚷ 1972(3)

Satisfaction of condition of probation requiring defendant to work diligently at lawful occupation could be precluded by downturn in economy to extent condition required defendant to maintain employment and, thus, condition would be modified to require defendant to work diligently at lawful occupation or actively seek employment. Godley v. State, App. 2 Dist., 659 So.2d 447 (1995). Sentencing And Punishment ⚷ 1972(3)

Imposition of condition on probation that probationer work diligently at lawful occupation and support any dependents to best of his ability did not have to be modified to require him to seek lawful employment. Bledsoe v. State, App. 5 Dist., 657 So.2d 1235 (1995). Sentencing And Punishment ⚷ 1972(3); Sentencing And Punishment ⚷ 1983(3)

Case would be remanded to trial court with instructions to amend employment provision of probation order stating that "you will work faithfully at suitable employment" to add words "to the best of your ability." Munson v. State, App. 2 Dist., 654 So.2d 1220 (1995). Sentencing And Punishment ⚷ 1972(3)

Requirement that, while on probation, defendant "work diligently at a lawful occupation" was not error. Dumas v. State, App. 5 Dist., 651 So.2d 699 (1995), opinion amended on rehearing. Sentencing And Punishment ⚷ 1972(2)

Trial court has authority to order defendant actively to seek full-time gainful employment during term of probation. Vezina v. State, App. 1 Dist., 644 So.2d 602 (1994). Sentencing And Punishment ⚷ 1976(2)

Trial court could not impose, as condition of community control sentence, that defendant have employment by specified date; trial court was limited to requiring probationer to work faithfully at suitable employment insofar as may be possible. Vezina v. State, App. 1 Dist., 644 So.2d 602 (1994). Sentencing And Punishment ⚷ 1976(2)

Trial court improperly imposed, as condition of community control sentence, requirement that defendant work no less than 35 hours per week and, if unemployed, seek employment on daily basis, since defendant would be in violation of condition if he should be employed but could work less than 35 hours per week, and condition would be modified to require that defendant work insofar as possible, and, if working less than 35 hours per week, seek full-time employment. Johnson v. State, App. 5 Dist., 636 So.2d 792 (1994). Sentencing And Punishment ⚷ 1972(2); Sentencing And Punishment ⚷ 1987

Probationer cannot be ordered to maintain full-time employment as condition of probation, and imposition of such requirement is sufficiently egregious to constitute fundamental error. White v. State, App. 1 Dist., 619 So.2d 429 (1993), review denied 626 So.2d 208. Criminal Law ⚷ 1042.3(4); Sentencing And Punishment ⚷ 1972(2)

Condition of probation requiring probationer to maintain full-time employment is sufficiently egregious to be fundamental error; since such factors as down-turn in economy could prevent completion of condition, more appropriate course would be to order probationer to seek gainful employment. Evans v. State, App. 1 Dist., 608 So.2d 90 (1992). Criminal Law ⚷ 1042.3(4); Sentencing And Punishment ⚷ 1972(2)

Trial court's requirement that defendant maintain full-time employment as condition of probation was sufficiently egregious to be equivalent of fundamental error to which defendant did not have to object in order to appeal. Walls v. State, App. 4 Dist., 596 So.2d 811 (1992). Criminal Law ⚷ 1042.3(4); Sentencing And Punishment ⚷ 1972(2)

It is proper to impose a probation condition requiring the probationer to "work diligently at a lawful occupation," but in order to prove violation of the work condition, the state must show that failure to maintain or acquire employment was willful and not caused by circumstances beyond the probationer's control. Winfield v. State, App. 1 Dist., 406 So.2d 50 (1981).

Sentencing And Punishment ⚷ 1972(2); Sentencing And Punishment ⚷ 1972(3)

108. —— Carnival business, employment or seeking employment

Prohibiting defendant from work in the carnival business as a condition of community control and probation was not reasonably related to the defendant's rehabilitation and was contrary to requirements of this section; the carnival business had been the defendant's sole livelihood for a considerable number of years and was not related to the crimes with which the defendant was charged and was not itself a criminal activity. Hussey v. State, App. 2 Dist., 504 So.2d 796 (1987), review denied 518 So.2d 1275. Sentencing And Punishment ⚷ 1972(2)

109. Unemployment compensation

Condition of probation that defendant draw no unemployment compensation while on probation was an unnecessary restriction upon the valid exercise of a valuable right. Bownes v. State, App. 4 Dist., 345 So.2d 787 (1977). Sentencing And Punishment ⚷ 1983(2)

110. Disclosure of revenue and assets

Requirement that prisoner in state correctional system shall disclose all revenue or assets as a condition of parole eligibility under § 944.485 did not result in prejudice to prisoner under First and Fifth Amendment guarantees of the United States Constitution. Panzavecchia v. Crockett, App. 1 Dist., 379 So.2d 1047 (1980). Constitutional Law ⚷ 1194; Constitutional Law ⚷ 4838; Criminal Law ⚷ 393(1)

111. Intoxicating substances—In general

A court's oral statement placing a defendant on "drug probation" is insufficient to put the defendant on notice of additional drug-related probation conditions. Ayoub v. State, App. 2 Dist., 901 So.2d 311 (2005). Sentencing And Punishment ⚷ 1918

Conditions of probation which prohibited defendant from using or being in possession of alcohol as well as condition of probation which provided for no early termination consideration were invalid. Washington v. State, App. 2 Dist., 686 So.2d 733 (1997). Sentencing And Punishment ⚷ 1980(2); Sentencing And Punishment ⚷ 1983(2)

Trial judge's statement at sentencing that defendant would serve "five years drug probation subsequent to prison" was insufficient to put defendant on notice of additional drug related probation conditions and thus, drug related special probation conditions would be stricken, except the random testing portion, as statutorily authorized, and the portion prohibiting defendant from consuming and possessing illegal drugs. Scott v. State, App. 2 Dist., 681 So.2d 738 (1996). Sentencing And Punishment ⚷ 1920

Trial court properly imposed probation conditions prohibiting ownership or possession of firearm and prohibiting visiting places where intoxicants, drugs, or other dangerous substances are unlawfully sold, dispensed or used. Miller v. State, App. 2 Dist., 664 So.2d 1066 (1995). Sentencing And Punishment ⚷ 1980(2); Sentencing And Punishment ⚷ 1981(2)

Probation condition prohibiting probationer from visiting places where intoxicants were illegally sold, dispensed or used was valid, though it was not orally pronounced at sentencing, as more precise definition of general prohibition, but portion of condition prohibiting excessive use of intoxicants had to be stricken. Chitty v. State, App. 2 Dist., 661 So.2d 26 (1994). Sentencing And Punishment ⚷ 1920; Sentencing And Punishment ⚷ 1980(2)

Portion of probation condition relating to excessive use of intoxicants was improper. Franklin v. State, App. 2 Dist., 658 So.2d 129 (1995). Sentencing And Punishment ⚷ 1980(2)

Trial court acted within its discretionary authority over probation and terms thereof in ordering as a condition of defendant's probation, on conviction for possession of cocaine, that he abstain from drinking any alcoholic beverages; court could reasonably have concluded that defendant might come to rely on or use alcohol as an intoxicant to excess as a substitute for the illegal drugs he had been abusing or, while under the influence of alcohol, succumb to his desire to abuse illegal drugs. Smith v. State, App. 1 Dist., 513 So.2d 1367 (1987). Sentencing And Punishment ⚷ 1980(2)

There was no error in imposing, as condition of probation, prohibition against defendant's consuming alcoholic beverages or frequenting establishments serving alcoholic beverages. Balser v. State, App. 5 Dist., 399 So.2d 67 (1981). Sentencing And Punishment ⚷ 1980(2)

Evidence that probationer had smoked marijuana was insufficient to disclose violation of probation condition that he should not use intoxicants to excess and should not visit places where intoxicants, drugs or dangerous substances are unlawfully used, notwithstanding suggestion that probationer had to be some place when he smoked the marijuana and, therefore, this was a place where drugs were being unlawfully used. Jones v. State, App. 2 Dist., 348 So.2d 942 (1977). Sentencing And Punishment ⚷ 2021

Terms of probation imposed upon defendant, convicted of obtaining property by worthless check, that defendant not "use intoxicants to excess," and that defendant "not use intoxicants," nor visit places where intoxicants, drugs or other dangerous substances are sold were not inconsistent with each other and were not unreasonable or unlawful. Heatherly v. State, App. 4 Dist., 343 So.2d 54 (1977). Sentencing And Punishment ⚿ 1980(2)

112. —— Specificity or vagueness, intoxicating substances

Probation condition imposed for drug violations which prohibited defendant from possessing any drugs or narcotics unless prescribed by physician was too vague, and therefore would be stricken. Levely v. State, App. 2 Dist., 685 So.2d 847 (1995). Sentencing And Punishment ⚿ 1980(3)

Probation condition which prohibited defendant from possessing "any drugs or narcotics unless prescribed by a physician" was stricken for being too vague. Hall v. State, App. 2 Dist., 661 So.2d 63 (1995). Sentencing And Punishment ⚿ 1980(3)

Court would strike condition of probation and community control which prohibited defendant from possessing "any drugs or narcotics unless prescribed by a physician," as that condition was too vague. Cooper v. State, App. 2 Dist., 660 So.2d 811 (1995). Sentencing And Punishment ⚿ 1980(3)

Court would strike condition of probation and community control which prohibited defendant from possessing "any drugs or narcotics unless prescribed by a physician," as that condition was too vague. Cooper v. State, App. 2 Dist., 660 So.2d 811 (1995). Sentencing And Punishment ⚿ 1980(3)

Probation condition prohibiting defendant from possessing "any drugs or narcotics unless prescribed by physician" would be stricken since it was too vague. Williams v. State, App. 2 Dist., 658 So.2d 1172 (1995). Sentencing And Punishment ⚿ 1980(3)

113. —— Notice, intoxicating substances

Defendant had constructive notice of statutory condition of probation that he was to submit to random drug testing upon request of his probation officer, thus supporting revocation of probation based upon positive test results of drug test and defendant's admission to using cocaine and marijuana. Phillips v. State, App. 2 Dist., 971 So.2d 255 (2008). Sentencing And Punishment ⚿ 1920

Probation condition requiring defendant to submit to random alcohol testing would not be stricken because statute provided notice of its imposition. Scott v. State, App. 2 Dist., 681 So.2d 738 (1996). Sentencing And Punishment ⚿ 1920

Because the word "intoxicant" is not materially different from and covers term "alcoholic beverage," sentencing court's use of words "no drugs or intoxicants, no bars or liquor stores" placed defendant on notice of substance of written condition of probation which required defendant to "totally abstain from the consumption of alcoholic beverages." McClendon v. State, App. 5 Dist., 659 So.2d 718 (1995). Sentencing And Punishment ⚿ 1921

114. —— Oral pronouncement, intoxicating substances

Probation condition imposed for drug violations which prohibited excessive use of intoxicants was a special condition, and was therefore rendered invalid by trial court's failure to orally pronounce such condition at sentencing. Levely v. State, App. 2 Dist., 685 So.2d 847 (1995). Sentencing And Punishment ⚿ 1920

Oral pronouncement of general condition of probation prohibiting defendant from using intoxicants to excess was not required. Caraway v. State, App. 2 Dist., 681 So.2d 723 (1996). Sentencing And Punishment ⚿ 1918

Conditions of probation prohibiting use of intoxicants to excess and requiring defendant to pay for random testing were special conditions required to be announced at sentencing. McNeal v. State, App. 2 Dist., 681 So.2d 715 (1995). Sentencing And Punishment ⚿ 1918

Conditions of probation prohibiting excessive use of intoxicants, requiring defendant to pay for random testing and requiring hourly accounting of defendant's activities were special conditions that were required to be orally announced at sentencing. Dykes v. State, App. 2 Dist., 681 So.2d 714 (1995). Sentencing And Punishment ⚿ 1918

Condition of probation prohibiting defendant from using intoxicants to excess, possessing drugs unless prescribed by physician, or visiting places where drugs are unlawfully sold or used need not be orally pronounced by sentencing court. Ringling v. State, App. 2 Dist., 678 So.2d 1339 (1996). Sentencing And Punishment ⚿ 1918

Conditions of probation prohibiting defendant from consuming any alcoholic beverages and visiting businesses where main source of income is sale of alcohol and requiring defendant to abide by curfew if directed by probation officer were invalid as they were special conditions that were not orally pronounced. Ringling v. State, App. 2 Dist., 678 So.2d 1339 (1996). Sentencing And Punishment ⚿ 1920

Probation conditions dealing with intoxicants and employment were general conditions of probation that did not have to be orally pronounced. Holmes v. State, App. 2 Dist., 675 So.2d 995 (1996). Sentencing And Punishment ⚷ 1918

Condition of probation prohibiting defendant from using intoxicants to excess was not statutorily prohibited and had to be orally pronounced to be valid. Leroux v. State, App. 4 Dist., 665 So.2d 1115 (1996). Sentencing And Punishment ⚷ 1918; Sentencing And Punishment ⚷ 1980(2)

Probation condition prohibiting use of intoxicants to excess is special condition which trial court must announce in open court. Johnson v. State, App. 2 Dist., 664 So.2d 1053 (1995). Sentencing And Punishment ⚷ 1918

Condition of probation prohibiting probationer from possessing drugs and narcotics unless prescribed by physician and from visiting places in which intoxicants, drugs, or other dangerous substances were unlawfully sold, dispensed, or used, was such "general prohibition" as did not have to be pronounced orally. Geeding v. State, App. 2 Dist., 662 So.2d 997 (1995). Sentencing And Punishment ⚷ 1918

In trial court's written conditions on probation of defendant convicted of burglary and grand theft, conditions requiring that he not use intoxicants to excess and that he not consume or possess alcohol were special conditions of probation and had to be orally pronounced; failure of trial judge to do so required that they be stricken. Hosie v. State, App. 2 Dist., 661 So.2d 909 (1995). Sentencing And Punishment ⚷ 1920

Conditions of probation involving the use of intoxicants and alcohol are special conditions and must be orally pronounced. Hosie v. State, App. 2 Dist., 661 So.2d 909 (1995). Sentencing And Punishment ⚷ 1918

Probation condition which prohibited defendant from visiting places where certain substances are unlawfully sold, dispensed, or used was valid as more precise definition of general prohibition and, as such, did not need to be orally pronounced at sentencing. Hall v. State, App. 2 Dist., 661 So.2d 63 (1995). Sentencing And Punishment ⚷ 1918; Sentencing And Punishment ⚷ 1980(2)

Probation condition prohibiting defendant from using intoxicants to excess was improper special condition, since it was not orally pronounced at sentencing. Hall v. State, App. 2 Dist., 661 So.2d 63 (1995). Sentencing And Punishment ⚷ 1920

Portion of condition of probation which stated that defendant "will not use intoxicants to excess" had to be stricken, since it was not orally pronounced at sentencing. Williams v. State, App. 2 Dist., 661 So.2d 59 (1995). Sentencing And Punishment ⚷ 1920

Court would strike condition of probation and community control providing that defendant would not use intoxicants to excess, as it was special condition of probation that was not orally announced at sentence. Cooper v. State, App. 2 Dist., 660 So.2d 811 (1995). Sentencing And Punishment ⚷ 1920

Probation condition providing that defendant shall not use intoxicants to excess was a special condition of probation which had to be orally pronounced at sentencing and since condition was not orally pronounced, it would be stricken. Williams v. State, App. 2 Dist., 658 So.2d 1172 (1995). Sentencing And Punishment ⚷ 1920

Portion of probation condition that prohibited excessive use of intoxicants was to be stricken where it was not orally pronounced at sentencing. Brown v. State, App. 2 Dist., 658 So.2d 1058 (1995). Sentencing And Punishment ⚷ 1920

Condition of probation prohibiting defendant from consuming alcohol, possessing alcohol, associating with persons who use alcohol, or frequenting places where alcohol was main source of business was special condition of probation required to be orally pronounced at sentencing. Callaway v. State, App. 2 Dist., 658 So.2d 593 (1995). Sentencing And Punishment ⚷ 1918

Condition of community control and probation prohibiting defendant from using intoxicants to excess was required to be stricken, where trial court did not announce it to defendant in open court. Curry v. State, App. 2 Dist., 656 So.2d 521 (1995), review granted 676 So.2d 412, review dismissed 682 So.2d 1091. Sentencing And Punishment ⚷ 1920

Special probation condition prohibiting the excessive use of intoxicants was invalid where condition was not orally pronounced at sentencing. Swanson v. State, App. 2 Dist., 656 So.2d 503 (1995), rehearing denied. Sentencing And Punishment ⚷ 1920

Probation condition prohibiting excessive use of intoxicants or possession of any drug or narcotics unless prescribed by physician was invalid and struck in that it was not orally pronounced at sentencing. Heathcoe v. State, App. 2 Dist., 654 So.2d 1258 (1995). Sentencing And Punishment ⚷ 1920

Condition of probation prohibiting defendant from using intoxicants to excess or possessing any drugs or narcotics was invalid, where condition was not orally pronounced at sentencing. Dexter v. State, App. 2 Dist., 654 So.2d 1248 (1995). Sentencing And Punishment ⚷ 1920

Condition of probation, that defendant was not to use intoxicants to excess, was special condition required to be orally pronounced at sentencing. Daughtery v. State, App. 2 Dist., 654 So.2d 1209 (1995). Sentencing And Punishment ⚷ 1918

Conditions of probation prohibiting defendant from using alcohol to excess and from consuming any alcoholic beverages, or visiting businesses where main source of income is sale of alcoholic beverages, would be stricken, because these special conditions were not pronounced at sentencing. Farrington v. State, App. 2 Dist., 654 So.2d 564 (1995), rehearing denied, amended on rehearing, review granted 663 So.2d 631, quashed 668 So.2d 598. Sentencing And Punishment ⚷ 1920

Probation condition barring excessive use of intoxicants had to be stricken since trial court failed to announce it in open court, and thereby prevented defendant from having opportunity to object to its imposition. Evans v. State, App. 2 Dist., 653 So.2d 1103 (1995). Sentencing And Punishment ⚷ 1920

Portions of special condition prohibiting defendant from consumption and possession of alcohol or illegal drugs, associating with people who use alcohol or illegal drugs, and frequenting places where alcohol is main source of business or where illegal drugs are used, that related to alcohol, were not orally pronounced, and so had to be stricken. Hamilton v. State, App. 2 Dist., 653 So.2d 1068 (1995). Sentencing And Punishment ⚷ 1920

115. —— Use to excess, intoxicating substances

Condition of probation that defendant, whose crime was not shown to be reasonably related to the use of intoxicants or illegal substances, not use intoxicants to excess or visit places where intoxicants, drugs, or other dangerous substances are unlawfully sold was a lawfully imposed valid general condition; portion of condition that defendant not use intoxicants to excess did not have to be orally pronounced. Carter v. State, App. 4 Dist., 677 So.2d 1349 (1996). Sentencing And Punishment ⚷ 1918; Sentencing And Punishment ⚷ 1980(2)

Condition of probation that prohibited defendant from using alcohol to excess could be imposed regardless of whether it directly related to circumstances of defendant's offense; condition was a standard condition applicable to any probationer under criminal procedure rules. Carter v. State, App. 4 Dist., 677 So.2d 1349 (1996). Sentencing And Punishment ⚷ 1980(2)

Special condition of probation prohibiting excessive use of intoxicants would be stricken, where condition was not pronounced orally at sentencing. Geeding v. State, App. 2 Dist., 662 So.2d 997 (1995). Sentencing And Punishment ⚷ 1920

Trial court could not prohibit probationer from using intoxicants to excess as condition of probation. Simmons v. State, App. 4 Dist., 662 So.2d 754 (1995). Sentencing And Punishment ⚷ 1980(2)

Court would strike condition of probation and community control providing that defendant would not use intoxicants to excess, as it was special condition of probation that was not orally announced at sentence. Cooper v. State, App. 2 Dist., 660 So.2d 811 (1995). Sentencing And Punishment ⚷ 1920

Condition of probation that defendant not use intoxicants to excess was a special condition of probation that had to be pronounced at sentencing, and trial court's failure to do so required that condition be stricken. Fielder v. State, App. 2 Dist., 658 So.2d 596 (1995). Sentencing And Punishment ⚷ 1920

Condition of probation prohibiting defendant from using intoxicants to excess was special condition required to be orally pronounced at sentencing. Callaway v. State, App. 2 Dist., 658 So.2d 593 (1995). Sentencing And Punishment ⚷ 1918

Probation condition that prohibited defendant from using intoxicants to excess was special condition which should have been orally pronounced, and so condition had to be stricken. Hamilton v. State, App. 2 Dist., 653 So.2d 1068 (1995). Sentencing And Punishment ⚷ 1920

Probation condition that prohibited probationer from using intoxicants to excess was "special condition of probation" that had to be orally pronounced at sentencing. Johnson v. State, App. 2 Dist., 652 So.2d 1258 (1995). Sentencing And Punishment ⚷ 1918

Probation condition of defendant convicted of attempted first degree murder with a firearm, requiring that he not use intoxicants to excess or visit places where intoxicants, drugs or other dangerous substances are unlawfully sold, dispensed or used, would be stricken to the extent it prohibited excessive use of intoxicants, since such prohibition was not orally pronounced at hearing, though remainder of condition would be affirmed, as it was more precise definition of general condition that need not be orally pronounced. Hall v. State, App. 2 Dist., 652 So.2d 1197 (1995), review granted 663 So.2d 632, quashed 668 So.2d 600. Sentencing And Punishment ⚷ 1921

Probation condition imposed on grand theft defendant, providing that defendant could not use intoxicants to excess, was invalid where condition was not orally pronounced at sentencing. Malone v. State, App. 2 Dist., 652 So.2d 902 (1995). Sentencing And Punishment ⚷ 1920

Special condition in written order of probation which proscribed use of intoxicants to excess had to be stricken; it was not statutorily authorized and had not been orally pronounced at defendant's sentencing hearing. Sheffield v. State, App. 2 Dist., 651 So.2d 160 (1995), review granted 663 So.2d 632, quashed 668 So.2d 600. Sentencing And Punishment ⚷ 1920; Sentencing And Punishment ⚷ 1980(2)

Written condition of probation that prohibited excessive use of intoxicants was required to be stricken, as it was not orally pronounced. Parsons v. State, App. 2 Dist., 650 So.2d 176 (1995), denial of post-conviction relief affirmed in part, reversed in part 672 So.2d 877. Sentencing And Punishment ⚷ 1920; Sentencing And Punishment ⚷ 1980(2)

Condition of probation prohibiting defendant from using intoxicants to excess was not valid where condition was not statutory condition of probation and was not announced in open court. Jaworski v. State, App. 4 Dist., 650 So.2d 172 (1995). Sentencing And Punishment ⚷ 1920; Sentencing And Punishment ⚷ 1980(2)

Condition of probation prohibiting defendant from using "intoxicants to excess" was special condition that was required to be pronounced orally at sentencing in order to be included in written order. Nank v. State, App. 2 Dist., 646 So.2d 762 (1994), rehearing denied. Sentencing And Punishment ⚷ 1918

116. —— Random testing, intoxicating substances

Conditions of probation, that defendant must not use intoxicants to excess; must submit to and pay for random testing for alcohol; shall not consume, possess, or associate with persons who use alcohol or frequent places where alcohol is main source of business; must submit to and pay for evaluation to determine whether or not he has any treatable alcohol problem; and must pay for any drug or alcohol treatment program, are special conditions of probation which must be orally pronounced at sentencing. Williams v. State, App. 2 Dist., 653 So.2d 407 (1995), rehearing denied, review granted 659 So.2d 1089, quashed 667 So.2d 191. Sentencing And Punishment ⚷ 1918

Conditions of probation prohibiting defendant from using intoxicants to the excess and requiring him to undergo random alcohol testing were special conditions of probation that were required to be orally pronounced. Hann v. State, App. 2 Dist., 653 So.2d 404 (1995), rehearing denied. Sentencing And Punishment ⚷ 1918

117. —— Possession of illegal narcotics, intoxicating substances

General condition of probation prohibiting possession of "any drugs or narcotics unless prescribed by a physician" applies only to illegal drugs and prescription drugs possessed without doctor's prescription, and does not authorize state to seek revocation of probation for possession of lawful, over-the-counter medication. Johnson v. State, App. 2 Dist., 701 So.2d 367 (1997). Sentencing And Punishment ⚷ 1980(3); Sentencing And Punishment ⚷ 2003

Portion of defendant's standard probation condition that prohibited the possession of drugs or narcotics unless prescribed by physician would be stricken as impermissibly vague. Garrison v. State, App. 2 Dist., 685 So.2d 53 (1996). Sentencing And Punishment ⚷ 1980(2)

Probation condition that prohibited probationer from possessing illegal drugs or visiting places where intoxicants were unlawfully sold was valid general condition of probation. Johnson v. State, App. 2 Dist., 652 So.2d 1258 (1995). Sentencing And Punishment ⚷ 1980(2)

Written sentencing form's special condition of probation, that defendant not use intoxicants to excess or possess any drugs or narcotics unless prescribed by physician, was required to be stricken; it was not standard statutory condition, and court failed to orally pronounce it. Lowell v. State, App. 1 Dist., 652 So.2d 975 (1995). Sentencing And Punishment ⚷ 1920

Probation condition prohibiting probationer from possessing "any drugs or narcotics unless prescribed by physician" was required to be stricken as vague; that prohibition could prohibit probationer from possessing over-the-counter cold medication or aspirin. Parsons v. State, App. 2 Dist., 650 So.2d 176 (1995), denial of post-conviction relief affirmed in part, reversed in part 672 So.2d 877. Sentencing And Punishment ⚷ 1980(3)

118. —— Restriction on frequenting drinking establishments, intoxicating substances

Condition of probation of defendant, who was convicted of uttering false, forged or altered check, that defendant "stay away from bars" fulfilled purposes of probation conditions. Brown v. State, App. 4 Dist., 406 So.2d 1262 (1981). Sentencing And Punishment ⚷ 1971(2)

119. Drug or rehabilitation programs—In general

Defendant's two discharges from treatment program required by condition of probation for burglary of dwelling did not amount to willful and substantial violation of probation; probation order did not require completion of program within specified period of time, and the state did not show that defendant was either unwilling or unable to complete program during his probationary term. Wilkerson v. State, App. 2 Dist., 884 So.2d 153 (2004). Sentencing And Punishment ⚷ 1977(3)

Probation condition requiring defendant to pay for random drug or alcohol testing would be stricken. Williams v. State, App. 2 Dist., 674 So.2d 885 (1996). Sentencing And Punishment ⚷ 1996

Probation officer's directive that probationer complete drug program was not a validly imposed court-ordered condition of probation and was not encompassed by requirement of condition that probationer comply with all instructions given by the officer; thus, probation could not be revoked for violation of directive that he complete drug program. Holterhaus v. State, App. 2 Dist., 417 So.2d 291 (1982). Sentencing And Punishment ⚷ 1977(2); Sentencing And Punishment ⚷ 2003

The parole and probation commission may order a parole violator into a community control program for a fixed period to be followed by a period of less restrictive supervision. Op. Atty.Gen., 83–79, Oct. 26, 1983.

Indigent alcoholics who were repeat violators of § 856.01 (repealed; see, now, § 856.011) could have been required to take antabuse as a condition of probation, if such medication is prescribed by a physician to arrest their ingestion of alcohol, if the necessary examination, treatment and medication can be provided by the department of health and rehabilitative services through an appropriate treatment resource under chapter 396, and if such condition of probation is designed to protect society and to rehabilitate the probationer. Op.Atty.Gen., 072–124, April 5, 1972.

120. —— Driving while intoxicated convictions, drug or rehabilitation programs

Under the authority of chapter 948, judges of state courts may require any person convicted of violating § 316.028 (repealed; see, now, § 316.193), relating to driving while intoxicated, to attend rehabilitation programs or courses as a term or condition of the violator's probation. Op.Atty.Gen., 072–351, Oct. 12, 1972.

Judges of municipal courts could have required any person convicted of violating § 316.028 (repealed; see, now, § 316.193), relating to driving while intoxicated or a validly enacted municipal ordinance counterpart of said section to attend rehabilitation programs or courses as a term or condition of probation where the probationary authority of the municipal court arose under a special act or the probationary authority arose under municipal home rule ordinance pursuant to chapter 167 and/or Const. Art. 8, § 2. Op.Atty.Gen., 072–351, Oct. 12, 1972.

121. —— Subsequent convictions, drug or rehabilitation programs

If a person pled guilty to driving while intoxicated under § 316.028 (repealed; see, now, § 316.193), and, as a term or condition of probation attended a rehabilitative DWI school or program, the judge could not then have found the defendant guilty of reckless driving pursuant to § 316.029 (repealed; see, now, § 316.192), and fined him without revoking his driver's license. Op.Atty.Gen., 072–352, Oct. 12, 1972.

122. —— Sufficiency of evidence, drug or rehabilitation programs

Evidence, consisting solely of hearsay reports as to defendant's conduct while attending a drug rehabilitation program, was not sufficient to support finding that defendant violated the terms of his probation where defendant categorically denied any misconduct. Curry v. State, App. 4 Dist., 379 So.2d 140 (1980). Sentencing And Punishment ⚷ 2021

When a defendant's probation is sought to be revoked because of his failure to successfully complete a designated rehabilitation program, some evidence must be submitted to show that the defendant was in some manner responsible for the failure. Curry v. State, App. 4 Dist., 379 So.2d 140 (1980). Sentencing And Punishment ⚷ 2021

123. —— Oral pronouncement, drug or rehabilitation programs

Evaluation and drug treatment, and successful completion of treatment, were special conditions of probation that had to be pronounced at sentencing. Parrish v. State, App. 1 Dist., 898 So.2d 1074 (2005). Sentencing And Punishment ⚷ 1918

Probation condition requiring defendant to pay for drug program was special condition of probation that had to be orally pronounced at sentencing. Sims v. State, App. 2 Dist., 688 So.2d 337 (1996), rehearing denied. Sentencing And Punishment ⚷ 1918

Special condition of probation requiring defendant "at his own expense" to enter and complete inpatient drug program did not conform to judge's pronouncement that defendant complete such program "at his expense to the extent he is able to meet that expense." Sims v. State, App. 2 Dist., 688 So.2d 337 (1996), rehearing denied. Sentencing And Punishment ⚷ 1921

Probation condition regarding alcohol treatment was special condition of probation, and thus, it was invalid when imposed without having been orally pronounced at sentencing. Sims v. State, App. 2 Dist., 688 So.2d 337 (1996), rehearing denied. Sentencing And Punishment ⚿ 1920

Condition of probation requiring defendant to pay for drug tests did not have to be stricken, although provision was not orally pronounced at sentencing; defendant requested that drug and alcohol counseling be made part of his sentence, court announced at sentencing that continued counseling would be a special condition of probation, and defendant's payment for drug test was implicit part of announced requirement for counseling. Filsaime v. State, App. 2 Dist., 679 So.2d 15 (1996), cause dismissed 682 So.2d 1099. Sentencing And Punishment ⚿ 1918

Portion of probation conditions which required defendant to pay for his drug and alcohol evaluation and testing was improper and could not be reimposed on remand where conditions were not orally announced by sentencing court. Ringling v. State, App. 2 Dist., 678 So.2d 1339 (1996). Criminal Law ⚿ 1192; Sentencing And Punishment ⚿ 1920

Condition of probation which required defendant to submit to random drug testing was valid special condition which need not be pronounced. Ringling v. State, App. 2 Dist., 678 So.2d 1339 (1996). Sentencing And Punishment ⚿ 1918

Written condition of probation that required defendant to undergo substance abuse treatment and/or education as directed by probation officer which was not orally pronounced at sentencing hearing was invalid, as requirement was special condition of probation not otherwise statutorily authorized. Vasquez v. State, App. 4 Dist., 663 So.2d 1343 (1995), review dismissed 666 So.2d 145. Sentencing And Punishment ⚿ 1920

Probation condition requiring probationer to submit to drug and alcohol evaluation and treatment, if necessary, was not erroneously imposed without oral pronouncement, in view of evidence that trial court stated, at sentencing, that defendant would need to be evaluated for drug treatment within 30 days and follow up treatment if necessary and for random urine screens while under supervision. Franklin v. State, App. 2 Dist., 658 So.2d 129 (1995). Sentencing And Punishment ⚿ 1918

Condition of probation and community control requiring defendant to submit at his own expense to evaluation and treatment programs was special condition that was required to be stricken when it was not announced orally in defendant's presence. Curry v. State, App. 2 Dist., 656 So.2d 521 (1995), review granted 676 So.2d 412, review dismissed 682 So.2d 1091. Sentencing And Punishment ⚿ 1920

Probation condition that required evaluation and treatment at defendant's expense for drug or alcohol problem was special condition that was not orally pronounced, and so had to be stricken. Hamilton v. State, App. 2 Dist., 653 So.2d 1068 (1995). Sentencing And Punishment ⚿ 1920

124. Mental health treatment

Condition of probation requiring probationer to undergo mental health evaluation and to complete successfully any treatment deemed necessary was special condition of probation, and, as it was pronounced orally at sentencing, it was properly included in written order. Kirkland v. State, App. 1 Dist., 666 So.2d 974 (1996). Sentencing And Punishment ⚿ 1918

Trial court erred in delegating its authority to a probation officer to make initial determination of whether need existed for treatment or counseling when sentencing defendant convicted for lewd and lascivious act upon child under the age of 16 rather than ordering diagnosis or evaluation itself to determine whether defendant was in need of treatment or counseling. Singleton v. State, App. 1 Dist., 582 So.2d 657 (1991). Constitutional Law ⚿ 2574; Sentencing And Punishment ⚿ 1988

Probation condition requiring that defendant submit to mental counseling "as directed by" his probation officer was not unlawful delegation of judicial authority to officer of executive branch; "as directed by" language of condition merely required that probation officer routinely supervise and monitor evaluation and counseling. Larson v. State, App. 1 Dist., 553 So.2d 226 (1989), approved in part, quashed in part 572 So.2d 1368. Constitutional Law ⚿ 2574

Order requiring the department of health and rehabilitative services to maintain defendant as a mentally disordered sex offender despite exhaustion of treatment violated the District Court of Appeal's decision in Florida Department of Health and Rehabilitative Services v. Gross, 421 So.2d 44 (Fla.3d DCA 1982) prohibiting imposition of such treatment as a condition of probation. Florida Dept. of Health and Rehabilitative Services v. Korvick, App. 3 Dist., 435 So.2d 351 (1983). Sentencing And Punishment ⚿ 1977(2)

125. Drivers' licenses—In general

Trial court could revoke defendant's driver's license for life as condition of probation after defendant was convicted of driving while intoxicated resulting in death, even though revocation extended beyond term of probation. Davis v.

State, App. 5 Dist., 688 So.2d 996 (1997). Sentencing And Punishment ⚷ 1979(2)

Department of Highway Safety and Motor Vehicles' revocation of driving privileges, for period of two years, of any person convicted of possession or sale of controlled substance may be imposed as condition of probation. Martin v. State, App. 1 Dist., 618 So.2d 737 (1993). Sentencing And Punishment ⚷ 1979(2)

Trial court did not have authority to suspend driver's license of defendant convicted of possession of cocaine as condition of probation, and could only direct Department of Highway Safety and Motor Vehicles to revoke license for a period of up to two years. Blair v. State, App. 2 Dist., 554 So.2d 1226 (1990). Automobiles ⚷ 144.2(5.1)

Court which was imposing conditions of probation on defendant convicted of possessing cocaine was without authority to actually suspend defendant's driver's license itself, and should, instead, have directed the Department of Highway Safety and Motor Vehicles to revoke the driving privileges for a period of one year. Ruise v. State, App. 1 Dist., 552 So.2d 270 (1989). Sentencing And Punishment ⚷ 1979(2)

Trial court had authority to establish as condition of probation that defendant convicted of sale or delivery of controlled substance not drive during his term of probation. Callahan v. State, App. 2 Dist., 550 So.2d 79 (1989). Sentencing And Punishment ⚷ 1979(2)

Where, as one condition of probation for defendant convicted of two counts of manslaughter by intoxication the trial court purported to revoke defendant's driver's license for life, court on appeal amended reference to license to constitute a condition of probation that during its term defendant should not drive motor vehicle and a recommendation to Department of Highway Safety and Motor Vehicles to suspend driving privileges for such time as appropriate under the law. Moreland v. State, App. 2 Dist., 442 So.2d 1002 (1983). Sentencing And Punishment ⚷ 1979(2)

126. —— Prohibition on driving, drivers' licenses

Trial court could impose probation conditions prohibiting defendant from driving or seeking hardship license during term of probation after defendant was convicted of driving while intoxicated resulting in death; although neither condition constituted criminal conduct, court could impose condition of probation reasonably related to offense or to future criminality. Davis v. State, App. 5 Dist., 688 So.2d 996 (1997). Sentencing And Punishment ⚷ 1979(2)

Trial judge may order as condition of probation that defendant not drive motor vehicle during term of probation if court finds that condition to be reasonably related to offense. Blair v. State, App. 2 Dist., 554 So.2d 1226 (1990). Sentencing And Punishment ⚷ 1979(2)

127. —— Suspension, drivers' licenses

Suspension of driver's license was proper condition of probation for defendant convicted of possession of cocaine. Ruise v. State, App. 1 Dist., 552 So.2d 270 (1989). Sentencing And Punishment ⚷ 1979(2)

128. —— Review, drivers' licenses

Issue of whether probation condition suspending defendant's driver's license had to be related to offense for which defendant was convicted was not preserved for appellate review absent objection by defendant to condition. Callahan v. State, App. 2 Dist., 550 So.2d 79 (1989). Criminal Law ⚷ 1042.3(4)

129. Traffic rules and regulations

Probation condition restricting defendant's driving speed to maximum of 35 miles per hour could not stand and would be modified to provide that defendant obey and observe all traffic laws, rules and regulations. Kominsky v. State, App. 1 Dist., 330 So.2d 800 (1976). Sentencing And Punishment ⚷ 1979(2)

130. Restriction on weapons possession—In general

Trial court properly imposed probation conditions prohibiting ownership or possession of firearm and prohibiting visiting places where intoxicants, drugs, or other dangerous substances are unlawfully sold, dispensed or used. Miller v. State, App. 2 Dist., 664 So.2d 1066 (1995). Sentencing And Punishment ⚷ 1980(2); Sentencing And Punishment ⚷ 1981(2)

Prohibiting possession of firearm was valid general condition of probation for defendants convicted of misdemeanors, insofar as they had been adjudicated guilty of felony in past. Johnson v. State, App. 2 Dist., 664 So.2d 1053 (1995). Sentencing And Punishment ⚷ 1981(2)

Because statute provides that convicted felons may not possess or control any firearm, condition of probation forbidding defendant "to possess, carry, or own any firearm" was valid whether or not it was orally pronounced at sentencing hearing. McClendon v. State, App. 5 Dist., 659 So.2d 718 (1995). Sentencing And Punishment ⚷ 1981(2); Sentencing And Punishment ⚷ 1981(3)

Condition of probation which prohibited convicted felon from possessing, caring or owning any weapons or firearms was proper. Brown v. State, App. 2 Dist., 658 So.2d 1058 (1995). Sentencing And Punishment ⚷ 1981(2)

Probation condition which prohibited ownership of firearm was proper. Franklin v. State, App. 2 Dist., 658 So.2d 129 (1995). Sentencing And Punishment ⚷ 1981(2)

Special condition of probation prohibiting ownership or possession of firearm was properly imposed. Heathcoe v. State, App. 2 Dist., 654 So.2d 1258 (1995). Sentencing And Punishment ⚷ 1981(2)

Special condition of probation prohibiting defendant from possessing, carrying, or owning any weapons without first obtaining consent of probation officer was stricken. Heathcoe v. State, App. 2 Dist., 654 So.2d 1258 (1995). Sentencing And Punishment ⚷ 1981(2)

Portion of probation condition implying that defendant may possess firearm with permission of his probation officer was not authorized, where defendant was convicted felon, who may not lawfully possess firearm. Stark v. State, App. 2 Dist., 650 So.2d 697 (1995). Sentencing And Punishment ⚷ 1981(2)

131. —— Weapons other than firearms, restriction on weapons possession

Probation condition requiring probationer to forfeit his brass knuckles was valid, though condition was not orally pronounced at sentencing, because statute, which provided that weapon of person arrested for carrying concealed weapon while committing or attempting to commit felony shall be forfeited without need for order of forfeiture, gave sufficient notice of forfeiture condition. Chitty v. State, App. 2 Dist., 661 So.2d 26 (1994). Sentencing And Punishment ⚷ 1918; Sentencing And Punishment ⚷ 1981(2)

Probation condition of defendant convicted of attempted first-degree murder with a firearm, requiring that he not possess, carry or own any weapons or firearms, would be affirmed to the extent it prohibited such activities with respect to firearms, but reference to weapons would be stricken. Hall v. State, App. 2 Dist., 652 So.2d 1197 (1995), review granted 663 So.2d 632, quashed 668 So.2d 600. Sentencing And Punishment ⚷ 1981(3)

132. —— Consent of probation officer, restriction on weapons possession

Costs and conditions of probation would be stricken to extent they were imposed without citation to statutory authority, without documentation or consideration of defendant's ability to pay, suggested that convicted felon may possess firearm with consent of his probation officer, and required defendant to pay for any drug and alcohol evaluations without oral pronouncement. Godwin v. State, App. 2 Dist., 676 So.2d 1012 (1996). Costs ⚷ 314; Sentencing And Punishment ⚷ 1920; Sentencing And Punishment ⚷ 1981(2)

Portion of probation order, which forbade defendant from carrying, possessing, or owning any weapon or firearm but for securing consent of his probation officer, which implied that felon can possess weapons otherwise prohibited with consent of his probation officer, was stricken. Crum v. State, App. 2 Dist., 664 So.2d 1051 (1995). Sentencing And Punishment ⚷ 1981(3)

Condition of probation that "you will not possess, carry, or own any weapons without first procuring consent of your Officer" does not imply that probation officer may consent to convicted felon's possession of weapons that are expressly prohibited by statute. Vasquez v. State, App. 4 Dist., 663 So.2d 1343 (1995), review dismissed 666 So.2d 145. Sentencing And Punishment ⚷ 1981(3)

Condition of probation that "you will neither possess, carry, or own any firearms, and you will not possess, carry, or own any weapons without first procuring consent of your Officer" was written in the conjunctive, and thus did not improperly imply that convicted felon may possess firearm with his probation officer's permission. Vasquez v. State, App. 4 Dist., 663 So.2d 1343 (1995), review dismissed 666 So.2d 145. Sentencing And Punishment ⚷ 1981(3)

Court would strike condition of probation and community control that prohibited carrying of weapons other than those statutorily enumerated; that was special condition of probation that was not orally announced at sentencing, and it implied that felon can possess weapons otherwise prohibited with consent of his probation officer. Cooper v. State, App. 2 Dist., 660 So.2d 811 (1995). Sentencing And Punishment ⚷ 1920; Sentencing And Punishment ⚷ 1981(3)

Probation condition imposed on convicted felon stating that "You will not possess, carry, or own any weapons without first procuring the consent" of probation officer would be stricken; condition implied that felon could possess weapons otherwise prohibited with the consent of his probation officer. Williams v. State, App. 2 Dist., 658 So.2d 1172 (1995). Sentencing And Punishment ⚷ 1981(3)

Condition of community control and probation prohibiting defendant from possessing firearms without consent of probation officer was required to be stricken, since convicted felon could not possess firearm lawfully. Curry v. State, App. 2 Dist., 656 So.2d 521 (1995), review granted 676 So.2d 412, review dismissed 682 So.2d 1091. Sentencing And Punishment ⚷ 1981(2)

Consent of probation officer does not permit felon to possess weapons otherwise prohibited. Green v. State, App. 2 Dist., 654 So.2d 1224 (1995). Weapons ⚷ 4

Condition of probation that improperly implied that convicted felon could possess firearm with his probation officer's permission would be stricken. Farrington v. State, App. 2 Dist., 654 So.2d 564 (1995), rehearing denied, amended on rehearing, review granted 663 So.2d 631, quashed 668 So.2d 598. Sentencing And Punishment ⚷ 1981(3)

Probation condition prohibiting possession while carrying weapon without probation officer's consent was invalid since defendant, as convicted felon, was prohibited from possessing or carrying firearm or concealed weapon, regardless of probation officer's consent. Johnson v. State, App. 2 Dist., 652 So.2d 1258 (1995). Sentencing And Punishment ⚷ 1981(2)

Probation condition prohibiting probationer from possessing, carrying or owning any weapons without first procuring consent of probation officer, as well as condition prohibiting probationer from using intoxicants to excess or possessing any drugs or narcotics unless prescribed by physician, were special conditions not announced in open court and, thus, had to be stricken. Howard v. State, App. 2 Dist., 652 So.2d 956 (1995). Sentencing And Punishment ⚷ 1920

Probation condition imposed on grand theft defendant, providing that defendant could not possess, carry, or own any weapons without first procuring consent of probation officer, was invalid; condition prohibited carrying of weapons other than those enumerated in statute providing valid general condition and was not orally pronounced at sentencing. Malone v. State, App. 2 Dist., 652 So.2d 902 (1995). Sentencing And Punishment ⚷ 1920; Sentencing And Punishment ⚷ 1981(2)

Probation condition imposed on grand theft defendant, providing that defendant could not possess, carry, or own any weapons without first procuring consent of probation officer, was invalid; condition implied that felon could, with consent of probation officer, possess weapons otherwise prohibited by another condition providing that defendant could not possess, carry, or own any firearms. Malone v. State, App. 2 Dist., 652 So.2d 902 (1995). Sentencing And Punishment ⚷ 1981(3)

Portion of probation condition that implied that probation officer could consent to defendant's possession of firearm was improper, and would be stricken. Geller v. State, App. 2 Dist., 651 So.2d 192 (1995), review granted 663 So.2d 631, quashed 668 So.2d 599. Sentencing And Punishment ⚷ 1981(3)

Condition of probation prohibiting convicted felon from owning or possessing firearm was valid except to extent that it implied that defendant's probation officer could consent to defendant's possession of firearm. Hart v. State, App. 2 Dist., 651 So.2d 112 (1995), review granted 659 So.2d 1089, quashed in part 668 So.2d 589. Sentencing And Punishment ⚷ 1981(3)

133. —— Special conditions, oral pronouncements, restriction on weapons possession

Trial court is required to orally pronounce special conditions of probation at time of sentencing. McClough v. State, App. 5 Dist., 669 So.2d 1099 (1996). Sentencing And Punishment ⚷ 1918

Probation condition requiring defendant to keep hourly accounting of all activities on daily log was special condition which had to be orally announced in open court. Burdo v. State, App. 3 Dist., 667 So.2d 874 (1996), review granted 676 So.2d 412, quashed 682 So.2d 557. Sentencing And Punishment ⚷ 1918

Trial court could not impose special conditions of probation without orally pronouncing them at sentencing. Bristol v. State, App. 2 Dist., 667 So.2d 486 (1996). Sentencing And Punishment ⚷ 1918

Special probation conditions that were imposed at sentencing but not orally pronounced had to be stricken. Thompson v. State, App. 2 Dist., 667 So.2d 447 (1996), habeas corpus dismissed 2006 WL 213868. Sentencing And Punishment ⚷ 1920

Condition of probation providing that probationer could not possess, carry, or own any weapons without first procuring consent of officer was special condition of probation that trial court was required to pronounce orally at sentencing hearing. Kirkland v. State, App. 1 Dist., 666 So.2d 974 (1996). Sentencing And Punishment ⚷ 1918

Special condition of probation must be pronounced orally at sentencing hearing or else it cannot be included in written order; however, "standard conditions of probation," meaning those listed in probation statute, may be included in written order even if they are not pronounced orally at sentencing hearing. Kirkland v. State, App. 1 Dist., 666 So.2d 974 (1996). Sentencing And Punishment ⚷ 1918

Trial court was required to orally pronounce special conditions of probation in order for such conditions to be valid. Turner v. State, App. 2

Dist., 666 So.2d 212 (1995). Sentencing And Punishment ⚷ 1918

Special condition of probation was improperly imposed where no oral announcement was made. Lawson v. State, App. 2 Dist., 666 So.2d 193 (1995). Sentencing And Punishment ⚷ 1920

Probation condition prohibiting the use of intoxicants to excess would be stricken since this was a special condition of probation requiring an oral pronouncement. Murphy v. State, App. 2 Dist., 666 So.2d 182 (1995). Sentencing And Punishment ⚷ 1920

Probation condition prohibiting possession, carrying or ownership of any weapons without first procuring consent of probation officer is special condition that must be pronounced at sentencing to be valid. Johnson v. State, App. 2 Dist., 664 So.2d 1053 (1995). Sentencing And Punishment ⚷ 1918

Condition placed on defendant's probation, that he not possess, carry, or own weapons other than firearms, which was added to prohibition against possessing, carrying, or owning firearms, was special condition that must be orally pronounced at sentencing. Johnson v. State, App. 4 Dist., 662 So.2d 755 (1995). Sentencing And Punishment ⚷ 1918

Condition of probation which stated that defendant was not to "possess, carry, or own any weapons without first procuring the consent of your officer," was improper, in sentencing for attempted second-degree murder; portion referring to weapons other than firearms was an invalid special condition not orally pronounced at sentencing, and remainder implied felon could possess weapons otherwise prohibited with consent of probation officer. Hall v. State, App. 2 Dist., 661 So.2d 63 (1995). Sentencing And Punishment ⚷ 1920; Sentencing And Punishment ⚷ 1981(3)

Special probation condition prohibiting defendant from possessing, carrying, or owning a weapon without first procuring consent of probation officer was invalid where condition was not orally pronounced at sentencing. Swanson v. State, App. 2 Dist., 656 So.2d 503 (1995), rehearing denied. Sentencing And Punishment ⚷ 1920

Condition of probation under which defendant was not to possess or own firearm had to be stricken, since defendant was not convicted felon and trial court failed to orally pronounce special condition. Rudnicki v. State, App. 2 Dist., 655 So.2d 1275 (1995). Sentencing And Punishment ⚷ 1920

Probation condition prohibiting possession of any weapon was "special condition of probation" that had to be orally pronounced. Johnson v. State, App. 2 Dist., 652 So.2d 1258 (1995). Sentencing And Punishment ⚷ 1918

Condition of probation precluding defendant from possessing, carrying or owning any weapons without first procuring consent of his officer was "special condition of probation" that was required to be pronounced at sentencing in order to be valid; there is no statutory prohibition as to possession of weapons. Parsons v. State, App. 2 Dist., 650 So.2d 176 (1995), denial of post-conviction relief affirmed in part, reversed in part 672 So.2d 877. Sentencing And Punishment ⚷ 1918

134. —— General conditions, oral pronouncements, restriction on weapons possession

No oral pronouncement was needed for general condition of probation under which defendant could not possess, carry or own firearm, upon being sentenced for attempted second-degree murder. Hall v. State, App. 2 Dist., 661 So.2d 63 (1995). Sentencing And Punishment ⚷ 1918

Condition of probation prohibiting defendant from owning or having in his care, custody, possession or control any firearm was general condition for which no oral pronouncement was needed. Callaway v. State, App. 2 Dist., 658 So.2d 593 (1995). Sentencing And Punishment ⚷ 1918

General prohibition of weapons or destructive devices, as condition of probation, was required to be orally pronounced at sentencing. Callaway v. State, App. 2 Dist., 658 So.2d 593 (1995). Sentencing And Punishment ⚷ 1918

Probation condition prohibiting possessing, carrying or owning firearms could be imposed, even though there had been no oral pronouncement regarding prohibition made at trial; it was general condition for which pronouncement was not required. Daughtery v. State, App. 2 Dist., 654 So.2d 1209 (1995). Sentencing And Punishment ⚷ 1918

Condition of probation prohibiting possession of firearm proscribed conduct which defendant, as convicted felon, was already legally prohibited from engaging in, and thus was a "general condition of probation" which was valid without having been pronounced in open court, but condition prohibiting possession of any weapon was a "special condition of probation" which was improperly imposed when it was not orally pronounced in open court. Mitchell v. State, App. 2 Dist., 654 So.2d 950 (1995). Sentencing And Punishment ⚷ 1920; Sentencing And Punishment ⚷ 1981(2)

General prohibition of possessing, carrying or owning any weapons, as opposed to firearms, would be stricken as condition of probation, since it was not orally pronounced at sentencing. Farrington v. State, App. 2 Dist., 654 So.2d 564 (1995), rehearing denied, amended on rehearing, review granted 663 So.2d 631, quashed 668 So.2d 598. Sentencing And Punishment ⚷ 1920

No oral pronouncement was required for general probation condition barring defendant from possessing, carrying, or owning firearms inasmuch as such conduct by person convicted of felony was prohibited by statute and condition constituted general probation condition; however, oral pronouncement was required for portion of condition barring defendant from possessing, carrying, or owning weapons and destructive devices. Evans v. State, App. 2 Dist., 653 So.2d 1103 (1995). Sentencing And Punishment ⚷ 1918

Probation conditions barring probationer from possessing, carrying or owning any firearms and from visiting places where intoxicants, drugs or other dangerous substances were unlawfully sold, dispensed or used were valid as more precise descriptions of general conditions, which did not have to be announced in open court. Howard v. State, App. 2 Dist., 652 So.2d 956 (1995). Sentencing And Punishment ⚷ 1918; Sentencing And Punishment ⚷ 1980(2); Sentencing And Punishment ⚷ 1981(2)

Written condition of probation prohibiting defendant from possessing, carrying or owning firearms was not required to be pronounced at sentencing; that was valid general condition, as felons may not possess firearms. Parsons v. State, App. 2 Dist., 650 So.2d 176 (1995), denial of post-conviction relief affirmed in part, reversed in part 672 So.2d 877. Sentencing And Punishment ⚷ 1918

District Court of Appeal would strike general prohibition of the possession of weapons, as opposed to firearms, where the condition was not orally pronounced at sentencing. Fitts v. State, App. 2 Dist., 649 So.2d 300 (1995). Sentencing And Punishment ⚷ 1138

135. —— Oral pronouncements, generally, restriction on weapons possession

Portion of probation weapons condition referring to destructive devices had to be orally pronounced. Holmes v. State, App. 2 Dist., 675 So.2d 995 (1996). Sentencing And Punishment ⚷ 1918

Even assuming that in-court explanation of special conditions of probation by probation officer at time of sentencing could be adequate substitute for court's oral pronouncement at time of sentencing, there was no evidence of such explanation on record; explanation was necessary for due process reasons and because a defendant must make contemporaneous objection to probation conditions at time of sentencing. Dean v. State, App. 4 Dist., 669 So.2d 1140 (1996). Criminal Law ⚷ 1126

Probation conditions barring defendant from carrying weapons, requiring him to maintain hourly accounting on a daily log of all his activities, and condition prohibiting him from use of intoxicants to excess, would be stricken, where they were not pronounced at sentencing. Green v. State, App. 2 Dist., 667 So.2d 432 (1996). Sentencing And Punishment ⚷ 1920

Condition of probation requiring probationer to support any dependents to the best of his ability was standard condition of probation that did not have to be pronounced orally at sentencing. Kirkland v. State, App. 1 Dist., 666 So.2d 974 (1996). Sentencing And Punishment ⚷ 1918

Conditions of probation that prohibited possession of weapons, prohibited excessive use of alcohol, and required defendant to pay for drug and alcohol abuse evaluation, treatment, and random testing, should have been orally pronounced at sentencing. Kirkland v. State, App. 2 Dist., 666 So.2d 185 (1995). Sentencing And Punishment ⚷ 1918

Written condition of probation that prohibited defendant, a convicted felon, from owning or possessing firearm, was valid despite fact that condition was not orally pronounced at sentencing hearing, as possession of firearm by convicted felon is statutorily prohibited. Vasquez v. State, App. 4 Dist., 663 So.2d 1343 (1995), review dismissed 666 So.2d 145. Sentencing And Punishment ⚷ 1920

Written condition of probation that prohibited defendant, a convicted felon, from owning or possessing any weapon without permission of probation officer was invalid, as limitation was not orally pronounced at sentencing hearing and it exceeded scope of statute. Vasquez v. State, App. 4 Dist., 663 So.2d 1343 (1995), review dismissed 666 So.2d 145. Sentencing And Punishment ⚷ 1920; Sentencing And Punishment ⚷ 1921; Sentencing And Punishment ⚷ 1981(2)

Condition of probation that defendant not possess, carry, or own any firearm was general condition that need not have been orally pronounced at sentencing. Johnson v. State, App. 4 Dist., 662 So.2d 755 (1995). Sentencing And Punishment ⚷ 1918

Trial court erred by prohibiting probationer from possessing, carrying, or owning weapons, except firearms, without consent of probation officer as condition of probation without pronouncing condition in open court. Simmons v. State, App. 4 Dist., 662 So.2d 754 (1995). Sentencing And Punishment ⚷ 1920

Sentencing court's failure to orally pronounce condition of probation that prohibits defendant from carrying weapon other than firearm while including it in written conditions of probation could be remedied on remand. McClendon v. State, App. 5 Dist., 659 So.2d 718 (1995). Sentencing And Punishment ⚷ 1920

Probation condition stating that defendant who was convicted of felony "will not possess, carry or own any firearms" was a general condition for which no oral pronouncement at sentencing was needed since statute made it unlawful for any person convicted of felony to own or possess firearm and thus, condition would not be stricken. Williams v. State, App. 2 Dist., 658 So.2d 1172 (1995). Sentencing And Punishment ⚷ 1918

Probation condition imposed on convicted felon, prohibiting the carrying of weapons other than those enumerated in statute prohibiting person convicted of felony from possessing firearms, would be struck since it was not orally pronounced at sentencing. Williams v. State, App. 2 Dist., 658 So.2d 1172 (1995). Sentencing And Punishment ⚷ 1920

Defendant, as convicted felon, was prohibited from possessing, owning, or carrying firearms, and so probation condition that prohibited same conduct was valid even though it had not been orally pronounced. Hamilton v. State, App. 2 Dist., 653 So.2d 1068 (1995). Sentencing And Punishment ⚷ 1918

Probation condition imposed on grand theft defendant, providing that defendant could not possess, carry or own any firearms, was valid, although not orally pronounced at sentencing. Malone v. State, App. 2 Dist., 652 So.2d 902 (1995). Sentencing And Punishment ⚷ 1918

Probation condition prohibiting possession or ownership of any weapon would be stricken, where condition was not orally pronounced at sentencing. Geller v. State, App. 2 Dist., 651 So.2d 192 (1995), review granted 663 So.2d 631, quashed 668 So.2d 599. Sentencing And Punishment ⚷ 1920

Conditions of probation prohibiting possession or ownership of any weapon and prohibiting excessive use of intoxicants were invalid due to lack of oral pronouncement of those conditions by trial court. Hart v. State, App. 2 Dist., 651 So.2d 112 (1995), review granted 659 So.2d 1089, quashed in part 668 So.2d 589. Sentencing And Punishment ⚷ 1920

136. Curfews

Written condition of probation that set curfew for defendant which was not orally pronounced at sentencing hearing was invalid, as curfew requirement was special condition of probation not otherwise statutorily authorized. Vasquez v. State, App. 4 Dist., 663 So.2d 1343 (1995), review dismissed 666 So.2d 145. Sentencing And Punishment ⚷ 1920

Probation conditions for defendant convicted of being felon in possession of firearm, which prohibited him from consuming alcohol or visiting establishments where alcohol is main source of income, and which imposed 9:00 p.m. curfew, would be stricken, as they constituted special conditions which were not orally pronounced at sentencing. Reed v. State, App. 2 Dist., 652 So.2d 912 (1995). Sentencing And Punishment ⚷ 1920

Written probation order could not establish 11:00 p.m. curfew when there was no mention of curfew at defendant's sentencing hearing. Zachary v. State, App. 2 Dist., 559 So.2d 105 (1990). Sentencing And Punishment ⚷ 1918; Sentencing And Punishment ⚷ 1921

Probation condition imposing 8 p.m. to 6 a.m. curfew on defendant was so harsh that it would counteract concept of rehabilitation and would be amended to provide for 11 p.m. to 6 a.m. curfew. Kominsky v. State, App. 1 Dist., 330 So.2d 800 (1976). Sentencing And Punishment ⚷ 1976(2)

Finding that petitioner had violated probation curfew restrictions was not supported by evidence when petitioner testified unequivocally that supervisor had lifted restrictions for date in question, and supervisor's testimony was not flatly contradictory thereto. Larocco v. State, App. 4 Dist., 276 So.2d 538 (1973). Sentencing And Punishment ⚷ 2021

137. Public service

Although trial court had authority to impose condition of public service as a condition of probation, trial court was without authority to require that probationer's public service be on a full-time employment basis. Fillastre v. State, App. 2 Dist., 387 So.2d 400 (1980). Sentencing And Punishment ⚷ 1982(2)

138. Armed forces

In posttrial posture, trial court may withhold adjudication or sentence or both and impose, as a condition of probation, requirement that defendant enter the armed forces. State v. Jogan, App. 3 Dist., 388 So.2d 322 (1980). Sentencing And Punishment ⚷ 1983(2)

A trial judge cannot release a prisoner for service in the armed forces of the United States. Op.Atty.Gen., 1943, p. 510.

139. Restitution—In general

Defendant convicted of driving under the influence and causing serious bodily injury to another could be required to pay restitution as condition of probation even though accident that led to his conviction rendered him paraplegic and even though state conceded that it was highly unlikely that defendant would ever be able to pay restitution. Brown v. State, App. 1 Dist., 645 So.2d 1066 (1994). Sentencing And Punishment ⚷ 1973(2)

Imposition of restitution as condition of community control 105 days after sentencing constituted illegal sentence where defendant did not agree to imposition of restitution as part of his presentencing plea agreement and restitution was not mentioned in written community control order. King v. State, App. 1 Dist., 611 So.2d 24 (1992). Sentencing And Punishment ⚷ 1887; Sentencing And Punishment ⚷ 1919

In setting the terms and conditions of probation, the trial court may require the probationer to make restitution for damage or loss caused by the offense in an amount to be determined by the court. Reynolds v. State, App. 1 Dist., 598 So.2d 188 (1992). Sentencing And Punishment ⚷ 1973(2)

Defendant who was convicted of writing bad check to supermarket could not be ordered to pay, as condition of probation, restitution ordered in other prosecutions for writing bad checks to same supermarket under statute permitting judge to order restitution to victim for damage or loss caused directly or indirectly by defendant's offense. Small v. State, App. 5 Dist., 587 So.2d 597 (1991). Sentencing And Punishment ⚷ 1973(2)

It was error for trial court to order defendant convicted of leaving scene of accident involving personal injuries, as condition of probation, to pay restitution to her employer or her insurance company, if insurance company reduced its claim to judgment and notified court, where restitution ordered could be construed to include not only damages resulting from defendant's criminal conduct of leaving scene of accident involving personal injuries, but also damages arising from accident itself. Williams v. State, App. 2 Dist., 505 So.2d 478 (1987), approved and remanded 520 So.2d 276. Sentencing And Punishment ⚷ 1973(3)

Conditions of probation requiring probationer to make restitution must generally be challenged in trial court before the issue may be raised on appeal. Young v. State, App. 2 Dist., 438 So.2d 998 (1983). Criminal Law ⚷ 1042.3(5)

Defendant, who returned all items that he personally took from dwelling but whose codefendant had sold some of items he took during burglary, was properly ordered, as condition of probation, to make restitution to victim for difference between value of goods stolen and goods recovered, plus interest, notwithstanding that all of goods that he stole were recovered. Woods v. State, App. 1 Dist., 418 So.2d 401 (1982). Sentencing And Punishment ⚷ 1973(2)

Defendant, following conviction and sentence for burglary and grand larceny, was, as a condition of probation, properly required to pay restitution, court costs and police academy costs, notwithstanding that defendant had previously been adjudicated insolvent. Pope v. State, App. 1 Dist., 368 So.2d 676 (1979). Sentencing And Punishment ⚷ 1973(2); Sentencing And Punishment ⚷ 1975(2)

Provision, within probation order, to effect that defendant would receive 18-month sentence if he violated condition of probation that he make restitution of medical expenses to victim became inoperative when court did not impose any sentence, but, rather, continued the probation after it was established that such a violation had occurred. Mayo v. State, App. 3 Dist., 346 So.2d 98 (1977). Sentencing And Punishment ⚷ 2039

140. —— Prerequisites, restitution

There is two-prong test for determining validity of condition of probation involving restitution: damage or loss must be causally related to offense for which it is imposed, and there must be significant relationship between loss and crime proven. Williams v. State, App. 1 Dist., 565 So.2d 849 (1990). Sentencing And Punishment ⚷ 1973(2)

141. —— Payment schedule, restitution

Establishment of payment schedule for restitution is judicial responsibility rather than supervisory function properly administered by probation officer. Jordan v. State, App. 1 Dist., 610 So.2d 616 (1992). Constitutional Law ⚷ 2574

142. —— Work requirements, restitution

Requirement that probationer work at least 60 hours per week so that he could make restitution payments to victims was proper. Spruill v. State, App. 5 Dist., 643 So.2d 1191 (1994). Sentencing And Punishment ⚷ 1972(2)

Trial court could not, as condition of defendant's probation, require defendant to maintain full-time and part-time employment in order to meet his restitutionary obligation, but could only require defendant to actively seek gainful employment; trial court's error was sufficiently egregious to be the equivalent of fundamental error, to which defendant did not have to make contemporaneous objection. Armstrong v. State, App. 5 Dist., 620 So.2d 1120 (1993). Criminal Law ⚷ 1042.3(4); Sentencing And Punishment ⚷ 1972(2)

143. —— Failure to pay, restitution

Special condition of defendant's probation, providing that defendant was to begin serving jail sentence if she failed to pay specified portions of total amount of restitution ordered by specified dates, was improper, and trial court would be directed on remand to amend order of probation to make clear that defendant would not be required to begin serving jail sentence unless and until it was determined that she had ability to make restitution payment, but willfully refused to do so. Daniels v. State, App. 1 Dist., 678 So.2d 860 (1996), rehearing denied. Criminal Law ⚷ 1192; Sentencing And Punishment ⚷ 1973(3); Sentencing And Punishment ⚷ 1976(3)

Special conditions of probationer's community control and probation which required probationer to remain in county unless permission was granted otherwise by state attorney's office was not abuse of discretion, in view of evidence that probationer's failure to make monthly restitution payments to victims began when his probation officer allowed him to move out of state. Spruill v. State, App. 5 Dist., 643 So.2d 1191 (1994). Sentencing And Punishment ⚷ 1967(2)

Defendant's probation could not be extended beyond maximum period of incarceration that was available for his offense, notwithstanding his inability to pay restitution as condition of probation during probationary period because of injury. Bono v. State, App. 1 Dist., 553 So.2d 293 (1989). Sentencing And Punishment ⚷ 1952

144. —— Unrelated offenses, restitution

Restitution that had been imposed for unemployment compensation fraud, but that was delinquent, could be imposed as condition of probation for unrelated offense of grand theft; trial judge reasonably concluded that requiring payment of delinquent restitution was necessary for rehabilitation and protection of public against future theft. Williams v. State, App. 1 Dist., 565 So.2d 849 (1990). Sentencing And Punishment ⚷ 1973(2)

145. —— Clarity of conditions, restitution

Restitution provision requiring that defendant "[p]ay restitution to victim as set forth in presentence investigation, and on schedule of probation officer" was improperly vague. Durrett v. State, App. 1 Dist., 530 So.2d 483 (1988). Sentencing And Punishment ⚷ 2199

146. —— Relationship to crime charged, restitution

Imposition of conditions on probation of defendant, who was on probation for dealing in stolen property when he violated terms of probation by driving under the influence of alcohol (DUI), that he abstain from consumption of intoxicants and from visiting establishments whose primary purpose was sale or consumption of intoxicants, and submit to random urinalysis, although perhaps not related to dealing in stolen property charge, was imposed, was reasonably related to preventing future criminality. Devine v. State, App. 5 Dist., 636 So.2d 179 (1994). Sentencing And Punishment ⚷ 1980(2); Sentencing And Punishment ⚷ 1996

Restitution for victim's loss of tools as result of theft of victim's truck being stolen could not be imposed as condition on probation for defendant convicted of grand theft of motor vehicle and possession of vehicle with altered vehicle identification number; defendant's admission that he purchased truck for $500 several weeks after it was stolen and his denial that there were tools in truck at time he acquired possession were uncontradicted, and there was no evidence that he was actual thief. Moore v. State, App. 5 Dist., 623 So.2d 842 (1993). Sentencing And Punishment ⚷ 1973(2)

Restitution for unrecovered property contained in stolen truck at time of theft was inappropriate where state did not present evidence that defendant was the actual thief or that he was linked to unrecovered property in any other way; truck was recovered approximately ten weeks after it was stolen, defendant's testimony that truck was in another's possession for at least five weeks after it was stolen was uncontradicted, and his possession was not sufficiently "recent" to qualify for presumption that he was thief based on possession of stolen property. Moore v. State, App. 5 Dist., 623 So.2d 842 (1993). Sentencing And Punishment ⚷ 2143

Requirement that defendant pay restitution as condition of probation for leaving scene of accident was improper since damages arising out of accident would have occurred with or without defendant committing the offense. Fykes v. State, App. 1 Dist., 599 So.2d 268 (1992). Sentencing And Punishment ⚷ 1973(2)

Restitution is to be imposed when damages or loss for which restitution is ordered is caused directly or indirectly by the offense. Fykes v. State, App. 1 Dist., 599 So.2d 268 (1992). Sentencing And Punishment ⚷ 2143

Condition of probation requiring defendant to pay restitution for items missing from victim's home was improper, where defendant was convicted only of stealing victim's automobile. Bayer v. State, App. 5 Dist., 597 So.2d 870 (1992). Sentencing And Punishment ⚷ 1973(2)

Defendant can be ordered to pay restitution only for damages caused directly or indirectly by act for which defendant is convicted. Bayer

v. State, App. 5 Dist., 597 So.2d 870 (1992). Sentencing And Punishment ⚿ 2143

Condition of probation for leaving scene of accident with injury or death and driving without a valid driver's license, requiring restitution for damages caused by the accident, was error where the damages were not sufficiently related to either of the offenses of which defendant was convicted. Ochoa v. State, App. 2 Dist., 596 So.2d 515 (1992). Sentencing And Punishment ⚿ 1973(2)

In determining amount of restitution payable by defendant convicted of grand theft, trial court improperly included items defendant was never specifically charged with having stolen and that were not found in his possession, and damages incurred during burglary of victim's home; no evidence linked defendant to actual burglary or to any of unrecovered items stolen during burglary, and there was six-month time lapse between defendant's arrest and burglary. Mansingh v. State, App. 1 Dist., 588 So.2d 636 (1991). Sentencing And Punishment ⚿ 2143

Whatever the breadth of judicial discretion in fashioning other conditions of probation, when condition of probation is that restitution be paid, payment may be ordered only for loss caused by offense for which defendant is being sentenced. Small v. State, App. 5 Dist., 587 So.2d 597 (1991). Sentencing And Punishment ⚿ 1973(2)

In order to sustain a restitution order which encompasses damage to victims for offenses a defendant is not charged with having committed, nor convicted of having committed, State must demonstrate a significant relationship between the loss or damage sustained by victim and defendant's acts in committing the offense for which he was charged and convicted. Faulkner v. State, App. 5 Dist., 582 So.2d 783 (1991). Sentencing And Punishment ⚿ 2145

Restitution order which encompassed damage suffered by victims of burglary unrelated to theft and sale of two rifles stolen from home lacked valid basis, except to extent that it compensated victims for loss of one rifle which was not recovered, where defendant pled nolo contendere to dealing in stolen property, specifically two rifles, and State failed to establish that defendant's dealing with the rifles caused or bore any significant relationship to loss of other items burglarized from victims' home. Faulkner v. State, App. 5 Dist., 582 So.2d 783 (1991). Sentencing And Punishment ⚿ 2143

Trial court could require defendant, who violated terms of his community control which was imposed after he was adjudicated guilty of burglary and dealing in stolen property, to pay restitution for offenses other than burglary and dealing in stolen property charges for which he was sentenced. Cogdell v. State, App. 5 Dist., 547 So.2d 256 (1989). Sentencing And Punishment ⚿ 2040

Defendant could not be required to pay restitution to theft victim as condition of probation, absent determination of whether victim's loss was either directly or indirectly caused by defendant's offense. Tucker v. State, App. 1 Dist., 529 So.2d 818 (1988). Sentencing And Punishment ⚿ 1973(2)

Defendant's probation was improperly conditioned upon compensation of victim of traffic accident for damages for accident where only crime defendant was convicted of was leaving scene of accident involving injury. Harrington v. State, App. 2 Dist., 516 So.2d 308 (1987), review dismissed 525 So.2d 881. Sentencing And Punishment ⚿ 1973(2)

Defendant could be ordered to pay $150 in restitution, as award bore significant relationship to offense of burglary of dwelling of which defendant had been convicted, even though theft charge to which defendant pled guilty had been nolle prossed by State. Lawson v. State, App. 1 Dist., 498 So.2d 541 (1986), review denied 506 So.2d 1042. Sentencing And Punishment ⚿ 2144

Ordering defendant to make restitution for injuries sustained by persons in automobile accident was proper condition of probation following plea of no contest to failure by one involved in accident to stop and render aid to injured person, where there was no question that defendant caused accident and injuries as result of his reckless driving. Bowling v. State, App. 5 Dist., 479 So.2d 146 (1985). Sentencing And Punishment ⚿ 1973(2)

Damage resulting from fire which occurred when defendant, during burglary of house, left lighted cigarette near her point of entry bore sufficient relationship to crime charged, in that the damage arose from defendant's criminal conduct, to allow a restitution provision in probation order. Roberts v. State, App. 5 Dist., 467 So.2d 439 (1985). Sentencing And Punishment ⚿ 1973(2)

Condition of probation imposed upon entry of guilty plea to depositing check with intent to defraud, that defendant make restitution to victims of crimes charged in subject indictment, as well as victims of crimes charged in two other indictments relating to same or similar offenses was properly imposed, even though condition was not related to specific crime charged in information under which defendant was placed on probation, where condition was reasonably related to crime charged and clearly had rehabilitative purpose. Rose v. State, App. 5 Dist., 434 So.2d 1014 (1983), petition for review denied 444 So.2d 418. Sentencing And Punishment ⚷ 1973(2)

In prosecution for leaving the scene of an accident involving an injury, imposition of restitution, as a condition of probation, for all damages resulting from the accident, not just those damages arising from the criminal act of leaving the scene, was improper. Riner v. State, App. 2 Dist., 389 So.2d 316 (1980). Sentencing And Punishment ⚷ 1973(2)

Offense with which defendant was charged, leaving scene of accident, did not result in or have any relationship to any damage or injury to victim, and no restitution condition of probation could be imposed. DiOrio v. State, App. 2 Dist., 359 So.2d 45 (1978). Sentencing And Punishment ⚷ 1973(2)

Where defendant was convicted of leaving scene of automobile accident resulting in injury to another person, and was placed on probation, court was not statutorily authorized to impose probation condition requiring that defendant pay specified amount to person with whose automobile his vehicle had collided, since such damage was not caused by criminal conduct of which defendant had been convicted. Fresneda v. State, 347 So.2d 1021 (1977). Sentencing And Punishment ⚷ 1973(2)

This section which allows sentencing court to require a defendant, as a condition of probation, to make restitution to the aggrieved party for damage or loss caused by defendant's offense does not authorize court to require defendant to make restitution in other unrelated cases for which defendant has not been convicted. Crowder v. State, App. 4 Dist., 334 So.2d 819 (1976), certiorari denied 342 So.2d 1101. Sentencing And Punishment ⚷ 1973(2)

Trial judge exceeded his authority in requiring that defendant, as a condition of his probation, make restitution in 20 cases unrelated to the offense for which he was convicted. Crowder v. State, App. 4 Dist., 334 So.2d 819 (1976), certiorari denied 342 So.2d 1101. Sentencing And Punishment ⚷ 1973(2)

147. —— Assessment, restitution

Assessment of restitution as condition of defendant's probation without first determining defendant's ability to pay was proper, where defendant did not offer any evidence of his inability to pay at sentencing, although he had ample opportunity to do so. Pentz v. State, App. 5 Dist., 642 So.2d 836 (1994). Sentencing And Punishment ⚷ 1973(2)

148. —— Amount of restitution

Written probation order requiring payment of $400 in restitution had to be modified to conform to court's oral pronouncement requiring probationer to pay $100 in restitution. Reiter v. State, App. 2 Dist., 674 So.2d 189 (1996). Sentencing And Punishment ⚷ 1921

Where offense of which defendant was convicted (petit theft) was theft of items having value of $300 or less, maximum value of items for which defendant could be ordered to pay restitution was also $300, even though evidence established that value of items defendant was originally charged with stealing was well in excess of $300. Peralta v. State, App. 5 Dist., 596 So.2d 1220 (1992). Sentencing And Punishment ⚷ 2164

Defendant cannot be required to pay restitution in excess of damages his criminal conduct caused. Mansingh v. State, App. 1 Dist., 588 So.2d 636 (1991). Sentencing And Punishment ⚷ 2160

Because victim's counseling had not been completed, trial court did not abuse its discretion in failing to fix amount of restitution defendant was required to pay as a condition of probation for counseling expenses incurred by victim assuming that, at a future appropriate time and upon application, trial court would determine amount of restitution to be paid and that duty could not be delegated. Weckerle v. State, App. 4 Dist., 579 So.2d 742 (1991). Constitutional Law ⚷ 2570; Sentencing And Punishment ⚷ 1973(2)

Trial judge did not err in failing to include specific amount of restitution in probation order at time of sentencing. Cogdell v. State, App. 5 Dist., 547 So.2d 256 (1989). Sentencing And Punishment ⚷ 1918

Trial court did not abuse its discretion in leaving determination of amount of restitution to be made to battery victim to future date given fact that victim had not fully recovered from injuries at time of sentencing; however, sentencing order lacked specificity regarding procedure for setting amount of restitution at some time in future, and thus, remand was required. McCaskill v. State, App. 1 Dist., 520 So.2d 664 (1988). Criminal Law ⚷ 1181.5(8); Sentencing And Punishment ⚷ 2199

Trial court was entitled to impose restitution as condition of probation at time of sentencing leaving determination of specific amount of restitution to be determined at a subsequent hearing. Villarreal v. State, App. 2 Dist., 516 So.2d 63 (1987). Sentencing And Punishment ⚷ 1973(3)

Requirement that burglary and petit theft defendant "pay one-half restitution as determined by probation officer," as condition of probation, was improper. Fazio v. State, App. 2 Dist., 509 So.2d 979 (1987). Sentencing And Punishment ⚷ 1973(2)

Burglary victim was damaged only to the extent of the value of used motorcycle parts stolen by defendant, and fact that victim's insurance coverage permitted victim to be paid in excess of that value did not permit trial court to order restitution in an amount in excess of the value of the used parts. Norman v. State, App. 1 Dist., 468 So.2d 1063 (1985), review denied 479 So.2d 118. Sentencing And Punishment ⚷ 2172

Where defendant made no objection to condition of restitution for damage or loss caused by his offense at time it was set, absence of judicial prescription of amount of restitution was not a defense against his probation revocation for violation of that condition. Wilson v. State, App. 1 Dist., 407 So.2d 1078 (1982). Sentencing And Punishment ⚷ 2006

Probation order requiring restitution of an amount equal to the full value of the aggregate theft committed by defendant and his codefendant did not constitute an abuse of discretion. Pollreisz v. State, App. 1 Dist., 406 So.2d 1297 (1981). Sentencing And Punishment ⚷ 1973(2)

Trial court erred when, in imposing conditions of probation, it required defendant to pay $6,000 in restitution to victim where defendant did not receive notice that restitution would be a condition of probation and there was nothing in record which would support conclusion that conduct of which defendant was convicted caused $6,000 worth of damage. Bradley v. State, App. 1 Dist., 406 So.2d 56 (1981). Sentencing And Punishment ⚷ 1917

Trial court did not err in including as a condition of probation that each of defendants convicted of conspiracy to aid or assist in the conduct of a lottery and aiding or assisting in conducting a lottery should pay restitution in the amount of $4,000 toward the cost of the investigation. Cuba v. State, App. 3 Dist., 362 So.2d 29 (1978), certiorari denied 378 So.2d 344, certiorari denied 378 So.2d 347. Sentencing And Punishment ⚷ 1973(2)

149. —— Orders, restitution

Absent evidence bearing on or specific finding of defendant's ability to pay, trial court's finding of violation of condition of probation requiring defendant to contribute $10 per month toward costs of his supervision would be stricken from order of revocation of probation. Abel v. State, App. 2 Dist., 383 So.2d 325 (1980). Sentencing And Punishment ⚷ 2028

150. —— Fair market value, restitution

Absent circumstances tending to show that fair market value does not adequately compensate theft victim or otherwise serve purpose of restitution, amount of restitution should be established through evidence of fair market value at time of theft. Mansingh v. State, App. 1 Dist., 588 So.2d 636 (1991). Sentencing And Punishment ⚷ 2172

For purposes of determining amount of restitution, fair market value may be established either through direct testimony or through production of evidence relating to all of four criteria: original cost, manner in which items were used, their general condition and quality, and percentage of depreciation. Mansingh v. State, App. 1 Dist., 588 So.2d 636 (1991). Sentencing And Punishment ⚷ 2172

There were no circumstances tending to show that fair market value would not adequately compensate grand theft victim or serve purpose of restitution and, thus, amount of restitution should have been established based on fair market value of stolen property at time of theft. Mansingh v. State, App. 1 Dist., 588 So.2d 636 (1991). Sentencing And Punishment ⚷ 2172

151. —— Minimum payments, restitution

Order requiring defendant, as condition of his probation, to make minimum monthly restitution payments of at least $300 would be modified on appeal, in order to strike the word "minimum" to avoid any suggestion that probation officer could require defendant to make higher monthly payments; defendant did not agree to delegate this authority to his probation officer. Armstrong v. State, App. 5 Dist., 620 So.2d 1120 (1993). Criminal Law ⚷ 1184(4.1)

152. —— Reservation of jurisdiction, restitution

In ordering periodic payments of restitution, trial court should have reserved jurisdiction to determine amount of those payments at hearing to be initiated by state and to be conducted after defendant began his term of probation. Wiley v. State, App. 4 Dist., 610 So.2d 70 (1992). Sentencing And Punishment ⚷ 2198

153. —— Modification, restitution

Court could modify sentence to set amount of restitution more than 60 days after sentence was imposed, where special conditions of original order required defendant to pay restitution in an amount to be determined. Gladfelter v. State, 618 So.2d 1364 (1993). Sentencing And Punishment ⚷ 2279

Probation officer exceeded his authority by increasing the monthly amount of restitution which probationer was required to pay. Jordan v. State, App. 1 Dist., 610 So.2d 616 (1992). Sentencing And Punishment ⚷ 1973(3)

154. —— Determination, restitution

Determination as to amount of restitution due from probationer must be made by trial court. Hamm v. State, App. 1 Dist., 403 So.2d 1155 (1981). Sentencing And Punishment ⚷ 1973(3)

155. —— Discretion of trial court, restitution

Trial court is not tied to fair market value as sole standard for determining amount of restitution, and may exercise discretion in determining that amount. Mansingh v. State, App. 1 Dist., 588 So.2d 636 (1991). Sentencing And Punishment ⚷ 2161

156. —— Ability to make restitution

It is improper for trial court to order immediate payment of restitution from defendant who has no immediate ability to pay. Edwards v. State, App. 5 Dist., 892 So.2d 1192 (2005). Sentencing And Punishment ⚷ 2134; Sentencing And Punishment ⚷ 2209

Probationer could be required to make restitution despite state's failure to establish any immediate ability on his part to pay total restitution order or any minimal installments, so long as order was based on probationer's future financial resources, within specified period or in specified installments. Ashlock v. State, App. 5 Dist., 632 So.2d 213 (1994). Sentencing And Punishment ⚷ 2134

Before person on probation can be imprisoned for failing to make restitution, there must be determination that that person has, or has had, ability to pay but has willfully refused to do so. Stephens v. State, 630 So.2d 1090 (1994). Sentencing And Punishment ⚷ 2003

Sentence that conditioned probation on defendant's making restitution to victim, and that provided for automatic imprisonment, without inquiry into defendant's ability to pay, if payment schedule was not followed, was illegal. Stephens v. State, 630 So.2d 1090 (1994). Sentencing And Punishment ⚷ 1973(2); Sentencing And Punishment ⚷ 2003

Requiring defendant and her codefendant jointly and severally to pay nearly $13,000 in restitution as condition to probation was unreasonable, where defendant effectively objected to amount of restitution and affirmatively introduced evidence in form of exact amount of her earnings that she did not have ability to pay amount imposed. Langston v. State, App. 4 Dist., 616 So.2d 597 (1993), review denied 626 So.2d 206. Sentencing And Punishment ⚷ 1973(2)

Before trial court imposed on defendant, as a condition of probation, that he pay child support per civil order, trial court should have made determination of defendant's present ability to pay current child support as well as unpaid arrearages. Ward v. State, App. 1 Dist., 511 So.2d 1109 (1987). Sentencing And Punishment ⚷ 1983(2)

That part of defendant's sentence which required him to make restitution as condition of parole would be vacated and assessment of $10 in costs would be stricken since defendant was indigent. Miller v. State, App. 4 Dist., 423 So.2d 623 (1982). Costs ⚷ 292; Pardon And Parole ⚷ 64.1

Revocation of probation for failure to make restitution or pay costs of supervision was improper where trial court had adjudicated defendant insolvent at time of entry of order of probation and there was no evidence presented concerning whether defendant was able to make restitution or pay costs. Grimsley v. State, App. 2 Dist., 408 So.2d 1075 (1982). Sentencing And Punishment ⚷ 2003

Ability to earn, even if it could be considered a factor in determining ability to pay, was not a basis for establishing a violation of restitution condition of probationary sentence absent evidence that defendant would have been hired at either of the job interviews set up for him and that being hired in either of those two positions would have resulted in defendant's being financially able to pay. Winfield v. State, App. 1 Dist., 406 So.2d 50 (1981). Sentencing And Punishment ⚷ 1973(3)

Defendant's probation could not be revoked for failure to pay restitution where the state failed to prove that the defendant had the financial ability to pay, but instead attempted to prove that the defendant had not actively pursued potential employment. Winfield v. State, App. 1 Dist., 406 So.2d 50 (1981). Sentencing And Punishment ⚷ 2003

Judgment revoking probation and imposing sentence following revocation would be reversed and proceedings would be remanded to trial court where record disclosed that trial court's primary concern in revoking probation was defendant's failure to pay medical costs incurred by victim, defendant's failure to pay such costs was not sufficient basis upon which to revoke his probation due to failure of state to establish defendant's solvency, and it was not established whether trial court would have revoked probation under remaining grounds or would have imposed remaining portion of term of imprisonment. Aaron v. State, App. 3 Dist., 400 So.2d 1033 (1981), review denied 408 So.2d 1095. Criminal Law ⚷ 1177.3(4); Criminal Law ⚷ 1181.5(8)

There must be a sufficient demonstration of ability to pay as well as a specific finding regarding ability to pay or else a holding that failure to make monthly payments is a violation of probation must be stricken. Smith v. State, App. 4 Dist., 380 So.2d 1175 (1980). Sentencing And Punishment ⚿ 1983(3)

Probationer's failure to make restitution payments to victim was not a "willful violation" of condition of probation where probationer did not have ability to make the payments. Smith v. State, App. 3 Dist., 377 So.2d 250 (1979). Sentencing And Punishment ⚿ 2003

It was a valid defense to technical violations of conditions of probation that defendant make payments on public defender's lien and make payments in restitution of her victims that defendant lost her job and was unable to make payments. Freiberger v. State, App. 4 Dist., 343 So.2d 57 (1977). Sentencing And Punishment ⚿ 2006

157. —— Indigency, restitution

In proceedings to revoke defendant's probation, state did not rebut defendant's testimony that he was an indigent, and therefore revocation of his probation could not be based on his failure to pay probation supervision costs. Parrish v. State, App. 3 Dist., 402 So.2d 530 (1981). Sentencing And Punishment ⚿ 2021

Probation could not be revoked for failure of probationer to abide by conditions of his probation requiring him to pay toward his cost of supervision, to pay restitution to victim, and to pay cost of defense and prosecution where, aside from fact that probationer was declared indigent by trial court, the record did not conclusively show that probationer had ability to make payments required of him as part of his probationary condition. Peterson v. State, App. 1 Dist., 384 So.2d 965 (1980). Sentencing And Punishment ⚿ 2003

158. —— Insolvency, restitution

A finding of a violation of the condition of probation requiring defendant to contribute $10 per month towards the cost of his supervision would be stricken from the order of revocation where defendant had been adjudicated insolvent 11 days prior to the revocation proceeding. Adamson v. State, App. 2 Dist., 383 So.2d 294 (1980). Sentencing And Punishment ⚿ 2028

159. —— Delegation, restitution

Determination of amount of restitution to be paid for each count of issuing worthless checks should have been made by trial court, and should not have been delegated to probation officer. Mendaros v. State, App. 1 Dist., 589 So.2d 386 (1991). Constitutional Law ⚿ 2574; Sentencing And Punishment ⚿ 2102

Determination of amount of restitution is a judicial responsibility which could not be delegated to probation officer. Buchanan v. State, App. 2 Dist., 483 So.2d 537 (1986). Constitutional Law ⚿ 2574

Trial court erred by delegating authority to a probation supervisor to determine amount of restitution. Henriquez v. State, App. 4 Dist., 463 So.2d 1178 (1984), quashed in part 485 So.2d 414. Sentencing And Punishment ⚿ 2197

Determination of defendant's ability to pay restitution was a judicial responsibility improperly delegated to defendant's probation officer. Ballance v. State, App. 1 Dist., 447 So.2d 974 (1984). Constitutional Law ⚿ 2574; Sentencing And Punishment ⚿ 2102

160. —— Destruction of property, restitution

Restitution could be ordered for damage done to automobile in effecting theft of stereo cassettes, stereo speakers, vehicle bug screen, and equalizer. Peralta v. State, App. 5 Dist., 596 So.2d 1220 (1992). Sentencing And Punishment ⚿ 2143

Defendant, who pled guilty to grand theft arising out of theft of a motorcycle, could be ordered to make restitution after motorcycle was destroyed as result of his careless driving while attempting to escape from police. Jones v. State, App. 4 Dist., 427 So.2d 398 (1983). Sentencing And Punishment ⚿ 2145

161. —— Lost profits, restitution

Defendant, who had entered into a rental agreement to pay $930 in regular rental payments for a television set, who made nine regular payments and then moved, taking the television set with her and leaving no forwarding address and making no further payments, and who was subsequently convicted by a plea of nolo contendere to charge of grand theft, could be required, as a condition of her probation, to make restitution for lost profits suffered by lessor of the television set; however, restitution could not exceed damage caused and, therefore, ordered restitution of $930 was required to be reduced by amount of regular payments made by defendant. Wilson v. State, App. 1 Dist., 452 So.2d 84 (1984), petition for review denied 461 So.2d 116. Sentencing And Punishment ⚿ 1973(3)

162. —— Medical care, restitution

Trial court was not authorized to impose, as condition of probation, requirement that defendant make restitution to county for medical care that county had duty to provide for injuries suffered in fall during incarceration in county jail. Comeau v. State, App. 1 Dist., 611 So.2d 68 (1992). Sentencing And Punishment ⚿ 1973(2)

163. —— Interest, restitution

Requirement that, as condition of probation, defendant pay 15% interest on restitution to victim of difference between value of goods stolen and goods recovered was not abuse of discretion. Woods v. State, App. 1 Dist., 418 So.2d 401 (1982). Sentencing And Punishment ⚿ 1973(2)

164. —— Excess to amount of damage, restitution

A probationer may not be required to make restitution in excess of the amount of damage caused by his criminal conduct but where criminal activity is undertaken in concert with others, the method of prorating any required restitution is a matter within discretion of trial judge. Pollreisz v. State, App. 1 Dist., 406 So.2d 1297 (1981). Sentencing And Punishment ⚿ 2178

In determining amount of restitution to be paid by probationer, trial court may not require payment in excess of amount of damage the criminal conduct caused the victim. Hamm v. State, App. 1 Dist., 403 So.2d 1155 (1981). Sentencing And Punishment ⚿ 1973(2)

Condition of probation requiring probationer to pay money to, or for benefit of, victim of his crime cannot require payment in excess of amount of damage which criminal conduct caused victim. Fresneda v. State, 347 So.2d 1021 (1977). Sentencing And Punishment ⚿ 1973(2)

165. —— Hearing following probation revocation, restitution

Restitution orders entered when defendant was sentenced upon probation revocation were required to be reversed, as defendant was not afforded opportunity to be heard. Strickland v. State, App. 2 Dist., 596 So.2d 1155 (1992), review denied 602 So.2d 942, certiorari denied 113 S.Ct. 1289, 507 U.S. 923, 122 L.Ed.2d 681. Criminal Law ⚿ 1177.3(4); Sentencing And Punishment ⚿ 358; Sentencing And Punishment ⚿ 2024

166. —— Aggrieved parties, restitution

Company which incurred costs to protect its vice-president and general manager who was threatened with injury unless he would transfer a certain employee was an "aggrieved party" to which defendant was properly required to pay restitution as a condition of probation. Ballance v. State, App. 1 Dist., 447 So.2d 974 (1984). Sentencing And Punishment ⚿ 1973(3)

Condition of probation which required that defendant, who was charged with second-degree murder of his wife with a firearm and who pled guilty to a lesser included offense of manslaughter, to pay the mother of his deceased wife $1,500 in restitution as a compromise figure for $3,000 which she either loaned or gave to defendant and his wife for purchase of furniture was improper and would be stricken; defendant's mother-in-law could not be considered an "aggrieved party" within meaning of this section with respect to the money for furniture and, even if assuming that the money from mother-in-law was a loan, not a gift, defendant's debt was not "caused by his offense" within meaning of the statute. Purvis v. State, App. 2 Dist., 442 So.2d 1085 (1983). Sentencing And Punishment ⚿ 1973(3)

167. —— Notice, restitution

Defendant is not entitled to advance notice before trial court imposes restitution, but where no prior notice is given to defendant, and he objects to, or otherwise contests, the restitution order, the trial judge must suspend the sentencing hearing for a reasonable time and allow the defendant to be heard on issues relevant to restitution. Reynolds v. State, App. 1 Dist., 598 So.2d 188 (1992). Sentencing And Punishment ⚿ 2181; Sentencing And Punishment ⚿ 2194

Where restitution was ordered at same time defendant was placed on probation at sentencing hearing, defendant was not provided with reasonable notice of proposed restitution or afforded adequate opportunity to be heard on amount of restitution. Milton v. State, App. 1 Dist., 453 So.2d 137 (1984). Sentencing And Punishment ⚿ 1906; Sentencing And Punishment ⚿ 1917

It was error to set amount of restitution defendant would be required to pay as condition of probation without holding hearing with prior notice to defendant. Edwards v. State, App. 2 Dist., 422 So.2d 24 (1982). Sentencing And Punishment ⚿ 1906; Sentencing And Punishment ⚿ 1917

When defendant has not been furnished prior notice of proposed restitution order as condition of probation and he objects to restitution as probation condition, he must be given opportunity to be heard, along with reasonable time to prepare. Miller v. State, App. 4 Dist., 407 So.2d 959 (1981). Sentencing And Punishment ⚿ 1906; Sentencing And Punishment ⚿ 1917

When requiring a defendant to pay restitution as condition of probation, defendant must be provided with notice of proposed restitution and given an opportunity to be heard on the amount and amount of restitution ordered may not be in excess of damage criminal conduct caused victim. Bradley v. State, App. 1 Dist., 406 So.2d 56 (1981). Sentencing And Punishment ⚿ 1917; Sentencing And Punishment ⚿ 1973(2)

By failing to notify defendant of its intention to prove that her work efforts were unsatisfactory, the state in proceeding to revoke probation for failure to pay restitution did not give the defendant an opportunity to prepare and present an appropriate defense to the charge; due process required that the probation revocation be based only on the violation alleged. Winfield v. State, App. 1 Dist., 406 So.2d 50 (1981). Sentencing And Punishment ⚿ 2013

Reversal of probation order was required where restitution was ordered without any prior notice that restitution was to be considered. Hamm v. State, App. 1 Dist., 403 So.2d 1155 (1981). Sentencing And Punishment ⚿ 1917

Where defendant was not denied opportunity to be heard but, rather, chose to silently accept court's resolution of questions concerning amount of restitution and his ability to pay that amount, order of restitution would not be reversed merely because trial court did not furnish defendant with advance notice that restitution might be imposed as condition of probation; receding from inconsistent statements in Stokes v. State, 377 So.2d 766, Kroenke v. State, 366 So.2d 46, DiOrio v. State, 359 So.2d 45, and Latti v. State, 364 So.2d 828. Goodson v. State, App. 2 Dist., 400 So.2d 791 (1981). Criminal Law ⚿ 1177.3(4)

Before restitution could properly be made condition of probation, defendant was entitled to notice and hearing as part of process by which amount of restitution was determined by court. Maples v. State, App. 5 Dist., 397 So.2d 1146 (1981). Sentencing And Punishment ⚿ 1917

In prosecution for grand larceny, failure to give defendant prior notice on issue whether restitution would be made condition of probation denied him opportunity to be heard on such issue, and thus imposition of restitution as condition of probation was improper. Reeves v. State, App. 2 Dist., 372 So.2d 1016 (1979). Sentencing And Punishment ⚿ 1906; Sentencing And Punishment ⚿ 1917

Notice of proposed restitution as condition of probation must be provided a defendant and an opportunity afforded him to be heard on amount of damage or loss. Blincoe v. State, App. 1 Dist., 371 So.2d 595 (1979). Sentencing And Punishment ⚿ 1917

Defendant was not entitled to reversal on asserted ground that he had not been provided notice and an opportunity to be heard regarding amount of restitution as a condition of probation, where defendant and his counsel were present when restitution was imposed but they failed to object or otherwise present the issue to the trial court so that it was impossible to determine from record that notice had not been given. Pope v. State, App. 1 Dist., 368 So.2d 676 (1979). Criminal Law ⚿ 1042.3(4)

Imposition of requirement that defendant make restitution, as a condition of probation, was error where defendant had not been given notice of proposed restitution order and an opportunity to be heard. Latti v. State, App. 2 Dist., 364 So.2d 828 (1978). Sentencing And Punishment ⚿ 1917

Before ordering restitution as condition of probation, trial judge should give defendant notice of proposed restitution order and allow defendant opportunity to be heard as to amount of damage or loss caused by his offense. Fresneda v. State, 347 So.2d 1021 (1977). Sentencing And Punishment ⚿ 1906; Sentencing And Punishment ⚿ 1917

168. —— Plea bargain, restitution

Fact that victim was not interested in restitution was not a clear and compelling reason not to order restitution as condition of probation for defendant who pled guilty to grand theft; defendant specifically agreed to restitution as a condition of his plea, and agreed to pay an amount of restitution higher than that charged by the state in the information. State v. Castro, App. 3 Dist., 965 So.2d 216 (2007), review denied 978 So.2d 159. Sentencing And Punishment ⚿ 1973(2)

Restitutionary probation condition was valid condition imposed upon open plea of guilty to charge of tampering with evidence where plea agreement indicated that parties contemplated that trial court would have option of including restitution as condition of probation, defendant negotiated for, and took full advantage of, nol pros of count charging him with leaving scene of accident and where defendant made no objection to trial judge's understanding that defendant was to pay restitution to accident victims. Adamo v. State, App. 4 Dist., 496 So.2d 252 (1986). Sentencing And Punishment ⚿ 1973(2)

Defendant convicted of grand theft of food commodities could not be required to make restitution for improperly distributed food products other than those distributed to the individuals named in the informations filed against him, regardless of fact that losses were all sustained by same victim. Barnes v. State, App. 2 Dist., 489 So.2d 1182 (1986). Sentencing And Punishment ⚿ 2145

Absent defendant's acknowledgement of theft in unrelated case and agreement to make restitution, all as part of plea bargain in which defendant pled nolo contendere to charge of grand theft on understanding that another information charging grand theft in unrelated case would be nolle prossed, trial court was precluded from requiring restitution for nolle prossed case as condition of probation. Bass v. State, App. 4 Dist., 462 So.2d 572 (1985), petition for review denied 475 So.2d 696. Sentencing And Punishment ⚷ 1973(2)

Where defendant, as part of plea bargain, acknowledged his responsibility for charges to be dismissed and agreed to make restitution to victims of dismissed charges, as well as to victims of crimes to which he pleaded guilty, a condition of probation requiring complete restitution was properly imposed. Argote v. State, App. 3 Dist., 433 So.2d 1013 (1983). Sentencing And Punishment ⚷ 1973(2)

Where plea agreement did not contain anything except two-year maximum term of imprisonment, defendant was sentenced to two years with last 18 months thereof suspended, defendant was subsequently placed on probation, and trial court subsequently imposed condition on probation that defendant make restitution to burglary victim, imposing the condition on probation did not violate original plea agreement. Carmo v. State, App. 4 Dist., 378 So.2d 850 (1979). Criminal Law ⚷ 273.1(2)

169. —— Due process and equal protection, restitution

Probationer's agreeing to make restitution as condition of probation regardless of his ability to pay was invalid and violated due process, equal protection, and prohibition of imprisonment for debt. Hamrick v. State, App. 3 Dist., 519 So.2d 81 (1988). Constitutional Law ⚷ 1106; Constitutional Law ⚷ 3819; Constitutional Law ⚷ 4732; Sentencing And Punishment ⚷ 1973(2)

170. —— Hearings, restitution

Trial court erred in imposing restitution as condition of probation, with amount to be determined at later date, then subsequently entering restitution order based upon bill submitted by victim at sentencing hearing, without holding restitution hearing. Gardipee v. State, App. 2 Dist., 620 So.2d 255 (1993). Sentencing And Punishment ⚷ 1906

Trial court had affirmative duty to conduct hearing so as to determine credibility of witnesses or lack thereof with respect to evidence of amount of restitution imposed on defendant, and court could not rely on written statements of witnesses. Langston v. State, App. 4 Dist., 616 So.2d 597 (1993), review denied 626 So.2d 206. Sentencing And Punishment ⚷ 2192

Requirement of restitution in order of probation was invalid, where trial court agreed to provide restitution hearing, as timely requested by defense counsel, but none was held. Reynolds v. State, App. 1 Dist., 598 So.2d 188 (1992). Sentencing And Punishment ⚷ 1906; Sentencing And Punishment ⚷ 1973(2)

Court erred in order modifying probation by imposing restitution without benefit of hearing. Bowers v. State, App. 2 Dist., 591 So.2d 311 (1991). Sentencing And Punishment ⚷ 1923

Prior to any restitution being paid, trial court would be compelled to conduct hearing to determine amount and manner of restitution payment and only trial court may determine that amount. Cogdell v. State, App. 5 Dist., 547 So.2d 256 (1989). Criminal Law ⚷ 1192

Inasmuch as defendant has right to appeal any order setting amount of restitution growing out of sentencing hearing, better procedure is for trial judge to set amount of restitution at sentencing hearing absent a clear reason for not doing so. Cogdell v. State, App. 5 Dist., 547 So.2d 256 (1989). Sentencing And Punishment ⚷ 2197

Where defendant was given opportunity to be heard on amount of restitution determined to be owing as a condition of probation and objected not to the amount, but to the propriety of the court requiring restitution on dismissed charges, he could not complain on appeal that amount determined was wrong. Argote v. State, App. 3 Dist., 433 So.2d 1013 (1983). Criminal Law ⚷ 1043(3)

If a defendant contests proposed restitution condition at sentencing hearing, he is entitled to continuance of hearing for a reasonable time in order to allow adequate preparation to be heard on issue. Wilson v. State, App. 1 Dist., 407 So.2d 1078 (1982). Criminal Law ⚷ 590(1)

Where defendant was not given notice prior to sentencing hearing that restitution was possibility and he objected to order of restitution, ends of justice would be best served by remanding cause to trial court to afford him hearing before it entered condition relative to restitution. Miller v. State, App. 4 Dist., 407 So.2d 959 (1981). Criminal Law ⚷ 1181.5(8)

Rule that trial judge must suspend sentencing hearing for reasonable time and allow defendant to be heard on issues relevant to restitution where trial judge prior to sentencing hearing does not furnish defendant notice that restitution is possibility and defendant objects or otherwise contests order of restitution will be applied only prospectively to cases in which order of probation is entered after date of decision establishing such rule. Miller v. State, App. 4 Dist., 407 So.2d 959 (1981). Courts ⚷ 100(1)

Ordering defendant to pay restitution in amount of $1,039 to victim was not error, despite claim that damages were $994 and that defendant was not afforded an opportunity to be heard thereon, where prosecutor explained that victim had an expense of $45 for which he had no receipt, but was prepared to testify concerning such expenditure, and both defendant and his attorney agreed to higher figure after trial judge stated that probation would be conditioned upon payment of full amount of damages. Ethridge v. State, App. 1 Dist., 383 So.2d 778 (1980). Sentencing And Punishment ⚷ 1887

Trial court's imposition of restitution as a condition of probation was improper, where defendant was given no notice that a restitution condition would be imposed, but, rather, condition was proposed for first time at defendant's sentencing hearing, and defendant was not afforded a hearing to establish that offense with which he was charged had relationship to damage to victim and to establish amount of damages or loss caused by his offense. Stokes v. State, App. 2 Dist., 377 So.2d 766 (1979). Sentencing And Punishment ⚷ 1917

171. —— Sufficiency of evidence, restitution

Amount of restitution, $2,343.54, ordered as condition of probation for offense of attempted criminal mischief was not fundamental error, even though jury found that value of damages to property was greater than $200 but less than $1,000; testimony and evidence presented at trial provided factual basis for amount ordered, and amount was not egregious. Gliszczynski v. State, App. 5 Dist., 654 So.2d 579 (1995). Criminal Law ⚷ 1042.3(4); Sentencing And Punishment ⚷ 1973(2)

Imposition of restitution in amount of $14,716.17 upon grand theft defendant was error where store's general manager stated in his sworn complaint that defendant had removed approximately $2,500 from store's cash receipts, much of the documentary evidence on which state relied was subject to hearsay rule and failed to meet strict requirements for admissibility under "business records" exception, and witnesses who testified on store's behalf could not determine precisely what portion of its losses above $2,500, if any, resulted from defendant's offense; state did not carry its statutory burden of establishing, by preponderance of evidence, that defendant caused store damage or loss in amount ordered. House v. State, App. 1 Dist., 614 So.2d 677 (1993). Sentencing And Punishment ⚷ 2187; Sentencing And Punishment ⚷ 2188(2)

Under statute applicable at time of 1990 offense, any decision not to order restitution had to be supported by reasons stated in detail in the record. Shaddix v. State, App. 1 Dist., 599 So.2d 269 (1992). Sentencing And Punishment ⚷ 2195

In establishing restitution payable, State had burden of demonstrating by preponderance of the evidence that victims' claims were directly or indirectly caused by commission of the offense in question. Bianco v. State, App. 4 Dist., 594 So.2d 861 (1992). Sentencing And Punishment ⚷ 2187

Restitution provisions in order of probation imposed on defendant who pled guilty to multiple counts of grand theft involving claims of fraud and misappropriation of funds arising out of contracts for construction and sale of homes by defendant's company were erroneous as to two of the numerous victims; evidence did not show that the two victims' additional mortgage and rental expense were caused by defendant's crime, nor should restitution be required as to items which contract did not require defendant to provide or which did not result in additional expense to homeowner. Bianco v. State, App. 4 Dist., 594 So.2d 861 (1992). Sentencing And Punishment ⚷ 1973(3)

Evidence did not support trial court's assessment of restitution in grand theft prosecution; evidence showed only how long victim had owned each item and its original purchase price. Mansingh v. State, App. 1 Dist., 588 So.2d 636 (1991). Sentencing And Punishment ⚷ 2188(4)

Order requiring defendant convicted of grand theft to make restitution in amount of $16,800 as condition of probation was not supported by evidence; State only proved damages to victims in amount of $1,200. Morel v. State, App. 2 Dist., 547 So.2d 341 (1989). Sentencing And Punishment ⚷ 1902

Absent evidence of probationer's ability to pay $10 per month for probation supervision, a condition of his probation, trial court could not properly find a violation of the condition. Marshall v. State, App. 2 Dist., 400 So.2d 567 (1981). Sentencing And Punishment ⚷ 2021

Violations of conditions of probation that probationer pay costs of supervision and of extradition would be stricken from order revoking probation where evidence was insufficient to establish that probationer was able to pay those costs. Deluca v. State, App. 4 Dist., 383 So.2d 751 (1980). Sentencing And Punishment ⚷ 2021

Revocation of probation would be affirmed, but in absence of evidence that probationer was able to pay costs of supervision and fact that he did not admit violation, case would be remanded for deletion of finding that probationer violated condition requiring payment of costs of supervision. Brooks v. State, App. 2 Dist., 376 So.2d 898 (1979). Criminal Law ⚷ 1181.5(8); Criminal Law ⚷ 1182

In probation revocation proceeding, evidence was sufficient to support finding that defendant had the ability to pay fine which he had failed to pay. McKinnon v. State, App. 5 Dist., 376

So.2d 275 (1979). Sentencing And Punishment ⚿ 2021

In absence of evidence that defendant was able to make payments required as condition of probation, finding that he violated such condition was improper. Robbins v. State, App. 4 Dist., 318 So.2d 472 (1975). Sentencing And Punishment ⚿ 2021

172. —— Guilty pleas, restitution

Defendant was estopped from raising alleged illegality of restitution ordered as condition of his probation, where defendant agreed to pay restitution in amount imposed by trial court in order to avoid being sentenced as habitual felony offender. Armstrong v. State, App. 5 Dist., 620 So.2d 1120 (1993). Criminal Law ⚿ 1137(1)

Defendant was estopped from raising alleged illegality of restitution as condition of probation, where restitution ordered was contemplated by plea agreement. Bradley v. State, App. 3 Dist., 602 So.2d 980 (1992). Criminal Law ⚿ 1137(2)

Trial court could revoke probation for failure to pay any amounts required to be paid as condition of that probation without specifically finding that defendant had financial ability to make payments where defendant pleaded guilty to violation of probation. Douglas v. State, App. 1 Dist., 433 So.2d 12 (1983). Sentencing And Punishment ⚿ 2029

173. —— Waiver, restitution

Condition of probation requiring defendant, who pleaded guilty to grand theft of automobile, to pay additional amount of restitution for value of items missing from victim's home, was not illegal or so egregious as to constitute fundamental error, and therefore defendant waived his right to appeal that condition by failing to raise contemporaneous objection. Bayer v. State, App. 5 Dist., 597 So.2d 870 (1992). Criminal Law ⚿ 1042.3(4)

Issue of trial court's alleged failure to consider defendant's ability to pay restitution as a special condition of probation was waived, where defendant expressed willingness to make restitution at change of plea hearing and did not protest amount imposed at sentencing or otherwise object based on his financial circumstances. Bishop v. State, App. 5 Dist., 564 So.2d 629 (1990). Sentencing And Punishment ⚿ 1973(2)

174. —— Estoppel, restitution

Defendant who pled guilty to leaving scene of an accident with injuries in exchange for three-year term of probation that included special condition of restitution was estopped from raising alleged illegality of the condition. Pollock v. Bryson, App. 2 Dist., 450 So.2d 1183 (1984). Criminal Law ⚿ 273.2(1)

175. —— Review, restitution

Record did not support trial court's finding, as a basis for striking restitution as condition of probation for defendant who plead guilty to grand theft, that the allegation of loss was not established, reasonable or credible, but rather was inflated, and probably perjurious, given that trial court did not conduct a restitution hearing, and no evidence was presented below from which the trial court could have reached any of these conclusions. State v. Castro, App. 3 Dist., 965 So.2d 216 (2007), review denied 978 So.2d 159. Sentencing And Punishment ⚿ 1902

If judge imposes previously unannounced probation conditions upon resentencing, following remand, then such conditions may be attacked as if they had been pronounced at original sentencing hearing. Justice v. State, App. 5 Dist., 658 So.2d 1028 (1995), on rehearing, review granted 666 So.2d 143, quashed 674 So.2d 123. Criminal Law ⚿ 1193

Defendant waived right to object to amount of monthly restitution ordered by trial court as condition of defendant's probation, where defendant failed to raise contemporaneous objection at sentencing hearing. Armstrong v. State, App. 5 Dist., 620 So.2d 1120 (1993). Criminal Law ⚿ 1042.3(4)

176. Charitable contributions

Trial court was not authorized to impose as condition of defendant's probation that he make contributions to certain organization in county. Allen v. State, App. 5 Dist., 676 So.2d 491 (1996). Sentencing And Punishment ⚿ 1983(2)

Trial court lacked authority to impose, as condition of probation in firearm case, that defendant make $2,500 contribution to named charity. Antosh v. State, App. 3 Dist., 510 So.2d 1158 (1987). Sentencing And Punishment ⚿ 1983(2)

177. Child support

Trial court abused its discretion in finding probationer had violated condition of probation by being behind on child support payments, where trial court found probationer violated probation by failing to provide support for child who was different from child named in affidavit of violation of probation. Reed v. State, App. 2 Dist., 865 So.2d 644 (2004). Sentencing And Punishment ⚿ 1983(3)

Trial court was justified in imposing on defendant, who pleaded nolo contendere to aggravated battery by use of deadly weapon on his estranged wife, as a condition of probation, requirement that he pay child support per civil order given provisions of this statute which expressly authorizes sentencing court to impose nine conditions of probation in every case and which provides as one of enumerated conditions that probationer be required to support his legal dependents to the best of his ability. Ward v. State, App. 1 Dist., 511 So.2d 1109 (1987). Sentencing And Punishment ⚷ 1983(2)

178. Electronic monitoring device

Defendant's failure to continually submit to electronic monitoring was not valid basis to revoke his community control, where such monitoring never became valid condition of community control; relevant statute did not give Department of Corrections authority to impose electronic monitoring as condition of community control, and community control order indicated that monitoring could be imposed when recommended by court, which never made such order. Anthony v. State, App. 2 Dist., 854 So.2d 744 (2003). Sentencing And Punishment ⚷ 1976(2)

Defendant's failure to wear electronic monitoring device could not serve as basis for revocation of community control where requirement that defendant wear device was imposed by community control officer, not by trial judge. Carson v. State, App. 4 Dist., 531 So.2d 1069 (1988). Sentencing And Punishment ⚷ 2003

Subsection (2)(d) of this section giving Department of Corrections discretion to require electronic monitoring of offenders sentenced to community control does not elevate Department's discretion to level of authority to create and impose "condition" of community control. Carson v. State, App. 4 Dist., 531 So.2d 1069 (1988). Sentencing And Punishment ⚷ 1976(2)

179. Polygraphs

Alleged violation of probation condition requiring that defendant "undergo psychiatric/mental health counseling" with specified sex offender counselor, based on defendant's failure to submit to polygraph testing as required by his counselor, could not be basis for revocation of probation, given that sex crime occurred prior to amendment of statute requiring annual polygraph testing for persons placed on sex offender probation for crimes committed on or after October 1, 1997. Lane v. State, App. 5 Dist., 762 So.2d 560 (2000). Sentencing And Punishment ⚷ 2003

Physician-imposed requirement that a polygraph be introduced into a treatment program for crimes committed before October 1, 1997 date, as to which persons placed on sex offender probation for crimes committed on or after that date are required to submit to annual polygraph testing under 1997 statute, cannot be the basis for a revocation of probation by one who balks at compliance. Lane v. State, App. 5 Dist., 762 So.2d 560 (2000). Sentencing And Punishment ⚷ 2003

Upon conviction for lewd assault on child, defendant could be required to take polygraph at reasonable intervals and to respond to questions that concern noncriminal conduct so long as results of polygraph would not be offered in evidence; probationer could only refuse to answer such questions if it was within his Fifth Amendment right to do so, and state could then elect to require answer by eliminating threat of prosecution; abrogating *Hart v. State,* 633 So.2d 1189. Cassamassima v. State, App. 5 Dist., 657 So.2d 906 (1995), certification denied. Criminal Law ⚷ 393(1); Sentencing And Punishment ⚷ 1996

180. Habitual offenders

Defendant is not precluded from agreeing to split sentence condition in which habitual offender sentence is imposed only on the probationary portion of the sentence and not on the imprisonment portion, notwithstanding its "hybrid" characteristics. Dunham v. State, App. 4 Dist., 683 So.2d 507 (1996), review granted 675 So.2d 120, approved 686 So.2d 1356. Sentencing And Punishment ⚷ 1887; Sentencing And Punishment ⚷ 1934

Trial court could not include as condition of probation and community control that defendant would be sentenced as habitual offender upon violation, since there was no notice of intent to habitualize at time of original sentencing or in original plea agreement. Anderson v. State, App. 4 Dist., 665 So.2d 367 (1996). Sentencing And Punishment ⚷ 1917

Written notice of intent to habitualize, a requirement for inclusion of condition of probation that defendant would be sentenced as habitual offender upon violation, was fulfilled by plea agreement in which defendant agreed that she would be subject to sentencing as habitual offender upon violation of probation or community control if she otherwise qualified as habitual offender, and court's pronouncement of this condition at sentencing. Anderson v. State, App. 4 Dist., 665 So.2d 367 (1996). Sentencing And Punishment ⚷ 1373; Sentencing And Punishment ⚷ 1983(2)

There was nothing inherently or per se illegal about sentence of community control coupled with determination that defendant was habitual felony offender. King v. State, App. 2 Dist., 597 So.2d 309 (1992), review denied 602 So.2d 942. Sentencing And Punishment ⚷ 1400; Sentencing And Punishment ⚷ 1873

181. Duration of probation

Trial court could not include special condition of probation that defendant may not be considered for early termination of probation, since statute allowed probationer to be brought before court at any time to be commended and possibly discharged from further supervision, based on facts and circumstances that developed during term of probation. Arriaga v. State, App. 4 Dist., 666 So.2d 949 (1996), rehearing denied. Sentencing And Punishment ⚷ 1983(2)

Trial court may not through probation condition divest Department of Corrections of its authority to recommend early termination of probation. Jones v. State, App. 2 Dist., 666 So.2d 191 (1995). Sentencing And Punishment ⚷ 1960

Condition of probation which provided that probationary term of defendant could not be terminated early and that defendant was required to participate in sex offender program impermissibly attempted to divest Department of Corrections of its authority to recommend early termination of probation and was stricken. Jones v. State, App. 2 Dist., 666 So.2d 191 (1995). Sentencing And Punishment ⚷ 1977(2); Sentencing And Punishment ⚷ 1983(2)

Trial court had no authority to sentence defendant to serve total sentence of six years and nine months, probation, community control and jail combined, when the statutory maximum punishment for possession of cocaine, a third-degree felony, was five years. Colon v. State, App. 4 Dist., 660 So.2d 373 (1995). Controlled Substances ⚷ 100(2)

Because total sanction for offense of aggravated assault, which was third-degree felony, could not exceed five years, defendant given prison sentence of four and one-half years could not receive probation in excess of six months. Villabol v. State, App. 2 Dist., 595 So.2d 1057 (1992), review denied 604 So.2d 489. Sentencing And Punishment ⚷ 1945

182. Violation of conditions of order—In general

It is impermissible to enhance the conditions and terms of a defendant's probation unless the trial court determines that defendant committed a willful and substantial violation of the conditions of probation. King v. State, App. 5 Dist., 990 So.2d 1191 (2008). Sentencing and Punishment ⚷ 1985

Defendant, who pleaded guilty to attempted sexual battery upon a child under 12 years of age and was sentenced to a five-year prison term followed by a ten-year sex offender probationary term, could not be found to have violated probation while he was still in prison; defendant's probation had not yet commenced, and he had not committed any crime or engaged in any act of misconduct while incarcerated that would demonstrate his unfitness as a probationer. King v. State, App. 5 Dist., 990 So.2d 1191 (2008). Sentencing and Punishment ⚷ 2006

Test on appeal of probation revocation is whether evidence is sufficient to satisfy conscience of court that condition of probation has been violated. Ordonez v. State, App. 4 Dist., 408 So.2d 760 (1982), review denied 419 So.2d 1200. Criminal Law ⚷ 1134.70

Where a defendant makes reasonable efforts to comply with probation conditions, his failure to do so may not be willful. Shaw v. State, App. 5 Dist., 391 So.2d 754 (1980). Sentencing And Punishment ⚷ 2003

Defendant's probation could not properly be revoked solely on basis of his expressed intention to violate its conditions. Blue v. State, App. 2 Dist., 377 So.2d 1016 (1979). Sentencing And Punishment ⚷ 2003

Where defendant was placed on probation, with condition of probation inserted at urging of his counsel, he could not thereafter be held to have violated probation upon sole ground that he was not proper candidate for probation under special condition. Donneil v. State, App. 3 Dist., 377 So.2d 805 (1979). Sentencing And Punishment ⚷ 1965

It was improper to rest finding of probation violation solely upon hearsay evidence. Robbins v. State, App. 4 Dist., 318 So.2d 472 (1975). Sentencing And Punishment ⚷ 2021

Upon duly finding that a parolee has violated the conditions of his parole, the parole and probation commission may enter a new parole order containing different and more restrictive conditions than those in the original parole order, including extension of the parole period within and not to exceed the statutorily prescribed limits. Op.Atty.Gen., 83–79, Oct. 26, 1983.

183. —— Providing address, violation of conditions of order

Failure of defendant, who pleaded guilty to attempted sexual battery upon a child under 12 years of age, to provide, while he was still imprisoned, a suitable address where he would reside upon his parole did not violate the sex offender probationary condition that prohibited him from living within 1,000 feet of certain designated locations; neither the condition of defendant's probation nor the sex offender statute requiring its imposition required defendant to give a suitable address prior to his release from prison or, for that matter, any address at all. King v. State, App. 5 Dist., 990 So.2d 1191 (2008). Sentencing and Punishment ⚷ 1971(3)

184. —— Harmless error, violation of conditions of order

Violation of three conditions of probation was sufficient basis for revocation, and erroneous finding by trial court that defendant had also violated another condition of probation was harmless clerical error, and thus no abuse of discretion was shown. Landry v. State, App. 5 Dist., 380 So.2d 1191 (1980). Criminal Law ⚷ 1177.3(4); Sentencing And Punishment ⚷ 2003

185. —— Educational requirements, violation of conditions of order

Where evidence showed that probationer made one feeble attempt to return to high school and, by his own admission, refused to comply with reasonable requirements of institution which resulted in termination of his relationship with school, probationer's violation of special condition of probation that he obtain high school diploma or general equivalency diploma had to be characterized as substantial and thus two tests of violative conduct were met, consisting of willful and substantial violation, sufficient to support revocation of probation. Ordonez v. State, App. 4 Dist., 408 So.2d 760 (1982), review denied 419 So.2d 1200. Sentencing And Punishment ⚷ 2003

186. Community service

Special probation condition allowing defendant to use community service hours to work off court costs was not authorized by statute. Garrison v. State, App. 2 Dist., 685 So.2d 53 (1996). Sentencing And Punishment ⚷ 1975(3)

Special probation condition requiring that defendant complete 100 hours of community service and specifying that he complete ten hours per month would be affirmed; monthly requirement did not alter that portion of the sentence imposed. Garrison v. State, App. 2 Dist., 685 So.2d 53 (1996). Sentencing And Punishment ⚷ 1982(3)

If probation is imposed as portion of sentence, monetary conditions may not be converted to community service hours. Burgess v. State, App. 2 Dist., 683 So.2d 1099 (1996). Sentencing And Punishment ⚷ 1965

Court was not authorized to convert mandatory costs to community service. Burgess v. State, App. 2 Dist., 683 So.2d 1099 (1996). Costs ⚷ 292

Trial court lacked authority to impose probation condition providing that defendant could perform 50 hours of community service in lieu of costs of supervision. Rasik v. State, App. 4 Dist., 683 So.2d 1097 (1996). Sentencing And Punishment ⚷ 1982(2)

Probation condition requiring probationer to perform 50 hours of community service work which was not orally pronounced at sentencing had to be stricken, as condition was not imposed in every case but was special condition. Chitty v. State, App. 2 Dist., 661 So.2d 26 (1994). Sentencing And Punishment ⚷ 1920

Community service sentence was improper as condition of probation for indigent defendant; moreover, imposition of community service time in lieu of imposition of trust fund costs was not appropriate. Houston v. State, App. 4 Dist., 540 So.2d 943 (1989). Sentencing And Punishment ⚷ 1982(2)

187. Violation of law during liberty—In general

Obedience to criminal statutes is not special condition of probation, and due process does not require defendant to receive verbal notice of this obligation before it is used as reason to revoke probation; all persons have constructive notice of state's criminal statutes. State v. Green, App. 2 Dist., 667 So.2d 959 (1996). Constitutional Law ⚷ 4732; Sentencing And Punishment ⚷ 1918

Any error in denying motion to dismiss charge that defendant had violated condition of probation, which required him to live honorably, by committing two batteries on his wife on ground that such condition was too vague and uncertain was harmless, in light of fact that such misconduct violated condition of probation that defendant live within the law and in view of fact that he had specific notice of the misconduct charged. Norris v. State, App. 4 Dist., 383 So.2d 691 (1980), petition for review denied 388 So.2d 1116. Sentencing And Punishment ⚷ 2004

Probation may be revoked solely upon conviction by jury of a subsequent crime, provided the subsequent conviction is valid. Egantoff v. State, App. 2 Dist., 208 So.2d 843 (1968), certiorari denied 218 So.2d 164. Sentencing And Punishment ⚷ 2004

Where probation order required defendant to live and remain at liberty without violation of any law, defendant's conviction in municipal court of crime of possession and sale of lottery tickets contrary to city ordinance sustained order revoking probation. Caston v. State, 58 So.2d 694 (1952). Sentencing And Punishment ⚷ 2004

188. —— Jurisdiction, violation of law during liberty

There was no jurisdictional impediment to prohibit trial court from entertaining affidavit of probation violation for conduct which occurred while appeal from probation order was pending and imposition of terms of probation was stayed pending review, from accepting defendant's plea to violation of terms and conditions of probation order and from subsequently sentencing him, following dismissal of defendant's appeal from order or probation and issuance of mandate affirming his conviction. Loeb v. State, App. 3 Dist., 387 So.2d 433 (1980). Sentencing And Punishment ⚷ 2010

189. —— Sufficiency of evidence, violation of law during liberty

Testimony that probationer entered home and attempted to take victim's purse established the elements of burglary and was sufficient to show violation of probation requirement "to live and remain at liberty without violating any law." Holt v. State, App. 5 Dist., 385 So.2d 1133 (1980). Sentencing And Punishment ⚷ 2021

Where allegation charging probationer with shoplifting in violation of condition of probation was neither admitted nor proved, trial court could not properly find that probationer violated that condition or base revocation of probation upon such a finding, and, inasmuch as other charged violations were technical, order of revocation must be reversed. McKeever v. State, App. 2 Dist., 359 So.2d 905 (1978). Sentencing And Punishment ⚷ 2021

190. —— Notice, violation of law during liberty

A person on probation does not need an official document to advise him that commission of a felony such as unlawful importing of cocaine while on probation constitutes a violation of such probation. Willner v. State, App. 3 Dist., 350 So.2d 1108 (1977). Sentencing And Punishment ⚷ 2004

191. Delegation to probation officers or supervisors—In general

Trial court's special condition of probation requiring defendant to pay costs of investigation in amount to be determined by his probation officer was improper as trial court is not authorized to delegate to probation officer responsibility of determining defendant's ability to pay costs and rate of such payment. McClough v. State, App. 5 Dist., 669 So.2d 1099 (1996). Constitutional Law ⚷ 2574; Sentencing And Punishment ⚷ 1975(2)

Although trial court may not delegate judicial duties to probation officer, it may delegate authority to exercise incidental discretion, such as supervision of counseling for probationer, provided that exercise of discretion is used for rehabilitative purposes. Evans v. State, App. 1 Dist., 608 So.2d 90 (1992). Constitutional Law ⚷ 2574

Trial court did not improperly delegate judicial responsibility to nonjudicial officer by conditioning defendant's probation on "the receipt of alcohol and/or drug evaluation and counseling as directed by the probation officer"; court itself clearly determined need for and mandated drug evaluation counseling and left only ministerial details of that requirement to probation officer's discretion. Langston v. State, App. 1 Dist., 551 So.2d 1268 (1989). Constitutional Law ⚷ 2574

Condition of probation that defendant undergo alcohol, drug and psychological evaluation and counseling "as directed by" his probation officer did not unlawfully delegate to the officer the judicial responsibility of setting terms and conditions of probation. Rowland v. State, App. 1 Dist., 548 So.2d 812 (1989). Constitutional Law ⚷ 2574

Although only the court can set conditions of probation, judge cannot personally supervise, and judge's delegation to probation supervisor of task of giving specific instructions necessary for effective and successful supervision is proper. Draper v. State, App. 5 Dist., 403 So.2d 615 (1981). Constitutional Law ⚷ 2574

192. —— Church programs, delegation to probation officers or supervisors

Condition of community control imposed upon juvenile adjudicated delinquent requiring him to "get with the pastor" of his mother's church and enroll in any and all of church's youth programs improperly delegated to pastor of church judicial function of determining programs best suited to meet delinquent's rehabilitation needs. L.M. v. State, App. 1 Dist., 587 So.2d 648 (1991). Constitutional Law ⚷ 2570; Infants ⚷ 225

193. —— Restitution, delegation to probation officers or supervisors

Trial court improperly required restitution to be paid at rate determined by defendant's probation officer, since no one but judge may set payment schedule for amounts owed in restitution. Hillman v. State, App. 5 Dist., 636 So.2d 181 (1994). Constitutional Law ⚷ 2574; Sentencing And Punishment ⚷ 1973(2)

Condition of probation is invalid if it delegates to probation officer the right to determine rate of repayment of restitution. Thomas v. State, App. 1 Dist., 635 So.2d 1009 (1994). Constitutional Law ⚷ 2574

Probation officer lacked authority to set payment schedule for restitution ordered against probationer; rather, payment schedule had to be set by court. Ashlock v. State, App. 5 Dist.,

632 So.2d 213 (1994). Constitutional Law ⚷ 2623; Sentencing And Punishment ⚷ 2102

After probation order directing defendant to pay restitution was found facially invalid as improperly delegating to probation officer right to determine rate of repayment, it was incumbent upon circuit court to conduct hearing and determine payment schedule. White v. State, App. 1 Dist., 627 So.2d 599 (1993). Criminal Law ⚷ 1192

Trial court could not delegate authority to set amount of monthly payments required as condition of probation to probation officer. Green v. State, App. 1 Dist., 620 So.2d 1126 (1993). Constitutional Law ⚷ 2574; Sentencing And Punishment ⚷ 1801

Portion of condition of probation that allowed probation officer to determine amount of restitution defendant was required to pay was improper; only court, not probation officer, could establish restitution pay schedule. Casto v. State, App. 5 Dist., 615 So.2d 792 (1993). Constitutional Law ⚷ 2574; Sentencing And Punishment ⚷ 1973(2)

Trial court's delegation to probation officer of determination of amount of restitution was clear error and error was not remedied by trial court's offer to hold hearing should defendant disagree with probation officer. Walls v. State, App. 1 Dist., 609 So.2d 83 (1992). Constitutional Law ⚷ 2574; Sentencing And Punishment ⚷ 1916

Defendant's failure to object to trial court's delegation to probation officer of determination of amount of restitution did not bar consideration of issue on appeal; trial court's order of restitution in amount to determine by probation officer constituted unlawful delegation of judicial responsibility to nonjudicial officer and failure to object did not confer authority to violate law in this manner. Walls v. State, App. 1 Dist., 609 So.2d 83 (1992). Constitutional Law ⚷ 2574; Criminal Law ⚷ 1030(2); Criminal Law ⚷ 1042.3(4)

Trial court improperly delegated its authority to probation officer to determine amount of restitution in criminal matter. Gilbert v. State, App. 5 Dist., 600 So.2d 557 (1992). Constitutional Law ⚷ 2574; Sentencing And Punishment ⚷ 2102

Determining amount of restitution is purely judicial function to be exercised by trial court and may not be delegated to probation officer. Shaddix v. State, App. 1 Dist., 599 So.2d 269 (1992). Constitutional Law ⚷ 2574

It was improper to delegate to probation officer responsibility of directing payment of restitution. Bowers v. State, App. 1 Dist., 596 So.2d 480 (1992). Constitutional Law ⚷ 2574; Sentencing And Punishment ⚷ 2102

Authority to determine amount of restitution for defendant's offense could not be delegated to defendant's probation officer. Bowen v. State, App. 5 Dist., 590 So.2d 1067 (1991). Constitutional Law ⚷ 2574; Sentencing And Punishment ⚷ 1973(2)

Trial court which ordered defendant to make restitution and which stated that "the probation people will figure out what the medical bill was and let you know what this is when you get out of prison" and which thereafter entered an order nunc pro tunc to the date of sentencing specifying the amount of restitution and the persons and organizations to which it was to be paid improperly delegated its duty to determine the amount of restitution to the probation officer. Robinson v. State, App. 1 Dist., 586 So.2d 88 (1991). Constitutional Law ⚷ 2574; Sentencing And Punishment ⚷ 2197

Although defendant did not object to court's delegation to probation officer of authority to determine amount of restitution, that failure to object did not confer on the court the authority to violate the law by delegating a judicial function to the probation officer. Robinson v. State, App. 1 Dist., 586 So.2d 88 (1991). Constitutional Law ⚷ 2574; Sentencing And Punishment ⚷ 2102

It is reversible error for court to explicitly order probation officer to determine amount of restitution. Robinson v. State, App. 1 Dist., 586 So.2d 88 (1991). Criminal Law ⚷ 1177.3(4)

Trial court improperly delegated judicial functions by allowing probation officer to set restitution payment schedule and determine amount of restitution. Ashe v. State, App. 1 Dist., 582 So.2d 759 (1991). Constitutional Law ⚷ 2574; Sentencing And Punishment ⚷ 2102

Determination of amount of restitution is a nondelegable judicial responsibility as is determination of defendant's ability to pay, i.e., by establishing rate of payment. Ashe v. State, App. 1 Dist., 582 So.2d 759 (1991). Constitutional Law ⚷ 2570

Amount of restitution to be paid by a defendant must be determined by the court, and not delegated to a probation or parole officer, and thus trial court's order that defendant "make restitution as determined by probation and parole" was required to be remanded to enable trial court to determine amount of restitution. Showers v. State, App. 1 Dist., 570 So.2d 377 (1990). Criminal Law ⚷ 1181.5(8); Sentencing And Punishment ⚷ 2197

Condition of probation order which required defendant to make restitution "according to a plan and schedule as directed by your Probation Officer" was clearly wrong and was required to be stricken. Williams v. State, App. 4 Dist., 556

So.2d 799 (1990). Sentencing And Punishment ⚷ 1973(2)

Trial court was not permitted to delegate to "Probation and Parole" issues regarding restitution when trial court sentenced defendant to split sentence, with condition of probationary period that defendant make restitution as directed by "Probation and Parole." Gray v. State, App. 1 Dist., 535 So.2d 721 (1988). Constitutional Law ⚷ 2574; Sentencing And Punishment ⚷ 1973(2)

Facts that trial judge's oral pronouncement of sentence and sentencing order adopted specific restitution recommendations from defendant's presentence investigation report did not constitute an unlawful delegation of judicial responsibility to defendant's probation officer. Bell v. State, App. 1 Dist., 535 So.2d 645 (1988). Constitutional Law ⚷ 2574

It is reversible error for trial court to delegate a judicial responsibility to a probation supervisor, and trial court erred in ordering defendant to pay restitution as directed by his probation officer, contrary to West's F.S.A. § 948.03(1)(e), requiring reparation or restitution to be determined by court. McDonald v. State, App. 2 Dist., 478 So.2d 113 (1985). Criminal Law ⚷ 1177.3(4); Criminal Law ⚷ 1177.3(5); Sentencing And Punishment ⚷ 2197

Trial court's duty to determine the amount of restitution to be made by defendant convicted of leaving the scene of an accident resulting in injury to a person and driving with a suspended driver's license could not be delegated to probation officer. Huffman v. State, App. 1 Dist., 472 So.2d 469 (1985), review denied 482 So.2d 348. Sentencing And Punishment ⚷ 2197

Where juvenile was convicted of battery, and as condition of community control was ordered to make restitution for damages to victim's vehicle "under terms and conditions specified by H.R.S.," trial court committed error by delegating determination of such terms and conditions to H.R.S. M.A.R. v. State, App. 5 Dist., 433 So.2d 29 (1983), petition for review denied 441 So.2d 632. Infants ⚷ 224

On defendant's conviction of aggravated battery, trial court erred in delegating authority to supervisor to determine amount of restitution to be made as condition of probation, and case would be remanded with instructions to hold evidentiary hearing as to amount of restitution to be made. Cisneros v. State, App. 3 Dist., 422 So.2d 1087 (1982). Constitutional Law ⚷ 2572; Criminal Law ⚷ 1181.5(8); Sentencing And Punishment ⚷ 1973(3)

Portion of trial court's order, following his conviction for aggravated assault, requiring defendant "to make restitution as determined by his probation supervisor" was improper in that it unlawfully delegated a judicial responsibility to a nonjudicial officer. Fletcher v. State, App. 2 Dist., 405 So.2d 748 (1981). Constitutional Law ⚷ 2574; Sentencing And Punishment ⚷ 2102

Trial court improperly requested probation and parole commission to determine amount of restitution due from probationer to victim. Hamm v. State, App. 1 Dist., 403 So.2d 1155 (1981). Constitutional Law ⚷ 2574; Sentencing And Punishment ⚷ 2102

It was improper for trial judge to delegate to probation supervisor authority to determine amount of restitution defendant was required to pay. Cada v. State, App. 4 Dist., 382 So.2d 405 (1980). Constitutional Law ⚷ 2574; Sentencing And Punishment ⚷ 2197

It was improper for trial judge to delegate to defendant's probation supervisor the authority to determine the amounts of restitution that defendant would be required to pay. Cothron v. State, App. 2 Dist., 377 So.2d 255 (1979). Constitutional Law ⚷ 2574; Sentencing And Punishment ⚷ 1973(2)

194. Collection of moneys

The parole and probation commission may assist the court in the collection of moneys ordered as a condition of probation, but does not have the authority to maintain a bank account to facilitate in the collection and disbursement of said funds. Therefore all funds should be deposited with the clerk of the appropriate court, and disbursed through the clerk's office. Op.Atty.Gen., 073–283, Aug. 14, 1973.

195. Presentence investigation

Where, after trial court accepted defendant's negotiated guilty plea, the terms of which were that defendant would be placed on probation following a presentence investigation, defendant left the state and failed to appear before the official conducting his presentence investigation and where defendant finally appeared for sentencing on the charges some one and one-half years later, it was not within the power of the court to enter an adjudication of guilty as of the date of defendant's plea and then revoke defendant's probation and sentence him to two years in state prison upon a finding that he had violated the terms of his probation by refusing to report for the presentence investigation. Malloy v. State, App. 2 Dist., 380 So.2d 501 (1980). Sentencing And Punishment ⚷ 2010

196. Investigation expenses

Probationary terms of defendant's sentence could not be modified to impose special condition that defendant pay $94,000 toward cost of investigation of his case after it was determined that equipment, which defendant was to turn over to State to pay costs of State's investigation, was worth less than its previously estimated value, where there was no evidence that prior to hearing on motion to modify probation, State had established total costs of investigation. Carrandi v. State, App. 3 Dist., 560 So.2d 245 (1990). Sentencing And Punishment ⚷ 1987

Probation condition which assessed against defendant expenses incurred by city of Havana in investigation relating to defendant's sale of cannabis was proper. Milton v. State, App. 1 Dist., 453 So.2d 137 (1984). Sentencing And Punishment ⚷ 1975(2)

197. Imprisonment or incarceration—In general

Special condition that defendant accused of possession of cocaine serve six months of his five-year probationary term on community control was impermissible upward departure from recommended guideline sentence of any nonstate prison sanction. Levy v. State, App. 1 Dist., 666 So.2d 925 (1995). Sentencing And Punishment ⚷ 802

Sentence imposing two years of community control, with special condition that defendant spend 51 weeks in county jail as part of that two-year period, did not depart from recommended guidelines sentence of 12 to 30 months' incarceration or community control. Reese v. State, App. 5 Dist., 535 So.2d 676 (1988). Sentencing And Punishment ⚷ 1946; Sentencing And Punishment ⚷ 1976(2)

Sentence of two-year term of community control with condition that 364 days of the sentence be served in the county jail, imposed upon defendant convicted of sexual offenses against a minor, was permissible as the imprisonment which was a condition of the community control was not to be in the state prison. Distefano v. State, App. 1 Dist., 526 So.2d 110 (1988). Sentencing And Punishment ⚷ 1976(2)

Term of imprisonment as condition of probation is permissible but should be rehabilitative and not punitive, and should not have effect of negating parole policy of state, and thus maximum period of incarceration which may be imposed as condition of probation is up to, but not including, one year. Webb v. State, App. 5 Dist., 392 So.2d 35 (1980). Sentencing And Punishment ⚷ 1976(2)

Trial courts have general authority to require incarceration as a condition of probation for felony offenses pursuant to the general condition provisions of statute. Adams v. State, App. 5 Dist., 387 So.2d 498 (1980). Sentencing And Punishment ⚷ 1976(2)

Trial courts have a general authority to require incarceration as a condition of probation for felony offenses. McGowan v. State, App. 3 Dist., 362 So.2d 335 (1978). Sentencing And Punishment ⚷ 1976(2)

Probation condition imposing jail time during probationary period was valid. Pace v. State, App. 4 Dist., 335 So.2d 11 (1976). Sentencing And Punishment ⚷ 1976(2)

Trial court has general authority to require incarceration as condition of probation for felony and misdemeanor offenses. State v. Jones, 327 So.2d 18 (1976), on remand 330 So.2d 189. Sentencing And Punishment ⚷ 1976(2)

Trial court may place defendant on probation and include, as condition, incarceration for a specific period of time within maximum sentence allowed. State v. Jones, 327 So.2d 18 (1976), on remand 330 So.2d 189. Sentencing And Punishment ⚷ 1976(2)

A period of incarceration may be made a condition of a term of probation. Brown v. State, App. 4 Dist., 302 So.2d 430 (1974). Sentencing And Punishment ⚷ 1976(2)

198. —— Additional punishment, imprisonment or incarceration

Defendant convicted of attempted handling and fondling of child under 16 years of age could not be sentenced to four years' probation and, as special condition of probation, to 16 months' incarceration; probationary split sentence exceeded statutory five-year maximum sentence for offense, and court could not impose more than 364 days of incarceration as special condition of probation. Nase v. State, App. 2 Dist., 746 So.2d 469 (1997). Infants ⚷ 20

State Supreme Court's proscription of incarceration which equals or exceeds one year as part of split sentence alternative applies only to sentencing techniques of § 948.01 authorizing courts to place defendant on probation whenever punishment by imprisonment for misdemeanor or felony is prescribed and this section providing that enumerations or specific kinds of terms and conditions of probation are not exclusive of court adding others. Riley v. State, App. 2 Dist., 407 So.2d 967 (1981). Sentencing And Punishment ⚷ 1936

199. —— What constitutes, imprisonment or incarceration

Under statute governing terms and conditions of probation and community control, which limits incarceration as a special condition thereof to 364 days, both county jail and probation and restitution center are included in definition of "incarceration," and thus sentence of additional 364 days in restitution center following 364 days in county jail was illegal. Berry v. State, App. 2 Dist., 636 So.2d 555 (1994), decision approved in part, quashed in part 647 So.2d 830. Sentencing And Punishment ⚷ 1976(2)

Both county jail and probation and restitution centers are included in definition of "incarceration" for purposes of statute providing that "incarceration" as condition of probation or community control may not exceed 364 days. Solis v. State, App. 2 Dist., 622 So.2d 584 (1993). Sentencing And Punishment ⚷ 1976(1)

200. —— Length of term, generally, imprisonment or incarceration

Trial court erred when it sentenced defendant to remain in probation and restitution center "until he doesn't need it anymore." Solis v. State, App. 2 Dist., 622 So.2d 584 (1993). Sentencing And Punishment ⚷ 1944

Sentencing error of one day was rendered moot by defendant's completion of term of imprisonment. Williams v. State, App. 4 Dist., 591 So.2d 295 (1991). Criminal Law ⚷ 1134.26

Imposition of 364–day county jail term plus two-year term of community control was not illegal sentence under applicable sentencing guideline which set a range of any nonstate prison sanction or community control of one to three and one-half years incarceration. Stinson v. State, App. 5 Dist., 590 So.2d 31 (1991). Sentencing And Punishment ⚷ 1936

Ten-year period of incarceration imposed as condition of probation was unlawful. Dunn v. State, App. 5 Dist., 398 So.2d 493 (1981). Sentencing And Punishment ⚷ 1976(2)

A lengthy prison term which has the effect of precluding parole before the term expires should not be imposed as a condition of probation. Spencer v. State, App. 3 Dist., 395 So.2d 1263 (1981). Sentencing And Punishment ⚷ 1976(2)

A lengthy prison term which has the effect of precluding parole before the term expires should not be imposed as a condition of probation. Cooney v. State, App. 3 Dist., 376 So.2d 926 (1979). Sentencing And Punishment ⚷ 1976(2)

Trial court order withholding adjudication of guilt and placing defendant on probation for five years, on condition that he spend ten months in county jail, was valid and in accord with law. Lewis v. State, App. 4 Dist., 298 So.2d 540 (1974). Sentencing And Punishment ⚷ 1976(2)

201. —— Maximum term, length of term, imprisonment or incarceration

Sentence of "five years, on probation of which two of them will be served in the Department of Corrections," violates Florida statute limiting period of incarceration to be served as condition of probation to 364 days. Davie v. State, App. 5 Dist., 632 So.2d 1090 (1994). Sentencing And Punishment ⚷ 1976(2)

"Special condition" of probation that defendant convicted for attempted handling and fondling of child under 16 serve five years in prison was illegal; incarceration imposed as condition of probation could not exceed 364 days. Randolph v. State, App. 2 Dist., 626 So.2d 1006 (1993). Sentencing And Punishment ⚷ 1976(2)

Period of incarceration imposed as condition of probation cannot exceed 364 days or sentence will be considered illegal. Marin v. State, App. 3 Dist., 624 So.2d 808 (1993). Sentencing And Punishment ⚷ 1976(2)

Trial court erred in sentencing defendant to two years community control with special condition that he spend 364 days in county jail and, upon release, enter probation center and stay "until he doesn't need it anymore"; defendant could not be sentenced to more than 364 days incarceration as condition of probation or community control. Solis v. State, App. 2 Dist., 622 So.2d 584 (1993). Sentencing And Punishment ⚷ 1976(2)

Trial court may not impose probationary period which exceeds statutory maximum sentence for underlying offense. Barnes v. State, App. 1 Dist., 614 So.2d 26 (1993). Sentencing And Punishment ⚷ 1946

Incarceration imposed as condition of probation could not exceed 364 days. Rosa v. State, App. 5 Dist., 592 So.2d 769 (1992). Sentencing And Punishment ⚷ 1976(2)

Villery sentence of 365 days in prison exceeded by one day sentencing limit for special condition of probation. Williams v. State, App. 4 Dist., 591 So.2d 295 (1991). Sentencing And Punishment ⚷ 1976(2)

Special probation condition of nine years' incarceration in county jail was invalid. Harris v. State, App. 4 Dist., 576 So.2d 426 (1991). Sentencing And Punishment ⚷ 1976(2)

Defendant, convicted of second-degree misdemeanor, could be placed on probation for more than 60 days, to maximum of six months, with 60–day incarceration as condition of probation. Smith v. State, 484 So.2d 581 (1986). Sentencing And Punishment ⚷ 1943; Sentencing And Punishment ⚷ 1976(2)

Requirement that defendant serve period of incarceration as condition for probation was not improper, notwithstanding fact that period of incarceration required equaled maximum allowable sentence for the offense. Smith v. State, App. 1 Dist., 448 So.2d 20 (1984), approved 484 So.2d 581. Sentencing And Punishment ⚷ 1976(2)

Maximum term of incarceration which may be imposed as condition of probation may not equal or exceed one year. Smith v. State, App. 2 Dist., 396 So.2d 206 (1981). Sentencing And Punishment ⚿ 1976(2)

Order of two years incarceration as special condition to defendant's five-year term of probation for grand theft was illegal. Scheurer v. State, App. 4 Dist., 396 So.2d 194 (1980). Sentencing And Punishment ⚿ 1976(2)

Trial court erred in imposing eight-year term of imprisonment as special condition of 12 years of probation. Spencer v. State, App. 3 Dist., 395 So.2d 1263 (1981). Sentencing And Punishment ⚿ 1976(2)

Incarceration as a condition of probation which exceeded one year was unlawful. Warmble v. State, App. 3 Dist., 393 So.2d 1164 (1981), review denied 402 So.2d 613. Sentencing And Punishment ⚿ 1976(2)

Imposing a mandatory prison term of ten years as a condition of probation, thereby rendering petitioner ineligible for parole consideration and thereby divesting the parole board of its exclusive authority to parole a defendant on a prison sentence, was improper and required reversal of the sentence and remand of the cause for imposition of a new sentence. Geter v. Wainwright, App. 3 Dist., 380 So.2d 1203 (1980), dismissed 392 So.2d 1381. Criminal Law ⚿ 1181.5(8); Sentencing And Punishment ⚿ 1976(2)

Six years' imprisonment, as a condition of 15 years' probation, was too long, and, thus, could not be imposed as a condition. Olcott v. State, App. 2 Dist., 378 So.2d 303 (1979). Sentencing And Punishment ⚿ 1976(2)

202. —— Appeal, length of term, imprisonment or incarceration

Issue of propriety of length of incarceration imposed as condition of probation should be raised in the first instance in the trial court. Brown v. State, App. 2 Dist., 407 So.2d 295 (1981). Criminal Law ⚿ 1042.3(4)

Trial court's imposition of long prison term as condition of probation was fundamental error, which prisoner could collaterally attack in motion for postconviction relief, although prisoner had taken no appeal from imposition of sentence, where there were no appellate decisions in state which questioned propriety of long prison term as condition of probation until after trial court had placed prisoner on probation. Hamm v. State, App. 2 Dist., 380 So.2d 1101 (1980), dismissed 383 So.2d 1203. Criminal Law ⚿ 1556; Sentencing And Punishment ⚿ 1976(2)

203. —— Intermittent imprisonment, imprisonment or incarceration

This section providing for terms and conditions of probation is sufficiently broad to allow imposition of intermittent imprisonment and payment of fine as conditions of probation. State v. Williams, App. 2 Dist., 237 So.2d 69 (1970). Sentencing And Punishment ⚿ 1974(2); Sentencing And Punishment ⚿ 1976(2)

204. —— Credit for time served, imprisonment or incarceration

When a trial court sentences a probationary term on some of a defendant's convictions consecutively to an incarcerative term on other offenses, the defendant is entitled to credit for the time he served in prison on the incarcerative portion of his sentence against the total sentence imposed after revocation of probation on the probationary portion of his sentence. Doty v. State, App. 1 Dist., 851 So.2d 827 (2003). Sentencing And Punishment ⚿ 2041

Defendant was entitled to credit for time served against incarceration imposed as condition of probation. Springer v. State, App. 5 Dist., 616 So.2d 1105 (1993). Sentencing And Punishment ⚿ 2041

Where court ordered defendant to serve 90 days in county jail as special condition of probation, with a credit for 15 days time served, credit was to be applied to defendant's release date under the special condition, not to the term of probation which began on date that term was imposed. Granfelt v. State, App. 4 Dist., 560 So.2d 401 (1990). Sentencing And Punishment ⚿ 1943; Sentencing And Punishment ⚿ 1976(3)

Placement in correctional center as condition of probation was "incarceration," requiring sentence credit to be given to probationer on remand if trial court decided to revoke probation. Jackson v. State, App. 5 Dist., 449 So.2d 309 (1984). Sentencing And Punishment ⚿ 1171

Trial court is required to award sentence credit for any time during which defendant is incarcerated as condition of probation. Jackson v. State, App. 5 Dist., 449 So.2d 309 (1984). Sentencing And Punishment ⚿ 1167

205. —— Prior probation periods, imprisonment or incarceration

It was improper to order term of imprisonment, imposed as condition of probation, to commence upon completion of prior probationary period without probationer's having been charged with any violations of such probation. Vihinen v. State, App. 4 Dist., 368 So.2d 626

(1979). Sentencing And Punishment ⚷ 1976(3)

206. Revocation of probation—In general

Term of probation had already expired before affidavit alleging violations of probation was filed, and thus revocation of probation was improper; earlier attempt to extend probation without proper notice and hearing was invalid. Gearhart v. State, App. 5 Dist., 885 So.2d 415 (2004). Sentencing And Punishment ⚷ 2010

Probationer, who has accepted the conditions of his or her probation, is not permitted to challenge one of the conditions of probation after probation has been revoked for a violation of that condition; receding from *Mathis v. State,* 683 So.2d 634 (Fla. 4th DCA 1996). Matthews v. State, App. 4 Dist., 736 So.2d 72 (1999). Criminal Law ⚷ 1134.70

Where the greater weight of the evidence supports a trial judge's finding that a probationer has violated a condition of probation, the decision whether to revoke probation is a matter which rests in sound discretion of trial judge. Goley v. State, App. 5 Dist., 584 So.2d 139 (1991). Sentencing And Punishment ⚷ 2001

Probation was improperly revoked for violation of condition which was not included in order placing defendant on probation. Sutton v. State, App. 3 Dist., 348 So.2d 626 (1977). Sentencing And Punishment ⚷ 2003

207. —— Failure to enter program, revocation of probation

Probationer's absence from two sessions of sex offender counseling, without more, did not give rise to willful and substantial violation of condition of probation that required probationer to enter, participate in, and successfully complete sex offender treatment, where probationer missed sessions because of hospital and dentist appointments, and probationer testified that he had shown sex offender therapist notes from doctors for absences, and that he believed therapist had excused his absences. Reed v. State, App. 2 Dist., 865 So.2d 644 (2004). Sentencing And Punishment ⚷ 1977(3)

Where evidence supports finding that a defendant has capacity to understand and the intelligence to be a willing participant in a mentally disordered sex offender program and has determined not to cooperate in such a program as a condition of probation, the trial court will be sustained in revoking probation. Cardoso v. State, App. 3 Dist., 421 So.2d 589 (1982). Sentencing And Punishment ⚷ 2003

208. —— Use of intoxicants or narcotics, revocation of probation

Trial court was justified in revoking defendant's probation on ground that he used intoxicants to excess in violation of condition of probation. Harvey v. State, App. 1 Dist., 399 So.2d 1134 (1981), review denied 411 So.2d 382. Sentencing And Punishment ⚷ 2003

Probationer's admission to probation supervisor that he had used heroin was sufficient to sustain revocation of probation for violation of probation condition proscribing use of narcotic drugs. Johnson v. State, App. 5 Dist., 378 So.2d 108 (1980). Sentencing And Punishment ⚷ 2021

209. —— Possession of weapons, revocation of probation

At probation revocation hearing, trial court properly found a violation of condition of defendant's probation that defendant would not possess a weapon or firearm without prior consent of his probation officer where, at the revocation hearing, State proved that a police officer had legally stopped defendant driving his car and spotted a rifle in plain view on the car floorboard and that defendant's probation officer had not given prior permission to possess the weapon. Tackett v. State, App. 2 Dist., 413 So.2d 117 (1982). Sentencing And Punishment ⚷ 2021

210. —— Failure to testify against others, revocation of probation

Where at arraignment it was agreed pursuant to plea negotiation that defendant would testify truthfully against other persons involved, but such agreement to testify was not made condition of probation, probation was improperly revoked upon his refusal to testify against another person. Morgan v. State, App. 2 Dist., 341 So.2d 201 (1976). Sentencing And Punishment ⚷ 2003

211. Notice—In general

Notice of probation conditions is required because defendants placed on probation normally do not see probation order until they report to probation office sometime after sentencing. Hart v. State, App. 2 Dist., 651 So.2d 112 (1995), review granted 659 So.2d 1089, quashed in part 668 So.2d 589. Sentencing And Punishment ⚷ 1917

Because defendant must make contemporaneous objection to probation conditions at time of sentencing, defendant must be informed of conditions being imposed. Hart v. State, App. 2 Dist., 651 So.2d 112 (1995), review granted 659 So.2d 1089, quashed in part 668 So.2d 589. Sentencing And Punishment ⚷ 1918

A defendant must be given notice of a proposed restitution order and be allowed to be heard as to the amount of damages or loss caused by his offense. Wilson v. State, App. 1

Dist., 407 So.2d 1078 (1982). Sentencing And Punishment ⚷ 2181

Trial judge may notify defendant prior to sentencing hearing that restitution is possibility and if he does so and affords defendant opportunity to be heard, trial court may then impose restitution as condition of probation, but if trial judge does not furnish defendant notice prior to sentencing hearing and defendant objects or otherwise contests order of restitution, trial judge must suspend hearing for reasonable time and allow defendant to be heard on issues relevant to restitution. Miller v. State, App. 4 Dist., 407 So.2d 959 (1981). Sentencing And Punishment ⚷ 1917

Defendant must be placed on notice as to what he must do or refrain from doing while on probation. Norris v. State, App. 4 Dist., 383 So.2d 691 (1980), petition for review denied 388 So.2d 1116. Sentencing And Punishment ⚷ 1918

Fundamental fairness requires that a defendant be placed on notice as to what he must do or refrain from doing while on probation. Hines v. State, 358 So.2d 183 (1978). Sentencing And Punishment ⚷ 1918

Before defendant's probation may be revoked, he must have been put on notice as to what he must do or cannot do as special conditions of the probation; such concept of notice to defendant is an essential element of "due process." Morgan v. State, App. 2 Dist., 341 So.2d 201 (1976). Sentencing And Punishment ⚷ 1917

212. —— Constructive and actual notice

Defendant was given constructive notice of condition of probation regarding working diligently at lawful occupation and supporting any dependents to the best of his ability and, thus, he could not attack that condition on appeal. Crawford v. State, App. 2 Dist., 616 So.2d 1158 (1993). Sentencing And Punishment ⚷ 1972(3)

Imposition of $1.00 per month payment to corporation as condition of community control and probation, which was not orally pronounced at sentencing but was included in written community control and probation orders, would be reversed since there was no statutory authorization for charge and defendant was thus not on constructive or actual notice of that condition. Johnson v. State, App. 1 Dist., 598 So.2d 282 (1992). Criminal Law ⚷ 1177.3(4); Sentencing And Punishment ⚷ 1921

213. —— Record or evidence, notice

Record did not indicate that trial court entered its order, conditioning probation on payment of attorney fees and courts costs with notice and hearing required by F.S.A. § 27.56; therefore, order assessing attorney fees and costs would be vacated. Smith v. State, App. 2 Dist., 441 So.2d 1162 (1983), quashed 468 So.2d 984. Sentencing And Punishment ⚷ 1917

In fulfilling statutory duty under § 948.02 (renumbered; see, now, § 945.26) of notifying a defendant of terms and conditions of probation it was not unreasonable for probation supervisor to use an office, rather than a home visit, to formally explain terms of probation and to deliver a copy of terms thereof; hence, defendant's repeated refusal to come to probation office, insisting that supervisor make home visits, furnished valid grounds for revocation, notwithstanding that defendant, who had been warned that he would be brought to court if he failed to come to the office, was never officially notified that failure to carry out instructions of his probation supervisor would warrant revocation. Mobley v. State, App. 3 Dist., 348 So.2d 373 (1977). Sentencing And Punishment ⚷ 1918; Sentencing And Punishment ⚷ 2005

214. —— Presumptions, notice

It is presumed that officials of the Department of Offender Rehabilitation carry out their statutory duty under § 948.02 (renumbered; see, now, § 945.26) to notify defendant concerning terms and conditions of probation; such presumption can only be overcome by affirmative evidence establishing that the Department did not so perform its duty; when such a showing is made and defendant is not otherwise advised of his probationary condition by the court, probation may not be revoked unless defendant is charged with violating the probationary conditions by committing a crime. Mobley v. State, App. 3 Dist., 348 So.2d 373 (1977). Sentencing And Punishment ⚷ 1988; Sentencing And Punishment ⚷ 2006

215. Forms

An unmarked condition on a standard probation form is not explicitly or implicitly part of the agreement. Mastick v. State, App. 3 Dist., 409 So.2d 203 (1982). Sentencing And Punishment ⚷ 1920

Unmarked condition on standard probation form is not, explicitly or implicitly, part of agreement between the parties. Croteau v. State, 334 So.2d 577 (1976). Sentencing And Punishment ⚷ 1920

216. Plea bargain—In general

Defendant entering into negotiated plea did not waive his right to contest on appeal illegal portion of probation order providing that he could perform 50 hours of community service in lieu of costs of supervision, as a defendant cannot acquiesce in illegal sentence. Rasik v.

State, App. 4 Dist., 683 So.2d 1097 (1996). Criminal Law ⚿ 1026.10(4)

Once defendant voluntarily and intelligently agrees without objection to terms and conditions of probation as part of negotiated plea, he cannot later attempt to have particular conditions set aside as being invalid and also demand that order of probation remain otherwise intact. Pollock v. Bryson, App. 2 Dist., 450 So.2d 1183 (1984). Criminal Law ⚿ 273.2(1)

Fact that defendant, who had initially been placed on probation for five years on condition that he spend 100 days in jail, was subsequently sentenced to five years' imprisonment, with credit for time served, on revocation of his probation did not violate agreement under which defendant had agreed to plead guilty and state had agreed to a "cap of one year with credit for time served, probation and adjudication up to court." Pugh v. State, App. 4 Dist., 379 So.2d 398 (1980). Sentencing And Punishment ⚿ 2041

217. —— Withdrawal of plea, plea bargain

Defendant's ignorance of restraints inherent in sex offender probation did not rise to level of good cause to withdraw his no contest plea to lewd or lascivious assault upon child under 16 years of age, where plea agreement allowed for punishment far greater than sex offender probation. Boutwell v. State, App. 5 Dist., 776 So.2d 1014 (2001). Criminal Law ⚿ 275.5(2)

218. —— Subsequent violation or revocation, plea bargain

If defendant pleads guilty pursuant to plea bargain and court places him on probation, court may sentence him to term in excess of provisions of original bargain if he violates his probation. Johnson v. State, App. 2 Dist., 378 So.2d 335 (1980), certiorari denied 402 So.2d 9. Sentencing And Punishment ⚿ 2036

Where court granted defendant probation when plea bargain did not require it, and court warned defendant of consequences of violation of probation, defendant could not complain when sentence was imposed in excess of plea bargain upon revocation of probation. Johnson v. State, App. 2 Dist., 378 So.2d 335 (1980), certiorari denied 402 So.2d 9. Sentencing And Punishment ⚿ 2036

So long as order of probation was within terms of plea agreement, court had fulfilled the plea bargain and events which brought about revocation of probation opened new chapter in which court was able to mete out any punishment within limits prescribed for the crime. Johnson v. State, App. 2 Dist., 378 So.2d 335 (1980), certiorari denied 402 So.2d 9. Sentencing And Punishment ⚿ 2038

219. Presumptions, generally

There is rebuttable presumption of rational connection between condition of probation and proper objective sought to be achieved by probation, which presumption probationer should have burden to overcome in proceeding instituted for that purpose in trial court. Bentley v. State, App. 5 Dist., 411 So.2d 1361 (1982), review denied 419 So.2d 1195. Criminal Law ⚿ 1144.17

It should be presumed that sentencing judge imposed conditions of probation to protect public and to increase probability that defendant will obey law in future. Bentley v. State, App. 5 Dist., 411 So.2d 1361 (1982), review denied 419 So.2d 1195. Criminal Law ⚿ 1144.17

220. Summary judgment

Rule governing court's consideration of motion for summary judgment requires that any opposing affidavits to motion for summary judgment be mailed at least five days prior to scheduled hearing or be hand delivered to opposing counsel at least two days prior to hearing. Harris v. Wilson, App. 1 Dist., 656 So.2d 512 (1995), rehearing denied, review granted 666 So.2d 143, approved 693 So.2d 945. Judgment ⚿ 185.1(1)

221. Statement of reasons

This section authorizing imposition of conditions of probation does not require that trial judge specify his reasons for imposing conditions of probation, but cautious judge may see fit to do so in event appellate court undertakes to review for substance and reasonableness. Bentley v. State, App. 5 Dist., 411 So.2d 1361 (1982), review denied 419 So.2d 1195. Sentencing And Punishment ⚿ 1916

Condition of probation that probationer "stay away from bars" was not unconstitutionally vague. Brown v. State, App. 4 Dist., 406 So.2d 1262 (1981). Sentencing And Punishment ⚿ 1980(2)

222. Orders—In general

In certain instances, condition of probation which is statutorily authorized or mandated may be imposed and included in written order of probation although omitted from oral pronouncements at sentencing. Jackson v. State, App. 5 Dist., 902 So.2d 193 (2005), rehearing denied, review denied 913 So.2d 596. Sentencing And Punishment ⚿ 1918

General conditions of probation not orally pronounced at sentencing may nevertheless be validly imposed by subsequent timely written order of probation. Jones v. State, App. 1 Dist., 876 So.2d 642 (2004). Sentencing And Punishment ⚿ 1920

General conditions of probation may be imposed either orally, or in writing, or both. Jones v. State, App. 1 Dist., 876 So.2d 642 (2004). Sentencing And Punishment ⚷ 1919

Due process requires that statutory condition of probation be either orally pronounced or included in a written order. Perez v. State, App. 4 Dist., 805 So.2d 76 (2002).

Form probation order used by county did not give defendant sufficient notice of special conditions of probation to make oral pronouncements by court unnecessary, particularly as conditions imposed were not even part of general conditions of probation promulgated by Supreme Court and varied in some respects from special conditions listed in Supreme Court's form order as conditions which can be checked off or filled in; conditions imposed required defendant to attend and successfully complete rehabilitation program, to submit to drug evaluation and treatment, to pay for random drug test to which defendant was to submit at probation officer's request, and to not use or possess alcoholic beverages for any purpose. Dean v. State, App. 4 Dist., 669 So.2d 1140 (1996). Sentencing And Punishment ⚷ 1918

Written order of probation must conform to oral pronouncement. Ashe v. State, App. 1 Dist., 582 So.2d 759 (1991). Sentencing And Punishment ⚷ 1921

Written order of probation, which contained special condition of payment of one dollar per month to local program, did not conform to oral pronouncement and, accordingly, would be revised on remand. Ashe v. State, App. 1 Dist., 582 So.2d 759 (1991). Criminal Law ⚷ 1181.5(8); Sentencing And Punishment ⚷ 1921

Probation order which violated ruling that general sentences may not be imposed, was required to be corrected to reflect that probation imposed applied only to one offense, or apportion total probation among two offenses concerned. Leonardi v. State, App. 5 Dist., 548 So.2d 811 (1989), approved 567 So.2d 408. Sentencing And Punishment ⚷ 1923

Where order which vacated three-year probationary term, which was excessive but unlawful only to extent of excess, and which placed defendant on probation for one year contained perfunctory recital that defendant had not violated conditions of his probation, such language was not court's ruling on hearing respecting probation violations, and in view of deputy clerk's minutes clearly reflecting two separate rulings by the court, defendant was not entitled to reversal of judgment that he had violated conditions of his probation. Peyton v. State, App. 3 Dist., 383 So.2d 737 (1980). Sentencing And Punishment ⚷ 2028

Order, which revoked probation and which recited that defendant had violated certain condition of probation though judge had announced that he was not satisfied that a violation of such condition had occurred, had to be corrected to eliminate the statement that defendant had violated such condition. Allen v. State, App. 5 Dist., 383 So.2d 674 (1980). Sentencing And Punishment ⚷ 2030

An order putting on probation for five-year period an accused who paid fine for keeping gaming table, and authorizing court to vacate probation for cause and to impose sentence which might have been imposed in first instance, was void from its inception. Ex parte Bosso, 41 So.2d 322 (1949). Sentencing And Punishment ⚷ 2037

223. —— Oral pronouncement, orders

Court erroneously included nine special conditions in its written probation order which were not orally announced by court at sentencing. Brown v. State, App. 2 Dist., 561 So.2d 1248 (1990). Sentencing And Punishment ⚷ 1921

Inclusion of special conditions of probation in written order that were not orally pronounced at sentencing hearing mandates reversal and remand for correction of written order to conform to oral pronouncement. Rowland v. State, App. 1 Dist., 548 So.2d 812 (1989). Criminal Law ⚷ 1177.3(4); Sentencing And Punishment ⚷ 1921

Inclusion in written order of special conditions of probation that were not orally pronounced at sentencing hearing required reversal of written order of probation and remand for correction, so that written order of probation conformed to oral pronouncement. Williams v. State, App. 2 Dist., 542 So.2d 479 (1989). Criminal Law ⚷ 1181.5(8)

Condition of probation requiring probationer to leave county by certain time of day was not unenforceable despite fact that condition was not reduced to writing in order of probation, where probationer was clearly apprised of condition at hearing where he was present, and acknowledged that condition. Jacobsen v. State, App. 2 Dist., 536 So.2d 373 (1988). Sentencing And Punishment ⚷ 1919

In reducing order which revoked probation to writing, trial court incorrectly found defendant to have violated all six counts of affidavits, rather than the limited findings orally made at hearing. Burton v. State, App. 4 Dist., 382 So.2d 835 (1980). Sentencing And Punishment ⚷ 2028

224. —— Remand, orders

Where written order contained several special conditions of probation which had not been orally announced at sentencing, remand was appropriate for trial court to conduct new sentencing hearing so that it could properly announce and imposed any conditions that it felt appropriate; it was not necessary to simply strike the unannounced conditions. Burdo v. State, App. 3 Dist., 667 So.2d 874 (1996), review granted 676 So.2d 412, quashed 682 So.2d 557. Criminal Law ⚷ 1181.5(3.1)

On remand after reversal of payment provision of order of probation, trial court was also required to resolve discrepancy between oral and written employment condition contained in order. Millard v. State, App. 5 Dist., 656 So.2d 258 (1995). Criminal Law ⚷ 1192

225. —— Specificity, orders

Sentencing court's imposition of probation condition, which stated that defendant who pleaded guilty to unlawful sexual activity with a minor could not view, own, or possess obscene, pornographic, or sexually explicit material, was improper, as the condition was not specific as to the defendant's specific deviant behavior; although the defendant had adequate notice of what was prohibited based upon the statutory language and the sentencing court's statements, the written order of probation should have been more specific and related to the defendant's particular deviant behavior pattern. Taylor v. State, App. 2 Dist., 821 So.2d 404 (2002). Sentencing And Punishment ⚷ 1983(2)

Condition of probation ordering defendant to "abide by previously ordered conditions of probation" should have explicitly stated specific cumulative conditions of probation, where defendant's extensive criminal record showed repeated instances of violation of different conditions of probation. Gaal v. State, App. 1 Dist., 599 So.2d 723 (1992). Sentencing And Punishment ⚷ 1918

226. —— Separate orders

Trial court improperly issued general order of probation for separate offenses; court was required to enter separate order of probation for each offense. Ford v. State, App. 5 Dist., 528 So.2d 538 (1988). Sentencing And Punishment ⚷ 1913

227. —— Subsequent orders

Where violation of probation was based on alleged sexual battery in which defendant used a gun and two technical violations were also involved, where defendant did not question violation of probation and findings of court as to sexual battery but appeal of order revoking probation was directed solely at technical violations, and where evidence was overwhelmingly supportive of trial court's findings regarding sexual battery, appeal solely on basis of technical violations was frivolous and would be dismissed. McKinnon v. State, App. 5 Dist., 376 So.2d 275 (1979). Criminal Law ⚷ 1131(4)

An order of the parole and probation commission placing a parole violator in community control supersedes and replaces the original parole order. The commission does not have to formally revoke the original release order because it is forfeited or suspended, subject to reinstatement, on the finding a parole violation took place; however, the commission could adopt conditions from the original parole order compatible with statutes pertaining thereto, in its new order placing the parolee into a community control program. Op.Atty.Gen., 83–79, Oct. 26, 1983.

228. Sentences—In general

Incarceration as a condition of probation does not constitute a "sentence." Smith v. State, App. 1 Dist., 448 So.2d 20 (1984), approved 484 So.2d 581. Sentencing And Punishment ⚷ 1976(1)

While defendant was placed on probation for five years conditioned on his serving one year in the county jail, and while he now asserted that he was entitled to gain time under § 951.21 as a county prisoner, imposition of a short term of imprisonment as a special condition of probation is not a "sentence." Adams v. State, App. 5 Dist., 387 So.2d 498 (1980). Sentencing And Punishment ⚷ 1976(1)

When incarceration is imposed as a condition of probation, such incarceration constitutes a condition of probation and not a sentence. McGowan v. State, App. 3 Dist., 362 So.2d 335 (1978). Sentencing And Punishment ⚷ 1976(1)

229. —— Gain time credit, sentences

Department of Corrections (DOC) had legal authority to forfeit credit for gain time upon revocation of defendant's probation, and the DOC's forfeiture of gain time could not be countermanded by the court, although court had told defendant in plea agreement that he would receive 15 years gain time. Jones v. State, App. 5 Dist., 782 So.2d 552 (2001). Prisons ⚷ 247; Sentencing And Punishment ⚷ 2041

Where defendant, who pled guilty to robbery, was sentenced to ten years' probation with special condition that he serve five years in state prison, transcript of sentencing proceeding strongly suggested that trial judge intended that defendant would be eligible for parole within six months but department of corrections took position that, under sentence as imposed, defendant was entitled to gain time against the five-year period and was not eligible for parole, sentence was to be vacated. Cooney v. State, App. 3 Dist., 376 So.2d 926 (1979). Sentencing And Punishment ⚷ 1976(3)

230. —— Departure, sentences

To extent that written probation order, which stated that defendant's failure to make restitution of medical expenses to victim of offense of breaking and entering with intent to commit assault and battery would result in a prison term, departed from judge's statement at hearing that such a failure would result in a two-year sentence, the order controlled; imposition of five-year sentence on revocation of probation in proceeding in which it was alleged that defendant had failed to make restitution and had committed three acts of larceny was proper. Mayo v. State, App. 3 Dist., 346 So.2d 98 (1977). Sentencing And Punishment ⚷ 1921

231. —— Consecutive or concurrent sentences

Sentencing defendant to 22 years' imprisonment for second-degree murder with further proviso that probation would commence upon release from prison and run for balance of sentence was illegal, since term of probation was not definite and certain. Maynard v. State, App. 5 Dist., 561 So.2d 449 (1990). Sentencing And Punishment ⚷ 1944

232. Entry of terms and conditions

It is a proper practice for court to approve and enter in its minutes the terms and conditions under which an offender is granted probation. Pickman v. State, App. 3 Dist., 155 So.2d 646 (1963), certiorari denied 164 So.2d 805. Sentencing And Punishment ⚷ 1918

233. Extension

Trial court has no authority to extend period of probation beyond maximum permissible sentence for underlying offense. Colon v. State, App. 4 Dist., 660 So.2d 373 (1995). Sentencing And Punishment ⚷ 1952

Absent any finding of a violation of probation in proceeding in which it was found that probationer's failure to make restitution payments to victim was not a willful violation because defendant did not have ability to make payments, circuit court was without authority to extend the probationary period. Smith v. State, App. 3 Dist., 377 So.2d 250 (1979). Sentencing And Punishment ⚷ 1923

Section 948.06 providing for revocation, modification, or continuance of probation after notice and hearing to defendant and a finding that defendant violated his probation is the only authority for extension of the period of probation. Patrick v. State, App. 1 Dist., 336 So.2d 1253 (1976). Sentencing And Punishment ⚷ 1950

Where court in previous action acted without authority in extending defendant's period of probation without giving notice or hearing to defendant on State's charge of violation of probation, a conviction based on violation of the improperly extended period of probation was reversed. Patrick v. State, App. 1 Dist., 336 So.2d 1253 (1976). Criminal Law ⚷ 1177.3(4)

This section which sets forth eight specific terms and conditions of probation which court may include in its order of probation and authorizes court to modify terms and conditions at any time within probation period does not authorize extension of period of probation. Patrick v. State, App. 1 Dist., 336 So.2d 1253 (1976). Sentencing And Punishment ⚷ 1950

234. Objections—In general

Defendant had no basis or need to object to special conditions of probation at his sentencing hearing, where trial court simply announced that defendant was sentenced to 30 months in prison, followed by five years' probation, and no reference was made in open court to any special conditions of probation. Olvey v. State, App. 2 Dist., 609 So.2d 640 (1992), decision clarified on rehearing. Sentencing And Punishment ⚷ 1918

Issue whether special condition of probation could be imposed was properly presented for consideration on the merits, where defendant's counsel made specific objection when trial court announced the condition. Walker v. State, App. 1 Dist., 461 So.2d 229 (1984). Criminal Law ⚷ 1042.3(4)

It was for trial court to make initial ruling on defendant's challenge to conditions of his probation. Myers v. State, App. 1 Dist., 426 So.2d 986 (1983). Sentencing And Punishment ⚷ 1922

235. —— Jurisdiction, objections

In order to challenge on appeal the terms and conditions of probation, defendant must state of record any objections at the time that probation is imposed, but when trial court lacks jurisdiction to impose probation, or another fundamental error occurs, no objection of record is required. Young v. State, App. 2 Dist., 438 So.2d 998 (1983). Criminal Law ⚷ 1042.3(4)

236. —— Waiver, objections

Defendant who pleaded guilty to sexual offense, and whose plea agreement included the standard conditions of probation which prohibited him from living or having unsupervised contact with minors within 1,000 feet of places where children congregate or from working in such environments, waived any objection to those conditions by signing the agreement. Nelson v. State, App. 1 Dist., 780 So.2d 294 (2001). Criminal Law ⚿ 273.4(1)

Condition of probation prohibiting defendant from possessing drugs or narcotics unless prescribed by a physician, though vague, did not constitute fundamental error, and defendant therefore waived any challenge to that condition by failing to contemporaneously object to its imposition. Williams v. State, App. 2 Dist., 681 So.2d 817 (1996). Criminal Law ⚿ 1042.3(4); Sentencing And Punishment ⚿ 1980(2)

Probationer waived objection to imposition of condition on his probation that he not use intoxicants to excess or visit places where intoxicants, drugs or other dangerous substances were unlawfully sold, dispensed or used, where he received written copy of condition at original sentencing and was orally told that same conditions would apply at his subsequent sentencing five years later, and did not object to condition at either time; thus defendant had either actual or constructive notice of condition. Bledsoe v. State, App. 5 Dist., 657 So.2d 1235 (1995). Sentencing And Punishment ⚿ 1917

Defendant's failure to object to probation condition that was not announced orally at sentencing hearing did not result in waiver of issue. Kelly v. State, App. 2 Dist., 552 So.2d 312 (1989). Criminal Law ⚿ 1042.3(4)

237. —— Fundamental error, objections

Order imposing term of incarceration for cocaine charges that exceeded one year as a special condition of his probation was serious and patent error, requiring reversal for resentencing despite failure to object. Graham v. State, App. 2 Dist., 753 So.2d 607 (2000). Criminal Law ⚿ 1042.3(4)

Contemporaneous objection is not prerequisite to appeal an illegal condition of probation or condition of probation that is so egregious as to be equivalent of fundamental error. Evans v. State, App. 1 Dist., 608 So.2d 90 (1992). Criminal Law ⚿ 1042.3(4)

Trial court's error in failing to order diagnosis or evaluation of defendant who was convicted for lewd and lascivious act upon child under the age of 16 was preserved even in absence of contemporaneous objection at sentencing proceeding. Singleton v. State, App. 1 Dist., 582 So.2d 657 (1991). Criminal Law ⚿ 1042.3(4)

238. —— Illegal conditions, objections

Contemporaneous objection rule is inapplicable to illegal condition of probation. Cassamassima v. State, App. 5 Dist., 657 So.2d 906 (1995), certification denied. Criminal Law ⚿ 1042.3(4)

239. —— Timely appeal and preservation of appeal rights, objections

Defendant failed to preserve for appellate review issue of whether the three special conditions of his probation should be stricken because they were not orally pronounced at sentencing, where defendant made no objection to these conditions at the trial level and made no motion to amend the probation order addressed to the trial court, and conditions did not constitute fundamental error. Barfield v. State, App. 5 Dist., 762 So.2d 564 (2000). Criminal Law ⚿ 1042.3(4); Criminal Law ⚿ 1044.1(1)

Defendant's failure to object to trial court's imposition of prosecution costs and public defender fees prevented review of his challenges to these conditions on appeal; prosecution costs and public defender fees imposed as conditions of probation were neither illegal nor so egregious as to amount to fundamental error. Holmes v. State, App. 4 Dist., 658 So.2d 1185 (1995). Criminal Law ⚿ 1042.3(4)

Probationer was required to object to condition imposed upon his probation to preserve his right to appeal, as condition, that he not use intoxicants to excess or visit places where intoxicants, drugs, or other dangerous substances were unlawfully sold, dispensed or used, was not illegal or so egregious as to be equivalent to fundamental error. Bledsoe v. State, App. 5 Dist., 657 So.2d 1235 (1995). Criminal Law ⚿ 1042.3(4); Sentencing And Punishment ⚿ 1980(2)

Defendant convicted of being felon in possession of firearm failed to preserve for appellate review his challenges to orally pronounced probation conditions, where he failed to object to the conditions and they were not so egregious as to be the equivalent of fundamental error. Reed v. State, App. 2 Dist., 652 So.2d 912 (1995). Criminal Law ⚿ 1042.3(4)

Defendant's failure to preserve appellate review of his challenges to orally pronounced probation conditions by objecting to them in trial court will not be overlooked by District Court of Appeal where the conditions are not so egregious as to be equivalent of fundamental error. Reed v. State, App. 2 Dist., 652 So.2d 912 (1995). Criminal Law ⚿ 1042.3(4)

To contest conditions of probation on appeal, defendant must preserve issue by objecting at time conditions are imposed, unless conditions are illegal or so egregious as to be equivalent of fundamental error. Devine v. State, App. 5 Dist., 636 So.2d 179 (1994). Criminal Law ⚿ 1042.3(4)

Conditions of probation limiting consumption of alcohol or requiring substance abuse screening are not type of conditions, namely, conditions which are illegal or so egregious as to be equivalent of fundamental error, which may be appealed in absence of contemporaneous objection. Devine v. State, App. 5 Dist., 636 So.2d 179 (1994). Criminal Law ⚷ 1042.3(4)

Defendant, who was on probation for dealing in stolen property, failed to timely object to conditions placed on his probation after he violated terms of probation by driving under the influence of alcohol (DUI), that he abstain from consumption of intoxicants and from visiting establishments whose primary purpose is sale or consumption of intoxicants, and submit to random urinalysis, and thus could not contest conditions on appeal. Devine v. State, App. 5 Dist., 636 So.2d 179 (1994). Criminal Law ⚷ 1042.3(4)

If defendant believes that trial court's imposition of probation is improper, defendant must make timely objection. McCarthren v. State, App. 5 Dist., 635 So.2d 1005 (1994). Sentencing And Punishment ⚷ 1922

Defendant must make contemporaneous objection to preserve his rights on appeal with regard to condition of probation unless the probation condition is egregious. McCarthren v. State, App. 5 Dist., 635 So.2d 1005 (1994). Criminal Law ⚷ 1042.3(4)

Defendant failed to preserve for appellate review issue regarding imposition of special condition of community control where defendant lodged no objection to condition. Weaver v. State, App. 5 Dist., 587 So.2d 654 (1991). Criminal Law ⚷ 1042.3(4)

Although special condition of probation prohibiting defendant, a licensed physician, from writing medical prescriptions while on probation was improper because it was not reasonably related to defendant's rehabilitation and did not provide a standard of conduct essential to protection of the public, case could not be remanded for correction of error, because defendant failed to make a contemporaneous objection to the condition. McPike v. State, App. 2 Dist., 473 So.2d 291 (1985). Criminal Law ⚷ 1042.3(4)

Defendant failed to preserve for appellate review issue whether trial court erred in requiring defendant to make restitution to city for investigative expense where, at sentencing hearing, after defense counsel stated that he objected to court costs going to the city, and after court responded that it would reconsider if defense counsel could show where it was illegal, defense counsel stated that he had no objection and that what he was trying to get to was the precedent being set, and stated no other legal ground or specific objection on the record. Clemmons v. State, App. 1 Dist., 456 So.2d 1224 (1984). Criminal Law ⚷ 1043(1)

Defendant who made no objection to imposition of conditions of his probation would not be allowed to raise on appeal the propriety of the condition that he not live with a member of the opposite sex who is not a relative without permission of his probation officer. Young v. State, App. 2 Dist., 438 So.2d 998 (1983). Criminal Law ⚷ 1042.3(4)

When, at sentencing, trial court proposes conditions under which it will offer probation, defendant should, if he feels conditions laden him with burdens too grievous to be borne, forthrightly object to them at that time and place. Bentley v. State, App. 5 Dist., 411 So.2d 1361 (1982), review denied 419 So.2d 1195. Sentencing And Punishment ⚷ 1922

Ordinarily, criminal defendant is not required to object to conditions of probation in order to preserve them for appellate review. Miller v. State, App. 4 Dist., 407 So.2d 959 (1981). Criminal Law ⚷ 1042.3(4)

Objections to sentence with respect to conditions of probation must first be raised before trial court. Barlow v. State, App. 5 Dist., 390 So.2d 165 (1980). Criminal Law ⚷ 1042.3(4)

Defendant who failed to challenge in trial court condition of probation order providing that defendant would have to pay ½ of total restitution to victims as directed by probation officer, was not entitled to raise issue on appeal of criminal convictions. Barlow v. State, App. 5 Dist., 388 So.2d 349 (1980). Criminal Law ⚷ 1042.3(4)

240. —— Acceptance of conditions, objections

Defendant waived any objection to sex offender probation conditions, where defendant waited until after he violated one of the conditions to challenge validity of conditions. State v. Thurman, App. 5 Dist., 791 So.2d 1228 (2001). Sentencing And Punishment ⚷ 1922

Defendant's failure to object to conditions of probation requiring him to submit to urinalysis testing and prohibiting him from using intoxicants in excess constituted acceptance of those conditions. Rowland v. State, App. 1 Dist., 548 So.2d 812 (1989). Sentencing And Punishment ⚷ 1922

Defendant could not be heard to complain on appeal that he was denied notice and hearing prior to imposition of restitution as condition of probation where he accepted such condition without objection. Seymour v. State, App. 2 Dist., 432 So.2d 770 (1983). Criminal Law ⚷ 1042.3(4)

241. —— Correction of sentence, objections

Alleged error in condition of order of probation requiring defendant to pay one half of total restitution to victims of his assault would not be heard on appeal where defendant did not direct motion to trial court to correct illegal sentence. Barlow v. State, App. 5 Dist., 390 So.2d 165 (1980). Criminal Law ⚷ 1044.1(1)

242. Rejection of probation

Defendant is not required to accept probation and may reject court's attempt to effect his rehabilitation by conditions of probation rather than by straight term of imprisonment. Bentley v. State, App. 5 Dist., 411 So.2d 1361 (1982), review denied 419 So.2d 1195. Sentencing And Punishment ⚷ 1821

Defendant's legal right is to not receive sentence of confinement in excess of statutory maximum, and if he feels proffered probation with conditions is more onerous than maximum confinement permitted by law, he should reject offer of probation. Bentley v. State, App. 5 Dist., 411 So.2d 1361 (1982), review denied 419 So.2d 1195. Sentencing And Punishment ⚷ 1821

243. Oral pronouncement—In general

Failure to orally pronounce at adjudicatory hearing community control condition that juvenile delinquent not possess or carry weapon unless permission was obtained from court warranted amending condition to forbid possession of firearm, electric weapon, or concealed weapon, as such conduct is statutorily forbidden by juvenile convicted of delinquent act that would be felony if committed by adult. C.C.B. v. State, App. 4 Dist., 782 So.2d 473 (2001). Infants ⚷ 230.1

General conditions of probation contained in order of probation form are not required to be orally pronounced at sentencing, but special conditions of probation must be pronounced. Torres v. State, App. 2 Dist., 712 So.2d 1169 (1998). Sentencing And Punishment ⚷ 1918

Standard probation condition published in rules of criminal procedure requires no oral announcement. Garrison v. State, App. 2 Dist., 685 So.2d 53 (1996). Sentencing And Punishment ⚷ 1918

Conditions of probation that were not orally pronounced at sentencing were nonetheless permissible to extent they were substantially same as conditions of form probation order of which appellant had constructive notice prior to sentencing. Wallace v. State, App. 2 Dist., 682 So.2d 1139 (1996), rehearing denied. Sentencing And Punishment ⚷ 1918

Trial court's written probation order, which completely restricted defendant from driving on street, had to be corrected to reflect probation condition that trial court orally pronounced at sentencing, which condition was that defendant not drive on portion of street running past victim's house, in prosecution for aggravated stalking. Lawley v. State, App. 1 Dist., 680 So.2d 472 (1996). Sentencing And Punishment ⚷ 1921

Court could impose probation conditions not orally pronounced where three challenged conditions were among 11 standard or general conditions of probation listed in order of probation form contained in rule, and remaining condition was also general condition of probation. Frey v. State, App. 2 Dist., 679 So.2d 37 (1996), review granted 687 So.2d 1303, approved 708 So.2d 918. Sentencing And Punishment ⚷ 1918

Various probationary conditions not orally pronounced at sentencing could not thereafter be imposed upon defendant. Walker v. State, App. 2 Dist., 662 So.2d 1352 (1995). Sentencing And Punishment ⚷ 1920

Trial court's imposition of special conditions of probation without announcing those conditions at sentencing was improper. Jones v. State, App. 2 Dist., 661 So.2d 50 (1995). Sentencing And Punishment ⚷ 1920

Sentencing court was required to announce any special conditions of probation at sentencing. Walker v. State, App. 2 Dist., 660 So.2d 332 (1995). Sentencing And Punishment ⚷ 1918

Imposition of written conditions of probation which were not orally pronounced at sentencing was error requiring resentencing. Harris v. State, App. 1 Dist., 655 So.2d 1179 (1995). Sentencing And Punishment ⚷ 1921

Special condition of probation must be orally announced at sentencing. Reyes v. State, App. 2 Dist., 655 So.2d 111 (1995). Sentencing And Punishment ⚷ 1918

Trial court must pronounce in open court special conditions of probation. George v. State, App. 2 Dist., 624 So.2d 824 (1993). Sentencing And Punishment ⚷ 1918

Failure to orally pronounce special probation conditions at time of resentencing when probation was reimposed did not require striking of probation conditions where those conditions had been orally pronounced at defendant's original sentencing. Jones v. State, App. 1 Dist., 622 So.2d 1153 (1993). Sentencing And Punishment ⚷ 1918

Reimposition of conditions of probation without announcing them orally in court warranted striking of special conditions as invalid. Duchesne v. State, App. 2 Dist., 616 So.2d 172 (1993). Criminal Law ⚷ 1184(4.1); Sentencing And Punishment ⚷ 1920

Trial court is not always required to orally announce conditions of probation. Gaal v.

State, App. 1 Dist., 599 So.2d 723 (1992). Sentencing And Punishment ⚷ 1918

244. —— Special conditions, oral pronouncement

Defendant's financial responsibility for drug testing, drug treatment, and curfew conditions, as set forth in Drug Offender Probation Standard Conditions, were "special conditions" of probation and were required to be orally pronounced at sentencing, where such conditions were not enumerated in applicable statutes or rule of criminal procedure. Cole v. State, App. 4 Dist., 932 So.2d 1123 (2006). Sentencing And Punishment ⚷ 1918

Condition of written probation order that required defendant to make monthly payments of $1 to nonprofit treatment program was not orally pronounced at sentencing hearing, and payment requirement was not included in statutory list of general conditions for which no pronouncement is required, and thus payment condition had to be stricken from probation order, but payment condition could be reimposed after defendant was given appropriate notice and opportunity to be heard. Jackson v. State, App. 5 Dist., 902 So.2d 193 (2005), rehearing denied, review denied 913 So.2d 596. Sentencing And Punishment ⚷ 1917; Sentencing And Punishment ⚷ 1920

Although requirement that defendant convicted of burglary of occupied structure submit to random drug testing and treatment was general condition of probation that did not require oral pronouncement at sentencing hearing, requirement that defendant pay for testing and treatment was special condition, and failure to orally pronounce such special condition at sentencing hearing required that special condition portion of condition be stricken, and special condition could not be reimposed. Jackson v. State, App. 5 Dist., 902 So.2d 193 (2005), rehearing denied, review denied 913 So.2d 596. Sentencing And Punishment ⚷ 1918; Sentencing And Punishment ⚷ 1920

Special conditions of probation that are not announced orally during sentence hearing must be stricken, and may not be reimposed at resentencing, unless statutory exceptions exist. Jackson v. State, App. 5 Dist., 902 So.2d 193 (2005), rehearing denied, review denied 913 So.2d 596. Sentencing And Punishment ⚷ 1920

Conditions of probation contained in written sentencing order, prohibiting defendant from frequenting bars, requiring defendant to obtain mental health counseling, requiring defendant to attend alcohol/drug rehabilitation programs, and requiring defendant to submit to drug tests, were special conditions required to be orally pronounced at time of sentencing, rather than general conditions not required to be orally pronounced, even though statute defining general conditions provided that enumeration of certain general conditions did not prevent court from adding others; catch-all provision did not convert all unlisted conditions into general conditions. England v. State, App. 5 Dist., 879 So.2d 660 (2004). Sentencing And Punishment ⚷ 1918

The condition imposed upon defendant, that he pay for alcohol and drug testing, was a special condition of probation that had to be pronounced orally to be properly imposed on a probationer. Holmes v. State, App. 1 Dist., 866 So.2d 144 (2004). Sentencing And Punishment ⚷ 1918

Written conditions of probation requiring defendant to pay for random drug testing, to observe curfew, to report daily to probation officer if not employed, and to undergo substance abuse treatment and drug awareness course were special conditions of probation which had to be stricken for failure of trial court to pronounce them orally at sentencing. Bunn v. State, App. 4 Dist., 687 So.2d 879 (1997). Sentencing And Punishment ⚷ 1920

Condition of probation/community control requiring defendant to keep hourly log was special condition that was required to be orally pronounced at sentencing. Head v. State, App. 2 Dist., 687 So.2d 281 (1997). Sentencing And Punishment ⚷ 1918

Special condition of probation imposed on defendant which was not orally pronounced at sentencing had to be stricken. Melton v. State, App. 2 Dist., 685 So.2d 853 (1995). Sentencing And Punishment ⚷ 1920

Where sentence is reversed because trial court failed to orally pronounce at sentencing any special conditions of probation reflected in written sentence, court must strike unannounced conditions and cannot reimpose them upon resentencing. Burdo v. State, 682 So.2d 557 (1996). Criminal Law ⚷ 1192

As contained in written report of probation, conditions requiring probationer to observe curfew, report daily to his probation officer if not employed, and enroll in Drug Awareness Course were "special conditions" that had to be stricken when they were not orally pronounced at sentencing, as those conditions were not among general probation conditions set out by statute or rule. Ealy v. State, App. 4 Dist., 681 So.2d 914 (1996). Sentencing And Punishment ⚷ 1920

Probation conditions that are not set out by statute or rule are "special conditions" that must be pronounced during sentencing in open court. Ealy v. State, App. 4 Dist., 681 So.2d 914 (1996). Sentencing And Punishment ⚷ 1918

If special conditions of probation are not orally pronounced at sentencing, trial court must strike unannounced conditions. Ealy v. State, App. 4 Dist., 681 So.2d 914 (1996). Sentencing And Punishment ⚷ 1920

245. —— Requirements or procedures, oral pronouncement

To comply with requirement that special conditions of probation be orally pronounced, trial courts must inform defendant in open court of substance of each special condition in manner sufficient to give defendant opportunity to object at time to any condition which defendant believes is inappropriate. Vasquez v. State, App. 4 Dist., 663 So.2d 1343 (1995), review dismissed 666 So.2d 145. Sentencing And Punishment ⚷ 1918

Although trial judge need not read and explain each and every special condition of probation or community control to a defendant, some procedure must be utilized so that defendant, before sentencing is completed, is aware of and understand conditions of his probation and can object to them; in all cases in which court is considering probation as an option, easiest manner of complying with requirement is to furnish copy of proposed probation conditions to defendant and his counsel at sentencing; counsel should then be given sufficient time to explain conditions to defendant, and defendant should be required to sign appropriate acknowledgement in open court; if defendant is unwilling to accept appropriate conditions, then court is free to exercise its discretion as it pleases. Cleveland v. State, App. 5 Dist., 617 So.2d 1166 (1993). Sentencing And Punishment ⚷ 1918

To meet "pronouncement in open court" requirement for special conditions of probation, it is sufficient for trial court to inform defendant in open court of substance of each special condition in manner sufficient to give defendant opportunity to object at that time to any condition which defendant believes is inappropriate; there is no requirement that trial court read verbatim to each defendant every special condition contained in defendant's order of probation. Olvey v. State, App. 2 Dist., 609 So.2d 640 (1992), decision clarified on rehearing. Sentencing And Punishment ⚷ 1918

246. —— Restitution, oral pronouncement

Probation condition requiring processing fee for each payment of restitution, costs, and/or fees was discretionary and had to be pronounced orally; moreover, as Department of Corrections had statutory authority to impose fee, trial court had no authority to do so. Powell v. State, App. 2 Dist., 681 So.2d 722 (1996). Sentencing And Punishment ⚷ 1918; Sentencing And Punishment ⚷ 1975(2)

247. —— Due process, oral pronouncement

To satisfy minimum requirements of due process, trial court must sufficiently apprise defendant of substance of each special condition of probation so that defendant has opportunity to object to any condition which defendant believes is inappropriate. Nank v. State, App. 2 Dist., 646 So.2d 762 (1994), rehearing denied. Constitutional Law ⚷ 4732

Due process requires special conditions of probation to be pronounced in open court in manner sufficient for defendant to know of the conditions and to have an opportunity to object to them. Olvey v. State, App. 2 Dist., 609 So.2d 640 (1992), decision clarified on rehearing. Constitutional Law ⚷ 4732

248. —— Purpose, oral pronouncement

Purpose of requiring trial court to orally pronounce special conditions of probation is to notify defendant of conditions so defendant has opportunity to object to their imposition. Bledsoe v. State, App. 5 Dist., 657 So.2d 1235 (1995). Sentencing And Punishment ⚷ 1918

249. —— Statutorily authorized conditions, oral pronouncement

Condition of written probation order that required defendant to submit to warrantless searches of his person, residence, and property was statutorily authorized condition, and thus such condition did not have to be orally pronounced at sentencing hearing to be validly imposed. Jackson v. State, App. 5 Dist., 902 So.2d 193 (2005), rehearing denied, review denied 913 So.2d 596. Sentencing And Punishment ⚷ 1918

Imposition of statutorily mandated conditions of sex offender probation requires no oral pronouncement at sentencing. Woodson v. State, App. 5 Dist., 864 So.2d 512 (2004), review granted 879 So.2d 626, review dismissed 889 So.2d 823. Sentencing And Punishment ⚷ 1918

Community control condition that juvenile delinquent participate in mental health assessment and follow recommended treatment was valid, even though condition was not orally pronounced at adjudicatory hearing; statute specifically mandates that community control program for adjudicated delinquent include rehabilitative component. C.C.B. v. State, App. 4 Dist., 782 So.2d 473 (2001). Infants ⚷ 223.1

Community control conditions that juvenile delinquent obey reasonable rules and regulations imposed by probation officer and that juvenile promptly and truthfully answer all questions by officer and carry out all instructions court or officer may give were valid, even though conditions were not orally pronounced at adjudicatory hearing; statute authorizes placement of juvenile in community control program under supervision of authorized agent of Department of Juvenile Justice. C.C.B. v. State, App. 4 Dist., 782 So.2d 473 (2001). Infants ⚷ 223.1

Other than conditions which are statutorily authorized or mandated by probation or community control statutes, another category of conditions which need not be orally pronounced is that conduct which is proscribed by statute; publication in Laws of Florida or Florida Statutes gives citizens constructive notice of consequences of their actions. W.J. v. State, App. 4 Dist., 688 So.2d 954 (1997). Sentencing And Punishment ⚷ 1918

Statutorily authorized condition of probation or community control may be included in written order without being orally pronounced at sentencing. Brock v. State, 688 So.2d 909 (1997). Sentencing And Punishment ⚷ 1918

General conditions of probation/community control contained in statutes or on forms attached to rules need not be orally pronounced at sentencing. Head v. State, App. 2 Dist., 687 So.2d 281 (1997). Sentencing And Punishment ⚷ 1918

Defendant placed on drug offender probation is on constructive notice that some or all of the standard conditions of probation listed in statute may be imposed, and oral pronouncement of those conditions is not required, nor is oral pronouncement required for conditions identical to those contained in the Supreme Court's "Form Order of Probation," but other conditions must be stricken if not orally pronounced. Tory v. State, App. 4 Dist., 686 So.2d 689 (1996). Sentencing And Punishment ⚷ 1918

Condition of probation, which prohibited probationer from entering establishments whose primary business was sale of alcoholic beverages, was special condition not statutorily authorized under probation statutes, and thus it was invalid when imposed without having been orally pronounced at probationer's sentencing for bookmaking. Steward v. State, App. 4 Dist., 677 So.2d 1369 (1996). Sentencing And Punishment ⚷ 1920

Probation conditions prohibiting defendant from owning firearm, required defendant to pay for drug testing, and prohibited defendant from visiting places where intoxicants or drugs are unlawfully sold or used did not have to be orally pronounced to be valid, where those actions were statutorily prohibited. Leroux v. State, App. 4 Dist., 665 So.2d 1115 (1996). Sentencing And Punishment ⚷ 1918; Sentencing And Punishment ⚷ 1965

All conditions of probation must be orally pronounced at time of sentencing unless conditions are statutorily authorized or are otherwise based on statute which will provide defendant with constructive notice. Hayes v. State, App. 4 Dist., 665 So.2d 339 (1995). Sentencing And Punishment ⚷ 1918

All conditions of probation must be orally pronounced at time of sentencing unless conditions are statutorily authorized or otherwise based on statute which will provide defendant with constructive notice. Vasquez v. State, App. 4 Dist., 663 So.2d 1343 (1995), review dismissed 666 So.2d 145. Sentencing And Punishment ⚷ 1918

Defendants have notice of all probation conditions contained in statute; therefore, there is no obligation to orally pronounce these conditions. Hart v. State, App. 2 Dist., 651 So.2d 112 (1995), review granted 659 So.2d 1089, quashed in part 668 So.2d 589. Sentencing And Punishment ⚷ 1918

The only general conditions of probation for which oral pronouncement is unnecessary are those contained within the statutes, not those contained in approved probation order. Hart v. State, App. 2 Dist., 651 So.2d 112 (1995), review granted 659 So.2d 1089, quashed in part 668 So.2d 589. Sentencing And Punishment ⚷ 1918

Condition of probation prohibiting defendant from visiting where controlled substances were unlawfully sold, dispensed or used was statutorily authorized and could be included in written order of probation without being orally pronounced at sentencing. Zeigler v. State, App. 4 Dist., 647 So.2d 272 (1994). Sentencing And Punishment ⚷ 1918; Sentencing And Punishment ⚷ 1980(2)

Special condition of probation which is statutorily authorized may be included in written order of probation without being orally pronounced at sentencing, but special condition which is not statutorily authorized must be pronounced orally at sentencing before it may be included in written probation order. Zeigler v. State, App. 4 Dist., 647 So.2d 272 (1994). Sentencing And Punishment ⚷ 1918

Condition of probation which is statutorily authorized may be included in written order of probation even if not orally pronounced at sentencing. Nank v. State, App. 2 Dist., 646 So.2d 762 (1994), rehearing denied. Sentencing And Punishment ⚷ 1921

Special condition of probation not statutorily authorized is required to be pronounced orally at sentencing before it can be included in written probation order. Nank v. State, App. 2 Dist., 646 So.2d 762 (1994), rehearing denied. Sentencing And Punishment ⚷ 1918

All special conditions of probation must be orally pronounced at sentencing; only those standard conditions of community control/probation which are statutorily listed may be included in written order even if not pronounced orally at sentencing. Shacraha v. State, App. 4 Dist., 635 So.2d 1051 (1994). Sentencing And Punishment ⚿ 1918; Sentencing And Punishment ⚿ 1921

Trial court's failure to orally pronounce written probation condition requiring defendant to report to probation office within 72 hours of his release from prison was not error; reporting requirement was merely administrative mechanism for enforcement of probation rather than substantive matter, and statute provided constructive notice which, along with opportunity to be heard and to raise objections at sentencing hearing, satisfied requirements of procedural due process. Gaal v. State, App. 1 Dist., 599 So.2d 723 (1992). Constitutional Law ⚿ 4732; Sentencing And Punishment ⚿ 1918

250. —— Conditions not announced orally, oral pronouncement

Trial court's failure to orally pronounce conditions of probation and community control orders requiring defendant convicted of possession of oxycodone and battery of a person 65 years of age or older to submit to and pay for evaluation and treatment for alcohol and illegal drugs entitled defendant to have conditions stricken; conditions were special conditions, and trial court announced only that defendant would be subject to evaluation for substance abuse. Ayoub v. State, App. 2 Dist., 901 So.2d 311 (2005). Sentencing And Punishment ⚿ 1920

Conditions of probation and community control orders requiring defendant convicted of possession of oxycodone and battery of a person 65 years of age or older to "submit to search and seizure of person, automobile and residence at any reasonable time by your probation officer without a warrant" did not need to be orally pronounced at sentencing. Ayoub v. State, App. 2 Dist., 901 So.2d 311 (2005). Sentencing And Punishment ⚿ 1918

Differences between oral pronouncement and written order as to supervision conditions violated by probationer required remand for the trial court to resolve the discrepancy and, if necessary, to correct the record as to the actual oral pronouncement of the conditions that were violated. Williams v. State, App. 2 Dist., 886 So.2d 1078 (2004). Criminal Law ⚿ 1181.5(8)

Record on appeal did not support trial court's conclusion, in denying defendant's motion to correct illegal sentence, that probation condition requiring defendant to obtain mental health counseling was mandatory, so as to excuse sentencing court's failure to orally pronounce condition, even though statute defining general conditions of probation required such counseling for defendants convicted of sexual battery of a child; attached judgment reflected that defendant was convicted of sexual battery on a person 12 years or older, and did not establish that the victim was a child. England v. State, App. 5 Dist., 879 So.2d 660 (2004). Sentencing And Punishment ⚿ 1920

Probationary condition imposed against defendant for conviction for burglary, possession of a short-barreled shotgun, theft of a firearm, and resisting an officer was struck on appeal upon finding that trial court failed to orally pronounce condition at sentencing. Russman v. State, App. 5 Dist., 869 So.2d 635 (2004). Sentencing And Punishment ⚿ 1920

Failure to orally pronounce at adjudicatory hearing community control condition that juvenile delinquent not associate with any person under supervision of Department of Juvenile Justice or Department of Corrections warranted striking of condition; although this condition was listed in rules of juvenile procedure form, condition was not addressed in statute addressing powers of disposition in delinquency case. C.C.B. v. State, App. 4 Dist., 782 So.2d 473 (2001). Infants ⚿ 230.1

Failure to orally pronounce at adjudicatory hearing community control condition that probation officer has discretion to take away any non-essential activities or privileges from juvenile delinquent warranted striking of condition, where there was no statutory authority for such condition. C.C.B. v. State, App. 4 Dist., 782 So.2d 473 (2001). Infants ⚿ 230.1

Condition of probation that is statutorily authorized does not have to be orally announced at the sentencing hearing. Maddox v. State, 760 So.2d 89 (2000). Sentencing And Punishment ⚿ 1918

General condition of probation prohibiting possession of "any drugs or narcotics unless prescribed by a physician" was not required to be orally announced at sentencing. Johnson v. State, App. 2 Dist., 701 So.2d 367 (1997). Sentencing And Punishment ⚿ 1918

Conditions of probation that were not orally pronounced at sentencing would be stricken on appeal. Wilson v. State, App. 2 Dist., 685 So.2d 844 (1995). Sentencing And Punishment ⚿ 1920

Conditions of community control which were not pronounced orally would be stricken. Cardi v. State, App. 2 Dist., 685 So.2d 842 (1995). Sentencing And Punishment ⚿ 1920

State's failure to orally inform probationer that he must complete community service within 90 days from his release from jail mandated striking that condition of probation. Mathis v.

State, App. 4 Dist., 683 So.2d 634 (1996). Sentencing And Punishment ⚷ 1920

Probation condition requiring probationer to waive extradition should violation of supervision occur had to be stricken since it was special condition which was not orally pronounced. Reiter v. State, App. 2 Dist., 674 So.2d 189 (1996). Sentencing And Punishment ⚷ 1920

Appellate court would strike those portions of probation conditions that were not statutorily mandated because they were not orally pronounced at sentencing. Miller v. State, App. 2 Dist., 664 So.2d 1066 (1995). Sentencing And Punishment ⚷ 1920

Trial court improperly imposed two special conditions of probation without announcing those conditions at sentencing. Nisbett v. State, App. 2 Dist., 660 So.2d 813 (1995). Sentencing And Punishment ⚷ 1920

Trial court erred in imposing five special conditions to probation relating to weapons and destructive devices, excessive use of intoxicants, consumption and possession of alcohol and payment for evaluation and treatment, where conditions were not announced at sentencing. Williams v. State, App. 2 Dist., 655 So.2d 1205 (1995). Sentencing And Punishment ⚷ 1918

A written probation order may not impose conditions of probation that were not orally pronounced at sentencing. Harris v. State, App. 1 Dist., 655 So.2d 1179 (1995). Sentencing And Punishment ⚷ 1920

Trial court could not impose condition of probation that was not orally pronounced at sentencing. Green v. State, App. 2 Dist., 654 So.2d 1224 (1995). Sentencing And Punishment ⚷ 1920

Conditions of probation trial court did not orally pronounce were required to be stricken. Emond v. State, App. 2 Dist., 652 So.2d 419 (1995), review granted 660 So.2d 715, quashed 668 So.2d 599. Sentencing And Punishment ⚷ 1920

Trial court could not impose "special condition" of probation without orally pronouncing it at sentencing. Geller v. State, App. 2 Dist., 651 So.2d 192 (1995), review granted 663 So.2d 631, quashed 668 So.2d 599. Sentencing And Punishment ⚷ 1918

In defendant's sentence for driving while licensed suspended, tampering with evidence and possession of marijuana, probation condition forbidding defendant from possessing weapons and firearms without first obtaining permission from his probation officer, and condition forbidding defendant from using intoxicants to excess and visiting places where they were unlawfully used or dispensed, were improperly imposed because they were not announced in open court. Gilbert v. State, App. 2 Dist., 647 So.2d 853 (1994). Sentencing And Punishment ⚷ 1918

Trial court erred in imposing 70 hours of community service as condition of community control, where condition was not orally pronounced at sentencing. Handy v. State, App. 4 Dist., 643 So.2d 1143 (1994), rehearing and rehearing en banc denied, review denied 651 So.2d 1194. Sentencing And Punishment ⚷ 1918

Imposing special conditions when placing defendant on probation that were neither orally pronounced at sentencing hearing nor statutorily authorized was error. Nunez v. State, App. 2 Dist., 633 So.2d 1146 (1994). Sentencing And Punishment ⚷ 1920; Sentencing And Punishment ⚷ 1965

Special conditions of probation would be stricken, where they were not orally pronounced at sentencing, and thus defendant had no opportunity to object to their imposition. Dycus v. State, App. 2 Dist., 629 So.2d 275 (1993). Sentencing And Punishment ⚷ 1920

Defendant was entitled to striking of three special conditions listed in written order of community control; trial court did not pronounce those conditions in open court. George v. State, App. 2 Dist., 624 So.2d 824 (1993). Sentencing And Punishment ⚷ 1920

Special conditions not pronounced orally by trial court must be struck. George v. State, App. 2 Dist., 624 So.2d 824 (1993). Criminal Law ⚷ 995(8); Criminal Law ⚷ 1184(4.1)

Conditions of probation regarding use of intoxicants, drugs, or dangerous substances and visiting places where they are unlawfully sold, dispensed, or used and regarding drug evaluation and treatment within 30 days of release from prison were improper where conditions were not pronounced orally at sentencing. Crawford v. State, App. 2 Dist., 616 So.2d 1158 (1993). Sentencing And Punishment ⚷ 1920

Conditions of probation not orally pronounced at sentencing would be reversed, notwithstanding any actual knowledge defendant might have had of the conditions. Olvey v. State, App. 2 Dist., 609 So.2d 640 (1992), decision clarified on rehearing. Criminal Law ⚷ 1177.3(4); Sentencing And Punishment ⚷ 1918

Special condition of probation will be stricken from written probation record if trial court fails to pronounce condition orally at sentencing. Walls v. State, App. 1 Dist., 609 So.2d 83 (1992). Sentencing And Punishment ⚷ 1920

Condition of written probation order, although not precisely phrased as condition, was stricken, where condition was not orally pronounced at sentencing. Walls v. State, App. 1

Dist., 609 So.2d 83 (1992). Sentencing And Punishment ⚿ 1920

Special condition of probation not orally pronounced at sentencing could not properly be included in written probation order. Williams v. State, App. 2 Dist., 601 So.2d 635 (1992). Sentencing And Punishment ⚿ 1921

251. —— Conformity to written order, oral pronouncement

Trial court's oral pronouncement of probation controlled over its written probation order, where trial court orally pronounced that prior probation order imposed on defendant on his conviction for custodial sexual battery would remain in full force and effect, but trial court's written probation order included several additional conditions to those imposed in prior probation order, such that trial court improperly deviated from its oral pronouncement. Harder v. State, App. 1 Dist., 14 So.3d 1291 (2009). Sentencing and Punishment ⚿ 1921

Trial court's oral pronouncement at hearing on alleged probation violation that probation stemming from conviction for grand theft would automatically terminate if defendant filed proof with probation officer that restitution and costs of supervision had been paid controlled over court's subsequent written order, which stated that probation may terminate when restitution was paid in full and all other terms and conditions were met. Manning v. State, App. 1 Dist., 890 So.2d 531 (2005). Sentencing And Punishment ⚿ 2009

Remand was required for correction of scrivener's error in connection with imposition of costs of extradition upon criminal defendant, where sentencing court's oral pronouncement was correct but written judgment for fines and costs did not identify such sum as costs of extradition. Bass v. State, App. 2 Dist., 873 So.2d 569 (2004), denial of post-conviction relief affirmed 932 So.2d 1170. Criminal Law ⚿ 1181.5(8)

Words spoken at sentencing hearing need not be precisely repeated in written order if words place defendant on notice of general substance of each condition and provide defendant with opportunity to object to the special condition. McClendon v. State, App. 5 Dist., 659 So.2d 718 (1995). Sentencing And Punishment ⚿ 1139

Oral conditions of probation prevail over inconsistent written conditions of probation. Peterson v. State, App. 5 Dist., 623 So.2d 637 (1993). Sentencing And Punishment ⚿ 1921

Trial court could not impose special conditions of probation in a written order which were not orally pronounced at sentencing. Turchario v. State, App. 2 Dist., 616 So.2d 539 (1993). Sentencing And Punishment ⚿ 1921

Handwritten condition of probation contained in written order of probation had to be stricken from order, where trial court did not pronounce orally this condition at sentencing. Carter v. State, App. 2 Dist., 606 So.2d 680 (1992). Sentencing And Punishment ⚿ 1921

252. —— Community control conditions, oral pronouncement

Community control condition that juvenile delinquent live and reside in home of parent and accept reasonable controls and discipline in that home did not need to be orally pronounced at disposition hearing; condition fell within statute authorizing placement of juvenile in community control program in his own home under such reasonable conditions as court may direct. W.J. v. State, App. 4 Dist., 688 So.2d 954 (1997). Infants ⚿ 225

Community control conditions requiring juvenile delinquent not to change residence without prior consent of counselor and to cooperate and maintain contact with counselor were valid, despite fact that they were not orally pronounced; statute authorized placement of juvenile in community control program in his home, to say that there could be no change of residence without consent was same as saying that juvenile could not unilaterally modify his sentence, and cooperating with counselor was necessary component of being under community control. W.J. v. State, App. 4 Dist., 688 So.2d 954 (1997). Infants ⚿ 225

Community control conditions requiring juvenile delinquent to attend school every day, to attend each assigned class, and to abide by rules and regulations of school authorities did not need to be orally pronounced; statute provided that community control program for adjudicated delinquent must include rehabilitative program such as requirement of participation in school, and language of this condition was merely explicit clarification of extent to which condition of school was imposed. W.J. v. State, App. 4 Dist., 688 So.2d 954 (1997). Infants ⚿ 225

To extent that community control condition prohibiting juvenile delinquent from possessing firearms or weapons prohibited possession of nonelectric, nonconcealed weapon, it had to have been orally pronounced; condition would be limited to proscription of possession of firearm, electric weapon, or concealed weapon, and any broader construction of condition would be stricken. W.J. v. State, App. 4 Dist., 688 So.2d 954 (1997). Infants ⚿ 225

Since statute prohibited any person under age 21 from having alcoholic beverages in his possession, court was not obligated to orally pronounce that portion of the community control condition for juvenile delinquent. W.J. v. State,

App. 4 Dist., 688 So.2d 954 (1997). Infants ⚷ 225

To extent that community control condition prohibited juvenile delinquent from possessing controlled substances lawfully obtained pursuant to valid prescription, it would be stricken. W.J. v. State, App. 4 Dist., 688 So.2d 954 (1997). Infants ⚷ 225

Fact that community control condition for juvenile delinquent was on form, containing no general or standard conditions applicable to most community control orders and requiring trial judge to affix mark next to condition in order to activate it, did not relieve court of obligation to orally pronounce it, if it was not explicitly authorized by statutory chapter governing juvenile proceedings or did not involve conduct which was prohibited by another statute. W.J. v. State, App. 4 Dist., 688 So.2d 954 (1997). Infants ⚷ 225

253. —— Objections, oral pronouncement

Defendant's failure to object at trial to imposition of special conditions of probation which were not announced at oral pronouncement of sentence or otherwise allowed by statute did not preclude him from challenging conditions on appeal. Felty v. State, App. 2 Dist., 616 So.2d 88 (1993), review granted 626 So.2d 205, quashed on other grounds 630 So.2d 1092. Criminal Law ⚷ 1042.3(4)

Trial court's pronouncement of sentence of four and one-half years community control was proper, although written judgment and sentence of two years community control had been filed previously; previous sentence was not orally pronounced, and defendant failed to object to sentence at sentencing hearing. Armstead v. State, App. 1 Dist., 612 So.2d 623 (1993). Sentencing And Punishment ⚷ 1921

254. —— General conditions, oral pronouncement

Submission to random drug testing and treatment is general condition of probation that does not require oral pronouncement at sentencing hearing. Jackson v. State, App. 5 Dist., 902 So.2d 193 (2005), rehearing denied, review denied 913 So.2d 596. Sentencing And Punishment ⚷ 1918

Condition of probation requiring defendant to pay costs of urinalysis, breath testing, or blood testing was not a general condition exempt from requirement that special conditions of probation must be pronounced at sentencing. Parrish v. State, App. 1 Dist., 898 So.2d 1074 (2005). Sentencing And Punishment ⚷ 1918

On resentencing juvenile defendant, trial court could impose general conditions of probation without oral pronouncement, but would be required to give defendant oral notice of conditions concerning payment for evaluation and treatment of drug and alcohol problems. Lunn v. State, App. 2 Dist., 675 So.2d 648 (1996). Sentencing And Punishment ⚷ 1918

Probation conditions which were general conditions contained in form order of probation did not have to be orally announced. Gilchrist v. State, App. 2 Dist., 674 So.2d 847 (1996). Sentencing And Punishment ⚷ 1918

"General conditions of probation" which need not be orally pronounced at sentencing hearing include conditions contained or derived from statutes such as those dealing with firearms. Vasquez v. State, App. 4 Dist., 663 So.2d 1343 (1995), review dismissed 666 So.2d 145. Sentencing And Punishment ⚷ 1918

In trial court's written conditions on probation of defendant convicted of burglary and grand theft, condition prohibiting him from visiting places where certain drugs or other dangerous substances were sold did not need to be orally pronounced because it was a general condition prohibiting association with persons engaged in criminal activities. Hosie v. State, App. 2 Dist., 661 So.2d 909 (1995). Sentencing And Punishment ⚷ 1918

Whether probation conditions are special or general is bright line between conditions that must be orally pronounced at sentencing and those for which no oral pronouncement is necessary. Hart v. State, App. 2 Dist., 651 So.2d 112 (1995), review granted 659 So.2d 1089, quashed in part 668 So.2d 589. Sentencing And Punishment ⚷ 1918

Condition of probation prohibiting probationer from visiting places where intoxicants were illegally sold was valid as more precise definition of general prohibition and, as such, was not required to be orally pronounced. Parsons v. State, App. 2 Dist., 650 So.2d 176 (1995), denial of post-conviction relief affirmed in part, reversed in part 672 So.2d 877. Sentencing And Punishment ⚷ 1918; Sentencing And Punishment ⚷ 1980(2)

Probation condition which proscribed visiting places where intoxicants, drugs, or other dangerous substances are unlawfully sold, dispensed or used, was valid, even though the condition was not orally pronounced at sentencing, as the condition was a more precise definition of a general prohibition. Fitts v. State, App. 2 Dist., 649 So.2d 300 (1995). Sentencing And Punishment ⚷ 1918

Condition of probation requiring probationer to work diligently to support his dependents to best of his ability was authorized by statute and, thus, was general condition that did not have to be orally pronounced in open court. Jennings v. State, App. 2 Dist., 645 So.2d 592 (1994).

Sentencing And Punishment ⚷ 1918; Sentencing And Punishment ⚷ 1983(2)

255. —— Discretionary costs or monetary payments, oral pronouncement

Trial court erred in requiring probationer, without pronouncement in open court, to pay $2 discretionary cost as condition of probation. Simmons v. State, App. 4 Dist., 662 So.2d 754 (1995). Costs ⚷ 314

Special condition of probation requiring defendant to make monetary payment would be stricken on appeal because trial court failed to pronounce condition orally at sentencing. Brown v. State, App. 1 Dist., 651 So.2d 227 (1995). Sentencing And Punishment ⚷ 1920

Special condition contained in each sentence requiring defendant to pay state one dollar per day for cost of his electronic monitoring during period of his community control had to be vacated where condition was not orally pronounced at sentencing, although it appeared in sentencing documents, and trial court failed to reference statutory authority for the imposition of those costs. Brooks v. State, App. 5 Dist., 649 So.2d 329 (1995). Costs ⚷ 314; Sentencing And Punishment ⚷ 1920

256. —— Possession of weapons, oral pronouncement

Probation condition prohibiting carrying of weapons other than those enumerated in statute was special condition of probation required to be orally pronounced at sentencing. Weber v. State, App. 2 Dist., 691 So.2d 1 (1995). Sentencing And Punishment ⚷ 1918

Special condition of probation that prohibited defendant from possessing, owning or carrying weapons and destructive devices was invalid when it was not pronounced orally at sentencing. Washington v. State, App. 2 Dist., 686 So.2d 733 (1997). Sentencing And Punishment ⚷ 1920

Probation condition for drug violations which prohibited defendant from carrying any weapons, including those not specifically enumerated in statute governing carrying of weapons by felons, was a special condition, and was therefore rendered invalid by trial court's failure to orally pronounce such condition at sentencing. Levely v. State, App. 2 Dist., 685 So.2d 847 (1995). Sentencing And Punishment ⚷ 1920

Conditions of probation, that probationer not procure weapon without consent of probation officer, and pay balance of victim costs and trust fund payments imposed by original probation order, were state law that did not have to be orally pronounced, since probationer was on constructive notice that he must comply with Florida law. Mathis v. State, App. 4 Dist., 683 So.2d 634 (1996). Sentencing And Punishment ⚷ 1918

Sentencing court's failure to pronounce condition of probation orally at sentencing did not preclude condition prohibiting possession of weapons, firearms, or destructive devices, in light of fact that condition was general condition contained in form probation order set forth in rule of which defendant had constructive notice prior to sentencing. Gant v. State, App. 2 Dist., 682 So.2d 1137 (1996), rehearing denied. Sentencing And Punishment ⚷ 1918

Trial court was not required at sentencing to orally pronounce probation conditions relating to alcohol and possession of weapons where those conditions were among those set forth in rule on form for order of probation. Martinez-Button v. State, App. 2 Dist., 681 So.2d 1184 (1996). Sentencing And Punishment ⚷ 1918

Because probation restrictions against firearms and weapons are contained in general condition of probation, that condition need not be pronounced orally by trial court. Williams v. State, App. 2 Dist., 681 So.2d 817 (1996). Sentencing And Punishment ⚷ 1918

Lack of oral pronouncement of probation condition which ordered probationer not to possess, carry, or own any weapons without consent of his probation officer warranted remand. Charlton v. State, App. 4 Dist., 662 So.2d 771 (1995). Criminal Law ⚷ 1181.5(8); Sentencing And Punishment ⚷ 1920

Oral pronouncement was required for probation condition ordering defendant not to possess, carry or own any of weapons without consent of his probation officer. Weinshenker v. State, App. 4 Dist., 662 So.2d 770 (1995), habeas corpus denied 1996 WL 537625. Sentencing And Punishment ⚷ 1918

Condition of probation, precluding defendant from possessing, carrying or owning any weapons without first procuring consent of probation officer, was to be stricken where it was not announced in open court. Brown v. State, App. 2 Dist., 658 So.2d 1058 (1995). Sentencing And Punishment ⚷ 1920

Condition of parol, that defendant could not carry any weapons or destructive devices, could not be upheld in absence of an oral pronouncement to that effect at sentencing. Daughtery v. State, App. 2 Dist., 654 So.2d 1209 (1995). Sentencing And Punishment ⚷ 1920

Portion of condition of probation preventing probationer from possessing weapons or firearms was valid general condition that did not have to be orally pronounced in open court. Jennings v. State, App. 2 Dist., 645 So.2d 592 (1994). Sentencing And Punishment ⚷ 1918; Sentencing And Punishment ⚷ 1981(2)

257. —— Criminal locations, oral pronouncement

Oral pronouncement was not required for probation provision prohibiting defendant from visiting "places where controlled substances are unlawfully sold, dispensed or used." Weinshenker v. State, App. 4 Dist., 662 So.2d 770 (1995), habeas corpus denied 1996 WL 537625. Sentencing And Punishment ⚿ 1918

Condition of probation that defendant not visit places where controlled substances are unlawfully sold, dispensed, or used was valid, even though it was not announced in open court; condition was more explicit clarification of statutory condition of probation that offender may not associate with persons engaged in criminal activities and, thus, condition need not have been pronounced in open court. Jaworski v. State, App. 4 Dist., 650 So.2d 172 (1995). Sentencing And Punishment ⚿ 1918

Condition of probation prohibiting probationer from visiting places where intoxicants were illegally sold was valid as precise definition of general prohibition and, thus, did not have to be orally pronounced in open court as special condition of probation. Jennings v. State, App. 2 Dist., 645 So.2d 592 (1994). Sentencing And Punishment ⚿ 1918; Sentencing And Punishment ⚿ 1980(2)

Trial court erred in imposing probation conditions forbidding defendant from using intoxicants to excess and visiting places where they are unlawfully used, or possessing weapons without first obtaining permission from his probation officer, where these conditions were not announced in open court. Dunbar v. State, App. 2 Dist., 633 So.2d 1136 (1994). Sentencing And Punishment ⚿ 1918

Special condition of parole prohibiting defendant from using intoxicants to excess or visiting places where intoxicants, drugs, or other dangerous substances were unlawfully sold, dispensed, or used was improper where it was not announced in open court. Gregory v. State, App. 2 Dist., 616 So.2d 174 (1993). Sentencing And Punishment ⚿ 1980(2)

Probation condition prohibiting defendant from using intoxicants to excess or visiting places where intoxicants or drugs were sold illegally had to be stricken where trial court did not pronounce it in open court. Carter v. State, App. 2 Dist., 606 So.2d 680 (1992). Sentencing And Punishment ⚿ 1920

258. —— Remand for correction, oral pronouncement

Where written judgment contained several probation conditions not orally announced at sentencing, remand was required for resolution of discrepancy between record of oral pronouncement and written order. Justice v. State, App. 5 Dist., 658 So.2d 1028 (1995), on rehearing, review granted 666 So.2d 143, quashed 674 So.2d 123. Criminal Law ⚿ 1181.5(8)

Remand was required to correct written sentence to conform to oral pronouncement of ten years probation for one attempted robbery count, where trial judge misspoke twice when orally pronouncing sentences in regards to sentence for attempted robbery, but followed misstatements both times by stating that he was sentencing defendant to ten years probation for attempted robbery, but written sentence showed 15 years in prison to be followed by ten years probation for that count. Moiter v. State, App. 2 Dist., 644 So.2d 154 (1994). Criminal Law ⚿ 1181.5(8)

Apparently inadvertent omission of hospital from oral announcement at sentencing hearing of victims to whom restitution had to be paid as condition of probation created discrepancy between oral and written judgment, warranting remand for resolution of discrepancy, rather than merely striking that condition from written judgment. Elmore v. State, App. 5 Dist., 636 So.2d 183 (1994). Criminal Law ⚿ 1181.5(8); Sentencing And Punishment ⚿ 1921

Trial court's failure to orally pronounce special conditions of probation at sentencing constituted a "discrepancy," and sentence would be vacated and case remanded for resolution of discrepancy. Cleveland v. State, App. 5 Dist., 617 So.2d 1166 (1993). Criminal Law ⚿ 1181.5(8); Sentencing And Punishment ⚿ 1921

259. —— Accounting, oral pronouncement

Condition of community control requiring defendant to maintain hourly accounting of all activities on daily log was special condition that was required to be stricken when court failed to orally announce it to defendant in open court. Curry v. State, App. 2 Dist., 656 So.2d 521 (1995), review granted 676 So.2d 412, review dismissed 682 So.2d 1091. Sentencing And Punishment ⚿ 1920

Conditions of community control, that drunk driving defendant maintain hourly accounting of her activities on daily log which would be submitted to community control officer, and that she participate in self-improvement programs, were special conditions of probation which had to be orally pronounced at sentencing. Shacraha v. State, App. 4 Dist., 635 So.2d 1051 (1994). Sentencing And Punishment ⚿ 1918

260. —— Drug evaluation or testing, oral pronouncement

Trial court was precluded from issuing a written order of probation that required defendant to submit to random drug testing at his own expense without orally pronouncing at sentencing the requirement that defendant bear the cost of such testing. Jones v. State, App. 2 Dist., 846 So.2d 662 (2003). Sentencing And Punishment ⚿ 1920

Condition of probation requiring defendant to pay for either alcohol or drug testing was "special condition" that needed to be orally pronounced at sentencing. Torres v. State, App. 2 Dist., 712 So.2d 1169 (1998). Sentencing And Punishment ⚿ 1918

Requirement that defendant pay for random drug testing was a special condition of probation that had to be orally announced. Porchia v. State, App. 5 Dist., 705 So.2d 1050 (1998), approved 716 So.2d 766. Sentencing And Punishment ⚿ 1918

Written probation condition which was more broad than oral pronouncement of terms of probation as it pertained to possession and consumption of alcohol and association with persons who use alcohol was improper. Fennell v. State, App. 2 Dist., 694 So.2d 873 (1997). Sentencing And Punishment ⚿ 1921

Written probation condition which required defendant to submit to and pay for drug or alcohol evaluation and successfully complete any recommended treatment program , which had not been orally announced, was improper, and could not be reimposed on remand. Fennell v. State, App. 2 Dist., 694 So.2d 873 (1997). Sentencing And Punishment ⚿ 1920

Probation condition requiring random drug and alcohol testing is a general condition and need not be orally pronounced at sentencing, nor must it relate to defendant's present criminal conduct or future criminality. Diaz v. State, App. 2 Dist., 691 So.2d 589 (1997). Sentencing And Punishment ⚿ 1918; Sentencing And Punishment ⚿ 1996

Portion of probation condition requiring defendant to "pay for" random urinalysis, breathalyzer, or blood tests was special condition of probation required to be orally pronounced at sentencing. Weber v. State, App. 2 Dist., 691 So.2d 1 (1995). Sentencing And Punishment ⚿ 1918

Trial court was not required to orally pronounce probation condition requiring probationer to pay costs of random drug and alcohol tests; one of court's standard conditions of probation required submission to random testing for alcohol and drugs, probationer's attorney orally waived reading of standard conditions, and trial court did orally inform defendant that, "you will pay any fees for evaluation, referral, and treatment." Wines v. State, App. 5 Dist., 690 So.2d 684 (1997). Sentencing And Punishment ⚿ 1918

Special condition of probation requiring defendant to pay for costs for urinalysis, breath test and blood tests, that was not orally pronounced, was required to be stricken. Watts v. State, App. 4 Dist., 688 So.2d 1018 (1997). Sentencing And Punishment ⚿ 1920

Condition of probation/community control requiring defendant to pay for blood, alcohol, breathalyzer and urinalysis testing was special condition required to be orally pronounced before imposition. Head v. State, App. 2 Dist., 687 So.2d 281 (1997). Sentencing And Punishment ⚿ 1918

Special conditions of probation which required defendant to pay for testing and treatment for alcohol and controlled substances were invalid where they were not pronounced orally. Washington v. State, App. 2 Dist., 686 So.2d 733 (1997). Sentencing And Punishment ⚿ 1920

Condition of probation order requiring defendant to submit to random drug testing as directed by his probation officer is general condition of probation, and therefore need not be orally announced. Jackson v. State, App. 5 Dist., 685 So.2d 1386 (1997). Sentencing And Punishment ⚿ 1918

Condition of probation order which requires that defendant who is subject to random drug testing pay for testing is special condition of probation which, to be valid, must be orally announced, even though condition of random testing is general condition and need not be announced. Jackson v. State, App. 5 Dist., 685 So.2d 1386 (1997). Sentencing And Punishment ⚿ 1918

Defendant convicted of sexual activity with child by person in custodial authority could not be required to pay for random testing for alcohol, drug, or controlled substance use, imposed as condition of probation, as condition had not been orally pronounced at sentencing; while there was a statute providing constructive notice to all defendants that random testing could be imposed as condition of probation, statute did not address payment for that testing. McConn v. State, App. 2 Dist., 685 So.2d 1331 (1996). Sentencing And Punishment ⚿ 1920

Trial court could not impose special condition of probation that defendant submit to random urinalysis, breath alcohol tests, or blood tests, where that condition was not orally announced at sentencing hearing. Snowden v. State, App. 1 Dist., 685 So.2d 974 (1996). Sentencing And Punishment ⚿ 1920

Probation condition imposed for drug violations which required defendant to pay for random urinalysis, breathalyzer or blood tests was a special condition, and was therefore rendered invalid by trial court's failure to orally pronounce such condition at sentencing. Levely v. State, App. 2 Dist., 685 So.2d 847 (1995). Sentencing And Punishment ⚷ 1920

Special condition of probation, which ordered defendant to submit at his own expense to drug and alcohol evaluation, was required to be orally announced and, where evaluation requirement was pronounced but clause requiring defendant to pay for evaluation was not, clause portion would be stricken. Garrison v. State, App. 2 Dist., 685 So.2d 53 (1996). Sentencing And Punishment ⚷ 1920

Condition of probation that defendant pay costs of random drug testing was not condition of probation approved in Rules of Criminal Procedure and was thus required to be orally pronounced at sentencing. Sanford v. State, App. 4 Dist., 684 So.2d 269 (1996). Sentencing And Punishment ⚷ 1918

Costs that trial court imposed for evaluation, referral, and monitoring in connection with substance abuse program would be stricken because court failed to announce them as a special condition of probation; they could not be reimposed. Frasier v. State, App. 5 Dist., 683 So.2d 623 (1996). Costs ⚷ 314

Special condition of probation that defendant pay for random drug testing was to be stricken for failure to orally pronounce it at sentencing. Wallace v. State, App. 2 Dist., 682 So.2d 1139 (1996), rehearing denied. Sentencing And Punishment ⚷ 1920

Probation condition requiring defendant to pay for random drug testing was special condition that had to be pronounced orally at sentencing, and sentencing court's failure to do so required that condition be stricken on appeal. Gant v. State, App. 2 Dist., 682 So.2d 1137 (1996), rehearing denied. Sentencing And Punishment ⚷ 1920

Portion of probation order that required defendant to pay for drug evaluation and treatment programs was properly stricken as a special condition not announced orally in defendant's presence at sentencing. Curry v. State, 682 So.2d 1091 (1996). Sentencing And Punishment ⚷ 1920

Probationer would not be required to observe portion of probation order referring to destructive device and would not be required to pay for random tests for alcohol or drugs; neither of those conditions were orally pronounced before imposition of probation sentence. Cherubin v. State, App. 2 Dist., 682 So.2d 173 (1996). Sentencing And Punishment ⚷ 1920; Sentencing And Punishment ⚷ 1975(2)

Probation conditions requiring defendant to pay for random drug testing and to pay for evaluation of alcohol abuse, and requiring evaluation to determine need for inpatient drug treatment, were special conditions of probation which were not orally pronounced and, thus, those conditions would be stricken. Norton v. State, App. 2 Dist., 681 So.2d 1186 (1996). Sentencing And Punishment ⚷ 1920

Special probation conditions requiring defendant not to consume any alcohol, to pay for random testing for alcohol, and to submit to and pay for evaluation to determine whether he had any treatable alcohol problem would be stricken because trial court did not announce these conditions at sentencing. Scott v. State, App. 2 Dist., 681 So.2d 738 (1996). Sentencing And Punishment ⚷ 1920

Random substance abuse testing probation condition applied to defendant and did not need to be orally pronounced because statute put him on notice. Scott v. State, App. 2 Dist., 681 So.2d 738 (1996). Sentencing And Punishment ⚷ 1918

Condition of probation requiring defendant to pay for random drug testing had to be stricken for not being orally pronounced at sentencing. Caraway v. State, App. 2 Dist., 681 So.2d 723 (1996). Sentencing And Punishment ⚷ 1920

Probation condition requiring probationer to submit to random testing was general condition and therefore could be imposed without oral pronouncement; however, portion of probation condition requiring probationer to pay for alcohol and drug testing was special condition of probation which had to be orally pronounced. Powell v. State, App. 2 Dist., 681 So.2d 722 (1996). Sentencing And Punishment ⚷ 1918

Requirement that defendant pay for substance abuse testing and evaluation was a special condition of probation that had to be announced at sentencing hearing. Aguirre v. State, App. 2 Dist., 680 So.2d 566 (1996). Sentencing And Punishment ⚷ 1918

Requiring defendant to pay for random testing for alcohol or controlled substances unless waived by probation officer was improper as probation condition since it was not orally pronounced at sentencing and that language was not contained in statute governing terms and conditions of probation or community control. Hill v. State, App. 2 Dist., 679 So.2d 842 (1996). Sentencing And Punishment ⚷ 1920; Sentencing And Punishment ⚷ 1975(2)

Probation provision for random drug and alcohol testing was general condition of probation that need not be orally pronounced, but portion of condition requiring defendant to pay for testing was special condition of probation, as was requirement that defendant "waive extradition should a violation of supervision occur." McDaniels v. State, App. 2 Dist., 679 So.2d 840 (1996). Sentencing And Punishment ⚷ 1918

Probation condition which required defendant to pay for random drug and alcohol testing was special condition which required oral pronouncement. Mardy v. State, App. 2 Dist., 678 So.2d 451 (1996). Sentencing And Punishment ⚷ 1918

Probation condition that required defendant to pay for random drug testing was stricken, as it was not orally pronounced and was not included in standard conditions of probation. Bailey v. State, App. 1 Dist., 677 So.2d 1358 (1996). Sentencing And Punishment ⚷ 1920

It was error for trial court to require defendant to pay for random drug testing as condition of probation where condition was not orally pronounced. Carter v. State, App. 4 Dist., 677 So.2d 1349 (1996). Sentencing And Punishment ⚷ 1920

Special probation condition providing that defendant pay for random urinalysis, breath alcohol or blood tests was not orally pronounced at sentencing, as required to impose such condition, and trial court could not seek to reimpose that condition on remand. Vickers v. State, App. 2 Dist., 677 So.2d 974 (1996). Criminal Law ⚷ 1192; Sentencing And Punishment ⚷ 1920

Probation condition that required probationers to pay for alcohol and drug testing and that was not orally pronounced had to be stricken; while submitting to alcohol and drug screening is standard condition of probation, requiring probationer to pay for the screening is special condition. Brown v. State, App. 2 Dist., 677 So.2d 395 (1996). Sentencing And Punishment ⚷ 1920

Failure of trial court to orally pronounce condition of probation calling for breathalyzer and blood testing, which are statutorily authorized as random testing, does not necessarily require that it be stricken from written order of probation on that basis. Fernandez v. State, App. 4 Dist., 677 So.2d 332 (1996), review dismissed 683 So.2d 485. Sentencing And Punishment ⚷ 1920

Requirement in written order of probation that defendant pay costs of random testing as condition of probation was improper, where it was not orally pronounced, and statute enumerating possible terms and conditions of probation did not specifically provide for defendant to be financially responsible for testing. Fernandez v. State, App. 4 Dist., 677 So.2d 332 (1996), review dismissed 683 So.2d 485. Sentencing And Punishment ⚷ 1920

Costs and conditions of probation would be stricken to extent they were imposed without citation to statutory authority, without documentation or consideration of defendant's ability to pay, suggested that convicted felon may possess firearm with consent of his probation officer, and required defendant to pay for any drug and alcohol evaluations without oral pronouncement. Godwin v. State, App. 2 Dist., 676 So.2d 1012 (1996). Costs ⚷ 314; Sentencing And Punishment ⚷ 1920; Sentencing And Punishment ⚷ 1981(2)

Where trial court did not orally pronounce that defendant was required to pay for drug evaluation or tests or orally order evaluation for alcohol use, those aspects of probation conditions had to be stricken. Holmes v. State, App. 2 Dist., 675 So.2d 995 (1996). Sentencing And Punishment ⚷ 1920

Probation condition requiring defendant to submit to random alcohol testing did not have to be orally pronounced because statute provided notice of its imposition. Holmes v. State, App. 2 Dist., 675 So.2d 995 (1996). Sentencing And Punishment ⚷ 1918

District Court of Appeal would strike portion of special condition of defendant's probation order requiring defendant to pay for cost of random drug testing, which portion was not orally pronounced at sentencing, without prejudice to State to seek reimposition on remand. Hinkle v. State, App. 2 Dist., 675 So.2d 621 (1996). Criminal Law ⚷ 1192; Sentencing And Punishment ⚷ 1920

Portion of probation condition requiring defendant to pay for random drug and alcohol testing was not contained in statute and was special condition of probation which would be stricken due to trial court's failure to announce payment requirement. Gilchrist v. State, App. 2 Dist., 674 So.2d 847 (1996). Sentencing And Punishment ⚷ 1920

Portion of probation condition providing for random drug and alcohol testing was general condition of probation and did not have to be orally pronounced. Gilchrist v. State, App. 2 Dist., 674 So.2d 847 (1996). Sentencing And Punishment ⚷ 1918

Probation condition which required probationer to submit to random blood, breathalyzer, and urinalysis examinations was standard condition of probation which was applicable to any probationer and, therefore, did not have to be orally pronounced. Reiter v. State, App. 2 Dist., 674 So.2d 189 (1996). Sentencing And Punishment ⚷ 1918

Portion of probation condition which required probationer to pay for random blood, breathalyzer and urinalysis examinations had to be stricken, where payment requirement was not mentioned at sentencing hearing and was not standard probation condition. Reiter v. State, App. 2 Dist., 674 So.2d 189 (1996). Sentencing And Punishment ⚷ 1920

Random drug and alcohol testing was general condition of probation set out in pertinent statute; thus, trial court did not err in imposing condition without orally pronouncing it at defendant's sentencing. Williams v. State, App. 2 Dist., 673 So.2d 536 (1996). Sentencing And Punishment ⚷ 1920

Condition of probation requiring defendant to pay for random drug and alcohol testing was improperly imposed, where that condition was not set out in pertinent statute or orally pronounced at sentencing. Williams v. State, App. 2 Dist., 673 So.2d 536 (1996). Sentencing And Punishment ⚷ 1920

Condition of probation for drug violator, that he submit and pay for evaluation to determine whether he had treatable problem with alcohol or other legal drugs, was required to be stricken; it had not been orally pronounced at time of sentence. Daughtery v. State, App. 2 Dist., 654 So.2d 1209 (1995). Sentencing And Punishment ⚷ 1920

Probation of drug defendant could be conditioned upon his paying for random testing for presence of alcohol or controlled substances; condition had been orally pronounced by trial court. Daughtery v. State, App. 2 Dist., 654 So.2d 1209 (1995). Sentencing And Punishment ⚷ 1918

Probation condition imposed on grand theft defendant, requiring defendant to submit to random alcohol testing, was valid, although condition was not orally pronounced at sentencing. Malone v. State, App. 2 Dist., 652 So.2d 902 (1995). Sentencing And Punishment ⚷ 1920

Probation condition imposed on grand theft defendant, requiring that defendant pay for random alcohol testing was invalid where condition was not orally pronounced at sentencing. Malone v. State, App. 2 Dist., 652 So.2d 902 (1995). Sentencing And Punishment ⚷ 1920

Words "at your own expense" would be stricken from condition of probation requiring defendant to submit to random alcohol and drug testing at his own expense, since requirement that testing be conducted at defendant's own expense was not orally pronounced at sentencing; requirement was not authorized by statute and thus was special condition which was required to be orally pronounced at sentencing. Luby v. State, App. 2 Dist., 648 So.2d 308 (1995). Sentencing And Punishment ⚷ 1920; Sentencing And Punishment ⚷ 1996

Condition of probation ordering defendant to submit, at his own expense, to drug and alcohol evaluation was special condition that was required to be orally pronounced at sentencing, in order to be included in written order. Nank v. State, App. 2 Dist., 646 So.2d 762 (1994), rehearing denied. Sentencing And Punishment ⚷ 1918

Under statute providing that court may include, as condition of probation, requirement that probationer submit to random testing as directed by correctional probation officer to determine presence or use of alcohol or controlled substances, testing was a standard condition of probation which did not have to be orally pronounced and which could be imposed regardless of whether it was directly related to circumstances of probationer's offense; however, such requirement was neither orally pronounced nor set forth in written probation order in instant case and, thus, probationer could not be found in violation of probation for failure to submit to urinalysis as ordered by probation officer. Paterson v. State, App. 1 Dist., 612 So.2d 692 (1993). Sentencing And Punishment ⚷ 1920; Sentencing And Punishment ⚷ 1996

Requirement in written order of probation that defendant must undergo random drug screening would not be stricken, even though such condition was not pronounced in open court, where statute authorized imposition of such condition in every case, and thus provided constructive notice to defendant. Tillman v. State, App. 2 Dist., 592 So.2d 767 (1992). Sentencing And Punishment ⚷ 1921

261. —— Notice, oral pronouncement

Sentencing court was not required to orally pronounce probation conditions of which defendant had constructive notice. Hill v. State, App. 2 Dist., 679 So.2d 842 (1996). Sentencing And Punishment ⚷ 1918

Probation conditions concerning weapons, intoxicants, and employment did not have to be orally pronounced because the order of probation form in criminal procedural rules provided notice of those conditions. Brown v. State, App. 2 Dist., 677 So.2d 395 (1996). Sentencing And Punishment ⚷ 1918

Since probationer had sufficient notice of challenged probation conditions in order of probation form, those conditions did not have to be orally pronounced. Reiter v. State, App. 2 Dist., 674 So.2d 189 (1996). Sentencing And Punishment ⚷ 1918

Defendant had constructive notice of condition of probation which he challenged because it was not orally pronounced at sentencing; thus, trial court did not err in failing to orally pronounce condition. Williams v. State, App. 2 Dist., 673 So.2d 536 (1996). Sentencing And Punishment ⚷ 1920

Conditions of probation included in probation order form approved by Florida Supreme Court and found in Rules of Criminal Procedure should provide defendants with sufficient constructive notice to make oral pronouncements of those conditions unnecessary. Emond v. State, App. 2 Dist., 652 So.2d 419 (1995), review granted 660 So.2d 715, quashed 668 So.2d 599. Sentencing And Punishment ⚷ 1918

Defendant had constructive notice of statutory probation condition requiring submission to tests to determine use of alcohol or controlled substance and, thus, condition was effective, even though not orally pronounced at sentencing hearing. Nunez v. State, App. 2 Dist., 633 So.2d 1146 (1994). Sentencing And Punishment ⚷ 1920; Sentencing And Punishment ⚷ 1996

When special conditions of probation are imposed for first time, conditions can be orally explained using language which is different from language in order of probation; so long as oral pronouncement is sufficient to place defendant on notice of general substance of each special condition and gives defendant opportunity to object, minimum requirements of due process are satisfied. Olvey v. State, App. 2 Dist., 609 So.2d 640 (1992), decision clarified on rehearing. Sentencing And Punishment ⚷ 1918

262. —— Use of intoxicants, oral pronouncement

Probation condition that defendant would not use intoxicants to excess was special condition of probation required to be orally pronounced at sentencing. Weber v. State, App. 2 Dist., 691 So.2d 1 (1995). Sentencing And Punishment ⚷ 1918

Probation conditions for defendant convicted of being felon in possession of firearm, which prohibited him from using intoxicants to excess and possessing unprescribed drugs or narcotics, would be stricken, as they constituted special conditions which were not orally pronounced at sentencing. Reed v. State, App. 2 Dist., 652 So.2d 912 (1995). Sentencing And Punishment ⚷ 1920

Portion of probation condition prohibiting defendant from using intoxicants to excess must be stricken, where trial court failed to announce condition in open court, preventing defendant from having opportunity to object to its imposition. Stark v. State, App. 2 Dist., 650 So.2d 697 (1995). Sentencing And Punishment ⚷ 1920

Probation condition proscribing the use of intoxicants to excess would be stricken by District Court of Appeal, where condition was not orally pronounced at sentencing. Fitts v. State, App. 2 Dist., 649 So.2d 300 (1995). Sentencing And Punishment ⚷ 1920

Condition of probation that defendant not use intoxicants was not orally announced at sentencing and, thus, would be reversed. Henning v. State, App. 4 Dist., 648 So.2d 1262 (1995). Criminal Law ⚷ 1177.3(4); Sentencing And Punishment ⚷ 1920

Portion of probation condition prohibiting probationer from excessive use of intoxicating substances was special condition and, thus, was rendered invalid by trial court's failure to pronounce condition in open court. Jennings v. State, App. 2 Dist., 645 So.2d 592 (1994). Sentencing And Punishment ⚷ 1920; Sentencing And Punishment ⚷ 1980(2)

Probation conditions that probationer not possess or use alcohol, visit places where alcohol is sold, dispensed, or used, or associate with persons who use alcohol must be orally announced at sentencing in order to be valid given that alcohol related conditions are not statutorily authorized. Peterson v. State, App. 2 Dist., 645 So.2d 84 (1994). Sentencing And Punishment ⚷ 1918

Alcohol-related conditions of written probation order, which generally prohibited defendant from using or being with persons who used alcohol, were invalid when not orally pronounced at sentencing. Peterson v. State, App. 2 Dist., 645 So.2d 84 (1994). Sentencing And Punishment ⚷ 1920

Condition of probation prohibiting defendant from visiting places where intoxicants, drugs or other dangerous substances were unlawfully sold, dispensed or used was valid, general condition which need not be pronounced in open court; condition was more precise defining of conduct prohibited under statute which stated as acceptable condition of probation that defendant not associate were persons engaged in criminal activities. Tomlinson v. State, App. 2 Dist., 645 So.2d 1 (1994), rehearing denied. Sentencing And Punishment ⚷ 1980(2)

Condition of probation prohibiting defendant from using intoxicants to excess was special condition which trial court was required to announce in open court, giving defendant opportunity to object to its imposition. Tomlinson v. State, App. 2 Dist., 645 So.2d 1 (1994), rehearing denied. Sentencing And Punishment ⚷ 1918; Sentencing And Punishment ⚷ 1980(2)

Special probation condition relating to defendant's use of intoxicants must be stricken, where trial court did not orally pronounce it in open court. Pagan v. State, App. 2 Dist., 637 So.2d 959 (1994). Sentencing And Punishment ⚷ 1920

Condition of probation that defendant not use intoxicants to excess or visit places where intoxicants, drugs or other dangerous substances are unlawfully sold, dispensed or used was invalid on the ground that it was not statutorily authorized and trial court did not pronounce it orally at sentencing hearing. Quinonez v. State, App.

2 Dist., 634 So.2d 173 (1994). Sentencing And Punishment ⚷ 1918; Sentencing And Punishment ⚷ 1980(2)

Trial court's oral pronouncement regarding probation condition dealing with use of intoxicants and drugs, indicating to defendant that he was to maintain drug-free activity and attend any drug counseling that Department of Corrections indicated that would be helpful, satisfied requirements of making clear to defendant general substance of condition. Brown v. State, App. 2 Dist., 613 So.2d 558 (1993). Sentencing And Punishment ⚷ 1918

263. —— Consecutive or concurrent sentences, oral pronouncement

Oral pronouncement of nine-year prison sentence on one count and ten-year concurrent sentences of probation on other counts was ambiguous, and, thus, remand was required for clarification; neither written sentences nor oral pronouncement made clear any plan for probationary terms to run concurrently with each other and consecutive to prison term. Nobles v. State, App. 2 Dist., 605 So.2d 996 (1992). Criminal Law ⚷ 1181.5(8); Sentencing And Punishment ⚷ 1941

264. —— Waiver, oral pronouncement

Failure to orally pronounce that probationer was required to pay for drug screens unless payment was waived by his probation officer resulted in striking of that probation condition. Franklin v. State, App. 2 Dist., 658 So.2d 129 (1995). Sentencing And Punishment ⚷ 1920

265. Conformity to oral pronouncement—In general

Written conditions of probation must conform with those which were orally pronounced. Roundtree v. State, App. 4 Dist., 661 So.2d 1249 (1995). Sentencing And Punishment ⚷ 1921

Inclusion in written order of special conditions of community control and probation that were not orally pronounced at sentencing required reversal of written order and its remand for correction to reflect only conditions orally pronounced at sentencing or those allowed by statute. Gentry v. State, App. 2 Dist., 614 So.2d 8 (1993). Criminal Law ⚷ 1181.5(8); Sentencing And Punishment ⚷ 1921

Trial court's imposition of restitution as condition of probation was erroneous, where court failed to orally pronounce condition at sentencing. Boone v. State, App. 1 Dist., 608 So.2d 564 (1992). Sentencing And Punishment ⚷ 1920

Written order of probation must conform to oral pronouncement at sentencing. Astolfo v. State, App. 2 Dist., 598 So.2d 314 (1992). Sentencing And Punishment ⚷ 1921

Special condition of probation not pronounced orally at sentencing hearing may not be included in written order. Cumbie v. State, App. 1 Dist., 597 So.2d 946 (1992), denial of habeas corpus affirmed in part, reversed in part 991 F.2d 715, certiorari denied 114 S.Ct. 650, 510 U.S. 1031, 126 L.Ed.2d 608. Sentencing And Punishment ⚷ 1921

Written sentencing order could not contain special conditions of probation that had not been orally pronounced at sentencing hearing. Flowers v. State, App. 1 Dist., 595 So.2d 263 (1992). Sentencing And Punishment ⚷ 1921

Probation condition that had not been orally pronounced by trial court was not part of sentence. Knight v. State, App. 2 Dist., 593 So.2d 1202 (1992). Sentencing And Punishment ⚷ 1920

Written probation order imposing condition that directed payment of one dollar per month as fee varied from trial judge's oral sentencing pronouncement and could not stand. Coupe v. State, App. 1 Dist., 591 So.2d 304 (1991). Sentencing And Punishment ⚷ 1921

Written sentence imposing restitution was improper, as restitution condition was not part of oral pronouncement at sentencing hearing. Williams v. State, App. 1 Dist., 588 So.2d 660 (1991). Sentencing And Punishment ⚷ 1921

Written sentencing or probation order must conform to trial court's oral pronouncement. Beaver v. State, App. 1 Dist., 588 So.2d 659 (1991). Sentencing And Punishment ⚷ 1921

Written condition of probation, that defendant have no contact with victim or "any witnesses," which allegedly conflicted with oral pronouncement that defendant was not to have contact with victim or "witnesses that testified against [him]," would be construed for sake of clarity logically to mean that defendant was not to have contact with victim or State's witnesses. Siplin v. State, App. 2 Dist., 584 So.2d 599 (1991). Sentencing And Punishment ⚷ 1921

266. —— Standard conditions, conformity to oral pronouncement

Standard conditions of probation listed in statute may be included in written order even if they are not pronounced orally at sentencing hearing. Cumbie v. State, App. 1 Dist., 597 So.2d 946 (1992), denial of habeas corpus affirmed in part, reversed in part 991 F.2d 715, certiorari denied 114 S.Ct. 650, 510 U.S. 1031, 126 L.Ed.2d 608. Sentencing And Punishment ⚷ 1921

267. —— Remand for correction of nonconforming sections, conformity to oral pronouncement

Remand was required where trial court's written sentence conflicted with its oral sentence; trial court orally imposed concurrent one-year sentences of probation with time served in county jail as a condition of probation, but its written order sentencing defendant failed to make jail a condition of probation. Richardson v. State, App. 2 Dist., 761 So.2d 1232 (2000). Criminal Law ⚷ 1181.5(8)

Written sentencing or probation order must conform to trial court's oral pronouncement, and where written order contains discrepancies, case must be remanded for correction. Vilicic v. State, App. 1 Dist., 637 So.2d 978 (1994). Criminal Law ⚷ 1181.5(8); Sentencing And Punishment ⚷ 1921

Written order of probation could not include condition not mentioned at sentencing hearing and, accordingly, would be reversed and remanded solely for deletion of additional requirement. Catholic v. State, App. 4 Dist., 632 So.2d 272 (1994). Sentencing And Punishment ⚷ 1921

Remand was required due to discrepancy between oral pronouncement of amount of restitution and written probation order. Brown v. State, App. 1 Dist., 605 So.2d 588 (1992). Criminal Law ⚷ 1181.5(8); Sentencing And Punishment ⚷ 1921

Reversal and remand for correction of written order to conform to oral pronouncement was required where trial court's oral pronouncement sentence did not include special condition of probation contained in written order. Pyle v. State, App. 1 Dist., 596 So.2d 744 (1992). Criminal Law ⚷ 1181.5(8); Sentencing And Punishment ⚷ 1921

Written probation order contained special condition not orally pronounced at sentencing regarding alcohol/substance abuse screening and counseling and would have to be corrected. Brown v. State, App. 1 Dist., 596 So.2d 507 (1992). Criminal Law ⚷ 1181.5(8); Sentencing And Punishment ⚷ 1921

Inclusion of special conditions of probation in written order which were not orally pronounced at sentencing hearing requires reversal and remand for correction of written order to comport to oral pronouncement. McCollun v. State, App. 1 Dist., 586 So.2d 490 (1991). Criminal Law ⚷ 1181.5(8)

268. —— Nonconforming conditions, conformity to oral pronouncement

Probation condition stating probationer waived all extradition rights and process during his term of supervision and agreed to comply and return to state, and the court of jurisdiction, upon official instruction to do so was special, rather than general condition, and thus had to be struck for failure of court to orally pronounce condition at sentencing. Queen v. State, App. 5 Dist., 832 So.2d 956 (2002). Sentencing And Punishment ⚷ 1920

Trial court's written probation order improperly required defendant to submit to breathalyzer or blood tests at any time requested by her officer; although trial court pronounced in open court requirement to submit to urinalysis, it did not include pronouncement of breathalyzer or blood tests. Dobrowolski v. State, App. 4 Dist., 663 So.2d 678 (1995). Sentencing And Punishment ⚷ 1920

Direction to stay away from five specified areas failed to conform with oral pronouncement that defendant stay away from areas known to be high drug use areas, to be defined by probation officer, and, thus, direction was not appropriate condition of probation for defendant who pled nolo contendere to sale of controlled substance. Wheatley v. State, App. 1 Dist., 629 So.2d 896 (1993). Sentencing And Punishment ⚷ 1921; Sentencing And Punishment ⚷ 1967(2)

Trial court's failure at sentencing hearing to orally pronounce that court costs were imposed on defendant as condition of probation constituted a discrepancy requiring probation to be vacated and remanded for resolution of discrepancy. Thomas v. State, App. 5 Dist., 625 So.2d 962 (1993). Criminal Law ⚷ 1181.5(8); Sentencing And Punishment ⚷ 1921

Requirement that defendant not use "dangerous substances" should not have been included as condition of his probation imposed pursuant to nolo contendere plea to charge of aggravated assault with deadly weapon, since it was not included in oral conditions of probation, it was not related to or connected with crime, and it was vague. Peterson v. State, App. 5 Dist., 623 So.2d 637 (1993). Sentencing And Punishment ⚷ 1918; Sentencing And Punishment ⚷ 1980(2)

Written order as to restitution as condition of probation was required to conform to conditions as pronounced at sentencing. Shaddix v. State, App. 1 Dist., 599 So.2d 269 (1992). Sentencing And Punishment ⚷ 1921

269. —— Modification of nonconforming conditions, conformity to oral pronouncement

Written conditions of defendant's probation were required to be modified to conform to oral pronouncements at sentencing, to clarify that portion of conditions restricting use of intoxicants and requiring breath and blood tests applied only to extent they were imposed incident to treatment based on ordered substance abuse evaluation. Swinford v. State, App. 4 Dist., 651 So.2d 225 (1995). Sentencing And Punishment ⚷ 1921

Special condition of probation that was not pronounced orally at sentencing hearing could not be contained in written order, requiring that condition requiring chemical testing of defendant "at your own expense" be revised on remand to eliminate words "at your own expense," which was not within standard conditions of probation in statute. Cumbie v. State, App. 1 Dist., 597 So.2d 946 (1992), denial of habeas corpus affirmed in part, reversed in part 991 F.2d 715, certiorari denied 114 S.Ct. 650, 510 U.S. 1031, 126 L.Ed.2d 608. Sentencing And Punishment ⚷ 1921

Written order of probation would be conformed to delete conditions that were not pronounced in open court, including prohibitions against use of intoxicants, visiting places where alcoholic beverages are served, visiting known high drug areas, and undergoing drug or alcohol treatment. Tillman v. State, App. 2 Dist., 592 So.2d 767 (1992). Sentencing And Punishment ⚷ 1921

270. —— Striking nonconforming conditions, conformity to oral pronouncement

Scrivener's error in written order providing for 71.7-month sentence on 29 counts of grand theft had to conform to 71.1-month sentence orally imposed. Reyes v. State, App. 3 Dist., 888 So.2d 95 (2004), review denied 904 So.2d 431. Sentencing And Punishment ⚷ 1139

Probation condition requiring probationer to participate in self-improvement programs determined by court or his officer was neither statutorily authorized nor contained within general conditions or probation, and thus had to be struck because it was not orally pronounced at sentencing. Queen v. State, App. 5 Dist., 832 So.2d 956 (2002). Sentencing And Punishment ⚷ 1920

Probation condition stating probationer waived all extradition rights and process during his term of supervision and agreed to comply and return to state, and the court of jurisdiction, upon official instruction to do so was special, rather than general condition, and thus had to be struck for failure of court to orally pronounce condition at sentencing. Queen v. State, App. 5 Dist., 832 So.2d 956 (2002). Sentencing And Punishment ⚷ 1920

Where unannounced conditions of probation appear in written order, but those conditions were not orally pronounced at sentencing hearing, the striking of challenged conditions, not remand for resentencing, is appropriate remedy. Vasquez v. State, App. 4 Dist., 663 So.2d 1343 (1995), review dismissed 666 So.2d 145. Criminal Law ⚷ 1181.5(8); Criminal Law ⚷ 1184(4.1)

Any special conditions of probation that do not conform to those pronounced at sentencing, other than those authorized by statute, should be stricken. Bell v. State, App. 4 Dist., 652 So.2d 1192 (1995). Sentencing And Punishment ⚷ 1921

Even in absence of contemporaneous objection, illegally imposed conditions of probation could be stricken, and thus District Court of Appeal would strike monthly assessment for county "First Step," and would reverse imposition of public defender's fee and remand for noticed hearing, at which hearing lower court was required to eliminate any discrepancies between its oral pronouncement of conditions and written probation order. Sweet v. State, App. 5 Dist., 644 So.2d 176 (1994). Criminal Law ⚷ 1042.3(4); Criminal Law ⚷ 1181.5(8)

Portion of written sentencing order instructing defendant that as condition of probation he could not frequent places where alcohol is the main source of business would be stricken, as order did not accurately reflect oral pronouncement which did not contain such instruction. Richardson v. State, App. 2 Dist., 620 So.2d 257 (1993). Sentencing And Punishment ⚷ 1921

Conditions of written community control order requiring hourly accounting of all of defendant's activities on daily log, and payment of $2 to two organizations had to be stricken where those conditions were not announced orally at sentencing and were not standard conditions of probation/community control. Vincent v. State, App. 1 Dist., 600 So.2d 1292 (1992). Sentencing And Punishment ⚷ 1921; Sentencing And Punishment ⚷ 1983(2)

Conditions of probation not pronounced in open court would be deleted. Forsythe v. State, App. 2 Dist., 597 So.2d 423 (1992). Sentencing And Punishment ⚷ 1920

Probation condition which required that probationer not use intoxicants to excess nor visit places where intoxicants, drugs or other dangerous substances are unlawfully sold, dispensed, or used would be deleted from written order, where record reflected that condition was not pronounced in open court; moreover, it did not appear from record that condition was reasonably related to grand theft offense or to probationer's rehabilitation. Demmons v. State, App. 2 Dist., 596 So.2d 731 (1992). Sentencing And Punishment ⚷ 1921

Special condition of probation which was not orally pronounced would be ordered stricken. Ochoa v. State, App. 2 Dist., 596 So.2d 515 (1992). Criminal Law ⚷ 1192

Special conditions of probation which did not conform to oral pronouncement at sentencing hearing were required to be stricken. Labar v. State, App. 2 Dist., 584 So.2d 37 (1991). Sentencing And Punishment ⚷ 1921

271. —— Nonconformities not material, conformity to oral pronouncement

There was no error in that certain conditions of probation pertaining to alcohol or substance abuse screening differed slightly in wording from those orally pronounced, where defendant made no objection and was on constructive notice of the conditions as enumerated in statute. Shaddix v. State, App. 1 Dist., 599 So.2d 269 (1992). Sentencing And Punishment ⚷ 1921

272. —— Alcohol testing, conformity to oral pronouncement

Requirement that defendant submit to blood, breathalyzer, and urinalysis examinations as condition of probation was not required to be orally pronounced at sentencing, since such requirement was authorized by section of probation statute authorizing "random testing." Hayes v. State, App. 1 Dist., 585 So.2d 397 (1991), review denied 593 So.2d 1052. Sentencing And Punishment ⚷ 1918

273. Resentencing

Remand for resentencing was required for trial court to exercise its discretion regarding whether electronic monitoring was warranted as condition of probation for defendant who had been convicted of custodial sexual battery; electronic monitoring was currently required by statute, but at time of defendant's offense, trial court had discretion to impose electronic monitoring as condition of defendant's probation, and it was unclear whether trial court believed that electronic monitoring was mandatory for defendant, or if trial court used its discretion in imposing electronic monitoring. Harder v. State, App. 1 Dist., 14 So.3d 1291 (2009). Criminal Law ⚷ 1181.5(8)

Where sentencing court imposed probation conditions in written order that were not orally pronounced at sentencing, court was not required to strike such conditions on remand, but could resentence defendant, if court made intention to include conditions known to defendant and gave defendant opportunity to reject probation. Justice v. State, App. 5 Dist., 658 So.2d 1028 (1995), on rehearing, review granted 666 So.2d 143, quashed 674 So.2d 123. Criminal Law ⚷ 1192

274. House arrest

"House arrest" was permissible condition of probation and defendant's probation could be revoked for failure to remain confined to residence after he had received two-year term of community control followed by ten years probation in exchange for plea of guilty to charges of aggravated assault and aggravated battery. Villabol v. State, App. 2 Dist., 595 So.2d 1057 (1992), review denied 604 So.2d 489. Sentencing And Punishment ⚷ 1976(3); Sentencing And Punishment ⚷ 2003

Probationary condition of "house arrest," precluding defendant from leaving his house without written permission, could not exceed two years as condition of community control. Villabol v. State, App. 2 Dist., 595 So.2d 1057 (1992), review denied 604 So.2d 489. Sentencing And Punishment ⚷ 1971(1); Sentencing And Punishment ⚷ 1976(2)

275. Timeliness of challenge

Attack on conditions of probation was too late, where it came only after a violation was charged, some 20 months after the original order of probation. Gallagher v. State, App. 5 Dist., 421 So.2d 581 (1982). Sentencing And Punishment ⚷ 1922

276. Certiorari

Trial court may modify probation conditions it has previously imposed at any time, as long it does not enhance penalty or add new conditions. Wanner v. State, App. 2 Dist., 746 So.2d 478 (1999). Sentencing And Punishment ⚷ 1985

Mere modification of restitution payees does not impose any new obligation upon defendant who has previously been ordered to pay restitution. Wanner v. State, App. 2 Dist., 746 So.2d 478 (1999). Sentencing And Punishment ⚷ 2197

Payment of fine and intermittent imprisonment imposed by trial court as conditions of probation on nolo contendere plea to charge of manslaughter did not constitute deviation from essential requirements of law which would justify treating attempted appeal by state from such conditions of probation as petition for certiorari. State v. Williams, App. 2 Dist., 237 So.2d 69 (1970). Criminal Law ⚷ 1024(9)

277. Review

Having failed to object to imposition of conditions of probation, which were orally pronounced at sentencing, probationer was not entitled to appellate review as to those conditions, so long as conditions complained of were not illegal and their imposition did not constitute fundamental error. Steward v. State, App. 4 Dist., 677 So.2d 1369 (1996). Criminal Law ⚷ 1042.3(4)

District Court of Appeal did not need to review special probation condition prohibiting defendant from consuming any alcoholic beverages, or reverse such otherwise invalid condition, where defendant failed to object, but where cause otherwise required remand, trial court would be requested to reconsider such special condition. Nelson v. State, App. 4 Dist., 669 So.2d 1145 (1996). Criminal Law ⚷ 1042.3(4); Criminal Law ⚷ 1192

Defendant is not required to make contemporaneous objection to conditions of probation which are illegal in order for objection to such conditions to be raised on appeal. Hughes v. State, App. 4 Dist., 667 So.2d 910 (1996), rehearing denied, review denied 676 So.2d 413. Criminal Law ⚷ 1042.3(4)

Any appeal attacking validity of specific condition of probation should be from adverse ruling in trial court. Bentley v. State, App. 5 Dist., 411 So.2d 1361 (1982), review denied 419 So.2d 1195. Criminal Law ⚷ 1023(16)

In event trial court, at sentencing, imposes conditions of probation upon defendant over defendant's clear objection, defendant must appeal from original probation order rather than attacking imposition of condition after its breach, and in event conditions are held improper by appellate court, cause should be remanded to trial court for reconsideration of sentence in light of trial court's inability to impose conditions it considered proper and needed; overruling Wilkinson v. State, 388 So.2d 1322 (1980). Bentley v. State, App. 5 Dist., 411 So.2d 1361 (1982), review denied 419 So.2d 1195. Criminal Law ⚷ 1181.5(2); Sentencing And Punishment ⚷ 1922

Contention that decision of district court of appeal that terms and conditions of probation had been sufficiently set forth was in conflict with this section relating to terms and conditions of probation did not give Supreme Court jurisdiction under constitution to review the decision on certiorari. Pickman v. State, 164 So.2d 805 (1964). Courts ⚷ 216

278. Costs—In general

Sentencing court lacked authority to impose law enforcement investigative costs as a special condition of probation, absent request by state that investigative costs be imposed or any documentation supporting imposition of investigative costs. Pazo v. State, App. 5 Dist., 684 So.2d 898 (1996). Sentencing And Punishment ⚷ 1916

Requirements that defendant pay investigative costs and make payment to crimes compensation fund as conditions of probation would be affirmed on appeal, notwithstanding state's concession of error, where there were no objections to imposition of those costs when they were imposed. Gomez v. State, App. 4 Dist., 684 So.2d 879 (1996). Criminal Law ⚷ 1042.3(4)

While defendant normally would not be able to renege on costs that were agreed to, record was ambiguous as to what defendant actually agreed to, and thus special conditions of probation, which required defendant to pay investigative and court costs, would be stricken, where defendant pled nolo contendere and agreed to plea agreement that included "standard costs of probation," but court itself indicated that court costs and investigative costs were "special conditions" of probation, not general conditions or what might be construed as standard costs. Jackson v. State, App. 5 Dist., 680 So.2d 1102 (1996). Sentencing And Punishment ⚷ 1921

Sentencing court could not impose special condition of probation requiring separate monthly payments to both Correctional Officer Training Fund and Criminal Justice Training Trust Fund; the two funds had been merged ten years earlier. Hester v. State, App. 5 Dist., 679 So.2d 884 (1996). Sentencing And Punishment ⚷ 1975(3)

Charging defendant $60 to be paid to non-profit organization supervising probation was within statutory limit of one dollar per month for five-year term of probation; however, statutory language did not authorize across-the-board $60 charge in all cases. McRae v. State, App. 5 Dist., 679 So.2d 14 (1996), rehearing denied. Costs ⚷ 304

Trial court orally waived cost of supervision and, therefore, probation condition requiring defendant to pay $50 per month toward cost of supervision would be stricken. Nieves v. State, App. 5 Dist., 678 So.2d 468 (1996). Sentencing And Punishment ⚷ 1921

Although portion of probation order assessing $609 for depositions was authorized, that amount was reduced on appeal by $200, which was amount defendant was assessed pursuant to statute pertaining to additional court costs. Bailey v. State, App. 1 Dist., 677 So.2d 1358 (1996). Sentencing And Punishment ⚷ 1975(3)

On remand, trial court could enter judgment, as opposed to monthly installments, for payment, as condition of probation, of public defender fees, statutory court costs, and cost of prosecution, in prosecution in which trial court originally improperly required defendant to pay those sums in equal monthly installments, contrary to judge's oral pronouncement that judgment for those fees would be imposed. Mosley v. State, App. 4 Dist., 677 So.2d 27 (1996), rehearing denied. Criminal Law ⚷ 1192

Trial court could not impose as special condition of probation that defendant pay sum to county First Step Program. McClough v. State, App. 5 Dist., 669 So.2d 1099 (1996). Sentencing And Punishment ⚷ 1975(2)

District Court of Appeal struck assessment of court costs ordered as condition of community control where trial court did not orally announce statutory authority supporting costs and written order of community control did not delineate any statutory basis. Martin v. State, App. 2 Dist., 667 So.2d 931 (1996). Costs ⚷ 314

Special condition of probation imposing cost for criminal justice education was discretionary and required oral pronouncement. Turner v. State, App. 2 Dist., 666 So.2d 212 (1995). Sentencing And Punishment ⚷ 1918; Sentencing And Punishment ⚷ 1975(2)

Probation condition requiring defendant to pay for evaluation and treatment of any alcohol or drug problem would be stricken since this was a special condition of probation which was not orally pronounced at sentencing. Murphy v. State, App. 2 Dist., 666 So.2d 182 (1995). Sentencing And Punishment ⚷ 1920

Sentencing court could not impose as condition of probation requirement of community service in lieu of costs of supervision of probation; any authority to exempt individual from paying all or part of his costs of supervision belonged initially to Department of Corrections. Kionka v. State, App. 4 Dist., 660 So.2d 419 (1995). Sentencing And Punishment ⚷ 1982(2)

Judge's statement at sentencing that defendant would have to pay specified sum for "court costs" did not encompass costs associated with defendant's participation in work program imposed as condition of probation, for purposes of requirement that conditions of probation be orally announced at sentencing. Hayes v. State, App. 1 Dist., 585 So.2d 397 (1991), review denied 593 So.2d 1052. Sentencing And Punishment ⚷ 1918

Sentencing court has discretion to impose payment of costs as condition of defendant's probation, even though there has been no adjudication of defendant's guilt and defendant is not liable for costs automatically as "convicted person." Clinger v. State, App. 5 Dist., 533 So.2d 315 (1988). Sentencing And Punishment ⚷ 1975(1)

Imposition of $4,500 in court costs as condition of probation in amended sentence without any increase in term of jail or prison time was not impermissible enhancement of punishment, even though costs were not assessed in original sentence. Johnson v. State, App. 1 Dist., 502 So.2d 1291 (1987). Sentencing And Punishment ⚷ 2332

Requirement that defendant pay $5,000 in court costs on reasonable monthly basis within term of probation as condition of probation which was determined without regard to actual costs or any estimate thereof was improper. Scott v. State, App. 2 Dist., 459 So.2d 1176 (1984). Sentencing And Punishment ⚷ 1975(2)

Requirement in order placing indigent defendant on probation that he pay his court costs as a condition of probation was proper. McGeorge v. State, App. 5 Dist., 386 So.2d 29 (1980). Sentencing And Punishment ⚷ 1975(2)

Requirement that indigent defendant repay court costs to county as condition of probation did not violate his constitutional rights. State v. Byrd, 378 So.2d 1231 (1979). Sentencing And Punishment ⚷ 1975(2)

Defendants who entered into plea negotiations and freely agreed to pay their pro rata share of the cost of the investigation as a condition of probation could not challenge that provision on appeal. Brenner v. State, App. 3 Dist., 337 So.2d 1007 (1976), rehearing denied 341 So.2d 287, certiorari denied 348 So.2d 944. Criminal Law ⚷ 1026.10(4)

279. —— Ability to pay, costs

Special condition of probation ordering that defendant would be responsible for paying costs of unsuccessful appeal, even though he was pronounced indigent, was stricken. Bailey v. State, App. 1 Dist., 677 So.2d 1358 (1996). Sentencing And Punishment ⚷ 1975(2)

No request was made by state attorney or any other agency nor did trial court consider defendant's financial resources, as required to impose probation condition that defendant pay amount for prosecution/investigative costs, but appropriate agency could seek to impose those costs on remand. Vickers v. State, App. 2 Dist., 677 So.2d 974 (1996). Sentencing And Punishment ⚷ 1975(2)

When trial court imposes special condition of probation that defendant pay costs of investigation, ability of defendant to pay costs of investigation must be determined at time of imposition. McClough v. State, App. 5 Dist., 669 So.2d 1099 (1996). Sentencing And Punishment ⚷ 1975(2)

Trial court improperly imposed special condition of probation requiring defendant to pay cots of investigation where trial court made no inquiry into defendant's ability to pay such costs and state failed to present any evidence to support its claim for costs. McClough v. State, App. 5 Dist., 669 So.2d 1099 (1996). Sentencing And Punishment ⚷ 1975(2)

Defendant should not have been ordered to pay $200 for costs of prosecution as condition of his probation following six months in jail, pursuant to his plea of nolo contendere to charge of selling cocaine; circuit court assessed costs of prosecution without any evidence of actual amount or defendant's financial ability to pay. Wyatt v. State, App. 4 Dist., 654 So.2d 613 (1995). Sentencing And Punishment ⚷ 1975(2)

Finding of a violation of condition requiring payment of court costs was subject to being stricken from order of revocation inasmuch as defendant was indigent and there was no showing of his ability to pay those costs. Abelson v. State, App. 2 Dist., 367 So.2d 633 (1979). Sentencing And Punishment ⚷ 2003

In proceeding in which defendant was convicted of buying, receiving or concealing stolen property, ordering payment of court costs as a condition of probation was not error, though defendant had been adjudged indigent at arraignment. Arnold v. State, App. 1 Dist., 356 So.2d 862 (1978). Sentencing And Punishment ⚷ 1975(2)

280. —— Notice, costs

Order of probation could not require defendant to pay investigative costs, where defendant was afforded neither sufficient notice of intent to seek imposition of those costs nor opportunity to be heard before they were imposed. Daniels v. State, App. 1 Dist., 678 So.2d 860 (1996), rehearing denied. Sentencing And Punishment ⚷ 1917

Defendant was entitled to notice of right to object to amount of public defender's fee imposed as probation condition; although state argued that notice was not required since defendant had agreed to pay fee in written plea agreement, amount of fee was not part of agreement, nor was there express waiver of right to contest amount. Nieves v. State, App. 5 Dist., 678 So.2d 468 (1996). Sentencing And Punishment ⚷ 1917

Probation condition requiring probationer to pay costs of prosecution and make payment to county drug fund, which was not orally pronounced at sentencing, had to be stricken; although imposition of such costs was statutorily permitted, probationer was not given notice of their imposition and was thus denied opportunity to object to amount. Chitty v. State, App. 2 Dist., 661 So.2d 26 (1994). Sentencing And Punishment ⚷ 1920

Discretionary court costs of two dollars were improperly imposed as probation condition without giving defendant notice and opportunity to be heard and, thus, costs were stricken. Heathcoe v. State, App. 2 Dist., 654 So.2d 1258 (1995). Sentencing And Punishment ⚷ 1917

Costs imposed upon defendant as a special condition of probation were required to be stricken, where the costs were imposed without adequate notice or opportunity to object. Bishop v. State, App. 5 Dist., 564 So.2d 629 (1990). Costs ⚷ 314

Trial court erred in ordering, as condition of probation, that defendant pay court costs and attorney's fees without affording defendant notice of court's intent to impose such condition and without ascertaining defendant's ability to pay. Boudreaux v. State, App. 1 Dist., 553 So.2d 376 (1989), jurisdiction accepted 559 So.2d 1140, quashed 572 So.2d 1372, on remand 578 So.2d 457. Sentencing And Punishment ⚷ 1975(2)

Court costs could not be imposed on defendant as condition of probation, without giving defendant proper notice and opportunity to object. Tucker v. State, App. 1 Dist., 529 So.2d 818 (1988). Sentencing And Punishment ⚷ 1917

281. —— Oral pronouncement, costs

Defendant who pleaded guilty to unlawful sexual activity with a minor was properly required to pay for the cost of drawing a DNA blood sample, even though that probation condition was not orally pronounced at sentencing; it was a statutory requirement that the defendant pay for the cost of the DNA sample, regardless of whether it was orally pronounced. Taylor v. State, App. 2 Dist., 821 So.2d 404 (2002). Sentencing And Punishment ⚷ 1920

In imposing conditions of probation, trial court erred in failing to orally announce all discretionary costs and fees. Wines v. State, App. 5 Dist., 690 So.2d 684 (1997). Sentencing And Punishment ⚷ 1920

Sentencing court could not impose special condition of probation assessing "Drug Testing Fee," where assessment was not separately announced at sentencing. Hester v. State, App. 5 Dist., 679 So.2d 884 (1996). Sentencing And Punishment ⚷ 1920

Requiring defendant to pay cost which was not announced at sentencing was invalid condition of probation. Ringling v. State, App. 2 Dist., 678 So.2d 1339 (1996). Sentencing And Punishment ⚷ 1920

Assessment of statutorily mandated $2 per month surcharge to Department of Corrections as probation condition was not required to be orally pronounced at sentencing. Nieves v. State, App. 5 Dist., 678 So.2d 468 (1996). Sentencing And Punishment ⚷ 1918

Trial court did not orally pronounce probation condition that defendant pay assessment to criminal justice education by municipalities and counties fund, as required to impose such condition, but state could seek to reimpose that cost upon remand. Vickers v. State, App. 2 Dist., 677 So.2d 974 (1996). Criminal Law ⚷ 1192; Sentencing And Punishment ⚷ 1920

On appeal, District Court of Appeal would strike conditions of probation that did not conform to trial court's oral pronouncements, including condition requiring defendant to inform her employer of her probationary status, portion of condition requiring defendant to pay public defender fees, statutory court costs, and cost of prosecution in monthly installments, and assessment of fee for county resolution criminal justice trust fund. Mosley v. State, App. 4 Dist., 677 So.2d 27 (1996), rehearing denied. Sentencing And Punishment ⚷ 1921

Sentence condition requiring defendant to pay $48, which was not orally pronounced, was not authorized. Nesbitt v. State, App. 5 Dist., 656 So.2d 259 (1995). Sentencing And Punishment ⚷ 1920

282. —— Proper form and statutory authority, costs

Trial court could not order Department of Corrections to pay for convicted sex offender's sex offender treatment program, imposed as a condition of sex offender probation; statute governing sex offender probation and community control required offenders to pay for their own treatment, and ordering Department to expend funds in a particular manner violated doctrine of separation of powers. Department of Corrections v. Grubbs, App. 2 Dist., 884 So.2d 1147 (2004). Constitutional Law ⚷ 2545(3); States ⚷ 111

Trial court erred in failing to cite to statutory authority for probation conditions requiring probationer to pay court costs, investigative costs, processing fee for administrative probation status, and $1 per month to organization. Wines v. State, App. 5 Dist., 690 So.2d 684 (1997). Sentencing And Punishment ⚷ 1918

Court costs could not be included in order of probation, in absence of any statutory authority authorizing sentencing court to impose such costs. Hayes v. State, App. 2 Dist., 686 So.2d 602 (1996). Costs ⚷ 292

Nonrecurring processing fee included in order of probation, which was to be imposed on defendant in event he obtained administrative probationary status after completing one half of his probation, was not authorized by statute and was stricken. Jackson v. State, App. 5 Dist., 685 So.2d 1386 (1997). Sentencing And Punishment ⚷ 1975(2)

Trial court's failure to state statutory authority for imposing court costs on defendant as condition of order of probation/community control required that condition be stricken. Melton v. State, App. 2 Dist., 685 So.2d 853 (1995). Sentencing And Punishment ⚷ 1975(2)

Assessment of costs, in order of probation, must be stricken where record does not contain citation to proper statutory authority supporting such assessment. Levely v. State, App. 2 Dist., 685 So.2d 847 (1995). Sentencing And Punishment ⚷ 1975(2)

Sentencing court was required to cite statutory authority when imposing law enforcement investigative costs as a special condition of probation. Pazo v. State, App. 5 Dist., 684 So.2d 898 (1996). Sentencing And Punishment ⚷ 1918

Condition of probation requiring defendant to pay court costs without statutory reference was improper. Ringling v. State, App. 2 Dist., 678 So.2d 1339 (1996). Sentencing And Punishment ⚷ 1975(2)

Portion of probation order that imposed 4% surcharge was stricken, as it was imposed without statutory authority. Bailey v. State, App. 1 Dist., 677 So.2d 1358 (1996). Sentencing And Punishment ⚷ 1975(2)

Trial court improperly imposed, as probation condition, amounts for court improvement fund, since amounts were not authorized under any existing statute, either as fine or cost. Vickers v. State, App. 2 Dist., 677 So.2d 974 (1996). Sentencing And Punishment ⚷ 1974(2); Sentencing And Punishment ⚷ 1975(2)

Trial court did not recite statutory authority for imposing probation condition of public defender lien and attorney cost, as required to impose such condition, but error could be corrected on remand. Vickers v. State, App. 2 Dist., 677 So.2d 974 (1996). Criminal Law ⚷ 1192; Sentencing And Punishment ⚷ 1920

Since order of probation gave no statutory authority for imposition of court costs and fine, those probation conditions had to be stricken. Reiter v. State, App. 2 Dist., 674 So.2d 189 (1996). Sentencing And Punishment ⚷ 1920

Trial court's assessment of court costs in the amount of $300 as a condition of probation would be stricken since trial court did not orally announce statutory authority supporting the costs and the judgment and sentence did not delineate the statutory basis for assessment of this lump sum. Miller v. State, App. 2 Dist., 664 So.2d 1066 (1995). Sentencing And Punishment ⚷ 1918

Provisions of order of probation which directed defendant to pay to rehabilitation organization $12 each year he was on probation and to pay $500 in court costs were stricken where record contained no citation to proper statutory authority supporting assessment of such costs. Crum v. State, App. 2 Dist., 664 So.2d 1051 (1995). Sentencing And Punishment ⚷ 1920

Payment of fine and court costs which court imposed as probation condition would be stricken because court failed to provide statutory authority for imposition of such costs. Martin v. State, App. 2 Dist., 659 So.2d 479 (1995). Costs ⚷ 314; Sentencing And Punishment ⚷ 1974(2); Sentencing And Punishment ⚷ 1975(2)

Trial court lacked authority to impose costs to County Board of Commissioners as condition of probation, where those costs were assessed without any citation to statutory authority. Holmes v. State, App. 4 Dist., 658 So.2d 1185 (1995). Sentencing And Punishment ⚷ 1975(2)

Costs imposed on defendant as condition of community control and probation could not be imposed without providing statutory reference. Curry v. State, App. 2 Dist., 656 So.2d 521 (1995), review granted 676 So.2d 412, review dismissed 682 So.2d 1091. Costs ⚷ 314

Trial court could not improve special condition in each sentence requiring defendant to pay costs where trial court failed to reference statutory authority for the imposition of costs. Brooks v. State, App. 5 Dist., 649 So.2d 329 (1995). Costs ⚷ 314

Condition of probation ordering defendant to pay one dollar per month to certain organization would be stricken, since no statutory authority was referenced for imposition of such costs. Luby v. State, App. 2 Dist., 648 So.2d 308 (1995). Sentencing And Punishment ⚷ 1975(2)

Court costs imposed on defendant as special condition of probation were stricken without prejudice where record did not reflect authority for imposing such costs; state could seek reimposition with citation of proper authority. Martin v. State, App. 2 Dist., 640 So.2d 1241 (1994). Sentencing And Punishment ⚷ 1975(2)

Trial court properly imposed statutory costs as condition of community control sentence. Johnson v. State, App. 5 Dist., 636 So.2d 792 (1994). Sentencing And Punishment ⚷ 1975(2)

Payment of $200 as additional cost associated with defendant's participation in work program was not statutorily authorized and, thus, payment was not appropriate condition of probation for defendant who pled nolo contendere to sale of controlled substance. Wheatley v. State, App. 1 Dist., 629 So.2d 896 (1993). Costs ⚷ 303; Sentencing And Punishment ⚷ 1975(2)

283. —— Procedures, costs

Condition of probation that defendant pay certain costs must be imposed with the same procedures used to impose costs of prosecution against convicted defendants. Reyes v. State, App. 2 Dist., 655 So.2d 111 (1995). Sentencing And Punishment ⚷ 1916

284. —— Court improvement program, costs

Requiring defendant to pay $50 for court improvement fund as condition of probation was invalid. Ringling v. State, App. 2 Dist., 678 So.2d 1339 (1996). Sentencing And Punishment ⚷ 1975(2)

Statute authorizing conditions of probation does not authorize local assessment for court improvement program in case involving violation of state statute. Reyes v. State, App. 2 Dist., 655 So.2d 111 (1995). Sentencing And Punishment ⚷ 1975(2)

285. —— Request by agency, costs

In imposing conditions of probation, trial court should not have assessed investigative costs absent request or supporting documentation for such costs from state. Wines v. State, App. 5 Dist., 690 So.2d 684 (1997). Sentencing And Punishment ⚷ 1916

Defendant convicted of driving while intoxicated resulting in death could not be required to pay investigative costs as condition of probation, where there was no request by state that investigative costs be imposed, or any documentation supporting imposition of such costs. Davis v. State, App. 5 Dist., 688 So.2d 996 (1997). Sentencing And Punishment ⚷ 1975(2)

Probation condition assessing costs of prosecution pursuant to statute would be stricken where there was no record that state requested costs or presented documentation to support assessment as required by statute. Nieves v. State, App. 5 Dist., 678 So.2d 468 (1996). Sentencing And Punishment ⚷ 1916

Probation condition assessing $100 for costs of prosecution was invalid in absence of express request by specific agency with adequate supporting documentation. Heathcoe v. State, App. 2 Dist., 654 So.2d 1258 (1995). Sentencing And Punishment ⚷ 1975(2)

286. —— Amount, costs

Statute requires that costs imposed as condition of probation be actual costs, rather than set at arbitrary figure. Smith v. State, App. 1 Dist., 401 So.2d 1176 (1981). Sentencing And Punishment ⚷ 1975(3)

287. Public defender lien

Portion of probation order imposing $450 public defender's lien was stricken, as defendant was not informed that he had right to challenge that assessment. Bailey v. State, App. 1 Dist., 677 So.2d 1358 (1996). Sentencing And Punishment ⚿ 1920

Although trial judge erred in imposing a public defender lien as a condition of defendant's parole, defendant was properly sentenced under sentencing guidelines, and thus, was not entitled to parole, rendering question moot. Boyett v. State, App. 2 Dist., 452 So.2d 958 (1984), adopted 467 So.2d 997. Pardon And Parole ⚿ 62

Order revoking probation must be reversed, where trial judge failed to consider fact that probationer had failed to pay his public defender lien only because he was indigent and unable to make the payment, even though his defense was that he thought he had paid more than the amount shown in the public defender's records. Baran v. State, App. 5 Dist., 381 So.2d 323 (1980). Sentencing And Punishment ⚿ 2006

288. Attorneys' fees

Trial court's imposition of attorney fees as condition of probation was improper, where court had stated at sentencing that such fees were not being imposed as condition of probation. Walker v. State, App. 2 Dist., 662 So.2d 1352 (1995). Sentencing And Punishment ⚿ 1975(2)

Trial court was not precluded from recommending imposition of attorney fees as condition of defendant's parole. Williams v. State, App. 2 Dist., 453 So.2d 516 (1984). Pardon And Parole ⚿ 64.1

948.031. Condition of probation or community control; public service

(1) Any person who is convicted of a felony or misdemeanor and who is placed on probation or into community control may be required as a condition of supervision to perform some type of public service for a tax-supported or tax-exempt entity, with the consent of such entity. Such public service shall be performed at a time other than during such person's regular hours of employment.

(2) Upon the request of the chief judge of the circuit, the Department of Corrections shall establish a public service program for a county, which program may include, but shall not be limited to, any of the following types of public service:

(a) Maintenance work on any property or building owned or leased by any state, county, or municipality or any nonprofit organization or agency.

(b) Maintenance work on any state-owned, county-owned, or municipally owned road or highway.

(c) Landscaping or maintenance work in any state, county, or municipal park or recreation area.

(d) Work in any state, county, or municipal hospital or any developmental services institution or other nonprofit organization or agency.

Laws 1976, c. 76–70, § 1; Laws 1983, c. 83–131, § 17; Laws 1987, c. 87–226, § 77; Laws 1989, c. 89–308, § 30.

Historical and Statutory Notes

Amendment Notes:

Laws 1983, c. 83–131, § 17, designated subsec. (1), provided for community control therein, and added subsec. (2).

Laws 1987, c. 87–226, was a reviser's correction bill amending subsec. (2)(d).

Laws 1989, c. 89–308, § 30, eff. Oct. 1, 1989, in subsec. (2), in par. (d), substituted "developmental services institution" for "major state retardation facility".

Library References

Sentencing and Punishment ⚷1982, 2082 to 2084.
Westlaw Topic No. 350H.
C.J.S. Criminal Law § 567.

Research References

Treatises and Practice Aids

16 Florida Practice Series § 7:11, Special Conditions of Probation.

Notes of Decisions

1. Validity

Sections 775.091 and 948.031 providing for imposition of community service as part of conditions of probation were not without limitation, so as to be unconstitutional; §§ 775.091 and 948.031 could only be applied in context of probation as part of sentence pursuant to conviction of criminal offense, and in all circumstances, maximum community service that could be imposed was limited to period of probation imposed under maximum penalty authorized for that offense. White v. State, App. 1 Dist., 539 So.2d 1160 (1989). Sentencing And Punishment ⚷ 1825

2. Construction and application

References to community service work, found in § 316.193, § 775.091 and this section indicate that such service is to be considered either as extra sanction or as additional condition of probation, and not as substitute for some other type of punishment. State v. Muoio, App. 2 Dist., 438 So.2d 160 (1983). Sentencing And Punishment ⚷ 2049

Although trial court had authority to impose condition of public service as a condition of probation, trial court was without authority to require that probationer's public service be on a full-time employment basis. Fillastre v. State, App. 2 Dist., 387 So.2d 400 (1980). Sentencing And Punishment ⚷ 1982(2)

3. Orders

An order of the parole and probation commission placing a parole violator in community control supersedes and replaces the original parole order. The commission does not have to formally revoke the original release order because it is forfeited or suspended, subject to reinstatement, on the finding a parole violation took place; however, the commission could adopt conditions from the original parole order compatible with statutes pertaining thereto, in its new order placing the parolee into a community control program. Op.Atty.Gen., 83–79, Oct. 26, 1983.

4. Violation of order

County court lacked jurisdiction to sanction defendant for failing to perform community service, 19 months after defendant had been ordered to perform 150 hours of community service at the rate of 15 hours per month, upon adjudication of guilt following her plea to misdemeanor marijuana possession, where maximum amount of time to which defendant could have been sentenced was one year; court was divested of jurisdiction over defendant upon expiration of probationary period. West's F.S.A. §§ 775.082(4)(a), 775.091, 893.13(6)(b), 921.187(1)(a), Rivera v. State, App. 3 Dist., 939 So.2d 116 (2006), rehearing denied, review granted 965 So.2d 123, review dismissed as improvidently granted 985 So.2d 1092. Sentencing And Punishment ⚷ 1948; Sentencing And Punishment ⚷ 1982(3)

5. Burden of proof

The state did not establish that defendant willfully and substantially violated special condition of his probation for drug offenses that required him to perform 100 community-service hours at rate of five hours per month; probation order did not specify a beginning or end date for defendant to complete his community-service hours, and at time that his probation was revoked, defendant had over two years remaining on his term, which was enough time for him to complete 100 hours of community service at rate of five hours per month. Bowser v. State, App. 2 Dist., 937 So.2d 1270 (2006). Sentencing And Punishment ⚷ 1982(3)

6. Jurisdiction of county court

County court lacked jurisdiction to sanction defendant for failing to perform community service, 19 months after defendant had been ordered to perform 150 hours of community service at the rate of 15 hours per month, upon adjudication of guilt following her plea to misdemeanor marijuana possession, where maximum amount of time to which defendant could have been sentenced was one year; court was divested of jurisdiction over defendant upon expiration of probationary period. West's F.S.A. §§§§ 775.082(4)(a), 775.091, 893.13(6)(b), 921.187(1)(a), Rivera v. State, App. 3 Dist., 939 So.2d 116 (2006), rehearing denied, review granted 965 So.2d 123, review dismissed as improvidently granted 985 So.2d 1092. Sentencing And Punishment ⚿ 1948; Sentencing And Punishment ⚿ 1982(3)

948.032. Condition of probation; restitution

If a defendant is placed on probation, any restitution ordered under s. 775.089 shall be a condition of the probation. The court may revoke probation if the defendant fails to comply with the order. In determining whether to revoke probation, the court shall consider the defendant's employment status, earning ability, and financial resources; the willfulness of the defendant's failure to pay; and any other special circumstances that may have a bearing on the defendant's ability to pay.

Laws 1984, c. 84–363, § 5; Laws 1993, c. 93–37, § 11.

Historical and Statutory Notes

Amendment Notes:

Laws 1993, c. 93–37, § 11, eff. Oct. 1, 1993, reenacted § 948.032, and made nonsubstantive changes, for the purpose of incorporating the amendment to § 775.089 in a reference thereto.

Section 16 of Laws 1993, c. 93–37, provides:

"This act shall take effect upon becoming a law, except that sections 1–12 and section 14 of this act shall take effect October 1, 1993, and shall apply to offenses committed on or after October 1, 1993."

Constitutional Provisions

Art. 1, § 11, provides:

"No person shall be imprisoned for debt, except in cases of fraud."

Cross References

Mitigation of sentence for restitution, see § 921.185.

Library References

Sentencing and Punishment ⚿1973, 2003, 2082 to 2084, 2087.

Westlaw Topic No. 350H.
C.J.S. Criminal Law §§ 567, 576, 2152.

Research References

Treatises and Practice Aids

16 Florida Practice Series § 7:35, Revocation of Probation or Community Control--Grounds for Revocation--Revocation After Commencement of Probation or Community Control--Failure to Pay Court-Ordered Costs or Restitution.

16 Florida Practice Series § 8:32, When Restitution is Disputed: Restitution Imposed After Evidentiary Hearing--Ability to Pay.

United States Supreme Court

Bankruptcy, restitution obligation discharge, see Kelly v. Robinson, U.S.Conn.1986, 107 S.Ct. 353, 479 U.S. 36, 93 L.Ed.2d 216.

Notes of Decisions

---

1. Significant relationship to offense

Requirement of restitution as condition of probation was proper in case of defendant, who had pled guilty to three counts of burglary based on unlawful entering of dwelling to commit theft; victims' damages, i.e., value of their stolen property, bore significant relationship to convicted offense. Rousseau v. State, App. 1 Dist., 496 So.2d 830 (1986), on rehearing 489 So.2d 828, approved and remanded 509 So.2d 281. Sentencing And Punishment ⚷ 1973(2)

2. Ability to make restitution

Trial court did not abuse its discretion by finding that probationer willfully violated condition of his probation by failing to make sufficient restitution payments, even if probationer could not afford to pay the $1,200 monthly restitution payment originally ordered; probationer was capable of paying more monthly restitution than the $100 to $150 he did pay. Oliver v. State, App. 5 Dist., 880 So.2d 794 (2004), rehearing denied. Sentencing And Punishment ⚷ 1973(3)

Revocation of probation for failure to pay restitution due to unemployment was abuse of discretion where trial court failed to determine whether probationer had the ability to pay restitution and that she willfully refused to do so; evidence was that probationer was capable of being gainfully employed at the time of the fourth hearing, was employed by seventh hearing, but not whether she had ability to work or to pay restitution from the beginning of probation up to fourth hearing. Cherry v. State, App. 2 Dist., 718 So.2d 294 (1998). Sentencing And Punishment ⚷ 2003; Sentencing And Punishment ⚷ 2021

Revocation of probation for failure to make restitution or pay costs of supervision was improper where trial court had adjudicated defendant insolvent at time of entry of order of probation and there was no evidence presented concerning whether defendant was able to make restitution or pay costs. Grimsley v. State, App. 2 Dist., 408 So.2d 1075 (1982). Sentencing And Punishment ⚷ 2003

Defendant's probation could not be revoked for failure to pay restitution where the state failed to prove that the defendant had the financial ability to pay, but instead attempted to prove that the defendant had not actively pursued potential employment. Winfield v. State, App. 1 Dist., 406 So.2d 50 (1981). Sentencing And Punishment ⚷ 2003

Judgment revoking probation and imposing sentence following revocation would be reversed and proceedings would be remanded to trial court where record disclosed that trial court's primary concern in revoking probation was defendant's failure to pay medical costs incurred by victim, defendant's failure to pay such costs was not sufficient basis upon which to revoke his probation due to failure of state to establish defendant's solvency, and it was not established whether trial court would have revoked probation under remaining grounds or would have imposed remaining portion of term of imprisonment. Aaron v. State, App. 3 Dist., 400 So.2d 1033 (1981), review denied 408 So.2d 1095. Criminal Law ⚷ 1177.3(4); Criminal Law ⚷ 1181.5(8)

3. Willful nonpayment of restitution

Restitution can be a condition of probation and willful nonpayment of restitution can be a violation of probation that warrants incarceration. Smith v. State, App. 2 Dist., 933 So.2d 723 (2006). Sentencing And Punishment ⚷ 1973(2); Sentencing And Punishment ⚷ 2003

948.033. Condition of probation or community control; criminal gang

Effective for a probationer or community controllee whose crime was committed on or after October 1, 2008, and who has been found to have committed the crime for the purpose of benefiting, promoting, or furthering the interests of a criminal gang, the court shall, in addition to any other conditions imposed, impose a condition prohibiting the probationer or community controllee from knowingly associating with other criminal gang members or associates, except as authorized by law enforcement officials, prosecutorial authorities, or the court, for the purpose of aiding in the investigation of criminal activity.

Added by Laws 2008, c. 2008–238, § 21, eff. Oct. 1, 2008.

Library References

Sentencing and Punishment ⚷1971, 2082 to 2084.
Westlaw Topic No. 350H.
C.J.S. Criminal Law § 567.

Research References

Treatises and Practice Aids

16 Florida Practice Series § 7:17, Criminal Gang Probation and Community Control.

948.034. Terms and conditions of probation; community residential drug punishment centers

(1) On or after October 1, 1993, any person who violates s. 893.13(1)(a)1., (1)(c)2., (1)(d)2., (2)(a)1., or (5)(a) may, in the discretion of the trial court, be required to successfully complete a term of probation in lieu of serving a term of imprisonment as required or authorized by s. 775.084, former s. 921.001, or s. 921.002, as follows:

(a) If the person has not previously been convicted of violating s. 893.13(1)(a)1., (1)(c)2., (1)(d)2., (2)(a)1., or (5)(a), adjudication may be withheld and the offender may be placed on probation for not less than 18 months, as a condition of which the court shall require the offender to reside at a community residential drug punishment center for 90 days. The offender must comply with all rules and regulations of the center and must pay a fee for the costs of room and board and residential supervision. Placement of an offender into a community residential drug punishment center is subject to budgetary considerations and availability of bed space. If the court requires the offender to reside at a community residential drug punishment center, the court shall also require the offender to comply with one or more of the other following terms and conditions:

1. Pay a fine of not less than $500 nor more than $10,000 pursuant to s. 775.083(1)(c).

2. Enter, regularly attend, and successfully complete a substance abuse education program of at least 40 hours or a prescribed substance abuse treatment program provided by a treatment resource licensed pursuant to chapter 397 or by a hospital licensed pursuant to chapter 395, as specified by the court. In addition, the court may refer the offender to a licensed agency for substance abuse evaluation and, if appropriate, substance abuse treatment subject to the ability of the offender to pay for such evaluation and treatment. If such referral is made, the offender must comply and must pay for the reasonable cost of the evaluation and treatment.

3. Perform at least 100 hours of public service.

4. Submit to routine and random drug testing which may be conducted during the probationary period, with the reasonable costs thereof borne by the offender.

5. Participate, at his or her own expense, in an appropriate self-help group, such as Narcotics Anonymous, Alcoholics Anonymous, or Cocaine Anonymous, if available.

(b) If the person has been previously convicted of one felony violation of s. 893.13(1)(a)1., (1)(c)2., (1)(d)2., (2)(a)1., or (5)(a), adjudication may not be withheld and the offender may be placed on probation for not less than 24 months, as a condition of which the court shall require the offender to reside at a community residential drug punishment center for 180 days. The offender must comply with all rules and regulations of the center and must pay a fee for the costs of room and board and residential supervision. Placement of an offender into a community residential drug punishment center is subject to budgetary considerations and availability of bed space. If the court requires the offender to reside at a community residential drug punishment center, the court shall also require the offender to comply with one or more of the other following terms and conditions:

1. Pay a fine of not less than $1,000 nor more than $10,000 pursuant to s. 775.083(1)(c).

2. Enter, regularly attend, and successfully complete a substance abuse education program of at least 40 hours or a prescribed substance abuse treatment program provided by a treatment resource licensed pursuant to chapter 397 or by a hospital licensed pursuant to chapter 395, as specified by the court. In addition, the court may refer the offender to a licensed agency for substance abuse evaluation and, if appropriate, substance abuse treatment subject to the ability of the offender to pay for such evaluation and treatment. If such referral is made, the offender must comply and must pay for the reasonable cost of the evaluation and treatment.

3. Perform at least 200 hours of public service.

4. Submit to routine and random drug testing which may be conducted during the probationary period, with the reasonable costs thereof borne by the offender.

5. Participate, at his or her own expense, in an appropriate self-help group, such as Narcotics Anonymous, Alcoholics Anonymous, or Cocaine Anonymous, if available.

(c) If the person has been previously convicted of two felony violations of s. 893.13(2)(a)1. or (5)(a), adjudication may not be withheld and the offender may be placed on probation for not less than 36 months, as a condition of which the court shall require the offender to reside at a community residential drug punishment center for 360 days. The offender must comply with all rules and regulations of the center and must pay a fee for the costs of room and board and residential supervision. Placement of an offender into a community residential drug punishment center is subject to budgetary considerations and availability of bed space. If the court requires the offender to reside at a community residential drug punishment center, the court shall also require the offender to comply with one or more of the other following terms and conditions:

1. Pay a fine of not less than $1,500 nor more than $10,000 pursuant to s. 775.083(1)(c).

2. Enter, regularly attend, and successfully complete a substance abuse education program of at least 40 hours or a prescribed substance abuse treatment program provided by a treatment resource licensed pursuant to chapter 397 or by a hospital licensed pursuant to chapter 395, as specified by the court. In addition, the court may refer the offender to a licensed agency for substance abuse evaluation and, if appropriate, substance abuse treatment subject to the ability of the offender to pay for such evaluation and treatment. If such referral is made, the offender must comply and must pay for the reasonable cost of the evaluation and treatment.

3. Perform at least 300 hours of public service.

4. Submit to routine and random drug testing which may be conducted during the probationary period, with the reasonable costs thereof borne by the offender.

5. Participate, at his or her own expense, in an appropriate self-help group, such as Narcotics Anonymous, Alcoholics Anonymous, or Cocaine Anonymous, if available.

(d) An offender who violates probation imposed pursuant to this section shall be sentenced in accordance with s. 921.002.

(2) On or after October 1, 1993, any person who violates s. 893.13(1)(a)2., (2)(a)2., (5)(b), or (6)(a) may, in the discretion of the trial court, be required to successfully complete a term of probation in lieu of serving a term of imprisonment as required or authorized by s. 775.084, former s. 921.001, or s. 921.002, as follows:

(a) If the person has not previously been convicted of violating s. 893.13(1)(a)2., (2)(a)2., (5)(b), or (6)(a), adjudication may be withheld and the offender shall be placed on probation for not less than 12 months, as a condition of which the court may require the offender to comply with one or more of the following terms and conditions:

1. Pay a fine of not less than $250 nor more than $5,000 pursuant to s. 775.083(1)(c).

2. Enter, regularly attend, and successfully complete a substance abuse education program of at least 40 hours or a prescribed substance abuse treatment program provided by a treatment resource licensed pursuant to chapter 397 or by a hospital licensed pursuant to chapter 395, as specified by the court. In addition, the court may refer the offender to a licensed agency for substance abuse evaluation and, if appropriate, substance abuse treatment subject to the ability of the offender to pay for such evaluation and treatment. If such referral is made, the offender must comply and must pay for the reasonable cost of the evaluation and treatment.

3. Perform at least 50 hours of public service.

4. Submit to routine and random drug testing which may be conducted during the probationary period, with the reasonable costs thereof borne by the offender.

5. Participate, at his or her own expense, in an appropriate self-help group, such as Narcotics Anonymous, Alcoholics Anonymous, or Cocaine Anonymous, if available.

(b) If the person has been previously convicted of one felony violation of s. 893.13(1)(a)2., (2)(a)2., (5)(b), or (6)(a), adjudication may not be withheld and the offender may be placed on probation for not less than 18 months, as a condition of which the court shall require the offender to reside at a community residential drug punishment center for 90 days. The offender must comply with all rules and regulations of the center and must pay a fee for the costs of room and board and residential supervision. Placement of an offender into a community residential drug punishment center is subject to budgetary considerations and availability of bed space. If the court requires the offender to reside at a community residential drug punishment center, the court shall also require the offender to comply with one or more of the other following terms and conditions:

1. Pay a fine of not less than $500 nor more than $5,000 pursuant to s. 775.083(1)(c).

2. Enter, regularly attend, and successfully complete a substance abuse intervention program of at least 80 hours provided by a treatment resource licensed pursuant to chapter 397 or by a hospital licensed pursuant to chapter 395, as specified by the court. In addition, the court may refer the offender to a licensed agency for substance abuse evaluation and, if appropriate, substance abuse treatment subject to the ability of the offender to pay for such evaluation and treatment. If such referral is made, the offender must comply and must pay for the reasonable cost of the evaluation and treatment.

3. Perform at least 100 hours of public service.

4. Submit to routine and random drug testing which may be conducted during the probationary period, with the reasonable costs thereof borne by the offender.

5. Participate, at his or her own expense, in an appropriate self-help group, such as Narcotics Anonymous, Alcoholics Anonymous, or Cocaine Anonymous, if available.

(c) If the person has been previously convicted of two felony violations of s. 893.13(2)(a)2., (5)(b), or (6)(a), adjudication may not be withheld and the offender may be placed on probation for not less than 24 months, as a condition of which the court shall require the offender to reside at a community residential drug punishment center for 120 days. The offender must comply with all rules and regulations of the center and must pay a fee for the costs of room and board and residential supervision. Placement of an offender into a community residential drug punishment center is subject to budgetary considerations and availability of bed space. If the court requires the offender to reside at a community residential drug punishment center, the court shall also require the offender to comply with one or more of the other following terms and conditions:

1. Pay a fine of not less than $1,000 nor more than $5,000 pursuant to s. 775.083(1)(c).

2. Enter, regularly attend, and successfully complete a prescribed substance abuse treatment program provided by a treatment resource licensed pursuant to chapter 397 or by a hospital licensed pursuant to chapter 395, as specified by the court. In addition, the court may refer the offender to a licensed agency for substance abuse evaluation and, if appropriate, substance abuse treatment subject to the ability of the offender to pay for such evaluation and treatment. If such referral is made, the offender must comply and must pay for the reasonable cost of the evaluation and treatment.

3. Perform at least 150 hours of public service.

4. Submit to routine and random drug testing which may be conducted during the probationary period, with the reasonable costs thereof borne by the offender.

5. Participate, at his or her own expense, in an appropriate self-help group, such as Narcotics Anonymous, Alcoholics Anonymous, or Cocaine Anonymous, if available.

(d) If the person has been previously convicted of three felony violations of s. 893.13(2)(a)2., (5)(b), or (6)(a), adjudication may not be withheld and the offender may be placed on probation for not less than 30 months, as a condition of which the court shall require the offender to reside at a community residential drug punishment center for 200 days. The offender must comply with all rules and regulations of the center and must pay a fee for the costs of room and board and residential supervision. Placement of an offender into a community residential drug punishment center is subject to budgetary considerations and availability of bed space. If the court requires the offender to reside at a community residential drug punishment center, the court shall also require the offender to comply with one or more of the other following terms and conditions:

1. Pay a fine of not less than $1,500 nor more than $5,000 pursuant to s. 775.083(1)(c).

2. Enter, regularly attend, and successfully complete a prescribed substance abuse treatment program provided by a treatment resource licensed pursuant to chapter 397 or by a hospital licensed pursuant to chapter 395, as specified by the court. In addition, the court may refer the offender to a licensed agency for substance abuse evaluation and, if appropriate, substance abuse treatment subject to the ability of the offender to pay for such evaluation and treatment. If such referral is made, the offender must comply and must pay for the reasonable cost of the evaluation and treatment.

3. Perform at least 200 hours of public service.

4. Submit to routine and random drug testing which may be conducted during the probationary period, with the reasonable costs thereof borne by the offender.

5. Participate, at his or her own expense, in an appropriate self-help group, such as Narcotics Anonymous, Alcoholics Anonymous, or Cocaine Anonymous, if available.

(e) If the person has been previously convicted of four felony violations of s. 893.13(2)(a)2., (5)(b), or (6)(a), adjudication may not be withheld and the offender may be placed on probation for not less than 36 months, as a condition of which the court shall require the offender to reside at a community residential drug punishment center for 360 days. The offender must comply with all rules and regulations of the center and must pay a fee for the costs of room and board and residential supervision. Placement of an offender into a community residential drug punishment center is subject to budgetary considerations and availability of bed space. If the court requires the offender to reside at a community residential drug punishment center, the court shall also require the offender to comply with one or more of the other following terms and conditions:

1. Pay a fine of not less than $2,000 nor more than $5,000 pursuant to s. 775.083(1)(c).

2. Enter, regularly attend, and successfully complete a prescribed substance abuse treatment program provided by a treatment resource licensed pursuant to chapter 397 or by a hospital licensed pursuant to chapter 395, as specified by the court. In addition, the court may refer the offender to a licensed agency for substance abuse evaluation and, if appropriate, substance abuse treatment subject to the ability of the offender to pay for such evaluation and treatment. If such referral is made, the offender must comply and must pay for the reasonable cost of the evaluation and treatment.

3. Perform at least 250 hours of public service.

4. Submit to routine and random drug testing which may be conducted during the probationary period, with the reasonable costs thereof borne by the offender.

5. Participate, at his or her own expense, in an appropriate self-help group, such as Narcotics Anonymous, Alcoholics Anonymous, or Cocaine Anonymous, if available.

(f) An offender who violates probation imposed pursuant to this section shall be sentenced in accordance with s. 921.002.

(3) Whenever the authorized provider for substance abuse treatment pursuant to this section is the same provider that conducts the substance abuse evaluations, that provider must submit a quarterly statistical report that shall be reviewed by the Department of Children and Family Services to ensure that excessive referrals to treatment have not been made. A programmatic and statistical report must be submitted annually to the Department of Children and Family Services by each provider authorized to provide services under this section.

(4) For the purposes of this section, multiple violations of any provision of chapter 893 which are pending before the court for sentencing at the same time and from the same criminal episode shall be considered as one violation.

(5) The Department of Corrections, in consultation with the Department of Children and Family Services, shall adopt rules as necessary to implement the provisions of this section relating to program standards and performance objectives of community residential drug punishment centers.

Laws 1993, c. 93–59, § 4; Laws 1994, c. 94–107, § 7. Amended by Laws 1997, c. 97–102, § 1685, eff. July 1, 1997; Laws 1997, c. 97–194, § 34, eff. Oct. 1, 1998; Laws 1998, c. 98–204, § 19, eff. Oct. 1, 1998; Laws 2000, c. 2000–320, § 8, eff. Oct. 1, 2000; Laws 2005, c. 2005–128, § 24, eff. July 1, 2005.

Historical and Statutory Notes

Amendment Notes:

Laws 1994, c. 94–107, a reviser's bill, in subsecs. (1) and (2), corrected citations in order to conform the statutes to the changes in internal cross references within § 893.13.

Laws 1997, c. 97–102, eff. July 1, 1997, removed gender-specific references applicable to human beings from volume 4 of the Florida Statutes without substantive changes in legal effect.

Laws 1997, c. 97–194, § 34, eff. Oct. 1, 1998, in subsecs. (1) and (2), corrected citations.

Laws 1998, c. 98–204, § 19, in subsecs. (1) and (2), deleted references to chapter 396; and, in subsecs. (3) and (5), substituted "Department of Children and Family Services" for "Department of Health and Rehabilitative Services".

Laws 2000, c. 2000–320, § 8, in subsec. (1)(c), following "s. 893.13" deleted "(1)(a)1., (1)(c)2., (1)(d)2."; and in subsecs. (2)(c), (2)(d), and (2)(e), following "s. 893.13" deleted "(1)(a)2.,".

Laws 2005, c. 2005–128, § 24, reenacted subsecs. (1) and (2) for the purpose of incorporating the amendment to § 893.13 in references thereto.

Laws 2005, c. 2005–128, § 25, provides:

"This act shall take effect July 1, 2005, and shall apply to offenses committed on or after that date."

Library References

Sentencing and Punishment ⚷1974, 1977, 1982, 1996, 2082 to 2084.

Westlaw Topic No. 350H.
C.J.S. Criminal Law § 567.

Research References

ALR Library

55 ALR 3rd 812, Review for Excessiveness of Sentence in Narcotics Case.

Forms

Florida Pleading and Practice Forms § 96:55, Order of Probation--Drug Offenders.

Florida Pleading and Practice Forms § 96:58, Order of Community Control--Drug Offender or Sexual Offender.

Treatises and Practice Aids

16 Florida Practice Series § 1:43, Sentencing Alternatives.

16 Florida Practice Series § 1:62, Costs, Assessments, Surcharges, and Fines--Community Service Alternative to Fine; Fine Disposal.

16 Florida Practice Series § 7:13, Drug Offender Probation.

16 Florida Practice Series § 7:20, Probationary and Community Control Time Periods.

16 Florida Practice Series § 1:100, Scoresheet Manipulation.

Notes of Decisions

---

1. Validity of probation

Trial court erred in sentencing defendant to concurrent terms of five years drug offender probation for battery on a law enforcement officer, resisting arrest with violence, and criminal mischief; defendant was not convicted of any of the drug related offenses listed in drug offender probation statute, and therefore could not be sentenced to drug offender probation. Ellis v. State, App. 4 Dist., 816 So.2d 759 (2002). Sentencing And Punishment ⚷ 1977(1)

Six previous convictions for sale of cocaine precluded application of drug offender probation to current conviction for sale of cocaine.

State v. Royal, App. 4 Dist., 763 So.2d 503 (2000). Sentencing And Punishment ⚷ 1872(3)

Probation as a drug offender was impermissible for felony driving while license was suspended or revoked, even though the defendant received a concurrent sentence for cocaine possession and even though the defendant apparently suffered from a drug addiction; the drug offender probation statute did not apply, and drug addiction was not a valid reason for downward departure from the guidelines sentence. State v. Lazo, App. 2 Dist., 761 So.2d 1244 (2000), review denied 790 So.2d 1105. Sentencing And Punishment ⚷ 864; Sentencing And Punishment ⚷ 1858

Sentence of two years of community control, successful completion of a substance abuse treatment program, participation in a drug abuse self-help group, $1500 fine, and 200 hours of required community service was not improper departure sentence for possession of cocaine. State v. Brown, App. 4 Dist., 723 So.2d 857 (1998). Chemical Dependents ⚷ 12; Controlled Substances ⚷ 100(2); Sentencing And Punishment ⚷ 1943

2. Basis for departure

Drug offender probation sentence on defendant's guilty plea to burglary and robbery was not reasonably related to defendant's rehabilitation, as required to be valid, where defendant did not agree to the probation, and the record did not disclose whether the probation was related to the crime, or to other criminal conduct or future criminality. Andrew v. State, App. 4 Dist., 988 So.2d 158 (2008). Sentencing And Punishment ⚷ 1977(2)

Defendant who has a felony conviction of a non-drug related offense is not eligible to receive an alternate sentence under statute governing terms and conditions of probation in a community residential drug punishment center for defendants committing certain drug offenses. State v. Langdon, App. 4 Dist., 978 So.2d 263 (2008). Sentencing And Punishment ⚷ 1872(2)

Defendant's postconviction claim that split sentences for burglary and possession of burglary tools were illegally imposed as part of drug offense was not refuted by record, in that "Drug Offender" notation appeared adjacent to lines of sentences imposed, and thus, remand was required for evidentiary hearing or denial supported by documentation conclusively showing defendant was not entitled to relief. Jackson v. State, App. 3 Dist., 908 So.2d 1133 (2005). Criminal Law ⚷ 1181.5(3.1)

Statute permitting court to sentence person who violates specific subsections of controlled substance delivery statute to a term of probation in lieu of imprisonment did not apply to mandatory minimum three-year term of imprisonment for delivery of cocaine within 1000 feet of a school, which was set forth in a section of the controlled substance delivery statute not listed in the sentencing statute. State v. Crews, App. 2 Dist., 884 So.2d 1139 (2004), on remand 2005 WL 6067013. Sentencing And Punishment ⚷ 1848

Trial court was precluded from entering a departure sentence, on defendant's adjudication of guilt for possession of marijuana, to three years probation with special condition that he complete outpatient treatment, without making a determination of how many prior violations defendant had for possession of a controlled substance or whether a bed was available at a residential facility, given that if defendant had even one qualifying violation, trial court would have been required to order defendant to reside at a community residential drug punishment center. State v. Harper, App. 2 Dist., 792 So.2d 1243 (2001). Sentencing And Punishment ⚷ 987

Resentencing on defendant's conviction for possession of cocaine was warranted following sentencing court's reference during hearing to incorrect authority as basis for its departure from guidelines scoresheet recommendation, which effectively precluded State from contesting court's sentence or building record to support argument; court's subsequent written citation to proper authority on guidelines scoresheet rendered record unclear as to which authority sentence was based upon. State v. Williams, App. 4 Dist., 759 So.2d 1 (1998). Criminal Law ⚷ 1181.5(8)

3. Oral pronouncement

As contained in written report of probation, conditions requiring probationer to observe curfew, report daily to his probation officer if not employed, and enroll in Drug Awareness Course were "special conditions" that had to be stricken when they were not orally pronounced at sentencing, as those conditions were not among general probation conditions set out by statute or rule. Ealy v. State, App. 4 Dist., 681 So.2d 914 (1996). Sentencing And Punishment ⚷ 1920

Probation conditions that are not set out by statute or rule are "special conditions" that must be pronounced during sentencing in open court. Ealy v. State, App. 4 Dist., 681 So.2d 914 (1996). Sentencing And Punishment ⚷ 1918

If special conditions of probation are not orally pronounced at sentencing, trial court must strike unannounced conditions. Ealy v. State,

App. 4 Dist., 681 So.2d 914 (1996). Sentencing And Punishment ⚷ 1920

4. Vacation of sentence

Sentence to drug offender probation for conviction of possession of cocaine was to be vacated, where sentences defendant received for sale of cocaine and possession of cocaine were intertwined, and defendant was ineligible to drug offender probation for sale of cocaine due to his previous six convictions for selling cocaine. State v. Royal, App. 4 Dist., 763 So.2d 503 (2000). Criminal Law ⚷ 1181.5(1)

5. Enumerated offenses

Trial court that sentenced defendant for grand theft and burglary of a conveyance could not impose drug offender probation, despite trial court's finding that defendant's offenses were related to his drug addiction; defendant's offenses were not among those enumerated in the then-effective version of the drug offender probation statute. Morris v. State, App. 4 Dist., 2010 WL 289201 (2010). Sentencing and Punishment ⚷ 1844; Sentencing and Punishment ⚷ 1856

Sentencing court could not impose drug offender probation regarding conviction for carrying a concealed weapon or firearm, which was not a drug-related offense set forth in statute governing drug offender probation. Beals v. State, App. 4 Dist., 14 So.3d 286 (2009). Sentencing and Punishment ⚷ 1864

A defendant may not be sentenced to drug offender probation unless he has been convicted of an enumerated drug offense or he has specifically agreed to such probation in a plea agreement, however a court may impose special conditions of probation which are desirable for rehabilitation. Andrew v. State, App. 4 Dist., 988 So.2d 158 (2008). Sentencing And Punishment ⚷ 1963; Sentencing And Punishment ⚷ 1977(1)

A court may not impose drug offender probation other than for the violation of a drug-related offense listed in the drug offender probation statute. Epperson v. State, App. 4 Dist., 955 So.2d 642 (2007). Sentencing And Punishment ⚷ 1848

Grand theft was not an enumerated drug-related offense for which drug offender probation could be imposed. Epperson v. State, App. 4 Dist., 955 So.2d 642 (2007). Sentencing And Punishment ⚷ 1856

Uttering a forged check and fraudulent use of a credit card were not enumerated offenses subject to drug offender probation. Whitmore v. State, App. 2 Dist., 910 So.2d 308 (2005). Sentencing And Punishment ⚷ 1846; Sentencing And Punishment ⚷ 1851

Trial court could not sentence defendant to drug-offender probation for driving while license suspended, and thus appellate court would reverse and remand for resentencing; offense was not enumerated offense subject to drug-offender probation. State v. DeMille, App. 2 Dist., 890 So.2d 454 (2004). Sentencing And Punishment ⚷ 1858

A defendant must be convicted of a specifically enumerated drug offense to qualify for a drug offender probation sentence. Parker v. State, App. 1 Dist., 839 So.2d 736 (2003), rehearing denied. Sentencing And Punishment ⚷ 1977(1)

Conviction for grand theft, an offense which is not a specifically enumerated drug offense, does not qualify for a drug offender probation sentence. Parker v. State, App. 1 Dist., 839 So.2d 736 (2003), rehearing denied. Sentencing And Punishment ⚷ 1977(1)

6. Postconviction motions

The imposition of drug offender probation and related conditions, when the trial court lacks authority to do so, is cognizable in a postconviction motion to correct illegal sentence. Epperson v. State, App. 4 Dist., 955 So.2d 642 (2007). Sentencing And Punishment ⚷ 2254

948.0345. Community service alternative to fine; fine disposal

Fines imposed pursuant to s. 948.034(1) and (2) shall be disposed of pursuant to s. 938.23(2). If the court finds that an offender is financially unable to pay all or part of the fine, the court may order the offender to perform community service for a specified additional period of time in lieu of payment of that portion of the fine which the court determines the offender is unable to pay. The court shall take into consideration the amount of the unpaid portion of the fine and the reasonable value of the services; however, the court shall not compute the reasonable value of services at a rate less than the federal minimum wage at the time of placing the offender on probation.

Laws 1993, c. 93–59, § 6. Amended by Laws 1997, c. 97–271, § 45, eff. July 1, 1997.

Historical and Statutory Notes

Amendment Notes:

Laws 1997, c. 97–271, § 45, eff. July 1, 1997, in the first sentence, "s. 938.23(2)" for "s. 893.16(2)".

Library References

Sentencing and Punishment ⚷1974, 1982, 2082 to 2084.

Westlaw Topic No. 350H.
C.J.S. Criminal Law § 567.

Research References

Treatises and Practice Aids

16 Florida Practice Series § 1:62, Costs, Assessments, Surcharges, and Fines--Community Service Alternative to Fine; Fine Disposal.

948.035. Residential treatment as a condition of probation or community control

(1) If the court imposes a period of residential treatment or incarceration as a condition of probation or community control, the residential treatment or incarceration shall be restricted to the following facilities:

(a) A Department of Corrections probation and restitution center;

(b) A probation program drug punishment treatment community;

(c) A community residential facility which is owned and operated by any public or private entity, excluding a community correctional center as defined in s. 944.026; or

(d) A county-owned facility.

(2) It is the intent of the Legislature that a county jail be used as the last available alternative for placement of an offender as a condition of probation. However, this shall not create a right of placement for the probationer, nor shall it restrict judicial discretion in ordering such treatment or incarceration.

(3) Prior to admission to such a facility or treatment community, the court shall obtain an individual assessment and recommendation on the appropriate treatment needs pursuant to the Community Control Implementation Manual which shall be considered by the court in ordering such placements. Placement in such a facility or center, or in the phase I secure residential phase of a probation program drug punishment treatment community, shall not exceed 364 days. Early completion of an offender's placement shall be recommended to the court, when appropriate, by the facility or center supervisor, by the supervising probation officer, or by the program manager. The Department of Corrections is authorized to contract with appropriate agencies for provision of services.

Laws 1985, c. 85–288, § 15; Laws 1989, c. 89–526, § 37; Laws 1990, c. 90–287, § 10; Laws 1991, c. 91–225, § 11; Laws 1991, c. 91–280, § 4. Renumbered from 948.03(7) and amended by Laws 2004, c. 2004–373, § 20, eff. July 1, 2004.

Historical and Statutory Notes

Amendment Notes:

Laws 2004, c. 2004–373, § 20, renumbered former subsec. (7) of § 948.03 as this section, and changed paragraph and subparagraph designations to subsection and paragraph designations; and in subsec. (3), deleted a reference to chapter 953 in the first sentence, and deleted the former fourth and fifth sentences which had read, "However, with respect to the placement of a probationer pursuant to chapter 953, such placement shall not be completed until satisfactory completion of the drug treatment program. Termination for cause from such a program shall be pursuant to s. 953.25(4).".

Library References

Sentencing and Punishment ⚷1977, 2082 to 2084.

Westlaw Topic No. 350H.

C.J.S. Criminal Law § 567.

948.036. Work programs as a condition of probation, community control, or other court-ordered community supervision

(1) Whenever an offender is required by the court to participate in any work program under the provisions of this chapter, enters into the pretrial intervention program pursuant to s. 948.08, or volunteers to work in a supervised work program conducted by a specified state, county, municipal, or community service organization or to work for the victim, either as an alternative to monetary restitution or as a part of the rehabilitative or community control program, the offender shall be considered an employee of the state for the purposes of chapter 440.

(2) In determining the average weekly wage, unless otherwise determined by a specific funding program, all remuneration received from the employer shall be considered a gratuity, and the offender shall not be entitled to any benefits otherwise payable under s. 440.15, regardless of whether the offender may be receiving wages and remuneration from other employment with another employer and regardless of his or her future wage-earning capacity. The provisions of this section do not apply to any person performing labor under a sentence of a court to perform community services as provided in s. 316.193.

Laws 1988, c. 88–122, § 70; Laws 1989, c. 89–526, § 37; Laws 1990, c. 90–337, § 8; Laws 1991, c. 91–280, § 4; Laws 1997, c. 97–102, § 1877. Renumbered from 948.03(8) and amended by Laws 2004, c. 2004–373, § 21, eff. July 1, 2004.

Historical and Statutory Notes

Amendment Notes:

Laws 2004, c. 2004–373, § 21, renumbered former subsec. (8) of § 948.03 as this section and changed paragraph designations to subsection designations; and in subsec. (2) substituted a reference to this section for a reference to this subsection.

Library References

Sentencing and Punishment ⚷1972, 1982, 2082 to 2084.

Westlaw Topic No. 350H.

C.J.S. Criminal Law § 567.

Research References

Forms

Florida Pleading and Practice Forms § 87:1, Definitions.

Florida Pleading and Practice Forms § 87:5, Persons and Employments Covered.

Treatises and Practice Aids

9 Florida Practice Series § 6:4, What Employers Provide Workers' Compensation Coverage in Florida?

9 Florida Practice Series § 6:24, Not an Employee: Prisoners, Inmates, and Those Doing Community Service Labor Under Court Sentence.

16 Florida Practice Series § 7:11, Special Conditions of Probation.

17 Florida Practice Series § 31:2, What Employers Provide Workers' Compensation Coverage in Florida?

948.037. Education and learning as a condition of probation or community control

(1) As a condition of community control, probation, or probation following incarceration, the court shall require an offender who has not obtained a high school diploma or high school equivalency diploma or who lacks basic or functional literacy skills, upon acceptance by an adult education program, to make a good faith effort toward completion of such basic or functional literacy skills or high school equivalency diploma, as defined in s. 1003.435, in accordance with the assessed adult general education needs of the individual offender. The court shall not revoke community control, probation, or probation following incarceration because of the offender's inability to achieve such skills or diploma but may revoke community control, probation, or probation following incarceration if the offender fails to make a good faith effort to achieve such skills or diploma. The court may grant early termination of community control, probation, or probation following incarceration upon the offender's successful completion of the approved program. As used in this subsection, "good faith effort" means the offender is enrolled in a program of instruction and is attending and making satisfactory progress toward completion of the requirements.

(2) A juvenile on community control who is a public school student must attend a public adult education program or a dropout prevention program, pursuant to s. 1003.53, which includes a second chance school or an alternative to expulsion, if the school district where the juvenile is enrolled offers such programs, unless the principal of the school determines that special circumstances warrant continuation in the regular educational school program.

(3) If a juvenile on community control attends a regular educational school program because a public adult education program or dropout prevention program, which includes a second chance school or an alternative to expulsion, is not available in the school district, the identity of the juvenile on community control, the nature of the felony offense committed by the juvenile, and the conditions of community control must be made known to each of the student's teachers.

Laws 1992, c. 92–310, § 23; Laws 1997, c. 97–234, § 27; Laws 2000, c. 2000–387, § 1045. Renumbered from 948.03(9) and amended by Laws 2004, c. 2004–373, § 22, eff. July 1, 2004.

Historical and Statutory Notes

Amendment Notes:

Laws 2004, c. 2004–373, § 22, renumbered former subsec. (9) of § 948.03 as this section, and changed paragraph designations to subsection designations; and in subsec. (1), inserted "the court shall" following "following incarceration,".

Library References

Sentencing and Punishment ⚷1982, 2082 to 2084.
Westlaw Topic No. 350H.
C.J.S. Criminal Law § 567.

Research References

Treatises and Practice Aids

16 Florida Practice Series § 7:11, Special Conditions of Probation.

948.038. Batterers' intervention program as a condition of probation, community control, or other court-ordered community supervision

As a condition of probation, community control, or any other court- ordered community supervision, the court shall order a person convicted of an offense of domestic violence, as defined in s. 741.28, to attend and successfully complete a batterers' intervention program unless the court determines that the person does not qualify for the batterers' intervention program pursuant to s. 741.325. The batterers' intervention program must be a program certified under s. 741.32, and the offender must pay the cost of attending the program.

Laws 2001, c. 2001–50, § 6. Laws 2001, c. 2001–50, § 6. Renumbered from 948.03(12) and amended by Laws 2004, c. 2004–373, § 25, eff. July 1, 2004.

Historical and Statutory Notes

Amendment Notes:

Laws 2004, c. 2004–373, § 25, renumbered former subsec. (12) of § 948.03 as this section, and deleted "Effective July 1, 2002," at the beginning of the last sentence.

Library References

Sentencing and Punishment ⚷1977, 2082 to 2084.
Westlaw Topic No. 350H.
C.J.S. Criminal Law § 567.

Research References

Treatises and Practice Aids

16 Florida Practice Series § 7:11, Special Conditions of Probation.

948.039. Special terms and conditions of probation or community control imposed by court order

The court may determine any special terms and conditions of probation or community control. The terms and conditions should be reasonably related to the circumstances of the offense committed and appropriate for the offender. The court shall impose the special terms and conditions by oral pronouncement at sentencing and include the terms and conditions in the written sentencing order. Special terms and conditions may include, but are not limited to, requirements that the offender:

(1) Attend an HIV/AIDS awareness program consisting of a class of not less than 2 hours or more than 4 hours in length, if such a program is available in

the county of the offender's residence. The offender shall pay the cost of attending the program.

(2) Pay not more than $1 per month during the term of probation or community control to a nonprofit organization established for the sole purpose of supplementing the rehabilitative efforts of the Department of Corrections.

Added by Laws 2004, c. 2004–373, § 26, eff. July 1, 2004.

Library References

Sentencing and Punishment ⚷1960 to 1983, 2082 to 2084.
Westlaw Topic No. 350H.
C.J.S. Criminal Law §§ 567, 2151 to 2152.

Research References

Treatises and Practice Aids

16 Florida Practice Series § 7:11, Special Conditions of Probation.

948.04. Period of probation; duty of probationer; early termination

(1) Defendants found guilty of felonies who are placed on probation shall be under supervision not to exceed 2 years unless otherwise specified by the court. No defendant placed on probation pursuant to s. 948.012(1) or s. 948.034 is subject to the probation limitations of this subsection. A defendant who is placed on probation or community control for a violation of chapter 794 or chapter 827 is subject to the maximum level of supervision provided by the supervising agency, and that supervision shall continue through the full term of the court-imposed probation or community control.

(2) Upon the termination of the period of probation, the probationer shall be released from probation and is not liable to sentence for the offense for which probation was allowed. During the period of probation, the probationer shall perform the terms and conditions of his or her probation.

(3) If the probationer has performed satisfactorily, has not been found in violation of any terms or conditions of supervision, and has met all financial sanctions imposed by the court, including, but not limited to, fines, court costs, and restitution, the Department of Corrections may recommend early termination of probation to the court at any time before the scheduled termination date.

Laws 1941, c. 20519, § 24; Laws 1943, c. 21775, § 5; Laws 1974, c. 74–112, § 10; Laws 1979, c. 79–77, § 1; Laws 1983, c. 83–131, § 18; Laws 1983, c. 83–228, § 3; Laws 1991, c. 91–280, § 5; Laws 1992, c. 92–76, § 1; Laws 1993, c. 93–59, § 5. Amended by Laws 1997, c. 97–102, § 1686, eff. July 1, 1997; Laws 2004, c. 2004–373, § 31, eff. July 1, 2004.

Historical and Statutory Notes

Amendment Notes:

Laws 1943, c. 21775, § 5, amended the first sentence by inserting "more than two years" following "shall not extend" and the proviso.

Laws 1974, c. 74–112, § 10, rewrote this section which formerly provided:

"The period of probation shall not extend more than two years beyond the maximum term for which the defendant might have been sentenced; provided, however, that if, during the period of probation of any case, it appears to the court that further supervision would be beneficial to the probationer or to society, the court may, by proper order, extend the supervision period, within the limits of time hereinabove specified. Upon the termination of the period of probation, the probationer shall be released from probation and shall not be liable to sentence for the crime for which probation was allowed. During the period of probation the probationer shall perform the terms and conditions of his probation."

Laws 1979, c. 79–77, § 1, deleted the first two sentences and added the last sentence to subsec. (2) dealing with recommendations of early termination of probation. The first two sentences of subsec. (2) formerly provided:

"The Parole and Probation Commission may discharge the offender prior to the expiration of his term of probation; however, the commission shall notify the court in writing prior to such discharge. If the court does not set the matter for hearing to be held within 30 days from the date of such notice, the offender may be discharged."

Laws 1983, c. 83–131, § 18, changed the statute reference in the second sentence [now the third sentence] of subsec. (1).

Laws 1983, c. 83–228, § 3, in subsec. (1), interpolated the second sentence; and in subsec. (2), substituted "offense" for "crime" in the first sentence.

Laws 1991, c. 91–280, § 5, eff. Oct. 1, 1991, rewrote the section.

Laws 1992, c. 92–76, § 1, eff. Oct. 1, 1992, in subsec. (1), added the third sentence.

Laws 1993, c. 93–59, § 5, eff. Oct. 1, 1993, in subsec. (1), inserted reference to § 948.034.

Laws 1997, c. 97–102, eff. July 1, 1997, removed gender-specific references applicable to human beings from volume 4 of the Florida Statutes without substantive changes in legal effect.

Laws 2004, c. 2004–373, § 31, in subsec. (1), substituted a reference to § 948.012(1) for a reference to § 948.01(6) in the second sentence.

Law Review and Journal Commentaries

Probation in Florida. Vernon W. Clark, 14 U.Fla.L.Rev. 213 (1961).

Sentence. Thomas A. Wills, 20 U.Miami L.Rev. 264 (1965).

Library References

Sentencing and Punishment ⚷1943 to 1947, 1953.

Westlaw Topic No. 350H.
C.J.S. Criminal Law §§ 2153, 2155.

Research References

ALR Library

13 ALR 4th 1240, Power of Court, After Expiration of Probation Term, to Revoke or Modify Probation for Violations Committed During the Probation Term.

141 ALR 1225, Imposition or Enforcement of Sentence Which Has Been Suspended Without Authority.

Treatises and Practice Aids

16 Florida Practice Series § 7:11, Special Conditions of Probation.

16 Florida Practice Series § 7:20, Probationary and Community Control Time Periods.

16 Florida Practice Series § 7:24, Modification or Recision of Probation or Community Control--After Violation.

16 Florida Practice Series § 7:25, Modification or Recision of Probation or Community Control--Early Termination of Probation/Community Control.

22 Florida Practice Series App. A, Florida Rules of Criminal Procedure.

United States Supreme Court

Probationer, self incrimination involved in disclosure to probation officer, see Minnesota v. Murphy, U.S.Minn.1984, 104 S.Ct. 1136, 465 U.S. 420, 79 L.Ed.2d 409, rehearing denied 104 S.Ct. 1932, 466 U.S. 945, 80 L.Ed.2d 477, on remand 348 N.W.2d 764.

Notes of Decisions

Waiver 11

---

1. Construction and application

Amended statutory probation limitation of this section was not applicable to defendant, convicted of selling personal property subject to lien without consent of lienholder and transferring motor vehicle without delivery of title, where offenses were committed prior to effective date of amended act, and thus defendant's sentence to five years' probation was proper, where such probation term fell within permissible limits of this section in effect at time acts were committed. Helmig v. State, App. 1 Dist., 330 So.2d 246 (1976). Sentencing And Punishment ⚷ 1828

2. Postponement of sentence

Even though defendant had pled guilty to charge of possession of a hallucinogenic drug of more than five grams, whereas he was guilty only of possession of less than five grams of such drugs, defendant had not suffered from any erroneous sentence, where trial judge had entered an order withholding adjudication of guilt and imposition of sentence and had placed defendant on probation for three years. Farhat v. State, App. 1 Dist., 293 So.2d 723 (1974). Criminal Law ⚷ 273.2(1)

Barring certain exceptions, sentence cannot be postponed indefinitely or for any considerable period. Yates v. Buchanan, App. 3 Dist., 170 So.2d 72 (1964). Sentencing And Punishment ⚷ 377

3. Maximum duration of probation

Probation statute does not authorize sentence of more than six months' probation for defendant convicted of second-degree misdemeanor. Purvis v. Lindsey ex rel. State, App. 4 Dist., 587 So.2d 638 (1991). Sentencing And Punishment ⚷ 1946

Defendant convicted of misdemeanors of DUI-property damage and of leaving scene of accident involving property damage could not be placed on probation for three years for each misdemeanor count inasmuch as maximum permissible sentence for misdemeanor was one year. Tollefson v. State, App. 1 Dist., 525 So.2d 957 (1988). Sentencing And Punishment ⚷ 1945

Trial court erred in placing defendant on two years probation for commission of two misdemeanors, and period of probation was properly limited to six months. Bell v. State, App. 2 Dist., 479 So.2d 308 (1985). Sentencing And Punishment ⚷ 1943

Defendant, who was sentenced to one-year period of probation upon conviction of second-degree misdemeanor, and who failed to appeal sentence even though longest permissible period of probation allowable for such violation was six months, could raise issue of unlawful length of penalty even after period for direct appeal had elapsed by way of appeal from revocation of probation based upon alleged violations occurring nine months after sentence was originally imposed; defendant served period of probation equal to maximum which could have legally been imposed upon him without being charged with violation, and remainder of probation period was void and could not serve as basis for further sentence or probation by trial court. Bouie v. State, App. 2 Dist., 360 So.2d 1142 (1978). Criminal Law ⚷ 1134.70; Sentencing And Punishment ⚷ 2006

One-year probation imposed upon defendant, who was allowed as result of a plea bargain to plead nolo contendere to second-degree misdemeanor of receiving stolen goods, maximum term for which was 60 days, was in excess of maximum provided by this section, which permits court to place defendant on probation for six months in a misdemeanor case and modification of probation term was therefore required. Alderman v. State, App. 2 Dist., 356 So.2d 928 (1978). Sentencing And Punishment ⚷ 1946

Provision of this section that defendants found guilty of misdemeanors who are placed on probation shall be under supervision not to exceed six months unless otherwise specified by the court does not authorize trial court to place a defendant who has been adjudicated guilty of a misdemeanor upon probation for unlimited period of time. McNulty v. State, App. 1 Dist., 339 So.2d 1155 (1976). Sentencing And Punishment ⚷ 1946

On conviction of aggravated assault, court could not extend period of probation beyond maximum permissible sentence of five years. Watts v. State, App. 2 Dist., 328 So.2d 223 (1976). Sentencing And Punishment ⚷ 1945

4. Excessive probation

Order of probation setting forth term of five years' probation for loitering and one year probation for petit theft would be vacated and cause remanded for imposition of new probationary terms, since both loitering and petit theft are second-degree misdemeanors for which the maximum probationary term is six months. Holloway v. State, App. 2 Dist., 393 So.2d 1185 (1981). Sentencing And Punishment ⚷ 1945

Imposition of five years probation for crime of petit larceny as second-degree misdemeanor was fundamental error because it exceeded the maximum probationary term for a second-degree misdemeanor, which is six months. Corraliza v. State, App. 3 Dist., 391 So.2d 330 (1980), petition for review denied 399 So.2d 1141. Sentencing And Punishment ⚿ 1943

Sentence of seven and one-half years in prison to be followed by nine and one-half years on probation imposed upon defendant, who pleaded guilty to breaking and entering with intent to commit grand larceny, a second-degree felony with a maximum punishment of 15 years in prison, was illegal and would be modified by reducing probationary period to seven and one-half years. Wright v. State, App. 4 Dist., 345 So.2d 782 (1977). Sentencing And Punishment ⚿ 1844

Since elimination of the provision formerly contained in this section that probation cannot extend more than two years beyond the maximum possible sentence limits the power of the courts to impose a period of probation beyond the maximum permissible sentence, except where expressly provided by law, the 17-year period of probation placed on defendant for his conviction of breaking and entering with intent to commit a felony, which offense carries a maximum sentence of 15 years, was improper. Magnin v. State, App. 2 Dist., 334 So.2d 638 (1976). Sentencing And Punishment ⚿ 1946

Sentence of 30 months probation for simple assault, a second-degree misdemeanor, was excessive; maximum period for which sentence of probation could be imposed was 790 days. McBride v. State, App. 4 Dist., 311 So.2d 752 (1975). Sentencing And Punishment ⚿ 1943

Two years plus 60 days was maximum period for probation for misdemeanor in second degree; accordingly, imposition of probation period of two and one-half years was excessive, requiring reduction to statutory maximum. Weldon v. State, App. 3 Dist., 287 So.2d 133 (1973), appeal dismissed 298 So.2d 419. Sentencing And Punishment ⚿ 1943

5. Commencement of probation

Trial court properly determined, on remand for resentencing, that defendant's term of probation began to run from date of original sentencing where defendant was originally sentenced to nonreporting probation and the sentence, on remand, imposed reporting probation. State v. McGraw, App. 3 Dist., 487 So.2d 359 (1986). Sentencing And Punishment ⚿ 1940

Defendant's term of probation began when his parole expired, not when he was released on parole from prison, and thus trial court had jurisdiction to entertain proceedings for revocation of defendant's probation. Johnson v. State, App. 2 Dist., 419 So.2d 752 (1982), petition for review denied 427 So.2d 737. Sentencing And Punishment ⚿ 1941

Where minutes recited that court placed defendant on probation for two years to run after release on other charges and probation order put defendant on probation for two years to begin on expiration of any prison sentence then being served and where concurrent sentences then being served were revoked but defendant was shortly thereafter resentenced, probation period began to run upon his release from resentence and could be revoked less than two months thereafter for failure to report to probation supervisor in accordance with parole condition. Roy v. State, App. 2 Dist., 207 So.2d 52 (1967), certiorari dismissed 211 So.2d 554. Sentencing And Punishment ⚿ 2006

6. Extension of probationary period

Formal order of probation, which consisted not of words spoken from bench nor of reporter's record of those words, but rather of written, signed, filed and recorded order, could not be impeached and its two-year period extended to three years by reference to transcript of proceedings, and thus, more than two but less than three years later, judge had no jurisdiction to revoke and extend probation. Watt v. State, App. 1 Dist., 323 So.2d 621 (1975). Sentencing And Punishment ⚿ 1913

Where there was prompt pronouncement of year sentence but it was not put into effect for period of several years thereafter, there was in effect probation but an illegal one where defendant was not placed in custody of parole commission, and period during which sentence was not put into effect extended beyond two-year period beyond the year sentence. Yates v. Buchanan, App. 3 Dist., 170 So.2d 72 (1964). Sentencing And Punishment ⚿ 1930; Sentencing And Punishment ⚿ 1950

7. Expiration of probation

Upon expiration of probationary period, court is divested of all jurisdiction over probationer unless prior to that time the processes of the court have been set in motion for revocation or modification of probation. Gardner v. State, App., 412 So.2d 10 (1981); Shankweiler v. State, App., 427 So.2d 215 (1983); Brooker v. State, App., 207 So.2d 478 (1968).

Sentencing probationer for violating probation, after term of probation had expired, was a violation of due process and fundamental error which could be raised for first time on appeal as it was equivalent of convicting person of nonexistent crime. Hebb v. State, App. 4 Dist., 714 So.2d 639 (1998). Constitutional Law ⚿ 4733(1); Criminal Law ⚿ 1042.3(4); Sentencing And Punishment ⚿ 2010

Condition of probation which provided that probationary term of defendant could not be terminated early and that defendant was required to participate in sex offender program impermissibly attempted to divest Department of Corrections of its authority to recommend early termination of probation and was stricken. Jones v. State, App. 2 Dist., 666 So.2d 191 (1995). Sentencing And Punishment ⚿ 1977(2); Sentencing And Punishment ⚿ 1983(2)

Rule providing that probationer could not be sentenced, based upon violation of probation, after probationary period had come to end, did not extend to procedure under which prosecution for physical abuse of spouse had been deferred while defendant performed condition of domestic violence deferred prosecution agreement calling for attendance at counseling sessions for total of 12 months; deferred prosecution differed from sentence following probation in that defendant had not entered plea to charge, jeopardy had never attached and under agreement prosecution would make final decision concerning disposition of charge after completion of program. State v. Fitzgerald, App. 2 Dist., 640 So.2d 214 (1994). Sentencing And Punishment ⚿ 2090

Special condition of probation providing that defendant could not be considered for early termination of probation would be stricken, as trial judge was not authorized to divest Department of Corrections of its authority to recommend early termination of probation; moreover, trial judge was not empowered to prevent Circuit Court in the future from exercising its authority to discharge probationer. Baker v. State, App. 2 Dist., 619 So.2d 411 (1993). Constitutional Law ⚿ 2545(1); Sentencing And Punishment ⚿ 1983(2)

Where additional counts which were added to affidavit of violation after expiration of defendant's probationary period constituted new and untimely filed charges of delivery of cocaine and delivery of heroin, trial court was divested of jurisdiction to consider them along with original, timely filed counts of actual or constructive possession of firearm, cocaine and heroin. Clark v. State, App. 4 Dist., 402 So.2d 43 (1981). Sentencing And Punishment ⚿ 2010

Once term of probation has expired, court lacks jurisdiction to entertain application for revocation of probation based upon violation which occurred during probation period unless, during term of probation, appropriate steps were taken to revoke or modify probation. Clark v. State, App. 4 Dist., 402 So.2d 43 (1981). Sentencing And Punishment ⚿ 2010

Affidavit and warrant charging defendant with violation of probation nine months after one-year period of probation was imposed came too late where underlying offense was second-degree misdemeanor for which longest permissible period of probation allowable was six months; warrant was filed after date lawful period of probation would have expired. Bouie v. State, App. 2 Dist., 360 So.2d 1142 (1978). Sentencing And Punishment ⚿ 2010

Probation violation cannot be charged after probation period has expired. Bouie v. State, App. 2 Dist., 360 So.2d 1142 (1978). Sentencing And Punishment ⚿ 2010

Where probation period had already ended prior to revocation of probation, trial court lacked jurisdiction to impose further sentence. Streeter v. State, App. 3 Dist., 211 So.2d 32 (1968). Sentencing And Punishment ⚿ 2032

Even if illegal order suspending defendant's sentence could be construed as order placing defendant on probation, he could not be legally sentenced when, after expiration of maximum statutory period of probation, he pleaded guilty to violation of probation. Coleman v. State, App. 3 Dist., 205 So.2d 5 (1967). Sentencing And Punishment ⚿ 2010

After expiration of probationary period, court had no jurisdiction to extend period of probation, where no affirmative action had been taken during probationary period to set in motion the processes of court for revocation or modification of probation. Pickman v. State, App. 3 Dist., 155 So.2d 646 (1963), certiorari denied 164 So.2d 805. Sentencing And Punishment ⚿ 1948

Court did not lose jurisdiction of a defendant by termination of his period of probation, but it had authority to sentence him for offense of which he was convicted, where warrant for defendant's arrest because of violation of probation was issued within period of probation, even though such warrant was not served until a date subsequent to termination of probation. Carroll v. Cochran, 140 So.2d 300 (1962). Sentencing And Punishment ⚿ 2010

In proceeding for revocation of probation, court was without jurisdiction to consider affidavits of charges made and filed subsequent to termination of period of probation, and such affidavits should have been quashed as incompetent. State ex rel. Ard v. Shelby, App. 1 Dist., 97 So.2d 631 (1957). Sentencing And Punishment ⚿ 2019

8. Early termination of probation

Trial court that sentenced defendant, who was convicted for at least the third time of driving under the influence (DUI) and driving while license suspended, to 11 months and 29 days in county jail followed by five years of probation could not impose a special condition of probation calling for no early termination of probation; trial court could not divest Department of Corrections of its authority to recommend early termination, or prevent circuit court from exercising its discretion to discharge defendant in the future. Murphy v. State, App. 2 Dist., 976 So.2d 1242 (2008). Constitutional Law ⚷ 2545(4); Sentencing And Punishment ⚷ 1983(2)

Where trial court imposes probationary period with special conditions and further offers early termination of that probation upon successful completion of all such conditions, the early termination provision is not self-executing; if and when special conditions are completed before natural expiration of probationary sentence, either defendant or Department of Corrections must advise court that all such conditions have been satisfied and request early termination, and once court has confirmed that all special conditions have been fulfilled it will then terminate probation. Hepburn v. State, App. 3 Dist., 780 So.2d 326 (2001). Sentencing And Punishment ⚷ 1953

Trial court had jurisdiction to terminate probationary period imposed for violation of sexual battery statute, upon defendant's motion for early termination of probation. Krug v. State, App. 3 Dist., 689 So.2d 391 (1997). Sentencing And Punishment ⚷ 1953

9. Violation of probation

A violation of probation must be set in motion prior to the termination of the period of probation. Vidaurre v. State, App. 2 Dist., 8 So.3d 1206 (2009). Sentencing and Punishment ⚷ 2010

A violation of probation must be set in motion prior to the termination of the period of probation. Jones v. State, App. 4 Dist., 954 So.2d 675 (2007). Sentencing And Punishment ⚷ 1948

10. Revocation of probation

Motion to revoke probation must be filed during probationary period in order for court to have jurisdiction to revoke. State v. Fitzgerald, App. 2 Dist., 640 So.2d 214 (1994). Sentencing And Punishment ⚷ 2010

Revocation of probationary term for crime of grand theft was subject to being affirmed where revocation proceedings were completed prior to expiration of probationary term. White v. State, App. 2 Dist., 410 So.2d 588 (1982). Sentencing And Punishment ⚷ 2010

Jurisdiction was not vested in trial court to revoke probation imposed on charge of resisting arrest without violence where term of probation expired before time affidavits initiating revocation process were filed. White v. State, App. 2 Dist., 410 So.2d 588 (1982). Sentencing And Punishment ⚷ 2010

Where provisions of this section which were in effect when defendant committed offense for which he was placed on probation permitted period of probation to extend up to two years beyond maximum term for which a defendant might be sentenced, and where defendant was subject to maximum five-year sentence, trial court which revoked defendant's probation acted within statutory limits in sentencing defendant to five years in prison, the last two years suspended, to be followed by three-years' probation. Adams v. State, App. 1 Dist., 330 So.2d 505 (1976). Sentencing And Punishment ⚷ 2038

Probation may be revoked solely upon conviction by jury of a subsequent crime, provided the subsequent conviction is valid. Egantoff v. State, App. 2 Dist., 208 So.2d 843 (1968), certiorari denied 218 So.2d 164. Sentencing And Punishment ⚷ 2004

11. Waiver

Where defendant agreed to and benefited from probation granted as substitute for bail or incarceration, he waived right to attack by appeal sentence thereafter imposed. Rodriguez v. State, App. 3 Dist., 441 So.2d 1129 (1983), petition for review denied 451 So.2d 850. Criminal Law ⚷ 1137(1)

12. Jurisdiction

Although court order revoking petitioner's probation, being invalid because based on misdemeanor convictions obtained in violation of right to counsel, could not justify continued jurisdiction of state court over petitioner, the warrant sworn out for petitioner's arrest, even though based solely on the invalid convictions, was sufficient for state court to retain jurisdiction over petitioner as a probationer, notwithstanding fact that technically petitioner's probationary period had ended, and proper disposition of case by federal habeas corpus court was to remand petitioner to custody of state for reconsideration of question whether he violated his probation. Clay v. Wainwright, 1972, 470 F.2d 478. Habeas Corpus ⚷ 794.1

Trial court lacked jurisdiction to find defendant in violation of his community control, as to his five year probation for the offense of possession of cocaine, where that term of probation had already ended before the violation took place. Vidaurre v. State, App. 2 Dist., 8 So.3d 1206 (2009). Sentencing and Punishment ⚷ 1948

Trial court lacked jurisdiction to conduct violation of probation hearing involving defendant who was given 18 months of drug offender probation, even though affidavit of violation was filed less than 18 months after defendant's probation was reinstated following a previous violation; probation was not extended when it was reinstated, and 18-month period had expired before affidavit of violation was filed. Jones v. State, App. 4 Dist., 954 So.2d 675 (2007). Sentencing And Punishment ⚷ 1948

Upon expiration of a probationary period the court is divested of all jurisdiction over the person of the probationer unless in the meantime the processes of the court have been set in motion for revocation or modification of the probation. Rivera v. State, App. 3 Dist., 939 So.2d 116 (2006), rehearing denied, review granted 965 So.2d 123, review dismissed as improvidently granted 985 So.2d 1092. Sentencing And Punishment ⚷ 1948

County court lacked jurisdiction to sanction defendant for failing to perform community service, 19 months after defendant had been ordered to perform 150 hours of community service at the rate of 15 hours per month, upon adjudication of guilt following her plea to misdemeanor marijuana possession, where maximum amount of time to which defendant could have been sentenced was one year; court was divested of jurisdiction over defendant upon expiration of probationary period. West's F.S.A. §§ 775.082(4)(a), 775.091, 893.13(6)(b), 921.187(1)(a), Rivera v. State, App. 3 Dist., 939 So.2d 116 (2006), rehearing denied, review granted 965 So.2d 123, review dismissed as improvidently granted 985 So.2d 1092. Sentencing And Punishment ⚷ 1948; Sentencing And Punishment ⚷ 1982(3)

Upon expiration of a probationary period the court is divested of all jurisdiction over the person of the probationer unless in the meantime the processes of the court have been set in motion for revocation or modification of the probation. Rivera v. State, App. 3 Dist., 939 So.2d 116 (2006), rehearing denied, review granted 965 So.2d 123, review dismissed as improvidently granted 985 So.2d 1092. Sentencing And Punishment ⚷ 1948

County court lacked jurisdiction to sanction defendant for failing to perform community service, 19 months after defendant had been ordered to perform 150 hours of community service at the rate of 15 hours per month, upon adjudication of guilt following her plea to misdemeanor marijuana possession, where maximum amount of time to which defendant could have been sentenced was one year; court was divested of jurisdiction over defendant upon expiration of probationary period. West's F.S.A. §§ 775.082(4)(a), 775.091, 893.13(6)(b), 921.187(1)(a), Rivera v. State, App. 3 Dist., 939 So.2d 116 (2006), rehearing denied, review granted 965 So.2d 123, review dismissed as improvidently granted 985 So.2d 1092. Sentencing And Punishment ⚷ 1948; Sentencing And Punishment ⚷ 1982(3)

Trial court lacked jurisdiction to proceed with violation of probation hearing where trial court erroneously sentenced defendant to more than six months' probation for second-degree misdemeanor defense, and affidavit of violation of probation was filed more than six months after defendant was placed on probation. Purvis v. Lindsey ex rel. State, App. 4 Dist., 587 So.2d 638 (1991). Sentencing And Punishment ⚷ 2010

On appeal from conviction of selling personal property subject to lien, without consent of lienholder, and transferring motor vehicle without delivery of title, the District Court of Appeal was unable to review propriety of term of probation, given nature of crimes for which he was convicted, as sentencing was peculiarly function of trial court. Helmig v. State, App. 1 Dist., 330 So.2d 246 (1976). Criminal Law ⚷ 1156.6

Where defendant pleaded guilty to breaking and entering with intent to commit misdemeanor, so that court could have imposed maximum sentence of five years or placed him on probation for maximum of seven years, court did not have jurisdiction to withhold imposition of sentence from day to day and term to term, and then, 12 years later, to revoke order illegally suspending sentence and impose sentence. Helton v. State, 106 So.2d 79 (1958). Sentencing And Punishment ⚷ 1808

948.05. Court to admonish or commend probationer or offender in community control

A court may at any time cause a probationer or offender in community control to appear before it to be admonished or commended, and, when satisfied that its action will be for the best interests of justice and the welfare of society, it may discharge the probationer or offender in community control from further supervision.

Laws 1941, c. 20519, § 25; Laws 1983, c. 83–131, § 19.

Historical and Statutory Notes

Amendment Notes:

Laws 1983, c. 83–131, § 19, provided for offenders in community control.

Cross References

Construction of law, see § 949.04.

Law Review and Journal Commentaries

Sentence. Thomas A. Wills, 20 U.Miami L.Rev. 264 (1965).

Library References

Sentencing and Punishment ⚷1953, 1988.
Westlaw Topic No. 350H.
C.J.S. Criminal Law § 2155.

Research References

Treatises and Practice Aids

16 Florida Practice Series § 7:25, Modification or Recision of Probation or Community Control--Early Termination of Probation/Community Control.

Notes of Decisions

Discharge of probationer 3
Judicial authority 1
Residence of probationer 2
Review 4

---

1. Judicial authority

Trial court that sentenced defendant, who was convicted for at least the third time of driving under the influence (DUI) and driving while license suspended, to 11 months and 29 days in county jail followed by five years of probation could not impose a special condition of probation calling for no early termination of probation; trial court could not divest Department of Corrections of its authority to recommend early termination, or prevent circuit court from exercising its discretion to discharge defendant in the future. Murphy v. State, App. 2 Dist., 976 So.2d 1242 (2008). Constitutional Law ⚷ 2545(4); Sentencing And Punishment ⚷ 1983(2)

Once a person begins serving new sentence after revocation of previous probation, he is beyond reach of original trial judge. Roy v. State, App. 2 Dist., 207 So.2d 52 (1967), certiorari dismissed 211 So.2d 554. Sentencing And Punishment ⚷ 2001

2. Residence of probationer

A court placing on probation a defendant who is to reside in Florida has no authority to order the probationer not to report to or be under the supervision of Florida parole and probation commission. The statutes mandatorily require that when a defendant is placed on probation, he is to be under the supervision and control of said commission unless he is permitted to reside in another state under the compact set forth in § 949.07. The court may thereafter terminate that supervision pursuant to the terms of this section. Op.Atty.Gen., 072–223, July 13, 1972.

Where a defendant is placed on probation and is not permitted to reside in another state pursuant to the compact set forth in § 949.07, the court placing him on probation has the authority to so frame the order of probation so as to permit the probationer to travel to, but not to reside in, another state on a temporary basis. If the original order of probation does not so permit, court has the authority to later amend the terms and conditions thereof in such manner as to allow the probationer to do this. Op. Atty.Gen., 072–223, July 13, 1972.

The only authority which a court has to allow a probationer to reside in another state is that granted by the compact set out in § 949.07. That compact provides that before granting such permission, opportunity shall be granted to the receiving state to investigate the home and prospective employment of the probationer. The compact further unequivocally provides that the receiving state will assume the duties of visitation and supervision over probationers of a sending state. The result is that when a court places a defendant on probation with permission to reside in another state, this must be done under the terms of said compact and the court has no authority whatever to order that the receiving state not investigate or supervise the probationer. Nevertheless, if the court later becomes satisfied that discharging the probationer from supervision in the other state will be for the best interests of justice and the welfare of society, then the court may discharge him from such supervision under the authority of this section. Op.Atty.Gen., 072–2223, July 13, 1972.

3. Discharge of probationer

Where trial court imposes probationary period with special conditions and further offers early termination of that probation upon successful completion of all such conditions, the early termination provision is not self-executing; if and when special conditions are completed before natural expiration of probationary sentence, either defendant or Department of Corrections must advise court that all such conditions have been satisfied and request early termination, and once court has confirmed that all special conditions have been fulfilled it will then terminate probation. Hepburn v. State, App. 3 Dist., 780 So.2d 326 (2001). Sentencing And Punishment ⚷ 1953

Trial court could not include special condition of probation that defendant may not be considered for early termination of probation, since statute allowed probationer to be brought before court at any time to be commended and possibly discharged from further supervision, based on facts and circumstances that developed during term of probation. Arriaga v. State, App. 4 Dist., 666 So.2d 949 (1996), rehearing denied. Sentencing And Punishment ⚷ 1983(2)

Trial judge is not empowered to prevent circuit court from in future exercising its authority to discharge probationer. Jones v. State, App. 2 Dist., 666 So.2d 191 (1995). Sentencing And Punishment ⚷ 1960

Special condition of probation providing that defendant could not be considered for early termination of probation would be stricken, as trial judge was not authorized to divest Department of Corrections of its authority to recommend early termination of probation; moreover, trial judge was not empowered to prevent Circuit Court in the future from exercising its authority to discharge probationer. Baker v. State, App. 2 Dist., 619 So.2d 411 (1993). Constitutional Law ⚷ 2545(1); Sentencing And Punishment ⚷ 1983(2)

4. Review

Order denying motion for early termination of period of probation which had been previously and lawfully imposed was nonappealable. Ziegler v. State, App. 3 Dist., 380 So.2d 564 (1980). Criminal Law ⚷ 1023(16)

Advisability, as opposed to legality, of a particular sentence is not subject to appellate review. Ziegler v. State, App. 3 Dist., 380 So.2d 564 (1980). Criminal Law ⚷ 1134.75

INDEX

TO

TITLE XLVII—CHAPTERS 900 TO 985

CRIMINAL PROCEDURE AND CORRECTIONS

SEE VOLUME CONTAINING END OF TITLE XLVII.

END OF VOLUME